CONTROLLER'S HANDBOOK

Controller's Handbook

Edited by

SAM R. GOODMAN

Executive Vice President—
Finance and Administration
The Baker & Taylor Company

JAMES S. REECE

Professor of Policy and Control
Graduate School of Business Administration
The University of Michigan

Dow Jones-Irwin   Homewood, Illinois   60430

ISBN 0-87094-157-7
Library of Congress Catalog Card No. 77–91319
Printed in the United States of America

3 4 5 6 7 8 9 0 K 5 4 3 2

Preface

The last ten years have seen remarkable expansion of the controller's role in almost all corporations. No longer is this person's job essentially that of a chief accountant: Today the controller is called upon by top management for data, analysis, and advice related to a vast array of decision-making activities. This handbook is designed to assist controllers in meeting the requirements of their demanding and challenging positions.

A handbook is no substitute for current reading. Accordingly, the controller needs to meet his or her obligation of keeping abreast of current developments by reading management periodicals and new books. However, a well-organized handbook also helps the controller meet the needs of the job. As an accurate and up-to-date compendium of current knowledge, *Controller's Handbook* has the advantages of compactness and comprehensiveness. It is a convenient place for the controller to refresh his or her memory on topics to which first exposure occurred some time ago, and to begin a search for relevant concepts and techniques on any particular topic. As a codification of the state of the art as of the publication date, this handbook limits the need for further search to only the most recent publications.

Such is the purpose of this volume. This handbook is not intended as an elementary text on the duties of a controller. Rather, the presumption is that the reader is an experienced financial manager with a broad knowledge of the field of controllership who will use the handbook to review and update individual understanding of specific topics as the need arises.

To help achieve this purpose, the chapters of this book are written either by business practitioners or by consultants and university people who have extensive first-hand contacts with financial executives. To the extent that academic theories are practicable, they are described, and their translation into workable procedures and policies is documented. Consistent with this approach, one of the editors is an experienced financial executive and the other is a professor who not only teaches, but also writes and consults in this field.

Before describing the structure of this handbook, it is appropriate to mention what is *not* contained herein. Because the duties of the controller in a given company are a function of such variables as its size, its organizational structure, and the management style of its top managers, some controllers may have responsibilities that are not covered in this book. The reader should know that this handbook is one of four in a series on the responsibilities of persons reporting to a company's chief financial officer. The other three books are *The Treasurer's Handbook, The Modern Accountant's Handbook,* and *The Information Systems Handbook* (all published by Dow Jones-Irwin). Thus a controller responsible for, say, management of receivables will find that topic covered in *The Treasurer's Handbook;* preparing the corporate annual report is the topic of several chapters in *The Modern Accountant's Handbook;* and controlling the data-processing resource is covered in depth in *The Information Systems Handbook.* These examples illustrate that noncoverage of a topic in *Controller's Handbook* is probably the result of a decision that inclusion in another handbook was more appropriate, either to permit greater depth of coverage or because of a judgment that in most major corporations a particular area of responsibility typically is assigned to a person whose title is other than "controller."

The 46 chapters of this handbook have been grouped into five major sections. Part I, "The Broad Role of Controllership," begins with a chapter describing in general the broadened scope of the modern controller's responsibilities, followed by chapters dealing more specifically with the controller's role in strategic planning and data processing. Part II, "Cost Systems," begins with an overview of cost concepts and terminology; this chapter is especially important because, although in practice terminology is used rather sloppily, in this handbook we try throughout to use terminology consistently as defined in Chapter 4. The remainder of Part II deals with cost behavior and cost-volume-profit charts, different kinds of costing systems (job, process, and variable), and problems in cost determination (prime and overhead).

In Part III, "Financial Analysis for Management Decisions," the focus changes from data gathering to data analysis for specific kinds of decisions: acquisitions, capital expenditures, lease versus buy, make versus buy, pricing, and inventory levels. Part IV, "Measuring Financial Responsibility," begins with an overview of responsibility accounting, and then goes into detail on issues surrounding expense centers (including discretionary expenses), profit centers (including transfer pricing), and investment centers (including ROI).

The concluding Part V, "The Management Control Process—Planning, Budgeting, and Performance Analysis," deals with a host of matters important to the ongoing management of profitability: long-range planning; budgeting; management reports; variance analysis; intracompany performance comparisons; incentive plans; measuring marketing's performance; standard cost controls; physical distribution control; inventory controls; controlling R&D; project management; controlling advertising costs; and controlling administrative costs. This section ends with chapters dealing with control in environments becoming increasingly important in the world of business: service organizations and multinational corporations.

Each chapter of this book ends with a list of Additional Sources of information on that chapter's topic. These added references, most of which were selected by the editors, may either: (1) expand upon a subject which the author appropriately dealt with only briefly; (2) present a perspective or point-of-view which differs somewhat from the author's; (3) provide a more theoretical or academic approach to the subject; or (4) give additional examples of how companies have implemented a concept. For the most part, these additional references appear in books or periodicals whose intended audience is managers, rather than those publications that are aimed more at university researchers. Although each author has approved the list of Additional Sources for his chapter, an author does not necessarily endorse the approaches or viewpoints contained in all of the references for his chapter.

Editing this handbook has been a more difficult and lengthier endeavor than we would have anticipated: Coordinating the work of 45 authors to produce a book that is both authoritative and cohesive involves problems that must number as some power of 45. But the satisfaction to us has also been great. We have learned from our authors, as we know our readers will. Indeed, it is hard to imagine any one person being able to write effectively and credibly all 46 chapters contained herein. So to our 45 authors go our thanks for their conscientiousness, patience, and willingness to share their insights and experience with others.

On behalf of ourselves and the contributing authors, we also wish to express our appreciation to our editorial assistant, Bonnie Bucks, and to our typist, Jill Kruse. The professional and alert manner with which they approached their tasks has saved us many headaches. These two women share our pride in the high quality of this handbook, as well as our relief that it is at last completed.

June 1978   SAM R. GOODMAN
                                                     JAMES S. REECE

Contributing Authors

ANDERSON, ROY A. (Chapter 6*)—Chairman of the Board, Lockheed Aircraft
Corporation

APPLEBY, HARRISON H. (Chapter 39)—Principal, Touche Ross & Company

AXELSON, CHARLES F. (Chapter 36)—Vice President, Chief Financial Officer,
Lawry's Foods, Inc.

BIEDERMAN, HARRY R. (Chapter 6*)—Senior Economic Advisor, Corporate
Planning and Analysis Office, Lockheed Aircraft Corporation

BLATZ, LEO G. (Chapter 2)—Vice President and Controller, The Singer Company

BOARDMAN, LANSDALE (Chapter 3)—Manager, Coopers & Lybrand

BOHNSACK, JOHN F. (Chapter 35)—Manager, Distribution Services, Housewares and Audio Business Division, General Electric Company

BRUHA, GEORGE R. (Chapter 8*)—Manager, Arthur Andersen & Co.

DEAN, JOEL (Chapter 20)—President, Joel Dean Associates, and Professor of
Business Economics, Columbia University

DUDICK, THOMAS S. (Chapters 23, 37, and 40)—Manager, Ernst & Whinney

DUNCAN, IAN D. (Chapters 9 and 19)—doctoral candidate in business administration, University of Western Ontario

ENRIGHT, RICHARD D. (Chapters 10 and 32)—Consultant for Accounting
Problems, Allentown, Pennsylvania

GOERLING, HELMUT K. (Chapters 13 and 31)—President, Davis and Goerling,
Inc.

GOODMAN, SAM R. (Chapter 1)—Executive Vice President—Finance and
Administration, The Baker & Taylor Company, Division of W. R. Grace &
Co.

GRAHAM, ROBERT L. (Chapter 11)—Comptroller and Treasurer, Digital Communications Corporation

---

* Denotes coauthor.

GRAMEN, S. ROBERT (Chapter 8*)—Manager, Arthur Andersen & Co.

HEIMLICH, C. ROGER (Chapter 12*)—Assistant Corporate Controller–Financial Information Programs, Cummins Engine Company, Inc.

HERTZ, DAVID B. (Chapter 16)—Director, McKinsey & Co., Inc.

HINES, PAUL G. (Chapter 45)—Senior Vice President, Corporate Development and Control, E. F. Hutton

JACK, D. MICHAEL (Chapter 12*)—Managerial Accounting Director, Cummins Engine Company, Inc.

JOHNSON, L. W. (Chapter 42)—Manager, Program Control, Aerospace Division, Control Data Corporation

KRAUS, DAVID (Chapter 34)—Principal, McKinsey & Company, Inc.

MCKAY, DONALD N. (Chapter 44)—Director of Budgets and Profit Planning, Phelps Dodge Corporation

MCNESBY, EDWARD J. (Chapter 4)—Manager of Cost Systems, General Foods Corporation

MATHEWS, MURRAY R., JR. (Chapter 30)—Vice President, Control, National Medical Care, Inc.

MINKIN, JEROME M. (Chapter 43)—Director, Operations Planning and Control, Schering Division, Schering-Plough Corporation

MOLZ, PHILIP J. (Chapter 25)—Vice President, Financial Administration International, Abbott International Ltd.

MURDY, J. L. (Chapter 15)—Vice President and Comptroller, Gulf Oil Corporation

MURRAY, LAWRENCE M. (Chapter 28)—Assistant Corporate Controller, Carborundum Company, Europe, Africa, & Middle East Operations.

NIBLOCK, EDWARD G. (Chapter 29*)—deceased; formerly Financial Planner, Xerox Corporation

PERE, ROBERT J. (Chapter 14)—formerly Group Vice President and Group Controller, W. R. Grace & Company

PYHRR, PETER A. (Chapter 24)—Pyhrr Associates, Inc.

RACHLIN, ROBERT (Chapter 27)—Director of Group Operations, American Management Associations

RAY, MARION W., JR. (Chapter 41)—Assistant Treasurer, The Hearst Corporation

SANDALLS, WILLIAM T., JR. (Chapter 29*)—Treasurer, Baybanks, Inc.

SCOTT, GEORGE M. (Chapter 46)—Professor of Accounting, College of Business Administration, The University of Oklahoma

SHANK, JOHN K. (Chapter 29*)—Arthur Young Professor of Accounting, Ohio State University

SOUR, PETER K. (Chapter 38)—Group Controller, Equipment & Transportation, Dravo Corporation, and Vice President, Finance, Union Mechling Corporation

SWALLEY, RICHARD W. (Chapter 5)—Accounting Manager, Firestone Plastics Company

TANZOLA, FRANK J. (Chapter 33)—Senior Vice President and Corporate Controller, U.S. Industries, Inc.

---

* Denotes coauthor.

TURK, JOHN O. (Chapters 17 and 18)—Controller, Dixie/Marathon Division, American Can Company

VENDIG, RICHARD E. (Chapter 26)—Manager, Audit Services Department, S. D. Leidesdorf & Company

WALKER, CHARLES W. (Chapter 22)—Management Consultant, Newsom, Earle & Walker

WEISS, NEIL S. (Chapter 21)—Professor, Graduate School of Business, Pace University

WILSON, RALPH O., JR. (Chapter 7)—Assistant Controller, Dravo Corporation

Contents

Managing the Computer Function: *Computer Managers Need Guidance in Staff Administration. Keeping the Programming under Control. Scheduling for Operations.* Computer People and Their Relations with Others: *Outside Help Is Not an Instant Solution. The Relationship between the Computer Team and General Management.*

Center Manufacturing Overhead. Relating Overhead to Product. Further Considerations: *Degree of Sophistication. Common Overhead Costs. Old and New Facilities. Start-Up and Idle Capacity. Financial Analysis. Methodology Change. Manufacturing Overhead Rate and Unit Cost Misconceptions. Trends.*

The per Unit Problem. Replacement Costing. Synchronous Use Valuation. Capacity Costing. Example 1: Capacity Costing in Asphalt Paving. Exhibit 2: Costing Bank-Teller Services. Summary.

part one

The Broad Role of Controllership

1

The Changing Scope of
the Controller's Function

Sam R. Goodman*

The discussion which follows is an attempt to critically examine the current role of the controller, as well as to contrast this role with that of the treasurer. It is the rare corporation which enjoys the professional relationship of tranquility between the two functions. In fact, sweetness and light are rarely found commodities because of the potential conflicts which exist between the two areas. Nevertheless, each serves a vital purpose, and each position must be carefully analyzed because changes are currently taking place within the financial sphere which call for a searching reexamination of the role of the controller and of his or her colleague, the treasurer. In order to best understand the ramifications of the changes which are taking place, it is best to view them in the light of the total financial organization.

THE GROWTH OF A BUSINESS

Whether a business is a "one-person show" or a large corporation with thousands of owners, its nucleus is money. Finance is the heart of every enterprise—no matter what its size or nature. Every business invests—and reinvests—in plant and equipment, materials, and

---

* Dr. Goodman is Executive Vice President—Finance and Administration of The Baker & Taylor Company, Division of W. R. Grace & Co., New York. This chapter is based on his monograph, *Organizing the Treasurer-Controller Function for Effective Financial Management*, © 1971 by Prentice-Hall, Inc.

services. The "dividends" on the investment are whatever the business has left after it meets expenses and sets aside funds for reinvestment. If earnings are high enough, the corporation shares its earnings with the stockholders who have invested in the company. The sole proprietor retains all profits as a personal dividend for risking time, energy, and capital in the enterprise.

The proprietorship and the giant corporation each have money problems. Both must base their operating plans on financial considerations. Each business defines its goals in financial terms and lays plans according to its financial capabilities. Their problems are alike in principle, different only in scale.

The typical business concern was once owned and run by one person. Perhaps this person had a small manufacturing concern, employing a dozen or so people. At first the owner personally handled most financial and accounting duties, as well as the other management activities required by the operation. By tracing the growth of a small business to corporate status, we see the important part finance played in the evolution.

The Crucial First Years

Our hypothetical firm probably had a tough time getting started. The widely held American dream—"to be my own boss"—prompts up to 400,000 individuals to establish their own businesses each year. But the word "establish" is misleading. About 335,000 firms cease operating each year. Some 380,000 other firms change hands.

Not surprisingly, a study by the Small Business Administration shows that a lack of financial acumen is a major cause of business failures. In a carefully selected sample of 81 small enterprises, the SBA found that more than half the firms had an initial capital investment of less than $3,000. The initial investment ranged from $12 to $37,000. According to the SBA report, this wide variation represents two different types of owners:

> . . . there are a smaller number of businessmen, in the traditional sense of the word, who realize that a business needs an adequate capital investment to begin operations. At the other extreme are those with just a few dollars, who decide to go into business either as an alternative to unemployment or in a kind of reckless gambling spirit. These are the people who, knowing nothing about business,

open on a shoestring in the blind hope that they will be able to make a go of it.[1]

Sixty percent of the total invested in the firms initially was equity capital, mainly cash and savings supplied by the owners themselves.

The SBA observed the 81-firm sample closely during the first two years after each business began. Four businesses failed within two months of their openings; 28 more closed at some time during the first year. At the end of two years, 40 of the 81 firms were out of business. Only eight of these closed for nonfinancial reasons. The rest failed either to make money or to manage their financial affairs properly. Bad locations, competition, adverse economic conditions, and other factors kept some of the businesses in the red. Many of the enterprises, however, could have continued with the proper financial management.

The owners made many fatal financial management errors. They overextended themselves in granting credit to customers; they bought in small quantities at high prices; they borrowed too heavily; they began with too little capital; they failed to maintain sufficient working reserves.

The Start of Expansion

But the small manufacturing concern that grew into a big corporation survived the first two years. The original owner obviously had better luck—or knew more about financial management—than the 40 who failed in the SBA sample. No doubt the owner knew the operating side of his or her business equally well.

Suppose the successful firm's growth really began when the owner decided to add a new product to the line. The owner undoubtedly based the decision to begin producing the product on some form of "market research" (but maybe on nothing more than a hunch that the new product would sell). Unless specialized, outside help was sought, the owner used whatever engineering knowledge he or she possessed to design the product.

Adding the new product to the line meant hiring more workers, so the owner put on the "personnel director's" hat. New equipment

---

[1] Kurt B. Mayer and Sidney Goldstein, *The First Two Years: Problems of Small Firm Growth and Survival* (Washington, D.C.: Small Business Administration, 1961), p. 53.

was needed, so the owner negotiated with a local bank for a loan and became the firm's "finance officer."

Even after acquiring several "management" employees, the head person very likely held on to nearly all management authority. To promote the new product, the owner became the "sales promotion director" and supervised the training of new employees. The owner was both the "sales executive" and the firm's only "sales manager" (and sold a little, too). In line with the duties as finance officer, the owner was the "chief accountant," "controller," and "treasurer."

The Developing Need for Management Help

With an expanding business, the owner found it increasingly difficult to find time to really manage the firm. Pressure built up fastest in the finance and accounting area. The new product brought more customers, more sales volume, and more credit problems. Even with the help of a bookkeeper, the "chief accountant" was hard-pressed to keep track of accounts receivable. To get proper sales coverage, the "sales manager" authorized expense accounts for the salespersons, which added to the accounting chores. The new production workers meant more payroll accounting and reporting work, and the additional revenue from sales activities required more attention to tax records. The owner could no longer be "finance officer," "controller," "treasurer," and "chief accountant." To be able to give more time to management, the owner added a credit manager, a payroll clerk or two, and other bookkeepers or accountants.

The Finance Function Grows

The added personnel gave the owner what he or she wanted—for a while. But after a time the owner began to feel that valuable time was lost making routine accounting decisions. The credit manager, the accountants, and even the payroll clerks were coming to the owner constantly for decisions. It was fairly obvious that the "finance department" was experiencing growing pains. To make certain of this diagnosis, the owner drew a chart of the firm's finance function which was something like the organization shown in Exhibit 1.

The owner's suspicions were confirmed. The finance function in the small but growing concern was underorganized. *Everyone reported directly to the owner.* Something had to be done to free the owner from the time-consuming duties that resulted from this inefficient organization. After a great deal of study, the owner named an accounting manager or chief accountant and devised the organizational plan shown in Exhibit 2.

Not a very great change? Not on paper, anyway. But it was a big step to take for a person who had had *all* of the responsibility and authority. More important, the new organizational plan gave the finance function—and the firm—room to grow.

EXHIBIT 1
Original Finance Organization

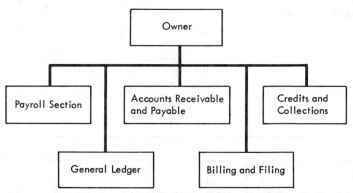

The implications are clear. The owner continued to handle the most important financial matters but leaned heavily on the new chief accountant to take care of more routine matters. Gradually, the accounting and financial duties expanded. New accounting systems were implemented to keep pace with the additional duties. Meanwhile, the business grew larger. Due to the sheer size of the operation, the owner soon found it impossible to make all important financial decisions alone. The chief accountant's help was asked in evaluating investment proposals, and the owner gradually learned to reply on the chief accountant's advice. The expanding business was demanding increased attention in other areas, so the owner made the chief accountant the controller. The new controller was responsible for most financial management and planning. For all practical purposes, the controller replaced the owner as "finance officer."

Of course, for the finance function to grow, the business had to grow. As the owner got out of accounting and controllership activities, more responsibility was delegated to sales and production specialists. To expand sales and production required more capital, and *all* performance is measured in dollars. To pave the way for the firm's overall growth, the finance function first had to take on new responsibilities.

Somewhere along the line, the original owner sold shares of ownership in the business to help finance its expansion. Perhaps it was at this time that the owner first realized the need for a top-level assistant to give advice on financial matters. But maybe it was after

EXHIBIT 2
Growing Finance Organization

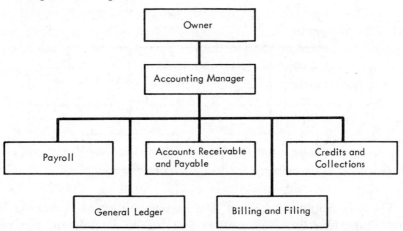

the business was incorporated, *after* the stock offering. Perhaps then the new board of directors, owning a major portion of the newly issued stock, advised the president to begin building a finance organization. Chances are that one of the directors, or another major shareholder, became treasurer or controller.

At any rate, the president retained a controlling interest; he or she may be chairman of the board as well as president. Several vice presidents report to the president (including a vice president for finance). The board of directors helps establish company goals and policy and advises the president on important problems. The business is financially accountable to its shareholders, to the state that authorized its incorporation, and to the Securities and Exchange Commission.

Finance played a major role in bringing the business to its present status, and the new character of the enterprise puts even heavier demands on the finance function.

WITHIN THE FINANCIAL ORGANIZATION

Whether a business is small or large, finance permeates all its activities. Production schedules, sales goals, new product research and development—all have financial aspects. In fact, the fundamental nature of *all* business activities is economic. Money is the foundation of all production and marketing efforts. Finance makes it possible for a proprietor—or a corporation—to make and sell goods or services. This is what makes any business a risk—the fact that there is money to be lost or gained. Finance negotiates with lenders and investors to give the enterprise the money it risks. At the same time it attempts to minimize the risk, to insure a profitable return on the investment.

The Functions of the Finance Department

In corporations (which account for some 85 percent of all business done in this country), the nature of the duties and responsibilities of finance depend largely on the grant of authority given by the board of directors. Under the corporate form of doing business, overall responsibility and authority rest with the board. It delegates this authority to the people charged with managing the day-to-day affairs of the business—the president, treasurer, controller, and other company officers.

Both the board of directors and those associated with the finance activities in a given company are primarily concerned with money. It follows that the finance department generally operates more closely with the board than most other departments. Take the matter of dividend payments to stockholders, for instance. Obviously, finance is directly concerned. But while finance executives may recommend the amount and nature of dividend payments, while their departments may prepare and disburse dividend checks, finance executives do not determine the amount of the payment. In this matter—as in many others—finance executives merely advise the board; it makes the ultimate decision. Similarly, the board decides what percentage of earnings the company shall retain for reinvestment, the size and composition of stock distributions, and so on. It generally authorizes the sale or purchase of capital assets of more than a specified value. In nearly all companies, finance executives merely advise the board on such matters, recommend this course of action or that. In many matters, finance executives have delegated authority from the board to act on their own. If a particular problem is outside their area of responsibility—one for the board of directors to handle—finance executives can only evaluate proposals and make a recommendation to the board. The board then makes the final decision and directs the president, the finance executive, or other company officers to carry it out.

Setting Financial Goals

In most companies, responsibility for financial planning and management belongs to the chief finance officer, who may have the title of vice president for finance, controller, or treasurer. In large companies the task may be divided among several officers but coordinated by the chief financial executive.

With the help of all those in the finance department, financial officers analyze past and present company programs. They define trends in sales volume, production cost, administrative expense, earnings, capital outlay, and return on investment. They interpret these trends in light of their probable effect on company operations and recommend to top management (and to the board of directors) short- and long-range plans based on their studies. They prepare annual operating budgets as well as long-range capital expenditure proposals.

The responsibilities of finance are not confined to analysis of conditions within the company. The company operates within the framework of the general economy. All company financial planning must allow for economic and political events likely to have an impact on company operations. Financial planning includes forecasting the general outlook for the country, for the industry, and for the particular company; it takes into account the probable effect of anticipated political events and government policies and programs. To give a complete picture, finance must supply other officers and the board of directors with an analysis that includes forecasts of labor conditions, wage rates, material costs, general marketing conditions, competitive forces, and technological advances.

Evaluating Alternatives

Working within the limits imposed by the board of directors, finance evaluates the countless investment proposals that come to the attention of top management. In deciding whether to invest in new equipment, buy a new building, or select a new supplier for a critical component, a company is faced with an almost infinite variety of alternatives. It generally tries to make the investments that offer the greatest return.

Suppose the problem is whether or not to replace an expensive piece of production equipment. The machine performs satisfactorily, but new models are capable of turning out more work in the same time with less scrap loss. Downtime has increased on the present equipment, with lost production as a result. But the equipment *is* paid for, and the depreciation charged against it over the years does not approach the cost of the new, more advanced models. On the other hand, the new equipment would mean savings in labor and materials, not to mention reduced downtime and lower maintenance costs.

There's no room for intuition or guess here. The suggestion to replace the machine may have come from the production superintendent, who is primarily interested in increased production. From his or her viewpoint, the proposal looks good. But to evaluate the proposal properly, all the facts must be translated into terms clear to everyone—dollars. What is the total cost to purchase, install, operate, and maintain the new equipment? How does this compare with the cost of operating and maintaining the present machine?

Here is where finance enters the picture. Financial executives know top management's general attitude toward the proposal because they understand the company's financial goals. They convert all aspects of the proposal into their money equivalents and recommend a course of action. In most cases, the choice is clear, because finance makes its decision after studying all possible courses of action. Only then does it make a recommendation. This recommendation takes company policy, available capital, and company objectives into consideration. The recommendation from finance generally answers the all-important question: "Which alternative will yield the best return on the investment?"

Acquiring Capital

Before management gives the go-ahead on an investment proposal, it must be assured that finance can obtain the necessary capital. Where does a company find capital? The answer to this question gives another insight into the broad scope of finance's responsibilities.

Capital generated within the enterprise:

1. Net cash flow from sales less operating costs, dividend payments, and debt payments.
2. Savings in operating expenses (by reducing inventory levels, stepping up production efficiency, or increasing collections).
3. Funds obtained by liquidating company-held assets.

Capital obtained from outside sources:

1. Short- and long-term borrowing.
2. Increasing equity capital by the sale of preferred or common stock.

In fulfilling its most important responsibility—administering the funds used to run the business—finance necessarily gets involved in nearly all company activities. By pinpointing waste in this operation or that, by recommending new methods that result in savings, finance may very well find the funds needed to buy that new machine, start construction on a new plant or warehouse, or expand sales coverage. And if the capital comes from savings in operating costs, the company pays nothing to outsiders for using the funds.

Of course, there are times when a company must go outside for capital. Say the company wants to revamp an entire plant or finance a merger with another firm. It needs immediate capital, and far more than savings in operating costs can produce. Its objective is to obtain the necessary capital at the lowest possible cost. The decision may be left solely to the finance executive, but he or she is more likely to analyze several sources of funds and present management with alternative plans for acquiring the capital—along with a recommendation.

To make a valid recommendation—or to reach a sound decision —finance executives must know the prevailing money market and know where to find funds at the lowest cost; they must also know the financial community and understand how it works. Whether recommending a straight long-term loan or a new stock issue, they must know all the implications—how their recommendation will affect other investment proposals, whether or not it agrees with the firm's tax planning, and what it will do to the existing capital structure.

Financial Control

Once a firm invests in a new machine or process, or acquires a new holding, it must make the investment pay off. In a sense, control is linked to every other finance responsibility. A company can control its expenditures only by planning them in advance; budgeting is a planning measure primarily, but a control and follow-up device as well. Finance "controls" when it questions waste or inefficiency, or when it suggests an improved production method. It may turn up needed capital in the process, but its main purpose is to increase the rate of return on the existing investment.

In nearly every company activity, from the planning stages to completion and beyond, financial management records progress, seeking constant assurance that things are progressing according to plan. Repeated over and again in all operations, control and follow-up become an integral part of each company activity. And by controlling continuing activities, finance helps steer the company toward its overall goals. With internal audits and cost accounting techniques, it appraises results; it suggests ways of improving performance. If necessary, it recommends that top management modify company goals, or change plans to cope with changing economic conditions.

CONTROLLERS' AND TREASURERS' FUNCTIONS

In the following sections, we will consider how the financial functions typically are distributed between the treasurer and the controller. We include the treasurer's roles in this Handbook for two reasons. First, in many companies some of the jobs described below as falling under the treasurer's responsibility are in fact the controller's responsibility. In other words, the treasurer-controller dichotomy in business is not nearly so clear as is, say, the marketing-manufacturing dichotomy. Second, it is important for controllers to have a good working knowledge of what tasks are performed by their financial executive colleague, the treasurer.

Functions of the Treasurer

The treasurer in a business corporation is the financial executive who is essentially responsible for all the functions which are classified under the general heading of "money management." As we have noted, this means that treasurers serve chiefly as the custodian of a corporation's funds. They retain the corporate funds in trust for the benefit of the corporation and disburse funds only when authorized.

In many companies, treasurers serve in other corporate capacities, such as a director, or as a vice president of finance. In smaller companies they also serve as a controller. The position of controller exists primarily among larger companies. The two positions are closely related: the treasurer is responsible for money management activities; the controller serves as chief accountant and financial planner.

Duties Assigned the Treasurer by Bylaws. An examination of the bylaws of many corporations shows a wide variety of functions delegated to the treasurer. This is due to the differences in the general organization of many corporations. The following are the duties usually assigned to the treasurer by the bylaws. This list is comprehensive; in many corporations, some of the powers listed here may be delegated to the controller, secretary, or internal auditor, rather than to the treasurer.

1. Supervising, having custody of, and assuming responsibility for all funds and securities of the corporation.
2. Maintaining bank accounts in designated banks.
3. Making books and records available to any of the directors during business hours.
4. Preparing statements on the company's financial condition for all regular meetings of the directors, and a complete report at the annual meeting of stockholders.
5. Receiving monies due to the corporation.

6. Maintaining records giving a full account of monies personally received and paid for by the corporation.
7. Signing certificates of shares in the capital stock of the company (together with the president or vice president).
8. Signing all checks, bills of exchange, and promissory notes, with such other officer as the board of directors may designate.
9. Advising the corporation on financial matters.
10. Maintaining custody of the stock book, and preparing the dividend payments.
11. Preparing and submitting tax reports.
12. Performing all other duties connected with the office, and any duties that the board of directors may assign.

Duties Assigned the Treasurer by Directors, Committees, and Officers. Bylaw provisions are often brief, and many of the treasurer's duties are delegated by special action of the board of directors or of its committees, and by direction of higher executive officers, such as the president and the chairman of the board. These duties are either of a temporary character, usually terminating in a report to the board, or are of a general nature, representing permanently assigned functions.

Typical functions delegated by special authorization and assignment are investigation for the development of pension plans and group insurance plans; examination of companies in which the corporation contemplates purchasing an interest; arranging for listing the company's securities on the stock exchange; and investigation of the feasibility of stock offerings.

The Treasurer's Major Areas of Responsibility. These include the following:

1. *Provision of capital.* Establishing and executing programs for providing capital needed by the business, including procurement of capital and maintaining required financial arrangements.
2. *Investor relations.* Establishing and maintaining an adequate market for the company's securities and maintaining liaison with investment bankers, financial analysts, and shareholders.
3. *Short-term financing.* Maintaining adequate sources for the company's current borrowing from commercial banks and other lending institutions.

4. *Banking and custody.* Maintaining banking arrangements for receiving, holding, and disbursing the company's monies and securities, plus responsibility for the financial aspects of real estate transactions.

5. *Credits and collections.* Directing credit granting and collection of accounts and supervising arrangements for financing sales, as through time payment and leasing plans.

6. *Investments.* Investing the company's funds as required and establishing and coordinating policies to govern investment in pension funds and similar trusts.

7. *Insurance.* Providing coverage as required.

Of course, most of the details of the day-to-day work of carrying out these responsibilities are delegated to members of the treasurer's staff, with the treasurer concentrating on supervising the staff and on broader financial policy matters. Similarly, many companies have one or more assistant treasurers. In some large corporations, especially where the treasurer performs the function of controller, an assistant treasurer heads up the accounting department.

Functions of the Controller

The controller is the financial executive of a large or medium-sized corporation who combines the responsibilities for accounting, auditing, budgeting, profit planning, performance reporting, tax control, and other corporate activities.

The control that controllers exert is based on the word "control" in the indirect sense of making decisions and controlling action toward enabling the company to make profits. The purest example of the controllership principle in common practice is in budgetary control, which includes all kinds of appraisal and measurement. Strictly speaking, only line managers "control"; the controller is a staff person, except in the role of manager of the controller's office. In fact, the term controller has evolved from "comptroller," which in turn is based on the French noun compte; "account." Thus the title "controller" historically relates to accounting, not to "control."

The Office of Controller. Although relatively new in American corporations, the office of controller continues to increase in importance. Legal statutes recognize the existence of the office of controller. The Securities Act of 1933 provides that the registration statement filed with the Securities and Exchange Commission must be signed by the controller of the issuing corporation or by its principal accounting officer, as well as by its other principal officers.

In some corporations, the office of controller is not an elective one; the controller is employed like any other department head. In other corporations, the board of directors elects the controller, whose duties are outlined in the corporate bylaws. In still other corporations, the office of controller is established by act of the executive committee, and the powers and duties are prescribed by resolution of the committee. Some organizations specify the controller's duties in an order signed by the president.

Duties Assigned the Controller. The controller's duties, as assigned by the bylaws, by resolution, or by executive order, usually require the controller to:

1. Serve as the chief accounting officer in charge of the company's accounting books, accounting records, and forms.
2. Audit all payrolls and vouchers and have them properly certified.
3. Prepare the company's balance sheet, income accounts, and other financial statements and reports, and give the president a complete report covering results of the company's operations during the past quarter and fiscal year to date.
4. Supervise the preparation, compilation, and filing of all reports, statements, statistics, and other data that the law requires or that the company president requests.
5. Receive all reports from agents and company departments that are needed for recording the company's general operations or for directing or supervising its accounts.
6. Maintain general control over the accounting practices of all subsidiary companies.
7. Supervise the enforcement and maintenance of the classification of accounts and any other accounting rules and regulations that any regulatory body prescribes.
8. Endorse for the company any checks or promissory notes for deposit, collector, or transfer.
9. Countersign all checks that the treasurer draws against funds of the company or its subsidiaries, except as otherwise provided by the board.
10. Approve the payment of all vouchers, drafts, and other ac-

counts payable when required by the president or any other persons designated.

11. Countersign all warrants that the treasurer draws for the deposit of securities in the company's safe-deposit boxes or withdrawal therefrom.
12. Appoint the internal auditor and staff and set their salaries.
13. Compose a budget showing the company's future requirements as shown by its accounts and the requisitions of the general manager and other officers.
14. Supervise all records and clerical and office procedures for departments of the company and its subsidiaries.
15. Perform any other duties and have any other powers that the board of directors may occasionally prescribe and that the president may assign.

Other Responsibilities Placed on Controllers. The controller's office is often responsible for tax matters, insurance of corporate property, leases, and office management. In some companies, the controller has charge of all service departments such as telephone, messenger service, janitors, filing, mailing, and similar matters.

The controller frequently serves on various committees such as the finance committee, investments committee, pension board, budget committee, insurance committee, and special committees of various kinds.

The functions of the controller cover a broad field and relate to the activities of all departments, including the treasurer's department. Primarily the controller wields a check on disbursements and receipts of the treasurer. The controller may approve vouchers before payment, and frequently prescribes the methods for keeping accounts in the treasurer's office.

The controller performs a quasi-official duty in supplying the president or the treasurer with statistical data drawn from the accounting records and from other sources, as a basis for current or future financing of the corporation. Included also as controllership activities are the application of electronic data processing to accounting systems and procedures, and the installation and coordination of paperwork flow.

Controllers sometimes act in an advisory capacity, with their recommendations carried out by the executives in charge of the departments concerned. Controllers may recommend accounting procedures for various branches, with implementation left to each branch manager. They frequently cooperate with the sales manager in compiling data for the production budget. They usually work with the factory superintendent or sales executive, as appropriate, to see that purchases remain as low as possible, consistent with production or sales requirements.

Assistant Controller. The assistant controller is charged with assisting the controller in special areas. The qualifications of the assistant controller should supplement those of the controller. If a controller's chief training is in accounting, the assistant should be qualified in cost standards, statistics, budgets, or other areas requiring special experience.

Many companies have more than one assistant controller. A company with two assistant controllers may put one in charge of general accounts and budgetary procedures and the other in charge of cost accounting. A company with three assistant controllers may delegate accounts and accounting methods to one, standards and statistics to another, and budgeting and forecasting to the third.

An assistant controller, in turn, delegates responsibility to supervisors for a certain amount of the routine work. The aim is to relieve the controller of as much detail as possible by apportioning much of the work among subordinates. This leaves the controller free to concentrate on procedures and policy matters.

NEW DIRECTIONS FOR FINANCIAL MANAGEMENT

During the last ten years, profound changes have taken place which represent a basic switch in management thinking relative to the role of the financial function. Problems are becoming more and more complex; and, moreover, the ramifications of these problems are so potentially severe as to tax the imagination of a conventional treasurer and controller. We find, for example, that it is extremely difficult to try any longer to discern a distinct boundary in the jobs of various executives. It is not uncommon today for controllers to participate in data processing or in management information systems design. Because finance is becoming recognized as such a major decision function in business, it is also much more common to see senior officers of companies originate from within the ranks of the financial function.

One of the major reasons for this is that financial officers have developed during their careers degrees of judgment which have been tempered by discipline and objectivity. The field of accounting and finance, for example, is no longer the staid, well-defined area which it was once thought to be. Accounting rules are changing almost daily. Financial instruments used to raise capital are being innovated almost as rapidly. Both the controller and the treasurer are being called upon to render economic judgment as well as custodial financial judgment.

Many more complexities are being generated by changes in current tax laws, and these complexities are of such magnitude that it must strain the abilities of the financial officer responsible for tax procedures. Changes in Internal Revenue rulings, for example, in the areas of capitalization versus expense for capital projects, are changing almost daily, and what was once an accepted rule of thumb may no longer be valid in today's changing tax environment. For example, the revenue service is much more stringent about what portion of a capital project may be expensed for tax purposes.

New problems which have been created by the social demands of society upon the corporation can change the nature and motivations of many of our corporate actions. Pollution control, for example, may strain the patience of a traditional financial executive. Nonproductive capital projects may now be required to be completed; and, moreover, rather than generating a positive cash flow for a corporation, they may, in fact, serve no other purpose than to satisfy a newly created social goal for corporate behavior. In addition, new forms of social legislation such as Medicare and Medicaid are increasing the complexity of the recording of social obligations of companies. In fact, the traditional profit and loss statement as we know it may someday be relegated to a historical wastebasket. It may be necessary and also desirable in the future to have a profit and loss statement based upon profit-oriented operations and a separate profit and loss statement to record the expenses incurred by performing social obligations of the corporation. The two, added together, would comprise the income statement of the overall corporate entity.

Other financial problems have been created by the multiplicity of demands on the financial area for statistical data to be reported to various services. Not only does the Federal Trade Commission require data but the Department of Agriculture, the Department of Commerce, and other various governmental functions have gotten in line for data. In addition to these purely governmental functions, quasi-governmental organizations have also assumed an inviolate role of confidant. The voluntary reporting of data to quasi-governmental and industrial agencies is becoming big business. It is not uncommon for organizations such as The National Industrial Conference Board, the Financial Executives Institute, Lionel Edie & Company, and other meritorious organizations to often request information from financial executives. Because of the nature of relationships which exist between corporations and these organizations, it is often difficult to ignore requests for information, especially when anonymity is promised.

Another aspect which is changing the future direction of the financial function is the increasing involvement of the function in internal decision-making affairs. These affairs may have little to do with finance, per se. They may deal with the complexities of administration of union wage negotiations, the ever-present potentials for mergers and acquisitions, the explosion of internal information to various arms of the corporation, and the upset to traditional thinking which has come about as a result of the revolution that the computer and data input have brought to the corporate sphere. The financial executive is being cast more and more in the light of the executive who is to appraise the probabilities of future occurrences. By the same token, the financial executive is being required less and less to report the historical objectivity of what has happened. It is becoming increasingly true in the field of finance that yesterday is dead; the challenge is to shape tomorrow.

We are becoming increasingly confronted by esoteric concepts such as financial planning through model building and applications of operations research to aspects of accounting and to portfolio management; and, moreover, we are being confronted by a younger executive who has been increasingly impatient with the willingness of traditional financial management to tolerate inactivity and to perpetuate custom.

One of the most crucial decisions that is being faced by the financial manager today is the degree to which the financial area should proceed in mechanization and computerization. It is all too easy to state that the computer is a rapid multiplier, or divisor, or adder; it is more than these things. It is a giant, efficient garbage can. The difference, however, is that this particular garbage can can cost a large amount of money, and it is the rare financial executive who calculates the financial trade-off in transferring traditional manual functions to the garbage can. Computers, per se, create new layers of overhead. Those new layers of overhead in turn create new peripheral expenses such as the paper supplies which must support the machine operation. One should be patently convinced only after having evaluated the financial trade-off in computerization that the movement to computer-based input is necessary at all. One very large company which was instrumental in developing the entire computer concept a generation ago has now turned full circle and is beginning to remove some of its financial programs from the computer because they have found that it is faster and, in some cases, more accurate to do the job manually than it had been doing prior to the changeover.

Lastly, in the field of new directions, the financial executive is becoming increasingly needed in various other operating areas of the company. The discipline of finance as well as the objectivity form a fine base for adventurers into other decision-making functions within a company. It was observed once by Lynn Townsend, the president of the Chrysler Corporation, that no function and no executive was more important than the financial executive. In more recent times, this thought has been echoed by Robert Townsend, the former president of Avis, in his books and in his seminars. The challenge then is to create well-rounded financial executives who are capable of taking off their blinders, of removing the rubber bands from their shirts, and tossing off the green eyeshades and substituting instead the various dresses and mentalities which accompany the all-around executive required for today's environment.

The Changing Role of the Controller

Traditionally, controllership is a type of staff function which in the past has been rather well defined by many organizations. Essentially the function of the position is to maintain some type of system of control and measurement of the historical operations of the business. The word "control," however, does not imply control in the literal sense, because one of the major responsibilities which controllers have in the past shied away from is the very exercise of control in decision making. For the most part they have played shy and permitted various other executive areas in line management to make major decisions. What has been overlooked by traditional controllers is the very fact that because of the unique nature of their position within the corporation, they are in a very special niche to observe and moreover to influence the magnitude and direction of profit.

Controllers, in exercising their responsibility as it has been traditionally defined, must be familiar with details in all facets of the business. The controller is the one special individual in the company who probably has, other than the chief executive officer, the best knowledge of products, manufacturing facilities, pricing, and competitive conditions. It has become increasingly important for controllers to accept responsibility in the specialty areas of data processing and communications equipment. More frequently now controllers are major speakers for corporate policy in representations to governmental agencies, to unions, and to interested professional organizations.

Of all individuals within the firm, the controller should be in the unique position to possess the mentality of appreciating profit response from various functional areas. In this manner, it is natural for the controller to be the most cost-conscious individual within a firm and yet maintain the posture of constructive suggestion. Cost consciousness does not of itself imply miserly, short-term, unconstructive thinking. Cost consciousness can be a dynamic vehicle by which the chief executive officer, with the guidance of the controller, can motivate the balance of the organization to augment the profit planning routine of a company. Cost consciousness and the conservation of resources is not simply a vehicle which should be exercised during times of economic hardship; plans for long-range cost reduction are as much a part of daily corporate activity as are profit planning and budgeting and the measurement and achievement for its goals. Long-range cost reduction is a subject worthy of special attention and should be considered as an equal and worthy partner of profit planning. In fact, one of the most ideal circumstances would be the concurrent use of both a profit plan and a cost-reduction plan for correlative periods of time and the augmentation of each of these plans by a special force appointed by the chief executive officer. Profit planning in a vacuum breeds inefficiency; long-range cost reduction in a vacuum breeds negativism. A combination of constructive profit planning and cost-reduction programming can bring positive results which can motivate and inspire all areas of the company.

In the new role, the controller is being increasingly cast as an internal quantitative consultant who, through various techniques, discipline, and objectivity can assist many other areas of the company to optimize their programs. It is the controller who is in the best position to advise the marketing area of levels of geographic and customer profitability, and the efficiency or inefficiency of media and promotion policy. The controller is also in an ideal position to advise the manufacturing area relative to the efficient use of directly applied manufacturing costs as well as the utilization of manufacturing period expenses.

Controllership, in essence, is on the threshold of the next venture into specialization of that function. It is no longer enough to have a single staff controller, or, in fact, even a division controller. Decision making is largely based upon quantitative input, and all areas of the company must make decisions in order to insure profitability. It is only a matter of time until we will see the creation of new forms of controllership such as a marketing controller, an advertising controller, a manufacturing controller, and a distribution controller. In terms of an analogy, it is not much different from visiting your medical practitioner. It is rare today to be able to enjoy the folksiness of a general medical doctor. Most often as patients we are referred to specialists in certain areas. This same course of events is now evolving for the function of controllership. The controller will, over a period of time, become a specialist who will cross traditional corporate organizational lines and who will participate fully in the decision-making function of individual areas.

The Marketing Controller Concept

The marketing controller concept was a natural evolution in the financial function which recognized the changing nature of the controller's duties. Although the idea was first proposed by Dr. Arnold Corbin of New York University in 1964, it was not until a year later that the Nestlé Company first implemented the idea. Like most changes in organizational concepts, the idea of the marketing controller was not the type of change which could succeed unless it was wholeheartedly accepted by the marketing area. The concept called for financially trained individuals to assist marketing personnel by employing decision theory to such problems as product pricing, promotional evaluation, geographic profitability, and sales force efficiency. Additionally, product life cycle theory was integrated into marketing/financial planning.

Candidates for such positions were recruited from both within Nestlé and from such companies as SCM and Revlon. The particular traits sought in candidates for the position included not only an empathy for the marketing concept but also a lack of rigidity in approach to financial problems. Over a period of time a marketing controller was assigned to the Coffee Marketing Division and subsequently to the remaining product divisions.

One of the unique features of the concept was the establishment of a *dual* reporting authority. The marketing controller reported directly to the general manager of the division *and* to the corporate financial officer. Years earlier, in a study conducted by the then Controllers Institute (now the Financial Executives Institute) which looked into reporting relationships of plant controllers, it was concluded that there is nothing wrong with one person's reporting to two persons *if the two persons "talk to each other."* Indeed, the foundation stone of the concept rests upon such a base. Without such a foundation, I doubt if the concept could survive.

Over time, marketing controllers were also assigned to functional manufacturing and physical distribution areas and met with equal success. As the financial officer for the company, the greatest concern I had was that of well-intentioned corporate people making "motherhood" decisions in a vacuum which might have onerous consequences for the total company. An example of one such decision which I feared is the type exemplified by a physical distribution manager who decides to raise customer service levels from, say, 94 percent to 96 percent. The innocuous, seemingly benefit-minded decision could have disastrous consequences on factory production, inventory levels, cash requirements and receivables. The marketing controller presence allayed some of these concerns.

Concurrently, with the assistance of the Marketing Science Institute in Cambridge, Massachusetts, an investigation into the marketing and financial relationships in selected large consumer-oriented companies was begun. The study was completed in 1967 and concluded that the marketing controller concept was entirely feasible. Since then, companies such as Bristol-Myers, Avon, DuPont, and American Cyanamid have adopted elements of the concept including relevant costs and an ROI approach to solving marketing problems. In addition, the Boston Consulting Group has seized upon the integration of "Product Life Cycles" as an element of marketing planning. Certainly, experience thus far appears to validate the initial optimism for the marketing controller concept.

The New Role of the Treasurer

The other side of the financial coin is that of treasurership. The position was grounded in pure finance, and the basis for the job was the concentration in procuring capital. In addition, the treasurer for the most part has been concerned with cash management and banking relations and sometimes credit and collection and insurance. In most recent times, treasurership has been augmented by increasing attention to a host of activities surrounding the task of pension fund administration.

In essence, if looked upon in the contrasting shadow of staff versus line, it may be said that the treasurer is something more of an operating executive and somewhat less than a staff executive if compared to the controller. The main function of the controller is to report. This is the controller's primary responsibility regardless of whether in the light of the foregoing discussion we agree with this description or not. Treasurers, however, are operating executives in the sense that their main function is not to report something which happened yesterday. Their obligation is day-to-day money management; and as such, they are not concerned with whether a debit equals a credit. Instead, as the guardian of all capital activities, they are designers of the capital structure of firms, and it is their mission to maintain adequate corporate/lending institution relationships which may affect sources of borrowing. One of the major decision areas confronting treasurers in their recent job evolution is the investment of corporate funds, whether they be long term or short term. This type of investment may take the form not only of excess cash to be invested in a recognized market but also in the granting of credit to customers. Credit is every bit as much a marketing tool as may be the media or promotion policy which is exercised by the marketing function. Through the treasurer, installment selling, financing through subsidiaries, questions of foreign exchange, and possibly lease-versus-purchase decisions are all funneled and evaluated.

In the exercise of their duties, it is clear that treasurers are exercising some degree of a public relations function. They need to deal frequently with the financial fraternity. They must also have immediate access to the senior levels of management of a company and must be in a position whereby they can communicate readily to the board of directors. One of the problems that has arisen to compound and confound the evolution of the position of treasurer is the changing motivation of business and the changing methodology of corporate communications. The sophistication of financial reporting and the increasing penetration into corporate activity of various interested parties also makes mandatory the attendance of the treasurer and/or the chief financial officer at such briefings. It is a reasonable question to ask whether the position of the treasurer as it is traditionally structured is sufficient to achieve all of the objectives of corporate communications and the optimization of operating capital. In the evolving status of financial management, it is also probable that corporations in the future will have two treasurers: one to deal with operating problems and the other to deal with problems of communications with interested parties.

Future Evolution of the Controller

If we were to look differently at financial management and examine what part of that function is involved in decision making and what part in the implementation of various decisions, it would become clear that contradictions have entered the picture. Decision making in the area of finance is, for the most part, vested in the chief executive officer of the company and through the chief financial officer and/or the treasurer. Decision implementing activities, however, may be vested in any of the foregoing but also includes the controller. In most recent years controllers are being increasingly called upon to make decisions, also. It is their prerogative, within generally accepted accounting principles, to influence both the magnitude and the direction of profit, within reason. The decision as to corporate policies regarding inventories, expenses versus capitalization, research and development, advertising, and depreciation are all types of decisions which would be within the province of the controller and which may have more of an immediate effect on profit than the overt action of operating line executives.

Organizing the Change

If not properly understood, information technology has the potential of drowning controllers in their own numbers. Change is imminent; change is good; and, further, change is sure to come. If controllers will not adapt to new forms of systems control and data technology, they will become remembered over a long period of time as the financial dinosaurs. In order to survive, they must, in effect, assume the posture of an internal quantitative consultant who will assume the responsibility for the entire process of gathering, processing, reporting, and disseminating all relevant information which is required by the various parties within a corporation. The foregoing is not meant to imply a similarity with the so-called "management information system." I distinguish between the two by the broad scope of executive wisdom and decision-making intuition found in the former; whereas I look upon the latter as a more mechanized function, more easily recognizable in the form of computerized data output than as a process of thinking. I am suggesting that in effect, a *corporate command post* be established to act as the headquarters for all relevant quantitative information within a firm. I am further suggesting that the controller is the logical candidate to serve as the "chief intelligence officer" who will act as the disseminator and creator of information. In effect, what is being suggested is that controllers, in particular, consider their role as that of total corporate data communications. The philosophical essence of the job should be shifted from that of traditional reporting of yesterday to the supplying of pertinent information for estimating tomorrow. In the past, leading financial writers such as Robert Beyer have stated that the controller "is closer to and understands better than perhaps anyone else the entity which is the core of the problems—a system by which information is transmitted to the various management levels." The assignment to the controller of the simple exercise of a management information system is short-changing the magnitude of the problem. The organizational and conceptual change suggested here goes far beyond the scope of such an assignment. The solution to the reorganization problem would probably require a new approach to corporate organization. In its essence, controllers would have to make clear the fact that their responsibility is manifold. Their responsibility for traditional custodial accounting, for cost accounting, for data processing, for budgeting, should all be clearly identified and supplemented by a separate unit which, for want of a better description, might be considered to be *"intelligence gathering and control."*

Rather than accepting the passive historical role which has been

EXHIBIT 3

Position Description for
Controller
Johns-Manville Corporation

The Vice President for Finance delegates responsibility to the Controller as follows:

ACCOUNTING

Accounts

1. To prepare the accounts of the corporations, except such as the Vice President may entrust to other responsibilities.

2. To recommend what accounting can best be performed by the Accounting Department, and what by other responsibilities.

3. To allocate income and expenditures among classifications and responsibilities.

4. To allocate general expense among operating divisions.

Expenditures

5. To verify the propriety of disbursement to be made at Headquarters.

Statements

6. To prepare financial statements for publication in the form prescribed by the President.

7. To prepare such detailed statements of the transactions and properties of the enterprises as will assist others to improve the earnings of the enterprises.

8. To recommend the nature of the published financial statements of the corporations.

Relations with Others

9. To provide for furnishing information to guide and assist personnel engaged in accounting and cost work throughout the enterprises.

10. To observe generally the manner of performance of accounting by other responsibilities, and to make recommendations for needed improvements.

General

11. To pursue such other accounting studies and duties as the Vice President may direct.

ANALYSIS

Financial Appraisal

12. To appraise proposed expenditures, where required and not otherwise provided for, or at the request of the President, Senior Officer or Senior Operating Vice President; and to advise as to their financial desirability.

13. To appraise the financial results of operations and the benefits received from expenditures made in the enterprises and reported thereon.

Financial Methods

14. To prescribe methods of financial analysis and to maintain such manuals of practice as will be useful.

15. To observe the manner of performance of financial analysis by the operating divisions and to recommend needed improvements.

Profit Planning and Budgets

16. To prescribe the methods and procedures to be followed in profit planning and the budgetary control of expenditures.

17. To appraise proposed profit plans for the President, where not otherwise provided for, and to consolidate corporate profit, action and growth plans.

18. To prepare forecasts of earnings, cash and investment for the corporation, and to determine annually the amount of general expense to be charged to each division during the year.

Services to Others

19. To supply financial service and assistance required by the President, and by vice presidents and department managers who are not in an operating division.

Government Business

20. To develop and recommend policies and procedures that will govern the extent to which J-M divulges cost and price information to contractors or agencies of the Federal Government and to provide general assistance, appropriate to a financial responsibility, when requested by division, research and other personnel dealing with these outside parties.

General

21. In accordance with the principles prescribed by the President, to establish the prices at which one division will sell products to another division, subject to the authority of division general managers to establish such prices by agreement.

22. To pursue such other studies or duties relating to financial analysis, profit planning or budgets as the Vice President may direct.

EXHIBIT 4

Position Description for
Controller
P. R. Mallory & Co. Inc.

BASIC FUNCTIONS

The duties of the Controller shall be to maintain adequate records of all assets, liabilities and transactions of the Corporation; to see that adequate audits thereof are currently and regularly made; and, in conjunction with other officers and employees, to initiate and enforce measures and procedures whereby the business of the Corporation shall be conducted with the maximum safety, efficiency and economy. His duties and powers shall extend to all subsidiary corporations, and, so far as the President may deem practicable, to all affiliated corporations.

The Controller is the chief accounting officer of the Company. In addition to his responsibility for maintaining all accounting records, the Controller's duties include the development, analysis, and interpretation of statistical and accounting information to appraise operating results in terms of costs, budgets, policies of operations, trends, and increased profit possibilities.

Has those additional responsibilities and authorities normally associated with an officer of the Corporation.

DUTIES AND RESPONSIBILITIES

1. To initiate, prepare, and issue standard practices relating to accounting policies and cost procedures as are necessary to ensure that adequate accounting records are maintained of all assets, liabilities, and transactions of the Company and that suitable systems are followed in compilation of product, manufacturing, distribution, and administrative costs.

2. To ensure that controls are adequate and current so that corrective action can be taken where necessary at the earliest possible moment.

3. To properly record financial transactions covered by minutes of the meetings of the Board of Directors.

4. Share the responsibility to see that properly qualified men occupy the positions of operating unit Controller.

5. To prepare and interpret financial statements, cost data, and management control reports of the Company. In cooperation with the Vice President–Finance, assist other executives in appraising their activities in terms of financial results, pointing out significant trends in operations as indicated by analysis of the reports; and assist the executives in determining future policies based on applying sound business judgment to the conclusions deduced from such facts.

6. To maintain a continuing internal auditing program.

7. To cooperate with public accountants appointed as auditors in the execution of their program of independent auditing.

8. To establish or approve procedures and methods for taking and costing of all inventories.

9. To review and approve procedures for handling cash and property so as to protect the Company from loss through negligence or dishonesty.

10. To maintain adequate records of authorized appropriations, and check against the appropriations the sums expended pursuant thereto.

11. In conjunction with other officers and department heads, to review and approve budgets covering all divisions and activities of the Company.

12. To coordinate clerical and office methods, records, reports, and procedures throughout the Company and its subsidiaries, and arrange for the development of standards for office and clerical activities, forms, equipment, and supplies for use throughout the Company. Develop clerical cost programs to insure that accounting and related records are maintained at lowest possible expense to the Company and its subsidiaries.

13. To supervise the activities of the Corporate Accounting, Internal Audit, Systems and the Budgetary Control departments.

ORGANIZATION RELATIONSHIPS

1. The Controller reports to the Vice President–Finance.

2. Has a functional relationship through the Vice President–Finance and President to the Presidents or General Managers of the divisions and subsidiaries and through them to the Treasurers/Controllers of those divisions and subsidiaries.

3. Maintains such relationships outside of the Company as are necessary to enhance the Company name and reputation.

traditional with finance, it is suggested that controllers assume a much more vigorous posture in dealing with fellow executives. If approached in a constructive manner, there is no reason why controllers cannot *impel* improved decisions. Their world should include the design and implementation of sales force incentive plans, advice and counsel in pricing, timing, and strategy as well as optimizing media and promotional programs.

One of the last frontiers for the investigation and improvement of cost control within corporate operation is that of physical distribution. The controller is in a unique position to take advantage and fill the void created by the information vacuum in that area. Methodology which will assist in appraising the efficiency and effectiveness of physical distribution operations will close the gap in corporate standards of performance which has existed ever since physical distribution became common a few decades ago. It is forcing a rethinking of traditional corporate organization. It has already created the position of a product manager. Hopefully, in the future it will include the creation of a specialized position which might be called the marketing controller.

Exhibits 3 and 4 illustrate contemporary position descriptions for controllers in well-known large companies.

ADDITIONAL SOURCES

"The Controller: Inflation Gives Him More Clout with Management." *Business Week,* August 15, 1977, p. 84.

Fox, Harold. "The Marketing Controller as Planner." *Managerial Planning,* July–August 1974, p. 33.

Gerstner, Louis V., and Anderson, M. Helen. "The Chief Financial Officer as Activist." *Harvard Business Review,* September–October 1976, p. 100.

Hill, Lawrence W. "The Growth of the Corporate Finance Function." *Financial Executive,* July 1976, p. 38.

Orr, George W. "The President's Job Is Easier." *Management Accounting,* June 1975, p. 25.

Robertson, George C. "The Operating Controller: Quarterback for Business." *Financial Executive,* May 1975, p. 18.

Silverman, Gary W. "Financial Training Rises to the Top." *Financial Executive,* November 1975, p. 32.

The Controller as a Corporate Strategist

Leo G. Blatz*

Corporate Strategy

Before considering the role of the controller as a corporate strategist, it is necessary to define corporate strategy as well as to establish some distinctions whereby corporate strategy differs from such other activities as long-range planning and multiyear budgeting. As the term is used here, corporate strategy can be defined as a planning process wherein the future direction and activity of a business is set forth in rather broad terms. Corporate strategy would also include the setting of corporate goals and objectives. Corporate goals and objectives can be established in conventional financial terms or they can deal with such nonfinancial considerations as market share, product leadership, or corporate image.

This concept of corporate strategy is broader in scope and less specific in terms of tactics than is long-range planning. Long-range planning will typically focus on a period of five years or longer and attempt to formulate plans and programs that will lead to the attainment of objectives that are embodied in corporate strategy.

Multiyear budgeting covers a narrower time span—typically two or three years. Here, the tactical programs of the long-range plan are refined still further and the expected results are set forth in financial terms. At least in the first year of the budget period, finan-

---

* Mr. Blatz is Vice President and Controller, The Singer Company, New York.

cial results are defined rather precisely to provide a reference point against which actual results can be compared.

There are several ways in which companies determine their corporate strategy. It sometimes happens, especially in smaller companies, that corporate strategy evolves from the efforts and experience of one person, usually the owner or chief executive of the business. Some companies use a committee approach for determining corporate strategy. In other companies, corporate strategy may be compiled and formulated by a senior staff member. This planning executive is usually a business generalist who gathers data from various sources both within and without the company and seeks to chart a corporate direction that will be consistent with the overall goals of the enterprise. In any case, the final responsibility for corporate strategy must reside with the chief executive of the enterprise. It is common for corporate strategy to be presented by the chief executive to the board of directors to get their reaction, and —hopefully—their advance support for the chief executive's stewardship of the company's affairs.

The Role of the Controller

Irrespective of how the planning function is organized in a company, the controller has a key role to play. The controller's role can be defined very broadly as providing data for the operation of the planning function.

Here, as in most forms of human endeavor, there is a right way and a wrong way to do it. To be effective, controllers must be part of the management team. This means that they assume a share of the responsibility for running the business, take part in management deliberations, and are parties to key decisions. At no time do controllers assume the attitude of being "noninvolved keepers of the score." It means also that controllers provide information in a constructive manner, being objective at all times. When the inevitable differences of opinion arise, they must avoid taking sides or slanting information.

Too many controllers have fallen into the practice of going to the boss when things are going well, proudly displaying the results and basking in the glow of the boss's pleasure. When things are going badly, these misguided controllers go to the boss with the results and say, "Look what they have done to you." Quite naturally, these actions are resented by the other members of the management team; and these controllers soon find themselves left out of important deliberations. They become less and less informed about what is really going on in the business. Consequently, the quality of financial reporting suffers, their services to other members of the management team are less useful, and they have failed to take their rightful place in the organization.

Data Inputs for Corporate Strategy

There are many kinds of data that the controller can furnish to the planning function. These many kinds of data can be put into two generic categories: evaluating alternatives, and measuring and comparison.

Evaluating Alternatives. The first category is the kind of data that helps to quantify alternatives. Sooner or later in the development of corporate strategy, choices have to be made. One of the key tools for developing corporate strategy is the projecting of financial impact of various alternative strategies. Many companies have found the use of a "corporate model" or other computer-based projection techniques to be a highly useful and timesaving approach to financial projections. It is possible to establish financial criteria for a base period which would represent recent historical data or a forecast that enjoys a high degree of credibility. Against this base period various assumptions can be applied such as rates of sales growth, rates of profit margin, return on assets, return on equity, or just about any ratios that are appropriate to a given situation. The resulting projections will provide an approximate idea of future financial results. The use of several sets of assumptions will also provide a sort of sensitivity analysis to indicate which aspects of a program are more critical or less critical. Once the base period data base is in place, any number of projections and analyses can be accomplished in a fraction of the time needed to do them by manual methods. It is here that the controller makes a vital contribution.

Projecting the impact of alternative strategies can be difficult. There are times when projections must be based on data that are sketchy and incomplete. The sources of data may often be outside the accounting system of the company, and the projections often go beyond conventional methods for budgeting and financial forecasting. It follows that financial data for planning purposes will sometimes be imperfect. However, imperfect data are better than no data. It is part of the controller's job to point out the weaknesses in the information that he or she provides and to spell out the assumptions upon which such information is built, so that the persons using the data can be aware of data limitations and can be guided accordingly.

There may be times when it is desirable to present a range of data showing the best case and the worst case and explaining why such an approach is used. So long as the people who make the decisions are aware of these weaknesses and assumptions, the information is useful.

Financial projections in the planning process are especially valuable when they replace decision making that is intuitive, emotional, or politically motivated. Few managers really want to make such unprofessional decisions. Such decisions usually occur when there is a vacuum of information. This is an indication that the controller has either been excluded from the planning process or for some reason has not made a proper contribution.

Examples of financial projections for planning purposes include the following:

1. In considering a potential acquisition, it is customary to prepare "pro forma" financial statements that will show the financial condition of the proposed new entity. Controllers as corporate strategists go beyond these conventional accounting procedures. They will prepare financial projections to indicate the benefits that may be expected from the proposed merger. These benefits can accrue to the combined enterprise in many ways. Typically, the benefits appear in such areas as combining parallel distribution systems, reduced central expenses, complementary product lines, and so on. The potential benefits can be identified by asking the basic question, "Why do we want to make this acquisition?"

   Having identified the benefits expected from the acquisition, controllers as corporate strategists will prepare a financial quantification. They will carefully explain the assumptions made. They will set forth any weaknesses they feel are inherent in the projections, explaining the reasons for such weaknesses.

2. In the case of divestments, the advantages to the divesting company are usually quite evident, but they should be care-

fully analyzed to be sure that there will be no future surprises in the form of fixed overheads previously absorbed by the divested operation or new expenses that must be incurred to provide services previously performed by the divested operation.

3. In corporate strategies involving product-line changes, the controller can make a unique contribution. The sales and profits from the new product line must be carefully projected. Particular attention should be directed to the cost of advertising campaigns, employee training programs, dealer assistance programs, and other types of expense incident to the introduction of new products.

In evaluating new product-line proposals, a sensitivity analysis is often useful. Such an analysis will show, in financial terms, which will happen if estimates of sales volume or other basic factors are high or low by varying degrees, usually expressed as percentages.

Financial projections connected with product-line strategies should not be limited to the new product line. The effect on existing or discontinued product lines must also be carefully analyzed. The analysis must go beyond the marketing effect. The impact at the manufacturing level should also be considered. Such factors as obsolescence of inventories and tooling, underabsorbed factory overheads, and so on, can have a critical impact on product-line strategies.

Measuring and Comparison.   The second generic category of information which the controller contributes in setting corporate strategy is the more conventional type of financial reporting that uses techniques of measuring and comparison.

This aspect of the controller's role can usually be a product of the company's regular accounting system. It consists of measuring, in financial terms, the results of corporate strategies that have been put into effect. These measured results are compared to expected results, and variations are fed back for analysis and corrective action. Very often this process of measurement, feedback, analysis, and early corrective action can make the difference between failure and success in the implementation of corporate strategy.

It might be thought that this measuring-comparison function is a normal by-product of the company's ongoing control process, but that is not necessarily the case. The results that apply to a given corporate strategy could be spread over a number of divisions, product lines, or profit centers of the company. Conversely, the applicable results could be included in a large reporting segment where they would not be readily apparent. In either case, a certain amount of analysis or combination is needed to bring the subject clearly into focus.

Consider the case of a company that introduces a new product line. The corporate strategy calls for this new product line to be marketed by the company's retail outlets in some market segments and through dealers in other market segments. The product is launched with full advertising and promotional support, but sales results after the first few months are below the projections made when the strategy was developed. An analysis of the sales results compared to planning projections indicates that direct retail sales are slightly better than projected and all of the short-fall is in the dealer channel. A task force is quickly formed, and representatives of the company are dispatched to visit major dealer outlets to try to determine what is the problem. The feedback from these visits reveals one common observation: the dealer salespeople are not pushing the new product. They do not demonstrate it to prospective customers, and many of them appear to be afraid of it. It is obvious that in the organization of the new-product introduction, the training of dealer sales personnel was overlooked. A systematic program of visiting dealer locations and conducting training seminars is quickly organized; and what appears to be a new-product failure is turned into a success through the techniques of measurement, comparison, analysis, and corrective action.

Another example concerns the company whose corporate strategy is to increase market share for a particular product. The controller prepares a projection of the incremental profit that might be expected from various levels of additional sales volume and the results look attractive. But the chief marketing executive objects: "In order to reach those sales levels, I have to have better prices." The head of manufacturing also objects: "I can't produce that kind of volume with our present plant." Obviously, further study is required. The problem is then referred to the manufacturing engineering staff. Upon analyzing the problem, the engineers conclude that the reason for the capacity problem in the factory can be isolated to a series of operations in one department to fabricate parts for a critical assembly.

Having identified the cause of the production problem, the engineers study it further and arrive at a proposed solution. By acquiring more up-to-date equipment for the bottleneck department, production can be increased and the labor cost of the product can be reduced significantly, but a substantial capital investment is required.

Now a new projection is required. The controller factors in the new assumptions of increased production, lower unit labor cost, lower selling price, and additional capital investment. The new projection indicates that the incremental profits will provide a very satisfactory return on the capital investment. It is determined that the company has adequate resources to finance the program, and it is approved.

In due course the new equipment is installed, an aggressive promotion program is initiated, and the marketing people happily report that the corporate objectives as to sales volume and market share have been achieved. But in the company's income statement, the news is not nearly so good. Incremental profits are only a fraction of what was expected.

At this point the comparison phase begins. Sales volume is indeed equal to the projection. Product pricing is in accord with the assumptions. The cost of the promotion campaign did not exceed planning estimates. The manufacturing cost, however, is higher than expected, and the savings in unit labor cost from the new equipment cannot be found.

The manager of the department where the new equipment is located reports that the equipment is working well, but the flow of parts from earlier operations has been so sporadic that the manager hasn't been able to make long enough production runs to realize the labor efficiency that is possible with the new equipment. Representatives of the industrial engineering and material control departments are asked to analyze the problem of parts supply. They conclude that certain operation sequences and shop order quantities that were adequate for the lower levels of output in the past are no longer appropriate.

The correction of these problems is a relatively simple matter once they have been identified through a process of measurement, comparison, analysis, and corrective action.

Controllers' Qualifications for Their Role

Controllers are uniquely qualified for the role of corporate strategists. The execution of their day-to-day responsibilities brings them into contact with every aspect and function of the business. After all, there is virtually nothing that happens in a business that does not have financial consequences; and for controllers to understand the forces behind the financial results, they must have a broad overall familiarity with the operations of the business. This kind of background is extremely valuable to the corporate strategist.

By professional training controllers have the habit of organizing ideas and impressions in an orderly manner and forming logical conclusions. They are inclined to test basic premises and challenge assumptions. They are not likely to take things for granted. Their educational backgrounds must, of course, provide them with a basic understanding of accounting. Additionally, they should have had broad academic exposure to other disciplines of management, such as marketing, data processing, production control, and so forth. The educational background of successful controllers should also include some basic philosophical studies aimed at broadening their intellectual horizons and teaching them to think in a clear, logical, thorough, and disciplined manner.

The succession of job assignments that lead to a controllership position should ideally include exposure to the important functions of the business, such as manufacturing, marketing, engineering, or whatever activities are critical to a particular business. Certainly, a controller's experience should include both the operating side of the enterprise and the staff functions, to provide an understanding of the interaction between these functions that is so essential to a successful company.

Advantages to the Controller

Performing the role of corporate strategists can have significant personal advantages to controllers and to those subordinates who

may participate from time to time. Their knowledge and understanding of the company are necessarily broadened. They will benefit from exposure at the highest level of the corporation, and their
contributions to the success of the enterprise will ultimately be
recognized and rewarded. The same kinds of benefits accrue to the
controller's subordinates as they receive on-the-job training for their
future responsibilities and have the opportunity for their own
talents and efforts to be recognized as they participate in the controller's role as a corporate strategist.

Advantages to the Business

There are some obvious advantages to the business when controllers perform the role of corporate strategists. For all of the reasons set forth earlier, the company will benefit from the direct contributions of the controller. There are also significant indirect
benefits. The effective controller is available to other members of
the management team on an informal consulting basis, and the
value of their contributions is enhanced by the controller's guidance.
If we accept the basic premise that a business exists to provide a
reasonable financial return to its owners, be they shareholders,
partners, or an individual, then everything that is done by the
people who run the business is important to the extent it leads to
the near- or long-term financial return to the owners. Therefore, the
accurate measurement of financial effects before things happen,
while they are happening, and after they have occurred must necessarily be a tremendous advantage to the success of the enterprise.

In Summary

Controllers have a key role to play in the development and implementation of corporate strategy. They provide information that
is both basic to the formulation of sound corporate strategy and
essential to its successful implementation. In many ways they are
uniquely qualified for this role. In the development and implementation of corporate strategy, as in other forms of endeavor,
success leads to rewards. Thus, significant benefits will accrue from
the controller's role as a corporate strategist—benefits to the controller, to the controller's associates, and to the business.

ADDITIONAL SOURCES

Andrews, Kenneth. *The Concept of Corporate Strategy.* Homewood, Ill.: Dow Jones-Irwin, 1971.

Ansoff, H. Igor. *Corporate Strategy.* New York: McGraw-Hill, Inc., 1965.

———, ed. *Business Strategy.* New York: Penguin Books, Inc., 1969.

Christensen, C. Roland; Berg, Norman A.; and Salter, Malcolm S. *Policy Formulation and Administration.* 7th ed. Homewood, Ill.: Richard D. Irwin, Inc., 1976.

Gilmore, Frank F. "Formulating Strategies in Smaller Companies." *Harvard Business Review,* May–June 1971, p. 71.

Haner, F. T. *Business Policy, Planning, and Strategy.* Cambridge, Mass.: Winthrop Publishers, Inc., 1976.

Mintzberg, Henry. "Strategy-Making in Three Modes." *California Management Review,* Winter 1973, p. 44.

Newman, William H., and Logan, James P. *Strategy, Policy, and Central Management.* 7th ed. Cincinnati: South-Western Publishing Co., 1976.

Uyterhoeven, Hugo E. R.; Ackerman, Robert W.; and Rosenblum, John W. *Strategy and Organization: Text and Cases in General Management.* Rev. ed. Homewood, Ill.: Richard D. Irwin, Inc., 1977.

The Controller and
the Business Computer

Lansdale Boardman*

In recent years there has been a significant split of opinion between those controllers who have made the company's computer function an important part of their responsibilities and those who have regarded this EDP area as far too technical for a member of general management. This author believes strongly that the controller must be involved significantly in the company's management controls over the use of business computers. This statement applies equally where an EDP function reports directly to the controller and where he or she is an active member of a committee which guides it.

The point basically is that certain very important controllership responsibilities are carried out through substantial reliance on the computer. Much of the routine of cost and financial measuring and reporting to management is performed through computer processing of figures and printing of reports. Much of the detail supporting financial analyses for management decision purposes is also obtained by EDP procedures.

Controllers cannot be satisfied that these computer-produced figures are dependable unless they have solid knowledge that EDP goals and actual practices are well conceived. Equally, controllers cannot be satisfied that the EDP costs chargeable to their function are under adequate control unless they have assured themselves that the economics of the computer function make good sense.

These comments are far from revolutionary, but their importance

---

* Mr. Boardman is a Manager in Coopers & Lybrand's New York office.

is immense because of the demonstrated ability of the computer to trap management into situations leading to expensive and painful failures. Management must delegate all the many details of EDP work to appropriate professionals, but the "horror stories" which we have all heard are evidence that it is easy to confuse proper delegation of the handling of details with a complete management abdication of responsibility.

How the Controller Can Add Outside Judgment to EDP Management

Controllers obviously will not get into data processing lingo such as "bytes," "nanoseconds," "program loops," and "relocatable libraries," but they must stay involved in basic policy development and revision.

Electronic data processing is an area where immense improvements in some office functions have permitted the EDP professionals to sell some company managements the "romance" of easy and rapid improvements in corporate information. The controller must grasp the responsibility for warning all members of the decision-making team that oversimplification is especially easy and tempting in the computer world. A typical example of this is the presentation to the company board of directors of a new random-access inventory system. An outline of such a system is briefer and easier to understand than an outline of a sequentially updated inventory system—even the terminology is cleaner. But the actual details of designing and installing the random-access system are substantially more complex. Unless the company's top EDP professional is unusually conservative, it is likely to be the controller's task to get the unpleasant details out on the table, so that longer installation schedules and increased costs can be faced and valued in relation to the real benefits of the random-access procedures.

A painful aspect of the whole subject of computerization, from the point of view of the controller, is that it appears as if the entire subject is in a state of extremely fluid change. The fact is that significant changes are occurring only in some special areas—for example, telecommunications—where systems being designed currently for installation 18 months hence show important differences from advanced systems already in use a couple of years ago. In most areas of equipment and of systems design, the changes are evolutionary, so that newer facilities are producing more and better results, rather than producing a whole new environment (although your friendly equipment salesperson may feel there is great economic pressure to persuade you that each new device is a major revolution). Even the minicomputers are changing our approaches significantly only in the area of programming, but they are not eliminating the need for documentation, backup files, and control totals—all of which are old computer problems.

The point to be emphasized here is that the business judgment areas are not greatly in flux. In order to exercise a steadying hand on the work of the EDP people, the controller does not have to embrace a multitude of new concepts each year. The most important topics in this judgment area are the guidance of feasibility studies (to plan the economic and practical benefits of proposed procedures) and the supervision of project controls (to be sure that a given implementation effort does not get away from its targets for time, cost, and effectiveness). The basic principles have not really changed in the last ten years, and the discussion of these two subjects later in this chapter will detail the importance of the controller's contribution to the thought processes of the EDP professionals.

The controller's guidance to the data processing people can be very constructive in showing them how to create policies which avoid the errors which others have made repeatedly. Much of this chapter is essentially devoted to discussion of what might be called "standard" mistakes—inappropriate staffing, insufficient controls, underestimation of the complexity of problems, ineffective communication with top management—to name a few. Furthermore the controller can get at the truth in such areas without knowing complete details of the peculiarities of application of EDP procedures to the industry's specific needs. Experience can be cited showing, for example, that the same type of guidance improved the company operations in two widely separate industries—a suburban newspaper and a fabricator of steel furniture—by developing improved middle-management communication to accelerate the issuance of data processing reports.

A Word about the Basics

Before a discussion is launched covering the specifics of the guidance the controller should give to the computer professionals, a brief survey is needed of the basics of the business computer world

—primarily to contradict some common misconceptions. The worst misunderstanding is the common idea that equipment is the pre-eminent consideration. When the subject of EDP arises, your friends ask you what kind of equipment your company uses. They do not ask the truly basic question, which is what kind of systems concept or approach your company uses to get results from the equipment.

The systems structure is not the tangible identification of tapes or disks or card sizes. Rather, it is the intangibles, such as the determination of what information is included in each of the important files used. It is the flow of data through the whole man-machine system—branches, warehouses, clerical functions, computer checking, manual correction of errors rejected, computer posting to master files, computer resequencing, computer calculations, computer report printing, report distribution, user reaction to reports, and so on. It is the whole concept of what to do with various kinds of exceptions, which may be kicked out of the computer process for manual handling or may be specially handled by the computer process. It is the whole concept of the reporting cycle, which may vary according to the different types of information the system is handling—monthly, weekly, daily, or "real time." It is the whole structure of product codes, customer codes, employee codes, and so forth, and the ways in which they have been designed to group appropriate classes of transactions.

The function of programming also is often misunderstood by business executives, as it relates to the whole scheme of things. People often speak to me about "the program," as if there were only one important program in a given business system. In a moderate-sized business system there are dozens of programs, and in a large system there are hundreds. For example, a payroll system is not just a program to figure pay and write checks. There is probably a program to check the incoming attendance hours data for errors, another program to calculate straight-time, overtime, and gross pay, another to determine or select deductions and determine net pay, another to write the checks and stubs, another to summarize labor distribution (or perhaps a large group of such reports), another for labor productivity or efficiency, another to report dues deductions to the union, another to put raises and other changes on the master file, and still others for quarterly and annual tax reports. The list can become very long if there are various classes of employee and various types of operation at different plants.

People often think that solving a problem starts with talking to a programmer. A program cannot be effectively written until system design work has been thought through carefully. This has to include appropriate consideration of the limitations and problems of the groups who are supplying data which are used by a program, and appropriate study of the needs of departments who use the results produced by a program. Design also includes working out the answers to technical questions concerned with the arrangement of data within each record in a file, and concerned with the sequence of records in a file, and sometimes concerned with machine process-time limitations (so that the wrong programming approach will not cause the job to require excessive hours), and sometimes concerned with special problems, such as machine halts to be required when improper conditions are found in the data. Thus, problem-solving starts with investigation by a systems analyst, whose personal qualifications will be discussed later.

The controller does not need to achieve a detailed understanding of a vast amount of technical information about computers in order to exercise valuable judgment. In the area of equipment, a few paragraphs will review all that is required. Each paragraph is related to the diagram in Exhibit 1.

EXHIBIT 1
Typical Computer Equipment Related to Operator's Duties

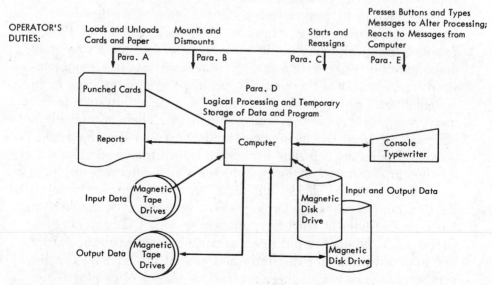

Note: Paragraph references are to the accompanying text describing the basics.

A.   Data are carried into the computer and out again by "peripherals." Card readers accept data in the form of patterns of punched holes in cards. Similar readers handle punched paper tape. There are punches to prepare corresponding forms of output data. Reports are put out on paper by printers.

B.   More voluminous data are "read into" the equipment or "written out" by magnetic tape drives, working with patterns of magnetized dots which represent characters and numbers to the machine. When information is posted to a magnetic tape file, the latest master file is read into the computer, and the new information is used to produce revised or updated records which are then written out on a new tape file. This leaves the content of the previous file unchanged.

C.   Voluminous data may also be handled on magnetic disk files. The computer can get information from a disk by reading records in sequence from the beginning to the end, as is necessary with magnetic tape, or it can be directed to determine where the record is for a specific product or customer, so that the data can be referenced directly. It is important to note that when a disk master file is updated by certain procedures, the previous status of the record is changed directly, unlike the techniques used with magnetic tape.

D.   The "central processing unit" (CPU) and the internal "core" memory are used together for temporary storage of information and processing of it in accordance with arithmetic and logical steps directed by the program also temporarily stored in the core memory.

E.   Operators are "paraprofessionals" who have precise knowledge in a few specialized areas but are not expected to have more than a general appreciation of programming and of system design. They load cards into the reader and mount and dismount tapes and disks when directed by written operator instructions. They react to messages typed by the computer console typewriter. They push buttons to start, alter, or interrupt the processing. Their work is outlined across the top of Exhibit 1.

Now that we have covered the need for the controller's concern, and the types of judgment the controller can exercise, and have touched on the nature of the equipment, the remainder of this chapter will cover specific areas where the controller can expect to provide guidance to the EDP professionals—project planning and control, management of the computer function, and relations with other groups in the company and outside.

PROJECT PLANNING AND CONTROL

Computer Projects Can Run Wild

Although controllers will usually find many reasons for having great respect for their company's computer professionals in terms of their knowledge of voluminous technicalities and in terms of their ingenuity in taking advantage of newly developed concepts, they should remember that cases are not too rare where administrative control of EDP situations has been almost completely lost. For example, in one case a sizable securities brokerage firm entered a merger to rescue another firm and got into serious difficulties primarily because the first firm did not increase its physical machine capacity until the last minute. In another instance a large manufacturer implemented excellent new systems on a new generation of computer, but this did not completely eliminate reliance on some continuing use of an older computer system. Recent observations of the shakedown of a substantial new system being installed by a service organization have indicated that last-minute revisions required to make an important program work are causing substantial delays—essentially because the manager was not sufficiently "humble" about the complexity of the system's requirements and the need for rigorous tests of the programs before the target date. Another organization got into continuing difficulties because they chose to be an early user of a new computer without getting adequate assurance of the dependability of the equipment; they spent months trying to live with magnetic tape drives which intermittently suffered variations in motor speed which stretched the magnetic tape, thereby destroying the readability of files.

New projects are always with us in nearly all business computer functions. This is unlike some other areas of business where the installation of a new procedure or a new production line is followed by a few years of routine operations, with only minor changes and refinements. This is not to say that computer people make a whole project out of a relatively simple thing such as changing the social security tax rate in a payroll system. It is to emphasize that computer people and the members of departments using their services are frequently developing major improvements in existing functions, or that computer people are mechanizing the handling of new functions, either to obtain cost savings or to provide better management information. Also there are projects to install a new generation of equipment which appears to handle current work faster or better.

Commercial EDP Projects Differ Vastly from Engineering Jobs

A business computer project is significantly different from a computer project aiming to solve mathematical or engineering problems, and the controller can protect computer people from serious policy errors by assuring that the distinction is understood by management. Since this point has been frequently misunderstood, it warrants some further elaboration. The arithmetic in a business system is nearly always very elementary, whereas scientific problems frequently require higher mathematics procedures; on the other hand, the logic necessary to classify transactions appropriately for business purposes is often extremely complex and studded with complicated exceptions. In many scientific problems, it is entirely possible to eliminate many exceptions simply by identifying them as "bad" readings (of doubtful accuracy) and eliminating them from all computations. In business the computer output is often extremely voluminous—not because of bad design, such as overly detailed reports, but because many checks and invoices must be written to maintain the company's relations with suppliers, employees, and customers, and because fine-detailed information (e.g., cost sheets) is needed for the work of senior clerks and junior levels of management.

The distinction drawn above is valid, but there are times when the waters are muddied by the fact that business use is made of certain special-purpose applications of "scientific" computer procedures. These can appear in economic analyses, perhaps in least squares projections, or in return on investment or discounted cash flow calculations. Also there are times when "management science" or "operations research" studies are used as the basis for special business decisions.

One problem in this area concerns staffing. Because the computer can serve as an extremely powerful calculation tool, management may feel that a person with mathematics or engineering background will be valuable in business computer systems design work. To the extent that mathematics has taught a person to think rigorously, this is fine; but there is real danger that the person who likes mathematics will be impatient with the picayune exceptions that are frequent in business, so that he or she refuses to design the system to handle them.

The other problem in this area is the greater need for controls in business computer applications, the need for both human and automated controls to prevent errors from causing grossly incorrect results. The business system needs the use of input control total procedures, essentially the same as batch tapes used with bookkeeping machine activity. There is need for "input edit" to identify improper items, both the common errors and the unusual ones, much as such transactions are caught and questioned by an experienced senior clerk in a manual system. There is need for thorough planning to discipline the reasonably prompt re-entry of items previously rejected as erroneous. This type of checking and control is less needed in mathematical systems.

Feasibility Studies Can Present Incomplete Results

A study of the practical and economic feasibility of a significant change in a business computer system is necessary to determine the wisdom of committing money and personnel to carrying it out. Obviously, this applies equally to the addition to the system of a new application or function, or to the substitution of new equipment. It is only in the case of a minor change in a program that work should be authorized on the basis of a less formal analysis of the practicality of the idea, plus a mere intuitive feel for the economic effects.

The area where the controller should be deeply interested is the formal feasibility study, because it is typically insufficiently researched and often presents underestimated costs. The impact on future activity in the controller's area can be immense if an incomplete system is installed in such a way as to interfere with good operating procedures. By the same token, the possible cost overruns for systems design and programming talent or for additional equipment can be substantial, whether they are incurred in a crash effort to rescue a poorly designed system or merely represent the differential between realistic costs and originally overoptimistic budgets.

A good feasibility study should start with an amount of fact-finding which is surprising (in its range and detail) to those who have not had experience in such work. The purpose of the new system or application should be stated in detail, not merely that we intend to do all payroll work, for example, but specification of the different classes of payroll gross calculation to be covered, the different taxing authorities for whom deductions must be processed, the whole range of other deductions which must be handled, the exceptions which must be flagged, the reports which are required for financial purposes, for cost purposes, and for regulatory submission. The difficulty and cost of a job cannot be reasonably appraised on the basis of a general statement of scope. A computer analyst needs a detailed written list of "requirements" before a plan of action can be set up that is of appropriate magnitude.

The fact-finding must also include comprehensive figures on the volumes of data to be handled. This means not only the number of records or cases in the master file (e.g., for customers or for products) but also the volumes of transactions of various types which must be handled. In most billing situations these transaction volume figures can vary substantially from season to season, and it is probably necessary to specify the extent of daily peaks—perhaps on Monday or Tuesday when the customers' mail hits the system. In the case of teleprocessing systems there can be substantial peaks on an hourly basis—midmorning activity can be far above the average hourly rate for a whole day.

Lengthly investigation has to be extended to obtain specifics about special problems, such as alternate sources of input to a system. For example, a wire and cable manufacturer had to do careful planning to get rush-order invoices (hand-typed outside of the computer system) properly and promptly included in the various sales analyses. Similarly, the analyst must use determination and imagination to develop a reasonable coverage of all the many kinds of exception which the system must handle. There also has to be assurance that the fact-finding has included substantial contact with the various people who must provide data to the system and with those who must be adequately served by the reports produced. At a domestic copper mine, a real problem was observed when a somewhat theory-oriented systems analyst built a system on the basis of what the analyst knew mine-management people should need, without holding any meaningful exchanges with various members of middle management to determine the impact of special situations unique to the company's orebody and to gain an understanding of the human preferences and limitations of the managers involved.

The controller has an opportunity to protect the data processing function from embarrassment by asking probing questions to see that people have really done their "homework" and have not oversimplified the situation in order to avoid the hard work of devising complex solutions. People are subject to a real temptation to redefine a problem to fit a preconceived solution, that is, a temptation to refuse to admit that certain queer exceptions will occur occasionally, or a temptation to insist that computerization is to be accompanied, for example, by a most unlikely agreement on the part of marketing management that the complex of trade and promotional discounts and district overrides will be simplified. Where an equipment salesperson is trying to offer a computer with a lower rental than the competition, the salesperson is most likely to use this approach in recommending a system design, but it is also quite possible for company systems analysts to fall into the trap.

Certainly controllers can insist that the problem requirements be fully defined. They can refuse to accept broad-brush descriptions of the company's needs. They can point out that if the logical situations and sequences of functions have not been written up, they have not been defined.

Closely related to the problem definition is the creation of a proposed system to develop the required results. This includes a specification of the various computer and manual steps, with estimates of the machine-hours and man-hours involved. The controller will also want to check to make sure that system design activities include identification of alternatives and discussion of their implications. This will likely include studies of schedules, frequency of posting to master files and processing, and size of batches. In many cases this will include consideration of the benefits and of the costs of random-access processing.

Analysis of costs will naturally attract the controller's attention, and the controller will do well to guide middle management toward pessimistic assumptions. The financial appraisal should not start with an accumulation of costs but with a moderately detailed installation schedule, because this is a basic factor, especially in determining the totals of various salary items. These items include the man-months of professionals devoted to a number of tasks: system design, detailed program specification writing, program coding and initial testing, devising synthesized test cases for all possible good and bad situations, analyzing results of such tests and determining what program revisions should be made, creating reference documentation of the EDP group and for the users in other departments, final live tests, conversion of master files from old formats into the new system, and finally, parallel runs and system acceptance. If costs are estimated on a "broad-brush" basis, without such a detailed schedule or plan of action, the total financial provisions can be grossly underestimated.

In recent years there has been increasing opportunity for significant savings through use of equipment purchase, third-party leases, and special financing, as compared with the classic form of direct lease. The controller is particularly qualified to comment on whether these alternatives are fully enough considered.

There are other areas where one should try in any way possible to exercise vigilance to catch omissions in EDP system cost determinations. For example, in a certain small department store, initial planning for an integrated computer system never came properly to grips with the cost of the large number of point-of-sale terminals (i.e., modified cash registers) that would be needed because their sales methods required departmental cashiering (rather than permitting centralized checkout). Similar problems occur when planning is made for data transmission from widely scattered sales offices and warehouses, and the number of peripherals (local devices) is an important financial consideration.

The same kind of omissions of complete thought can cause overstatements of the savings to be achieved by a new system. Initial plans may come up with desirable salary reductions through the transfer of large numbers of clerks to functions elsewhere. Only lengthy analysis will bring out the fact that some of the savings are not realistic. Cases have been seen where some of the billings have to remain typewritten rather than computerized, because of the complexities of foreign trade paperwork. A case was noted in a book publisher's prebilling operation where the function of a group of clerical checkers could not truly be drastically reduced, because in actuality the group was devoting as much time to paper distribution as it was to proofread checking.

Experience has shown that the most painful cost overruns tend to occur in projects where the total timetable is more than nine months to a year. In these big jobs, the controller might do well to provide an especially large cushion for contingencies.

Implementation Requires Continuing Control

The implementation of a project starts out requiring more of the same investigation that was emphasized in the discussion of a feasibility study—more fact-finding, digging deeper, and crystallizing all the petty details that in a manual system are handled by the senior clerks. This includes determining the frequencies of special circumstances, such as nonstandard customer instructions on invoices. In one organization this was far from simple, as frequency percentage estimates from the billing manager, the shipping manager, an order editor, and the sales analysis supervisor ranged from 5 percent to 40 percent; actual sampling had to be used to determine whether to design the system so that this situation would be routine or would be an exception.

Report formats are another area for extended investigation. The feasibility study may have properly determined report content, and draft formats may have been used to gain acceptance by users of the general plan. However, when it comes to getting ready to write programs, the report layouts must be precise and frozen. Each user must be checked to be sure that the user does not have an objection which demonstrates a factor which the system should not omit. Each user must be convinced that the reports are convenient for the user's purposes, so that when the system goes on line there will be cooperation rather than sniping.

The systems analysts must also write detailed specifications covering the logical decisions to be formed in each program, along with associated documentation, such as layouts for records in magnetic tape files and magnetic disk files. Under certain circumstances they will also produce "decision tables" showing in a tabular form that the program action for each possible alternative combination of events has been precisely defined. Clearly this is a technical area, where the controller would not get involved in specifics; but one certainly can check that the fact-finding which leads to this is being done and not brushed off, and that analysts are devoting man-weeks of effort and are developing adequate documentation to assure that all members of the EDP team have access to the necessary facts.

It is almost impossible to overemphasize the need for documentation. Sometimes the worst effects of lack of documentation are primarily felt only after a lapse of years, as in a case where a company's complex program for printing customer statements was not supported by explanatory literature. Later the actual "source program" was physically lost, and the company was completely dependent on copies of the "object program" which could not possibly be altered to meet changing business needs. The only way the organization got out of this situation was by waiting until a transition was made to an entirely new system.

In addition to the report layouts and program specifications discussed above, proper documentation should include charts showing the flow of data from computer function to computer function, and record structure layouts. The format of all these papers is not important, and some variation resulting from personal preferences of the professionals is acceptable. The important need is that the information be comprehensive and correct—precisely correct. The controller may well want to ask for specific assurances that it is checked and double-checked. Even a superficial review may quickly pick up a significant absence of documentation. For example, an outside auditor was reviewing the EDP functions of a moderate-sized plant and asked the EDP manager to lead him through the several volumes of documentation. The auditor noted that the papers through which he was riffling did not mention the accounts receivable function; his inquiry brought the answer, "That's the application we have not yet documented."

The controller should realize that the EDP manager may have to be sold on the need for a large amount of persistence to get good documentation. One cannot just command that the papers be created and expect to receive them in a few weeks. The data processing professionals can generate many good excuses for omitting this work: a revision was so urgent that we did not have time to document it; the programmer on the job is so brilliant that he or she cannot be bothered with petty paperwork; the budget for the job was set without provision for the man-hours of talented people (not clerks) needed; the program was written in COBOL language which has features which can make the assembly list self-explanatory (unless the programmer chooses to omit the necessary captions and notations); and so on.

With their financial backgrounds, controllers may sometimes be rudely surprised by the fact that some EDP people can build a system without any emphasis on controls. A painful example of this was recently seen in a system developed by a computer service bureau for the back-office work of small securities brokers. There was no control relating input transaction cards to the broker submitting them, with the result that when an operator dropped the cards on the floor and mixed them up, some items were posted to the files of the wrong brokers without the bureau being aware of the errors until some of their clients complained bitterly.

Without going through all the details of a system, controllers can assure themselves as to whether there is a general "atmosphere" of control. All input data should come through a control section or desk, with batch totals logged on work sheets or blotters. All output reports should have their totals approved by the control section before release. All adjustment transactions should be funneled through the control desk, since adjustments in an EDP system are like adjustments in a manual system—more likely to have errors than routine transactions. The control clerk is likely to catch duplicate corrections of an error and should also be responsible for assuring that corrections of items previously rejected are resubmitted in a timely manner. Although this may require careful planning of manual and EDP details, it is an important matter; the financial press recently reported that a large company had a "float" of some $5,000,000 of accounts receivable rejected items, where lack of close follow-up was eventually the cause of a large write-off.

In some situations the controller can make an immensely important contribution by assuring that a competent member of each significant user department is a member of the system design and implementation team. The users must understand that they are to provide large amounts of information upon request by the EDP people, and this means man-days of time. More importantly, the users must share in the responsibility for "putting the show on the road." A case was observed of a large system installation in a major bank, where implementation dragged until there was finally an understanding that initiative had to be supplied by users, not merely by the computer team.

Wisdom Is Needed when the Schedule Starts to Slip

Project control has to mean that management has dependable mechanisms for knowing whether the planned implementation is on time or whether the magnitude of delays is known, and also whether the system will actually work. First, let us consider the matter of timeable or schedule. This must be a detailed write-up of jobs or "events" to be completed with specification of man-weeks or man-months of effort required for each and with notation of calendar target dates. The controller will be concerned to assure the company that this plan is based on details and not on intuition, and that the estimates of time reflect personal commitments on the part of the EDP groups and user groups responsible.

Some managers have strong enthusiasms for specific formats for a schedule. A well-annotated Gantt chart or a formal typewritten tabulation will serve. The use of PERT charts or critical path procedures can work well for getting a meeting of minds during the initial planning stage. They can also be an excellent selling tool, because they imply mathematically dependable controls. However, some question can be raised as to whether PERT charts are a convenient tool for necessary follow-up on detailed performance and for rigorous analysis of the impact of schedule slippages as they may occur. The important fundamental is whether the schedule is general or based on detailed facts. In one company the causes of difficulty were pinpointed by the discovery that the very professionally prepared PERT chart was not based on any detailed fabric of facts and responsible agreements.

Project control also includes the use of good judgment in handling situations when there has been schedule slippage—or when slippage is threatened. Computer management may have come up through a career path which primarily afforded programming experience, so that guidance from the controller in the area of project management will be valuable. The controller has likely gained the perspective of experience directly in the control of status of projects in accounting procedure development or special accounting investigations, as well as indirectly in the appraisal of ongoing engineering projects or plant improvement programs in connection with budgetary and financial management duties. (See also Chapter 42.)

Under schedule pressures it is easy for middle management to invert priorities. Cases have been observed where an implementation team under pressure started programming on some "easy" programs before the systems flow was really defined, on the mistaken theory that it was good to get some programming done early even though it might be ill conceived. In one instance the final steps of implementation included creation of a brief formal training course for certain clerical groups with whom the new system would interact closely. When problems made it hard to find the man-hours of systems analyst's time available to create the course, a decision to go ahead anyway with only informal training resulted in a substantially more difficult start-up of the new system. In another case a system included some random-access processing and it was discovered during the last weeks before conversion that this program would take a 30-hour chunk of processing time. Since the conversion date had been promised to all members of top management, the implementation team chose to hold to the planned schedule and hope that their strongest programmer would be able to modify the offending complex program and test it adequately in a month to bring the computer hours down to a manageable level.

If a project is in difficulty, the manager may be tempted to underestimate the cost of completing it, simply because the manager does not wish to have top management cancel it. The controller can bring pressure to assure that any revised estimate is adequately realistic.

The pressures of schedule problems can cause people to decide on shortcuts which cause confusion. In one "horror story" the team handling initial actual runs of a complex financial analysis program learned from the users that under certain conditions the logic of the program was improper. A revision of the program was correctly created, but the previous version was kept on file, and the team thought that they remembered which version applied to which conditions. Because of time pressures, the versions were not identified, and on two occasions ten-hour computer runs were wasted through the use of the wrong version. The technically correct way to handle a problem such as this is not the controller's responsibility. The controller's concern is with keeping some control over the emotional excitement of the installation team and their temptation to make technical changes without keeping formal records. A lesser case of the same problem can arise when an EDP analyst finds that a new problem can be solved by the direct use of an existing program without modification, but without consideration of the simple fact that the report caption printed by the program has nothing to do with the new purpose, leading to confusion on the part of users of the report (who may not get the word that the report title is misleading).

A standard shortcut under pressure is the omission of significant parts of documentation. This occurs very frequently when a systems analyst correctly determines the content of a needed program modification and a programmer creates and tests the modification perfectly; neither person writes up a paragraph describing the change because they have understood each other so clearly that it seems totally unnecessary, "and besides they do not have time for such frills." The standards result of this is that a year later, when job turnover or special assignments have made another analyst and programmer responsible for a further change to meet new company requirements, they start out unaware of the change; when they find that the program somehow no longer is consistent with the original specification, they must engage in what amounts to archaeological research to find out what the program then does.

Other documentation omissions are also a frequent class of shortcut under pressure. There are cases where the precise structure of one file was changed for good reason, but the file layout forms were not amended; at a later date a new program was developed for a special use of the file, and found to be unworkable because it depended on the file being in the original format. A different form of omission concerned a group of well-designed control totals required to tie together a complex group of reports. The control totals served their purpose excellently, except that the absence of reference literature on the proper arithmetic reconciliation of the totals forced all checking to be performed by highly skilled employees, when the job should have been delegated to conscientious clerks using instructions, reference lists, and a few special forms.

On occasion, middle management may decide on a change of the scope of a project in order to meet schedule deadlines, but without reporting the decision to top management. For example, one broker's system for commodity margin accounts absorbed the customers of another house in merger, without providing for the identification of "regulated" as distinct from "nonregulated" accounts, required by government authorities. When the results became obvious, a large amount of clerical and computer work had to be reworked on an overtime basis. This case, like others mentioned before, is not a situation where the controller should be checking out the detailed systems design work; but it is an area where the controller can be checking that the people directly responsible are working with enough time to sit back and rethink their own plans occasionally, and that they are in good communication with the key knowledgeable people in the departments using the results of the computer processes.

A final topic in the area of project control is proper formal reporting to top management on the interim status of each important computer project. One common error in this area is the omission of any reports to management, other than brief verbal reviews. The other common error is the provision for reports which serve to boast of the technical competence of the EDP professionals but do not convey specific details as to targets slipping and corrective actions being taken. The ideal report should be rather spare and brief. In the case of a large financial organization, a key improvement in their previously amorphous implementation controls was the development of status reports which cited significant targets met and targets missed, with condensed comments, and with notation of nearby due dates for top-management decisions which were essential to subsequent steps in the projects.

Quality Control Means Excellent Testing

Sufficient quality control in the area of project management is a subject that deserves special attention. Many of the horror stories of computer problems can be directly ascribed to limited testing of the programs before efforts were made to use a new system with actual data. The controller can protect the company against last-minute crises by asking probing questions in the months before the target date as to whether testing is taken for granted or is a matter for conscientious and rigorous study.

As a starter, one will find that all programmers do some testing. They like to satisfy themselves that the computer actually runs to the "end of job," which means that it gets to the end of all of the input files and that it prints appropriate grand totals. They like to demonstrate that the program repeats the proper page headings at the top of each page of the report with nice neat consecutive page numbers. Unfortunately they do not like to save their test data in a permanent folder, so that a systems analyst can go over it later to see what situations are demonstrated and what cases are not included.

A fundamental rule is that testing should be controlled by a systems analyst, not by the programmer who wrote the program. The programmer will include cases to demonstrate that the program handles the situations which the programmer understood must be expected. A good analyst will put in all the cases which could come up in the data files which the program uses. This can catch situations which the programmer did not understand when the specifications for the program were read, and it may catch situations which were not really covered in the specifications except perhaps by implication.

A well-designed test contains a small number of cases for hypothetical (or "synthetic") products, customers, employees, or shop operations, plus a somewhat larger number of cases for exceptions. It must contain not only normal exceptions but also the rare ones which "cannot happen"—the cases which the clerks are supposed never to permit in the input tickets or cards, and the cases which the programs earlier in the system flow will normally reject (but will not be caught when adjustment items are inserted later in the series of computer runs without benefit of the checking performed by programs early in the flow). The total number of test cases is never in the thousands. It may be only a dozen; more often it is 30 or 60 items; in a very complex situation a test may contain nearly 200 imaginary customers. Volume is not important, as such, since one case can demonstrate a specific result and a duplicate is not needed. In many circumstances, two cases are needed to demonstrate the results in the presence of a given factor and in the absence of it.

Emphasis is needed on careful documentation of a synthetic test. This is to provide systems analysts with an opportunity to rerun a test after a later revision in a previously accepted program. It also permits later reconsideration of the results when an unusual possibility is brought up for discussion. If it is found that the special case is not represented in the test data, it can be added to the test files and the results will be dependable evidence of how the system truly works.

A common form of testing is known as "live testing," the use of a file or files of recent actual transactions to demonstrate that a new or revised program is working properly. Often this requires fewer man-hours of effort to prepare. Certainly it requires less intellectual study. Obviously, it will quickly demonstrate that there is trouble if an exception in the data causes the program to stop in midprocess. Also it is a good way to check on the machine-time requirements of a program—if a test with 10,000 items takes 17 minutes of machine time, a production run with 100,000 items will probably require almost three hours.

Despite the appeal of live testing, the synthetic test has important benefits which the controller may need to emphasize to the systems analysis manager. Each exception in a synthetic test can be easily found and studied. In a live test, it is easy to overlook the fact that a certain exception occurred and was handled wrongly by the machine. Furthermore a live test is not likely to contain every one of the more rare exceptions. For example, if the maintenance department in a plant has different rules for Sunday premium pay from the production departments, the live-test data may not happen to contain both kinds of Sunday work in a given week.

Even if a synthetic test is designed without proper inclusion of one or two surprising exceptions, it will aid the implementation team in cleaning up most of the errors in programs before live tests are run. This can result in large savings of computer time when live tests are run as a reassurance that all procedures are correct. Situations have been seen in a variety of systems where live tests of difficult programs required repeated eight-hour runs of data to clean up successively a group of unrelated errors which had not been seen previously because of lack of rigorous synthetic testing. There are also cases where a good job of synthetic testing is followed by a live test demonstration of an error; the benefit of the synthetic test work here is that it minimizes the hours of study and diagnosis necessary to get at the cause of the error. The systems analyst and the programmer can eliminate from investigation each of the possible causes for which the synthetic data contain a clear demonstration of how the program works, thus localizing the areas of program logic which must be restudied. Obviously, the controller's responsibility is not to audit the tests in detail but to inquire as to whether test documentation is visible and to ask for examples of the ingenuity and diversity of cases therein.

Even after system installation is completely accepted, the benefits of good test documentation continue to accrue. In any system, failures will occur during production operations, and these must be dealt with promptly. Reference to synthetic test results will again eliminate many aspects of a program which do not need to be restudied, so that the team investigating a failure can concentrate their attention on a narrower range of possibilities, such as a new type of transaction, a computer operator error, a bad spot in the physical tape of one of the magnetic tape files, or an error in a "parameter" card which directs a choice between options in a program. Another benefit is the ease of rerunning synthetic tests after a revision has been made in a going system; this can protect against embarrassments, such as a situation where a revision was made correctly in a large jobs-in-process analysis report, but a minor oversight caused the suppression of printing of one column throughout the entire report.

MANAGING THE COMPUTER FUNCTION

Computer Managers Need Guidance in Staff Administration

There are a number of aspects of the routine administration of the management information systems or data processing function where the professional EDP manager may need practical guidance from the controller. This is not to suggest that the controller should insert himself into the daily operations, but it is to recommend that a careful eye be kept on the month-to-month decision making and the evolution of policy.

Staff qualifications is an area where unfortunate policies seem to become accepted. At the higher professional levels, EDP people seem to have high intelligence, good verbal skills, and personal charm—all important and necessary attributes. However, these need to be balanced by other traits. Meticulousness and determination are essential. This is not to say that a top manager needs to personally check all the details, but he must be vehemently eager to pursue the staff to be sure that they are dotting every "i" and crossing every "t"; and he must have an intense awareness that an item that looks like a minor technicality can stop a system completely.

Data processing people need to have a willingness to accept some inconvenience in their work, like working late when deadlines are slipping, or documenting petty and routine facts just as carefully as they attack new and fascinating technological concepts. Management must be careful to avoid hiring people who have a tendency to be "royal" about their professional prerogatives—for example, a strong programmer who rebels against being assigned to write a minor program when less skilled staff members are fully scheduled, or one who resists "program maintenance" work (the revision of old programs) because he or she regards the writing of new programs as more "creative." The same vanity can be found among systems design people; perhaps it explains why they do not get into synthetic test work as often as they should.

Ability to write down the facts crisply is another important trait for effective data processing people. At times one will find employees who literally rebel against documenting programs and changes as concepts are developed, by simply never getting around to writing up the plans. Ability to handle verbal English is far from synonymous with ability to produce clear written English. The use of technical jargon simply makes this problem worse: the use of technical language is in part a matter of pride in ability to juggle esoteric terms; at times, however, it is a matter of inability to use plain English equivalents.

At higher levels of professional work, controllers may find that their guidance is particularly valuable in protecting the company against the hiring or promotion of managers lacking breadth of judgment. If an EDP person has "tunnel vision" and concentrates on the aspects of a project which especially attract his or her attention, factors may be overlooked which should have been included in the development of a course of action. This can occur in relatively obvious situations, like the omission of analysis of computer running time (e.g., when random-access procedures are made part of the solution to a problem), expanding a 10-hour monthly run into a 24-hour process. It can equally appear in more subtle situations such as including in the current system some measures of flexibility so that unexpected future corporate developments can be handled without major upset. A simple example of this would be providing spaces to accept substantial changes in product number patterns which might be needed as a result of future mergers or acquisitions.

Mathematical ability and experience sounds like a valuable qualification, and of course it is where the system design or programming does contain significant use of higher mathematics. However, a great majority of business computer applications contain only simple arithmetic. The problem is that commercial work contains a large number of untidy and very unexpected exceptions, and the scientific mind can impatiently demand that good discipline would eliminate the odd products and queer customers from the work, instead of accepting the need to develop procedures which will not fail when the unusual sales department request comes in.

What may be called the "administrative attitude" is also important in computer work, possibly because the work demands people whose background and training are primarily technically oriented. Since controllers use administrative talents in directing the evolution of practices and policies of substantial groups of clerical employees in and near their own function, they are particularly qualified to guide the approaches of the data processing management. For example, there is the need for "cleaning up" currently when minor roughnessess in procedures are recognized or minor errors are detected, with the attitude of intending to make next month's and next year's operations moderately smoother. Perhaps the best case in point is the perennial problem of improvement of documentation of procedures. If data processing people regard additions to documentation as a major project, they will not get around to them until all other projects are pretty well completed—if ever. They should understand that significant improvement can be achieved by adding a page here, and correcting a page there, as they happen to be important to the work of one week or another.

The people problem of staff morale and staff promotion has its difficulties in EDP as it does elsewhere. Many of the professionals are essentially creative workers, and they are likely to be emotional rather than stolid. Staff mobility can vary surprisingly. There are some employees in operations or in programming who are capable of growing into excellent systems analysts, given the right training assignments and guidance. But there are others who cannot develop the broader judgment needed, or who cannot learn how to communicate effectively with members of other departments who may not normally require skill in explaining their work and needs to others. In this area where decisions can be unfortunately based almost entirely on technical skills, the controller's understanding of people can be a valuable form of guidance.

Keeping the Programming under Control

The application of good judgment in the setting of policies for the management of programming is another area where the controller's attention can pay dividends. This involves the work of systems analysts who define what each program is to accomplish, and the work of programmers who write each program according to the problem definition presented by the analysts. The distinction between the two functions sounds legalistic, but if it is ignored, the organization is likely to find troubles arising.

Fundamentally programmers must be intelligent and meticulous persons. They must be content to spend many hours in solitary work, simply because interruptions break up the complex trains of thought which they must build. Analysts must be persons of similar intelligence who are able to define in writing precisely what is needed. Often they must be able to get the necessary facts by talking with clerical people who know their work well but are unable to conceptualize and verbalize the rules which they use. Analysts have to have the patience, tact, ingenuity, and perseverance to get at the working rules by cross-questioning the clerks about how they handle appropriate specific examples.

If analysts do not do this work thoroughly, programmers find, as they build the structure of program logic, that there are possibilities for which they have not received direction. At this point, they are likely to make assumptions as to what the company wants, but the chances are that assumptions that seem very reasonable to them do not reflect what the company needs. This results in another "computer error," which could have been avoided if supervision had devoted special attention to the completeness of the work of the analyst rather than to the competence of the programmer.

On some occasions it is possible to skirt this problem area by using a programmer-analyst, who has both programming experience and systems analysis abilities. This sounds like a panacea, but it is not. In the first place, programmer-analysts are rather rarely found. In the second place, their work can have weaknesses. Such persons are likely to shortcut the use of proper documentation: they do not feel like writing down the problem definition completely because it is already in their minds as they work out the program. Also it is likely that such workers will find a narrow solution to the company problem because their assignments have not ranged over the whole pattern of the company system, with the result that they are not aware of other aspects of the problem.

While the controller will not wish to get into EDP technicalities, such as the choice of "programming language" or decisions as to whether to solve a problem by writing one complex program or to take it in stages using two programs of moderate difficulty, his ideas about policy for staff qualifications will be valuable. He will also wish to assure himself that EDP supervision is documenting the communication between analyst and programmer. Often a verbal "clarification" by the analyst to the programmer actually is found to be an undocumented change in written specifications.

Estimating the man-days of programming necessary for a moderate revision—or for a whole project—is an area where a good professional can normally come up with pretty dependable figures. However, general management must understand that in specific cases the estimate can be wildly out of line, either because of a misunderstanding of one aspect of the problem or because of simple bad luck. Probably the most important contribution the controller can make is to provide a bias against overoptimistic estimates, which are very likely to be made if the estimator is under some pressure to avoid facing the fact that the problem has significant difficulties.

Programming is a field where relatively high rates of staff turnover are normal. This requires that policies be set which will facilitate program "maintenance" (revisions to handle new company needs, or to correct previously unnoted errors) by employees who did not write the originals. This means that there should be formal "programming standards" controlling matters of nomenclature and format and use of options available in the software provided by the manufacturer. This lends further emphasis to the need for complete documentation, so that a new programmer does not need to reinvent the wheel. Finally, this shows again the importance of preserving test data as demonstration of what the program accomplishes before revision, and as a means of demonstrating that after revision it continues to accomplish what is necessary.

Scheduling for Operations

The scheduling of routine computer operations is surprisingly difficult. Variations in volume of items to be processed are common and often are very large, either from day to day, or from season to season. Delays in submission of the last batch of input transactions can back up related steps in a schedule, although the responsibility may be in the hands of departments completely independent of the computer group. The bad luck of a program failure shortly before the end of a long process run can also affect deadlines badly.

This occurred during preparation of monthly statements for a commodities brokerage operation after seven hours of processing of a job normally requiring eight hours; because of the way the program was written, the entire job had to be run again, adding a full seven hours delay at the time of a schedule peak. Frequent difficulties with schedules can cause EDP supervision to ask top management for additional costly equipment.

Controllers can keep an eye on the reasonability of the whole schedule-planning process. They can improve liaison so that predictions of volume are based on complete facts. They may influence other departments responsible for input paperwork so that the "cutoff" of transactions is handled in a disciplined way. They can ask leading questions about long-running programs to assure that they are protected with "checkpoint restart" procedures, so that recovery after a failure does not require reprocessing of all the files but only rerunning of data from a point shortly before the occurrence of the failure. This procedure can be a protection, regardless of whether the failure of operations was due to an equipment malfunction or due to some rare and unexpected situation in the input data.

COMPUTER PEOPLE AND THEIR RELATIONS WITH OTHERS

It has already been indicated that the controller can improve the effectiveness of the EDP function by aiding liaison with other departments concerned with proposed projects or with everyday operations. Further consideration of these "people problems" is warranted, in the areas of auditing, outside assistance, and other members of general management.

The difference in scope and purpose between the work of internal auditors and of outside auditors is noteworthy in its relationship with EDP. Although both are concerned with some verification of specific data and some review of controls, the outside auditor is interested in areas where errors or potential for errors could significantly affect the published financial statements, where the internal auditor is concerned with the dependability of monthly and weekly reports covering the effectiveness of small parts of the operations of the whole organization for use by middle management as well as senior executives.

Controllers may find that they need to urge internal auditors to gain a detailed understanding of the EDP system. In a large regional commercial bank, members of the internal audit group were competent and aggressive in their coverage of all operational functions except the computer. As is well known, there has been substantial reconsideration of philosophy in the audit of insurance companies (whether by regulatory bodies or by independent accountants), because they had practically excluded the computer functions from their scope. The controller may need to help sell the audit function to the EDP manager so that he or she can understand the auditor's concern with internal controls over the origination and processing of transactions and of changes in reference master files. The controller may also have occasion to push for improvement of internal checks so that there is adequate separation of duties between clerical people, machine operations, and programming, respectively.

Detailed discussion of audit procedures is not appropriate here, since entire volumes have been devoted to the subject of applicability of test decks, computer program packages written by audit firms, and forms of questionnaire for internal control reviews. However, since some practitioners recommend actual audit study of the precise details of individual programs, the controller may wish to discourage undue emphasis on this approach: unless a program is relatively simple, it is not realistic for auditors to believe that they can be certain that they understand every logical detail (especially if fraud is a possibility) even after a full week of desk-checking the list of instructions. Furthermore, it is only possible in rare cases for auditors to keep control of a key program, so that they are certain that the precise logic found therein during review, for example, in August was also the logic in use in March and in November.

Outside Help Is Not an Instant Solution

Many companies have displayed an innocent eagerness to believe that the promised help of an outside organization would cure their computer problems. Most commonly the promises of equipment salespersons are accepted in simple trust. In actual fact, the various representatives of a computer manufacturer can and do give excellent advice, but actual providing of man-weeks of detailed work is rare, unless a special contract has been signed. A company must take the heavy responsibility of making its own computer plans work, and it may be the controller's duty to get this fact across to members of general management who may have played golf with someone whose boasts made it sound easy. A case in point was a suit by a food wholesaler against a major computer manufacturer, citing the confusion and business losses suffered because they believed the salesperson's simple promise that he would make the system work.

The use of consultants is recommended to aid in the formulation of major computer plans or to assist an organization in making an installation which is beyond the range of their experience, with the important proviso that the relationship is defined and followed closely. There must be a plan, well understood by the consultant and by company management, as to target dates, responsibilities assumed by the consultant and by specific company departments, and the scope and limitations of the joint activity. If the situation has not been worked out and crisply specified in writing, the results can be profoundly disappointing. Magazine articles and whole books have been written on the consulting relationship, and they are just as applicable for data processing projects as they are for production control systems or complete management reorganizations.

In recent years a specialized form of outside EDP assistance has been developed which is usually called "facilities management," where a contractor agrees to use his or her own staff to assume full responsibility for computer operations, program maintenance, and even the planning of systems improvements. Like consulting arrangements, this needs good definition of who is responsible for what. There is also a requirement, which the controller is well qualified to fill, that liaison be promoted between company departments who must work with the EDP function and the contractor's employees. If this is not followed, situations will arise from time to time where the responsibility is not well defined and no one has "grabbed the ball." It can be easy for members of middle management to assume that anything related to EDP is up to the contractor.

The use of computer service bureaus for business data processing is a broad and diffuse subject, ranging from the use of a standard "package" of programs for normal payroll work, to the use of special procedures developed only for company use, to the rental of machine time for the processing of company work through company programs. These paragraphs are not intended to touch on the use of service bureaus for mathematical computations. The important generalization is that any service bureau function must be kept under company management and control. The relationship should be initiated only after enough reference checks are made to assure the competence and responsiveness of the service bureau people, because there will be times when the work requires more than routine attention. If the plan involves conversion to a new system at the bureau, special inquiry should be made as to the helpfulness of the bureau personnel during the necessarily difficult periods of such a transition. For the relationship to continue to work properly, it is essential that a member of the company staff be assigned full responsibility for all liaison.

Where the company is using a service bureau package such as payroll, which is generally applicable to many industries, the controller's concerns are simply that his or her people have a general understanding of how the system works and that they maintain excellent control totals for hours, master rates, deductions, and so on. Where the company plans use of a service bureau package developed for the needs of a specific industry, there are important additional considerations: the system is not likely to be flexible to meet the special requirements of any one unique organization; the transactions must be presented in the form that the system demands; any special information needs must be met by manual procedures or by creation of a company EDP system which takes data from the package and reanalyzes it. These limitations in an industry package will almost always be somewhat confining; certainly the controller should be certain that they are carefully appraised before a contract is signed.

If a service bureau is hired to develop and run special computer procedures for the company, the job should be as carefully defined as any implementation discussed earlier, spelling out transaction volumes, exceptions, fundamental logic, schedule limits, controls, and so on. Equally, there is great need for heavy testing before routine runs start; the necessity for this is emphasized by the fact that the service bureau team may be unfamiliar with your industry, and certainly is not accustomed to peculiarities of terminology and practice within the company.

A somewhat simpler relationship with a service bureau arises when the contract is merely to rent computer time either for testing a new system before company equipment is delivered or to handle special or seasonal overloads of work. An important consideration is the competence of the bureau computer operators, and a technical requirement is precise compatibility between bureau equipment and company equipment, so that files and programs can be operated at either location without special attention. Since this type of relationship may be set up with an organization that is not normally acting as a service bureau but is merely renting out idle time of its house equipment, it may be necessary to check as to the availability of adequate desk space for work by company programmers and analysts, if they are revising and debugging programs under circumstances where dependence on messenger service to carry test materials would be cumbersome in the presence of multiple reruns to correct errors or demonstrate expanded concepts.

Controllers should find that their judgment is called for in analyzing the financial and contractual aspects of the service bureau relationships. The expected procedures for billing should be clearly understood; this may include a periodic minimum, and a rate for volume (in items or hours) above the minimum. There should be a means for handling the cost of later revisions in a package, without a complete reopening of the contract. The language should clearly specify who is responsible for the cost of correcting errors or recreating lost data. If the bureau has written programs for the company, there should be no misunderstanding as to who owns them, if the company later decides to bring the function into its own house. A corresponding provision in the case of a package should specify what happens if the bureau goes out of business, so that the company can retrieve its records and can use the package programs to continue vital company functions.

The Relationship between the Computer Team and General Management

Over the years since commercial use of the computer has been accepted, there have been many times when general management assumed that EDP could produce magic overnight. When this is followed by intense pressure on the data processing employees to produce the demanded results, the results have commonly been confusion and gross errors. The basic fact of life is that EDP is very flexible at the time a system is being conceived, but very rigid after the system has been frozen into precise file structures to which all the programs are dovetailed. The simple truth is that if a sales analysis system is designed for use of the company's five-digit product code number, and if the company later acquires a related product line which already has a six-digit product code firmly imbedded in blueprints, catalogs, and customer manuals, it will require a major systems change to bring the new line into the existing computer system.

The controller is in an excellent position to serve as liaison between the computer professionals on the one hand and associates in general management on the other hand. If union negotiations are in process, any discussion of new methods of paying employees or new rules for pension computations should be reviewed by the EDP group before they finally accepted by the negotiating team, so that consideration of the costs will not stop at appraisal of the additional disbursements but will also include the cost of computer system revisions which may be necessary. If new marketing plans are being developed, the computer professionals should be alerted promptly to any need for consideration of revisions in billing or commission procedures which might arise from, for example, new complexities in trade discounts offered. Similar liaison is necessary as changes in manufacturing processes are considered, so that the data processing operation will be able to stay abreast of new procedures affecting cost analysis or inventory management. This is not to suggest that the substance of a major management decision should be changed to make things easier for the computer professionals, but merely to recommend that it is wise to give the EDP people time to get ready for new needs and to give them opportunities to suggest changes in format of information which may make the computer procedure revisions less costly.

The most common problem in areas such as those mentioned is management insistence on tight deadlines for computer changes to meet early company commitments, for example, a new billing procedure required for a sales promotion which has an obvious seasonal deadline. It may seem reasonable to be tough-minded and let the EDP group work some overtime since they are well paid, but that kind of overwork has often caused employee fatigue, leading to poor judgments in technical matters, possibly then leading to serious failures of the data processing system to produce necessary information and paperwork. The controller should be able to anticipate such situations before they become crises, and the controller can also serve as a buffer between the computer groups and the top-management group when their respective needs are in conflict.

Implicit in all of this is the controller's opportunity to promote understanding of EDP by general management—not only the valuable powers of EDP but also its very real limitations. At the same time the controller can promote the ability of the computer professionals to convey their important ideas to management in reasonable business English instead of in technical jargon.

ADDITIONAL SOURCES

Allen, Brandt. "Embezzler's Guide to the Computer." *Harvard Business Review,* July–August 1975, p. 79.

Alter, Steven L. "How Effective Managers Use Information Systems." *Harvard Business Review,* November–December 1976, p. 97.

Axelson, Charles F. "How to Avoid the Pitfalls of Information Systems Development." *Financial Executive,* April 1976, p. 25.

Gibson, Cyrus F., and Nolan, Richard L. "Managing the Four Stages of EDP Growth." *Harvard Business Review,* January–February 1974, p. 76.

Goldstein, Robert C., and Nolan, Richard L. "Personal Privacy versus the Corporate Computer." *Harvard Business Review,* March–April 1975, p. 62.

Lucas, Henry C. *Computer Based Information Systems in Organizations.* Chicago: Science Research Associates, Inc., 1973.

McFarlan, F. Warren; Nolan, Richard L.; and Norton, David P. *Information Systems Administration.* New York: Holt, Rinehart and Winston, Inc., 1973.

————, and Nolan, Richard L., eds. *Information Systems Handbook.* Homewood, Ill.: Dow Jones-Irwin, 1975.

Martin, R. Keith. "The Financial Executive and the Computer: The Continuing Struggle." *Financial Executive,* March 1977, p. 26.

Murdick, Robert G., and Ross, Joel E. *Information Systems for Modern Management.* Englewood Cliffs, N.J.: Prentice-Hall, Inc., 1975.

Sanders, Donald H. *Computers in Business: An Introduction.* New York: McGraw-Hill, Inc., 1975.

Wooldridge, Susan, and London, Keith. *The Computer Survival Handbook.* Boston: Gambit, Inc., 1973.

part two

Cost Systems

4

Basic Cost Concepts and Terminology

Edward J. McNesby*

BASIC COST CONCEPTS

Definition of Cost

Cost is defined as measurement, in monetary terms, of the amount of resources used for some purpose or objective, such as a commercial product[1] offered for general sale or a construction project. Resources include raw materials, packaging materials, labor hours worked, fringe benefits, salaried support staff, purchased supplies and services, and the capital tied up in inventories, land, buildings, and equipment.

Definition of Cost Objective

A cost objective is defined as the purpose for which costs are measured. For example, the manufacture of a unit of product may be a cost objective; the manufacture *and sale* of that unit is another cost objective. Cost objectives can also be organization units; for example, the personnel department can be thought of as a cost objective.

The uses of cost objectives ordinarily fall into two major areas.

---

* Mr. McNesby is Manager of Cost Systems for General Foods Corporation, White Plains.

[1] "Products" is understood to mean either goods or services.

One of these is for the preparation of financial reporting statements for shareholders, the public, the Securities and Exchange Commission, and other regulatory bodies. For example, product cost objectives are needed to value finished goods inventories and to measure the cost of goods sold. The other is management accounting uses: to assist in budgeting operations, to help analyze the performance of responsibility centers, and to help estimate the future costs that should result from many kinds of business decisions.

Distinction between Cost and Expense

Basically, a *cost* is incurred when something is purchased and the Cash or Accounts Payable account is credited. In this context, *purchased* means the acquisition of resources such as materials, labor, or other services in exchange essentially for cash or a promise to pay in kind in the definable future. If the purchase will provide future benefits, the debit is to an asset account. In that sense, assets are *capitalized costs* or *unexpired costs*. On the other hand, if the benefits are received immediately, the debit is to an expense account. Thus, expenses are *expired costs*.

As assets represented by capitalized costs or unexpired costs give up their benefits, they are "written off" or expensed and in that manner are converted to *expired costs*. The mechanism for expensing fixed assets is called *depreciation*. For intangible assets, it is called *amortization*. For natural resources, it is called *depletion*. Those production costs that are capitalized in finished goods inventory expire when a sale is recorded; the expense account is *Cost of Goods Sold*.

The criterion for determining when a cost becomes an expense is the *matching concept*. Under this concept, a cost becomes an expense in the same period in which the cost helped to generate revenues. In other words, revenues and the expenses associated with generating those revenues are matched in the same fiscal time period.

PURPOSES OF HISTORICAL COST INFORMATION

Financial Reporting Statements

Historical cost information provides the base for the dollar amounts that are shown on the balance sheet for inventories of raw materials, work in process, and finished goods, and on the income statement for the cost of goods sold. These amounts must be accurate and must help to present fairly the financial condition of the company being reported. They are subject to review and certification by the firm's public accountants as a fair representation to the public and the shareholders on the published financial condition of the business. The firm's credit standing, stock value, reputation, and enduring viability depend on an unqualified certification of the financial statements.

Historical cost information also is used to prepare annual and quarterly reports for submission to the Securities and Exchange Commission. Firms whose stock is traded on organized securities exchanges, such as the New York Stock Exchange, are required to file Form 10-K each year and Form 10-Q each quarter. These reports usually contain more detail than the firm's annual report to stockholders and its press release of quarterly earnings, respectively.

Historical cost information also is used for reports required to be filed with regulatory bodies other than the Securities and Exchange Commission. The most obvious agency is the Internal Revenue Service and its municipal, county, and state counterparts. Income tax returns filed with these agencies are subject to audit. In order to avoid penalties, it makes good business sense to make sure that costs reflected on the returns are fully supported by historical cost records. Some companies, such as utilities and transportation companies, must also file reports with state and federal regulatory bodies which oversee their operations and are involved in rate setting.

Management Uses

Historical cost information finds its most profitable use in management's selection of the most beneficial of available alternate courses of action. Among these uses are the following:

1. To assist in budgeting for operations, where the past is used as a guide to the future.
2. To help analyze the performance of responsibility centers.
3. To help estimate future costs for many kinds of decisions and analyses, such as:
   a. Pricing decisions.
   b. Make-or-buy decisions and lease-or-buy decisions.
   c. Break-even analysis.

d. Capital budgeting analyses and decisions.
e. Optimization models.

For example, suppose that a firm is considering introducing a new product into the market. Taking into consideration historical costs, the cost of that product must be estimated based on the types and quantities of raw materials or component parts needed, the labor crew size, composition and wage-rate level required, the amount of variable overhead such as power needed to manufacture each unit of product, and the fixed costs to furnish the facilities and staff needed to house, service, and administer the manufacture of the new product. Then the cost estimate can be used to determine a selling price by adding a markup sufficient to maintain or improve on the firm's rate of return on investment.

As another example, consider a firm that is in a growth position. The volume of sales is increasing, and additional production facilities may be desirable. Certain questions must be answered. Should additional production capacity be acquired by investing in the necessary assets and labor force? Or should the facilities be leased? Or should product be arranged for through subcontracting for its manufacture? Where should the additional production volume be generated geographically?

In order to answer these questions, the cost of production must be predetermined for each of the alternate considerations, again using historical costs as an aid in cost estimating. The estimated costs should be segregated between variable costs and fixed costs so that the total cost at various volume levels can be predicted with reasonable accuracy.

Once a course of action has been decided on, the estimated costs on which the decision was based should be converted into standards and budgets. Actual costs resulting from the implementation of the decision then can be compared to the standards and budgets. If this comparison yields significant unfavorable differences, corrective action should be taken promptly either in the form of improved production efficiency, increased selling prices, or some offsetting action in other areas of the business that will halt the unexpected drain on the firm's profits.

DIFFERENT WAYS OF CLASSIFYING COSTS

In practice, cost terminology is used rather imprecisely. In fact, there are several quite different ways to think of costs, each involving a different cost concept and its own terminology. Some of these ways of classifying costs are described below.

By Traceability to a Cost Objective

Direct costs are those that are traceable to, or caused by, a single cost objective. *Indirect costs* are those that are associated with two or more cost objectives jointly. Thus, a plant manager's salary is a direct cost of the plant. If the plant manufactures more than one type of product, the plant manager's salary is an indirect cost of any one of those products. However, if the plant manufactures just one type of product, the plant manager's salary is a direct cost of that product. These examples illustrate the important fact that for the terms "direct" or "indirect" to be meaningful, it must be clear what specific cost objective one has in mind; that is, costs are direct or indirect with respect to specified cost objectives.[2]

By Accounting Treatment of the Cost

Period costs are expensed in the period in which the cost is incurred. *Product costs* (sometimes called inventoriable costs) are the costs of manufactured goods which are capitalized in inventory, and thus are unexpired, until the goods are sold. For audited statements and tax reporting, product costs must be *full manufacturing costs*. The full manufacturing (or "factory") cost of a product is the aggregate of its direct manufacturing costs plus a fair share of its indirect manufacturing costs. Full factory cost also is called *absorption cost*.

Capital costs, which also like product costs are unexpired, are the the costs of plant and equipment which originally are capitalized at the expenditure made for their acquisition, and thereafter are systematically written off or depreciated as the plant and equipment give up their benefits.

By Behavior of the Cost with Respect to Volume

Variable costs are those that tend to increase proportionately with volume, such as raw materials, online direct labor, and the power costs directly associated with running manufacturing equip-

---

[2] In practice, if no cost objective is explicitly stated, "direct" and "indirect" usually refer to manufacture of a unit of product.

ment. *Nonvariable* or *fixed costs* are those that do not vary with volume, such as the plant manager's salary and the depreciation of plant and equipment. *Semivariable costs* are those that vary with volume but not proportionately, such as the salaries of shift supervisors. Semivariable costs can be segregated into their variable and nonvariable components for purposes of profit planning and breakeven analysis, using techniques such as the method of least squares. (See Chapter 6.)

It should be noted that although in practice many people use "direct costs" and "variable costs" as synonyms, these terms in fact relate to quite different cost concepts. This "sloppy" usage probably occurs because most of the direct costs of a product (a ubiquitous cost objective) are variable (increase in total in proportion to volume increases). For example, the term "direct costing systems" is frequently used; but strictly speaking, these should be called "variable costing systems." (See Chapter 13.)

By Time Period for Which Cost Is Computed

Historical costs are those that have been incurred in past periods. *Budgeted costs* are those that are expected to be incurred in future periods, short term and long term. It is useful to be able to express these costs not only in terms of the dollar level for the future period but also in terms of constant dollars by using a selected past period as a constant dollar base, or base period.

By Management Function

Manufacturing costs cover the costs of the range of activities from procurement of materials to the point where plant management relinquishes control of the finished goods. Manufacturing costs include expenditures for materials and supplies; direct, supervisory, and indirect payroll, including related employee fringe benefit costs; depreciation; power; repairs; taxes; and all other expenses incurred on behalf of manufacturing and plant storage operations.

Marketing costs are the costs incurred after the plant management relinquishes control of the finished goods, in distributing, promoting, advertising, and selling those goods to customers. These costs include the operation of distribution warehouses, freight from plant to distribution warehouse and then to customer (if terms are f.o.b. customers), media advertising, trade and consumer promotional offers, and the field sales force.

Administrative costs are those associated with the general management of the firm, and include senior executives such as the president and staff, as well as the staff offices (accounting, legal, personnel, and so on.)

Financial costs are the costs associated with using external sources of funds to finance the firm. Accounting reports the cost of debt funds—that is, interest. At present, financial accounting does not report a cost for equity capital, since this cost is not amenable to precise and purely objective determination. However, some companies do "impute" an equity cost for internal management reports; this cost is combined proportionately with debt cost to arrive at a "weighted-average cost of capital." Interest *income,* in a sense, is a negative financial cost, and is therefore sometimes offset against interest expense in financial reports. In many financial reports, financial costs are "buried" in the "general and administrative" cost caption.

By Degree of Managerial Influence

Costs are accumulated in centers of responsibility, in line with the responsibilities that are assigned to each manager. *Controllable costs,* therefore, are those costs that are subject to significant influence by a responsibility center manager. (The definition of noncontrollable costs is analogous.) Note that "controllability" is not an inherent trait of a cost; the term "controllable" must relate to controllability in a specified responsibility center. For example, a given cost may not be controllable by Manager A but may be controllable by A's immediate superior.

However, all costs are controllable by *some* manager, even though certain costs may be difficult to assign managerial responsibility for. Where these difficulties are encountered, agreement should be reached by the manager affected as to who will carry the ultimate cost responsibility. A prime example concerns maintenance costs. Usually maintenance costs at point of incurrence are collected in a center of responsibility assigned to a maintenance manager. As repair and maintenance work is carried out, usually on job orders originated by production department managers, the maintenance costs are transferred to the production centers on a cost per hour basis plus out-of-pocket maintenance supplies.

An effective way to handle maintenance cost responsibility is to consider preventive maintenance programs as a cost controllable by the maintenance manager, and to treat charged-out repair order costs as a cost controllable by the recipient of the maintenance service.

By Ability to Set the Proper Amount when Budgeting

Committed costs are those *sunk* costs, such as property taxes and depreciation of capital facilities, for which acquisition commitment has already been made and the decision point for avoidance has passed.

Discretionary costs are, first, those of a nonrecurring nature for which final commitments have not yet been made and that consequently can be postponed until future fiscal periods or canceled outright. Examples of this type of discretionary costs include research and development projects, roof repair (if the roof is not leaking), and repaving of parking lots. Second, discretionary costs are those of a normal recurring operating nature that represent functions that are necessary for the operation and maintenance of facilities but can be changed in amount by management decision aimed at improving organizational and methods effectiveness. Examples of this type of cost include support activities such as legal, accounting, and personnel offices. Discretionary costs also are sometimes called *programmed* or *managed costs*. The key concept inherent in these discretionary costs is that it is not possible to "scientifically" determine the *right* amount to spend; rather, the appropriate amount to spend is a matter of judgment.

Engineered costs, on the other hand, are those that *can* be scientifically or mathematically predetermined because a clear, provable input-output relation exists. An example of an engineered cost is direct labor, where a certain number of labor tending hours is required in relationship to the machine's rated output. Similarly, in most instances raw materials usage is an engineered cost.

Specialized Cost Concepts

The term *differential costs*, which are sometimes called *incremental* or *relevant costs*, applies to costs that are different under one set of conditions than they would be under another set of conditions. In the specific case of a consideration involving a proposed change in the volume of output, the differential cost *per unit* of output is essentially the same as what economists call marginal cost (and what accountants call variable cost).

Opportunity cost is the value of the sacrifice (usually expressed in terms of foregone profit) incurred when the choice of one course of action requires that an alternative course of action must be given up. This concept comes into play when some resource is constrained. For example, when a firm is at capacity and chooses to make Product B instead of Product A, the lost contribution margin (variable margin) from Product A is an opportunity cost of the decision to make Product B instead.

DEVELOPMENT OF FULL COST

The *full cost* of a cost objective is a measure of *all* the resources used for that objective. The most common cost objective for which full costs are developed is the manufacturing cost of a product. As for any cost objective, the full cost of a product is the sum of its direct costs and a fair share of its indirect costs. These full costs can be thought of as being "built up" from various cost elements.

Basic Buildup

The most basic elements of the costs of products[3] are called *prime costs*. Prime costs consist of direct materials and the direct labor needed to convert the raw materials to finished products. Identification of these prime costs represents the first basic step in building up full costs.

The next step in cost buildup is to add variable manufacturing overhead to prime costs in order to arrive at variable manufacturing costs.[4] Variable costs are sensitive to the volume of manufacturing activity. They will rise when the volume of production rises and fall when this volume falls. The costs change in proportion to the

---

[3] Again, "products" may be either goods or services. In this section, we treat producing products as the cost objectives. However, the process is essentially the same for determining the full cost of *any* cost objective: Full costs = Direct costs + Fair share of indirect costs.

[4] This assumes that the product's direct material and direct labor costs are variable with volume, which is usually the case.

changes in volume. Variable manufacturing overhead usually includes costs such as electricity used to power production equipment and certain supplies needed on the production lines. (A full explanation of systems focusing on variable costs will be found in Chapter 13).

The final step in the full-cost buildup is to add nonvariable factory overhead to the variable manufacturing costs in order to arrive at *full cost* or "factory door" cost. Full cost also is termed "inventory cost," because generally accepted accounting principles call for inventories to be costed at full cost. Full cost also is called "absorption cost," because it entails "absorbing" all factory overheads onto individual units of product.

In order to aid in establishing a selling price for a product, costs other than manufacturing costs also are allocated to each type of product. These nonmanufacturing costs include costs such as marketing, research and development, and general/administrative costs. For purposes of break-even analysis, nonmanufacturing expenses also are segregated into variable and nonvariable components. Most nonmanufacturing expenses will be found to be nonvariable, but some will tend to vary in proportion to the volume of sales, such as selling commissions, sales discounts, sales returns and allowances, and transit warehousing.

Measurement of Prime Costs

Direct material costs are measured in terms of quantity and price. Quantity measurements involve the determination of how much of each type of material is put into production. There are several ways to do this. The selection of the "right" method takes into consideration the degree of accuracy desired and the attendant administrative and clerical expense. A few of the methods of direct material quantity measurement are: (1) a pallet ticket system; (2) a physical inventory of the quantities of materials on hand at the beginning of the period plus receipts during the period, minus a physical inventory of the quantities of materials on hand at the end of the period; and (3), measuring devices such as controlled scales and flow meters.

The direct material prices that are applied to the quantities used are taken from the books of account and supplementary inventory records. These records usually are designed to calculate the average cost per unit of direct materials that are available for use in production.[5]

Direct labor costs also are measured in terms of quantity and price. Quantity, in this case, is direct labor hours worked. Price is the worker's hourly wage rate. Hours worked are derived from time-cards or other payroll records of hours worked by each employee. This is accompanied by an assignment card, usually maintained by the supervisor, which indicates the number of hours worked on each cost objective. The particular employee's wage rate is taken from the payroll records. Fringe benefit costs per hour should be added to the wage rates, expressed either as a separate rate per hour or as a percentage of wages earned based on hours worked. The fringe benefit rate should be an annual average in order to avoid direct labor cost distortions because of fringe benefit seasonality peaking that could result from such erratic influences as vacation pay, social security contributions, and Christmas bonuses.[6]

Allocation of Indirect Costs

Indirect manufacturing costs, also called "factory overheads," are allocated to products in developing full manufacturing costs. The total indirect manufacturing costs are divided by production volume in order to determine an *overhead* or *burden rate*. The volume used for this purpose should be representative of a normal level of capacity utilization. (See Chapter 11, "Determining 'Normal' Production Volume.")

This assignment of indirect costs to products is done for two purposes. One is to value finished goods inventories at full manufacturing costs in order to comply with generally accepted accounting principles. This is based on the principle that indirect manufacturing costs, as well as prime costs, add value to a manufactured product, and assets are supposed to be valued at "cost." The second purpose is to assure that full consideration is given to recovering all costs, not just direct costs, in setting product selling prices at a

---

[5] The details of costing direct materials and labor differ if a company uses a *standard* cost system rather than an actual cost system. See Chapter 23, "Standard Cost Control for Manufacturing Costs." Chapter 10, "Determining Standard Material and Labor Costs," is also applicable.

[6] Notwithstanding the fact that fringes on direct labor really are a part of direct labor cost, as described here, many companies treat fringes on direct labor as part of factory overhead.

level that should return a satisfactory margin of profit to the firm.

Overhead or burden rates usually are predetermined. This is done by dividing the planned production volume for the year into the annual budget for indirect manufacturing expenses. There are two reasons for using annualized predetermined, or standard, overhead rates rather than actual overhead cost rates each interim period, whether that period is monthly or quarterly. One reason is that it facilitates timeliness in reporting interim results. The other is that it eliminates seasonality in the overhead rate; otherwise, goods produced in a low-volume month would be costed at a higher cost than those in a high-volume month. Product costs in interim periods would be distorted and would represent misleading information for business decisions, particularly those having to do with funding of product promotional activities. Similarly, in a job shop, pricing decisions might be affected, with a tendency to raise prices as volume is falling, perhaps thereby accelerating the volume decline.

In determining the overhead rate, the following steps should be followed:[7]

1. Classify each cost center, or center or responsibility, into one of three categories: production, service, or general. Production cost centers are those that are directly engaged in converting direct materials to finished goods. Service centers exist to provide services to the various factory departments, including production centers. Examples of service cost centers are maintenance, plant engineering, quality control, and production planning and scheduling. Two other service centers usually defined are "occupancy," which is not a physical department but just an account in which costs such as rent and heat are accumulated, and "general," which includes the plant superintendent's office and perhaps other plant administrative functions.

2. Identify the manufacturing overhead costs directly incurred by each cost center, where possible. For example, depreciation on equipment in Department X can be identified directly with that department. (This is an example of a cost which is *indirect* with respect to products, and is therefore called "overhead," but is *direct* with respect to a given department.)

3. To the extent that service centers provide services directly to

---

[7] For details, see Chapter 12, "Manufacturing Overhead Allocations."

production centers, assign the service center costs to each production cost center serviced based on services specifically scheduled to be rendered.

4. Make direct assignments of general cost center costs to production centers wherever possible.

5. Allocate all indirect costs still remaining in the service and general cost centers on whatever basis seems to make the most sense. In determining such bases, managers of these service centers should be consulted. However, it probably serves no useful purpose to attempt to reach a maximum degree of precision because allocations are necessarily arbitrary. An alternate method is to allocate the indirect costs to products on some "common denominator" basis such as variable manufacturing conversion cost expected to be incurred at planned volume levels for each product. This latter method may be preferable if a plant contains a great variety of products and manufacturing operations.

6. Determine a measure of volume for each production center.

7. Divide the volume into the total of overhead costs which have been assigned to each production center in order to determine each production center's overhead rate. This rate is then used to "apply" or "absorb" overhead onto products passing through the production center.

To the extent that budgeted indirect manufacturing costs and planned volume for each cost center differ from actuals, overhead spending variances and under- or overabsorbed volume variances will arise. These are described more fully in Chapters 12 and 32.

COST ACCOUNTING SYSTEMS

A *cost accounting system* is a system that accumulates costs and assigns them to cost objectives. Most frequently, the cost objective is a unit of product; hence some managers refer to these systems as "product costing systems."

A cost accounting system has four central objectives. The first is *accuracy* of cost data. Accuracy is one of the benefits usually derived from computerized cost systems. Accuracy is vital because cost data often are the basis for business decisions which affect whether the firm will generate earnings satisfactory to the owners.

The second objective is *timeliness* of cost information. This means that the cost system must make available cost data used for business decisions and statutory reporting requirements quickly. For example, cost data that measure manufacturing performance by comparing actual costs to standards must be reported to the plant manager in time for the manager to take prompt corrective action wherever it is needed.

The third objective of a cost accounting system is *flexibility*, which means that the system must be capable of being tapped to answer different cost-related questions. The system should provide management with information needed to develop a profitable plan of operations. It should generate information needed to keep operations on the planned path to desired profits by evaluating cost performance effectiveness. It should indicate whether selling prices can yield desired profit margins and, as pointed out previously, it should provide cost data when needed for use in pricing decisions, make-or-buy decisions, break-even analyses, capital budgeting analyses and decisions, and optimization models.

The fourth objective of a cost accounting system is to carry out the first three objectives at *reasonable administrative cost.*

To realize these objectives, the system should be entirely free of nonessentials. Every operation of the system should have a productive business use or meet a statutory requirement. So doing will keep to a minimum the amount of clerical and supervisory personnel, computer and associated peripheral equipment usage, office space, supplies, and communications needed to operate the system.

Different Cost Accounting Systems

There are three basic types of product costing systems:

1. Full costing (or full absorption costing) systems;
2. Variable ("direct") costing systems; and
3. Full absorption costing systems with flexible budgets.

Each of these systems normally makes use of standards and budgets for cost control purposes.

The development of full costs in a *full costing system* was discussed earlier in this chapter.

Variable costing systems frequently are referred to as direct costting systems, which is a misnomer because certain nonvariable costs are usually also chargable directly to a particular product. A variable ("direct") costing system treats only *variable* manufacturing costs as *product* costs and charges only these costs to product inventory. *Fixed* or nonvariable manufacturing costs are treated as *period* costs; they are expensed in the period incurred. (Refer to Chapter 13 for complete treatment of variable costing systems.)

A system using *full absorption standard costs with flexible budgets* is designed to take advantage of planning and control features of both full costing and variable costing. Full costing is used for cost accounting purposes. Flexible budgets are used for planning and control of manufacturing costs. A flexible budget classifies each type of expense according to how it reacts to increases or decreases in product volume. In other words, it separates variable and fixed costs in operating budgets and in product costs. Consequently, total costs can be estimated with reasonable accuracy by multiplying planned product volumes for the fiscal period by standard unit variable costs and adding to that total the fixed costs budgeted for the same period. It also permits budget allowances to be granted to manufacturing managers in accordance with the levels of production activity at which their departments actually operated.

Another way of classifying cost systems is by whether they are *job order* systems or *process* systems. As the name implies, a job order costing system collects the cost for *each* physically identifiable job or batch of work as it moves through the factory (or other productive process, as for a construction job). On the other hand, a process costing system collects costs for *all* products worked on during an accounting period; unit costs are determined by averaging— that is, dividing total costs of the product in the period by the number of units produced. These systems are described in detail in Chapters 7 and 8, respectively.

Finally, cost systems may be *actual* cost systems or *standard* cost systems. Actual cost systems as the name implies, charge units of product with the *actual* costs incurred in making these products. Standard cost systems charge products with the costs that *should have been incurred*—that is, with their predetermined standard costs. Development of cost standards for prime costs is discussed in Chapter 10. Most companies use a predetermined or standard factory overhead rate in their costing procedures, regardless of whether prime costs are actual or standard amounts. Overhead rate determination is presented in detail in Chapters 11 and 12.

SUMMARY

"Cost" is a very slippery word in that many different adjectives are used in front of this word, each of which relates to a quite different cost concept. Recognizing that precise usage often is not found in practice, in this chapter we have attempted to be precise in relating cost terminology and concepts. Other chapters in this book will use cost terminology in the sense in which terms have been defined in this chapter. For ease of future reference, a glossary follows.

GLOSSARY OF COST-RELATED TERMS

Absorption costs—see Full costs.

Amortization is the mechanism for writing off (expensing) intangible assets. (The term is also commonly applied to tangible assets, such as tooling, dies, and molds.)

Assets—see Capitalized costs.

Capital costs are the costs of plant and equipment, originally capitalized, and then systematically written off as the plant and equipment give up their benefits.

Capitalized costs is the formal name for *assets*. These costs are incurred when something is purchased, and the purchase will provide future benefits; therefore they are also called "unexpired costs." The debit is to an asset account, and the Cash or Accounts Payable account is credited. As the benefits are "released," the capitalized cost is "written off." (See Expired costs.)

Committed costs are those costs which are the inevitable consequences of commitments previously made; also called "sunk costs."

Controllable costs are those costs subject to significant influence by a responsibility center manager.

Cost is a measurement, in monetary terms, of the amount of resources used for some purpose.

Cost accounting system is a system which collects costs and assigns them to cost objectives.

Cost objective is a technical name for the purpose for which costs are measured.

Cost of goods sold is the expense account to which finished goods inventory costs are charged when they expire on recording of a sale. (In custom job shops, there usually is no finished goods inventory, and the credit is to work in process.)

Depletion is the mechanism for writing off (expensing) natural resources assets.

Depreciation is the mechanism for writing off (expensing) fixed assets.

Differential costs are those costs that are different under one set of conditions than they would be under another set of conditions. They are also called "relevant" or "incremental" costs.

Direct costing systems—see Variable costing systems.

Direct costs are items of cost which are traceable to or caused by a single cost objective.

Discretionary costs are those costs for which the "right" level is a matter of judgment.

Engineered costs are those costs for which the "right" amount can be "scientifically" determined, because a clear input-output relation exists.

Expenses—see Expired costs.

Expired costs is the formal name for *expenses*. These costs may be incurred when something is purchased, and the purchase provides benefits which are essentially received immediately. The debit is to an expense account, and the Cash or Accounts Payable account is credited. Expenses also occur when previously capitalized or unexpired costs (i.e., assets) "expire" (give up their benefits); in this case we say the asset is "written off" or "expensed."

Fixed costs—see Nonvariable costs.

Full costing systems (also called "absorption costing systems") value products at full costs; i.e., both variable production costs and allocated fixed production overhead are included. (Contrast with Variable costing systems.)

Full costs of a cost objective are the sum of its direct costs plus a fair share of its indirect costs.

Incremental costs—see Differential costs.

Indirect costs are associated with two or more cost objectives jointly.

Inventory costs—see Full costs.

Job costing systems collect the cost of each physically identifiable job or batch of work as it moves through the factory (or other productive process, as for a construction job).

Managed costs—see Discretionary costs.

Marginal costs are those costs per unit of output that are different for one volume level of output than for another. They are essentially the same as variable costs per unit.

Matching concept is the criterion used in determining the accounting period in which a cost becomes an expense; this is in the same period in which the cost helped generate revenues.

Noncontrollable costs are those costs not significantly influenced by a responsibility center manager.

Nonvariable costs are those which, in total, do not vary with volume. They commonly are called "fixed costs."

Opportunity cost is the value of the sacrifice, usually expressed in terms of foregone profit, incurred when the choice of one course of action requires that an alternative course of action be given up.

Overhead is another term for factory indirect costs.

Period costs are costs which are expensed in the same period in which the cost is incurred.

Prime cost is the sum of direct material cost plus direct labor cost.

Process costing systems do not directly collect unit costs of products, but rather determine average product unit cost by dividing total product costs by the number of equivalent units of production.

Product costs are the costs of manufacturing goods, which are capitalized in inventory until the goods are sold.

Programmed costs—see Discretionary costs.

Relevant costs—see Differential costs.

Semivariable costs vary with volume, but less than proportionately, and can be segregated into variable and fixed components.

Variable costing systems treat only variable manufacturing costs as product costs, and treat fixed manufacturing costs as period costs.

Variable costs increase in total proportionately with volume. (Variable costs *per unit* are constant.)

ADDITIONAL SOURCES

Anthony, Robert N. "The Rebirth of Cost Accounting." *Management Accounting*, October 1975, p. 13.

————, and Reece, James S. *Management Accounting Principles*, chaps. 15, 16. 3d ed. Homewood, Ill.: Richard D. Irwin, Inc., 1975.

Fremgen, James M. *Accounting for Managerial Analysis*, chap. 2. 3d ed. Homewood, Ill.: Richard D. Irwin, Inc., 1976.

Horngren, Charles T. *Cost Accounting: A Managerial Emphasis*. 4th ed. Englewood Cliffs, N.J.: Prentice-Hall, Inc., 1977.

Matz, Adolph, and Usry, Milton F. *Cost Accounting: Planning and Control*. 6th ed. Cincinnati: South-Western Publishing Co., 1976.

Mayer, Harry O. "Cost Accounting Standards." *Management Accounting*, October 1975, p. 17.

Neuner, John J. W., and Deakin, Edward B. *Cost Accounting: Principles and Practice*. 9th ed. Homewood, Ill.: Richard D. Irwin, Inc., 1977.

Shillinglaw, Gordon. *Managerial Cost Accounting*. 4th ed. Homewood, Ill.: Richard D. Irwin, Inc., 1977.

5

Analyzing Cost Behavior

Richard W. Swalley*

The Importance of Cost Analysis

A major objective of cost analysis is to provide internal management with proper and necessary information so that intelligent and timely decisions can be made regarding planning, coordinating, and controlling operations. The cost system is not complete if it is designed only to supply historical data to meet this objective. The data need to be supplied in a manner such that cost analysis is a logical and timely extension of the system.

A typical example of this is the use of a standard cost system. Basically, standards are set based on past production and cost performance, tempered for future expectations. At the end of the month, variances are generated based on actual performance. If these variances are significant, the system has automatically signaled either a potential problem needing investigation or a potential opportunity to capitalize upon, in the case of some "favorable" variances.

Further cost analysis is required, however, as part of that system in order to determine what happened to create the variances and solve the problem. Results of operations can only be evaluated properly by looking at the individual costs in depth.

If cost behavior is analyzed constantly by its various components,

* Mr. Swalley is Accounting Manager for Firestone Plastics Company, Pottstown, Pennsylvania.

it is possible to predict with a reasonable degree of accuracy what the variances will be before they are even generated, and to advise management what steps to take before the fact in order to minimize unfavorable variances or to maximize favorable variances, thus improving the profit potential of the company.

In the case of an unexpected drop in orders, if management is forced to reduce its production for the next month, a good cost analyst would immediately advise management what costs can be reduced (variable costs) and by how much, and at the same time inform them of what costs will not be reduced regardless what the level of production is (fixed costs). This is "responsible reporting"— imperative if a business is to be run profitably and responsibly.

In order to do this, it is necessary that the nature of cost elements be thoroughly understood at all levels of management, not simply in the accounting department.

Nature of Cost Elements

Essential to utilizing various analytical techniques of cost analysis is the recognition and understanding of the manufacturing cost elements involved. These are generally categorized as direct material, direct labor, and overhead.

Direct materials are those materials which become an integral part of the product being produced and are significant enough in cost to be ascertainable on a per unit basis. Normally, these costs will vary in direct proportion to production—that is, they are variable costs. Direct labor is the physical time and corresponding dollars spent in converting the raw materials into a finished product. Although this expense does vary with production, it is not always possible to eliminate the expense proportionately when volume decreases; for example, union contracts may require pay for eight hours despite the fact that a production worker may have only five hours of actual working time at his or her regular production job. The dollars paid for the time not spent on direct production, however, should be charged to overhead expense as indirect labor, or through another special account so that records can show readily how much these idle-time costs are.

Overhead generally covers all the other costs in the manufacturing process, including employee benefits, indirect materials, supervision, electricity and fuel charges, depreciation, taxes and insurance on plant assets, and so on. Some of these costs by their nature are fixed total dollars, that is, they will not as a rule increase or decrease regardless of the volume produced. Depreciation on equipment and buildings, taxes and insurance, real estate rentals, and salaries paid for supervisory, administrative, and managerial personnel are good examples of fixed expenses.

Variable overhead costs are those costs which generally vary with production volumes. This includes overtime premiums paid (clock card or salary), materials used in the production process but not easily identifiable on a per unit basis, operating supplies necessary to keep the plant running but which do not become a part of the finished product, and so forth.

Some costs are a combination of fixed and variable elements and generally will not vary in direct proportion to the volume of production. Maintenance of machinery and equipment, for example, requires a certain amount of normal maintenance activities regardless of whether machines are operating near capacity or well below capacity. As production increases, however, it is likely that maintenance will increase, although not necessarily in direct proportion to volume. In addition, there are certain expenses such as supervision, process control, quality control, and so on, which are fixed to a certain level of production, but should production exceed that level, another increment of fixed expense is required in order to maintain effective operations.

Each cost must be analyzed individually, and sometimes with different analytical tools, in order to be able to predict with some degree of accuracy what the costs will be if decisions are to be made relative to the entire operation.

ANALYZING BEHAVIOR OF DIRECT MATERIALS AND DIRECT LABOR

Direct Material

In most cases, direct material is the easiest cost element to analyze. Everything produced is made of some material. In order to manufacture a product, a formula, bill of materials, or specification sheet is prepared to determine the quantities of various materials required to produce a certain volume of output. Acceptable percentages of material for normal waste and/or dissipation are generally added as a separate item in order to have a reasonable guide against which to measure performance. Actual material usage is compared with predetermined usage, and any gains or losses are analyzed to determine why performance differed.

Since materials may be added into the process in several steps, the analysis should look to the various steps to determine where the variances occurred. One way of providing these data is to follow the flow of material from one department to the next, requiring reports to be prepared showing receipts of material and shipments of completed material into the next stage. Direct material variances through any one department or stage of process should be brought to the attention of department managers, production managers, or process engineers who can determine why discrepancies exist and take proper action to construct methods for reclamation, reduction of dissipation, and so forth.

Direct Labor

Direct labor cost analysis is somewhat more difficult than direct materials. While direct materials will almost always vary in direct proportion to output, there are many industries where direct labor is relatively fixed within ranges of productivity.

Time and motion studies are exceptionally valuable in ascertaining costs of production labor. Where jobs are specialized with one individual performing basically the same function eight hours a day, the engineers performing the studies can relate production with hours and the accountants can readily provide a cost per unit produced. If piece rates can be set based on these studies, it makes cost analysis even easier.

In many industries, where an individual is assigned several machines to keep running simultaneously, the direct labor cost can fluctuate on a per unit basis, since orders may not warrant running all the machines. While accountants do not run the plant, they should point out to management the per unit effects on direct labor costs where volumes are altered. This can be done rather well by preparing an analysis relating machine usage, personnel requirements, and labor dollars expended, and then following up with comments as to why costs per unit increase or decrease.

Where new projects are undertaken, where technological changes take place, or where a single standard labor time is utilized to determine standard direct labor costs, it is advisable for accountants to assume that a learning effect is present and to apply learning-curve theory to their work. Simply stated, it has been found on certain repetitive jobs, worker performance has a definite rate of improvement; for example, when under an 80 percent theoretical learning curve, with each doubling of cumulative experience, the cumulative average per unit cost for items subject to the learning curve drops by 20 percent.

Example: Assume that Product A is introduced in 1978, with an anticipated volume of 10,000 units per year. In 1978, the total costs for Product A subject to the learning curve are $500,000, or an average of $50 per unit. Industrial engineers have judged that an 80 percent learning curve is appropriate. The following table projects costs (in constant dollars) for 16 years, or 160,000 cumulative units of experience:

Years since Introduction	Cumulative Quantity	Average Cumulative Unit Cost*	Average Unit Cost for Increment	Average Annual Decrease
1.................	10,000	$50.00	$50.00	—
2.................	20,000	40.00	30.00†	$20.00
4.................	40,000	32.00	24.00	3.00‡
8.................	80,000	25.60	19.20	1.20
16.................	160,000	20.48	15.36	0.48

* For cost elements subject to the learning curve. Some cost elements, such as amortization of tooling costs, are not subject to learning.
† Since the first 20,000 units cost $800,000 (20,000 × $40), and the first 10,000 units cost $500,000, then units 10,001–20,000 cost $300,000, or an average of $30 per unit.
‡ ($30 − $24) ÷ 2 years = $3.

While the example above deals with all costs subject to learning effects (which are not limited solely to direct labor), the reader can easily imagine a similar calculation restricted to labor hours. For example, assume the table in the example applies only to labor at $5 an hour. The key column is the middle one; we would then have cumulative average labor time of ten hours for the first 10,000 units, eight hours for the first 20,000, and so on.

Numerical calculations such as those in the example can be prepared on a new product. If the learning rate is known for similar products, the opportunity of knowing how the direct labor costs will behave on new products aids in establishing costs and prices. Formulas are available to calculate the average time required to produce the total units desired, and also to calculate the marginal time required to produce the next units. Since time can be easily converted to money, the value of this type of analysis is evident in determining, projecting, or controlling direct labor costs on a new product or when frequent hiring of new people is required.

ANALYSIS OF OVERHEAD

Overhead is essentially a "grab bag" of all costs except direct material and direct labor (prime costs). As such, the engineering method employed in analyzing prime costs is not advised in analyzing most overhead costs, since the cost of doing such an analysis can be prohibitive. Historical costs, therefore, usually provide the best basis for overhead analysis.

Certain steps should be taken in order to assure that the historical costs will provide representative and accurate figures upon which to base an analysis for decision-making purposes. Total raw cost data (as opposed to departmental cost charges) should be used when analyzing certain costs, in order to save time and confusion that adds little to the accuracy of the analysis. The distribution of electricity to departments based on floor space, production, or number of employees, for instance, is useful only in an analysis of departmental costs. Even then such a distribution should be used only with full knowledge that without meters in each department, or highly sophisticated engineering studies of departmental equipment's horsepower, the distribution cannot be completely accurate.

A complete set of statistics should be established and updated monthly including machine-hours, direct labor hours, direct labor dollars, direct material usage, number of clock card employees, number of salaried employees, production units, and so on.

Exhibit 1 is a list of some relevant and vital statistics. Direct labor hours, for example, are delineated by regular hours, replacement hours, and increased production hours. Replacement overtime hours are necessitated by personnel who called in sick. A close analysis shows what months show heavy needs for this type of overtime. If possible, inventory could be built during other months so that certain machines could be shut down during these periods, thereby reducing costs.

Average outside temperature could also be a major factor in projecting utility costs, that is, oil, coal, or electricity requirements

EXHIBIT 1
Comparative Statistics

Month	No. of Direct Labor Personnel	Direct Labor Hours				Direct Labor Dollars			
		Regular Hours	Overtime		Total	Reg. Hrs. W/O OT Prem.	Overtime Premium		Total
			Replace	Incr. Prod.			Replace	Incr. Prod.	
January	620	25,040	1,000	4,960	31,000	$123,040	$2,000	$9,920	$134,960
February	614	24,400	400	3,168	27,968	111,872	800	6,336	119,008
March	622	28,200	320	1,240	29,760	130,944	704	2,728	134,376
April	618	27,120	160	-0-	27,280	120,032	352	-0-	120,384
May	612	24,784	16	-0-	24,800	109,114	32	-0-	109,146
June	612	24,800	-0-	-0-	24,800	109,120	-0-	-0-	109,120
July	615	25,720	320	2,480	28,520	125,488	704	5,456	131,648
August	620	14,840	40	1,240	16,120	70,928	88	2,728	73,744
September	621	28,504	16	-0-	28,520	125,488	35	-0-	125,523
October	621	25,880	160	2,480	28,520	125,488	352	5,456	131,296
November	625	25,660	480	3,720	29,860	131,384	1,056	8,194	140,634
December	628	26,480	640	3,720	30,840	135,692	1,406	8,194	145,292

Month	Equivalent Days Worked		Machine-Hours Worked	Units Produced	Maintenance Expense	Electricity Expense	Average Outside Temperature	Depreciation Expense
	Regular	Overtime						
January	21	4.0	6,000	100,000	$3,800	$10,400	20°	$10,000
February	20	2.6	5,424	83,800	3,315	9,540	20	10,000
March	23	1.0	5,760	94,500	3,430	10,100	35	10,000
April	21	0.2	5,088	80,400	3,172	8,500	50	10,000
May	20	-0-	4,800	80,100	3,292	7,795	65	10,000
June	22	-0-	4,200	66,000	2,880	7,500	70	10,000
July	21	2.0	5,520	88,400	3,462	9,720	75	10,000
August	12	1.0	3,120	50,600	2,318	5,770	75	10,000
September	23	-0-	5,520	91,200	3,520	9,555	60	10,000
October	21	2.0	5,520	90,400	3,695	9,660	50	10,000
November	21	3.0	5,760	94,600	3,735	9,840	45	10,000
December	22	3.0	6,000	97,200	4,155	10,200	25	10,000

for heating during winter months or for air conditioning during summer months.

Many other statistics could and should be listed, such as kilowatt-hours and cost per kilowatt-hour, peak demand kilowatt-hours and cost of same, pounds of steam produced per gallon of oil, gallons of oil used, and purchase price per gallon of oil. Every item that affects cost of operation is pertinent and should be tracked as closely as possible so that changes are easily pinpointed and readily explained by the proper, responsible individuals.

Unusual factors affecting the statistics should be noted and adjustments made so that when a relationship between an overhead cost item and the basic statistic is established, it is a true relationship, not distorted by an unusual occurrence. Technological changes naturally have a definite impact on costs and require constant updates in order to analyze costs with a reasonable degree of accuracy.

Price or rate changes should be adjusted so that when costs over a period of time are used they reflect the same rates to compare with the basic statistic, that is, when a rate change is effective, past costs should be adjusted to reflect this change before the analytical tools shown later in the chapter are used. This is especially necessary for costs having a fixed element and a variable element. If this is not done in a period of rising costs, the fixed element could be shown as something other than it actually is, unless it too had the same rate increase applied to it. After the initial relationship has been determined, any variable rate increase can be applied to project total costs or to determine if actual costs are in line in any time period.

After the set of accumulated statistics has been prepared, manufacturing costs should be compared with each of the individual independent variables to ascertain what kind of relationship exists. Probably the easiest way to see if there is a relationship between two variables is to visually compare the list of statistics to various costs and choose the ones most closely related to plot on graph paper. Exhibit 2 shows several plottings which appear to have a good relationship.

Statistical Scattergraphs. After the plots are prepared, with costs on the vertical axis and corresponding determinant variables (i.e., activity measures or volumes) on the horizontal axis, visual inspection of the points on the graphs will indicate which variable the respective cost is most likely to follow. A straight line can then

EXHIBIT 2
Plots of Cost-Volume Relationships

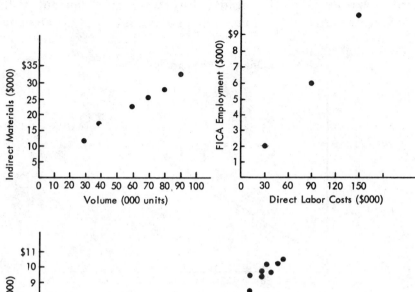

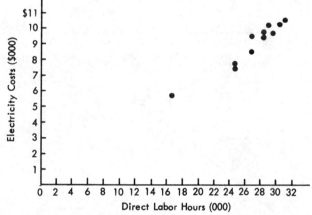

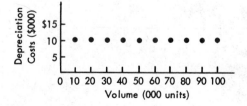

be drawn to fit the trend of the points. Where a cost is semivariable (i.e., has fixed and variable components), the line will intersect the vertical axis at the point considered to be the fixed element. If the cost is truly variable, this line will, of course, intersect at the origin.

EXHIBIT 3
Visual Fitting of a Line to a Scattergraph

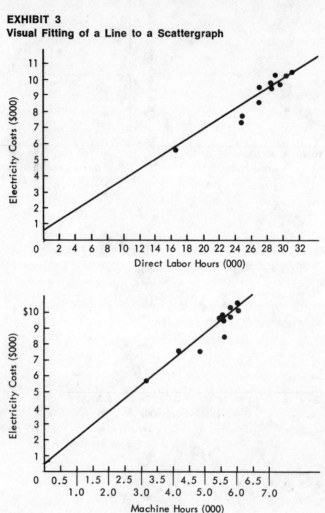

If the line runs completely horizontal, the cost will be fixed, at least relative to the variable with which it is matched. Electricity costs are shown on Exhibit 3 plotted against both direct labor hours and machine-hours. Both appear to have possibilities in projecting the variable and fixed elements of this cost. (Note that the fixed component is less than $1,000; it may "truly" be zero, since the lines in Exhibit 3 are only visual approximations.)

A straight line algebraically is written $y = a + bx$, where y is the vertical axis showing costs; a is the point of intersection of the line with the vertical (y) axis; x is the horizontal axis, showing the determinant variable (volume of production, machine-hours, etc.); and b is the variable rate (slope).

A plot of electricity costs shown in Exhibit 3 compared to machine-hours, with a straight line drawn through the points, indicates that fixed costs (a) are about $600 and the variable rate (b) is approximately $1.633 to $1.657 per machine-hour. This is calculated from the hand-drawn graph using the straight-line formula, setting a equal to $600 and solving for b, based on two points of the historical data presented:

$$y = a + bx$$
$$y = \$600 + bx$$

High = January: $10,400 = $600 + $b \cdot$ 6,000 machine-hours
$\qquad b = \$1.633$ per machine-hour
Low = August: $ 5,770 = $600 + $b \cdot$ 3,120 machine-hours
$\qquad b = \$1.657$ per machine-hour

The straight line represents an average of past occurrences based on a line drawn by the preparer. In many cases, this visual approximation is sufficient to establish the fixed and variable elements of many costs.

A further refinement of this straight-line technique of cost analysis is the "method of least squares," or "linear regression." Before we discuss this, however, it should be pointed out that it is possible to calculate the fixed costs and variable rate in a simple mathematical manner, utilizing the historical data required to prepare the graphs and the straight-line formula. This is called the "high-low points method."

High-Low Points Method

This method is also based on the formula for a straight line, $y = a + bx$, but solves for the variable rate first by comparing the high and low costs to their corresponding variables.

Exhibit 4 shows this method in detail. The fixed expenses are $754 per month, and the variable rate is $1.6076 per machine-hour.

Although there is a discrepancy between the hand-drawn scatter-graph method and the high-low points method as presented, this may not be considered significant. It is difficult to say which is more accurate. Both are relatively simple techniques and have their uses. The high-low points method utilizes only two points from the historical experience, that is, it draws a straight line through the high point and low point and discards all other activity. Indiscriminate use of these two points could prove erroneous if other factors are not considered carefully.

EXHIBIT 4
High-Low Points Method (machine-hours and electricity costs from Exhibit 1)

	Machine-Hours	Electricity Costs
High...........	$6,000 = x_h$	$\$10,400 = y_h$
Low...........	$3,120 = x_l$	$5,770 = y_l$
	$2,880 = (x_h - x_l)$	$\$ 4,630 = (y_h - y_l)$

$y = a + bx$ x = corresponding units
y = total cost x_h = units @ high cost
y_h = high cost x_l = units @ low cost
y_l = low cost a = fixed cost
                       b = variable rate

$$b = \frac{y_h - y_l}{x_h - x_l} = \frac{\$10,400 - \$5,770}{6,000 - 3,120} = \frac{\$4,630}{2,880} = \$1.6076$$

$y_h = a + b(x_h)$ or $y_l = a + b(x_l)$
$\$10,400 = a + \$1.6076(6,000)$ $5,770 = a + \$1.6076(3,120)$
$a = \$754$ $a = \$754$

Fixed costs = \$754 per month
Variable rate = \$1.6076 per machine-hour

Least Squares Method

The least squares method is a refinement of both the above methods. It provides the most accurate formula for a straight line by minimizing the sum of the squares of the vertical distances from the actual costs to the straight line projected from the formula.

When this method is utilized on machine-hours and electricity costs, the fixed costs are \$526 per month and the variable cost is approximately \$1.6308 per machine-hour. Two methods to calculate this line are presented in Exhibit 5. Method 2, solving by simultaneous equations, shows again the use of the straight-line formula.

In the method of least squares, as in the statistical scattergraph and high-low points methods, costs were directly associated with one corresponding variable. This is the ideal situation. It is most probable, however, that the behavior of a particular cost element is much more accurately analyzed if more than one corresponding (independent) variable is analyzed.

Multiple Regression Analysis

Multiple regression analysis allows the accountant to analyze the behavior of costs when more than one corresponding variable determines a particular cost. The intent is to place a dollar value (here, for electricity) on two or more measures of volume (here, machine-hours and number of personnel) so that, given a production schedule requiring a certain number of machine-hours and direct labor hours, for example, the total costs can be predicted with a relatively high degree of accuracy.

Electricity costs, for example, may be a function of machine-hours and the number of employees or the number of days worked.

EXHIBIT 5
Least Squares Method No. 1

	x Machine-Hours	x_1 Deviation from Average	y Total Costs	y_1 Deviation from Average	x_1^2	$x_1 y_1$
January............	6,000	+ 774	$ 10,400	$+1,352	599,706	$ 1,046,448
February..........	5,424	+ 198	9,540	+ 492	39,204	97,416
March............	5,760	+ 534	10,100	+1,052	285,156	561,768
April.............	5,088	− 138	8,500	− 548	19,044	75,624
May..............	4,800	− 426	7,795	−1,253	181,476	533,778
June.............	4,200	−1,026	7,500	−1,548	1,052,676	1,588,248
July.............	5,520	+ 294	9,720	+ 672	86,436	197,568
August...........	3,120	−2,106	5,770	−3,278	4,435,236	6,903,468
September........	5,520	+ 294	9,555	+ 507	86,436	149,058
October..........	5,520	+ 294	9,660	+ 612	86,436	179,928
November........	5,760	+ 534	9,840	+ 792	285,156	422,928
December........	6,000	+ 774	10,200	+1,152	599,076	891,648
	62,712		$108,580		7,755,408	$12,647,880
Average =	5,226		$ 9,048.33			

$$\text{Variable rate} = \frac{\Sigma x_1 \cdot y_1}{\Sigma x_1^2} = \frac{\$12,647,880}{7,755,408} = \$1.6308 \text{ per machine-hour}$$

Fixed expenses = Average total costs − (Average hours × Variable rate)
= \$9,048.33 − (5,226 × \$1.6308)
= \$526 per month

EXHIBIT 5 *(continued)*
Least Squares Method No. 2

	x Machine- Hours	y Total Cost	x² (000 omitted)	xy (000 omitted)
January.............	6,000	$ 10,400	36,000	$ 62,400
February...........	5,424	9,540	29,420	51,745
March.............	5,760	10,100	33,178	58,176
April.............	5,088	8,500	25,888	43,248
May...............	4,800	7,795	23,040	37,416
June..............	4,200	7,500	17,640	31,500
July..............	5,520	9,720	30,470	53,654
August............	3,120	5,770	9,734	18,002
September.........	5,520	9,555	30,470	52,744
October...........	5,520	9,660	30,470	53,323
November.........	5,760	9,840	33,178	56,678
December.........	6,000	10,200	36,000	61,200
	62,712	$108,580	335,488	$580,086

Solve by simultaneous equations:

1. $\Sigma y = Na + b\Sigma x$
2. $\Sigma xy = a\Sigma x + b\Sigma x^2$

1. $\$108,580 = 12a + b(62,712)$
2. $\$580,086,000 = a(62,712) + b(335,488,000)$

a = Fixed costs = \$526 per month
b = Variable rate = \$1.6308 per machine-hour

In order to determine costs based upon two variables, the problem is solved by three equations:

$$y = aN + b \cdot x + c \cdot z$$
$$\Sigma xy = a\Sigma x + b\Sigma x^2 + c\Sigma xz$$
$$\Sigma yz = a\Sigma y + b\Sigma xz + c\Sigma z^2$$

Where:

x = machine-hours.
y = electricity costs.
z = number of employees (or number of days worked).
a = fixed costs.
b = variable rate per machine-hour.
c = variable rate per number of employees (or number of days worked).
N = number of observations.

Matrix algebra is useful when there are a few observations to contend with and the numbers are not large. Showing the mathematics of the calculation is beyond the scope of this chapter. We will simply state that, using these historical data:

Month	Machine-Hours (000)	No. of Employees	Electricity Costs ($000)
January............... 3	3	$21
February.............. 1	1	8
March................. 4	3	28
April................. 6	5	37

One can determine that the data imply that electricity costs are $3,500 fixed per month, plus $7 per machine-hour *and* —$1,500 per employee.[1] Using this formula, at any combination of anticipated machine-hours to be worked and personnel to be utilized, electricity costs can be approximated.

Computer programming of multiple regression techniques affords the accountant the opportunity to analyze costs based on any number of variables and to introduce "dummy" variables to account for conditions which affect costs but which are hard to quantify. For example, it is probable that if a plant is located in an area where the summers are hot and the plant is air-conditioned, the effects of air-conditioning costs based on degree-days can be ascertained. Likewise, winter months requiring heat costs can also be entered into the equation based on temperature. The possibilities of using computer programming and multiple regression analysis in cost analysis are almost limitless, and should be looked into thoroughly.

Whatever the method utilized in analyzing costs, it is extremely important that costs be charged into the system in a manner that enables managers properly to control expenses for which they are responsible, while at the same time providing the necessary data for the cost analyst constantly to update the delineation of costs in order to report to top management what costs are likely to be at various stages of production and sales.

THE CHART OF ACCOUNTS

Fixed costs should be charged to an account within a group of accounts in the ledger designated as fixed expenses. Variable costs

---

[1] The negative cost per employee would suggest that the more people there are, the fewer machines, and hence lower electricity costs.

should likewise be charged to an account within a group of accounts designated as variable expenses. Semivariable expenses should be further separated into fixed and variable components and charged accordingly. Exhibit 6 shows a very simple chart of accounts to illustrate this point.

In the case of an electric bill, for instance, there is a definite amount of fixed expense independent of production, hours worked, and so on. Each month the bill should be split, charging the fixed portion, as estimated through the various methods explained earlier, into an account separate from the other (variable) portion.

In the case of overtime for direct labor, the straight-time portion of wages paid should be charged to the direct labor account, and the overtime premium charged to an account called Overtime Premium—Direct Labor. Overtime as a result of replacement time required for personnel out sick should also be charged to a separate account. Often overtime premium for all personnel is lumped together in one account, making it difficult to analyze.

All salary overtime, where applicable, should be charged into a separate overtime account in order to determine fully the impact on variable costs as a result of working longer hours than normally required. Here too, if supervisors receive overtime for replacing other salaried employees who are sick or on vacation, this overtime should be charged to a separate account. If this is done, it will enable management to determine when the economics warrant an additional supervisor or technician, that is, when weekly or monthly overtime costs are such that they are higher than the costs involved in hiring an additional salaried employee. Without a separate account, there is no automatic device that will indicate that other, more economic methods might be necessary.

Employee benefits, likewise, should be split as to their fixed or variable nature. Insurance premiums and pension funds requirements are generally a fixed monthly charge for each employee. These normally are not reduced during a short layoff period as determined by the labor contract. Vacation pay is usually determined by past earnings over a stated period of time, and in some cases is fixed again by contract as to how much an individual is entitled to, even if that individual should leave sometime within the fiscal year.

On the other hand, social security, holiday pay, worker's compensation, and unemployment compensation benefits generally vary directly with the number of employees and their wages. As such, these expenses should be categorized in a manner consistent with the type of analysis that would best indicate to management when cost reductions are feasible.

Maintenance expenses should also be delineated as to the fixed and variable portions. There is little doubt where an industry has

EXHIBIT 6
Chart of Accounts

Account No.	Description
Volume-related (0–500);	
0– 50	Direct labor
51–100	Indirect labor
101–125	Supervision
126–140	Clerical
141–160	Overtime premium—Direct labor
161–180	Overtime premium—Indirect labor
181–200	Overtime premium—Salaried
201–220	Employee benefits—Direct labor
201	Social Security
202	Unemployment Compensation
203	Vacation
204	Holiday
221–240	Employee benefits—Indirect labor
241–260	Employee benefits—Salaried
301–350	Maintenance
351–400	Utilities
351	Electric power—Machines
361	Gas—Ovens, etc.
362	Gas—Boilers
401–500	Other
Fixed (501–999):	
501–520	Supervision
521–540	Clerical
541–560	Employee benefits—Direct and indirect labor
551	Employee benefits—Pensions
552	Employee benefits—Insurance
561–580	Employee benefits—Salaried
561	Employee benefits—Pension
562	Employee benefits—Insurance
563	Employee benefits—Taxes
601–650	Maintenance
601	Maintenance—Contracts
602	Maintenance—Oiling, Greasing, etc.
651–699	Utilities
651	Utilities—Heat
652	Utilities—Lighting
653	Utilities—Machine Maintenance
701–750	Depreciation
751–800	Taxes
801–850	Insurance
851–900	Long-Term Leases

many machines to contend with that a preventive maintenance program is in effect. This includes normal oiling, greasing, replacing worn parts, and so forth, and should be considered as relatively fixed in nature. That maintenance required as a result of increased usage should be classified as variable expense.

Electricity required to light the factory, to keep the temperature at a certain level, or to keep motors running in certain machinery to prevent major problems are all examples of fixed elements of what is normally (but erroneously) considered entirely variable expenses. These portions of the expense should be coded to a fixed expense account and the balance charged to a variable expense account.

On a departmental statement prepared for managers' use to control expenses in their department, by separating the variable from the fixed portion department managers know exactly which expenses they need to control based on the production schedule they are required to meet. They can be prepared to answer questions relative to their performance and even make suggestions relative to the overall profitability of the firm by pointing to some fixed expenses which could possibly be reduced if production does not increase. (See, also, Chapter 23, "Standard Cost Control for Manufacturing Costs.")

An overall production statement for management should differentiate between those expenses that middle management can be called upon to control and those expenses which are directly related to decisions made at the top level. Depreciation, for instance, is generally the result of top management's decision to purchase capital equipment. They are responsible for securing funds for that investment and seeing that a proper payout is calculated to substantiate that investment. Middle management suggests; top management acts. Depreciation, therefore, is an expense which should be reported to top management.

Taxes, also, are top management's responsibility. Real property taxes are generally dependent upon the chosen location and as such are more or less determined at the initial inception of any business. Subsequent assessment increases can be challenged by top management alone. Likewise, personal property taxes are determined by investment in equipment, inventories, and so on, which are the responsibilities of top management.

EXHIBIT 7
Cost of Goods Manufactured Report (January)

Volume: 100,000

	Monthly Expense	Cost per Unit
Volume-related expenses:		
Material...................................	$ 38,400	$0.384
Direct labor.................................	$ 99,200	0.992
Variable overhead:		
Indirect labor............................	$ 22,100	
Overtime premium: Direct labor...........	23,840	
Overtime premium: Indirect labor.........	4,870	
Overtime: Salaried.......................	1,650	
Employee benefits: Direct, indirect........	10,720	
Employee benefits: Salaried..............	115	
Maintenance.............................	3,750	
Utilities.................................	9,650	
Supplies.................................	1,420	
Total variable overhead.................	$ 78,115	0.781
Total variable expenses.............	$215,715	$2.157
Fixed expenses:		
Manufacturing:		
Supervision.............................	$ 40,100	
Clerical.................................	8,300	
Employee benefits: Direct, indirect........	33,210	
Employee benefits: Salaried..............	8,300	
Maintenance.............................	1,250	
Utilities.................................	750	
Total manufacturing fixed...............	$ 91,910	
Other fixed:		
Depreciation.............................	$ 85,000	
Taxes...................................	7,000	
Insurance...............................	1,000	
Research and development.................	26,250	
Long-term leases.........................	4,380	
Total other.............................	$123,630	
Total fixed expenses...............	$215,540	
Total cost of goods manufactured.............	$431,255	

Long-term leases or rental on equipment, warehouse space, automobiles, and so forth, should be charged to accounts that are shown on top management's statements since no long-term lease could be entered into without top management's sanction. Charges for short-term requirements, however, such as leasing a delivery truck while major maintenance is being performed on a company's vehicle, should be charged to the department involved.

Research and development departmental charges should be shown as a separate item on prepared statements in such a manner that top management, who normally have direct control over these expenditures, are held accountable for them.

The chart of accounts should be detailed in such a way as to produce operating statements that clearly enable the cost analyst to pinpoint what the effects of volume changes, increased rates, increased capital investment, and so on, will have on the overall profitability of the organization without an enormous amount of work. Exhibit 7 shows a simple operations report prepared in a manner conducive to relatively easy cost analysis. The ease of preparing a statement at various levels of manufacturing is self-evident. Likewise, the break-even point can be readily calculated.

SUMMARY

There are many available techniques of analyzing cost behavior. All of these as presented have been with us for a long time, but any technique needs constant updating. New-product development, new-process developments, technological changes, all require a fresh look at the methods employed in order to derive the most advantageous technique for management to make the decisions which ultimately determine the success or failure of a business.

With the availability of sophisticated computer technology, multiple regression analysis allows the cost analyst to determine how costs are dependent upon multiple elements of the entire production process.

As the accountant becomes more aware of this very valuable tool, the chart of accounts should be altered in order to sectionalize those variable costs which are dependent upon known variable factors. Other variables dependent upon other factors such as labor union contracts, labor laws, and so forth, should be sectionalized also. The chart of accounts then works for the cost analyst and at the same time provides a firm basis for preparation of statements.

The chart of accounts, the subsequent reports prepared from the records, and the analysis of cost behavior are all part of a whole system. It is extremely important that they are all tied together logically and provide timely data, inexpensively so that management can run their business effectively and efficiently.

ADDITIONAL SOURCES

Abernathy, William J., and Wayne, Kenneth. "Limits of the Learning Curve." *Harvard Business Review,* September–October 1974, p. 109.

Bump, Edwin A. "Effects of Learning on Cost Projections." *Management Accounting,* May 1974, p. 19.

Corcoran, A. Wayne. *Mathematical Applications in Accounting,* chaps. 6, 7. New York: Harcourt, Brace and World, 1968.

Dopuch, Nicholas; Birnberg, Jacob G.; and Demski, Joel. *Cost Accounting: Accounting Data for Management's Decisions,* chap. 23. New York: Harcourt Brace Jovanovich, Inc., 1974.

Elliott, W. Larry. "Cost Behavior: A Dynamic Concept." *Management Accounting,* March 1974, p. 33.

Hirschmann, Winfred B. "Profit from the Learning Curve." *Harvard Business Review,* January–February 1964, p. 125.

Horngren, Charles T. *Cost Accounting: A Managerial Emphasis,* chap. 25. 4th ed. Englewood Cliffs, N.J.: Prentice-Hall, Inc., 1977.

Lyon, George C. "Fixed Characteristics of Variable Costs." *Management Accounting,* October 1973, p. 27.

Morse, Wayne J. "Learning Curve Cost Projections with Constant Unit Costs." *Managerial Planning,* March–April 1974, p. 15.

Shillinglaw, Gordon. *Managerial Cost Accounting,* chaps. 3, 18. 4th ed. Homewood, Ill.: Richard D. Irwin, Inc., 1977.

6

Using Cost-Volume-Profit Charts

Roy A. Anderson
Harry R. Biederman*

Cost-volume-profit analysis (CVP) or "break even" is not new. Break-even charts have been traced to two engineers, Knoeppel and Hess, in the first decade of the twentieth century.[1] As for ancient break-even thoughts, Adam Smith reminds us that:

> . . . Democritus, who wrote upon husbandry about two thousand years ago, and who was regarded by the ancients as one of the fathers of the art, thought they did not act wisely who enclosed a kitchen garden. The profit, he said, would not compensate the expense of a stone wall; and bricks (he meant, I suppose, bricks baked in the sun) mouldered with the rain, and the winter storm, and required continual repairs.[2]

Although one of the oldest applications of management science, CVP retains its popularity. In a survey made by the authors in the mid-1970s[3] (which will be referred to a number of times in this

---

* Mr. Anderson is Chairman of the Board; and Dr. Biederman is Senior Economic Advisor, Corporate Planning and Analysis Office, Lockheed Aircraft Corporation, Burbank.

[1] R. M. Soldofsky, "Accountants' vs. Economists' Concepts of Break-Even Analysis," *N.A.A. Bulletin*, December 1959. He gives credit for this information to Ned Chopin.

[2] Adam Smith, *The Wealth of Nations* (New York: The Modern Library, Random House, Inc., 1937), p. 153.

[3] R. A. Anderson and H. R. Biederman, "How Industry Uses Break-Even Analysis," in *The Treasurer's Handbook*, eds. J. Fred Weston and Maurice C. Goudzwaard (Homewood, Ill.: Dow Jones-Irwin, Inc., 1976), chap. 14.

chapter), we found that 72 percent of those replying employed the technique, and less than 5 percent had reduced their use over the past ten years.

COST-VOLUME-PROFIT CHARTS

As the name suggests, cost-volume-profit analysis examines the relationship of costs and profits to the *volume* of business. It goes without saying—and in the name "cost-volume-profit" it has, in fact, gone without saying—that revenues are also related to volume.

Essentially the analysis divides total costs into fixed and variable components and plots these costs and revenues against the volume of business. Revenue per unit exceeds variable costs per unit and is able to make some contribution toward recovering fixed costs. The volume at which all of the fixed costs as well as the variable costs are recovered is the break-even point. Interest in this particular volume, that which is necessary to just recover costs, is sufficiently great that the popular name for the process remains "break-even analysis."

Exhibit 1A is a typical break-even chart. The assumptions have been adapted from a manufacturing plant of electromechanical equipment. In summary, fixed costs are $750,000 of which $100,000 is depreciation. Variable costs are $3.50 per unit, and the price is $6.00 per unit. Fixed costs are shown as a horizontal line, a fixed amount regardless of the volume of production. Variable costs which increase proportionately with volumes are added to the fixed costs. The result is a total cost line. Revenues are zero when the volume is zero and are assumed to increase proportionately with volume. Break-even volume in this example is at 300,000 units per month.

The difference between the price per unit of $6.00 and the variable cost per unit of $3.50 is $2.50; each unit sold provides that "contribution margin" to be applied against the fixed costs. The contribution margin divided into the fixed cost is a way of finding the break-even quantity:

$$Q_b = \frac{F}{P - V}$$

EXHIBIT 1
Four Ways to Depict Break Even

Premises for Exhibit 1:
Price (P) .... $6.00 per unit
Variable costs (VC) .... $3.50 per unit
Fixed costs (FC) $750,000
   Including depreciation $100,000
Relevant volume .... 100,000—450,000 units
Relevant Period .... January 1–September 30,
                                                  recent year

A. Standard Form — Horizontal Fixed Costs;
   Volume in Physical Units

B. Standard Form — Horizontal Fixed Costs;
   Volume in Dollars

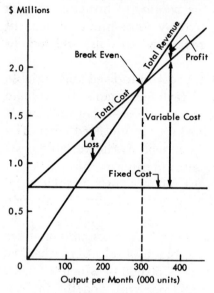

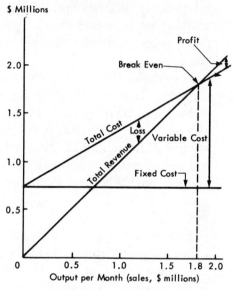

C. <u>Contribution</u> to Fixed Costs and
   <u>Profits</u> Form — Volume in Physical Units

D. Profit/Volume (P/V) Form —
   Volume in Dollars

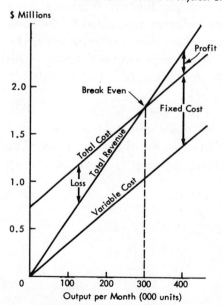

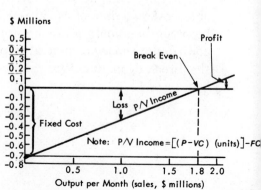

Note: P/V Income = $[(P-VC)\,(\text{units})] - FC$

where:

$$Q_b = \text{break-even quantity.}$$
$$F = \text{fixed costs.}$$
$$P = \text{price per unit.}$$
$$V = \text{variable cost per unit.}$$
$$P\text{-}V = \text{contribution margin.}$$

In the example,

$$Q_b = \frac{\$750{,}000}{\$6.00 - \$3.50} = \frac{\$750{,}000}{\$2.50} = 300{,}000 \text{ units}$$

The total profit for any quantity can be computed by finding the total revenue and subtracting total costs:

$$I = TR - TC$$
$$I = (P \times Q) - (V \times Q + F)$$

where:

$$I = \text{total profit (income).}$$
$$TR = \text{total revenue.}$$
$$TC = \text{total cost.}$$
$$Q = \text{quantity.}$$

In the example, for a quantity of 400,000, that is, 100,000 units beyond break even,

$$I = (\$6.00 \times 400{,}000) - (\$3.50 \times 400{,}000 + \$750{,}000) =$$
$$\$250{,}000$$

That is also the difference between the quantity being considered (Q) and the break-even quantity (Q_b) times the contribution margin:

$$100{,}000 \times \$2.50 = \$250{,}000$$

The other charts in Exhibit 1 illustrate other ways of presenting the same information. Exhibit 1B is the same as 1A, except that volume has been expressed in dollar sales volume terms rather than units. When a variety of products is being produced, a dollar measure of volume is often preferable to a physical measure. Either can be used with these charts.

Exhibit 1C changes the order of "stacking" of fixed and variable costs. In this case, variable costs are plotted on the bottom and fixed costs are added to arrive at the total cost curve. An advantage of plotting the information this way is that the fixed costs are depicted as being overcome by the contribution margin; the total revenue curve rises faster than the variable cost curve and eliminates the initial fixed cost loss.

Exhibit 1D, the profit/volume or P/V version, is a favorite for examination of alternate product and pricing strategies. It too shows the fixed costs being overcome by volume times the contribution margin, but this is all incorporated in one line. The total fixed cost is plotted as a negative amount at the origin. It is reduced by the contribution margin times the volume. The line that is plotted is the sum of the contribution margin times unit volume less the fixed cost:

$$[(\text{Price} - \text{Variable cost per unit}) \times \text{Volume in units}] - \text{Fixed cost}$$
$$[(\$6.00 - \$3.50) \times 400{,}000] - \$750{,}000 = \$250{,}000$$

The line that is plotted is called the P/V income, and the slope of the line is the P/V ratio. This is the ratio of the contribution margin to the price. In this case, it is $\$2.50/\$6.00 = \$0.417$. There will be $\$0.417$ addition to profit or reduction in loss for each additional dollar of volume.

Assumptions and Limitations

Exhibit 2 lists the assumptions and limitations of the linear CVP analysis. Each assumption turns out also to be a limitation because it constrains the generality of the approach.

CVP analysis is useful because it presents clearly and simply the elements of profit planning. This is illustrated in Exhibit 1. The assumptions that follow underlie the neat linear relationships in that figure. Since linear assumptions are not realistic in all cases, this raises questions about the application of the simplest form of CVP to some problems. It is safe to say that the CVP analysis can be modified to overcome linearity and most other limitations, to the degree that is desirable. There comes a point, however, where the modifications should not be made and other management tools should be called upon to compliment CVP. For example, if major nonlinearities exist and affect results, they should be included and the linear assumptions modified. The introduction of time value of money on the other hand is in most cases better left to capital budgeting approaches rather than incorporating that into CVP.

EXHIBIT 2. Assumptions and Limitations of CVP Analysis

Assumption/Limitation	*Comment*
1. The analysis is valid for a limited range of values—the "relevant range"—and a limited period of time.	1. Failure to observe these limits would lead to working with data that are not realistic. Observing the limits solves most problems with CVP. Linear relations often exist for limited changes in volume; and nonvolume changes such as technology, tastes, and factor prices can more safely be assumed to be constant over short periods.
2. Costs can be categorized as fixed or variable.	2. Semifixed costs present a problem that can be solved by segregating fixed and variable postures, smoothing steps, or explicitly showing nonlinear ties. (See separate fixed-variable cost discussion.)
2a. Variable costs change proportionately with volume within the relevant volume range.	2a. & 2b. There is a danger that linear cost and revenue relationships may be used when nonlinearities are significant. The typical economists' curves are contrasted with break even in Exhibit 3. Nonlinear curves often have optimum quantities; linear ones do not.
2b. Fixed costs are constant within the relevant volume range.	
3. Revenues change proportionately with volumes	3. Price is constant for all volumes within the relevant range.
4. There is a constant product mix.	4. Data should be adjusted for any shifts in product mix.
5. There is no significant change in inventories (i.e., in physical units, sales volume equals production volume).	5. Costs and revenues are related to the same volume. Data should be adjusted if inventories change markedly.
6. Changes in volume alone are responsible for changes in costs and revenues.	6. There are other influences (see 1 above) on costs and revenues, but they are lessened if narrow time and volume limits are applied. (See scatter diagram discussion.) CVP helps in profit planning, but is not a full business plan.
7. Appropriate data can be found.	7. Data are not readily available. Fixed assets are not recorded in amounts on a replacement cost basis. Inflation adjustments can be made. Costs are not classified as fixed or variable in normal accounting records. Cost analysis is necessary.
8. The analysis is deterministic.	8. Uncertainty and a probabilistic approach can be introduced. This will change decisions in some cases.*
9. Operating leverage questions can be dealt with in the CVP framework.	9. This should be supported with capital budgeting approaches that consider the time value of money.

* A lucid explanation of fundamentals is Robert K. Jaedicke and Alexander A. Robichek, "Cost-Volume-Profit Analysis under Conditions of Uncertainty," *The Accounting Review*, October 1964, pp. 917–26.

Fortunately, the simple linear cases are often realistic and the basic CVP analysis can be applied just as Exhibit 1 suggests. This is particularly true when the range of volumes and time period limitations are recognized and adhered to.

The linear break-even assumptions are in contrast to the economists' assumption of continually changing prices and unit costs, as shown in Exhibit 3. In the economists' total revenue curve, on the left, the increase and then decline in total revenue is due to a lower price being associated with larger quantities. At first the decline

EXHIBIT 3
Nonlinear and Linear Break Even

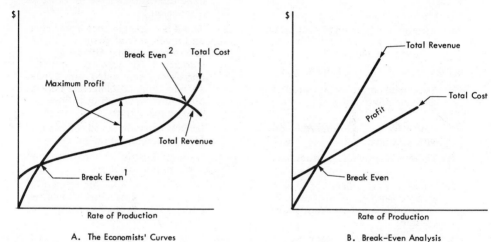

A. The Economists' Curves

B. Break-Even Analysis

brings a disproportionately large increase in sales and total revenue increases—the demand curve is "elastic." With further price reductions the increase in sales is less than proportional to the decrease in price and total revenue falls—demand is "inelastic." On the cost side, movements in opposite directions of fixed and variable costs per unit shape the curve. Except for small volumes, the declining fixed costs per unit are more than offset by rising variable costs per unit. The sum of variable and fixed unit costs rises and so does total cost as output increases. The output at which total revenue most exceeds total cost is the point of maximum profit. There is no similar point for the linear break-even curves; the larger the volume, the greater the profits, within the range of volumes considered. Cost studies have found that most businesses are operating in a range of relatively constant unit costs. As a result, the break-even analysis' constant unit cost curve is more useful than the economists' cost curves.

As for prices, the characteristics of competition faced by a product are the key to whether prices need to be lowered for greater volume. It is clear, however, that there is stability in many prices as quantities change substantially. For limited periods and quantities, a variation in quantity produced without a change in price is frequently a realistic assumption. It is also true, however, that businesses are often concerned about price-quantity relationships. So, either linear or nonlinear revenue curves may be appropriate in a given case. A pricing example below combines the two.

Costs

Differential Costs. Chapter 4 is devoted to "Basic Cost Concepts and Terminology;" therefore only a few summary remarks on this subject are necessary here. There is an emphasis on differential costs in CVP analysis; a key question is, do costs differ (vary) or remain fixed as volume changes? In addition, the contribution margin (price — variable cost) is identified in CVP and some contribution analysis is almost unavoidable (Exhibit 1C). Since CVP is to be used for decisions about the future, future costs—or for near-term matters, current costs—rather than historical costs are relevant. (Chapter 4 says that historical costs are used for break-even analysis, and they are; but costs of the period affected by the decision *should* be used.) The opportunity cost concept—the cost of a factor of production is its value in its best alternative use—is also applicable. Labor and material and most overhead costs are current opportunity costs, since they are market prices paid by all users. In periods of frequent price and wage changes, even those costs may not represent labor and material costs during the period being considered. Analyses in both constant dollars and in inflated dollars help clarify issues.

Accounting records are apt to be farthest from current and future costs in measuring depreciation. The book value of depreciation is usually a poor measure of the value of capital consumption by a business. The acquisition costs may be many years old and far from replacement costs; also the method of computing depreciation may not represent the change in value of a fixed asset during an accounting period. (In generally accepted accounting principles, depreciation is intended to be an allocation of original cost to the periods of benefit derived from an asset; it is not intended to represent a decrease in an asset's market value.) An estimate of the difference in the market value of an asset if it is sold now or a year from now is a better measure of the annual cost of a fixed asset. If the experimental 1976 SEC requirements for replacement costing receive wide applicability, current depreciation values will be more readily available. While it is not at all uncommon to use book depreciation as one of the fixed costs, it is seldom a good measure for use in decision making.

Fixed, Variable, and Semifixed Costs. CVP is obviously short-run analysis. Both the range of volumes and the time to which the relationships apply are limited. Economists have been fond of pointing out that in the short run there are fixed and variable costs, but in the long run all costs are variable. In CVP application a category of semifixed (or semivariable) costs appears. Many of these are steplike functions. Such costs can accommodate an increase in volume up to a point; then they must be augmented. When this category of costs is recognized, the economists' statement should be modified to say that in the short run there are fixed, variable, and semifixed costs, while in the long run there are only variable and semifixed costs.

Fortunately, many short-run costs fall clearly into the fixed or variable categories. Variable costs—costs that (in total) increase proportionately with volume—usually include raw material incorporated into a final product, fuel and utilities necessary to the production process and various other materials consumed. For some products and services direct labor varies with volume, while for others there is a fixed requirement for labor if the production process is to take place at all. Purchased parts and components are variable costs in cases of hardware production.

Fixed costs—those which (in total) do not vary with volume—are likely to include fuel and utilities related to occupancy, insurance and taxes, interest, depreciation, some of the supervisory labor, and all of the managerial labor.

Semifixed costs increase with volume, but not proportionately, and that upsets linear assumptions. Some such costs increase in steps as noted above. Others combine fixed and variable features and, if these two elements can be separated, that eliminates a semifixed cost. For example, selling expense may be partly fixed, and partly variable. Housekeeping expenses are usually partly fixed regardless of the volume of production, and partly related to the volume. The same is true of large-scale computer operations.

Other examples of semifixed costs can be found in indirect activities such as industrial relations, finance, intermediate level managers, tool control, scheduling, marketing, office services, telephone and telegraph, travel, security, professional outside services, and product distribution.

Our survey of firms showed fixed and variable costs do present problems for CVP analysis. (There were 116 replies in total, but not everyone replied to all questions.) We found the following:

	Number Agreeing
The segregation of costs into fixed and variable:	
a. Is an essential step in our break-even work.............. 77	
b. Has not been a preoccupation with us; we are concerned with total revenues and total costs and do not apply break-even analyses requiring a division into fixed and variable costs............................. 16	
c. Is a difficult and involved process........................ 25	
d. Is a relatively easy process............................... 28	
e. Can best be accomplished by understanding the nature of each cost element and judging whether it is fixed or variable...................................... 66	
f. Can best be accomplished by statistical analyses (linear regression) that derive an intercept as a fixed cost and the slope as variable cost................. 10	

In answer to the question of what problems have given most trouble with break even, "Difficulties in separating total costs into fixed and variable costs," outranked the second problem (linear assumptions) by 43 to 31. Respondents' comments emphasized that many costs were semivariable and that there was difficulty in obtaining management agreement on how costs should be classified.

Linear relationships like those in Exhibit 1 are simple, easy to work with, and easy to understand. It is possible, however, to show the nonproportional variations in costs in an analysis. Exhibit 4 shows the effects of quantity buying on material costs (the area just above total fixed costs), and of double and three-shift operations on variable costs. Important discontinuities should be displayed. On the other hand, where linear approximation do not distort the re-

EXHIBIT 4
Semivariable Costs

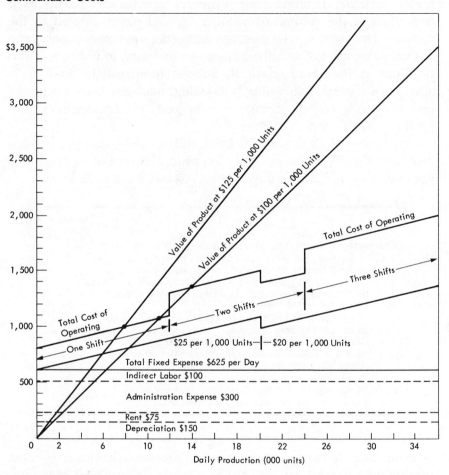

* Break-even points.
Source: Alvin A. Hass, "Profitability (or Loss) at a Glance," *Modern Plastics*, February 1972 (McGraw-Hill, Inc.).

sults, smoothing step costs and the use of judgment or statistical methods (discussed in the next section) to separate the fixed and variable portions of semifixed costs are ways of converting semifixed costs to fixed and variable costs.

Judgment or Scatter Diagrams? The survey found that the most common way of deciding whether a cost is fixed, variable, or semifixed is by attempting to understand the nature of each cost element and making a judgment as to how it relates to volume.

Only 10 out of 77 respondents said that the segregation of costs could best be accomplished by a scatter diagram analysis that interprets the intercept of a line fitted to the data as a fixed cost and the slope as the variable cost. That approach is illustrated in Exhibit 5.

EXHIBIT 5
Scatter Diagram Approach to Fixed and Variable Costs

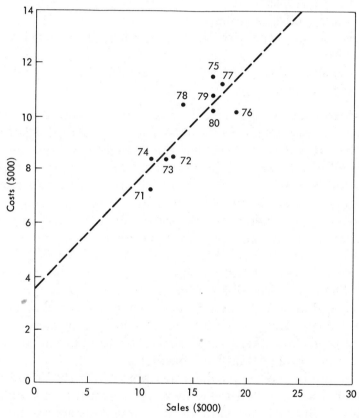

Note: 71 is 1971; 76, 1976, etc.

A scatter diagram may be applied to total costs or to some cost segment like labor, fuel, direct manufacturing costs, data processing, sales effort, and so forth. Exhibit 5, adapted from Raun,[4] plots assumed total cost over a number of years against dollar sales

---

[4] Donald L. Raun, "The Limitations of Profit Graphs, Breakeven Analysis, and Budgets," *The Accounting Review,* October 1964, p. 930.

volume. One way of interpreting the results would be that the intercept with the *y*-axis of the "least squares" line is the level of fixed costs, and the slope is the variable costs per dollar of sales.[5] The general formula is:

$$y = a + bx$$

where:

y = the total cost.

x = volume of sales in dollars.

a = is the intercept with the *y*-axis, which is the level of fixed costs.

b = the slope of the line, which is the variable cost per dollar of sales volume.

In this particular case, the fixed costs would be $3,712.67 and the variable cost per dollar of sales $0.41: $y = \$3{,}712.67 + \$0.41x$.

In Exhibit 5 it is obvious that the change in volume does not explain all of the variation in costs. If it did, the points would all fall on the line. It is also clear that volume does explain much of the change in costs, about three fourths in this case. That it does not explain more should not be surprising, since the analysis violates a number of the assumptions listed earlier. Relevant range is forgotten: the sales data fall between $10,000 and $20,000, but the interpretation of fixed and variable costs extends the data to the origin. The time covered is certainly not limited to a short period like a year. Rather it covers a decade during which technology and prices changed. Even if the assumptions had been more carefully adhered to, factors other than volume doubtless have affected cost, but the relationship would have been closer.

In defense of the scatter diagram approach, it should be noted that if data are adjusted to be more homogeneous, this approach can provide insights. Assumptions that some costs are fixed or variable may be thrown into question by the data. Disagreements about the nature of different cost elements may be narrowed by using statistical information. Expert judgment, which is the alternative to a statistical approach, is, after all, usually an individual's integra-

---

[5] This method of relating two variables by fitting a straight line to the points on a scatter diagram is called linear regression, a correlation analysis technique. The line is fitted so that the sum of the squares of the vertical distances of the points from the fitted line is a minimum. The points on such a "least squares" line are the most probable values of the quantity being measured on the vertical axis. See Fredrick C. Mills, *Statistical Methods,* 3d ed. (New York: Henry Holt & Co., 1955), pp. 249–50.

tion of such information with adjustments for unusual events in the past and new departures in the future.

APPLICATIONS

The kinds of businesses that find applications for CVP seem unlimited. Journals specialized in banking, education, medical care, publishing, insurance, and mail order are among those that have dealt with CVP in recent years. That is not surprising since CVP is potentially helpful to any business that has a fixed-cost hurdle in the path of profits.

The kinds of problems posed to CVP also grow, but more slowly. In the survey of business firms mentioned earlier, we found that the most popular uses of CVP were to estimate profits and losses at different volumes and to make decisions about undertaking or discontinuing an operation. Pricing alternatives and contribution analysis were the next most popular uses, followed by analyses of cash break even, profitability of different segments of the business, product mix, and operating leverage.

Most applications may be at the level of the firm, a facility, a line of business, or a product. A number are described below.

Finding the Break-Even Point and Profits over the Relevant Volume

Knowing and obtaining the volume necessary to break even—to have total revenues that will cover total costs—is a matter of concern to almost every business at some time.

A sad example is the sportsmen's emporium of Abercrombie and Fitch. After 84 years of business, which included supplying safari gear to Theodore Roosevelt and equipping Admiral Byrd for his Antarctica expedition, the company filed for reorganization under Chapter XI of the Bankruptcy Act. Its treasurer explained, "We just didn't do enough business to support the overhead we have now."[6]

Exhibit 1 illustrates the identification of the break-even point and also shows the effect of volume on either side of that point.

Cash Break Even

The cash impact of the volume of business is often more important than accrual profits. There are noncash sums in both revenues

---

[6] *New York Times,* August 7, 1976, p. 1.

EXHIBIT 6
Cash and Full-Cost Break-Even Comparison

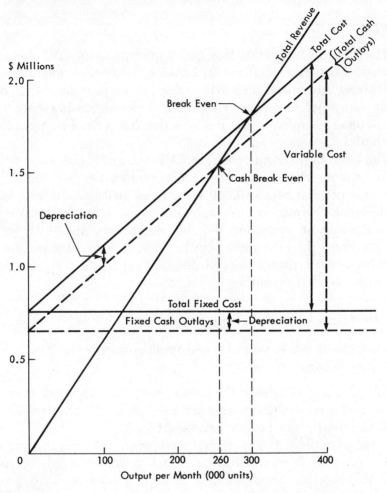

and costs, but the most obvious item is depreciation. By excluding depreciation from fixed costs, a first approximation of the cash break even can be obtained. A firm may operate well below its break-even point and still be above its cash break even.

This form of the break-even chart is shown by a dashed cost line on Exhibit 6. It is based on the same assumptions as Exhibit 1. Excluding the $100,000 of depreciation from the fixed costs results in a cash break even of 260,000 units per month, compared to a full-cost break even of 300,000 units.

Multiple Product, Multiple Plant Companies

A single break-even analysis can be made for a company consisting of several plants, each selling several product lines. A single analysis for such a firm would assume a constant mix of products and unchanging cost and price relationships among the products. But some of the most important CVP problems deal with the profitability of individual product lines. These problems require the development of an individual product break-even analysis at each plant location.

This may be approached as follows.[7] For each *total* sales volume for the company as a whole, identify a portion of sales with each product line at each plant. Identify fixed and variable costs at the plant level associated with the volume of sales of each product line. Fixed costs that are at the company level and common to all activities—company-wide overhead—need not be allocated to plants or product lines. This procedure will provide the data for a break-even chart for each product line at each plant location. The P/V chart (Exhibit 1D) provides a very useful form. An illustration for two products at one plant is shown in Exhibit 7. The fixed costs, the profitability in terms of contribution to overhead or profits per dollar of sales (the P/V ratio), the break-even point, and profit or loss for any value of sales are all displayed. Alternate pricing, investing, or other strategies may be examined. To go from a single product to the total company profits, a cascade approach is used as illustrated below.

At sales of $1 million for the company:

The contribution of Product A to Plant 1's overhead and profits (Sales = $200,000)..........	+$70,000
The contribution of Product B to Plant 1's overhead and profits (Sales = $150,000)..........	+ 40,000
Less Plant 1's fixed cost.........................	− 90,000
Plant A's contribution to company overhead and profits...	+ 20,000
The same steps for Plant 2 yield a contribution to company overhead and profits.................	+ 50,000
Total contribution to company overhead and profits of Plants 1 and 2........................	+ 70,000
Less company-wide fixed costs....................	− 50,000
Equals company's profit..........................	$20,000

[7] For a detailed case involving multiple product lines and locations refer to W. Warren Haynes and William R. Henry, *Managerial Economics,* 3d ed. (Dallas: Business Publications, Inc., 1974), pp. 318–26. Another interesting multiproduct case is in Robert N. Anthony and James S. Reece, *Management Accounting: Text and Cases,* 5th ed. (Homewood, Ill.: Richard D. Irwin, Inc., 1975), pp. 548–53.

EXHIBIT 7
CVP Charts for Two Product Lines in One Plant of a Company with Multiple Products and Plants

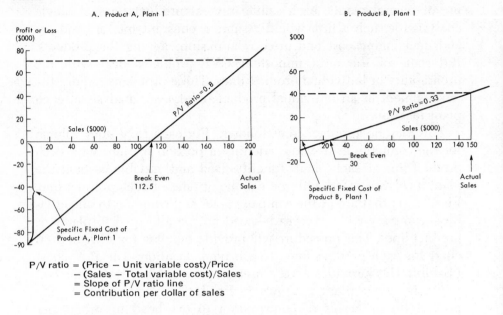

A. Product A, Plant 1

B. Product B, Plant 1

P/V ratio = (Price − Unit variable cost)/Price
 − (Sales − Total variable cost)/Sales
 = Slope of P/V ratio line
 = Contribution per dollar of sales

A Price Discrimination Strategy

An example of pricing presented by Donald Snook, Jr.[8] illustrates several points. He describes a private clinic operating at 50 percent of capacity. Its patient visits per year total 6,000; and at an average price per visit of $10, revenues total $60,000. Total costs are $61,000, of which $25,000 is fixed and $36,000 variable. The variable costs result from the 6,000 "units" (patient visits) costing $6 per unit. The clinic is now sustaining a loss of $1,000 per year. It has an offer of 3,000 additional visits per year from a local union if the rate is reduced to $8 per visit for that group.

Exhibit 8 shows the loss without the union's incremental 3,000 visits, and the profit with them. The interesting aspects of the case is that by accepting a fee ($8) that more than covers the variable cost ($6) but does not cover total cost ($61,000 ÷ 6,000 = $10.17) at the original volume, the clinic covers full cost and makes a profit. The contribution margin for the 3,000 incremental visits is $8 —

---

[8] Donald Snook, Jr., "Break-Even Analysis Gives Manager Flexibility and Control in Making Decisions," *Hospital Financial Management,* September 1975, pp. 58–62.

$6 = $2. The deficit at 6,000 visits was $1,000, and the first 500 added visits with a contribution of $2 each can overcome that. The remaining 2,500 incremental visits added $5,000 of profits. Another way to look at this is in terms of fixed and variable costs per unit. The variable cost is a constant $6. The per visit (allocated) fixed cost fell from $25,000 ÷ 6,000 = $4.17 at 6,000 visits to $25,000 ÷ 9,000 = $2.78 at 9,000 units. The total cost per visit fell from $10.17 to $8.78, and the clinic would have broken even if 9,000 patients had paid that price ($8.78). Adding to the volume of business at a price that does not cover full cost at a low volume may lower fixed

EXHIBIT 8
Added Business at Less than Total Cost

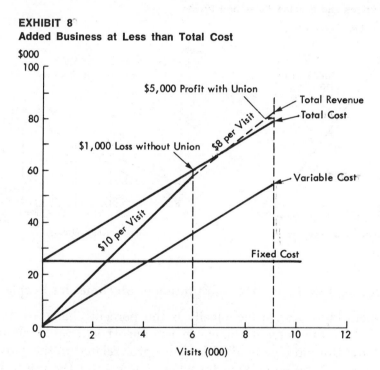

costs per unit enough to result in profits at the higher volume. Of course, recognizing the need for a work load over which to spread fixed costs is nothing new. But it is sometimes omitted in contribution discussions, which often emphasize the acceptability for a brief time of business that covers variable costs and some but not all fixed cost. The additional business may in fact lower the average fixed cost so the lower price covers full cost.

General Pricing Strategy

A more general examination of the effect of price changes is shown in Exhibit 9. Changes in the price result in different slopes of the revenue line and different break-even quantities. As Haynes and Henry[9] point out, the demand for each quantity can be estimated and the price that maximizes profit can be identified. In this case, the price of $6 yields the highest profit of the three prices considered.

EXHIBIT 9
Alternate Prices and Related Sales and Profits

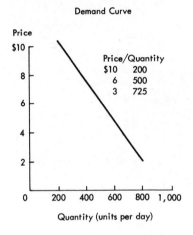

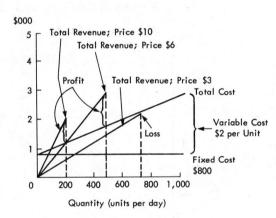

Operating Leverage—The Substitution of Machines for People

Operating leverage technically is the percent change in profits divided by the percent change in volume. It is a profit elasticity measure. But more generally, the concept is related to the substitution of plant and equipment for labor. The greater the use of fixed assets and the less of labor, the greater the operating leverage in most cases. This is because variable costs per unit of output typically decrease with the use of more capital equipment. An increase in volume will generally result in a greater increase in profits for the more capital-intensive plant than for the more labor-intensive plant, because total variable costs will rise less for one than the other.

Exhibit 10 is an example of the application of break-even analysis

---

[9] Haynes and Henry, *Managerial Economics*, p. 200.

to the question of whether or not to substitute equipment for labor. It is a real problem faced by a military electronics equipment manufacturer several years ago. The circuit board component of a disposable acoustical device could be made manually or with an automated line. The manual assembly would require 25 employees, and the automated assembly, only 6. The setup for the manual line would cost $25,000, and for the automated line an additional $50,000 (i.e., $75,000 in total). At a price of $14.50, break even for

EXHIBIT 10
Automated versus Manual Production

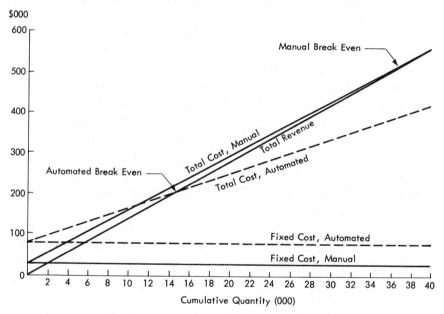

the manual process was 36,000 units and for the automated system, 14,479 units.

The automated system costs less than the manual one at relatively low quantities and seemed well worth installing. In other cases, the fixed costs required to automate often involve an added risk, and the investment is only justified if there are prospects of a large sales volume. That is not a problem here. At relatively small volumes the automated system pays for itself.

This conclusion is reinforced by the fact that in this case the whole cost of the automation is written off by the break-even point.

Its full fixed cost—not just its depreciation—is included in the $75,000. This is a limited production rather than a continuous production case, since the volume is represented by cumulative quantity rather than the rate of production. Limited production is discussed more fully below.

Dominant Fixed Costs

A review of applications of CVP brings to light many cases in which all, or nearly all, costs are fixed. Entertainment events fall into this class. For example, in 1976 Hollywood's film festival, Filmex, broke even for the first time.[10] Costs did not vary with attendance, but revenues did. In fact, there were grants that resulted in revenues that were fixed as well as revenues that were variable. The curves looked something like Exhibit 11. If the fixed revenue is omitted and the total revenue starts at the origin, a similar picture can be drawn for other individual theatrical presentations. The concern about breaking even in the theater goes back to classical Greek drama which had high costs of production because of their choruses.

Banks' costs are mostly fixed; a banker tells us:[11] "It can reasonably be assumed that all costs are fixed relative to the volume of deposits, except for the interest paid on deposits. The interest paid on deposits is directly proportional to the amount or volume of deposits, while over a wide relevant range of deposits, other costs do not vary appreciably. Thus costs such as personnel costs, occupancy costs, equipment costs, and the cost of borrowed funds are assumed to be relatively fixed (constant) over a reasonably wide volume range of deposits."

An analysis of the insurance industry arrives at a similar conclusion, "With the exception of commissions to brokers, the variable costs incurred by an insurance agency tend to be relatively insignificant in amount."[12]

These examples in which fixed costs dominate might raise the question about cases where all or nearly all costs are variable. They

---

[10] *Los Angeles Times*, April 24, 1976, pt. II, p. 7.

[11] Charles H. Eggleston, "Break-Even Analysis and the Bank," *Bankers Magazine*, Winter 1972, pp. 59–63.

[12] Louis F. Biagioni, "Profitability Analysis in the Independent Insurance Agency," *CPCU Annals*, December 1974, pp. 271–76.

EXHIBIT 11
Filmex Break Even

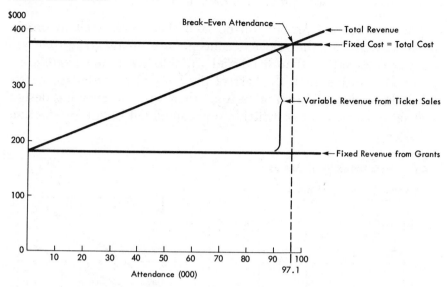

exist—research assistants, services provided by individuals out of
their homes—but are not of interest since the price must cover the
variable cost in each transaction, and there is no problem of adequate volume to overcome the nonexistent fixed costs.

Limited Production: Nonrecurring and Recurring Costs

Rate of production in units, or dollars, is the usual measure of
volume in a CVP analysis. This measure is appropriate when the
production is expected to go on for an indefinite period and the
quantities to be produced are essentially unlimited. Most manufacturing and service businesses are of this nature. But not all! Airplanes, special-purpose machines, cranes, elevators, ships, books,
plays, and innumerable job shop orders for special items are examples of limited production. Here is what one economics text says of
these cases:

> The traditional laws of production are oriented to the problem of
> infinitely continued production. . . . Many production decisions,
> however, involve a given volume or period of production. For
> example, the firm is to print 10,000 copies of a book or produce 300

planes of a certain type. . . . The traditional theory does not directly cope with production for a finite run. . . .[13]

Cases of limited production do lend themselves well to break-even analysis, but the relevant concepts are *nonrecurring and recurring costs* rather than fixed and variable costs, and *cumulative production* rather than the rate of production. In order to undertake a limited production of an item, there are nonrecurring design and setup costs, most of which are accumulated before production

EXHIBIT 12
An Aircraft Break-Even Analysis

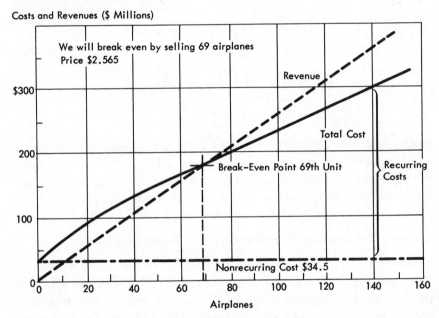

Costs and Revenues ($ Millions)

starts. These must be recovered by sales if the operation is to be profitable. Recurring costs are expended during the production phase.

Exhibit 12 shows the break-even planning for an actual aircraft program. The nonrecurring cost of $34.5 million covers preproduction costs—those which are necessary to design, develop, perform

[13] G. S. Stigler, *The Theory of Price*, 3d ed. (New York: Macmillan, Inc., 1967), p. 171. Stigler credits Alchian and Hirshleiger in this section.

tests, build mock-ups, and provide production tooling. The recurring costs include not only manufacturing and procurement but also support activities such as redesign and sustaining engineering and tooling.

Note the departure from linear assumptions in the recurring costs. The curve shows that there are decreasing costs per unit as the cumulative quantity increases. Behind these decreasing costs is the "learning curve," or really a family of learning curves, for assembly, subassembly, and various fabrication and processing stages in the production process. Learning curves usually take the form of a constant percent reduction in man-hours with a doubling of output. Thus an 80 percent curve is one that shows 80 percent of the original man-hours required in an operation as output increases from 1 to 2 planes or from 2 to 4 planes or from 200 to 400 planes. On an arithmetic grid the curve is a hyperbola; on a double logrithmic grid it is a straight line.

While the nonrecurring cost curve in Exhibit 12 could be approximated by a straight line, the losses for quantities less than break even would be understated and gains beyond break even overstated if a linear approximation were used. There are similar discrepancies whenever linear approximations are used for nonlinear realities in break-even analyses, but the learning curve is so much a part of aircraft cost-estimating that it is very likely to be included in break-even work.

The ideas of fixed and variable costs and nonrecurring and recurring have similarities, but are quite different in terms of costs included. Direct labor and material which are typically variable costs are included in both nonrecurring and recurring costs. Similarly, those overhead items that are usually fixed costs are included in both recurring and nonrecurring costs. The criteria for sorting costs differ in cases of continuous production as opposed to limited production. In the latter, the question is related to the preproduction or production phase of the work. In both cases the question is whether the volume—rate of production on one case, cumulative production in the other—will be sufficient to overcome the hurdle of costs that do not vary with quantity.

More than one third of the businesses we surveyed engaged in limited production runs. This suggests the recurring and nonrecurring approach to break-even merits more attention than it usually receives.

There is an interesting relationship between break-even analysis of limited production quantities and the most popular capital budgeting technique, the payback method. While a payback usually does not explicitly discount cash flows, it is concerned with the *time* for a project to recover its investment. More exactly, it is concerned with the time for net cash flow to recover from a negative position to zero. Break-even analysis, on the other hand, emphasizes the *quantity* that must be sold to break even. The two points are the same: the break-even quantity will be sold at the time the net cash position reaches zero. This is true in principle, although some accounting reconciliations may be necessary.

Exhibit 13 is the same as the previous exhibit, except for the

EXHIBIT 13
Break-Even and Payback Analyses

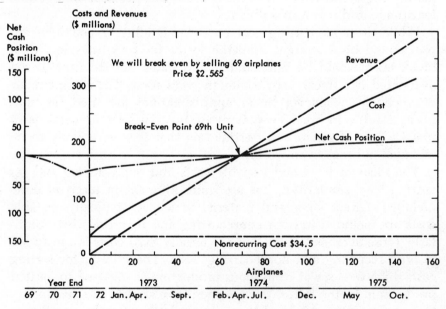

overlay of net cash flow information. The small positive cash flow by the end of 1969 is due to prepayments that were expected by that time. The time scale is arbitrary prior to the delivery of the first ten aircraft. The fact that break even and payback are different views of the same event in the case of limited production is well illustrated by this case.

SUMMARY AND CONCLUSIONS

There are, of course, objections to payback as a capital budgeting technique. It fails to take into account the time value of money specifically and in its preference for an early payback may favor a project with a lower present value than another. Management would make a mistake in relying on such a technique exclusively; but there is value in this lucid portrayal of the depth and shape of the negative cash position and the time until the firm is again at a cash break-even point. This useful approach should be supplemented by others that take into account the time value of money and additional elements of a complete business plan.

Similarly, there are objectives to CVP. It often simplifies in an attempt to present the essence of an issue. Exhibit 2 summarized some of these simplifying assumptions. There are other analyses that should supplement a break-even chart; but that is not to deny that break-even analysis will provide valuable insights and identify crucial issues. The complexities that are eliminated can be reintroduced in part by refining the CVP analysis and in part by adding other analyses. Thus, cost-volume-profit analysis remains an important technique to assist management in profit planning.

One final note on behalf of CVP. While its greatest claim is that it helps cut through complexities to clarify issues, it also fosters the applications of managerial accounting principles. Such concepts as contribution analysis, differential costs and revenues, and opportunity costs are usually the appropriate ones for business decisions. CVP encourages an understanding and use of these concepts.

ADDITIONAL SOURCES

Anderson, Lane K. "Expanded Breakeven Analysis for a Multi-Product Company." *Management Accounting*, July 1975, p. 30.

————, Roy A., and Biederman, Harry R. "How Industry Uses Break-Even Analysis," chap. 14 of *The Treasurer's Handbook*. Edited by J. Fred Weston and Maurice C. Goudzwaard. Homewood, Ill.: Dow Jones-Irwin, 1976.

Christenson, Charles J.; Vancil, Richard F.; and Marshall, Paul W. *Managerial Economics: Text and Cases*, chap. 3. Rev. ed. Homewood, Ill.: Richard D. Irwin, Inc., 1973.

Eggleston, Charles H. "Break-Even Analysis and the Bank." *Bankers Magazine*, Winter 1972, p. 59.

Fremgen, James M. *Accounting for Managerial Analysis,* chap. 13. 3d ed. Homewood, Ill.: Richard D. Irwin, Inc., 1976.

Hartl, Robert J. "The Linear Total Revenue Curve in Cost-Volume-Profit Analysis." *Management Accounting,* March 1975, p. 49.

Haynes, W. Warren, and Henry, William R. *Managerial Economics,* pp. 318–26. 3d ed. Dallas: Business Publications, Inc., 1974.

Hilliard, Jimmy E., and Leitch, Robert A. "Cost-Volume-Profit Analysis under Uncertainty: A Log Normal Approach." *The Accounting Review,* January 1975, p. 69.

Jaedicke, Robert K., and Robichek, Alexander A. "Cost-Volume-Profit Analysis under Conditions of Uncertainty." *The Accounting Review,* October 1964, p. 917.

Larimore, L. Keith. "Break-Even Analysis for Higher Education." *Management Accounting,* September 1974, p. 25.

Neuner, John J. W., and Deakin, Edward B. *Cost Accounting: Principles and Practice,* chaps. 16, 20. 9th ed. Homewood, Ill.: Richard D. Irwin, Inc., 1977.

Raun, Donald L. "The Limitations of Profit Graphs, Breakeven Analysis, and Budgets." *The Accounting Review,* October 1964, p. 930.

Snook, Donald, Jr. "Break-Even Analysis Gives Manager Flexibility and Control in Making Decisions." *Hospital Financial Management,* September 1975, pp. 58–62.

7

Job Order Cost Systems

Ralph O. Wilson, Jr.*

Job order cost systems, or more modernly, *specific order cost systems,* are used when knowing the cost of projects, individual units, or groups of identical units is required and production is done on separate and distinct jobs or lots of product. Each job is assigned a number, to which the cost of the material, labor, and overhead necessary to complete the specific project or order of finished goods is accumulated.

The best illustration of the mechanics of the job order process is the *job cost sheet,* which was manually posted and summarized prior to the advent of the computer, and is still utilized by small operations. While this illustration is based on a manually posted system, most companies now use a computer, and the job cost sheet has been replaced by job cost *data bases* for labor, material, and overhead, with appropriate software for summarization and report writing.

In a job cost system, the cost of each job is recorded on a job cost sheet, which generally contains separate sections for labor, materials, and overhead. The job cost sheet shown in Exhibit 1 contains one column for material cost and one for labor cost; usually several such columns are provided to furnish additional details. For example, the job cost sheet for a shipbuilder might contain material columns for steel, engines, hardware, and so on, and labor columns for functions such as cutting, handling, and welding. The

* Mr. Wilson is Assistant Controller, Dravo Corporation, Pittsburgh, Pennsylvania.

EXHIBIT 1
Job Cost Sheet

"A" MANUFACTURING COMPANY

Customer _____   Job Order Number _____

Description _____   Date Started _____

Quantity Ordered _____   Date Completed _____

Quantity Completed _____

		DIRECT MATERIALS		DIRECT LABOR			OVERHEAD	
Date	Regn.	Type	Amount	Week Ending	Hours	Amount	Week Ending	Amount
	TOTAL			TOTAL			TOTAL	

Cost Summary

	Amount	Actual Unit Cost	Estimated Unit Cost	(Over)/Under- estimate
Direct Materials	_____	_____	_____	_____
Direct Labor	_____	_____	_____	_____
Overhead	_____	_____	_____	_____
Total Job	_____	_____	_____	_____

Explanation of Variance: _____

_____

_____

purpose of the job cost sheet (or the job cost data base, if a computer is used) is cost segregation. It should be designed with a view to its ultimate utilization of furnishing the cost information required to control cost on projects or jobs in progress and to provide historical cost for management bidding/pricing decisions. The collection of cost sheets, or information in the data base, constitutes a subsidiary record supporting the Work in Process account in the general ledger.

Some examples of "jobs" for which a job order system would be appropriate are as follows:

Heavy manufacturing:	One or more turbines.
	One or more towboats or ships.
	The equipment for an ore benefication plant.
Light manufacturing:	An order of chairs for a furniture factory.
	An order of printing for a printer.
	A lot of castings for a foundry.
Construction:	A dam, a bridge, or a section of a highway.
	A house or group of houses.
	The plumbing or electricity for a house or group of houses.
Service industry:	Design and construction management for a nuclear power plant.
	Performance of a corporate audit by a certified public accounting firm.
	Washing the windows in a building.
	Repairing an automobile.

It is evident from these examples that the value of a "job" can vary from a few dollars to multimillions of dollars, and the time period can vary from hours to years.

Job versus Process Costing

Job order costing differs from process costing systems in that *unit costs* in the process system are average costs for a period of time. Companies manufacturing homogeneous products on a continuous basis, such as cement, beer, paper, petroleum products, chemicals.

and steel, use the process cost system. Also, certain public utilities like electric power, gas, water, and steam heat cost their products by the process method.

In continuous process production, a product ordinarily moves from raw material to finished form through a sequence of departments or cost centers. A department or cost center is one operation or a series of operations where a specific step in the completion of the product is performed. The department or cost center provides the basis for process costing. Costs are accumulated by the department for a time period such as a week or a month, without any attempt to associate cost with *individual* units of product. At the end of the period the total costs collected for the department are divided by the physical output of the department to obtain the average unit cost for the product in that department. The average unit cost times the number of units transferred becomes, in effect, the cost of the material entering the succeeding department or the cost of the products put into finished good inventory, if the product is complete.

The process system not only provides information on unit cost but if the proper organizational structure is present, it will measure performance within each area of production responsibility. Cost of production reports show the cost of labor, material, and overhead used to process an average unit through each department and the average cost of each unit of finished product. (The chapter following this one deals entirely with process costing systems.)

The choice of whether to use a job order or process cost system is determined in most cases by the project, type of product, and the production process. Job order systems are mandatory for construction, heavy manufacturing, and most service industries. Homogeneous products require process cost systems. Light manufacturing sometimes provides an option where either method may be used. Although the job order system requires more record keeping with resulting higher cost, it should be used whenever there are identifiable units with reason to expect significant cost variances between units or groups of units.

It should not be assumed, of course, that a company will use only one of these systems throughout the company. For example, companies using the process method for their primary production often use a job order cost system for controlling unique or "one-shot" efforts such as capital expenditure projects, major repairs, and so on.

Job Cost Example

A hypothetical example of an application of job order costing is a joint venture of several contractors to bid on and perform a major construction project. The contractors jointly prepare a proposal and bid for the project utilizing their joint knowledge and resources. When they are successful in being awarded a contract, they form a separate legal entity (the joint venture) to perform the work. The joint venture partners make advances to, or investments in, the joint venture to provide working capital. The joint venture's accounting system then becomes essentially a job order cost system with one job.

The partners assign a management team to the joint venture, and all costs of salaries, fringe benefits, and so on of this team are paid by the joint venture. The joint venture hires labor, both direct and indirect, to perform the project and pays all costs related to labor. It purchases and pays for the equipment, material, and supplies required by the project. It also contracts with subcontractors to provide labor, materials, and services that can be furnished more economically by them. Any services provided by the partners to the project are billed to the joint venture and are paid by the joint venture. The joint venture issues invoices to the owner/customer for the performance of the contract and receives payment from the owner/customer.

At the end of the contract, after the surplus equipment and supplies have been sold, all of the cost of the project and all of the revenue received from the owner/customer have been recorded in the joint venture. After returning the partner's advances/investments, the profit or loss on the contract is distributed among the partners. In effect, this is what job order costing is all about: the bringing together of all of the cost information related to a specific order of work.

SYSTEM PARAMETERS

Managers' Requirements

Before the features of a job cost system are established, the organization's managers must be considered. Remember, a very simple system will meet all normal accounting requirements, so any further sophistication of the system is for the benefit of its users. A sophisticated system which is designed, implemented, and imposed by the accounting group or controller's office is notoriously ineffective.

Systems are not capable of controlling organizational performance; however, they do provide information to the managers who *are* in a position to interpret and take action. If the managers view the data as helpful and use the information properly, the cost system works. If, on the other hand, managers do not perceive the system as helpful—which may happen because they were not given training in how to use the system—the system will be circumvented or ignored and will become worthless.

Traditionally, organizations seldom invest much effort in training managers to use cost control systems or in trying to adapt cost control systems to the users' management "styles." Instead, most organizations spend much time in designing, refining, and improving the technical aspect of their systems. The result is that while cost control systems continually become more precise, accurate, and technologically sophisticated, the users' comprehension declines and the information provided by the system is not used by the manager. The cost control system and the way that it is used constitute a potentially powerful tool for influencing individual behavior. Performance of all levels of management is generally evaluated at least in part on cost control system information. Since performance evaluation is the basis for most management remuneration policies, managers generally want to understand and be affiliated with good cost control systems.

Top management must be dedicated to the cost control system. The system must be consistent with management's style and strategy. If a proposed system does not support management's style and strategy, either management must be committed to a change or the system must be modified. Top management must be the system's sponsor and be prepared to actively and visibly use the cost information furnished. The cost system should be an internal part of management planning, coordination, and control procedures so that accomplishment of goals can be measured. Good performance must be rewarded and poor performance corrected.

Middle management is the principal user of the information provided by any cost control system. They are dedicated to the system and use the information for the day-to-day control of operations. They are not only interested in accomplishing goals but in how the goals are achieved. To illustrate, holding the line on or reducing overhead expense might be detrimentally accomplished by deferring or eliminating needed maintenance work. Middle-management reports highlight this type of information along with other cost variances. The requirements of middle management for sufficiently detailed information to optimize operations must be met.

First-level management, usually the supervisor, job superintendent, or project manager, is the source for the majority of cost system input and is the primary user of the most detailed information provided by the system. In addition to input for cost information, first-line supervisors must measure and report units of production or percent of completion accomplished if meaningful reports are to be prepared. The cost system provides first-level management with an "early warning" function of surfacing problems before those problems reach the crisis state, provided the system is understood and utilized. First-level managers need today's results today; however, as a practical matter, they usually receive results weekly.

All levels of management must participate with the controller's office in setting the parameters of a cost system. The key to a good cost control system is having all levels of management understand the system's objectives and its mechanics. All levels must be convinced that the system is practical, consistent with management objectives, and that it will provide accurate, timely, useful information with reasonable cost and effort.

Coding Structure

The base requirements of any cost system are to make it simple, understandable, flexible, current, accurate, inexpensive, and efficient. In a job order cost system the three areas that usually complicate the system and cause misunderstandings are the detailed segregation of labor and material into the various operations performed; confusion relating to the splits between direct and indirect labor and direct and indirect material; and overhead allocations.

A chart of accounts or coding structure provides a standard designation of each element involved in a job and is used in estimating and pricing as well as recording and analyzing of job cost. The code structure must relate to the natural phases of production or construction and unit performance for each code must be measurable. One problem is that many of us get carried away and es-

tablish an excessive number of codes: we say we *might* need the
information, and that it is always easier to add two detailed items
together than to attempt later to develop the needed detail.

It must be remembered, however, that the accuracy of the system is a function of the quality of the inputs. If the person making
the original data input has to make an estimate, or is arbitrary in
making segregations of time and material because of coding requirements that are not congruent with the various tasks, nothing
in the system can later improve these data. The key is to have codes
which have understandable descriptions, with examples whenever
confusion is possible.

6071: Concrete Spillway

6071.011	Plant (Air, Water, Electricity, etc.)
6071.012	Batch and Mix Concrete—Purchase Aggregate
6071.013	Haul Concrete
6071.014	Place Concrete
6071.015	Screed Finish
6071.016	Float Finish
6071.017	Steel Trowel Finish
6071.018	Point and Patch
6071.019	Horizontal Construction Joints
6071.021	Cure and Cleanup
6071.024	Build in Place Wood Forms
6071.025	Shop Fabricate Reusable Wood Forms
6071.026	Set and Strip Wood Forms
6071.027	Shop Fabricate Special Wood Forms
6071.028	Set and Strip Special Wood Forms
6071.033	Purchase and Assemble Special Steel Forms
6071.034	Set and Strip Special Steel Forms
6071.037	P.V.C. Water Stop
6071.038	Drains
6071.039	Foundation preparation
6071.042	Other Specials

The simplest coding structure would be (1) labor, (2) material,
and (3) overhead. The illustration is an example of a more complex
coding structure for placing concrete in a dam spillway. In this
example, the major code 6071 indicates a direct cost (a 6,000-series
number) for bid item 71, Concrete Spillway. The next three-digit
intermediate code (after the decimal) represents the operational
breakdown of bid item 71 used for estimating and cost control. In
addition, the two-digit minor code (not shown) represents subcoding
for Labor (.01), Material (.02), Specific Plant (.03), Equipment

Rental or Depreciation (.04), Supplies (.05), Subcontractors (.06) and General Overhead (.07).

When the chart of accounts or coding system is established, it will form the heart of the job cost system, and hence all users must be consulted before the coding structure is made final. Pricing estimators must use the same coding system in preparing estimates. The detail must be significant, meet management's needs, and the detail segregation must relate to the natural phases of operations and be readily discernible to those who prepare input.

Any numbering sequence can be used for job identification. The individual job is usually determined by customer orders; however, the system must have sufficient flexibility to permit combining several customer orders into one job order if dictated by efficient production scheduling. When items are manufactured for stock, the number of units included in a job should match natural economic production lots, taking into consideration job setup cost and inventory carrying cost.

Reports

The standard format of the reports emanating from the job cost system should be tailored to each management level's interest and ability to understand. To be effective, control reports must provide adequate (from the user's point of view) and accurate data, and they must be frequent and timely. Each report should be a part of an integrated system of periodic reports. A performance report to the first-line level of management must support a segment of the performance report to each higher level of management. The reports should fit the organization chart of the company and follow definite lines of authority and responsibility. For each level, it is important for reports to be incisive and to encourage "management by exception." Reporting should highlight priority information and reduce the complexity of reports by approximating (rounding off), summarizing (showing totals and subtotals), and comparing (actual versus budget). Reports reflecting only actual dollar amounts have little value for lower level managers; units of production, unit cost, and comparisons to estimates or budgets must be included. The reports should be reviewed from time to time to be sure they continue to be used and meet user requirements.

SYSTEM UTILIZATION

The job cost accounting system and its related job cost data base are utilized to furnish information for:

Internal and external financial reporting;

Current job cost control;

Budgets and forecasts; and

Historical costs for pricing and future estimating.

Cost information is used for internal financial reports (as contrasted to job cost reports) to management. These reports are specifically formatted to highlight management objectives and are frequently in a format comparable with the formats of external reports for stockholders, the public, and the various regulatory agencies. Although all of these reports have different formats and objectives, and are subject to differing interpretations, all must flow from, and have a basic commonality with, the job cost system. All external reports are reviewed by public accountants who must certify that they are in accordance with generally accepted accounting principles applied on a consistent basis.

Current job cost control is aided by the job order cost system by maintaining unit cost figures on a day-to-day basis so that if any one item is higher than estimated, it may be examined and corrected while the job is still in process. By spotting cost overruns while the job is in its early stages, permitting early correction of problems, management may be able to effect substantial reductions in final cost. First-line managers need daily feedback highlighting developing problems in their area of control. They can then manage by exception and concentrate their efforts on the troubled area.

One of the fallacies of this type of managing by exception is that sometimes items with large potential for savings are overlooked just because they were estimated high and do not show up on the exception report. Some provision must be made for periodic review of large unit items with potential for savings, even though these tasks are being performed within their estimated cost.

Budgets are more useful when they are prepared in detail, permitting later comparison with actual cost detail. Detailed budgeting motivates managers to really plan their operations, rather than taking a "broad-brush" approach to both planning and budgeting. Production schedules control light manufacturing companies' budgets, while heavy manufacturing and contractors prepare their budgets and control costs by using actual cost to date, committed cost, and estimated cost to complete. Good budgets highlight potential problem areas and motivate management to concentrate its efforts on maximizing profits.

The most important function of budgeting is that it forces the manager to plan and be committed to that plan for the budget time period. Effective budgets are prepared by operating management with the assistance of staff in the controller's office. Operating management must be committed to the budget. If the controller's office prepares the budgets, operating management can always say, "Those financial people prepared the budget and since they do not know anything about operations, how are we expected to meet their budget?"

Historical job unit costs and production rates provide management with accurate data upon which to formulate future pricing. Of course, historical job costs must be evaluated and adjusted to reflect changes caused by differences in job characteristics, inflation of labor and material costs, and changes in productivity. Although most sales prices are established by competition, it is imperative that management understand and utilize historical cost in creating marketing strategies. Adjusted historical cost plays an important role in establishing price/volume/profit ratios so that various price positions can be evaluated and the proper marketing trade-offs made to maximize overall company profits while getting the job or sale at a competitive price.

Using appropriate operational cost coding for estimating and costing enhances management's ability to review past performance and prepare accurate estimates of future job costs. When the amount of data and the frequency of use justify it, historical data are maintained in computerized data banks with extensive sorting capabilities and are frequently updated to include latest actuals. Data banks also include special notes relating to special circumstances, production errors, and so forth, enabling management to take advantage of improved methods or to avoid problems on future jobs.

JOB COSTING COMPONENTS

The basic components for manufacturing and service industry job order cost systems are material, labor, and overhead; equipment and subcontractors are added for the construction industry. Manu-

EXHIBIT 2
Job Cost-Flowchart

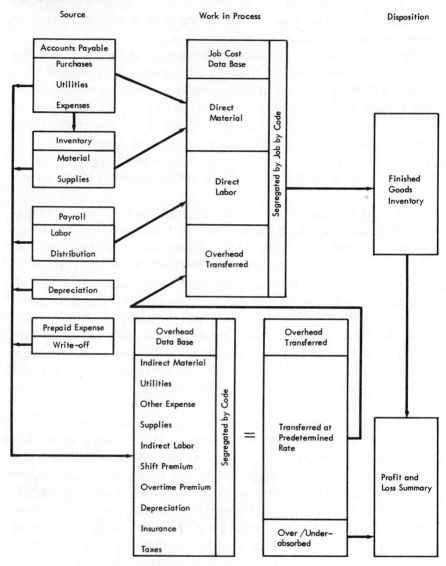

facturing costs flow from materials (inventory and purchases), payroll, and overhead accounts to the work in process accounts (a job cost data base) to a finished goods inventory account or, in some cases, directly to cost of sales. A diagram of these cost flows is shown in Exhibit 2.

Materials

The materials account is a perpetual inventory account which receives and controls the amount of raw materials ("direct materials") and consumable supplies ("indirect materials") on hand. As materials are issued for specific job use, the costs are transferred to the appropriate job in the job cost data base.[1] Costs of supplies which cannot be identified with specific jobs (indirect materials) are transferred to the overhead account. For example, the grease issued from supplies inventory in an auto repair shop will be used on several jobs, and the time involved in measuring and recording the exact amount used on each job would be ridiculous in comparison to the value of the grease transferred.

Of course, accounting for these materials transactions requires that the company have an established policy as to materials inventory valuation. The benefits of Lifo, Fifo, average cost, and standard inventory prices must be considered when this policy is established.

Heavy manufacturing and construction contractors usually charge materials purchased specifically for a major job directly to the job, bypassing the materials inventory account. These companies normally maintain a separate "committed cost" data base, wherein the committed costs of direct materials and subcontracts are recorded at the time the purchase order or subcontract is written. The committed cost is then compared to the original estimated cost, and an immediate analysis is prepared showing the effect of the transaction on job profits.

Labor

Payroll records are required to pay the employees and for the preparation of payroll tax returns, insurance reports, and other labor-based forms. To get cost information for the job cost data base, we need a distribution of how the time of each employee was spent. In addition to the job number, the operation the worker performed (as defined in the job code structure) is needed; for example, on a house construction contract, excavating for footings, finishing concrete floor, or laying bricks for a fireplace. The key to the accuracy of the labor portion of the job cost system relies on

---

[1] Recall that for a small company, this data base may consist of a set of manually prepared job cost sheets, one for each job.

the person who makes the time distribution. This can be the supervisor, the worker (approved by the supervisor), or a timechecker (checked by the supervisor). Again, it must be stressed that this first level of management must understand the system and its benefits if it is to operate correctly.

Direct labor that is identified with a specific job is transferred to the job cost data base for that job. Indirect labor, which (by definition) cannot be identified with specific jobs, is transferred to overhead. For example, the amount of wages for a welder is transferred to the job on which the welder works, but the wages of a storekeeper cannot be identified by jobs (or at least it is not worthwhile trying to do so), and therefore is transferred to overhead.

A simple distribution of "gross wages earned" is a satisfactory measure of labor costs. However, several alternative methods are available. One method includes payroll taxes, hospitalization, insurance, union welfare and pension funds, and all other fringe benefits. This gives emphasis to the total cost of a unit of labor. Another method is to use average rates rather than the specific rates actually paid to the individual employee, to eliminate variations due to using different labor categories, for example, second-year apprentices versus first-year apprentices or journeymen. This method saves time by simplifying calculations and reducing errors in labor distribution.

Overtime and shift premiums are particularly difficult to allocate; for example, does one charge overtime to the job that caused the overtime, if one knows, or to the job on which the overtime was worked? Most companies charge overtime and shift premiums to overhead.

One of the first-line management's prime functions is to control labor; therefore, they need information on labor cost with variances to estimates or standards as quickly as possible. For operating purposes, labor reports grow stale very rapidly. Many cost systems include separate daily reports for labor.

Overhead

Manufacturing overhead normally comprises all manufacturing expense other than direct materials and direct labor. Some overhead expenses such as depreciation and supervision are fixed and do not fluctuate with volume changes, while other overhead expenses such as utilities and consumable supplies are variable and do fluctuate with volume changes. Sufficient subfiles (codes) must be established in the overhead data base so that individual overhead expenses can be monitored and controlled.

A relationship between overhead incurred and the product produced must be established. For an optimum system, overhead should relate directly to the base on which the overhead is applied. Imagination seems to be the only limiter on determining acceptable methods. Overheads are transferred to jobs on the basis of machine-hours, total man-hours, cost of material, specific man-hours, labor dollars, units of product, total project cost, total project revenue, and, sometimes, combinations of two or more of the above. If more than one basis is used for allocation, separate congruent pools of overhead expense must be maintained. The key is to have a method that is reasonably equitable, correlates well with the incurrence of cost, is understood by all levels of management, and uses data readily available in the data base.

Complex systems that once were regarded as too burdensome and expensive with hand-posted methods can be readily implemented with a computer, and should be considered if they correlate well to actual cost and are better understood by management.

In service industries, most jobs are of short duration, with longer jobs accounted for on a percentage-of-completion method of accounting. In many service companies, overhead is not allocated to individual jobs but is maintained and controlled by an autonomous overhead control systems. For example, consulting engineers normally deduct job direct labor and direct materials from job revenues to account for individual job gross profit or net fees. Total overhead expense for the period is then deducted to give net income from operations. Due to the importance of overhead expense, which may run as high as 50 percent of revenue, it is budgeted and rigidly controlled separately from job cost.[2]

Due to the time lag after the end of an accounting period before the period's actual overhead rate can be determined, a predetermined, rather than an actual, rate for application of overhead is used. This enables management to know with reasonable accuracy the total cost for jobs completed and in process on an ongoing

---

[2] One reason that overhead for a professional service firm may be high is that professionals' nonbillable time is treated as overhead expense.

basis. To obtain the rate for applying overhead to jobs, the budgeted overhead expense for the year, or other planning period, is
divided by the anticipated base. These values are generally revised
each year during the preparation of the budget.

Use of a predetermined rate facilitates timely preparation of
interim cost and financial statements throughout the year. It is also
used so that overhead can be charged to jobs at a rate that eliminates the fluctuations in job costs which would result from spreading fixed overhead costs over varying levels of periodic production
(i.e., from seasonality). The use of a predetermined overhead rate
is also helpful to management in preparing bids on contract work
and in quoting firm prices on special jobs.

Since overhead is applied on the basis of annual estimates, a
balance may remain in the overhead account at the end of any
period. When production fluctuates seasonally, little overhead is
applied in a month of low production but much is applied in a
month of high production. The overhead expense is likely to be incurred more or less evenly over the year, particularly to the extent
that many overhead costs, such as depreciation, rent, property
taxes, and insurance, are fixed, and are typically recorded uniformly
over the months; for example, the annual property tax payment is
treated as though it were 12 monthly installments. Production
fluctuations leave a debit balance in overhead after a period of low
production and a credit balance after a period of high production.
Expenses and production volume are apt to vary from budgets and
estimates, which may result in a balance in either direction. Regardless of cause or nature, the balance in overhead is called an
overhead variance. More specifically, the balance is called "underabsorbed overhead" if a debit balance and "overabsorbed overhead" if a credit balance.

During the year, the overhead variance is usually carried as a
balance sheet item. If the variance is major and is caused by an
error in the rate, the variance should be allocated to cost of goods
sold, work in process, and finished goods. At the end of the year,
overhead variances are generally written off to cost of goods sold on
the assumption that they arise because of errors in the rate, and the
amounts attributable to inventories are not material. As a practical
matter, a special account called Overhead Transferred or Overhead
Absorbed is often established for the transfer to job cost so that the
overhead expense account retains the total overhead expense which
is offset by the overhead transferred or absorbed account.

Equipment and Subcontracts

Equipment required to perform a construction contract is a major cost item for the construction contractor. The cost of owning, maintaining, and operating equipment is charged to individual jobs, and the cost of major equipment is segregated by the operations performed; for example, a crane may be charged to excavation, handling steel, placing concrete, and so on.

Most construction contractors have an equipment "pool" (account) to which depreciation, insurance, taxes, and major repairs are charged. The pool is "relieved" of this cost by transferring cost to the jobs using the equipment at standard rates. A special account called "Equipment Transferred" or "Equipment Absorbed" is often established to record the transfer to job cost so that the equipment cost account retains the total equipment cost, which is offset by the equipment transferred or absorbed account. Monthly, daily, and hourly rates are established by estimating the total cost of the equipment (depreciation, insurance, taxes, and major repairs) and dividing by the estimated chargeable life of the equipment. The chargeable life of the equipment takes into account the idle time due to the seasonal nature of the industry and downtime for repairs. At the end of the year, under- or overabsorbed equipment variances are generally written off to profit and loss due to the sunk nature of such cost.

Jobs normally are charged with the full cost of equipment operators, maintenance mechanics, maintenance supplies, and fuel. They also are charged for all uninsured equipment losses and any damages resulting from abuse or improper operation.

Cost of special equipment purchased for a specific job may be charged directly to job cost with credit given to the job when the equipment is sold. Thus the job is charged with the full cost of this special equipment. If the special equipment is not sold at the end of the job, an appropriate salvage value must be established and credit given to the job.

Subcontractors are used by general contractors to do specialty work. For example, the home builder generally subcontracts the plumbing, brickwork, electrical, and landscaping. The subcontractor furnishes supervision, labor, direct materials, supplies, and equipment to perform a given segment of the job which is defined in a formal subcontract agreement. The general contract terms are usually passed through to the subcontractor so that the subcontractor has the same rights and restraints the owner established with the general contractor. Subcontract costs are segregated into the same operations (codes) that the general contractor would have used had it performed the work itself except that the subcontractor usually does not furnish the general contractor with a separate cost for actual labor, material, equipment, and overhead.

In large manufacturing and construction jobs in progress for extended periods of time, profits may be taken to the profit and loss account either when the contract is completed or on a percentage-of-completion basis. The completed contract basis has the advantage of conservatively delaying profit-taking until actual profits are known. Using this method for tax-reporting purposes helps cash flow by delaying tax payments to the end of the job. Losses are taken as soon as they can be anticipated; however, this is not permissible for taxes. The principal disadvantage of the completed contract method is that profits flow to the profit and loss account erratically with frequent and substantial fluctuations.

The percentage-of-completion method smooths out the flow of profits to the profit and loss account, as profits are taken to this account in each accounting period as work progresses. Most percentage-of-completion methods use the ratio of actual cost divided by total estimated cost, multiplied by total estimated profit, to determine profit earned to date. The principal disadvantage of this method is that in the early stages of the job, management is traditionally optimistic and too much profit is taken to the profit and loss account. This causes embarrassment when profits previously taken must be reduced. Users of the percentage-of-completion method require accurate cost forecasts reasonably prepared by a knowledgeable management. (Incidentally, a firm can use percentage of completion for its internal or shareholder reporting but still use completed contract for tax reporting.)

Standard costs (discussed in Chapter 23) can be applied to a job cost system in the manufacturing industries, but it is generally not used in the construction and service industries because of the diversity of the job operations and the lack of common, repeatable operations.

REPORTING

The job cost report formats in Exhibit 3 illustrate methods used to communicate cost information to management. The construction industry report formats (A, B, C, and D) for constructing a portion of a steel processing plant, illustrate report formats used by three levels of management. The following is a glossary of terms used in column headings for report formats A, B, C, and D:

Base estimate: Original estimate of quantity (units) and cost of work to be performed.

Revised estimate: Original estimate plus or minus change orders from the customer or a redistribution due to change in construction method, for example, change from direct labor to subcontract.

Installed [this] period: Quantities (units) of work performed, labor cost, and material and subcontractor cost committed in the current period.

Installed (committed) to date: Same as installed (this) period on a "to-date" (i.e., cumulative) basis.

E.T.C. forecast: Estimated cost to complete, the quantities and dollar amounts for future activities or expenditures not yet committed. The source for this information is the project engineer in collaboration with the job engineer, assisted by the cost engineer. Information here reflects the effect of latest engineering reports, vendor quotes, and other information that affects the final forecast cost for each code.

Forecast total: The sum of installed (committed) to date and E.T.C. forecast to complete.

Gain or loss: Computed—revised estimate minus forecast total.

Variance: Difference in gain/loss this report versus last report.

Estimated unit cost: Originally estimated unit cost for each item of work.

Installed unit cost: Actual unit cost for each item of work.

Report format A, to top management, has been summarized to five items: total direct cost, total backcharges and extras, total indirect cost, home office overhead, and contingency. This report compares the forecasted total cost with the revised estimated cost and highlights the gain or loss to date. This short form allows management to review a large number of jobs quickly.

Report format B, which accompanies format A to top management, is a summation of 15 major categories of work (only 7 of which are shown in Exhibit 3). This report indicates the gain or

EXHIBIT 3
Construction Industry Job Cost Reports

Report Format A

Description	Base Estimate	Revised Estimate	Committed to Date	(E.T.C.) Forecast	Forecast Total	Gain/Loss
Total direct codes, 0100–7999						
Total backcharges and extras codes, 8000–8999						
Total indirect codes, 9000–9979						
Overhead code, 9980						
Contingency code, 9990						
Total cost						

Report Format B

Range Code	Range Description	Base Estimate	Revised Estimate	Committed to Date	(E.T.C.) Forecast	Forecast Total	Gain/Loss	Variance
0100–0299	Site preparation							
0300–0899	Foundations and concrete							
0900–1899	Structures							
1900–3899	Mechanical equipment standard							
3900–4899	Mechanical equipment job related							
4900–5899	Piping							
5900–6599	Electrical							

Report Format C

Code	Description	Base Estimate	Revised Estimate	Installed Period	Installed (committed) to Date	Forecast (E.T.C.)	Forecast Total	Gain/Loss
0100	Clearing site	S$	S$ HR L$ LE		S$ HR L$ LE	HR L$	S$ HR L$ LE	S$ HR L$ LE
0200	Facilities	S$	S$ M$ ME	M$ ME	M$ ME	S$ M$	S$ M$ ME	S$ M$ ME
0300	Excavation		HR L$ LE	HR L$ LE	HR L$ LE	HR L$	HR L$ LE	HR L$ LE

Report Format D

Code	Description	Base Estimate	Revised Estimate	Installed Period	Installed (committed) to Date	Forecast (E.T.C.) Known	Forecast (E.T.C.) Unknown	Forecast Total	Gain/Loss	Estimate Unit Cost	Installed Unit Cost
0300	Excavation		HR CY L$ LE	HR CY L$ LE	HR CY L$ LE	HR CY L$		HR CY L$ LE	HR CY L$ LE	HR/CY L$/CY	
0311	Excavation, backfill, spoil area-07	CY S$	CY M$		S$ SE			S$ SE CY M$	S$ SE CY M$	M$/CY	
	Item total	$	$	$	$	$		$	$		

loss for each major category and highlights variances from the last report. The two reports (22 lines of information) combine to keep top management aware of the current status of each job.

Middle management is the principal user of format C reports, which are summarized on the "100" code level (about 75 categories of cost). For each category of cost, the report shows labor hours (HR), labor dollars (L$), labor escalation (LE), subcontract dollars (S$), subcontract escalation (SE), material dollars (M$), and material escalation (ME) in each column of the report. This report highlights the gains and losses for each element of cost for the "100" code level categories of work.

The detailed report, format D, is used by on-site management, home office project management, and the cost department. The detail coding (several hundred possible segregations) included in this report is the lowest level accumulated in this job cost system. In addition to the cost elements included in report format C, this report includes estimated, installed, and forecasted quantities (CY = cubic yards) of work performed and estimated and installed unit cost.

The above reports were designed as working tools for each level of management in accordance with their needs. However, all are available to other levels on a request basis; for example, top management may request detailed cost data for specific jobs or specific cost categories when required for managerial decisions.

Labor Control

In a service industry, people are generally the service company's most important asset. Since labor and labor-related expenses comprise the majority of service company costs, controlling labor and labor-related expense is the key to success in this industry. Due to this characteristic, service industry report formats are predominately labor oriented.

If we use consulting engineering companies as an example of the service industry, we find that they earn their revenue by selling the services and expertise of their people. Generally, they bill a client for technical salaries (engineers, drafters, etc.) times a multiplier to recover employee benefits, overhead, and profit. There are many variations in contract terms, such as cost times a multiplier that includes the fee; cost times a multiplier plus a fixed fee; lump sum;

guaranteed maximums; incentive targets; and various combinations. Overhead expenses are usually not allocated to job cost and are deducted from gross profit or net fees.

To equate the various types of contracts and to provide a basis for overhead comparisons, an equivalent base must be established. Technical salaries (engineers, drafters, etc.) are the most commonly used equivalent base. An alternate base, revenue earned, is used by some companies; however, revenue is oftentimes distorted when flow-through costs (items invoiced to clients without markup) vary from normal patterns. Consulting engineering firms are usually organized so that the project manager has complete control of the project and reports directly to the division vice president. Department managers (civil engineering, mechanical engineering, etc.) furnish people to the project manager to perform the work; however, they retain control of the people and their related indirect expense. They also report directly to the division vice president.

Two separate control systems are established. The one for direct labor and direct material, a job order cost system, is controlled by the project manager. The second system, for overhead expense, is controlled by the functional department managers (civil engineering, mechanical engineering, administration, accounting, and so on.)

Jobs are evaluated on the basis of gross profit or net fee contribution to overhead and net operating profit. Contribution is usually expressed as a percentage of technical salaries charged to the job. The project manager's reports are formatted to highlight contribution by function, and include service labor (technical salaries), expense (flow-through cost), revenue earned on service labor, contribution, and the percent contribution on technical salaries. Sufficient detail is available so that the project manager can determine individual time spent on specific drawings when required. A key here is drawing status and average man-hours per drawing. Detail at this level includes work performed by individual employees. Division management receives condensed contribution reports for all jobs controlled by the division.

Report format E (Exhibit 4) illustrates a typical project cost and process report used by division management. Top management's report is a contribution exception report that lists only those jobs that do not produce an acceptable contribution percentage. This emphasis on the jobs with below-average contribution directs

EXHIBIT 4
Report Format E

PROJECT COST AND PROGRESS REPORT

Report No. _____
Project No. _____
Project Mgr. _____

Run Date _____ Page _____
Period Ending _____

	Current Period							Job to Date	Total
	Total Hours	Regular Hours	O/T Hours	Premium Hours	Current Est./Hours	Hours To Date	Hours Remaining	Direct Cost	Revenue
Project summary:									
Total engineering.............	0.0	0.0	0.0	0.0	0.0	0.0	0.0	0.00	0.00
Total design.................	0.0	0.0	0.0	0.0	0.0	0.0	0.0	0.00	0.00
Total other technical support.....	0.0	0.0	0.0	0.0	0.0	0.0	0.0	0.00	0.00
Total other support services.......	0.0	0.0	0.0	0.0	0.0	0.0	0.0	0.00	0.00
Total labor...................	0.0	0.0	0.0	0.0	0.0	0.0	0.0	0.00	0.00
Total billable expenses...........								0.00	0.00
Total non-billable expenses.......								0.00	0.00
Total expenses...............								0.00	0.00
Total job....................	0.0	0.0	0.0	0.0	0.0	0.0	0.0	0.00	0.00

Direct Cost		Current Period	Job to Date	% Completed	Current Total Estimate
	Services	0.00	0.00	0.0	0.00
	Expenses	0.00	0.00	0.0	0.00

Revenue		Current Period	Mo. %	Job to Date	% Completed	Current Total Estimate
	Services	0.00	0.0	0.00	0.0	0.00
	Expenses	0.00	0.0	0.00	0.0	0.00

Contribution	Current Period	Job to Date	Current Total Estimate	Original Estimate
Amount	0.00	0.00	0.00	0.00
Percent of Labor	0.0	0.0	0.0	0.0

Note: 0.00 indicates dollar amount (actual report is in whole dollars).
0.0 indicates hour or percentage figure.

EXHIBIT 5
Report Format F

DIVISIONAL INCOME STATEMENT

Division _____ For Period Ended _____ Issued _____

		Current Period				Year to Date			
		Actual	% Payroll Cost	Budget	Variance	Actual	% Payroll Cost	Budget	Variance
	Contract Revenues and Cost								
1	Service revenues	0.00	0.0	0.00	0.00	0.00	0.0	0.00	0.00
3	Total service revenue	0.00	0.0	0.00	0.00	0.00	0.0	0.00	0.00
4	Payroll cost to produce line 3	0.00	0.0	0.00	0.00	0.00	100.0	0.00	0.00
5	Net service revenue	0.00	0.0	0.00	0.00	0.00	0.0	0.00	0.00
6	Data processing revenue	0.00	0.0	0.00	0.00	0.00	0.0	0.00	0.00
7	Reprographics revenue	0.00	0.0	0.00	0.00	0.00	0.0	0.00	0.00
8	Other revenue	0.00	0.0	0.00	0.00	0.00	0.0	0.00	0.00
9	Total revenue from expense and other	0.00	0.0	0.00	0.00	0.00	0.0	0.00	0.00
10	Cost of billable expense	0.00	0.0	0.00	0.00	0.00	0.0	0.00	0.00
11	Cost of nonbillable expense	0.00	0.0	0.00	0.00	0.00	0.0	0.00	0.00
12	Net revenue (expenses)	0.00	0.0	0.00	0.00	0.00	0.0	0.00	0.00
13	Net contribution	0.00	0.0	0.00	0.00	0.00	0.0	0.00	0.00
	Divisional Overhead								
16	Salaries (see ① on format G)	0.00	0.0	0.00	0.00	0.00	0.0	0.00	0.00
17	Expenses (see ② on format G)	0.00	0.0	0.00	0.00	0.00	0.0	0.00	0.00
18	Total (see ③ on format G)	0.00	0.0	0.00	0.00	0.00	0.0	0.00	0.00
19	Profit (loss) before allocations and taxes	0.00	0.0	0.00	0.00	0.00	0.0	0.00	0.00
20	Intradivisional allocation	0.00	0.0	0.00	0.00	0.00	0.0	0.00	0.00
21	Corporate allocations	0.00	0.0	0.00	0.00	0.00	0.0	0.00	0.00
22	Total allocated expenses	0.00	0.0	0.00	0.00	0.00	0.0	0.00	0.00
24	Net profit (loss) before taxes	0.00	0.0	0.00	0.00	0.00	0.0	0.00	0.00
25	Allocated federal and state taxes	0.00	0.0	0.00	0.00	0.00	0.0	0.00	0.00
26	Net income	0.00	0.0	0.00	0.00	0.00	0.0	0.00	0.00

Note: 0.00 indicates dollar amount (report is in whole dollars).
0.0 indicates percentage figure.

EXHIBIT 6
Report Format G

DIVISIONAL JOB COSTS
AND OVERHEAD

Division _____   Center Number _____   Period Ended _____ Issued _____

| | Current Period | | | | Year to Date | | | |
	Actual	% Payroll Cost	Budget	Variance	Actual	% Payroll Cost	Budget	Variance
Job Costs								
Labor	0.00	0.0	0.00	0.00	0.00	0.0	0.00	0.00
Out-of-Pocket expenses	0.00	0.0	0.00	0.00	0.00	0.0	0.00	0.00
Total	0.00	0.0	0.00	0.00	0.00	0.0	0.00	0.00
Overhead								
Salaries and fringe benefits:								
General, administration, and clerical	0.00	0.0	0.00	0.00	0.00	0.0	0.00	0.00
Marketing and proposals	0.00	0.0	0.00	0.00	0.00	0.0	0.00	0.00
Professional development	0.00	0.0	0.00	0.00	0.00	0.0	0.00	0.00
Research development and standards	0.00	0.0	0.00	0.00	0.00	0.0	0.00	0.00
Unassigned time	0.00	0.0	0.00	0.00	0.00	0.0	0.00	0.00
Total salaries	0.00	0.0	0.00	0.00	0.00	0.0	0.00	0.00
① Total salaries and fringe benefits	0.00	0.0	0.00	0.00	0.00	0.0	0.00	0.00

Expenses:

Services of others	0.00	0.00	0.0	0.00	0.00	0.0
Travel expenses	0.00	0.00	0.0	0.00	0.00	0.0
Advertising and sales promotion	0.00	0.00	0.0	0.00	0.00	0.0
Recruitment and moving expenses	0.00	0.00	0.0	0.00	0.00	0.0
Communication costs	0.00	0.00	0.0	0.00	0.00	0.0
Reprographics	0.00	0.00	0.0	0.00	0.00	0.0
Data processing	0.00	0.00	0.0	0.00	0.00	0.0
Automated drafting	0.00	0.00	0.0	0.00	0.00	0.0
Incentive compensation	0.00	0.00	0.0	0.00	0.00	0.0
Supplies	0.00	0.00	0.0	0.00	0.00	0.0
Depreciation—equipment	0.00	0.00	0.0	0.00	0.00	0.0
Other building cost	0.00	0.00	0.0	0.00	0.00	0.0
Other equipment cost	0.00	0.00	0.0	0.00	0.00	0.0
Insurance expense	0.00	0.00	0.0	0.00	0.00	0.0
Miscellaneous	0.00	0.00	0.0	0.00	0.00	0.0
Professional development	0.00	0.00	0.0	0.00	0.00	0.0
② Total expenses	0.00	0.00	0.0	0.00	0.00	0.0
③ Total overhead	0.00	0.00	0.0	0.00	0.00	0.0

Note: 0.00 indicates dollar amount (report is in whole dollars).
0.0 indicates percentage figure.
A double ** is printed next to variances that exceed 10 percent.

management's attention and concentrates its efforts toward improving results on the jobs that are not producing satisfactory results.

Overhead Control

Overhead expenses are accumulated in expense codes similar to the following:

Administrative—Time	Professional Development—Time
Administrative—Expense	Professional Development—Expense
Unassigned—Time	Nonbillable Travel Expense
Unassigned—Expense	Office Space Rent
Employee Education—Time	Equipment Depreciation
Employee Education—Expense	Supplies
Local Communication Cost	Professional Services
Recruitment—Time	Professional Societies
Recruitment—Expense	Technical Research—Time
Employee Moving Expenses	Technical Research—Expense

Overhead report formats for first-level management, the section heads, include only those items of overhead expense over which the section head has control. Appropriate comparisons to budgeted expenses and their relationship to section technical salaries are included. At this level, individual expenses are detailed by employee.

Department manager's reports include a summary cost of all sections in the department including those costs not controllable by the section and department, plus the individual section reports. Comparisons to budgeted expenses and their relationship to department technical salaries are included. Lowest normal detail furnished in this area is total expense for the period by code by section.

Divisional reports are a summary of departmental reports with variances from predicted expenses highlighted for the division and for each department. Report formats F and G (Exhibits 5 and 6) are illustrative of divisional summary income statements and divisional job cost and overhead summaries. Departmental managers' explanation of major variances are a part of this report.

Top management receives total company overhead expense with appropriate comparisons to budget and the technical salary base.

Exception reports list, by expense codes, all expenses that are more than 10 percent higher or lower than the predicted percentage of the technical salary base by department. This allows expenses to increase when the technical salaries increase without setting off alarms, and signals the need for expense reductions when the technical salary base declines without equivalent expense reductions. In many cases, knowing that the firm is not spending the budgeted amounts is just as important as knowing where it overspent. For example, a consulting engineering firm would not want to fall behind in employee education or technical research, which might give an advantage to competitors.

This group of reports, specifically formatted for a consulting engineering company, is designed to furnish all levels of management with the information required to manage the various activities of the company. All lower level reports are available to higher levels of management on a request basis. (For additional information on control in professional service firms, see Chapter 45.)

Manufacturing cost report formats are tailored to the needs of their particular industries as were the reports for the construction and service industries we discussed here. In manufacturing, other elements of cost are as important, or more important, than those we illustrated. In manufacturing, some of the items often highlighted are machine production rates, setup time, handling time, material usage, waste, idle time, and so on. Each report is, however, custom-made to fit the requirements of the individual industry and company. Superior report formats can only be established by close cooperation and consultation with the users, the various levels of management.

SUMMARY

The focal points of this chapter are the concepts and principles required in a job order cost system and the cooperative relationships and joint efforts required to insure management utilization of the information provided by the system. Discussion about debits, credits, and general mechanics of operating the system has been minimized because they are well covered in most cost accounting books.

Users' participation in planning, implementation, and utilization of the system is vital to a successful system. The user must understand the system, the input, the internal mechanics, and the output, and be convinced that the information furnished is meaningful, accurate, timely, and will assist in managing the business. The first and most important step in creating a cost system is communication with all levels of management and the establishment of mutual goals. Once a commonality of goals is achieved and management enthusiasm is generated, a successful system will be forthcoming.

Editors' Note: Having been exposed in this chapter to the costs systems needed for controlling projects, the reader may also want to consult Chapter 42, "Project Management Systems."

ADDITIONAL SOURCES

Clough, Richard H. *Construction Project Management.* New York: John Wiley & Sons, Inc., 1972.

Dellinger, Roy E. "Job Cost Reporting for Construction Companies." *Cost and Management,* July–August 1974, p. 24.

Fremgen, James M. *Accounting for Managerial Analysis,* chap. 4. 3d ed. Homewood, Ill.: Richard D. Irwin, Inc., 1976.

Horngren, Charles T. *Cost Accounting: A Managerial Emphasis,* chap. 4. 4th ed. Englewood Cliffs, N.J.: Prentice-Hall, Inc., 1977.

Neuner, John J. W., and Deakin, Edward B. *Cost Accounting: Principles and Practice,* chap. 2. 9th ed. Homewood, Ill.: Richard D. Irwin, Inc., 1977.

Niles, Timothy J., and Dowis, Robert H. "Accounting for New Plant Construction." *Management Accounting,* July 1974, p. 35.

Shillinglaw, Gordon. *Managerial Cost Accounting,* chap. 2. 4th ed. Homewood, Ill.: Richard D. Irwin, Inc., 1977.

8

Process Costing Systems

George R. Bruha and S. Robert Gramen*

Cost Accounting Objectives

The primary objective of any cost accounting system is to provide for the accumulation of costs to permit meaningful managerial analysis and interpretation for decision making, and to enable accurate financial reporting. This objective is met by designing the system to provide accurate, pertinent, and timely information in three areas:

1. *Product costing*—for the pricing of product and service lines and various other analytical purposes.
2. *Inventory valuation*—to meet internal and external financial reporting requirements.
3. *Cost control*—over the production and operating activities.

To meet these needs the controller must design and implement a cost accounting system that will express in monetary terms the operating and production activities of the company and the flow of items, products, and personnel costs into, through, and out of a company. It is a procedure which "shadows" the actual operations or production processes by costing transaction activity and by providing (as a part of an integrated system) cost accounting, planning, and reporting information for management decision-making

---

* Dr. Bruha and Mr. Gramen are Managers with Arthur Andersen & Co., Detroit.

purposes to the various accounting, planning, and reporting sub-systems in a timely and accurate manner.

In designing a good cost accounting system, the controller must first clearly understand the company's products, production processing technologies, and the reporting environment of the industry in which the company operates. This understanding will permit the tailoring of the cost accounting and reporting system to the particular product and process environment. This chapter discusses the characteristics of production organizations that can employ *process cost accounting systems* and further summarizes the principles of the design and use of such systems.

The Required Environment

The two most commonly defined types of cost collection systems are job order and process cost systems. Job order costing is the appropriate costing system where production is scheduled, performed, and costs are accumulated on the basis of a job order or lot. This type of cost accumulation is appropriate for jobs which are custom designed or unique or, generally, jobs whose costs are clearly distinguishable by the time of completion of the job. A job cost collection system is more common when there is a diverse line of products. In a job order system each job or lot is treated as independent of all others. Unit costs may be calculated when production of the job or lot is complete. The unit cost is computed by dividing the total cost accumulated for the job by the number of output units. (For further details, see the preceding chapter.)

An industry for which the use of a process cost system is appropriate is one where the work is characterized as being stable within a continuous, recurring manufacturing process. There is a continuous flow of a large number of homogeneous products without reference to specific orders or lots. In such an industry the end products are homogeneous and there is no necessity to associate costs with specific jobs, lots, or orders. Process costing is found, for example, in the steel, food-processing, chemical, glass, cement, textile, and petroleum industries.

Exhibit 1 illustrates the production process for Plastics, Inc., a hypothetical company that would use a process cost accounting system. Plastics, Inc., produces extruded plastic sheet and formed products such as buckets, covers, automotive interior components,

EXHIBIT 1

PLASTICS, INC.
Production Flow

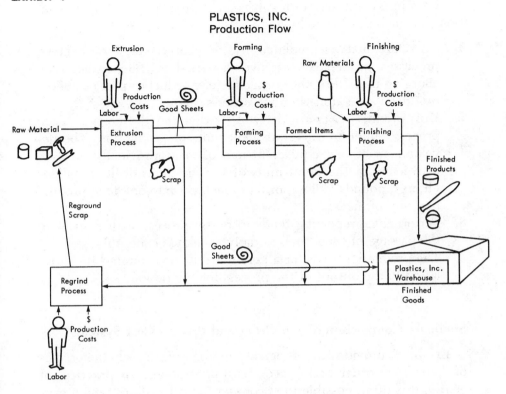

and so on. They have an extrusion process and subsequent job operations to form, trim, grind, and finish parts. The trimmed edges and uneven sheets from the extrusion process and trim scrap from forming are broken up and reground. Bad pieces are reported as scrap upon inspection and are reclaimed in regrind for use as raw material. A scrap credit is allowed for scrap pieces and trim in costing the final product. Production counts or weights are taken before all operations and as finished units are transferred to finished goods inventory. Note that not all of the finished products go through all processes. Some sheet is taken from the extrusion process directly to finished goods. Also, additional raw materials (chemicals and coloring) are added in the finishing process. A process cost system can be developed to effectively "model" this production process and provide the cost accounting data required by management.

Overview of Process Costing Concepts

The process cost system involves an approach to cost accumulation that includes the following steps:

1. Costs are first accumulated by, or charged to, cost centers, processes, or departments over a period of time, rather than charging them directly to specific jobs or lots of product being produced, as is done in a job order system.
2. Unit product costs are derived by dividing the costs in each process center by the equivalent units of production. The development of that equivalent unit of measure usually involves conversion of the input units of various items such as gallons (liters), pounds (kilos), or feet (meters) into one final production unit of measure.
3. Performance reporting tends to be by process with respect to the passage of time, such as daily, weekly, or monthly.
4. The production costs for a period are then accounted for in relation to the output of the process for the period.

Summary Comparison of Job Order and Process Cost Systems

Exhibit 2 provides a comparison of the primary characteristics of "pure" job order and process costing systems. In practice, of course, it is often possible to encounter hybrid systems which contain elements of both job order and process cost systems.

EXHIBIT 2
Comparison of Process and Job Collection Characteristics

	Job System	Process System
Production is scheduled, performed, and charges made to jobs or lots...	Yes	No
Charges are made to processes and time periods...........	No	Yes
Homogeneous product.......................................	No	Yes
A better system for a diverse product line.................	Yes	No
Performance reporting is by job, and sometimes also by department or operation.................................	Yes	No
Performance reporting is by process with respect to time...	No	Yes
Product-profitability determinations are possible by comparing actual cost to planned cost......................	Yes	Yes
Routings or process sheets are available..................	Not always	Yes
Generally end product produced for stock.................	No	Yes
Higher investment in equipment; lower labor cost..........	No	Yes

It is important to understand the strengths and weaknesses of either a pure process or job cost collection approach. However, selection of the appropriate cost collection system is not an either-or decision based on the relative strengths and weaknesses of these two approaches. Rather, systems design involves selecting the appropriate approach for the production process and tailoring that approach to a particular environment and its characteristics.

The primary strength of a process cost collection system is that it is relatively simple to calculate unit costs if there is an actual cost accumulation requirement and a homogeneous product is produced. It is usually easier to use standard costs in a true process situation because:

1.   There is less product diversity and therefore fewer standards.
2.   Bills of material tend to be required at only one or two levels.
3.   There are fewer intermediate stocking and count points.
4.   Routings are made up of fixed process steps and are therefore relatively stable.

Also, process cost collection systems tend to be less expensive because of the presence of fewer process operations, fewer products, and consequently fewer pieces of cost information to keep track of. Once something starts into production, management usually cannot confuse the issue by splitting lots, using alternate material, or changing schedules. If adequate measurement capability exists, performance reporting tends to be less voluminous and can be made an integral part of daily, weekly, and monthly financial statement presentations.

A weakness of a process cost collection system is that if products are not homogeneous, reported costs must be prorated among the various products in order to determine the actual product cost. If work in process is significant (often it is not), the inventory calculation may be difficult or inaccurate because the measurement of work in process is difficult. As the number of products using the same process grows, or the length of the production runs increases, actual unit cost collection becomes less accurate for individual products. The calculation of material usage variances (which are almost always significant) requires special consideration in that expensive special measuring devices may be required to measure input accurately, and cutoff points between products may be difficult to establish. If the above comparisons cannot be made to calculate the material usage variance, extensive physical inventories must be taken.

APPLICATION OF PROCESS COSTING CONCEPTS

In its most straightforward application the process cost system is indeed simple. In the case where all materials enter at the start of the process, all products exit at the end of the process, and the "production pipeline" is clear at the end of the accounting period, the application of the process cost system is trivial. Unit product costs (i.e., the costs of the finished product per pound, square foot, etc.) are determined by dividing the total costs for the period (material, labor, and overhead) by the units of finished product.

However, in practice this simple case is not frequently encountered. Instead, the process cost system must be developed to recognize factors such as:

Work in process at the beginning and end of the accounting period and the determination of equivalent units;

Materials or other costs added during the production process;

Costs transferred from one department to another;

Allocation of costs to scrap and bad units; and

Normal spoilage versus unusual spoilage.

The development of a process costing system that will adequately meet management's requirements requires that these factors be incorporated in the design and application of the process costing approach.

Work in Process and the Determination of Equivalent Units

The continuous nature of the production process implies that in many instances there will be work in process inventories at the beginning and end of the period. This presents a costing problem, for how are these partially complete units going to be treated in computing unit cost?

The process costing approach is based on the *homogeneity assumption*. This assumption is that each unit completed is considered to have received the same treatment as all other units. That is, each completed unit contains the same amount of direct materials and has had the same amount of direct labor and factory overhead applied to it. In general, all units at the same stage of completion are considered to contain the same amount of each cost element. This notion provides the key to the treatment of the work in process inventories which invariably exist in the process.

If in addition to the homogeneity assumption, all manufacturing cost elements—direct materials, direct labor, and overhead—are assumed to be incurred evenly over the process, then the critical realization is that from a cost viewpoint, 100 units in beginning inventory which are 10 percent complete are the exact equivalent of 10 units in beginning inventory which are 100 percent complete. In either case, 100 units 10 percent complete or 10 units 100 percent complete, the number of *equivalent units* in beginning inventory is 10. Similarly, if there is no beginning inventory, 200 units are started in a period, and all 200 units are 60 percent completed at the end of the period, then the equivalent-unit production for the period is 120 units. That is, the expected cost for the period equals the cost that would have been expected to be incurred if 120 units had been started and completed in the period. Again, the assumption made in these examples is that costs are incurred evenly over the entire production process.

In order to calculate unit cost in a process costing system, the equivalent-unit production for the period must be determined. The following equation is useful in determining a period's equivalent-unit production, the validity of which should be self-evident:

> Equivalent units in beginning inventory
> + Equivalent production units
> = Equivalent units transferred out of the process
> + Equivalent units in ending inventory

Knowledge of any three variables in the above equation permits the calculation of the fourth. Usually, the unknown variable is the equivalent-unit production for the period.

For example, assume the following data were collected for a particular period:

> Beginning inventory (20% complete).................. 1,000 tons
> Units transferred out of the process................. 18,000 tons
> Ending inventory (30% complete)..................... 2,000 tons

What is the equivalent production for the period? A solution is readily obtained using the identity and the equivalent unit concepts:

Equivalent units in beginning inventory...................... 200 tons
+ Equivalent production....................................... + (unknown)
= Equivalent units transferred out of the process............. = 18,000 tons
+ Equivalent units in ending inventory....................... +   600 tons

Thus, the equivalent production for the period is 18,400 tons.

Unfortunately the preceding example is deceptively simple and was used primarily to introduce the concept of equivalent units, the essence of process costing. A complexity is introduced when we drop the assumption that manufacturing cost elements are incurred evenly over the process. For direct material this assumption is not realistic, since this cost element is usually added at a discrete point in the production process. Often direct materials are added only at the beginning of the production process, but in some processes they may be added at more than one point. For instance, Material A may be added at the beginning of the process and Material B may be added at the midpoint. Thus, any unit of production that is started will be complete as to Material A, but any unit that is less than 50 percent complete will have no Material B, and any unit that is more than 50 percent complete will be complete as to Material B. Therefore, the number of equivalent-production units will be different for Material A and Material B.

For example, consider a process where Material A is added at the beginning of the process, Material B is added at the midpoint of the process, and conversion (the application of direct labor and manufacturing overhead) occurs uniformly throughout the process. We are given the following information for a production period:

Beginning inventory (20% complete)............................ 1,000 tons
Units transferred out of the process........................... 18,000
Ending inventory (30% complete)................................ 2,000

The problem is to determine the number of equivalent-production units.

Diagrammatically this process may be represented as shown in Exhibit 3.

The equivalent-production calculations for Materials A and B and for conversion are as follows:

Material A:
Equivalent units in beginning inventory..................... 1,000* tons
+ Equivalent production..................................... + (unknown)
= Equivalent units transferred out of the process........... = 18,000 tons
+ Equivalent units in ending inventory...................... + 2,000* tons
    * Note that, as shown in Exhibit 3, the beginning and ending inventory are complete as to Material A.

EXHIBIT 3
Diagram of a Production Process

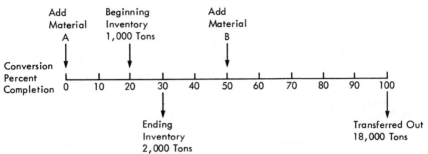

The equivalent production for Material A is 19,000 units (tons).

Material B:
    Equivalent units in beginning inventory...................... 0 tons*
    + Equivalent production..................................... + (unknown)
    = Equivalent units transferred out of the process............ = 18,000 tons
    + Equivalent units in ending inventory...................... 0 tons*
        * Note that, as shown in the diagram, neither the beginning nor the ending inventory
contain Material B.

The equivalent production for Material B is 18,000 units (tons).

Conversion:
    Equivalent units in beginning inventory...................... 200 tons
    + Equivalent production..................................... + (unknown)
    = Equivalent units transferred out of the process............ = 18,000 tons
    + Equivalent units in ending inventory...................... +   600 tons

The equivalent production for conversion is 18,400 units (tons).

It should be emphasized that a separate equivalent-production figure must be calculated for each cost that varies in a unique way. Costs that are applied in an identical manner in the production process can be grouped, and a single equivalent-production unit figure can be calculated. Direct labor and manufacturing overhead, for instance, often are incurred at the same rate and therefore are grouped. Direct labor and manufacturing overhead together are called conversion costs.

Transferred-In Costs of Prior Department

Most production processes involve two or more departments. Diagrammatically, product flows through a production process may be represented as one of the three flows shown in Exhibit 4.

EXHIBIT 4
Production Processes

A. Departments in Series

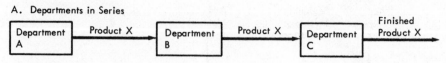

B. Parallel Departments Early in Process

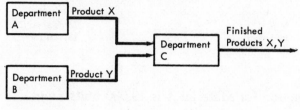

C. Parallel Finishing Departments

A department's cost is usually composed of one or more of the following: direct material, direct labor, and manufacturing overhead. In the department in which these costs are incurred, unit costs are developed for each cost that varies in a unique way. In subsequent departments all of these costs are combined and allocated as an aggregate. For example, assume the flow is as represented in part A of Exhibit 4: direct material, direct labor, and manufacturing overhead costs are incurred in all departments. In Department A separate costs are developed for materials and conversion. All the costs are then transferred to Department B. In Department B all the costs from Department A should be handled together as one cost—transferred-in cost. Thus, in Department B an equivalent unit figure for transferred-in cost is calculated.

Cost Allocation

If the reader is not familiar with the mechanics of Fifo and weighted-average inventory costing techniques, a review should be made before continuing with this section.

The following describes the five basic steps in the systematic allocation of cost to ending work in process inventory and to units transferred out:

Step 1. *Physical flow.* Determine the physical flow of units regardless of their stage of completion. Are all the units accounted for?

Step 2. *Equivalent-production units for the period.* Calculate the equivalent-production units for the period for each uniquely varying cost.

Step 3. *Total cost to account for by element.* Determine the total cost-by-cost element to be allocated between ending work in process inventory and units transferred out.

Step 4. *Cost per equivalent unit.* Calculate the cost per equivalent unit, taking into consideration the specified inventory costing method, Fifo or weighted average.

Step 5. *Total cost of inventories.* Using the unit costs calculated in Step 4, determine the cost associated with ending work in process inventory and the cost associated with the units transferred out of the process. These two costs, ending work in process and transferred out, should be equal to the total costs computed in Step 3.

This five-step approach provides a systematic method for cost allocation in a production process environment.

An Illustration. To illustrate this five-step approach, assume conversion takes place evenly over the prduction process. Material A is added at the beginning of the production process, and Material B is added when conversion is 60 percent complete. Beginning work in process is 600 units, which are 70 percent complete as to conversion and have accumulated costs as follows:

Material A	$ 240.00
Material B	480.00
Conversion	1,084.20
Total	$1,804.20

Ending work in process is 800 units, 30 percent complete as to conversion. During the period, 12,000 units were completed and 12,200 units were started. Costs added were:

Material A	$ 6,160.00
Material B	9,120.00
Conversion	27,067.80
Total	$42,347.80

Diagrammatically this process may be represented as shown in Exhibit 5.

EXHIBIT 5
Diagram for Five-Step Illustration

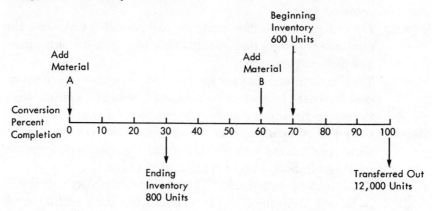

Below are shown the calculations for computing the cost of goods transferred out and ending inventory, first using weighted-average costing and then using Fifo costing:

Weighted-Average Method

	(Step 1) Physical Flow
Beginning inventory	600
+ Additions	12,200
= Transferred out	12,000
+ Ending inventory	800

Material A

	(Step 2) Equivalent Units	(Step 3) Total Cost	(Step 4) Weighted-Average Unit Cost	(Step 5) Total Allocated Cost
Beginning inventory	600	$ 240.00 ⎫	$0.50 = $\dfrac{\$ 6,400}{12,800}$	
+ Additions	12,200	6,160.00 ⎭		
= Transferred out	12,000		$0.50	$6,000.00 (d)
+ Ending inventory	800		$0.50	400.00 (e)
		$6,400.00 (a)*		$6,400.00

* Small letters in parentheses are used as cross-references to the cost summary below.

Material B

	(Step 2) Equivalent Units	(Step 3) Total Cost	(Step 4) Weighted-Average Unit Cost	(Step 5) Total Allocated Cost
Beginning inventory........	600	$ 480.00⎫	$0.80 = $\dfrac{\$ 9,600}{12,000}$	
+ Additions...............	11,400	9,120.00⎭		
= Transferred out..........	12,000		$0.80	$9,600.00 (f)
+ Ending inventory.........	0		$0.80	0.00 (g)
		$9,600.00 (b)		$9,600.00

Conversion

	(Step 2) Equivalent Units	(Step 3) Total Cost	(Step 4) Weighted-Average Unit Cost	(Step 5) Total Allocated Cost
Beginning inventory........	420	$ 1,084.20⎫	$2.30 = $\dfrac{\$28,152}{12,240}$	
+ Additions...............	11,820	27,067.80⎭		
= Transferred out..........	12,000		$2.30	$27,600.00 (h)
+ Ending inventory.........	240		$2.30	552.00 (i)
		$28,152.00 (c)		$28,152.00

Step 1 consists of accounting for beginning inventory units and units started in production. These units, if none are lost, must either be in ending inventory or have been transferred out. Step 2 consists of calculating the equivalent-production units in beginning inventory, in ending inventory, and transferred out. Then using the equivalent unit equation we solve for the equivalent production for the period. Step 3 determines the total cost to be allocated to units transferred out and units in ending inventory. This cost consists of the cost in beginning inventory and the cost added during the period.

Step 4 consists of calculating the weighted-average unit cost. The weighted-average unit cost is calculated by taking the total cost and dividing by the number of equivalent units with which the total cost is associated. For example, Material A weighted-average unit cost is determined by dividing $6,400 ($240 + $6,160) by 12,800 units (600 units + 12,200 units). The total cost determined in Step 3 is allocated to ending inventory and units transferred out on the basis of the weighted-average unit cost calculated in Step 4. This allocation is shown in Step 5.

The following cost summary provides a useful check to determine that all costs are allocated:

	Total Cost to Be Allocated		Total Allocated Cost	
Material A..........	$ 6,400.00 (a)	Transferred out:		
Material B..........	9,600.00 (b)	Material A..........	$ 6,000.00 (d)	
Conversion.........	28,152.00 (c)	Material B..........	9,600.00 (f)	
	$44,152.00	Conversion.........	27,600.00 (h)	$43,200.00
		Ending inventory:		
		Material A..........	$ 400.00 (e)	
		Material B..........	0.00 (g)	
		Conversion.........	552.00 (i)	952.00
				$44,152.00

Using the Fifo method, the calculations are as follows:

Fifo Method

	(Step 1) Physical Flow
Beginning inventory......................	600
+ Additions.............................	12,200
= Transferred out.......................	12,000
+ Ending inventory......................	800

Material A

	(Step 2) Equivalent Units	(Step 3) Total Cost	(Step 4) Fifo Unit Cost	(Step 5) Allocated Cost
Beginning inventory...........	600	$ 240.00	$0.40	
+ Additions..................	12,200	6,160.00	0.505	
= Transferred out.............	12,000			$5,996.00 (d)
+ Ending inventory...........	800		0.505	404.00 (e)
		$6,400.00 (a)		$6,400.00

Material B

	(Step 2) Equivalent Units	(Step 3) Total Cost	(Step 4) Fifo Unit Cost	(Step 5) Allocated Cost
Beginning inventory...........	600	$ 480.00	$0.80	
+ Additions..................	11,400	9,120.00	0.80	
= Transferred out.............	12,000			$9,600.00 (f)
+ Ending inventory...........	0		0.80	0.00 (g)
		$9,600.00 (b)		$9,600.00

Conversion

	(Step 2) Equivalent Units	(Step 3) Total Cost	(Step 4) Fifo Unit Cost	(Step 5) Allocated Cost
Beginning inventory...........	420	$ 1,084.20	$2.58	
+ Additions....................	11,820	27,067.80	2.29	
= Transferred out.............	12,000			$27,602.40 (h)
+ Ending inventory...........	240		2.29	549.60 (i)
		$28,152.00 (c)		$28,152.00

Cost Summary

	Total Cost to Be Allocated		Total Allocated Cost	
Material A..........	$ 6,400.00 (a)	Transferred out:		
Material B..........	9,600.00 (b)	Material A..........	$ 5,996.00 (d)	
Conversion........	28,152.00 (c)	Material B..........	9,600.00 (f)	
	$44,152.00	Conversion........	27,602.40 (h)	$43,198.40
		Ending inventory:		
		Material A..........	$ 404.00 (e)	
		Material B..........	0.00 (g)	
		Conversion........	549.60 (i)	953.60
				$44,152.00

The results of Steps 1, 2, and 3 are the same using Fifo costing as they were using weighted-average costing. Step 4 consists of calculating the unit cost associated with beginning inventory and the unit cost associated with the production for the period. The unit cost associated with beginning inventory is calculated by dividing the total cost associated with beginning inventory by the equivalent units in beginning inventory. Thus, Material A beginning inventory cost is $0.40 ($240 ÷ 600); Material B is $0.80 ($480 ÷ 600); and conversion is (approximately) $2.58 ($1,084.20 ÷ 420). The unit cost associated with the production for the period is calculated by dividing the cost added during the period by the equivalent production for the period. Thus, Material A unit cost is $0.505 ($6,160 ÷ 12,200); Material B, $0.80 ($9,120 ÷ 11,400); and conversion, $2.29 ($27,067.80 ÷ 11,820).

Cost is then allocated on a Fifo basis. The result of this allocation is shown in Step 5. Again, the cost summary provides a useful check that all costs are allocated and provides a summary of costs for work in process inventory and ending inventory.

Cost Allocation for Bad Units

When resources are combined in the production process, there is no guarantee that only good, salable output units will result. Usually there will be scrap, lost or defective output units, or loss through shrinkage, dust, evaporation, smoke, and so forth. In some cases, scrap can be recovered to provide a salable or reusable raw material item. When this is the case, the value of the "bad" unit should be deducted from the costs of the production center. For units lost through dust, evaporation, and so on, there is no reusable value.

Often some bad units—scrap, defective, or lost units—are expected or planned. There are two reasons for these planned or expected bad units. One is the inherent nature of the process. For example, suppose a 4- by 5½-foot piece of sheet metal is needed for a process but that sheet metal is only available in 4- by 6-foot pieces. The sheet must be trimmed, resulting in a 4- by ½-foot piece of scrap. The second reason for planned or expected bad units is that even though from a technical standpoint it is possible to eliminate all bad units, from a cost-benefit standpoint it would be uneconomical to eliminate them. The increase in cost necessary to obtain greater control would exceed the cost associated with the bad units which would be avoided.

Some bad units are not planned or expected. Bad units can occur because the process is not operating at the planned efficiency. Planned or expected bad units, those which arise under efficient operating conditions, are considered normal. Bad units that result because of inefficient operating conditions are considered abnormal.

The previous equation used to calculate a period's equivalent-unit production must be adjusted to accommodate normal and abnormal bad units. The identity used when normal and/or abnormal bad units exist is:

> Equivalent units in beginning inventory
> + Equivalent production units
> = Equivalent units transferred out of the process
> + Equivalent normal bad units
> + Equivalent abnormal bad units
> + Equivalent units in ending inventory

Of course, knowledge of any five variables in this equation permits the calculation of the sixth. Usually, the unknown variable is equivalent production units.

For example, assume the following facts: beginning inventory, 80 percent complete, is 2,000 units; and ending inventory, 30 percent complete, is 1,000 units. Inspection occurs at the end of the process. There were 22,000 units that passed inspection this period. Seven hundred twenty units were inspected and found defective. Normal spoilage is 3 percent of the number that pass inspection. All material is added at the beginning of the process and conversion takes place evenly over the production process.

We need to determine the equivalent production for the periods. A solution is readily obtained, therefore, by using the above identity:

Materials:
Equivalent units in beginning inventory.................... 2,000 units
+ Equivalent production................................... + (unknown)
= Equivalent units transferred out of the process.......... = 22,000 units
+ Equivalent normal bad units............................. +   660 units
+ Equivalent abnormal bad units........................... +   60 units
+ Equivalent units in ending inventory.................... + 1,000 units

Thus, the equivalent production for materials is 21,720 units.

Conversion:
Equivalent units in beginning inventory.................... 1,600 units
+ Equivalent production................................... + (unknown)
= Equivalent units transferred out of process.............. = 22,000 units
+ Equivalent normal bad units............................. +   660 units
+ Equivalent abnormal bad units........................... +   60 units
+ Equivalent units in ending inventory.................... +   300 units

Thus, the equivalent production for conversion is 21,420 units.

The costs associated with normal bad units and abnormal bad units are treated differently. Since normal bad units are an inherent part of the production process, their cost is reallocated to the good units with which they are inherently associated. Abnormal bad units are not inherently a part of the production process; they are a result of inefficient operations and may be thought of as an unfavorable variance. The cost of abnormal bad units is usually expensed in the period in which the abnormal bad units were identified.

Thus for cost allocation purposes when normal and/or abnormal bad units exist the following general approach is used:

1. Treat all bad units, both normal and abnormal, as if they are good and allocate costs in the manner described in the previous section, "Cost Allocation."

2. The costs associated with the normal bad units should be re-allocated to the good units with which they are inherently associated.
3. The costs associated with the abnormal bad units should be expensed.

The following three examples will help interpret point 2. These examples are depicted in Exhibit 6. In Example 1, assuming a Fifo flow, the units in beginning inventory underwent inspection this period. Hence there are identified normal bad units associated with the units that were in beginning inventory and transferred out. The units that were started and transferred out this period also underwent inspection, and thus there are identified normal bad units associated with them. The units that are in ending inventory are only 50 percent complete as to conversion and have not been inspected; thus, during this period, these units do not have identified normal bad units associated with them. Therefore, all the costs allocated to the normal bad units are reallocated to the units transferred out.

In Example 2, again assuming a Fifo flow, the units in beginning inventory underwent inspection this period; thus, there are identified normal bad units associated with units that were in beginning inventory and transferred out. The units that were started and transferred out this period also underwent inspection, and thus there are identified normal bad units associated with them. The units that are in ending inventory also have normal bad units associated with them because they have undergone inspection this period. Thus, the normal bad units are associated with all the units transferred out (8,000 units) and the units in ending inventory (400 units). Moreover, $8,000 \div (8,000 + 400)$ of the cost allocated to the normal bad units is reallocated to the units transferred out, and $400 \div (8,000 + 400)$ of the cost allocated to the normal bad units is reallocated to the units in ending inventory.

In Example 3, the units in beginning inventory underwent inspection in a prior period; thus, normal bad units identified with this period are not associated with the units that were in beginning inventory and transferred out. The units that were started and transferred out this period underwent inspection, and thus this period there are identified normal bad units associated with them. The units that are in ending inventory also have normal bad units associated with them because they have undergone inspection this

EXHIBIT 6
Treatment of Normal Bad Units

Example 1

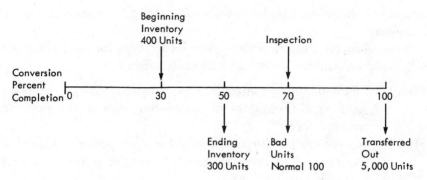

Example 2

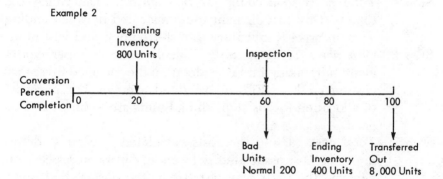

Example 3

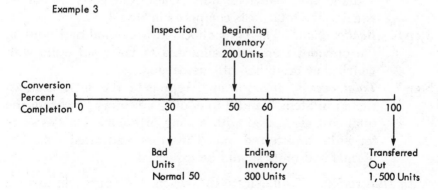

period. Thus $(1,500 - 200) \div [(1,500 - 200) + 300]$ of the cost allocated to the normal bad units is reallocated to the units transferred out, and $300 \div [(1,500 - 200) + 300]$ of the cost allocated to the normal bad units is reallocated to the units in ending inventory.

The following describes the seven basic steps for cost allocation when normal and/or abnormal bad units exist:

Step 1. *Physical flow.* Determine the physical flow of units regardless of their stage of completion. Are all the units accounted for?

Step 2. *Equivalent-production units for the period.* Calculate the equivalent-production units for the period for each uniquely varying cost.

Step 3. *Total costs to account for by element.* Determine the total cost-by-cost element to be allocated between ending work in process inventory, transferred out, and bad units.

Step 4. *Cost per equivalent unit.* Calculate the cost per equivalent unit, taking into consideration the specified inventory costing method, Fifo or weighted average. For purposes of allocation in this step, all bad units are to be treated as good.

Step 5. *Total cost.* Using the costs calculated in Step 4, determine the cost associated with ending work in process inventory, the units transferred out, the normal bad units, and the abnormal bad units. These four costs should be equal to the total costs computed in Step 3.

Step 6. *Reallocation.* The costs allocated to normal bad units in the previous step are reallocated to the good units with which they are inherently associated.

Step 7. *Total cost of inventories.* Aggregate the total cost assigned in Steps 5 and 6 to ending inventory to obtain the total cost associated with ending inventory. Do the same for units transferred out. The costs associated with abnormal bad units should be expensed.

An Illustration. To illustrate this seven-step approach, assume conversion takes place evenly over the production process. Material A is added at the beginning of the production process. Material B is added at the end of the production process. Inspection occurs when conversion is 90 percent complete. Beginning work in process inventory is 2,000 units which are 80 percent complete as to conversion and have these costs:

Material A	$2,200
Material B	0
Conversion	2,400
Total	$4,600

Ending work in process inventory is 1,000 units, 95 percent complete as to conversion. During the period, 20,000 units were completed and 19,300 units were started with these added costs:

Material A	$21,230
Material B	10,000
Conversion	29,430
Total	$60,660

Units not passing inspection included 200 "normal" defects and 100 "abnormal" ones.

EXHIBIT 7
Diagram for Seven-Step Illustration

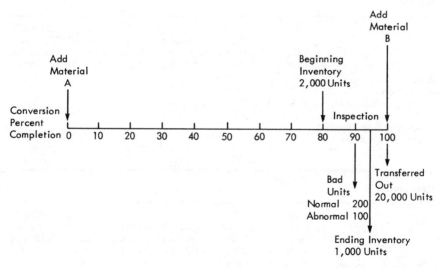

Diagrammatically the process may be represented as shown in Exhibit 7. We are required to compute the cost of goods transferred out and ending inventory using weighted-average costing:

	(Step 1) Physical Flow
Beginning inventory......................	2,000
+ Additions..............................	19,300
= Transferred out.........................	20,000
+ Normal spoiled units...................	200
+ Abnormal spoiled units................	100
+ Ending inventory.......................	1,000

Material A

	(Step 2) Equiv-alent Units	(Step 3) Total Cost	(Step 4) Unit Cost All Good	(Step 5) Total Cost	(Step 6) Real-location	(Step 7) Total Allocated Cost
Beginning inventory....	2,000	$ 2,200⎫	$1.10			
+ Additions............	19,300	21,230⎭				
= Transferred out......	20,000		1.10	$22,000	$210*	$22,210 (d)
+ Normal spoiled.......	200		1.10	220		
+ Abnormal spoiled....	100		1.10	110		110 (e)
+ Ending inventory.....	1,000		1.10	1,100	10	1,110 (f)
		$23,430 (a)		$23,430	$220	$23,430

* Rounded $\left(\dfrac{20,000}{21,000} \times \$220\right)$.

Material B

	(Step 2) Equiv-alent Units	(Step 3) Total Cost	(Step 4) Unit Cost All Good	(Step 5) Total Cost	(Step 6) Real-location	(Step 7) Total Allocated Cost
Beginning inventory....	0	0⎫	$0.50			
+ Additions............	20,000	$10,000⎭				
= Transferred out......	20,000		0.50	$10,000		$10,000 (g)
+ Normal spoiled.......	0					
+ Abnormal spoiled....	0					— (h)
+ Ending inventory.....	0					— (i)
		$10,000 (b)		$10,000		$10,000

Conversion

	(Step 2) Equiv-alent Units	(Step 3) Total Cost	(Step 4) Unit Cost All Good	(Step 5) Total Cost	(Step 6) Real-location	(Step 7) Total Allocated Cost
Beginning inventory....	1,600	$ 2,400⎫	$1.50			
+ Additions............	19,620	29,430⎭				
= Transferred out......	20,000		1.50	$30,000	$257*	$30,257 (j)
+ Normal spoiled.......	180		1.50	270		
+ Abnormal spoiled....	90		1.50	135		135 (k)
+ Ending inventory.....	950		1.50	1,425	13	1,438 (1)
		$31,830 (c)		$31,830	$270	$31,830

* Rounded.

Cost Summary

	Total Cost to Be Allocated	Cost Allocated		
		Transferred Out	Ending Inventory	Abnormal Bad Units
Material A...........	$23,430 (a)	$22,210 (d)	$1,110 (f)	$110 (e)
Material B...........	10,000 (b)	10,000 (g)	— (i)	— (h)
Conversion..........	31,830 (c)	30,257 (j)	1,438 (l)	135 (k)
	$65,260	$62,467	$2,548	$245

Steps 1 through 5 are similar to those in the previous five-step illustration, given that the normal and abnormal bad units are treated as good units. Step 6 consists of the reallocation of the costs allocated to normal bad units in Step 5. The costs allocated to normal bad units are to be reallocated to the good units with which they are associated. Inspection occurs when conversion is 90 percent complete. As beginning inventory units are only 80 percent complete, they were inspected this period; and since ending inventory is 95 percent complete, all units in ending inventory and all units transferred out were inspected this period. Thus the cost associated with the normal bad units is reallocated to ending inventory and the units transferred out on the basis of the number of units in ending inventory and transferred out. Thus for Material A, 1,000 ÷ 21,000 of the cost associated with normal bad units is reallocated to ending inventory, and 20,000 ÷ 21,000 of the cost associated with normal bad units is reallocated to units transferred out. For Material B there is no problem, because there is no Material B associated with the units when inspected; thus, there is no Material B associated with the bad units. Conversion costs associated with normal bad units are reallocated on a 1,000 to 20,000 ratio to ending inventory and units transferred out respectively.

MANAGERIAL CONTROL

Accounting Entries

Once the process of allocating costs to the units produced and in ending inventory is completed, the required accounting entries follow logically. Costs must be accumulated by producing department for each cost element to be allocated in a unique way. Thus, accounts would be established in each department for the following types of costs:

Materials.

Labor.

Overhead.

Machine usage.

Completed production.

At the end of the period the costs accumulated in these accounts are then allocated to:

Finished goods.

Work in process.

Abnormal spoilage.

Exhibit 8 is a summary of the journal entries resulting in the eventual valuation of finished goods and work in process. Each entry is related to an economic event and requires a source document to "capture" the data related to that event.

Standard Costs

As with any other type of cost accounting system, predetermined standard costs can be used in a process cost system to enhance management's ability to use the system to control operations. The significant disadvantage of reporting only actual costs for control purposes is the extreme difficulty in pinpointing where excessive costs are being incurred. It is much easier to compare actual performance to a quantified standard or estimate than to look at actual cost figures and try to determine if they are out of line and by how much.

Materials price variances can be calculated within a process system just as in any other system. Normally the price variance will be calculated at the time materials are purchased (i.e., debited to Materials Inventory), and the standard cost is charged to Work in Process when materials are issued. The labor and overhead variances are calculated as usual, with the rate variance calculated as the cost per hour worked compared to the standard rate, and the efficiency variance based on the cost per unit of final product compared to standard. (For more details on variance analysis, see Chapter 32.)

Exhibit 9 summarizes the cost flow through the process cost system for the Plastics, Inc., example discussed earlier and illus-

EXHIBIT 8. Summary of Process Costing Accounting Entries

Economic Event	Source	Entry	Comments
1. Material input to work in process from stores.			
a. Measured in.	Instrumentation, a pick list, or a material requisition.	Dr.—WIP. Cr.—Stores.	Material is never actually recorded in WIP except where it moves from one operation to the next with a count point between. In that case the debit would be to Work in Process. Period-end WIP in a given operation must be estimated or, if insignificant, ignored.
b. Input exploded from production counts.	Production counts.	Dr.—Finished Goods. Cr.—Stores.	
2. Labor.	Time cards or journal entries charging labor costs to processes or operations.	Dr.—Machine or operation cost pool. Cr.—Labor clearing. Dr./Cr.—Labor variance if standard labor instead of machine manning is used.	The machine or operation cost pool is charged to WIP based on standard labor hours or as part of a machine rate. The latter method is used much the same as an overhead rate. The latter method is used where labor costs are insignificant relative to the total cost of the operations cost pool.
3. Other conversion costs.			
a. Process or operation related costs.		Dr.—Machine or operation cost pool. Cr.—Payables, reserve for depreciation, etc.	These costs relate directly to a machine or operation and are charged to production along with labor, using a machine rate and machine time charged to a job or batch.
b. General manufacturing overhead.		Dr.—WIP. Cr.—Manufacturing Overhead pool.	
4. Machine usage.	Time required to complete job or batch per the standard process sheet or based on the actual time to flow through a process.	Dr.—WIP. Cr.—Machine or operation cost pool.	
5. Completed production.	Production count.	Dr.—Finished Goods. Cr.—WIP. Dr./Cr.—Yield and mix variances.	

EXHIBIT 9

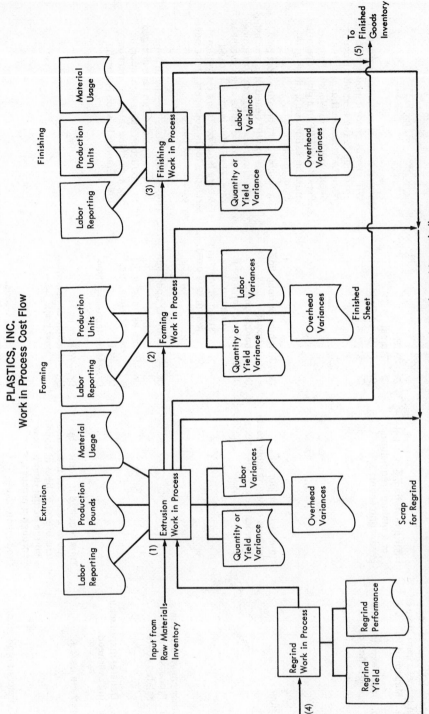

PLASTICS, INC.
Work in Process Cost Flow

(1) Sheet plastic is made from poly-vinyl and/or regrind.
(2) Sheet plastic is formed as a job.
(3) Product is trimmed, ground, and polished.
(4) Scrap trim and sheet is sent to regrinding.
(5) Sheet and finished products flow to Finished Goods Inventory.

trated in Exhibit 1. Exhibit 9 shows material variance. Since the material price variance is isolated when materials are purchased, the variance in Exhibit 9 is a quantity or yield variance, the calculation of which will now be described.

Quantity or Yield Variance. If a process results in there being normal bad units, the standard costs associated with the good units should reflect a factor for the costs of these bad units, including a credit for any recoverable value. Abnormal spoilage, however, is identified as a quantity or yield variance.

The calculation of this variance is illustrated in the following example, which assumes:

$$\text{Standard cost of raw material} = SCRM = 29 \text{ cents per pound}$$
$$\text{Scrap credit value} = SCV = 5 \text{ cents per pound}$$

Standard yield	=	Y =	78.0%
Flash loss		= FL =	7.0
Expected scrap	=	ES =	15.0
			100.0%

The standard cost of the output per pound is equal to the difference between the standard cost of the raw material and 15.0 percent of the scrap value per pound, divided by the yield. Expressed as a formula, the standard cost per pound of output is:

$$[SCRM - (SCV)(ES)] \div Y = [\$0.29 - (\$0.05)(0.15)] \div 0.78$$
$$= [\$0.29 - \$0.0075] \div 0.78 = 36.22 \text{ cents per pound}$$

Assuming for illustrative purposes that there were 20,000 pounds of input and 18,000 pounds of output, then we have:

	Weight (lbs.)	Yield %	Standard Material Cost	Scrap Credit Weight (lbs.)	Amount
Actual input............	20,000		$5,800		
Actual yield.............	18,000	90.0	6,520	600	$ 30
Standard yield..........	15,600	78.0	5,650	3,000	150
Variance...............	2,400	12.0	$ 870	2,400	$120

Therefore, the standard cost of the actual output in this example is $6,520 (18,000 pounds @36.22 cents per pound). The favorable yield variance of $870 (2,400 pounds @36.22 cents per pound) is partially offset by a scrap-credit variance of $120 (2,400 pounds @5 cents per pound); that is, because there were 2,400 pounds less scrap generated, scrap revenues of $120 were foregone.

Ideally, direct measurements of actual output, input, and scrap provide the data for calculating the yield variance. However, in many situations it is too costly or impractical to obtain all three measurements for each unit of product. It may be feasible to use vendor-supplied data for actual input weight if the scrap occurs at the first operation. It may also be desirable to accumulate physically the scrap for many units of product and calculate the scrap credit at the end of a run or shift.

If the raw material involves ingredients that are already mixed together when purchased, such as crude oil or raw milk (butterfat and skim), the use of sampling and quantitative analysis techniques will be necessary to determine the actual amount of each ingredient used.

PRACTICAL CONSIDERATIONS

Naturally, in designing a process cost system the practical requirements of the business involved must be considered. The following sections discuss some of the practical problems involved in implementing a process cost system.

Establishing Measuring Points

In process industries it is often difficult to measure the input and production of the product, and hence it is difficult to report material usage and movement accurately. For example, measurement is often complicated by the physical characteristics of the product; the difficulty of evaluating changes in moisture content of a material is an example.

In some industries, the consistency of the product flowing in pipes is not such that it can be measured effectively. Some chemicals have a corrosive effect on meters or other equipment utilized to measure flow and consequently accurate measurement is difficult. In some mixing situations, materials are added using shutoff values, measuring cans, and other imprecise means. It may be impractical or impossible to get usage information other than by reading measuring gauges or meters on tanks at fixed intervals, or by taking frequent physical inventories to determine usage through disappearance.

In a closed process, a gallon (or any other volume unit of measure) of output expands as its temperature rises and/or its pressure is lowered. If production reporting is based on gallons, variances will often occur solely due to temperature and/or pressure differences between the input materials and output product. A conversion factor must be developed to translate input material at one temperature and/or pressure to equivalent output at a different temperature and/or pressure.

In the food-processing and paper industries, variations may occur in the moisture content of output due to evaporation, equipment problems, and operator errors. Expensive measurement devices and sampling procedures may be required to determine accurately the actual moisture content in the finished product. In industries such as plastics and paper, computer-controlled scanning and test devices have been developed to conduct repetitive measurements of temperature, thickness, width, consistency, and other characteristics, resulting in dramatic improvements in quality and product cost. The need for this degree of sophistication should be based upon the materiality of the cost element being measured within the total product cost. An economic comparison of the cost of measuring versus the potential savings from measuring more accurately should be made to determine if improved or additional measuring devices are warranted.

Measurement is usually undertaken at a point in the process where most or all of the input or transferred product passes. This is often a point between two responsibility centers or physical work centers. Accurate measurement is necessary to establish proper inventory valuation between two different processes or departments and to provide accurate performance measurement of actual cost incurrence in comparison to the standard cost for a process.

Different Units of Measure

A potential reporting problem related to countability and measurement occurs when material is purchased in one unit of measure, is issued to production under another unit of measure, and possibly completes the production process under a third unit of measure. When it is not practical to use the same unit of measure throughout the process, a conversion factor must be used to convert reported input and output to the same unit of measure. Examples of this type of situation include the following:

Unit of Measure Conversion	Type of Material
Purchased in pounds and issued in pieces	Steel plate, aluminum, plastic, paper
Purchased in pounds and issued in feet	Copper wire, steel rod

A conversion factor must also be developed when the material changes in size and form during the conversion process, and a size unit of measure, such as gallons or feet (as opposed to pounds), must be used:

Production Process	Conversion Factor Requirement
Chemical and food processing.........	Conversion of gallons of raw material at one temperature and pressure to equivalent gallons of output at a different temperature and pressure, to pounds and/or to packages
Papermaking.........................	Pulp and waste paper at a specified moisture content to equivalent pounds of a given basis-weight paper
Extrusion of electrical conduit.........	Conversion of unextruded, raw core to finished core (e.g., 1 foot of raw core = 1.12 feet of finished core)

The actual physical characteristics of the material, such as volume, length, thickness, and density, will vary from assumed characteristics used to develop the conversion factor. At best, the conversion factor represents a good overall average of past historical experience. To the extent that current characteristics depart from historical experience, the conversion factor will be inaccurate and distortions will occur in the material usage variance amounts.

Valuing Work in Process

The entire work in process inventory of a company might fit the process environment, or process flows may only apply to certain cost centers or departments. In either case, there are three preliminary questions to be asked relative to valuing work in process in a process situation:

1. Is the dollar amount of work in process significant at the end of an accounting period? Quite frequently the work in process amount is small, particularly where the inventory is contained within a single flow (i.e., single series of operations) without any staging points. Significance may depend on the ending balance relative to the total amount of inventory which has passed through work in process during the accounting period.
2. Can work in process or the flow into and out of work in process be physically measured fairly easily at period end using some form of instrumentation?
3. Can the quantities in work in process be established by knowing that a process capacity is either completely full or empty? This would be possible in a process involving a product in liquid form where the content of tanks and piping systems would be known beforehand.

If work in process is insignificant or easily determined, valuation is very simple. However, problems arise in valuing work in process when work in process is significant, when physical measurement is difficult, and when any of the following conditions exist:

1. Input to work in process is calculated based on an explosion of production output. This occurs where input is not metered or charged in some manner to a production job, lot, or batch.
2. There are staging points in the process, and the product characteristics and instrumentation are such that staged amounts are difficult to count.
3. Yield loss is significant throughout the process, and it is difficult to record the loss until a lot or batch is completed, or at least until it moves through a count point.
4. Instrumentation is inaccurate.
5. Many process systems use production jobs, lots, or batches to control the properties or quality of the output. When a job is completed, a costly setup for the next job may be required. If significant, setup may be treated as a direct cost and included in the standard unit cost versus charging it to manufacturing overhead. The volume over which setup is spread is difficult to determine.

6. There are a large number of orders in process, and physical control over usage on particular production orders is difficult. Examples include the conversion of wood to small wood products such as cabinets or mill work, and in the conversion of paper in roll form to a large variety of sizes, shapes, and colors in the form of products such as school tablets, notebook fillers, and pads.

SUMMARY

Certain manufacturing environments involve a continuous, recurring process with raw material and the other elements of production entering the process in a fixed manner. The process results in the production of a homogeneous end product without reference to specific orders or lots. In these cases, the process cost "model" is the appropriate approach to be used in developing cost information for the purposes of product costing, inventory valuation, and cost control.

The process costing approach involves the accumulation of production costs by cost center, process, or department for a period of time. At the end of the time period the unit costs can be determined for the finished product as well as any units remaining in production. The product costs can then be allocated between the finished and incomplete units. This allocation is completed based on the homogeneity assumption. This assumption provides that each unit completed contains the same amount of direct material and has had the same amount of direct labor and factory overhead applied. All units in work in process at the end of the time period and at the same stage of completion are considered to contain the same amount of any given cost element. The homogeneity assumption permits the statement of work in process at the end of the period in equivalent units of finished products. Thus the total production costs for the period can be allocated over these equivalent units by class of production cost to provide values for the finished goods and work in process inventories at the end of the period.

In developing the process cost model, standard costs can be employed. Unit costs are adjusted to reflect the cost of bad or spoiled units. The cost of normal spoilage (less any salvage value) is treated as a cost of production and is added to the cost of the good units. The cost of abnormal spoilage is recognized as a quantity or yield variance and is expensed in the period.

In designing and installing a process cost system, the specific environment in which the system will operate must be evaluated. The development of a usable and workable system requires the consideration of a number of practical factors. The ability to measure product quantities and flows at any given point in the process must be evaluated; the materiality of work in process units at various points may determine whether or not there is a need to measure this quantity; or the measurement of output in units which differ from those used for input may have to be incorporated in the design.

The key to the design of a process cost system is to understand thoroughly the production process itself, the mechanics of the process costing approach, and the management needs to be met by the system. This will permit the development of a cost accounting system which accurately reflects the events of the production process and meets management's needs.

ADDITIONAL SOURCES

Franke, Reimund. "A Process Model for Costing." *Management Accounting*, January 1975, p. 45.

Fremgen, James M. *Accounting for Managerial Analysis*, chap. 4. 3d ed. Homewood, Ill.: Richard D. Irwin, Inc., 1976.

Horngren, Charles T. *Cost Accounting: A Managerial Emphasis*, chaps. 18, 19. 4th ed. Englewood Cliffs, N.J.: Prentice-Hall, Inc., 1977.

Neuner, John J. W., and Deakin, Edward B. *Cost Accounting: Principles and Practice*, chaps. 3, 4. 9th ed. Homewood, Ill.: Richard D. Irwin, Inc., 1977.

Shillinglaw, Gordon. *Managerial Cost Accounting*, chap. 10. 4th ed. Homewood, Ill.: Richard D. Irwin, Inc., 1977.

9

Joint- and By-Product Costing

Ian D. Duncan*

The petroleum, lumber, and meat-packing industries, and many other manufacturing concerns produce more than one product from the processing of a single raw material. Indeed, one may argue that *all* manufacturing processes produce more than one product. This is true even for the so-called single-product manufacturing firms.

Is this last statement contradictory? No. The point is that by virtue of producing a single product which is marketable, scrap or waste is also produced. In most cases, the costs associated with producing this scrap are *not* separated out, and the total manufacturing costs are applied to the so-called main product. The cost of producing the scrap is really quite small and hence negligible.

In some cases, however, it is possible either to sell this secondary product as it is, or to use some further manufacturing process and transform it into a marketable product. In these cases where the "waste" or "scrap" is sold, some sort of allocation of costs, such as raw materials and direct labor, is necessary in order to arrive at a product cost for the secondary product.

Some common examples where the manufacturing process produces two recognizable products simultaneously, or where a single raw material input is common to all finished products, are found in Exhibit 1.

---

* Mr. Duncan is pursuing a doctorate degree in business administration at the University of Western Ontario. He was formerly a Research Associate with the Society of Management Accountants of Canada.

Up to this point we have used the terminology of "scrap" or "secondary" product to describe a simultaneously produced product. This terminology, however, should be considerably sharpened and refined. By introducing the terms *joint product* and *by-product* this is accomplished. Each of these will be discussed in some detail later in the chapter; however, it is essential to define them and differentiate between them at this point.

When a group of individual products is simultaneously produced, with each product having a significant relative sales value, the outputs are usually called *joint products*. The exact point in a manufacturing process where two or more products can be distinguished is denoted as the *split-off point*. This split-off point can

EXHIBIT 1
Examples of Main and Secondary Products

Raw Material	Products Produced	
	Main Product	Secondary Product
Steel rod	Screws, nails	Metal fragments
Live cattle	Various cuts of meat	Trimmings, hides
Trees	Lumber	Sawdust particles, woodchips

be either when the manufacturing process is complete (i.e., when the raw materials have been converted into finished goods) or alternatively at some intermediate point in the manufacturing process.

By-product is a term which is applied to products produced simultaneously that have a very minor sales value (or no sales value) as compared with that of the major or chief product.

The thrust of this chapter is the distinction between the necessary allocation of costs associated with joint products and by-products for purposes of income determination, and the irrelevance of allocated costs in management decisions regarding the further processing or selling as-is of simultaneously produced products. In this regard, various methods of cost allocation for joint costs will be discussed, as well as the accounting techniques for by-product costs. The irrelevance of allocated costs in managerial decision making will be illustrated with an example.

A LOOK AT JOINT PRODUCTS

Some examples of joint products can be found in Exhibit 1. The definition of joint products given in the introduction clearly differentiates between joint products and by-products. The salient points regarding joint products according to this definition are the following:

Produced simultaneously (with respect to common raw material inputs and common manufacturing processes); and

Each product has a significant relative sales value.

Using these two points as decision criteria, it is clear that many products (or for that matter, services) qualify under the classification of joint products. This "jointness" may be associated with the complete transformation from raw materials into finished goods or it may be characteristic of only part of the complete transformation process.

All costs associated with the manufacture of joint products, up to the point in the production process where they are clearly differentiable as distinct products, are called joint-product costs or simply *joint costs*. In these instances, one can clearly establish a cost factor associated with the inputs required to produce multiple products. The cost associated with the manufacture of each individual product, however, is part of an indivisible sum (i.e., a joint cost).

It is the job of the management accountant to make a decision regarding the allocation (or nonallocation) of joint costs for the purposes of inventory valuation and product profitability determination. In this section, three methods of allocating joint costs will be examined. These are the following:

Sales-value method.

Physical-unit method.

Average-unit-cost method.

These methods will be explained and illustrated using a common example. Therefore, it will be possible to observe their relative differences in terms of cost allocation.

The following example will serve as a means of illustrating the various allocation methods. It is very general and admittedly quite simplified as compared with the real world. However, increasing the "realism" of the example would only cloud the issue at hand and be detrimental to understanding the problem.

Example 1

The PLR Company Limited is a manufacturing company that produces "widgets" and "gizmoes." These are joint products and require no further processing after the joint manufacturing process. Therefore, we have the following production model:

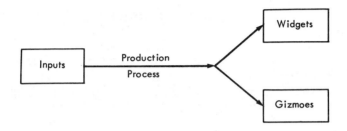

The total cost of inputs and production for one year is $1,000, all of which is a joint cost. The result of the production process is 600 widgets and 400 gizmoes. Widgets sell for $1 each, and gizmoes sell for $2 each. The production model can therefore be detailed as follows:

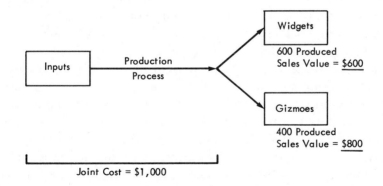

Sales or Market-Value Method. The first method of allocating joint materials and processing costs that will be discussed is the so-called *sales or market-value method.* Under this method, the criterion for allocating joint costs is the relative sales value associated

EXHIBIT 2
Sales-Value Method of Cost Allocation

Joint Products	Sales Value	Proportion of Total Sales Value	Proportion of Joint Costs Allocated to Each Product
Widgets..............	$ 600	6/14	6/14 × $1,000 = $ 429
Gizmoes.............	800	8/14	8/14 × $1,000 = 571
	$1,400		$1,000

If we assume that all that is produced is sold within the year, the income statement would be as follows:

PLR COMPANY LIMITED
Income Statement

	Widgets	Gizmoes	Total
Sales.........................	$600	$800	$1,400
Cost of goods sold.............	429	571	1,000
Gross profit....................	$171	$229	$ 400

with each individual product. Therefore, the costs are allocated to the products on the basis of their ability to earn revenue. The assumption is that if a higher selling price exists for one product as compared with another product, then the production costs associated with that product must also be higher.

The mechanics of this method as applied to the example are found in Exhibit 2. An income statement on a product basis for one year is also presented in this exhibit. Note that with this method the gross profit percentage is the same on each of the joint products, that is, approximately 29 percent.

Physical-Unit Method. This method of allocating costs uses a physical measure such as weight, volume, length, and so on as the criterion for allocating joint costs. The joint products should therefore be measured in terms of a basic unit such as pounds, gallons, meters, and so on. It should be noted that this method of allocation does not try to relate costs to the revenue-producing ability of the joint products as did the sales-value method. The income statement in Exhibit 3 clearly illustrates this point. For this reason, in certain circumstances it may *not* be the most meaningful method of cost allocation. A caution is therefore necessary regarding its general application.

It is assumed in Exhibit 3, which illustrates this method, that a widget weighs 2 pounds and a gizmo weighs ½ pound. Note the

EXHIBIT 3
Physical-Unit Method of Cost Allocation

Total weight of widgets......................	(600 × 2) = 1,200 pounds
Total weight of gizmoes.....................	(400 × 1/2) = 200
Total number of pounds produced...........	1,400 pounds

Joint Products	Total Weight (lbs.)	Proportion of Total Weight	Proportion of Joint Costs Allocated to Each Product
Widgets.............	1,200	12/14	12/14 × $1,000 = $ 857
Gizmoes............	200	2/14	2/14 × $1,000 = 143
	1,400		$1,000

Assume again that all that is produced is sold within the year. The income statement under this method is therefore as follows:

PLR COMPANY LIMITED
Income Statement

	Widgets	Gizmoes	Total
Sales.........................	$ 600	$800	$1,400
Cost of goods sold...........	857	143	1,000
Gross profit.................	$(257)	$657	$ 400

high profit on gizmoes and the loss on widgets. Both of these may be quite unrealistic.

Average-Unit-Cost Method. The last method of joint-cost allocation that will be dealt with here is the *average-unit-cost method.* This method is similar to the physical unit method just discussed in that both methods' allocations are based upon physical measures rather than revenue-generating ability. Therefore, drawbacks associated with the physical unit method are not eliminated under the average-unit-cost method.

Under the average-unit-cost method, total manufacturing joint costs are divided by the total number of physical units produced. This yields an average cost associated with the production of each unit of product regardless of its physical characteristics.

In Exhibit 4, an illustration similar to that given for the previous two allocation methods is presented. Note that all the profit is gained on the sale of the gizmoes, while the widgets are at the break-even point. This situation may also be unrealistic.

Different methods of allocation of joint costs have been illustrated and discussed. Perhaps the most important message in all this is that the allocation of joint costs is a completely arbitrary

EXHIBIT 4
Average-Unit-Cost Method of Cost Allocation

Total number of widgets........................	600	
Total number of gizmoes.......................	400	
Total products manufactured...................	1,000	

Joint Products	*Units Produced*	*Proportion of Total Units Produced*	*Proportion of Joint Costs Allocated to Each Product*
Widgets...............	600	6/10	6/10 × $1,000 = $ 600
Gizmoes..............	400	4/10	4/10 × $1,000 = 400
	1,000		$1,000

Assume as before that all that is produced is sold within the year. The income statement under this method is therefore as follows:

PLR COMPANY LIMITED
Income Statement

	Widgets	*Gizmoes*	*Total*
Sales.........................	$600	$800	$1,400
Cost of goods sold.............	600	400	1,000
Gross profit...................	$ 0	$400	$ 400

process. Apportioning joint costs to products in a meaningful manner is more than difficult for any purpose. Some might argue, and justifiably so, that it is impossible.

Input Basis. Those who feel that the problems associated with the arbitrariness of the allocation of joint costs cannot adequately be overcome suggest an alternate course of action: the gross profit should be calculated on an *input* basis rather than on a finished (intermediate) product basis up to the so-called split-off point. The products themselves are inseparable up to this point. It should be noted that costs incurred after the split-off point should be assigned to their respective products.

Exhibit 5 illustrates this alternative approach as applied to the example.

In Exhibit 6, a summary of the various treatments of joint costs is presented. As was stated previously, the gross profit per product is an arbitrary figure subject to manipulation within certain bounds by management. What is clearly unalterable is the fact that a company gross profit of $400 resulted from the difference in total revenues of $1,400 and total incurred costs of $1,000. It is on this existing certainty that the last method discussed (input basis) bases its argument.

EXHIBIT 5
Profit Margin Calculated on an Input Basis

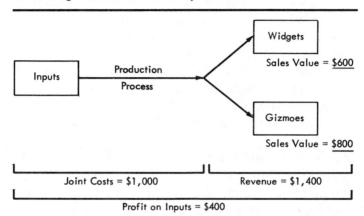

Therefore, gross profit on an input basis is $400.

PLR COMPANY LIMITED
Income Statement

Sales.............................	$1,400
Cost of goods sold................	1,000
Gross profit......................	$ 400

Whatever the allocation procedure selected however, one should not be lulled into believing that one has performed the impossible with a formula and sharpened pencil.

Realizable Value for Inventory Valuation. While the input basis circumvents the artificial and arbitrary allocation of joint costs and is quite satisfactory for the income statement, difficulty arises when a company does not sell all that it produces in the year

EXHIBIT 6
A Comparison of the Various Treatments of Joint Costs

	Sales-Value Method		Physical-Unit Method		Average-Unit-Cost Method		Input Basis
	Widgets	Gizmoes	Widgets	Gizmoes	Widgets	Gizmoes	
Sales....................	$600	$800	$ 600	$800	$600	$800	$1,400
Cost of goods sold.......	429	571	857	143	600	400	1,000
Gross profit or loss per							
product..............	$171	$229	$(257)	$657	$ 0	$400	$ 400
Total gross profit...........	$400		$400		$400		$ 400

and management must carry products in inventory at a specific value. The input basis does not allow for the individual valuation which is needed for the reporting of inventories on the balance sheet. Clearly, any of the allocation methods previously discussed would yield an inventory valuation. Alternatively, a company wishing to avoid the "sin" of joint-cost allocation may choose to carry inventories of jointly manufactured products at sales or *realizable values* or at *net realizable values*. Net realizable value is the sales value minus any costs which are only associated with selling the product.

Using either the realizable value or net realizable value, one does not even consider joint costs. However, a criticism of this approach is that the profit is recognized before it is received. Inventories are traditionally carried at cost, and profit is not recognized until a sale has taken place. Under this approach, as inventories increase in size, profits also increase. If there is very little difference between the sales value and cost value of inventories (i.e., low-margin products), and if the inventory size is relatively stable, this criticism is somewhat overcome.

A variation on the realizable-value method is to determine a realistic profit margin that is in line with that of other company products and to record inventory values at the net realizable value *minus* this independently determined profit margin. In this case, the profit margin on different joint products can take on different values. Under the sales-value method, on the other hand, a common profit margin was associated with each of the products.

It is important to recognize that there is *no attempt* under the net-realizable-value approach to explicitly allocate the *actual joint costs* of production, and this is the key difference between this approach and the allocation approaches which were discussed earlier.

A LOOK AT BY-PRODUCTS

A definition of by-products was given in the introduction to this chapter. From this definition, the characteristics of by-products can be seen as the following:

Produced simultaneously; and

Very *minor* sales value (or no sales value) as compared with the major product.

The main difference, therefore, between joint products and by-products is not in the nature of their production but rather in their relative sales values. Those by-products which have *no* sales value are usually considered as scrap. Some by-products which have a sales value that is very, very low as compared with the main product may also be referred to as scrap.

The point is that the division between joint products, by-products, and scrap products is not a black-and-white situation. Rather, the classification depends upon the specific circumstance. (In any event, by-products and scrap are accounted for in basically the same way.)

As in the case of joint products, by-products can be one of two possible types:

1. Those that are salable *without* the necessity of further processing after the so-called split-off point; and
2. Those that *do* require processing after the split-off point in order to be salable.

One can easily establish the total cost of the inputs to a manufacturing process which produces a main product and one or more by-product. However, as in the case of joint products, difficulty exists when one tries to ascertain the actual cost of manufacturing the main product and the by-product(s) on an individual basis. This problem is, however, not quite so crucial in this case since by-products are usually very minor contributors, both in terms of quantity and sales value, when compared to the main product. Therefore, the nature and characteristics of by-products should be kept in mind by the management accountant when he or she starts to consider the use of expensive human resources to devise very refined by-product accounting techniques. In short, the more refined and expensive accounting methods should be carefully weighed in terms of benefits derived before they are introduced.

As the above discussion would suggest, there are numerous methods of accounting for by-products. In most cases, however, the income statement differences will be insignificant. All the accounting methods can be classified into one of two broad classifications. These are the following:

1. Accounting methods which *do not* attempt to assign a specific cost to the by-products for income determination or inventory valuation; and

2. Accounting methods which *do* attempt to assign some portion of the total manufacturing joint costs to the by-product.

We will use a simplified example to help illustrate numerically the relative income statement differences in the various accounting methods.

Example 2

The ABX Company Limited is a manufacturing company that produces a product known as *ABX*. Besides producing this main product, a salable by-product known as *BX* is also produced from the manufacturing process.

Therefore, the following production model exists:

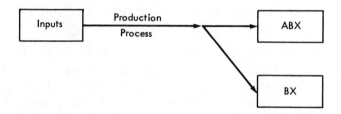

The total cost of inputs and production for one year is $10,000. The process yields 9,000 units of ABX and 1,000 units of BX as by-product. ABX is a product that sells for $3 per unit, and the BX by-product sells for $0.10 per unit. The above production model can be described in more detail as follows:

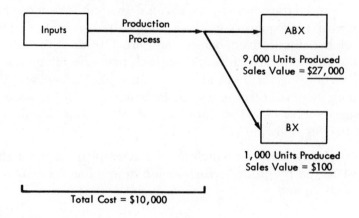

It is assumed that all that is produced is sold in the year. Note that BX is definitely a by-product because of its low relative sales value.

Methods Which Do Not Cost the By-Product

Under the first classification of accounting methods—those which *do not* attempt to assign a specific cost to the by-products—the actual revenue that is received from the sales of by-products can be included on the income statement as any of the following:

1. Other income.
2. Additional sales revenue.
3. A deduction from the cost of goods sold for the main product.
4. A deduction from the total manufacturing costs of the main product.

The above methods for the treatment of by-product revenues are illustrated in Exhibit 7.

EXHIBIT 7
Accounting for By-Products—Classification 1 (a comparison of alternative methods)

ABX COMPANY LIMITED
Income Statement

	Methods (described below)			
	(1)	*(2)*	*(3)*	*(4)*
Sales................................	$27,000	$27,000	$27,000	$27,000
Additional revenue				
(2) (by-products)...................		100		
Total...........................	$27,000	$27,100	$27,000	$27,000
Cost of goods sold:				
Manufacturing costs................	$10,000	$10,000	$10,000	$10,000
By-product revenue (4).............				(100)
Cost of goods sold....................	$10,000	$10,000	$10,000	$ 9,900
By-product revenue (3)...........			(100)	
Cost of goods sold (net)..............			$ 9,900	
Gross profit on sales.................	$17,000	$17,100	$17,100	$17,100
Other income (1)				
By-product revenue...............	100			
Income............................	$17,100	$17,100	$17,100	$17,100

Methods:
(1) Other income.
(2) Additional sales revenue.
(3) Deduction from cost of goods sold.
(4) Deduction from total manufacturing costs.

Methods Which Cost the By-Product

Methods of accounting for by-product revenues which fall into the second classification—those that *do* attempt to assign some portion of the total manufacturing costs to the by-product—reduce the cost of manufacturing the main product by either:

1. The net realizable value of the by-products produced; or,
2. The net realizable value minus a reasonable profit margin.

EXHIBIT 8
Accounting for By-Products—Classification 2

ABX COMPANY LIMITED
Income Statement

	Methods (described below)	
	(1)	*(2)*
Sales—main product.....................	$27,000	$27,000
Cost of goods sold:		
Manufacturing costs (total)............	$10,000	$10,000
Net realizable value of by-product (1).......................	(100)	
Net realizable value minus profit on by-product (2)..............		(90)
Cost of goods sold......................	$ 9,900	$ 9,910
Gross profit on sales of main product............................	$17,100	$17,090
Sales of by-product.....................		$ 100
Cost of goods sold (by-product).........		90
Gross profit on sales of by-product...........................		$ 10
Income................................	$17,100	$17,100

Methods:
(1) Net-realizable-value approach.
(2) Net realizable value minus reasonable profit margin.

It should be noted that both of these approaches are in contrast to Method 4 (deduction from the total manufacturing costs of the main product) under the first classification, which used the actual revenue received from by-product sales as the deduction. Under this second classification, on the other hand, the by-product is assigned a value or cost for inventory purposes. Any unsold by-product at the year-end can be carried on the balance sheet as inventory.

If it is assumed in the example that the selling costs of the by-product are negligible, then its *net realizable value* is $100. Neither a profit nor a loss is recognized on the sale of the by-product in this case. If it is assumed that a "reasonable profit" is $10, then the net realizable value minus a reasonable profit is $90. This can be considered as the "cost" of manufacturing the by-product. Exhibit 8 illustrates these alternate approaches.

DECISION MAKING AND JOINT COSTS

There are two main decisions that management may be required to make regarding joint products and by-products. These are:

1. Should the joint product or by-product be sold as-is, or processed further?
2. What selling price is required for the joint product or by-product so that an "acceptable" profit is achieved?

Up to this point in the chapter, discussion has concentrated on accounting for by-products and joint products from the point of view of inventory valuation and income reporting. All that has been said regarding the allocation of joint costs is quite *irrelevant* when one must make a decision regarding the further processing of a joint product or by-product. This point of irrelevance should be clearly understood.

The Further-Processing Decision

A joint product or by-product results from a manufacturing process undertaken because of a previous management decision. In other words, previously spent costs are sunk costs. The decision whether to sell a joint product or by-product as-is or to process it further should be made by comparing the realizable revenue before further processing with the realizable revenue after further processing, minus the additional processing costs; that is, the *differential income* is the relevant decision variable.

For instance, in Example 1, widgets have a sales value at the split-off point of $600. If further processing, costing $500, resulted in a product with sales value of $1,200, then the widget should be processed further. The differential income resulting from processing the product further is $100 ($600 differential revenue less $500 differential costs). If further processing is not the alternative decided upon, then $100 would be forgone by the company. Historical joint costs and the way they are allocated clearly do not influence the decision at all. In fact, if they are considered and used in the evaluation of various alternatives, an erroneous decision may result. This point becomes clearer when one reconsiders the numerical examples illustrating the various allocation methods summarized in Exhibit 6.

In summary, then, the decision rule with regard to the further processing question is:

> Process a product further as long as the incremental revenue exceeds the additional costs involved with the additional processing.

The Pricing Decision

If a company is in a position to set its own prices or if it has power to negotiate prices, then clearly the question of how to price the joint product or by-product must be answered by company management. Allocated joint costs are also *irrelevant* for this management decision. As was previously illustrated in the chapter, a change in an allocation method can change an acceptable profit to a significant loss.

The decision to accept a certain price for a by-product or joint product should not be considered in isolation from the prices received for the main product or other joint products respectively. The *total* revenues received from the joint outputs should be compared with the *total* cost of inputs and production. Profit should be calculated therefore on an "input basis" rather than on an individual joint- or by-product basis. This approach, which was illustrated previously in the section dealing with joint products, is the decision rule with regards to Question 2.

ILLUSTRATIVE CASE STUDY

The following case, which is taken from *Management Accounting: Text and Cases* (5th edition) by Robert N. Anthony and James S. Reece, illustrates the irrelevance of allocated joint costs in management decision making.

Craik Veneer Company*

The sales manager of the Craik Veneer Company received from the Groton Company an offer to buy one million feet per month of sound "backs" of $\frac{1}{24}$-inch birch veneer[1] at $8 per thousand surface feet. The sales manager wanted to accept the offer, but the production manager argued that it should not be accepted because the cost of production was at least $10 per thousand feet and probably more.

The Craik company manufactured rotary cut birch veneer from high-grade yellow birch logs bought in Vermont. Selected sections called "blocks" were cut out of those logs, the length of the block varying from 84 inches to 98 inches, depending on the length along the grain of the veneer being produced. These blocks, as cut for the lathe, cost an average of $200 per thousand board feet. A thousand board feet, log measure, was an amount of logs which, being sawed, would produce a thousand board feet of lumber. (A board foot is one square foot one inch thick.) After being cut, the blocks were put in vats filled with hot water and left there for 24 to 48 hours until the entire log was heated through.

Manufacturing Process

In the rotary veneer process, a block was put in a lathe in which a knife longer than the block, with a heavy frame, guide bars, and pressure bars, was brought against the side of the block so that it cut off a thin slice of wood the entire length of the block. The process was similar to unrolling a large roll of paper held on a horizontal shaft. The process could be controlled with skillful operation so it would produce veneer of uniform thickness. The Craik company produced principally $\frac{1}{24}$-inch veneer, and for the purposes of this case it may be assumed that all of its product was $\frac{1}{24}$-inch.

The sheet of veneer from the lathe, for instance from a 98-inch block, was brought onto a clipping table approximately 60 feet long. This table had rubber belts on its upper surface which moved the veneer along to the clipper. At this point the veneer was like a long sheet of paper moving along the table, the veneer being 98

[1] Veneer is a term applied to thin leaves or layers of wood. Generally veneer is made of valuable wood and is laid over a core of inferior wood.

inches along the grain. The clipper was a long knife extending entirely across the table. The clipper operator was one of the most
highly skilled workers in the plant. Constantly inspecting the sheet
of veneer, he first took one cut to get a straight edge. If the next
section of the sheet was of high quality, he advanced the sheet
not over 3 feet 8 inches, depending on customers' requirements. If
the sheet showed a defect within 3 feet 8 inches, he made his cut
just short of the defect. A worker called the "off bearer" piled these
sheets on a hand truck reserved for high-grade or "face" veneer. If
the defect was a knot, the clipper operator then advanced the sheet
enough to clear the knot and took another cut, making a piece of
waste possibly 3 inches wide. If he decided that a section of the
sheet was not of face quality, he cut it off for "backs," either 3 feet
8 inches or in lesser widths. Backs were put on another hand truck.

The clipper operator thus separated the whole sheet of veneer
into faces, backs, and waste. The faces consisted of pieces of veneer
98 inches long along the grain and anywhere from 6 inches to 3
feet 8 inches wide. The sound backs were of the same size. The
waste went to a chipper and was then burned. The term "faces"
came from the fact that these veneer sheets were substantially perfect and could be used on the exposed parts of furniture or on the
best face of plywood.[2] The backs had minor defects and were so
called because they were used on the back of plywood panels. The
quality required for faces was established by specifications and by
the custom of the industry. The dividing line between sound backs
and waste was similarly established. The Craik company had a
reputation for using high-grade logs and for producing a high grade
of veneer both on faces and backs.

Groton Company's Offer

The Groton Company's product design department had developed two new lines of furniture, one in blond modern and one
in colonial, in which the table tops, dresser tops and panels, drawer
fronts, and other exposed parts were of birch veneer over lower-
grade birch or poplar cores, with table legs, dresser frames, and so
on, of solid birch. The Groton people knew that while all sheets of

---

[2] Veneer is a single thin sheet of wood. Plywood consists of several sheets (three,
five, or nine) glued together with the grain of alternate courses at right angles to
add to the strength.

backs contained defects, 50 to 60 percent of the area of backs as produced by Craik were of face quality. They had discovered that by buying backs 84 inches to 98 inches long they could cut clear face-quality veneer into lengths that would match their use requirements: enough 54 inches for their longest dresser tops and enough of other lengths down to 14-inch drawer fronts. The remainder of the veneer that was not of face quality could be used for such purposes as making plywood for drawer bottoms. The methods developed in the product design department had been tested by cutting up several carloads of backs bought from Craik and by the manufacture and sale of the furniture.

On the basis of this experience the Groton Company offered Craik $8 per thousand feet for one million feet per month of sound backs in $1/24$-inch birch veneer for the next 12 months.

Cost Information

The Craik company cut an average of 12,000 board feet of logs a day in one eight-hour shift. With the high quality of logs it bought, it got a yield of 18,000 surface feet of $1/24$-inch veneer per 1,000 board feet cut; this graded on the average 50 percent faces and 50 percent backs.

Labor and factory overhead costs together averaged $8 per thousand surface feet of veneer; selling costs averaged $1.50. Both the cost of the blocks and operating costs for the heating, lathe turning, and clipping operations were joint costs; backs had to be produced in order to get the faces. The remaining operations in drying, a slight amount of reclipping, storing, and shipping were in a sense separate costs as the operations were done on backs separately, although with the same equipment. The labor and factory overhead costs through clipping averaged $6.75 per 1,000 surface feet of veneer; those for drying and later operations, $1.25.

The selling price for $1/24$-inch birch faces 84 inches to 98 inches long was $40 per thousand surface feet. Face veneer 84 inches to 98 inches had a high price because it could be used on large surfaces, such as flush birch doors that require lengths up to eight feet. The veneer shorter in length along the grain, made from recutting backs, had a somewhat lower price because it could not be used for these purposes. Unlike faces, the price of backs fluctuated widely. Sometimes Craik could get $10 per thousand feet, but the insistence of the production manager on $10 had led to the accumulation of a heavy inventory of backs. Faces were easy to sell and were shipped essentially as fast as they were produced.

More effort was required to sell backs than to sell faces, although both were sold to the same customers by the same sales force. Sometimes buyers of faces were required to take a percentage of backs in order to get a carload of faces. For these reasons the offer of the customer was attractive to the sales manager.

Discussion of Offer

When the production manager was first informed by the sales manager of the offer of $8 per thousand surface feet, the production manager contended that "Your salespersons are so lazy, they would give veneer away if nobody watched them." The production manager went on to say:

> If a birch block cost $200 per thousand and we get 18,000 feet of $\frac{1}{24}$-inch-thick veneer from every thousand board feet of the block, the cost of the block to be allocated to a thousand feet of veneer, whether backs or faces, is $200 divided by 18,000 feet, or about $11.11 per thousand feet. Simple arithmetic proves that selling backs at $8 per thousand doesn't even pay for the material, let alone labor and overhead.

The sales manager countered that this argument was fallacious:

> Allocating the cost of the block to the veneer in this manner implies that backs are as valuable as faces, which is not the case. The $11.11 material figure for a thousand feet of veneer that you get is merely an average of the value of faces and backs. The material for faces is worth considerably more per thousand feet than this figure; the material for backs is worth considerably less.

The sales manager suggested that the proper procedure was to allocate the cost of the block to faces and backs in proportion to the amounts for which the products were sold. Using this method, the ratio that the revenue of one of the two grades of veneer bore to the revenue received from both grades of veneer would be applied to the total cost of the block, the result representing the cost to be allocated to that particular grade. To illustrate this method, assume a block of a thousand board feet cost $200, and the selling prices and quantities of faces and backs are as shown in the following table:

Grade	$\frac{1}{24}$-Inch Veneer in Feet	Sales Revenue per 1,000 Feet	Net Value	Percent of Total	Cost Applicable to Each
Faces...........	9,000	$40	$360	83.3%	$166.67
Backs..........	9,000	8	72	16.6	33.33
	18,000		$432	100.0%	$200.00

The material cost applicable to each product, then, per thousand feet of $\frac{1}{24}$-inch veneer would be $166.67/9,000 feet $\times$ 1,000 feet, or $18.52, for faces; and $33.33/9,000 feet $\times$ 1,000 feet, or $3.70, for backs.

The production manager again argued that this did not represent the true material cost, which was the same for both products, and added:

> Under your method the material cost allocated to either faces or backs would be a function of their relative selling prices. If the selling price of faces fell from $40 per thousand to $20 per thousand and the price of backs remained the same, you would then charge much more material cost to backs, and much less to faces. Your method of allocating cost doesn't make sense.

The sales manager at this point said:

> O.K., if you don't think that method is justified, then let's treat backs as a by-product. I think you'll agree that we would prefer to be making faces all the time, yet we can't. As long as we manufacture faces, we're going to produce backs as an undesirable consequence. Now if we consider backs as a by-product, we can charge all block costs to faces. The net proceeds from the sale of backs, after allowing for all conversion, selling and administrative expenses, can be credited to the raw material cost of faces. All profits and losses of the business would be borne by the main product.

The production manager, however, pointed out again that the cost of material allocated to faces would still be a function of the selling price of backs and, furthermore, there would be some difficulty in trying to value inventories at the end of an accounting period; and that any profits arising from the sale of backs would be hidden, since it would be included in the credit to faces. "It is important to determine the profit or loss being realized on the sale of backs so we can establish a firm sales policy," he said.

Because of their inability to resolve this question, the production manager and the sales manager consulted the president of the Craik Veneer Company, who, in turn, asked the controlled to examine the cost situation to determine whether the $8 per thousand surface feet of $\frac{1}{24}$-inch backs would, or would not, result in a profit.

Comments on the Case

In this case, the sales manager must decide whether or not to accept the offer made by the Groton Company of "$8 per thousand feet for one million feet per month of sound backs in $\frac{1}{24}$-inch birch veneer for the next 12 months."

It is impossible to determine "the" cost of faces and backs. Each individual in the case is arguing for a method that is useful to that person and that would lead to the adoption of a preferred policy. No cost allocation method determines a "real," "actual," or "true" cost in this sort of situation.

More important than the choice of an allocation method is educating the organization to understand the method's limitations, whichever method is adopted. If the sales manager holds back on inventory rather than sell them "below cost," this is a mistake. It can perhaps be corrected by changing the definition of "cost," but a sounder approach is to have everyone understand the limitations of whatever definition is used.

Backs may be considered as a true by-product, and there are advantages in costing them as such. It may, however, be desirable to use an estimate of the sales value of backs over the next year or so, rather than to use the by-product accounting method that credits the actual sales value of each transaction to faces. This method implies that the price of faces must be high enough to yield a satisfactory profit for the whole enterprise, which is in accord with the facts.

The difference between material costs and other costs is that material costs are entirely joint, whereas certain labor and overhead costs can be traced directly to backs. These further processing costs, amounting to $1.25 per thousand surface feet, whatever the system, should be charged to backs and segregated in such a way that the incremental cost of completing backs is known. In addition, if the company actually incurs incremental selling costs of $1.50 per thousand surface feet of backs, this cost is relevant in deciding whether to accept Groton's offer. The amount of these costs beyond the split-off point is the absolute minimum selling price of backs; that is, $2.75, assuming incremental selling costs of $1.50 per thousand surface feet. If the price should ever get this low, the backs material should be discarded or burned rather than being finished into salable product. Using an estimated sales realization rather than the actual realization gives the sales manager a pricing target, and would show how much of the profit or loss resulted from the sales manager's ability to sell above or below the target figure.

The following factors should be considered by the sales manager of the Craik Veneer Company in his decision concerning the acceptance of the Groton Company offer:

1. Because the selling costs have averaged $1.50 per thousand and more effort is required to sell backs than faces, the sales manager should not accept the offer if he thinks he can get more than $9.50 ($8.00 offer + $1.50 selling costs) per thousand for backs through having the sales force push the sale of backs. Again, the $1.50 figure is relevant here only if it will actually save the company this much in its selling costs. If the sales force are not on commission, and no selling expense is saved (such as laying off salespersons) by taking the Groton Company's offer, then the Craik sales manager should not accept the Groton offer if he thinks he can sell all available backs at anything above $8 per thousand surface feet.
2. He should consider the size of the heavy inventory of backs on hand and whether or not there is any possibility of not being able to sell these backs at a reasonable price of $8 or more.
3. He should consider the effect on customer relations of sometimes requiring them to take a percentage of backs in order to get a carload of faces.
4. He should consider alternative uses of backs such as having the Craik Company make plywood, or of having Craik cut up backs and make smaller sizes of face veneer, as the Groton Company plans to do with the backs.

It is only after *these* factors are considered and evaluated that the sales manager can make a decision which is beneficial to the company.

It should be emphasized again that allocated joint costs are relevant only for inventory valuation and income reporting. They have no bearing on this or any managerial decision.

CONCLUSION AND SUMMARY

This chapter has been an in-depth look at joint- and by-product costs. One should be aware of the differences between joint products and by-products and how these differences influence the associated accounting procedures.

Several methods of joint-cost allocation were presented and illustrated in detail. Also, the various accounting methods for handling by-product costs were explained. These methods, it must be emphasized, are only of use for purposes of inventory valuation and income determination.

Managerial decisions concerning the further processing of a joint product or by-product should be based on a comparison of incremental revenue and incremental costs. The decision should favor further processing as long as the incremental revenue exceeds the incremental costs. Managerial decisions concerning the acceptability of profit margin for by-products and/or joint products should be based upon "input basis" profit calculations.

ADDITIONAL SOURCES

Anthony, Robert N., and Reece, James S. *Management Accounting Principles,* pp. 348–50. 3d ed. Homewood, Ill.: Richard D. Irwin, Inc., 1975.

Butler, John J. "Joint Product Analysis." *Management Accounting,* December 1971, p. 12.

DeCoster, Don T.; Ramanathan, Kavasseri V.; and Sundem, Gary L. *Accounting for Managerial Decision Making.* Los Angeles: Melville Publishing Co., 1974.

Dickey, Robert I., ed. *Accountants' Cost Handbook.* 2d ed. New York: The Ronald Press Co., 1960.

Dopuch, Nicholas; Birnberg, Jacob C.; and Demski, Joel. *Cost Accounting: Accounting Data for Management's Decisions,* chap. 14. New York: Harcourt Brace Jovanovich, Inc., 1974.

Horngren, Charles T. *Cost Accounting: A Managerial Emphasis,* chap. 17. 4th ed. Englewood Cliffs, N.J.: Prentice-Hall, Inc., 1977.

Matz, Adolph, and Usry, Milton F. *Cost Accounting Planning and Control*, chap. 8. 6th ed. Cincinnati: South-Western Publishing Co., 1976.

Neuner, John J. W., and Deakin, Edward B. *Cost Accounting: Principles and Practice*, chap. 5. 9th ed. Homewood, Ill.: Richard D. Irwin, Inc., 1977.

Shillinglaw, Gordon. *Managerial Cost Accounting*, chap. 11. 4th ed. Homewood, Ill.: Richard D. Irwin, Inc., 1977.

10

Determining Standard Material and Labor Costs

Richard D. Enright*

A standard cost is a tool. Like many other tools it can be extremely sophisticated or extremely simple. The degree of sophistication which this tool should possess is determined by the needs and capabilities of its users. The users of the standard cost tool are the people responsible for the management of the enterprise.

In this chapter an attempt will be made to illustrate how such a tool is made or developed. We will cover the various ingredients needed and also the question of responsibility for the various operations required to determine and maintain standard costs. The conclusion of this chapter will cover the use of standard cost principles in nonmanufacturing areas. Chapter 32, "Variance Analysis of Operating Results," will show the end benefits of standard costs.

USES OF STANDARD COSTS

There are three principal ways managers use standard costs: for measuring, for production, and for analysis. It is extremely important to keep these uses or purposes of standard costs in mind as the standard costs are determined.

---

* Mr. Enright has an accounting consulting practice in Allentown, Pennsylvania.

The Measuring Tool

The most common use of standard costs is as a measuring device. The performance of supervision is measured against the costs which should have been incurred according to the applicable standard costs.

Most large companies now use standard costs as the "yardstick" against which manufacturing supervision is measured or judged. In this setting—the engineered expense environment of manufacturing—a good, sound, and reasonable standard cost system probably comes as close as possible to being objective in the evaluation of performance. However, the reverse is probably also true. A poor standard cost is a highly subjective basis for evaluating performance. An observation at this point is that nonmanufacturing supervision is seldom evaluated as objectively. Perhaps this chapter will help improve this situation.

Two subsidiary questions arise when discussing the measurement aspect of standard costs. The first of these is the desirable "tightness" of the standards. The two extremes are: to set the standards so high that only a work force of bionic men or women could reach them; or to set the standards at or slightly below the historical average performance. The first is justified on the theory that unrealistic goals will insure maximum effort; the second is justified because it will presumably prevent mistakes or criticism caused by undue optimism.

It is doubtful that goals never reached insure anything but frustration; and goals based upon average performance seem to have a bias against improvement which could be fatal. The standard costs should be set at a level that "reasonably good supervision of reasonably good employees using the equipment and facilities available" will attain. Agreed—this is hardly precise, but it is about the best that can be done. Perhaps it could be stated another way: "Achievement of the standard costs should result in a commendation for the supervisor, but not a medal."

The second subsidiary question deals with the "exactness" of the standards. The author once worked for a supervisor who would complain constantly about "measuring with a micrometer in order to cut it off with a big bucksaw." Be reasonable. Since a standard is a theoretical number, it can be as exact as the calculator/computer will allow; but exactness in excess of the ability to measure actual performance is a waste. Standard costs for products measured in tons should not be determined in ounces. Also to be considered is the cost effect of increased exactness: if the next decimal point of the standard does not change, the cost per finished unit at least $0.01, it probably should not be used.

The Prediction Tool

In the author's judgment, the quality of a standard cost system is determined by its value as a prediction tool. If the standard costs have been properly determined, then it should be possible to predetermine the cost of a new product or service. Granted that if the present product is wicker baskets and the new product is battleships this may not hold true. However, in the real world the new product is most likely using mostly the same equipment and facilities as the present products, and a good standard cost system should be able to predict with reasonable accuracy the performance and therefore the cost. This predictive ability should apply to changes in run size, dimensions, or almost any other variation from the present products as well.

This is important because of the tremendous input this feature of standard costs can make to one of the most important and frequent management decisions—establishment of the selling price. True, many individual prices have little or no correlation to costs; but it is also true that in the long run prices must exceed costs or the firm will cease to exist. It is even important to know the magnitude of the loss in those cases of products sold at a loss to gain entry into a market or to satisfy customer requirements when the customer is purchasing other profitable products. This loss represents an investment, and the investment can only be judged if its amount (the loss) and the benefits both are known.

The ability of standard costs to predict is also essential to the determination of capacity requirements. In the planning (budgeting) process there must be a step to determine that the facilities and equipment on hand are sufficient to handle the anticipated volume. Good standard costs based upon knowledge of required machine/man-hours and materials are used in this process. In a related area, firms working at or near capacity can use the standard cost information as a basis for improving overall profitability by dropping some of the least profitable products. This is a complex problem which requires the maximum of good information and, at times, relatively sophisticated tools such as linear programming.

Of course, the staff or work force requirement can also be determined by a good standard cost system. This is another use of standard costs in the planning function. Being over- or understaffed is very costly, causing extra unemployment taxes, various fringe benefits, idle time, short shipment, overtime, and so on. Control of these costs could be critical.

The Analytical Tool

Good standard costs are usable in many analytical studies which the firm must perform. These cover such areas as investing in additional or replacement equipment or facilities, make-or-buy decisions, and determining which equipment should be shut down in slow periods. In several chapters of this Handbook, the reader will see opportunities to use either present or *future* standard costs in various decision-making and analytical contexts.

In summary, standard costs perform a multitude of services in the decision-making process. They cannot eliminate judgment from the process, but by providing a maximum amount of facts they can be a great assistance to that judgment. In the next two sections, we will consider in some detail the "how" of determining standard costs.

DETERMINING LABOR STANDARDS

Before getting into the how and why of determining the standard costs of labor, it is appropriate that we define some terms. These are terms which seem to be extremely difficult to define, but unless there is a working definition it is not possible to discuss intelligently the subject of standard costs.

First, what is a *direct cost?* In the context of this chapter, by "direct cost" we shall mean "a cost incurred in the hope of directly increasing the quantity or quality of specific salable goods or services"; that is, our cost objective will be a company's products. Note that the definition does not depend on the nature of the cost but on the *purpose* or object of the cost. For example, a machinist's labor costs in a machine shop are not automatically direct. The machinist may spend some time on maintenance or research projects, for example; these costs are indirect with respect to specific products. The important question is, what did you hope to accomplish with this cost? Further, it should be noted that purpose is "salable" products, not products for sale. Time spent manufacturing samples, for example, would definitely qualify as direct time.

What, then, is an *indirect* cost? An indirect cost will be defined as "a cost incurred in support of the direct cost operations." For example, the janitorial operations are indirect because they do not increase the quantity or quality of salable products; but they do, presumably, affect the ability of the direct cost operation to improve the quantity/quality of specific salable products. Supervisors, utilities, and occupancy expenses usually fall into the indirect category.

Variable costs are, of course, costs which vary with some measure of activity. In a manufacturing operation, these represent costs which vary as production volume increases (or decreases). In practice, variable costs correlate extremely well with direct costs; that is, most of the items which are classified as direct will also be classified as variable. In fact, the correlation is so close that the terms are often used interchangeably, even though they are conceptually different. (There is a whole cost accounting system commonly called "direct costing," which is misnamed: the system is really "variable costing.") For example, maintenance costs may very well vary with the production level, but they are certainly not costs incurred in the hope of directly increasing the quantity or quality of specific salable products. Similarly, setup or startup costs are an example of direct costs which are not variable.

Fixed costs, then, are costs which do not vary with production volume. Actually, in a sense there are no fixed costs since, given enough time, all costs can be altered. The phrase usually is narrowed to be "costs fixed in the short run" or an equivalent concept. Fixed costs correlate closely with indirect costs, but again they do not correlate exactly. Depreciation on a machine only usable for one product would be an example of a cost both direct and fixed.

This chapter will deal with those costs which are variable, whether they be direct or indirect, and with any fixed costs which are also direct. The reason for this selection is that these are the costs which should relate in some way to what and/or how much is being produced; therefore, they should be incorporated into the standard cost of the products to be produced. Going back to the idea at the beginning of this chapter, these are the costs to be measured, or predicted, or analyzed.

The other costs (indirect fixed) are only of interest to standard costing when an attempt is made to allocate them to man-hours, machine-hours, and so on, in order to approximate full costs. This allocation is not part of the scope of this chapter. In fact, the author feels this should only be attempted where absolutely necessary, as, for example, when the producer is working on some type of cost-reimbursement contract, such as a cost-plus-fixed-fee contract with the government.

Standard Times

The initial step in determining standard labor costs is to determine the amount of time required to perform the various operations in the manufacture of the product. This is one of those places where some accountants have loaded down their cost systems with excessive detail. Each product manufactured does not have a complete set of operations of its own; rather, the operations involved in the manufacture of all the products tend to be similar. The secret is to break the operations down to their fundamental elements. Using as an example a paper-converting operation (waxing, printing, extruding, laminating, etc.), we shall see how this works.

Exhibit 1 illustrates the type of equipment which may be available to the paper converter mentioned above. The first section gives the physical characteristics of the various machines. Since the standard costs are to be developed based upon the "facilities and equipment available," these data become the parameters around which the system is built.

The next several sections provide information concerning the various times and/or speeds possible with this equipment. There are three steps involved in the operation of all the machines. These steps are setup, roll changing, and running. (The special case of the printer is only another type of setup.) It should be noted, however, that what influences the times involved in these steps is determined by various factors. A look at the running speeds indicates that there are three possible determinants involved based upon the particular

EXHIBIT 1
Operating Information for Machines (paper converter)

	Waxer	Wax Laminator	Glue Laminator	Extruder	Printer	Winders/ Slitters (3)
Maximum roll width.	90″	50″	45″	60″	36″	56″
Maximum roll diameter on.	60″	30″	36″	48″	54″	45″
Maximum roll diameter off.	50″	40″	40″	54″	45″	55″
Setup time (hours).	0.10	0.15	0.20	0.05	0.50*	0.10
Each additional color.					0.10	
Each slit.						0.05
Time per roll-on.	0.17	0.20	0.10	0.15	0.10	0.15
Time per roll-off.	0.13	0.10	0.10	0.05	0.12	0.10
Plus each slit.						0.03
Running speed (fpm):						
1–3 lbs. added.	800	500	250	400		
4–8 lbs. added.	600	400	175	300		
9–12 lbs. added.	600	400	125	200		
One color.					300	
Two colors.					270	
Three colors.					240	
Four colors.					210	
Five colors.					180	
Six colors.					150	
Basis weight on 60 +.						750
Basis weight on 46–60.						600
Basis weight on 31–45.						500
Basis weight on 0–30.						400
Weekly machine-hours.	168	168	40	48	120	504
Shifts.	3	3	1	1	3	3

* If the press has not been run for a period of time in excess of eight hours, there is an additional four hours setup required for warming up. This warming up also consumes 300 linear feet of base paper.

machine. These determinants are (1) the pounds of material added per basis weight, (2) the number of colors to be printed, and (3) the basis weight on the machine.

Basis weight is a term referring to the weight of 3,000 square feet of paper (foil cellophane). Therefore, 3 pounds of wax added means 3 pounds per 3,000 square feet and a basis weight of 60 pounds means that every 3,000 square feet of the roll weighs 60 pounds.

The first question an accountant is likely to ask at this point is, "How in blazes am I supposed to know all these details about a lot of complicated machinery?" The answer is, "You ask." If the firm has an industrial engineer, you can get help. Industrial engineers have all this information, probably in greater detail than required because they built their standards on these same general principles. For example, they probably have a set of instructions covering the way to perform each of these operations plus the times which should be involved. Talk with, ask of, demand of, and confer with the industrial engineers. In a very real sense standard costs are a dollarization of industrial engineering standards. It is to the benefit of the cost accountant, and the industrial engineer, to open and maintain a dialogue.

If there is no industrial engineer, then *someone* in the manufacturing department is performing this function. This person may be as systematic as an industrial engineer, or may be "flying by the seat of his pants." In either case, this person is the best source available, so you can get help. Be extremely careful how the questions are phrased. The information desired is not that product A can be produced at 500 pounds per hour and Product B at 1,000 pounds per hour. Standard costs have been built upon this type of information, but such standards do not meet the requirements for predictability and analysis established in the introduction. Rather, the information required is why twice as much Product B can be produced as Product A. The answer to this is absolutely necessary if the standard costs are to have any validity as a prediction tool.

Because this person is probably not accustomed to thinking like a cost accountant or an industrial engineer, it is extremely important that questions be phrased properly. As is the case in almost any learning process, the name of the game is ask the right questions properly. Be patient and skeptical—and *polite*. Do not hesitate to ask the same question again and again, perhaps rephrased slightly. The answers are coming from one who will probably be measured by these standard costs. Also, remember that neither participant in the dialogue has a detailed grasp of the other's discipline.

Obviously, there are problems involved if there is no industrial engineer as a source, but the problem may be a blessing in disguise. The lack of an industrial engineer forces a dialogue between the cost accountant and the manufacturing personnel. This dialogue must be opened sooner or later if the standard costs are to be utilized. The tool will be used only if the other managers have faith in its accuracy and reliability. It is the cost accountant's job to create this faith. Changing the standards because the information collected from the industrial engineer and/or manufacturing was faulty does not tend to create this faith. To repeat: ask the right question, properly; be patient and skeptical, and polite.

There is one method for the cost accountant to gather this information not mentioned before. It is called observation. The author has spent many hours observing the operations of various machines. It can frequently be an eye-opening experience. Try it.

Other Factors

Exhibit 2 represents various information obtained from the same sources as above, plus purchasing and/or material handling. The information falls into three groups which will be discussed below.

Because the product is normally sold by weight, all of the cost

EXHIBIT 2
Material Characteristics

	Paper A	Paper B	Wax	Glue	Poly-ethylene	Ink
Pounds per inch of width:						
60" diameter 3" core	20.00	30.00	4.32	45.00	25.00	1.50
54" diameter 3" core	16.14	24.21	3.49	36.32	20.18	1.21
50" diameter 3" core	13.84	20.76	2.99	31.14	17.30	1.04
48" diameter 3" core	12.74	19.11	2.75	28.66	15.92	0.96
45" diameter 3" core	11.20	16.80	2.42	25.20	14.00	0.84
40" diameter 3" core	8.84	13.26	1.91	19.89	11.05	0.66
36" diameter 3" core	7.16	10.74	1.55	16.11	8.95	0.54
30" diameter 3" core	4.96	7.44	1.07	11.16	6.20	0.37
27" diameter 3" core	4.00	6.00	0.86	9.00	5.00	0.30
24" diameter 3" core	3.14	4.71	0.68	7.06	3.92	0.24
21" diameter 3" core	2.40	3.60	0.52	5.40	3.00	0.18
18" diameter 3" core	1.76	2.64	0.38	3.96	2.20	0.13
15" diameter 3" core	1.20	1.80	0.26	2.70	1.50	0.09
12" diameter 3" core	0.74	1.11	0.16	1.66	0.92	0.06
9" diameter 3" core	0.40	0.60	0.09	0.90	0.50	0.03
6" diameter 3" core	0.14	0.21	0.03	0.32	0.18	0.01
Loss factors:						
Waxer	3%	2%				
Wax laminator	4	3				
Glue laminator	5	4				
Extruder	2	1				
Printer (1–3 colors)	6	5				
Printer (4 colors)	7	6				
Printer (5 colors)	8	7				
Printer (6 colors)	9	8				
Winder (unprinted)	4	3				
Winder (printed)	8	7				
Trim factors:						
Unprinted	2"	1"				
Printed	4	2				

standards must be expressed in weight (pounds). The first section of Exhibit 2 gives the means for determining the roll weights involved in calculating the cost for roll changes. Naturally there will be no rolls of ink, but there will be rolls containing ink, so this item is included at its equivalent roll weight.

The second section gives various loss factors which it is felt are not reasonably avoided. These would be a result of such problems as the quality of materials available, the condition of the machinery, and the carefulness of the work force and/or supervision. Inspection could also be a part of this loss.

The third section covers the fact that it is not possible to properly wax, print, and so forth, the full width of the roll. For example, there may be a tendency to build up at the edges. The loss is expressed as additional inches required. To illustrate, a printed roll of paper A would have to start 34 inches wide to have a finished roll of 30 inches.

Machine Time to Man-Hour Conversion

Once these physical characteristics of the machines, personnel, and materials have been established, it is necessary to start converting the machine-hour data into "people" hours, because labor costs are payments to and/or for people.

Exhibit 3 illustrates the required work force needed to keep all the machines running simultaneously. The roll-wrapping operation is a manual chore not requiring machinery, and the figure of 5.00 represents an approximation of the force needed when all machines

EXHIBIT 3
Standard Work Force (paper converter)

		Force Required All Machines Running				
	Press Operator	A Machine Operator	B Machine Operator	Press Helper	Machine Helper	Roll Wrapper
Waxer...................		1.00			0.50	
Wax laminator...........		1.00			0.50	
Glue laminator..........		1.00			0.50	
Extruder................		1.00			0.50	
Printer.................	1.00			2.00		
Winder/slitter (3)........			3.00		1.00	
Roll wrapping...........						5.00
Total work force....	1.00	4.00	3.00	2.00	3.00	5.00

are operating. The actual requirements would depend upon the specific products involved. It is further assumed that because of the distance between machines, the helpers on the first two machines cannot assist with the next two. The industrial engineer and/or manufacturing supervisor can provide this information. However, be sensitive to attempts to "pad" the personnel requirements.

Having established the requirements, the next step is to determine how many machine-hours should be used for the purpose of determining standard costs. Exhibit 1 listed the number of machine-hours it is anticipated will be used on a weekly basis. The source for this information is the sales/production figures as used in the company operating budget. Remember the standard costs will be predictive. This means if the amount to be produced is known, the amount of machine-hours required can be known.

Assuming the company has a production plan, this plan should probably be the basis for the machine-hours used in the standard costs. In fact, if this information is available and *not* used as the basis, there should be an extremely good reason. The advantage of this as a basis is that it ties the standard costs into the plan in such a way that it is easy to analyze the effects on total profit of failures to reach the sales/production plan. Increases in the sales from the plan, for example, could cause an increase in overtime premium. The total effect of this sales increase cannot be known until this and other factors have been plugged into the analysis.

If there is no company plan with sufficient detail to be used as a basis, the best advice would be to develop such a plan and/or set the machine-hours at a level which will minimize as far as possible variances caused by changes in the sale/production volume beyond the control of the manufacturing department.

Hourly Machine Rates

Once the standard machine-hours to be used are known, the next step is to man the machines, cost the people, and develop a rate per machine hour. Exhibits 4A to 4F show how this is done. Starting with Exhibit 4A, the waxer and wax laminator, we shall follow this operation step by step.

Exhibits 1 and 3 tell us each waxing machine should run 168 hours (24×7) per week and the work force requirement for each

EXHIBIT 4

A. Wax Laminator and Waxer Machine-Hours Rate

	Hourly Rate	Man-Hours per Week	Shifts per Week	Employees Required	Dollars per Week	Dollars per Machine-Hours (168 hours)
A operator................	$5.00	168	3	4	$ 840.00	$5.00
Shift differential...........	0.10	112	2		11.20	0.07
Overtime premium........	2.50	8			20.00	0.12
Hourly fringes.............	0.40	168			67.20	0.40
Percentage fringes........					87.12	0.52
Per worker fringes.........					40.00	0.24
Total A operator......	$6.34	168	3	4	$1,065.52	$6.35*
Machine helper...........	$2.00	84	3	2	$ 168.00	$1.00
Shift differential...........	0.10	56	2		5.60	0.03
Overtime premium........	1.00	8			8.00	0.05
Hourly fringes.............	0.40	84			33.60	0.20
Percentage fringes........					18.16	0.11
Per worker fringes.........		—	—	—	20.00	0.12
Machine helper total...............	$3.02	84	3	2	$ 253.36	$1.51
Grand total................	$5.23†	252	3	6	$1,318.88	$7.86

* Differs from $1,065.52 ÷ 168 = $6.34 owing t) rounding.
† This is the weighted-average rate for the operator-helper combination.

B. Glue Laminator

	Hourly Rate	Man-Hours per Week	Shifts per Week	Employees Required	Dollars per Week	Dollars per Machine-Hours (40 hours)
A operator................	$5.00	40	1	1	$200.00	$5.00
Shift differential...........	0.10	0			0.00	0.00
Overtime premium........	2.50	0			0.00	0.00
Hourly fringes.............	0.40	40			16.00	0.40
Percentage fringes........					20.00	0.50
Per worker fringes					10.00	0.25
Total A operator......	$6.15	40	1	1	$246.00	$6.15
Machine helper...........	$2.00	24	1	0.5	$ 48.00	$1.20
Shift differential...........	0.10	0			0.00	0.00
Overtime premium........	1.00	4			4.00	0.10
Hourly fringes.............	0.40	24			9.60	0.24
Percentage fringes........					5.20	0.13
Per worker fringes		—	—	—	5.00	0.13
Machine helper total...............	$2.99	24	1	0.5	$ 71.80	$1.80
Grand total................	$4.97*	64	1	1.5	$317.80	$7.95

* Weighted-average rate.

EXHIBIT 4 (continued)
C. Extruder

	Hourly Rate	Man-Hours per Week	Shifts per Week	Employees Required	Dollars per Week	Dollars per Machine-Hours (48 hours)
A operator................	$5.00	48	1	1	$240.00	$5.00
Shift differential...........	0.10	0			0.00	0.00
Overtime premium........	2.50	8			20.00	0.42
Hourly fringes.............	0.40	48			19.20	0.40
Percentage fringes........					26.00	0.54
Per worker fringes.........					10.00	0.21
Total A operator......	$6.57	48	1	1	$315.20	$6.57
Machine helper...........	$2.00	24	1	0.5	$ 48.00	$1.00
Shift differential...........	0.10	0			0.00	0.00
Overtime premium........	1.00	4			4.00	0.08
Hourly fringes.............	0.40	24			9.60	0.20
Percentage fringes........					5.20	0.11
Per worker fringes.........					5.00	0.10
Machine helper total...............	$2.99	24	1	0.5	$ 71.80	$1.49
Grand total................	$5.38*	72	1	1.5	$387.00	$8.06

* Weighted-average rate.

D. Breakdown of Direct and/or Variable Standard Labor per Press Machine-Hour

	Hourly Base Rate	Man-Hours per Week	Shifts per Week	Employees Required	Dollars per Week	Dollars per Machine-Hours (120 hours)
Press operator	$6.00	124	3	3	$ 744.00	$ 6.20
Shift differential...........	0.10	84	2		8.40	0.07
Overtime premium........	3.00	4			12.00	0.10
Hourly fringes.............	0.40	124			49.60	0.41
Percentage fringes........					76.44	0.64
Per worker fringes.........					30.00	0.25
Total press operator costs..............	$7.42	124	3	3	$ 920.44	$ 7.67
Press helper................	$3.00	240	3	6	$ 720.00	$ 6.00
Shift differential...........	0.10	160	2		16.00	0.13
Overtime premium........	1.50	0			0.00	0.00
Hourly fringes.............	0.40	240			96.00	0.80
Percentage fringes........					73.60	0.61
Per worker fringes.........					60.00	0.50
Press helper total................	$4.02	240	3	6	$ 965.60	$ 8.04
Grand total................	$5.18	364	3	9	$1,886.04	$15.71

EXHIBIT 4 (concluded)
E. Winders

	Hourly Rate	Man-Hours per Week	Shifts per Week	Employees Required	Dollars per Week	Dollars per Machine-Hours (504 hours)
B operator.................	$4.00	504	3	12	$2,016.00	$4.00
Shift differential...........	0.10	336			33.60	0.07
Overtime premium........	2.00	24			48.00	0.10
Hourly fringes.............	0.40	504			201.60	0.40
Percentage fringes........					209.76	0.42
Per worker fringes.........					120.00	0.24
Total B operator......	$5.22	504	3	12	$2,628.96	$5.23*
Machine helper...........	$2.00	168	3	4	$ 336.00	$0.67
Shift differential...........	0.10	112			11.20	0.02
Overtime premium........	1.00	8			8.00	0.02
Hourly fringes.............	0.40	168			67.20	0.13
Percentage fringes........					35.52	0.07
Per worker fringes.........					40.00	0.08
Machine helper total...............	$2.96	168	3	4	$ 497.92	$0.99
Grand total................	$4.65†	672	3	16	$3,126.88	$6.22

* Differs from $2,628.96 ÷ 504 = $5.22 owing to rounding.
† Weighted-average rate.

F. Roll Wrapping

	Hourly Rate	Man-Hours per Week	Shifts per Week	Employees Required	Dollars per Week
Wrapper....................	$1.00	544	3	11	$ 544.00
Shift differential...........	0.10	264			26.40
Overtime premium........		104			52.00
Hourly fringes.............	0.40	544			217.60
Percentage fringes........					62.24
Per worker fringes.........					110.00
Wrapper total........	$1.86	544	3	11	$1,012.24

machine is one A operator, plus one machine helper shared between the machines. Payroll records and/or labor contracts tell us that A operators are paid $5 per hour and machine helpers $2 per hour. All employees receive 10 cents per hour additional for working the second or third shift, and all employees receive a premium of 50 percent of their base rate for work in excess of 40 hours per week.

By a careful analysis of the fringe benefits, we have determined that they can be classified into three groups as follows:

1. *Hourly fringes.* These are not too common, but it is certainly conceivable to have a union welfare plan which requires the employer to contribute to the fund a flat amount per hour worked.
2. *Percentage fringes.* A good example of this type is the social security tax. Unless the employee passes the base, this is a flat percentage of total wages received.
3. *Per worker fringes.* Frequently group insurance plans, pen- · sion plans, and health and welfare plans call for a flat amount per person on the work force. Unless your work force is extremely low paid, the federal and state unemployment tax falls into this category because of the low taxable base.

Of course, in practice a group insurance plan may have elements of all three types; but careful analysis should be able to break these plans apart. Also to be considered are factors to cover potential turnover (for example, unemployment taxes).

Referring to Exhibit 4A, it can be seen how all these data are incorporated into the standard labor rate per machine-hour. Running around the clock will require four A operators each working 42 hours to man the equipment. The alternative of three employees working 56 hours apiece would require more overtime and probably a loss in morale and efficiency. The $5 A operator's rate times 168 hours equals $840. Then since two thirds of the hours (112) are multiplied by the shift differential of $0.10, this equals $11.20. Eight of the hours (4 people, 2 hours each) are worked under the overtime premium condition—8 hours × ($5 × 50 percent) = $20. The hourly fringe cost of 40 cents multiplied by 168 equals $67.20. A percentage fringe cost of 10 percent of actual wages paid (base plus shift plus overtime premium) equals the $87.12, and a per worker cost of $10 per week equals $40. These labor costs total $1,065.52, which, when divided by 168 man-hours, gives an average cost of $6.34 per hour of A operator's time.

The determination of machine helper costs is exactly the same, except the base rate is $2 and the employees and man-hours are cut in half because there is only ½ helper per machine (see Exhibit 3). All of this results in a standard labor cost of $7.86 per machine-hour.

How was this rate determined? It was determined by integrating a variety of information from industrial engineering through payroll into a meaningful number. This is the procedure for all standard cost determination: integrating information collected from a variety of sources.

Now referring to Exhibit 4B, the glue laminator will be costed. There are two factors involved here. Overtime premium is not part of the A operator's costs; and because the extruder runs 48 hours, the glue laminator has been charged with ½ a helper for 48 hours because the helper will have to work the 8 additional hours. A lively debate could be started over this decision. The entire cost of the eight hours could have been charged to the extruder (see Exhibit 4C), but this would have had the effect of penalizing extruded products because of their good volume. Instead, the decision made penalizes glue laminated product costs for their low volume, which seems more reasonable. Another alternative could be to combine the costs of both machines as we did in Exhibit 4A and derive a common rate. This would be appropriate if both machines were capable of the same tasks. For the moment, at least, we will stick to the Exhibit 4B rate of $7.95 per machine-hour.

Exhibit 4C shows a rate of $8.06 per machine-hour. Since no new principles are involved in this calculation, we do not need to spend any more time on this.

Glancing at Exhibit 4D reveals a new type of problem. Exhibit 1 states that there is a weekly start-up time of four hours to warm up the press. Exhibit 4D shows how this is handled. The costs cover 124 press operator man-hours, but the rate per machine-hour of $15.71 is derived using 120 machine-hours.

The calculation in Exhibit 4E of the winder/slitter rate of $6.22 per machine-hour involves nothing new.

Exhibit 4F, covering the roll-wrapping operations, is a different situation. First, there is no machine-hour rate as such, since roll wrapping is a manual operation. Also, because there is no machine to operate, there is a possibility to shift the work load to the first shift, avoiding the shift differential, and to consider the advantages/disadvantages of adding people or paying overtime. The real limits to this shifting would be space, both for the employees and for the storage of the production from the second and third shifts. Exhibit 4F assumes some of this shifting, and arrives at a cost of $1.86 per man-hour. (The reader is expected to be able to solve the problem of finding $1 per hour workers.)

Labor Efficiency

There is one area left before standard labor costs can be completely determined. This is the area of efficiency. Exhibit 5 illustrates the efficiency to be assumed for the converting plant. Some of the areas covered are coffee breaks, for which the employees are paid, and various downtimes. The first two listed downtimes would be the responsibility of the scheduler or materials handler. They represent time lost because certain material deliveries were not properly coordinated. Because these are standard costs, they should represent conditions not easily remedied. An example would be lack of space or inadequate advance notice. Downtime caused by just poor scheduling should not be included in the standards.

Machine failure would be the responsibility of the maintenance crew, and again represents conditions not easily remedied (old machinery, machine always running such as the waxer), rather than poor performance. Personal time is a nebulous area, but the point is, how far can it reasonably be controlled? That is the level to build into the standards.

The resulting efficiency figures derived, ranging from 0.945 to 0.979, will be built into the standard times below for each product.

Before going into the actual labor costs of specific products, it would be beneficial to consider the following. An immense effort has been spent in preparatory work, but it was necessary and beneficial because it enables us to be sure all the possible factors have

EXHIBIT 5
Efficiencies Used in Standard Costs

	Waxer and Wax Laminator	Glue Laminator	Extruder	Printer	Winder/ Slitter	Roll Wrapping
Budgeted hours..........	336.00	40.00	48.00	120.00	504.00	544.00
Coffee breaks...........	(4.20)	(0.50)	(0.60)	(0.80)	(6.30)	(6.80)
Downtimes:						
For product............	(2.00)	(1.00)	(0.50)	(0.30)	(3.00)	(1.00)
For material...........	(0.20)	(0.50)	(0.10)	(2.90)	0.00	(0.10)
Machine failure..........	(0.30)	(0.10)	(0.10)	(1.00)	(0.90)	0.00
Personal time...........	(0.30)	(0.10)	(0.70)	(1.00)	(0.80)	(3.10)
Adjusted hours..........	329.00	37.80	46.00	114.00	493.00	532.10
Efficiency = Adjusted hours ÷ Budgeted hours........	0.979	0.945	0.958	0.950	0.978	0.978

been considered. For example, the steps required to this point have involved consideration of the following:

Crew sizes.
Worker's efficiency.
Scheduling efficiency.
Downtime.
Machine capacities.
Labor rates and policies.
Fringe benefits.

A Standard cost system built without consideration of these factors would be a house built on quicksand.

Product Labor Costs

Now the standard labor costs of specific products can be determined. Exhibit 6 shows how this is done. First is the description of the desired finished product, which in this example is a roll 11 inches wide by 12 inches in diameter of paper A waxed to a basis weight of 40 pounds from a starting basis weight of 30 pounds.

In the first section of Exhibit 6 is a listing of certain information which is determinable because of all the preparatory work previously done. First, there is the base yield of 1.333 for the waxer. This was determined by dividing the basis weight desired off the waxer by the basis weight of the paper put on the machine ($40 \div 30 = 1.333$). Next comes a figure of 0.970 for a run yield. This comes from Exhibit 2 (100 percent $-$ 3 percent loss factor = 97 percent or 0.970). There is no trim on the waxer, so the trim yield is 1.000. The total yield is the product of the base yield times the run yield ($1.333 \times 0.970 = 1.293$). In summary, what the total yield tells us is that for every 1,000 pounds of paper consumed there should be 1.293 pounds of waxed paper. The column labeled "Finished Yield" represents the effect of all the operations subsequent to this operation. In other words, of the 1.293 pounds of wax paper produced above, only 1.187 (1.293×0.918) will actually ever be wrapped for sale.

For the winder/slitter operation, the base yield is a 1.000 because there is no change in basis weight, and Exhibit 1 tells us that that run yield will be 0.960. Exhibit 2 also tells us that there will be 2 inches of trim required and Exhibit 1 tells us that the maximum roll widths are 90 inches for the waxer and 56 inches for the

EXHIBIT 6

Standard Costs per Hundredweight (paper A 30-pound basis weight waxed to 40-pound basis weight; finished roll width, 11- by 12-inch diameter; quantity, 20,000 pounds [200 cwt])

	Base Yield	Run Yield	Trim Yield	Total Yield	Finished Yield	Roll-On Width	Roll-On Dia.	Roll-On Wt. (cwt.)	Set-up Time	Roll-On Time	Roll-Off Time	Run Speed	Efficiency Factor	Labor Cost per Hour
Operation 1, waxer	1.333	0.970	1.000	1.293	0.918	46	60	9.20	0.10	0.17	0.13	600	0.979	$7.83
Operation 2, winder/slitter	1.000	0.960	0.956	0.918	1.000	46	45	4.14	0.25	0.15	0.19	500	0.978	6.22
Operation 3, roll wrap	1.000	1.000	1.000	1.000		11	12	0.26	0.00	0.40			0.978	1.86
Total	1.333	0.931	0.956	1.187		46			0.35					

Operation 1:

Setup time per cwt.	= 0.10 ÷ 200.000	= 0.001 ÷ 1.293	= 0.001
Roll-on time per cwt.	= 0.17 ÷ 9.200	= 0.018 ÷ 1.293	= 0.014
Running time per cwt.	= 60.00 ÷ 600 × 30 × 46	= 0.073 ÷ 1.293	= 0.056
Roll-off time per cwt.	= 0.13 ÷ 4.140	= 0.031 ÷ 1.000	= 0.031
		= 0.102 ÷ 0.979	= 0.104 hour per cwt. This operation ÷ 0.918 = 0.113 hour per cwt. finished product.

Operation 2:

Setup time per cwt.	= 0.25 ÷ 200.000	= 0.001 ÷ 0.918	= 0.001
Roll-on time per cwt.	= 0.15 ÷ 4.140	= 0.036 ÷ 0.918	= 0.039
Running time per cwt.	= 60.00 ÷ 500 × 40 × 46	= 0.065 ÷ 0.918	= 0.071
Roll-off time per cwt.	= 0.19 ÷ 0.260	= 0.073 ÷ 1.000	= 0.073
		= 0.184 ÷ 0.978	= 0.188 hour per cwt. This operation ÷ 1.000 = 0.188 hour per cwt. finished product.

Operation 3:

Roll-on time per cwt.	= 0.40 ÷ 0.260	= 1.538 ÷ 1.000	= 1.538
		= 1.538 ÷ 0.978	= 1.573 hour per cwt. This operation ÷ 1.000 = 1.573 hour per cwt. finished product.

Total Labor Cost per Cwt.

	Waxer	Winder	Roll Wrap	Total
After Operation 1	0.81	0.00	0.00	$0.81
After Operation 2	0.88	1.17	0.00	2.05
After Operation 3	0.88	1.17	2.93	4.98

winder. Obviously the winder is the determining machine, so the standard roll width must be 46 inches ($11 \times 4 + 2$-inch trim), and the trim yield must be 0.956 ($44 \div 46$). Because there are no further yields other than 1.000, the finished yield is 1.000 for the winder/slitter.

The roll width column was explained above. The roll diameter was determined as follows. Since there is no previous operation, the waxer should take the largest diameter possible (60 inches from Exhibit 1). Exhibit 1 also shows that the waxer can handle rolls-off up to 50-inch diameter; however, the winder cannot handle rolls greater than 45 inches, so 45 inches must be the standard roll size off the waxer and on the winder.

Roll weights are determined using Exhibit 2 as follows. Paper A on the waxer at 60-inch diameter is (46 inches $\times 20$) or 920 inches (9.20 inches per hundredweight). Off the waxer and on the winder the paper is a mixture of wax and base paper so the calculation is as follows (refer to Exhibit 2):

$$\frac{(11.20 \times 30) + (2.42 \times 10)}{40} = 9.0 \times 46 = 414 \text{ or } 4.14$$

per hundredweight

The roll weight finished of 26 pounds is actually for a set of four rolls, and is calculated the same as above.

The next four columns come from Exhibit 1 (except for roll wrapping). The efficiency factor is derived from Exhibit 5, and the hourly costs from Exhibits 4A to 4F.

All of the preparatory work previously done enables us to have all this basis data on hand whenever a standard cost must be calculated.

The next section of Exhibit 6 shows the calculation of machine-hours necessary to manufacture this particular product. Using the waxer as an example, we see that the calculation done in steps is as follows:

1. Setup time per occurrence divided by the order (run) quantity, and then by the total yield, gives the standard setup time adjusted per hundredweight of product off the waxer.
2. Roll-on time per occurrence divided by the roll weight on, and then by the total yield, gives the standard roll-on time adjusted per hundredweight of product off the waxer.

3. Running time is determined by the formula 60,000 ÷ speed in fpm × basis weight on × the width, and then adjusted by the total yield, which gives the standard running time adjusted per hundredweight off the waxer.
4. Roll-off time is similar to 2 above, except that total yield is 1.000 because logically the yield factors have already happened before the roll is removed.

The total of 1–4 above is then divided by the efficiency factor to give the standard hours per hundredweight off the waxer. In order to obtain the standard waxer hours per hundredweight "out-the-door," the standard hours off the waxer must be divided by the product of all the total yields for subsequent operations. In Exhibit 6 the standard waxer hours are 0.104 per hundredweight off the waxer and 0.113 "out-the-door."

The last step in determining standard labor costs is to multiply the hourly cost rate by the appropriate hours. In Exhibit 6, for example, $7.83 × 0.104 hours = $0.81 per hundredweight and $7.83 × 0.113 hours = $0.88 per hundredweight. Note that the cost of the waxer operation expressed per hundredweight of product changes as the product moves through subsequent operations.

Now it has been determined that the direct labor cost of this product at standard is $4.98 per hundredweight of product finished (ready for shipment). However, what is not so obvious is the wealth of by-product type information which has been generated which can be used for scheduling, predicting, or analyzing purposes. Some samples follow:

Pounds of paper A required for run = 16,849 (20,000 ÷ 1.187).
Pounds of wax required for run = 5,611 (16,849 × 0.333).
Waxer hours required = 22.60 (200 × 0.113).
Winder hours required = 37.60 (200 × 0.188).
Roll wrap hours required = 314.60 (200 × 1.573).

Exhibit 7 shows the standard labor costs for a laminated product. The significant difference is the handling of two rolls on for every roll off. Yield factors influenced by the type of paper are assumed to be determined by the least favorable yield when there are both types of paper involved.

This completes our illustration of labor costs for the moment,

EXHIBIT 7

Standard Costs per Hundredweight (paper A [25-lb. basis weight] glue laminated to paper B [30-lb. basis weight] with 2-inch glue; finished roll width, 9 x 24-inch diameter; order size, 5,000 pounds)

	Base Yield	Run Yield	Trim Yield	Total Yield	Finished Yield	Roll-On Width	Roll-On Dia.	Roll-On Wt. (cwt.)	Set-up Time	Roll-On Time	Roll-Off Time	Run Speed	Efficiency Factor	Labor Cost per Hour
Operation 1, glue laminator	1.036	0.950	1.000	0.984	0.909	38	36	(A) 272	0.20	0.10	0.10	250	0.945	$7.95
Operation 2, winder/slitter	1.000	0.960	0.947	0.909	1.00	38	40	(B) 408	0.25	0.15	0.19	600	0.978	6.22
Operation 3, Roll wrap	1.000	1.000	1.000	1.000	1.00	9	24	439	0.00	0.40	0.00		0.978	1.86
Total	1.036	0.912	0.947	0.895				148						

Operation 1:

Setup time per cwt.	0.20 ÷ 50.00	= 0.004		= 0.004
Roll-on time per cwt. A.	0.10 ÷ 2.72	= 0.037	÷ 0.984	= 0.038
Roll-on time per cwt. B	0.10 ÷ 4.08	= 0.025	÷ 0.984	= 0.025
Running time per cwt.	600.00 ÷ 250 × 55 × 38	= 0.115	÷ 0.984	= 0.117
Roll-off time per cwt.	0.10 ÷ 4.39	= 0.023	÷ 1.000	= 0.023

0.207 ÷ 0.945 = 0.219 hour per cwt. This operation ÷ 0.909 = 0.241 hour per cwt. finished product.

Operation 2:

Setup time per cwt.	0.25 ÷ 50.00	= 0.005	÷ 0.909	= 0.006
Roll-on time per cwt.	0.15 ÷ 4.39	= 0.034	÷ 0.909	= 0.037
Running time per cwt.	600.00 ÷ 600 × 57 × 38	= 0.046	÷ 0.909	= 0.051
Roll-off time per cwt.	0.19 ÷ 1.48	= 0.128	÷ 1.000	= 0.128

0.222 ÷ 0.978 = 0.227 hour per cwt. This operation ÷ 0.978 = 0.227 hour per cwt. finished product.

Operation 3:

Roll-on time per cwt.	0.40 ÷ 1.48	= 0.270	÷ 1.000	= 0.270

0.270 ÷ 1.000 = 0.270 ÷ 0.978 = 0.276 hour per cwt. This operation ÷ 0.978 = 0.276 hour per cwt. finished product.

Total Labor Cost per Cwt.

	Glue Laminator	Winder	Roll Wrap	Total
After Operation 1	1.74	0.00	0.00	$1.74
After Operation 2	1.92	1.41	0.00	3.33
After Operation 3	1.92	1.41	0.51	3.84

because it is necessary to review the determination of standard material costs so the entire picture comes into focus.

DETERMINING MATERIAL STANDARDS

The first step in the discussion of material standards will be a review of the direct/indirect concepts defined in the beginning of the section dealing with labor standards and how they relate to materials. In the materials context: (1) direct material is a material consumed in the hope of directly increasing the quantity or quality of specific salable products (the paper, wax, and glue in Exhibits 6 and 7); (2) indirect material is material consumed in support of the direct cost operations (janitorial supplies, heating fuel, lubricant for the waxer, etc.); (3) variable material is material which will be consumed in proportion to the production of specific products (the lubricant for the waxer might be such a material); and (4) fixed material is material which tends to have a constant consumption level regardless of the production volume (the start-up loss of base paper on the press could be considered such a material—see Exhibit 1; it is also direct material). This section will deal with all variable material costs and all direct material costs. As explained under labor costs, the indirect fixed costs are not within the scope of this chapter.

Determining standard material costs is a function of two elements, quantity consumed and price. Because the price is often dependent on quantity, we will begin with the determination of quantity. The labor cost determination above discussed this problem briefly. In the discussion of Exhibit 6, it was mentioned that the 20,000 pounds order required 16,849 pounds of paper A. Since the product specification called for a product which was to be 75 percent paper ($30 \div 40$), it follows that only 15,000 pounds of paper will ever be sold to the customer. In short, 1,849 pounds (11 percent) of the paper required is lost. The determination of standard material costs requires the capability to determine what this loss should be and why.

To acquire this capability, it is necessary to start asking questions. To reiterate, it is important to ask the right question, properly and to be patient, skeptical, and polite. To whom should these questions be addressed? The sources of information would include manufacturing personnel, purchasing people, material handlers, industrial engineers, and the suppliers. In addition, many suppliers (vendors) and/or their trade associations have printed information available concerning various characteristics of their products.

Which factors and/or characteristics are likely to have an effect on any particular material as used in any particular operation in order to create any specific product cannot be adequately covered within the scope of this chapter. We will only list a number of areas which, based upon the author's experience, can affect material losses or waste yields. Hopefully, this list will come close enough to those factors of importance to the reader to be helpful. The list follows:

1. The quality of materials received is such that losses are inevitable (i.e., bad spots). Assuming better quality is available at a higher price, this is a subject tailor-made for the type of analysis a good standard cost system can provide.
2. The condition of the machinery which will work on the material. If the condition is improvable either by better maintenance or capital investments, another subject for analysis is presented.
3. The carefulness of the work force. When determining standard costs, consideration should be given to the possibility of improvement with "reasonably good management." Again if extra care means slower production, analysis is in order.
4. Inspection. Analysis can determine the optimum level desired.
5. The capacity of the machines. The trim loss discussed above would be an example of losses incurred by the inability of a machine to perform. (The machines are unable to wax, print, etc., the full roll width.)
6. Overruns causing lost materials. If quantity specifications are tighter than production's ability to control, there is a loss.
7. Overweight. In industries which sell their product in predetermined quantities, a loss factor can be caused because of the inability of the packaging machinery to control the quantity packaged. This is another version of 5 and 6 above.

After discussions with the other personnel involved, it is necessary to make the judgments required concerning yields or losses and to set up a standard yield. Exhibit 2 has established these standard yields for demonstration purposes.

The next area to consider is the standard price to be used in the standard costs of products. This is probably the most difficult area to determine because of the large element of judgment required. Before attempting to set these prices, it would be useful to return to the bases of standard costs as discussed in the introduction. Those bases were the purpose which standard costs can serve. Those bases and how they apply to this are as follows:

1. *Measurement.* This means the standard price should be set at the level prudent management would pay. If storage facilities are scarce or poor (likely to cause deterioration over a period of time), then the standard price should reflect the price for the quantity which can safely be stored.
2. *Predictability.* In order for the standards to be predictable, it is required that the assumptions used be understood and stated. The primary assumption is the production level anticipated by the operating plan for the relevant time period. This knowledge allows for the ability to predict the effects on costs to be expected from changes in the plan. If production of product A is doubled, what effect will this have on the purchase price of the relevant raw materials?

   It is important to remember that the standard price must include *all* costs incurred in getting the material to the manufacturing center. This certainly would include shipping, but might also include the costs of refinements, modification, and inspection as well.

   Once the groundwork has been laid, the standard purchase price is developed as in Exhibit 8. In Exhibit 8 can be seen those elements which must be considered in establishing standard purchase prices. Some comments about the various columns follow:

1. Budgeted consumption is derived from the planned units to be produced.
2. Premanufacturing yield covers losses caused by evaporation, unavoidable damage in spoilage, inspection (assuming that all rejects are chargeable to the vendor), cutting of smaller pieces from larger ones, and so on.
3. Budgeted purchases are Column 1 ÷ Column 2.
4. Reorder points, delivery time, and number of shipments are the parameters around which the purchase quantity and inventory standards are built.
5. Average inventory is a check that the storage facilities can handle the purchase quantities and therefore the purchase price built into the standard. The available information also al-

EXHIBIT 8
Standard Purchase Prices for the Year

Material	Budgeted Consumption (pounds)	Premanu- facturing Yield	Budgeted Purchases	Reorder Point	Delivery Time (weeks)	No. of Shipments	Average Inventory	Purchase Quantity	Standard Price	Standard Freight	Standard Inspection	Total Standard Cost	Total Adjusted Standard Cost
Paper A.........	90,000	1.000	90,000	3,600	1	50	2,769	1,800	$0.19	0.02	0.04	$0.25	$0.25
Paper B.........	66,000	1.000	66,000	1,400	1	25	1,452	2,640	0.24	0.02	0.04	0.30	0.30
Raw wax.........	19,000	1.000	19,000	900	2	12	962	1,583	0.07	0.00	0.00	0.07	0.07
Wax additive...	1,900	1.000	1,900	180	4	4	274	475	1.11	0.00	0.00	1.11	1.11
Wax catalyst...	600	1.000	600	60	4	2	162	300	0.14	0.10	0.00	0.24	0.24
Glue...........	6,000	0.950	6,316	3,000	13	8	1,822	790	0.77	0.04	0.00	0.81	0.85
Polyethylene...	11,000	0.960	11,458	1,600	6	13	720	881	0.34	0.11	0.05	0.50	0.52
Ink...........	4,000	0.700	5,714	500	3	10	456	571	3.75	0.00	0.00	3.75	5.36

lows the calculation of maximum inventories (Reorder point +
Purchase quantity − [Weekly consumption × Delivery time]),
which is another check on the adequacy of facilities.

6. Standard price and standard freight reflect the costs associated
with the item in the purchase quantity amount.

7. Standard inspection covers the variable and/or direct costs associated with inspecting, modifying, or storing of the product.
These costs would be based upon standard costs for the inspecting, modifying, or storing.

8. Total standard cost and total adjusted standard cost reflect all
the items above as adjusted for premanufacturing yields.

There remains untouched one broad area in the standard cost of
materials. That area is the formula, batch, mix, or recipe. This condition exists any time two or more raw materials are combined. For
example, baking operations would have many formulas or recipes.
Exhibit 8 gave three ingredients from which the wax used in our
examples will be constructed.

Exhibit 9 shows that the cost of materials plus mixing labor
equals $0.22 per pound ready for use by the waxer or wax lami-
nator. Note that there are yields involved here, including the catalyst yield of 0.000, and the labor involved has an efficiency factor
of 0.978. This completes the development of the standard material
cost.

UNIT PRIME COSTS

Exhibits 10 and 11 show the combination of direct labor and
material costs—sometimes referred to as "prime costs." These fig-

EXHIBIT 9
Wax Formula

Ingredient	Pounds per Batch	Mixing Yield	Finished Pounds Batch	Total Adjusted Standard Cost Pound	Standard Material Cost Batch	Standard Material Cost per Pound Finished
Raw wax..........................	190	0.950	180	$0.07	$13.30	$0.07
Wax additive....................	19	0.900	17	1.11	21.09	0.11
Wax catalyst....................	6	0.000	0	0.24	1.44	0.01
Total material............	215	0.916	197	$0.17	$35.83	$0.19
Labor costs.....................	3 hours roll wrap labor—3 × $1.86 ÷ 0.978				5.70	0.03
Grand total.....................					$41.53	$0.22

ures complete the buildup of standard costs started with Exhibits 6 and 7. Scanning these illustrations, it is apparent that there is a wealth of information available. It is this wealth of information, the by-products of the standard cost determinations, that makes standard costs a tool of prediction and analysis as well as measurement.

For example, the standards provide information useful to sched-

EXHIBIT 10
Standard Costs per Hundredweight (paper A waxed, 30/40; width 11 inches, diameter, 12 inches; quantity, 20,000 pounds)

	Operator 1 Waxer	Operator 2 Winder	Operator 3 Roll Wrap	Total (finished)
Base yield........................	1.333	1.000	1.000	1.333
Run yield.........................	0.970	0.960	1.000	0.931
Trim yield........................	1.000	0.956	1.000	0.956
Total yield..................	1.293	0.918	1.000	1.187
Roll-on information:				
Width..........................	46	46	44	11
Diameter.......................	60	45	12	12
Weight (cwt.)..................	9.20	4.14	0.26	0.06
Machine information:				
Setup time (hrs.)...............	0.10	0.25	0.00	
Roll-on time (hrs.).............	0.17	0.15	0.40	
Running speed (fpm)...........	600.00	500.00		
Roll-off time...................	0.13	0.19		
Labor cost per hour.............	$ 7.83	$ 6.22	$ 1.86	
Setup time hours per cwt........	0.001	0.001		
Roll-on time...................	0.014	0.039	1.538	
Running time...................	0.056	0.071		
Roll-off time..................	0.031	0.073		
Total time this operation.....	0.102	0.184	1.538	
Efficiency factor...............	0.979	0.978	0.978	
Adjusted total this operation.................	0.104	0.188	1.573	
Labor costs this operation..........	$ 0.81	$ 1.17	$ 2.93	
Labor costs prior operation........	0.00	0.88	2.05	
Labor costs end operation..........	$ 0.81	$ 2.05	$ 4.98	$ 4.98
Paper A this operation.............	$ 19.33			$21.06
Wax this operation.................	5.67			6.17
Total material this operation..	$ 25.00			$27.23
Material prior operation...........	0.00	$ 27.23	$ 27.23	
Material costs end operation.......	$ 25.00	$ 27.23	$ 27.23	$27.23
Total costs this operation..........	$ 25.81	$ 1.17	$ 2.93	
Total cost prior operation..........	0.00	28.12	29.29	
Total cost end operation..........	$ 25.81	$ 29.29	$ 32.22	$32.22
Machine-hours required...........	22.60	37.60	314.60	
Paper A required..................	16,849			
Wax required.....................	5,611			

EXHIBIT 11

Standard Costs per Hundredweight (paper A glue laminated to paper B, 25/55/57; width 9 inches; diameter, 24 inches; ordered size, 5,000 pounds)

	Operator 1 Glue Lam.	Operator 2 Winder	Operator 3 Roll Wrap	Total (finished)
Base yield........................	1.036	1.000	1.000	1.036
Run yield........................	0.950	0.960	1.000	0.912
Trim yield........................	1.000	0.947	1.000	0.947
Total yield..................	0.984	0.909	1.000	0.895
Roll-on information:				
Width...........................	38	38		
Diameter.......................	36	40		
Weight (cwt.)....................	4.08 and	4.39	1.48	
Machine information:				
Set up time (hrs.)................	0.20	0.25		
Roll-on time (hrs.)..............	0.10	0.15	0.40	
Running speed (fpm.)...........	250.00	600.00		
Roll-off time (hrs.).............	0.10	0.19		
Labor cost per hour..............	$ 7.95	6.22	1.86	
Setup time hours per cwt........	0.004	0.006		
Roll-on time.....................	0.063	0.037	0.270	
Running time....................	0.117	0.051		
Roll-off time....................	0.023	0.128		
Total time this operation.....	0.207	0.222	0.270	____
Efficiency.......................	0.945	0.978	0.978	
Adjusted total this operation..................	0.219	0.227	0.276	____
Labor costs this operation..........	$ 1.74	$ 1.41	$ 0.51	
Labor costs prior operation.........	0.00	1.92	3.33	
Labor costs end operation..........	$ 1.74	$ 3.33	$ 3.84	____
Paper A this operation.............	$ 11.53			
Paper B this operation.............	16.62			
Glue this operation.................	3.11			____
Total material this operation...................	$ 31.26			
Material prior operation............	0.00	$ 34.39	$34.39	____
Material costs end operation.......	$ 31.26	$ 34.39	$34.39	
Total cost this operation...........	$ 33.00	$ 1.41	$ 0.51	
Total cost prior operation...........	0.00	36.30	37.71	____
Total cost end operation...........	$ 33.00	$ 37.71	$38.22	
Machine-hours required...........	12.05	11.35	13.80	
Paper required.....................	5,586			
Glue required......................	201			

uling (machine-hours required) and purchasing (wax required). Also, the inventory values after each operation are available ("Total cost end operation"). In short, not only is the cost known but also a great deal about why the costs are what they are is known; and changes in quantity, roll size, running speeds, and so forth, can be substituted freely to enable an accurate prediction of costs under different circumstances.

SPECIAL PROBLEMS AND GREY AREAS

Now that the fundamentals of standard cost determination have been covered, it is appropriate to look at some of the wrinkles possible in standard cost development.

Direct Fixed Costs

The first area would be the direct nonvariable cost. That is a cost specifically caused by a product or group of products, but which does not increase or decrease in proportion to the production of such a product. Whenever possible, such a cost should become part of the standard cost of the product or products. Do not be a purist in these matters. The criterion for inclusion or exclusion should be the chance of management making a faulty decision. Generally speaking, exclusion runs greater risks than inclusions.

An example of such a cost would be the start-up process involving the printer, as explained in Exhibit 1. All printed costs should carry some share of this cost. In the calculation of machine-hour rates (Exhibit 4D), the labor costs are automatically spread to all printed products because the divisor (machine-hours) is less than man-hours. The material can also be spread as follows:

$a.$ $\dfrac{12 \text{ inches} \times 300 \text{ feet} \times \text{Width}}{432{,}000} = \text{Weekly waste pounds.}$

$b.$ $\dfrac{\text{Machine-hours required}}{504 \text{ budgeted machine-hours}} = \text{Percent of } (a) \text{ chargeable to this job.}$

$c.$ $(a) \times (b) \div$ Pounds paper required this operation $=$ Start-up loss yield.

$d.$ $100 -$ Loss factor (Exhibit 2) $- (c) =$ Run yield this operation.

The formula itself is not important. There are even some flaws in the assumptions behind it. What is important is that it gives a reasonable (not exact) basis for spreading this direct fixed cost to the products which cause it, which is preferable to burying it in the manufacturing overhead.

Joint Products and By-Products

Another special problem is the joint-product, by-product, reusable waste area. Basically there are two methods for handling such matters. One method is to credit standard costs for some value (usually market value) for the production of the second product. This is mixing apples and oranges and will lead to standard cost confusion. The market value of the second product is a marketing problem and should not be mixed with manufacturing problems.

The other method is to determine the standard cost of the product using the same thinking as above. Using Exhibit 11 as a basis, assume that the "waste" from Operation 1 has a value either as scrap or another product. In effect this means there is no waste in Operation 1, or the run yield is 1.000. In this case the labor cost for Operation 1 (refer to Exhibit 7) would be: 0.004 setup + 0.037 roll-on + 0.025 roll-on + 0.115 running + 0.023 roll-off = 0.204 hours $\times$ \$7.95 = \$1.62 per hundredweight. The material costs would be \$25.00 $\times$ 25/55 $\div$ 1.036 = \$10.97 for paper A; \$30.00 $\times$ 30/55 $\div$ 1.036 = \$15.80 for paper B; and \$0.85 $\times$ 3.6 $\div$ 1.036 = \$2.95 for the glue; resulting in \$29.72 per hundredweight total material costs. The total cost after operation 1 is then \$1.62 plus \$29.72 or \$31.34 per hundredweight, compared to the \$33.00 in Exhibit 11. This same cost also applies to the scrap, waste, and so forth, which is marketed or used. The total cost of the primary product will now be \$36.40 per hundredweight, not \$38.22. (See Chapter 9 for further discussion of joint- and by-product costing.)

Learning Curves

Learning curves are another subject deserving mention. The learning-curve concept states that the more often a task is performed, the faster it will be performed. In fact, this improvement can be predicted within reasonable accuracy. Industrial engineering uses this concept in developing manual operating standards, such as roll changes or assembling. Applying the concept to determining standard costs involves the validity of the performance standards. For example, the learning curve indicates that if there is no change in personnel or methods, the standard time for roll changing should be reducing each year. However, new personnel, new methods, perhaps new products will destroy the pattern. Also operations which are machine-paced usually are not subject to the learning curve: if the maximum speed is 600 fpm, the learning curve will not make it go 700 fpm.

Where the curve is most applicable is an assembly-type operator's job involving long runs of the same products. By studying how long it takes to produce the first unit of product, it is possible to determine the time it should take to produce the 100th, 1,000th, 10,000th, and so forth, which enables the standard hours to be used for costs to be based upon the 100th, 1,000th, or 10,000th product with confidence. (See Chapter 5.)

Classification Difficulties

One last grey area worth discussing is the "neither-fish-nor-fowl" category. This refers to costs which are direct and/or variable but are hard to classify either as labor or material. For example, if rent were paid on machine-hours or units produced, this cost should be included in the product cost. If it were by machine-hour, it would be added to the machine-hour rate, whereas if it were paid by unit produced, it would be treated similar to material costs. Electricity consumed in running machinery could be another example of this. The criterion for inclusion or exclusion is the same as for the fixed direct costs above: What gives the management the most useful "actionable" information?

Who Sets the Standards?

The standard cost "tool" is a tool with many uses ranging from the measurement of plant performance through the establishment of selling prices to the determination of the products to be manufactured and/or sold. Because there are so many uses involving so many departments or functions, it follows that the ultimate responsibility for setting the standards must be with the president or his or her equivalent in the organization.

Now it would be most unusual for presidents to actually involve themselves in the myraid of decisions and personnel required in setting standards. They must of necessity delegate this responsibility to someone else. This someone should be the controller or equivalent. There are several reasons why the controller is the best choice for coordinating all the people and making the judgments between competing claims from different functions, users, and so on. Some of these reasons are as follows:

1. The controller should be the least biased of all possible choices. The controller is best able to judge objectively the competing claims of sales and manufacturing, for example.
2. In a firm with multiple locations, the controller can best assure that the "yardstick" is the same at each location.
3. The controller will be responsible for the preparation of measurement, prediction, and analytical reports. It follows that the controller should be the final judge, subject to the president's approval, of the components of these reports.
4. Ideally the controller and the accountants under the controller at the plant level should be free of undue influence from the operating departments in their thinking. This is an extremely delicate area but it is very important to the whole concept of standard costs. If the controller or any of the controller's people, whether the relationship is a solid or a dashed line, are coerced by the users and/or "judgees" of the standards into setting standards contrary to the controller's honest opinion, then a certain element of objectivity is lost. Nonobjective standards are a fraud and a dangerous tool. There should be lively, spirited, wide-open discussion whenever a difference exists, but it should be understood that only the controller can "coerce" the plant accountant; all the others must convince the controller, and only the president can "coerce" the controller. And if coercion is necessary very often there should be a serious effort made to determine why.

In coordinating the standard-setting task, the controller must deal with a variety of functions and people. First controllers must be in touch with the industrial engineering function. It is this function which provides much of the bare bones of the performance standards. Other sources of bare bones information are purchasing agents, material handlers, and the supervisor level of supervision. The importance and role of these functions were covered in the "how to" sections above.

All of this "bare bones" information must be integrated into the big picture; or it may have to be modified to fit into this picture. This requires the coordination with the sales/marketing area, and perhaps with research and capital expenditure plans. The people involved here are probably plant managers, sales and marketing directors, research directors, divisional presidents, and the budget director.

Obviously this coordination will result in many differing viewpoints. Controllers and their people must be able to weigh intelligently these viewpoints and resolve the questions as correctly as possible in an uncertain world. The objective is to set the standards so the maximum usefulness is obtained. This usefulness is to be weighed against the following criteria:

1. The ability to measure performance fairly.
2. The ability to predict future performance.
3. The ability to serve as an aid to meaningful analysis.

NONMANUFACTURING APPLICATIONS

Most major and many smaller firms are using standard costs for their manufacturing operations, but very few firms have developed similar tools as aids to their nonmanufacturing supervisors. This is a tragic state of affairs. All recent studies of the American economy indicate a major shift towards nonmanufacturing activity. This shift is both external in the sense that service-oriented industries are growing faster than manufacturing-oriented industries, and internal in the sense that a greater percentage of individual firms' costs or expenses are represented by nonmanufacturing costs such as marketing, advertising, accounting, and research. Supplementing this shift is the tremendous growth in government and other nonprofit service agencies.

Unfortunately, except for rare instances, these nonmanufacturing functions are not subject to the type of measurement, prediction, and analysis that standard costs provide for manufacturing. Probably the chief cause of this problem is the difficulty in developing input/output relationships, which are key to the standard cost concept. Manufacturing operations have tangible measuring points (units produced). Many of the other areas do not have such clear output measures. However, controllers must attempt to develop standard costs or an equivalent for these operations if they wish to fulfill their role of providing management with a maximum of "actionable" information. Too much of the total operating costs are in nonmanufacturing areas for these costs to be ignored. The challenge must be accepted.

The author has developed such a system covering the delivery costs for a fleet delivery operation. The system is described in the article, "Standard Costs for Delivery Systems," published in *Management Accounting*, January 1974. The type of questions which had to be asked and answered in developing this system (remember how important it is "to ask the right questions properly") are repeated here because hopefully this will aid others in developing similar systems for nonmanufacturing areas:

Question 1: What is the measuring unit? In manufacturing it would be pounds produced, or units produced, or perhaps a specific job or contract. In delivery it was determined to be one trip. In other areas it will be something else. The important thing is that a basic measuring unit must be found.

Question 2: What causes costs? In the converting plant examples above it was run size, roll size, or manufacturing specifications. In delivering it was the miles to be traveled, the amount to be unloaded, the number of stops required, and whether the driver had to sleep away from the shipping point. Again, whatever the function, these equivalent causes must be found.

Question 3: What are the performance factors required? This is the roll change, running speed, setup, trim yields, and so forth, in manufacturing. In delivery it was the speed, unloading time, stop time, breakdowns and lodging time. Equivalent factors exist for any operation.

This is the type of questioning which must be performed if nonmanufacturing operations are to be measured properly. Both nonmanufacturing and manufacturing operations must be brought under standard costs if controllers are to perform their duties to determine what the profits are, what they should be, why they are not as they should be, and what can be done about them.

ADDITIONAL SOURCES

Fremgen, James M. *Accounting for Managerial Analysis*, chap. 9. 3d ed. Homewood, Ill.: Richard D. Irwin, Inc., 1976.

Horngren, Charles T. *Cost Accounting: A Managerial Emphasis*, chap. 7. 4th ed. Englewood Cliffs, N.J.: Prentice-Hall, Inc., 1977.

Neuner, John J. W., and Deakin, Edward B.   *Cost Accounting: Principles and Practice,* chaps. 7, 8, 11. 9th ed. Homewood, Ill.: Richard D. Irwin, Inc., 1977.

Pickerill, Ron W., and Guthrie, Art.   "Calculation of Average Labor Rates in a Cost Accounting System: A Better Way?" *Cost and Management,* January–February 1976, p. 24.

Piper, Roswell M.   "Engineering Standards and Standard Costs." *Management Accounting,* September 1976, p. 44.

Reuter, Vincent G.   "Work Measurement Practices." *California Management Review,* Fall 1971, p. 24.

Shillinglaw, Gordon.   *Managerial Cost Accounting,* chap. 6. 4th ed. Homewood, Ill.: Richard D. Irwin, Inc., 1977.

11

Determining "Normal" Production Volume

Robert L. Graham*

In any business there has to be a balance established between physical capacity levels on the one hand and customer sales volume on the other. With more and more corporations concentrating on the return-on-investment concept for measuring performance, it is imperative that manufacturing enterprises balance the ability to produce with the demand for the product. Since inventory levels contribute a very large share of the assets employed, the art of forecasting what the production budget should be for the coming year is one of the most important analyses that a company will undertake. With the cost of money at record levels, common sense dictates that expected sales should be the starting point in balancing production output, rather than producing at full capacity and hoping that the sales force can market eventually at a reasonable price that will recover full costs and hopefully produce a profit.

It also has to be recognized that in many product areas delivery is the key in obtaining the order, and that inventory in excess of orders is not, in itself, something to be entirely avoided. The overall goal of any company should be to produce at a level that will minimize investment in inventory, while still attempting to smooth out the peaks and valleys which naturally arise in business. This volume level is defined as *normal volume*.

* Mr. Graham is Comptroller and Treasurer of Digital Communications Corporation, Gaithersburg, Maryland.

WHAT IS CAPACITY?

Capacity can be defined as the fixed amount of plant, machinery, and personnel to which management has committed itself and with which it expects to conduct the business. Volume (or activity) is the variable factor in business. It is related to capacity by the fact that volume attempts to make the best use of existing capacity.

There are three generally accepted capacity levels which, depending on the business one is in, will have varying degrees of usefulness. These are theoretical capacity, practical capacity, and normal capacity.

The *theoretical capacity* of a facility is its capacity to produce at full speed without interruptions. This theoretical capacity is achieved only if the facility produces output 100 percent of the time.

Because it is highly improbable that any facility can operate at theoretical capacity, allowances must be made for unavoidable interruptions such as time lost for repairs, setup, rework, materials delays, holidays, vacations, Sundays, and so on. These allowances reduce theoretical capacity to a level called the *practical capacity* level. The sum of these reductions might look as follows, starting from the 100 percent or theoretical number:

Theoretical capacity	100%
Less:	
Vacation (two weeks)	4
Holidays (10 days)	4
Sundays (52 days)	14
Downtime, setup, changeover, repair, etc.	8
Total reductions	30%
Practical capacity	70%

The range of these reductions varies with the industry involved, and also depends a great deal on whether the business is highly capital intensive (e.g., electricity generation) or labor intensive (e.g., component hand assembly). The major point to remember is that none of the above reductions has yet addressed the chief external cause of capacity change—lack of customer orders.

To address this, a company then takes the second step in its capacity review: it further lowers its practical capacity by forecasting the average demand for its product over the coming period. An example would be not operating the third shift, which in itself would reduce volume by 33 percent from the practical capacity level.

An example of the three capacity levels calculated for a sample machining department, together with cost data for each level, is shown in Exhibit 1.

In viewing the cost differences generated by the changing volume levels in Exhibit 1, most businesses would ignore the theoreti-

EXHIBIT 1
Calculation of Capacity per Annum

XYZ COMPANY

		Annual Hours	Capacity Level
	Cost Center—Machining		
	One-Machine—Three-Shift Operation		
I.	Calculation of Capacity:		
	24 hours per day × 5 workdays × 52 weeks =	6,240	Theoretical
		2,080	@ 100%
		per shift	
	Less allowances:		
	Vacation shutdown = 10 days × 24 hours =	(240)	
	Holiday shutdown = 10 days × 24 hours =	(240)	
	Standard downtime, = 1 hour per shift ×		
	changeover, repairs 3 × 240 days =	(720)	
	Subtotal	5,040	Practical
		1,680	@ 80%
		per shift	

Note that practical producing capacity due to shutdowns, and so forth, reduced theoretical by 20 percent. Assume one unit can be produced per working hour; therefore, annual practical production would be at 5,040 units. Assume the sales department forecasts orders of approximately 3,375 units for the coming period and management does not stock inventory. A further allowance must be made to get to normal volume as follows:

$$5,040 \text{ units} - 3,375 \text{ units} = 1,665 \text{ excess units}$$
$$\times 1 \text{ hour per unit standard}$$
$$\overline{1,665 \text{ excess hours}}$$

Practical volume above..........	5,040	
Excess hours....................	1,665	
Subtotal...................	3,375	Normal @ 54%

Normal volume is then set at 54 percent for the coming period, or a shutdown of one shift.

II. *Cost per Hour Summary:*

	Normal	Practical	Theoretical
Machine-hours.........................	3,375 hrs.	5,040 hrs.	6,240 hrs.
Fixed overhead........................	$24,960	$24,960	$24,960
Variable overhead $6 per hour..........	20,250	30,240	37,440
Total..............................	$45,210	$55,200	$62,400
Rate per machine-hour.................	$13.40	$10.95	$10.00

cal cost level as being not attainable, although it is the ultimate or "super standard" for which to strive.

Determining Theoretical Capacity

The meaning of this term may in itself bring on confusion, in that a steel company would think in terms of tons of steel per period, an automobile manufacturer in terms of cars produced, a textile producer in terms of yards of cloth manufactured, and so forth. By contrast, a job-shop machining company working in many varied types of units would have difficulty in that the capacity in output of finished products is quite meaningless because the output is not homogeneous. Here, output must be expressed in more universal terms. The units commonly used are *available hours*.

Whatever the industry, this output potential is a good general measure of capacity because it can be converted fairly easily to a physical-capacity equivalent in terms of the number of machines and direct labor hours required. Breaking these required output hours down into various lower classifications gives the data needed to work with in developing a plant layout. One then needs to translate everything into physical units of capacity—number of actual machines and people by operation. In doing this, two factors must be considered carefully: the plant efficiency factor and the scrap factor.

Through the *plant efficiency factor* one recognizes that because of schedule delays, breakdowns, maintenance, and so on, a portion of the available hours cannot be used for generating salable output. The *scrap factor* takes into account the fact that for any real production process, some bad parts will be produced; this will cause more time to be used and, hence, will require more capacity in hours. These allowances are determined by actual records or engineered standards as discussed later in this section.

We then can come up with a projected capacity in physical producing units as follows:

Assumed output...	100 motors per week
Standard machine or labor hours/unit..................	5.5 hours per unit
Total theoretical capacity needed......................	550 hours per week
Plant efficiency factor.................................	80%
Adjusted capacity hours (theoretical capacity ÷ 0.80)...	688 hours
Scrap factor...	3%
Total theoretical capacity needed (adjusted capacity ÷ 0.97)...	709 hours

If we expect to work on a one-shift basis (40 hours), the number of machines and/or employees needed working at 80 percent efficiency with 3 percent scrap would be 709 ÷ 40 or 17.73 units. Capacity, however, comes in "chunks," and therefore one would go to 18 full units and expect some idle capacity, or to 17 units and try to make up the difference with a small amount of overtime.

Since most businesses are going concerns and already occupy a building, the following section on the plant layout needed to accommodate needed capacity may already have been dictated. But, in essence, the question of needed capacity boils down into various financial and physical restrictions. These restrictions may be from state or federal laws on the number of square feet allowed per employee, or union regulations on layout and job descriptions, and so forth. Essentially, in an existing building the options are limited and it is assumed that one makes the best of the situation unless economics dictate the construction of a new facility. One must provide a building that will contain enough of the severest restriction—namely square footage. The problem then is to lay out the appropriate type of line within the restriction, having previously decided what will be made versus purchased,[1] how many shifts will be utilized, and what may be provided for future capacity.

Basic Layout Types

The two types of layouts used to fit available capacity into a building are (1) *process* or *functional layout* and (2) *product* or *line layout*. When process layout is used, machines or workers are arranged in functional groups. In other words, all the milling machines would be grouped in one area, as would all the inspectors, assemblers, and so on. The parts take various routings as dictated by their design requirements. Parts are then moved from operation to operation in batches or lots and stored at each work station to await their turn. Additionally, some parts may need to be machined, while others may be purchased fully machined and moved directly into assembly.

When product or line layout is used, machines and labor are arranged according to the sequence of operations required to fabricate and assemble. Since each of the operations constitutes a specific task, parts move in a continuous nature. All parts start at the

---

[1] See Chapter 19 for details on "Make-or-Buy Decisions."

first department and end at the last; the parts go through all operations without any skipping. Under product layout, the basic organization of the layout is dictated by the product and not the function. The variety of products manufactured will usually dictate the type of layout chosen, and often many plants have layouts of both types. Line layout is found most commonly in high-volume/ standard type products, with a stable demand and continuous supply of material.

Such factors as the location of the different operations, material handling problems, operation sequence analyses, block diagrams, line balancing techniques, and other more advanced analyses must be considered and should be researched by consulting an expert in the field.[2]

Work Standards and Allowances

In a previous section in discussing adjustment of theoretical capacity to practical capacity, brief mention was made of allowances for nonproductive time. In this section we will expand somewhat on this topic, focusing on the labor aspect of nonproductive time.

A work standard is made up of the following:

    (1) Normal time (= actual work time)
+ (2) Allowance for personal time
+ (3) Fatigue allowance
+ (4) Allowance for measured delays normal to job
= (5) Total standard time

The most difficult aspect in setting any standard, in order to utilize the above formula, is determining just what "normal time" is. As previously noted, it is called "the actual work time on a unit of production." However, the world is full of people with extremely varied capabilities. The foremost rule in setting the normal work time per task is to make sure that approximately 95 percent of the people who perform that task can attain the normal time. But how does one determine what that 95 percent standard is? Obviously, if we had the time and the money we could test everyone and obtain a very convenient statistical distribution and yield the answer. This is, of course, very impractical.

---

[2] See, for example, Elwood S. Buffa, *Modern Production Management,* 4th ed. (New York, John Wiley & Sons, Inc., 1973), chapters 9–14.

The technique most widely used is to test a few people—some experienced and some relatively inexperienced. To the observed time per unit for each person tested it is necessary to add a performance rating factor assessed by an unbiased observer. The purpose of this factor is to enable taking a relatively small sample of actually observed times and translating it into what is considered an average time that 95 percent of the work force can attain. For instance, assume the observed time is one hour per unit. The performance rater estimates that the particular worker observed produces, or has the capability to produce, at 20 percent faster than average. The performance rater would, therefore, set the standard at one hour divided by 80 percent or 75 minutes per unit. On the other hand, had the performance rater observed a relatively uncoordinated worker who required one hour, the rater might judge that this worker was 20 percent slower than the average and, therefore, would set the standard at one hour times 80 percent, or 48 minutes per unit.

The other major method of determining normal time is for the industrial engineer to break down the job into its different elementary movements; and with the use of standardized data tables and experienced estimates, the industrial engineer very arbitrarily assigns a standard to each element and then adds these to get the total standard time. Although more scientific in nature, it of course meets with disapproval from most of the employees because the worker has not participated at all. Another basic disadvantage is the cost. In the trade this approach is known as "work factor analysis" or "time and motion study."

After determining normal time by one of the above-mentioned techniques, one must then determine what types of allowances must be built in. The first allowance for personal time is self-explanatory as to a person's basic biological needs for a drink of water and use of the washroom.

The second type of personal allowance is the fatigue allowance. This allowance varies considerably from industry to industry, and is related to the physical strain of the job. The most popular and almost universally granted fatigue allowance is the "coffee break." On top of this, depending upon the industry, one would add rest periods, for example, to ward off eyestrain in an assembler or back strain in a miner. This rest period could run from 5 minutes per hour to as high as 30 minutes per hour in some cases. Union contracts or state and federal laws usually dictate the allowance factor.

The last type of allowance is the measured delay type. Examples would be the setup time per machine, a machine that must be cleaned every hour, and so on. These types of allowances are predictable and are an integral part of the business and not related to biological factors. Actual time records and/or work measurement techniques are used to determine such allowances.

To summarize this section, an example of a total standard time calculation for a machine shop is shown:

(1)	Normal time by stopwatch:	6.0 minutes per unit
+ (2)	Personal time:	6 minutes per hour (10%) = 0.6 minutes per unit
+ (3)	Fatigue time:	48 minutes per day (10%) = 0.6 minutes per unit
+ (4)	Setup time:	48 minutes per day (10%) = 0.6 minutes per unit
= (5)	Total standard:	7.8 minutes per unit

As a final point, one must realize that any supervisor has an informal standard in mind based on experience. When the term "production standard" or "time standard" is used with either white-collar or blue-collar jobs, one assumes that it has been formalized.

DETERMINING NORMAL VOLUME

The primary step in forecasting normal volume is to obtain a reasonable forecast of customer orders from the marketing/sales department. Normal volume should be determined for the business as a whole and then broken down by cost centers and departments as required. This will immediately expose any large imbalances by cost center since seldom are departments within an operation perfectly balanced. This is especially true in companies with a broad product mix and customer base. A sample new-order forecast is shown in Exhibit 2.

It becomes readily apparent when viewing Exhibit 2 that the production manager would be in a crisis state if production had to match deliveries. Therefore, the production manager's first task is to produce a reasonable production schedule that smooths out the peaks and valleys and allows relatively stable work flow and work force, and yet still meet customer delivery requirements. The production manager should start by averaging the yearly needs for

EXHIBIT 2
New-Order Forecast 1978

XYZ COMPANY

		First Quarter		Second Quarter		Third Quarter		Fourth Quarter		Total 1978	
No.	Name	Units	Dollars	Units	Dollars	Units	Dollars	Units	Dollars	Units	Dollars
A	Assemblies........	250	$ 12,500	250	$ 12,500	500	$ 25,000	500	$ 25,000	1,500	$ 75,000
B	Mixers...........	450	45,000	450	45,000	450	45,000	450	45,000	1,800	180,000
C	Filters...........	1,000	150,000	2,000	300,000	500	75,000	500	75,000	4,000	600,000
D	Joints...........	750	150,000	100	20,000	100	20,000	100	20,000	1,050	210,000
E	Switches.........	1,000	250,000	—	—	1,000	250,000	—	—	2,000	500,000
	Totals ($)........		$607,500		$377,500		$415,000		$165,000		$1,565,000

each product into a total matrix which will minimize overloads between departments and, hopefully, keep idle time and layoffs at a minimum. A sample production plan in hours, mating capacity with production needs and smoothing out deliveries, is shown in Exhibit 3. The capacity levels are calculated utilizing Exhibit 1 capacity.

After preparing Exhibit 3, the production manager must make some basic business decisions as to how to accomplish building the existing production plan for the year, armed with the knowledge of what present practical capacity levels are.

In the machining department, it is apparent that the present capacity level of 15,120 machine-hours is sufficiently close to the smoothed-out estimate of machine capacity to assume that no further capacity decisions should be required to accomplish a goal. However, a very extreme change in the mix of the business toward more of Product E at ten hours per unit and away from Product A at two hours per unit could cause a major problem and change in plans as the year progresses.

The assembly department, however, is a completely different matter, and will require immediate attention to avoid its becoming a "bottleneck" to the smooth flow of production to and from the other departments. The yearly shortage is 22,280 assembly hours or approximately four more workers for each of the three shifts.[3]

The test and ship department is likewise in a serious position, although it is one of excess facilities rather than overload. In this department the annual excess is 9,020 hours, or approximately five workers (say, two excess on two of the shifts and one excess on one of the shifts.)

Demand-Capacity Imbalances

The production manager has several alternatives that are open to solve imbalance problems. The following actions might be taken in an overload situation:

1. *Working overtime.* In our example the production manager would have two additional days available per week, although

---

[3] Exhibit 3 assumes a 40-hour week per worker and 10½ weeks per quarter; hence, 420 hours per worker per quarter, or 1,680 per year. Thus 22,280 ÷ 1,680 equals 13 workers, or 4 workers more on two shifts, and 5 more on one of the shifts.

EXHIBIT 3
Production Plan in Hours (three shifts)

XYZ COMPANY—1978

Machine Standard Hours per Unit	Department	Quarter (1) Hours Required	(2) Hours Required	(3) Hours Required	(4) Hours Required	1978 Total Hours Units	Hours
	Machining						
2	Product A........	750	750	750	750	1,500	3,000
4	Product B........	1,800	1,800	1,800	1,800	1,800	7,200
6	Product C........	6,000	6,000	6,000	6,000	4,000	24,000
8	Product D........	2,100	2,100	2,100	2,100	1,050	8,400
10	Product E........	5,000	5,000	5,000	5,000	2,000	20,000
	Subtotal.........	15,650	15,650	15,650	15,650		62,600
	Three-shift capacity—12 machines.....	15,120	15,120	15,120	15,120		60,480
	Assembly						
2	Product A........	750	750	750	750	1,500	3,000
4	Product B........	1,800	1,800	1,800	1,800	1,800	7,200
6	Product C........	6,000	6,000	6,000	6,000	4,000	24,000
8	Product D........	2,100	2,100	2,100	2,100	1,050	8,400
10	Product E........	5,000	5,000	5,000	5,000	2,000	20,000
	Subtotal.........	15,650	15,650	15,650	15,650		62,600
	Three-shift capacity—8 workers per shift.....	10,080	10,080	10,080	10,080		40,320
	Test and Ship						
1	Product A........	375	375	375	375	1,500	1,500
2	Product B........	900	900	900	900	1,800	3,600
3	Product C........	3,000	3,000	3,000	3,000	4,000	12,000
4	Product D........	1,050	1,050	1,050	1,050	1,050	4,200
5	Product E........	2,500	2,500	2,500	2,500	2,000	10,000
	Subtotal.........	7,825	7,825	7,825	7,825		31,300
	Three-shift capacity—8 workers per shift.....	10,080	10,080	10,080	10,080		40,320

the overtime premium after 40 hours would have to be taken into account.

2. *Subcontracting.* If, after consultation with management, it is felt that outside help is needed due to a lack of immediate space, machinery, or people, the production manager may have the overload work done by an outside firm. Normal volume would then be present capacity.

3. *Purchase additional equipment/space.* If management agrees, and the machinery lead time or training of operators can be accomplished within a reasonable period, additional capacity should be purchased. This increases the normal volume figure and, hence, capacity.

4. *Introduce an additional shift.* In cases where the department may only be working one or two eight-hour shifts, it may be easier and less expensive to start up another full or partial shift.

5. *Transfer between departments.* Where departments are fairly compatible, a quick solution is to utilize idle facilities or space in one department to increase the capacity of another.

Any of the above choices is available, and the most suitable one should be chosen after economic and social (people) analyses determine the necessary compromises needed. Such situations as union rules, availability of subcontractors, or a labor force shortage may make the production manager choose one which at first glance does not appear as the best solution.

In an excess capacity situation, some alternatives are as follows:

1. Sell excess equipment.
2. Lay off or transfer people.
3. Redirect the sales department to look for additional opportunities.
4. Become a subcontractor for someone else.

Each of the preceding means of dealing with imbalance situations has built-in advantages and disadvantages associated with it. Some of these pluses and minuses that should be considered are summarized as follows.

When using overtime, the advantage is one of continuing to utilize experienced people with the same fixed cost of plant and machinery. This advantage can be offset by the immediate increased cost of the premium dollars, and also a possible reluctance on the part of the people to work overtime when needed due to fatigue, family obligations, and so on.

The pluses of subcontracting are highlighted by the fact that it creates dual sourcing of vendors for critical parts while, at the same time, it creates a comparison of outside- versus in-plant costs. However, the experience curve for the outside vendor and the volume purchased may lead to higher prices, especially if the vendor needs nonrecurring money for items such as tooling. Also, control over quality or proprietary processes is minimized.

By purchasing additional equipment and space, the immediate gain is increased capacity and continual control over the manufacture of the product with the additional volume capabilities creating marginal revenue on the increased output. The obvious losses that accrue immediately are the additional training and debugging costs associated with any new setup, and the possible increase in supervision costs in the short run.

When introducing an additional shift, it presupposes an adequate supply of labor for what could be termed "other than normal working hours." If there are adequate employees available willing to work these shifts, the gain from utilizing the same plant and equipment fixed costs is readily evident. However, a second- or third-shift premium payment, and sometimes lesser efficiency, may tend to offset these pluses. Also, the increased use of the machinery may cause higher maintenance costs and downtime.

Transferring work between compatible departments increases the skills and morale within the company, while at the same time holding idle costs at a minimum. The disadvantages would be mainly in the area of availability when needed, and again, the experience curve for additional training. It should be a short-term solution only.

As for the excess capacity situation, when cutting back capacity and the people associated with it, the technique should be one of getting as much of a plus as possible out of the negative situations which are always hard to deal with. Selling excess equipment and laying off the people should be the last resort after exhausting all additional volume opportunities. The disadvantages are evident. One can only try to find a buyer for the machinery and jobs for the employees, while still trying to absorb the idle fixed costs. Thus alternatives (3) and (4) are usually more attractive, though pursuing them may require the need for short-term contribution pricing, rather than pricing based on recovering fully absorbed costs plus a profit.

Cutbacks of any type may be traumatic and should be taken only after all means of obtaining additional work for the short run have been entirely exhausted. In many cases, marginal-cost pricing may help pay for the fixed costs in the short run, thereby decreasing the "panic" types of cutbacks and enabling the business to pursue a gradual phase out of excess capacity.

Other Bases

The method shown for determining normal volume used the machine-hour approach as the base. However, the same method is used to compute direct labor and direct material as the absorption base. In these cases, the present work force would be the present capacity by department. Individual labor standards would be used to compute the normal volume needed. Material standards would be spread over time, depending on the lead time in receiving the material from vendors and the inventory stocking policies in the firm. The normal-volume method has obvious benefits which accrue to the purchasing department, in that once determined by type of product, the needs may be bought in terms of annual buys, blanket orders for a period, dual sourcing, and so forth.

All of the above results in a smoother flow of material at a lower cost to the firm by helping the vendors in their planning process and avoiding many small buys at higher prices. Also, premium prices for rushed deliveries are minimized. Late material deliveries can be a significant cost problem in terms of labor efficiency since it is extremely difficult to cut back working hours in all but rare instances and still maintain a loyal work force. Nothing devastates smooth production and morale more than sitting around waiting for a $0.05 resistor so that a $100,000 unit can be finished and shipped. Normal-volume planning should reduce these holdups to a minimum.

As a final note to this section, it should be pointed out that normal-volume planning is a continuous policy. It must be updated in a disciplined manner—monthly, quarterly, and so forth—to adjust quickly for any large variations from the original annual forecasts. Volume and mix changes in business need to be identified quickly so that substitutions of products can take place. Management must always heed the classic saying of "the only thing sure in life is death and taxes." Day-to-day planning is a must to tune production to the annual goal.

Overall Normal-Volume Uses

Once normal volume has been determined, many other practical uses of it for the controller arise. Some of the primary uses are described below.

Basis of Annual Operating Budget. The normal activity level is the core from which all other budget calculations are derived. Sales units are converted into production units, and inventory change decisions become the balancing item. The largest overhead expense in many businesses is the indirect labor and staff functions. A successful business must have a minimum staffing level to carry on these support functions adequately but, at the same time, add to the base only when the volume of real work calls for it (not just because total volume has increased at the shipment level).

As an example, purchasing's work load will not necessarily double just because shipments go up 100 percent. If increased volume is attributed to the same product mix, chances are that the purchasing department will only have to write orders *in larger amounts* rather than more orders. The number of people in purchasing is related to the number of orders placed, and not the dollar amount of material bought. The shipping and receiving departments, however, would find themselves more closely aligned with total volume changes. Budget preparation time for a service group should include a review of its own volume before additions are made or reductions recommended. However, it is usually the sum of the support functions that can get expenses out of line. Therefore, in many medium-sized to large businesses a total relationship of direct to indirect personnel is monitored, with this ratio targeted at, say, 1.5 to 1 or 2 to 1.

The remaining expenses related to payroll are then computed, along with costs such as building and utilities, operating supplies, material costs and depreciation, to form a total financial budget.

Many other related budgets are then computed such as the cash flow and capital equipment. Capital equipment budgets tend to be longer in lead time than other purchases and, hence, it becomes very important—especially in a growing business—never to run out of needed capacity and thereby allow a competitor with more foresight to grow because of your inability to deliver. A long-range normal-volume approach tends to commit capital funds rationally and in time, with a planned growth and/or replacement level in tune with all other company budgets. This avoids panic buying at usually higher prices for expedited delivery.

Midpoint of the Flexible Budget. Normal volume techniques are used to derive the annual budget base as described above. The annual budget then becomes the midpoint of all flexible budget calculations for both absorption base and expense levels. Once these bases are derived, the second step in setting up a flexible budgeting system is to match expenses to the various volume levels of activity. These expenses are categorized into three main categories: fixed costs, semivariable costs, and variable costs:

1. Fixed costs are cost items whose amount is unrelated to volume within a certain time span and physical asset capacity, for example, depreciation, building lease costs, insurance, and property taxes.
2. Semivariable costs exhibit both fixed and variable characteristics, for example, indirect labor, utilities, and repair costs.
3. Variable costs vary dollar for dollar with volume, for example, expenses for fringe benefits, direct labor, and production materials that directly correlate with changes in volume.

The computation of fixed and variable costs is readily ascertainable for the most part. However, semivariable costs must be split into their respective fixed and variable amounts.

After choosing the normal production base and classifying the applicable expenses into fixed and variable components, it is a simple procedure to set up a flexible budget matrix within the variations from the desired norm. We chose to set budgets from the 75 percent to 125 percent level of normal volume as being the most practical. In addition, a time horizon on fixed costs was set at one year. Exhibits 4 and 5 give an example of a departmental flexible overhead budget.

Exhibit 4 is developed by dividing the individual variable expense categories by the direct labor base forecasted for the department, representing the 100 percent baseline level. The variable

EXHIBIT 4
Flexible Overhead Budget Formulation

	Baseline Level 100%		
	Fixed Expenses	Variable Expenses	Variable Rate per Direct Labor Dollars
Semivariable costs:			
Indirect labor..........................	$121,500	$121,500	$0.1676
Labor related..........................	16,250	16,250	0.0224
Supplies and repairs....................	2,600	2,600	0.0036
Other expenses and credits.............	1,500	1,500	0.0020
Employee related......................	500	500	0.0007
Subtotal..............................	$142,350	$142,350	$0.1963
Fixed costs:			
Rent, insurance, taxes, depreciation..........................	141,500	—	—
Total...............................	$283,850	$142,350	$0.1963

1. The fixed component of semivariable costs is assumed to be 50 percent of the normal (100 percent) budget level.
2. Direct labor dollars, multiplied by variable rate per direct labor dollar, plus fixed expense, equals budgeted overhead.
3. Normal volume is 725,000 direct labor dollars.

expense column was originally developed by assuming that the fixed portion of semivariable expenses in this department was 50 percent of the total.

Once the variable rate per direct labor dollar is determined by expense category, the balance of the flexible budget matrix appearing in Exhibit 5 is developed by multiplying the direct labor base at the 75 percent or 125 percent level by the factors shown in Exhibit 4 and adding the applicable fixed expense portion to establish a new budget.

Target for Sales Goals and Pricing Policies. Since the sales department supplies the order forecast which is used in developing the normal-volume base, an interesting "feedback" develops in which the normal-volume calculation yields excess capacity information. Hence, the sales personnel are then put in the position of usually being forced to review again the forecast, especially as to filling the "gaps" or excess capacity lines.

A very effective way of accomplishing this increased volume is through marginal-cost pricing techniques or outside contracting of other firm's products. As long as the subcontract work does what is intended and will not hurt existing production lines or become an "end in itself," this is an effective way of allowing sales to play a

EXHIBIT 5
Flexible Overhead Budget

	Baseline Level		
	75%	100%	125%
Direct labor base.........................	$543,750	$725,000	$906,250
Semivariable costs:			
Indirect labor............................	$212,633	$243,000	$273,388
Labor related............................	28,430	32,500	36,550
Supplies and repairs....................	4,558	5,200	5,863
Other....................................	2,586	3,000	3,313
Employee related.......................	881	1,000	1,134
Subtotal.................................	$249,088	$284,700	$320,248
Fixed costs:			
Rent, depreciation, taxes, insurance.....	141,500	141,500	141,500
Total budgeted expense.............	$390,588	426,200	$461,748
Internal overhead rate (rounded)...........	72%	59%	51%
Variable expenses.........................	$106,738	$142,350	$177,898
Fixed expenses...........................	$283,850	$283,850	$283,850
Fixed overhead rate.......................	52.20%	39.15%	31.32%
Variable overhead rate....................	19.63%	19.63%	19.63%

very important role in keeping costs down. The danger to be avoided is having the sales department concentrate too much on marginal business, since by definition the lower prices make orders somewhat easier to obtain. A plant full of products that will not absorb full overhead and general staff costs can only lead to eventual disaster. Most sales departments have standards of performance calculated on total dollar orders received. Therefore, it is essential that "planned" marginal business be segregated in the sales budget as a separate line item called "planned investments" or some other appropriate term which will highlight the amount taken. Constant review is needed to assure management that marginal-cost pricing is not being abused.

As a final note, many larger firms do not pursue "in-house" business from other divisions or plants which can be an immediate source of orders. It is amazing how little many purchasing departments in larger companies sometimes know about the general capabilities of their related divisions, especially if the company is run on a very decentralized basis. This can be an immediate source of marginal or support orders in the short run to help an overload in another plant. The lower costs then benefit the entire company as a whole.

Basis for Standard Costs. Unless a drastic change in business takes place, standard costs are usually calculated for a fiscal period of one year. The annual operating budget provides a planned volume and expense level which automatically translates into burden rates. These fixed burden rates can then be used in the calculation of all full standard costs utilized in the business. This will tend to level out the peaks and valleys which normally occur over the year by setting rates only annually, and utilizing an over-underabsorbed account in the interim. This facilitates interim inventory pricing, unit cost control, and pricing for quotes. A unit produced in October is then compared with a unit produced in May on the same overhead baseline.

Determination of the Break-Even Point. After preparation of the annual budget and flexible overhead budget based on normal-volume calculations, it becomes an easy matter to prepare gross break-even analyses for the business as a whole. The break-even sales formula is computed as follows:

$$\text{Break-even sales volume} = \frac{\text{Total fixed expenses}}{1 - \dfrac{\text{Total variable expenses}}{\text{Total sales volume}}}$$

After determining the "break-even sales," this number is then compared with the "normal sales" in the budget to determine the percentage of normal volume at which the firm must operate to break even:

$$\frac{\text{Break-even sales volume}}{\text{Normal (budget) sales volume}}$$

$$= \text{Percent normal capacity to break even}$$

Break-even analyses offer wide applications for economic model exercises such as considering alternatives, testing proposed actions, shifting of fixed and variable costs (old versus new plant, as an example), and changes in sales mix, prices, and quantities. Many controllers will construct the above calculations in graphic form which, to the nonfinancial manager, may be easier to understand and would preclude the necessity of any arithmetic calculations.[4]

Final Comment on Usage. As a final thought, the process of determining normal volume utilizes plantwide participative man-

---

[4] See Chapter 6, "Using Cost-Volume-Profit Charts," for a more detailed discussion of break-even analysis.

agement techniques. Sales determines orders; production determines schedules and accounting prepares the overall financial
model. Annual goals are then set with a team-planning approach,
thereby avoiding as much as possible the daily "fire-fighting" behavior in which many organizations find themselves. Once technologies are established, it is then very easy to assist managers in
planning, even longer range planning (i.e., three- and five-year
plans). Managers will even find the time available since the automatic control systems will tend to help them manage by exception
rather than by crisis.

All models must have a margin of error built into the goals. The
importance is the planning process itself rather than necessarily
how close to final budget one comes. Planning is continuous in
nature which, in itself, will tend to make attainment of the budget
more probable.

LONG-RANGE VOLUME CONSIDERATIONS

The bulk of the discussion on normal volume and capacity up to
this point has dealt with what is known as the "short run," or usually one fiscal year for a firm. However, for many firms the "short
run" may be defined in periods of up to three to five years, and,
hence, normal volume must be considered over a longer planning
period. This is especially true for many of the large defense contractors where a contract could be a multiyear buy starting with
prototypes and containing options of up to five years on production
quantities. The firm that wins the contract must have available
facilities to handle the high-volume production years, and the business is characterized by program phase ins and phase outs over the
"long run." All of the techniques described earlier in determining
normal volume still apply with two major differences:

1. All work is built to customer orders and, therefore, there are no
    inventory buildup decisions to make; and
2. The volume swings may be tremendous between years, depend-
    ing on the available funding level; these swings are accom-
    panied by high fixed-cost investment and long start-up cycles.

The normal-volume calculation changes from one of forecasting
orders to obtain production bases (since orders are 90 percent

known), to timing the production volume with many unknowns as to the production standards, costs, schedules, and so forth, which are still mainly estimates or may have been proven only on a few prototypes. A slip of a couple of months in the schedule could change production volume between years substantially. With this in mind, after gearing up for a large contract or a few large contracts, the alternate opportunities if funding does not materialize are few in nature and, therefore, some level of factoring may be necessary. A common technique is to spread actual backlog at its 100 percent value, but to factor projected orders at say 90 percent, 80 percent, or some other safety factor. On programs that are in the

EXHIBIT 6
Long-Range Marketing Forecast

SPARROW AIRCRAFT COMPANY
(dollars in millions)

System/Opportunities		1978	1979	1980	1981	1982	Five-Year Total
X14:	Domestic—possible......	$70.0	$40.0	$ 30.0	$ 20.0	$ 10.0	$170.0
	100% budget..........	70.0	40.0	30.0	20.0	10.0	170.0
X14:	Foreign—possible........	—	—	50.0	70.0	100.0	220.0
	50% budget...........	—	—	25.0	35.0	50.0	110.0
X14A:	Domestic—possible......	—	30.0	40.0	50.0	60.0	180.0
	80% budget.............	—	24.0	32.0	40.0	48.0	144.0
X14A:	Foreign—possible........	—	—	—	20.0	30.0	50.0
	10% budget...........	—	—	—	2.0	3.0	5.0
X15:	Design—possible........	10.0	10.0	20.0	30.0	30.0	100.0
	30% budget............	3.0	3.0	6.0	9.0	9.0	30.0
	Total possible.............	$80.0	$80.0	$140.0	$190.0	$230.0	$720.0
	Total budget factored.....	73.0	67.0	93.0	106.0	120.0	459.0

bid stage, it might be prudent to assume that on the average one in three realistically may be captured, and hence these are factored at 33 percent probability.

Exhibit 6 depicts a five-year new order plan for a custom business, showing both the possible and probable (factored) budget numbers. Exhibit 7 shows the budget, translating orders into sales and adding current backlog. The basis for sales assumes a 12-month program on each system, with half of the shipments in the year of order and the other half in the following year. This assumes equivalent units to be built at $\frac{1}{12}$ per month. Overall labor loading and material projections are then calculated for five years. For simplicity the following cost matrix was used:

Sales.................................. 100%
Profit................................. 10
Total cost............................ 90
G&A................................... 15
Manufacturing cost.................... 75
Direct labor.......................... 15
Overhead............................. 25
Material.............................. 35

Manloading assumes an average labor rate of $5 per hour and total work hours, per man-year, at 1,728 (48 weeks × 40 hours = 1,920 × 90 percent efficiency = 1,728 work hours). Indirect employees will be set at 75 percent of direct employees.

After viewing the buildup from $61.5 million to $113.0 million of sales, management would probably set normal capacity at some-

EXHIBIT 7
Long-Range Sales and Manloading

	System	1978	1979	1980	1981	1982	Total
		SPARROW AIRCRAFT COMPANY					
		(dollars in millions)					
Sales:							
X14:	Domestic—possible....	$35.0	$55.0	$35.0	$25.0	$ 15.0	$165.0
	100% budget.........	35.0	55.0	35.0	25.0	15.0	165.0
	backlog........	25.0					25.0
X14:	Foreign—possible......	—	—	25.0	60.0	85.0	170.0
	50% budget.........	—	—	12.5	30.0	42.5	85.0
X14A:	Domestic—possible....	—	15.0	35.0	45.0	55.0	150.0
	80% budget.........	—	12.0	28.0	36.0	44.0	120.0
X14A:	Foreign—possible......	—	—	—	10.0	25.0	35.0
	10% budget.........	—	—	—	1.0	2.5	3.5
X15:	Design—possible......	5.0	10.0	15.0	25.0	30.0	85.0
	30% budget.........	1.5	3.0	4.5	7.5	9.0	25.5
	Total budget sales........	$61.5	$70.0	$80.0	$99.5	$113.0	$424.0
Manloading:							
Direct labor—15%.............		9.2	10.5	12.0	14.9	17.0	
Wage rate—$5 per hour........							
Hours needed (in 000s)........		1,840	2,100	2,400	2,980	3,400	
Hours per man-year (1,728)....							
Direct employees needed.....		1,065	1,215	1,389	1,725	1,968	
Indirect @ 3/4 direct..........		799	911	1,042	1,294	1,476	
	Total manloading........	1,864	2,126	2,431	3,019	3,444	
Material purchases:							
35% of sales..................		21.5	24.5	28.0	34.8	39.6	

where around \$90 to \$100 million sales as the most realistic, but would provide a total capacity to handle as much as 20 percent over budget. Training of personnel, other sources of material supply, layout of production lines, and so on, would be started in the 1978–79 period to assure having the capability needed in 1981–82 and beyond. At the same time, contingency plans for a cutback of 20 percent (should the foreign buys not materialize) must also be considered. The major point to be remembered in long-range planning is that the planning exercise itself is most important. If there is no destination mapped out, one can never know one's lost. Planning tries to *create* a future and *cause* things to happen, rather than merely reacting to things as they occur.

SUMMARY

The overall goal of any company should be to produce at a level that will minimize investment in inventory, while still attempting to smooth out the peaks and valleys of business. This volume level is defined as "normal volume."

Normal volume is calculated by starting with the theoretical capacity in output hours and calculating allowances such as holidays, machine breakdowns, and vacations. The output with built-in allowances is then called practical volume. This practical volume is adjusted further to normal volume by addressing the levels of customer orders expected, and further adjusting planned output to meet this demand.

Work standards measurement and plant layout play a significant role in determining what the allowances will be.

The normal-volume calculations will yield "bottleneck" departments or sections with excess capacity available, which have to be analyzed as to what actions may be taken to smooth out capacity. Such actions as working overtime, subcontracting, adding another shift or selling excess assets are some of the ways utilized to relieve the imbalances.

Normal-volume determinations have many other uses in that they become the core of the annual operating plan, the midpoint of the flexible budget, the basis for standard costs, and the baseline for break-even point analyses.

The short run for most businesses is usually stated as one fiscal year but, in some situations, the normal volume calculation should be extended to cover from three to five years, especially for large system contractors who manufacture airplanes, tanks, ships, and all other producers of a large single-product nature characterized by a high fixed-cost investment with little opportunity for change if demand slumps.

ADDITIONAL SOURCES

Buffa, Elwood S. *Modern Production Management.* New York: John Wiley & Sons, Inc., 1973.

Grinnell, D., Jacque. "Activity Levels and the Disposition of Volume Variances." *Management Accounting,* August 1975, p. 29.

Wycoff, David W. "Direct and Idle-Time Cost Accounting." *Management Accounting,* December 1974, p. 36.

12

Manufacturing Overhead Allocations

D. Michael Jack and C. Roger Heimlich*

Manufacturing overhead is all manufacturing cost *other* than prime costs (direct material and direct labor). Allocation of overheads is the process by which such costs are associated with the products or services (cost objectives) which an organization provides.

Manufacturing overheads are allocated to provide product costs for financial reporting and managerial decision-making purposes. More than one allocation method may be required to satisfy different needs. The allocations process is a periodic analytic exercise which first associates overhead costs with the production departments and products which cause or benefit from these costs, and then applies the costs to products produced.

This chapter directly addresses the process of overhead allocation to manufactured products, but the concepts and methods discussed here are also generally applicable to organizations providing services.

USES OF ALLOCATED OVERHEAD

Inventory Valuation

The accounting concept of matching costs with revenue for the accounting period in which the revenue is realized requires that

* Mr. Jack is Managerial Accounting Director, and Mr. Heimlich is Assistant Corporate Controller–Financial Information Programs, both for Cummins Engine Company, Inc., Columbus, Indiana.

manufacturing overheads, as well as prime costs, be recorded as inventory assets during the period between production and sale. This requirement dictates that overheads be allocated to products in some manner which permits matching of these costs with products sold. Tax regulations and accounting principles permit some latitude in the determination of the overhead expenses which are to be inventoried and those which may be recognized as expenses of the period in which they were incurred. Maximizing those costs treated as period costs will have the effect of deferring income realization and thus deferring taxation with consequent favorable cash flow effect.

Precision in allocation of overheads to specific products is not required for valuing inventories. Simply allocating total plant overhead costs to products proportionate to their direct labor content is a generally acceptable and widely used method. However, this method has little value for managerial purposes.

Contract Costing

The process of allocating costs to products or projects produced under a contract may differ significantly from that required for other purposes. The principal reason for the difference is that many overheads may be applied directly to the contract, precluding the timing problems encountered in the "matching" process and the difficulties of applying fixed costs to varying quantities of product produced during an accounting period. In other words, the contract may, for costing purposes, be treated as a single product produced within a single accounting period.

Much governmental procurement is on a contractual basis. In the United States, the Cost Accounting Standards Board[1] was established by the Congress in 1970 to promulgate cost accounting standards to be used uniformly by federal agencies and their contractors.

It will generally be advantageous to the contractor to employ allocation methods that will support association of a maximum amount of cost to the project, an objective contrary to the usual one for financial reporting purposes.

---

[1] Cost Accounting Standards Board, 441 G Street, N.W., Washington, D.C. 20548.

Costs of Products and Services

Accurate determination of the cost of products is necessary to support many important managerial decision-making processes. Some of these are described below.

Pricing. Knowledge of precise costs is valuable information in determining selling prices. Use of plantwide overhead rates to allocate costs to products for pricing purposes may result in prices that do not adequately cover long-term costs for some products. Recognition of this circumstance in the marketplace (i.e., by customers) can cause shifts in product sales mix that will yield lower than expected profit margins.

Make versus Buy. Decisions to make products rather than buy them (or vice versa) require precise costs for both options. Knowledge of the fixed and variable portions of overhead is also essential. Use of invalid information for this purpose can result in incorrect decisions that have significant financial impact on the firm. (See Chapter 19 for a detailed treatment of make-or-buy decisions.)

Capacity Allocation. When demand exceeds capacity, potentially significant financial benefits can accrue from allocating the available capacity to those products which yield the highest profit margins per unit of capacity. Identification of those products with higher margins requires accurate costs.

Capacity Expansion. Evaluation of proposals to add capacity for specific products requires detailed knowledge of the fixed and variable unit costs of the incremental capacity in order to support rational decision analysis.

Sale Efforts. Knowledge of profit contribution from each product can assist in determining the amount and allocation of marketing resources in a manner that will optimize total contribution to profit.

Product Cost Control. Meaningful allocation of overheads to products can support product cost control efforts. A control process requires periodic measurement and comparison with standards or prior measurements. Overhead cost allocation is an analytic process performed from time to time. Use of allocated overheads for cost control purposes may require more frequent application of the process than is needed for other purposes. Caution: Apparent changes in product costs determined by applying previously determined overhead rates are generally *not* useful for overhead cost control purposes.

Responsibility Center Control

Effective control of the efficiency of both service and production centers requires that all costs supporting their activities be associated with them. The process of allocating overheads to products generally requires allocation of cost to responsibility centers as an intermediate step in the process, and consequently these intermediate allocation results may be used for control purposes. Again, one must remember the caution that only the results of analysis, not the application of previously determined rates, have significant value for this purpose.

Allocation Process Considerations

The purposes for which overheads are being allocated is an important determinant in defining the process to be used in allocating them. Another determinant is the materiality of overheads relative to total product costs. If prime costs constitute the bulk of product costs, the benefits of precise allocation of overheads may not be commensurate with the cost of developing and operating the allocation process. Smaller firms may find that allocation based upon the judgment of knowledgeable management will meet their requirements adequately.

In determining the nature of the cost allocation process to be employed, consideration must be given to the classification of costs into categories that will be allocated by different methods. Typical of the issues which must be addressed is whether most overheads vary proportionately with the labor content of products, thus permitting reasonable allocation of overhead as a rate per unit of labor activity. If some overheads vary proportionately with material value or weight, it may be necessary to determine overhead rates based on these factors in addition to, or even instead of, the more usual labor-based rates. Further possible refinements include determination of separate overhead rates for different kinds of materials from which products are manufactured. Such refinements offer the possibility of more precise allocation of overheads to products, but at the expense of more time-consuming and costly processes to determine the various overhead rates and apply them to products inventoried or sold.

Judgment must be exercised in determining the allocation precision required and thus the sophistication required of the allocation process. The path to application of more complex allocation processes should be evolutionary, both to substantiate the inadequacy of a simpler approach before a more costly alternative is elected and to permit development of the necessary analytic skills and disciplines required to support the more precise process.

DEFINITION AND MEASUREMENT OF MANUFACTURING OVERHEAD

Precise definition of the costs which comprise manufacturing overhead and of the information required to determine their magnitude for the purpose of overhead allocation is necessary to support description and operation of the allocation process.

Manufacturing Overhead Defined

Total company costs for a period of time may be divided into four broad categories: financial, general and administrative, selling, and manufacturing (see Exhibit 1). The manufacturing cost category can then be independently subdivided based upon a number of different classification methods (see Chapter 4). The two-way classification by behavior and traceability as depicted in Exhibit 1 provides the structure within which manufacturing overhead can best be defined.

An adequate operational definition of manufacturing overhead is *all manufacturing costs other than prime costs.* Aggregation of the two-way classifications of Exhibit 1 can be used to define useful cost categories as follows:

Traceability/Behavior	Cost Classifications	
Direct/variable	Prime cost	
Indirect/variable	Variable overhead ⎫	Total manufacturing
Direct/fixed ⎫	Fixed overhead ⎭	overhead
Indirect/fixed ⎭		

EXHIBIT 1
Cost Categorization

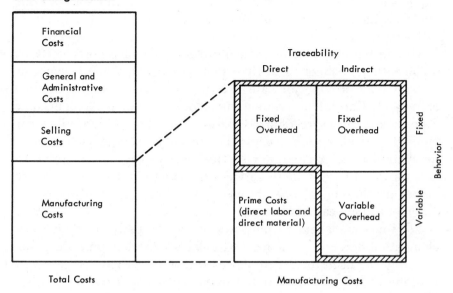

The classification of costs as manufacturing costs rather than selling or G&A costs, as well as classifications within the manufacturing cost category, are subject to some discretion. For instance, some order-entry and order-processing costs might be classified as either selling or manufacturing costs, perhaps dependent upon the functional organization in which the process is located. General plant management might, at least in part, be classed as a G&A expense rather than a manufacturing expense. Within the manufacturing cost category, materials or supplies that are consumed in the process of manufacturing may be treated as overhead even though they are fully variable and can be directly associated with specific products. Existing classification criteria should be reviewed to determine whether changes are required to support meaningful manufacturing overhead allocation.

Overhead Cost Determination

Overhead costs are collected through the accounting system or estimated by use of a model of the accounting system to predict future costs. A model of the accounting system, frequently ill defined, underlies the application of a budgeting process. Flexible budgets are well-defined (but not necessarily accurate) accounting models which recognize the behavior of costs within a range of activity.

The accounting system basically classifies and reports costs by organizational element and by expense category. Some accounting systems may provide for categorization of some costs by product or project. Careful determination of organizational elements and expense categories recognized within the chart of accounts can facilitate the allocation process. For instance, charge-back systems for maintenance or computer services can provide direct information on the usage of these services by various production departments, precluding the need to use informal records or management judgment to allocate such costs.

For some management purposes it may be useful to define cost elements differently than for historical accounting purposes, thus dictating the need for different measurement methods. An example is the use of depreciation based upon replacement cost of productive assets for pricing purposes.

Projected overhead costs for a future period during which they will be applied to products will be required to meet most needs. Estimation of costs for the future period requires precise definition of the quantity of production (not sales, if inventory level changes are a possibility) for that future period upon which the estimation of costs is to be based. Use of estimates of actual production may result in variation from period to period in unit overhead because of changes in the amount of fixed overhead which is applied to each unit. Such variation usually cannot and should not be reflected in pricing or cost control decisions. The use of smoothed "normal" volumes (see Chapter 11) is frequently elected to avoid these aberrations.

Some decisions based upon product cost should utilize differential cost rather than full cost. When production is below capacity, differential cost per unit is the same as variable cost per unit. Separation of fixed and variable overhead cost in the measurement and subsequent allocation processes will provide variable overhead rates for this purpose. The extra effort required to maintain the separation of fixed and variable costs throughout the allocation process may well pay off in the form of better management decisions.

THE BASIC ALLOCATION PROCESS

The basic overhead allocation process is composed of three distinct tasks. They are:

1. Association of overheads with cost centers and/or cost pools.
2. Allocation of service center costs to production centers or cost pools.
3. Assignment of costs from production centers and cost pools to products.

The diagram in Exhibit 2 depicts this process.

EXHIBIT 2
The Overhead Allocation Process

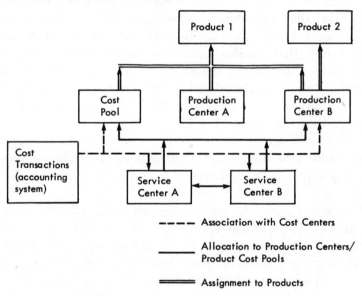

- - - - Association with Cost Centers

———— Allocation to Production Centers/ Product Cost Pools

======= Assignment to Products

Cost Collection Elements

Overhead costs are collected within cost centers or cost pools as the initial step in the process of assigning them to products. In practice, costs centers are frequently organizational units, but they need not be. Cost pools are collection media which are defined for special purposes.

Production Cost Center.   An area of activity in which products are processed, and which is homogeneous either with regard to the kinds of products processed or to the kind of equipment utilized, is called a *production cost center*. Ideally, overhead costs should vary directly, though not necessarily proportionately, with a single measure of the level of activity within the center.

Service Cost Center. An area of activity that provides support services to production cost centers, but in which products are not processed, is called a *service cost center*. Maintenance, materials handling, and inspection activities are examples of service activities. "Artificial" service cost centers to accumulate plantwide expense such as building depreciation, real estate taxes, and general heating and lighting costs may be useful.

Product Cost Pool. A cost collection category defined in terms of product characteristics rather than in terms of manufacturing activities is called a *product cost pool*. For instance, if procurement, handling, and storage costs are related to the value of material purchased rather than to the manner in which the material is processed, these costs should be collected in a cost pool and applied proportionately to material value. If these costs differed significantly for various types of materials, separate cost pools could be established for each type.

Costs are allocated from one service center to another, and from service centers to production cost centers or pools, by means of *allocation* bases. They are assigned to products by means of *activity* bases.

Allocation Bases. A measurable characteristic to which the magnitude of a particular service provided is related is called an *allocation basis*. For example, personnel services provided to cost centers may vary directly with the total number of people employed by the center, while maintenance services might be related to total hours of machine operation. If the latter figure were not available, power consumption for machine operation might be a suitable *surrogate allocation basis*.

Activity Bases. A measure of the activity of a production cost center, or within a product cost pool, with which overhead costs vary directly and for which the contribution of each product processed within the center to the total level of activity can be determined, is called an *activity basis*. For a given production center, overheads could vary with the total weight of material processed. If the weight of each product processed is determinable, then weight would likely be the activity basis of choice for that center.

A Simple Case

In the simplest case, all production departments are treated as a single production cost center, in which case all service departments support this single production cost center. Total overhead may then be allocated to products on a single basis, say, direct labor dollars. The overhead rate is calculated as follows:

$$\text{OH} = \frac{\text{Total overhead dollars}}{\text{Total direct labor dollars}}$$

The overhead rate will typically be calculated from values derived from estimates of overhead costs and labor activity for some future period of production.

Production Volume Determination. A typical situation would be to determine an overhead rate late in the current year for application during the following year. To determine the level of production to be used for determination of next year's overhead rate, the actual production of each type of product (or homogeneous group of products) for the past few years, the estimated total production for the current year, and the forecast of production for the next few years might be utilized. The pattern of production levels for each product over these several years, both historical and forecast, would be "smoothed" using an analytic or judgmental method to provide "normal" estimates of production volumes for the following year. Note that these normal volumes will almost certainly differ from both forecast volumes and the actual volumes which will eventually be produced. (Determination of normal volumes is covered in Chapter 11.)

Labor Activity Determination. The dimension of the labor activity variable to be used as the basis for allocating overhead to product must first be decided upon. The first consideration is that a value for the variable must be available for each product produced. For example, actual direct labor cost per unit cannot be used for overhead application to products if the cost accounting system only provides *standard* direct labor cost per unit.

A second consideration is the inherent property of the overhead rate determination method to apply variation in the activity level variable to the overhead amount applied to the product. If actual direct labor cost per unit is selected as the dimension of the labor activity variable, and if the unit labor cost actually experienced is only 95 percent of the amount estimated for the purpose of determining the overhead rate, then only 95 percent of the estimated total overhead will be applied if the normal volume is actually produced. This result would be correct for those elements of overhead that actually vary proportionately with labor cost produced. However, overhead cost elements such as all fixed costs, material handling costs, and others which do not vary proportionately with direct labor would not be adequately covered by the total amount of overhead applied under these circumstances. Appropriate determination of the dimension of the labor activity variable can minimize the amount of overhead over- or underapplied, but such differences will almost always occur. (Calculation and analysis of overhead variances is treated in Chapter 32).

If a standard cost system is employed and includes standard direct labor cost per unit, this value might well be selected as the labor activity base. The per unit direct labor costs would then be extended by the estimated volumes for each product to determine the total expected direct labor dollars—the denominator for the overhead rate fraction.

Overhead Expense Determination. With volumes for each product specified and an estimate of labor activity available, estimated total overhead cost for the next year can be estimated. The estimation process will be similar to the budgeting process. If normal volumes differ from forecast volumes which would be employed to determine budgets for use as responsibility reporting standards, then a separate determination of expense at the normal volumes would be required. As in the responsibility budgeting process, changes in production method, salaries and wage rates, and other factors which affect overhead costs must be considered in arriving at a reasonably accurate estimate of total overhead. If the purpose of the rate is to assign to products only inventoriable overhead, then obviously only those overhead elements which are inventoriable should be included.

Overhead Rate Application. Once the overhead rate has been determined, it can be applied to products produced by extending the number of standard direct labor dollars in the products manufactured by the overhead rate, which will be a certain number of dollars per direct labor dollar. The overhead amount may be determined in this manner for individual products or for total production during the period; however, care must be taken in determining the meaning of the value computed.

The foregoing discussion outlines a procedure to determine a plantwide overhead rate for a future period. Similar procedures are widely used. The following cautions are pertinent to use of such a plantwide rate:

1. Application to specific products is meaningful only if the products produced and the processes by which they are produced are relatively homogeneous; if this is not the case, then use of departmental overhead rates and other refinements is indicated.
2. If actual volumes differ from the volumes used to determine the overhead rate, the overhead applied can be expected to differ from actual overhead incurred for several reasons, including incorrect application of fixed costs and behavior of overhead cost elements that are related to factors other than direct labor cost.
3. If assumptions used to determine estimated overhead costs, such as energy costs, prove to be invalid, calculated overhead amounts will err similarly.
4. Overhead cost estimates utilizing overhead cost elements appropriate for one purpose, such as determination of inventoriable overhead produced, may be invalid for another purpose, such as full costing for product pricing purposes.

THE DETAILED ALLOCATION PROCESS

Having considered a simple case of overhead allocation, the following sections describe the manufacturing overhead allocation process in more detail. We now assume a complete, thorough allocation is required and also assume the end objective is to determine product cost. To reiterate a point made earlier, the same principles can also be used to determine the cost of a service or a project. The amount of detail work done will vary with the need for accuracy and the effect on total product cost.

Reporting Systems

The time and effort required to allocate manufacturing overhead and the results of that allocation depend heavily upon how the accounting system classifies and reports costs. It is essential, therefore, that consideration be given to the manufacturing overhead allocation process whenever any responsibility reporting or other cost accounting system is designed. To facilitate allocation, systems should be designed to identify the cost of services performed by one department for another or expenses incurred by one department incident to another.

Maintenance costs, for example, are a significant part of total manufacturing overhead costs of any capital-intensive manufacturing operation. Yet, some accounting systems only track maintenance cost by expense account number within the maintenance department. This may be sufficient for responsibility accounting or for measuring the performance of the maintenance department's manager, but it does little to support maintenance expense allocation.

One refinement which could be made in this case would be to charge maintenance time and material directly to the using department, and credit a contra account in the maintenance department for the same amount. One of two basic methods could be used to value maintenance time. The first is to charge the straight-time rate of the maintenance employee. If Department A required ten hours of work, the charge to Department A would be $80, given an $8 per hour straight-time wage rate. The other method is to charge a predetermined hourly rate which includes maintenance supervision and miscellaneous expenses (e.g., minor repair parts or supplies) as well as the rate for the maintenance employee. Department A would be charged $150 in this case, assuming the same $8 base rate and adding $7 to cover maintenance supervision and other expenses.

Another refinement is to accumulate time and material by the using department number as subsidiary information within the maintenance department. The using department would not be directly charged in this case.

Machine number could be used instead of, or in addition to, using department number in either of the above refinements. This would provide extremely useful data if machine-hour overhead rates are to be developed.

Similar approaches can be used for other support areas. Consideration should also be given to overhead rate development in determining the number of production departments. To illustrate this point, assume a machine-press production area consists of heavy- and medium-duty presses each producing different parts. Instead of one department for all presses, consider using two departments—one for medium-duty and one for heavy-duty presses. Involved in the decision are judgments regarding the actual ability to segregate most costs between the two proposed departments, the impact on responsibility accounting for the area, the amount of precision needed in the overhead rates, and, most importantly, the significance (or materiality) of the difference in the overhead rates if the machine-press area is treated as two departments rather than as a single cost center.

Another key to meaningful cost allocation is to ensure the base data used are accurate; doing this is the first step in determining overhead rates. Review the cost accumulation system for discipline and integrity. If there is a maintenance charge-off system, for example, verify it is being used correctly and that "bogus" or "favorite" charge numbers (i.e., those that might be used for idle time) are not being used excessively. Check departmental amounts for incorrect or significant nonrecurring charges. Ascertain that data in supporting systems, such as depreciation from a fixed assets system, are complete and accurate.

Review all data used for reasonableness and completeness before allocating. This will save a substantial amount of time should an error be discovered later in the allocation process.

Expenses Not Accumulated by Department or Project

Expenses not accumulated by department should be assigned directly to the production cost center or product cost pool whenever possible. (These expenses usually are not accumulated by department because they are considered "noncontrollable" by department heads.) Natural gas usage for a heat-treating or smelting operation, for example, can be determined from meter readings for the specific area. This portion of the natural gas cost then can be excluded from the remainder which will probably have to be allocated on some surrogate basis. Depreciation on machinery and equipment in the production cost center can be determined by reference to depreciation on the specific machines in the department. If formal accounting records are not kept by department, plant or process engineering should be able to provide a list of at least the major equipment by cost center.

Whenever these types of expenses are not directly assignable, they should be allocated to product, production, and service cost centers proportionate to their causal factors. Following are examples of some of the more typical expenses not accumulated by department which need to be allocated on this basis:

Salary and Wage-Related Benefits.[2] These benefits, often called "fringes," may include payroll taxes; holiday pay; vacation pay; medical, life, and other insurance premiums; pensions; and paid absence time. The most effective method of allocating these costs is to express them as a percent of total salary or wages and then allocate them to each cost center based upon the total salary and wages in the cost center. If the benefits vary significantly by class of employee (i.e., hourly or salary), it may be necessary to develop a different fringe benefit rate for each class. A further refinement is to allocate a portion (e.g., payroll taxes) as a percentage of wages and the remainder on head count (e.g., medical insurance).

Depreciation. Depreciation on machinery and equipment in departments *other than* production cost centers should be assigned to the support areas by reference to specific assets in the area. Depreciation on machinery and equipment which cannot be assigned to any specific area should be assigned to the common overhead pool. (Allocation of this pool will be covered later.)

Building depreciation should be assigned to each cost center on the basis of square feet. Square feet by cost center can be determined by plant or process engineering. Most likely, the sum of the square feet by area will be less than total building floor space, because of common areas such as rest rooms, vending areas, aisles, and unused floor space. Depreciation per square foot for allocation purposes can be determined in one of two ways:

Method A:

$$\frac{\text{Building depreciation}}{\substack{\text{Total floor space identifiable} \\ \text{with specific areas}}} = \substack{\text{Building depreciation} \\ \text{rate per square foot of} \\ \text{specific use}}$$

Method B:

$$\frac{\text{Building depreciation}}{\text{Total building square feet}} = \substack{\text{Depreciation rate per} \\ \text{building square foot}}$$

[2] Many companies treat these "fringe" costs for production workers as part of direct labor cost, rather than as an overhead item, as described here.

Method A is preferable when the difference between identified and floor space is slight or the difference could be allocated with minimum effect on the final result. Method B is preferable when the difference is significant and the common floor space cannot be rationally allocated on identified square footage. This would be the case when a large amount of floor space is simply unassignable because of building layout and usage. Depreciation on common floor space can be assigned to the common overhead pool. Idle floor space—a portion of a building which could be used for manufacturing or warehousing but is currently not being used—should be separately identified and not treated as common floor space in either Method A or B.

If a plant consists of numerous buildings, an average depreciation rate per square foot for the entire plant should be used. This method is much simpler and prevents distortion in product cost arising simply because of where the activity is located. Exceptions would be made for special-purpose buildings or cost-plus contract pricing considerations.

Asset-Related Insurance and Taxes.   Insurance and tax expense can be divided into building related, equipment related, and inventory related. Building-related costs can be allocated in proportion to square feet. Equipment-related costs can be allocated in proportion to the gross book value of machinery and equipment by area.

Inventory-related property taxes vary significantly by state. The magnitude of this cost influences its treatment in overhead allocation. Alternative methods are to allocate it based on value of direct material purchases, to allocate it on average inventory value by product or cost center, or to include it as part of the common overhead cost pool.

A work sheet such as the one illustrated in Exhibit 3 can prove very useful for developing depreciation, taxes, and insurance expenses by cost pool; reconciling to the total cost to be allocated; and providing a source of common reference data for special studies.

Utilities.   A reasonable approach in the allocation of utility costs is to attempt to identify them to the extent possible by specific cost centers on a causal basis. As mentioned at the beginning of this section, it is often possible to identify specific usage of natural gas, for example, by particular production cost centers. If direct metering is not possible, plant or process engineering should be able to provide an estimate of usage.

EXHIBIT 3

COMPANY X
Manufacturing Overhead Rate Development
Depreciation, Taxes, and Insurance Worksheet
(thousands)

Department* No.	Department* Description	Machinery and Equipment		Building			Taxes and Insurance		
		Gross Book Value	Depreciation	Floor Space	Depre-ciation†	Total Depreciation	On Equipment‡	On Buildings§	Total
100	Receiving	$ 10	$ 2	10	$ 1	$ 3	$ —	$ 1	$ 1
110	Receiving inspection	113	81	2	—	81	1	—	1
· · ·	· · ·	· · ·	· · ·	· · ·	· · ·	· · ·	· · ·	· · ·	· · ·
510	Casting	2,156	752	50	5	757	22	3	25
520	Machining	3,030	1,958	50	5	1,963	30	3	33
530	Assembly	810	300	100	10	310	8	6	14
· · ·	· · ·	· · ·	· · ·	· · ·	· · ·	· · ·	· · ·	· · ·	· · ·
700	Finished goods stores	150	90	200	20	110	2	12	14
· · ·	· · ·	· · ·	· · ·	· · ·	· · ·	· · ·	· · ·	· · ·	· · ·
	Totals	$15,763	$9,072	900	$90	$9,162	$158	$54	$212

* Project number, product, or cost pool could be used instead of, or in addition to, department number.
† Allocated on a basis of $0.10 per square foot.
‡ Allocated on a basis of 1 percent of gross book value.
§ Allocated on a basis of $0.06 per square foot.

If natural gas is used both for heating and production processes, first determine the amount used for production processes and then allocate the remainder on square feet of floor space (or perhaps cubic feet of space). The process-related amount, of course, should be assigned directly to the applicable cost centers.

Electricity costs may be the most difficult to allocate because of multiple rate structures (which consider peak demand as well as usage) and the difficulty in quantifying usage. Assistance of the plant or process engineering department again will be necessary to allocate electrical costs meaningfully. Metered usage, machine horsepower and shifts utilized, engineering estimates, or substation KVA ratings are surrogates which can be used to allocate process-related electrical costs to cost centers. More than one such surrogate can be used: one can be used to allocate the fixed portion and another to allocate the variable portion of electricity costs, for example. Lighting costs can be allocated in proportion to square feet of space lighted.

The same logic can be used for water and sewage. Identify specific high-usage areas and assign the estimated cost of that usage to the area. The remainder can be allocated by any number of methods. However, the cost involved is usually not significant and can therefore be assigned to the common overhead cost pool.

A work sheet similar to the one in Exhibit 3 is helpful in summarizing and documenting the utility cost allocation.

Data Processing. Data processing operations cost can be allocated to using departments by using rates for file storage and computer time. Systems and programming time can be allocated to using departments based on predetermined rates which cover supervision, debugging expense, and other systems and programming departmental expenses. Separate rates should be established for programming man-hours and systems man-hours. (See Chapter 25 for further details on support department charge-back systems.)

Transportation and Related Charges. It is preferable to include freight-in and import duty on purchased parts as part of the direct material cost of a purchased part. If it is impractical to do so, a means of allocating these costs must be developed. There are several suggested alternative approaches.

One approach is to allocate transportation and related charges to product based on purchase cost. This is the simplest method, but could result in distortions if there is not a direct correlation between purchase cost and transportation cost. It also results in spreading of import duty over all products, instead of only to the particular imported materials.

Another approach is to refine the method just described by categorizing material into different segments by similarity of weight, cost, and source. Have the purchasing or transportation department determine an estimated average transportation and related cost for each category. Either this estimate may be used or, if the total estimate and the actual (or budgeted) amounts are different, the actual can be prorated in proportion to the estimated costs.

Transportation and related costs can also be assigned to the production cost centers which first use the purchased materials. This approach, however, may result in distortion if several different types of products are processed by the cost center. The cost center activity base would not correctly assign representative shares of transportation cost to each type of product.

Shrinkage and Obsolescence. Inventory shrinkage and obsolescence can be treated in much the same way as transportation and related costs. The main difference would be to segregate material by the propensity to suffer inventory loss, instead of by weight or source. Bulk materials, for example, may be more subject to shrinkage than individual parts, and should therefore be assigned a higher share of shrinkage cost than other products.

An analysis of the annual physical inventory results or of interim adjustments to perpetual inventories will indicate which materials are most likely to suffer shrinkage. If the shrinkage actually occurs as part of the production process, shrinkage expense should be allocated to the applicable production cost centers. If it is more a function of the type of material or of the manner of accounting for the material in inventory, then allocation by material category is more rational.

Allocation of Cost Center Manufacturing Overhead

In the section above, noncontrollable costs—those not normally charged to any particular responsibility department—were allocated to service cost centers, production cost centers, or directly to the product cost pool. The next step in the allocation process is to allocate service cost center expenses, including any assigned noncontrollable expenses, to production cost centers or to product cost pools.

This normally involves a multiple-step operation because many of the service cost centers support not only production departments but also other service departments. The allocation of overhead among service departments which mutually support each other may be performed through the use of matrix algebra to determine the precise overhead allocation. By considering materiality, the allocation basis used, and the primary order of services rendered, however, the sequence in which to allocate service cost center expenses can generally be determined, and the allocation can be done without resorting to sophisticated mathematical techniques.

The allocation process should begin with the departments which are most general in nature and which support other manufacturing service departments as well as production cost centers. The last service departments allocated should be those which directly support the production cost centers and which have little to do with the other service departments.

Assign on a Services-Rendered Basis. Allocation should be based on services normally rendered for (or expenses incurred incident to) other service departments or production cost centers. This allocation is generally more meaningful if the services rendered represent services to be rendered over a long period of time—say, two or more years. Allocation using this longer term basis prevents some of the distortions that arise because of a short-term emphasis in a particular area.

Expenses of the machine maintenance department, for example, will probably be allocated on the time and material spent in each department. However, if a particular production department has incurred (or is expected to incur) an extraordinarily disproportionate amount of maintenance department expenses and time, the allocation should be adjusted to recognize the abnormality. Similarly, industrial engineering may concentrate on specific production areas at given points in time, but in the long run may spend their time in direct proportion to the standard hours incurred in each area.

All expenses in a support department do not need to be allocated on the same basis. Major expenses in each department should be analyzed to determine for what area they are incurred and to identify the most appropriate allocation base.

Assign on a Meaningful Surrogate Basis. When it is not possible to allocate expenses on a specific, identifiable services-rendered basis, it is often possible to find a meaningful substitute which is indicative of the services rendered. Total department head count, for example, may be a reasonable basis for allocation of certain personnel and payroll department expenses. Another illustration is the allocation of plant management (area management and general supervisor) to production departments in proportion to the number of supervisors.

Judgmental Allocation of Common Manufacturing Overhead. Some departmental expenses can only be allocated on a basis determined by individual judgment. The plant manager's departmental expenses cannot be related to any production cost center on other than a judgmental basis. Miscellaneous activities performed by manufacturing overhead departments for nonmanufacturing departments, but not charged to those departments, are another example of manufacturing overhead which must be allocated judgmentally. A specific example of this type of activity is janitorial services performed for administrative, marketing, or basic research areas by the plant janitors.

Common overhead also includes the noncontrollable (nondepartmental) costs which cannot be allocated on any specific basis (e.g., common floor space).

There are two basic common overhead allocation approaches. One is to allocate each of these types of overhead expense individually to service and production departments. The other is to accumulate these as common overhead and allocate the total. The first approach allows more flexibility in choosing the most suitable allocation basis for each item of overhead—for example, asset values for property insurance or space utilized for utilities. The latter approach requires less work and makes the common expenses easier to identify when special analysis of product cost or product cost centers is required.

Because the allocation is judgmental by definition, and because the impact on product cost is usually insignificant, the recommended method is to combine common items and allocate them on a single basis. Some of the common bases which can be used are as follows:

Product Cost Excluding Common Overhead. The term "product cost" in this case consists of direct material, direct labor, and assigned manufacturing overhead. Common overhead can be expressed as a percent of total product cost and added to the cost of a product. To illustrate, assume Product X has direct material cost of $5, direct labor cost of $1, and an assigned manufacturing overhead of $4, for a total of $10 per unit. If the common overhead rate is 5 percent of assigned product cost, the common overhead for Product X is $0.50 ($10 × 5 percent); so the total manufacturing cost is $10.50.

This basis offers the least variation in total product cost. It assumes that common costs are basically costs of doing business and, therefore, would fairly be shared by each product by allocating on this basis. On the other hand, it is a more cumbersome and time-consuming effort. Moreover, by definition the allocation is arbitrary so there is no rationale to support the "fair-share" concept. Rather the allocation is really on an "ability-to-bear" or minimum variance concept.

Production Cost Center Manufacturing Expense, Production Cost Center Head Count, or Direct Labor. In these similar methods, common overhead is simply allocated in proportion to one of these bases. There is little theoretical argument to support this approach. It is, however, a simple and straightforward way by which to allocate the common overhead.

Sometimes, because of either the inordinate effort required or simply the lack of any supporting data, it may not be possible to allocate a major expense on a reasonable basis. The major expense, then, becomes the same as common overhead. Utility costs could be one example of this type of expense. In this case it may be wise to have separate categories of so-called common overhead so that each category can be allocated on a different and more appropriate base.

Allocation Suggestions. Exhibit 4 gives suggested methods for allocating manufacturing overhead to production cost centers or other cost pools. This process is shown schematically in Exhibit 5, while examples of the actual work papers which could be used are shown in Exhibit 6.

A few clarifying statements may be helpful:

1. There is no substitute for good judgment in deciding what allocation basis to use and how much time and effort should be spent developing the basis. The decision depends upon the precision required and the significance of the cost to be allocated. In some instances, it may be useful to verify or determine allocation basis by the use of scatter diagrams or regression analysis.

2. Numerous steps can be used in the allocation process. To illus-

EXHIBIT 4
Suggested Allocation Methods

Support Department	Allocation To	Allocation Method
Plant manager	Immediate staff	Percent of time spent with each functional area; total head count in each area
	All departments	Head count in each department
Personnel (employee relations, benefits, safety, etc.)	All departments	Head count in each department; time spent by department
Plant security	All departments	Square feet or head count within area assigned to each guard
Controller's office:		
Payroll	All departments	Head count; total payroll dollars in each department
Cost and budgets	Product	Cost of production by product
Building maintenance	All departments (with significant floor space)	Square feet; square feet within type of building if cost is significantly different by type of building
Plant utilities	All departments (with significant usage)	Engineering estimates of services provided; square feet for heat or lighting
Special maintenance projects (carpenters, plumbers, rearrangement expenses)	All departments (with recurring significant usage)	Time and material; full-time assignment of special maintenance employees
Janitorial services	All using departments	Square feet; square feet within areas assigned to each janitorial force or individual janitor
Machine maintenance (including vehicle maintenance)	All using departments or cost centers	Time and material; full-time assignment of maintenance employees; number of work orders
	Product	Time and material; assignment of maintenance employees
Tool room	All using departments or cost centers	Time and material; number of requisitions
	Products	Time and material; number of requisitions
Process (manufacturing) engineering	Production cost centers	Time and material; full-time assignment of process engineering personnel
	Products	Time and material; full-time assignment of personnel
Industrial engineering	All departments or cost centers for which standards are established	Total standard hours earned by department; analysis of time spent in each area; full-time assignment of personnel
	Products	Total standard hours incurred by product; cost of production

EXHIBIT 4 *(continued)*

Support Department	Allocation To	Allocation Method
Order administration (and product specifications)	Products	Assignment of order administration personnel; analysis of man-hours spent by type of product
	Product cost centers (those completing salable items)	Assignment of personnel by product line; analysis of time spent by product
Purchasing, material scheduling, and expediting	Direct material categories	Analysis of amount of time and expenses related to each category; assignment of purchasing agents and amount of materials and materials personnel purchased by category
	Production cost centers (those first using the purchased material)	Analysis of time spent acquiring material for each cost center; time spent by category of material related to material used by each cost center
Receiving and raw and in-process stores	Direct material categories	Analysis of man-hours spent and floor space used by category; identification of special facilities or equipment by material category (e.g., bulk storage tanks); amount of material purchased by category; number of shipments received
	Production cost centers (those first using the purchased materials)	Analysis of time and facilities invested for each cost center; expense by category of material related to the material related to the material used by each cost center
Production scheduling and control	Production cost centers	Analysis of time spent by center; number of setups; number of production orders; number of material requisitions; number of direct labor operations; assignment of personnel
	Product	Analysis of time spent by product; number of orders scheduled; number of direct labor operations
Material movement (material handling)	Production cost centers	Analysis of personnel and material handling equipment requirements; amount of quantity of material transferred among departments; assignment of material handling personnel
	Product	Analysis of personnel and equipment requirements; amount or quantity of material used by product; assignment of personnel
Production inspection	Production cost centers	Assignment of inspection personnel; value of products produced; standard labor hours produced
Area management (superintendents and general supervisors)	Production cost centers	Percentage time spent by cost center; number of supervisors; total cost center head count

Note: Any of the above can be included in the common overhead cost pool and allocated to product or production cost centers as described in the text.

EXHIBIT 5
Allocation Schematic

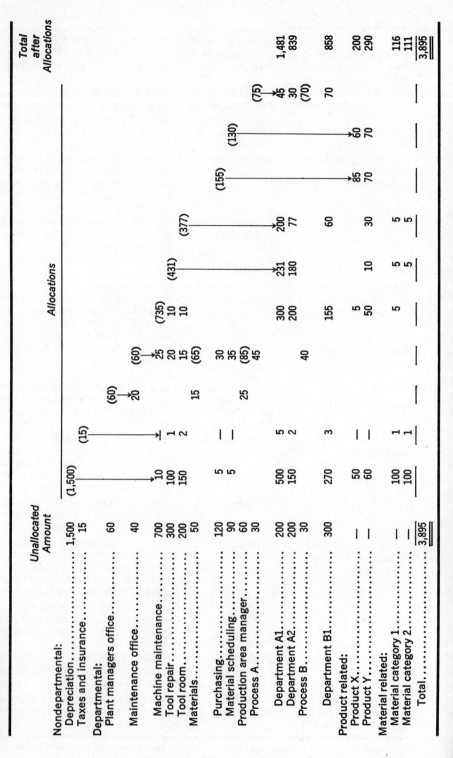

EXHIBIT 6
Example of Allocation Worksheet

DEPARTMENT XX
Gidget Final Assembly Overhead
($000)

Source	Budget Statement		Adjustments		Corrected Amount and Allocations		Adjustments
	Variable	Fixed	Variable	Fixed	Variable	Fixed	
Department XX direct overhead:							
Salary and wages	121	30	—	18	121	48	Supervisors excluded from budget statement.
Operating supplies	5				5		
Tools	10	2	(2)		8	2	Tools charged in error to this department instead of to Department 22.
Maintenance	5	5			5	5	
Scrap	3	—			3		
Other	—	2			—	2	
Total	144	39	(2)	18	142	57	
Direct allocations:							
Fringes					24	12	
Depreciation (Schedule D)						30	
Taxes and insurance (Schedule D-1)						3	
Utilities						2	
Support department allocation:							
Area management (Schedule A-1)					1	30	
Maintenance (Schedule A-2)					72	15	
⋮							
Total overhead					360	240	
Rate based on direct labor activity base of $150					240%	160%	

trate, a plant manager's office expense may be allocated to the office expense of each of the immediate staff (e.g., materials director). Their expenses, including the allocated expense, must be allocated to each department within their area before their departmental expenses can be allocated. For example, the materials director's office expense must be allocated to purchasing, material scheduling, and other departments before each of those is allocated. This process is depicted in Exhibit 5.

3. Allocation of departmental expenses based on the assignment of personnel in the department refers to the assignment of the non-supervisory personnel in the department. Allocation of industrial engineering based on the assignment of personnel, for example, means the expense of the industrial engineering department should be allocated proportionately over the number of industrial engineers assigned to each area.

4. Even the assignment of expense of one department may require multiple steps. Again using industrial engineering as an illustration, it may be reasonable to allocate industrial engineering expense to each major manufacturing process area based on the assignment of industrial engineers in that area. However, another step may be needed to allocate the area industrial engineering expense to specific production cost centers within that area.

5. More than one allocation basis may be used to allocate the expenses of any given department. For example, if both maintenance material and labor are accumulated in the machine maintenance department, it may make more sense to allocate maintenance material to the using departments based on maintenance material usage, and the remainder of the expense to using departments based on time spent by the machine maintenance personnel in each department.

6. It is preferable *not* to allocate common overhead. By definition the allocation is arbitrary and, depending upon the use, can be very misleading. If it is necessary to allocate common overhead, the amount allocated should be clearly identified.

7. Manufacturing overhead should be divided into variable and fixed components, and that distinction should be maintained throughout the entire allocation process. This facilitates various analyses where the fixed-variable distinction is important; for example, break-even analysis and make-or-buy decisions.

8. Discuss allocation alternatives with the head of each service

center. They often will have excellent suggestions for allocation bases.

Relating Overhead to Product

To this point the discussion has been concentrated on the allocation of manufacturing overhead to production cost centers and cost pools. In most cases the end objective of the overhead allocation process is to develop a per unit product cost. Therefore, an appropriate activity basis (or bases) must be chosen to relate aggregate costs to individual units.

Activity Bases. This section includes descriptions of potential activity bases, any one or more of which could be used to apply manufacturing overhead cost to a specific unit. First, however, we should consider the criteria for choosing activity bases. The activity basis should:

1. Reasonably reflect the differences in manufacturing overhead incurred for different products passing through the same cost center or benefitting from the same cost pool.
2. Be useful in projecting long-term changes in aggregate cost. In other words, the activity base and associated rate should be capable of being used to project total manufacturing overhead incurred if the product's volume were to be expanded significantly.
3. Be readily available or easily attainable from plant operating data.
4. Not be subject to significant changes which would make the overhead rate developed incorrect.
5. Not be so small in relation to the associated overhead that a relatively minor change in the activity base would result in a major change in unit product manufacturing overhead applied.

Activity bases include the following:

Direct Labor Hours. Direct labor hours are generally readily available and are an appropriate basis for labor-intensive operations such as assembly work. Use of a rate based on hours does not reflect economic increases (i.e., inflation), however, while a rate based on direct labor dollars would. The choice would depend on the labor content of manufacturing overhead and how that labor cost changes with direct labor rate changes. For example, if manufacturing overhead is 75 percent indirect labor, and if all labor—both direct and indirect—receives a wage rate increase at the same time, a manufacturing overhead rate based on direct labor dollars would be more appropriate.

Many cost accounting systems have more than one type of direct labor hour available. For any one unit, standard (budget) hours, the latest time-study (current standard) hours, and actual hours may be available. The manner in which these change during the year, and how manufacturing overhead changes with them, have to be considered in order to determine which is best to use as an activity base. Generally, the latest time-study hours are the most reasonable because, among other reasons, they are more stable than actual hours, more clearly related to units produced than actual hours, and reflect operations improvements which standard hours do not.

Direct Labor Dollars.   Many of the pros and cons of direct labor hours also apply to direct labor dollars. The primary exception is wage-rate change, which was discussed above. Another advantage of direct labor dollars may be convenience; it is often simpler in analytical studies to work only in dollars instead of both dollars and hours.

Direct Material Cost.   This is usually an appropriate basis for expenses such as freight-in, receiving costs, purchasing, inventory taxes and insurance, stores, and other inventory-related costs. It may not be valid for machining or assembly operations and cannot be used to identify incremental overhead costs associated with those operations. Either standard direct material cost or actual direct material cost may be used as the base. As with direct labor, the choice would depend on how the expenses to be associated with direct material change with changes in unit direct material costs.

Units.   A unit activity base is appropriate for overhead costs which are roughly the same on a per unit basis for a particular series of operations, and where alternative activity bases would give a widely varying cost per unit for the same series of operations. To illustrate, the cost of scheduling, expediting, and preparing a customer's order for shipment may be the same on a per unit basis. On the other hand, the direct material cost or direct labor content of the unit shipped may vary greatly from unit to unit, making them inappropriate activity bases for assignment of the customer-related costs just described.

Machine-Hours. Machine-hour rates can be used in very capital-intensive operations where direct labor is quite small on a per unit basis, or where the operating costs of different machines in the production department vary widely depending on the type and size of machine. To illustrate, some manufacturing processes are so automated that the only function of a direct labor classified employee is to monitor the operation or to load and unload the line. The so-called direct labor hour per piece for that operation may be too small and subject to too much change (in percentages terms) to reasonably and consistently relate manufacturing overhead to product. Machine-hours may be more consistent and meaningful.

As another illustration, a production department may consist of large and small presses, each producing different parts. Separate machine-hour rates could be developed for the large and small presses which recognize the inherent difference in operating costs between the two types of machines.

Other. Other activity bases are limited only by imagination, degree of sophisticated desired, and data available. For example, square inches plated, quantity (pounds or gallons) of material processed, and indirect labor hours per piece are but a few of the other activity bases which could be used.

Development of Rate. Development of the overhead rate, once all overhead is allocated and the activity base is chosen, is simple. The rate is simply the total allocated cost in the particular pool divided by the total activity for the same period of time. For example, if the total allocated overhead for production Cost Center A is $25,000 and (assuming direct labor hours is the activity base) total direct labor hours are 1,000, the overhead rate for Cost Center A is $25 per direct labor hour. A product produced by Cost Center A requiring two hours per piece would have a unit overhead cost of 2 hours × $25 per hour or $50.

Note, however, that this product may pass through other cost centers and, hence, would have a total overhead cost equal to the sum of the unit overhead costs computed in each cost center. Different activity bases could be used for each department. The table following shows how total overhead cost for a product could be calculated:

Product Z Unit Overhead Cost

Cost Center	Activity Base	Cost Center Rate	Product Z Reqt. per Unit	Product Z Unit OH Cost
Production Department A	Direct labor hours	$25 per hr.	2.0 hrs.	$50.00
Production Department B	Direct labor hours	$10 per hr.	3.0 hrs.	30.00
Material Class F	Material cost	5%	$100	5.00
—	Unit	$ 3.50 per unit	1 unit	3.50
		Total Product Z unit overhead cost.............		$88.50

There are several pitfalls which must be kept in mind when rates are developed:

1. Material overhead rates must be developed by material category to recognize differences in relative material cost per weight or size, ordering and receiving practices, and inventory turnover. Product Y, for example, may cost the same as Product Z, but have ten times the bulk and weight. Moreover, Product Z may be individually ordered and inspected, whereas Product Y is ordered on a blanket order in large quantities and only spot-checked upon receipt. On the other hand, both products could have the same cost, size, and weight, but one could have a high inventory turnover and the other a low turnover. Therefore, the use of one material overhead rate to cover such costs as purchasing, receiving inspection, stores, and inventory associated costs would distort the actual overhead cost incurred for each type of material.

2. If a production cost center's manufacturing overhead rate is expressed as a percent of the total direct labor for that cost center, application of that overhead rate to a wage other than the cost center average may give misleading results.

3. If direct material or direct labor manufacturing overhead rates are based on standard costs, erroneous results are possible if those rates are applied to actual direct material and direct labor costs and vice versa.

4. High- and low-volume parts produced by the same cost center may have different overhead costs incurred for them than the costs that would be indicated by use of one cost center rate. The high-volume parts, for example, may be produced in capital-intensive operations with large lot sizes, while low-volume parts are pro-

duced in labor-intensive operations in low lot sizes (high setup cost per piece).

In summary, a manufacturing overhead rate is simply a means of applying manufacturing overhead cost to each unit of product produced. Rates should be verified by extending the volumes times activity bases times the manufacturing overhead rates and summing the results. The total should agree with the total overhead to be allocated or an error has occurred in the allocation process.

FURTHER CONSIDERATIONS

Degree of Sophistication

The most important factor influencing the degree of sophistication is the need for or use of the rate. What is the purpose of the allocation? Who will use the information? How will it be used? The objectives must be clearly in mind before the allocation methodology can be determined.

Other factors influence the level of accuracy and detail needed. The size of the operation and the type of variety of products produced, for example, would influence allocation methods. A one-plant, one-product operation would probably have a simple overhead allocation process, while a multiplant, multiproduct operation would have a more sophisticated process—particularly if the industry were highly competitive. In general, the degree of sophistication should increase as the number and variety of products increases.

The manufacturing process itself affects the allocation process. A company having both high overhead, capital-intensive operations and low overhead, labor-intensive operations will no doubt have a more refined allocation process than a company with only labor-intensive operations. Basically, the level of detail required varies with the number of different types of manufacturing processes.

Still another factor affecting the amount of effort expended in overhead allocation is the sensitivity of the final result. If manufacturing overhead is a small portion of total product cost, it may not pay to spend a great amount of time determining product manufacturing overhead. Likewise, if the majority of manufacturing overhead cannot be allocated on a specific and meaningful basis, it may not make sense to spend an inordinate amount of time allocating minor overhead items. In other words, the effect on the final result, in either absolute dollars or percentage difference in product cost, should guide the amount of analysis performed to allocate manufacturing overhead.

Common Overhead Costs

Any time one plant produces more than one product, common costs will be incurred. The amount of common cost in any one product will, of course, vary with the type of product and the manufacturing process. Awareness of the relative amount of common overhead in the manufacturing overhead allocated for any planning or analysis study is necessary to properly identify the relevant costs.

Old and New Facilities

Whenever the same product is produced at more than one plant, management has a tendency to compare unit product costs. Even if the same manufacturing overhead allocation methodology is used at each plant, costs will most likely differ. A major difference may arise from the difference in facilities cost. Thus, the difference in cost may be primarily caused by the difference in depreciation expense between an old and a new facility rather than by operating efficiency. This should be made clear to nonfinancial users of cost allocation data.

Replacement Cost.   An alternative approach would be to use replacement cost as the basis for depreciation. However, there may be reasons to use replacement cost other than to eliminate the difference in product cost for old versus new facilities. Development of product cost including allocation of depreciation on asset replacement cost could be beneficial in various make-or-buy, capacity expansion, strategic planning, and pricing decisions.

Start-Up and Idle Capacity

The method of handling start-up or idle capacity costs in manufacturing overhead allocation goes back to the basic question: Why is overhead being allocated?

In a start-up situation, management usually wants to know what the cost of the product is versus budgeted cost, and also what the indicated mature cost of the product is. This means start-up expenses should be properly identified and allocated, but segregated in the allocation work papers (or even in the rates) to facilitate analysis.

Idle capacity should be treated as common manufacturing overhead unless it can be attributed to a particular product. Even then, it should only be assigned to the product if the nature of the product and product volume are such that the idle capacity is necessary at times for that particular product because of business cycle or seasonality factors.

Financial Analysis

Financial analysis needs are too varied to be satisfied only by product cost rates. Detail such as shown in Exhibit 6 is helpful in analytical studies because it allows flexibility in revising certain elements of the rates or in using portions of the rate to project expense levels in a similar operation.

As an illustration, to estimate cash flow for a particular product, depreciation expense must be distinguishable from other product overhead. With some foresight, depreciation expense can be segregated in the manufacturing overhead rate detail. As another example, segregation of salary and wages will enable an easier projection of personnel requirements if a particular product line were to be expanded.

Methodology Change

Be prepared to explain changes in methodology to users of the allocated overhead. Change for the sake of change which results in significantly different results will cause credibility problems. Users (e.g., management, marketing, customers, financial analysts, pricing) will tend to disregard the results of a long and arduous overhead allocation if changes in the results cannot be explained logically and rationally.

Manufacturing Overhead Rate and Unit Cost Misconceptions

Many users of per unit product manufacturing overhead costs do not understand that, although overhead accounting procedures cause overhead costs to *appear* to be variable, in fact unit overhead costs consist of *both* variable *and* fixed elements. In an analysis of *long-term* alternatives, it may be appropriate to treat total overhead as being variable with volume; but in an analysis of short-term alternatives, one should focus only on the overhead costs which are variable with short-run volume changes.

The manufacturing overhead rates are based on expense level assumptions, volume assumptions, and allocation assumptions. Any change in these assumptions will change the rate. Again, the point is that rates cannot be used blindly. They must be modified whenever any of the underlying assumptions are modified.

A misconception related to the overhead variability misconception is that the activity base generates the manufacturing overhead. This is, at best, only partly true. An activity base is merely the best method of relating allocated manufacturing overhead to a product. To illustrate, assume a manufacturing overhead rate is $20 per direct labor hour and that the product produced requires 2.0 labor hours per unit. The unit manufacturing overhead cost would be 2.0 hours × $20 per hour or $40. A common mistake is to assume a 0.5-hour reduction in the labor hours required to produce the product would reduce unit manufacturing overhead cost by $10 (0.5 hours × $20 per hour). Indeed, the manufacturing overhead cost per hour may have increased because of an addition of more automated equipment to obtain the reduction in direct labor hours.

Rates can be used effectively as long as the user understands they are a rough approximation of the real world. It is the responsibility of controllers to understand how rates are to be used so that they can provide relevant information and guidance to the user.

Trends

Several trends are worth mentioning because they may influence the methodology used for manufacturing overhead allocation. The astute controller will be aware of these trends and make changes to his overhead allocation process accordingly.

Capital versus Labor. Manufacturing is becoming more and more capital intensive, a well-known trend. Obviously, this weakens the traditional labor activity basis for manufacturing overhead rates. Even the direct labor concept is changing from the traditional definition of labor which can be directly associated with a given product. Now, direct labor may consist of personnel assigned to monitor or do routine maintenance on completely automated lines. Their time cannot really be directly associated with individual units of product because the line may run at different rates, or because the workers' time on a relative basis may be insignificant to the total manufacturing overhead cost incurred to operate the line. Meaningful manufacturing overhead rates will have to be based on other activity bases such as machine-hours or units.

Government Regulations. Defense contractors are acutely aware of the changes in manufacturing overhead allocation methodology required by the Cost Accounting Standards Board. It appears these requirements will become even more stringent and specific. The IRS has also become more specific as to which costs should be allocated to inventory versus treated as period costs. Multinational companies may find increased government pressure to better identify manufacturing costs associated with various products to improve segment or product profitability reporting by geographic territory, or to justify transfer prices upon which duty or excise taxes are collected.

Society. Basic changes in society will have an impact on manufacturing overhead levels. Shorter workweeks, for example, may require companies to increase basic manufacturing capacity or change manufacturing processes. Increased automation to relieve workers of menial tasks has been a trend for some time. Job redesign to give workers more latitude on what tasks they perform or to broaden the scope of the job from merely production or assembling of one component to the complete assembly of a product has changed the cost structures and activity bases.

Energy. Scarcity of natural resources also has had, and will continue to have, more of an impact on operating methods and cost structures. Natural gas shortages, for example, force companies to curtail production or change to more costly manufacturing methods. Scarcity has also forced costs of utilities and indirect materials up at a much higher rate than labor-related costs. Therefore, utilities and materials are gradually becoming a higher proportion of total manufacturing overhead.

Environmental and Ecological. Costs of complying with government environmental regulations are also changing manufacturing overhead cost structures in numerous ways. Again, utility costs are higher as utility companies pass through costs of added environmental controls. Within a manufacturing concern, manufacturing methods may need to be changed to comply with environmental standards. The requirements of Occupational Safety and Health Act (OSHA) also add to manufacturing overhead costs. Added safety equipment on machines and noise control, for example, adds to the depreciation expense associated with some manufacturing processes.

ADDITIONAL SOURCES

Dearden, John. *Cost Accounting and Financial Control Systems,* chap. 2. Reading, Mass.: Addison-Wesley Publishing Co., Inc., 1973.

Fremgen, James M. *Accounting for Managerial Analysis,* chap. 5. 3d ed. Homewood, Ill.: Richard D. Irwin, Inc., 1976.

Horngren, Charles T. *Cost Accounting: A Managerial Emphasis,* chaps. 15, 16. 4th ed. Englewood Cliffs, N.J.: Prentice-Hall, Inc., 1977.

Livingstone, John L. *Management Planning and Control: Mathematical Models.* New York: McGraw-Hill, Inc., 1970.

Matz, Adolph, and Usry, Milton F. *Cost Accounting Planning and Control,* chaps. 9–11. 6th ed. Cincinnati: South-Western Publishing Co., 1976.

Neuner, John J. W., and Deakin, Edward B. *Cost Accounting: Principles and Practice,* chaps. 9, 10, 12. 9th ed. Homewood, Ill.: Richard D. Irwin, Inc., 1977.

Report on the Feasibility of Applying Uniform Accounting Standards to Negotiated Defense Contracts. Washington, D.C.: U.S. Government Printing Office, January 1970.

Shillinglaw, Gordon. *Managerial Cost Accounting,* chap. 8. 4th ed. Homewood, Ill.: Richard D. Irwin, Inc., 1977.

13

"Direct" (Variable) Costing

Helmut K. Goerling[*]

Costs are expenditures of money in exchange for specific benefits. The cost of a coat provides beneficial protection from inclement weather. In business, costs provide goods and services to the enterprise necessary for its operations.

Costs are incurred for one of two fundamentally different purposes:

1. *For production of goods and services (what the customer actually gets).* These costs relate specifically to producing *individual* units of goods and/or service offered for sale by a business. They occur, therefore, in direct proportion to sales or manufacturing activity; they are volume dependent, that is, *variable*.[1]

2. *Time/capacity costs (period costs).* These costs support the business as such, rather than individual units of goods or service. They are essential to the very existence of an enterprise. Therefore, they are a function of time and capacity during the period or periods a business plans to operate. While the amount of these expenditures is determined by general expectations of total volume *levels* or planned *capacity*, these costs are *not* ex-

[*] Mr. Goerling is President of Davis and Goerling, Inc., management consultants in Chicago.

[1] Many people refer to these costs as "direct" costs (and similarly to fixed costs as "indirect"). However, as pointed out in Chapter 4, direct and variable costs (and indirect and fixed costs) are not synonymous conceptually.

pected to change with each individual unit of activity; that is, they are nonvariable or *fixed*.

No serious dispute ever surrounded the treatment of variable costs. These costs in any cost system are specifically identified and measured by product or service.

But time/capacity costs (or "fixed overhead costs," as they are frequently called) suffered a quite different fate. By definition, any attempt to prorate or average time costs over all units sharing in their benefits (facility rent, supervision, or similar costs) must be recognized as what it is: a procedure which shows fixed time/capacity costs on a per unit basis as if they were variable and escapable with unit-volume change. This includes all techniques of full costing: overhead absorption (burdening) and allocation and distribution of joint costs, no matter how complex, logical, or mathematically precise the techniques may be.

The above premise does not deny that it is desirable to identify the total ("full") cost of a single unit. This is often useful for pricing purposes, or for identifying "weak" products which can no longer be consistently sold at a price in excess of their full costs. But this full-cost approach violates the fact that costs are incurred for the two fundamentally different purposes stated at the outset: unit of activity as opposed to time and capacity.

Variable costing[2] methods deal with costs in their two basic characteristics:

Expenditures which are identifiable in units of product and service.

Enterprise or time costs which are not affected by each individual unit of product or service sold, but which provide basic operating capability and capacity.

The discussion below will focus on three major points: absorption (full) costing, conventional variable costing systems, and profit contribution statements. But first, we must be clear on terminology, particularly the fixed-variable cost dichotomy.

---

[2] The first article describing these methods appeared in 1936 and referred to the methods as "direct costing." That name has stuck, even though the conceptually correct name should be "variable costing." Rather than perpetuate the misnomer, we will use "variable costing" in this chapter.

Terminology Note

If, in the course of this discussion, the reader feels some confusion regarding terminology, he or she is referred to Chapter 4, where all recurrent cost-related terms in this Handbook are explained. Diagrams illustrating some terms related to cost-volume relationships appear in Exhibit 1, below.

As pointed out in detail in Chapter 6, "Using Cost-Volume-Profit Charts," certain assumptions underlie graphs such as those in Exhibit 1. The two most important assumptions are these:

1. The cost-volume relationship is valid only within a specified time period. (Most frequently, this period is one year—but un-

EXHIBIT 1
Graphic Illustration of Cost Behavior

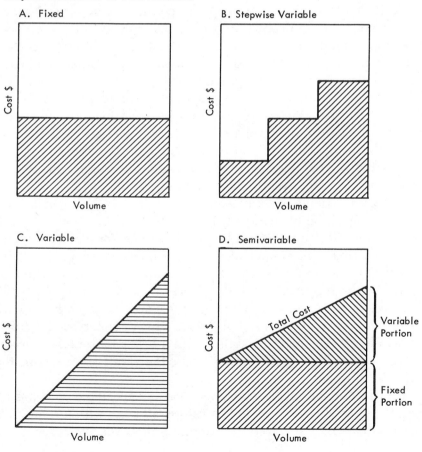

fortunately, usually such graphs are not labeled to indicate the time period of validity.) Over a long enough period of time, *all* costs are likely to vary. Conversely, the shorter a period for which a decision has to be made, the more likely that costs will not vary but will behave in a fixed manner.

2. The graph is valid only within the "zone of applicability" or "relevant range" (range of expected business activity). This "ballpark" estimate of business activity is most important because, as business activity goes beyond the upper limits of this zone, fixed costs are likely to increase significantly. The reverse also holds true; namely, as business declines below the lower limit, fixed costs must be reduced noticeably to retain or regain profitability of the business.

Variable costs, while in concept are constant on a *per unit* basis, in fact are likely to decline on a per unit basis as volume exceeds the upper limit of the zone of applicability, reflecting certain "economies of scale." (Indeed, if *economists* treated marginal costs the way accountants treat variable costs—constant on a per unit basis—many diagrams in economics texts would have to be redrawn!) Greater efficiencies achieved in operations and favorable volume discounts for purchased goods and services will tend to lower the "true" rate per unit of variable costs. However, within a reasonably narrow relevant range, a straight-line approximation of total variable costs is both adequate and useful.

Stepwise variable costs illustrate this principle best, since their zones of applicability are clearly defined by the "risers" on the steps. For instance, if a supervisor is limited (by policy or union contract) to supervising a maximum of 10 workers, the need for the 11th laborer will incrementally increase the cost of supervision (a second supervisor is required). But this increase in cost generates additional capacity (up to 20 workers or 9 more) without further increase in supervisory costs. This means cost of supervision (supervisors) has a zone of applicability with a lower limit of 11 workers and an upper limit of 20 workers. As either limit is exceeded, the cost will change.

It is also important to remember that any specific cost is not always fixed or always variable. Therefore, all costs within a business must be carefully analyzed to determine their specific behavior so that all costing can be based on cost behavior as actually experienced.

Profit versus Contribution Margin. To avoid possible misunderstanding, the following definitions will apply within this discussion:

$$\text{Profit} = \text{Sales revenue less variable costs less fixed costs}$$
$$P = SR - VC - FC$$
$$\text{Contribution} = \text{Sales revenue less variable costs}$$
$$C = SR - VC$$

These two statements can be combined to show:

$$\text{Contribution} = \text{Fixed costs plus profit}$$
$$C = FC + P$$

This last formula displays the use of contribution: first, all fixed costs must be paid; then profit will be generated (after break even) at the *rate* of the per unit contribution margin.

When the discussion is limited to *manufacturing costs,* the terms *gross profit* and *contribution margin* will be used, as follows:

$$\text{Gross profit} = \text{Sales revenue less variable manufacturing costs less fixed manufacturing costs}$$
$$GP = SR - VMC - FMC$$
$$\text{Contribution margin} = \text{Sales revenue less variable manufacturing costs}$$
$$CM = SR - VMC$$

Once again, note that:

$$\text{Contribution margin} = \text{Fixed manufacturing costs plus gross profit}$$
$$CM = FMC + GP$$

With these concepts and terms in mind, we can now proceed to discuss costing systems.

COSTING SYSTEMS

Absorption (Full) Costing

To determine the cost of individual units of goods or service, cost accounting first charges variable costs—material, labor, and variable overhead. But a problem arises when the attempt is made to prorate to individual units the time/capacity costs (fixed overhead), which are incurred *in total* regardless of unit volume. The proponents of this technique argue that this must be done to meet the full costing requirements of generally accepted accounting principles and income tax reporting. While this is true, as we point out in detail in Chapter 31, "Profit versus Profitability: Preparing Meaningful Management Reports," *internal* accounting and reporting procedures frequently can usefully depart from shareholder or tax reporting requirements.

To achieve equitable distribution of time/capacity costs, a measurable, direct time or cost element must be found which presumably occurs in all product units in the same proportion as that in which overhead should be allocated. When a single element (such as direct labor dollars or hours, machine-hours, or material consumed) seems to yield illogical or inequitable results, combinations or completely different bases for overhead allocations are selected. Next, volume for these allocation bases is projected. Total planned period costs divided by volume estimates provide the allocation rates (also called "overhead rates," "absorption rates," and "burden rates"). These rates are applied to the allocation base (e.g., direct labor dollars) for each product.

The process of fixed overhead allocation to individual products or units of production has four major shortcomings:

1. These costs cannot be directly charged to individual units of product because they cannot be identified or measured by unit. Therefore, any method of cost absorption (cost allocation) is based on one or more assumptions and is thus arbitrary.
2. The amount of fixed overhead charged per unit combines a variety of different types of costs such as plant supervision, maintenance, production scheduling, equipment rental or depreciation, building depreciation, property taxes, heat and light, and many more. As a result, any absorption method destroys cost *visibility* since it summarizes a variety of costs which then appear in a lump-sum overhead absorption figure.
3. Most importantly, the allocation of fixed period costs to individual units of production makes these costs *appear* as if they were variable (so much per unit). As a result, overhead amounts appear to be volume dependent: as volume rises, overhead appears to increase, even though actual expenditures have not changed at all. Conversely, as volume declines, overhead

appears to fall even though actual costs remain unchanged. Too often, managers (and even some accountants) forget that *absorbed* overhead, which *looks like* a variable cost, is not the same thing as "real" fixed overhead costs.

4. Absorption requires a volume projection (sales or production forecast). As shortages influence an economy, volume becomes a function of supply rather than demand. This means that sales forecasts are determined by the ability of a business to obtain (make or buy) a product rather than by its capability to sell (as in a surplus economy). Shortages in primary or derivative raw materials or limited transportation capacity (fuel shortage, lower speed limits, too few trucks) make the absorption costing volume assumption difficult due to the uncertainty of volume that can be realized.

Finally, it must be noted that this volume dependence makes fully absorbed per unit product costs poor management decision tools if changes of volume are involved. For instance, assume Product A costs a total of $3 per unit; the cost includes $1 raw material (directly variable, identifiable, and measurable), $1 direct labor (also directly variable), and $1 allocated fixed costs (fixed overhead). Assume also that Product A sells for $4 per unit. This leads to the obvious assumption that the sale of one more unit of Product A results in a gross profit increase of $1. Obviously, profit can only be generated after all fixed costs (total amount) have been paid. Thus, when a manager is trying to estimate the profit impact if volume increases, say, 100 units, he or she cannot simply expect this to be 100 times $1 gross profit. The increase in volume also changes the base of allocation. This in turn will affect the distribution of fixed costs to units resulting in proportionately lesser per unit cost allocation of period costs. Inversely, in case of a volume decline of 100 units, the impact on profit would be in excess of 100 times the $1 gross profit due to a comparable underabsorption situation. In fact, producing and selling an incremental unit of Product A will increase profit by $2, its contribution margin.

Variable Costing Systems

"Cost system" generically refers to the structured accounting for all business costs. Since business costs are incurred for specific benefits either (1) to be consumed in the current period (expenses) or (2) for benefits to be realized in future periods (assets), cost systems must provide appropriate sets of rules and standard procedures to separate costs accordingly.

Cost System Taxonomy.   Cost system taxonomy (classification) is determined by two basic criteria:

1.   Whether the system employs cost targets (standards); and
2.   Treatment of time/capacity costs (period costs).

As their name indicates, *actual* (or custodial) *cost systems* deal with known expenditures (costs actually incurred). By necessity, this makes them backward-looking (history oriented). By contrast, *standard* (or performance) *cost systems* employ the capability to compare preestablished targets (quotas, budgets, standards) to actual results as they become known. This makes them forward-looking (future oriented) as far as the planning of operations is concerned; and result oriented through their capability to measure results against plan. In other respects, actual and standard cost systems are very similar and employ identical concepts of accounting.

Actual cost systems are generally preferred in custom job-shop operations. The reasoning here states that since all work is done to different (usually the customer's) specifications—that is, the tasks are nonrepetitive—no standards can be established in advance. This holds even if bidding for the job is required—and that obviously means that some sort of projection has been made. (See Chapter 7, "Job Order Cost Systems.")

Standard cost systems force managers to plan their work in advance (at least in theory). This capability allows better balancing of capacity and activity and provides direction and stability to business operations. Accountants have long (and successfully) argued for standards to be in effect at least for one year. Yet during the last decade, business dynamics have undergone dramatic changes. Inflationary pressures caused cost increases so great as to render standards virtually meaningless within a few months; consumer tastes have proven more fickle to shorten average brand product life from seven years in the early 1960s to less than four years most recently; and shifting from surplus to shortage of product and/or capacity (or vice versa) has played havoc with forecasts of sales or supply and their coincident impact on business costs. Contemporary standard cost systems, therefore, must have the capability to adjust standards quickly (literally overnight) and to retain several standards during the same year, each properly identified by the date it became effective, and the date it was updated as changing conditions demanded new plans.

Differences in accounting treatment of fixed manufacturing overhead further define cost systems. Allocating fixed manufacturing costs (overhead) to units of production is, as we have said, a popular technique resulting in so-called full cost. If absorption costing is not used, the cost system is referred to as a "variable" or "direct" cost system, so called because it assigns to products only their directly variable manufacturing costs. *Contribution costing* goes one step further: it determines the contribution a unit of product makes towards funding fixed costs and profit by charging *all* (not just manufacturing) variable costs to each product.

Exhibits 2 and 3 contrast absorption (full) and variable costing systems. We described the mechanics of full costing in the previous section, so Exhibit 2 is self-explanatory.

Variable Costing Systems. Variable costing systems (Exhibit 3) differ from absorption cost systems in one basic assumption: it is reasoned that fixed manufacturing overhead costs are simply *period* costs which must be incurred merely to be in business. Typically, period costs do not change with changes in activity (volume) as they must be committed in advance (before the period starts). So why (the reasoning continues) should there be a difference between an office building (the cost of which would be treated as a period cost) and the fixed costs of a manufacturing plant (which would be absorbed under "traditional" costing systems)? Variable cost systems therefore treat all fixed period costs alike, whether they are manufacturing or nonmanufacturing costs. As a result, product costs are calculated per unit on a *variable-cost basis only;* fixed manufacturing costs are then shown in their entirety as an expense of the *time period* in which they were incurred, without attempt to attribute them to individual units of product.

It is obvious that this variable costing approach has a major impact on inventory valuation. Since unit costs in a standard variable cost system do not include a provision for fixed manufacturing costs, inventories are valued at a lesser amount. However, after making an initial downward adjustment in Retained Earnings to reflect the elimination of fixed manufacturing costs from Inventory, variable

EXHIBIT 2
Cost Flow in Full-Absorption Cost Systems*

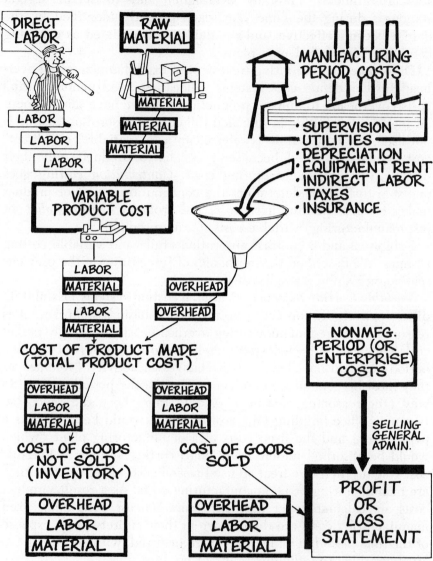

Copyright 1972 by Helmut K. Goerling.

* For simplicity, this diagram assumes that all manufacturing overhead is fixed in nature. In practice, of course, some costs commonly called "overhead" are variable: power to operate productive machinery is one example.

EXHIBIT 3
Cost Flow in Non-Absorption (Variable) Cost Systems*

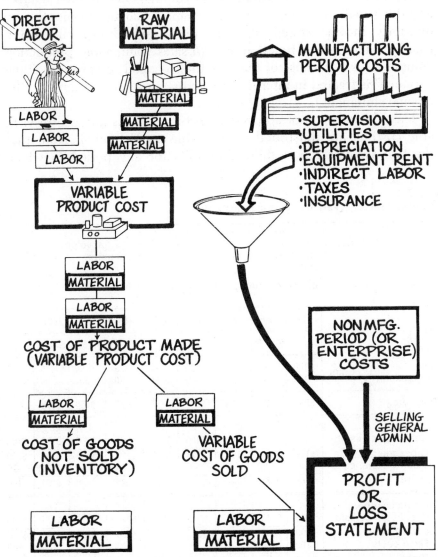

Copyright 1972 by Helmut K. Goerling.

*Again, as in Exhibit 2, for simplicity here we assume that all manufacturing period (over-head) costs are fixed for the relevant time period.

costing has the very desirable attribute of making (internally) reported profit a function *solely* of sales volume. On the other hand—and this usually comes as a surprise to most managers—monthly or quarterly income statements prepared using absorption costing usually make profit a function of *both* sales volume *and* production volume. This is because of the way the so-called "overhead volume variance" is treated in interim statements (as a direct charge to the income statement).

This phenomenon of absorption costing, and its absence in variable costing, are illustrated in the table on Exhibit 4. Note that the two systems report different profits for any period in which

EXHIBIT 4
Full versus "Direct" (Variable) Costing Illustration

Assume:	Unit price $= \$5$	N = Normal volume
	Unit variable costs $= \$3$	$= 100$ units
	Fixed costs $= \$100$	
	Full cost per unit $= \$3 + \dfrac{\$100}{100 \text{ units}} = \$4$	

	(1)	(2)	(3)	(4)	(5)	(6)	(7)	(8)	(9)
	S = P			S > P			S < P		
Sales (S) units	100	80	110	115	90	125	90	75	100
Production (P)	100	80	110	100	80	110	100	80	110
Revenue	$500	$400	$550	$575	$450	$625	$450	$375	$500
Full costing:									
Cost of goods sold	$400	$320	$440	$460	$360	$500	$360	$300	$400
Gross margin	$100	$ 80	$110	$115	$ 90	$125	$ 90	$ 75	$100
Volume variance*	—	(20)	10	—	(20)	10	—	(20)	10
Profit	$100	$ 60	$120	$115	$ 70	$135	$ 90	$ 55	$110
Variable costing:									
Cost of goods sold	$300	$240	$330	$345	$270	$375	$270	$225	$300
Contribution	$200	$160	$220	$230	$180	$250	$180	$150	$200
Fixed costs	100	100	100	100	100	100	100	100	100
Profit	$100	$ 60	$120	$130	$ 80	$150	$ 80	$ 50	$100

Observe   S = P, no profit difference; S > P, greater profit with variable costing; S < P, greater profit with full costing.

Compare columns (1) and (9): same sales, but different profits with full costing; same profits with variable costing. The same phenomenon is demonstrated by comparing (5) and (7).

*Overhead volume variance, caused by underabsorbing fixed costs (if P < N) or overabsorbing them (P > N). For example, in column (2), production volume (80 units) is 20 units below normal volume (100 units); since each unit (at normal volume) was to absorb $1 of fixed costs, costs are underabsorbed by $20, reducing the period's profit by that amount.

sales volume (S) and production volume (P) are not equal (in physical units). By comparing Columns 1 and 9, for example, one can see that with full costing a manager could improve a plant's *apparent* profitability in the period by increasing production. While this might appear (to a manager's unwitting superior) to represent "good" or "improved" performance, in fact it is not, since it costs money to carry the resultant buildup in inventory.

Contribution Systems

Contribution systems are also nonabsorption cost systems. That means that product cost is calculated using variable costs only. Fixed manufacturing costs are treated as period expenses. In this respect, contribution systems are quite similar to variable cost systems.

But here the similarity ends: variable cost systems limit themselves to separating *manufacturing* costs into their variable and fixed components. Nonmanufacturing costs are treated in a conventional manner—shown as period costs "below the (gross margin) line." It is here that contribution cost systems do make an important difference. First of all, they separate all costs incurred in a business into three groups:

1. Variable manufacturing costs;
2. Other variable costs (e.g., sales commissions); and
3. Fixed costs.

By separating costs according to their behavior, contribution cost systems have several unique capabilities:

1. They have built-in break-even analysis capability (see Chapter 6).
2. They reflect costs as those costs *actually* behave (because no absorption allocation or proration is employed).
3. They lend themselves best for (internal) responsibility statements, since they identify all costs which are direct (relevant, pertinent) to a task (product, function) and therefore are under the jurisdiction of one manager.

Summary of Cost Systems

Both actual or standard cost systems can employ the concepts of absorption costing or variable costing, or can be (if only rarely) contribution systems. Contribution systems are usually budget or planning oriented, and would, therefore, be performance systems rather than custodial in nature. Of course, in practice, terminology is often less than precise. For example "standard cost" systems are often assumed to be also "absorption cost" systems. Correctly, cost systems need a double title, such as "standard-absorption" or "actual-variable." This point is illustrated in Exhibit 5.

EXHIBIT 5
Cost Systems Terminology

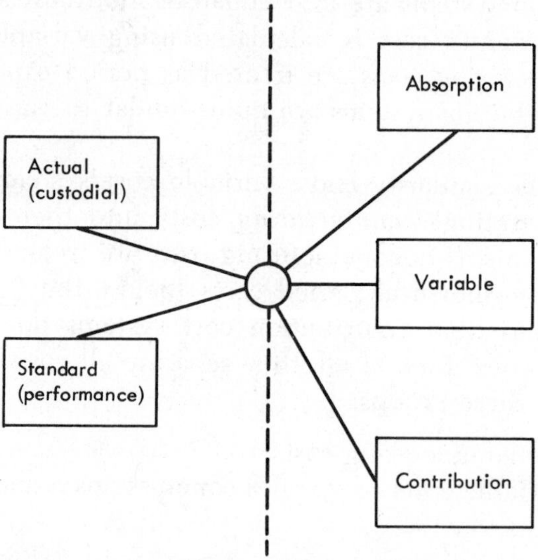

COMPARISON OF FULL-COST AND VARIABLE-COST SYSTEMS

Cost accounting has the most important accounting task from the manager's point of view: the job of telling decision makers precisely how much a product, a service, a function, a project, or a venture costs. It is conceivable that this definition of purpose is overly simplistic. But apparently cost accounting is not very successful in view of the question asked by frustrated managers again and again: "Please, tell me how much this *really* costs.

Many answers have been offered to this question. In fact, it fathered cost accounting in the first place. This is regrettable, since the question is improperly asked. As a result, attempts to provide a single answer to this question are doomed to failure because two assumptions are missing:

1. The precise set of circumstances against which the question is asked. For instance, volume assumptions, manufacturing process, sourcing, risk of obsolescence, warranties, and so on, must be made explicit.
2. How the recipient will use the answer. This could include anything from product costing through make-versus-buy analysis, market development, return-on-investment calculations for equipment or plants, to profit projections or reports to stockholders.

These assumptions play a major role in determining the economic impact of unit transactions. Throughout the following discussion we will bear them in mind. Because of the importance of this issue, variable and absorption costing must be compared in detail.

Inventory Valuation and Reported Profit

The difference in dealing with fixed manufacturing overhead (Exhibits 2 and 3) yields different product costs. In absorption cost systems, products are costed to include an allocated portion of these fixed manufacturing costs; variable cost systems charge only variable product costs to each unit. Therefore, the two methods result in a substantial difference in the valuation of inventory. Full costing calculates a higher unit cost, with the results we will now describe.

If a unit of inventory is made in one period but not sold in that same period, the overhead cost in its inventory value constitutes a cost deferral. The same transaction in a variable cost system results in only the variable product cost being capitalized in inventory, while the fixed overhead is charged against the profit and loss statement for the current period. Thus, inventory changes affect profit calculation. Increases in the physical size of inventory under absorption costing will result in more fixed costs being capitalized in inventory, and higher reported profit for the period than if variable costing were used. This is illustrated in Columns 7–9 in Exhibit 4, where sales (in units) was less than production, and hence there was an inventory buildup.

On the other hand, in a period of inventory decrease, the reverse would be true. Variable cost systems will show higher profits because they are charging only *that* period's fixed production costs to the income statement, whereas a full costing system is "uncapitalizing" more fixed factory costs (some—if not all—actually incurred in *prior* periods) than it is capitalizing in inventory. Columns 4–6 of Exhibit 4 illustrate this phenomenon.

To reiterate—because the point is not widely recognized among managers: variable costing makes gross margin (and other things being equal, profit after S, G&A expenses) solely a function of the quantity of goods *sold;* whereas in full costing, gross margin (after adjustment for overhead volume variance) is impacted *both* by the period's sales volume *and production volume.* Since most managers intuitively think of profits' being generated solely by sales and not being affected by the period's production volume, variable costing is the more "natural" method to use for internal reporting purposes.[3]

Normal Volume and the Concept of Conservatism

As we have observed, per unit prorations of overhead costs are volume dependent: a "normal-volume" assumption must be made in order to assign fixed costs to units of product. Therefore, any bias that affects this volume estimate requires careful evaluation.

"Conservatism" is a stated accounting concept. It requires financial officers to prepare conservative statements. This concept dates back to the mid-thirties, when it was formulated in the wake of the stock market crash of 1929. There was a necessity at that time to rebuild the public's confidence in business as an investment opportunity. However, the allocation of overhead requires a business to estimate its volume base for the forthcoming year. Conceivably, the financial officer in recognition of the conservatism concept might override a sales forecast prepared by the market manager and use a lower number as the volume base. The impact will obviously increase the per unit average of manufacturing overhead; if significant, this could tend to push the price (to maintain acceptable profit margins) beyond the market price established by competition. Needless to say, this in turn would impair the product's chances of achieving the volume forecast prepared by the sales department.

---

[3] It can be argued that it is also more "natural" for shareholder reporting. However, GAAP require assets to be valued at cost, and accountants (rightly) view fixed manufacturing costs as part of the cost of work in process or finished goods inventories.

Most controllers would scoff at the idea of this occurring. However, it must be noted that most product cost sheets do not show the volume base which was used in calculating overhead costs per unit. Therefore, visibility is minimal. It should be noted at this time that there can be no objection to conservatism on the controller's part in evaluating projected sales; however, a word of caution is in order to urge avoidance of making changes in the sales forecast/allocation base without making this change known and visible.

Ratio of Direct to Indirect Costs

The ratio of direct to indirect costs plays an important role in absorption systems. As volume falls, direct product costs are proportionately lower than indirect manufacturing costs, and absorption rates based on direct costs (or a part thereof) can rapidly increase. As such, any inadequacies built into the allocation formulas become greatly amplified. (Overhead rates of more than 200 percent are not impossible or even rare, but obviously may render any allocated amount highly questionable). If management is not alert to the cause of the increase in per unit overhead, there might be a tendency to increase prices as volume falls—likely accelerating the volume downturn.

Contribution Statements

To make operating statements useful and meaningful to managers, the expanded and refined definitions of relevant costs and cost behavior are applied. This means that these statements can be prepared for individual products or services, and entire product lines or divisions; and they can be consolidated into the corporate profit and loss statement.

In this connection, it is obvious that the base of observation shifts and, as a result, so does the definition of direct costs. For instance, the salary of a product manager is *indirect* to individual units of his or her product but *direct* to the product line in total. Similarly, the division general manager's salary is *indirect* to any one of the division's product lines but is *direct* to the total division. Finally, corporate staff services are indirect to individual products and divisions but obviously direct to the total corporation (as opposed to some other business).

EXHIBIT 6

PRODUCT CONTRIBUTION STATEMENT
For Period_____

Budget sales units		Unit of Measure		
		Per Unit	**Amount**	**%**
Net proceeds from sales				

Variable cost of goods sold
  Raw material
  Direct labor				

V D P E Royalties A I R X Freight-out charges R R O P Public warehouse expenses I E D E Spoiled goods A C U N Cash discounts B T C S Distributors' discount L T E Commissions E S Total VDPE				
Variable product contribution				

F D P E   Product administration
I   I   R X   Product advertising
X R O P   Promotions
E E D E   Market research
D C U N   Product development
    T C S   Manufacturing direct
        T E   Special sales representatives
          S   Permanent product exhibits
             Total FDPE				

Direct product contribution Less provision for contingency				
Net direct product contribution (*product manager's responsibility*)				

F C P E   Administration
I   O E X   Factory period costs
X R R P   Factory variances
E P I   E   Sales expense
D O O N   Institutional advertising
    R D S   Public relations
    A   E   Company-owned warehouse
    T   S   Research
    E   Interest
            Total FCPE				

Net profit (loss)				

Contribution statements (Exhibit 6) are oriented specifically to the job of managing the business and are based on clear definitions of individual managers' responsibilities, purposes of costs, cost behavior, and interim reporting concepts.

Individual Managers' Responsibilities.   For responsibility center reports to be equitable and useful, they should reflect the basic notion that managers should not be held accountable for factors which are not controllable within their spheres of responsibility. Therefore, contribution statements should separate controllable and noncontrollable costs: those items that managers can decide upon, versus those costs that are imposed upon them by their superiors or allocated from corporate overhead.

Implementing this concept frequently requires a revision of the existing chart of accounts and department numbers. When businesses were simple (but beyond the capability of one person to run them), conventional task identification referred to marketing, manufacturing, engineering, and finance as the primary tasks within a business. However, as the complexity or product lines and business increased, task identification became vague, since manufacturing might be involved in producing a large number of products. Also, functions such as "truck operations" should probably be made part of a function titled "Delivery of Goods to Purchaser" and include, in addition, the cost of preparing shipping orders, bonding of drivers, insurance of goods while in transit, and all other identifiable delivery expenses. Without such clear identification of the task to be accomplished and all costs necessary to accomplish it, value analysis cannot be executed from accounting statements.

As another example, we would regroup the chart of accounts for Material Handling and Storage as follows:

Direct Material Handling and Storage Cost
    Labor
    Equipment Availability
    Equipment Maintenance
    Warehouse Space
    Warehouse Utilities
    Warehouse Security
    Insurance
    Pilferage/Spoilage
    Risk of Obsolescense

Indirect Material Handling and Storage Cost
  Cost of Capital
  Property Taxes
  Real Estate Taxes
  Inventory Taxes

Additional identifiers may be necessary for control and analysis to identify specific products, product lines, services or projects which benefit directly, exclusively, or uniquely by specific items of cost. Further it is possible that one product line is marketed to more than one industry, possibly through different channels. Also, the exploration and establishment of foreign markets for domestic products will incur specific costs which should be separately identifiable, rather than proportioned to the sum of domestic and foreign product sales. Therefore, costs may need to be identified to industry, market, or region. Absorption or allocation methods have no place in this sort of cost identification.

Purposes of Costs. Type and purpose are most important identifiers. They indicate the type of cost incurred or the purpose for which money flowed out of a business. Generally, charts of accounts include in their list of cost types items (sometimes called "line items") such as salaries, wages, insurance, utilities, rent, taxes, and many more. To make identification precise and simple, numbers are frequently assigned to each type of cost. A partial conventional list might look as follows:

3. Movable Equipment Costs
     31. Lift Trucks
          311   Rental/Lease
          312   Depreciation
          313   Maintenance/Repair
          315   Insurance
          319   Other
     32. Automobiles
          321   Rental/Lease
          322   Depreciation
          323   Maintenance/Repair
          324   Gas/Oil
          325   Insurance
          329   Other

33. Trucks
    311   Rental/Lease
    332   Depreciation
    333   Maintenance/Repair
    334   Gas/Oil
    335   Insurance
    336   Tolls
    337   Truck Drivers' Meals
    339   Other

Lists of this type presumably contain one title for each significant or routine type of cost. In that context, note account titles such as "other," "miscellaneous," or "unidentified" which are included in many charts: here visibility is not provided but deliberately clouded. Obviously, money is *not* spent for "other," but the true reason or purpose is lost. Often it is argued that these accounts are set up to avoid unnecessarily long charts of accounts. However, as a rule of thumb, I believe that items of more than $100 or which occur repeatedly should not be encoded "other."

Cost identification is important. Planning, execution, and evaluation are all hampered if cost visibility is clouded. Therefore, charts of accounts should not be left solely to accountants to design; operating managers must get involved. Also, if cost details are needed for some purposes, then the chart of accounts is where they must be defined and provided for.

Example:

		Auto rental
		Auto lease
		Gas
		Oil
Auto expense	versus	Lubrication
		Tune-up
		Tires
		Repair
		Insurance
		License

Of course, having the details does not mean that all details must be printed on every report every time unless specifically requested or needed. But the details should be available in the cost system data base.

Cost Behavior. Contribution statements separate costs as follows (and as illustrated in Exhibit 6):

1. Variable direct product expenses (VDPE), regardless of where they might appear on the conventional profit and loss statement. When VDPE is subtracted from revenue, we have variable product contribution.
2. Fixed direct product expenses (FDPE), those costs which specifically benefit the product, service, or function being reported upon. These costs would disappear if this product or function were to be eliminated. Variable product contribution minus FDPE gives direct product contribution. Thus, the difference between revenue and all direct costs, both variable and fixed, becomes the direct contribution or impact on profit that is under the control of one product manager.
3. Fixed corporate period expenses (FCPE) are shown below the direct contribution line merely as an estimate of the fair share of corporate indirect costs which should be borne by this product. These costs are noncontrollable, that is, not under the control of the manager who has prime responsibility of revenues and costs on this statement and, therefore, have been segregated so as not to confuse evaluation of performance.

By separating costs according to their behavior and relevance, contribution statements have the several unique capabilities earlier alleged: built-in break-even analysis capability; reflection of "true" cost behavior (because no allocations are employed); and they lend themselves best for (internal) responsibility statements, since they identify all costs which are relevant to a product, task, or function, and therefore are under the jurisdiction of one manager.

Interim Reports. Progress or interim reports under contribution-type reporting are prepared differently from the conventional formats. As long as fixed period costs are essentially committed in their entirety *up to a year in advance,* it could be improper to report quarterly (or monthly) progress showing profit that is predicated on revenues received during only one quarter (month), because few product lines are void of at least some seasonality. With this in mind, fixed costs will be earned in other than equal quarterly (monthly) installments. Also, profit really cannot be generated in a business at all until such time that all fixed costs have been paid for.

EXHIBIT 7

INTERIM REPORT FOR FIRST QUARTER		
Net sales revenue		$9,535,000

Variable direct product expenses:
  Variable cost of goods sold
  Freight and warehousing
  Sales commission
  Cash discounts
	$2,522,000
	518,000
	1,310,000
	125,000
		
		$4,475,000

Variable product contribution		$5,060,000 ←

Fixed direct product expenses as
  budgeted for the year:
  Product administration
  Product advertising
  Promotions
  Market research
  Product development
	
	$ 240,000
	821,000
	313,000
	150,000
	198,000
		
		$1,722,000

Fixed corporate period expenses
  as budgeted for the year:
  Administration
  Manufacturing
  Selling
  Interest
  Institutional advertising
	
	$ 831,000
	572,000
	1,260,000
	465,000
	950,000
		
		$4,078,000

Total fixed expenses for the year		$5,800,000
Estimated fixed expense not yet recovered		$ (740,000)
Planned recovery first quarter (40%)		$2,320,000 ←
Potential profit to plan First quarter earnings per share (1,000,000 shares outstanding)		$2,740,000 ← $2.74 per share

The Interim Report Format in Exhibit 7 allows clearest possible visibility of progress on an annual target and can be used for quarterly or monthly increments.

SUMMARY

Absorption (full) costing, though required for shareholder and income tax reporting, has serious shortcomings as an *internal* reporting technique. Foremost of these disadvantages are (1) it is potentially misleading because it makes fixed factory overhead costs *appear* to be variable; and (2) it makes profit in interim reports a function of both sales and production volumes, rather than solely sales volume.

Variable costing addresses these two weaknesses. Moreover, if variable costing is carried one step further to the notion of contribution statements, it facilitates visibility of those items controllable by individual responsibility center managers, and therefore results in a more equitable and useful internal reporting system.

ADDITIONAL SOURCES

McCormick, Edmund J.   "Sharpening the Competitive Edge for Profits." *Financial Executive*, April 1975, p. 22.

Mullis, Elbert N.   "Variable Budgeting for Financial Planning and Control." *Management Accounting*, February 1975, p. 43.

Neuner, John J. W., and Deakin, Edward B.   *Cost Accounting: Principles and Practice*, chap. 17. 9th ed. Homewood, Ill.: Richard D. Irwin, Inc., 1977.

Shillinglaw, Gordon.   *Managerial Cost Accounting*, chap. 4. 4th ed. Homewood, Ill.: Richard D. Irwin, Inc., 1977.

Swalley, Richard W.   "The Benefits of Direct Costing." *Management Accounting*, September 1974, p. 13.

Treacy, John E.   "For Direct Costing in the Steel Industry." *Management Accounting*, June 1977, p. 44.

part three

Financial Analysis for Management Decisions

14

Selecting and Evaluating Potential Acquisitions

Robert J. Pere*

Purpose

The rewards of a well-executed acquisition program are substantial. This chapter will deal both with the requirements for a successful program and with the many potential pitfalls. The latter are emphasized because they are less obvious and readily overlooked in the eagerness to obtain the benefits.

This chapter is written mainly from the buyer's viewpoint. The seller will also find it informative, as it lists pitfalls which the buyer may consider negative factors in the seller's business. The section on "Benefits" may reveal values to the buyer which might not be obvious to the seller.

Benefits of Acquisitions

The main objective of acquiring an operation is to increase the profitability (normally long term) of the buyer's business. In examining a potential acquisition, consideration should be given to possibilities such as the following for increasing profitability.[1] These are only illustrative examples, which the reader can amplify to fit a company's particular situation.

---

* Mr. Pere was formerly Group Vice President and Group Controller at W. R. Grace & Company, with responsibilities for acquisitions and other special studies.

[1] In this chapter, "profitability" is used synonymously with "earnings per share."

1. It may be more advantageous to a company's stockholders to use unneeded cash or an unused line of credit to acquire another company rather than to increase dividends. The resulting increase in earnings per share may more than outweigh the capital outlay. Moreover, increased earnings should increase the common stock price, which normally is more advantageous to a shareholder on an after-tax basis than would be an increase in dividends.

2. Frequently it is more advantageous to use an exchange of stock when the buyer's shares have a higher price/earnings ratio than the seller's. If the transaction can be treated as a pooling of interests, the buyer can afford to pay more than the seller's shares command in the open market and will increase earnings per share, as long as the excess over market value is less than the price/earnings ratio. A simple example illustrates this phenomenon. Assume the following:

	Buyer *Co. A*	*Seller* *Co. B*
Current price per share..................	$50	$50
Projected earnings per share.............	$ 2	$ 3
Projected price/earnings ratio...........	25	16.7

    Under these conditions, Company A can pay up to $75 per share to acquire Company B's stock without diluting the earnings per share (or, equivalently, increasing the P/E ratio).

3. Using a deferred payment plan, where much of the purchase price will be paid from the acquisition's future earnings, can increase profitability of an acquisition by avoiding interest charges on funds that otherwise would have to be borrowed to help finance the acquisition.

4. If it can be arranged, paying a basic amount plus a bonus ("kicker") based on future earnings has a number of advantages. The most obvious is that the earnings will not have been overestimated when considering the purchase price. Additionally, when it is desired to retain the acquiree's former owner/managers in the business, this can be used as an incentive to continue, or improve upon, past performance. There is, however, a danger in such arrangements. The seller may be dissatisfied with the additional controls imposed by being part of

a larger organization, feeling that these controls are only increasing expenses and consequently reducing earnings and the kicker payments. Similarly, the buyer may feel frustrated from being constrained to observe local autonomy, or from taking the blame for causing lower kicker payments.

5. It is occasionally possible to find a firm which can be partially or totally liquidated at a profit, which would provide funds to acquire a larger and/or more profitable company. These special situations can exist either because they have not been discovered by other investors, or due to conservative accounting practices which undervalue the balance sheet (e.g., Lifo inventory valuation, accelerated depreciation, indefinitely deferred taxes, and so on).

6. In an acquisition, some of the objectives may be to obtain the rights to patents, brand names, or the technological or management skills of the employees. (But see below for pitfalls.)

7. Particularly in consumer products, the acquirer may have a strong market position in its local geographical market but face a substantial entry cost to expand into other areas. An acquisition in another such area may represent a more economical alternative to a "grass roots" expansion effort. (A word of caution: These attempts to avoid "threshold" costs have recently been under attack by the FTC.)

8. A number of possibilities may exist for improvement in production efficiencies. The acquirer may have excess plant capacity available which could be utilized if the acquired company's sales volume could be added and its plant closed. If both firms are producing two or more products, a specialization could provide longer production runs by allocating production between the two. Similarly, it may be feasible to abandon the less efficient of the two plants and expand the more efficient one, with a resultant decrease in overall production costs.

9. Although to some people "synergism" is just a slick word, in fact in some instances two companies' resources can be combined with the effect that "the whole is greater than the sum of the (formerly separate) parts." Such synergism can arise from management talent, purchasing knowledge, personal contacts, or sales contacts in the acquired company that will benefit the acquirer's current performance.

10. The use of the new acquisition's financial resources, such as excess cash or special financing arrangements (e.g., low-cost municipal loans), to invest in new profitable projects may increase the acquiring company's profitability.

11. Conversely, the acquirer's ability to contribute to the acquired company financing which is needed for expansion but which is unavailable to the acquiree in the money markets, may make an acquisition attractive.

12. In certain countries there are income tax exemptions, including capital investment credits and possibly export credits, for foreign companies willing to invest. These tax benefits can provide an additional incentive for the acquirer. Even domestically, sometimes low interest rate loans are available to bring industry to a certain region. Similarly, tax-loss carryforward for an acquirer in a related industry may be available, which can reduce the financing needs in a turnaround situation.

Alternatives to Acquisition

It may be possible to obtain the objectives of an acquisition without acquiring the owners' equity of the candidate firm. The following alternatives may be considered:

1. *Acquisition of the assets of the company.* This limits the outlay to those assets required for the desired products, brand name, or additional capacity. Further, responsibility is avoided for any contingent or undisclosed liabilities.

2. *Licensing agreements.* These can be much cheaper than acquiring assets or equity, when seeking technology or brandname use. This technique is applicable where a limited geographical area is to be covered or a product's future is limited or uncertain, since the benefits to the licensee are usually less than those pertaining to an equity interest. This arrangement can also be used in the acquisition program as a way of becoming more familiar with the products and markets before deciding on full acquisition.

3. *Joint ventures.* These are a possibility when the potential acquisition does not wish to sell all, or part, of the current operation but is unable to finance expansion into new markets.

While there have been some successful long-term joint ventures, there is a danger of the ventures falling out in the long term. The venturer contributing the know-how easily forgets that he or she could never have made the success without the other's funds, distribution system, or whatever. This technique is, however, useful for short-term operations (e.g., products with a short remaining life, such as fad items).

4. *Sales agencies.* These can be considered where the objective is to round out the product line or where the agent has a distribution system in place which the acquiring company would find expensive to duplicate.

Acquisition Policy

While some firms have been successful in expanding profitably by considering every opportunity presented, it is safer to develop an acquisition policy which will concentrate on certain types of prospects. By limiting the alternatives, much time is saved but, more importantly, many errors can be avoided. In developing a policy, the later section on pitfalls should be also useful. The special problems of foreign acquisitions are described in a still later section.

The first step in developing an acquisition policy is organization. It is highly important to assemble a team which includes the chief executive officer; otherwise, much work and money might be spent on evaluation of potential candidates that will not be supported in a recommendation to the board of directors. The organization should be centralized in order to prevent duplication of effort. In some large companies, it is not unknown to have two divisions competing for the same acquisition. There might also exist differing acquisition objectives in any decentralized organization. The overall comparison of alternative return on investment opportunities is also facilitated. The team should include financial and tax experts, marketing and production personnel as well as attorneys, and, of course, when technical know-how is the objective, R&D people. Some companies find it desirable to include an outside director to counterbalance the enthusiasm of the management team. This choice depends on the quality of such individual, as well as the selection of the whole management team. The outside director may prove to be a rubber stamp, due to lack of a feeling of responsibility, preoccupation with principal work, or loss of touch with—or lack of knowledge of—current business practices or technology.

For the development of the specific acquisition policy the following areas should be considered:

1. *Affinity with current operations.* The acquiring company's managers will be better able to control and assist the acquired company when they are familiar with the business. Such affinity could be in technology, production equipment, markets and marketing techniques, or any combination thereof. In urging affinity as a principle basis for setting acquisition policy, it is not intended to be too literal. History abounds with examples of the mistakes of a too-narrow definition: railroads that did not realize they were in the public transportation business; motion-picture producers who fought television; and even carriage makers who sponsored legislation against the horseless carriage. In fact, the possibility of abandoning, at least partially, the current product lines in favor of those offering better future potential should never be overlooked.

2. *Affinity of management techniques and objectives.* Where the purchaser is a large public corporation and the seller is a closely held private company, this affinity will not normally exist at the time of acquisition but should be created as rapidly as possible, unless it is intended to replace the management of the acquired firm.

3. *Profitability.* This criterion should take precedence over size as the main criterion for evaluating a prospective acquisition. The prestige of size can be a temptation which may result in lesser profitability.

4. *Extent of the acquisition program.* A realistic maximum should be placed on this extent. Overleveraging (too high a debt/equity ratio) can be dangerous. Naturally, this limit should be revised as the financial condition of the acquiring company changes.

5. *Establishment of a desired rate of return.* Setting this rate is difficult. Some parameters normally involved are the company's historical rate; the rate earned by others in the business; the rate earned by another company in the industry which has been judged "well managed"; and—most importantly—the company's cost of capital and alternative uses of those capital investment funds.

An integral part of acquisition policy is the plan to finance acquisitions. This will depend on conditions specific to the acquirer: one with a high price/earnings ratio will prefer exchanges of stock; those whose stock is undervalued will prefer cash; in either case, the availability of excess cash, or credit, may be the overriding consideration. Usually it is advisable to keep flexible on these matters, since what the buyer prefers to do is not necessarily acceptable to the seller.

With regard to the desires of the seller, another policy consideration is involved. The management of the prospect may be dissatisfied with the terms offered, or even opposed to any sale. If the acquisition is expected to benefit the acquirer substantially and the offering price seems to be reasonable, the candidate firm's stockholders can be approached directly with a tender offer. This technique is more expensive than having the management's concurrence, as stockholder lists must be obtained (and frequently by litigation), mailings must be made either to solicit stock or proxies, and so on. In addition, if the effort is successful, the acquiring company will be in possession of a company with an alienated management. Nevertheless in some instances this tactic may be beneficial.

It should be noted that federal law requires the purchaser of 5 percent or more of the equity of a company to make such fact public and state his or her intentions. In this manner the management of the prospective acquisition is forewarned of any attempts to buy control in the open market.

The Search for Potential Acquisitions

The balance between in-house and outside assistance in finding potential acquisitions is largely a factor of the size of the acquiring company. In any event, the acquirer should maintain centralized control of the efforts, since its objectives are paramount.

An initial study of the various markets which show the most promise of future growth will be of distinct advantage, not only in identifying those acquisition candidates most worthy of consideration but also in evaluating the desirability of continuing efforts in the acquirer's own business. This study can be rather economically accomplished by a review of the current literature of those who supply investment advice: for example, Moody's, Standard and Poor's, Dun and Bradstreet, Value Line, and stock brokers with a good in-house investment research capability. Such information can be used as input into simple computer models designed to provide a rapid comparative ranking of the fields and specific companies according to how well they fit the acquirer's investment objectives (e.g., earnings per share, ROI, debt/capitalization ratio, and so on).

While in-house efforts are essential to establish the areas to be searched, using outside assistance in finding candidates for acquisition helps assure that all firms in such areas are brought to the attention of the searcher's management. In particular, information on privately held firms' statistics is not always available to the public. Among the sources of information on such companies are commercial banks, investment bankers, stock brokers, and professional merger consultants, who in their roles as finders usually have access to otherwise private information. In addition, business opportunities advertisements in newspapers and trade magazines, placed either by the acquiring company or by the prospective acquisition, can be used to identify candidates.

In all cases, an initial agreement should be made on the magnitude of the finder's fee to be paid. Normally this will be a percentage of the purchase price which decreases as the magnitude of the price increases. These rates change with the economic climate.[2] Thus, it will be wise to seek advice before establishing the offered rate. Such advice may be obtained from bankers, attorneys, consultants, or even from personal friends who are actively engaged in acquisitions.

A particular word of caution is warranted in the use of outsiders to search for the potential acquisition. There are some finders who will approach the acquirer with supposed opportunities, and then, after ascertaining interest, will see if the prospect is also interested. In this manner, they may collect a double fee and represent both sides to the transaction. The acquiring firm should make sure that anyone approaching it actually represents the prospect.

Evaluation of the Potential Acquisition

The evaluation stage is one of the most critical, since it will form the basis for the two most important decisions: whether to proceed

---

[2] At the writing of this chapter, such fees varied from 5 percent of acquisition cost for $1 million or less, to 1 percent (on a step basis) for $5 million acquisitions (e.g., 5 percent for the first $1 million, 4 percent for the next $1 million, and so on).

with negotiations; and what price to pay. Since, except for the special short-term gain previously noted, the objective is to increase long-term profitability of the acquirer, the three most important parts of the evaluation are: (1) a forecast of the future market (including price competition) for the prospect's products; (2) an analysis of the prospect's fixed and variable costs, tied to the market forecast in order to project the future stream of earnings; and (3) an evaluation of the candidate firm's management's ability to achieve these projections. A checklist of other items to be considered, or detail behind these three major considerations, is presented later in this section.

Market Analysis. If the market to be entered is different from the acquirer's either from a geographic or product-line standpoint, it will be wise to conduct some market research before coming to a conclusion on the future volume and price levels to be expected. While some information can be gained by reviewing articles and books on the subject, it will be prudent to have a study made by professionals familiar with the particular market.

In arriving at a sales forecast, it is important that consideration be given to the individual products. Most products have a life cycle, and it is essential to know in which phase each product is. It is also important to identify and evaluate competition.

While looking at the total market for the various products, one would normally be discouraged to find that the market in total is declining. There are special cases, however, where entering such a market can be quite profitable, even in the long term. This is true when there is a trend to concentration in the industry, with the larger, more efficient companies expanding, with the decline in general market volume borne by the demise of the smaller, less efficient producers.

An examination of the prospect's new products under development is also important to the marketing evaluation. The history of such product development may give some insight into the management's view of such programs and their success in developing and introducing new products.

Financial Analysis. In making the financial analysis, it may be necessary to restate the figures in order to have them consistent with the accounting practices of the acquirer. This may be due to differences between proprietorship accounting (choice of accounting practices to avoid taxes) and publicly held practice (choice which gives highest earnings per share). In addition, there is the possibility that the acquisition has been "prepared" for sale by showing a constant earnings growth pattern through the choice of legitimate alternative accounting practices. (For more detail on this, see the later section on pitfalls.)

At the risk of repeating other chapters, it should be particularly observed that the analysis of fixed and variable costs must take into account the following:

1. Future price-cost relationships may be altered by increased competition or other factors.
2. Product mix may be changing and therefore so may be overall margins.
3. The prospective acquisition may be operating close to capacity and, therefore, may require an additional capital investment (with resultant increased depreciation) to meet the projections.
4. The change in reporting and control requirements, particularly when a smaller company joins a large one, may impose extra costs in both the clerical and management areas.

In making the evaluation based on improved earnings per share, the accounting requirements of the SEC and the Financial Accounting Standards Board must be explored. The most important accounting distinction is between pooling of interests and treatment as a purchase. Normally, each will affect the reportable earnings per share differently. The ability to treat the transaction as a pooling of interests avoids the necessity of capitalizing and then amortizing "goodwill." As this Handbook goes to press, the FASB is reconsidering the entire acquisition accounting issue, and hence we will not discuss the currently applicable principles as set forth in *Accounting Principles Board Opinions No. 16* and *17*. It should be mentioned, however, that under *APB Opinion No. 16* the choice of pooling of interests or purchase accounting is fixed by the structure of the purchase agreement, not by a discretionary accounting policy decision. This is an area where utilizing outside accounting expertise is a necessity prior to the signing of a letter of intent.

Current accounting practice (*APB Opinion No. 18*) also requires in most cases that the equity method of accounting be used if a minority interest in excess of 20 percent has been acquired. This means that the owner of the minority interest must take into its income its pro rata share of the profits or losses of the company in which it has an interest, whether or not the profits are received as dividends. The other half of this accounting entry is to increase (or, for losses, decrease) the investment account.

The following are also desirable portions of the financial investigation. The degree to which this information can be gathered may depend on the current management's willingness to divulge the information.

1. *Product-line profitability.* This information can yield much interesting information, not only for evaluating future profitability but also for identifying the need for product pruning.
2. *The possibility that the industry may be cyclical.* At present, they may be at the peak of the cycle.
3. *The seasonal nature of the industry.* This may reveal possibilities for the addition of counterseasonal products.
4. *Differences between the acquirer's and acquiree's industries.* Normally, it is considered that good managers can operate in any industry. This is generally true, but only if they recognize that there are some differences that must be learned. More specifically:
   a. Where the dominant product cost is a raw material traded on a world exchange (e.g., agricultural or mineral raw materials), there is a necessity for knowledge of hedging operations.
   b. Capital goods manufacturers may find it difficult to consider advertising in the same light as capital investment when they are entering a consumer-product market.
   c. Entry into defense or other government-associated industries can pose new problems for those not familiar with government procurement procedures.
   d. There are some industries, notably petroleum, where there is a wide variety of products that can be made from the same raw material. Maximizing profits requires keeping abreast of the markets daily, providing flexibility in the production process and its scheduling, and using mathematical models such as linear programming to make product-mix decisions.
5. Estimates of future cash flows, including the need to invest in capital assets and the requirements to service debt.
6. Appraisal of inventory and capital assets for obsolescence.

7. Reviews of independent and tax audits for prior years.
8. Reviews of all employment contracts, profit sharing, stock-option and bonus plans, as well as union contracts and history of labor strife.

Management Ability.   Where it is intended to keep the current management, and in many cases where the plan is to replace it, an evaluation of the staff should be made. This is particularly important when the acquired company is family owned or is otherwise closely held. In addition to the norms of good management competence, an evaluation of the following specific points will be wise:

1. Will the acquisition's managers be able to adapt to being a part of a larger company with possibly different objectives from those they have been following?
2. Will they be able to grow with the expansion plans contemplated? The talent to grow a company from humble beginnings to a sales volume of, say, $15 million to $20 million, does not assure that further growth will not tax their abilities. Superior entrepreneurial ability and the capability to manage by delegation often do not occur in the same individual.
3. Is there extensive nepotism? This may have damaged the morale of the rest of the staff or caused inefficiencies. Also, the plan to replace top management may result in losing an even larger percentage of the staff than planned.
4. What change in incentive is likely to take place after the acquisition? In the closely held company, the acquisition is likely to create a top management that is independently wealthy, causing a reduction in "hunger" for success.
5. Is there a second level of management ready, or at least in training, to take over the top positions?

The best insurance against facing future management problems is to have a successor management available in the wings. Assuming that it is planned to continue with the present management, one or two experienced managers can be employed by headquarters to oversee and learn the intricacies of the new acquisition (but with staff authority only). This may seem to be an expensive way to insure against management failure, but in the long run it may pay for itself. Depending on the relative sizes of the acquirer and the acquisition, such staff members could be "understudying" more than one subsidiary. Perhaps one of the most useful functions of such headquarters staff individuals would be to follow up on the weaknesses discovered during the acquisition evaluation procedure. It is not unusual to find that specific problems identified in the evaluation are promptly forgotten after the acquisition has been consummated.

There are various legal investigations that should be made before, or, if not acceptable to the acquisition's management, shortly after the closing. In the latter case, adequate escrow should be provided to meet the shortcomings. More specifically, the following investigations need to be undertaken:

1. An independent accounting audit.
2. Title searches and encumbrances.
3. Adequacy of insurance coverage.
4. Zoning regulations and the availability of land for expansion.
5. Pollution and environmental problems.
6. Availability of utilities.
7. Leases held, or given, with terms and conditions.
8. Terms and conditions of all long-term contracts, whether sales, purchase, or sales agencies.
9. Patents and trademarks in use and their expiration dates, as well as pending applications.
10. Pending lawsuits with an appraisal of their outcome.
11. Stock ownership of subsidiaries.

This legal checklist is furnished here not to preempt the attorney's function in an acquisition, but rather to emphasize that there are many legal problems that warrant the use of an experienced attorney in the acquisition process. In fact, it is strongly recommended that no documents be signed before receiving such counsel. This is important, not only from the standpoint of protection from the economic pitfalls but from the legal pitfalls as well. Also, the antitrust laws and their application are so complex that expert counsel is required.

Further Steps after the Evaluation

In many cases, all of the evaluation steps cannot be made before the negotiations because of the unwillingness of the prospective acquisition to reveal complete details prior to assurance that the acquirer has a legitimate interest. Full use should be made of any public information in such cases, and indeed in any case, to assure that information supplied is consistent and credible. In order to protect the acquirer against evaluation errors, it is normal to enter into a "letter of intent" agreement specifying that the buyer agrees to buy subject to certain conditions. Among these are substantiation of the financial representations made and the various evaluation checks not already carried out. The most important clause is that the purchase is subject to the approval of the acquirer's board of directors. This enables the purchaser to withdraw completely, or renegotiate terms, if anything untoward is discovered, or unexpectedly develops, before final agreement is reached.

At this stage, it must be kept in mind that there must be a public announcement of the negotiations if the acquirer's sales volume is in excess of $250 million and the potential acquisition has sales of more than $10 million. This FTC requirement tends to offset the advantages of the letter of intent in three ways:

1. The FTC may start an investigation, or seek a temporary restraining order, which may discourage either, or both, parties from further negotiations.
2. Competitors are advised that the prospective acquisition is available.
3. The employee morale of the potential acquisition may deteriorate.

A fourth disadvantage, normally applicable to foreign acquisitions only, is that the potential acquisition's management may wish to keep the transaction confidential from the tax authorities.

The final closing agreement should provide for certain warranties by the seller that asset values have not been overstated; all liabilities have been disclosed; all long-term contracts have been revealed; all titles to property have been properly presented; and that no adverse developments have recently occurred. To back these warranties, it should be provided that a portion of the payment be kept in escrow for a reasonable period of time (normally one to three years, depending on the nature of the risks involved).

As for arriving at a target price for the acquisition, we have previously stated the relevance of ROI and price/earnings ratio considerations. The shrewd seller will try to discern the "suitor's" criteria, as well as considering his or her own reasons for selling, in determining the final asking price. Naturally, both buyer and seller must recognize the realities of the current economic situation as well. If the potential acquirer's long-range forecasts project good results from the acquiree, then the "optimistic" buyer has a negotiating advantage over a pessimistic seller; but such forecasts on the part of the seller do not give this same advantage.

Pitfalls to Be Avoided

The pitfalls encountered in acquisitions are often so obvious that one would not think anyone capable of falling into them. As with most mistakes, they have a way of being more obvious with hindsight. While the pitfalls listed below may seem incongruous, each one in fact represents an actual case. The danger in these pitfalls is not so much in making an unwise acquisition as it is in paying too great a price, or in not having (or not following through on) a plan to overcome the weaknesses revealed. Either of these latter pitfalls is likely to nullify the objective of improving profitability of the acquirer.

Perhaps the most frequent mistake is to pay too high a price for an acquisition which has been "prepared" for selling. Such preparation can be a matter of timing (choosing the peak of a business cycle in which to negotiate), or of manipulation of the accounting policies to improve the historical financial record. Protection against the former is gained from the market analysis.

The manipulation of the accounting policies can be accomplished by a number of means, even under generally accepted accounting principles. The most typical are choices in matching income with expense in such a manner as to give the appearance of a growth record, as follows:

1. Items charged to expense in earlier years, which logically could have been deferred.
2. Accelerated depreciation, causing high charges in the earlier years and smaller charges currently.
3. Ultraconservative provisions for inventory obsolescence in early years, which produce "windfall" profits later when such stock is used or sold.
4. Insufficient current provision for obsolete inventories, depreciation on fixed assets, doubtful accounts, or contingent liabilities,

such as pending lawsuits, tax claims, warranty liability, and accident claims.

5. Continuing to carry on portions of the business that are in a loss position rather than facing the necessity of writing off the assets.
6. Currently capitalizing items that logically could be expensed.
7. Changes in accounting practice:
    a. Lifo to Fifo inventory valuation.
    b. Appraisal write-up of fixed assets.
    c. Earlier billing dates.
    d. Accelerated to straight-line depreciation.
    e. Slower amortization rates of goodwill, patents, or other intangible assets.

In addition to an acquisition candidate's having been "prepared" for sale, the following pitfalls have been observed.

1. The acquired company may now find that its financial resources have improved to the point that it can invest in projects not previously possible. If the parent's management does not have sufficient expertise in the new subsidiary's field, the normal investment control procedures at headquarters may permit such projects to go ahead, even though an in-depth "informed" analysis would reveal that they are not sufficiently profitable to meet the parent's investment criteria. Examples are research and development projects, major advertising campaigns, and expansion projects.[3]
2. It is sometimes forgotten that reputation in a limited geographical market is no assurance that the acquired firm is capable of going national.
3. The acquiree's desire to produce top-quality products may not be matched by a market for such quality.
4. Unfamiliarity of the acquirer with the nature of the acquisition's business may act to the detriment of the profitability of the acquisition. For example, those accustomed to evaluations

---

[3] In one actual instance, "Company X" took its first step into a services industry by acquiring a small, successful firm. The acquired firm had limited financial resources, and therefore had needed bank credit to finance its new "deals." After the acquisition, the acquired operation successfully got funds from the parent for new ventures, but its profit evaporated. A subsequent analysis revealed that the former profitability was due to the bank's refusing financing on questionable deals. Thus the acquired firm's former "success" was more the result of astute bankers than it was of the firm's management capability.

of investment in capital equipment may not realize that the decision to invest in advertising or research and development are analogous. Those not experienced in the necessity to hedge principle raw material purchases markets may feel that such practice is unwarranted speculation.

5. The historical reputation of the acquisition's brand name may favorably—but unjustifiably—predispose the buyer. Qualities may have deteriorated, the market may have changed, or the company may have hurt its reputation while trying to increase current profits in preparation for selling out.

6. The potential acquisition may be too small for the larger corporate climate. The management of a large company tends to impose more formal and centralized reporting and control procedures than may be necessary to insure the continued profitability of the prospect. In addition, the necessity for conforming to audit standards, or to governmental agency or stock exchange regulations, may place too heavy a burden on the smaller operation.

7. A special danger exists in the service industries (e.g., advertising, real estate, management consulting, restaurants, hotels, travel bureaus, and so on) where the profitability may depend heavily on the personnel acquired and their continuance with the firm.

8. The belief that a team spirit will automatically develop, once the acquisition is part of the larger company, is usually not true. The local management does not automatically change its goals or method of management. Thus, what had been thought to be a simple procedure of improving performance by calling attention to poor practices, by offering the benefits of synergism with sister companies, or by suppressing individual unit benefits to the overall good of the parent, is not automatically realized. (One new acquisition actually had a top-management meeting to consider the parent's demand that it turn over its excess cash to the centrally managed cash pool.) While such problems would seem to be a matter of self-defeating efforts and completely illogical, one must consider the mental attitudes of the acquired managers who are no longer "the" top management, or of the subordinates who do not know if or when they may be dismissed. Candor in plans can help, but not completely overcome, this problem. The most persuasive argument, if backed

by actual performance, is that the new atmosphere generates increased personal opportunity for all.

At all stages in the evaluation, it is important not to lose sight of the original objectives being sought in the company's acquisition policy. If the criteria have been well thought out, there is little danger of being carried away by impulse. At the same time, one should be flexible enough to change these criteria if careful consideration seems to warrant this. Obviously, this is part and parcel of the management process.

Postacquisition Policy

Postacquisition policy is essential to success. The important issue is autonomy versus central management. It is almost inevitable that the acquisition's management will feel a loss of autonomy despite promises or intentions to the contrary. They will have to fit into corporate planning and reporting requirements that may be completely strange and, possibly, felt to be useless. This built-in friction should be planned for either by an indoctrination or personnel-replacement program. In the event that there is little affinity between the businesses of the acquirer and the acquisition, it will be wise to add an expert in the new area to the acquiring company's headquarters staff. This individual should be given sufficient latitude to help avoid the imposition of inappropriate disciplines upon the acquired company. It is sometimes felt that local autonomy, combined with central approval of major capital expenditures, will serve to avoid the possibility of local management's investing unwisely from a total corporate standpoint. While such central control is useful to be sure that the local management has thought through its plans, lack of headquarters expertise in each individual business can make the actual approval a more or less automatic exercise.

The postacquisition policy should also include steps to reassure the acquired firm's employees below the top management. The trauma of working in a new environment is not confined to the top level but is very real to all (even when not justified). Perhaps the most persuasive point that can be made, preferably in personal meetings, is the increased opportunity for personal advancement presented to each employee by association with a larger company.

Unless this is actively pursued with a program of internal promotion, there will be a distinct loss of morale.

Special Pitfalls Involved in Foreign Acquisitions

Perhaps the two most important difficulties in acquiring and managing foreign acquisitions are the language barrier and the differences in business practices.

While the language barrier is most obvious, it is frequently felt soluble by the employment of a competent translator. To those who do not speak a second language, or even those who have a working knowledge of another language, it is common to find that the idea persists that there are precise equivalents of American words in everyone's language. A brief encounter with doing business in another country, even in Great Britain, should provide adequate evidence to the contrary. Since communication is one of the prime tools of management, this language barrier cannot be underestimated. Understanding of the problem, on both sides, must exist or negotiations and/or agreements can dissolve into acrimony on breaches of faith, nonperformance of obligations, or even insubordination.

Differences in business practices can be substantial, including differences in accounting practices, nepotism and cronyism, tax evasion, bribery, and kickbacks. One must understand the history of the specific country before outright condemnation of practices which are normally repugnant to the American ethic. In many cases these practices have been fostered by repressive governments which have attempted to despoil the population by extracting every penny possible in taxation as well as a tradition of support for the close-knit family as a protection from poverty. While an American firm may not condone these practices, it must be recognized that if one wishes to do business in these countries, one may be at a competitive disadvantage without conforming to the local mores. For example, it is quite possible for a firm to pay additional taxes (above the legal rate), since some foreign tax authorities will ordinarily assume that tax declarations are false; in one instance a foreign subsidiary with a loss was assessed income taxes.

Some other problems presented by a foreign acquisition include the following:

1. Knowledge of, and expertise in, the need to hedge against risks of monetary exchange fluctuations. As with future commodity transactions, there may be an inclination to consider this a matter of speculation, but the profitability of the acquisition may be seriously impaired if the risk of devaluation or revaluation is not properly insured by currency "swap" contracts.

2. Special government regulations and practices. An investigation of these with regard to business operations is always recommended. Specifically:

   a. Possibility of expropriation.

   b. Ability to export capital or profits.

   c. Need for government approval for foreign investment. The establishment of a joint venture may be the only solution, for example, in certain far eastern countries, due to restrictions. In this connection, investigation should be made of so-called nontariff protectionism. These barriers to free trade can take the form of import quotas, export subsidies, import surcharges, special local specifications on quality or labeling, local subsidies to special industries, delays in processing clearance of imported goods, and so forth. These nontariff barriers can be either a hindrance or a help, depending on which side of the barrier one sits.

   d. Differences in tax laws which allow deductions for expenses not generally recognized in the United States (notably amortization of goodwill or depreciation on reappraisals).

3. Lack of local management's understanding of regulations with regard to U.S. financial reporting requirements.

4. Insurance needs. These are generally underestimated, particularly in the field of product liability.

5. The risk that one has acquired a large percentage of the local market, without realizing how small this is in monetary terms.

6. Latent nationalism which will resist either cooperation with headquarters or sister companies.

7. A disparity of accounting concepts. While previously mentioned, the risk that a foreign concern may have made little attempt to match income with expenses to produce an income statement which is meaningful is even higher than with a domestic one. This results from a concentration on cash flow rather than profit and loss. There may be two sets of books: one for the owners and one for the tax collector. The use of a

public accounting firm, familiar with local practices, can assist in the evaluation. Postacquisition treatment must also be considered, since it is the future stream of earnings that is being purchased. There are a number of legitimate charges (royalties, export commissions, management fees, and so on) that may be acceptable to obtain the same local tax rate.[4]

As mentioned previously, the neglect of such pitfalls can block what otherwise would be an excellent acquisition—and the benefits can be greater in foreign than domestic acquisitions, provided a plan is devised and implemented to correct any problems after acquisition.

Several problems are presented in foreign acquisitions by U.S. government laws on investment and income taxes, controlled by special regulations of the Internal Revenue Service. Since both laws have been in an almost constant state of flux in recent years, it will be wise to consult the most recent regulations before taking any action. Also, acquiring companies should be aware that both regulations are subject to many special conditions depending on percentage ownership, tier of ownership, local tax practices, and classification of the foreign country's economy (e.g., developed, underdeveloped, and so on).

A very special problem is posed by prospective acquisitions located in countries with rampant inflation (notably, many in Latin America), where monetary exchange corrections are made only sporadically (and reluctantly), and then in relatively large amounts. More specifically, the problem is caused by evaluating earnings at the "official" exchange rate, when there is little reason to believe that this represents reality. While such practice reflects generally accepted accounting principles, it does not satisfy management's need for effective financial analysis of a proposed acquisition.

In such cases, it is recommended that an inflation index be constructed to restate dollar earnings to a more realistic base. The lack of accurate demographic statistics in these same countries may require resort to an index of the history of the price fluctuations of the company's purchases. While this runs the risk of assuming that the purchasing is being done efficiently, it is preferable to no ad-

---

[4] Investments in "Controlled Foreign Corporations" receive special U.S. tax treatment; see "Subpart F Income" regulations, and consult tax counsel.

justment. In making these restatements, the eventual accounting requirements should be kept in mind. More specifically, any devaluation will be reported on a balance sheet basis with the change in net working capital being the major consideration. Thus, income will be affected by an exchange gain or loss based on the current assets less the current liabilities.

In this connection, postacquisition policy should provide for a negative working capital position. Since exchange losses are recognized on the U.S. books based on net working capital, a devaluation in terms of the dollar will result in a reportable profit on exchange if the working capital is negative. It will also be wise to adopt the same accounting practices used for analysis in the management control of the new acquisition. The separation of operating results from inflation is equally important after acquisition. (See Chapter 46 for additional discussion of controls in international operations.)

ADDITIONAL SOURCES

Cheek, Logan M. "Corporate Expansion: Predicting Profitability." *Financial Executive*, March 1975, p. 38.

Currie, Edward M. "Acquisition Costing and the Bargaining Area." *Management Accounting*, September 1974, p. 29.

Heath, John. "Valuation Factors and Techniques in Mergers and Acquisitions." *Financial Executive*, April 1972, p. 34.

Howell, Robert A. "Plan to Integrate Your Acquisitions." *Harvard Business Review*, November–December 1970, p. 66.

Kitching, John. "Winning and Losing with European Acquisitions." *Harvard Business Review*, March–April 1974, p. 124.

Levinson, Harry. "A Psychologist Diagnoses Merger Failures." *Harvard Business Review*, March–April 1970, p. 139.

Levitt, Theodore. "Dinosaurs among the Bears and Bulls." *Harvard Business Review*, January–February 1975, p. 41.

McCarthy, George D., and Healy, Robert E. *Valuing a Company: Practices and Procedures*. New York: The Ronald Press Co., 1971.

MacDougal, Gary E., and Malek, Frederic V. "Master Plan for Merger Negotiations." *Harvard Business Review*, January–February 1970, p. 71.

Parker, John M. "The Key Role of Property Appraisals in Mergers and Acquisitions." *Financial Executive*, September 1972, p. 20.

Rockwell, Willard F. "How to Acquire a Company." *Harvard Business Review*, September–October 1968, p. 121.

Seed, Allen H. "Why Corporate Marriages Fail." *Financial Executive*, December 1974, p. 56.

Shad, John S. R. "The Financial Realities of Mergers." *Harvard Business Review*, November–December 1969, p. 133.

Swigart, James A. "Corporate Acquisitions: Taxable or Tax-Free?" *Management Accounting*, November 1975, p. 40.

Troubh, Raymond S. "Purchased Affection: A Primer on Cash Tender Offers." *Harvard Business Review*, July–August 1976, p. 79.

Weston, J. Fred, and Brigham, Eugene F. *Essentials of Managerial Finance*, chaps. 18, 23. 4th ed. Hinsdale, Ill.: The Dryden Press, 1977.

———, and Goudzwaard, Maurice B., eds. *Treasurer's Handbook*, chaps. 44, 45. Homewood, Ill.: Dow Jones-Irwin, 1976.

15

Analyzing Capital Expenditure Proposals

J. L. Murdy*

Maintenance, renewal, and expansion of productive assets continues to be one of the most fundamental management tasks in business. Since this responsibility is so fundamental, it is also one of the most demanding.

Initially, good managers address this issue in the context of the long-range planning and capital budgeting processes.[1] During the long-range planning process and subsequent preparation of the annual capital budget, funding capacities are assessed and resources are allocated to those renewal and expansion projects which most clearly conform with the company's priorities. Very quickly, however, the problem becomes focused in consideration of specific capital expenditure proposals.

This chapter will deal with specific project proposals based on the assumptions that valid long-range plans are already developed for the company and that an annual capital appropriation and expenditure program has been approved by the board of directors.

CAPITAL BUDGETING SEQUENCE

To begin our consideration of capital expenditure proposal analysis, we will first discuss the internal sequence of proposing, reviewing, and approving.

---

* Mr. Murdy is Vice President and Comptroller of Gulf Oil Corporation, Pittsburgh.

[1] The author addresses this matter further in Chapter 17 of J. Fred Weston and Maurice B. Goudzwaard, eds., *The Treasurer's Handbook* (Homewood, Ill.: Dow Jones-Irwin, Inc., 1976).

Proposing

Assuming a multiple-subsidiary or multiple-division organization, most proposals will have been initiated at the operating subsidiary level. Although many companies concentrate their project review capabilities at the home office, the most effective organizational arrangement provides strong development and review abilities at the subsidiary level, while looking to corporate review for broader policy interpretation and coordination where interdivisional issues exist. Hopefully, this does not sound too idealistic. The simple fact of the matter is that mature operating management should insist on thorough review at the subsidiary level rather than submitting an essentially unchallenged proposal to corporate headquarters where staff review is necessarily more removed and generally less sympathetic.

Exhibit 1 shows diagrammatically the sequence of steps in the capital expenditure proposal process.

Processing Approach. Before discussing capital expenditure proposal review techniques, it may be helpful to consider briefly the mechanical aspects of presenting and processing a project. To do this, we should begin with a simple listing of those expenditures which should be subject to evaluation and review disciplines. Following is such a suggested list:

> All significant items accounted for as property, plant, and equipment, including leased assets requiring capitalization under the Financial Accounting Standards Board's rules.
>
> Equity investments in other entities.
>
> Long-term loans and advances to associated companies and ventures.
>
> Major expensed research and exploration programs.

Each of these involves a substantial commitment of company funds which needs to be considered within a system of sound fiscal controls.

Instructions and forms should exist in each company to control capital proposal processing. Although different terms are used to describe this format, it is commonly referred to as the authority for expenditure or "AFE."

Approval of a capital plan or budget generally does not constitute approval to expend funds on specific projects. This approval is

EXHIBIT 1
Capital Expenditure Proposal Sequence

Subsidiary or Division Level

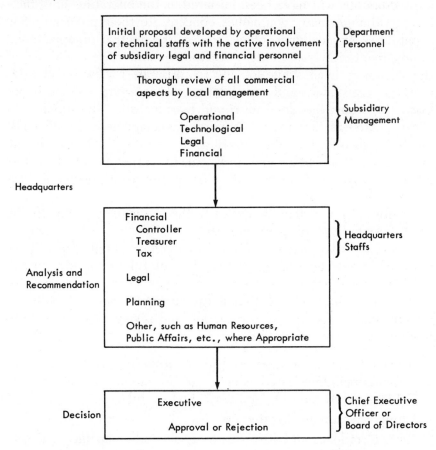

obtained through submission of project AFEs. Exhibit 2 is an example of an AFE form which will be used as the outline of much of the following discussion. Without laboring through a line-by-line discussion of this form, it may be helpful to highlight the purposes this form is intended to fulfill:

Identification of budget category and status.

Brief description of the project.

Basis of capital estimate along with key assumptions and economic premises.

EXHIBIT 2

AUTHORITY FOR EXPENDITURE

ALL DOLLAR AMOUNTS IN THOUSANDS   DATE:

AFE NUMBER

50211

COMPANY & SUB–ELEMENT:	BUDGET DATA:				
	MANDATORY ☐ MAINTENANCE ☐ DISCRETIONARY ☐			BUDGETED $	
				TRANSFER $	
				ADDITION $ _____	
	CATEGORY:			TOTAL $	

NAME & DESCRIPTION:

BASIS OF CAPITAL ESTIMATE:

KEY ASSUMPTIONS & BASIS OF ECONOMICS:

INVESTMENT ITEMS		CURRENT REQUEST	REQUIREMENT OVER LIFE
CAPITAL	NEW MONEY	$	$
	TRF'D ASSETS		
WORKING CAPITAL			
OTHER			
TOTAL INVESTMENT		$	$

ECONOMIC INDICATORS		BASE CASE	EXPANDED CASE	INCREMENTAL CASE
R O C E	FIRST FIVE YEARS	%	%	%
	SECOND FIVE YEARS	%	%	%
	THIRD FIVE YEARS	%	%	%
PAYOUT PERIOD:				
INITIAL EXP. ( )		YRS.	YRS.	YRS.
START UP ( )		YRS.	YRS.	YRS.
DCF RATE		%	%	%

EFFECT ON CORPORATE NET INCOME (LOSS) AFTER U. S. INCOME TAX

	YEAR	AMOUNT		YEAR	AMOUNT
(1)	19_____	$_____	(6)	19_____	$_____
(2)	19_____	$_____	(7)	19_____	$_____
(3)	19_____	$_____	(8)	19_____	$_____
(4)	19_____	$_____	(9)	19_____	$_____
(5)	19_____	$_____	(10)	19_____	$_____

SECONDARY EFFECT

POSITIVE ☐   NEGATIVE ☐

EXPLANATION: _____

_____

_____

_____

APPROVALS – ★SPONSOR

★		FINAL APPROVAL & DATE

EXHIBIT 2 *(continued)*

AUTHORITY FOR EXPENDITURE – PAGE 2

AFE NUMBER

50212

%

ANNUAL RETURN ON CAPITAL EMPLOYED

SENSITIVITY ANALYSES:

			PAYOUT (INITIAL EXP.)
INVESTMENT		DCF	
INCREASE	%		
OTHER:			
VOLUME			
DECREASE	%		
OTHER:			
PRICE			
DECREASE	%		
OTHER:			

			PAYOUT (INITIAL EXP.)
OPERATING EXPENSE		DCF	
INCREASE	%		
OTHER:			
OTHER FACTORS			

CONTINGENT CONSIDERATIONS AND ADDITIONAL COMMENTS:

Clear identification of investment scope and expected economic returns.

Effect on corporate net income over critical periods in the investment and return cycle.

Document appropriate approval sequence.

Chart return on employed capital over the life of the asset and identify the most significant sensitivity issues.

Provide an opportunity for supplementary discussion of related benefits or exposures which are not readily quantifiable or identifiable.

Although there are no inflexible rules in this regard, administration of the capital budget and AFE process is most commonly aligned with the controller function. This arrangement is particularly sensible since monitoring capital commitments and expenditures is basic to the fiscal control process. In addition, some of the most critical determinants used in this process are based on financial statement treatment. And, of course, controller-oriented analytical approaches are directly applicable to capital project evaluations.

Classification. A particularly helpful step in project analysis is to classify a project as being mandatory, maintenance, or discretionary. *Mandatory* identifies funds for which the company is either legally or contractually committed. Such projects commonly involve expenditures required to meet environmental criteria or to provide the facilities necessary to produce products covered by long-term contracts. Determining the mandatory nature of a project is an extremely critical review point. If a project is truly mandatory, it is subjected to a different type of critique. Almost by definition, mandatory projects will not meet normal profitability criteria tests. Judicious selection of least-cost alternatives is a critically important management function which pays excellent dividends from efficiencies which allow more cash flow to be devoted to higher return discretionary spending.

Before discussing maintenance projects, it is worth a few moments' reflection to stop and consider the kind of challenge mandatory projects should receive. Since mandatory proposals invariably involve interpretations of contractual provisions or regulations, the corporate legal department should be expected to show considerable initiative in considering appropriate solutions. Although it is not possible to list all the kinds of circumstances which may make a certain investment mandatory, general rules can be adopted to insure that this classification is not abused. In administering the proposal review program, controllers should satisfy themselves that legal interpretations are obtained in writing following a thorough discussion of the issues and alternatives with involved operating, legal, technical, and financial personnel.

Maintenance capital proposals generally include the normal renewal necessary to maintain existing plant and equipment. As a practical matter, the challenge on maintenance type capital investments is generally less subjective since the needs are usually apparent. Partial replacement of existing facilities is generally a more cut-and-dried decision. The controller's review in these cases will normally emphasize contracting and bidding approaches as well as paying special attention to salvage values and similar effects to obtain some realization from the facilities being scrapped or abandoned.

Discretionary projects are funds intended to enhance economic return, generally through expansion of the existing productive or market base or by investment in new products, new regions, or new businesses. Discretionary spending is growth oriented and demands the finest thinking from each management area.

Although these distinctions seem quite apparent, in actual practice it is often difficult to categorize a given project clearly. At times, a mandatory project proposal may be expanded to provide an incremental profit opportunity. Similarly, a new profit opportunity may also solve an environmental exposure. Capital maintenance and renewal will also frequently allow some technological advance that yields an economic return. These factors should be recognized when they occur, but it is still quite important to identify the driving motivation behind a given investment proposal.

Reviewing

Commercial Aspects. The most essential substantive step in evaluating capital expenditure proposals begins with determining the inherent commercial aspects of the project under consideration. It is hard to overemphasize the importance of this concept since the effectiveness of subsequent review techniques is predicated on a clear understanding of the business purpose to be served by a given project. Unless operating, legal, planning, and financial personnel come to a common understanding on this first and most basic step, an effective coordinated project evaluation is not possible.

Capital expenditure proposals are usually significant business microcosms in themselves. As a result, they will generally have the following four commercial aspects:

Operational.
Technological.
Legal.
Financial.

Although this outline appears separative, it is important to realize that all aspects interact and, therefore, each proposal must be looked at from a broad management, total business point of view. Not infrequently this simple principle is missed. As a result, in those cases reviews tend to be very structured with the operator leaving the legal and financial considerations to those respective staff groups without considering the business totality of a given proposal. Similarly, some accountants and attorneys content themselves with a narrow review of "the numbers" or the "legal form" without feeling a strong responsibility to comment on overall commercial validity. Later sections in this chapter will deal with each of the four major commercial aspects while placing major emphasis on the area of financial review.

Now let us make a more extensive consideration of commercial aspects which must be looked at in conducting an effective business review of capital expenditure proposals at subsidiary and headquarters levels.

Operational and Technological.   The first question which needs to be identified clearly and answered is so basically simple that it is often missed:

"What business purpose is the project proposed to accomplish?"

Obviously, there can be any number of answers to this first question. By way of example, the answer could be any of the following:

Needed to meet existing contractual supply commitments.

Needed to meet environmental standards.

Part of a planned program to modernize existing productive capacity in order to provide cost-competitive products to existing markets.

An element in planned expansion into new marketing areas or new product lines.

Acquisition of additional mineral reserves to maintain or expand position for future period operations.

Operational purposes need to be clearly established and key aspects quantified. These include production systems, volumes, costs, licenses, logistics, and efficiencies. An essential part of most productive facility projects is an explanation of the technology which will be used. Obviously, the financial reviewer is seldom knowledgeable enough to provide an effective challenge of technology. However, as a general rule, situations which involve new technology are usually less predictable than projects which will employ existing technology. Therefore, when technological change is proposed, added concern should be focused on legal arrangements, insurance protection, financing flexibility, and license warranties.

Proposals to produce products must be followed by a prudent assessment of where and how those products will be marketed. This often involves marketing studies which should satisfy management on the questions of realistic volumes, prices, sales terms, and distribution channels. Each of these aspects required candid scrutiny. Some important points on the checklist are:

1. Comparison of projected volumes with relevant past and present experiences:
   a. Within the company.
   b. Competitor experience.
   c. Market share.
   d. Market growth.
   e. Capacity utilization.
2. Pricing premises should be tested against company and competitor experience as well as:
   a. Price versus cost (full and incremental) to assess gross profit margins.
   b. Regulatory factors where governmental controls may be present.
   c. Historical pricing volatility.
3. Sales terms need to be compared with company experience and competitive practices:
   a. Changing industry trends.
   b. Credit exposure and control.

4. Distribution channels should be realistically assessed, especially, if new or expanded channels must be used:
   a. Approach: retail, jobber, agents, and brokers.
   b. Commission, discount practices.
   c. Distribution costs.
   d. Alternative logistics.

From the operating point of view, effective analysis of a capital expenditure proposal requires a hard look at the basic rationale of the specific project along with serious consideration and quantification of possible alternatives. This is much easier said than done. Projects which represent an extension of existing businesses using current technology and process design are certainly easier to analyze and are more comfortably accepted by management compared to new product or new technology proposals. Recognizing this, the analysis process should avoid beating the familiar to death while gingerly sidestepping the analytical difficulties of coming to grips with a new type of commercial proposition.

New ideas require critical assessments of organizational capability. Following is a checklist of considerations which need to be answered to executive management's satisfaction:

How widely is the new process applied in competitor operations?

Will the new technology or new product line require hiring new personnel or can the current personnel contingent handle this project?

What threats of economic or technical obsolescence are already known?

Are share of market and market growth assumptions consistent with current patterns?

All of these questions require candid answers which are often best obtained through face-to-face discussions rather than relying on stacks of written reports. In the entire process of reviewing capital expenditure proposals, particular attention should be paid to keeping documentation and commentary as concise as possible. We are all familiar with the glossy, bound portfolios which so often are received in promotion of an internal project. Such strong selling techniques would be much better reserved for dealing with potential customers rather than being expended in intramural "selling."

Legal. Legal review is an extremely critical element in most capital project proposals. Although it is somewhat presumptuous to list legal review points in the context of controller-oriented analysis, the following outline may be helpful in scoping considerations common to most proposals:

Legal substance:
  Regulatory implications.
  Conformance with general commercial practices.
  Compliance with overriding contractual commitments.
  Protection against risk or competitive infringement.
  Optimum legal vehicle (partnership, corporation, undivided interest, asset ownership).
  Warranties, rights, responsibilities, claims, and so on.

Legal form:
  Contract format.
  Compliance with company policies.
  Clear definitions or formulas if the proposal involves cost- or profit-sharing with outside parties.
  Approach and mechanics for settling disputes.
  Prescribed remedies for defaults or windup in the event circumstances do not develop as originally conceived.

It is not uncommon to find that legal review is self-limiting to form only. This is a critical failing. Valid legal review includes careful attention to substance and general business prudence as well as to the niceties of good legal technique.

A sound capital expenditure analysis system places major emphasis on effective legal review. In this sense, participation and clearance by counsel are absolutely essential ingredients rather than simply necessary evils. Counsel should be involved from the earliest stages of conceptualizing and negotiating a business arrangement right through to its finalization and closing. The old cliche, "An ounce of prevention is worth a pound of cure," contains the basic wisdom of controlling human events and, therefore, commercial events. It is a wise caution to realize that prevention is even better when it comes in doses of more than an ounce.

Although all management elements must work as a team in reviewing capital expenditure proposals, it is a fundamental fact of commercial life that one of the closest alliances should exist between the financial group and the counsel's office. These two groups have a commonality of interests in so many respects that each has a serious responsibility to see that mutual involvement is encouraged throughout the review process. Contrary to popular belief, "nit-picking" points from the general counsel may prove to be some of the most important considerations in a given business arrangement.

Financial Analysis

Without minimizing the importance of operational, technological, and legal reviews, the balance of this chapter will concentrate on financial aspects, since those are generally the controller's special responsibilities.

Financial review should be addressed in its three most significant phases:

Quantification.
Profitability studies.
Financing arrangements.

Exhibit 3 shows in diagram form the key elements in each of these phases.

Investment Constituents. The first step in analyzing a capital expenditure proposal is to quantify clearly its scope of investment. Depending on the type of proposal, this step can be comparatively easy or quite complex. Quantification of an investment should include total company outlays, including investments in noncash working capital, and financing exposure, if the project includes outside guarantees or other contractual undertakings. If an investment is being made in whole or in part with assets other than cash or cash equivalents, reviews should be based on the fair market value of assets invested.

For example, a proposal to replace warehousing facilities for standard manufactured products on an existing site will not require very extensive review to be satisfied that the investment in site, structure, and equipment has been completely quantified. There are few unusual undertakings in such a project and, since it represents replacement rather than expansion, there is little or no increase in noncash working capital. Similarly, the project has no further contingencies or investment exposures. Since the project will be

EXHIBIT 3
Financial Review Phases

Investment Constituent
Quantification

Property, plant, and equipment
Noncash working capital =
    Inventories
    + Receivables
    − Related trade liabilities
Guarantees, warranties, and other
    financial or operating exposures

Profitability Studies

Financial projections
    Earnings, net of tax
    Cash flow, net of tax
    Sensitivity ranges
Investment decision criteria
    Return on capital employed
    Return on equity
    Payout
        From initial investment
        From start-up of operations
    Discounted cash flow
    Present value

Financing Arrangements

General company funds
Special funding
    Asset exchange
    Project financing
    Guarantees
    Deferred revenue sources

funded entirely from existing cash resources, there are no unusual financing considerations.

In contrast to such a simple proposal, a one-of-a-kind joint-venture processing facility for highly radioactive materials has investment constituents which are extremely difficult to quantify. To elaborate, the following outline may be illustrative:

Property, plant, and equipment:

The site may require an extensive buffer zone to satisfy environmental, regulatory, and public-affairs requirements or pressures. Since some of these factors are necessarily judgmental and subjective, there may be significant uncertainties in estimating the costs of site acquisition and preparation.

Facility design is largely experimental and subject to constantly evolving regulatory and licensing changes.

Backup systems and other safeguards may not be subject to realistic assessment pending design finalization.

Because of such uncertainties, contractors will not bid on a fixed-price basis; therefore, estimates must be used without any assurances that cost overruns will be containable.

Noncash working capital:

Depending on proposed contracting approaches and assumed radioactive materials values, inventories, receivables, and payables can fluctuate widely.

Uncertain cyclical processing patterns may require periodic stockpiling or variable credit terms.

Other exposures:

In this type of project, other financial exposures are extensive and must be adequately considered in describing the investment base. First, there are exposures inherent in joint-venture activities. If a general partnership form of agreement is used, each partner is potentially liable for much more than his or her proportionate interest in the venture. Because of this fact, serious attention needs to be paid to assessing the financial capability of each participating partner. Depending on the scope of uncertainties, it would not be wise for two or more partners of widely differing financial capacity to take on major projects. Similar difficulties can arise if the various partners have significantly different tax-paying positions. A so-called 50/50 partnership is really an economic misnomer if each partner is not in essentially the same tax-paying position. This point is often missed in conceptualizing a new venture but becomes extremely critical in negotiating specific terms and subsequent sharing of operating costs and capital replacement.

Joint venture facilities are often funded through guaranteed borrowings or borrowings supported by throughput agreements.

Since these arrangements involve complex operating, legal, and financial undertakings, an effective review should satisfy all concerned parties that terms and conditions are operationally realistic, legally secure, and financially sound.

Profitability Studies. In addressing the review of capital expenditure proposals, each company must choose those profitability or economic return criteria which will be given special attention in assessing the desirability of various projects. Rather than try to pick one economic measurement, management is wise to look at a full array of possible profitability measures to see whether a given project appears attractive from several dimensions. Without attempting to list all possible measures, the following constitutes a practical, workable list which stands up well in actual experience:

ROCE—return on capital employed.

ROE—return on equity.

Payout.

DCF—discounted cash flow.

NPV—net present value.

Invariably, one or another among this list seems to attract more attention from a given management group, but none can be ignored if a project is to be severely challenged.

This chapter will not attempt to analyze specific formula for each criterion. The Appendix to this chapter provides an example of profitability analysis instructions. Several of the books listed under "Additional Sources" at the end of this chapter also contain thorough descriptions of the calculations involved in these techniques. Here, we will attempt to assess the significance of these criteria and suggest appropriate responses to each.

First it is important to realize that the utility of these essentially financial criteria should be apparent to all participants in the capital project proposal and review system. Only a myopic operating management insists an investment is "the thing to do regardless of what *your* numbers show." Obviously, if an investment opportunity is attractive, its validity can be demonstrated and reasonably quantified.

To consider the utility of various profitability analysis criteria, it may be helpful to go back to the basic motivation for investment. *Money should be invested to yield an attractive return within a reasonably current time frame without undertaking avoidable or imprudent risk*. This is such an obvious truism that parts of it are often missed when one is confronted with the high complexity of many investment opportunities in today's commercial environment.

In the context of this truism, each profitability measurement may be judged for its relevancy.

ROCE tells what *average* return an investment will yield over its operating life. This is particularly useful in the sense that ROCE is a common criteria for stock analysis and long-range planning purposes. However, it is imperfect since it does not time-weight returns and is not a useful measure of investment liquidity.

ROE is also helpful in the sense that it conforms with stock analysis critique, but it suffers from the same time-weighting imperfection noted for ROCE.

Payout addresses the issue of having cash at risk over a period of time, but it does not consider postpayout period returns which are the primary goal of any investment. However, its usefulness in assessing the cash-risk period should not be overlooked, especially since long payout periods subject any investment to increased conjecture and uncertainty and therefore to greater risk.

DCF and *NPV* take account of the time value of money. Accordingly, many people argue that these discounting techniques are the only conceptually valid methods of evaluating a project's economics. However, these techniques ignore the "real-world" emphases on the impact a capital project may have on return on investment and earnings per share.

Financing Arrangements. Funding capital expenditures is normally a responsibility of corporate financial management rather than a matter related to individual projects. The treasurer is charged with responsibility for selecting the most appropriate means of financing various funding requirements within a company. For this fundamental reason, project profitability analysis should not be confused with the choice of one mode of financing versus a different mode when comparing the economic attractiveness of different capital projects. Stated another way, a low-return project should not benefit from any enhancement in presentation on the assumption that it will be project financed, while another project will be covered with general purpose funds.

Recognizing this critical principle, it is nevertheless important to identify how a project is to be funded. Special funding should be noted in the AFE presentation, and relevant particulars should be considered during the evaluation process by all interested parties. This is especially important if asset exchange is involved.

There may be instances which justify some variation from this fundamental principle. For instance, risk aspects of a particular project may be so significant that management will not approve the proposal unless those risks can be appropriately shared with third parties through some form of project financing or special-purpose funding. In other circumstances, project financing may provide a unique opportunity to obtain funds at rates more attractive than through general-purpose borrowings, or even to obtain funds that would not be available at all if the project did not exist. Tax-exempt pollution control bonds are a common example of this type of occurrence. In such cases, unattractive project economics are actually enhanced through project financing, since funds raised at very favorable rates cannot be otherwise realized.

Postcompletion Capital Project Evaluations

Postcompletion evaluations of capital projects is an integral aspect of effective fiscal monitoring. Because this topic is covered in the following chapter, this chapter will not attempt to deal with this ancillary aspect of review, other than to note its importance and remind readers that evaluation is in fact a continuing process which needs constantly to relate past experiences to current project proposals. Based on postcompletion reviews, effective checklists should be developed to assist current appraisals approaches.

Conclusion

In summing up this discussion of capital expenditure review, three considerations are key. First, projects have to be looked at from a total business viewpoint. This requires active involvement by all management elements. Second, sound mathematical and analytical techniques should be used to assist the decision-making process, but the inherent limitations of those techniques need to be recognized. Third, the entire process of recommendation and evaluation requires dedication to realism. Pet projects and pet proposers cannot be allowed to dominate the consideration of the critical commercial aspects of capital renewal and expansion.

APPENDIX

I. METHODS OF PROFITABILITY MEASUREMENT

    A. *General*

        All profitability indicators are to be calculated after U.S. and foreign income taxes. The estimated amounts and timing of tax liabilities are to be used when calculating the payout, discounted cash flow rate (DCF), and net present value (NPV); but the income tax expense for financial reporting purposes, including deferred taxes, is to be used for the return on capital employed (ROCE) and effect on corporate net income calculations. Financing costs incurred by the company in providing investment funds for the project normally are not to be included in the computations, except for the effect on corporate net income calculations.

    B. *Profitability Indicators*

        1. *Return on Capital Employed (ROCE)*

            The ROCE is the average income (loss) divided by the average net investment. Where an average loss is incurred, a negative ROCE is to be reflected. For the company's purposes, the ROCE is to be calculated on a calendar-year basis for the first five years, second five years, and third five years, respectively, of the project's life. Preoperational years are included in these time frames, starting with the year of first significant disbursement of funds. Average income is the sum of the project's annual net incomes (losses), after consideration of interperiod tax allocations, for each five-year period divided by five. Preoperational revenues and expense and interest income arising from actual company loans to the project are to be included in the computation of income, but gains or losses on residual values are normally excluded. Minor income and expense items prior to the year of first significant disbursement of funds are to be reflected in the year of first significant expenditure. The average net investment is the sum of the yearly weighted average net book values (investment less accumulated depreciation or other recovery of company investment) for each five-year period divided by five.

2. *Payout Periods*

    Payout periods measure the elapsed time required for a project's cumulative net cash flow to become and remain positive from (*a*) the date of the first significant disbursement of funds, and (*b*) the start-up of operations. Where the company enters into a noncancelable operating lease or a take-or-pay agreement which is not part of the investment financing plan, the amount of the company's total fixed commitment shall be included in the payout calculations. Also, where the company is the recipient of revenue under a noncancelable lease or take-or-pay arrangement, the fixed revenue amount is also to be included in the payout calculations.

3. *Effect on Corporate Net Income (loss)*

    The company's share of the project's net income or loss, as it will be reflected in the company's consolidated financial reports, is to be reported for the initial ten calendar years of the project, including preoperational years. Depreciation, actual interest paid on loans, income taxes, gains or losses on exchange or sale of assets, and so forth, are included in the calculation on the basis of accounting entries actually anticipated to be made. Interperiod tax allocations required under *APB Opinion No. 11* will apply. Net income (loss) shall reflect only the project's impact on the division undertaking the project and will not include any secondary effects accruing to any other corporate element.

4. *Discounted Cash Flow Rate (DCF)**

    DCF calculates the interest rate which discounts the estimated cash inflows of a project to a present value equal to the present value of estimated cash outflows. Calculations are made on a calendar-year basis using

---

* *Editors' Note:* Some companies (and most textbooks) refer to this rate as the "internal rate of return" of a project. This rate is the discount rate which makes a project's NPV equal to zero.

year-end discount factors. Where project revenues and expenses occur in the same calendar year as the initial investment outlay, the net amount is considered the year "zero" cash outflow.

5. *Net Present Value (NPV)*

   NPV is the present value of all cash inflows less the present value of all cash outflows. When the NPV is utilized, it will be calculated over a range of several representative discount rates.

II. PREPARATION OF PROFITABILITY REVIEW

A. *General*
   1. *Forecast Data*
      a. Forecast data should represent the "most probable" estimates of investment, realizations, expenses, and so forth, and give appropriate consideration to the effects of inflation and local economic conditions. Volume, price, and expense forecasts will be based on market price projections. Construction costs should be based on definitive estimates to the extent possible.
      b. For major plant construction projects where a significant part of the funds must be committed before definitive costs or profitability are available, an AFE is to be submitted for the specific, limited commitment. Preliminary economics for the entire project are to be prepared based on available estimates in sufficient detail to identify major investment items and future decision points. Subsequent requests for additional funds will be accompanied by updated economics for the project.
   2. *Basis of Evaluations*
      a. Investment proposals may be evaluated on a freestanding or an incremental basis, as determined by the type of project being evaluated.
      b. In a freestanding project, the proposed investment is usually independent of any existing in-

vestment, except for source material and supply investment per II. B. 8., and is, therefore, evaluated on its own merits.

c. In an incremental project, which normally involves the expansion or modification of an existing facility or business, the expanded project (proposed case) is to be compared with existing operations (base case) to develop the incremental profitability. Profitability indicators are usually presented for the base and proposed cases, as well as for the incremental case. When the profitability of the existing operations is acceptable or when it is such an integral part of the business that the alternative of disposing of the facilities is remote, an incremental evaluation alone can be presented; but the reason(s) for not including the base and proposed cases should be clearly indicated. Justification for a proposed investment to modify or expand an existing facility should not be based on a comparison of the proposal with some alternative modification or expansion plan. However, the alternatives considered and their relative profitability should be discussed in the Narrative Section.

3. *Expenditure Overruns and Changes in Scope*
When supplemental AFE's are submitted, the funds requested are to be segregated between funds applicable to overruns and funds applicable to changes in scope. Separate AFE forms are to be completed for each component of the supplemental request.

B. *Composition of Investment*
1. *Investment* consists of the total asset commitment or exposure to a project, including property, plant, equipment, working capital, maintenance capital, contingent liabilities, and other costs such as financing leases and intangible assets capitalized in accordance with accounting policies. Undefined capital outlays assumed for future general plant improvements and maintenance are included, but are not assumed to be income generating. Investments, loans, and loan guar-

antees for less than wholly owned projects are described in II. D.

2. *Working capital* is to be based on the needs of the particular type of business. Loans to cover temporary cash shortfalls represent additional working capital requirements.

3. *Existing property, plant, and equipment* dedicated exclusively to a project is to be included in the investment at its net fair market sales value (i.e., net of selling expenses and the tax effect from any capital gain or loss) or, if this is not determinable, at its net book value. In calculating the effect on corporate net income, the actual accounting entries anticipated will govern the basis to be used.

4. *Exchange of assets.* The fair market sales value of the asset given in exchange is considered to be the cost of the asset acquired.

5. *Contingent liabilities* associated with the financing plan for the investment, such as loan guarantees, throughput agreements, and take-or-pay agreements (i.e., commitments to pay even if product or service is unavailable—a "hell-or-high-water" clause) represent potential outlays by the company and are included in the project's investment to the extent of the third-party loan which they secure. In the ROCE, this investment is reduced annually in accordance with the actual loan repayments by the loan recipient or other fulfillment of the commitment. In the payout and DCF, the contingent liability is treated as a company cash outlay in the year it is incurred. Subsequent reductions in the actual liability are considered as cash inflows to the company. In calculating the company's income where a loan guarantee or long-term commitment securing a third-party loan is involved, interest income should also be considered as a company receipt to parallel the actual interest on the loan as paid by the loan recipient and reflected in the project's profit or loss.

6. *Financial leverage* to the company is the use of third-party financing for a portion of the investment of a

project which results in the company's receiving a share of the project's income (or loss) proportionately greater than its share of the project's investment requirements.

   a.   Balance sheet leverage exists in those instances where the third-party financing is accorded off-balance-sheet treatment for the company's consolidated accounts and thus the project's total assets are not all included in the company's employed capital. However, such financing arrangements are usually structured in such a manner that the company commits its credit backing to the project through guarantees, commitments, or some other form of support and usually remains exposed in the event of default.

   b.   Economic leverage is the true shifting of project risk to a third party without recourse and is present only in those situations where (1) the company has no legal obligation or commitment to the project other than the equity, loans, or assets it has contributed to the project; and (2) the company provides no form of financing security; and (3) the company has no future exposure or obligation to repay the loan or satisfy a claim in the event the project is unable to do so. In summary, the borrowing must truly be without recourse.

   c.   For profitability analysis purposes, both balance sheet leverage and economic leverage must exist before leveraged economics may be considered.

   d.   The prior approval of the corporate comptroller is required before leveraged economics may be presented.

   e.   In those instances where leveraging is permitted, total project economics on an unleveraged basis must also be presented.

7. *Investment grants* and other capital investment incentives are to be treated as a reduction in the project's investment.

8. *Existing and planned investments* in fixed assets, to

be partially utilized by the proposed project as a source of materials or services, are not to be included in the project's investment, but the project is to be charged for the materials or services as described in II. C. 1.

9. *Residual values* of fixed assets are normally disregarded in the calculation of the profitability measurements unless they have a material effect on the economics and can be forecast with a substantial degree of certainty. Recovery of working capital, and any fixed asset residual values to be included under these guidelines, should be recognized in the year following the last year of the project's life.

C. *Cost Valuations*

1. *Raw materials and services* are to be charged to the project on the basis of market prices. Where such agreements have not been made, the following guidelines apply.

   a. *Raw materials and products,* either produced by the company or purchased from third parties, which will be used in a proposed project are to be charged to the project at estimated market prices for the relevant time period.

   b. *Transportation* is charged at alternative-use values, or operating costs plus a return on investment, for transportation facilities owned by the company and at market cost for transportation facilities not owned by the company. For major projects where specialty transportation to service the facilities will be constructed by the company or obtained under long-term financial leases, the construction costs or capitalized lease costs will be included in the investment and the annual operating expenses charged against revenue.

   c. *All other significant raw materials and major services* are to be valued at market prices.

2. *Depreciation*

   For ROCE, depreciation is based on the methods and useful lives to be used for financial reporting purposes. The net fair market sales values of existing assets dedicated exclusively to a project are depreciated over their remaining useful lives in accordance with corporate depreciation policies. For the effect on corporate net income computations, the anticipated depreciation charges to the company's consolidated accounts are to be used. In calculating income taxes for payout, DCF, and NPV, the appropriate tax bases, depreciation methods, and depreciable lives should be used. Tax depreciation on existing assets is based on the assets' actual bases and remaining lives.

3. *Overhead*

   Incremental overhead is charged to projects for those expenses incurred locally and need not include corporate headquarters' charges.

4. *Income Tax*

   a. Income taxes for projects within the United States are based on the current and anticipated statutory state and federal tax rates. Any applicable investment tax credit is included in the tax calculation. Pretax losses are reduced to an after-tax basis only if tax benefits are assured in the company's overall tax situation.

   b. For projects outside the United States, all foreign and U.S. income taxes are to be recognized. The profitability analysis should be prepared and presented on a "stand-alone" basis in which foreign income taxes and U.S. income taxes, as applicable, are charged to the project at the anticipated statutory rates. To the extent they can be utilized, tax credits arising from foreign taxation of a project's earnings may be used to offset that project's statutory U.S. tax in the economics. Operational losses, for both foreign and U.S. tax purposes, are reduced to an after-tax basis only if the losses would actually reduce the company's foreign income taxes in that country and the tax benefits are assured in the company's overall U.S. tax situation.

   c. For ROCE and the effect on corporate net income, the annual tax provision is the tax expense to be recognized for financial reporting purposes, reflecting the interperiod tax allocation requirements of *APB Opinion No. 11*. For payout, DCF, and NPV, the estimated tax liabilities to be incurred should be used to calculate after-tax cash flows. The time interval between the date of creation of an income tax liability and the actual payment may generally be ignored.

D. *Less Than Wholly Owned Projects*

1. Generally, the company's profitability, as measured by economic indicators, is the same as that of the project. However, the individual circumstances of a particular investment proposal may alter this general relationship; in such cases, the results to the company are to be reported using the overall project results as an intermediate step of the analysis. The comptroller department should be consulted in these instances. Additional considerations to be taken into account when the proposal is a foreign project are indicated in II. E.

2. When the company loans funds, guarantees debt, or incurs other forms of contingent liabilities in excess of its equity ownership in such projects, the unpaid balance of this additional commitment is included as part of the company's investment for the calculation of economic indicators.

3. For those projects whose investment and profits or losses are included in the company's financial statements by way of accounting consolidation, the economic evaluation is made in accordance with the normal guidelines for a wholly owned project, except for adjustments to recognize the minority interest.

4. For those projects where the company's investment and profits are accounted for on a nonconsolidated equity basis, the company's ROCE income is its share of the project's earnings, adjusted to conform to corporate accounting policies, plus interest income to the company's net of withholding taxes, less dividend taxes in the years that dividends are available for distribution. Interest expense arising from direct loans

by the company or a third party is to be charged to the project's earnings prior to calculating the company's share of such earnings. The average net investment for the ROCE is based on the annual carrying value of the investment on the company's consolidated balance sheet plus contingent liabilities outstanding. Undistributed earnings, net of applicable dividend taxes, are part of net investment. In calculating payout, DCF, and NPV, the company's cash outflow includes equity investments, advances, and contingent liabilities. Cash inflow to the company consists of repayments of the investment, reduction of the contingent liabilities, interest net of withholding taxes, and cash available for dividends net of dividend taxes.

5. For those projects where the company's investment and profits are accounted for on a cost basis, the ROCE income consists of dividend and interest income to the company. Investment consists of the company's asset commitment (equity, loans, advances, and contingent liabilities) less capital dividend distributions, loan and advance repayments, and reduction of contingent liabilities. The DCF, payout, and NPV are computed on the basis of the company's disbursements and receipts of cash and the guideline provisions for the handling of contingent liabilities as outlined in II. B. 5. Supplemental economics should also be presented indicating the profitability of the specific project itself, if applicable.

E. *Foreign Projects*
1. Foreign projects should be valued on the basis of cash invested and contingent liabilities incurred by the company and cash fully available and repatriable to the company. Therefore, local accounting procedures, legal restrictions on profit distributions and repatriation of funds, currency regulations, availability of foreign exchange, withholding taxes on interest and dividends, and political and economic considerations and trends must be considered in foreign projects. The ROCE income is generally based on actual

accounting results, as adjusted to conform to corporate accounting policies, reduced by withholding taxes on interest and dividends. For payment, DCF, and NPV, cash flow to the company is the U.S. dollar equivalent of cash available for distribution, net of applicable taxes, assuming the funds are remitted as interest or dividends.

2. Forecast data for receipts and disbursements of funds in local currencies should be developed initially in the local currency and translated to dollars at the projected exchange rates.

ADDITIONAL SOURCES

Also see Additional Sources for Chapter 17.

Anthony, Robert N., and Reece, James S. *Management Accounting Principles*, chap. 19. 3d ed. Homewood, Ill.: Richard D. Irwin, Inc., 1975.

Chapin, Troy A. "Selling DCFR." *Management Accounting*, December 1975, p. 45.

Day, James E. "A Screening Model for Investment Proposals." *Management Accounting*, January 1975, p. 48.

Donaldson, Gordon. "Strategic Hurdle Rates for Capital Investment." *Harvard Business Review*, March–April 1972, p. 50.

Fremgen, James M. *Accounting for Managerial Analysis*, chaps. 16, 17. 3d ed. Homewood, Ill.: Richard D. Irwin, Inc., 1976.

———. "Capital Budgeting Practices: A Survey." *Management Accounting*, May 1973, p. 19.

Horngren, Charles T. *Cost Accounting: A Managerial Emphasis*, chaps. 12, 13. 4th ed. Englewood Cliffs, N.J.: Prentice-Hall, Inc., 1977.

Jones, David A. "Capital Budgeting: Mixing Up the Balance Sheet." *Financial Executive*, April 1976, p. 45.

Lerner, Eugene M. and Rappaport, Alfred. "Limit DCF in Capital Budgeting." *Harvard Business Review*, September–October 1968, p. 133.

Neuner, John J. W., and Deakin, Edward B. *Cost Accounting: Principles and Practice*, chap. 21. 9th ed. Homewood, Ill.: Richard D. Irwin, Inc., 1977.

Oakford, Robert V. *Capital Budgeting: A Quantitative Evaluation of Investment Alternatives.* New York: The Ronald Press Co., 1970.

Quirin, G. David. *The Capital Expenditure Decision.* Homewood, Ill.: Richard D. Irwin, Inc., 1967.

Shillinglaw, Gordon. *Managerial Cost Accounting,* chaps. 14, 15. 4th ed. Homewood, Ill.: Richard D. Irwin, Inc., 1977.

Sihler, William W. "Presenting Capital Expenditure Requests to Management." *Financial Executive,* April 1973, p. 72.

Weston, J. Fred, and Brigham, Eugene F. *Essentials of Managerial Finance,* chap. 11. 4th ed. Hinsdale, Ill.: The Dryden Press, 1977.

———, and Goudzwaard, Maurice B., eds. *Treasurer's Handbook,* chaps. 15–17. Homewood, Ill.: Dow Jones-Irwin, 1976.

16

Incorporating Risk in Capital Expenditure Analysis

David B. Hertz*

UNCERTAINTY AND RISK

An investment's intrinsic worth is measurable in terms of the stream of values (including salvage) it returns to the investor over its useful life. The prospective worth of a capital investment, therefore, can be evaluated by the stream of net returns (in whatever form) that is expected to be forthcoming once it has been made. The investment inputs and returns usually (but not always, or necessarily) are measured in monetary units. As shown in the preceding chapter, the times at which the various parts of the investments are made and at which the returns are anticipated need to be taken into account in order to compare the values of a dollar spent or received today with those that may be spent or received in the future. Discounting future cost and values at some suitably chosen rate of interest is used to relate a projected stream of investment costs to a projected stream of earnings in order to provide either (1) a measure of the internal rate of return of the investment (IRR) or (2) a measure of the present value of the difference between the two streams at some chosen rate of interest (NPV).

The Nature of Uncertainty

However, virtually all of the elements of the IRR or NPV analyses are subject to the uncertainties of the unknown future. To illus-

* Mr. Hertz is a Director of McKinsey & Co., Inc., New York.

ILLUSTRATION 1*
Bidding Five Times, with a 20 Percent Chance of Winning Each Time

Chance of Winning Contract Exactly	*Is*
No time......................	0.3277
One time.....................	0.4096
Two times....................	0.2048
Three times..................	0.0512
Four times...................	0.0064
Five times...................	0.0003

* Explanatory Note to Illustration 1.

The calculations for Illustration 1 are as follows:

Let $P(W) =$ Probability of winning $= 0.2$, and $P(L) =$ Probability of losing $= 0.8$. Two rules and the combination formula will be utilized.

Rule 1. Multiplication rule of probabilities:
   If the probability of event A is $P(A)$ and the probability of event B is $P(B)$, and the events are independent of each other, then the probability that *both* will happen is:

$$P(AB) = P(A) \times P(B)$$

Rule 2. Addition rule of probabilities:
   If the probability of an event A is $P(A)$ and the probability of an event B is $P(B)$, and the events are mutually exclusive, then the probability that one *or* the other will happen is:

$$P(A + B) = P(A) + P(B)$$

Combinations of M:
   If M denotes the number of combinations of n things taken p at a time,

$$M = \frac{n!}{p!\,(n-p)!}, \text{ where } n! = 1 \times 2 \times 3 \times \cdots \times n.$$

Calculations:

No time: $L, L, L, L, L = [P(L)]^5 = (0.8)^5 = \underline{0.3277}$

One time: W, L, L, L, L, etc. $= [P(L)]^4[P(W)] = (0.8)^4(0.2) = 0.08192$

$$M = \frac{5!}{1!4!} = 5 \qquad\qquad (5)(0.08192) = \underline{0.4096}$$

Two times: W, W, L, L, L, etc. $= [P(L)]^3[P(W)]^2 = (0.8)^3(0.2)^2 = 0.02048$

$$M = \frac{5!}{2!3!} = 10 \qquad\qquad (10)(0.02048) = \underline{0.2048}$$

Three times: W, W, W, L, L, etc. $= [P(L)]^2[P(W)]^3 = (0.8)^2(0.2)^3 = 0.00512$

$$M = \frac{5!}{3!2!} = 10 \qquad\qquad (10)(0.00512) = \underline{0.0512}$$

Four times: W, W, W, W, L, etc. $= [P(L)][P(W)]^4 = (0.8)(.2)^4 = 0.00128$

$$M = \frac{5!}{4!1!} = 5 \qquad\qquad (5)(0.00128) = \underline{0.0064}$$

Five times: $W, W, W, W, W = [P(W)]^5 = (0.2)^5 = \underline{0.0003}$

trate the necessity for taking these uncertainties into account, consider a situation in which a company bids on a series of contracts. The costs of preparing and submitting a bid are known to be $10,000, and the possible (NPV) *gross* return (not including the bid cost) is known to be $50,000. In other words, the payoff is five to one, *if* a contract is obtained. Thus, if the chances of getting a contract are one in five (20 percent)—that is, if one could bid five times on a similar (in size, payoff, and chances of winning) contract —one or more of those should come through with reasonable certainty (but interestingly enough, there would be a 33 percent chance that even in five trials the bidder would win none). The actual chances for winning zero to five times work out as shown in Illustration 1.

If now we take these chances of winning and multiply by the gross amount to be gained in each instance, we should find that the company expects to break even, which is intuitively understandable since the payoff is five to one on odds of one in five. This is shown in Illustration 2.

ILLUSTRATION 2

Chance of Winning Contract Exactly	Is	Gross Profit	Chance Times Gross Profit
No time..........................	0.3277	$ 0	$ 0
One time........................	0.4096	50,000	20,480
Two times.......................	0.2048	100,000	20,480
Three times.....................	0.0512	150,000	7,680
Four times......................	0.0064	200,000	1,280
Five times......................	0.0003	250,000	75
Total expected profit..			$50,000*

* Individual numbers add to $49,995 rather than $50,000 due to rounding.

It will not matter how often the company bids; it still will have the *same* expectation of breaking even, under these conditions of uncertainty and payoff. When bidding once, there is an 80 percent chance that the $10,000 bid cost will be lost; when bidding five times, there is a 33 percent chance that $50,000 (cost of five bids at $10,000 each) will be entirely lost. Although there is a chance (20 percent) that on *one* bid the investor will be rewarded with a return of 400 percent [($50,000 − $10,000) ÷ $10,000 = 400 percent], most prudent managers probably would seek more than an expected value of zero (0.2 × $40,000 + 0.8 × −$10,000 = $0) even before going ahead with a single bid. In other words, the uncertainty of winning (one chance in five) combined with the risk (80 percent) of losing the stake of $10,000 ordinarily would be too great to compensate for the size of the anticipated net gain ($50,000 minus the $10,000 bid cost). This simple situation illustrates why the prudent executive should seek to understand not only the investment stakes and the anticipated returns from a specific investment but also the uncertainties and risks surrounding that investment.

The future always is uncertain. None of the expected events upon which the business executive builds analyses for investment decisions is absolutely certain. Of course, the amount or nature of the uncertainty will vary, depending upon the kind of event under consideration and the length of time before that event is expected to come to pass. Tomorrow's weather is less uncertain than the weather on a specific date two years hence; next year's sales of a well-established product are far less uncertain than those of a new and untried product not yet out of the laboratory.

The end results of past business transactions are measured by a set of accounts that relate one to the other—sales revenue, costs of raw materials, labor, and overheads for a specific product or a set of specific products, for example—providing profit and loss statements matched to balance sheet changes and giving a measure of return on the investment related to those transactions.

The historical data that enter these transaction records, of course, are generally expected to be approximately accurate. Even these data are subject to some uncertainty, but ordinarily this is not sufficient to call the results into question. The anticipated returns on future investments are evaluated by the same kind of accounting analyses as used to record historical operations. However, there is a very major difference: the data that purport to describe the expected transactions are now predictions or projected estimates. The actual outcomes of investment decisions based on such predictions and evaluations hinge on the particular combination of values that critical variables (e.g., sales volume or manufacturing cost) really do take in the future. Often the best that the manager can say about such variables as they are projected into the future is that they are likely to be wide ranging—in other words, highly uncertain. Knowledge of the uncertainties underlying the estimates used in such analyses is crucial information for the decision maker.

Two potential investments having the same "best (subjective) estimate" values for future profitability and return on investment are *not* equivalent if one investment alternative has a much wider range of possible outcomes than the other—that is, if the uncertainty surrounding the best estimates is very different. (This will be illustrated in detail later in this chapter.) Thus, decision makers should be able to differentiate among opportunities not only on the basis of their expected outcomes but also on the uncertainties surrounding these outcomes. If they do not have this latter information, they will not be able to judge adequately the nature of a particular investment risk. Therefore, the uncertainties inherent in the future surrounding each of the significant inputs in an investment analysis need to be understood clearly. The manager needs to have the uncertainties in these factors quantified. For example, the uncertainty of a sales estimate can be represented by either a table, a pie chart, a histogram, or a cumulative probability distribution. (See Exhibit 1.)

The forms most often used to express the uncertainties about future outcomes are the histogram and the cumulative probability distribution. The shape of the histogram reflects the certainty (or its converse, the ignorance) of the estimator as to the outcome of an event. For example, in a situation where manufacturing costs are significant, if cost estimates are well known from past experience to be reliable, the shape will peak sharply above the most likely value; but if there is considerable uncertainty, the shape will resemble a plateau (Exhibit 2). In this way, explicit recognition is given to the uncertainty attached to a variable in the projected investment account. The histogram, or other form of distribution, provides a portrayal of the *specific estimated probabilities* within which the variable will fall, given ranges of values. Knowledge of the estimated uncertainties surrounding key variables permits better evaluation of the risks entailed by specific investment alternatives.

The Nature of Risk

A consensus of dictionary definitions of *risk* is "exposure to the chance of injury or loss, and the degree of probability of such loss." Managers are well aware of the fact that all investments involve a greater or lesser degree of risk—either by virtue of the size of the potential loss (a loss that could bankrupt a business will be viewed

EXHIBIT 1
Four Ways of Representing a Probability Distribution

1. Table

Range of Sales (million tons per annum)	5 – 10	10 – 15	15 – 20	20 – 25	25 – 30
Probability of Sales Being in This Range	0.10	0.30	0.40	0.15	0.05

2. Pie Chart   3. Histogram

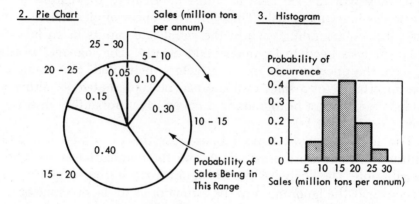

4. Cumulative Probability Distribution

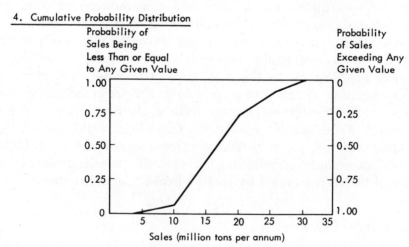

EXHIBIT 2

The Shape of the Probability Distribution Reflects the Accuracy of the Estimate

A. Probability distribution of a cost that can be estimated accurately

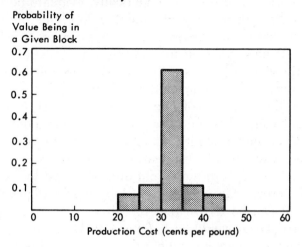

Probability of
Value Being in
a Given Block

Production Cost (cents per pound)

B. Probability distribution of a cost that cannot be estimated accurately

Probability of
Value Being in
a Given Block

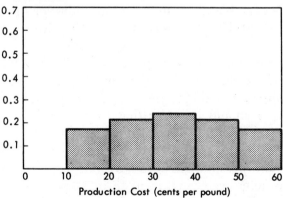

Production Cost (cents per pound)

in a different light than one which simply could reduce earnings by a few percent) or because of the likelihood of such loss (the greater the size of potential loss, the more critical for the decision maker becomes the probability of its occurrence). Most business executives, either intuitively or analytically, evaluate both of these elements of risk: magnitude of potential loss and probability of loss. But whether or not the executive, investor, or decision maker evaluates risk and takes it into account in making investment choices, if the risk *truly* does exist, then it is present whether he or she does or does not try to do anything about it.

Another difficult aspect of taking account of risk in investment decisions is the fact that the variability of economic outcomes may be greater than the variability of factors leading to those outcomes. For example, assume an investment of $4,000 is expected to yield a $1,000 annual pretax return over out-of-pocket cost for seven years. Given a 32 percent tax rate, straight-line depreciation and no salvage value, it can be shown that the after-tax discounted internal rate of return (IRR) would be 11.6 percent. However, if the investment lasts only six years instead of seven (a $\frac{1}{7}$ or 14 percent change from the original estimate), then the return drops to 9.1 percent (a 22 percent reduction from 11.6). Similarly, if the pretax return turns out to be $800 annually (a 20 percent reduction), then the IRR falls to 6.5 percent, or only 56 percent of the original estimate. As this simple example illustrates, the variability of the return over ranges of uncertainty in the elements of the investment can be very significant.

For another example, in a simplified conventional analysis of an investment, where the "best-guess" estimates of the input elements are to be compared with the best (optimistic) and worst (pessimistic) cases, it should be clear that there is no way to make a prudent decision. Using a simple ROI measure, we obtain the results shown in Illustration 3. What is significant here is not so much the fact that the possible ROIs range from 0 to 56.6 percent (although if the range were, say, from 18 to 22 percent for the worst to best cases, the uncertainty involved probably would be acceptable). Rather, it is significant that the chances a specific ROI will occur are completely unspecified. It should make a great deal of difference to the decision maker to know that (1) 0 percent ROI has a 1 in 100 chance of occurring, while at least 20 percent ROI could occur one in two times, and 56.5 percent ROI, 1 in 20 times;

ILLUSTRATION 3

$$ROI = \frac{(Price \times Unit\ sales) - (Costs)}{Investment}$$

Best-Guess Estimates	Likely Ranges
Price = $5.00	$5.00 to $5.50
Costs = $800,000	$700,000 to $875,000
Sales = 200,000 units	175,000 to 225,000 units
Investment = $1,000,000	$950,000 to $1,100,000

Best-guess: $\dfrac{5.0 \times 200,000 - 800,000}{1,000,000} = 20\ percent\ ROI$

Worst case: $\dfrac{5.0 \times 175,000 - 875,000}{1,100,000} = 0\ percent\ ROI$

Best case: $\dfrac{5.5 \times 225,000 - 700,000}{950,000} = 56.6\ percent\ ROI$

versus (2) 0 percent ROI at 1 in 15 chances, at least 20 percent ROI, 1 in 10 times, and 56.5 percent ROI, 1 in 100 times. Even with the same range of ROI outcomes, the prospects for each of these investments would look entirely different when the probabilities of the outcomes are considered.

Coping with Risk

Only the most naive investors act as though there were no risk in every investment. At the very least they make one or more of the following adjustments to aid in their decision whether to make what they consider a risky investment. However, as described, each of these has shortcomings.

More Accurate Forecasts. Reducing the error in estimates is a worthy objective. But no matter how many estimates of the future go into a capital investment decision, when all is said and done, the future is still the future. Therefore, however well we forecast, we are still left with the certain knowledge that we cannot eliminate all uncertainty.

Empirical Adjustments. Adjusting the factors influencing the outcome of a decision is subject to serious difficulties. We would like to adjust them so as to cut down the likelihood that we will make a "bad" investment, but how can we do that without at the same time spoiling our chances to make a "good" one? And in any case, what is the basis for adjustment? We adjust, not for uncertainty, but for bias.

For example, construction estimates are often exceeded. If a company's history of construction costs is that 90 percent of its estimates have been exceeded by 15 percent, then in a capital estimate there is every justification for increasing the value of this factor by 15 percent. This is a matter of improving the accuracy of the estimate. But suppose that new-product sales estimates have been exceeded by more than 75 percent in one fourth of all historical cases, and have not reached 50 percent of the estimate in one sixth of all such cases? Penalties for overestimating are very tangible, and so management is apt to reduce the sales estimate to "cover" the one case in six—thereby reducing the calculated rate of return. In doing so, it is possibly missing some of its best opportunities.

Revising Cutoff Rates. Selecting higher cutoff rates for protecting against uncertainty is attempting much the same thing. Management would like to have a possibility of return in proportion to the risk it takes. Where there is much uncertainty involved in the various estimates of sales, costs, prices, and so on, a high calculated return from the investment provides some incentive for taking the risk. This is, in fact, a perfectly sound position. The trouble is that decision makers still need to know explicitly what risks they are taking—and what the odds are on achieving the expected return.

Three-Level Estimates. A start at spelling out risks is sometimes made by taking the high, medium, and low values of the estimated factors and calculating rates of return based on various combinations of the pessimistic, average, and optimistic estimates (as we did in Illustration 3). These calculations give a picture of the range of possible results, but do not tell the executive whether the pessimistic result is more likely than the optimistic one—or, in fact, whether the average result is much more likely to occur than either of the extremes. So, although this is a step in the right direction, it still does not give a clear enough picture for comparing alternatives.

Selected Probabilities. Various methods have been used to include the probabilities of specific factors in the return calculation. L. C. Grant discussed a program for forecasting discounted cash flow rates of return where the service life is subject to obsolescence and deterioration. He calculated the odds that the investment will terminate at any time after it is made depending on the probability distribution of the service-life factor. After calculating these factors for each year through maximum service life, he then determined an overall expected rate of return.[1]

Edward G. Bennion suggested the use of game theory to take into account alternative market growth rates as they would determine rate of return for various alternatives. He used the estimated probabilities that specific growth rates will occur to develop optimum strategies. Bennion pointed out:

> Forecasting can result in a negative contribution to capital budget decisions unless it goes further than merely providing a single most probable prediction. . . . [With] an estimated probability coefficient for the forecast, plus knowledge of the payoffs for the company's alternative investments and calculation of indifference probabilities . . . the margin of error may be substantially reduced, and the businessman can tell just how far off his forecast may be before it leads him to a wrong decision.[2]

Note that both Grant's and Bennion's methods yield an expected return, each based on only *one* uncertain input factor—service life in the first case, market growth in the second. Both are helpful, and both tend to improve the clarity with which the executive can view investment alternatives. But neither sharpens up the range of "risk taken" or "return hoped for" sufficiently to help very much in the complex decisions of capital planning.

There are two kinds of risks to be taken into account:

1. The risk implicit in the wider range of outcomes (the difference between the ranges 0 to 56 percent and 18 to 22 percent in the previous example): This is one of greater risk of low return coupled with *possibly* higher returns for the former, and a high degree of comfort or safety (i.e., freedom from risk) with the latter.

2. The risk of a greater probability of an unfavorable outcome. A contract bid that has only one chance in three of not being won is inherently less risky—at the same bidding cost—than one that has four chances out of five of not being won.

In either of these kinds of cases, in order to understand the nature of the risks, it is necessary to attach some numerical probabilities to each of the outcomes in order to develop an average for

---

[1] "Monitoring Capital Investments," *Financial Executive*, April 1963, p. 19.

[2] "Capital Budgeting and Game Theory," *Harvard Business Review*, November–December 1956, p. 123.

ILLUSTRATION 4
Bidding Five Times—Total Cost $50,000

Chance of Winning Contract Exactly	Is	Gross Profit	Net Profit	Chance Times Net Profit
No time......................	0.3277	$ 0	—$ 50,000	—$16,385
One time.....................	0.4096	50,000	0	0
Two times....................	0.2048	100,000	50,000	10,240
Three times..................	0.0512	150,000	100,000	5,120
Four times...................	0.0064	200,000	150,000	960
Five times...................	0.0003	250,000	200,000	60
Expected net profit.......				$ 0*

* Individual numbers add to —$5 rather than $0 due to rounding.

these outcomes, weighted by the probability of their occurrence. (See Illustrations 1 and 2.) This average then will be the *expectation* or expected value of the particular investment. Thus, to calculate the expected value of the contract bids in Illustration 2, we should determine the payoff for each of the six possible outcomes, as shown in Illustration 4.

This particular business opportunity cannot in the long run be expected to yield a profit, and in the short run could yield a substantial loss. However, there is *some* probability of winning a contract that could make the investment attractive. That probability presumably will vary from manager to manager, depending on a manager's "risk preference" or "risk aversion" viewpoints—in other words, on what is formally called the manager's *utility function.*

In the remainder of this chapter, we will deal in depth with two of the notions we have thus far introduced. In the next section we will discuss how to deal *systematically* with a decision maker's risk preference—that is, a decision maker's relative feelings about the *attractiveness* of the various outcomes which might result from an investment decision. Then we will deal with "decision trees" and a technique called "Monte Carlo Simulation," which are used in structuring and analyzing *complex* investment (and other) decisions, where a number of uncontrollable factors can influence the eventual outcome of an investment decision.

UTILITY, RISK PREFERENCE, AND RISK AVERSION

In the situation described above, the cost of making the bid was $10,000 and the gross return was $50,000 ($40,000, net of bid costs).

This is equivalent to a lottery in which there is only one prize, $50,000, and in which a ticket costs $10,000. We have seen, as we would expect, that a one-in-five chance of winning leads to a break-even "expectation" along with a substantial "risk" of loss. This situation is equivalent to a capital investment that has been reduced to "certain" or "for sure" costs and returns, with only the chance of success remaining as the element that will cause management to decide whether or not to proceed. The net present value of the costs could be $100,000,000 rather than $10,000; the net present value of the returns, $500,000,000 rather than $50,000; but the *basic* structure would not be altered: that is, managers would still have to decide what risks they would be willing to take—what probabilities of success would they require before they made a decision to proceed—and this could vary with the size of the business opportunity.

The Utility Function

Clearly, if the chances of achieving the estimated return (i.e., winning the lottery) were 100 percent (i.e., certain), the only issue

ILLUSTRATION 5

Contract	Loss	Probability of Loss	Return	Probability of Return
A.................	$10,000	0.8	$50,000	0.2
B.................	10,000	0.6	50,000	0.4
C.................	10,000	0.4	50,000	0.6
D.................	10,000	0.0	50,000	1.0

would be whether there were some better certain return available. On the other hand, a one-in-five chance of winning *might* not appeal to a manager. So the question is, how can one determine what probability of achieving a specific return would appeal to a given manager, knowing that this must be a matter of individual choice (one manager might require almost 100 percent certainty, while another might be willing to risk a slightly better chance than one in five)?

In Illustration 5 we show a range of probabilities—from 20 to 100 percent chance of winning—which may be considered to apply to alternative contract opportunities. If these were four mutually exclusive choices, clearly the manager would rank them from D to A in descending order (i.e., D is a "sure thing," while A has only one-in-five chances of being successful). But, how can we determine, on a general basis, whether the manager would choose *any* given investment on the basis of the kind of data available here (known costs, returns, and probabilities of success)?

Consider any probability (P) of the successful $50,000 return on the investment. Then the probability of losing $10,000 will be $(1 - P)$. Suppose the manager already had incurred a debt of $5,000 to the contracting party and was offered the $-$10,000/$50,-000 contract *possibility* in return for cancellation of the debt. At what value of P would the manager *just* be willing to do this? Or, to put it another way, at what value of P would the manager not

ILLUSTRATION 6

Sure Loss or Profit	Choice of P in $-$10,000/ $50,000 Contract to Just Compensate for Loss or Profit
$-$ 5,000.	0.3
$-$ 2,000.	0.5
0 (doing nothing).	0.6
$+$ 4,000.	0.8
$+$ 10,000.	0.9

care *whether* he continued to owe the $5,000 *or* took a chance on losing $10,000 or winning $50,000? Suppose the answer was that P should be 0.3 for the manager not to care. This is equivalent to the statement that "the manager is *indifferent* between (1) a sure loss of $5,000 or (2) a 30 percent probability of grossing $50,000 along with a 70 percent probability of losing $10,000."

Now let us drop the assumptions that the manager owes the contracting party $5,000. Suppose the manager is offered this contract and must choose whether to do it or not—what would the manager require P to be? Assume at this point the manager says 0.6. We could continue asking for the manager's choice of P for other values of sure losses (debts), say, $2,000, and sure profits of, say, $4,000 and $10,000, which would make the manager indifferent between (1) taking the sure amount or (2) gambling on winning the contract with probability P of success. The results might be summarized as shown in Illustration 6.

Note that a debt (sure loss) of $10,000 should be equivalent to a value of P of 0; that is, the decision maker is indifferent between (1) a sure loss of −$10,000 and (2) a probability $P = 0$ of winning the −$10,000/$50,000 gamble. Similarly, a sure profit of $50,000 could only be reasonably expected to require a P of 1.0, since if $P = 1.0$ the decision maker will win the −$10,000/$50,000 gamble. To describe these decisions in general terms, so that this manager's preferences for risk or gain can be applied in other situations, we note the following: The assessed values of P can be used as an index of the manager's attitude toward risk—called "preference" or "utility value." For example, we can say that an outcome with economic consequences of a $5,000 loss has a utility value of 0.3, whereas a gain of $10,000 has a utility value of 0.9. Illustration 7 shows all of

ILLUSTRATION 7

Sure Loss or Profit	Utility Value
−$10,000	0.0
− 5,000	0.3
− 2,000	0.5
0	0.6
+ 4,000	0.8
+ 10,000	0.9
+ 50,000	1.0

these values, based on the five assessments we got from the manager, plus the utility of 0 for the worst outcome and of 1.0 for the best—these latter two utilities being self-evident, without questioning the manager. These seven points can be plotted, and a smooth "utility curve" drawn through them, as shown in Exhibit 3.

It should be noted that although we used probabilities of winning the −$10,000/$50,000 "reference gamble" as units of utility, this is only one way of labeling the utility scale (vertical axis). For example, the utility of −$5,000 could be called 30, provided that the other utilities were similarly rescaled (e.g., utility of $10,000 = 90). The important thing is that the utility scale show *relative* preferences for outcomes; for example, that the utility for $10,000 be three times the utility of −$5,000, whatever utility units— "utiles"—are used. If investors are consistent in their feelings about risk, that is, if they follow the same utility curve for all decisions, this curve can be used to discriminate among alternative risky investments. Also, the units of the horizontal axis can be of whatever values—for example, IRR, NPV, ROI, ROS—that may be relevant

EXHIBIT 3
A Utility Curve

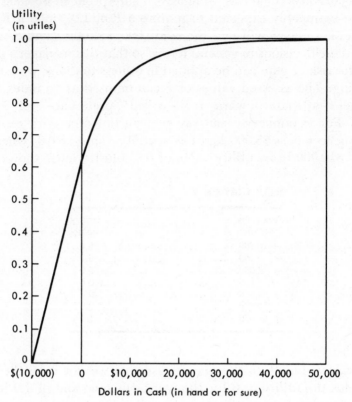

Utility
(in utiles)

1.0

0.9

0.8

0.7

0.6

0.5

0.4

0.3

0.2

0.1

0

$(10,000)   0 $10,000   20,000   30,000   40,000   50,000

Dollars in Cash (in hand or for sure)

to the investor's decisions, and can span any range of values that may be useful. But the resulting utility curves must, of course, reflect a manager's *relative* preferences for greater or smaller gains or losses.

Risk Aversion and Risk Preference

The curve shown in Exhibit 3 is that of a highly "risk-averse" investor. For example, the increase in utility (to the investor) of avoiding a loss of $10,000 (going from −$10,000 to $0) is 0.6 units; whereas going from $0 to $50,000 increases the investor's utility only 0.4 units (1.0 − 0.6). This risk-averse curve describes an investor who would require a probability of 60 percent or more of winning the $50,000 contract of Illustration 1 (at a cost of $10,000) compared to doing nothing ($0 for sure).

A "risk-prone" or risk-preferring investor would simply require lower probabilities of success to make trade-offs against doing nothing. Illustration 8, along with Exhibit 4, show a different decision maker's choice of probabilities in the −$10,000/$50,000 situation (to just compensate for the sure loss or profit as before), and exemplifies the fact that a concave utility curve (Exhibit 3) is risk averting, while a convex utility curve is risk preferring (Exhibit 4). This investor would accept the gamble on the −$10,000/$50,000 contract, rather than do nothing, at *any* odds above 1 in 10.

ILLUSTRATION 8

Sure Loss or Profit	Choice of P in −$10,000/ $50,000 Contract to Just Compensate for Loss or Profit	Utility
−$10,000	0.00	0.00
− 5,000	0.05	0.05
− 2,000	0.08	0.08
0	0.10	0.10
+ 4,000	0.15	0.15
+ 10,000	0.20	0.20
+ 50,000	1.00	1.00

Using Utility Curves

Exhibit 5 illustrates a utility curve showing an investor's risk-averse preferences for return on investment (ROI). In this instance, the investor equates a −5 percent yield with 0 utility and a 25 percent yield with a utility value of 1. Given a correctly derived utility curve, investors, if they act logically and consistently, will rank their preference for investments in order of their respective utilities; further, the manner in which the utilities are derived means that the utility of a *risky* alternative is equal to its expected utility.

Let us develop a decision-making example. An illustrative set of three alternative plant investments ranges from $18,000,000 to $45,000,000, the yield from each of which depends upon the growth of the market for the product under consideration. (See Illustration 9.) The expected utility and the investor's optimum course of action on each of these alternatives now can be determined from the ROI utility curve of Exhibit 5 and the probabilities of each of the market sizes indicated above. "Expected utilities" are calculated in Illustration 10; these are computed the same way as is any expected value.

EXHIBIT 4
Utility Curve of a Risk-Preferring Investor

Utility
(in utiles)

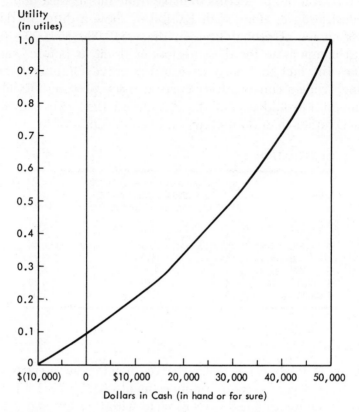

Dollars in Cash (in hand or for sure)

Thus, the 0.60 expected utility of the $25,000,000 investment is the highest; this investment is the most attractive to this investor given his or her attitude toward risk at a particular point in time (as reflected in Exhibit 5).

Practicality of Utility Curves

The derivation of this kind of utility curve is useful for analyzing the kinds of behavior managers may display in the face of risky capital investments. On the other hand, it is not a simple matter to obtain a consistent utility curve from a manager, nor is it possible to say that such a curve is stable over even short periods of time. It should be obvious that the "state of the economy," the condition of a balance sheet, even a particularly satisfactory (or unfortunate)

EXHIBIT 5
Investor's Utility Curve of ROI

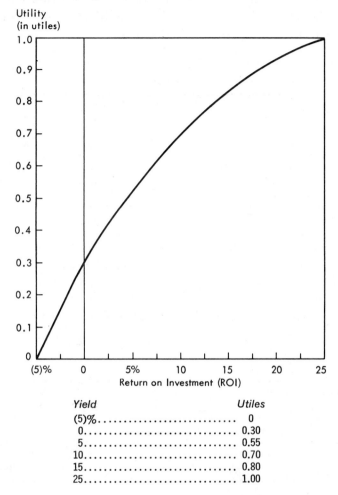

Yield	Utiles
(5)%............................	0
0...............................	0.30
5...............................	0.55
10..............................	0.70
15..............................	0.80
25..............................	1.00

transaction, might well change the manager's attitude toward risk.

Further, most managers do not feel comfortable in dealing with the idea of picking probabilities for a gamble which make it equivalent to "sure" results. One risky action may not be equivalent to another in a manager's mind (although in terms of utility they may be the same)—for example, a horseracing bet versus a new plant versus a government contract bid. A decision may be one that should reflect the preferences of multiple decision makers, but there is no simple or consistent way to combine these preferences into a single "corporate" utility curve. It is not possible to make consistent interpersonal comparisons of utility. Risky investments whose utilities *are* determinable do not combine additively unless the utility curve is a straight line (so-called "linear preference," which is "play-

ILLUSTRATION 9
Return on Investment for Alternative Plants

	Growth of Market		
	High	*Moderate*	*Low*
Probabilities....................	⅓	⅓	⅓
Investment:			
1. $18,000,000...............	5%	5%	5%
2. 25,000,000...............	15	10	0
3. 45,000,000...............	25	3	−5

ing the averages" rather than being either risk averse or risk preferring). That is, the utility of an Investment A and an Investment B combined is *not* equal to the utility of Investment A plus the utility of Investment B in any of the curves above.

On the other hand, the derivation of utility curves may help determine what decisions are *so* risky that ordinary calculations of

ILLUSTRATION 10

For investment:

1. Expected $U_{(1)} = (\frac{1}{3} \times U_{5\%}) + (\frac{1}{3} \times U_{5\%}) + (\frac{1}{3} \times U_{5\%})$
   $= U_{5\%} = 0.55$ utiles
2. Expected $U_{(2)} = (\frac{1}{3} \times U_{15\%}) + (\frac{1}{3} \times U_{10\%}) + (\frac{1}{3} \times U_{0\%})$
   $= (\frac{1}{3} \times 0.8) + (\frac{1}{3} \times 0.7) + (\frac{1}{3} \times 0.3) = 0.60$ utiles
3. Expected $U_{(3)} = (\frac{1}{3} \times U_{25\%}) + (\frac{1}{3} \times U_{3\%}) + (\frac{1}{3} \times U_{-5\%})$
   $= (\frac{1}{3} \times 1.0) + (\frac{1}{3} \times 0.45) + (\frac{1}{3} \times 0) = 0.48$ utiles

profit expectation do not provide straightforward answers. Where this is the case, an unraveling of policy considerations may result from the application of the ideas of utility curves and thereby permit better investment decisions to be made. These ideas provide the essential rationale for investment diversification. However, most capital investments are decided on the basis of their expected monetary value (EMV), plus such nonmonetary considerations that may be pertinent.

Diversification is most effective when the investor can choose

ILLUSTRATION 11

Investment	Possible Loss	Probability of Loss	Possible Gain	Probability of Gain
A	$90,000	0.30	$150,000	0.70

Expected value$_A$ = $(-90,000 \times 0.3) + (150,000 \times 0.7) = \$78,000$

| B | B-1 | $45,000 | 0.30 | $75,000 | 0.70 |
| | B-2 | $45,000 | 0.30 | $75,000 | 0.70 |

Expected value$_B$ = $-(45,000 + 45,000) \times 0.3 + (75,000 + 75,000) \times 0.7 = \$78,000$

more than one risky investment whose outcomes are significantly independent of one another. Illustration 11 shows two choices: either two investments together B-1 and B-2), or a single investment (A); the choice is to be made by an investor with the utility curve shown in Exhibit 6.

EXHIBIT 6
Utility Curve

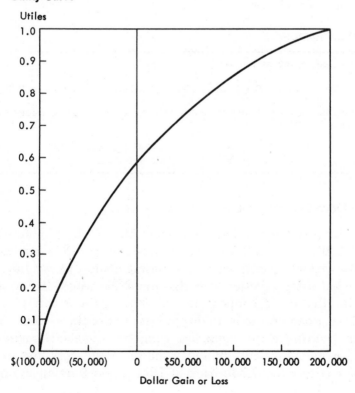

Since B-1 and B-2 are independent investments, the probability of a $90,000 loss—that is, losing $45,000 on both of the investments—is (0.3×0.3) or 0.09; the probability of a $30,000 gain (i.e., lose on either B-1 or B-2, gain on the other) is $(0.3 \times 0.7) + (0.3 \times 0.7)$ or 0.42; and the probability of a $150,000 gain is (0.7×0.7) or 0.49. (Note that $0.09 + 0.42 + 0.49 = 1.00$, consistent with the laws of probability.)

The utility for Investment A, from the curve in Exhibit 6, is shown in Illustration 12. Note that the risk-averse investor prefers B, even though the expected gain of the alternatives is the same (i.e., $78,000). This can be explained intuitively if we note that by diversifying between two smaller, independent investments, the investor does not change his or her *expected* gain but does reduce its variance—that is to say, the investor takes less risk of making a loss and has a surer chance for a gain. However, it should also be noted that the investor has *reduced* the chances to achieve the highest gain (from 0.70 to 0.49). Since the investor is risk averse (a convex utility curve), it is to be expected that the less-risky situation of Investment B will be preferred.

ILLUSTRATION 12

The utility of Investment A is:

$$U_A = U_{-90,000} \times 0.3 + U_{+150,000} \times 0.7 = (0.1 \times 0.3) + (0.95 \times 0.7) = 0.70;$$

whereas, the utility of Investment B (with the same expected value as A, that is, $78,000) is:

$$U_B = U_{-90,000} \times 0.09 + U_{+30,000} \times 0.42 + U_{+150,000} \times 0.49$$
$$= (0.1 \times 0.09) + (0.75 \times 0.42) + (0.95 \times 0.49) = 0.79$$

Other Decision Methods

For the investments discussed under the heading "Using Utility Curves," Illustrations 9 and 10, the risk-averse utility curves gives the $25,000,000 investment as the wisest choice, as we have seen. Now, what if the investor feels that he or she would like to look at the *worst* that could happen (the *minimum* gain or *maximum* loss) and make a decision so as to do the best under these worst circumstances (*maximize* the *minimum* gain, the so-called *maximin* criterion; or its equivalent, *minimize* the *maximum* loss, the so-called *minimax* criterion)? Look back at Illustration 9 as an example of how to apply the maximin criterion. The worst that could happen would be for the market growth to be low; if it were low, the best decision would be investment (1), with a 5 percent ROI. Thus, the maximin criterion leads the decision maker to proceed with investment (1).

On the other hand, the decision maker might wish to *maximize* the *maximum* gain (the *maximax* criterion), which would lead to the optimistic conclusion that (3) is the best choice, with a one-third chance of achieving 25 percent ROI. Finally, the manager might wish to weigh the odds on the maximum and minimum gains (i.e., multiply the maxmium payoff for a given decision by a weight for that payoff and add to it the minimum payoff for that decision multiplied by a weight for that payoff) and provide a "mixed" (called Hurwicz) criterion for each investment that reflects relative pessimism and optimism about the future.

Whatever choice is made, there is a significant probability that the investor will wish that another choice was made; that is, the investor will regret the loss of the opportunity to do better. A criterion for making a decision that would minimize this regret or opportunity loss involves measuring the difference between the yield for a given decision and what *would* have been the yield for the best decision under a specific market growth (or state of nature). Thus, if in the Illustration 9 example the investor chose investment (2) and the growth turned out to be high, the investor's regret would be the difference between the 25 percent that could have been gotten by choosing (3) and the 15 percent that actually would be received under (2), or a 10 percent difference.

Illustration 13 tabulates these "regrets" (more formally, "oppor-

ILLUSTRATION 13

	Regret Criterion for Plant Investment if the Actual Outcome Is—			
And the Choice of Investment Is:	High Market Growth	Moderate Market Growth	Low Market Growth	Expected Regret*
1. $18,000,000............... 20%	5%	0%	8.3%
2. 25,000,000................. 10	0	5	5.0
3. 45,000,000................. 0	7	10	5.7

* The expected regrets are calculated as follows:
1. Expected regret = $\frac{1}{3} \times 20 + \frac{1}{3} \times 5 + \frac{1}{3} \times 0$ = 8.3 percent.
2. Expected regret = $\frac{1}{3} \times 10 + \frac{1}{3} \times 0 + \frac{1}{3} \times 5$ = 5.0 percent.
3. Expected regret = $\frac{1}{3} \times 0 + \frac{1}{3} \times 7 + \frac{1}{3} \times 10$ = 5.7 percent.

tunity costs") for all nine possibilities in Illustration 9. *Given* one of the three market growth outcomes, the best choice for that outcome has zero regret, and each of the other two choices has a regret which is the difference between its ROI outcome and the outcome if the *best* alternative had been chosen. Thus, the decision maker can see that investment (1) could give rise to the maximum individual regret (20 percent), as well as the maximum expected regret or opportunity loss (8.3 percent), while investment (2) provides the minimum expectation of such regret (5.0 percent).

Summary

In general, the capital investment problem can be structured, at a given point in time, as a matrix in which *the investment choices* (I_1, I_2, etc.) are subject to future situations (S_1, S_2, etc.) in the world (e.g., "states of the marketplace," or the occurrence of specific events—in other words, "states of nature"), each with some assumed or estimated probability of *occurrence* (P_1, P_2, etc., where $P_1 +$

ILLUSTRATION 14

States of nature		S_1	S_3	$-------$	S_n
Probabilities		P_1	P_2	$-------$	P_n
	I_1	O_{11}	O_{12}	$-------$	O_{1n}
	I_2	O_{21}	O_{22}	$-------$	O_{2n}
Investments	—	—	—	$-------$	—
				(Outcomes)	
	—	—	—	$-------$	—
	—	—	—	$-------$	—
	—	—	—	$-------$	—
	I_{1n}	O_{m1}	O_{m2}	$-------$	O_{mn}

$P_2 + \cdots + P_n = 1$), and yield outcomes (O_1, O_2, etc.) that depend on which state of nature actually comes about. (See Illustration 14). If the specific attitude of the investor toward risk can be determined (the investor's utility curve), the outcomes can be expressed in consistent units; and if the probabilities of the states of nature can be estimated, then the best course of action is to *maximize expected utility*.

The investor's attitude toward risk can be used to help make choices when a utility curve is not determined—for example, a maximax choice, a maximin choice, or a minimum regret choice.

These criteria exist because there is no *sure* way of dealing with the decision maker's attitudes, preferences, objectives, along with the uncertainties that inherently attach to the future.

If over the size range of the investment alternatives available the investor's attitude toward risk is one of "playing the averages" (e.g., the investor is indifferent between a sure gain of $X and a gamble with an expected value of $X), then the maximization of *expected monetary value* (*EMV*) is a useful criterion. Using this criterion the investor chooses that investment strategy that maximizes gain weighted by the probabilities on the states of nature (or, equivalently, minimizes the opportunity loss or regret, weighted similarly). The EMV decision strategy will lead to the same result as the minimization of opportunity loss. For example, the alternative plant strategy chosen by the latter criterion in Illustration 13 was Investment 2 with a minimum opportunity loss of 5.0 percent. Under maximum EMV, the results will lead to the same decision— invest (2), with an expected return of 8.3 percent:

1. $EMV_{(1)} = (\frac{1}{3} \times 5) + (\frac{1}{3} \times 5) + (\frac{1}{3} \times 5) = 5.0$ percent
2. $EMV_{(2)} = (\frac{1}{3} \times 15) + (\frac{1}{3} \times 10) + (\frac{1}{3} \times 0) = \underline{8.3 \text{ percent}}$
3. $EMV_{(3)} = (\frac{1}{3} \times 25) + (\frac{1}{3} \times 3) + (\frac{1}{3} \times -5) = \overline{7.7 \text{ percent}}$

To represent either EMV or expected utility, the decision problem may be effectively structured by means of a decision tree. This is discussed in the next section.

DECISION TREES—INCORPORATING PROBABILITY INTO INVESTMENT ANALYSIS

The decision paths to possible outcomes under alternative states of nature or external events can be described by a *decision tree*. The simplest case is one in which there is only one investment decision involving two or more alternatives and two or more states of nature —a "single-stage" decision. Exhibit 7 illustrates such a case with the data from the alternative plant investments and market conditions in Illustration 9. The decision tree simply makes explicit the decisions and the uncertain elements facing the investor. The expected monetary return (EMV) for each decision is calculated by tracing back the outcomes weighted by the probability of their occurrence to each *node* where chance (e.g., a competitor's action) or nature (e.g., rainfall during a growing season) takes over.

EXHIBIT 7
Use of Decision Tree to Analyze New Plant Investment Alternatives

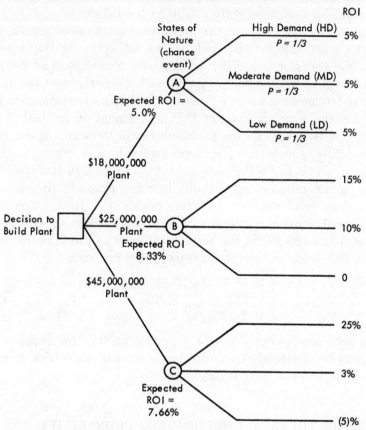

Multiple Decision Stages

The same methodology applies to the multistage investment problem, that is, one in which a series of decisions is required, the ultimate outcomes from which depend both on the various choices made and the uncertainties of future events or states of the world. The method requires that the EMVs be calculated back from the end of the tree to each chance event node, with the decision yielding highest EMV at the node then being selected for the immediately previous decision stage. This decision stage then is treated as though it were the end of the tree and "rolled back" to the preceding chance event nodes, where the appropriate preceding decision is once again selected. The process is continued through all decision stages until all decisions but one have been eliminated. This one will have the highest EMV.

The possible decisions for a two-stage plant investment and subsequent expansion under conditions of uncertainty as to whether additional market share will become available are as shown in Illustration 15. There are two key uncertainty factors in the future: (1) under expansion, will the company capture a greater market share (probability estimated at 20 percent), or only maintain its present share (probability 80 percent); and (2) with no expansion, can the present product sales mix be upgraded to increase profits (probability 10 percent) or not (probability 90 percent)? Other questions include sensitivity of the present values of the alternative decisions to changes in these probabilities and to postponement of the

ILLUSTRATION 15

1. At first decision point:
   A Large plant—$40 million investment
   B Small expandable plant—$25 million investment
   C No new plant—$0 investment
2. After three years—second decision point:
   B-1 Expand plant B—$15 million investment
   B-2 Do not expand
   C-1 Expand plant C—$25 million investment
   C-2 Do not expand

decision to expand beyond three years. The completed decision tree for this two-stage investment decision problem is shown in Exhibit 8. In order to reflect the time value of money, we will use net present value (NPV) as the decision criterion.

The first step in the calculation of the expected NPVs for the various decision points, after having laid out all the alternative possibilities along the branches of tree, is to determine the net present value (or other criterion that a manager may wish to use) using the accepted methods for determining that value (as described in Chapter 15). Thus, there are 16 paths through the decision tree in Exhibit 8. Each one has its own NPV at the end of the tenth year, depending upon the decisions taken at the starting year and at the third year (decision points 1 and 2 on the decision tree). Thus, for example, branch number (1) involves a $40 million outlay for a large plant, the assumption that an increased share of the market would ensue and would yield an NPV (if the assumption held true)

EXHIBIT 8
Two-Stage Decision Tree for Plant Investment

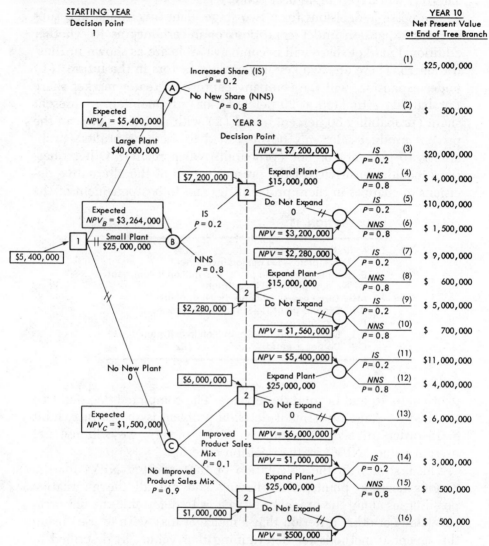

of $25 million. However, it is counterbalanced by the possibility of no new share of market—branch (2)—which would lead to over-investment and an NPV of only $500,000.

Therefore, "rolling back" from these end points, as before, the expected NPV of a decision to build a large plant in the starting year is:

Expected NPV_A = $(0.2 \times 25,000,000) + (0.8 \times 500,000)$
        $= 5,400,000$

Similarly, for the small-plant decision (B), working backwards to decision point 2 (which did not enter into the calculation relating to the large plant since there was only one decision to be made), we find the expected NPV for the second expansion to be:

Expected NPV_{B-2} = $(0.2 \times 20,000,000) + (0.8 \times 4,000,000)$
        $= 7,200,000$

which must be balanced against no expansion at decision point 2, or:

Expected NPV_{B-2} = $(0.2 \times 10,000,000) + (0.8 \times 1,500,000)$
        $= 3,200,000$

Thus, if we had reached decision point 2 along the branches from a decision to build a small plant and had achieved increased share of market, the best decision (as we look at it in the starting year) would be to expand. Therefore, the manager can discard the no-expansion possibility (indicated by the two lines "chopping off" that branch) and consider only expansion. However, the increased-share possibility only has a 20 percent chance of occurring; thus, the *no-increased-share branch* also must be considered, one of its alternate possibilities discarded, and the best result combined with the $7,200,000 expectation at decision point 2. As Exhibit 8 indicates, expansion branches (7) and (8) yield an NPV of $2.28 million; whereas the no-expansion branches (9) and (10) result in only $1.56 million, and therefore are discarded.

The possibilities of the small-plant expansion may now be combined to compare it with the other alternatives:

Expected NPV_B = $(7,200,000 \times 0.2) + (2,280,000 \times 0.8)$
        $= 3,264,000$

Similarly, for no new plant (possibility C), the expected NPV is caluculated at $1.5 million. Thus, the large-plant alternative has the highest expectation ($5.4 million) and should be chosen given a satisfactory degree of confidence in the assumptions.

The sensitivity of the decision to invest in the large plant (alternative A) to the assumption of a 20 percent probability of increased market share can be checked by substituting larger and smaller values for this event in the tree. It happens that any probability larger than 20 percent would increase the relative desirability of the large plant; and even at 10 percent probability of increased share, the large plant still remains the most desirable. To determine the sensitivity of the result to the timing of either the first or second decision, additional branches can be constructed to this tree that represent alternative timing possibilities.

As many stages and alternatives may be included in such a tree as seems desirable and practical to the manager. Weak strategies (in terms of their expected yields) can be "pruned out" to simplify the calculations. But the basic methodology remains the same, no matter what the size of the tree: (1) laying out in sequence all the alternatives; (2) assessing the chance events or states of nature that will affect them; (3) determining the payoff criterion at the end of each branch; (4) calculating the expected payoffs by rolling back through each chance event node to the relevant decision point; (5) selecting the strategies at the respective decision points with the highest payoff; (6) continuing to calculate through the chance event nodes; and (7) resulting eventually in an expected payoff that is equivalent to the decision maker to the entire problem depicted by the tree.

A decision tree permits the evaluation and comparison of monetary expectations (EMVs) under the general circumstance that the number of branches leading from chance event nodes is relatively small; otherwise a decision tree may become impractically unwieldy. This means that the distribution of chance events at those nodes is represented by only a few point estimates (e.g., 20 percent chance of increased and 80 percent chance of decreased market share). As a result of this "condensed" representation, the decision tree's expected value for the decision criterion may not be an adequate representation of the average that would result if more complete estimated distributions of these chance events were taken into account. A more complete representation for each alternative investment decision, or strategy, would be a probability-type distribution of the payoffs (such as NPV, payback, ROE, and so on). Using these representations to compare business opportunities provides a more complete insight into the nature of specific risky investments. This method of incorporating uncertainty into investment evaluations is called *risk analysis*, and will be discussed in the following section.

RISK ANALYSIS—DEVELOPING PROBABILITY
DISTRIBUTIONS OF INVESTMENT OUTCOMES

Risk analysis combines estimates of the probability distribution of each factor affecting an investment decision (whether monetary or not—for example, probabilities for varying amounts of rainfall might be used along with assessments of crop yields to combine with selling price probabilities to give estimates of cash crop possibilities), and then simulates the possible combinations of the values for each factor to determine the range of possible outcomes and the probability associated with each possible outcome.

Carrying Out a Risk Analysis

To carry out a risk analysis requires five basic steps as shown in Exhibit 9:

1. Describe in a flowchart the factors involved in the investment, over time, and their relationships to one another and to the period-by-period outcome of the investment from initiation to final disposal or to a chosen time in the future.
2. Estimate the range of value for each of the factors (e.g., range of selling prices, sales growth rate), and within that range the likelihood of occurrence (i.e., probability) of each value of the factor.
3. Estimate the relative dependence of the factors on one another, as shown in Exhibit 10—for example, by dividing the range of the nondependent factor (e.g., price) into a small number (three or four) of categories and determining the type of estimates described by Step 2 above for the dependent factor (e.g., sales) for each of those categories.
4. Select at random from the distribution of values for each factor one particular value (Exhibit 11). This random selection process, carried out by a computer, is called *Monte Carlo Simulation.* Then combine the values for all of the factors and compute the payoff (ROE, NPV, or other criterion) from that combination. We will use the discounted cash flow rate of return as our payoff or decision criterion. Where there are dependencies as described in Step 3 above, select a value at random from the independent distribution, and use this value to determine the dependent distribution belonging to the particular category of

EXHIBIT 9
Major Steps of Risk Analysis

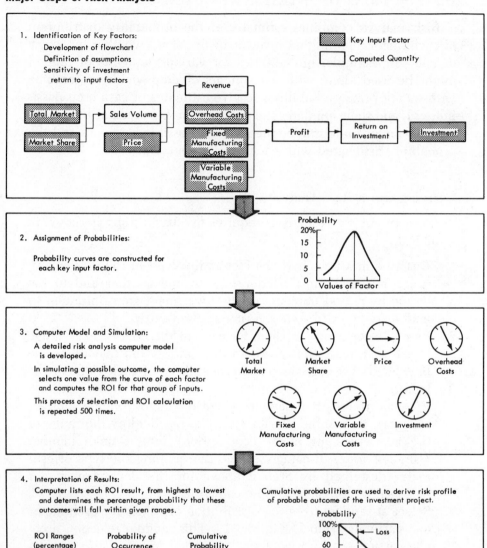

1. Identification of Key Factors:
   - Development of flowchart
   - Definition of assumptions
   - Sensitivity of investment return to input factors

   ▨ Key Input Factor
   ▢ Computed Quantity

   Total Market → Sales Volume → Revenue → Profit → Return on Investment ← Investment
   Market Share → Price → Overhead Costs, Fixed Manufacturing Costs, Variable Manufacturing Costs

2. Assignment of Probabilities:

   Probability curves are constructed for each key input factor.

   Probability
   20%
   15
   10
   5
   0
   Values of Factor

3. Computer Model and Simulation:

   A detailed risk analysis computer model is developed.

   In simulating a possible outcome, the computer selects one value from the curve of each factor and computes the ROI for that group of inputs.

   This process of selection and ROI calculation is repeated 500 times.

   Total Market   Market Share   Price   Overhead Costs

   Fixed Manufacturing Costs   Variable Manufacturing Costs   Investment

4. Interpretation of Results:

   Computer lists each ROI result, from highest to lowest and determines the percentage probability that these outcomes will fall within given ranges.

ROI Ranges (percentage)	Probability of Occurrence	Cumulative Probability
60 to 80	5%	5%
40 to 60	19	24
20 to 40	33	57
0 to 20	21	78
(20) to 0	14	92
(40) to (20)	(8)	100

   Cumulative probabilities are used to derive risk profile of probable outcome of the investment project.

   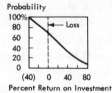

   Probability
   100%
   80
   60   ← Loss
   40
   20
   0
   (40) 0 40 80
   Percent Return on Investment

EXHIBIT 10
Relating Factors to Each Other in Risk Analysis

Example: Sales to Price

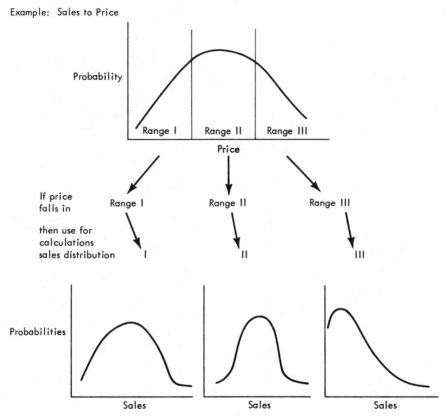

the independent distribution in which the category falls and
then select at random the dependent factor.

5. Repeat Step 4 (usually with a computer) above, over and over
again, to provide a large number (500–1,000 will usually suffice)
of outcomes that will define the odds of occurrence of each possible payoff value. (Each repetition of Step 4 is called a "trial.")

The process is one of simulating to the most practical extent the
way events might unfold in the future. Clearly the most extreme
events in each distribution would combine very seldom, having a
low likelihood of being randomly selected at the same time. Since
there are literally millions of possible *combinations* of values in the
usual investment analysis, the important point is to test the probabilities that various *specific* returns will occur. This is analogous

EXHIBIT 11
Risk Analysis

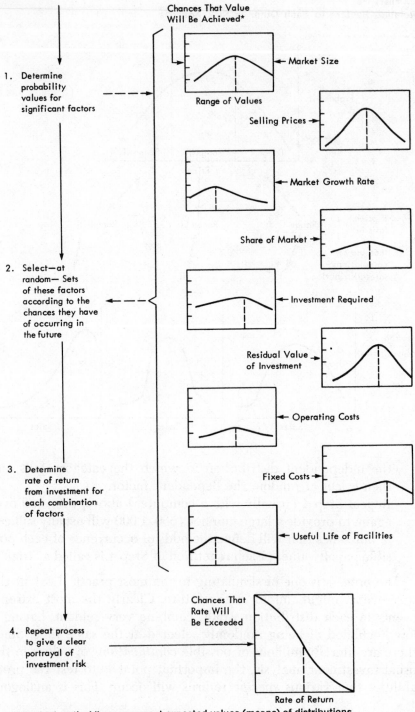

* Dashed vertical lines represent expected values (means) of distributions.

to finding out by recording the results of a great many throws of dice what percentage of "7s" (or other combinations) might be expected.

The types of distributions shown in Exhibits 1 and 2 are used to describe the various input factors. These are combined, as shown in Exhibit 11, to give an output of probability that a given rate of return will be achieved or exceeded. Exhibit 12 shows the DCF out-

EXHIBIT 12
End Results from Risk Analysis of Investment Project

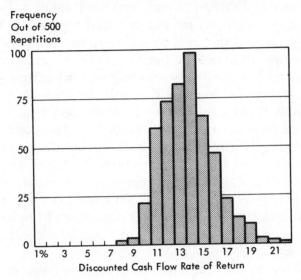

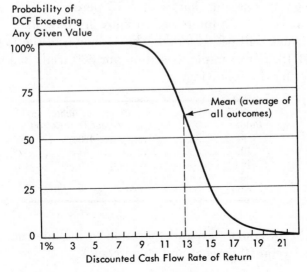

comes from 500 repetitions of an investment project and the cumulative frequency distribution of those outcomes. Standard computer packages are available from computer manufacturers and from time-sharing services to run such risk analyses.

Interpretation of Results

Exhibit 12 (top portion) shows how frequently various outcomes (measured in discounted cash flow rate of return percentages) occurred when 500 "trials" were performed using a Monte Carlo simulation approach. To review, *one* trial represents the outcome that would result if the "real world" were to correspond to a given set of assumptions about the future, that set of assumptions having been generated by randomly selecting one value from each of the nine probability distributions shown in Exhibit 11. For example, from Exhibit 12 we can see that 75 of the 500 trials resulted in a return of 12 percent—that is, 75/500 or 15 percent of the randomly generated sets of assumptions about the future resulted in a 12 percent return; and almost 20 percent of the trials (i.e., almost 100 trials) produced a DCF rate of return of 14 percent. Similarly, we can see that fewer than 5 of the 500 trials (i.e., 1 percent of the trials) resulted in a DCF return of 9 percent; and 1 percent or fewer of the trials produced returns of 8 percent, 20 percent, 21 percent, or 22 percent.

In addition to knowing how likely a *given* outcome is likely to occur (e.g., 15 percent chance of a 12 percent DCF return), the decision maker is also interested in knowing how likely it is that a given outcome will be *exceeded*. This is shown in the lower portion of Exhibit 12. For example, based on our 500 trials, we can say (in tabular form) the following:

% DCF Return	Chance of Achieving at Least That Return
5	100%
10	94
15	35
20	2
25	0

(We could, of course, expand the table to include more detail for returns between 10 percent and 20 percent.)

We can also say, based on our risk analysis, that the *expected* (average or mean) return from this project is about 13 percent. This is an especially interesting and important result, which illustrates one of the values of this analytical approach. For if we had taken the expected value *of each distribution* in Exhibit 11 (market size, selling prices, . . . , useful life of facilities), and used *those* nine values to calculate a DCF return for the project, the calculation would show a return of 17 percent. Thus, combining a series of "best estimates" for the nine factors does *not* give a realistic picture of the expected outcome of the project. In this case, the difference between the "true" expectation of a 13 percent return and the misleading 17 percent return calculated using the individual distributions' expected values could well mean the difference between rejecting or accepting the project (if, for example, the company used a 15 percent hurdle rate for projects of this type).[3] In sum, failure to deal systematically with the inherent uncertainties in the analysis of a project can lead to making the *wrong decision* on whether the project should be approved.

Let us now look further at the benefits of risk analysis.

Isolating Crucial Risk Determinants and Identifying Key Factors

The first step in risk analysis covers the identification of the significant factors that affect the ultimate outcome of the project and determination of which of these can be quantified with confidence. From the detailed flowchart of the economic process of the investment project that has been developed, the assumptions underlying the major input factors are spelled out and checked for validity. The preparation of this flowchart is often an illuminating exercise in itself, giving managers further insights into interrelationships they were formerly dealing with solely on an intuitive level.

After the key input factors have been established, a nonprobabilistic computer model is often constructed that provides early information on the sensitivity of the investment results to changes in the input factors. By analyzing sensitivity at this early stage, de-

---

[3] This phenomenon—the expected value of a function not being the same as the value of the function calculated using the individual distributions' expected values—can occur if the individual distributions are not "normal" distributions, or if the function is nonlinear. Both of these conditions hold here: the nine distributions in Exhibit 11 are not "normal," and the discounting calculation to arrive at DCF rate of return is nonlinear.

cision makers can gain valuable knowledge of the impact of each variable on the total project and can focus on improving the accuracy of the most important factors.

Computer Model and Simulation.   The detailed computer model that is usually used takes into account all of the significant uncertain input factors and the probabilities assigned to those factors, as well as the factors that are known for certain. As noted above, the computer selects at random within the predetermined range of values one particular value for each factor, combines the values, and computes the profitability of that situation. The computer then lists the range of possible outcomes in terms of such payoff measures as discounted cash flows, payback, and so on, together with the percentage of situations falling within given ranges. This information is put together in a *risk profile* of the investment (Exhibit 12). This risk profile provides a manager with the expected value of the investment and tells the manager the chance the project has of achieving each potential outcome, including the chance of achieving various levels of loss.

Risk profiles are derived for *each* investment opportunity. By comparing the shape and the relative position of these profiles to each other, managers can determine the differences in expected return, the possible variability of that return, and the relative risk of alternative investment opportunities. On the basis of this knowledge, they then can select investment projects that best meet corporate objectives.

Advantages of Risk Analysis

Risk analysis adds a number of distinctive features to other approaches for evaluating investment alternatives. First, risk analysis provides more information about investment projects. Instead of single estimates or expected values, the approach provides information on all the possible outcomes of a project, ranging from total loss to the highest expected rate of return. At the same time, the chance each value has of actually occurring is quantified and described by the risk profile, and the expected rate of return is identified.

Second, risk analysis allows management to make comparisons between investment alternatives with different risks and returns. Management is able to discriminate between investments by comparing the risk profiles of investment alternatives:

1. The expected rates of return, based on weighted probabilities of all possible returns, can be compared.
2. The shapes of the risk profiles provide information on the likelihood of variance from the expected rates of return, A "tight" probability distribution, or risk profile, indicates a small chance that the rate of return will vary greatly from the expected return.[4]
3. The relative position of two or more risk profiles to each other and to their axes indicates the degree of risk that each investment project will incur a loss.

ILLUSTRATION 16
Comparison of Two Investment Opportunities (selected statistics)

	Investment A	Investment B
Amount of investment	$10,000,000	$10,000,000
Life of investment (in years)	10	10
Expected annual net cash inflow	$ 1,300,000	$ 1,400,000
Variability of cash inflow:		
1 chance in 50 of being *greater* than	$ 1,700,000	$ 3,400,000
1 chance in 50 of being *less** than	$ 900,000	$ (600,000)
Expected return on investment	5.0%	6.8%
Variability of return on investment		
1 chance in 50 of being *greater* than	7.0%	15.5%
1 chance in 50 of being *less** than	3.0%	(4.0)%
Risk of investment:		
Chances of a loss	Negligible	1 in 10
Expected size of loss		$ 200,000

* In the case of negative figures (indicated by parentheses) "less than" means "worse than."

Risk analysis also allows the user to ascertain the sensitivity of the results of an investment project to each or all of the input factors. This makes it possible to determine the effect of added or changed information on the outcome of the investment project.

Comparing Opportunities. From a decision-making point of view, the most significant of the advantages of risk analysis is that it allows management to discriminate between measures of (1) expected return based on weighted probabilities of all possible returns; (2) variability of return; and (3) risks. Illustration 16

---

[4] The "tightness" of a probability distribution is characterized by the range between the minimum and maximum value of that distribution. The smaller the range, the tighter the distribution.

EXHIBIT 13
Comparative Risk Profiles of Two Investments

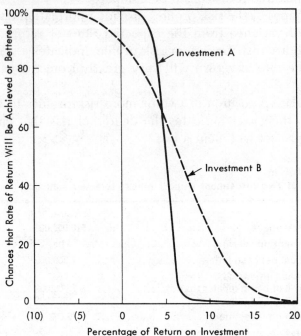

describes two alternative investments, A and B, showing the differences between these three measures. When these two investments are evaluated by risk analysis, the data tabulated in Illustration 16 and plotted in Exhibit 13 are obtained. From these data we see that:

1. Investment B has a higher expected return than Investment A (6.8 percent versus 5.0 percent).
2. Investment B also has substantially more variability than Investment A. There is a good chance that Investment B will earn a return which is quite different from the expected return of 6.8 percent, even possibly as high as 5.5 percent, or as low as a loss of 4 percent. Investment A is not likely to vary greatly from the expected 5 percent return; its return almost certainly will fall between 3.0 percent and 7.0 percent.
3. Investment B involves far more risk than does Investment A. There is virtually no chance of incurring a loss on Investment A. However, there is one chance in ten of losing money on Invest-

ment B. If such a loss occurs, its expected size is approximately $200,000.

Clearly, the risk analysis method of evaluating investments provides management with a maximum amount of information on which to base a decision. Investment decisions made only on the basis of maximum expected return are not unequivocally the best decisions, nor do they permit examination of the business opportunity in terms of risk-averse behavior or preference of managers. Whether an explicit utility curve is available or not, the risk analysis profile permits direct comparison, at all points of the return distribution, of the probabilities attached to the alternative investments.

Combining Risky Investments—Investment Strategy

An *investment strategy* may be defined as comprising a combination of individual business opportunities. The strategy can be described by the same attributes and in the same form as an individual risk opportunity. Thus, a strategy may be characterized by probabilistic profiles of profits, costs, and so on. To make strategies comparable for evaluation, investment and profit profiles should represent results over a common time period.

Since each of these characteristics typically is the sum of the corresponding characteristics of several opportunities, the combined attributes for the strategy often can be assumed to be distributed normally (for statistical reasons) in the typical "bell-shaped curve." The expected value of the attributes for any strategy then will be the sum of the expected values of the corresponding attributes of the opportunities included in that strategy, and the variance will be the sum of the corresponding variances. On the basis of such profiles, a strategy may be represented as a specific outcome of the expected return for some specific capital investment.

Each strategy or set of opportunities can be described as a point on a return versus investment graph. This point represents the expected values of the capital required and the returns generated as a result of following that strategy. Each of these values has a probability distribution associated with it. Combining these distributions and representing the uncertainties attached to profits and investment for a strategy produces an "oval of uncertainty" within which possible outcomes of the strategy will fall (Exhibit 14). Specifying different levels of risk—for example, one, two, or three standard deviations in the investment and profit dimensions—will result in ever larger concentric ovals containing all possible outcomes of that strategy with roughly 68, 95, and 99 percent certainty respectively. The decision maker, by choosing levels of risk acceptable for both the profit and investment requirement, then explicitly chooses a set of outcomes to be considered for a strategy.

EXHIBIT 14
Strategy Definition on Investment-Return Graph

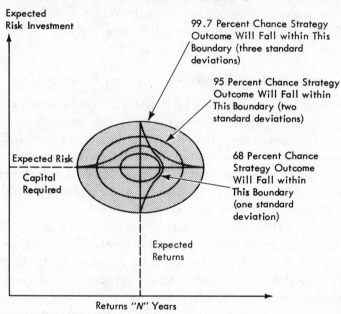

Increased expected profits of a particular strategy or combination of opportunities ordinarily will be directly related to higher investments. Additionally, both higher profits and higher investments usually entail greater risks. Where this is the case, the oval areas of uncertainty become larger profit expectations.

Measuring variability, or risk, of outcomes in terms of the probability distribution over the values which are likely to occur makes the problem of choosing between alternative strategies more complex. Strategies are no longer as easily distinguishable as when they were characterized by a single set of estimates of expected profit outcomes and capital requirements. The risk versus return trade-off now must be considered in conjunction with the return versus investment amount choice that traditionally is made.

Management, of course, would like to select a strategy that both maximizes results (i.e., profits) at acceptable risk-capital investment, and minimizes the uncertainty or risk. Seeking additional returns, however, often entails accepting additional uncertainty—that is, risk. If two strategies produce the same average profit results, the one that involves a lower risk-capital expenditure and/or involves less "variability" (or uncertainty as to the outcome) for the same yield clearly is a more desirable strategy. Conversely, of two strategies entailing the same risk, the one producing the higher expected profit return for equivalent risk investment obviously is the better strategy.

Based on this concept of suitable use of risk-capital investment, a set of available strategies can be reduced to only those that promise the most attractive return for a given level of risk investment. A suitable strategy will belong to this smaller group.

Selection from the group of attractive strategies will be guided primarily by available risk capital. But, within any range of investment, several strategies may seem attractive. And these may not, in fact, be clearly distinguishable from one another, on the basis of expectation in the face of uncertainty. Then, the "intangible" factors that always enter into investment choice must be expected to prevail.

Summary

The process for selecting a strategy based on probabilistic representation of the uncertainties underlying investments proceeds as follows:

1. Generate possible strategies as combinations of the set of business opportunities and evaluate their associated return/capital requirements profiles over a specific period.
2. For any possible level of capital investment over the planning horizon, identify those strategies promising highest expected returns. Strategies identified in this way are attractive in their use of available capital.

3. From among the attractive set, select that strategy (or combination of exploration opportunities) that best meets expected goals at an acceptable risk level. If the corresponding expected required capital exposure is too high, trade-offs must be made. This can be done easily by moving down in expected profit to a strategy in the attractive set having a lower expected risk capital requirement.

The final choice between investment, returns, and risk of alternative strategies will not be determined solely by the presentation of these outcomes, but bringing out the differences and sharpening understanding of the trade-offs as this process allows will certainly lead to more consistent and better strategic decisions.

ADDITIONAL SOURCES

Bierman, Harold; Bonini, Charles P.; and Hausman, Warren H. *Quantitative Analysis for Business Decisions*, chaps. 4, 5, 10, 21. 5th ed. Homewood, Ill.: Richard D. Irwin, Inc., 1977.

Christenson, Charles J.; Vancil, Richard F.; and Marshall, Paul W. *Managerial Economics: Text and Cases*, chaps. 4, 5, 10. Rev. ed. Homewood, Ill.: Richard D. Irwin, Inc., 1973.

Hammond, John S. "Better Decisions with Preference Theory." *Harvard Business Review*, November–December 1967, p. 123.

Hertz, David B. "Investment Policies That Pay Off." *Harvard Business Review*, January–February 1968, p. 96.

———. "Risk Analysis in Capital Investment." *Harvard Business Review*, January–February 1964, p. 95.

Hespos, Richard F., and Strassman, Paul A. "Stochastic Decision Trees for the Analysis of Investment Decisions." *Management Science*, August 1965, p. 244.

Lindley, D. V. *Making Decisions*. London: John Wiley & Sons, 1971.

Magee, John F. "Decision Trees for Decision Making." *Harvard Business Review*, July–August 1964, p. 126.

———. "How to Use Decision Trees in Capital Investment." *Harvard Business Review*, September–October 1964, p. 79.

Raiffa, Howard. *Decision Analysis*. Reading, Mass.: Addison-Wesley Publishing Co., Inc., 1968.

Rudisill, Edward L. "Analyzing Investment Risk." *Financial Executive*, September 1972, p. 24.

Schlaifer, Robert O. *Analysis of Decisions under Uncertainty.* New York: McGraw-Hill, Inc., 1969.

Thomas, Howard. *Decision Theory and the Manager.* London: Pitman Publishing Corp., 1972.

Weston, J. Fred, and Brigham, Eugene F. *Essentials of Managerial Finance,* chap. 12. 4th ed. Hinsdale, Ill.: The Dryden Press, 1977.

17

Establishing a Program for the Control of Capital Expenditures

John O. Turk*

When a company spends in excess of $100 million annually—in many cases, hundreds of millions of dollars—on capital investment, it is incumbent upon that organization to maintain good control over the outlay of those funds. It is important that the controls employed are good, efficient, and adequate to administer the program. However, concern should also be expressed about overcontrolling. A firm which does not spend heavily certainly does not need, nor does it want, as elaborate a system to monitor its expenditures as a company which spends very heavily. It is, therefore, necessary to tailor the type of control system fairly tightly with the real need there is for the system.

Another way of viewing this task of appropriate level of control is to consider the added benefit if more control were adopted. Do more controls, indeed, really give a better managerial grip on the project or program? On the other hand, does less control really remove the project or program from the scrutiny it deserves? This decision is a difficult one, but experience will go a long way in making the right decision. However, the type of control system for capital expenditures is not solely dependent upon the amount of money involved on a given project or total program; also the decision process itself is crucial. It is critical that appropriate levels of man-

---

* Mr. Turk is Controller of the Dixie/Marathon Division of American Can Company, Greenwich, Connecticut.

agement be aware both of the level of the capital program and also of any potential interrelationships between various projects. It is this overall awareness type of control which can make the total program more efficient.

In this chapter we will discuss where control should really commence. We will also take a brief look at the capital program from its birth and follow through with the steps of monitoring and controlling the program and its projects, not only in Year 1 but over a period of time. Although a particular capital program may be born in one specific year, the projects which compose that program may cease in that year or they may continue for several years thereafter. In order to establish not only good systems for monitoring and controlling projects but also in order to achieve professionalism and expertise in the analysis and evaluation of capital projects, it is absolutely necessary to maintain surveillance of each substantial project virtually from "birth" to "death."

Now that we have discussed when the monitoring of a capital investment project should terminate, when should monitoring and control originate? It is essential that the systems for following a capital project begin as soon as the project is conceived. This is necessary in order to assure that the project is required—that it does in fact satisfy a need. The first step of a good monitoring and control system is to establish that a real need does exist for a particular investment. In order to assure that this question is answered at the earliest possible time, it is important to develop a good system for planning the capital program. If a good planning system does not exist, many man-hours can be wasted chasing down details of a project prior to the involvement of the requisite individuals who should be involved or who are to make the ultimate decision.

PLANNING THE CAPITAL PROGRAM

Planning of the capital program should be the initial step in a company's financial planning cycle and must be a very integral segment of that cycle as the financial plan moves down the timetable toward completion. The financial plan should be viewed as a resource plan—that is, an identification of the resources available or required to meet the corporate commitment for growth. There are some rather preliminary steps that can be undertaken on the capital program prior to the formal initiation of the actual financial planning schedule itself. In order to understand how these initial steps can commence we should understand the broad general parts of a capital program.

Segmentation of the Capital Program

A major corporation can separate its capital program into two broad general categories of projects based upon the absolute dollar magnitude of those projects. The first grouping of projects might fall under the label of "ordinaries." Ordinaries can be further split between "specific ordinaries" and "blankets." Specific ordinaries may have a dollar magnitude of $50,000 or more, while blankets would consist of those projects under $50,000. Examples of this latter group are automotive, office furniture and fixtures, and small investments in plant and equipment. Specific ordinaries would depend upon the nature of the company's operations.

The second group of capital projects is then called "major projects." Projects within this particular area would cost in excess of $100,000 and by their sheer size would be the most important projects over which control should be exercised.[1] Having broken the capital program into three parts in this manner, we can identify the areas more readily which will require more or less control. Segmentation of the program into blankets, specific ordinaries, and majors recognizes a need to exercise more control over majors than specific ordinaries and blankets. However, although the dollar magnitude of blankets and specific ordinaries is not that great, it does not mean control should be nonexistent. It simply means that the timing and formality of the monitoring and reporting system need not be as elaborate or detailed as for major projects.

Now that the annual capital program has been divided into three components, we can plan accordingly. Since the blanket projects normally don't have a direct relation to volume or marketing needs, we can get an early start planning this portion of the total program. It should be our objective to have the blanket projects completed and approved prior to the beginning of the formal financial planning cycle.

---

[1] The "break points" here of $50,000 and $100,000 are illustrative, although they are in use in many major companies. Each company, of course, should choose its own break points based on its own perceived needs for authorization controls.

There is also a fairly good possibility that a number of the specific ordinary projects and maybe a couple of the major projects could also be investigated at an early date. This opportunity would arise if these projects were of a replacement or production-improvement nature.

Major projects would probably be the last to be tied up, both because of the amount of the investment and because of the likelihood that major projects will involve significant increases in volume or new product needs. Volume and new product requirements usually do not become "official" until after the formal financial planning cycle has commenced with the submission of anticipated sales volumes to production scheduling.

Planning Timetable

Exhibit 1 illustrates a typical capital program timetable at a plant location for a company whose fiscal year is on a calendar-year basis. As capital projects are being identified and detailed, it is also necessary to determine the expense portion of the project and the depreciation expense impact. The expense portion is an identification of incremental expense directly resulting from the particular project. Expenses are costs that have been or will be incurred but are not capitalized. It is essential that we identify those components of the capital program which impact other functional areas and in addition affect the income statement.

Exhibit 1 also identifies the type of approvals that should be received prior to actual commencement of acting on the proposals encompassed within the capital program. At the local level the capital program is approved by the engineering manager in conjunction with the general accounting services manager, and it is then approved on a top-line basis by the local operations manager and staff. After tentative approval by the division engineering manager on a preliminary basis, the program is then detailed and a full-blown presentation with all appropriate detail is made to the local operations manager. Once local ratification has been received, the program is then forwarded for divisional and ultimately corporate approval.

Once full approval for the capital program has been obtained, the first step in the control process has been accomplished. We now

EXHIBIT 1
Capital Program Timetable Calendar Year 1974

Date	Activity	Responsibility
May 1	Office furniture and fixture and automotive needs to project accounting.	Staff department managers
May 1	Blanket project requirements—that is, furniture and fixture, automotive, and plant and equipment consolidated by project accounting and project engineering.	Project accounting and control supervisor and project engineering manager
June 3	Production volumes to project engineering.	Production scheduling
July 8	Submit projects planned with financial justification to project accounting.	Project engineering manager
July 12	Complete listing of all projects.	Project engineering manager
July 16	Review top-line capital appropriations with engineering manager.	Project accounting and control supervisor
July 18	Review top-line capital appropriations plans with local management.	Project accounting and control supervisor
July 23	Submit capital appropriations for plants to division engineering manager.	Project accounting and control supervisor
July 30	Submit projects justified on categories other than financial payback to project accounting.	Project engineering manager
August 2	Submit expense portion of capital and depreciation expense to indirect cost department.	Project accounting and control supervisor
August 9	Review annual capital program in detail with local management.	General accounting services manager
August 23	Review annual capital program with division management.	Operations manager and staff
September 13	Submit annual capital program—appropriations and expenditures—to division headquarters for consolidation into total division capital program.	General accounting services manager
October 11	Submit capital additions, equipment disposals, and return-on-funds-employed data to headquarters.	General accounting services manager
November 15	Review total division capital program with corporate management.	Division controller

have a program that encompasses the most important projects for the fiscal year. The various approval levels that had to be satisfied were the initial phase in our system to monitor the capital program.

Types of Projects

The primary responsibility for the identification of capital projects lies with the project engineering manager (or a counterpart, dependent upon the organization). It is the project engineering manager working in conjunction with a counterpart in the controller's department who should determine the next segmentation of the capital program. We have already separated the program into blankets, specific ordinaries and majors. However, we must now identify those projects which can be justified on a financial basis; that is, implementation of a project that can be paid back financially from those that are warranted for other reasons. Those projects which have financial implications can be justified to management based upon the return on investment that those projects will provide. Projects which do not have a basis in financial return or payback also have a very important reason for being proposed. Such projects could be warranted due to quality improvement, safety, replacement, and so on. Projects such as these have an impact on the product/company from a nonfinancial basis which may very easily be for the betterment of the business or social consciousness.

Projects which have been justified on financial grounds require a somewhat separate and different controlling and reporting mechanism than other projects. By approving a project because it is going to give an adequate return on the investment, we accept the responsibility of following up to ascertain that in fact the projected return was actually realized.

As the capital program is being drawn up, it is the responsibility of the project accounting group to determine the financial return on projects which will pay themselves off. It is not sufficient for this group just to take the particular inputs—that is, volume, cost savings, and so forth—and determine the return on investment and payback period. Project accounting must question the validity of all inputs into the financial justification. When they issue a given return and payback, they are also issuing a certified statement that all components of the justification are in fact correct and legitimate. Such validation is necessary because the control and reporting systems are going to continually monitor those projects until they either pay back or until it can be determined that the projects will not pay off.

The basic foundation of the capital program has now been laid. Projects have been identified and categorized both as to dollar amount—less than $50,000, $50,000 to $100,000, and over $100,000 —and they have also been segmented as to whether they have a financial justification or not. Once these basic steps are completed, project engineering and project accounting can proceed to write up each project and then advance through the steps to achieve first plant and then headquarters approval of its program.

As each capital project is being written up, it is necessary to identify the expenditure of funds along with the appropriation requirements. This is necessary in order to determine the availability of capital funds to finance the program. Appropriation and expenditure requirements should be done on a quarterly basis in order to better control not only the capital projects themselves but also to control the need for funds.

Although the total program is approved by corporate management, it should be recognized that what they are approving is just that—the *total* capital program. The presentation that is made to management does not get into many details of the projects. In effect what is being approved is the general thrust of the program. In order to get the final authorization to appropriate and expend funds, a detailed capital project request must be issued and approved at appropriate levels. What is important to understand at this point is that general approval has been received and that permission has been granted to proceed into a more detailed investigation of the projects. We will review the detailed steps taken to get individual project approval later.

By reviewing the programs of the several groups/divisions that make up the company or corporation, top-level management is able to see the overall company capital program. Such an overview gives them the total perspective and allows them to consider the program in entirety to determine the following:

1. Are there any inconsistencies in the program?
2. Are different groups/divisions requesting the same or similar projects?
3. What are the overall benefits of the program?
4. Is the total program affordable? (If not, prioritization is required.)
5. How can the program best be financed?

These and many more considerations are the responsibility and input of top management as they consider the projects and programs presented to them for their concurrence or approval.

In fact, what the planning system brings to capital project planning is a distinction between informal general consent and formal detailed written approval. However, it is necessary to surpass successfully this initial informal control phase in order to continue with the blueprints of the project itself.

PROJECT EXPENDITURE CONTROL

Having gone through the elaborate system of planning, detailing, and gaining approval of the capital program, our work would be wasted or useless if we did not follow up with the details of the program once it had begun. It certainly is not sufficient nor does it gain anything for us if we spend three or four months developing the program, if we are not going to attempt to monitor it. There should be some relationship between the amount of time and effort consumed in developing the program and the degree of control we exercise in monitoring the program. A good guideline for this effort could be the number of dollars we have tied up in a particular project or program. In a time when funds are tight and interest rates are escalating rapidly, it is incumbent upon good managers to ensure that they direct funds in the most efficient manner to those efforts which will realize the best returns for the company in the future. Again the degree of control, monitoring, and reporting is directly dependent upon the type of project that is being implemented.

A project with a basis in financial justification would require similar controls as other projects during the building construction stage; however, once online, the type of monitoring and reporting changes quite dramatically. We will look into this later in the chapter.

When is the expenditure control system initiated for a capital project? As we stated earlier, the system of control over a capital project begins at the initial review stage within the planning cycle. Once the capital program has received final corporate approval, a different set of controls and reports of a formal nature should be available once work on a particular project is begun.

Project Approval

As each individual capital project is readied for approval, the degree and depth of both analytical review and effort is dependent

EXHIBIT 2
Authorization Schedule

CAPITAL PROJECTS, LEASE REQUESTS, AND DISPOSALS OF FIXED ASSETS	Division President or Corporate Staff Officer	Corporate Executive to Whom Operating Unit or Head-quarters Function Reports	Board of Directors
I. ORIGINAL AUTHORIZATION			
A. *$1,000,000 or More*			
1. *Capital projects*—$1,000,000 or more of capital funds *or* $2,000,000 or more of capital plus working funds.			X
2. *Leases* with an aggregate rental of $1,000,000 or more *or* any lease with an *annual* rental commitment of $200,000 or more.			X
B. *$100,000 to $999,000*			
1. Capital projects		X	
2. *Leases* with an aggregate rental between $100,000 and $999,000 provided annual rental commitment is less than $200,000		X	
C. *Less Than $100,000*			
1. Capital projects—Individual projects requiring *less than* $100,000 in capital funds (limited to the *total* funds approved in the annual program for each of the following categories: plant and equipment; office furniture and equipment; automobiles and trucks).	X		
2. Leases with an aggregate rental of less than $100,000	X		
II. EXPENDITURES IN EXCESS OF ORIGINAL AUTHORIZATION			
A. *Projects $100,000 or More*			
1. Up to 20% in excess of original authorization but *less* than $100,000	X		
2. Over either of the limits in (1) but *less* than $1,000,000		X	
3. $1,000,000 or more			X
B. *Projects under $100,000* Expenditures in excess of the *total* amount identified and approved for *each of the following categories:* plant and equipment; office furniture and equipment; automobiles and trucks		X	

upon the final level of approval that is required for the specific project. Exhibit 2 shows a typical authorization schedule.

In this approval schedule the capital projects are segmented between majors and ordinaries with ordinaries further separated between specific ordinaries and blankets. The level of funds involved is the overriding determinant in the final level of approval. The level of funds is determined both by the amount of noncurrent assets and the amount of working capital employed. Additionally, the level of approval is dependent upon original authorizations, overruns, and additions to the annual program. Recognizing not only the number of levels required for final formal approval but also the amount of funds involved is sufficient to warrant appropriate planning and control of the expenditures of a particular project. For example, a specific ordinary project could be haphazardly developed and request $50,000 in funds. Such a project, assuming it was identified in the annual program, would have to be signed by the division general manager. However, if there was an overrun on that project, the overrun could potentially have to be approved by not only the division general manager but might have to go all the way to the board of directors for final approval. With such risk apparent, it certainly behooves the project accounting group to do their "homework" well the first time. Additionally, it provides ample reason for instituting appropriate controls within the system. Recognizing the series of approvals that potentially have to be secured, how do we go about preparing the necessary documentation to achieve approval?

As discussed earlier, as the annual capital program is prepared for submission, a top-line summary of a given project is developed. Exhibits 3 and 4 are examples of the initial write-up of projects. The purpose of this form is to secure the approval of management to commit or expend funds on a particular capital project. The form is utilized both as input to the annual program as well as the preface for the detailed project request as it is developed for formal approval of the capital project.

This form provides a fairly good introduction to the essential ingredients of a project. By scanning this document we can determine the title, purpose, and description of the project as well as its net cost, financial justification, and the estimated rate of expenditures. The bottom of the form provides for all appropriate approval signatures.

EXHIBIT 3
Capital Project Request

8/31/77	
Date	

Project "Z"   —   15
Project Title & Number

ABC   —   Chicago, Illinois
Division & Location

New Request ☒   Supplement ☐
Expansion - Existing Product ☒ A
Purpose   ☐ B

PROJECT DESCRIPTION

SUMMARY OF INVESTMENT	
NEW CAPITAL FUNDS REQUIRED	$1,950,000
EXPENSE BEFORE TAXES	$ 50,000
LESS: TRADE-IN OR SALVAGE, IF ANY	—
Total This Request	$2,000,000
PREVIOUSLY APPROPRIATED	—
Total Project Cost	$2,000,000

FINANCIAL JUSTIFICATION	
ROFE (PBT BASIS) · 10-YR. AVERAGE	92.4%
PAYBACK PERIOD 10/77 FROM F1982 TO	3.9YRS.
NOT REQUIRED	☐
*BASED ON TOTAL PROJECT COST AND WORKING FUNDS OF	$3,137,000

ESTIMATED EXPENDITURE RATE	
QUARTER ENDING 12/31 F1978	$ 400,000
QUARTER ENDING 3/31 F1978	$1,000,000
QUARTER ENDING 6/30 F1979	$ 100,000
QUARTER ENDING 9/30 F1979	$ 500,000
REMAINDER	—

OTHER INFORMATION	
MAJOR ☒ SPECIFIC ORDINARY ☐ BLANKET ☐	
INCLUDED IN ANNUAL PROGRAM YES ☒ NO ☐	
PERCENT OF ENGINEERING COMPLETED	10%
ESTIMATED START-UP COSTS	$ 42,000
ESTIMATED START-UP DATE	6/78

LEVEL OF APPROVAL REQUIRED
☒ BOARD ☐ CHAIRPERSON ☐ EXEC. V.P. ☐ GEN. MGR.

SIGNATURES		DATE
DIRECTOR CORP. ENG.		
DIRECTOR B & A		
GENERAL MANAGER		
VICE PRESIDENT		
EXEC. VICE PRESIDENT		
PRESIDENT		
CHAIRPERSON		

For Division Use – Signatures	
NAME AND TITLE	DATE

EXHIBIT 4
Capital Project Request

	4/16/77
	Date

Project "B" — 13
Project Title & Number

XYZ — Chicago, Illinois
Division & Location

New Request ☒   Supplement ☐
Reduce Costs   ☐ A
Purpose   ☒ B

PROJECT DESCRIPTION

SUMMARY OF INVESTMENT		
NEW CAPITAL FUNDS REQUIRED	$	75,000
EXPENSE BEFORE TAXES	$	12,000
LESS: TRADE-IN OR SALVAGE, IF ANY	$	4,000
Total This Request	$	83,000
PREVIOUSLY APPROPRIATED		—
Total Project Cost	$	83,000

FINANCIAL JUSTIFICATION	
ROFE (PBT BASIS) · 10-YR. AVERAGE	61.7%
PAYBACK 12/78 F1983 PERIOD —————————————— FROM TO	4.0 YRS.
NOT REQUIRED	☐
*BASED ON TOTAL PROJECT COST AND WORKING FUNDS OF	$ 75,950

ESTIMATED EXPENDITURE RATE		
QUARTER ENDING 6/30 F1979	$	20,000
QUARTER ENDING 9/30 F1979	$	50,000
QUARTER ENDING 12/31 F1979	$	13,000
QUARTER ENDING F19		
REMAINDER		

OTHER INFORMATION		
MAJOR ☐ SPECIFIC ORDINARY ☒ BLANKET ☐		
INCLUDED IN ANNUAL PROGRAM YES ☒ NO ☐		
PERCENT OF ENGINEERING COMPLETED		25%
ESTIMATED START-UP COSTS	$	
ESTIMATED START-UP DATE		12/78

LEVEL OF APPROVAL REQUIRED

☐ BOARD ☐ CHAIRPERSON ☐ EXEC. V.P. ☒ GEN. MGR.

SIGNATURES		DATE
DIRECTOR CORP. ENG.		
DIRECTOR B & A		
GENERAL MANAGER		
VICE PRESIDENT		
EXEC. VICE PRESIDENT		
PRESIDENT		
CHAIRPERSON		

For Division Use – Signatures	
NAME AND TITLE	DATE

A financial justification is not applicable in all cases. If such is the case, this is identified. However, should a financial justification be necessary, this section of the form is filled out with data developed from supplementary work schedules. The "ROFE"—return on funds employed—and "payback" are prepared for every profit-increasing project which requires a total of $50,000 or more of new capital and funds. The return on funds employed is calculated over ten years of a project's life and draws a relationship between the total incremental funds required for a project and the incremental profit which the project is anticipated to generate. ROFE is calculated both before and after taxes. A project's payback period is the length of time it takes that project to return the funds invested. The period which is measured commences with the initial operational date of the project. (These concepts are covered in Chapter 15.)

In addition to the calculation of ROFE and payback, it is also necessary to utilize a discounted cash flow technique in order to recognize the time value of the funds tied up in the investment. This is necessary because the calculation of the payback period ignores the timing of the cash flows generated by the project. It is very significant if the heavier cash flows come in early or late, or even after the evaluation period has ended. The importance of timing is seen from the fact that the further out in time the inflow of cash is, the lower the present value of that income. (This is also discussed in Chapter 15.)

Exhibit 5 is an example of the supplementary work schedules required to provide the data for the calculation of ROFE and payback. Basically, this form is separated into the following four parts:

1. Net project cost detail.   3. Profit and loss.
2. Funds employed.   4. ROFE and payback calculations.

The net project cost is fairly self-explanatory. It identifies the gross capital outlay in addition to the expense (noncapital) portion of the project. This gross cost is reduced by salvage value, taxes on the expense portion, and the investment credit (if applicable). The funds employed section is made up of two sections—capital funds and working funds. Capital funds are the net project cost less cumulative depreciation. Working funds are cash, receivables, inventories, prepaid and deferred expenses, and current liabilities.

EXHIBIT 5
Financial Evaluation

ABC | Chicago, Ill. | Project Y | Project No. 15 | 4/16/77
Division | Location | Project Title | | Date — Supplement No.

PROJECT REQUEST DETAIL

PROJECT REQUEST DETAIL	1ST PER.	2D PER.	PER.	PER.	PER.
1. LAND	$ 100				
2. BUILDINGS	750				
3. MACHINERY & EQUIPMENT	500	$ 500			
4. ENGINEERING	200				
5. OTHER (EXPLAIN)					
6. NEW CAPITAL FUNDS REQ. (1 THRU 5)	1,550	$ 500			
7. ADD: EXPENSE BEFORE TAXES	75				
8. LESS: SALVAGE VALUE (OLD ASSET)	50				
9. TOTAL PROJECT COST*	$ 1,575	$ 500			
10. LESS: EXPENSE BEFORE TAXES	75				
11. NET PROJECT COST	$ 1,500	$ 500			

*Same as Project Request FUNDS EMPLOYED / PROFIT AND LOSS

	1ST PER. 6 mos.	2D PER. FY1979	3D PER. FY1980	4TH PER. FY1981	5TH PER. FY1982	6TH PER. FY1983	7TH PER. FY1984	8TH PER. FY1985	9TH PER. FY1986	10TH PER. FY1987	11TH PER. 6 mos.	10-YR. AVG.
12. NOT PROJECT COST (LINE 11)	$ 1,500	$ 2,000	$ 2,000	$ 2,000	$ 2,000	$ 2,000	$ 2,000	$ 2,000	$ 2,000	$ 2,000	$ 2,000	
13. DEDUCT DEPRECIATION (CUM.)	34	135	236	337	438	539	640	741	842	943		
14. CAPITAL FUNDS EMPLOYED	$ 1,466	$ 1,865	$ 1,764	$ 1,663	$ 1,562	$ 1,461	$ 1,360	$ 1,259	$ 1,158	$ 1,057		$ 1,462
15. CASH	$ 59	$ 126	129	131	131	131	132	132	132	132		124
16. RECEIVABLES	101	202	202	202	202	202	202	202	202	202		192
17. INVENTORIES	105	168	169	170	171	172	172	173	174	175		165
18. PREPAID & DEFERRED EXPENSE	(4)	(9)	(9)	(9)	(9)	(9)	(9)	(9)	(9)	(9)		(9)
19. LESS: CURRENT LIABILITIES	88	175	176	177	178	179	180	181	181	182		170
20. TOTAL WORKING FUNDS (15 THRU 19)	173	312	315	317	317	317	317	318	318	318		302
21. TOTAL NEW FUNDS EMPLOYED (14+20)	$ 1,639	$ 2,177	$ 2,079	$ 1,980	$ 1,879	$ 1,778	$ 1,677	$ 1,576	$ 1,476	$ 1,375		$ 1,764
PROFIT AND LOSS												
22. UNIT VOLUME	750	$ 1,500	$ 1,550	$ 1,600	$ 1,650	$ 1,700	$ 1,750	$ 1,850	$ 1,900	$ 1,950	$ 1,150	$ 1,735
23. GROSS SALES	$ 2,474	$ 5,625	$ 5,767	$ 5,935	$ 6,169	$ 6,375	$ 6,586	$ 6,801	$ 7,010	$ 7,218	$ 4,333	$ 6,429
24. DEDUCTIONS	224	530	545	601	620	644	666	689	703	728	438	639
25. NET SALES	$ 2,250	$ 5,095	$ 5,222	$ 5,334	$ 5,549	$ 5,731	$ 5,920	$ 6,112	$ 6,307	$ 6,490	$ 3,895	$ 5,790
26. COST OF GOODS SOLD	1,091	2,468	2,492	2,537	2,632	2,706	2,782	2,878	2,963	3,035	1,815	2,740
27. GROSS PROFIT	$ 1,159	$ 2,627	$ 2,730	$ 2,797	$ 2,917	$ 3,025	$ 3,138	$ 3,234	$ 3,344	$ 3,455	$ 2,080	$ 3,050
GROSS PROFIT % NET SALES	51.5%	51.6%	52.3%	52.4%	52.6%	52.8%	53.0%	52.9%	53.0%	53.2%	53.4%	52.7%
28. ADVERTISING EXPENSE	$ 1,118	$ 2,425	$ 1,055	$ 892	$ 627	$ 575	$ 599	$ 620	$ 666	$ 666	$ 401	$ 961
29. SELLING EXPENSE	75	190	190	190	190	195	200	200	200	200	110	194
30. GEN. AND ADMIN. COSTS	26	62	63	68	71	76	77	83	88	89	52	76
31. RESEARCH EXPENSE	43	15	15	15	15	13	13	13	13	13	8	18
32. START-UP COSTS	42											4
33. OTHER (EXPLAIN) EROS. PROD. X	25	50	50	50	50	55	55	55	60	65	45	56
34. PROFIT BEFORE TAXES	$ (170)	$ (115)	$ 1,357	$ 1,582	$ 1,964	$ 2,111	$ 2,194	$ 2,263	$ 2,342	$ 2,422	$ 1,464	$ 1,741
35. LESS: TAXES	$ (85)	$ (58)	$ 791	$ 791	$ 982	$ 1,056	$ 1,097	$ 1,132	$ 1,171	$ 1,211	$ 732	$ 871
36. ADD: INVESTMENT CREDIT	70											7
37. NET PROFIT	$ (15)	$ (57)	$ 678	$ 791	$ 982	$ 1,055	$ 1,097	$ 1,131	$ 1,171	$ 1,211	$ 732	$ 877
38. CUMULATIVE NET PROFIT	$ (15)	$ (72)	$ 606	$ 1,397	$ 2,379	$ 3,434	$ 4,531	$ 5,662	$ 6,833	$ 8,044	$ 8,776	$ 877
39. DEFERRED TAX	11	43	38	32	27							
40. CUMULATIVE DEFERRED TAX	11	54	92	124	151							
41. NEW FUNDS TO REPAY (38+40. LESS 21)	$ (1,643)	$ (2,195)	$ (1,381)	$ (459)	$ 651							

RETURN ON NEW FUNDS EMPLOYED · 10-YR. AVG.

		PAT (C÷A)	PBT (B÷A)
A - NEW FUNDS EMPLOYED (LINE 21)		$1,764	$1,764
B - PROFIT BEFORE TAXES (LINE 34)			$1,741
C - NET PROFIT (LINE 37)		877	
D - CALCULATED RETURN		49.7%	98.7%

PAYBACK YEARS FROM OPERATIONAL DATE

PART YEAR CALCULATION FOR FIRST PERIOD	0.5	YRS.
NUMBER OF FULL YEARS TO PAY BACK	3.0	YRS.
PART YEAR CALCULATION FOR LAST PERIOD	0.4	YRS.
TOTAL YEARS TO PAY BACK	3.9	YRS.

A given company should be able to develop a series of formulas for the calculations of the various components of working funds. Relationships with volume can be drawn for cash, receivables, inventories, and current liabilities. Such calculations can be developed on supplementary work sheets.

Once these forms have been completed, the project is ready for review prior to moving through the authorization process. When the appropriate level of approval has been attained, work on the project may commence.

A company should establish criteria on the evaluation tests in the case of profit increasing projects. Profit increasing projects should be segmented between cost reduction projects and business expansion projects. The separation is made because the risks of achieving anticipated results vary between these two kinds of projects. The greater the risk involved, the higher the return on investment (ROI) should be. In both instances payback should be keyed to the economic life of the new assets. Normally, the longer the economic life, the more acceptable a longer payback period becomes.

If the project is not to be based on a financial justification, the financial analytical work load is eased. However, more effort must be spent on the rationale for initiating the program. The project could be adapted for safety and convenience, product quality, or other reasons. If payback and ROI cannot be computed, it must be demonstrated that the improvement is clearly identifiable and desirable. Having separated projects between those with and without a financial justifications, we can now regroup all projects as we evolve an ongoing control system which is applicable to both types of projects.

The Project Step Sheet

As a project is forwarded for approval at its home location, a project estimate or "step sheet" is attached which readily identifies the detailed spending for construction in its logical component parts (Exhibit 6). This estimate is frequently called a step sheet because it provides a tracking of each stage or "step" the project goes through. This tracking is by cost component or "line item"—that is, equipment, labor, and materials.

This form is prepared by the project engineer and is reviewed

EXHIBIT 6
Project Step Sheet

I/E ET	Job #	Step	T O	Date Mo.–Da.	Description	Target Mo.–Yr.	Equipment	Labor	Material	Total
Prepared by_____ Fiscal Year ____1977____									
Title and Total Scope of Project									
I	5653	00	G	0407	Ventilate Sheet Metal Shop		1,500	600	1,400	3,500
I	5653	01	G	0407	Purchase and Install a Roof Ventilator		1,500		700	2,200
I	5653	02	G	0407	Install Sw. & Wiring for 5 HP Motor			200	300	500
E	5653	81	G	0407	Install Portable Hoods & Flex Ducts			300	200	500
I	5653	03	G	0407	Contingency			100	200	300
			G							
			G							
			G							
			G							
			G							
			G							
			G							
			G							

Job Numbers: 1000–5999 Capital (I)   Step Numbers: I jobs, I steps 01–79
              6000–8999 Expense (E)   I jobs, E steps 81–99
              9000–9998 Expense Transfer (ET)   E and ET jobs, all steps 01–99

with project accounting prior to the project's submission. This document, then, becomes the basis for controlling project spending since it is in a sense the budget for the project. The most important facet of control provided by the step sheet is the division of project spending into three integral parts—equipment, labor, and material. As the project is routed within the plant facility for approval, this breakout can be reviewed readily by management to determine its adequacy. The step sheet, as the basic control device, is backed up with a weekly Capital and Expense Status Report (Exhibit 7).

Capital and Expense Status Report

The computerized weekly Capital and Expense Status Report is issued to both project engineering and the project accounting department. Included in this report is a listing of commitments, actual expenditures (invoices paid, labor, stores withdrawals), and the

EXHIBIT 7
Capital Expense and Status Report

LABOR THROUGH   05/30
STORES THROUGH   06/04
INVOICES THROUGH   06/04

JOB STP CENTER ACCOUNT	DESCRIPTION	DATE	TOTAL	EQUIPMENT	LABOR	MATERIAL
5653	VENTILATE SHEET METAL SHOP	04/07	3,500.00	1,500.00	600.00	1,400.00
5653 01	PUR & INST A ROOF VENTILATOR	04/07	2,200.00	1,500.00		700.00
−34 001−02	PO 69196	05/15	1,020.00	1,020.00		
−34 001−02	PO 69196 V 101181	10/09	1,330.00	1,330.00		
−34 001−04	JT 090028	09/23	81.39			81.39
−34 001−04	JT 100028	09/28	2.72			2.72
−34 001−04	PO 72927	09/15	600.00			600.00
−34 001−04	PO 72927 V 101420	10/14	578.69			578.69
921−25 104−04	JT 110001	11/01	21.36		21.36	
921−26 104−04	JT 090001	09/27	26.70		26.70	
921−26 104−04	JT 090001	09/27	8.00		8.00	
921−26 104−04	JT 090001	09/27	16.02		16.02	
921−26 104−04	JT 090001	00/00	26.70		26.70	
921−26 104−04	JT 100001	10/04	29.38		29.38	
921−26 104−04	JT 100001	10/04	18.70		18.70	
921−26 104−04	JT 100001	10/04	24.02		24.02	
	PURCHASE ORDERS COMMITTED		21.31			21.31
	CHARGES ACTUALLY SPENT		2,163.68	1,330.00	170.88	662.80
	JOB STEP BALANCE		15.01	170.00	170.88−	15.89
5653 02	INST SW & WIRING FOR 5 HP MOTOR	04/07	500.00		200.00	300.00
	PURCHASE ORDERS COMMITTED					
	CHARGES ACTUALLY SPENT					
	JOB STEP BALANCE		500.00		200.00	300.00
5653 03	CONTINGENCY	04/07	300.00		100.00	200.00
	PURCHASE ORDERS COMMITTED					
	CHARGES ACTUALLY SPENT					
	JOB STEP BALANCE		300.00		100.00	200.00
	CAPITAL ESTIMATES		3,000.00	1,500.00	100.00	1,400.00
	CAPITAL COMMITMENTS		21.31			21.31
	CAPITAL CHARGES		2,163.68	1,330.00	170.88	662.80
	CAPITAL BALANCE		815.01	170.00	70.88−	715.89
5653 81	INSTALL PORTABLE HOODS & FLEX DUCTS	04/07	500.00		300.00	200.00
	PURCHASE ORDERS COMMITTED					
	CHARGES ACTUALLY SPENT					
	JOB STEP BALANCE		500.00		300.00	200.00
	EXPENSE ESTIMATES		500.00		300.00	200.00
	EXPENSE COMMITMENTS					
	EXPENSE CHARGES					
	EXPENSE BALANCE		500.00		300.00	200.00
5653	TOTAL JOB ESTIMATE		3,500.00	1,500.00	400.00	1,600.00
	TOTAL COMMITMENTS		21.31			21.31
	TOTAL CHARGES SPENT		2,163.68	1,330.00	170.88	662.80
	TOTAL JOB BALANCE		1,315.01	170.00	229.12	915.89

remaining balance of funds related to each segment of the project identified in the step sheet. This report reflects total commitments, total expenditures, and balance of funds remaining. The Capital and Expense Status Report provides a weekly update of the project's financial status both to engineering and to accounting, and as such is the primary report used for project control.

Project Reviews

Another control step which is fairly simple, but is essential when major commitments of funds are involved, is the timely review of projects. At a plant location it is good practice for project accounting to review on a timely basis each project in excess of $25,000 with the project engineer responsible. Reviews should be scheduled dependent upon the rate of construction and flow of commitments and expenditures. During such a review, a step-by-step analysis should be conducted to determine:

1. If there are any open commitments which should be canceled so that funds may be returned to either the step balance or to the contingency step for use elsewhere in the project, thus preventing any understatement in the project balance.
2. If any construction steps require additional funding to achieve completion and, if so, how this will affect the overall status of the project. If deemed necessary and feasible, funds could be transferred from the contingency step to cover the overrun step. This would reduce the contingency step balance and keep the total project in balance.
3. If specific construction steps don't require all the budgeted funds. If so, and if these funds are not needed in another step within the project, a possible underrun could occur.
4. If the project schedule is a target and if not, how that will affect the overall project.

Proper implementation of these reviews will provide early detection of any project's financial problems. In order for this system to work, clear understanding and open communication are essential.

The Major Project Control Manual

For major projects, a technique which is very useful is the compilation of a "Major Project Control Manual." The purpose of such a manual is to provide the engineering and accounting departments with all the necessary information to control a project's expenditures. The manual is a composition of pertinent data relating to all aspects of an individual project. Included within such a manual would be the following documentation:

1. Approved Capital Project Request.
2. Control estimate.

EXHIBIT 8
Financial Status Report (project ABC)

Step	Step Description	Control Estimate	Latest Estimate	Spent	Committed	Balance
01	Steamers	$199,800	$214,800	$187,200	$ 19,200	$ 8,400
02	Soakers	41,400	41,400	21,100	13,500	6,800
03	Pumps	11,700	11,700	6,200	—	5,500
04	Process pumps	16,700	16,700	—	15,400	1,300
05	Platform	3,700	3,700	—	3,700	—
06	Piping	81,000	81,000	1,200	63,100	16,700
07	Vapor collection	16,900	20,100	6,900	13,200	—
08	Auxiliary tanks	7,200	7,200	5,300	1,200	700
09	Dust collection	2,400	2,400	—	900	1,500
10	Dryer gas burner	89,300	89,300	34,500	51,700	3,100
11	Insulation	9,500	9,500	—	8,600	900
12	Electrical—wet	31,100	31,100	4,600	17,500	9,000
13	Roof vent fans	14,700	14,700	—	—	14,700
14	Concrete work	4,700	4,700	—	4,200	500
15	Painting	6,200	6,200	—	6,100	100
16	Electrical—dry	27,100	27,100	—	—	27,100
17	Engineering	13,700	13,700	11,200	—	2,500
18	Contingency	21,000	2,800	—	—	2,800
19	Surge bin	4,700	4,700	3,000	1,400	300
20	Instrumentation	14,700	14,700	—	12,800	1,900
	Capital	$617,500	$617,500	$281,200	$232,500	$103,800
81	Temporary construction	$ 3,700	$ 3,700	—	$ 1,500	$ 2,200
82	Remove and install instruments.	2,600	2,600	—	2,300	300
83	Concrete	2,200	2,700	—	2,700	—
84	Dryer conversion	34,300	34,300	—	25,000	9,300
85	Remove piping	3,400	3,400	—	—	3,400
86	Reset conveyors	3,400	3,400	—	2,500	900
87	Packaging conveyor	39,600	39,600	$ 10,800	5,700	23,100
88	Remove existing equipment	9,300	9,300	—	8,900	400
89	Contingency	4,000	3,500	—	—	3,500
90	Excess crew and overtime (P&L)	100,000	100,000	200	41,700	58,100
	Expense	$202,500	$202,500	$ 11,000	$ 90,300	$101,200
	Total	$820,000	$820,000	$292,200	$322,800	$205,000

Contingency balance:
Control estimate............... $ 25,000
To be transferred out.......... 18,700
Balance................. $ 6,300

Transfers:
1. $15,000 to Step 01—steamers
2. 3,200 to Step 07—vapor collection
3. 500 to Step 83—concrete

Construction and Financial commentary:
1. Construction start-up has been postponed for two weeks for the following reasons:
   a. Other production requirements must be filled.
   b. Plant X has been experiencing start-up problems which may affect our designs.
   The financial impact of this delay cannot be determined at this time.
2. Pipe fitters contract has not been settled. Piping costs could increase $30–40M.

EXHIBIT 9
Product X Capital Project—Flash Report No. 4 (project status)

	Control Estimate	Spent/ Committed	Balance
Capital..................	$617,500	$527,800	$ 89,700
Expense................	202,500	117,600	84,900
	$820,000	$645,400	$174,600

Percentage of funds spent/committed—79%.
Percentage physically completed—3%.

Commentary:
  Project remains in a hold status.

EXHIBIT 10
Capital Project Status Report (dollar amounts are thousands)

Projects	Date Authorized	Amount Authorized	Committed or Spent	Balance
Project A.................	01/18/75	$1,294*	$1,287	$ 7‡
Project B.................	06/02/75	797†	657	140‡
Project C.................	03/09/77	95	—	95‡
Project D................	02/10/77	35	18	17
Project E.................	04/01/77	25	14	11‡
Project F.................	03/20/76	45	37	8‡
Project G................	03/18/76	48	37	11‡
Project H................	03/09/76	55	7	48‡
Project I.................	05/04/76	55	55	—‡
Project J.................	10/19/76	50	24	26‡
Project K.................	02/29/77	50	50	—‡
Project L.................	04/02/77	55	11	44
Project M................	03/13/75	32	30	2‡
Project N................	09/11/76	25	6	19
Project O................	05/25/76	45	27	18‡
Project P.................	09/11/76	33	31	2‡
Project Q................	06/08/76	48	48	—
Project R................	10/19/76	48	47	1
Project S.................	01/12/77	35	4	31
Project T.................	01/26/77	45	4	41
Project U.................	02/22/77	45	12	33
Project V................	03/19/77	30	16	14
Project W................	04/02/77	45	31	14
Project X.................	02/11/77	28	—	28‡
Project Y................		333	173	160

  * Includes $49,000 authorized overrun.
  † Revised authorized amount reflects $95,000 return to Division and a $72,000 approved overrun.
  ‡ No change from last report.

EXHIBIT 11

			CARRY–OVER DATA			AUTHORIZATIONS				
☐ MAJOR ☐ ORDINARY } CAPITAL AUTHORIZATION and EXPENDITURE STATUS REPORT FY19_____ QUARTER ENDED _____										
PROJECT TITLE	F.V. OF AUTH.	CLASS·	AUTHORIZED AMOUNT	EXPENDED PRIOR YRS.	NET CARRY–OVER	JUNE QTR. ACT./EST.	SEPT. QTR. ACT./EST.	DEC. QTR. ACT./EST.	MARCH QTR. ACT./EST.	TOTAL ACT./EST.
	2	3*	4	5	6	7	8	9	10	11
TOTAL										

* R = REDUCE COST   N = EXPANSION – DEVELOPMENT PRODUCTS (new)   Q = QUALITY
  E = EXPANSION – ESTABLISHED PRODUCTS (existing)   S = SAFETY AND CONVENIENCE   O = OTHER

PAGE_____ OF _____

EXPENDITURES						EXPENDITURES (HIGHER) OR LOWER THAN AUTHORIZED		OUTSTANDING COMMITMENTS	COMPLETION DATE		
JUNE ACT./EST.	SEPT. QTR. ACT./EST.	DEC. QTR. ACT./EST.	MARCH ACT./EST.	SUBSEQUENT YRS. EST.	TOTAL ACT./EST.	ACTUAL	EST.		ORIG. EST.	ACT.	LAT. EST.
12	13	14	15	16	17	18	19	20	21	22	23

3. Current Capital and Expense Status Reports.
4. Direct cost, indirect cost, and start-up cost data per information request.
5. Financial Status Report.
6. Excerpts from engineer's weekly notes.
7. Construction schedule charts (Gantt charts).
8. Informational correspondence.
9. Outline of the special methods to be utilized in controlling the project.

Maintenance of such documentation should yield excellent control over a major project.

The Financial Status Report

In addition to the previously mentioned controls, local management maintains control through periodic reports which they require. A Financial Status Report (Exhibit 8) is usually issued on a monthly basis for major projects or specific ordinaries (over $50,000). This report gives management an overall top-line picture of how the project is progressing. This report is distributed by project accounting following a review of the data with the project engineer. The information contained in the report should cover the original control estimate, the latest estimate of funds required, funds committed to date, funds spent to date, and the remaining balance of the individual construction steps and the total project. (See Exhibit 8.) Accompanying this report should be appropriate commentary containing pertinent data affecting the financial status of the project.

The Weekly Flash Report

A weekly "Flash Report" covering major projects could be issued to post management constantly about the status of projects which have either long or short construction periods and a large amount of authorized funds. This top-line report (Exhibit 9) indicates the total funds authorized, funds committed and spent, and the remaining balance of funds available. Pertinent commentary could be included if the need warranted it.

EXHIBIT 12

_____ DIVISION

SUMMARY OF PAYBACK STATUS OF PROFIT-INCREASING CAPITAL PROJECTS ($100,000 or over)

AS OF _____

($000)

	NO. OF PROJECT	TOTAL FUNDS TO BE REPAID		AVERAGE ANNUAL CASH FLOW		PAYBACK YEARS		TEN-YEAR AVERAGE					
								NEW FUNDS		PBT		ROFE	
		ORIGINAL	ACT./LE.	ORIGINAL	ACT./LE	ORIGINAL	ACT/LE	ORIGINAL	ACT/LE	ORIGINAL	ACT/LE	ORIGINAL	ACT/LE
A – PROJECTS DECLARED PAID BACK IN FY____													
— ORIGINAL OBJECTIVE ACHIEVED OR EXCEEDED													
— MODIFIED OBJECTIVE ACHIEVED													
B – PROJECTS PAYBACK DECLARED UNATTAINABLE FY____													
C – PROJECTS PAYBACK CONTINUED UNDER REVIEW													
— AUTHORIZED PRIOR TO FY____													
— AUTHORIZED DURING FY____													
TOTAL													
TOTAL – ALL PROJECTS													

EXHIBIT 13

_____ DIVISION

PAYBACK STATUS REPORT OF PROFIT-INCREASING CAPTIAL PROJECTS ($100,000 or OVER)

AS OF _____

($000)

PROJECT DESCRIPTION					**FUNDS**				
			OPERATIONAL DATE		APPROPRIATIONS - INCLUDING SUPPLEMENTS				
EXISTING EXPANSION	PURP.*	FISC. YR. AUTH.	ORIG.	ACT./ LE	AMOUNT APPROP.	CAPITAL FUNDS	EXP. AFTER TAXES	WRK. FNDS. IN YR. OF PAYBACK	TOT. FUNDS TO BE REPAID
1	2	3	4	5	6	7	8	9	10
A. Projects Declared Paid Back in FY77									
Original Objective Achieved or Exceeded									
Project E									
Total									
Modified Objective Achieved									
Project B									
Total									
Total Projects Declared Paid Back									
B. Projects Declared Payback Unattainable in FY77									
Project A									
Total									
C. Projects Continued under Review									
Authorized Prior to FY77									
Project D									
Total									
Authorized during FY77									
Project C									
Total									
Total Projects Continued under review									
Grand Total All Existing Expansion Projects									

*PURPOSE: R–REDUCE COST; N–NEW PRODUCTS–DEVELOPMENT; E–EXISTING PRODUCTS–EXPANSION

EMPLOYED				FINANCIAL EVALUATION								
EXP.-ACT. OR LAT. EST. -INCL. SUPPLS.				NUMBER OF YEARS TO PAYBACK		TEN YEAR AVERAGES						
CAPITAL FUNDS	EXP. AFTER TAXES	WRK. FNDS. IN YR. OF PAYBACK	TOT. FUNDS TO BE REPAID			ROFE		PBT		NEW FUNDS		
				ORIG.	LAT.	ORIG.	LAT.	ORIG.	LAT.	ORIG.	LAT.	
11	12	13	14	15	16	17	18	19	20	21	22	

EXHIBIT 14
FY1978 Investment Status Report

FY1978 INVESTMENT STATUS REPORT

SUPPLEMENTARY SCHEDULE II

DIVISION _____

EXISTING LINE/NEW LINE INVESTMENT ANALYSIS

PROJECT DESCRIPTION	MARKET GROWTH					MARKET SHARE					VOLUME					PRETAX PROFIT				
	FY78		FY79			FY78		FY79			FY78		FY79			FY78		FY79		%
	CAP. PROJ. REQ.	ACT.	CAP. PROJ. REQ.	APF	LE	CAP. PROJ. REQ.	ACT.	CAP. PROJ. REQ.	APF	LE	CAP. PROJ. REQ.	ACT.	CAP. PROJ. REQ.	APF	LE	CAP. PROJ. REQ.	ACT.	CAP. PROJ. REQ.	APF	LE / CAPACITY UTILIZED

The Monthly Status Report

In order to keep local management apprised of the overall status of the capital program, a biweekly or monthly Status Report is issued (Exhibit 10). This report should reflect the financial status of each individual project—majors, specific ordinaries, and blankets over $25,000. The amount authorized, funds committed and spent, and the remaining balance available are the essential components of this document. In addition to the reports prepared for local management to keep them aware of the pace and expenditures of the annual capital program, two reports which are quite beneficial at the corporate level are also assembled.

The Corporate Report. Periodically the status of major, specific ordinary, and blanket projects is summarized for corporate management. On a quarterly basis a Capital Authorization and Expenditure Status Report should be developed to provide information on appropriation and expenditures (Exhibit 11). This report gives quarterly documentation and timing on a project-by-project basis of all activity within the three major categories of projects. On an annual basis an Annual Expenditure Status and Payback Report should be prepared (Exhibits 12–14). This report was alluded to earlier in the chapter when we were discussing the follow-up monitoring of a project even after it was completely operational.

When profit-increasing projects are prepared for routing through the approval process, we mentioned that ROFE and payback financial justification were developed. On an annual basis all payback projects should be reviewed to determine whether or not the original ROFE and payback criteria still apply. Projects could remain on target, could pay back sooner or later than anticipated, or might not pay back at all. It is only by annually monitoring all payback projects that we can determine this status. It is through such review and analysis of why the initial financial justification changed that we can learn to forecast better in the future.

SUMMARY

In this chapter we have reviewed the need for capital program and capital project control. Control commences with the annual planning of the capital program on a project by project basis. With corporate management's approval of the annual program, the wheels are set in motion to develop project documentation and move through the authorization system. Once approval has been received at the appropriate level dependent upon the level of funds requested, specific control steps are initiated. At the foundation of these controls is the step sheet, which accompanies the project through the approval process at the local plant level. The following are essential segments of a good and adequate control system:

1. Capital Program Planning Schedule.
2. Appropriate Authorization Schedule.
3. Capital Project Request Form.
4. Capital Project Financial Evaluation.
5. Capital Project Step Sheet.
6. Capital and Expense Status Report.
7. Financial Status Report.
8. Flash Report.
9. Monthly Status Report.
10. Quarterly Capital Authorization and Expenditure Status Report.
11. Payback Status Report.

Implementation of these controls (or, at a minimum, the most essential of the reports) should be a firm basis of a good monitoring and control system. Open and effective communication is an important component of any system of controls. Without clear lines of authority and communication, no system can be successful.

ADDITIONAL SOURCES

Also see Additional Sources for Chapter 15.

Bierman, Harold, and Smidt, Seymour. *The Capital Budgeting Decision.* 4th ed. New York: Macmillan Co., 1975.

Bower, Joseph L. *Managing the Resource Allocation Process.* Boston: Harvard Business School Division of Research, 1970.

Folger, H. Russell. "Ranking Techniques and Capital Rationing." *Accounting Review*, January 1972, p. 134.

Klammer, Thomas. "Empirical Evidence of the Adoption of Sophisticated Capital Budgeting Techniques." *Journal of Business*, July 1972, p. 387.

Mehler, Edmund W. "Capital Budgeting: Theory and Practice." *Management Accounting*, September 1976, p. 32.

Shuckett, Donald H., and Mack, Edward J. *Decision Strategies in Financial Management.* New York: American Management Associations, 1973.

Vandell, Robert F., and Stonich, Paul J. "Capital Budgeting: Theory or Results?" *Financial Executive,* August 1973, p. 46.

Weston, J. Fred, and Goudzwaard, Maurice B., eds. *Treasurer's Handbook,* chap. 17. Homewood, Ill.: Dow Jones-Irwin, 1976.

18

The Lease versus Purchase Decision

John O. Turk*

In this chapter we will examine "The Lease versus Purchase Decision" as follows: (1) review of the growth of leasing; (2) summary of Accounting Principles Board and Financial Accounting Standards Board pronouncements on leasing; (3) highlights of the impact of the alternative financing methods on the balance sheet; and (4) analysis of three ways to finance—cash purchase, lease, and bank note.

THE GROWTH OF LEASING

It has been estimated by *Fortune* magazine that if leasing continues to grow at its recent 20 percent rate, about one fifth of all new capital equipment that business puts into productive use will be leased.[1] Although no statistics are available on the leasing industry per se, the Comptroller of the Currency, who reports the detailed operations of national banks, indicates that there was a 23 percent increase in the book value of equipment leased by such banks in 1972. This increase brought the book value of this leased equipment to $1.1 billion. Additionally, according to the Comptroller of the Currency, the number of national banks involved in leasing activities doubled between 1968 and 1972, from 267 to 532.

What makes the national bank data even more significant is the

---

* Mr. Turk is Controller of the Dixie/Marathon Division of American Can Company, Greenwich, Connecticut.
[1] Peter Vanderwicken, "The Powerful Logic of the Leasing Boom," *Fortune*, November 1973, pp. 132–36, 190, 192, 194.

fact that analyses excluded those banks that operated through subsidiaries of bank holding companies. More than 40 bank holding companies have set up leasing subsidiaries following a 1971 Federal Reserve Board decision which permitted bank holding companies to take part in equipment leasing. These concerns have become, in some instances, very substantial factors in the leasing industry, with Citicorp Leasing, the leasing subsidiary of First National City Corporation of New York, becoming the world's largest leasing company.[2] On a total basis it has been estimated that 1974 saw over $11 billion in new equipment leased, and there are estimates that year-end 1975 saw the totality of equipment on lease in the neighborhood of $100 billion.

There are several reasons for this boom in leasing. One of the major factors responsible for the shift in the attitude of companies toward leasing is a trend away from the ownership ethic. "For years, the ownership ethic among businessmen was so strong that, except in the railroad industry where rolling stock has been leased for years, leasing was a thing that nice companies just didn't do," states Peter R. Nevitt, president of First Chicago Leasing Corporation, an affiliate of the First National Bank of Chicago. "Nowadays, executives have come to realize that use and not ownership is the crucial thing, and that leasing is just an alternative mode of financing."[3]

Another significant reason for the growth in leasing has been the aforementioned increasing participation by the banking industry. The banking industry seemed to give leasing a new character. In combination with this new esteem, the liquidity bind of 1969–70 got many corporate financial executives curious about new ways to finance. Consequently, as business turned up in the mid-70s, leasing grew hand in hand with the economy.

What Is Leasing?

When the need arises for a company to utilize fixed assets, the company must make a decision as to how those assets will be acquired. On the one hand, the company can go out and purchase the assets directly. They pay for them and they own them. On the

---

[2] Jonathan R. Laing, "Rent-a-Anything—More Companies Lease a Variety of Equipment Instead of Purchasing It," *The Wall Street Journal*, October 1, 1973.
[3] *Ibid.*

other hand, the company may elect not to purchase the assets but decide to rent them. They pay someone else a set fee for a set period of time to utilize the assets. But between ownership and rental there lies a vast, rather confusing and complicated area called "leasing."

In leasing, the user of the property (called the *lessee*) pays a rental type of charge (lease payment) to the owner of the property (called the *lessor*) for the right to use the asset. The lease payment represents the asset's depreciation, insurance, interest, and taxes —that is, costs associated with asset ownership. Also included in the lease payment is compensation for the profit and risk to which the lessor is entitled. In some instances the lessee may have to pay the insurance and taxes, dependent upon the arrangements made with the lessor. In other situations the lease payment might even include a maintenance agreement.

In the area between purchase and rental, where leasing lies amid controversy and confusion, there are various kinds of leases. Among these are sale-and-leaseback, lease with option to purchase, lease with option to terminate, net lease, and maintenance lease. Each of these is described briefly below.

Sale-and-Leaseback. Under this arrangement a company that owns an asset sells it to another and the latter leases it back to the firm from which they purchased the asset. The selling firm realizes an immediate increase in working capital, net of capital gains tax. This type of arrangement is beneficial when the company can utilize the funds received to earn a return greater than the cost of the funds.

EXHIBIT 1
Illustration of Lease with Option to Terminate

Year	Annual Lease Payments	Cumulative Lease Payments
1	$75,000	$ 75,000
2	75,000	150,000
3	75,000	225,000
4	75,000	300,000
5	17,863	317,863
6	17,800	335,663
7	17,800	353,463
8	17,800	371,263
9	17,800	389,063
10	17,800	406,863

Assumptions: Principal, $250,000; option to terminate at end of fourth year.

Lease with Option to Purchase. In this arrangement the lessee has the option to purchase the assets after a period of time during the lease agreement. Generally, the lease payments are neither accelerated nor is any extra lease payment charged if the option is exercised. The acquisition cost in this type of arrangement is not incurred, of course, until the option is exercised.

Lease with Option to Terminate. In some types of leasing plans the lessee is allowed to terminate the lease prior to the expiration date. In this situation there may be a cost for this cancellation option. The lease payments may be increased or accelerated. Exhibit 1 is an example of accelerated payments where the termination option is available after the fourth year. The significance of the impact of the termination option is obvious—that is, 74 percent of the total lease payment stream has been paid before the option can be exercised.[4]

Net Lease and Maintenance Lease. The basic difference between the net lease and the maintenance lease is that under the former the lessee pays the costs of maintenance and repair, taxes, insurance, and other related expenses; whereas in the latter instance the lessor provides maintenance service and pays the insurance.

If the option illustrated in Exhibit 1 had instead been a simple, straight lease agreement, the payment schedule shown in Exhibit 2 would have been in force:

EXHIBIT 2
Payment Schedule for Simple Lease

Year	Interest at 10 Percent	Amortization of Principal	Annual Lease Payment
1.................	$ 25,000	$ 15,686	$ 40,686
2.................	23,431	17,255	40,686
3.................	21,706	18,981	40,687
4.................	19,808	20,878	40,686
5.................	17,720	22,966	40,686
6.................	15,423	25,264	40,687
7.................	12,897	27,789	40,686
8.................	10,118	30,568	40,686
9.................	7,061	33,626	40,687
10.................	3,699	36,987	40,686
Total.............	$156,863	$250,000	$406,863

---

[4] The cost of the termination option in the illustration is $40,700. This is the difference between the net present values of the two payment streams in Exhibit 1 ($290,700 versus $250,000, when the streams are discounted at 10 percent).

Along with the various kinds of leasing there are many types of leasing arrangements. Among the most common types of these arrangements are: manufacturer to user, one manufacturer to another manufacturer, leasing company to a user, and finance company to user. These arrangements are self-explanatory and basically vary in what kind of lessor is utilized. One particular arrangement might be more beneficial, depending upon the company involved and the kind of property required.

Rationale for Leasing

The fundamental component of leasing is time. A lease defers the corporation's expenditure of capital and allows this capital to be utilized in the shorter run for uses other than asset acquisition. The corporation can use someone else's funds today while deferring its own funds for a project which the company feels is more utilitarian either now or at some future time.

While it is generally held that the main allure of leasing is convenience and flexibility, there are several more sophisticated reasons for the selection of leasing as an alternative of financing when it is generally the most expensive option.

Advantages and Disadvantages of Leasing

Various authors have delineated the advantages and disadvantages of leasing. We should take a look at some of these advantages and disadvantages and search out the rationale behind some of the considerations that are mentioned in order to gain a better insight into the thought process behind leasing.

The Federal Reserve Bank of Boston surveyed 60 manufacturers and found that the main stated advantage of leasing was that it conserved working capital, while the predominant disadvantage was its high cost. Exhibit 3 details the survey's findings.[5]

A given company certainly will view the lease-versus-purchase decision quite differently than another. For this reason the factors identified above could be viewed either as an advantage or disadvantage dependent upon the point of view adopted by a par-

---

[5] "Leasing's Role in Machinery Financing," *New England Business Review* (Federal Reserve Bank of Boston), September 1961, p. 2.

EXHIBIT 3
Considerations in Leasing: Survey of 60 New England Manufacturers

	Percent of Firms Citing
Advantages	
Conserves working capital	83
Eliminates equipment disposal	38
Has tax advantages	32
Preserves bank credit	30
Eliminates maintenance problems	26
Provides for temporary equipment need	25
Provides flexibility in operations	23
Is low cost	21
Disadvantages	
Is high cost	55
Does not build equity	43
Increases fixed obligations	42
Has tax disadvantages	8

ticular company. However, it might be beneficial for us to review a bit of the rationale behind some of the more frequently mentioned factors.

Conserves Working Capital. In this instance, a company can use the funds of the leasing service to obtain needed equipment immediately without tieing up its own funds with an immediate cash outlay. Internal funds could then be utilized to invest in a more profitable venture. Additionally, the working capital position would be improved because increased expenses would decrease taxable income and thereby taxes. This advantage would arise when lease payments were charged against operating expenses on a schedule more favorable than the depreciation which would be charged for acquired assets.

Eliminates Equipment Disposal. Not having ownership of the leased assets, the responsibility for disposal would rest in the leasing service. Another option along this same line is the hedge against obsolescence. If the lease is for an asset in an industry whose technology is changing rapidly, the lessee could ask for a cancellation clause if the equipment becomes obsolete.

Preserves Bank Credit. The inherent advantage here lies in the fact that the company does not have to go to a bank to obtain credit to purchase new assets. The benefits here are twofold. First, the company does not have to use up any of its line of credit. Second, since no loan was taken, the debt/equity position is unaffected (assuming the credit-line indenture does not call for treating lease obligations as long-term debt).

Is High Cost.   The cost usually is higher because the risk and services are provided by the lessor. The lessor must pay off the acquired asset, hedge against obsolescence, arrange financing, pay legal fees, make a profit margin, and so on. But aside from the quantitive considerations, there are also qualitative reasons why many companies feel the cost isn't really too high.

Does Not Build Equity.   By leasing rather than purchasing new assets, the company is not adding to its equity but rather adding to someone else's equity. The assets are not on their books but on the lessor's books. While in some respects, this is a disadvantage, it is also true that with the leased assets excluded from the company's balance sheet, the return on investment as calculated on a lower base of assets will appear higher than if the company owned the assets outright.

Increases Fixed Obligations.   Fixed obligations are increased since annual lease charges are incurred instead of the one-time cost of direct purchase. While this is quoted as a disadvantage, it is also an advantage to many companies who would rather have the annual fixed charges and could not otherwise afford the major acquisition.

By reviewing these few advantages and disadvantages in more detail we can see the real thought-provoking nature of the lease-versus-purchase decision. It is for this reason that it is necessary to thoroughly understand the ins and outs of the leasing decision. But before we delve into the intricacies of leasing from accounting and financial analyses viewpoints, it might be interesting to take a look at some attitudes about equipment leasing.

Opinions Relative to Leasing

In a privately printed speech, Alvin Zises surveyed the investment community's as well as other sources' attitudes toward equipment leasing. In order to place some general perspective on this subject, it might be appropriate to review some of the comments that have been documented by Mr. Zises.[6] In his speech, Mr. Zises referred to comments of several leading individuals and their feelings relative to the subject of leasing.

---

[6] Alvin Zises, "Equipment Leasing: Its Place in the Corporate Financial Design," privately printed speech, pp. 1–4.

Bennett R. Keenan of New England Merchants National Bank of Boston in a paper entitled, "Financing a Leasing Corporation," writes:

> A lease is not debt. . . . A lease has, to be sure, certain elements also found in debt. It lacks, however one feature of debt, at least, that to a creditor should explode any notion that a lease is debt. In the event of bankruptcy of the debtor, debt is normally recognized in fact as a claim; in bankruptcy of a lessee, this is not the case.[7]

Gordon D. Brown, vice president of the Bank of New York, has stated:

> Going back through the history of finance, you will find that questions were asked about the conditional sales contract when the straight mortgage was a more common security form. Only a few years ago the term loan was not considered sensible for a business or a bank. The lease is filling a current need for supplemental financing and is probably in about the same status as consumer financing and term loan were some 15–20 years ago.[8]

In 1959, Harvard Business School surveyed the investment community in one of the most extensive attitudinal studies about leasing and found:

> 90% of the respondents to the [financial] analysts' survey and 65% of the respondents to the corporate survey state that the use of long-term noncancellable leases makes it possible for a company to obtain a greater amount of credit than would be possible if debt financing were used.[9]

Another discussion within the context of the Harvard study indicated that the failure to use financing such as leasing could possibly force up the cost of incremental debt:

> Each increase in the rates of a company's senior debt likewise increases the comparative cost of incremental debt. The treasurer of a major oil company informed us that because his firm had not made sufficient use of junior financings like leasing, his company's rate of senior debt securities was higher than that of comparable companies and consequently, he claimed, the interest rates in his company's incremental debt securities were also higher. His conclusion was that his company, by paying a higher rate in incre-

---

[7] Ibid., p. 1.

[8] Ibid.

[9] R. F. Vancil and R. N. Anthony, "The Financial Community Looks at Leasing," *Harvard Business Review,* November–December 1959, pp. 120 and 121.

mental debt, was paying the rate equivalent for junior financing but did not have its benefit in the capital structure. The prudent use of equipment leasing, according to institutional investors and financial analysts, will not be treated as a debt burden because of its junior nature.[10]

ACCOUNTING TREATMENT OF LEASING

As was stated earlier in this chapter, the growth of leasing has been rapid in recent years. In an effort to keep the accounting profession contemporary with this growth in leasing, the Accounting Principles Board (APB) continuously updated financial thinking by issuing various opinions. It is the objective of this section to summarize some of the more general concepts on accounting treatment of leases as promulgated by the Accounting Principles Board (APB) and its successor, the Financial Accounting Standards Board (FASB).

Probably the first pronouncement relative to leasing was issued by the AICPA in *Accounting Research Bulletin No. 38* issued in 1949. The Accounting Principles Board (APB) during the ten-year span from 1963–73 issued four major *Opinions* and one minor *Opinion*. The major *Opinions* were *Nos. 5, 7, 27,* and *31* and were entitled as follows:

Opinion No. 5—"Reporting of Leases in Financial Statements of Lessees"

Opinion No. 7—"Accounting for Leases in Financial Statements of Lessors"

Opinion No. 27—"Accounting for Lease Transactions by Manufacturer or Dealer Lessors"

Opinion No. 31—"Disclosure of Lease Commitments by Lessees."

The APB's successor, the Financial Accounting Standards Board, issued *Statement No. 13,* "Accounting for Leases," late in 1976.

APB Opinion No. 5

The primary thrust of this opinion was: Does the acceptance of a noncancellable agreement to lease on a rental basis create assets

---

[10] Ibid.

and liabilities on the books of the lessee? It was the opinion of the APB that no assets or liabilities had to be indicated in the lessee's balance sheet as long as the lease agreement was not actually an installment purchase. If the agreement was an installment purchase, it had to be shown as such.

If the acquired property which is being leased is in fact an installment purchase, this disclosure must be so indicated by the appropriate presentation on the balance sheet: the leased property is shown as an asset, valued at the discounted amount of future lease payments, and this same amount is shown as a liability. The asset is then depreciated as though it were owned, without reference to the pattern of lease payments.

Since it is often difficult to determine the differentiation between leases of an installment purchase nature and those that are not, *Opinion No. 5* offered two criteria to aid in this decision process. First, if the initial lease term is materially less than the property's useful life, and the lessee has the option to renew the lease for the remaining useful life at substantially less than the fair market rental value; or, second, if the lessee has the right to acquire the property at a price substantially less than its fair market value, then the lease was to be considered in substance a purchase.

In summary of *Opinion No. 5*, we can say that it dealt essentially with the classification of leases as to their propriety as equity building or not. This *Opinion* also dealt with the disclosure required of such leases.

APB Opinion No. 7

Opinion No. 7 dealt with the other partner in the lease—the lessor. But before we delve into this *Opinion's* specifics, we should distinguish between the two methods utilized by lessors to book both expenses and revenues associated with leasing.

The two procedures available for the recording of lease related revenues and expenses are "the operating method" and "the financing method." The distinguishing factor between these two methodologies is the time factor. While the former method recognizes revenue as received and thus expenses all costs associated with the leased asset as they are incurred, the latter views the lease as a long-term item and spreads the income over the entire period of the lease. In both of these instances the APB made specific recommendations as to what types of lessors should follow which methodology.

In cases where the lessor significantly kept possession of the risks or rewards of ownership, the Board felt that the operating method be adopted. On the other hand, the APB recommended that the financing method be utilized when the risks or rewards of ownership were not retained by the lessor.

To summarize *Opinion No. 7,* we could state that it dealt basically with the accounting methods of handling leases in the financial statements. The operating method recognizes revenue and associated expenses as received and as incurred respectively. The financing method tends to defer income and expenses over the time of the lease.

APB Opinion No. 10

The Accounting Principles Board in *Opinion No. 10* dealt with an issue raised in *Opinion No. 5.* Whereas the former opinion discusses to some degree the relationship between lessees and lessors who are related in business, the latter opinion required the consolidation of the subsidiary into the parent when the subsidiary's principal business was leasing property and/or facilities to the parent or other affiliate or subsidiary.

APB Opinion No. 27

Accounting Principles Board *Opinion No. 27* was issued because of the great number of questions that had arisen over the application and interpretation of *Opinion No. 7.* More specifically this opinion attempted to clarify "when a manufacturer or dealer lessor should recognize a lease transaction with an independent lessee as if it were a sale." *Opinion No. 27* was presented in three sections— two-party lease transactions, participation by third parties, and transactions with related companies.

In the first section on two-party transactions, it was the opinion of the Board that leases are equivalent to sales when if at the time of entering into the agreement, the collectibility was reasonably certain, that there were no significant uncertainties and the lessee could obtain title at a reasonable market price or the term substantially equaled the economic life of the property. Additionally, under this situation it was felt that when there is a credit risk which is so high as to preclude reasonable assurance of collection, the lease transaction should not be recorded as a sale.

The third party becomes involved when a manufacturer or dealer lessor sells or assigns a lease or property subject to a lease. This assignment could be to an independent financing institution or to an independent leasing company. Basically, *Opinion No. 27* stated that assignment of a lease to a third party does not change the substance of whether it is an operating lease or an installment purchase, and hence the accounting for the lease should not ordinarily change.

In their treatment of transactions with related companies, the APB defined related companies to be "a subsidiary, corporate joint venture or other investee in which the manufacturer or dealer has a financial interest." It was felt that as long as the transaction meets all the criteria of leases equivalent to a sale, the participation of a related company does not void the determination that a sale has taken place.

APB Opinion No. 31

Opinion No. 31 was issued to gain further disclosure of desirable relevant information in the financial statements. The Board felt that sufficient information about noncapitalized leases should be disclosed in the financial statements to enable users to evaluate the impact of those data on the overall financial statements. *Opinion No. 31* required disclosure of the total rental expense entering into the net income calculation. Also required was disclosure of minimum future rental commitments on noncancellable leases, that is, leases that have an initial or remaining term of more than one year or is cancellable only upon the occurrence of some remote contingency or upon the payment of a substantial penalty.

FASB Statement No. 13

Because of inconsistencies in, and differences of opinion about, these APB *Opinions,* in 1973 the FASB began an extensive review of lease accounting, which resulted in issuance of *FASB Statement No. 13.*

Effective January 1, 1977, this *Statement,* "Accounting for

Leases," established lease reporting standards for both lessors and lessees, and superseded earlier *APB Opinions* on the subject. The *Statement* is comprehensive, and is over 100 pages in length. The primary thrust of the *Statement* was to establish very specific criteria for determining whether a lease is an operating lease or a capital lease—the same basic issue addressed in 1964 by *APB Opinion No. 5*. If a lease meets one or more of the following criteria, it must be classified as a "capital lease" by the lessee:

1. The lease transfers ownership of the property to the lessee by the end of the lease term;
2. The lease contains a "bargain purchase" option;
3. The lease term is equal to 75 percent or more of the estimated economic life of the leased property; or
4. The present value of the minimum lease payments equals or exceeds 90 percent of the excess of the fair value of the leased property over any related investment tax credit retained by the lessor.

The terms used in stating these criteria are elaborately defined in the *Statement*. Leases not meeting any of the criteria are "operating leases."

For a capital lease, the lessee records the asset and the obligation at an amount equal to the present value of the minimum lease payments during the lease term, excluding that portion of payments representing executory costs such as insurance, maintenance, and taxes to be paid by the lessor. In most cases, the discount rate used in determining this present value is the lessee's incremental borrowing rate—that is, the rate the lessee would have incurred to borrow the funds to purchase the leased asset on a secured loan with repayment terms similar to those called for in the lease.

From the lessor's standpoint, if a lease (except for "leveraged leases") meets one or more of the above criteria, *and* both of these criteria:

1. Collectibility of the lease payments is reasonably predictable; and
2. No important uncertainties surround the amount of unreimbursable costs yet to be incurred by the lessor under the lease;

then the lease is accounted for by the lessor either as a "sales-type lease" (if a manufacturer's or dealer's profit is earned by the lessor) or as a "direct financing lease." Otherwise, the lessor treats the lease as an operating lease. Sales-type or direct financing leases are capitalized by the lessor; the accounting entry essentially involves debiting a lease payments receivable account and crediting an inventory or similar asset account to reflect the "sale" of the leased asset.

The preceding brief summaries of the APB and FASB pronouncements on leasing were presented as background information, since one cannot ignore reporting implications when analyzing lease-versus-purchase decisions. These summaries reflect the complexity and diversity of opinion relative to this subject, and suggest the importance of seeking well-informed accounting counsel in lease-reporting matters.

LEASE VERSUS BUY: METHODOLOGY OF ANALYSIS

We have reviewed the growth in the use of lease financing and also have reviewed the history of the accounting treatment of leases. Through these reviews we should have developed a sufficient degree of understanding of leasing to enable us now to move into the development of a methodology by which we can identify a consistent operating framework for lease-versus-buy analysis.

Leasing Is a Financing Alternative

To begin with it is important that we recognize what the lease-versus-buy decision is. It is a financing decision; it is *not* an investment decision. The investment decision was made when it was determined that a particular asset was required and could be made available for use. The lease-and-buy options are simply two alternative methods to gain the use of the asset. This distinction is important here for two reasons:

1. We do not want to evaluate the investment decision all over again.
2. As a method of financing, leasing can be considered an alternate source of funds—that is, an alternative to debt, short-term borrowing, or equity.

(The investment and financing decisions should be kept separate *unless* the company is going to finance the investment [capital project] with debt that is only available *if* the investment is pursued. However, as a starting point, this is *not* the case.)

Once the decision to acquire an asset is made, the company must then determine the method of financing that investment. Factors that must be considered in selecting the proper financing method are:

1. Other borrowing commitments;
2. Availability of funds from lending sources; and
3. Company's current debt/equity ratio.

As each alternative financing method is investigated, the costs of the funds from the various sources must also be reviewed.

Other Borrowing Commitments. In reviewing the potential sources of financing, the company could be faced with a situation where it has already reached its credit line. If this is the case, this option might be closed unless an extension of the line of credit were achieved or other sources could be developed. In situations such as this the leasing option becomes quite viable.

EXHIBIT 4
Impact of Increasing Debt on the Debt/Equity Ratio

	Current	Proposed
Debt.....................................	$13	$16
Equity....................................	$39	$39
Debt/equity ratio.......................	1:3.0	1:2.4

Availability of Funds. The availability of funds from lending sources is another potential source of financing. However, the leasing alternative becomes viable should funds not be readily available in the marketplace. This occurrence could take place due to the above-mentioned other borrowing commitments, a tight-money situation, or an economic downturn.

Debt/Equity Considerations. Companies must recognize the impact of either increasing their debt or increasing their equity. The availability of debt is not only impacted by the two factors cited above (borrowing commitments and availability of funds) but also could be affected by the debt/equity ratio of the company. Without expounding on the pluses or minuses of different debt/equity ratios we can review the impact of adding additional debt.

Assume a hypothetical company's debt/equity ratio is 1 to 3, and assume further that the addition of long-term debt of $3 million would change this ratio to 1 to 2.4 (see Exhibit 4). Such a change might not be considered beneficial by either the shareholders or the financial community. On the other hand, the company has the option to increase owners' equity by $3 million. However, should the investment be of a cost reduction nature with the results as shown in Exhibit 5, earnings per share can be "diluted," which presumably will result in a decrease in the market price of each share. Note that if in this example the project had generated $250,000 in additional profit, the earnings per share would have remained at $10 and no dilution would have occurred.

EXHIBIT 5
Impact of Increasing Owners' Equity on Earnings per Share

	Current	Proposed
Profit.............................	$1,000,000	$1,200,000
Shares outstanding................	100,000	125,000
Earnings per share...............	$10.00	$9.60

The entire financing evaluation has an impact on the balance sheet. Exhibit 6 is a simplified version of the effects of leasing, cash purchase, and borrowing on the balance sheet, where it is assumed a $100,000 piece of equipment is acquired. The example also assumes that current accounting rulings would not require the lease to be capitalized, were that option chosen.

DCF Method

The discounted cash flow (DCF) method of analysis is required in order to perform an accurate lease-versus-buy analysis. This method of analysis utilizes the identification of after-tax cash flows for each alternative and also utilizes the discounting of cash flows to reflect the time value of money as integral components in the evaluation process. This is not to say that the profit impact of projects in the lease-versus-buy alternative is overlooked because we utilize a cash flow approach. The overall lease-versus-buy decision requires that the relative profit impact be an important consideration.

EXHIBIT 6
Balance Sheet Effect

Assets	Before Acquisition	After Leasing	After Cash Purchase	After Bank Loan
Current Assets:				
Cash..............................	$ 200,000	$ 200,000	$ 100,000	$ 200,000
Accounts receivable...............	200,000	200,000	200,000	200,000
Inventory.........................	300,000	300,000	300,000	300,000
Total Current Assets.........	$ 700,000	$ 700,000	$ 600,000	$ 700,000
Fixed Assets......................	1,000,000	1,000,000	1,100,000	1,100,000
Total Assets..............	$1,700,000	$1,700,000	$1,700,000	$1,800,000
Liabilities and Stockholders' Equity				
Liabilities:				
Current..........................	$ 200,000	$ 200,000	$ 200,000	$ 233,333
Long-term........................	300,000	300,000	300,000	366,667
Total Liabilities..............	$ 500,000	$ 500,000	$ 500,000	$ 600,000
Stockholders' Equity..............	1,200,000	1,200,000	1,200,000	1,200,000
Total Liabilities and Stockholders' Equity...	$1,700,000	$1,700,000	$1,700,000	$1,800,000
Working capital...................	$ 500,000	$ 500,000	$ 400,000	$ 466,667
Current ratio.....................	3.5 to 1	3.5 to 1	3.0 to 1	3.0 to 1
Liquidity ratio...................	2.0 to 1	2.0 to 1	1.5 to 1	1.71 to 1

Assumptions: Equipment cost, $100,000; lease, five years (lease not required to be capitalized); bank loan, three years.

Recognizing, then, that the investment decision on the particular asset was made when the company determined that the acquisition of the asset was desirable, we can now develop a methodology to follow in the determination of a lease decision or a buy decision.

There are two rather commonly utilized discounted cash flow methods for the lease-versus-buy evaluation. The "effective-cost-of-leasing method" develops a cost from a comparison of the cash flows of the lease option to the cash flows of the purchase option. The differences in the cash flows are identified, and an effective interest rate cost is generated. The cost of the lease is that interest rate at which the net present value of the cash flow differences is equal to zero.

The "net-present-value method," while it would give the same results for a given set of data as the cost-of-leasing method, is not quite as simple. In this methodology the cash flows are identified and dealt with separately. The cash flows are developed separately, and each stream is discounted at the company's projected cost of capital, with the total of each discounted stream of cash flows yielding the net present value for each alternative. The alternative having the lowest net present value of cash outlays is the one selected.

The effective-cost-of-leasing method is simpler and therefore preferable because it develops the differences in cash flows and thereby ignores common costs.

Steps in the Analysis. The lease-versus-buy decision can be investigated from the standpoint of which decision is the least costly. Therefore, the analysis which we will adopt must pursue that end. Our technique will follow these steps:

1. Develop separate cash flows for each financing alternative.
2. Determine tax deductibility of lease (rent) expense and determine applicability of investment credit.
3. Determine the present value of each cash flow.
4. Select the financing alternative which presents the lowest cost.

The steps of this methodology will be outlined through a series of exhibits in order to clarify the content of the lease-versus-buy analysis.

In the example presented in Exhibit 7 we have utilized the following assumptions:

1. Ten-year straight-line lease expense (i.e., equal payments at constant intervals) of $40,000 rent per year.
2. Tax rate of 50 percent.
3. After-tax opportunity cost of 10 percent.
4. $200,000 equipment cost.

The result of the cash flow work sheet on leasing in Exhibit 7 indicates a cumulative discounted cash outflow of $122,880.

Exhibit 8 should now be completed. This table should be filled out in the following manner:

Column 1: Identifies the periods of time for which the cash flow is developed.

Column 2: Shows the onetime outlay of capital to purchase the asset.

Column 3: Indicates the depreciation tax shield arising from the acquisition of the asset.

Column 4: Identifies the investment tax credit allowance (if applicable).

EXHIBIT 7

Cash Flow Work Sheet—Lease Financing (outflow of funds)

Year	Rent Expense	Tax Saving	Net Cash Cost	Present Value Factor, 10 Percent	Discounted Net Cash Flow	Cumulative DCF
0	—	—	—	1.000	—	—
1	$ (40,000)	$ 20,000	$ (20,000)	0.909	$(18,180)	$ (18,180)
2	(40,000)	20,000	(20,000)	0.826	(16,520)	(34,700)
3	(40,000)	20,000	(20,000)	0.751	(15,020)	(49,720)
4	(40,000)	20,000	(20,000)	0.683	(13,660)	(63,380)
5	(40,000)	20,000	(20,000)	0.621	(12,420)	(75,800)
6	(40,000)	20,000	(20,000)	0.564	(11,280)	(87,080)
7	(40,000)	20,000	(20,000)	0.513	(10,260)	(97,340)
8	(40,000)	20,000	(20,000)	0.467	(9,340)	(106,680)
9	(40,000)	20,000	(20,000)	0.424	(8,480)	(115,160)
10	(40,000)	20,000	(20,000)	0.386	(7,720)	(122,880)
Total	$(400,000)	$200,000	$(200,000)			$(122,880)

Column 5: The net of Column 2 minus Column 3 and Column 4.

Column 6: Identifies the after-tax opportunity cost of the funds invested.

Column 7: The result of discounting the net cash cost by the appropriate present value factor.

Column 8: Cumulative total of the discounted cash flows from Column 7.

In the example in Exhibit 7 we have utilized the same base case data as in Exhibit 6 with the additional assumptions due to the acquisition of a capital asset:

1. Depreciation over ten years, sum-of-the-years'-digits method.
2. No residual (or scrap) value.
3. Investment tax credit of 10 percent is applicable.

The results of Exhibit 8 indicate that the net discounted outflow of funds would be $109,917. Therefore, from this analysis we can move to Step 4 of our technique of analysis—selecting the financing alternative which presents the least cost.

We can review the lease option versus the purchase option first from an undiscounted point of view. The purchase alternative had a net cash cost of $80,000, while the leasing alternative had a net cash cost of $200,000. Without question, from this viewpoint the purchase option is the right choice ($120,000 less costly). However, if the decision were made solely within this context, there could potentially be an erroneous choice.

As was stated earlier one of the reasons why leasing is a costly alternative is due to the fact that the lessor shoulders all the risks of ownership and the lessee is not burdened with such risks. Therefore, a significant portion of the difference between purchasing and leasing ($120,000) can be attributed to these risks of ownership. A critical point here then is the cost of risk taking. Do the risks of ownership outstrip the incremental cost of leasing?

In our examples we applied an after-tax opportunity cost of 10 percent as our discounting factor. It is through this discounting technique that the risks of ownership inherent in the cash purchase option are brought to a more comparable basis to the lease option. As a result of the discounting procedure, the risk purchase alternative would generate a cash outflow of $109,917, while the leasing alternative realized an outflow of $122,880—a difference of $12,963

EXHIBIT 8
Cash Flow Work Sheet—Cash Purchase

Year	Cash Outlay	Tax Savings from Depreciation	Investment Tax Credit	Net Cash Cost	Present Value Factor	Net DCF	Cumulative DCF
0	$(200,000)	—	$20,000	$(180,000)	1.000	$(180,000)	$(180,000)
1	—	$ 18,182	—	18,182	0.909	16,527	(163,473)
2	—	16,364	—	16,364	0.826	13,517	(149,956)
3	—	14,545	—	14,545	0.751	10,923	(139,033)
4	—	12,727	—	12,727	0.683	8,693	(130,340)
5	—	10,909	—	10,909	0.621	6,774	(123,566)
6	—	9,091	—	9,091	0.564	5,127	(118,439)
7	—	7,273	—	7,273	0.513	3,731	(114,708)
8	—	5,455	—	5,455	0.467	2,547	(112,161)
9	—	3,636	—	3,636	0.424	1,542	(110,619)
10	—	1,818	—	1,818	0.386	702	(109,917)
Total	$(200,000)	$100,000	$20,000	$ (80,000)			$(109,917)

favoring outright purchase. A higher discount rate would have broadened this relatively narrow gap, while a lower discount rate might have given us a different decision.

Another method through which an asset could be acquired on a purchase basis would be by borrowing the required funds via a bank loan. This method is somewhat different from the examples presented in Exhibits 7 and 8. In this situation the bank loan financing (mortgage note) is directly associated with the investment. In other words, it is assumed that this incremental debt was available solely for the financing of this particular investment, and further assumed that this mortgage note does not change the cost of capital for funds other than this note.

Utilizing the same example as before, the cash flows under the leasing alternative would remain the same as in Exhibit 7. Exhibit 9 shows the cash flow work sheet for the bank loan alternative. In this instance we will assume the following relative to the bank loan:

1. Compensating balances not required.
2. Interest rate of 10 percent on the outstanding opening balance.
3. Term of loan to be ten years, repayable with interest in ten equal year-end installments.

In this example, as in the previous one, we require $200,000 to purchase additional assets. In this instance we have gone to a bank and borrowed the equivalent of the $200,000 discounted over the loan payoff period. In this case we will have to repay approximately $325,500 over the life of the loan in order to realize cash proceeds of approximately $200,000 to purchase the asset. The net cash flow of debt financing is derived from the net of the components in Exhibit 9:

Column 1: Year.

Column 2: Principal amount that is outstanding at the beginning of each year.

Column 3: Interest on the beginning principal at a 10 percent rate.

Column 4: The annual payment at $32,550 per year.

Column 5: Principal reduction is the balance of the $32,550 available to pay toward reducing the beginning balance after interest has been paid (subtracted).

Column 6: The ending principal—Column 2 (beginning principal) less Column 5 (principal reduction).

EXHIBIT 9

Cash Flow Work Sheet—Bank Loan

Year	Beginning Principal	Interest at 10 Percent	Payment	Principal Reduction	Ending Principal	Tax Savings from Interest	Discounted Tax Savings
1.........	$200,000	$ 20,000	$ 32,550	$ 12,550	$187,450	$10,000	$ 9,090
2.........	187,450	18,745	32,550	13,805	173,645	9,373	7,742
3.........	173,645	17,365	32,550	15,185	158,460	8,682	6,520
4.........	158,460	15,846	32,550	16,704	141,756	7,923	5,411
5.........	141,756	14,176	32,550	18,374	123,382	7,088	4,402
6.........	123,382	12,338	32,550	20,212	103,170	6,169	3,479
7.........	103,170	10,317	32,550	22,233	80,937	5,159	2,647
8.........	80,937	8,094	32,550	24,456	56,481	4,047	1,890
9.........	56,481	5,648	32,550	26,902	29,579	2,824	1,197
10.........	29,579	2,958	32,550	29,592	(13)*	1,479	571
Total.......		$125,487	$325,500	$200,013*		$62,744	$42,949

Net present value of this alternative: −$200,000 (initial outlay) + $20,000 (tax credit) + $70,083 (depreciation tax shield) + $42,949 (interest tax shield) = $(66,968).
* Extra $13 is due to rounding. (Exact annual payment would be $32,549.08.)
The true cost of this alternative is $82,538.

Column 7: Tax savings from interest expense—Column 2 multiplied by a 50 percent tax rate.

Column 8: The discounted tax savings—Column 7 multiplied by the 10 percent present value discount factor.

Basically, this alternative is the same as the cash purchase, except that there is the additional tax shield of $42,949 arising from the incremental interest. Thus the present value of this alternative is a net outflow of $66,968, making the bank loan the most economic means of acquiring the asset from a purely quantitative standpoint:

```
Lease................................ $122,880
Purchase...........................   109,917
Bank loan..........................    66,968
```

It must be emphasized, however, that Exhibit 8 is based on some very explicit assumptions which would be unusual in most such decisions—financing tied specifically to the investment which does not alter the company's overall cost of capital. In most instances these assumptions would not hold, and therefore an analysis showing an explicit interest tax shield would be invalid; normally only the first two alternatives would obtain.

As was stated earlier in the chapter, there are very critical qualitative factors which must be considered in conjunction with the quantitative factors delineated above. In this instance, although the bank loan would have been the least expensive mode of financing, it would have reduced the line of credit available to the company. By pursuing the lease option, the credit line would remain intact available for other needs. It is qualitative factors such as this that tender the lease alternative a viable one.

CONCLUSION

In this chapter we have reviewed the growth of leasing in today's economic environment. A review of the Accounting Principles Board and Financial Accounting Standards Board pronouncements on the accounting treatment of leasing has been presented in order for management to recognize the intricacies of leasing prior to becoming deeply involved in this mode of financing. A methodology has been presented for evaluating three alternative methods of financing: cash purchase, leasing, and investment-specific bank borrowing. Both the quantitative and qualitative factors of financing alternatives have been stressed. Understanding these methods and factors should enable the newcomer to commence an analysis in this area. Experience in using these techniques will lend additional sophistication that a specific project might warrant.

ADDITIONAL SOURCES

Batkin, Alan. "Leasing vs. Buying: A Guide for the Perplexed." *Financial Executive,* June 1973, p. 62.

Elliott, Grover S. "Leasing of Capital Equipment." *Management Accounting,* December 1975, p. 39.

Ferrara, William L. "Lease vs. Purchase: A Quasi-Financing Approach." *Management Accounting,* January 1974, p. 21.

Gustafson, George A. "Computers—Lease or Buy?" *Financial Executive,* July 1973, p. 64.

Hill, William H. "Should You Lease Company Cars?" *Financial Executive,* November 1973, p. 48.

Kasper, Larry J. "Evaluating the Cost of Financial Leases." *Management Accounting,* May 1977, p. 43.

Laing, Jonathan R. "Rent-a-Anything—More Companies Lease a Variety of Equipment Instead of Purchasing It." *Wall Street Journal,* October 1, 1973, p. 1.

Marcus, Robert P. "The Buy vs. Lease Decision Revisited." *Financial Executive,* December 1976, p. 34.

Mundrick, Daniel J. "Lease vs. Purchase in a Government Contract Environment." *Financial Executive,* June 1972, p. 22.

Ryan, Robert J. "Leveraged Leasing." *Management Accounting,* April 1977, p. 45.

Simon, William. "Leasing: What Should You Ask Your CPA?" *Financial Executive,* July 1977, p. 32.

Vancil, Richard F. *Leasing of Industrial Equipment.* New York: McGraw-Hill, Inc., 1963.

Vanderwicken, Peter. "The Powerful Logic of the Leasing Boom." *Fortune,* November 1973, p. 132.

Weston, J. Fred, and Goudzwaard, Maurice B., eds. *Treasurer's Handbook,* chap. 37. Homewood, Ill.: Dow Jones-Irwin, Inc., 1976.

19

Make-or-Buy Decisions

Ian D. Duncan*

In both manufacturing and service industries, "make-or-buy" decisions have always played and will continue to play a vital role in management decision making. The decision made by management, whatever it may be, will have a direct effect on the cash flows, and hence profitability, of the firm. While decisions made by management in this area are based substantially upon financial analysis of cost and investment figures, it is emphasized that consideration should also be given to relevant nonfinancial criteria.

The make-or-buy alternatives in terms of manufacturing industries are quite easy to formulate. A company involved in manufacturing may want to evaluate the feasibility of any of the following make-or-buy alternatives in connection with a specific component part:

1. If the part is being manufactured, evaluate the feasibility of buying it from outside.
2. If the product is being purchased from an external supplier, evaluate the feasibility of manufacturing it in-house.
3. If it is a new product, evaluate the feasibility of the "make" alternative and the "buy" alternative fully before making a choice.

---

* Mr. Duncan is pursuing a doctorate degree in business administration at the University of Western Ontario. He was formerly a Research Associate with the Society of Management Accountants of Canada.

In terms of service industries, the make-or-buy alternatives may not at first glance be as intuitively obvious. They do however, exist, and the decision criteria applicable to service industries generally follow those applicable to manufacturing concerns. The above alternatives can be restated in terms of service industries in the following way:

1. If the service is being completely supplied (i.e., made) by the service company, evaluate the feasibility of subcontracting part or all of the service to an outside company.
2. If the service is subcontracted (i.e., purchased) outside of the particular firm, evaluate the feasibility of the firm itself supplying all or part of the service.
3. If the offering of a new service is being considered by the firm, fully evaluate the feasibility of "making" the service (i.e., taking necessary steps to supply the service with in-house resources) and "buying" the service (i.e., subcontracting the supplying of the service to an external firm).

This chapter does not address the question "to make or to buy" with the intention of arriving at an all-inclusive and categorical decision favoring either of the alternatives. Rather, the objective of this chapter is both to provide a quantitative method of analysis for evaluating the apparent "make-or-buy" dilemma in financial terms and also to stimulate some thought about nonfinancial criteria and their importance in the decision.

INPUTS TO THE DECISION AND THE DECISION PROCESS

There are multiple criteria for a company to consider when deciding whether a particular product or component part should be manufactured in-house or purchased from a supplier. This also applies to service industries considering their "make-or-buy" alternatives in the context of service. These criteria may be either of a financial nature or, equally important, a nonfinancial nature. Further, some criteria may definitely favor the buying alternative while others may favor in-house manufacturing. Exhibit 1 illustrates this financial-nonfinancial nature, and lists examples of each type of decision criterion for each of the two possible alternatives, namely, making and buying.

EXHIBIT 1
Decision Criteria for the Make-or-Buy Problem

Criteria for Making

Financial Criteria

1. "Full cost" for the make alternative is less than that for the buy alternative.
2. "Full investment" for the make alternative is less than that for the buy alternative.
3. Analysis of the projected cash flows indicates that making is the preferred alternative.

Nonfinancial Criteria

1. The project to be initiated is of a confidential nature.
2. Moving the component or part from place to place is difficult or impossible.
3. It is easier to control final delivery dates.
4. The component part is very uncommon to the industry and complicated to make.
5. It is company policy to manufacture all components in-house.
6. Dependence on external manufacturers is undesirable and risky.
7. The required level of quality can only be achieved through your own manufacturing expertise and supervision.
8. You have adequate capacity to manufacture now and also meet any further requirements.

Criteria for Buying

Financial Criteria

1. "Full cost" for the buy alternative is less than that for the make alternative.
2. "Full investment" for the buy alternative is less than that for the make alternative.
3. Analysis of the projected cash flows indicates that buying is the preferred alternative.

Nonfinancial Criteria

1. The nature of the project favors buying from an outside supplier (e.g., patents on the production process or product.)
2. There is not sufficient time to develop in-house production facilities.
3. The company does not want to bear the effects of variation in demand.
4. It is company policy to purchase certain component parts.
5. Specialization in the industry may favor buying.
6. You have sufficient manufacturing capacity for now but cannot hope to meet future growth requirements.
7. The project is of a very "short run" nature and does not warrant the investment in self-manufacture.
8. The required level of quality is beyond the capabilities of your firm for various reasons—for example, high quality raw materials are not obtainable.
9. Outside suppliers can handle product guarantees more effectively.
10. Rapid technological advances in the industry favor buying.

From Exhibit 1, it is clear that cost studies and investment evaluations, while they are necessary and indeed very influential in the decision, cannot alone give a definitive answer to the make-or-buy question. One cannot simply disregard the numerous nonfinancial issues surrounding such a decision. In fact, not infrequently the nonfinancial considerations can actually outweigh the most detailed financial analysis. An example of this would be a situation where a financial analysis indicates that the best decision is to buy from an outside supplier, but the confidential nature of the product itself warrants any additional expense associated with in-house manufacture. This is but one such example.

The actual process involved in making the decision varies from company to company. Policies and procedures for handling the make-or-buy question may range from very informal decision making, involving perhaps the manager of manufacturing and an individual from the purchasing department, to a very formal analysis of the alternatives.

Make-or-buy decisions in terms of manufacturing industries, because of their complexity, should not be made in isolation from the essential business functions, that is, marketing, manufacturing, engineering, purchasing, and accounting. Input from these functional areas, both financial and nonfinancial, makes it possible for the make-or-buy question to be analyzed in terms of the effect upon the entire environmental framework of the organization.

The input of the internal or management accounting function, which is frequently one of the major participants in the analysis, is very important to the decision-making process. The accounting function provides both figures and financial analysis based upon information received from marketing, manufacturing, engineering, and purchasing. Exhibit 2 illustrates a formal decision-making process, utilizing inputs from the various functional areas (of a manufacturing organization), for evaluating the make-or-buy alternatives.

Note in Exhibit 2 that the responsibility for choosing between the two alternatives is made by a rather vague entity referred to as the "decision-making body." In reality, the responsibility for the actual make-or-buy decision is delegated to a particular level, department, or function within the structure of the organization. This responsibility center, as the exhibit illustrates, works in conjunction with the various other functions and is dependent upon their inputs for its ultimate decision.

EXHIBIT 2
Participants in the Make-or-Buy Decision

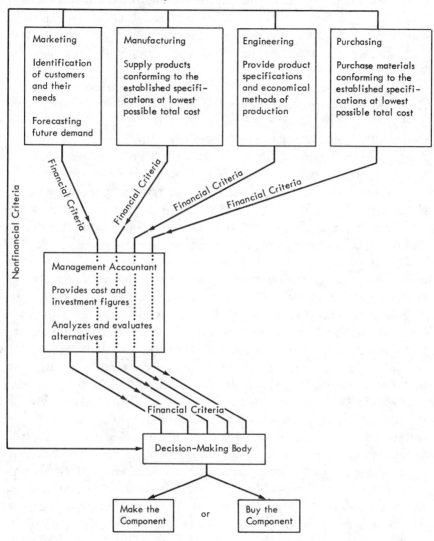

Financial Criteria Examined

Determining the Cash Flows. Referring back to Exhibit 1, we see that the important financial decision criterion is the analysis of projected cash flows for the making alternative and the buying alternative. The reliability of the make-or-buy decision, therefore, depends upon the accuracy of the respective cash flow estimates.

If it is assumed that the selling price of the component part, or, in the case of a service industry, the charge for the services rendered, is independent of the decision to make or buy, then only the cash outflows associated with each alternative need to be examined. The cash flow analysis takes into account the various cost and investment considerations connected with each alternative.

Clearly, it is crucial to the decision-making process that an accurate determination and subsequent analysis of the costs associated with each of the alternatives be carried out. Therefore, initially the quality and quantity specifications of the product being considered should be established. If these specifications change depending upon the particular alternative, then it is impossible to make meaningful comparisons and conclusions. The component specifications must remain fixed in order to make a valid appraisal of the situation at hand. Obviously, if one attempts to "compare apples and oranges," the results are meaningless.

The make-or-buy decision is a *specific* management decision and as such requires that the cost elements be identified with the cost objectives relevant to the decision—that is, to make the product or to buy from an outside source. In other words, cost determination is governed by the particular cost objective. For example, the valuation placed on the raw materials inventories as stated on the balance sheet is quite adequate for external reporting purposes, but it may have little bearing on the cost figure of such inventories that should be considered in the evaluation of the make-or-buy alternative. The balance sheet information, whether it be stated in terms of Lifo or Fifo, is of a historical nature, and the decision to be made will have future rather than past or present implications.

On the subject of determining the relevant costs, it is perhaps more functional to provide a few words of *caution* rather than try and give a detailed "prescription" for their specific determination. The above example illustrates a critical limitation on accounting data—namely, historical in nature. The allocation of overhead and certain joint costs for the purpose of determining and reporting net income places further limitations on the usefulness of such data for evaluating the make-or-buy decision.

Each of the alternatives—self-manufacture and buying from an external supplier—has particular investment elements associated with it. These elements are determined according to the specific investment objective. The evaluation must give consideration to these required investments which, for example, may be either in the form of facilities, equipment, or accounts receivable and payable.

What is the nature of the cost and investment data that should be considered? Several methods of analysis are suggested in the literature. Two methods, however, are found most often. The first method involves a comparison of the incremental operating costs and incremental investment considerations associated with making and buying the component or service. This approach fails to take into account a number of costs and investment considerations which are implicit to the decision. Increased administration costs, for example, and the opportunity costs associated with the use of existing facilities and equipment would be ignored by such an analysis.

The second method, on the other hand, takes into consideration the necessary investment and all additional costs, both direct and indirect, which are associated with the alternative on a long-term basis. In short, all costs and investment implicit to the decision are considered in the analysis, since in the long term they are all variable or differential costs. The longer this "long term"—5, 10, or 15 years—the more costs that will be differential.

It is this approach that the National Association of Accountants supports.[1] (It should be noted that this Statement deals only with manufacturing firms, however, and does not apply its findings to service industries.) The approach is referred to in the Statement as the *"full-*cost*–full-*investment" approach, and it is indeed applicable to both manufacturing and service industry decisions. The following passage from the Statement clarifies the position taken therein:

> On a short-term basis, the incremental or marginal cost and investment factors may be controlling; however, the Committee [on Management Accounting Practices] strongly emphasizes that make-or-buy evaluations must give consideration to the long-term implications based on *full* cost and *full* investment.[2]

As indicated in the above quote, the incremental approach to the make-or-buy decision is quite adequate for short-term projects, be they in the manufacturing industry or equally in the service industry. What, however, is "short term"—one month, two months,

---

[1] National Association of Accountants, *Statement No. 5: Criteria for Make-or-Buy Decisions* (New York, June 21, 1973).

[2] Ibid., p. 2.

or one year? This, unfortunately, cannot be categorically defined. Most managers, however, can distinguish the difference between short term and long term for their own particular situation. This is perhaps the most appropriate way to answer such a question. The critical issue in this is the realization that the planning schedule can only arbitrarily be split up into the long term and short term, and that some short-term decisions may have implications—perhaps not at first visible—for the longer term. The criteria, therefore, for using a full-cost–full-investment approach is the existence of possible long-term ramifications, resulting from the decision to make or buy. If the decision would indeed result in a commitment with long-term implications, a full-cost–full-investment analysis is essential.

Exhibits 3 and 4 list some examples of the more significant cost elements to be considered under each alternative when using the

EXHIBIT 3*
Full Costs in Make-or-Buy Decisions

Direct and Indirect Costs to Buy	*Direct and Indirect Costs to Make*
Administration	Administration
	Direct manufacturing costs
Engineering	Engineering
Freight and duties	Freight and duties
Inspection	
Insurance and taxes	Indirect manufacturing costs
Inventory carrying costs (but not the cost of investment in inventory, which is included as a part of total investment)	Inventory carrying costs (but not the cost of investment in inventory, which is included as a part of total investment)
Invoice cost	
Invoice processing	Invoice processing
	Manufacturing variances
	Material handling
Patterns, dies, and molds	Patterns, dies, and molds
Purchasing	Purchasing
Quality assurance	Quality assurance
Receiving and handling	
Research and development	Research and development
	Start-up costs
Tooling	Tooling
Plus	
Continuing costs relating to a capability to "make" which may not be readily eliminated by a decision to "buy"	

* National Association of Accountants, *Statement No. 5: Criteria for Make-or-Buy Decisions* (New York, June 21, 1973), p. 8.

full-cost–full-investment approach. These exhibits, however, are by no means exhaustive.

These two methods of evaluating the make-or-buy decision will become clearer when a simplified example is presented and analysed. Such an illustrative example is found at the end of this chapter.

Future Financial Considerations.   Under either alternative, consideration should be given to the possibility of any future costs which may become associated with the alternative. A fixed-price

EXHIBIT 4*
Investment in Make-or-Buy Decisions

Investment to Buy	Investment to Make
Accounts payable to suppliers	Accounts payable to suppliers
	Accrued payrolls
Inventory	Inventory
	Manufacturing facilities
Molds and dies	Molds and dies
Office and service facilities	Office and service facilities
Supplier credit terms	Supplier credit terms
Warehousing facilities	Warehousing facilities

Plus

Investment relating to a capacity to "make" which may not be readily eliminated by a decision to "buy"

* National Association of Accountants, *Statement No. 5: Criteria for Make-or-Buy Decisions* (New York, June 21, 1973), pp. 11, 12.

contract to buy from an outside supplier may be preferable during times of inflation since the supplier bears the adverse inflationary effects. Also, when there are possible drastic changes in technology or design from year to year, such as in the automobile industry, it may be less risky and less costly in the long run to buy from a supplier. The additional costs of manufacturing would result from machines having to be retooled each year so they could produce the new parts. These are just a couple of examples where the future must be considered as part of the evaluation of the alternatives.

Financial Analysis.   With any project, an important part of the analysis is the determination of the relative return on investment. Clearly, the time value of money must be given consideration in the analysis quite simply because money has value over time. Net-present-value analysis and internal-rate-of-return analysis are the two familiar methods employed for determining a relative return on the investment. (See Chapter 15.)

The following also need to be determined before the return can be calculated:

1. Time frame;
2. Cash flows;
3. Cost of capital; and
4. Risk involved.

Time frame is determined by the economic life of the project. The economic life in turn is determined from the shortest of the physical life, technological life, and product-market life.

Cash outflows for each alternative are determined from the cost analysis of each alternative. The resulting cash inflows associated with an alternative are determined by calculating the combined cost and investment outflow differential for that alternative as compared with the other alternative.

The cost of capital will vary from company to company. Probably, the after-tax cost will be between 10 and 15 percent.[3] The risk is usually an unquantified entity that varies from project to project. Consideration should however be given to the risk involved.

It is also desirable to know the effect of errors in estimates on the whole analysis. For example, how sensitive is the analysis to a 5 percent error in any of the estimates? These considerations should be kept in mind while carrying out the analysis.

Nonfinancial Criteria Examined

Referring again to Exhibit 1, note that there are several nonfinancial considerations for both the making and buying alternatives. To this point, the discussion has concentrated almost completely on the financial aspects of the make-or-buy decision. However, it should be reiterated that the final decision must incorporate *both* financial analysis and nonfinancial considerations.

Nonfinancial factors are, of course, numerous and unique to each individual company. They can stem from, or form a part of, com-

---

[3] Ibid., p. 14.

pany policy. Depending upon the actual significance of the non-financial criteria, the ultimate make-or-buy decision may be reversed from that reached after conducting a financial analysis. An example illustrating this was stated earlier in the chapter and another example is stated here to further clarify this point of discussion. Assume that after a financial analysis is completed, the best alternative is self-manufacture of a particular component. However, it is discovered that the company requires very high standards of quality which cannot be achieved in-house. Therefore, when all the criteria are examined, purchasing from an outside supplier at a higher cost is the better choice.

Further examples of these nonfinancial considerations are found in Exhibit 1 and will be briefly expanded upon in the following paragraphs.

If the project is of a confidential nature, either because of its own secrecy—for example, a government defense project—or because the processes involved are secret, then making would be the desired alternative. This concern for confidentiality can apply equally both to service firms, which may have a unique service to offer or a unique way of offering an existing service; and to manufacturing concerns; who may have developed some competitive advantage through a particular specialized process that would have to be made known to a supplier if a component part was to be purchased from such a source.

On the other hand, if certain processes, equipment, and/or products are protected by patents, then the product or service should be purchased. By selecting the buying alternative, the company avoids the strong possibility of legal implications. These would be undesirable since their long-run effect on the company would be quite unpredictable.

If the component or part is difficult or impossible to move from the supplier to the company, for example, either because of its being fragile, unusually large or its odd shape, then making is preferred.

It may be that the demand for a particular service or product exists now and is expected to increase rapidly within a time period of one month. Clearly such a short lead time may not be sufficient for facilities to be developed in-house, and hence buying, whether or not it is determined more costly from the financial evaluation, is the decision to make.

Certainly self-manufacture affords direct supervision of the project. This, in turn, enables easier control of final delivery dates, inventories, and any future changes. If such control is desired or needed, or if the component part is itself very uncommon and complicated to make, then the benefits derived from direct supervision may warrant self-manufacture.

Company policy to manufacture all components or parts in-house may be an attempt by the corporate management to give employees as much stability as possible in their jobs. The benefits of having this employment stability accrue also to management who are relieved of the task of employee recruitment. Thus making at slightly higher cost is (in the long run) the preferred alternative. Also, if the company employees are members of a union, it is pressure from the union which forces or constrains management to give consideration to employment stability. Hence, corporate policy would reflect this constraint in the form of self-manufacture. In this case, the benefits of making are quite obvious.

If, on the other hand, demand fluctuates and temporarily reaches unusually large quantities that cannot be met from self-manufacturing, then buying from a supplier to meet peak requirements may be preferred. Rather than hire people for a short time, corporate policy to maintain employment stability would dictate the buying alternative.

The dependence on external manufacturers always has associated with it a certain degree of risk and hence may be undesirable whatever the cost saving according to the financial evaluation. If the required level of product quality can only be achieved through self-manufacture and in-house quality control, then clearly buying is undesirable.

There should exist sufficient manufacturing capacity not only for the present but also for future growth requirements. If this required capacity cannot in any way be made available, then future considerations indicate that buying may be the appropriate decision.

Industry specialization may be such that it *cannot* be duplicated in-house. This fact, combined with the requirement of high quality, indicates a choice for outside suppliers.

Other nonfinancial considerations that can influence the make-or-buy decision are: the short-run nature of the project which may not warrant investment in self-manufacture; the handling of product guarantees by outside suppliers as compared to yourself; and the rapid changes in technology and your ability to handle these as compared with an outside supplier.

The important point that one should grasp from this discussion on nonfinancial criteria is that they are essential to the decision-making process. The actual criteria vary from company to company and, indeed, situation to situation within the same company. The implications of such considerations, however, should be evaluated fully before making a final decision.

CONCLUSION

One should realize from the preceding that there are a number of reasons why companies should buy products and/or manufacture products or, in the case of service industries, contract out for the service or supply the service themselves.

Cost studies alone, while they are necessary and helpful, do not supply the complete answer to the make-or-buy dilemma. The non-financial considerations are significant to the analysis and vary from company to company. The final decision is by no means easy and is not without a measure of uncertainty.

It is common knowledge that, over time, business does not remain static. Changes in technology, markets, competition, and economic conditions require that the "make-or-buy" decision be reviewed and reevaluated periodically.

The following illustrative example provides a clarification of the material discussed in this chapter.

AN ILLUSTRATIVE EXAMPLE

The Al-Rite Manufacturing Company has recently been considering the possibility of starting to manufacture a particular component (the ART) or buying it from a different outside supplier who offers a more competitive price than the present supplier. The present contract expired and negotiations carried on with suppliers by the company produced the following unit costs of buying:

```
Volume purchased................. 200,000 units
Cost (price) per unit................    $1.75
Freight and delivery
   charges per unit.................     0.25
       Total unit cost...............    $2.00
```

The contract for the above prices was of a three-year duration. This was with the understanding that volume purchased would increase annually by about 5 to 6 percent.

The following table presents full costs of buying for the three-year period:

	Year 1	Year 2	Year 3
Requirements.................	200,000 units	230,000 units	260,000 units
Costs to buy @ $2............	$400,000	$460,000	$520,000
Purchasing costs.............	20,000	21,000	22,000
Quality control costs........	50,000	52,000	55,000
Handling costs...............	25,000	28,000	31,000
Total incremental costs......	$495,000	$561,000	$628,000
Allocated costs:			
Administrative expense.......	$ 20,000	$ 24,000	$ 32,000
Full costs...................	$515,000	$585,000	$660,000

If the component was manufactured by the Al-Rite Company, the costs involved were determined to be:

Variable cost.........................	$1.50 (materials and labor)
Capacity cost*........................	0.25
Total standard cost.............	$1.75

* This is the cost assigned to the use of present (idle) facilities. It is a variable overhead, including such elements as power and supplies.

Unit material and labor costs were expected to increase 10 percent yearly. Start-up expenses are $30,000, and the costs of learning during the first year were estimated at $70,000.

The following table presents data for the make alternative:

	Year 1	Year 2	Year 3
Requirements.......................	200,000 units	230,000 units	260,000 units
Total variable costs @ $1.50			
(10% yearly increase)..............	$300,000	$379,500	$471,900
Support costs......................	20,000	25,000	30,000
Start-up costs.....................	30,000	—	—
Learning costs.....................	70,000	—	—
Total incremental costs........	$420,000	$404,500	$501,900
Present capacity costs.............	$ 50,000	$ 57,500	$ 65,000
Administrative costs...............	100,000	120,000	140,000
Full costs......................	$570,000	$582,000	$706,900

If the product component is purchased, there is no fixed investment as with self-manufacture. However, there is an investment in one month's supply of working capital, just as there is with self-manufacture. This is calculated as $\frac{1}{12}$ of the annual total variable costs of manufacturing, or $\frac{1}{12}$ of the cost to buy, as the case may be, and is increased each year by $\frac{1}{12}$ of the annual increment in each of these costs:

	Investment if Bought		
	Year 1	Year 2	Year 3
Working capital...........	$33,333	$5,000	$5,000

As well as the investment in one month's supply of working capital, there is a total investment in equipment of $195,000 if the product is manufactured within the company. This can be depreciated over the three-year life of the project using straight line with no salvage value. Initially, manufacturing space which is presently idle could be used for the facilities. This space, however, or one of an equivalent size, would be needed within the first year of self-manufacture for the expected expansion of present manu-

	Investment if Made In-House		
	Year 1	Year 2	Year 3
Equipment...............................	$195,000		
Additional investment in working capital...................................	25,000	$6,625	$7,700
Total incremental investment........	$220,000	$6,625	$7,700
Existing facilities.........................	200,000	—	—
Total investment....................	$420,000	$6,625	$7,700

facturing facilities. The capital cost of providing new facilities to meet expected expansion needs and to replace the area that would be used for self-manufacture is $200,000. Since this would result from self-manufacture only, the analysis must consider the value of the existing available facilities as part of the investment of the "make" alternative.

The complete analysis on a full-cost–full-investment basis is shown in Table A. In Table B an incremental analysis is shown.

TABLE A
Financial Analysis: Full-Cost and Full-Investment Analysis

	Prior to Year 1	Year 1	Year 2	Year 3
Capital investment to make...........	$ 420,000		$ 6,625	$ 7,700
Capital investment to buy............	33,333		5,000	5,000
A. Additional investment to make....	$ 386,667		$ 1,625	$ 2,700
1. Cash costs to make...........		$570,000	$582,000	$706,900
Depreciation expense*........		65,000	65,000	65,000
Total tax-deductible costs...................		$635,000	$647,000	$771,900
2. Tax shield (50%).............		$317,500	$323,500	$385,950
3. Net cash outflow to make (1) − (2).....................		252,500	258,500	320,950
4. Costs to buy.................		$515,000	$585,000	$660,000
After-tax cash outflow to buy (50%)..................		$257,500	$292,500	$330,000
B. Cash flow saved by making (4) − (3)......................		$ 5,000	$ 34,000	$ 9,050
Combined investment and cost cash flow differential (B) − (A).....................	$(386,667)	$ 5,000	$ 32,375	$ 6,350

If the initial investment under either alternative (make/buy) is made at the beginning of the first year of the project, and if the required rate of return after taxes is 15 percent, the net present value of the "make" alternative is calculated as follows:†

$$\text{NPV} = -\$386,667 + \$5,000(0.8696) + \$32,375(0.7561) + \$6,350(0.6575)$$
$$= -386,667 + 4,348 + 24,479 + 4,175$$
$$= -\$353,665$$

* Straight-line depreciation is used here only to maintain simplicity in the example. Normally a company would use accelerated depreciation for tax purposes, and it is depreciation reported for tax purposes (as opposed to shareholders) which provides the depreciation tax shield.
† Numbers in parentheses are appropriate 15 percent discount factors.

The NPV in the incremental analysis case (Table B), since it is greater than zero, indicates that the "make" alternative should be selected. However, the NPV in the full analysis case, since it is a large negative number, *clearly* indicates that the "make" alternative should be *rejected*. Which analysis should be accepted as valid?

The full-cost and full-investment analysis indicates the proper course of action, that is, select the *buy alternative*. This analysis is clearly appropriate since it takes into consideration all implications associated with the commitment of the firm to the *make* alternative over the three-year period (long term). In particular, the analysis in Table B ignores the fact that the "make" alternative will necessitate a $200,000 outlay for more manufacturing space during the

TABLE B
Financial Analysis: Incremental Cost and Investment Analysis

	Prior to Year 1	Year 1	Year 2	Year 3
Capital investment to make...........	$ 220,000		$ 6,625	$ 7,700
Capital investment to buy............	33,333		5,000	5,000
A. Additional investment to make....	$ 186,667		$ 1,625	$ 2,700
1. Cash costs to make...........		$420,000	$404,500	$501,900
Depreciation expense........		65,000	65,000	65,000
Total tax-deductible costs..................		$485,000	$469,500	$566,900
2. Tax shield (50%)..............		$242,500	$234,750	$283,450
3. Net cash outflow to make (1) − (2).....................		$177,500	$169,750	$218,450
Costs to buy.................		$495,000	$561,000	$628,000
4. After-tax cash outflow to buy (50%)..................		$247,500	$280,500	$314,000
B. Cash flow saved by making (4) − (3)......................		$ 70,000	$110,750	$ 95,550
Combined investment and cost cash flow differential (B) − (A)......................	$(186,667)	$ 70,000	$109,125	$ 92,850

Again, if the initial investment is made at the beginning of the first year of the project and if the required rate of return after taxes is 15 percent as in the "full" analysis case, the net present value of the "make" alternative is calculated as follows:

$$NPV = -\$186,667 + \$70,000(0.8696) + \$109,125(0.7561) + \$92,850(0.6575)$$
$$= -186,667 + 60,872 + 82,509 + 61,049$$
$$= +\$17,763$$

first year of self-manufacture, whereas this outlay is avoided if the "buy" alternative is chosen.

It is clear that a decision based upon an incremental analysis (positive NPV) can be disastrous for the firm over the long run. This approach ignores the full quantitative implications associated with the make alternative.

In sum, while an incremental approach may be applicable for "reversible" make-or-buy decisions in the short run, if such a decision involves a long-run capital commitment, the "full" analysis should be used.

ADDITIONAL SOURCES

Anthony, Robert N., and Reece, James S. *Management Accounting Principles*, chaps. 17, 18. 3d ed. Homewood, Ill.: Richard D. Irwin, Inc., 1975.

Duncan, Ian D. "Make-or-Buy Decisions." *Cost and Management,* September–October 1975, p. 44.

Gordon, Lawrence A.; Miller, Danny; and Mintzberg, Henry. *Normative Models in Managerial Decision-Making.* Special Study No. 9 of the Society of Industrial Accountants of Canada and the National Association of Accountants, 1975.

Gross, Harry. "Make-or-Buy Decisions in Growing Firms." *Accounting Review,* October 1966, p. 745.

Hubler, Myron J. "The Make-or-Buy Decision." *Management Services,* November–December 1966, p. 45.

National Association of Accountants. *Statement No. 5: Criteria for Make-or-Buy Decisions.* New York, June 21, 1973.

Roe, P. A. "Modeling a Make-or-Buy Decision at ICI." *Long Range Planning,* December 1972, p. 21.

Vancil, Richard F., ed. *Financial Executive's Handbook,* chap. 15. Homewood, Ill.: Dow Jones-Irwin, Inc., 1970.

20

Pricing Policies
for New Products*

Joel Dean†

Editors' Note: This chapter first appeared in the *Harvard
Business Review* in November 1950. Because of the unending
requests for reprints of the article, and because of its continuing validity, it was republished in the November–December 1976 *Harvard Business Review* as an "HBR Classic." This
newer printing includes a retrospective commentary by Mr.
Dean, in which he amplifies his earlier writing with insights
from the intervening years and in light of such developments
as inflation.

INTRODUCTION

How to price a new product is a top management puzzle that
is too often solved by cost-theology and hunch. This chapter suggests a pricing policy geared to the dynamic nature of a new product's competitive status. Today's high rate of innovation makes the
economic evolution of a new product a strategic guide to practical
pricing.

New products have a protected distinctiveness which is doomed

---

* Reprinted by permission of the Harvard University Press (collected in *Modern
Marketing Strategy,* E. C. Bursk and J. F. Chapman, eds., 1964). Copyright © 1950,
1976 by The President and Fellows of Harvard College.

† Mr. Dean is President of Joel Dean Associates and Professor of Business Economics at Columbia University.

to progressive degeneration from competitive inroads. The invention of a new marketable specialty is usually followed by a period of patent protection when markets are still hesitant and unexplored and when product design is fluid. Then comes a period of rapid expansion of sales as market acceptance is gained.

Next the product becomes a target for competitive encroachment. New competitors enter the field, and innovations narrow the gap of distinctiveness between the product and its substitutes. The seller's zone of pricing discretion narrows as his distinctive "specialty" fades into a pedestrian "commodity" which is so little differentiated from other products that the seller has limited independence in pricing, even if rivals are few.

Throughout the cycle, continual changes occur in promotional and price elasticity and in cost of production and distribution. These changes call for adjustments in price policy. Appropriate pricing over the cycle depends on the development of three different aspects of maturity, which usually move in almost parallel time paths:

1. *Technical maturity,* indicated by declining rate of product development, increasing standardization among brands, and increasing stability of manufacturing processes and knowledge about them.
2. *Market maturity,* indicated by consumer acceptance of the basic service idea, by widespread belief that the products of most manufacturers will perform satisfactorily, and by enough familiarity and sophistication to permit consumers to compare brands competently.
3. *Competitive maturity,* indicated by increasing stability of market shares and price structures.

Of course, interaction among these components tends to make them move together. That is, intrusion by new competitors helps to develop the market, but entrance is most tempting when the new product appears to be establishing market acceptance.

The rate at which the cycle of degeneration progresses varies widely among products. What are the factors that set its pace? An overriding determinant is technical—the extent to which the economic environment must be reorganized to use the innovation effectively. The scale of plant investment and technical research called forth by the telephone, electric power, the automobile, or air transport makes for a long gestation period, as compared with even such major innovations as cellophane or frozen foods.

Development comes fastest when the new gadget fills a new vacuum made to order for it. Electric stoves, as one example, have risen to 50 percent market saturation in the fast-growing Pacific Northwest, where electric power has become the lowest cost energy. Products still in early developmental stages also provide rich opportunities for product differentiation, which with heavy research costs holds off competitive degeneration. But aside from technical factors, the rate of degeneration is controlled by economic forces that can be subsumed under rate of market acceptance and ease of competitive entry.

By *market acceptance* is meant the extent to which buyers consider the product a serious alternative to other ways of performing the same service. Market acceptance is a frictional factor. The effect of cultural lags may endure for some time after quality and costs make products technically useful. The slow catch-on of the "electric pig" (garbage-disposal unit) is an example.

On the other hand, the attitude of acceptance may exist long before any workable model can be developed; then the final appearance of the product will produce an explosive growth curve in sales. The antihistamine cold tablet, a spectacular example, reflects the national faith in chemistry's ability to vanquish the common cold. And, of course, low unit price may speed market acceptance of an innovation; ball-point pens and all-steel houses started at about the same time, but look at the difference in their sales curves.

Ease of competitive entry is a major determinant of the speed of degeneration of a specialty. An illustration is found in the washing machine business before the war, where with little basic patent protection the Maytag position was quickly eroded by small manufacturers who performed essentially an assembly operation. The ball-point pen cascaded from a $12 novelty to a 49-cent "price football," partly because entry barriers of patents and techniques were ineffective. Frozen orange juice, which started as a protected specialty of Minute Maid, is speeding through its competitive cycle, with competing brands now crowding into the market.

At the outset the innovator can control the rate of competitive deterioration to an important degree by nonprice as well as by price strategies. Through successful research in product improvement he can protect his specialty position both by extending the life of his basic patent and by keeping ahead of competitors in product development. The record of the International Business Machines punchcard equipment illustrates this potentiality. Ease of entry is also affected by a policy of "stay-out" pricing (so low as to make the prospects look uninviting), which under some circumstances may slow down the process of competitive encroachment.

STEPS IN PIONEER PRICING

Pricing problems start when a company finds a product that is a radical departure from existing ways of performing a service and that is temporarily protected from competition by patents, secrets of production, control at the point of a scarce resource, or by other barriers. The seller here has a wide range of pricing discretion resulting from extreme product differentiation.

A good example of pricing latitude conferred by protected superiority of product is provided by the McGraw Electric Company's "Toastmaster," which, both initially and over a period of years, was able to command a very substantial price premium over competitive toasters. Apparently this advantage resulted from (a) a good product that was distinctive and superior and (b) substantial and skillful sales promotion.

Similarly, Sunbeam priced its electric iron $2 above comparable models of major firms with considerable success. And Sunbeam courageously priced its new metal coffeemaker at $32, much above competitive makes of glass coffeemakers, but it was highly successful.

To get a picture of how a manufacturer should go about setting his price in the pioneer stage, let me describe the main steps of the process (of course the classification is arbitrary and the steps are interrelated): (a) estimate of demand, (b) decision on market targets, (c) design of promotional strategy, and (d) choice of distribution channels.

Estimate of Demand

The problem at the pioneer stage differs from that in a relatively stable monopoly because the product is beyond the experience of buyers and because the perishability of its distinctiveness must be reckoned with. How can demand for new products be explored? How can we find out how much people will pay for a product that has never before been seen or used? There are several levels of refinement to this analysis.

The initial problem of estimating demand for a new product can be broken into a series of subproblems: (*a*) whether the product will go at all (assuming price is in a competitive range), (*b*) what range of price will make the product economically attractive to buyers, (*c*) what sales volumes can be expected at various points in this price range, and (*d*) what reaction will price produce in manufacturers and sellers of displaced substitutes.

The first step is an exploration of the *preferences and educability of consumers*, always, of course, in the light of the technical feasibility of the new product. How many potential buyers are there? Is the product a practical device for meeting their needs? How can it be improved to meet their needs better? What proportion of the potential buyers would prefer, or could be induced to prefer, this product to already existing products (prices being equal)?

Sometimes it is feasible to start with the assumption that all vulnerable substitutes will be fully displaced. For example, to get some idea of the maximum limits of demand for a new type of reflecting-sign material, a company started with estimates of the aggregate number and area of auto license plates, highway markers, railroad operational signs, and name signs for streets and homes. Next, the proportion of each category needing night-light reflection was guessed. For example, it was assumed that only rural and suburban homes could benefit by this kind of name sign, and the estimate of need in this category was made accordingly.

It is not uncommon and possibly not unrealistic for a manufacturer to make the blithe assumption at this stage that the product price will be "within a competitive range" without having much idea of what that range is. For example, in developing a new type of camera equipment, one of the electrical companies judged its acceptability to professional photographers by technical performance without making any inquiry into its economic value. When the equipment was later placed in an economic setting, the indications were that sales would be negligible.

The second step is marking out this *competitive range of price*. Vicarious pricing experience can be secured by interviewing selected distributors who have enough comparative knowledge of customers' alternatives and preferences to judge what price range would make the new product "a good value." Direct discussions with representative experienced industrial users have produced reliable estimates of the "practical" range of prices. Manufacturers of electrical equipment often explore the economic as well as the technical feasibility of a new product by sending engineers with blueprints and models to see customers, such as technical and operating executives.

In guessing the price range of a radically new consumers' product of small unit value, the concept of *barter equivalent* can be a useful research guide. For example, a manufacturer of paper specialties tested a dramatic new product in the following fashion: A wide variety of consumer products totally unlike the new product were purchased and spread out on a big table. Consumers selected the products they would swap for the new product. By finding out whether the product would trade even for a dish pan, a towel, or a hairpin, the executives got a rough idea of what range of prices might strike typical consumers as reasonable in the light of the values they could get for their money in totally different kinds of expenditures.

But asking prospective consumers how much they think they would be willing to pay for a new product, even by such indirect or disguised methods, may often fail to give a reliable indication of the demand schedule. Most times people just do not know what they would pay. It depends partly on their income and on future alternatives. Early in the postwar period a manufacturer of television sets tried this method and got highly erratic and obviously unreliable results because the distortion of war shortages kept prospects from fully visualizing the multiple ways of spending their money.

Another deficiency, which may, however, be less serious than it appears, is that responses are biased by the consumer's confused notion that he is bargaining for a good price. Not until techniques of depth interviewing are more refined than they are now can this crude and direct method of exploring a new product's demand schedule hold much promise of being accurate.

One appliance manufacturer tried out new products on a sample of employees by selling to them at deep discounts, with the stipulation that they could if they wished return the products at the end of the experiment period and get a refund of their low purchase price. Demand for foreign orange juice was tested by placing it in several markets at three different prices, ranging around the price of fresh fruit; the result showed rather low price elasticity.

While inquiries of this sort are often much too short-run to give any real indication of consumer tastes, the relevant point here is that even such rough probing often yields broad impressions of price elasticity, particularly in relation to product variations such as styling, placing of controls, and use of automatic features. It may show, for example, that $5 of cost put into streamlining or chromium stripping can add $50 to the price.

The third step, a more definite inquiry into the *probable sales from several possible prices,* starts with an investigation of the prices of substitutes. Usually the buyer has a choice of existing ways of having the same service performed; an analysis of the costs of these choices serves as a guide in setting the price for a new way.

Comparisons are easy and significant for industrial customers who have a costing system to tell them the exact value, say, of a forklift truck in terms of warehouse labor saved. Indeed, chemical companies setting up a research project to displace an existing material often know from the start the top price that can be charged for the new substitute in terms of cost of the present material.

But in most cases the comparison is obfuscated by the presence of quality differences that may be important bases for price premiums. This is most true of household appliances, where the alternative is an unknown amount of labor of a mysterious value. In pricing a cargo parachute the choices are: (*a*) free fall in a padded box from a plane flown close to the ground, (*b*) landing the plane, (*c*) back shipment by land from the next air terminal, or (*d*) land shipment all the way. These options differ widely in their service value and are not very useful pricing guides.

Thus it is particularly hard to know how much good will be done by making the new product cheaper than the old by various amounts, or how much the market will be restricted by making the new product more expensive. The answers usually come from experiment or research.

The fourth step in estimating demand is to consider the *possibility of retaliation by manufacturers of displaced substitutes* in the form of price cutting. This development may not occur at all if the new product displaces only a small market segment. If old industries do fight it out, however, their incremental costs provide a floor to the resulting price competition and should be brought into price plans.

For example, a manufacturer of black-and-white sensitized paper studied the possibility that lowering his price would displace blueprint paper substantially. Not only did he investigate the prices of blueprint paper, but he also felt it necessary to estimate the out-of-pocket cost of making blueprint paper because of the probability that manufacturers already in the market would fight back by reducing prices toward the level of their incremental costs.

Decision on Market Targets

When the company has developed some idea of the range of demand and the range of prices that are feasible for the new product, it is in a position to make some basic strategic decisions on market targets and promotional plans. To decide on market objectives requires answers to several questions: What ultimate market share is wanted for the new product? How does it fit into the present product line? What about production methods? What are the possible distribution channels?

These are questions of joint costs in production and distribution, of plant expansion outlays, and of potential competition. If entry is easy, the company may not be eager to disrupt its present production and selling operations to capture and hold a large slice of the new market. But if the prospective profits shape up to a substantial new income source, it will be worthwhile to make the capital expenditures on plant needed to reap the full harvest.

A basic factor in answering all these questions is the expected behavior of production and distribution costs. The relevant data here are all the production outlays that will be made after the decision day—the capital expenditures as well as the variable costs. A go-ahead decision will hardly be made without some assurance that these costs can be recovered before the product becomes a football in the market. Many different projections of costs will be made, depending on the alternative scales of output, rate of market expansion, threats of potential competition, and measures to meet that competition that are under consideration. But these factors and the decision that is made on promotional strategy are interdependent. The fact is that this is a circular problem that in theory can only be solved by simultaneous equations.

Fortunately, it is possible to make some approximations that can break the circle: scale economies become significantly different only with broad changes in the size of plant and the type of production methods. This narrows the range of cost projections to workable proportions. The effects of using different distribution channels can be guessed fairly well without meshing the choices in with all the production and selling possibilities. The most vulnerable point of the circle is probably the decision on promotional strategy. The choices here are broad and produce a variety of results. The next step in the pricing process is therefore a plan for promotion.

Design of Promotional Strategy

Initial promotion outlays are an investment in the product that cannot be recovered until some kind of market has been established. The innovator shoulders the burden of creating a market—educating consumers to the existence and uses of the product. Later imitators will never have to do this job; so, if the innovator does not want to be simply a benefactor to his future competitors, he must make pricing plans to recover his initial outlays before his pricing discretion evaporates.

His basic strategic problem is to find the right mixture of price and promotion to maximize his long-run profits. He can choose a relatively high price in pioneering stages, together with extravagant advertising and dealer discounts, and plan to get his promotion costs back early; or he can use low prices and lean margins from the very outset in order to discourage potential competition when the barriers of patents, distribution channels, or production techniques become inadequate. This question is discussed further shortly.

Choice of Distribution Channels

Estimation of the costs of moving the new product through the channels of distribution to the final consumer must enter into the pricing procedure since these costs govern the factory price that will result in a specified consumer price and since it is the consumer price that matters for volume. Distributive margins are partly pure promotional costs and partly physical-distribution costs. Margins must at least cover the distributors' costs of warehousing, handling, and order taking. These costs are similar to factory production costs in being related to physical capacity and its utilization, i.e., fluctuations in production or sales volume.

Hence these set a floor to trade-channel discounts. But distributors usually also contribute promotional effort—in point-of-sale pushing, local advertising, and display—when it is made worth their while. These pure promotional costs are more optional. Unlike physical-handling costs they have no necessary functional relation to sales volume. An added layer of margin in trade discounts to produce this localized sales effort (with retail price fixed) is an optional way for the manufacturer to spend his prospecting money in putting over a new product.

In establishing promotional costs, the manufacturer must decide on the extent to which the selling effort will be delegated to members of the distribution chain. Indeed, some distribution channels, such as house-to-house selling and retail-store selling supplemented by home demonstrators, represent a substantial delegation of the manufacturer's promotional job, and these usually involve much higher distribution-channel costs than do conventional methods.

Rich distributor margins are an appropriate use of promotion funds only when the producer thinks a high price plus promotion is a better expansion policy in the specialty than low price by itself. Thus there is an intimate interaction between the pricing of a new product and the costs and the problems of floating it down the distribution channels to the final consumer.

POLICIES FOR PIONEER PRICING

The strategic decision in pricing a new product is the choice between (a) a policy of high initial prices that skim the cream of demand and (b) a policy of low prices from the outset serving as an active agent for market penetration. Although the actual range of choice is much wider than this, a sharp dichotomy clarifies the issues for consideration.

Skimming Price

For products that represent a drastic departure from accepted ways of performing a service, a policy of relatively high prices coupled with heavy promotional expenditures in the early stages of market development (and lower prices at later stages) has proved successful for many products. There are several reasons for the success of this policy:

1. Demand is likely to be more inelastic with respect to price in the early stages than it is when the product is full grown. This is particularly true for consumers' goods. A novel product, such as the electric blanket or the electric pig, is not yet accepted as a part of the expenditure pattern. Consumers are still ignorant about its value compared with the value of conventional alternatives. Moreover, at least in the early stages, the product has so few close rivals that cross-elasticity of demand is low. Promotional elasticity is, on the other hand, quite high, particularly for products with high unit prices such as television sets. Since it is difficult for the customer to value the service of the product in a way to price it intelligently, he is by default principally interested in how well it will work.

2. Launching a new product with a high price is an efficient device for breaking the market up into segments that differ in price elasticity of demand. The initial high price serves to skim the cream of the market that is relatively insensitive to price. Subsequent price reductions tap successfully more elastic sectors of the market. This pricing strategy is exemplified by the systematic succession of editions of a book, sometimes starting with a $50 limited personal edition and ending up with a 25-cent pocket book.

3. This policy is safer, or at least appears so. Facing an unknown elasticity of demand, a high initial price serves as a "refusal" price during the stage of exploration. How much costs can be reduced as the market expands and as the design of the product is improved by increasing production efficiency with new techniques is difficult to predict. One of the electrical companies recently introduced a new lamp bulb at a comparatively high initial price, but they made the announcement that the price would be reduced as the company found ways of cutting its costs.

4. Many companies are not in a position to finance the product flotation out of distant future revenues. High cash outlays in the early stages result from heavy costs of production and distributor organizing, in addition to the promotional invest-

ment in the pioneer product. High prices are a reasonable financing technique for shouldering these burdens in the light of the many uncertainties about the future.

Penetration Price

The alternative policy is to use low prices as the principal instrument for penetrating mass markets early. This policy is the reverse of the skimming policy in which the price is lowered only as short-run competition forces it.

The passive skimming policy has the virtue of safeguarding some profits at every stage of market penetration. But it prevents quick sales to the many buyers who are at the lower end of the income scale or the lower end of the preference scale and who therefore are unwilling to pay any substantial premium for product or reputation superiority. The active approach in probing possibilities for market expansion by early penetration pricing requires research, forecasting, and courage.

A decision to price for market expansion can be reached at various stages in a product's life cycle: before birth, at birth, in childhood, in adulthood, or in senescence. The chances for large-volume sales should at least be explored in the early stages of product development research, even before the pilot stage, perhaps with a more definitive exploration when the product goes into production and the price and distribution plans are decided upon. And the question of pricing to expand the market, if not answered earlier, will probably arise once more after the product has established an elite market.

Quite a few products have been rescued from premature senescence by pricing them low enough to tap new markets. The reissues of important books in the 25-cent pocket book category illustrate this point particularly well. These have produced not only commercial but intellectual renascence as well to many authors. The patterns of sales growth of a product that had reached stability in a high-price market have undergone sharp changes when it was suddenly priced low enough to tap new markets.

A contrasting illustration of passive policy is the recent pricing experience of the airlines. Although safety considerations and differences in equipment and service cloud the picture, it is pretty clear that the bargain-rate coach fares of scheduled airlines were adopted in reaction to the cut rates of nonscheduled airlines. This competitive response has apparently established a new pattern of traffic growth for the scheduled airlines.

An example of penetration pricing at the initial stage of the product's market life, again from the book field, is Simon & Schuster's recently adopted policy of bringing out new titles in a $1, paperbound edition simultaneously with the conventional higher priced, cloth-bound edition.

What conditions warrant aggressive pricing for market penetration? This question cannot be answered categorically, but it may be helpful to generalize that the following conditions indicate the desirability of an early low-price policy:

- A high price-elasticity of demand in the short run, i.e., a high degree of responsiveness of sales to reductions in price.
- Substantial savings in production costs as the result of greater volume—not a necessary condition, however, since if elasticity of demand is high enough, pricing for market expansion may be profitable without realizing production economies.
- Product characteristics such that it will not seem bizarre when it is first fitted into the consumers' expenditure pattern.
- A strong threat of potential competition.

This threat of potential competition is a highly persuasive reason for penetration pricing. One of the major objectives of most low-pricing policies in the pioneering stages of market development is to raise entry barriers to prospective competitors. This is appropriate when entrants must make large-scale investments to reach minimum costs and they cannot slip into an established market by selling at substantial discounts.

In many industries, however, the important potential competitor is a large, multiple-product firm operating as well in other fields than that represented by the product in question. For a firm, the most important consideration for entry is not existing margins but the prospect of a large and growing volume of sales. Present margins over costs are not the dominant consideration because such firms are normally confident that they can get their costs down as low as competitors' costs if the volume of production is large.

Therefore, when total industry sales are not expected to amount to much, a high-margin policy can be followed because entry is improbable in view of the expectation of low volume and because it does not matter too much to potential competitors if the new product is introduced.

The fact remains that for products whose market potential appears big, a policy of stay-out pricing from the outset makes much more sense. When a leading soap manufacturer developed an additive that whitened clothes and enhanced the brilliance of colors, the company chose to take its gains in a larger share of the market rather than in a temporary price premium. Such a decision was sound, since the company's competitors could be expected to match or better the product improvement fairly promptly. Under these circumstances, the price premium would have been short-lived, whereas the gains in market share were more likely to be retained.

Of course, any decision to start out with lower prices must take into account the fact that if the new product calls for capital recovery over a long period, the risk may be great that later entrants will be able to exploit new production techniques which can undercut the pioneer's original cost structure. In such cases, the low-price pattern should be adopted with a view to long-run rather than to short-run profits, with recognition that it usually takes time to attain the volume potentialities of the market.

It is sound to calculate profits in dollar terms rather than in percentage margins and to think in terms of *percentage return on the investment required* to produce and sell the expanded volume rather than in terms of percentage markup. Profit calculation should also recognize the contributions that market-development pricing can make to the sale of other products and to the long-run future of the company. Often a decision to use development pricing will turn on these considerations of long-term impacts upon the firm's total operation strategy rather than on the profits directly attributable to the individual product.

An example of market-expansion pricing is found in the experience of a producer of asbestos shingles, which have a limited sale in the high-price house market. The company wanted to broaden the market in order to compete effectively with other roofing products for the inexpensive home. It tried to find the price of asphalt shingles that would make the annual cost per unit of roof over a period of years as low as the cheaper roofing that currently commanded the mass market. Indications were that the price would have to be at least this low before volume sales would come.

Next, the company explored the relationship between production costs and volume, far beyond the range of its own volume experience. Variable costs and fixed overhead costs were estimated separately, and the possibilities of a different organization of production were explored. Calculating in terms of anticipated dollars of profit rather than in terms of percentage margin, the company reduced the price of asbestos shingles and brought the annual cost down close to the cost of the cheapest asphalt roof. This reduction produced a greatly expanded volume and secured a substantial share of the mass market.

PRICING IN MATURITY

To determine what pricing policies are appropriate for later stages in the cycle of market and competitive maturity, the manufacturer must be able to tell when a product is approaching maturity. Some of the symptoms of degeneration of competitive status toward the commodity level are:

Weakening in brand preference—this may be evidenced by a higher cross-elasticity of demand among leading products, the leading brand not being able to continue demanding as much price premium as initially without losing position.

Narrowing physical variation among products as the best designs are developed and standardized—this has been dramatically demonstrated in automobiles and is still in process in television receivers.

The entry in force of private-label competitors—this is exemplified by the mail-order houses' sale of own-label refrigerators and paint sprayers.

Market saturation—the ratio of replacement sales to new equipment sales serves as an indicator of the competitive degeneration of durable goods, but in general it must be kept in mind that both market size and degree of saturation are hard to define (e.g., saturation of the radio market, which was initially thought to be one radio per home and later had to be expanded to one radio per room).

The stabilization of production methods—a dramatic innovation that slashes costs (e.g., prefabricated houses) may disrupt what appears to be a well-stabilized oligopoly market.

The first step for the manufacturer whose specialty is about to slip into the commodity category is to reduce real prices promptly as soon as symptoms of deterioration appear. This step is essential if he is to forestall the entry of private-label competitors. Examples of failure to make such a reduction are abundant.

By and large, private-label competition has speeded up the inevitable evolution of high-price specialties into commodities and has tended to force margins down by making price reductions more open and more universal than they would otherwise be. From one standpoint, the rapid growth of the private-label share in the market is a symptom of unwise pricing on the part of the national-brand sector of the industry.

This does not mean that the manufacturer should declare open price war in the industry. When he moves into mature competitive stages, he enters oligopoly relationships where price slashing is peculiarly dangerous and unpopular. But, with active competition in prices precluded, competitive efforts may move in other directions, particularly toward product improvement and market segmentation.

Product improvement at this stage, where most of the important developments have been put into all brands, practically amounts to market segmentation. For it means adding refinements and quality extras that put the brand in the elite category, with an appeal only to the top-income brackets. This is a common tactic in food marketing, and in the tire industry it was the response of the General Tire Company to the competitive conditions of the 1930s.

As the product matures and as its distinctiveness narrows, a choice must sometimes be made by the company concerning the rung of the competitive price ladder it should occupy—roughly, the choice between a low and a not-so-low relative price. A price at the low end of the array of the industry's real prices is usually associated with a product mixture showing a lean element of services and reputation (the product being physically similar to competitive brands, however) and a company having a lower gross margin than the other industry members (although not necessarily a lower net margin). The choice of such a low-price policy may be dictated by technical or market inferiorities of the product, or it may be adopted because the company has faith in the long-run price elasticity of demand and the ability of low prices to penetrate an important segment of the market not tapped by higher prices. The classic example is Henry Ford's pricing decision in the 1920s.

IN SUMMARY

In pricing products of perishable distinctiveness, a company must study the cycle of competitive degeneration in order to determine its major causes, its probable speed, and the chances of slowing it down. Pricing in the pioneering stage of the cycle involves difficult problems of projecting potential demand and of guessing the relation of price to sales.

The first step in this process is to explore consumer preferences and to establish the feasibility of the product, in order to get a rough idea of whether demand will warrant further exploration. The second step is to mark out a range of prices that will make the product economically attractive to buyers. The third step is to estimate the probable sales that will result from alternative prices.

If these initial explorations are encouraging, the next move is to make decisions on promotional strategy and distribution channels. The policy of relatively high prices in the pioneering stage has much to commend it, particularly when sales seem to be comparatively unresponsive to price but quite responsive to educational promotion.

On the other hand, the policy of relatively low prices in the pioneering stage, in anticipation of the cost savings resulting from an expanding market, has been strikingly successful under the right conditions. Low prices look to long-run rather than short-run profits and discourage potential competitors.

Pricing in the mature stages of a product's life cycle requires a technique for recognizing when a product is approaching maturity. Pricing problems in this stage border closely on those of oligopoly.

RETROSPECTIVE COMMENTARY

Twenty-five years have brought important changes and have taught us much, but the basics of pricing pioneer products are the same, only clearer. New product pricing, if the product is truly novel, is in essence monopoly pricing—modified only because the monopoly power of the new product is (*a*) restricted because buyers have alternatives, (*b*) ephemeral because it is subject to inevitable erosion as competitors equal or better it, and (*c*) controllable because actions of the seller can affect the amount and the durability of the new product's market power.

In pricing, the *buyer's* viewpoint should be controlling. For example, buyer's-rate-of-return pricing of new capital equipment looks at your price through the eyes of the customer. It recognizes that the upper limit is the price that will produce the minimum acceptable rate of return on the investment of a sufficiently large number of prospects. This return has a broad range for two reasons. First, the added profits obtainable from the use of your equipment will differ among customers and among applications for the same customer. Second, prospective customers also differ in the minimum rate of return that will induce them to invest in your product.

This capital-budgeting approach opens a new kind of demand analysis, which involves inquiry into: (*a*) the costs of buyers from displaceable alternative ways of doing the job, (*b*) the cost-saving and profit-producing capability of your equipment, and (*c*) the capital management policies of your customers, particularly their cost of capital and cut-off criteria.

Role of Cost

Cost should play a role in new product pricing quite different from that in traditional cost-plus pricing. To use cost wisely requires answers to some questions of theory: Whose cost? Which cost? What role?

As to whose cost, three persons are important: prospective buyers, existent and potential competitors, and the producer of the new product. For each of the three, cost should play a different role and the concept of cost should differ accordingly.

The role of prospective *buyers'* costs is to forecast their response to alternative prices by determining what your product will do to the costs of your buyers. Rate-of-return pricing of capital goods illustrates this buyer's-cost approach, which is applicable in principle to all new products.

Cost is usually the crucial estimate in appraising *competitors'* capabilities. Two kinds of competitor costs need to be forecasted. The first is for products already in the marketplace. One purpose is to predict staying power; for this the cost concept is competitors' long-run incremental cost. Another purpose may be to guess the floor of retaliation pricing; for this we need competitors' short-run incremental cost.

The second kind is the cost of a competitive product that is unborn, but that could eventually displace yours. Time-spotted prediction of the performance characteristics, the costs, and the probable prices of future new products is both essential and possible. Such a prediction is essential because it determines the economic life expectancy of your product and the shape of its competitiveness cycle.

It is possible, first, because the pace of technical advance in product design is persistent and can usually be determined by statistical study of past progress. It is possible, second, because the rate at which competitors' cost will slide down the cost compression curve that results from cost-saving investments in manufacturing equipment, methods, and worker learning is usually a logarithmic function of cumulative output. Thus this rate can be ascertained and projected.

The *producer's* cost should play several different roles in pricing a new product, depending on the decision involved. The first decision concerns capital control. A new product must be priced before any significant investment is made in research and must be periodically repriced when more money is invested as its development progresses toward market. The concept of cost that is relevant for this decision is the predicted full cost, which should include imputed cost of capital on intangible investment over the whole life cycle of the new product. Its profitability and investment return are meaningless for any shorter period.

A second decision is "birth control." The commercialization decision calls for a similar concept of cost and discounted-cash-flow investment analysis, but one that is confined to incremental investment beyond product birth.

Another role of cost is to establish a price floor that is also the threshold for selecting from candidate prices those that will maximize return on a new product investment at different stages of its life. The relevant concept here is future short-run incremental cost.

Segmentation Pricing

Particularly for new products, an important tactic is differential pricing for separated market segments. To enhance profits, we split the market into sectors that differ in price sensitivity, charging higher prices to those who are impervious and lower prices to the more sensitive souls.

One requisite is the ability to identify and seal off groups of prospects who differ in sensitivity of sales to price and/or differ in the effectiveness of competition (cross-elasticity of demand). Another is that leakage from the low-price segment must be small and costs of segregation low enough to make it worthwhile.

One device is time segmentation: a skimming price strategy at the outset followed by penetration pricing as the product matures. Another device is price-shaped modification of a basic product to enhance traits for which one group of customers will pay dearly (e.g., reliability for the military).

A similar device is product-configuration differentials (notably extras: the roof of the Stanley Steamer was an extra when it was a new product). Another is afterlife pricing (e.g., repair parts, expendable components, and auxiliary services). Also, trade channel discounts commonly achieve profitable price discrimination (e.g., original equipment discounts).

Cost Compression Curve

Cost forecasting for pricing new products should be based on the cost compression curve, which relates real manufacturing cost per unit of value added to the cumulative quantity produced. This cost function (sometimes labeled "learning curve" or "experience curve") is mainly the consequence of cost-cutting investments (largely intangible) to discover and achieve internal substitutions, automation, worker learning, scale economies, and technological advances. Usually these move together as a logarithmic function of accumulated output.

Cost-compression-curve pricing of technically advanced products (for example, a microprocessor) epitomizes penetration pricing. It condenses the time span of the process of cutting prices *ahead* of forecasted cost savings in order to beat competitors to the bigger market and the resulting manufacturing economies that are opened up because of creative pricing.

This cost-compression-curve pricing strategy, which took two decades for the Model T's life span, is condensed into a few months for the integrated circuit. But though the speed and the sources of saving are different, the principle is the same: a steep cost compression curve suggests penetration pricing of a new product. Such pricing is most attractive when the product superiority over rivals is small and ephemeral and when entry and expansion by competitors is easy and probable.

Impacts of Inflation

Continuous high-speed inflation has important impacts on new-product pricing. It changes the goal. It renders obsolete accounted earnings per share as the corporation's overriding goal—replacing it with maximization of the present worth (discounted at the corporation's cost of capital) of the future stream of real purchasing power dividends (including a terminal dividend or capital gain). Real earnings in terms of cash-flow buying power alone determine the power to pay real dividends.

Inflation raises the buyers' bench-mark costs of the new products' competitive alternatives. Thus it lifts the buyer benefits obtainable from the new products' protected distinctiveness (for example, it saves more wage dollars). It raises the seller's required return on the investment to create and to launch the new product. Why? Because his cost of equity capital and of debt capital will be made higher to compensate for anticipated inflation. For the same reason, inflation raises the customer's cutoff point of minimum acceptable return. It also intensifies the rivalry for scarce investment dollars among the seller's new-product candidates. Hence it probably tends to increase stillbirths, but may lower subsequent infant mortality. For these reasons, perennial inflation will make an economic attack on the problem of pricing new products even more compelling.

Pricing of new products remains an art. But the experienced judgment required to price and reprice the product over its life cycle to fit its changing competitive environment may be improved by considering seven pricing precepts suggested by this analysis:

1. Pricing a new product is an occasion for rethinking the overriding corporate goal. This goal should be to maximize the present worth, discounted at the corporation's cost of capital, of the future stream of real (purchasing-power) dividends, including a terminal dividend or capital gain. The Wall Street

traditional objective—maximizing the size or the growth of book earnings per share—is an inferior master goal that is made obsolete by inflation.

2. The unit for making decisions and for measuring return on investment is the entire economic life of the new product. Reported *annual* profits on a new product have little economic significance. The pricing implications of the new product's changing competitive status as it passes through its life cycle from birth to obsolescence are intricate but compelling.

3. Pricing of a new product should begin long before its birth, and repricing should continue over its life cycle. Prospective prices coupled with forecasted costs should control the decision to invest in its development, the determination to launch it commercially, and the decision to kill it.

4. Your new product should be viewed through the eyes of the buyer. Rate of return on customers' investment should be the main consideration in pricing a pioneering capital good: the buyer's savings (and added earnings), expressed as return on his investment in your new product, are the key to both estimating price sensitivity of demand and pricing profitably.

5. Costs can supply useful guidance in new-product pricing, but not by the conventional wisdom of cost-plus pricing. Costs of three persons are pertinent: the buyer, your rival, and the producer himself. The role of cost differs among the three, as does the concept of cost that is pertinent to that role: different costs for different decisions.

6. A strategy of price skimming can be distinguished from a strategy of penetration pricing. Skimming is appropriate at the outset for some pioneering products, particularly when followed by penetration pricing (for example, the price cascade of a new book). In contrast, a policy of penetration pricing from the outset, in anticipation of the cost compression curve for manufacturing costs, is usually best when this curve falls steeply and projectably, and is buttressed by economies of scale and of advancing technology, and when demand is price sensitive and invasion is threatened.

7. Penetration and skimming pricing can be used at the same time in different sectors of the market. Creating opportunities to split the market into segments that differ in price sensitivity and in competitiveness, so as to simultaneously charge higher prices

in insensitive segments and price low to elastic sectors, can produce extra profits and faster cost compression for a new product. Devices are legion.

ADDITIONAL SOURCES*

Arpan, Jeffrey S. "Multinational Firm Pricing in International Markets." *Sloan Management Review,* Winter 1972–73, p. 1.

Christenson, Charles J.; Vancil, Richard F.; and Marshall, Paul W. *Managerial Economics: Text and Cases,* chaps. 7, 8. Rev. ed. Homewood, Ill.: Richard D. Irwin, Inc., 1973.

Corr, Arthur V. "The Role of Cost in Pricing." *Management Accounting* November 1974, p. 15.

Deakin, Michael D. "Pricing for Return on Investment." *Management Accounting,* December 1975, p. 43.

Edelman, Franz. "Art and Science of Competitive Bidding." *Harvard Business Review,* July–August 1965, p. 53.

Fremgen, James M. *Accounting for Managerial Analysis,* chap. 15. 3d ed. Homewood, Ill.: Richard D. Irwin, Inc., 1976.

Fuss, Norman H. "How to Raise Prices—Judiciously—to Meet Today's Conditions." *Harvard Business Review,* May–June 1975, p. 10.

Hampel, Robert E. "Pricing Policies and Profitability." *Management Accounting,* July 1977, p. 53.

Levitt, Theodore. "Marketing Myopia." *Harvard Business Review,* September–October 1975, p. 26.

Reynolds, Alan. "A Kind Word for 'Cream Skimming.'" *Harvard Business Review,* November–December 1974, p. 113.

Roberge, Michael D. "Pricing for Government Contractors." *Management Accounting,* June 1973, p. 28.

Shapiro, Benson P. "The Psychology of Pricing." *Harvard Business Review,* July–August 1968, p. 14.

Shillinglaw, Gordon. *Managerial Cost Accounting,* chap. 16. 4th ed. Homewood, Ill.: Richard D. Irwin, Inc., 1977.

Walker, Arleigh W. "How to Price Industrial Products." *Harvard Business Review,* September–October 1967, p. 125.

---

* These sources were selected by the editors, and did not appear as a part of Mr. Dean's *Harvard Business Review* article.

21

Inventory Decision Models

Neil S. Weiss*

The primary purpose of inventory decision models is to answer two basic questions:

"What quantity of an item should be ordered or produced?" and "How often should an item be ordered or produced?"

To answer these questions, certain items of information are needed concerning such factors as demand, costs and lead times, and the stability or variability of these factors.

Demand

Fundamental to the establishment of any inventory control system is a forecast of demand. The simplest control systems assume a stable and uniform demand pattern over the forecast period. As long as these assumptions of stability and uniformity are not seriously violated, the basic control systems can be surprisingly serviceable. For example, if there is a marked seasonal pattern of demand, the control system can be changed for each season with new ordering criteria developed for each period. Similarly, if an upward trend in demand is expected, the ordering criteria in use can be revised at frequent intervals.

* Professor Weiss is a Professor in the Graduate School of Business of Pace University, Pleasantville, New York.

Costs

In any decision-making or operating system, the costs to be considered are those affected by (or incremental to) the decision. In inventory systems, there are three types of costs that must be considered: carrying costs, ordering or setup costs, and shortage costs. Generally the annual purchase cost of merchandise purchased need not be considered (except as it effects carrying costs), since this annual total is usually not influenced by inventory ordering or production policies. In other words, the number of units ordered during the year multiplied by the unit cost is the same, whether the total annual requirements are acquired in a few large batches or many smaller batches. However, where quantity discounts are involved, the relationships between order quantities and effective purchase prices must be considered. Furthermore, where prices are highly volatile, such as in the case of commodities, the material cost estimates may well be the primary cost variable to be considered.

Carrying Costs

Carrying costs are those costs involved in the holding of inventory. The primary component of this cost is the "imputed" interest on the investment in inventory. For example, if money is borrowed to obtain inventory, the interest on the loan during the inventory holding period would be one measure of the interest cost. If the inventory is financed by internally generated funds, the profit lost by inability to use the cash in profitable ways during the holding period would be another measure of financing cost. Finally, if the inventory is financed by the vendor, the extra cost over cash purchase would be a third measure of the cost.

Other components of the carrying cost include storage, insurance, obsolescence, spoilage, shrinkage, and theft. Considering all of the components, the total carrying cost may run as high as 20 percent or more of the inventory value.

Ordering or Setup Cost

For items which are manufactured by the company, there are various costs involved in the preparation for a production run. These include machine setup, paperwork, and other preparation costs.

Where the inventory is purchased, an ordering cost rather than a setup cost is involved. The ordering cost includes such items as order preparation and processing, evaluation of bids, other vendor contacts, receiving, handling, paying the vendor's invoice, and other items which vary with the number of orders processed rather than with the total quantity of inventory itself.

Understock Cost

By far the most difficult costs to measure are those costs involved in being understocked. The primary reason for this is the fact that the major components are "opportunity costs" rather than out-of-pocket costs. For example, the major aspects of understock costs include the cost of customer dissatisfaction due to inability to obtain the product or to delay in receiving it, the cost of a lost sale, or the cost of a lost customer for the current and future sales. Since accountants record only the costs of events that have occurred but do not record the opportunity costs of events which did not occur (e.g., a lost sale), it is very difficult to obtain hard data on understock costs.

In order to deal with this difficult problem, a number of approaches are possible. One approach involves an evaluation of the estimated losses in sales resulting from being out of stock for varying periods of time through statistical analysis, subjective judgment, or simple assumption. Another approach is to establish in advance an acceptable probability level for being out of stock. This level can be prescribed as a desired average level or as a maximum permissible level. At the other extreme, extensive analysis using surveys, simulations, and mathematical models may sometimes be used to estimate the individual components making up the total understock cost.

Order Lead Time

Lead time refers to the interval between the time an order is placed and the time the items are received. The approach to ordering that is often used involves determination of the time at which items are needed, and then, using the lead time interval, the point at which the order should be placed is found. In many cases the lead time will vary somewhat from order to order. In such situations the average lead time can be used to determine the order point. However, if a conservative policy is desired to reduce greatly the possibility of being out of stock, the longest estimated lead time may be used.

Safety Stock

Just as variability in the lead time interval requires adjustments due to the uncertainty involved, variable demand during the order or production cycle requires adjustments. In order to deal with periods in which demand is greater than average, an additional quantity of inventory known as the "safety stock" is introduced.

The size of the safety stock is based on two factors. The first is the degree of variability in demand, which is usually measured by the mean absolute deviation (MAD) or the standard deviation (σ). The second factor is the acceptable risk of being out of stock. In other words, one must determine the proportion of the time that management is willing to find itself out of stock when an item is demanded. The smaller proportion of time acceptable, the larger the safety stock needed.

There are two basic approaches to the determination of this risk. First, management may specify this risk level as an input to the inventory model based on judgment and experience. Second, the risk level may be calculated by appropriate evaluation of the relationship between the carrying cost and the understock cost. Where understock costs can be measured with reasonable accuracy, the second method is to be preferred. However, in many situations understock costs can be determined only by a rough approximation. When this is the case, it may be more meaningful to estimate an acceptable risk level directly than to estimate an understock cost which is used to calculate an appropriate risk level.

Illustration of Cost Interrelationships

Inventory models represent the prime example of "opposing cost models." These are models in which the relevant costs move in opposite directions so that it is impossible to control them individually and simultaneously. To illustrate this, observe in Exhibit 1 the movement of carrying costs and ordering costs as ordering quantities increase.

Notice that carrying costs increase as the order quantity grows, while the setup or ordering costs decrease. If one attempted to minimize carrying costs alone, very small order quantities would be recommended. However, this would require many orders or setups throughout the year, with the result that setup or ordering costs would be very high, more than offsetting the savings in carrying costs.

The general approach to dealing with opposing cost situations is to minimize the total of the costs involved instead of dealing with them individually. In Exhibit 1, this minimum level, indicated by an order quantity of Q^*, occurs at the point of intersection of the two costs. While this relationship does not hold true for all opposing cost models, it is a characteristic of the widely used "economic order quantity" model which will be used throughout this chapter.

EXHIBIT 1
Inventory Costs

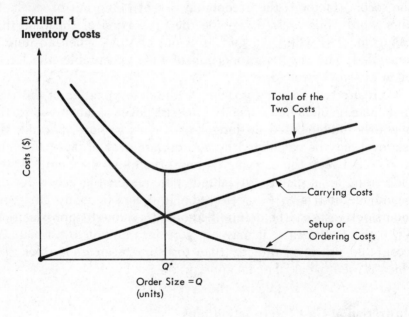

Fixed Quantity Systems

The most frequently used type of inventory control system is the "Q system" or "fixed quantity system." This type of system is characterized by the fact that a fixed order quantity, Q, is calculated, and whenever an order is to be placed, the fixed quantity is used.

As mentioned at the beginning of this chapter, inventory control systems answer two questions: "How much should be ordered?" and "When should the order be placed?" In Q systems the amount of the order is fixed, but the time of order placement varies from period to period, depending on the level of demand.

Generally, Q systems operate on the basis of two parameters, or fixed characteristics. These parameters are the order quantity, Q, and the reorder point. In other words, whenever the inventory level drops to the reorder point, an order is placed for the amount of the

EXHIBIT 2
Diagram of a Q System

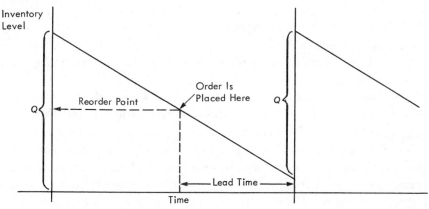

fixed order quantity, Q. Exhibit 2 illustrates these relationships. Some method of nearly continual monitoring is necessary to implement this type of system so that the reorder point will be recognized.

Determination of the Order Quantity

For the sake of simplicity, the approximate method of determining the Q-system parameters will be used here, followed by a discussion of the changes needed for the exact procedures. In many cases the results of the approximate method are quite close to those of the exact method so that these approximations are serviceable.

The first step is to determine the "economic order quantity" (Q). The formula for Q depends on a number of factors such as the assumed pattern of demand and the existence of shortages. The value of Q which minimizes the total cost function in Exhibit 1 is:

$$Q = \sqrt{\frac{2DS}{Ci}}$$

where:

Q = economic order quantity (shown as Q^* in Exhibit 1).
D = demand per year in units.
S = the setup or ordering cost per order.
C = cost per unit.
i = carrying cost, expressed as a percentage of inventory value (e.g., 20 percent = 0.20).

It should be pointed out that the relationships within the fixed order quantity formula provide insights into the inventory process. The presence of D in the numerator indicates that as demand increases, so does the order quantity. The same is true of the order cost. This is reasonable since an increased order cost would lead to placing fewer orders, which is accomplished by increasing the quantity ordered.

The presence of the carrying cost in the denominator indicates that as carrying costs increase, the quantity ordered, and the average inventory size, is decreased. This should be obvious.

Finally the presence of the square root sign is particularly important because it means that, for example, if demand increases, the order quantity should increase—but not in proportion to the increase in demand. Rather the increase in order quantity should be equal to the square root of the increase in demand. Thus, if demand were to double from one year to the next, the order quantity should increase to 1.41 times the preceding year's order quantity; that is, a 100 percent increase in demand increases the economic order quantity by only 41 percent.

Once the order quantity has been determined, the reorder point can be found. If demand and lead time are assumed to be constant, the reorder point is simply determined by finding the demand for inventory during the lead-time period; in symbols,

$$RP = D_{LT}$$

Safety Stock. However, demand is *not* usually known and constant. Therefore, it is necessary to introduce a safety stock to protect against situations in which demand during the lead-time period is greater than usual. It is important to note that *no* protection is needed with regard to unusually large demand above the reorder point. The reason for this is that the reorder point will be reached earlier than usual, and therefore a new order will be placed sooner.

This creates no extra risk of being out of stock. Only when demand is greater than usual *during* the lead-time period, or when the lead time is longer than usual, is there danger of such a risk.

Therefore, the safety stock is based on the variability in demand during the lead-time period. We can measure this variability by using the standard deviation (σ_{LT}). The standard deviation is one of the most widely used measures of variability of data around an average level of values. In the situation concerning the inventory model under discussion, the average level would relate to the normal level of inventory at the end of an inventory cycle. The standard deviation would then measure the degree to which the actual inventory level at the end of a cycle departs from the normal level. A large standard deviation would indicate that from period to period the ending inventory level varies quite a bit. Thus, the probability of being significantly out of stock at various times of the year would be quite high if no safety stock were to be provided.

The size of the safety stock is obtained by multiplying the standard deviation by a factor based on the appropriate risk of being out of stock. For example, if the demand pattern during the lead-time period is assumed to follow the normal probability distribution, and management is willing to be out of stock at most 5 percent of the time, the safety stock should be equal to 1.65 standard deviations.

The factor Z_α of 1.65 comes from tables of the normal distribution. Z represents the number of standard deviations below the average level which is necessary to provide the desired protection against unusual demand. The subscript α indicates that this value of Z is determined by selection of the appropriate or acceptable probability of being out of stock. (This is discussed below.)

EXHIBIT 3
Q System with Safety Stock

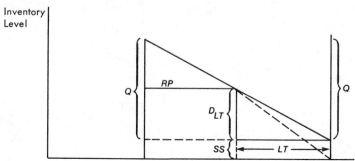

As Exhibit 3 indicates, the inventory cycle starts at the level consisting of the economic order quantity (Q), plus the safety stock (SS). The reorder point (RP) occurs when the inventory level falls to that point where the amount on hand consists of a normal supply for the lead time period (D_{LT}), plus the safety stock.

Thus, in this example, the reorder point would equal the average demand during the lead time plus the safety stock:

$$RP = D_{LT} + SS$$

or

$$RP = D_{LT} + Z_\alpha \cdot \sigma_{LT}$$

where:

RP = reorder point.
D_{LT} = average demand during the lead-time period.
SS = safety stock.
α = appropriate probability of being out of stock.
Z_α = corresponding multiplier based on the risk (α) of being out of stock.
σ_{LT} = standard deviation of demand during the lead-time period.

The following example illustrates a Q system with the possibility of shortages.

$$\text{Demand } (D) = 324 \text{ units per year}$$
$$\text{Unit cost } (C) = \$45$$
$$\text{Carrying cost rates } (i) = 20 \text{ percent per year}$$
$$\text{Order cost } (S) = \$50 \text{ per order}$$
$$\text{Understock cost } (U) = \$16 \text{ per unit per year}$$
$$\text{Lead time } (LT) = 1 \text{ month}$$
$$\text{Demand during } LT(D_{LT}) = \tfrac{1}{12} \cdot 324 = 27 \text{ units}$$
$$\text{Standard deviation } (\sigma_{LT}) = 15 \text{ units}$$

Management willingness to be out of stock $(\alpha) = 10$ percent of time at most:

$$Q = \sqrt{\frac{2DS}{Ci}} \qquad = \sqrt{\frac{2 \cdot 324 \cdot 50}{45 \cdot 0.20}}$$

$$Q = \sqrt{\frac{32{,}400}{9}} \qquad = \sqrt{3{,}600} = 60 \text{ units}$$

$$SS = Z_\alpha \cdot \sigma_{LT}$$

With a value of $\alpha = 0.10$, tables of the normal probability indicate that $Z_\alpha = 1.28$.

Therefore:

$$SS = 1.28 \cdot 15 = 19.2 \text{ units (rounded to 20 units)}$$
$$RP = D_{LT} + SS = 27 + 20 = 47 \text{ units}$$

Thus, the appropriate inventory policy would be to order 60 units whenever the inventory level falls to 47 units.

A second approach to this problem is to calculate the risk level α from a formula based on the relationship between the carrying and understock costs. Just as the formula for Q involves the balancing of the opposing costs of carrying and ordering, the formula for α involves the balancing of the opposing costs of carrying (or overstock) and shortage (or understock). The formula takes into account the fact that higher understock costs relative to carrying costs lead to lower acceptable levels of shortage. This formula is:

$$\alpha = 1 - \frac{U}{H + U} = 1 - \frac{16}{9 + 16} \qquad \text{(where } H = C \cdot i = \text{carrying cost)}$$

$$\alpha = 1 - \frac{16}{25} = 0.36 \text{ or 36 percent}$$

If these cost figures are accurate, they indicate that management has been unduly conservative in allowing only a 10 percent chance of being out of stock. In other words, management can reduce overall costs of inventory management by reducing its safety stock so that shortages occur 36 percent of the time instead of 10 percent of the time. The reduction in carrying costs in this situation will be as large, or larger than, the increase in shortage costs.

The revised results based on a value of $\alpha = 0.36$ are:

$$Z_\alpha = 0.36$$
$$SS = 0.36 \cdot 15 = 5.4 \text{ (rounded to 6, the next higher integer)}$$
$$RP = 27 + 6 = 33 \text{ units}$$

Thus, the safety stock is 14 units lower than before.

Fixed Interval Systems

A fixed interval system is a system in which orders are placed at fixed intervals or fixed *periods* (P) of time; thus, it is called the

"P system." As an example, it might be convenient to place orders at the end of each week rather than at the time a reorder point is reached. This is especially true when there are many products to be ordered from a single supplier or manufacturer.

In a sense, the P system is exactly the opposite of the Q system. In the Q system, the order quantity is a fixed amount while the reorder point varies depending on demand. In the P system, the reorder point is based on a fixed interval of time while the quantity to be ordered varies with demand. Thus, the approach to be used in the P system is to calculate the optimum order period and then to set up the approprate rule to allow calculation of the order quantities.

The approximate order quantity for the P system involves the same formula as in the Q system:

$$Q = \sqrt{\frac{2DS}{Ci}}$$

However, this value of Q is converted into the equivalent number of orders for the period by using the relationship

$$N = \frac{D}{Q},$$

where:

$N =$ number of orders to be placed during the period.

For example, if the demand (D) is 1,200 units for the year and the fixed order quantity is determined to be 100 units, then 12 orders would be placed during the year:

$$N = \frac{D}{Q} = \frac{1,200}{100} = 12 \text{ orders for the year}$$

This means that the ordering interval is $t = 1$ month, since

$$t = \frac{1}{N} = \frac{1}{12} \text{ year or 1 month.}$$

The P system can be represented diagramatically as shown in Exhibit 4,

EXHIBIT 4
Diagram of a P System

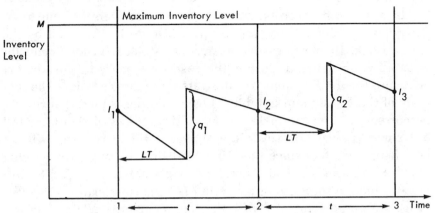

where:

  I_1 = inventory on hand at the first reorder point.
  I_2 = inventory on hand at the second reorder point.
  q_1 = quantity ordered at the first reorder point.
  q_2 = quantity ordered at the second reorder point.
  M = maximum inventory level. This value controls the order
         quantity q.
  LT = lead time.
  t = fixed order interval.

Exhibit 4 shows the movement of inventory levels over time, including two full cycles of inventory. At the start of each cycle an order is placed, with arrival of additional merchandise at the end of the lead-time period (LT).

Once the ordering interval t has been determined, the quantity to be ordered (q) is calculated by comparing the inventory on hand (I) with the maximum inventory level (M). Thus,

$$q_1 = M - I_1$$
$$q_2 = M - I_2, \text{ and so forth}$$

All that remains to complete the P system operating procedures is to calculate M. The value for M is calculated in a manner similar to the calculation of the reorder point in the Q system, in that it involves average demand plus a safety stock for unusually large demand.

The major difference between the two parameters (M and reorder point) concerns the period of protection to be provided by the safety stock. In the Q system, the safety stock is needed only for variability of demand during the lead-time period. This is not adequate for the P system. To illustrate this point, consider the diagram of the P system in Exhibit 4. Once an order is placed at time 1, no corrections can be made for heavy demand until time 2, a full order-period away. However, the impact of this correction will not be felt immediately since there is a lead time between the placing of an order and its arrival. Therefore, safety stock is needed to provide protection for a full order period (t) plus one lead time (LT). Thus, M can be compared with the reorder point (RP) as follows:

$$RP = D_{LT} + SS \qquad M = D_{(t+LT)} + SS$$
$$\text{where} \qquad\qquad \text{where}$$
$$SS = Z_\alpha \cdot \sigma_{LT} \qquad SS = Z_\alpha \sigma_{(t+LT)}$$

The P system can be illustrated by using the example given earlier in connection with the Q system. To repeat the facts:

$D = 324$ units per year.
$C = \$45$ per unit.
$i = 20$ percent per year.
$S = \$50$ per order.
$U = \$16$ per unit per year.
$LT = 1$ month.
$D_{LT} = \frac{1}{12} \cdot 324 - 27$ units; $\sigma_{LT} = 15$ units.

As before,

$$Q = \sqrt{\frac{2DS}{Ci}} = 60 \text{ units.}$$

Therefore, the number of orders per year,

$$N = \frac{D}{Q} = \frac{324}{60} = 5.4,$$

and the order interval

$$t = \frac{12}{N} \text{ months} = \frac{12}{5.4} = 2.22 \text{ months.}$$

Since $M = D_{(t + LT)} + SS$, we must determine the demand during a full order period plus a lead time:

Since $D_{LT} = 27$ units for 1 month,

$$D_t = 2.22 \times 27 \text{ units} = 60 \text{ units for } 2.22 \text{ months}$$

and

$$D_{(t+LT)} = 60 + 27 = 87 \text{ units}$$

The safety stock, $SS = Z_\alpha \sigma_{(t + LT)}$. In order to obtain the standard deviation for the period $t + LT$, it must be pointed out that standard deviations are not additive or proportional to time. Therefore, it is not correct to multiply $2.22 \cdot \sigma_{LT}$ to obtain the standard deviation for the order period. However, the variance, which is the square of the standard deviation (σ^2), does have the above properties. Thus, we can proceed as follows:

$$\sigma_{LT} = 15 \text{ units per month}$$
$$\sigma_{LT}^2 = 225 \text{ units}$$
$$\sigma_t^2 = 2.22 \cdot 225 = 500 \text{ units}$$
$$\sigma_{(t+LT)}^2 = 500 + 225 = 725 \text{ units}$$
$$\sigma_{(t+LT)} = \sqrt{725} = 26.9 \text{ units}$$

With a value of $\alpha = 0.10$, as before, $Z_\alpha = 1.28$, and

$$SS = 1.28 \cdot 26.9 = 34.4 \text{ (rounded to 35)}$$
$$M = D_{(t+LT)} + SS = 87 + 35 = 122$$

To summarize the operating procedures for a P system with the above parameters, every 2.2 months the inventory is determined, and an order is placed for the amount of the difference between $M = 122$ units and the quantity actually on hand at that time.

Other Systems

Variations on the above P and Q systems have been discussed in the literature on inventory models. One variation that has received wide attention is sometimes called the "s, S system." The first parameter(s) is similar to the reorder point (RP) in the Q system, and the second parameter (S) is similar to M in the P system. This approach can be diagramed as shown in Exhibit 5.

As in the P system, there is an order period (t) at the end of which the inventory is evaluated. When an order is placed, the quantity ordered is:

$$q = S - I$$

which is similar to the P system in which

$$q = M - I$$

The major change from the P system is the fact that it is not necessary to place an order at the end of each order period. Orders will be placed at the order date only when the inventory level (I) is below s, the first parameter. Thus, in the above diagram no order will be placed at date 1, since I_1 is greater than s. At date 2, I_2 is below s, and therefore an order will be placed for $S - I_2$ units. At 3, since I_3 is greater than s, no order will be placed.

EXHIBIT 5
Diagram of s, S System

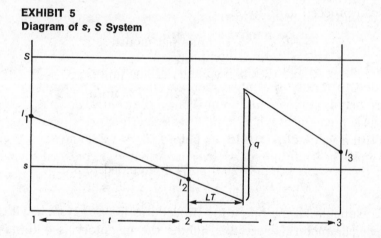

The calculations for s and S proceed in a similar manner to those for RP and M. The major difference lies in the fact that the periods of protection used in computing safety stock can vary from those used in Q and P systems.

Another way of relating the s, S system to the Q and P systems is as follows. If the order period t is made long enough, the inventory on hand will always be below s at the end of the period, so that an order will be placed every period and the system will become essentially the P system. If the time period is made short enough, at many order dates no order will be placed, but when the order is placed, the inventory will be just about at the value of s. Thus, since orders will be placed when the inventory drops to s, this parameter becomes the reorder point and the order quantity becomes a nearly constant amount equal to $S - s$. Since the system has a fixed reorder point s and a fixed order quantity $S - s$, it approximates the Q system in which

$$Q = S - s$$

and

$$RP = s$$

Multiple-Item Control Systems

Where a firm has a number of items or categories of inventory, each can be treated independently by using the procedures outlined above. In some situations, however, certain problems arise. Two of the more common are as follows. First, management may decide that the total investment in inventory resulting from the use of inventory models is unacceptably large, and that some method is needed to reduce this investment in an efficient manner. Second, there may be so many different items to be controlled that the costs of these procedures when applied to each item or category are prohibitive.

When the total inventory investment based on optimal inventory policies is unacceptably high, the adjustment procedure appropriate for reducing inventories involves a scaling down procedure in which the new order sizes are made proportional to the square roots of the estimated annual dollar sales. This can be illustrated through the following example.

Suppose a company has four categories of inventory. Based on an optimal ordering policy, the total (in dollar terms) of the economic order quantities for these four groups is $10,000. However, management believes this to be too high and sets an upper limit of $8,000. The esimated annual demand is as follows:

Category	Annual Demand
1	$10,000
2	6,000
3	16,000
4	18,000
Total	$50,000

Although it varies between categories, the average number of orders per year is five, resulting in a fixed order quantity of $10,000 per order for all four groups.

The calculations are shown in the following table:[1]

(1)	(2) Annual	(3)	(4) Percentages	(5) Order Size
Category	Demand	$\sqrt{\text{Demand}}$	(of Column 3)	(Column 4 × 8,000)
1...................	$10,000	$100	22.8%	$1,820
2...................	6,000	77.5	17.7	1,410
3...................	16,000	126.5	28.8	2,310
4...................	18,000	134.2	30.7	2,460
	$50,000	$438.2	100.0%	$8,000

It should be noted that this procedure is based solely on the estimates of annual demand for the products and does not involve the use of previously computed optimal order quantities.

The second problem to be dealt with concerns the cost of maintaining optimal inventory policies for many items. The approach discussed here is sometimes called the "ABC" inventory classification system. It is illustrated by Exhibit 6, which shows that only about 25 percent of the company's products account for the bulk of company sales: these are "Category A" products. On the other hand, the products in Category C, while large in number account for only a small percentage of sales. The implication of this analysis is that sophisticated optimal inventory policies need not be applied to those products in Category C. This step alone can provide substantial savings in costs of inventory procedures. Further gains can be made by using simplified versions of the inventory policies for those items in Category B.

It should be emphasized that this illustration represents a phenomenon that has been observed to occur in many different types of situations. However, the percentages given in this example are approximations and do not imply uniformity from case to case. Category A may include as little as 60 percent of total dollar sales or as much as 90 percent of the total.

---

[1] For the proof of this procedure see Martin K. Starr and David W. Miller, *Inventory Control: Theory and Practice* (Englewood Cliffs, N.J.: Prentice-Hall, Inc., 1962), pp. 92–97.

EXHIBIT 6
Illustration of ABC Analysis

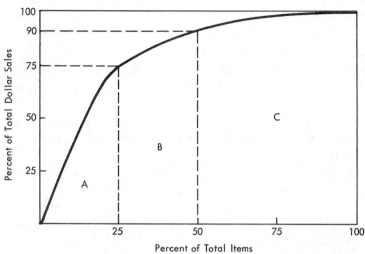

Summary

It should be emphasized that the models and techniques de-scribed in this chapter are based on assumptions that do not always reflect the actual situations faced by management. For example, all of our models have assumed a level demand; that is why inventory levels over time had a "sawtooth" pattern in Exhibits 3–5. There-fore, the informed manager may quite properly decide to override the decisions suggested by these models when the uniqueness of a situation suggests that the results of the models are inappropriate.

In summary, this chapter has attempted to provide the reader with those basic concepts and methods underlying most applied in-ventory control processes. No two systems will be identical, with wide variations in techniques and philosophies. However, knowl-edge of these basics will help to understand many of these systems.

ADDITIONAL SOURCES

Bierman, Harold; Bonini, Charles P.; and Hausman, Warren H. *Quan-titative Analysis for Business Decisions,* chaps. 17–19. 5th ed. Home-wood, Ill.: Richard D. Irwin, Inc., 1977.

Buffa, Elwood S., and Taubert, William H. *Production-Inventory Sys-tems: Planning and Control.* Rev. ed. Homewood, Ill.: Richard D. Irwin, Inc., 1972.

Carter, Albert G. "Computing Inventory ROI." *Management Accounting,* July 1973, p. 43.

Chase, Richard B., and Aquilano, Nicholas J. *Production and Operations Management.* Homewood, Ill.: Richard D. Irwin, Inc., 1977.

Deakin, Edward B. "Finding Optimal Order Quantity when Quality Discounts Are Offered." *Cost and Management,* May–June 1975, p. 40.

Goyal, S. K. "Costing for OR Inventory Models." *Cost and Management,* July–August 1973, p. 34.

Hoffman, Raymond A., and Gunders, Henry. *Inventories: Control, Costing, and Effect upon Income Taxes.* New York: The Ronald Press Co., 1971.

Lambert, Douglas M., and LaLonde, Bernard J. "Inventory Carrying Costs." *Management Accounting,* August 1976, p. 31.

Miller, Jeffrey G., and Sprague, Linda G. "Behind the Growth in Materials Requirements Planning." *Harvard Business Review,* September–October 1975, p. 83.

Schiff, Michael. "Credit and Inventory Management—Separate or Together?" *Financial Executive,* November 1972, p. 28.

Shycon, Harvey N., and Sprague, Christopher R. "Put a Price Tag on Your Customer Servicing Levels." *Harvard Business Review,* July–August 1975, p. 71.

Starr, Martin K., and Miller, David W. *Inventory Control: Theory and Practice.* Englewood Cliffs, N.J.: Prentice-Hall, Inc., 1962.

Thurston, Philip H. "Requirements Planning for Inventory Control." *Harvard Business Review,* May–June 1972, p. 67.

Weston, J. Fred, and Goudzwaard, Maurice B., eds. *Treasurer's Handbook,* chaps. 23, 24. Homewood, Ill.: Dow Jones-Irwin, Inc., 1976.

part four
Measuring Financial Responsibility

22

An Overview of Responsibility Accounting

Charles W. Walker*

About 25 years ago, Lawrence A. Appley, president of the then-young American Management Association was traveling around the country lecturing to management groups. The underlying theme of his talks was subsequently summarized in an Association publication, one section of which indirectly underscores the advantages inherent in responsibility accounting. This section follows:[1]

Kinds of Management Quality

Quality is relative. To evaluate the quality of something, it must be compared with something else of a similar nature. In order to appraise the quality of management, it seems necessary to describe certain types of management so that quality comparisons can be made.

The following list represents at least one kind of management classification that can be made, on the basis of the attitudes that prevail within a company toward the managerial job. Actually, it classifies the attitudes of the *top* managements of companies, because the entire management structure usually reflects the thinking of the top segment.

1. *Clear in Purpose and Sound of Action.* That industrial and

---

* Mr. Walker is a Management Consultant with Newsom, Earle & Walker, Greensboro, North Carolina; formerly Controller of Washington Mills Company, Winston-Salem.

[1] Lawrence A. Appley, *A Current Appraisal of the Quality of Management* (New York: American Management Association, 1952), p. 6.

business management which: *understands* the true nature and responsibilities of management; carefully and conscientiously *selects and develops* members of the management team in line with required qualifications and preparation; *is guided in its actions* by the firm belief that products and services it offers are means whereby the company's employees may render a genuine service to society with deep personal satisfaction.

2. *Sincere in Desire and Earnest in Effort.* That management which: *realizes* that there is something much broader in the nature and responsibilities of management than it now comprehends and *is seeking to discover it; recognizes* that the management team must be carefully selected and trained and is *trying* to do something about this; *is searching for* the true combination of the interests of management, employees, and society as a whole in a common goal.

3. *Unaware and Unfortunate.* That management which: is doing *a routine,* day-in-and-day-out, run-of-the-mill-job *without being particularly aware* of the tremendous forces and influences that are acting upon it and *without realizing,* or *taking measures to establish,* any other goal than distribution of product and service at a profit.

4. *Anti-Social and Outmoded.* That management which: is essentially *anti-social,* moved only by the single purpose of making money through shrewd manipulation of funds and the exploitation of human beings.

This fourth kind of management still exists. Such a management is usually found to be a "one-man show," where the owner-manager makes all decisions, does not trust subordinates, and therefore has no need for more than the most simple bookkeeping system. There is a limit to the degree of detail any individual can manage. Thus, the one-person management is doomed to failure because there can be no promise of growth.

On the other hand, the kind of management which is "clear in purpose and sound of action" is one whose company will out-produce, out-sell, out-profit, and out-service by a wide margin any competitor which is "antisocial and outmoded." However, obtaining this highest management ranking is not easy. Not unlike any major undertaking, any goal can be reached (including the moon) so long as a plan and program are developed and followed.

To begin with, to win appraisal as being of the highest quality, a management must do the following:

- Reduce to writing:

    A clear-cut, comprehensive statement of *why* the company is in business—*what its purpose is.*

    An official company statement of *the nature of management and its responsibilities.*

- Establish a current and effective means for *appraising the caliber of overall management,* of *individual members* of the management team, and of *potential managers.*

- Put into effect a *management program* that clearly spells out the objectives, procedures, and responsibilities in such a manner as to assure the teamwork needed to reach and remain at the top of its industry classification.

There are additional elements in an overall management program. However, we are concerned here with the means by which the *scorekeeping* is maintained. This scorekeeping system points out the mistakes that are made and in turn helps suggest corrective action. In short, we are interested in *responsibility accounting.*

ORGANIZATIONAL STRUCTURE

Delegation of Responsibility and Authority

We have already underscored the element of responsibility. Responsibility must be delegated and accompanied by commensurate authority. Responsibility and/or authority assumed outside an organized pattern generates chaos. The purpose of this overview of responsibility accounting is to outline a system of accounting which, through a series of interrelated reports, discloses to management at successive levels the performance of subordinate levels in terms of established management objectives.

While it is not the purpose here to prescribe organizational patterns, the soundness of the organization chart has a direct bearing on the results arising from the assignment of responsibility and authority. In this day of large companies, diversified either as conglomerates or as multiproduct plants, the problem of centralization versus decentralization evades the perfect solution. In structuring a company organization, many factors must be considered, including:

Corporate structure—holding company to subsidiaries to divisions to plants to individual departments.

Concentration of related products in individual plants.

Diversification of products within plants.

Extent to which intermediate products are transferred ("sold") between subsidiaries.

Extent to which the sales organization parallels (in terms of product lines) the manufacturing organization.

Geographical territories covered by operating units.

Line-staff relationships.

Executive incentive arrangements.

The resultant organizational structure thus suggests the degree to which authority and responsibility are to be delegated.

Perhaps the most difficult action an executive must take is the delegation of control to a subordinate. Everyone has the propensity for making mistakes, but not everyone has the capacity to profit by having made mistakes. Nevertheless, company and individual executive growth involve some degree of risk. We see today a wide range of degrees to which this delegation is exercised, from that of delegating only on a day-to-day basis to that of complete autonomy to the head of a plant, division, or subsidiary company. In the first instance, executives handicapped by day-to-day limitations can be regarded as "straw bosses," having no latitude for individual planning. In the last case, we can be certain that such a company is at the top and will remain there. Why? Because in this instance it is safe to assume that goals and general policies have been so established and spelled out that there can be no doubt of what is expected of each executive or department head. Further, the accounting reports in such situations will be designed so as to forewarn the "slipping" executive of the inevitable.

Functional Concept of Organization

No matter what the size of any functioning body may be, there must exist some form of structure if the body is to succeed and grow. In organizations, no group of key persons can hope to succeed as a unit when no visible, logical management linkage exists. The list of functions or activities that must be maintained is almost limitless. Therefore, they must be reduced to a workable number. Thus, we most frequently show what are commonly called *primary functions*. Stated another way, primary functions are those which have a part in the operating framework of the organization. Secondary functions, on the other hand, are those which ensure that the responsibility centers do their jobs and thus assure successful and profitable results for the operating entity. Exhibit 1 illustrates a list of primary functions which would apply to a typical organization engaged in manufacturing. While for the most part the functions would be assigned as listed under each indicated department, departures might occur in any given company.

Having determined the assignment of the primary functions, a chart of organization should be prepared in such a fashion as to indicate the line-staff relationships of the various departments. Such a chart differs slightly from a typical "chain of command" type of organization chart to enable the proper positioning of the assigned primary functions under each department. Exhibit 2 illustrates a typical functional organization chart. Sometimes a company will prepare a typical "chain of command" type of chart and separately list the primary functions shown in Exhibit 1. The listing of primary functions paves the way for the preparation of individual position descriptions.

Position Descriptions. As suggested earlier, unless executives enjoy a clear understanding of their respective scopes of responsibility and of the parameters of their authority, there is a strong likelihood that the organization as a whole will operate with a limited chance for success, and perhaps for survival. Therefore, position descriptions for all key positions in a company are not only helpful but are necessary. Quite often the task of preparing position descriptions is assigned to a single department, and in some instances to a single individual. The preparation by key managers of their own position descriptions is one of the best means of developing in their minds a clear understanding of their scope of responsibility and authority.

In the interest of general uniformity, an outline of the key sections of position descriptions should be developed and distributed to the management group. A small committee, usually the executive or management committee, should be assigned the task of reviewing and polishing the submitted descriptions. Exhibit 3 illustrates one form of position description, in this case for a controller. In addition to presenting a clear picture of the organizational structure, the organization chart showing primary functions, together with the position descriptions, set the stage for creating the pattern of responsibility accounting.

EXHIBIT 1
Primary Organizational Functions

Chief Executive Officer
  General policies
  Coordinate line and staff activities
  Profit guidelines
  Sales objectives
  Operating goals
  Executive salary guidelines
  Review and endorsement of capital expenditures
  Review and endorsement of all expense budgets

  Finance
    General accounting
    Fixed asset accounting
    Cash control
    Staff budgets
    Salary payrolls
    Governmental agency reporting
    Data processing
    Accounting systems
    Information scheduling
    Sales and profit projection summaries
    Credit management

  Industrial Engineering
    Time-study policies and procedures
    Plant layouts
    Material specifications
    Materials handling equipment layout
    Wage administration
    Functional responsibility for methods engineering

  Industrial Relations
    General personnel policies
    Supervisory recruitment
    Job descriptions—supervisory
    Separation and turnover analysis
    Personnel services
    Hospital and medical insurance coordination
    Functional responsibility for plant personnel departments

  Purchasing
    Raw materials
    General supplies
    Purchase expediting
    Price negotiations
    Salvage sales
    Raw materials—standard price projections
    Manufacturing materials—standard price projections
    Production machinery and equipment
    Office furniture and equipment
    Transportation equipment
    Functional responsibility for plant supply rooms

Vice President, Marketing
  General sales policies
  Major-customer relations
  Pricing guidelines
  Selling expense budgets and control
  Sales personnel performance standards

EXHIBIT 1 (*continued*)

Distribution
 Coordination of shipping, warehousing, customer service
  activities
 Traffic management
 Carrier contacts
 Distribution expense budgets and control

 Shipping and Warehousing
  Finished goods storage
  Order assembly
  Shipping
  Railcar and truck loading

 Customer Service
  Order editing
  Shipment scheduling
  Liaison with production scheduling
  Customer order correlation
  Customer follow-up

Marketing
 Sales forecasting
 Product pricing
 Catalog preparation
 Advertising
 Market research
 Product development
 Styling
 Product design specifications

 Field Sales
  Customer relations
  Sales promotion
  Sales aids
  Sales training

Vice President, Manufacturing
 Coordinate all line and staff production activities
 Production hiring, promotion, and separation policies

 Manufacturing Accounting
  Cost accounting
  Plant payrolls
  Supplies inventory control
  Inventory pricing, extending, summarizing
  Petty cash control
  Raw materials records
  Accounts payable processing
  Intraplant and interplant inventory transfer control
  Capital asset program audits

 Methods Engineering
  Work methods (or work simplification)
  Time and motion studies
  Material quality standards
  Production time standards
  Machine assignment standards
  Equipment layouts
  Materials handling layouts

EXHIBIT 1 (*continued*)

Personnel
  Applicant screening and testing
    Plant nonsupervisory personnel
    Plant and office clerical
  Employee indoctrination
  Employee training
  Job descriptions—production employees
  Merit-rating programs
  Plant safety and personal injury protection
  Medical and first aid
  Employee discipline rules
  Recreation programs
  Personnel services
  Community relations
  Personnel records

Quality Control
  Product inspection
    Incoming materials
    In process
    Finished goods
  Process inspection
    Methods
    Equipment
  Customer quality complaint follow-up
  Disposition of rejects

Production Scheduling
  Establishment of seasonal base-stock levels
  Conversion of customer orders to production schedules
    Raw materials
    Work in process
    Finished goods
  Materials requisitioning
  Materials receiving and stores
  In process, storage
  Inventories—primary count
  Interplant scheduling

Plant Engineering
  Manufacturing equipment design and specifications
  Building design, construction, and maintenance
  Capital asset programs
  Utilities design and operation
  Truck and auto maintenance
  Plant protection
    Fire and safety
    Security
  Plant housekeeping
  Yard and grounds maintenance and housekeeping

Plant Managers and Production Department Supervisors
  Production (output)
  Productivity
  Product quality
  Material usage
  Expense control
  Departmental housekeeping

EXHIBIT 1 *(concluded)*

Personnel
Hiring
Promotion
Transfer
Discharge
Safety observance
Discipline

Communication Flow.   A necessary adjunct to the charted organizational structure of a company is a reasonably defined communication flow of management information. Such a pattern should describe "clearing points" and the order in which responsible executives have access to, approve or disapprove, and recommend decisions or actions determined from the information.

For example, there often exists the possibility that certain process or product cost information may be misused. The primary purpose of a product cost is the setting of selling prices high enough to assure a fair profit. Often, however, costs are used for other purposes: make-or-buy decisions, comparisons of costs of the same or similar products made at two or more plants in the same company, break-even analyses, and so on. As another example, most companies publish two sets of financial statements: one for internal or management purposes, the other for external reporting to stockholders, bankers, and vendors. This is not to suggest two sets of books—just two types of format.

In both of these cases, the internal flow of data needs to be defined, since the manner in which the data are developed will, in most cases, be dissimilar, having been determined with differing purposes in mind. In addition to a pattern of distribution, some information needs to be denied to certain individuals because of the test of the "need-to-know" principle.

Departmentalization—Responsibility Centers

Regardless of the size or the complexity of an organization, departmentalization is a must, be the enterprise one of trading, service, or manufacturing. The pattern of departmentalization should be kept as simple as possible. Otherwise control can become unwieldy. Similarly, as has often been prescribed, an accounting system must be kept simple.

EXHIBIT 2
Functional Organization Chart (controllers' department)

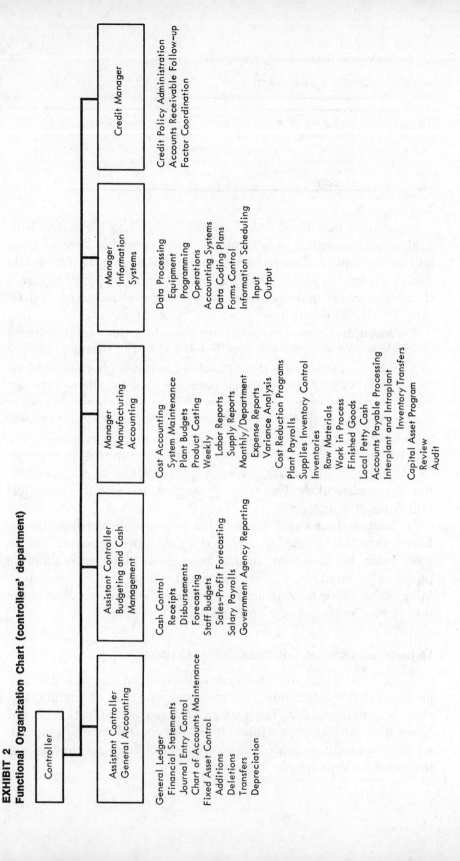

Controller

Assistant Controller
General Accounting

General Ledger
Financial Statements
Journal Entry Control
Chart of Accounts Maintenance
Fixed Asset Control
Additions
Deletions
Transfers
Depreciation

Assistant Controller
Budgeting and Cash
Management

Cash Control
Receipts
Disbursements
Forecasting
Staff Budgets
Sales–Profit Forecasting
Salary Payrolls
Government Agency Reporting

Manager
Manufacturing
Accounting

Cost Accounting
System Maintenance
Plant Budgets
Product Costing
Weekly
Labor Reports
Supply Reports
Monthly/Department
Expense Reports
Variance Analysis
Cost Reduction Programs
Plant Payrolls
Supplies Inventory Control
Inventories
Raw Materials
Work in Process
Finished Goods
Local Petty Cash
Accounts Payable Processing
Interplant and Intraplant
Inventory Transfers
Capital Asset Program
Review
Audit

Manager
Information
Systems

Data Processing
Equipment
Programming
Operations
Accounting Systems
Data Coding Plans
Forms Control
Information Scheduling
Input
Output

Credit Manager

Credit Policy Administration
Accounts Receivable Follow–up
Factor Coordination

EXHIBIT 3
Position Description

Title: Controller, Consumer Products Division

Primary Functions
1. Collection of all data necessary for compiling periodic financial statements.
2. Collection of all data necessary for reports as required for governmental agencies.
3. Coordination of data required for capital asset programs.
4. Coordination of data required for sales and profit budgets.
5. Coordination of data for cash flow projections.
6. Administration of cost accounting activities as required for integration with financial records.

General Objectives and Responsibilities
1. The maintenance of the general ledgers (through the computer). The preparation of periodic financial and other operating statements. The preparation of analyses of such statements. The analysis of financial data for special reports as required by operating management. Control of the chart of accounts.
2. The collection and submission of data via prescribed reports for various governmental agencies, such as the Bureau of the Census and taxing authorities, except those pertaining to the entire corporation.
3. Assistance to department heads in the preparation of data required for capital asset programs. The assembly of such data into chronological projections of cash requirements. The periodic follow-up of such programs to assure that original justifications have been satisfied.
4. Assistance to department heads in the preparation of data required for sales and profit budgets. The assembly of such data into projections in such detail as to enable comparisons of budgeted to actual results in such a manner as to facilitate assignment of responsibility and cause for departures from budget.
5. The establishment and maintenance of procedures required to facilitate reasonably accurate forecasts of division cash requirements for current and near future operations.
6. General administration of the standard cost accounting procedures to assure:
   Accurate predetermination of—
     Product costs
     Operating expenditures
   Accurate measurement of the utilization of company assets—cash, facilities, and personnel.
   Accurate valuation of inventories for balance sheet purposes.
7. General supervision of the taking, assembly, pricing, and extension of periodic physical inventories.
8. The calculation of weekly and monthly payrolls to the point of gross wages and salaries and the establishment of control totals for data processing of payrolls. The preparation of information pertaining to payrolls as required for periodic reports to governmental agencies.
9. The maintenance of control procedures to assure accurate processing of data on the computer.
10. The maintenance of fixed asset records to assure proper responsibility for custody of such assets.
11. The maintenance of accounts payable procedures to assure the prompt payment of vendor invoices.

A complete description would also include: a personnel table for the controller's office; a current expense budget; a listing of assets in the controller's department; a description of limits on his authority; a listing of the department's relationships to other departments; and a description of perquisites, hiring qualifications, and advancement opportunities.

Responsibility accounting suggests reporting of performance by centers of responsibility. An organization is made up of a group of responsibility centers, which are otherwise known (generically) as departments. A responsibility center often carries a second label in addition to its department name. Dependent upon its basic function to the entire organization, it may be classed as an expense,[2] profit, revenue, or investment center. In general, a responsibility center is a department, or, in some cases, a group of departments, under the authority and control of a *responsible manager*. Brief definitions of the various types of responsibility center will be helpful in understanding the principles of responsibility accounting.

Expense Centers.   There are really two types of expense centers —*standard expense centers* (sometimes also known as production centers) and *discretionary expense centers*. A standard expense center is generally one which, by changing or adding to the physical characteristics of a product, increases the value (material, labor or overhead) of the product being manufactured. These centers are discussed in detail in the next chapter.

A discretionary expense center generally is one which gives support to other responsibility centers. These support activities may or may not, by the allocation process, indirectly add value (in an accounting sense) to a product or service. They will add value if their expenses are allocated to products or services, and thus increase the "inventory value" of the products. Examples include the plant accounting, production scheduling, plant maintenance, and plant personnel departments.

If a discretionary expense center's services do not directly support production centers, the services are regarded as period expenses and thus are not capitalized in inventories. Examples include the legal, internal auditing, public relations, advertising, corporate accounting, and customer service departments. Discretionary expense centers are discussed in detail in Chapter 24, and a system for charging their services to other departments is described in Chapter 25.

---

[2] Expense centers are frequently referred to as "cost centers." Strictly speaking, a cost center is an entity with which costs are identified in the cost accounting system. A cost center need not have a manager responsible for it, or even be a "real" department; for example, some cost systems have an "occupancy" cost center that is simply a repository for the costs of rent, property insurance, and so forth. An expense center, on the other hand, is always a real department, with a manager responsible for its activities.

Revenue Centers. A revenue center has responsibility for generating a target level of sales revenues. Many companies treat district sales offices—and even individual salespersons—as revenue centers. Of course, the selling job requires incurrence of expenses for travel, entertainment, advertising, and so on. Revenue centers have budgets for these items, too. Thus revenue centers are also discretionary expense centers. However, these expenses are *not* subtracted from revenues: the resulting figure would not be profit, for the expense budget in a revenue center does not (by definition) include the cost of goods sold. If it did, then the center would be a profit center rather than a revenue center.

Profit Centers. A profit center is a responsibility center that by its efforts obtains a price for the company's products or services that exceeds the total cost of manufacturing and delivering these products or services. Put another way, these centers are held responsible for both revenues and expenses by measuring the centers' profits. These centers may be essentially self-contained independent businesses, or may be sales divisions which buy their goods at a standard cost from the company's factories and/or from outside suppliers.

Usually, profit centers obtain their revenues from customers outside the company. However, a profit center also may "sell" (transfer) goods or services to other responsibility centers at a value which exceeds the cumulative cost to the point of transfer. When such transfers occur between responsibility centers, intercompany profits appear in the accounting records. (In financial reports to outsiders, any internal profits must be eliminated and inventories valued at cost devoid of internal profits.) Of course, many profit centers make sales both within the company and to outside customers.

Investment Centers. These are responsibility centers in which profit is measured *and* in which this profit is related to the center's investment base, either by calculating return on investment (ROI) or residual income. From this definition it can be seen that since profit is measured for investment centers, in a sense these centers are profit centers. That is why many companies call them profit centers; but we feel it useful to distinguish investment centers from those profit centers in which the profits are not related to the centers' investment bases.

The concept of measuring profitability in terms of return on investment is increasing in popularity. As discussed in Chapter 27, there are many issues to be resolved by a company that has investment centers. The most difficult of these issues is deciding on a definition of what constitutes "investment."

ASPECTS OF RESPONSIBILITY ACCOUNTING

Responsibility accounting is one of several accounting processes in a firm, the others including accounting for financial reporting (to shareholders and other "outsiders"), accounting for the costs of goods and services (usually "full-cost" accounting), and differential accounting for special analyses (capital budgeting, make-or-buy decisions, and so on). Responsibility accounting is that type of management (i.e., internal) accounting that collects and reports both planned and actual accounting data *in terms of responsibility centers.*

The Management Control Process

Because of its focus on responsibility centers, responsibility accounting is the backbone of what is frequently called the *management control process.* This process includes two related activities—planning and control. Planning is deciding what to do and how and when to do it; control is assuring that the desired results are attained.

Although much of the management control process is conducted informally, most companies have a formal management control system, consisting of some or all of the following phases:[3]

Programming.

Budgeting.

Operating and accounting.

Reporting and analysis.

As shown in Exhibit 4, these phases form a loop which recurs in a regular cycle.

The *programming* phase is the one in which a company decides on the programs it will undertake (i.e., product lines, R&D programs, and so on) and the approximate amount of resources to be

---

[3] This terminology is that of Robert N. Anthony and James S. Reece, as used in *Management Accounting Principles* (Homewood, Ill.: Richard D. Irwin, Inc., 1975), chap. 20.

EXHIBIT 4
The Management Control Cycle

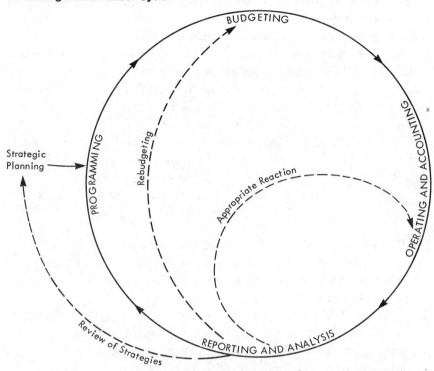

BUDGETING

Strategic
Planning

PROGRAMMING

Rebudgeting

Appropriate Reaction

OPERATING AND ACCOUNTING

Review of Strategies

REPORTING AND ANALYSIS

Source: Adapted from: Robert N. Anthony and James S. Reece, *Management Accounting Principles* (Homewood, Ill.: Richard D. Irwin, Inc., 1975), p. 460.

allocated to each program. Programming takes place within the context of strategic plans, and prior to the formulation of detailed operating budgets. In many companies, tentative programming decisions are made for several years out into the future, in which case the programming phase is often referred to as *long-range planning*.

In the *budgeting* phase of the management control cycle, program plans are detailed for the next year in monetary terms. The focus here is on responsibility centers rather than on programs per se. This is because responsibility center managers are the focus of control, and a given responsibility center may perform tasks related to several programs, but not perform *all* of the tasks for *any* program. For example, an automobile assembly plant may assemble Ford and Mercury automobiles—these are two different programs, but the plant is performing only one set of tasks (final assembly, as opposed to welding frames, building engines or transmissions, and so on.) Thus, by definition, responsibility accounting is intimately related to budgeting.

During the *operating and accounting* phase, records are kept of resources actually consumed (i.e., costs) and the revenues actually generated. These records should be structured so that data can be "captured" both by program and by responsibility center. Accordingly, the design of the responsibility accounting chart of accounts is important for this step of the control cycle.

The fourth, and most important, step is *reporting and analysis*. Without "closing the loop" with this step, the responsibility accounting process becomes a fairly futile exercise in data collection. As shown in Exhibit 4, the analysis of management reports may lead to four different types of "feedback":

1. Reports may indicate that a reexamination of corporate strategy is in order; for example, the company should cease making new investments in its traditional industry because indicated returns are inadequate.
2. Somewhat less dramatic, the reports may suggest the need to drop, change, or add programs next year; for example, the company should drop a certain product line because it can no longer compete effectively with imports.
3. Analysis of variances (actual-versus-budget differences) may suggest that the assumptions built into the budget were unrealistic, and the budget should be revised; for example, wildcat strikes unexpectedly caused a four-week shutdown of operations so that budget baseline is now fairly meaningless.
4. Reports of variances may indicate that some unanticipated problem needs correction—or some unanticipated opportunity needs to be further capitalized upon; for example, unfavorable material yield variances keep appearing, or a favorable selling price variance has shown up. (This short-term feedback to current operations, which we call "appropriate reaction," is the most familiar one to many managers.[4])

---

[4] Many authors call this feedback "corrective action," which obviously implies that a variance means there is some problem to be corrected. We prefer "appropriate reaction," to stress that *favorable* variances also should be investigated. However, it is in fact a rare company where favorable variances command anywhere near as much attention as unfavorable ones do.

Having seen this overview of the management control process, later in the chapter we will discuss in more detail the budgeting and periodic reporting aspects of management control. First, however, we will describe two aspects of responsibility accounting which are quite different from one another: first, the chart of accounts, which is a rather technical and precise topic; and second, behavioral aspects of responsibility accounting, which involve more qualitative and speculative considerations.

The Chart of Accounts

Essential to any accounting activity is a chart of accounts, which lists all accounts for the balance sheet and income statement. The arrangement of the accounts and an accompanying coding structure is important for both financial reporting and management accounting statement preparation activities. An example of an account's structure is shown in Exhibit 5.

Limited distribution of appropriate sections of the chart of accounts should be made to each operating unit of the company. Among the purposes to be served by this distribution are: an aid in the budgeting process; the provision for proper charging and segregation of expenses; and a measure of the degree of cost control being exercised over each account.

Fixed and Variable Costs. It is desirable when designing the chart of accounts to segregate accounts which tend to be variable costs from those which tend to be fixed. Of course, it is difficult to find any revenue or expense account which is either 100 percent fixed or 100 percent variable in nature. Arbitrary stands often are taken on either of the two classifications. In nearly every case, an account generally classed as variable is found to have a fixed element and, conversely, an account classed as fixed is found to have a variable element. These principles apply to a "going" business as opposed to a severely depressed business.

In a situation where a company is introducing the fixed-variable concept into budgeting (i.e., flexible budgets), the separation of some accounts into their properly proportioned fixed and variable elements will be difficult. For some accounts, an analysis of the elements or items to be charged can be useful in setting the line of demarcation. Precision is not important; reasonable judgment should suffice. For example, the power and light budget can be set

EXHIBIT 5
Example of a Coding Structure for an Expense Account

2xx–	*Other Payroll Related Costs*
21x–	*Direct Payments to Employees*
211–	Overtime Premiums
212–	Shift Premiums
213–	Attendance Premiums
216–	Vacation Pay
217–	Holiday Pay
22x–	*Payroll Taxes*
221–	F.I.C.A. Taxes
222–	Unemployment Benefit Taxes—Federal
223–	Unemployment Benefit Taxes—State
23x–	*Payroll Insurance*
231–	Workmen's Compensation Insurance
235–	Group Insurance Premiums
24x–	*Employee Benefits—Direct*
241–	Holiday Gifts
242–	YMCA Support
243–	Merchandise Discounts
244–	Employee Awards
245–	Educational Assistance
246–	Stock Purchase Supplement
247–	Relocation Expense
248–	Employee Meals
249–	Uniforms
26x–	*Employee Benefits—Indirect*
261–	Employment Services
262–	Company Newspaper
263–	Music
264–	Credit Union Expense
265–	Pension Plan Costs
266–	Employee Orientation Expense

Each account is defined in an accompanying document (not shown here). For example:

263–*Music:* The cost of equipment, records, tapes, and any other devices used for disseminating music in offices or plants. Includes fees paid to outside sources of music such as Muzak. Original equipment cost, if capitalized, is to be charged to balance sheet account 257, Office Furniture and Equipment, and depreciated accordingly.

up on a fixed-variable basis by determining the kilowatt demand of lights, elevators, auxiliary equipment, air-conditioning equipment, and heating (if electrical), all of which are generally fixed, and then determining the demand of motors and other devices using electricity for production equipment, usually considered variable. The proportionate relation of the two determines the base for dividing the total power budget into fixed and variable components.

Valid Account Matrix. When a company implements more so-phisticated degrees of financial control, there usually develops among department heads a tendency to request the use of more detailed expense accounts on the grounds that more specific identi-fication facilities better control. This is further aggravated because, somehow, department heads learn that certain accounts do exist and often try to justify their need for them. All this leads to more accounting detail than is actually necessary.

An effective device for exercising control over the availability of accounts is the *valid account matrix.* This is simply a table consist-ing of a listing across the top of the responsibility centers, and down the side a listing of the various expense accounts from the master chart of accounts. This table is usually created on cross-sectioned paper, and then authorized accounts are indicated by check marks in appropriate squares.

In the event the ledger is maintained on a computer, the matrix serves as a device for creating a master file of valid accounts. Thus, control is exercised by programming the computer to reject entries made to invalid accounts. The matrix is also useful in creating "authorized approval" lists. Under responsibility accounting, de-partment heads are entitled to protection against unauthorized charges to their departments. Also, it is assumed that with responsi-bility accounting, accounts over which the department head exer-cises no control are not budgeted or charged to a department. Thus, under a plan of authorized approvals, signatures are specified for approving purchase orders, receiving reports, invoices, time records, and other documents related to the expense charging procedures.

Behavioral Aspects of Management Control[5]

The purpose of management control in general, and responsi-bility accounting in particular, is to assure that managers obtain and use resources effectively and efficiently in the accomplishment of the organization's goals.

This process has a behavioral aspect and a technical aspect. The behavioral aspect is discussed at length in books on organizational behavior or social psychology. Although we shall provide here only a brief discussion, it is an essential one because the technical as-

---

[5] This section is adapted from Anthony and Reece, *Management Accounting Principles.*

pects are meaningful only if one understands that they are *intended to influence behavior*. The management control process in part consists of inducing the human beings in an organization to take those actions that will help attain the company's goals and to refrain from taking actions that are inconsistent with these goals. Although for some purposes an accumulation of the costs of manufacturing a product is useful, management cannot literally "control" a product, or the costs of making a product. What management does—or at least what it attempts to do—is control the actions of the *people* who are responsible for incurring these costs.

Behavior of Participants

Each person in an organization is called a *participant*. People become participants—that is, join an organization—because they believe that by doing so they can achieve their *personal* goals. Their decisions to contribute to the productive work of the organization once they have become members of it are also based on their perceptions that this will help achieve personal goals.

An individual's personal goals can be expressed as *needs*. Some of these needs are *material* and can be satisfied by the money a person earns on the job. Other needs are *psychological*. People need to have their abilities and achievements recognized; they need social acceptance as members of a group; they need to feel a sense of personal worth; they need to feel secure; they need the freedom to exercise discretion; they may need a feeling of power and achievement.

The relative importance of these needs varies with different persons, and their importance also varies with the same person at different times. For some people, earning a great deal of money is a dominant need; for others, monetary considerations are much less important. Only a relatively few people attach much importance to the need to exercise discretion or the need for achievement, but these few persons tend to be the leaders of the organization. The relative importance that persons attach to their own needs is heavily influenced by the attitude of their colleagues and of their superiors.

Incentives.   Individuals are influenced both by positive incentives and negative incentives. A *positive* incentive, also called a reward, is the satisfaction of a need, or the expectation that a need will be satisfied. A *negative incentive,* also called a punishment, is

the deprivation of satisfaction of a need, or the fear of such deprivation. Research on incentives tends to support the following:

Individuals are more strongly motivated by positive incentives
than by negative incentives.

Monetary compensation is an important incentive, but beyond
the subsistence level the amount of compensation is not necessarily as important as nonmonetary rewards. Nevertheless, the
amount of a person's earnings is often important indirectly as
an indication of how his or her achievement and ability are
regarded.

The effectiveness of incentives diminishes rapidly as the time
elapses between an action and the reward or punishment ad-
ministered for it. This is why it is important that reports on
performance be made available and acted on quickly. Management control cannot wait for the annual financial statements that appear three months or so after the year has ended.

Needs may be unconscious, or they may be expressed as aspirations or goals. Motivation is weakest when the person perceives
a goal as being either unattainable or too easily attainable.
Motivation is strong when the goal can be attained with some
effort and when the individual regards its attainment as important in relation to personal needs.

A person tends to accept reports of his or her performance more
willingly and to use them more constructively when they are
presented in a manner that can be regarded as objective, that
is, without personal bias.

Persons are receptive to learning better ways of doing things only
when they personally recognize the inadequacies of their present behavior.

Beyond a certain point, pressure for improved performance accomplishes nothing. This optimum point is far below the maximum amount of pressure that conceivably could be exerted.

Incentives take many forms. In some situations a quite simple
signal can be effective. For example, in the New York City government there was a project to sort out and discard files on those Medicaid cases that had been closed. These files occupied 1,200 file
cabinets. When the job started, each clerk was examining an average of 150 files a day, which was unsatisfactory. The supervisor

then made the following change: instead of discarding files in a common container, each clerk was asked to pile them in front of his or her work station. As the piles mounted, it became apparent to everyone how much work each clerk was doing. Production immediately increased to 300 files a day.[6]

At the other extreme, the reward can be that compensation is related to individual performance through a performance bonus. In view of the importance which many people attach to monetary compensation, this is a strong motivation indeed. (See Chapter 34.) In some cases it is too strong, for unless the basis for the bonus payment is very carefully worked out, incessant arguments will go on about equity of the bonus system. If, however, rewards are in the form of oral praise for good performance or criticism for poor performance, inequities in the numerical reports can be allowed for when interpreting the results.

Individuals differ in their needs and in their reactions to incentives of various types. An important function of managers at each level is to adapt their applications of the management control system to the personalities and attitudes of the individuals whom they supervise. Thus an impersonal system can never be a substitute for interpersonal actions; rather, the system is a framework that should be adapted by the manager to fit individual situations.

Goal Congruence.   Since an organization does not have a "mind of its own," the organization itself literally cannot have goals. The "organizational goals" often referred to are actually the goals of top management. Top management wants these organizational goals to be attained, but other participants have their own personal goals that *they* want to achieve. These personal goals are the satisfaction of their needs. In other words, participants act in their own self-interest.

The difference between organizational goals and personal goals suggests the central purpose of a management control system: the system should be designed so that actions that it leads people to take in accordance with their perceived self-interest are actions that are also in the best interests of the company. In the language of social psychology, the management control system should encourage *goal congruence;* that is, it should be structured so that the goals of participants so far as feasible are consistent with the goals of the organization as a whole.

---

[6] From *Management Accounting,* December 1972, p. 63.

Perfect congruence between individual goals and organizational goals does not exist. As a minimum, however, the system should not encourage individuals to act against the best interests of the company. For example, if the management control system signals that the emphasis should be only on reducing costs, and if managers respond by reducing costs at the expense of adequate quality or by reducing costs in their own responsibility centers by measures that cause a more than offsetting increase in costs in some other responsibility center, they have been motivated, but in the wrong direction. It is therefore important to ask two separate questions about any practice used in a management control system:

1.   What action does it motivate people to take in their own perceived self-interest, and
2.   Is this action in the best interests of the company?

Cooperation and Conflict.   The appearance of an organization chart implies that the way in which organizational goals are attained is that the top manager makes a decision and communicates that decision down through the organizational hierarchy, and then managers at lower levels of the organization proceed to implement it. It should now be apparent that this is *not* the way in which an organization actually functions.

What actually happens is that each subordinate reacts to the instructions of top management in accordance with how those instructions affect the subordinate's personal needs. Since usually more than one responsibility center is involved in carrying out a given plan, the interactions between their managers also affect what actually happens. For example, although the manager of the maintenance department is supposed to see to it that the maintenance needs of the operating departments are satisfied, if there is friction between the maintenance manager and an operating manager, the needs of that operating manager's department may, in fact, be slighted. For these and many other reasons, conflict exists within organizations.

At the same time, the work of the organization will not get done unless its participants work together with a certain amount of harmony. Thus, there is also cooperation in organizations. Participants realize that unless there is a reasonable amount of cooperation, the organization will dissolve, and the participants will then be unable to satisfy *any* of the needs which motivated them to join the organization in the first place.

An organization attempts to maintain an appropriate balance between the forces that create conflict and those that create cooperation. Some conflict is not only inevitable, it is desirable. Conflict results in part from the competition among participants for promotion or other forms of need satisfaction; and such competition is, within limits, healthy. A certain amount of cooperation is also obviously essential, but if undue emphasis is placed on engendering cooperative attitudes, the most able participants will be denied the opportunity of demonstrating their full potentialities.

Top-Management Sponsorship. A management control system will probably be ineffective unless subordinate managers are convinced that top management considers the system to be important. If a system is installed with no more management backing than the directive, "Let's have a good control system," then instead of being a part of the management process, the system becomes a paper-shuffling routine.

Action is a sure signal, probably the only effective signal, that top management is interested in the control system. Basically, this action involves praise or other reward for good performance, criticism of or removal of the causes for poor performance, or questions leading to these actions. If, in contrast, reports on performance disappear into executive offices and are never heard about again, the organization has reason to assume that management is not paying attention to them. And if management does not pay attention to them, why should anyone else?

Participation and Understanding. Control is exercised in part by establishing standards of expected performance and comparing actual performance with these standards. Whatever standard of good performance is adopted, it is likely to be effective as a means of control only if the people being judged agree that it is an equitable standard. If they do not agree, they are likely to pay no attention to comparisons between their performance and the standard; and they are likely to resent, and if possible reject, an attempt by anyone else to make such a comparison.

The best way to assure this agreement is to ask the people whose performance is to be measured to participate in the process of setting the standard. In order to participate intelligently, managers need to understand clearly what the control system is, what they are expected to do, what basis they are going to be judged on, and so on. Such an understanding probably cannot be achieved by written communication alone. Frequent meetings of supervisors for discussion and explanation are required.

The process of educating the individuals involved in the system is necessarily a continuous one. Not uncommonly, a system is introduced with a loud fanfare, works well for a time, and then gradually withers away in effectiveness as the initial stimulus disappears.

Focus on Line Managers. Since subordinates are responsible to their superiors, they should receive praise, criticism, and other incentives from their superiors. Staff people should not be directly involved in these motivation activities (except with respect to control of the staff organizations themselves). Line managers are the focal points in management control. Staff people collect, summarize, analyze, and present information that is useful in the management control process, and they make calculations that translate management judgments into the format of the control system. There may be many such staff people; indeed, the controller's department is often the largest staff department in a company. However, the significant decisions and control actions are the responsibility of the line managers, not of the staff.

Budgeting

As pointed out in the definition of responsibility accounting, this type of accounting involves a comparison of planned and actual results. The planned results in monetary terms are called *budgets*.

Chapter 30 deals in its entirety with the subject of preparing the annual budget. One approach to budgeting for discretionary expense centers is described in Chapter 24, and manufacturing budgets are discussed in Chapter 23. Thus in this chapter we will only highlight a few aspects of the budgeting process.

Budgeting for Support Departments. In business enterprises, much is said and done about performance in production areas. Many companies maintain well-organized industrial engineering programs, the principle activity of which is the determination of productivity standards. This function has often extended to the measurement of certain clerical activities, particularly those which are highly repetitious in nature. However, relatively little is done in staff and service areas to formulate a basis for acceptable performance and to measure actual performance in terms of expected levels of performance.

Occasionally, one finds a company which grants the manager of major operating units almost complete operating autonomy. This is to say that, within general corporate operating policies, such executives are left to their own devices to satisfy predetermined objectives. Thus, should these managers be less than satisfied with the services furnished from outside their own operating unit, they have complete freedom either to obtain such services from outside sources or to establish their own service departments. This puts pressure on any headquarters staff units to provide service that is as good or better than is available from outside service firms.

The staff departments are usually divided between those which support production departments and those which service general overhead departments. The general overhead departments commonly include sales, general administration, research and development, public relations, and others whose activities do not change the physical characteristics of products or add value in measurable increments to goods or services sold to outside customers. In a large organization, the staff departments might include: mechanical repair, electrical, plumbing or pipefitting, painting, carpentry, and sanitation, as well as payroll, production scheduling, plant or cost accounting, quality control, purchasing, and so forth.

Budgeting for staff and service departments is often difficult because of the "empire-building" tendencies inherent in these activities and the lack of control in the absence of precise product or service specifications. Again, outside "competition"—that is, other sources of services—tends to be an effective countervailing force to these tendencies, provided, of course, that responsibility centers are charged for services provided internally.

The question then arises as to the best method of charging the benefiting departments for the costs of these services. There are several ways of doing this, three of which bear comment: periodic allocation, periodic flat charge, or actual charging on the basis of man-hours or machine-hours consumed in furnishing services. Within those three general methods are found numerous variations. A brief description of each follows.

Period Allocation. This can be done weekly or monthly. At the time of budgeting some appropriate basis is chosen for allocation purposes. Possible allocation bases include direct labor dollars or hours, total labor dollars, number of employees, production floor space, horsepower of motors, replacement value of production equipment, and so on. Sometimes it is necessary to "weight" the allocation basis in the event all production centers are not budgeted to operate the same number of hours per week.

On the basis of the allocation method selected, each staff or service department's budget is allocated to the appropriate production departments. In turn, the allocated amounts become part of the budgets of those departments to which the budget allocations have been made. The allocations can be regarded as fixed charges or a combination of fixed and variable. Then, during each week or month, as actual expense charges or accruals are made to the respective staff-service departments, these costs are charged to the using or benefiting departments on the same allocation base as was employed during the budgeting process. To the extent that the using departments are more or less busy than was assumed in setting the allocation rates, then the service departments' costs may be (respectively) over- or underabsorbed.

Periodic Flat Charge. This method is the same as the periodic allocation method so far as budgeting goes. However, instead of allocating total *actual* expenses, only the amounts *budgeted* are charged out. Differences between total actual expenses and amounts charged out to using departments are charged to appropriate variance accounts. This method has the advantage of not passing on service department efficiencies or inefficiencies to the using departments.

Actual Usage Charge. Under this method, each staff or service department is treated as though it were an outside company selling its services to the producing departments. The steps involved in this method are as follows:

1. Each producing department estimates the amount of service it normally will require each week or month. These amounts are measured in terms of man-hours, or machine-hours, or a combination of the two.
2. The hours budgeted to be "purchased" are accumulated for each service department.
3. On the basis of hours expected to be sold, each service department determines its personnel and expense requirements (salaries and wages).
4. A budgeted hourly rate for service is calculated.
5. In turn, the expected "purchased" service hours are valued at

the calculated rates and the resultant amounts become part of the producing departments' budgets.

6. Records of hours furnished the producing departments are summarized each week or month, valued at the budgeted hourly rates and charges made by memo billings or journal entries. As in the case of the periodic flat charge method, the differences between total actual expenses and charges are transferred to appropriate variance accounts. (Chapter 25 deals in more detail with service department charge-back systems.)

Sometimes companies want to account for service departments' serving *each other*, as well as serving the producing departments. Still, it is desired to "budget out" all service department costs to producing departments. In this case the determination of allocation rates for charging the producing departments requires a special method of calculation. The approach involves creating a set of simultaneous equations and solving for hourly rates by means of matrix algebra. Those companies faced with this situation either have, or can obtain access to, a computer program with which such equations can be solved in a matter of seconds.

Cost Accounting for Responsibility Accounting

Techniques for measuring, controlling, reducing, and otherwise managing cost for profit improvement are perhaps more numerous than are techniques for financial reporting. It is far better to employ the "counting the cash in the bank" method of measuring financial results than to determine inventory values or cost of sales by a cost system which does not fit the particular industry, product line, or processing stages of a given company. In order to effectively implement a system of responsibility accounting, a company needs an acceptable system of cost accounting. The pattern for building up product costs on paper must parallel the actual stages employed through the manufacturing processes of the products. The same principle applies to costing services.

This chapter is not intended to cover the broad subject of cost accounting, which is discussed in Part II of this Handbook. However, some exposure to techniques will be necessary in order to support responsibility accounting. Imagination should enable the controller to adapt from one type to another as would be required for varying types of business endeavor. The nature of a business will suggest the system best suited to a given company.

When we speak of responsibility accounting, the existence of some pattern of *standards* of performance is acknowledged. This point generally implies the existence of a system having predetermined standard costs of products and/or services. In what follows, a full process-standard cost system completely integrated with the financial records is assumed.

Product costing begins with a basic, unchanging pair of ingredients: time and materials. The length of an hour never changes. Pounds, kilograms, inches, meters, gallons, liters, or kilowatt-hours do not change. Once the length of time and quantities of materials required to make a product are established, a product is specified. Any change in time or material causes a change in the specification of the product. A change in the equipment employed in manufacture may change the time requirement (usually a saving), as can a change in manual methods. More significant, however, are changes in the values (i.e., costs) of time and materials. It is here that the clarification of responsibility accounting begins. This is best accomplished through an understanding of a few basic points in the management of assets:

1. So long as a purchasing department exists, the production department managers' responsibilities for materials are in terms of physical quantities, not purchase prices.
2. The purchasing agent has the responsibility for obtaining the best possible prices (consistent with quality specifications) for those materials which go into a product.
3. The production department manager has the prime responsibility for the efficient utilization of the company's assets—materials, production equipment, and workers. The industrial engineering department serves in an advisory capacity in setting methods, time values, and size of work force.
4. The sales department has the responsibility for attempting to obtain orders of sufficient magnitude to keep the plants operating near or at capacity.
5. The maintenance department has the responsibility of keeping the machinery and equipment in good operating condition.
6. The personnel department must locate, interview, and screen candidates for employment. Also, the personnel department

must develop programs for the proper orientation of newly hired persons. Dependent upon the levels of technical skill required, industrial engineering may assist personnel in the development of training programs and methods.

7.   There are several pressures external to the company which require that certain departments alter their means of fulfilling assigned responsibilities:

   a.   New industries in the area, offering higher rates of pay, may alter a company's attitudes and practices with respect to rates of pay, fringe benefits, and other hiring practices.

   b.   Prices of materials may require the R&D or product development departments to consider modifications to existing products or even alternative materials.

   c.   Customers' likes and dislikes, styling trends, and "better mousetraps" can have devastating effects on product demand.

An understanding of the various forces on a company, both internal and external, brings into focus the importance of measuring company performance in segments which we call responsibility centers. But the terms of measurement must be such that the responsibility center managers receive an impartial measurement of their performance. The measuring devices—reports—to be of value, must be in terms which suggest corrective action.

Budget Revisions

The frequency of updating budgets and standard product costs is a matter which frequently poses a dilemma. The general rule of thumb is once a year. However there are a number of factors which require consideration of a different timetable:

1.   Price trends of raw and other manufacturing materials.
2.   General wage-rate changes.
3.   Major changes in certain overhead costs, such as fuel, power, machine repairs and repair parts.
4.   Major changes in the complement of production machinery and equipment.

Such factors, if not recognized, can lead to neglect in properly updating prices of finished products. Sometimes raw material price changes, labor rate changes, and changes in some overhead factors can, by simple mathematical computations performed by a computer, be carried into total product costs as frequently as is necessary. In these cases, the original standard costs and budgets are also retained, so that the system and its reports enable the tracking of cost and performance trends. This is important so that these data can be used in conjunction with other factors at the time of individual salary reviews and in consideration of promotions of individuals.

Return-on-Investment Pricing

Preparing profit budgets requires, of course, assumptions about the prices of the company's goods and services. Mention was made earlier of investment centers and of the popularity of evaluating profit performance on the principle of return on investment. Related to this, there is often found the need for a technique of determining acceptable selling prices which include an element of profit tied to a planned return on investment. This becomes somewhat cumbersome where the proportions of material, labor, variable, and fixed overhead costs vary widely within a company's product line. The projection of a constant profit level under such circumstances is further complicated when the product mix is subject to significant changes.

There are a number of methods for calculating suggested profit per unit for each item in the product line in a manner which, if resultant selling prices are acceptable and sales volume keeps manufacturing facilities operating at planned levels, will result in profit's remaining constant. One such method is briefly described below:

1. Select the investment base (assets, invested capital, owners' equity, etc.).
2. Determine the desired rate of ROI.
3. Multiply this rate times the investment base to determine the desired dollars of profit per year.
4. Select a principal operation or process through which all, or the majority of, products pass in manufacture, usually a nearly final operation or assembly.
5. Convert the annual profit amount to profit for a workable period of time—week or month. Be certain to make due allowance for normal periods of inactivity, as would occur for vacations, holidays, inventory taking, and major overhaul programs.

6. For the same period of time—week or month—determine the number of man-hours or machine-hours available or budgeted for the production center selected in Step 4.

7. Divide the dollars determined in Step 5 by the hours determined in Step 6. The result is the planned dollars of profit per hour.

8. For each unit of each product which passes through the selected production point, multiply the rate of profit per hour from Step 7 by the computed number of hours required to process the unit of product at that point.

The result obtained from this procedure is the suggested profit per unit of finished product. When added to all other costs—manufacturing, R&D, shipping and warehousing, and general administrative, the computed profit gives a suggested selling price. Thus, the sales department has a target price. When comparing company products with like products offered by competitors, price comparisons can be made and pricing strategies set.

Periodic Reporting

The value of any managerial procedure can be determined by its usefulness to the management team. No procedure on its own ever contributed to profit. On the other hand, for any business to become and/or remain profitable, a number of disciplines are required. Procedures generally constitute the pattern of discipline. A procedure for stimulating profitability usually is concerned with assembling a series of facts and figures which appear in varying formats on a set of reports.

The pattern of reports described below assumes that a series of conditions exist:

1. The organization illustrated is a representative small-to-medium conglomerate consisting of three divisions, four separate companies, and several plants that manufacture a variety of product lines. The organization chart, shown as Exhibit 2, shows the "chain-of-command" interrelationships of the various operating units.

2. A full process-standard cost accounting system, integrated with the financial records, is presumed. The standards used for budgeting are revised once a year, and there is a midyear review to determine whether midyear revisions are also needed. Physical

inventories of raw materials, work in process, and finished goods are taken every six months, except that physical inventories of certain categories of raw materials and finished goods are taken monthly.

3.   During the third month of each quarter are prepared: preliminary plans for sales and production; projected cash flow, balance sheet, and income statements; and an accompanying manufacturing plan, covering the *second* (as opposed to the next) future quarter, by months. At the same time the preliminary plans for the next quarter are reviewed, updated, and published. These plans are then incorporated into the statements that report actual results for the next three months.

4.   The scope of the series of reports follows closely that indicated by the organization chart. While departments are not shown on the chart illustrated, detail reporting begins at the department level. Then, as the reporting progresses toward the total-company level, department, plant, company, and division results are successively merged and summarized.

A typical report on operating profits is shown in Exhibit 6. We feel the format of this report is outmoded for *internal* reporting purposes. The same results, but presented in a format arising from responsibility accounting, are shown in Exhibit 7. This statement, along with the Report on Planned Profits (Exhibit 8), discloses the areas from which departures from planned results occurred and the reasons for these variances. The Report on Operating Profits shows the departures from standard budgets along with the planned or forecasted departures from standard budgets, the latter having been adjusted to current levels of operation.

Standard Budget.   Before elaborating on the significant features of the various reports in this illustrative situation, a brief explanation of the routine followed by this typical company is in order. The essential steps are described; more detailed actions are somewhat self-prescribed and are left to the imagination of the reader. At the outset, assuming that department heads have a reasonable understanding of their responsibilities, the stage is set for an annual program of setting standard operating budgets. A typical action program would require the following steps:

1.   Establish premises: The president, executive vice president, or the management committee establishes the following:
     a.   General operating levels (for each plant, if variations from

a norm are expected) expressed in days per week and hours and shifts per day, allowing for idle days for holidays, vacations, inventory taking, and so forth.

   b. Wages, including anticipated wage increases, restrictions on nonscheduled overtime.

2. Prepare/update list of production expense centers.

3. Prepare manning tables for hourly and salaried personnel, extended into dollars.

4. Prepare budgets of overhead for all departments, breaking amounts for each account into fixed and variable components.

5. Prepare overhead allocation data.

6. Prepare schedule of man- or machine-hours for all expense centers.

7. Allocate fixed and variable overhead to expense centers.

EXHIBIT 6

REPORT ON OPERATING PROFIT:
OUTMODED FORMAT
Month of_____, 1978

Gross sales:			
Floor coverings.................		$ 619,194.80	
Acoustical tile...................		750,118.30	
Textile products...............		578,030.70	
Total.......................			$1,947,343.80
Less:			
Returns.......................		$ 123,185.90	
Allowances....................		4,083.10	
Total.......................			127,269.00
Net sales........................			$1,820,074.80
Cost of sales:			
Beginning inventories.........	$2,649,180.22		
Materials purchases..........	642,276.41		
Labor.........................	226,685.79		
Overhead.....................	390,403.30		
Total available..........		$3,908,545.72	
Ending inventories............		2,618,430.92	
Cost of sales............			1,290,114.80
Gross profit......................			$ 529,960.00
Percent gross profit.........			29.12
Other expenses:			
Selling expense.................		$ 242,195.60	
General administrative expense.....................		103,850.73	
Total.......................			$ 346,046.33
Operating profit...................			$ 183,913.67
Percent operating profit...........			10.10%

8. Calculate man- or machine-hour rates of labor and overhead, fixed and variable.
9. Calculate product standard costs.
10. Prepare schedules of nonmanufacturing costs.
11. Prepare data for calculating target profit.
12. Prepare schedule of suggested selling prices for all finished products.

> *Note:* Appropriate interim reviews of budgets and final cost and selling price data are presumed. Also, completion of this work prior to the beginning of each fiscal year is a must.

Quarterly Budgeting. The second action program to be followed pertains to periodic sales, production, and profit budgeting. A quarterly timetable has been mentioned for this illustrative company. A suggested list of activities includes:

1. A meeting with an economist familiar with the market in which the company operates. The future outlook and the external influences which could warrant alternative approaches to marketing under anticipated influences are usually the key points discussed. Marketing and manufacturing executives should comprise the participants.
2. The direction of forecast development can stem from either manufacturing or sales. Generally, in a highly competitive industry manufacturing should lead, while in a more highly styled and lucrative industry, sales should lead. Assuming manufacturing leads, then a representative product mix in sufficient volume to utilize budgeted capacity for the number of "normal" working days in the second future quarter is prepared.
3. The sales department reviews the projected volume and suggests changes.
4. At the same time, the volume forecasted three months earlier for the immediate future quarter is reviewed and updated.
5. The projections for the two quarters are extended at standard cost and at suggested selling prices.
6. Responsible department heads then prepare for each month their best estimates of operating variances.
7. The accounting department then projects the data into the customary formats of financial statements—income statement, balance sheet, and statement of changes in financial position (funds flow statement).

EXHIBIT 7

REPORT ON OPERATING PROFIT: UNDER RESPONSIBILITY ACCOUNTING FORMAT
Month of _____, 1978

By Product Group	Total		Floor Coverings		Acoustical Tile		Textile Products	
	Actual	Plan	Actual	Plan	Actual	Plan	Actual	Plan
Gross sales—at suggested prices	$1,953,367.30	$1,998,200.00	$617,948.60	$598,200.00	$752,468.30	$800,000.00	$582,950.40	$600,000.00
Returns—at suggested prices	127,698.98	126,800.00	62,420.18	56,800.00	43,128.60	40,000.00	22,150.20	30,000.00
Net sales—at suggested prices	$1,825,668.32	$1,871,400.00	$555,528.42	$541,400.00	$709,339.70	$760,000.00	$560,800.20	$570,000.00
Variable cost of sales—at standard	816,206.33	814,488.00	222,211.37	227,388.00	319,202.87	319,200.00	274,792.09	267,900.00
Marginal profit—at standard	$1,009,461.99	$1,056,912.00	$333,317.05	$314,012.00	$390,136.83	$440,800.00	$286,008.11	$302,100.00
Fixed cost of sales—at standard	461,761.65	448,748.00	166,658.68	173,248.00	177,334.93	167,200.00	117,768.04	108,300.00
Gross profit—at standard	$ 547,700.34	$ 608,164.00	$166,658.37	$140,764.00	$212,801.90	$273,600.00	$168,240.07	$193,800.00
Percent standard gross profit	30.00	32.50	30.00	26.00	30.00	36.00	30.00	34.00
Price adjustments (decreases)	$ (5,593.52)	$ (10,500.00)	$ 4,208.40	$ —	$ (2,860.12)	$ (3,000.00)	$ (6,941.80)	$ (7,500.00)
Net sales—at actual prices	$1,820,074.80	$1,860,900.00	$559,736.82	$541,400.00	$706,479.58	$757,000.00	$553,858.40	$562,500.00
Departure from plan (decreases)	$ (40,825.20)	$ —	$ 18,336.82	$ —	$(50,520.42)		$ (8,641.60)	
Adjusted gross profit—at standard	$ 542,106.82	$ 597,664.00	$170,866.77	$140,764.00	$209,941.78	$270,600.00	$161,298.27	$186,300.00
Percent adjusted standard gross profit	29.78	32.12	30.53	26.00	29.72	35.75	29.12	33.12

By Plants	Total		Chemicals		Forest Products		Molded Plastics	
Variances on variable costs of production (unfavorable):	Actual	Plan	Actual	Plan	Actual	Plan	Actual	Plan
Materials—prices	$ 595.10	$ 2,350.00	$ 252.80	$ 1,850.00	$ (3,843.30)	$ (2,500.00)	$ 4,185.60	$ 3,000.00
—usage	(908.22)	(2,800.00)	1,212.48	(800.00)	—	(2,000.00)	(2,120.70)	—
—mix	(2,131.00)		(1,050.10)		—	—	(1,080.90)	—
—yield	2,357.60	6,600.00	185.80	(400.00)	1,221.20	5,000.00	950.60	2,000.00
Labor productivity	2,101.10	2,500.00	4,381.20	8,500.00	(4,130.10)	(6,000.00)	1,850.00	—
—payroll	(4,883.10)	(9,200.00)	(2,081.30)	(2,200.00)	720.10	(3,000.00)	(3,521.90)	(4,000.00)
—wage rates	(21,778.40)	(24,000.00)	(11,498.50)	(12,000.00)	(850.10)	—	(9,429.80)	(12,000.00)
Overhead—productivity	2,742.20	2,000.00	5,186.90	10,000.00	(4,796.80)	(8,000.00)	2,352.10	—
—spending	26,345.20	23,000.00	5,540.10	8,000.00	6,983.30	5,000.00	13,821.80	10,000.00
Total	$ 4,440.48	$ 450.00	$ 2,129.38	$ 12,950.00	$ (4,695.70)	$(11,500.00)	$ 7,006.80	$ (1,000.00)

Variances on fixed costs of production (unfavorable):

Overhead—spending	$ (1,500.00)	—	$ (8,212.00)	—	$ (1,500.00)	—	—	—
—volume	(15,087.30)	(15,000.00)	—	$ (6,000.00)	(2,053.00)	—	$ (4,822.30)	$ (9,000.00)
Total	$ (16,587.30)	$ (15,000.00)	$ (8,212.00)	$ (6,000.00)	$ (3,553.00)	$(11,500.00)	$ (4,822.30)	$ (9,000.00)
Total variances	$ (12,146.82)	$ (14,550.00)	$ (6,082.62)	$ 6,950.00	$ (8,248.70)		$ (2,184.50)	$(10,000.00)
Gross profit—at actual	$ 529,960.00	$ 583,114.00						
Percent actual gross profit	29.12	31.34						
Other operating costs:								
Selling expense	$ 242,195.60	$ 250,000.00						
General and administrative	103,850.73	102,500.00						
Total	$ 346,046.33	$ 352,500.00						
Operating profit	$ 183,913.67	$ 230,614.00						
Percent operating profit	10.10	12.39						

EXHIBIT 8

REPORT ON PLANNED PROFIT
Month of_____, 1978

Operating profit:

Plan..	$230,614.00
Actual...	183,913.67
Department from plan (unfavorable)........................	$(46,700.33)

Sources and causes of gain or loss:
Resulting from sales:

Volume..	$(14,949.09)
Selling prices..	4,906.48
Product mix...	(45,601.87)
Selling expenses..	7,804.40
Total..	$(47,840.08)

Resulting from purchasing:

Material prices...	$ (1,754.90)

Resulting from production:
Material:

Usage..	1,891.78
Mix..	(2,131.00)
Yield..	(4,242.40)

Labor:

Payroll..	4,316.90
Wage rates...	2,221.60
Overhead spending..	1,845.20
Productivity...	343.30
Total..	$ 4,245.38

Resulting from administration................................	$ (1,350.73)
Total departure from plan...................................	$(46,700.33)

Again, at appropriate points in the preparation schedule, management reviews and revisions are made. The data are then entered each month on financial statements to enable comparisons of actuals with planned or forecasted results of operations.

Ancillary Reporting Activities. One area of responsibility accounting is often neglected—capital expenditures. Such outlays are made for a number of reasons: introduction of new-product lines, compliance with regulations issued by governmental agencies, expansion of production facilities to increase output volume, reduction in manufacturing costs, and so forth. The cost-reduction segment of capital outlays should be subjected to careful scrutiny prior to inception and, sometimes more importantly, be given a post-installation review to assure that anticipated cost reductions are realized. (See Chapters 15–17.)

There are other reports which evaluate performance of a company or certain segments of a company. One of these is a report on the distribution function's costs that includes an evaluation of distribution methods to aid in determining the need for improvement in distribution methods and procedures. Another is a report which evaluates the relative profit contribution of major products or product groups. Trend analysis through the use of graphics is often helpful to decision making when using these reports. A similar report, but tracking the profit contribution of major customers, is also helpful.

Periodic Reports. To this point the organizational structure, translated into a system of reports on results compared to budgeted results, has been described. The Report on Planned Profits, Exhibit 8, is perhaps the key report from the standpoint of underlining departures from planned results by cause and responsibility. A simple report should be prepared for each lower level subdivision (responsibility center) of a company which has identifiable revenues from outside sources. Then, as reporting proceeds toward the consolidated results for the total company, subconsolidations are made at each level in accordance with the chain-of-command lines as exemplified on the organization chart.

This report compares actual operating profit with budgeted operating profit. It then details the variances as to cause and as to which responsibility center either performed better than budgeted or fell short of expectations. The report's line items and their identifications follow:

Responsibility assigned to the sales department:

1. *Volume.* A combination of two factors:
   a. Resulting from a higher or lower level of shipments than planned. This factor is determined by extending the difference between planned and actual net sales at suggested prices by the planned percent standard gross profit.
   b. Resulting from operating manufacturing facilities more or fewer hours than those set in the plan. It represents the standard fixed overhead per man- or machine-hour times those hours, all accumulated for the plant or responsibility center and compared to the planned variance. The difference is added to that determined for sales or shipments above.

   Note: That portion of the departure between planned

and actual operating profit attributed to volume is usually considered to be a responsibility of the sales department. There are times when the responsibility lies elsewhere in the organization. For example:

There may have been sufficient orders in-house to have enabled the plant or group of plants to run as budgeted. However, due to negligence in maintainance, key production equipment could have suffered a major breakdown requiring repairs over several days' time. Or, the purchasing department could have failed to ensure that certain materials were properly scheduled for arrival. Sometimes, external factors—strikes, acts of God, customer cancellations—can cause unplanned volume departures.

2. *Selling prices.* As mentioned earlier, the system of responsibility accounting illustrated includes the element of determining suggested selling prices. A number of factors, including competition, the offering of a new product which can be priced at a premium, and so on, generally prevent actual selling prices from matching the computed, suggested prices. Therefore, the budgeting activity includes a determination of the extent to which actual prices will vary from suggested prices. Actual events—a downturn in the market, justified increases, and so forth—will result in a departure from the forecasted price adjustments.

3. *Product mix.* In the planning activity, the sales department projects a representative mix of products to be shipped/invoiced in projected quantities. Extensions of these quantities at suggested selling prices and at standard manufacturing costs provide a standard gross profit and a percentage standard gross profit. Extensions of the actual units shipped/invoiced provide the same factors. When the actual units shipped are extended at the difference between planned and actual standard percent gross profit, a departure from planned operating profit due to a change from the planned product mix is disclosed.

4. *Selling expense.* At the time of setting or revising standard costs, a standard budget of selling expenses is developed. Any item of selling expense which is considered to be variable in nature is usually found to vary in some proportion to fluctuation in sales—salespersons' commissions, for example. On the other hand, there are times when sales efforts are more active

in an attempt to boost sagging sales, in the form of advertising and other promotional efforts. Therefore, sales department expenditures are more predictable over the short term. So, as part of the planning activity, using the annual "standard" budget, expenditures are estimated for each month in the next two future quarters. The difference between total planned and actual selling expense appears on this report.

Responsibility assigned to manufacturing:

1. *Material prices.* For the purpose of determining the materials segment of product standard manufacturing cost, the purchasing department is usually expected to develop a projection of the unit purchase price of each raw material or purchased part. Such price projections are usually expected averages for the year being budgeted. Prices also usually include a provision for freight required to land the materials at the company's plants. Since anticipated price changes are incorporated in the average, an estimate is made for each month's forecast of the difference between standard and actual costs of materials to be consumed each month. The variance between budgeted and actual price variances appears on this report. Sometimes, especially in companies with widely diversified products and with correspondingly widely diversified raw materials, such variances are detailed to major materials groups in separate, more detailed reports.

3. *Material usage.* Earlier the point was made that, so long as a purchasing department was held responsible for obtaining the best prices possible for materials, the production department manager's responsibility is limited to physical quantities. At times, unexpected sizable quantities of materials are set aside, or consumed in excess of the standard quantities prescribed in the bills of materials. Those materials set aside usually have failed to meet quality standards. Other excesses can occur in the form of spillage, improper mixture, and other off-standard occurrences. Under a plan of accounting which extends to process-standard cost accounting, it is necessary to convert these quantity variances to dollar amounts. This is accomplished in one of several ways. In some types of manufacture, intermediate products are carried through the various stages of manufacture under lot control. Thus, procedures for measuring the actual

yield in terms of expected yield lead to quantity departure measurement. In other situations, because work in process inventories are under ledger control, because responsibility center managers are held accountable for inventory losses, and because products are not under lot or batch control, department heads are expected to follow a procedure of reporting those quantity departures, if material in size. Then the accounting department values the items reported at their standard material and accumulated labor and overhead values. Only in rare cases are gains expected to occur, and only occasionally are losses forecasted. The actual losses are charged to a usage variance account and credited to the proper inventory account or to the quarterly profit and loss statement.

The remaining variances are self-explanatory. The budgeting of variance amounts is dependent on whether changes of certain levels of spending or productivity are anticipated. For example:

A wage rate change may be planned for some midpoint in an upcoming quarter. Assuming it was anticipated and allowed for when setting the standard budget, obviously variances in one direction will occur prior to the effective date of the change and in the other direction after the effective date. Therefore a determination of the variance should be made for each month and forecasted as a wage-rate variance.

A program of labor-force reduction through incentives, labor-saving equipment installations, or other efforts designed to reduce labor cost can suggest the planning for a payroll variance forecast.

There are a number of reasons that certain production centers can experience a variance, favorable or unfavorable, as a result of turning out production units at a rate per hour greater or less than standard. To the extent possible, such variances should be planned or forecasted. Productivity variances apply to both labor and overhead.

Under a fixed-variable concept of budgeting (also called flexible budgeting) and standard costing of products, actual expenditures are usually compared with a budget that has been adjusted to the actual level of operations, expressed as a percent of available or budgeted capacity. The differences remaining after this volume adjustment are classed as spending variances.

Beyond this budget adjustment, it is sometimes appropriate to forecast spending variances. Examples include an anticipated increase in rates to be charged by the power company, anticipated salary increases, anticipated major overhaul programs, a new plant roof, and so on.

Responsibility assigned to general administration, research and development, or any other nonmanufacturing groups: In these instances the approach would be similar to that which was described for selling expenses.

Under the described plan of responsibility accounting the Report on Planned Profits is considered the device by which the head of each profit center is informed of the degree to which subordinates have fulfilled their responsibilities in comparison to a budget. From this report, and then from the statement of operating profits, the statement of manufacturing expenses, the labor comparison report and other more detailed, more frequently prepared reports, responsibility center managers are kept informed of their progress.

A typical report on operating profits combines results by profit center and by production expense center. The three product groups are assumed to be marketed by three separate groups in the sales department. However, parts, subassemblies, and finished products, because of their manufacturing requirements, come from a different pattern of plant identification. Thus, profit contribution factors arising from sales efforts are identified by product groups, while profit contributions factors arising from plant management groups are identified as to the plants in which they occurred; that is, as mentioned previously, the programs (product groups) and responsibility centers do not coincide. Frequently, attempts are made to identify manufacturing variances to individual products or product groups. However, it has been found that the vast majority of occurrences of such variances are condition related and seldom product related. Occasionally a departure from standard can be tied to a product but is not necessarily caused by that product; it merely happened while a certain product was in process.

The elements of overhead expense which were incurred in manufacturing are illustrated in Exhibit 9, a statement of manufacturing overhead expenses. The elements of expense incurred or accrued for a given accounting period are listed. The first three columns list the standard budget amounts for a four-week month. During the par-

EXHIBIT 9

STATEMENT OF MANUFACTURING OVERHEAD EXPENSES
Molded Plastics Plant
Month of _____, 1978
Four Weeks—Operating Activity, 89.5 Percent

Normal Budget

Account	Total	Fixed	Variable @ 100%	89.5%	Spending Allowance
Variable—controllable expenses:					
Salaries and indirect labor:					
Salaries—supervision.........	$ 6,700.00	$ 4,600.00	$ 2,100.00	$ 1,879.50	$ 6,479.50
Salaries—clerical..............	5,900.00	2,400.00	3,500.00	3,132.50	5,532.50
Indirect labor.................	3,200.00	500.00	2,700.00	2,416.50	2,916.50
Total....................	$ 15,800.00	$ 7,500.00	$ 8,300.00	$ 7,428.50	$ 14,928.50
Payroll-related costs:					
Makeup pay..................	$ 800.00	$	$ 800.00	$ 716.00	$ 716.00
Shift premium...............	1,350.00		1,350.00	1,208.25	1,208.25
Overtime premium...........	2,475.00	300.00	2,175.00	1,946.63	2,246.63
Payroll taxes.................	5,800.00	600.00	5,200.00	4,654.00	5,254.00
Group insurance.............	1,480.00	175.00	1,305.00	1,167.97	1,342.97
Compensation insurance......	375.00	60.00	315.00	281.93	341.93
Total....................	$ 12,280.00	$ 1,135.00	$11,145.00	$ 9,974.78	$ 11,109.78
Supplies and utilities:					
Fuels........................	$ 2,475.00	$ 1,500.00	$ 975.00	$ 872.63	$ 2,372.63
Power and lights..............	4,350.00	1,350.00	3,000.00	2,685.00	4,035.00
Water........................	100.00	75.00	25.00	22.37	97.37
Expense supplies.............	36,000.00	4,000.00	32,000.00	28,640.00	32,640.00
Postage......................	450.00	350.00	100.00	89.50	439.50
Total....................	$ 43,375.00	$ 7,275.00	$36,100.00	$32,309.50	$ 39,584.50
General expense:					
Repairs and maintenance.....	$ 15,500.00	$ 1,500.00	$14,000.00	$12,530.00	$ 14,030.00
Dues and subscriptions.......	200.00	200.00			200.00
Travel and entertainment.....	750.00	500.00	250.00	223.75	723.75
Telephone and teletype.......	800.00	200.00	600.00	537.00	737.00
Miscellaneous................	750.00	250.00	500.00	447.50	697.50
Total....................	$ 18,000.00	$ 2,650.00	$15,350.00	$13,738.25	$ 16,388.25
Total variable—					
controllable........	$ 89,455.00	$18,560.00	$70,895.00	$63,451.03	$ 82,011.03
Fixed charges:					
Depreciation....................	$ 23,500.00	$23,500.00			$ 23,500.00
Taxes........................	1,200.00	1,200.00			1,200.00
Insurance....................	585.00	585.00			585.00
Total fixed—					
Noncontrollable........	$ 25,285.00	$25,285.00			$ 25,285.00
Total expenses.........	$114,740.00	$43,845.00	$70,895.00	$63,451.03	$107,296.03

Actual Expenses	Spending Variance (unfavorable)	Type	Summary of Variances (unfavorable)		
			Actual	Plan	Departure
$ 5,729.50	$ 750.00	**Materials:**			
4,332.50	1,200.00	Price....................	$ 4,185.60	$ 3,000.00	$ 1,185.60
2,466.50	450.00	Usage...................	(2,120.70)	—	(2,120.70)
$12,528.50	$ 2,400.00	Mix.....................	(1,080.90)	—	(1,080.90)
		Yield...................	950.60	2,000.00	(1,049.40)
		Total...............	$ 1,934.60	$ 5,000.00	$(3,065.40)
$ 523.82	$ 192.18				
960.09	248.16	**Labor:**			
1,965.67	280.96	Productivity.............	$ 1,850.00	—	$ 1,850.00
2,042.86	3,211.14	Payroll.................	(3,521.90)	$ (4,000.00)	478.10
1,447.15	(104.18)	Wage rate..............	(9,429.80)	(12,000.00)	2,570.20
353.49	(11.56)	Total...............	$(11,101.70)	$(16,000.00)	$ 4,898.30
$ 7,293.08	$ 3,816.70				
		Overhead:			
		Productivity.............	$ 2,352.10	—	$ 2,352.10
$ 1,787.44	$ 585.19	Spending...............	13,821.80	$ 10,000.00	3,821.80
4,038.46	(3.46)	Volume................	(4,822.30)	(9,000.00)	4,177.70
108.85	(11.48)	Total...............	$ 11,351.60	$ 1,000.00	$10,351.60
25,254.90	7,385.10	Total variance...	$ 2,184.50	$(10,000.00)	$12,184.50
339.00	100.50				
$31,528.65	$ 8,055.85				
$15,130.42	$(1,100.42)				
187.50	12.50				
397.95	325.80				
643.82	93.18				
479.31	218.19				
$16,839.00	$ (450.75)				
$68,189.23	$13,821.80				
$23,575.00	$ (75.00)				
1,125.00	75.00				
585.00					
$25,285.00					
$93,474.23	$13,821.80				

EXHIBIT 10

WEEKLY COST REPORT
Molded Plastics Plant
Week Ending _____, 1978

Department, Cost Center, Labor Class	Unit—Hours Absorbed	Operated	Normal	Labor Dollars Absorbed	Required	Actual	Labor Variances Productivity	Payroll	Total	Ratios Productivity	Total	Activity
Raw material storage.....	354.0	360.0	400.0	$ 1,239.00	$ 1,260.00	$ 1,381.20	$ (21.00)	$(121.20)	$(142.20)	1.017	1.115	0.885
Preparation:												
Mixing.............	392.6	400.0	400.0	1,570.40	1,600.00	1,590.10	(29.60)	9.90	(19.70)	1.019	1.013	0.982
Pellet..............	686.4	720.0	800.0	6,177.60	6,480.00	6,618.40	(302.40)	(138.40)	(440.80)	1.049	1.071	0.858
Total............				$ 7,748.00	$ 8,080.00	$ 8,208.50	$(332.00)	$(128.50)	$(460.50)	1.043	1.059	
Molding:												
Injection:												
Production.........	305.2	300.0	320.0	$ 3,204.60	$ 3,150.00	$ 3,025.00	$ 54.60	$ 125.00	$ 179.60	0.983	0.944	0.954
Complementary.....				564.62	555.00	610.50	9.62	(55.50)	(45.88)		1.081	
Blow:												
Production.........	192.8	200.0	200.0	2,814.88	2,920.00	3,110.20	(105.12)	(190.20)	(295.32)	1.037	1.105	0.964
Complementary.....				146.53	152.00	168.10	(5.47)	(16.10)	(21.57)		1.147	
Laminating:												
Production.........	86.7	80.0	160.0	1,586.61	1,464.00	1,390.40	122.61	73.60	196.21	0.923	0.876	0.542
Complementary.....				281.78	260.00	260.00	21.78	—	21.78		0.923	
Total............				$ 8,599.02	$ 8,501.00	$ 8,564.20	$ 98.02	$ (63.20)	$ 34.82	0.989	0.996	
Finishing:												
Production.........	496.4	520.0	600.0	$ 2,382.72	$ 2,496.00	$ 2,610.80	$(113.28)	$(114.80)	$(228.08)	1.048	1.096	0.827
Packing:												
Production.........	504.2	500.0	480.0	$ 2,142.85	$ 2,125.00	$ 2,310.40	$ 17.85	$(185.40)	$(167.55)	0.992	1.078	1.050
Complementary.....				428.57	425.00	410.80	3.57	14.20	17.77		0.959	
Total............				$ 2,571.42	$ 2,550.00	$ 2,721.20	$ 21.42	$(171.20)	$(149.78)	0.992	1.058	
Total plant:												
Production.........				$21,118.66	$21,495.00	$22,036.50	$(376.34)	$(541.50)	$(917.84)	1.018	1.043	
Complementary.....				1,421.50	1,392.00	1,419.40	29.50	(57.40)	(27.90)		1.020	
Total............	3,018.3	3,080.0	3,360.0	$22,540.16	$22,887.00	$23,485.90	$(346.84)	$(598.90)	$(945.74)	1.015	1.042	0.898

Material Gains (losses)

Usage.............	$(485.00)
Mix...............	182.60
Yield..............	(221.80)
Total.............	$(464.20)

Overhead Account	Spending Allowance	Actual	Spending Variance
Clerical wages..........	$ 1,142.80	$ 1,260.40	$(117.60)
Indirect labor..........	718.60	702.70	15.90
Makeup pay............	179.00	145.20	33.80
Shift premium..........	309.40	246.10	63.30
Overtime premium......	485.20	492.60	(7.40)
Expense supplies........	7,160.00	6,232.80	927.20
Repairs and maintenance..	3,165.00	3,792.30	(627.20)
Total................	$13,160.00	$12,872.10	$ 287.90

ticular month shown, the manufacturing facilities were operated at 92.5 percent of the budgeted capacity. Therefore, the variable increments for each account were adjusted to this level. To the adjusted variable elements the fixed increments were added to provide the spending allowance for each account. When compared to the actual expenses listed, the spending variance for each account is determined. Since the manager of a plant is presumed to possess an approved budget, the first four columns of figures may be omitted from the reports of manufacturing expenses. This statement is a summary of all manufacturing statements which are prepared for each of the operating and staff departments. Obviously, many of the accounts listed would not be applicable to all departments and, accordingly, departmental statements would bear fewer accounts.

Next is shown a Weekly Cost Comparison Report (Exhibit 10), which can be prepared and published weekly since most elements required for the report are available on a weekly timetable: payroll, production, repair and supply invoices, material usage and waste data. In fact, many companies which pay under an incentive plan prepare and publish productivity data on a daily schedule. Significant features pertaining to labor cost include:

1. *Unit-hours absorbed*—the number of man- or machine-hours which are required for the number of units of production turned out for the week.
2. *Unit-hours operated*—the actual man- or machine-hours worked or operated.
3. *Unit-hours normal*—the man- or machine-hours which were determined at the time the standard budgeting activity was under way.
4. *Labor dollars absorbed*—the standard labor dollar value of the production units made for the week.
5. *Labor dollars required*—the wages which should have been paid for the hours operated, had wage rates been at standard, had productivity been at the predetermined rates per hour, and had the number of workers been at standard.
6. *Labor dollars actual*—the straight-time wages paid for the week.
7. *Labor variance productivity*—the difference between labor dollars absorbed and labor dollars required. Stated another way it is the difference between absorbed unit hours and required unit hours, both at standard labor rates.

8. *Labor variance payroll*—the difference between labor dollars required and actual labor dollars. Sometimes this variance is separated into two variances, that caused by departures from standard rates of pay and that caused by departures from a standard number of workers.

A ratio-analysis approach enables performance comparisons between various expense centers through relationship to a common denominator—a base of 1.000. This approach is used in the last three columns of the Weekly Cost Report in Exhibit 10. The productivity ratio reflects the number of unit-hours which were employed to produce a standard hour's output, while the total ratio reflects the dollars of straight-time wages paid for each standard labor dollar's worth of production. The activity ratio shows the extent to which an expense center operated in balance with other expense centers and with the total plant. While overhead expense and cost details are summarized only once a month, the ratios serve to predict the productivity variance and the volume variance on overhead.

While this exhibit does not do so, the various line items (labor categories) can be broken down by the various job classifications if desired. This is often done on a temporary basis in cases where a problem requires attention and correction. The items of overhead expense and material yield factors are self-explanatory.

Timeliness. A plan of accounting may rate high in excellence from the standpoints of accuracy, completeness, and helpfulness to management; but this effectiveness can easily be destroyed by tardiness in publication of reports. While reporting timeliness is the primary responsibility of the accounting department, other departments have certain responsibilities tied to the generation of accounting data. These data include production reports, material usage reports, payroll information, order and sales statistics, purchase and vendor invoice information, and the like. While much of this information is outside the control of the accounting department, accounting can, through the application of flowcharting, PERT/critical path, and other techniques, establish timetables for the submission and processing of the needed data. Proper scheduling is of special importance if the company operates in-house computer facilities or even if a service bureau is employed. In summary, timeliness is dependent upon two elements—timetables and responsibility assignments.

EXHIBIT 11. Accounting Flow Diagram*

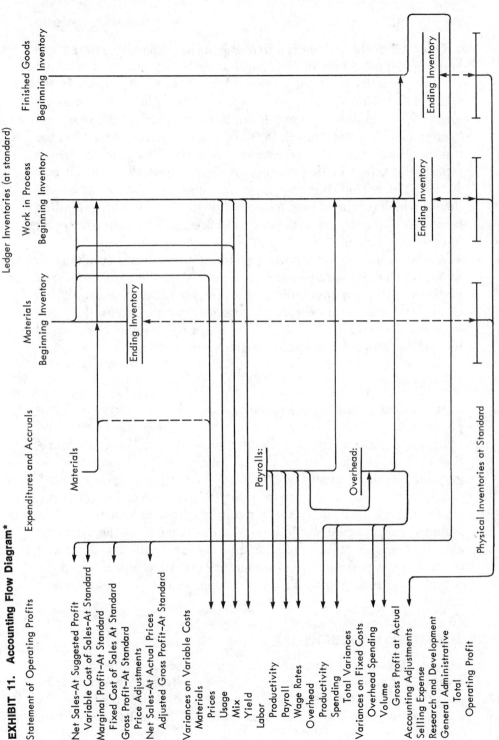

* This diagram would be accompanied by a narrative description—especially helpful to nonaccountants—which is not shown here due to space limitations.

Quite often the accounting department has difficulty gaining and keeping respect for its efforts. In most cases, ignorance of how accounting gets its job done is the culprit in such situations. If the head of a responsibility center understands what the accounting group does and how it assembles data that terminate in reports reflecting the performance of that company segment, much of the mystery disappears and cooperation improves. The procedures and reports illustrated in this chapter presume a process-standard cost system. The accounting flow diagram, shown as Exhibit 11 is one device which can be of help to a profit center head in understanding how data originate, are processed, and are carried to the statement of operating profits.

As the more detailed reports, pertaining to the lower subdivisions of an organization, are merged in various stages toward the report on the overall company, a form of "averaging" takes place and, as a result, favorable and unfavorable extremes become obscured. Therefore, these should be highlighted in narrative comments prepared by members of the accounting department.

Conclusion

In summary, business organizations today are too large, too complicated, and affected by too many external forces to be managed by a single person. The many activities which lead to the generation of a profit (or a return on the invested capital) must be organized according to a plan. Those top-management groups which delegate authority and responsibility should succeed if accountability is organized along the appropriate lines of command. The systems and procedures employed in measuring financial performance do not need to be confusing and appear mysterious. One fact persists: *every* person on the company's payroll has within grasp the potential for reducing profits or of adding to the planned financial results.

ADDITIONAL SOURCES

Anthony, Robert N. *Planning and Control Systems: A Framework for Analysis.* Boston: Harvard Business School Division of Research, 1965.

———, and Dearden, John. *Management Control Systems: Text and Cases,* chaps. 1–4, 12. 3d ed. Homewood, Ill.: Richard D. Irwin, Inc., 1976.

————, and Reece, James S. *Management Accounting Principles,* chaps. 14, 20. 3d ed. Homewood, Ill.: Richard D. Irwin, Inc., 1975.

Cammann, Cortlandt, and Nadler, David A. "Fit Control Systems to Your Managerial Style." *Harvard Business Review,* January–February 1976, p. 65.

Caplan, Edwin H. *Management Accounting and Behavioral Science.* Reading, Mass.: Addison-Wesley Publishing Co., Inc., 1971.

Dalton, Gene W., and Lawrence, Paul R. *Motivation and Control in Organizations.* Homewood, Ill.: Richard D. Irwin, Inc., 1971.

Lawrence, Paul R., and Lorsch, Jay W. *Organization and Environment.* Boston: Harvard Business School Division of Research, 1967.

Liao, Shu S. "Responsibility Centers." *Management Accounting,* July 1973, p. 46.

Lorange, Peter, and Scott Morton, Michael S. "A Framework for Management Control Systems." *Sloan Management Review,* Fall 1974, p. 41.

Shillinglaw, Gordon. *Managerial Cost Accounting,* chaps. 19, 24. 4th ed. Homewood, Ill.: Richard D. Irwin, Inc., 1977.

Vancil, Richard F. "What Kind of Management Control Do You Need?" *Harvard Business Review,* March–April 1973, p. 75.

Walker, Charles W. "Profitability and Responsibility Accounting." *Management Accounting,* December 1971, p. 23.

23

Standard Cost Control
for Manufacturing Costs

Thomas S. Dudick*

Material, direct labor, and overhead (burden), referred to by some as "engineered costs,"[1] are those costs that relate directly to the manufacturing process. When incurred during the accounting period, they are referred to as the cost of production or cost of manufacture. Exhibit 1, entitled "Production Cost Report," illustrates a report that summarizes the manufacturing costs for an entire manufacturing plant. At the time the product is sold, the terminology "cost of sales" or "cost of goods sold" is applied to the amount of cost relieved from inventory.

As with any reporting and control procedure, the focus of manufacturing cost control is the responsibility center and its manager. In manufacturing (as elsewhere), there is a hierarchy of these responsibility centers, starting with the vice president of manufacturing and extending through the plant manager, supervisor, general foreman, and foreman levels down to individual departments or work stations. Each such center is variously called a "standard cost center," an "engineered expense center," or simply a "cost center."[2]

* Mr. Dudick is Manager, Ernst & Whinney, New York.

[1] As pointed out in Chapter 4, for many manufacturing costs a clear input-output relationship exists, which can be used to determine the "right" amount of resources to input in order to achieve a given output. Because this input-output relationship is often established by industrial engineers, these costs are sometimes called "engineered costs."

[2] Some authors draw a distinction between an expense center and a cost center: the former is a responsibility center for purposes of control, while the latter is a cost identification center for accounting purposes. For example, in cost accounting there

(In addition to these "line" responsibility centers, there of course are also support departments such as tooling and production scheduling; but they tend to be discretionary expense centers, and control over their operations is discussed in the next chapter.)

General and administrative expenses, as well as marketing expenses, are sometimes referred to as "below-the-line" expenses (i.e., gross margin line). These are also often called "managed" or "discretionary expenses," because determining the "right" amount to spend is largely a matter of discretion or judgment. Although these costs are necessary for running the business, they are not directly associated with the manufacturing process; they are discussed in the next chapter.

This chapter will discuss the relative importance of the three elements of manufacturing cost in different types of businesses; it will explain various types of controls that can be used; and it will illustrate recommended report formats and procedures that can be employed.

Relative Importance of the Three Elements of Cost

The relative amount of emphasis placed on development of controls for labor, material, and overhead should be based on the magnitude of the particular element of cost. While, ideally, it would be well to fully control each of the three elements of cost—without favoring one element over the others—real-world conditions must be taken into account. Pressures of the modern business world just don't allow the ideal course of action to be pursued—the next best course is to place major emphasis on major items of cost.

To illustrate, let's consider three different companies, showing how different cost structures suggest different emphases on control:

	Company A	Company B	Company C
Material...........................	28%	59%	80%
Direct labor.......................	27	5	6
Overhead (burden)...............	45	36	14
Total manufacturing cost........	100%	100%	100%

can be an "Occupancy" cost center, which is a cost "pool" for collecting expenses such as rent, heat, and insurance; but it is not a "real" department (responsibility center).

It is obvious from the above that Company C, with 80 percent of its total manufacturing cost made up of material, warrants a good deal more emphasis in control of that element of cost than of direct labor and overhead, which, together, account for only 20 percent.

Company A's breakdown of costs indicates that there should be great emphasis given to controlling labor cost. With this high percentage of labor in the products of this company, it is evident that a good deal of labor is required in the fabrication process. If the

EXHIBIT 1

PRODUCTION COST REPORT

Plant _____   Year of _____ 19 __XX__

SUMMARY	MONTH		YEAR TO DATE	
	ACTUAL	BUDGET	ACTUAL	BUDGET
Sales Value of Production			7,987,100	
Material			3,711,540	
Direct Labor			746,823	
Total Prime Cost			4,458,363	
Indirect Labor–Prod'n. Depts.			128,560	
Indirect Labor–Service Depts.			538,607	
Labor Connected Expenses			321,289	
Non-Payroll Expenses			511,400	
TOTAL OVERHEAD			1,499,856	
TOTAL COST OF PRODUCTION			5,958,219	

OPERATING STATISTICS	% OF COST	% OF COST	% OF SALES VALUE	% OF SALES VALUE
Sales Value of Production	–		100.0	
Material	62.3		46.4	
Direct Labor	12.5		9.4	
Indirect Labor-Prod'n. Depts.	2.2		1.6	
Indirect Labor-Service Depts.	9.0		6.7	
Labor Connected Expenses	5.4		4.0	
Non-Payroll Expenses	8.6		6.4	
TOTAL COST	100.0		74.5	

COMMENTS:

EXHIBIT 1 (*continued*)

MATERIAL

Plant _____   Year of _19_ **XX**

	MONTH		YEAR TO DATE	
	ACTUAL	BUDGET	ACTUAL	BUDGET
Steel			381,269	
Purchased Fabricated Parts			731,969	
Purchased Components			2,598,302	
TOTAL MATERIAL COST			3,711,540	

DIRECT LABOR

DEPARTMENT		MONTH		YEAR TO DATE	
		ACTUAL	BUDGET	ACTUAL	BUDGET
Semi-Automatic Presses				283,151	
Automatic Presses				225,646	
Assembly and Test				238,026	
TOTAL DIRECT LABOR				746,823	

INDIRECT LABOR — PRODUCTION DEPARTMENTS

DEPARTMENT		MONTH		YEAR TO DATE	
		ACTUAL	BUDGET	ACTUAL	BUDGET
Semi-Automatic Presses				35,712	
Automatic Presses				39,965	
Assembly and Test				52,883	
TOTAL INDIRECT LABOR — PROD'N.				128,560	

EXHIBIT 1 (*continued*)

INDIRECT LABOR – SERVICE DEPARTMENTS

Plant _____   Year of 19 __XX__

DEPARTMENT		MONTH		YEAR TO DATE	
		ACTUAL	BUDGET	ACTUAL	BUDGET
General Manager's Staff				50,932	
Personnel				72,200	
Cost Accounting				39,370	
Material Control				86,679	
Engineering				45,356	
Quality Assurance				25,285	
Purchasing				27,278	
Maintenance				81,950	
Receiving and Shipping				109,557	
TOTAL INDIRECT LABOR-SV.				538,607	

LABOR CONNECTED EXPENSES

ACCOUNT NAME		MONTH		YEAR TO DATE	
		ACTUAL	BUDGET	ACTUAL	BUDGET
Overtime Premium				42,890	
Shift Premium				10,154	
Vacation Expense				27,166	
Unemployment Insurance				29,778	
Group Life Insurance				12,430	
Hospitalization				35,595	
Pension Expense				43,505	
Comp. and Liability Ins.				25,990	
Payroll Taxes				93,781	
TOTAL LABOR CONNECTED				321,289	

EXHIBIT 1 (concluded)

NON-PAYROLL EXPENSES

Plant _____   Year of ___ 19 __XX__

ACCOUNT NAME	MONTH		YEAR TO DATE	
	ACTUAL	BUDGET	ACTUAL	BUDGET
UTILITIES				
Water			4,000	
Gas			4,100	
Electricity			46,900	
Telephone			9,120	
Acetylene			275	
FACILITIES COST				
Rent			2,000	
Property Taxes			8,290	
Purchased Services			5,400	
Depreciation			195,100	
Insurance			2,817	
Fuel Oil			34,600	
SUPPLIES				
Stationery			5,900	
Postage			3,100	
Expendable Tools			20,700	
Maintenance Materials			65,700	
Lubricants and Chemicals			8,000	
Factory Supplies			4,200	
Die Maintenance and Amortization			58,648	
OFFICE EXPENSES				
Employment Expenses			4,750	
Subscriptions			500	
Dues and Memberships			500	
Computer Services			3,500	
Rental of Equipment			10,600	
Travel Expense			12,700	
TOTAL NON-PAYROLL EXPENSES			511,400	

labor is inefficient, spoiled products mean spoiled material and overhead as well.

Company B is a highly automated operation which fabricates metal parts. In this company, proper scheduling and maintenance of the equipment is the key to good cost control, since poor scheduling or machine breakdowns will mean excess labor cost because of waiting for material or for the equipment to become operable.

In this chapter we will first deal with the standard cost control of labor, and then of material. Finally, flexible budgets for control of overhead will be discussed.

CONTROL OF DIRECT LABOR

As modern industry becomes more and more competitive and automation increases, direct labor becomes smaller and smaller in relation to material and overhead. Frequently direct labor is less than 10 percent of manufacturing cost. Yet, in many such cases where labor is a minor element of cost, it receives substantially more attention than the other two elements. Standards are developed for each operation by element within the operation. Performance against actual is compared by operation, and by employee each day. Reams of paper are issued each day displaying this information to anyone who may be interested in reviewing masses of detail. When labor is one of the larger elements of cost, this detail *can* be helpful; but when material is a very substantial cost element, then the major thrust of control should be on the material.

Daily Labor Performance Report

Exhibit 2 illustrates some information extracted from a typical direct labor performance report for a machine shop.

In the company in which this report is produced, it is prepared on the computer and is distributed daily to each foreman. Although it is a daily report, it cannot be distributed until the day after the work has been completed, for obvious reasons.

A survey was made of the foremen receiving the reports to determine to what use the information shown was being put. The comments were as follows:

Comment No. 1: "There has been an improvement in timing. I used to receive the report two days late but I now receive it the following day. This is still not the answer. What good is it for me to approach an employee who was inefficient on an operation 24 hours ago? I have to catch inefficiencies on the spot. Find a way for me to monitor the efficiency of my 20 people on an hour-to-hour basis and I can do something about it, but don't ask me to review what 20 people did 24 hours after the fact."

Comment No. 2: "Yes, I use the report. It's good for my operation because the work is fairly standardized. I look the figures over to see if I have operators who are consistently inefficient. If I find some, and I frequently do, I speak to them. One time, I found an operator who was always working at about 100 percent efficiency. I checked, out of curiosity, and found he wasn't reporting his production correctly. This made me wonder if any others were doing the same. It would be almost a full-time job to find out but I have more important things to do."

Comment No. 3: "I stopped looking at these reports. Many of the standards are so out of date that the figures don't mean anything. Look at this one: How could an operator perform at 275 percent efficiency? It's obvious that something's wrong.

EXHIBIT 2

				DAILY DIRECT LABOR PERFORMANCE REPORT			
Dept.	Machine Shop				Date	July 28	
Operator	Part No.	Oper-ation	Quan-tity	Standard Hours per Piece	Actual Hours on Standard	Standard Hours Earned	% Effi-ciency
2701	516220	52	28	0.0209	2.10	0.59	
	502168	56	10	0.0714	1.40	0.71	
					3.50	1.30	37
1442	57180	31	125	0.0392	5.20	4.90	
	76140	52	23	0.0553	1.40	1.27	
	76140	58	23	0.0588	1.40	1.35	
					8.00	7.52	94
5387	619449	89	35	0.0424	3.50	1.48	
	619449	89	75	0.0424	3.50	3.18	
	619449	89	15	0.0424	1.00	0.64	
					8.00	5.30	66
3365	75185	120	38	0.1540	5.50	5.85	
	54987	190	5	0.6667	2.50	3.33	
					8.00	9.18	115
Total departmental efficiency......................... 86.8							

I'm not complaining. I know it costs money to keep revising all those standards. What I say is, let's cut out some of this kind of paperwork and save money. There must be cheaper ways of doing this job."

Comment No. 4: "No, I don't like the report. I tried to use it but found that my people were fudging production figures (even though we don't have an incentive pay plan). Here's one case right here. I know this bird doesn't achieve 95 percent efficiency. He's clever, though. If you checked back you would find that his charges to "off standard" are very high. He charges time to standard only when the job looks easy. Sure, I know I have to sign off on his timecards and make sure they're right, but I also have to get out the production or we won't have any customers."

Although several others interviewed conceded that the report was an excellent one, the general impression gained was that it was seldom referred to, because so many standards were going out of date faster than they could be revised, because the report was late, and because the mass of detail it contained could not be digested and used on a timely basis. A like survey made in another company using a similar report disclosed surprisingly similar results.

In pursuing the reporting of labor efficiency further and discussing it with the individuals interviewed, there was general agreement that corrective steps to make this daily report useful would be too expensive. One member of the group suggested:

> The accounting department uses standards for its cost system. Even if these are frozen for six months, why don't they price up production counts taken from the move tickets and give us a weekly summary showing the number produced, the standard allowed cost, and the actual direct labor cost? This would tell us on a weekly basis what the monthly variance report tells us at the end of each month. This way we'll know, week by week, how we'll stand on the monthly report, and we can take the necessary action.

In response to a question that was asked this same individual, "How can you do something about it when you don't know which operator was inefficient?" he replied:

> I know which of my operators are efficient and which are inefficient without paperwork six inches high to tell me. I also know which parts are giving me trouble and I'm constantly trying to correct

this. All I'm asking is that you cut out all this paperwork, and free up the industrial engineers so they can get out on the floor and clean up the methods. That's what industrial engineers are for—to help the factory with its problems, not create more. Is this asking too much?

Establishment of Standards and Measurement of Performance

Although the purpose of labor standards is to provide a means for monitoring labor performance to assure greater productivity, the process of establishing standards and controlling performance is not as clear-cut as might be expected. There are two reasons for this:

1. It is not always possible to standardize labor operations to the point that every operation is measurable against a standard.
2. Continual changes in methods of manufacture and interruptions in production flow, attributable to circumstances outside the control of the labor force, negate the use of standards in the affected areas.

As a result, one frequently finds that although labor performance may be 90 percent or better for those operations that are on standard, the percentage represented by "standard" work may account for only half of the total work performed. The level of efficiency for the other half—if it were measurable against standards —might well be at an efficiency as low as 20 percent. Obviously, to report performance of labor while on standard and to ignore performance when not on standard (as was done in Exhibit 1, incidentally), is misleading.

It becomes apparent that any measure made of direct labor cannot be localized within a narrow frame of reference—the big picture must be revealed. How this is done is illustrated in the example that follows.

Weekly Performance Report

The report in Exhibit 3 not only shows the performance while on standard work but it also provides information that will reflect overall performance in terms of the actual cost of direct labor per earned hour. The standard for performing a particular job is assumed to be 20 units per hour. In a week, 7,120 of these units were

EXHIBIT 3

	WEEKLY PERFORMANCE REPORT							
	Week Ending September 11							
	Performance While on Standard						Payroll Cost	
	Earned Hours	Ac- tual Hours	Effi- ciency	Indi- rect Hours	Total Actual Hours	Time on Stan- dard	Total Actual	Per Earned Hour
Standard.......	318	318	100%	144	462	69%	$1,656	$5.21
Actual..........	356	383	93	320	703	51	2,973	8.36

* Details normally shown on a supplementary report.

completed. The total earned hours were therefore 356 (7,120 divided by 20). The actual number of hours required to complete these 7,120 units was 383. The percentage efficiency was 93 percent (356 earned hours divided by 383 actual hours).

However, in addition to the 383 hours shown in Exhibit 3, an additional 320 hours were expended by the direct labor force in such tasks as material preparation, rework, and lost time because of poor material flow. When these 320 hours, which have been classified as indirect labor, are added to the 383 hours, the total "reconstituted" direct labor hours are 703. The revised efficiency percentage now becomes 51 percent (356 earned hours divided by 703). While it is helpful to the foreman to know that direct labor, while on standard, performed at 93 percent, it is more important to know that on an overall basis the efficiency was only 51 percent.

While efficiency percentages can be an important indicator of performance, they do not equate performance with dollars. Without a knowledge of the absolute dollars involved, it is entirely possible that much management time can be concentrated on improving an efficiency percentage by, say, 40 percent, which in terms of potential dollar savings might not be as significant as a 30 percent improvement in another department with a larger cost base.

An alternative to complete reliance on percentages is a combination of percent performance while on standard and total labor cost per earned hour. With total labor cost expressed in terms of cost per earned hour, the foreman can compare this cost with what the standard cost should be per earned hour, as summarized in the report shown in Exhibit 3.

Steps in Evaluating Performance. There are three basic steps to be followed in evaluating performance in this type of report. These are as follows:

1. Each succeeding week's results are compared with the standard. The standard is based on a normal-sized crew working a 40-hour week. Performance while on standard can reasonably be expected to attain 100 percent and even to exceed 100 percent with a bit of effort. The attainment of 356 earned hours was based on completion of good production amounting to this many earned hours but requiring some overtime. To attain this many earned hours required actual hours of 383, with the result that performance while on standard was 93 percent rather than an attainable 100 percent.
2. The standard shows that the labor force should have been on standard 69 percent of the time, but actual figures showed time on standard of only 51 percent. The excessive number of indirect hour charges was due to excessive rework and lost time because of delays in the flow of material. As a result, the actual payroll cost was substantially larger than it should have been.
3. To determine the trend of performance on a dollar denominator basis, the last column of the report shows the actual payroll cost per earned hour. This figure is $8.36 per earned hour as compared with a standard of $5.21. The excess cost is $3.15 per hour, which when multiplied by 356 earned hours is a total of $1,121 in excess cost for the week.

The standards that are used in developing this report and the steps enumerated above are furnished by the industrial engineering department. These can be developed through time studies, through predetermined tables or from adjusted historical data.

Use of the Data. Companies in which labor is an important element of cost should use standards and should prepare such a report at least for the major segments of the business. It is unfortunate that some companies that use standards prepare highly detailed reports listing the performance by employee for each day and for each operation without ever focusing on the larger picture that highlights trends and provides a more actionable basis for making management decisions.

A report of the type described above provides first-line supervision with a realistic tool for control in a format that highlights trends. However, no report can achieve control by itself. A report can only show performance and highlight poor areas—the foreman must take the corrective action.

CONTROL OF MATERIAL

Material is the most difficult element of manufacturing cost to account for. The reason is that actual usage, in many companies, is not known until an inventory is taken, usually at year-end. Some companies with more advanced computerized production and inventory control systems maintain perpetual inventories for all stockrooms. Such companies are able to determine the amount of inventory with a fair degree of accuracy throughout the year.

Although material accountability presents some real problems, the case for control is not hopeless. It will be found that although many items of material need to be accounted for, a small number of items will usually make up a large percentage of the total. (Determining these percentages is sometimes referred to as an "ABC analysis.") Even if a physical inventory is required in order to properly report material usage on a more frequent basis, this physical inventory need only cover the high-value items. This is the selective control technique.

Use of the Selective Control Technique

The experience of one company using the selective control technique can be used to illustrate how it works. An analysis indicated that 87 different material items were used in normal production and that 12 of these accounted for 52 percent of the value. Although a larger than 52 percent coverage would have been desirable (27 items accounted for 85 percent coverage), it was felt in the interest of economy and speed that only 12 items would be controlled at the outset. Arrangements were made with the factory to take an inventory of the 12 items each Friday shortly before the close of work. The stockroom would also furnish the financial group with figures showing the number of the items issued and returned to stock. These were furnished daily along with the number of units which were produced and accepted by the stockroom. Receipt of these figures on a daily basis permitted cursory checks to be made to detect unusually low or unusually high activity, a circumstance which resulted in the financial group's becoming more production oriented through questions which arose and which required answers by production personnel. Daily receipt of production and issue figures facilitated the accumulation of the figures during the week so the final day's production and issues needed only to be added to the prior four days' totals. As soon as the inventory information was available, each item was summarized and the material utilization percentage determined, as illustrated in Exhibit 4.

EXHIBIT 4

			WEEKLY MATERIAL UTILIZATION REPORT				
			(figures are in units)				
			Week Ending _____				
Part No.	Be-ginning Inventory	Issues to Floor	Returns	Ending In-ventory	Material Usage	Pro-duction	Utili-zation (%)
138819	98,000	18,045		26,000	90,045	82,812	92
144404	5,400	96,750		10,750	91,400	82,812	91
211362	3,500	63,500		67,000	51,891	77
223414	860	252,695	3,010	8,624	241,921	252,190	104
201134	8,000	378,510	6,000	3,080	377,430	252,170	67
199966	15,530	133,000		7,224	141,306	101,527	72
211633	14,217	33,400		26,307	21,310	19,683	92
198986	8,820	69,000	11,000		66,820	24,066	36
253007	1,550	35,650	21,130	3,000	13,070	5,689	44
244031	3,640	10,500	2,860	3,920	7,360	5,689	77
22306	2,000	8,150		1,000	9,150	5,589	61
23364	15,754	88,540	6,653	12,507	85,134	65,482	77

The beginning inventory is always the same as the preceding week's ending inventory—unless an error is found. Issues to the floor are added to the beginning inventory to determine the total amount of material available. This figure is reduced by returns to stock, which sometimes are high because they represent rejects due to poor workmanship by a preceding department. The adjusted amount is then reduced by the ending inventory to arrive at the amount of material used. This, divided into the output or production, results in a material utilization percentage.

Part 198986 in Exhibit 4 is illustrative of the use that may be put to this type of control. The beginning inventory amounts to 8,820 units; 69,000 units were issued to cover the next two weeks' production requirements. The 11,000 returns to stock represented defective parts which were returned to stock for rework. The entire amount of material available, less returns, was used in the production of 24,066 finished parts—a material utilization of only 36 percent. Investigation into this low percentage revealed that the quality of the parts which were issued from stock was generally poor (indicating poor inspection procedures).

The financial control group, as a result of this experience, began to watch for large returns to stock as a clue to repetition of this type of low utilization. To prevent similar problems in the future, rush production of parts such as 198986 was minimized by maintaining a min-max inventory in stock sufficient to take care of two or three weeks' production requirements. When issues would be made to the floor in the future, there was greater assurance that the parts would not be defective because adequate lead times were provided to all production areas within the company to eliminate rejections due to haste. Through watchfulness of the utilization figures, trends were monitored to determine what could be done to improve utilization. This report also provided a weekly analysis of inventory of the 12 dominant items. If an inventory remained too high and was untouched for four weeks in a row, questions were asked and frequently it was possible to obtain orders to reduce the inventory to tolerable limits. This eliminated later obsolescence and consequent write-offs. Incidentally, maintaining this type of report in units rather than in dollars eliminates a great deal of work in dollarizing the figures.

Inventory Taking Not Always Necessary

It is not always necessary to account for inventory changes to obtain effective material control. When the flow of the product and its components can be monitored so "unaccounted for disappearance" is not an important factor, an analysis of spoilage provides adequate control. This type of control is usually more economical than the weekly material utilization report. It is also more timely because spoilage information can be provided on an hourly basis if need be.

One of the companies whose material cost control procedures were studied prepared a daily spoilage report which showed the number of each unit rejected (except for minor items). If the defect could be reworked the spoilage quantity was adjusted and the rework cost noted. This report was issued each morning for the preceding day, with a short statement explaining major causes of an unusually high spoilage rate.

The information appearing on the daily report is summarized on a weekly basis by type of unit and the defect causing the rejection. Dollar values are then assigned and a listing is made in order of dollar magnitude of spoilage, with the highest cost items appearing at the top of the list. A specimen copy of this weekly report is shown in Exhibit 5. The part number rejected is shown as well as

EXHIBIT 5

| | | WEEKLY SPOILAGE REPORT
(dollar value of rejects)
Week Ending _____ | | | |
| | | Week's | | | |
Part No.	Used on Product No.	Scheduled Production	No. of Rejects	Type of Defect	Total Cost
603	78396	300	19	116	$ 625.38
301	69842	150	9	43	531.52
673	39461	75	8	52	503.61
498	21312	890	150	14	342.16
306	14398	250	14	16	221.03
403	31982	600	32	6	114.32
106	21699	300	25	55	98.14
198	4443	250	8	62	41.10
					$2,477.26
		This week's annualized total...............			$123,863.00
		Prior week's annualized total...............			114,132.75

the final product in which the part appears. The week's scheduled production is shown in order that a relationship might be made as to the magnitude of rejects. While a "Percent Rejects to Week's Scheduled Production" might be useful for this purpose, it was decided that every additional column adds to the cost of the report and to the preparation time. The next-to-last column shows the reject code, while the last column shows the dollar cost of the rejects. The total week's rejects of $2,477.26 is annualized (assuming 50 working weeks per year) to emphasize the magnitude of spoilage over a year's time. The prior week's annualized total is also shown for comparative purposes.

The report is closed out at the close of business on Tuesday and issued Wednesday morning. In a weekly meeting held on Wednesday shortly after distribution of the report, the quality assurance group and production foremen discuss the causes of spoilage and suggest remedies. Primary emphasis would be placed on the first three items which (in dollar terms) account for 67 percent of the rejects. If time permits, the fourth item, which accounts for another 14 percent, would be discussed. When appropriate, other parties such as the purchasing agent or material control supervisor might be called in on a discussion dealing with defects due to rough handling of parts or improper storage. Actual participation by these individuals has a more salutary effect than a telephoned complaint delivered in haste and received in haste—oftentimes accompanied by emotional reactions. The purpose of the midweek meeting is to permit action to be taken in the same week as the decisions and

EXHIBIT 6

WEEKLY SPOILAGE REPORT (units scrapped) Week Ending _____					
Assembly Operations	No. of Starts	Good Units	% Good to Starts	Cumulative % Good	Rejects
A. 1....................	100	99	99.0	99.0	1
2....................	99	98	99.0	98.0	1
3....................	98	95	96.9	95.0	3
4....................	95	75	78.9	75.0	20
5....................	75	65	86.7	65.0	10
B. 1....................	145	145	100.0	100.0	—
2....................	140	134	95.7	95.7	6
3....................	42	41	97.6	93.4	1
4....................	41	36	87.8	82.0	5

recommendations are made. The results are carefully reviewed in the following week's meeting to determine if the problems have been corrected.

Another company that assembles components which, once assembled cannot be taken apart for repair, summarizes weekly spoilage in units on a cumulative basis. The figures correspond with the sequence of operations and are illustrated in part A of Exhibit 6. At Assembly Operation 1, 100 units were started but one was rejected with the result showing 99.0 percent good. Operation 2 shows 99 starts with one rejected. Operation 3, with 98 starts (because two had already been rejected), resulted in three rejects or

96.9 percent good units. Operations 4 and 5 follow the same procedures.

The cumulative "Percent Good" shows the cumulative effect of losses all along the line. While in part A this figure is readily apparent from looking at the column headed good units and relating this to 100 starts at Operation 1, it is not always possible in actual practice to determine this figure in this manner. The reason is that all units started in each operation are not always completely processed and forwarded to the next operation in the same week. The illustration in part B would be more typical. In this example, the cumulative percentage good would be calculated as follows:

100.0 percent in Operation 1 multiplied by 95.7 percent in
Operation 2 = 95.7 percent
95.7 percent in Operation 2 multiplied by 97.6 percent in
Operation 3 = 93.4 percent
93.4 percent in Operation 3 multiplied by 87.8 percent in
Operation 4 = 82.0 percent

The significance of the cumulative percentage of rejects is that it highlights the total impact of accumulated spoilage. It appraises the overall effect of the rejects rather than looking at only a segment at a time. Referring back to part A of Exhibit 6, it should be little consolation to management to see that Operations 1, 2, and 3 are running better than 90 percent when only 65 percent of all units started are still good by the end of assembly operations.

This type of control highlights such losses without requiring time-consuming cost calculations. While application of costs to the units would better equate for relative values, it is questionable that the additional information obtained would justify the cost and possible delay in issuance of the conventional type report.

Material Control in Machine-Paced Operations

When a manufacturing process is paced by automatic equipment, and machine-hours rather than direct labor becomes the index of productivity, material control can be simplified by tying in productivity with the running time of the machines. Illustrative of this are the comparative weights of finished product per machine-hour, as shown in Exhibit 7. The part is a high-volume item which requires several punch presses. The weight of the finished parts is divided by the aggregate of the machine-hours of all the presses running a like part to arrive at "pounds of finished production per machine-hour."

This report covers a relatively inexpensive part made of steel. A part made of bronze or copper would show the pounds of production per machine-hour for each individual press running that part so that excess material usage caused by a particular press with a defective die or other defect would be quickly highlighted. While this type of report is not scientific by any means, it is basic in its simplicity, and an economical report for those companies producing certain types of products of relatively low unit value.

In a plastics operation, on the other hand, when the product is represented by such disparate items as trays, containers, cabinets,

EXHIBIT 7

PRODUCTION PER MACHINE-HOUR		
Part No. _____	Department _____	
Week Ending	*Number of Machine-Hours*	*Pounds of Finished Production per Machine-Hour*
2/7...............................	250	13.02
2/14..............................	310	13.40
2/21..............................	249	12.55
2/28..............................	361	12.70
3/7...............................	279	12.52
3/14..............................	214	10.22
Standard..........................	285	13.20

and other formed parts, the greater value and bulk warrant use of a more sophisticated type of reporting. In addition to the greater unit cost and bulk, output may not be as closely correlated with machine hours, particularly when an operator stops and starts the press each time it completes the cycle in order to remove the finished product. This is not true in all cases because many small plastic items are frequently formed on fully automatic presses.

To obtain more sophisticated material control, a simplified report is demonstrated in Exhibit 8. The total theoretical production of 14,761,094 shown under "rotary" indicates the number of units which should have been produced with a running time of 7,343 hours. The actual production of 13,705,000 is divided by the

EXHIBIT 8

| | | | | | Powder | | |
| | | | | | Consumption | | |

Press Type	Hours Running Time	Total Net Production	Total Theoretical Production	% Effi- ciency	Actual Pounds Powder Used	Theoretical Pounds Powder Used	% Utili- zation
Rotary.........	7,343	13,705,000	14,761,094	93	221,690	203,891	92
741 Stokes......	5,585	4,421,683	4,695,061	94	82,900	73,795	89
800 Stokes......	3,392	845,455	951,848	89	11,040	7,445	67
200 Stokes......	1,492	801,347	808,097	99	3,410	2,223	65

MATERIAL UTILIZATION REPORT
Plastic Molding

theoretical production to show the percentage efficiency of 93 percent. The theoretical amount of powder which should have been
consumed to make 13,705,000 units is shown to be 203,891 pounds.
Since 221,690 pounds were actually used, the percentage utilization
is 92 percent. Obtaining figures on actual usage of material might
entail taking into consideration changes in floor inventories, unless
records are kept on the actual amount of powder put into the press
hoppers. (If the material is brought into the presses automatically
from silos, then a different approach must be taken to account for
actual usage of material.)

The methods of control for material (as well as labor) must be
adapted to suit the needs of the specific company. No one method
can be applied universally to all companies or even to companies
within a specific industry. The methods that have been demonstrated in this chapter are only a few of the many different ones
that are available for use. Which one applies in a particular situation must be determined through good business judgment.

CONTROL OF MANUFACTURING OVERHEAD:
FLEXIBLE BUDGETS

Ideally, the overhead budget, like the material and direct labor
budget, would start with a forecast of sales. From this a production
budget would be prepared. The production budget would differ
from the sales forecast depending upon how much and what types
of products are already in inventory and what changes might be
planned in the inventory level. In some companies, sales forecasts

are not a sufficiently reliable basis on which to make production forecasts. For this reason an alternative approach is needed. This approach should recognize that the company is in business to sell certain services rather than specific products at precisely forecasted quantities.

When budgeting is based on the sale of services, you must recognize that you are selling such commodities as labor and machine time. Budgets would be developed for such types of services as assembly, plating, metal stamping, molding, milling, and drilling. For each of these, a range of activity and a range of expenses would be determined within a normal range of activity. Then, for a particular level of activity, the applicable level of expense would be determined. Should the activity change, the amount of budgeted expense would be correspondingly adjusted. This is known as flexible budgeting. Availability of a flexible budget permits the company to establish guidelines as to what its costs should be at various levels of activity. Should the level change, the budget formula allows for adjustments to the actual level. How this works will be discussed next.

The Flexible Budget

The flexible budget is not only a budgeting tool—it is used for determining the marginal contribution that various products make to profits as well as providing the mechanics for determining the break-even point of business. We will initially discuss the flexible budgeting technique as it applies to any cost category (including total manufacturing costs), and then will discuss the application to overhead control specifically. Let's first deal with the separation of fixed (nonvariable) and variable costs.

Separating Fixed (nonvariable) and Variable Costs. The classic method, usually given "top billing" in textbooks, is the *scatter diagram.* The principle followed in this method is to determine from historical data the relationship of expense to volume by plotting 12 to 15 months' data on graph paper. The vertical axis is used to represent the amount of expense while the horizontal axis represents the level of activity. Each month's expense is plotted with reference to both scales. Theoretically, the points representing the expenses should show a linear pattern—sloping from zero (if the expense is completely variable) to some value representing the amount of expense at the highest volume level that had been experienced during the period plotted. If the expense contains an element of fixed cost, the line will intersect the vertical axis above the zero point—that point representing the fixed costs. The slope of the line will show the variable portion of the expense. (See Chapter 5 for further details.)

In theory, the scatter diagram is a sound method for segregating the fixed and variable costs. However, in the real world of business, costs don't behave with quite the amount of precision that is required to make this method effective. Most businesses are subject to fluctuating levels of activity. When a factory, for example, is preparing for an increase in volume, certain departments such as production scheduling, inventory control, purchasing, industrial engineering, and personnel are working at high volume—while factory activity is still low.

The production control group will be busy analyzing the schedules and the stockroom personnel will be checking inventories to determine what items must be ordered. The purchasing department will be soliciting quotations from suppliers and placing orders. Some eight to ten (or more) weeks later, when the material has been received, the receiving personnel and stockroom employees will be busy storing the new material and preparing kits for issuance to the production lines.

Likewise, the personnel department will be recalling employees from layoff while the industrial engineers will be laying out and balancing the production lines.

All of the aforementioned departments will be operating at a high level of activity and incurring overtime while factory activity is relatively low. When everything has been readied and the volume of production rises, the service departments taper off in their activity.

As a result of this counteraction between the indirect and direct activities, the scatter diagram can become a hodgepodge of points that tell a very confusing story.

Those who are mathematically inclined will propose the *least squares formula* as the solution when the scatter diagram is difficult to use. When the basic data defy analysis through simple scatter diagraming, it is not likely to show any clearer results when the points are fitted to a complex formula. In fact, the data may be even further distorted because of the tendency of the least squares formula to unduly weight extreme items.

With the advent of the computer, there are many who look to the magic of electronic technology to work out a mathematical model that will provide the breakout of fixed and variable costs. The *computer* approach has all the disadvantages of the scatter diagram because it uses the same data. In addition, it would use techniques very similar to the least squares formula. The computer does not, at this time, provide the answer.

If a mathematical approach is to be followed, then the *low-high method* is superior to the three approaches thus far discussed. Under this procedure a certain amount of judgment is used in selecting two estimates of volume and expense within the normal range of activity. The use of this approach is demonstrated below in four steps:

Step 1. Assume that you drive your car within a range of 1,000 and 2,000 miles per month.

Step 2. When you drive 1,000 miles per month, assume that your monthly cost is $165. At a level of 2,000 miles per month let us suppose that this cost increases to $230.

Step 3. Putting the first two steps together, we arrive at the formula for ascertaining the variable cost per mile:

	Low	High	Difference
Miles per month.........................	1,000	2,000	1,000
Cost per month.........................	$165	$230	$65

The variable cost is determined by dividing the variation in mileage into the variation in cost: $65 divided by 1,000 miles. This gives us a variable cost of $0.065 per mile. The variable cost for the two levels, then, is:

Low	High
$65	$130

Step 4. The next step in arriving at the budget formula is the determination of the fixed cost per month. This is done by subtracting the variable costs shown in Step 3 from total costs in Step 2:

	Low	High
Total cost—Step 2................	$165	$230
Less variable cost in Step 3.......	65	130
Fixed cost.......................	$100	$100

Using the Budget Formula to Budget Overhead Costs at Various Levels. Continuing with our example of the automobile, let us now budget cost for the operation of our car for several levels between 1,000 and 2,000 miles per month:

Number of Miles	Fixed Cost per Month	Variable Cost at $0.065 per Mile	Total Budget
1,000..................	$100	$ 65	$165
1,200..................	100	78	178
1,400..................	100	91	191
1,600..................	100	104	204
1,800..................	100	117	217
2,000..................	100	130	230

A characteristic deficiency of all the methods discussed thus far is that the fixed cost is determined in a "lump"—department heads given overhead budget formulas for their departments would be somewhat confused if they were told that their fixed overhead expenses were "so many dollars per month" without knowing what was contained in this total. The next method, called the step method, overcomes this deficiency.

Under the *step method,* an overhead budget would be determined for each expense for various capacity levels—ranging, say, from 60 percent to 100 percent in increments of 5 percent. When activity in a particular month approaches one of these levels, the total budget for that capacity level is used. This method is quite sophisticated and requires that capacity levels be measurable. Measurability is not always possible when there is a multiplicity of diverse operations. Businesses considering the use of the step method should first assure themselves that they have fairly well standardized manufacturing processes and acceptable denominators for measuring activity levels. (See Chapter 11 for further discussion of volume measures.)

The method preferred by the writer might be called the *par-*

ticipatory approach. It consists of the identification of specific items of overhead cost as to their fixed and variable characteristics. This identification and classification process is accomplished with the direct participation of the department head responsible for controlling the overhead cost. Since indirect labor, with fringe benefits, accounts for probably 70 percent to 85 percent of all overhead, this item warrants use of an approach that is more analytical then graphs or mathematical formulas. If, therefore, a job-by-job analysis is made in determining the fixed and variable characteristics of each position, the semivariable factor can be ignored since it will automatically disappear. Once the indirect labor is disposed of, several major cost items can be classified with relative ease. These include depreciation and occupancy costs, which are fixed, and maintenance of equipment, which is generally considered variable with the use of the equipment.

The foregoing expenses usually account for as much as 85 percent to 90 percent of total overhead expense. The remaining 10 percent to 15 percent, which can be made up of from 30 to 50 items, can be dealt with on a fairly arbitrary basis—with little loss in overall accuracy, but with a saving of valuable time.

This method of separating fixed and variable costs has the advantage that it requires the involvement of department managers. By becoming involved, they will be more interested in controlling their costs because they will understand how the costs were budgeted, having been a party to the determination of the budget formula. Departmental budgets will then be more meaningful to them.

The Departmental Overhead Budget

Exhibit 9 illustrates how an overhead budget would be presented for a department. Although it was originally anticipated that the department would operate at a volume of 50,000 standard productive direct labor hours, the actual production level turned out to be 55,000 standard productive hours. This, then, became the level for which variable overhead expenditures were budgeted. Supplies, for which the variable allowance is 30.18 cents per standard productive hour, is shown as $16,600 (55,000 standard productive hours times 30.18 cents), compared with an actual expenditure of $16,010. Supervision is budgeted at $10,710 irrespective of whether the volume level is 50,000 or 55,000 hours because this is a fixed cost (within any anticipated range of volume).

Note that although this is an overhead report, information on direct labor is also included. This is often done to aid in the analysis of the report; for example, some overhead variances may be related to direct labor variances. (Of course, more detailed reports on labor —and materials—would be prepared, as discussed earlier in this chapter.)

EXHIBIT 9

DEPARTMENTAL OVERHEAD BUDGET

Month_____ Department_____

Activity Level—Standard Direct Labor Hours
Planned—50,000
Actual—55,000

| | Budget Formula | Current Month | | | Year-to-Date Variance |
		Allowed Budget*	Actual	Variance	
Direct labor dollars.... $	5.50 per hr.	$302,500	$303,100	$ (600)	$(1,760)
Fixed overhead:					
Supervision.........	2,677.50 per wk.	10,710	10,710	—	—
Variable overhead:					
Other indirect labor.............	$0.5573 per hr.	30,650	31,800	(1,150)	(5,070)
Tools and gauges...	0.4473 per hr.	24,600	24,650	(50)	120
Supplies............	0.3018 per hr.	16,600	16,010	590	(3,540)
Electricity..........	0.1333 per hr.	7,330	7,190	140	380
Total overhead..		$ 89,890	$ 90,360	$ (470)	$(8,110)
Total direct labor and overhead......		$392,390	$393,460	$(1,070)	$(9,870)

* Based on *actual* activity level. The variances therefore do not have a volume component. They are "spending" variances. (See Chapter 32.)

The variance column is the focal point for the department head to compare actual costs with budget. The unfavorable direct labor variance of $600 could have resulted from untrained help whose performance fell below standard. It might also have resulted from improper scheduling of production which caused production delays with the consequent downtime. The indirect labor variance could have been caused by a greater number of short runs than was anticipated. With this type of knowledge, the department head might, in the future, schedule longer runs to avoid this situation.

The year-to-date variance figures provide a perspective for department heads in determining whether they are improving or incurring greater variances. Whatever the cause, the department head must investigate the reason for the variance and take corrective action. The budget allowance, which is adjustable with volume, provides the tool for alerting the manager as to where corrective action is needed.

An advantage of the flexible budget for *control* purposes is that it reflects realistically the behavior of overhead costs, whereas absorption accounting does not. (This is because overhead rates used to absorb overhead into products treat fixed overhead as though it were variable.) With a focus on what costs should have been for the *actual* level of operations, factory management is not confused and/or frustrated by uncontrollable volume variances. Both superior and subordinate can focus on controllable overhead spending variances, without being distracted by reported variances reflecting the under- or overabsorption of budgeted fixed overhead costs. (Overhead volume variance is discussed in Chapter 32.)[3]

It should also be mentioned that although Exhibit 9 relates to manufacturing costs, the same principle can be applied to nonmanufacturing costs, provided that one is comfortable in assuming that certain costs *should* increase as volume increases.[4] For example, certain activities in staff offices such as personnel or accounting can legitimately be budgeted on a flexible budget basis.

Savings Resulting from Review of the Flexible Budget

It is sometimes not realized that development of a flexible overhead budget may provide some before-the-fact cost-savings insights, as well as providing useful after-the-fact reporting. For example, the general manager of manufacturing of one company, in reviewing the staffing of each department, as shown in the development of the budget formula, noted that there were some 11 sweepers in

---

[3] Of course, if top management feels plant management *is* responsible for volume fluctuations—for example, if the 10 percent volume increase shown in Exhibit 9 resulted from factory quality control efforts and responsiveness to customer delivery requests, rather than being attributable to more aggressive marketing efforts, then a case can be made for including the overhead volume variance in factory overhead reports.

[4] This is *not* the case, for example, with advertising expenses. Although management may *permit* more advertising as sales increase, there is no reason this cost *should* increase with sales—in fact, perhaps it should increase as sales fall.

two adjacent departments. As a result of this observation, an automatic sweeper was purchased and 9 of the 11 sweepers were eliminated.

The manufacturing vice president of another company, who was accustomed to seeing only total salary and wage information, without an individual job staffing breakdown, noted in his flexible budget that he had seven elevator operators. "Why," he asked himself, "in this day and age of automation, are we operating elevators manually?" As a result of this observation, automatic elevators were installed—with a payback within three years.

The manufacturing vice president of another company, who also had previously seen only total wage and salary figures by department, noted in his flexible budget report that five maintenance craftsmen were assigned to a three-year project to overhaul equipment at a total cost of $165,000. Although this executive had been party to the arrangement to undertake the project, his new overview prompted the question as to the desirability of replacing the equipment rather than rebuilding it. He now raised the question as to the cost of new equipment and found that it would be $225,000— $60,000 more than the cost of rebuilding. However, because of the automatic features of the new machinery, direct labor costs would be reduced by $40,000 annually. On the basis of these facts, which were sparked because of availability of a job-by-job analysis in the budget, the overhaul program was discontinued.

Preparing a budget logically and evaluating its contents in proper perspective can produce cost savings equal to, if not greater than, any of the savings achieved through comparing the actual costs against the budget.

Cost control techniques, then, should have for their purpose not merely the after-the-fact measurements—they should be designed to provide the professional manager of a business with the kind of overview of the operations and the breakdown of cost elements in such fashion that he or she can make sound decisions that will result in more profitable operations.

ADDITIONAL SOURCES

Amante, Joseph R., and Graham, Robert L. "Flexible Budgeting: A Defense Industry Approach." *Management Accounting*, February 1974, p. 37.

Anthony, Robert N., and Dearden, John. *Management Control Systems: Text and Cases,* chap. 5. 3rd ed. Homewood, Ill.: Richard D. Irwin, Inc., 1976.

Craig, Charles E., and Harris, R. Clark. "Total Productivity Measurement at the Firm Level." *Sloan Management Review,* Spring 1973, p. 13.

DeWelt, Robert L. "Labor Measurement and Control." *Management Accounting,* October 1976, p. 26.

Dudick, Thomas S. *Cost Controls for Industry.* 2d ed. Englewood Cliffs, N.J.: Prentice-Hall, Inc., 1976.

————, ed. *How to Improve Profitability through More Effective Planning.* New York: Wiley-Interscience, Inc., 1975.

————. *Profile for Profitability.* New York: Wiley-Interscience, Inc., 1972.

Friedman, Lawrence. "A Variable Budgeting System for Consumer Advertising." *Sloan Management Review,* Winter 1971, p. 77.

Horngren, Charles T. *Cost Accounting: A Managerial Emphasis,* chaps. 7, 8. 4th ed. Englewood Cliffs, N.J.: Prentice-Hall, Inc., 1977.

Liao, Shu S. "Three-Step Analysis Measures Productivity." *Management Accounting,* August 1975, p. 25.

Mullis, Elbert N. "Variable Budgeting for Financial Planning and Control." *Management Accounting,* February 1975, p. 43.

Piper, Roswell M. "Engineering Standards and Standard Costs." *Management Accounting,* September 1976, p. 44.

Shillinglaw, Gordon. *Managerial Cost Accounting,* chaps. 7, 20. 4th ed. Homewood, Ill.: Richard D. Irwin, Inc., 1977.

Sprigg, William T.; Hanson, Alan; and Steffens, Larry. "Controlling and Tracking Unit Costs." *Management Accounting,* November 1976, p. 47.

24

Discretionary Expense Centers and Zero-Base Budgeting

Peter A. Pyhrr*

PROBLEMS IN CONTROLLING DISCRETIONARY EXPENSES

The control of discretionary expense centers is one of the thornier problems which management faces. As has been pointed out earlier (Chapter 22), discretionary expense centers are those for which the expenses are not directly related to the production of physical goods. In a manufacturing environment, this would include such functions as production planning, maintenance, quality control, research and development, legal services, accounting—in short, any function whose costs are not in large part "engineered." In a service environment, almost all expenses are discretionary: thus budgeting and controlling these expenses is largely a matter of judgment. Given the growth of the service sector, both inside and outside of manufacturing, functions whose expenses are primarily discretionary are becoming more and more important.

Measuring Output

One of the most important features distinguishing a discretionary from an engineered expense center is the difficulty of measuring output of discretionary activities. While it is fairly simple to express the results of direct labor, raw materials, and other direct

---

* Mr. Pyhrr is President of Pyhrr Associates, Inc., Middletown, New Jersey.

factory costs in terms of number of units produced or dollar value of production, the same does not usually hold true for the results of discretionary expenses. How much, for example, do the accounting department or the new sophisticated computer contribute to corporate profits? Or more difficult yet, how much does the federal government contribute to secondary education, crime control, or national defense? These examples illustrate one of the most important aspects of discretionary expense activities: *it is almost impossible to put a dollar value on their outputs.* Indeed, in many cases it is difficult even to define in operational terms what their outputs are! What, for example, are the outputs of the Federal Communications Commission or of a corporation's legal department?

Even if the outputs of a discretionary expense center could be defined, there remains a major difference between discretionary and engineered expenses. In the case of the latter, a given amount of raw materials, direct labor, machine processing, and so forth (i.e., inputs) will result in one unit of production (output). The input-output relationship is very clear: one pound of steel, properly processed, makes one one-pound widget. There is no difficulty determining what became of the input—it is a physical part of the output. But how does the salary of another accountant affect the outputs of the accounting department? How does another hundred million dollars of antipoverty money from the government affect poverty?

In the case of many discretionary expenses, one cannot even look at the inputs and say which *direction* of cost change represents an improvement. Generally speaking, if more steel is sent through a factory, more widgets come out the other end. But if more money is spent on the legal department, does that mean that the firm will be sued less? If more money is spent on the general staff, will the nation have a better national defense? What happens if funding for research and development goes down 10 percent? In all of these cases, given that the amount spent (the input) goes up or down, one can say very little about how—if at all—the output will change.

Budget Comparisons

This leads to yet another problem. In a purely manufacturing environment, it makes sense to evaluate a manager on the basis of actual versus budgeted costs (inputs). If the budget for production of a million widgets is $3 million and a manager has produced a million widgets for $2.8 million, he or she has obviously done a good job if the widgets are up to specs. But if a manager were told to spend $3 million on research and development and came back a year later having spent only $2.8 million, one would be hard put to say whether or not the manager had done a good job. The distinction is that the first manager produced something tangible; there should be no question as to whether or not 1 million acceptable widgets were actually produced. But given the very tenuous connection between dollars going into the research and development pipeline and the value coming out, it is impossible to say whether the second manager "produced" the right amount of R&D. Obviously, if one does not know how costs affect output, it is not possible to measure outputs by measuring costs!

The research and development example in the previous paragraph illustrates yet another of the many problems in the administration of discretionary expense centers. Even if one assumes that the output of research and development can be measured (a rather tenuous assumption), and also that increasing the amount spent on R&D will produce more output, there remains the problem of *time lag*. Money spent today is not likely to produce results for several years. Managers, however, are usually evaluated on their performance for *this* year. Indeed, in many cases managers who spend (or authorize) the money for R&D will not be in their present position when the results come in. Thus, what one manager sows, another shall reap; this makes evaluation even more troublesome.

Managerial Evaluation

The discussion so far has focused on problems which arise from the fuzziness of output measures and from the inconvenient lack of a direct link between resources input and results output in many discretionary expense centers. As if these problems were not sufficient, there is yet another set of problems which discretionary expenses and discretionary expense centers pose to top management. These problems relate not so much to the nature of the functions themselves as to the skills, time, and orientation of the managers who must evaluate them.

It is very unlikely that the manager of several discretionary expense centers, for example, a vice president of administrative services, will be expert in all of the functions which report to him or her. This person may, for example, be unable to delve deeply into the data processing function without being drowned in EDP jargon and buzzwords. Professionals who deal with a technical specialty on a daily basis will always (one hopes!) be more on top of the field than the manager who spends only a small amount of time (if that) with technical concerns. This is true even if the manager in question is one whose early training and experience were in that particular field, let alone one who has never been exposed to it on more than a cursory level. What this means is that the manager cannot rely on his or her own understanding of each of the technical functions which he or she supervises when evaluating the performance of these functions. Even if the manager were technically competent in every discipline supervised, this person would probably not have the *time* to delve deeply into the operations of each function. This would be especially true for those managers who have a large number of functions reporting to them—vice presidents in charge of administration, for example. For reasons both of time and of skill, then, a manager is not likely to be able to control discretionary expense centers by means of detailed knowledge of their day-to-day operations.

There is also a more subtle reason why intuitive evaluation and control by top management is not likely to work. Top management's views of the adequacy of service functions may well be somewhat biased. A department which makes lower level users wait weeks or even months for its services may well give a vice president overnight service—especially if that particular vice president evaluates the adequacy of the department's output! This sort of red-carpet treatment may lead higher management into believing that discretionary expense centers are providing much better service than is actually the case.

Elements of Good Management Control

Now that we have examined some of the problems which may arise in administering (or attempting to administer) discretionary expense centers, let us look at some of the things which can be done to solve these problems. There are a number of elements which are important in a good management control system for the sorts of expense centers about which we have been talking. Some of these elements are (1) the selection of good managers to head up the discretionary expense centers; (2) maintaining the proper organizational climate; (3) looking for elements of engineered costs; and (4) looking beyond the costs to the policies and procedures which underlie them. It is also important to remember that performance, not just costs, has to be controlled in most cases. Below we shall examine some of these elements in more detail.

Good Managers. The first and most important element of a good management control system for discretionary expense centers is to have good managers heading up the expense centers. These managers should be capable both technically and administratively. Technical competence is necessary, since the head of each expense center is going to have to know what is going on in his or her department in order to control either performance or cost—let alone managing both so as to get "the most bang for the buck" (or cost effectiveness, for a more elegant term). The same reasons require that the manager should be a good administrator; the best technical competence in the world is useless if it is not channeled into activity which will achieve organizational goals. Unfortunately, the identification, training, and assignment of capable people is easier said than done; and there do not seem to be any simple (or even complex) rules to follow.

Organizational Climate. The second important element in a good system for the control of discretionary expense centers is a good organizational climate. A good climate does not necessarily mean that all coworkers are great friends or that all of them whistle while they work, but rather that the importance of the job to be done is recognized, and that people feel that costs matter. Good control of costs will be almost impossible if most employees (including management) feel that costs don't much matter, since the money doesn't really "belong" to anyone. As a sidenote, if the organizational system confers prestige according to how much money a department spends, the control of costs is not likely to be very successful. Again, all of this is easy to talk about and difficult to do; about the only thing which can be said on how to do it is that the climate must start at the top. The reason for this is fairly obvious: if top management is not concerned about costs, the level below them will not bother about costs either, and soon enough this attitude will spread through the entire organization.

Finding Engineered Costs. Another element in a good control system, this time easier to carry out, is attempting to find engineered costs within discretionary expense centers. For example, data processing may not be made up primarily of engineered expenses, but keypunching is not much different than manufacturing widgets. Similarly, although accounting is not an engineered expense center, much of the routine clerical work which is contained within it can be made into engineered costs. The trick here is to look for routine tasks which have easily identifiable inputs and outputs, and where the inputs determine (in large part at least) the outputs. Most discretionary expense centers contain at least some of these tasks; identifying them as engineered rather than discretionary allows management to get a firm grip on at least *that* portion of the total costs.

Task Review. We have seen that the costs and other inputs which go into a discretionary expense center do not necessarily have any direct relationship with the outputs which come out of those centers. One possible solution to the problem of controlling these costs then is to look not at the costs, but at what tasks are being performed. The activities of the expense center under consideration can be broken up to show just what each one accomplishes, and how much it costs. Ideally, then management could select from a smorgasbord of activities which it would like done, and fund just these. The methodology to perform this task evaluation, as well as addressing the broader questions of objectives, benefits and outputs, efficiency and effectiveness, and priorities, is a technique known as *zero-base budgeting*. Most of the rest of this chapter will be devoted to elaborating on this technique.

Control at Budget Time. One additional aspect of control should be mentioned before going into details of zero-base budgeting. Whatever budgeting system is used, zero based or incremental, the time to control discretionary costs is at *budget* time. Once the budget for the year has been set, the main function of management is not to make sure that the budget is being rigidly adhered to, but that the tasks which were to be accomplished are in fact being accomplished. It bears repeating that with discretionary expenses, the fact that actual cost equals budgeted cost does *not* necessarily mean that a good job has been done. Budgets for this sort of task represent an *allowance,* not a goal.

ZERO-BASE BUDGETING

The planning and budgeting process is the method that top management uses to allocate its internal resources; it provides the framework for management control during the operating year. The adequacy of the budgeting process will in large part determine management's ability to control operations effectively. Unfortunately, traditional budgeting systems tend to: be number oriented, rather than decision oriented; be cumbersome, rather than flexible; identify total dollars requested, rather than identifying spending priorities; and start with the current level of operation as an established base, rather than reevaluating all programs. Traditional budgeting systems provide a poor basis for control—especially for controlling changing situations which may quickly outmode the original budget.

The remainder of this chapter will review traditional budget techniques and problems, propose and describe a new budget technique called "zero-base budgeting," and then discuss the use of expense budgets for management control, all with particular emphasis on discretionary (nonengineered) costs. Throughout I use the term "budgeting" to be synonymous with the term "short-term planning." Budgeting refers to the one-year budget established by most companies, as opposed to long-term planning, which usually covers a three- to five-year period.

The Budgeting Process

The basic purpose of any budgeting process is to effectively allocate limited resources. To effectively budget, we must determine simultaneously the answers to two questions:

1. Where and how can we most effectively spend our money?
2. How much money should we spend?

We can always increase expenditures at the expense of profits, or decrease expenditures at some operating penalty.

To answer these questions, most corporations use current operating and expenditure levels as an established base. They then analyze only those desired increases (or occasionally decreases) from this established base, looking at only a small fraction of the total budget dollars. For the most part, these corporations do not ask:

Are the base activities efficient and effective?

What alternatives do we have?

Should current activities be eliminated or reduced in order to fund higher priority new programs or to improve profits?

One of the basic requirements of an effective budgeting process is to identify "actionable" or discretionary costs to top management. The budgeting process should provide this focus on discretionary costs so that management can concentrate its time on decision making that will impact profits and profitability.

Exhibit 1 illustrates the scope of management activities in in-

EXHIBIT 1
Scope of Management Activities

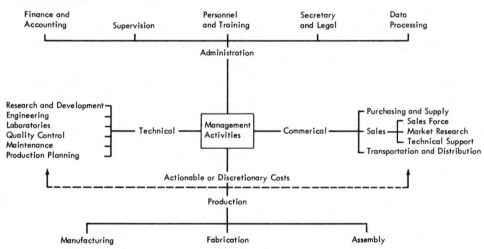

dustry. Administrative, technical, and most commercial portions of the budget (some transportation and distribution costs may be part of the standard cost system) are actionable or discretionary costs. Capital expenditures are also actionable costs. Direct labor, direct material, and some direct overhead associated with production operations are not truly actionable or discretionary costs, because there is usually no benefit from increasing these expenditures if no additional tangible output is produced. The budgeting effort for these direct costs is usually an engineering study with emphasis on minimizing unit costs, with the budget developed by multiplying units of output by standard unit costs. (See Chapter 10, "Determining Standard Material and Labor Costs," and Chapter 23, "Standard Cost Control for Manufacturing Costs.")

Although discretionary costs may be only a fraction of the total budget in a heavy manufacturing organization, the activities subject to zero-base budgeting techniques are usually the most difficult to plan and control, and yet they offer management the greatest lever to affect profits. For example:

1. Marketing and research and development programs determine the future course and growth of the organization.
2. Expenses for research and development, capital improvements, industrial engineering, production planning, and so on, can directly impact manufacturing technology and processes and can heavily influence direct manufacturing costs.
3. Arbitrary cost reductions in the service and support functions without full understanding of the consequences involved can create severe problems, with cost savings proving minor compared to the resulting production problems and increased direct manufacturing costs.
4. Service and overhead functions can be varied significantly over short periods of time.

If we were to identify and plot discretionary expenditures over a period of time, we would probably see a chart such as shown in Exhibit 2. As a *percentage* of sales, management would like to see actionable costs decrease as the sales volume increased. In plotting such a curve, we would see actual points falling above and below the average line. This indicates that we really have a range of variable expenses. This range may be significantly greater than prior history would indicate, especially during periods of economic stress.

During the budgeting process we want to identify the alternatives and consequences within this acceptable expenditure range. As we increase expenditures, we incur a profit penalty, but we receive operating and longer term benefits. As we decrease expenditures, we receive a profit benefit but incur operating and longer term penalties.

In any manufacturing organization, discretionary costs are significant, and they provide our major leverage for affecting both profits and profitability. The purpose of the budgeting process is to identify this expenditure range and the trade-offs between the

EXHIBIT 2
Actionable or Discretionary Costs versus Sales

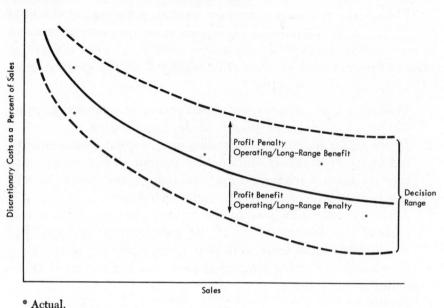

* Actual.

costs of current operations, development needs, and profit for top-management decision making and allocation of resources. An effective method to identify and evaluate these trade-offs is *zero-base budgeting.*

Traditional versus Zero-Base Budgeting

Exhibit 3 identifies the sequences of traditional budgeting versus zero-base budgeting. Both budget processes start from some long-term planning process, during which we define objectives, goals, strategies, and major programs. In the budget-development sequence, both budget processes start with an estimate of sales volume, from which we can calculate the cost of direct labor, materials, and overhead using standard costing procedures. During the latter stages of the budgeting process, these direct costs may be revised due to planned expenditures for capital, research, or manufacturing support that will impact these direct cost standards.

At this stage, the traditional budgeting procedures and zero-base budgeting part company. Under traditional procedures, we first

EXHIBIT 3
Traditional versus Zero-Base Budgeting

Budget Sequence	Traditional (numbers oriented)	Zero-Base (management oriented)
1. Long-term planning (3–5 years)	Objectives, goals, strategies	Objectives, goals, strategies
2. Budget development (1 year)	Develop sales forecast	Develop sales forecast
	Establish costs for direct labor, material, and overhead (standard costing systems)	Establish costs for direct labor, material, and overhead (standard costing systems)
(Actionable or discretionary costs)	Estimate costs of current activities	Evaluate current activities and alternatives
	Estimate costs of new activities	Identify and evaluate new activities and alternatives
	Detailed budgets developed	Establish priorities
3. Evaluation	Test against dollars / goals	Test against plan Establish trade-offs
4. Final product	Detail budget finalized	Budget and operating plan established Detailed budgets developed

estimate the costs of current activities. These are provided as a base and are usually not reevaluated. New activities are evaluated, and operating managers determine which new activities can be funded. Detail budgets are then established for each operation, combining current and new activities into a single budget by chart of accounts.

At this stage, any budget revision by top management forces a recycling of the budget development process and a revision of detail budgets. Management also has difficulty determining whether appropriate actions have been planned or budgeted to achieve the established goals. They must test the detailed budgets against dollar goals, and management typically has a difficult time evaluating alternative levels of expense because alternatives and consequences are not readily displayed.

Under zero-base budgeting, we evaluate current activities and alternatives *at the same time* we identify and evaluate new programs. Operating managers establish their priorities, and thus identify the trade-offs between expenditure levels and operating needs. New activities can be ranked higher than current activities, and thus achieve funding for new activities within current funding levels. It is then top management's responsibility to make the final evaluation and funding decisions.

Using zero-base budgeting, top management can readily test the budget against the plan since they are looking at an evaluation in priorities of activities rather than only detailed numbers. Management can identify trade-offs and consequences of alternative expenditure levels and establish the approved budget level. In the process, we get an operating plan as well as a budget. The budget is a product of operating decisions. All too often we make budget decisions first, which then become a rigid framework or strait jacket within which line managers must operate.

As the final step, after the budgets are approved, we can do the detail budgeting and fine-tuning of numbers. (Detail budgeting is typically ingrained into budgeting procedures. It is interesting to note that the company that developed zero-base budgeting eliminated the requirement for detail budgets because zero-base budgeting procedures provided all the control they desired.)

ZERO-BASE BUDGETING PROCEDURES

Zero-base budgeting is a two-step procedure. In the first step, managers analyze and describe each activity which their department carries out in a *decision package* or a series of decision packages. Packages are prepared for both current and new activities. In the second step, these decision packages must be evaluated and ranked. Management can then examine these packages and priorities, evaluate the trade-offs, and establish the budget.

Developing Decision Packages

Decision packages are the building blocks of the zero-base budgeting process. A decision package identifies a discrete function or operation for management evaluation and comparison to other activities. To make this evaluation, one must identify and analyze:

Objectives;
Consequences of not performing the function;

Costs and benefits;
Measures of performance; and
Alternative courses of action.

To break down their departments' activities into decision packages, managers should think in terms of three broad categories: service and support, capital expenditures, and overhead expenses directly associated with manufacturing.

Service and support packages focus on five kinds of subjects: people, projects or programs, services provided, services received, and cost reduction. People provide one of the most common subjects for decision packages, both because they spend money and because their wages and salaries create expenses. Personnel are likely to be the subject of decision packages in areas where (a) costs are primarily people related, (b) people perform several tasks and functions and a level of personnel-related effort can be identified, or (c) the functions of specific individuals can be condensed or eliminated. This is also an area where control is likely to be difficult, since managers have a natural tendency to protect the people working under them and are not likely to formulate packages which would facilitate cutting their staffs.

Projects or programs are likely to be package topics where expenses are generated by personnel and services provided, and where these expenses can be traced to a specific program. An example might be an automated inventory system. Services provided is a useful category whenever charges for a specific service can be determined. Services received is an appropriate category for a decision package whenever costs for services received are paid to sources external to a manager's area of activity. It should be noted, of course, that if these services are provided by other areas within the same organization, acceptance or rejection of such packages is liable to impact both the recipient and the provider of the services. Cost reduction is a useful category when the benefits of the reduction will not offset the costs during the first year.

The key to developing decision packages is the development of alternatives. Zero-base budgeting requires managers to develop two types of alternatives:

1. Different ways of performing the same function. (Alternatives might include make-versus-buy, centralization-versus-decen-

tralization, or an evaluation of different procedures or technologies.)

This is the easier of the two alternatives, and usually the first set
to be evaluated.

Once managers have chosen the way they consider best, they
should be asked to:

2. Determine alternative levels of effort for performing the same
   function.

Managers must identify a minimum level of effort, below which
they think the function should be discontinued. This level is usually
well below the current level of effort (i.e., 70–80 percent of the current level of funding). Additional levels of effort can be identified
as separate packages. Additional packages can bring the activity
up to its current level, or provide increases above the current level.

The most common questions at this point are:

Why should different levels of effort be identified? and

Why shouldn't managers choose the level of effort they think
necessary and recommend that level?

There are two reasons for identifying different levels of effort. First,
the functional-level managers are best equipped to identify and
evaluate different levels of effort. It should be the responsibility
of these operating managers to advise higher management of these
possibilities. The definition of a minimum level forces managers
into a thorough evaluation of alternatives and the identification of
the most important elements of their function. It then becomes
higher management's responsibility to evaluate the relative importance of functions and different levels of effort within each function. Second, limited expenditure levels would cause the complete
elimination of some functions if only one decision package at some
desired level of effort were identified. Such elimination might not
be desirable and practical. Moreover, higher management might
prefer to have the option of reducing levels of effort rather than
eliminating entire functions.

Let us walk through an actual example of decision package selection from a typical production planning department in an operation
which makes integrated circuits. The production planning manager
first identified three alternative ways to perform the production
planning function for which he or she was responsible:

A separate production planning department for Product X;

Having line foremen do their own planning; and

A combined production planning department for Products X, Y, and Z.

The production planning manager then evaluated these alternatives which were selected and decided which one would be the most effective way of accomplishing the production planning task. This sort of analysis of different ways of accomplishing the task in question allows managers to examine and challenge the ways in which they have been doing business.

In the example at hand, the manager did not prepare the decision packages at this stage of the analysis. Instead the manager proceeded to identify several levels of effort for performing the function. The first alternative way of performing the function (a separate production planning department for Product X) was then broken up into different levels. These were a minimum level (below the present operating level) plus two additional levels. These levels were:

1. Product X planning, minimum level: cost, $45,000. Four planners required to provide minimum planning support and coordination between marketing and manufacturing and to establish production schedules and reports. This level would involve reduced longer range planning, inventory control, and marketing support for special product modifications.
2. Product X planning, first increment above minimum level: cost, $15,000 additional. Add a long-range planner to increase forward planning of production and shipping schedule from two to four weeks, update in-process inventory reports daily rather than every other day (to aid inventory control), and assist marketing manager with customers who require special product modifications. (This is the current level of staffing.)
3. Product X planning, second increment above minimum level: cost, $15,000 additional. Add an operations research analyst to evaluate optimal length of production runs versus optimal inventory levels by stock number of product. Savings of 1 percent in production costs or 5 percent reduction in inventory level would offset this added cost.

These three levels of activity then became the decision packages for the production planning function.

EXHIBIT 4
Decision Package Form (page 1)

(1) Package Name Product X Planning (1 of 3: minimum level)	(2) Division Circuits	(3) Department Pdn. Planning	(4) Customer Center 205	(5) Rank 2

(6) Statement of Purpose

Provide minimum level of planning effort for Product X, with an estimated 5.8 million production units, to provide production and shipping schedules for the line foreman.

(7) Description of Actions (operations)

Maintain updated production and shipping schedules for two weeks in advance (currently maintaining schedules four weeks in advance).

Provide finished goods inventory level reports daily and in process inventory reports every other day (currently being done daily).

Maintain perpetual inventory system (computerized) on raw materials to maintain a two-week supply on hand and a two-week supply on order.

Two accounting clerks, two planners.

(8) Achievements/Benefits

Activity required for minimum maintenance of planning function to deliver products on schedule. Overtime and clerical effort reduced due to perpetual inventory system. Professional replaced with clerk for a savings of $6,000.

(9) Consequences of Not Approving Package

Elimination of planners would force line foremen to do their own planning (zero incremental cost for foremen); but excessive inventories, inefficient production runs, and delayed shipments would result in excessive sales loss.

(10) Quantitative Package Measures	1975	1976	1977	(11) Resources Required ($000)	1975	1976	1977	% 77/76
$ million NSB/planner	3.75	3.60	5.25	Gross $	45	60	45	75%
Average inventory/$ million NSB	10%	12%	12%	Net $	45	60	45	75%
Package cost/NSB	0.30%	0.33%	0.21%	People: Hourly	1	1	2	200%
Package cost/GPM	0.90%	1.1%	0.75%	Salary	3	4	2	50%

Manager ___John Adams___   Prepared By ___John Adams___   Date ___7/10/76___ Page 1 of __2__

Management now is presented with a range of alternatives. The planning function for Product X can be eliminated if all packages are disapproved or ranked so low that they don't get funded. Management can approve package "1 of 3" (minimum level) for $45,000. They can approve package "2 of 3" for $60,000 if management considers the long-range planner worth an additional $15,000. Management can approve "3 of 3" for $75,000 if management considers the operations research analyst worth that extra $15,000. Each of the three levels of effort can stand by itself, and management can evaluate its cost versus benefit.

EXHIBIT 4
Decision Package Form (page 2)

(1) Package Name Product X Planning (1 of 3: minimum level)	(2) Division Circuits	(3) Department Pdn. Planning	(4) Cost Center 205		(5) Rank 2	

(12) Alternatives (different levels of effort) and Cost	(14) Detail Costing			
	#	Account	1976	1977
Package 2 of 3 (cost $15K): Add back long-range planner. Increase forward planning of production and shipping schedules from two to four weeks, update in process inventory reports daily, assist marketing manager with special problem customers.		Wages	5.5	10.2
		Salaries	38.8	21.0
		Benefits	5.1	3.2
Package 3 of 3 (cost $15K): Add operations research analyst to evaluate optimal length of production runs versus optimal inventory level by color and size of product.				
	211	Maintenance		
	215	Matl./Supplies	2.3	2.6
	217	Depreciation	0.7	0.5
	401	Travel		
	415	Fees		
(13) Alternatives (different ways of performing the same function, activity, or operation)	501	Telephone	1.2	1.0
	502	Rent/Occupancy	2.5	2.5
1. Combine production planning for Products X, Y, and Z: Save two planners at $15,000 each (total of 12 planners for combined departments). Foremen of each product line fear lack of specialized service; peak workloads on all product lines coincide, creating an excessive burden on one supervisor to effectively manage; product departments are located in separate buildings and physical proximity of planning is desired.	503	Utilities	0.5	0.5
	710	Computer	3.0	3.0
2. Production planning performed by line foremen: (see consequences of not approving this package).				

		All other	0.5	0.5
Notes: NSB = net sales billed GPM = gross profit margin	Gross $		60.1	45.0
	Net $		60.1	45.0

(15) Quarterly Distribution				
	1	2	3	4
Gross	10	11	12	12
Net	10	11	12	12
Hrly.	1	2	2	2
Sal.	2	2	2	2

Page 2 of 2

The format used to display these packages is developed to insure that managers do the proper evaluation of their activities, and to communicate their evaluation to management. Exhibit 4 shows a two-page sample format. This example happens to be the first of the three packages. All the other packages would use the same form, focusing only on the additional $15,000 for each incremental package (levels 2 and 3).

These decision packages are prepared by the operating managers in each organization. This spreads the work load throughout the organization. These operating managers are best equipped to make this type of detailed evaluation, and they are the ones who will be held accountable for implementation and performance. The ranking process will entail reviewing and approving the decision packages, with top management requiring revisions in decision packages if they disagree with the analysis and proposals.

The Ranking Process

The second step of the zero-base budgeting process is the ranking process. The ranking process establishes priorities among the functions as displayed on the decision packages. If we wanted to limit our ranking severely, we could have only those managers preparing packages rank their own packages. However, this would put the burden on the division manager to establish the trade-offs among industrial engineering, production planning, and maintenance—as well as sales and administrative functions. At the other extreme, we could have one ranking for the entire division or corporation. As a realistic compromise (depending primarily on organizational size), we would probably stop the formal ranking process at some intermediate organizational level—such as plant manager.

Where we stop the formal ranking process depends on two considerations: the volume of packages and the ranking procedures used. In any large organization, it would be impossible for top, or even intermediate-level managers to review in detail and rank *every* decision package. This problem has a two-pronged solution: (1) concentrating management's attention on lower priority or discretionary items around which funding levels or cutoffs will be determined; and (2) limiting the number of consolidation levels to which the packages will be merged.

Concentrating management's attention on discretionary items implies that for each level of management which reviews the rankings of packages, there shall be some sort of expected funding level. Those packages which are ranked as essential (i.e., very high priority), and thus would be funded under almost any circumstances, need be given only a cursory review by top management, since it will normally be middle management's responsibility to have reviewed these packages in detail. Those packages which may or may not be funded should receive most of the attention—these are the packages about which decisions are going to have to be made. At each level of management, of course, the expected funding level will be higher, and so at each level most of the time and attention will be paid to those packages about which funding decisions will have to be made. There is no point quibbling about whether a given package should be ranked 4th or 7th if all of the top 25 are likely to be funded; in the same circumstance, it may be fairly important whether a given package is ranked 23rd or 27th.

Limiting the number of consolidation levels means that lower level management combines many of the packages, and top management need only look at entire programs rather than individual positions. This has the advantages of saving top management's time, and of delegating decisions to those managers who are closest to the action. It has the disadvantage of preventing review of the detailed elements which have gone into the funding levels suggested for the consolidated packages. The consolidation procedure is depicted in Exhibit 5.

EXHIBIT 5
The Process of Consolidation

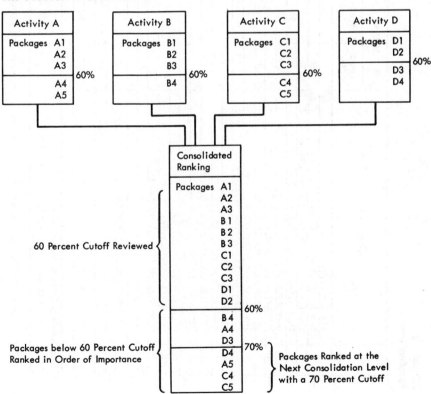

EXHIBIT 6
Ranking Form

Rank	Package Name	1976 Resources Gross $	1976 Net $	1976 People Hrly./Sal.	1977 Resources Gross $	1977 Net $	1977 People Hrly./Sal.	Cumulative Level Gross $	Cumulative Net $	%*
1	Quality Control (1 of 3)	175	175	11/3	90	90	6/1	90	90	
2	Product X Planning (1 of 3)	60	60	1/4	45	45	2/2	135	135	
3	Routine and Preventive Maintenance (1 of 2)	150	150	10/2	105	105	7/1	240	240	
4	Industrial Engineering (1 of 4)	90	90	2/6	41	41	1/2	281	281	
5	Administration	23	23	1/1	25	25	1/1	306	306	
6	Product X Planning (2 of 3)			/	15	15	/1	321	321	
7	Relocate Test and Assembly				45	45	/	366	366	71%
8	Industrial Engineering (2 of 4)			/	35	35	/3	401	401	80%
9	Routine and Preventive Maintenance (2 of 2)	9	9	1/	50	50	3/1	451	451	82%
10	Maintenance Scheduler				10	10	1/	461	461	82%
11	Quality Control (2 of 3)				83	83	5/1	544	544	97%
12	Industrial Engineering (3 of 4)				20	20	1/1	564	564	100%
13	Quality Control (3 of 3)				30	30	2/1	594	594	105%
14	Product X Planning (3 of 3)				15	15	/1	609	609	108%
15	Records and File Clerk	6	6	1/	6	6	1/	615	615	109%
16	Industrial Engineering (4 of 4)				15	15	/1	630	630	112%
17	Computerized Scheduling Model				10	10	/	640	640	114%
				/			/			
	Nonrecurring 1976 Expense	50	50	/			/			
	1976 Expense	563	563	/			/			

Sample Calculation:

$$\frac{640}{563} = 114\%$$

Cost Center or Organization Ranked: Manufacturing Support: Product X	Manager Bill Williams	Prepared By: Joe Schmidt	Date 7/25/76	Page 1 of 1

*1977 Cumulative Net $ as a % of Total 1976 Budgeted Net $ for corresponding organizations. (In this case, 1977 Cumulative Net $ as a % of $563.)

How the ranking is carried out also helps determine whether the volume of packages is or is not a problem. The alternatives here split into those having to do *with whom,* and those concerning *how.* Who should do the ranking; an individual or a committee? How should the ranking be done; by physically sorting packages or by assigning weights? At higher levels the expertise required to rank different packages from different units may well require the committee approach. When using a committee (and in general, when the number of packages is greater than about 50), it is usually easier to assign rankings by voting (assigning weights) rather than sorting. There are three possible voting procedures:

1. Each member gets one vote on some fixed scale (e.g., 0–50), with either the average or the total points determining the rankings.
2. Each member votes on several criteria (with either equal or weighted values), and the total points determine the ranking.
3. A combination of the first two, with the first used for preliminary ranking and the second for detailed ranking around the cutoff level.

The sample ranking form shown in Exhibit 6 merely displays the priorities of the decision packages. This example shows a ranking prepared by the plant manager. The plant manager established priorities among packages prepared by:

Production planning (packages 2, 6, and 14).

Quality control.

Industrial engineering.

Maintenance.

Special item: Relocate test and assembly (no. 7).

The ranking form in this example also displays a cumulative column. If we funded packages 1 through 14, we would approve a budget of $609,000, which would put us at 108 percent of current year's spending.

The Profit Plan

The final funding decisions for those activities using zero-base budgeting are determined by establishing the cutoff level on each ranking (e.g., packages 1–14 funded, package 15 and all lower ranked packages not funded). To make the final funding decisions, management must incorporate the zero-base budgeting analysis into the total cost picture in order to develop its profit plan. Management will develop its profit plan by merging the income and expense plans as shown in Exhibit 7.

The sales plan or forecast and the resulting budgets for direct labor, material, and overhead are normally the first to be finalized. Given a specified state-of-the-art in the manufacturing process, the relationship between sales and direct manufacturing costs is reasonably inflexible, with inventory levels being the only major variable that management can manipulate to affect profits (which in turn depends on the accounting methods used for materials, supplies, goods in process, and finished goods). Therefore, the

EXHIBIT 7
Developing the Profit Plan

Revenues	*(minus)*	*Expenses*		*(equals)*	*Pretax Income*
Sales		Direct labor		Standard	
Other		Direct material	}	cost ⟶	Inflexible
income		Some direct overhead			
		Manufacturing service and support	}		
		Department and division overhead		Zero-base	
		Corporate overhead	}	budgeting ⟷	Flexible
		Research and development			

major flexibility in management's arsenal to impact the profit plan are the activities displayed in the decision package rankings, with longer term profits heavily affected by the packages approved for marketing, research and development, industrial engineering, and so on.

The corporation's profit plan will be put together by consolidating such plans from many organizational units. Profit plans will usually be established for profit centers, product lines, or departments. These plans are then consolidated, along with some division overhead, into the corporate profit plan. This consolidation is an iterative decision-making process where management can be guided by models or historical trends in establishing profit levels for each organizational unit. However, profit problems from one organization, major new expenditures on product development or new facilities, and overall corporate profit objectives, force top management to evaluate the profit plans of individual product departments against corporate profit needs as well as against each department's profit objective. In times of profit pressure, it is not unusual "to rob Peter to pay Paul" by further reducing the budget in an organization that has already met its profit objective. Management can continually revise the budgets by revising the cutoff level on any or all rankings, satisfied that the reductions have eliminated or reduced the least important activities to the corporation, or can revise its profit objectives if the consequences associated with further budget reductions are unacceptable or unrealistic.

Implementation Problems

There are three general requirements for the successful implementation of a zero-base budgeting system: (1) support from top management, (2) effective design of the system, and (3) effective management of the system. Zero-base budgeting, like many other general systems, can be effectively killed by lack of support from top management. Strong leadership from the top, such as was provided in Georgia by Governor Jimmy Carter, is essential. The importance of good design and good management of the implementation is self-evident.

Three categories of implementation problems should be expected when a zero-base budgeting system is introduced. These are (1) fears and administrative problems; (2) decision-package formulation problems; and (3) ranking-process problems.

There are four common difficulties in the category of fears and administrative problems that management should expect when zero-base budgeting is first implemented:

1. Managers are often apprehensive of any process which forces decision making and requires detailed public scrutiny of their activities.
2. Administration and communication problems arise because more managers become involved in the zero-base budgeting process than in traditional planning and budgeting activities.
3. Formalized policy and planning assumptions are often nonexistent or inadequate. If they are adequate, they may not be communicated properly to lower level managers.

4. First-year time requirements may exceed the time spent in
    traditional planning and budgeting, and therefore raise ques-
    tions about the unwieldiness of zero-base budgeting procedures.
    Calendar time is not usually extended, but the zero-base analy-
    sis requires extensive time and effort. However, in subsequent
    years, time requirements may actually be reduced well below
    the time required by traditional budgeting.

The zero-base budgeting requirement for analysis of job functions
and establishing priorities is often viewed as an extremely dangerous and upsetting process by those managers who place high
priority on survival. Many of these managers have learned to survive
by keeping low profiles or "keeping their noses clean." Zero-base
budgeting forces an examination of what these managers are doing
and how they are doing it. They may therefore be expected to op-
pose the implementation of the process and to try to sabotage it
during implementation. This fear of scrutiny of activities seems to
be more pronounced in government than in industry, and more
common in poorly managed organizations than in well-managed
ones. There is no pat answer to this problem; it is one reason why
top-management support is so essential.

Administration and communication problems are inevitable at
first. Many of the managers who participate in zero-base budgeting
are not "financial types," and have not previously participated in
planning or budgeting activities. This also increases the problems
in auditing and controlling the process. Many of these problems
are inevitable when implementing a new and different system for
the first time. By anticipating and planning for these sorts of
problems, their impact can be reduced.

One of the benefits of zero-base budgeting is that it highlights
the lack of coordination among activities and the lack of planning
assumptions. These factors should be anticipated by top management *before* the zero-base budgeting process is begun. Managers
responsible for implementing the process within each organization
need to identify both the assumptions required and any specific
studies or alternatives which they wish various activity managers
to consider. If this is not done, assumptions underlying the different
proposals will not be consistent, coordination will be inadequate,
and many managers will not consider different activities from the
status quo.

The first year's planning and budgeting time requirements will probably exceed those of more conventional planning and budgeting systems. This is because zero-base budgeting is a sufficiently different technique that much of what it requires must be done for the first time. As the process becomes more routine and managers become more accustomed to it, the time required will decrease considerably.

Procedures for formulating decision packages and for ranking them have already been discussed. Since these are the two aspects of zero-base budgeting which differ most from more conventional systems, it is only to be expected that these would also be the aspects with which managers have the most problems. Guidance from the top and practice are the primary cures.

Management Control

The ability for management to control its operations effectively will be primarily established by its budgeting process. Traditional control systems center around the reporting of budget variances (i.e., actual expense versus budget). Although these budget variances are significant when comparing sales and bottom-line profit variances, these budget variances are not always meaningful when looking at budget variances of discretionary expense departments and programs. These variances may actually be misleading if work loads decrease—being "on budget" may not indicate good performance.

There are two major problems inherent in traditional control procedures:

1.   Control is based on numerical budget variances of actual-versus-budgeted expense, and does not traditionally include a formalized evaluation or measurement of *performance* (outputs) of individual departments or programs.
2.   Changing situations often outmode the budget, and management has a difficult time evaluating performance against the original budget or revising the budgets to fit the new situation.

That these problems exist is not surprising, because traditional budget procedures are heavily number oriented and do not provide management with adequate visibility to look "underneath the numbers" as to meaningful performance measures or potential alternatives available.

Zero-base budgeting allows management to hold all activities and operations to the performance that each one commits to in its decision packages—as well as to a budget. The summation of approved packages for each expense center or budget unit provides the budget framework for the reporting of actual costs and budget variances. The analysis provided by each decision package is usually a much deeper analysis of an expense center (which may contain several activities or programs) thar previously existed, and aids management in evaluating the reason for cost or performance variances. Typical reporting systems that indicate only cost and people variances from either budget or the previous forecast can be augmented by the standard reporting of work load and performance measures for those activities having readily definable measures.

Unfortunately, as we have seen, many of the overhead, service, and support activities do not have readily measurable work load and performance measures that lend themselves to a standard reporting format. The evaluation and control of these activities is not determined by budget variances (which can usually be readily controlled by varying the staffing levels) but by the performance and effectiveness of these activities. Management can determine the performance and effectiveness of these activities through special reviews or performance auditing. With the advent of zero-base budgeting, these reviews can be started with a review of the approved packages for each organization, followed by a status report on actual accomplishments versus commitment, problems, corrective action proposed or being undertaken, new programs, and changes in the environment or organizational requirements that were not anticipated in the operating plan and budget. In addition to such a review, performance auditing can be conducted by individual managers or teams of managers, or by an internal audit staff as part of their normal audit procedures.

Major changes implemented using zero-base budgeting techniques during the operating year have the same foundation for implementation and control of the revised plans and budgets as the original process provided for the original plans and budgets. Reductions based on eliminating or revising decision packages merely revise the road map for management to follow in implementing the revised plan, and allow holding of all activities and operations to a revised budget and a revised set of work load and performance measures. Increased budgets to meet new situations can be handled by preparing new decision packages, revising packages, or merely approving additional packages for funding. The detailed revisions allow management to identify organization changes, changes in services provided by service and support activities, and the consequences of such changes.

Zero-base budgeting thus provides a powerful operating tool for management to adjust operations and resources to keep abreast of a rapidly changing environment. Zero-base budgeting provides three strengths that enable management to adjust rapidly to changing situations:

1. A well-analyzed and documented baseline (performance as well as budget), with an existing set of priorities from which management can determine the actions required.
2. An efficient procedure for management to follow to identify the specific actions required, including changes in the assumptions and guidelines during the planning and budgeting process, budget reductions, and organizational changes.
3. A detailed identification of the consequences of the actions taken, which the procedure assuring management that the least important activities were eliminated or reduced, or the most important activities added.

If the required changes result from cost overruns or developing new activities and programs, zero-base budgeting allows management to review the previously budgeted activities to determine if they should be reduced to provide the funding required.

Should Zero-Base Budgeting Be Done Every Year?

There is no simple "yes" or "no" answer to the question of whether zero-base budgeting should be done every year. After going through the process the first time, an organization will decide whether the process should be repeated or not. If so (and this is the more common decision), there are three reasons to continue the process the second year rather than at some future time. These are:

1. The results and analysis of the first year will probably need improvement;

2. Managers will probably not have learned the process thoroughly yet, and the type of analysis required will not have become an ingrained way of thinking; and

3. Many departments may want to expand the analysis more deeply than was possible on a first attempt.

Once the process has been repeated the second year, management will have to decide how often to repeat it. In general, the process need not be repeated every year if the following two conditions are met:

1. Management is satisfied that operations are both effective and efficient.

2. The environment is reasonably stable.

If zero-base budgeting is not repeated every year, the budgets for the in between years can be set by reviewing the old decision packages, developing new ones for new activities and modifying rankings as necessary. This enables the organization to avoid incremental budgeting without having to go through the entire zero-base budgeting process.

Summary

Returning to our original purpose—to provide top management with an effective budgeting and decision-making tool to effectively allocate resources, particularly where discretionary costs are involved—I think that the zero-base budgeting approach can:

1. Identify the range of expenses for each activity and program within which top management can make its funding decisions;

2. Explicitly identify the consequences of various funding levels within this range, assuring that the highest priority activities are funded first; and

3. Provide a basis for effective management control, and a basis from which to react to subsequent changes during the operating year.

Zero-base budgeting is no panacea to problems of discretionary expense center control, but it certainly is an improvement over the way these problems are frequently dealt with—through incremental budgeting, which really is to "give in" to the problem rather than addressing it.

ADDITIONAL SOURCES

Anthony, Robert N., and Dearden, John. *Management Control Systems: Text and Cases,* chap. 5. 3d ed. Homewood, Ill.: Richard D. Irwin, Inc., 1976.

Cheek, Logan M. *Zero-Base Budgeting Comes of Age.* New York: American Management Associations, 1977.

Clark, Lindley H. "Zero-Base Budgeting, Advocated by Carter, Used by Many Firms." *Wall Street Journal,* March 14, 1977, p. 1.

Davis, K. Roscoe. "Budgeting by Level of Activity." *Managerial Planning,* May–June 1975, p. 10.

Pyhrr, Peter A. *Zero-Base Budgeting.* New York: John Wiley & Sons, Inc., 1975.

———. "Zero-Base Budgeting." *Harvard Business Review,* November–December 1970, p. 111.

———. "ZBB Across the Board." *Conference Board Magazine,* November 1977.

Stonich, Paul J. "Zero Base Planning—A Management Tool." *Managerial Planning,* July–August 1976, p. 1.

———. *Zero-Base Planning and Budgeting.* Homewood, Ill.: Dow Jones-Irwin, 1977.

"What it Means to Build a Budget from Zero." *Business Week,* April 18, 1977, p. 160.

25

Service Department Charge-Back Systems

Philip J. Molz*

Most large companies run their business on the basis of decentralized operating units. Nevertheless, for reasons of efficiency and effectiveness, they may provide their operating organizations with certain types of services which are centralized. When this is the case, the following question must be answered: *Should the operating units be charged for these centralized services?*

Basically, centralized services may be classified in the following types:

1. Central services over which the operating unit has no control (examples: accounting, industrial relations, legal).
2. Central services that the operating unit must accept, but for which the amount of service is partially controllable by the unit (examples: data processing, research and development).
3. Central services which the operating unit may decide to use or not (example: data processing).

Most companies do not use charge-back systems for services in the first category. The cost of these services may or may not be *allocated* to operating units as part of a "headquarters" overhead allocation; but charge-back (in the sense used in this chapter) implies a transaction- or time-based charge for services rendered, as op-

---

* Mr. Molz is Vice President, Financial Administration International, Abbott International Ltd., North Chicago, Illinois. At the time of writing this chapter, he was Controller, Latin American Group, Xerox Corporation.

posed to an arbitrary allocation procedure, however equitable that procedure may be felt to be. However, it is quite common for at least some of the services in the second category and all in the third to be charged back to the using departments based on these units' actual usage of the centralized services.

In this chapter we will look at charge-back systems in the context of data processing, based on the author's experience at Xerox. While EDP services constitute a common application of charge-back systems, the reader should recognize at the outset that the same issues and methodologies apply with little (if any) modification to word processing centers; publications departments; public relations, legal, or in-house consulting departments; or any other service group which is delivering a service that could be purchased on the outside rather than provided by an in-house group.

"Pros" and "Cons" of Charge-Back

There is no clear "yes" or "no" answer to the question "should users be charged for services provided by other organizations in the company?" Let's first take a look at some of the "cons":

1. One obvious drawback is the cost of administering a charge-back system. This cost must, of course, be balanced by the savings resulting from better control and increased user cost awareness.
2. Any form of charge-back system will engender budget games; however, this is also true of other management control devices.
3. There is usually a negative attitude toward paying for in-house service.
4. Since centralized services are not directly controllable by the operating manager, there is often the strong feeling that these services should not be charged to the operating manager.

In the case of Xerox, the arguments in favor of a charge-back system far outweighed the negative arguments. Here are some of the "pros":

1. One principal argument for some form of charge-back system is the philosophical belief in a decentralized style of management, where the end user of computer resources is given the authority and responsibility for the effective and efficient allocation of resources.

2. The system requires the user to plan his needs better in order to make firmer commitments to the central computer group.
3. A charge-back system forms a better basis for motivating and evaluating the performance of both user and service organizations.
4. By eliminating the "free resource" aspect of a no-charge system, the need for a top-management committee to ration and prioritize computer resources is eliminated.
5. Users who must pay for the application are likely to be more selective in the applications proposed, as well as eliminate applications no longer serving the needs of the business.

A charge-back system of any kind assumes that managers make rational, economic decisions; that they are provided with accurate and understandable data; and that they are motivated to choose the best alternative. Although these assumptions may generally hold, nevertheless a company may choose to provide a centralized service as a free resource until potential users are familiar with the service's potential benefits. For example, when computers were first introduced in many companies, no charge-back system was used, so that operating managers would be encouraged to explore the possibility of using the computer for work formerly done manually or for special analyses that otherwise would not be undertaken at all. However, this puts the EDP manager (or some committee) in the position of rationing computer time. Frequently this free-resource approach is followed by an EDP overhead allocation procedure, to make operating managers aware of the magnitude of data processing costs, which in turn may lead the managers to question both the total computer operation costs and their allocated share of these costs. Charge-back systems often are the next (and final) evolutionary stage in this process of resolving the centralized EDP cost issue.

Lesson 1: *Despite the problems associated with a charge-back system, the pros appear to outweigh the cons.*

TYPES OF CHARGE-BACK SYSTEMS

Cost-Based Systems

A cost-based charge-back system is one which, collectively, charges the units using computer services with all of the computer division's costs. The intent of such a system is to make the user aware of the costs of being provided with the service.

The best way to accomplish this purpose is by an actual charge to the user's budget, rather than by a mere "memo" notification. The computer division's efforts will be focused on controlling its costs. Of course, the bill to the user will motivate the user to control costs by controlling usage of computer services.

In the case of computing services, the major difficulty in a cost-based system is the high percentage of fixed costs in the short term and the fact that additional capacity is added in large, fixed chunks. These cost parameters mean that a large portion of the cost charged a user for application is a recovery of computer-center fixed costs rather than a recovery of out-of-pocket costs specifically identifiable with the user's application.

The bill for a given application should vary according to changes in computer configurations, changes in the volume of applications, other changes in the run environment, and so on. These fluctuations usually require complex allocation algorithms and often result in complicated and volatile billings. As utilization increases, fixed costs are spread over more applications, thus reducing unit costs, but encouraging faster movement toward full capacity and a large incremental increase in costs. Similarly, as utilization declines, unit costs increase, thus driving additional marginal applications from the system and further increasing unit costs.

Another problem with systems aimed at charging all of the computer division's *actual* costs to its users is that if the computer operation is not run efficiently, the users are penalized for this inefficiency, rather than the computer center being penalized. This problem is the same as if one manufacturing unit supplied another department with a certain machined part, and the "making unit" charged the "buying unit" actual full costs instead of a standard cost. While this problem is quickly recognized when setting transfer prices for tangible goods, it is sometimes overlooked when pricing intangible services within the company.

Standard Cost Systems

The above difficulties can be partially overcome by a standard cost system and a two-stage charge-back procedure. The latter consists of (1) a flat monthly charge based on budgeted fixed costs, and (2) a variable charge based on budgeted usage. The variable charge would increase to a fully loaded charge when budgeted volume was exceeded, thereby encouraging users to meet budget estimates. If usage is below budget, the user must still absorb the fixed costs necessary to provide the budgeted capacity.

This sort of system (which is also proposed for transfer prices of tangible goods in Chapter 26) has the advantage of making fixed costs "appear fixed" and variable costs "appear variable"; that is, it portrays accurately to the user the true economics of the decision. The system should also discourage budget games and encourage accurate budgeting, since the user realizes only marginal gains by "padding" the budget.

One important drawback to a cost-based or standard cost system is that it does not provide an *external* standard against which to measure the effectiveness and efficiency of the computer division. The division can be motivated to meet a cost goal, but historical costs alone may not be a sufficient basis for setting this goal. Cost as a percentage of sales has been used by some companies as an external guide, but this is at best a very rough standard due to the difficulty of finding a similar company against which to compare performance. This drawback is addressed in some companies by using market-price charges, and treating the computer operation as a profit center.

Partial Charge-Back Systems

The partial charge-back system attempts to ration the computer resources' usage without necessarily providing the user with a true cost of the resource and without necessarily breaking even. The significant characteristic and advantage of such a system is that the rate structure is established with a view towards simplicity, ease of understanding, and consistency of charges for a given application over an extended period of time. The rate structure typically embodies policy decisions concerning the manner in which the structure will motivate the users (that is, priority pricing, lower rates for computer-bound jobs, and so forth).

Market-Price Systems

In a market-price system, as the name implies, the rate structure is set in relation to the external market price of computer service bureaus. As such, the system provides a convenient, external measure of the performance of the internal computer division. Of course, this system has no cost allocation problems; the computer division is measured on the difference between its revenues and its costs, which are determined independently.

The market-price system does have several important difficulties or drawbacks:

It is almost impossible to establish an exact market price. Computer service is not yet a commodity market (although it shows signs of moving in that direction) and service bureau rates vary greatly depending on configuration, quality of service, charging factors, and so on. Therefore, disagreements over what constitutes a competitive rate are inevitable.

A true market does not really exist. For example, in Xerox, the Information Systems Division (ISD) has a captive market and incurs little selling expenses. This is somewhat offset by higher potential service levels due to reliance on in-house customers.

Nevertheless, a market-price system is heavily dependent on policies which aim to approximate an arm's-length bargaining process.

From the user's viewpoint, the system disguises the corporation's true cost economics. To the user, all costs appear variable, and the user is motivated to "pad" the budget and then realize cost savings which are not real from a corporate standpoint.

The central computer division may focus efforts on increasing profits by increasing revenues rather than by reducing costs. Where the user does not exercise the appropriate check, the computer division may find that increasing revenues is an easier way for making up a budget deficit than reducing costs. This expansionary bias is reinforced by the fact that improved computer division efficiency will often result in reduced revenues as well as reduced costs, with the resulting unfavorable impact on the division's profit commitment.

Lesson 2:   *Regardless of what charge-back system is selected, the main point is that it be easily understandable.*

WHICH CHARGE-BACK SYSTEM SHOULD ONE USE?

The choice of methodologies is basically a strategic question. Each of the charge-back systems described above is conceptually sound, each has certain natural strengths, and each has weaknesses which must be overcome through policies and administration of the system.

In the final analysis, the best system for your company depends on the company's objectives and the preference of management. For example, in the case of the Xerox Corporation, the policy on the charge-back system reads in part: "Provide users with a true indication of the market value of services being given," and "establish a quantitative management performance measurement of ISD [Information Systems Division] service operations by comparison to commercial organizations." These objectives clearly establish the supremacy of the market-price system in addressing Xerox's major purposes for the charge-back system.

Lesson 3:   *The kind of charge-back system finally chosen will depend mainly on the company's objectives, needs and management style.*

Key Points of Xerox's Charge-Back System

The market-price system presently in force at Xerox is characterized by the following basic policies:

Computing *must* be purchased from Xerox's Information Systems Division (ISD).

All computing services are established on a price basis that is competitive with "quality" outside service bureau vendors.

Customers are charged for specific services on the basis of actual utilization of those services.

Equal prices are charged to all ISD customers for similar services.

Prices are set up on the basis of charge per unit of service.

The reader should view Xerox's system as an illustration, rather than necessarily as a model. Again, the basic policies and charge-back rate structure should be tailored to the company's own needs and management's preferences.

The "Frosting on the Cake"

The company atmosphere, management's style, the timing of implementation, and so on, all play an important role in considering the advisability of a charge-back system.

Xerox has always been a fast-growing company, and people in the company have become accustomed to frequent organizational and procedural changes. Nevertheless, the creation of an information systems division several years ago was a change of such magnitude that it created quite a stir within the corporate organization.

Because most divisions and groups used to have their own computer facilities and services, the new organization was perceived as more rigid and probably more costly. The basic idea for creating ISD was to dissociate more clearly business problems from computer problems, by decentralizing to the users the decision making for computer-based information systems, as well as by centralizing in one provider the necessary computer technology and professional skills.

The reorganization involved personnel movements which, of course, contributed to the feeling of uncertainty and uneasiness on the part of many people, especially users, towards the new ISD organization. Before people had a chance to get used to the new organizational setup, the charge-back system was installed and, as one of our executives put it, it was "the frosting on the cake."

The following section will examine the software development process, which is the most important interface between ISD and users' organizations. Constant cooperation is required between both groups. The charge-back system makes very explicit the frontier between ISD programmers and the users' systems analysts and it thus contains some potential people problems or threats.

Lesson 4:   *Some organizations and people can adapt to changes better than others—it is important to review and understand the atmosphere in preparation for any changes.*

BEHAVIORAL IMPLICATIONS OF CHARGE-BACK SYSTEMS

In the development of a new computer-based information system, the analysts have to work closely with the programmers if a given project is to be completed successfully. A charge-back system might not encourage such essential cooperation if the organization is structured so that systems analysts and programmers work for different organizational units.

The different allegiances between analysts, who are on the user's side, and programmers, who are on the EDP service's side, are amplified by the charge-back, which puts a dollar sign on that relationship. This tends to reinforce the "wall" separating the two groups. For fear of having to absorb more of the development costs, specifications are examined by user systems analysts as carefully as would a legal counsel. In some cases in Xerox, "underground" programmers had been actually hired directly by the users because it was less expensive than using ISD programmers. Also, unfortunately there were a few mistakes in the first bills to users, and so trust and confidence in the charge-back system for programming services were shaken. These are not significant as such, but they illustrate how the charge-back system can threaten the essential teamwork between analysts and programmers.

The charge-back system can also influence the function of the analysts in relation to the user group. It increases their responsibility toward the end users to provide accurate estimates of development costs for major projects. Some end users may express fear of being pulled into a project following optimistic cost estimates established by their analysts. Many analysts may feel that the charge-back would generate tremendous pressures on their middle position: they are squeezed between their customers' needs (the end users) and their dependence on a programming work force which they do not control. For instance, there is no assurance that a given programmer will stay on a given job.

For the systems analysts as well as the programmers, the partition between both functions causes some concern about their career paths. In the past, programmers who were getting tired of the routine coding job could get closer to the business problems raised by a project; they could, after a while, become analysts. A few years later, as an analyst a programmer could be promoted to some higher function within the computer organization where knowledge of both the computer and business side of things would be helpful.

Under the present system at Xerox, to become an analyst a programmer would have to change from a service operation to a user organization. As a senior analyst it seems difficult to join an end-user organization for lack of operating experience. Passing to ISD means a change of organization again. Therefore, ISD cannot nurture within its organization people who have been exposed to both business and computer experiences.

The separation between programmers and analysts might cause some concern. The accent put on that separation by the charge-back system will do little to alleviate that problem. But the problem really is one of organizational structure, not the charge-back system.

Lesson 5: *Awareness of potential problem areas is the first step—subsequent solutions are usually found.*

Are there any positive factors to offset these apprehensions? Fortunately, yes. First of all, the "wall" between programmers and analysts is in practice not as high as it might appear on the organization chart. In actuality, programmers and analysts might report to different organizations, but at Xerox they work side by side in the same physical location in most cases.

Second, analysts are required to make sure that all end-users' needs are satisfied. It is true that the charge-back system has increased the incentive for systems analysts to write as complete specifications as possible. This does have the advantage of bypassing phases in the analysis process and makes more certain that a short-term gain of time will not cause more serious delays and costs in the long run.

Finally, the software development manager has an excellent opportunity now of managing the total Xerox programming work force in a manner more consistent with the corporation's overall interest. For instance, trade-offs can be made better than in the past in terms of allocation of skills between projects of different degrees of difficulty, urgency, and importance.

Lesson 6: *Physical location of programmers and analysts may be more important than where they are on the organization chart.*

Advantages of Central Computing Services to the User

In one important respect, a central computing service, even with a charge-back system procedure, provides a much better level of service than before. In the past, although they had control of their own computer, users were frequently subject to capacity constraints. Also, there was a continual need to justify large, incremental capital expenditures in order to continue to provide the desired level of service and performance. Subject to the user's budget limitations, the user is now free to spend as much on computing as deemed necessary to support operations.

Lesson 7:   *Point out to the user the many important advantages of a central service facility.*

Controller Approval

At Xerox, each year prior to the operating units' budget preparation, ISD submits a rate structure proposal to the corporate controller. Since the rate structure can have important effects on the usage of the computer resources, it is essential that proper consideration be given to the incentives built into the rate structure. The structure should include both a list of all chargeable elements, as well as the rates at which they will be charged during the upcoming budget year. For example, for processing jobs there will be charges per second of CPU time, for minutes of core storage time, per thousand accesses to external memory (tape or disk), per tape setup, per thousand cards read, per thousand lines printed, and so forth.

The presentation of the rate structure proposal should also highlight all changes from the previous year's chargeable elements and rates. Appropriate justification for these charges should be included in the proposal. For instance, the computer services organization may wish to regulate its work load by offering a priority discount rate structure depending on the urgency or time of delivery of the users' requirements.

The next step in the rate-setting process should be a thorough review of the proposed rate structure by the controller's staff. Particular attention should be focused on the justifications for any changes.

At the same time as the rate structure is being determined, the computer services organization should perform a review and an update of its application profiles in conjunction with its users. This review should be conducted in terms of utilization of chargeable resources in physical units (that is, CPU time, number of pages, maximum core requirements, and so on).

Lesson 8:   *Be as specific as possible in the development of a rate structure in order to minimize future disagreements.*

After approval of the rate structure and review of the profiles, updated profiles are recomputed by the computer organization in terms of dollars, and subsequently submitted to the users. The users are then able to utilize the profiles in preparing their annual operating plans and budgets, in which they state their intended utilization of computer resources and the anticipated costs.

At Xerox, the planned utilization of ISD resources is supported by so-called "transfer agreements," which are signed agreements between the services organization and the users. Once these agreements are finalized, ISD is able to prepare its own annual operating plan or budget. End-of-year time constraints may require some overlap in the last phases of the budget preparation, but the essential factor is to provide the users with updated profiles in time to utilize them for budget preparation.

Lesson 9:   *Signed agreements between the services organiza-tion and users can avoid many problems in charges and service during the budget year.*

Computer Division–User Conflicts

It is natural that there will be times where significant disagreements arise between the computer organization and a user. One means of handling such disputes is the establishment of a "grievance committee." This grievance committee, whose job is to settle inter-organizational disputes concerning charges, quality of service, disposition of cost savings, budget adjustments (possibly arising from unplanned investments beneficial from an overall corporate viewpoint), and so on, should probably report to the company controller. It should be composed of individuals sensitive to both computer and financial aspects of a question, and who have the capability of trading off conflicting arguments to the best interest of the company on a case-by-case basis. In the area of interorganizational disputes, the committee should have decision-making and policy-setting powers independent of the computer and users' organizations.

The committee should be sufficiently accessible to ensure that every important grievance is heard. In this regard, a once-a-month formal meeting of the committee and representatives of the computer and users' organizations might be a good way to ensure discussion of serious problem areas.

Lesson 10: *The existence of a "grievance committee" can help settle interorganizational disputes and be an essential "sound-off" board for users.*

Major Development Projects

Major development projects should be managed in the context of a matrix organization. For instance, a programmer reports functionally to the software development manager, while the project manager assumes responsibility for his utilization and evaluation on a specific project.

The project manager should provide to the software development manager a formal evaluation of each programmer's project performance. In turn, the software development manager will explicitly take into account the impact of the programmer's assignment changes on the continuity of the team effort. At a minimum, the head programmer should stay with major projects as long as desired by the project manager.

Companies differ in their approaches to development project charges. In some instances, if the project is approved, no development charge is made, and only post development computing costs are subject to charge-backs. The drawback in this approach is that it makes a project appear less expensive to the proposing user than it really is to the company.

To avoid this phenomenon, a development charge must be made. How to handle this charge has all the complications of any arm's-length contract arrangement for a one-shot effort. Whether the arrangement is largely a cost-reimbursement one or a fixed-price agreement depends on such factors as uncertainties in the development effort and the forecasting ability of the computer group. Needless to say, user-proposers tend to favor a fixed-price arrangement, whereas a cost-reimbursement agreement is more to the liking of the computer division.

User "Leverage"

The best way to give leverage to the users in the discussion of the contract terms, either for development efforts or recurring processing, is to allow users to contract services outside. Some companies do precisely that.

At Xerox, it was decided not to give this authorization to users. Naturally, this means that ISD has the difficult task of showing and convincing users that its charge-back system is based on competitive rates and services. As long as an impartial party (like the controller's office) makes certain that this is the case, users are generally satisfied that billed rates are reasonable.

Lesson 11: *Find some means to make sure that the user is satisfied that the rates are reasonable lest the charge-back system backfire.*

Handling Budget Variance Cost Savings

Since computing costs are to a certain extent discretionary expenses, the incentive to cut costs should come only at budget-setting time. (See Chapter 24.) During the budget year, the incentive for the user should be to meet projections; therefore, budget variance cost "savings" should be "trapped" in the user's operating statements. The controller should ensure that the appropriate systems are in place to identify and trap these budget variances. The controller should also make sure that appropriate real cost-saving targets are built into the user's budget. Similarly, even though the rate structure is set to provide break-even operations (or perhaps a profit) for the computer operation, there should be an incentive for EDP managers to "beat" their overall budget and be appropriately rewarded for so doing.

AUDITING THE CHARGE-BACK SYSTEM

Xerox has found it highly valuable to have a management audit of its current charge-back system and policies. In order to obtain a truly impartial review, after implementation of the new system, they solicited assistance of a study team from the Harvard Business School. The basic objectives of the study were to:

Evaluate the current pricing structure.

Determine how the new pricing procedure affected users.

Determine how the new pricing method affected providers of services.

Recommend modifications of the present system, where appropriate.

Lesson 12:   *As with any system, continual monitoring is essential to ensure that "it's working."*

Survey Interviews

Interviews were conducted by this study team which used open-ended questions designed to identify and examine each person's specific role in the charge-back system and his experience to date in operating within the framework of the system. Here are some examples of questions which might be asked.

Issues concerning the company as a whole:

1. How is the company organized? Profit centers? Expense centers? and so on.
2. What are the goals and objectives of the company (both explicit and implicit)?
3. How are organizational goals factored into operational objectives? What is the role of budgets? How is performance evaluated and rewarded?
4. How does the charge-back system work in practice? Is the system taken seriously?
5. How is the computer resource commitment tied into the planning/budgeting process?
6. What is the level of user awareness in the organization? Cost awareness? Applications awareness? Impact of decentralized systems concept on users?

Issues concerning the charge-back system:

1. What are management's objectives for the charge-back system? Control? Motivation? Evaluation? Coordination?
2. How does the process work? What is the bargaining process? How is market price determined? Who has the power? Who has final decision authority?
3. Does the transfer pricing mechanism adequately reflect the underlying economics of the decision? Are incremental costs highlighted? What about the fixed-cost/variable-cost relationships?
4. What are the motivational aspects of the system? What are users and suppliers likely to do given the pricing mechanism? Are these actions/reactions consistent with the company ob-

jectives? Are potential disasters perhaps created by the pricing system?

5. What is the impact of the policy of denying users outside access to computer resources (or, what is the impact of permitting users to go to the outside)?

6. How do users and suppliers perceive the user-buyer/seller relationship? Are there potential problems in this interface in addition to the transfer price problem?

7. What are the long-run/short-run trade-offs involved?

8. Does the administration of the charge-back system cost more than it is worth?

9. Does the user understand the pricing mechanism? Can the user really perform the resource allocation decision?

10. What mechanism does the system use for voicing user dissatisfaction?

11. How are priorities determined? Is system pricing used in balancing user priorities?

12. How is the system affected by change (for example, decline/increase in usage or new equipment)?

13. Who gets the benefit of improved efficiency? Are cost savings trapped or do they become a discretionary pool of funds?

14. Must the central computing facility service all user demands? How does it handle peak and overload conditions? How are these costs factored into the transfer price?

The study team's experience led to the following conclusion:

Lesson 13:   *Questions should be asked in person rather than by written questionnaire—the survey will then result in more meaningful answers.*

Results

As one might imagine, the results of the survey showed quite a variety of attitudes toward the charge-back system. First, let us summarize the more prevalent opinions before making some generalizations about the different reactions.

Neutral.   One category of comments was basically neutral in the sense that, to a number of people, the charge-back system had no effect, either bad or good, on the attitudes and working habits. Following are typical examples of this group's reactions:

It was too soon to appreciate how good or bad the charge-back system was because there was no history attached to the figures.

The charges which passed from ISD to the user were not composed of "real" dollars but rather were "funny" money, because they remained within the company's boundaries.

Opposed. There were quite a few opinions against the system. Of course, some of these may well represent a "normal" reaction on the part of people to be against any new system—a natural resistance to change. In any case, here are some typical reactions:

The charge-back system is not worth the cost of administering it.

The system takes everybody's time and does not help to manage or control.

It was detrimental to the company as a whole since it would stress immediate "penny" savings to the detriment of longer term "pound" economies.

Charge rates were too high and not truly competitive.

The charge-back system would encourage people to play games with their budgets, using the computer budget as a cushion to stay within the overall budget figure.

There was no control, so to speak, over ISD since official corporate policy forbade users to go to the outside for "cheaper" servies.

In Favor. People in favor of a charge-back system presented the following arguments:

It developed a cost awareness on the part of users.

It provided users with a true indication of the market value of services rendered.

It also allowed users to better allocate their resources within their budget.

It permitted measurement of computer service performance against the outside competition of vendors of computer services.

Better utilization of the computer created an incentive for providers to sell more services in order to bring revenues back up to budget.

The charge-back system provided managers at all levels with a useful management tool.

General Comments

This will come as no surprise, but the positions taken by individuals toward the charge-back system, and the strength of their conviction for or against the system, varied primarily according to the following factors:

Users were generally opposed to the institution of a charge-back system; people in computer services were generally in favor.

Within the user groups, systems analysts tended to be less opposed than end users.

Again in the case of the users, opposition to the charge-back system seemed to increase the higher the "rank" of the user.

The share of the user's budget represented by computer service expenses is another element of the user's sensitivity to charge-back.

The more a user feels committed to an overall budget figure, the stronger the user's reaction is to an increased computer bill and the stronger the incentive to understand the system and reduce the amount of the bill.

Lesson 14: *What is important is not whether someone is "for" or "against" the new system, but why.*

User Reactions to Charges

Most users interviewed expressed dissatisfaction with the charges billed to them by ISD, which may come as no surprise. There are several factors, however, which seem to explain the general feeling of dissatisfaction:

The charge-back system had forced computing costs to become much more visible; they had been pulled out of hidden niches in the operating units and aggregated in one place.

Since they were no longer directly responsible for computing expenses, users were more inclined to complain.

The loss of hands-on control of the resource with the formation of a central computing facility heightened the users' sensitivity.

The fact that the user must pay budget dollars to cover costs over which he has limited control contributed to the complaint-generating atmosphere.

It must be stressed at this point that the pressure on ISD to control costs was a definite, positive aspect of the system. This pressure provides a needed check and balance to ensure that efforts to reduce costs are maintained.

User Views of Service

In general, the users expressed willingness to pay the price, provided they received the level of service required. This does not mean to imply that complaints about either cost or service are likely to disappear.

Xerox's PPICS (Production, Planning and Inventory Control System), for example, which can virtually shut down manufacturing operations if it does not process on time, pinpoints the critical nature of central computer service requirements. If the plant managers should lose faith in ISD's ability to provide the required service, they will resort to manual systems, which admittedly would duplicate ISD's work and are less than optimal solutions, but which the plant managers feel they can control.

The nature of service is an extremely difficult one to define. As long as users are denied the hands-on control afforded by possession of their own computer and are denied access to alternative suppliers, they will feel somewhat frustrated by the possibility to get "service" from a central computer facility.

The difficulty in defining "quality of service" presents an important problem in the context of a charge-back system. ISD performance evaluation, for example, is based principally on its performance in relation to its profit commitment. Of course, an important secondary goal is its service to users. These two goals can and often do conflict. For instance, if ISD improves the efficiency of a user's system, thereby enabling faster turnaround time and lower costs, ISD's revenues (and profit) will suffer. ISD, therefore, has an incentive to keep all cost savings and, conversely, is inclined to pass on to users any cost inefficiencies through higher rates.

One user summarized the feeling by indicating that the system was a one-way commitment: "We commit budget dollars—but get no service commitment in return." His point may be oversimplified, but it is important that the computer organization remain aware of the dangers involved in the conflict between a very "hard" profit target and a "soft" or ill-defined service objective.

Lesson 15:   *Both costs and service must be well-defined and agreed upon.*

General Conclusions from Survey

The following conclusions emerged from Xerox's attitude survey of its charge-back system:

It was felt that the strong initial reactions on the part of most users was basically due to short-term resistance and would disappear once the charge-back system was understood and functioning properly.

There was definitely a strong increase in cost awareness on the part of both users and providers of computer services.

Users' demands for quality service increased.

On the negative side, there was evidence of "cheating;" that is, some users actually went to outside services (contrary to company policy).

The system can backfire fast if the users do not receive good service.

Lesson 16:   *Let the system settle in and work for a while before taking an attitude survey.*

Of course, many companies will not want to use an outside consultant or business school study team to audit user reaction to a charge-back scheme. The important thing is not that such a survey be done by outsiders, but that it be done. The disadvantage of using a consultant for this purpose is cost; the advantage is the greater aura of objectivity an outsider has over, say, a study team from the controller's office (especially if the EDP manager reports to the controller).

CONCLUSION

The author's experience at Xerox with respect to charging operating units for services performed by a central service facility may be summarized as follows:

A charge-back system has very significant advantages.

The system should be tailor-made to each company's particular needs and kept simple.

Proper attitudes and understanding must be developed before implementation.

The system must be continually monitored and changed where necessary.

As each month passed, more Xerox managers agreed that the "go" decision for a charge-back system was the right overall company decision. But there was a commitment by management to continue to look for better ways to provide service to its operating units and customers.

ADDITIONAL SOURCES

Cushing, Barry E. "Pricing Internal Computer Services: The Basic Issues." *Management Accounting*, April 1976, p. 47.

McFarlan, F. Warren, and Nolan, Richard L., eds. *The Information Systems Handbook*, chap. 8. Homewood, Ill.: Dow Jones-Irwin, 1975.

Nolan, Richard L. "Controlling the Costs of Data Services." *Harvard Business Review*, July–August 1977, p. 114.

26

Profit Centers
and Transfer Prices

Richard E. Vendig*

PROFIT CENTERS

Profit may generally be defined as the excess of revenues over expenses for a specified period of time for a particular accounting entity. A *profit center* is a segment of a business, such as a division, that is accountable for the excess of revenues over expenses. An expense center, on the other hand, is a segment of a business for which no attempt is made to measure profit. (See Chapters 23 and 24 for detailed discussions of expense centers.) With the profit or expense center concepts, a segment of a company is regarded as a somewhat "independent" business with a manager who may have final responsibility for revenues (under the profit center concept), expenses (under both the profit center and the expense center concepts), or profit plus the assets employed to maintain operations of the division (investment center concept—See Chapter 27).

When the results of operations for a responsibility center are measured in terms of profit, the responsibility center is called a *profit center*. Thus the utilization of the profit center concept by a particular company represents both upper management's desire to delegate authority within the organization, and a means of motivating its managers and evaluating their performance in terms of profit.

---

* Richard E. Vendig, CPA, is a Manager in the Audit Services Department of the New York office of S. D. Leidesdorf & Co.

Some Practical Considerations regarding Profit Center Organization

As managers are delegated authority to make decisions, both the speed and quality of these decisions should be enhanced since the person most familiar with a situation is making the decision. If managers are being evaluated in terms of profits, their awareness of profits is enhanced and they will be motivated to improve them. Performance measurement is expanded to include the effects of a manager's decisions relating to both revenues and expenses, rather than one or the other.

However, suboptimization of total company profits may result since there may be (1) too much emphasis on short-run profits, and managers as a result may tend to minimize certain important expenditures such as for maintenance and training; (2) friction and competition between previously cooperative units may increase substantially; and (3) optimization of each profit center's indicated profit does not guarantee that the company's overall profits will be optimized. (These points will be discussed later in this chapter.)

As the size of a company, the type and number of its products, and the number of locations of the company's facilities increase, the need to decentralize and establish a profit center organization increases. Management will become less able to identify the relevant day-to-day details of the business and therefore will delegate the day-to-day decisions to the respective managers. For this delegation to work effectively, certain personnel and system requirements must be met. Competent divisional[1] (responsibility center) managers are needed. A management information system that provides reliable information for planning, controlling, and coordinating profit centers is required; and upper management must know how to use this information system and its resultant reports to meet their objectives. Within the information system certain problems may exist relating to measurement of profit, as discussed in the next section.

Problems in Profit Center Measurement

Since profit centers are segments of a company and are not in fact independent entities, and because transfers ("interdivisional

---

[1] We will use the term "division" generically to mean *any* profit center in a company having two or more profit centers. In practice, these organizational units are variously called "groups," "divisions," "business units," or even "departments."

sales") of goods and services are likely to occur between profit centers, certain problems are likely to occur relating to accounting for nontraceable costs and transfers between profit centers.

First, consider the problem of nontraceable costs. Nontraceable costs are costs common to more than one profit center. Some writers on profit centers argue that nontraceable costs such as corporate overhead should be charged to a profit center on a basis that reflects consumption of a particular service; or if this method is not feasible, these costs should be allocated on some reasonable basis. The rationale for this point of view is that if the profit center were in fact an independent company, it would have to incur some of these costs currently being incurred at "headquarters."

However, others argue that since nontraceable costs may be allocated on an arbitrary basis, they tend to obscure analysis for purposes of performance evaluation and decision making; these costs therefore have little justification for being allocated. These people ask if it is not really certain that these costs apply to a particular profit center, why allocate them? These costs should be applied to the entity as a whole. In the sale of a product to an outside customer, the price set by either upper management, the market or both in effect determines which products shall carry the burden of covering nontraceable costs and how much each product will carry. This thought is consistent with the view that common costs are a "handicap" of the firm as a whole and not of a single profit center. Nontraceable costs are common costs by definition; and at a divisional level, it may be questioned whether anyone should be charged with them.

In practice, a company must decide which of these points of view should be reflected in its calculation of a profit center's income. This decision should be made on the basis of a judgment as to which approach will result in the most positive motivation on the part of a profit center manager. Also, some companies have imaginatively avoided making a choice by showing *two* profit figures on profit center reports, one *before* considering allocated joint costs and the other *net* of such allocations. In theory, the former is used in evaluating the profit center manager, while the latter is used to identify the income of the profit center viewed as a hypothetical independent economic entity.

Second, since profit centers may buy and sell both internally and externally, the gathering of management information, the making of decisions, and the evaluation of decisions may become somewhat complex in contrast with an "ideal" accounting entity that has no intracompany purchases or sales. Intracompany transfers make it necessary to maintain a workable arrangement for pricing the intermediate goods and services transferred from one segment (responsibility center) to another. The practice is referred to as *transfer pricing*.

TRANSFER PRICING

An intracompany transfer can be thought of as an "arm's-length transaction" between two responsibility centers. The selling unit and the buying unit both have vested interests involved. While the selling unit is interested in covering as much of its cost as possible, the buying unit is interested in obtaining its needed intermediate product as cheaply as possible. If no outside source exists, the buying unit is still faced with the question of whether it is better to buy the intermediate product from another responsibility center capable of producing it or to manufacture it itself. The transfer price, therefore, must be equitable to both parties, and it is arrived at by negotiation between the parties.

Objectives of Transfer Pricing

Transfer pricing helps management to measure the economic performance of each responsibility center of the company. In addition it should motivate the responsibility center's manager to make sound decisions that not only increase the profits of the profit center but also the profits of the firm as a whole.

For accounting purposes, all intracompany transfers could be recorded at cost. But if this method were employed, it would not be possible to implement the profit center concept in a meaningful way. Only when a price other than cost is provided for each product which moves from segment to segment before it is sold to outside customers can a measure of the contribution to profit for the particular segment be obtained. Even if transfers of intermediate products take place in amounts small to the company, if these amounts are significant to the responsibility center, they will have a material (though not overwhelmingly significant) effect on the performance evaluation of a profit center.

Thus, where profit responsibility is delegated to the heads of various profit centers, transfer prices at other than cost are essential for the preparation of meaningful performance reports for each profit responsibility center. If the prices of products sold from one unit to another are dependent upon the divisional manager's abilities to negotiate prices and control costs and contribute to either a profit or loss for the division, then the results of operations will clearly be a measure of performance.

The transfer pricing system permits each segment of the company the opportunity to earn a profit from intracompany transfers proportionate to the operations it performs. A segment is not guaranteed a profit. The possibility of incurring a loss should exist, just as it exists with sales to outside customers.

Practical Problems Related to Intracompany Selling

If an active outside market exists for the intermediate product, the purchasing unit should have the opportunity to buy the product outside the company if the intracompany price is unsatisfactory to it. The decision of where the product is to be obtained, whether produced within the company or purchased from outside the company, is known as a *sourcing decision*. This sourcing policy of the buying unit's being able to buy in-house or outside would tend to place the buying segment on an equal footing with the selling segment in negotiating a price. The seller must meet the competitive outside price or lose the business. He or she does not have a captive customer and must therefore be responsive to this customer. However, this practice may be counter to overall company objectives. The *buying* unit may have lower costs buying outside than if it bought within the company, but this decrease in the buyer's costs may not be sufficient to offset the adverse effects of lower volume in the manufacturing (i.e., selling) unit.

Another problem is that intracompany selling can lead to friction between the segments of a company. Competition, manipulation, disappointment, frustration, and distrust may undermine needed cooperation between segments. As one author puts it:

> If a manager is to be judged by the reported profitableness of his division, pressure is on him to do two things: (i) take whatever steps seem indicated to maximize the profits of his division, regardless of their effect on other divisions, or on the company as a whole;

(ii) apply himself to manipulating the profit-measurement procedures to his individual advantage at the expense of other division
heads less concerned or less influential.[2]

A formal structure of transfer price administration is required in
order to resolve the above problems and possible disputes; otherwise top management may be forced to become involved with "um-
piring" functions. This, in turn, might increase costs by requiring
more executive time or by causing a misallocation of executive time.
However, if negotiations for transfer prices were on a periodic basis,
semiannually or annually, excessive use of executive time may be
avoided.

As a result of the foregoing problems, procedures for arbitration
and negotiation must be established, and a sourcing policy must be
set as to when a buying segment must purchase from within the
company rather than from outside it. This policy should force the
buying segment to purchase from the manufacturing segment only
when the incremental loss to the selling division will be greater
than the incremental savings that the buying division will realize
by purchasing from a less-expensive external source. Similar guidelines must be established for the producing division if it wishes to
sell its entire output externally rather than internally. A system of
negotiation and arbitration within prescribed measures is the key to
resolving these problems.

To preclude the manipulation of profit measurement procedures,
the use of objective accounting personnel and practices (as direct
or variable costing) in the determination and establishment of such
procedures is mandatory. Also, a set of prescribed or negotiated
rules as to the measurement of controllable (traceable) costs and
controllable (traceable) capital employed would also limit the extent of possible manipulation.

Pricing Considerations

Should the transfer prices be based on arbitrary markup (over
cost) percentages? If our goal is a responsibility center's profit-
performance measurement and evaluation, and the intermediate
products have an external market, the prices for these transfers

---

[2] Howard C. Greer, "Divisional Profit Calculation—Notes on the 'Transfer Price'
Problem," *NAA Bulletin,* July 1962, p. 6.

should have some relationship to the external market price. However, the internal manufacturing segment (selling unit) does not incur any significant advertising expenses or distribution costs when selling internally; thus, the manager of the buying division may expect a transfer price less than the going market price per unit. The problem is determining how much less the cost per unit should be. Objectivity and equity may be difficult to implement even when a market price exists.

If an outside market does not exist, the negotiations may tend toward nonsense. For such an intermediate product (no outside market), the managers of the buying and selling units may start "negotiations" at extremely divergent prices since there is no market price to act as a focal point. In this instance, the transfer price could be based on cost plus a charge for capital employed. This concept will be amplified later in this chapter under the caption "A Three-Part Transfer Price."

In economics, the price of a particular good or service is determined by the point of intersection of its supply and demand curves. But in practice, how many companies can estimate what quantity of product will be sold at one price, let alone at all possible prices?[3] Without a demand schedule the methods of economics, its equations, and its graphs are not applicable.

The concept that probably underlies the actions of most responsible business executives is that of satisfactory profit, or satisfactory return on investment; that is, they have a notion of a fair or reasonable profit that should be earned in their business and strive to earn such a profit.[4] The reasonable-profit concept leads to what is known as *full-cost pricing*.

The full-cost pricing method usually entails computing the full cost of the product and adding to this a profit margin, determined either as a percentage of cost or as a percentage of the investment involved in making the product. The relevant costs are full costs, which are those costs used directly in the manufacture of a product plus a fair portion of those costs used indirectly in the manufacture of a product. If the profit allowance is determined as a return on a measure of capital employed in the manufacture of a product, this practice would be consistent with the overall objective of earning

---

[3] Robert N. Anthony and James S. Reece, *Management Accounting Principles*, 3d ed. (Homewood, Ill.: Richard D. Irwin, Inc., 1975), pp. 467–68.

[4] Ibid.

a satisfactory return on investment. But what costs are incurred in the manufacture of a product?

The price with a full-cost approach would cover not only the traceable variable and fixed costs incurred in production (direct costs) but also the variable and fixed costs incurred which provide for the ability to produce (indirect costs). The transfer price represents a composite of the costs involved. The individual costs represent uses of scarce resources for the production of a product. The transfer price thus far discussed covers only the full cost of the product; what about profit? Within the framework of intracompany transfers, the "profits" of a selling profit center become a cost of the buying center, and of any subsequent profit center in the "chain" of profit centers dealing with the ultimate end item. To the entity *as a whole*, however, a transfer price will not affect the profits of the entity, though it may affect the decisions to be made when using accounting information incorporating a transfer price.

To this point, the classification of costs has been rather general, and nothing has been said as to what system of accounting should be used for them. Since the transfer price is to be applied in decision-making and performance evaluation functions, direct (variable) costing appears very applicable. (See Chapter 13.) Thus, the essential characteristic required of costs to be included within the transfer price is that they be traceable to the responsibility center. The transfer price, by a full-cost approach, would cover all variable and fixed traceable costs incurred within a responsibility center for the production of an intermediate good. Arbitrary cost allocations (as discussed earlier) will impact the determination of cost-based transfer prices and may have a negative effect on motivating a profit center manager and therefore should be avoided.

To summarize the pricing considerations in an intracompany transaction, "the manufacturing division sells to the sales division at an agreed-upon price, which beside covering the cost of materials, labor and overhead, must also include in its overhead charge an amount to cover interest on investment,"[5] or profit.

CASE ILLUSTRATION

The following case is presented as a basis for evaluating several alternative methods of transfer pricing. Based on the weaknesses of

---

[5] David Solomons, *Divisional Performance: Measurement and Control* (Homewood, Ill.: Richard D. Irwin, Inc., 1968), p. 162.

the alternatives discussed, a method is proposed which entails a modification of the full-cost approach to transfer pricing. This method would operate in a negotiated transfer price environment, and would enhance meaningful interpretation of performance evaluation and the control functions of a firm. While reading the case keep in mind that the evaluation of a segment's performance should be in terms of the activity that was budgeted for it or in terms of its planned objective.

The Argentine Drug Caper[6]

Bill Powell, the general manager of the International Division of the Hawlsey Drug Company, finds himself faced with an extremely difficult competitive situation in Argentina. A Japanese competitor is underpricing him on his major product, Alzan, in the Argentine market; and he is faced with the total loss of all Argentine sales for this product.

Alzan is manufactured in one of Hawlsey Drug's U.S. plants, from which the International Division purchases it. The plant is an integral part of one of the domestic divisions of the company.

Bill's problem, as he sees it, is a matter of meeting his competitor's price. Alzan and the Japanese competitive product are basically equal from the standpoint of quality and performance. Both suppliers' delivery and credit terms are similar. The basic financial facts are as follows:

```
Prices:
  Alzan (a pill)....................................... $1.00 per gross
  Japanese Pill....................................... $0.60 per gross
Hawlsey's annual volume:
  5,000,000 gross plus an estimated
    15% annual growth factor
Manufacturing cost:
  (including transportation)......................... $0.70 per gross
```

Bill's initial reaction to this situation was that he could not afford to meet the competitive price of $0.60 (since his division would then show a loss of $0.10 per unit) and that he must therefore drop the product. He then remembered, somewhat vaguely, a discussion he got involved in while attending an executive development program. The discussion revolved around the idea that manufacturing costs were best thought of as consisting of two separate compo-

---

[6] This case was written by Prof. William L. Ferrara of The Pennsylvania State University College of Business Administration and is used here with his permission.

nents, that is, fixed and variable. The fixed costs had been described as a "kind of handicap" which a company tried to overcome by generating a sufficient "contribution" to cover these fixed costs and hopefully also to provide a profit. This contribution was defined as the difference between sales and variable costs.

Bill wondered if these concepts might be applicable to his situation. As the result of a cable to the company's main office in Atlanta, Bill found that Hawlsey did not separate variable and fixed costs in its cost accounting system. However, a cost analyst estimated that $0.30 of the $0.70 per gross manufacturing cost represented allocations of fixed costs.

Based on the above information, Bill realized that the standard variable costs per gross were $0.40. Based on the variable costs, then, there was a potential for a contribution of $0.20 per gross if the competitive price was met. With these facts in hand, Bill went to Atlanta to discuss his problem with the headquarters pricing staff.

In Atlanta, all agreed that the company's other products collectively were covering fixed costs and that capacity was available for the foreseeable future to produce sufficient amounts of Alzan. All also agreed that the competitive price had to be met and that it could be met without any adverse effects and with a $0.20 per gross contribution. Bill Powell went home satisfied that he could retain his Argentine Alzan business at a price which would be profitable to Hawlsey Drug Company.

A few months later, Bill noticed that reports concerning the profitability of South American sales were getting worse and worse. He could not understand this, since everything seemed to be going well from a volume and cost point of view.

Bill decided that he had to uncover the causes of his poor showing, so he started to analyze in detail the profit report for South America. To his surprise, he found that the headquarters accounting staff was charging his Argentine sales of Alzan with a manufacturing cost of $0.70 per gross rather than $0.40. His anticipated contribution of $0.20 per gross was, in effect, being turned into an accounting loss of $0.10 per gross. An expected annual contribution of $1,000,000 ($0.20 × 5,000,000 gross) was being turned into a loss of $500,000 ($0.10 × 5,000,000 gross) by a group of accountants!

Bill then tried to explain his poor South American showing at a special meeting of the company's executive committee. They could not understand his explanation and, like the accountants, discussed only the "full cost" of manufacturing. Bill left the meeting muttering to himself, "I make a sound profitable decision and the accounting department makes me look like a fool. I guess they and the executive committee are really telling me to give up the Argentine market for Alzan."

Preliminary Comments on the "Caper"

In the above case, the major problem centers on the mistaken concept that a course of action that is profitable for the total company will automatically appear profitable from the standpoint of the manufacturing division or the distribution division. The environment in this case is a contributing factor in that the divisions have no available competitive markets for products bought from or sold to other divisions in the company. Thus, since no market values exist, transfer prices must be based upon costs. These factors appear to be the primary cause for confusion.

Specifically, the accountants and executives of Hawlsey Drug Company neglected the very basic nature of fixed costs and treated them in the International Division's income statement as variable costs.[7] This treatment of fixed costs by the accounting department both (1) distorts the profit picture of the Argentine segment and (2) destroys the credibility of accounting data in the eyes of Bill Powell.

Full-Cost Transfer Pricing

The facts from the preceding case relevant to the full-cost method of transfer pricing are:

Previously stated:
    Units involved.................................... 5,000,000 gross
    Manufacturing costs transferred:
        Variable.. $0.40 per gross
        Fixed... $0.30 per gross
    Competitive sales price........................... $0.60 per gross
Additional data:
    Argentine marketing costs:
        Variable.. $0.002 per gross
        Fixed... $5,000 per year

---

[7] This, of course, is always the effect of full-cost accounting as used in "generally accepted accounting principles."

Under the full-cost method, the price of the units transferred would be determined by deriving a total unit cost, that is, adding the variable costs plus fixed costs transferred per gross ($0.40 + $0.30 = $0.70).

In Exhibit 1, the effect of using the full-cost method can be observed. When fixed costs are unitized, in accounting statements they "look like" variable costs, and hence there is a tendency to regard them as being, in fact, variable. They thus tend to lose their fixed-cost trait as a "handicap." If fixed costs are not unitized and were treated as fixed (i.e., a lump-sum charge rather than a pro-rated variable amount per unit), the Argentine division would have shown at least a positive marginal contribution. As it is, this segment shows only a "Division net contribution" of minus $515,000.

Exhibit 1
Illustrative Divisional Income Statement
Argentine Market—Full-Cost Transfer Price

Sales (5,000,000 @ $0.60)...............................		$3,000,000
Costs:		
Manufacturing costs (5,000,000 @ $0.70)............	$3,500,000	
Marketing:		
Variable (5,000,000 @ $0.002)......................	10,000	
Fixed...	5,000	3,515,000
Division net contribution..............................		$ (515,000)

These fixed-variable cost concepts are most important, not only for planning but also for performance evaluation. By unitizing fixed costs to derive a full-cost transfer price, not only does the distinction between fixed and variable costs become obscure but the application of incremental analytical techniques also becomes difficult.

Though the fixed costs of the selling division are treated as variable costs by the buying division, they remain as fixed costs to the company as a whole. This inconsistency can lead to suboptimal decisions. The buying division manager will only buy the intermediate product if the final sale price is great enough to cover the transfer price plus any additional costs he may incur. The total effect from the transaction may in fact be to increase total company profit, but the full-cost transfer price could conceal this fact and thus motivate a manager to forego an opportunity that is in the best interests of the company because it does not *appear* to be in his division's best interest. An additional defect of the full-cost transfer price is that no element of profit is considered for the producing unit. This tends to negate the profit center concept, especially where the producing division transfers a significant part of its output.

Variable-Cost Transfer Pricing

The apparent logical alternative to address the potential for sub-optimization inherent in full-cost transfer pricing is the use of variable costs only. In this way the performance report of the buying division (e.g., the Argentine market) will report profits measured in accordance with the profit contribution concept which was used to make the decision to meet the $0.60 competitive price. Bill Powell could then say, "I made a sound and profitable decision and the accounting department reported the facts properly." Exhibit 2 shows how the variable-cost method of transfer pricing affects divisional profit calculations.[8]

Exhibit 2
Illustrative Divisional Income Statement
Argentine Market—Variable-Cost Transfer Price

Sales (5,000,000 @ $0.60)...........................		$3,000,000
Variable costs:		
Manufacturing (5,000,000 @ $0.40).................	$2,000,000	
Marketing (5,000,000 @ $0.002)...................	10,000	2,010,000
Contribution.......................................		$ 990,000
Fixed costs:		
Marketing.......................................		5,000
Division net contribution...........................		$ 985,000

Unfortunately, the variable-cost method places too much emphasis on the short run, as indicated by use of contribution ideology and the absence of a charge for fixed manufacturing costs. With the variable-cost method (except for the division which sells its output to outside customers), all other divisions involved with intracompany transfers are in effect regarded as being expense centers. The resulting defect is similar to that pointed out earlier in regard to full-cost transfer pricing, where the profit center concept was said to be negated for the producing division due to the lack of an ele-

---

[8] The variable-cost method is considered to be an operational approximation to the marginal-cost method. For some further thought on this notion, see Gordon Shillinglaw, *Managerial Cost Accounting*, 4th ed. (Homewood, Ill.: Richard D. Irwin, Inc., 1977), chap. 26.

ment of profit in the transfer price. Under the variable-cost method, the problem is exaggerated, since neither profit nor fixed costs are considered in the transfer price.

In succeeding paragraphs, a combination of full-cost and variable-cost transfer pricing known as a two-part transfer price will be illustrated. This combination seems to place both short- and long-term considerations in proper perspective and could easily yield results that would satisfy Bill Powell, the accounting department, and the executive committee, as well as the domestic division which manufactures Alzan.

A Two-Part Transfer Price[9]

The domestic division which manufactures Alzan would justifiably feel disadvantaged if the International Division paid only a variable cost of $0.40 per unit for products which required the incurrence of fixed manufacturing costs. On the other hand, Bill Powell seems to be on the right track when he asks for recognition of the distinction between variable and fixed costs in measuring his division's profitability. A two-part transfer price, consisting of the standard variable cost to manufacture plus a *lump-sum* share of budgeted fixed manufacturing cost, could accommodate both divisions. Furthermore, the two-part transfer price could engender long- and short-run divisional decision making which would be simultaneously beneficial to the divisions as well as to the company as a whole.

Variable costs are directly related to production and should be a part of the transfer price. Since the buying (International) division has no control over the efficiency or inefficiency of operation of the selling (domestic) division, its profit performance within the company should not reflect efficiencies or inefficiencies of the selling division. Therefore, only variable costs at *standard* should be included within the transfer price. Including variable cost at standard rather than at actual in the transfer price should tend to motivate the manufacturing segments to operate as efficiently as possible in

---

[9] Two-part transfer pricing is essentially the same technique recommended by C. F. Schlatter for the distribution of service department costs to producing departments. See his *Advanced Cost Accounting* (New York: John Wiley & Sons, Inc., 1939), chap. 2. Shillinglaw, *Managerial Cost Accounting, pp.* 864–67, and Solomons, *Divisional Performance*, pp. 198–205, have done much in recent years to popularize the two-part transfer price.

order to produce a favorable variance and favorable evaluation in terms of variable costs.

Fixed costs tend not to vary with volume and represent capacity employed in the manufacture of an item or the ability to produce an item. From the standpoint of the selling division, if another division desires to have them produce an item for it, it is only reasonable that the buying division be charged for a proportion of the capacity costs incurred. As with the variable cost portion of the transfer price, the lump-sum portion should be based on standard (i.e., budgeted) fixed costs, not actual fixed costs.

But in determining this lump sum, what measure of capacity would be fair to the interested parties? First, the buying division would only be willing to include in the transfer price a proportionate amount of the capacity costs directly traceable to the manufacturing segment. Since the allocation of nontraceable fixed costs can only be accomplished on an arbitrary basis, the manager of the buying division would not want costs included in the transfer price which may not be truly attributable to that segment. Second, the buying and selling divisions would want a measure of capacity which is realistic. As a guideline to arriving at a fair measure of capacity, one can refer to the average operating level assumed by the designers when they were considering how large to construct the plant. Actual capacity could then be established as a percentage above or below this design norm, based on a practical assessment of *de facto* utilization. Traceable fixed costs would be assigned in terms of a proportion of budgeted traceable fixed costs equal to the ratio of capacity used or budgeted for the transferred items.

If current average expected use materially differs from the planned average operating level as specified by the designers, the managers of the divisions involved should determine via negotiation the proportion of fixed costs to be assigned to transferred items. The designer's planned average operating level or an estimate of the average capacity should act as a focal point for meaningful negotiation. Otherwise, the managers of the buying and selling divisions may start negotiations at extremely divergent amounts.

To prevent the buying division from treating these fixed costs as variable costs, they should be included in the transfer price as a lump-sum payment. By being included as a lump-sum payment, fixed costs maintain their characteristic nature as being a "handicap" which must be overcome by an adequate contribution. To add emphasis to the "handicap" nature of the fixed costs, they could be transferred at the beginning of each operating period on a budgeted basis. If monthly or quarterly statements are desired, the annual fixed cost charge could be treated as an amortizable deferred charge.

The transfer price now includes variable costs at standard (so as not to transfer the efficiencies or inefficiencies in the manufacturing division to the buying division) and a lump-sum payment representing a portion of traceable budgeted fixed costs based on the expected average operating level of the selling unit and the expected demand of the buying unit. The latter is or should be determined as a part of the annual budgetary process in negotiation between buying and selling units and, after negotiation, represents a committed cost to the buying profit center.

For purposes of illustration, assume the same situation exists as discussed in the case example using the full-cost method. Here fixed costs will be treated as a lump-sum payment to be included in the transfer price. The amount of this lump-sum payment has been determined via negotiation between the parties (buying and selling units) as a proportion of the traceable budgeted fixed costs of the producing unit based on capacity utilized for the transferred items. The transfer price also includes variable costs.

In Exhibit 3, both short-term factors (variable costs) and long-term factors (fixed costs) are considered. An evaluation of a profit center's performance could therefore be made for either or even for both simultaneously. Thus, within any planning period it is possible to make knowledgeable decisions on a variable cost basis, since the fixed costs are committed (i.e., Bill Powell would have met the competitive price in the short run, since he already was committed

Exhibit 3
Illustrative Divisional Income Statement
Argentine Market—Two-Part Transfer Price

Sales (5,000,000 @ $0.60).............................		$3,000,000
Variable costs:		
Manufacturing (5,000,000 @ $0.40).................	$2,000,000	
Marketing (5,000,000 @ $0.002).....................	10,000	2,010,000
Contribution..		$ 990,000
Fixed costs:		
Manufacturing (lump-sum fixed costs		
transferred).....................................	$1,500,000	
Marketing...	5,000	1,505,000
Division net contribution............................		$ (515,000)

to paying his division's share of the supplying division's budgeted fixed costs). For decisions beyond the current planning period, the segments have information for making long-term decisions because fixed costs are shown separately (i.e., Bill Powell had good information to use in long-term decision making).

The buying division will be able to avoid the lump-sum charge only if it decides it will not buy; but once the commitment to buy is made via the budgetary process, the fixed costs should be considered committed for the planning period while the variable costs may still be considered avoidable by altering plans with sufficient notice during the planning period. With sufficient notice and an ability of the producing division to find alternative uses for capacity, some or all of the fixed costs originally considered transferred to a division could also be made avoidable. If all capacity costs are not "sold" by the internal selling division (i.e., idle or unsold capacity exists), it will be forced to look for an alternative buyer for its unutilized capacity.

To enhance the two-part transfer price discussed, and yet preserve the integrity of the profit center concept, a charge for the use of capital employed should be included in the transfer price. This creates a three-part transfer price.

A Three-Part Transfer Price

Assume that capital employed can be attributed to the Argentine market as follows:

a. Capital employed directly in the Argentine market—$50,000.
b. Argentine market's share of capital employed in the manufacturing division—$100,000.

With a 10 percent desired return on capital employed, the charge for the use of capital is 10 percent of $150,000 or $15,000. Although top management sets the rate of capital charge, the users of capital determine the amount of capital employed in essentially the same manner as the lump-sum charge for traceable fixed costs. Thus, the capital charge should be considered traceable.[10]

---

[10] A capital charge based on traceable assets employed is used to avoid arbitrary allocations of nontraceable assets employed. Further research may be needed in this area of determining how, if at all, nontraceable cost and assets should be included in the capital charge via, for example, a required rate of return which is higher than the desired rate of return for the firm as a whole, which includes all nontraceable costs and assets.

Exhibit 4 illustrates how the three-part transfer price can be built into a divisional income statement. As can be seen, Exhibit 4 is the same as Exhibit 3 down to the "Division net contribution" line. At that point, the "Capital charge" is deducted in order to yield "Division residual income," which can best be described as division earnings or loss in excess of the desired return on the assets used in generating those earnings.

The three-part transfer price thus keeps separate the three distinct pieces of a transfer price which can be exceedingly useful in evaluating both long- and short-range situations. In the present context, Bill Powell would have seen that meeting the competitive

Exhibit 4
Illustrative Divisional Income Statement
Argentine Market—Three-Part Transfer Price

Sales (5,000,000 @ $0.60).............................		$3,000,000
Variable costs:		
Manufacturing (5,000,000 @ $0.40).................	$2,000,000	
Marketing (5,000,000 @ $0.002).....................	10,000	2,010,000
Contribution...		$ 990,000
Fixed costs:		
Manufacturing....................................	$1,500,000	
Marketing..	5,000	1,505,000
Division net contribution............................		$ (515,000)
Capital charge—10%:		
Manufacturing....................................	$ 10,000	
Marketing..	5,000	15,000
Division residual income............................		$ (530,000)

price yielded a positive marginal contribution of $990,000, even though the $0.60 price would not have fully covered the fixed cost commitment of $1,505,000 or the capital charge of $15,000. However, Bill Powell would have also seen that retaining the market by meeting the price yielded an opportunity to ultimately cover the committed fixed costs and capital charge via a change in pricing tactics by competition and/or the annual market growth rate of 15 percent. This analytical approach is certainly the kind of thinking to be fostered by managements and supported by internal accounting procedures.

Bill Powell and others in similar situations would still have a problem if their efforts were to be evaluated solely in terms of absolute values, such as the negative "Division net contribution" or

"Divisional residual income." To offset—and perhaps eliminate—such a problem, the three-part transfer price should be coupled to a schedule of relative values, such as variances from budget, for performance evaluation purposes. A way of doing this is shown in Exhibit 5. Managerial decisions that result in minimal or negative profitability will be judged less harshly if the background to or reasons for the decision are apparent. The budget column supplies the needed information in this case.

Generality of the Three-Part Transfer Price. Practically every knowledgeable accountant and manager today recognizes the utility

Exhibit 5
Illustrative Divisional Income Statement
Incorporating a Three-Part Transfer Price

	Budget		*Actual*	
Sales...		XX		XX
Transfers to other divisions				
(includes three parts).........................		XX		XX
Total revenues....................................		XX		XX
Less variable costs:				
Transfers in @ standard.........................	XX		XX	
This division's.................................	XX	XX	XX	XX
Contribution......................................		XX		XX
Less traceable fixed costs:				
Transfers in....................................	XX		XX	
This division's.................................	XX	XX	XX	XX
Division's net contribution........................		XX		XX
Less capital charge:				
Transfers in....................................	XX		XX	
This division's (based on traceable assets				
employed)....................................	XX	XX	XX	XX
Division residual income..........................		XX		XX

of a distinction between variable and fixed costs and perhaps also the utility of a charge for the use of capital. The three-part transfer price simply says in effect that if this utility is so great, why not embody it in accounting systems concerning the assignment of costs among the various divisions of the firm? The basic nature of each element of cost will not be obscured, and if fixed costs are assigned to using divisions in lump-sum amounts, the often-heard comment, "You are ignoring fixed costs!" will be eliminated.

Rather than an additional illustration tailored specifically to the previous data presented for the International Division of Hawlsey

Drug Company, Exhibit 5 is a general illustration summarizing the previous comments. With it, it is easy to imagine how a division, either buying or selling, would be evaluated in terms of the budgeting process and in the light of the three-part transfer price.

SUMMARY AND CONCLUSION

When a market price for items involved in intracompany transfers is not available, a three-part transfer price has great utility. Intracompany buying divisions should be satisfied as long as appropriate recognition is given to the basically distinct cost categories and especially if performance is evaluated in terms of variances from budget. Intracompany selling divisions should also be satisfied, since they would be given appropriate credit for costs incurred including an element of profit via a capital charge. Management and accounting systems specialists should be satisfied, since the three-part transfer price inclines divisions toward appropriate consideration of long- and short-run facets of decision making.

However, if a market price is available for an intermediate good which is involved in an intracompany transfer, it is a focal point at which the buying and selling units may start negotiations. It is readily available and would represent the ceiling price for transfers. Market prices should be reduced by selling and bad debt costs since these costs are generally not incurred on internal sales.

Transfer pricing systems are needed if profit centers are to be established within a company. Unfortunately, transfer pricing may be extremely difficult to implement and may require a great deal of top management's time and discretion to resolve arguments, such that other forms of performance evaluation possibly would be employed.

ADDITIONAL SOURCES

Abdel-Khalik, A. Rashad, and Lusk, Edward J. "Transfer Pricing—A Synthesis." *The Accounting Review,* January 1974, p. 8.

Anthony, Robert N., and Dearden, John. *Management Control Systems: Text and Cases,* chaps. 6, 7. 3d ed. Homewood, Ill.: Richard D. Irwin, Inc., 1976.

————, and Reece, James S. *Management Accounting Principles,* chap. 20, 3d ed. Homewood, Ill.: Richard D. Irwin, Inc., 1975.

Barrett, M. Edgar. "Case of the Tangled Transfer Price." *Harvard Business Review,* May–June 1977, p. 20.

Dearden, John. "Appraising Profit Center Managers." *Harvard Business Review,* May–June 1968, p. 80.

Dickey, Robert I., ed. *Accountants' Cost Handbook.* 2d ed. New York: The Ronald Press Co., 1960.

Ferrara, William L. "The Contribution Approach." *NAA Bulletin,* December 1964, p. 19.

Goetz, Billy E. "Transfer Prices: An Exercise in Relevancy and Goal Congruence." *The Accounting Review,* July 1967, p. 435.

Granick, David. "National Differences in the Use of Internal Transfer Prices." *California Management Review,* Summer 1975, p. 28.

Greer, Howard C. "Divisional Profit Calculation—Notes on the 'Transfer Price' Problem." *NAA Bulletin,* July 1962, p. 6.

Holstrum, Gary L., and Sauls, Eugene H. "The Opportunity Cost Transfer Price." *Management Accounting,* May 1973, p. 29.

Horngren, Charles T. *Cost Accounting: A Managerial Emphasis,* chap. 22. 4th ed. Englewood Cliffs, N.J.: Prentice-Hall, Inc., 1977.

Hirshleifer, Jack. "Economics of the Divisionalized Firm." *Journal of Business,* April 1957, p. 96.

————. "On the Economics of Transfer Pricing." *Journal of Business,* July 1956, p. 172.

Onsi, Mohamed. "A Transfer Price System Based on Opportunity Cost." *The Accounting Review,* July 1970, p. 535.

Shillinglaw, Gordon. *Managerial Cost Accounting,* chap. 26. 4th ed. Homewood, Ill.: Richard D. Irwin, Inc., 1977.

Solomons, David. *Divisional Performance: Measurement and Control.* Homewood, Ill.: Richard D. Irwin, Inc., 1968.

Vendig, Richard E. "A Three-Part Transfer Price." *Management Accounting,* September 1973, p. 33.

Watson, Spencer C. "A Vote for R&D Profit Centers." *Management Accounting,* April 1975, p. 50.

27

Investment Centers and ROI

Robert Rachlin*

The preceding chapter dealt with the concept of profit centers, and with the issues of transfer pricing attendant to implementation of a profit center measurement and control system. In this chapter, we consider the broadest concept of responsibility center measurement—investment centers.

Difference between Profit Centers and Investment Centers

Whereas in a profit center approach an earnings figure is attributed to a responsibility center, the investment center concept deals also with the investment needed and/or utilized in the generation of those earnings.[1] These earnings and investments can be looked upon either in total to determine the impact and/or relationship of earnings to investment, or in terms of the incremental earnings that are generated from incremental investment. To focus on it in another way, with investment centers we consider, "How much investment is needed to support anticipated earnings?" or "How much earnings can be expected from a given amount of investment?"

It must be recognized that increased earnings do not necessarily

---

* Mr. Rachlin is Director of Group Operations for the American Management Associations, New York.

[1] *Editors' Note:* Although we, along with management accounting textbooks, maintain this definitional distinction between profit centers and investment centers, many practitioners refer to *both* types of responsibility center simply as "profit centers."

mean favorable performance. These earnings may require a dispro-portionate amount of investment to generate them, and when mea-sured by the investment added, they may actually constitute a lower return on investment. Earnings alone do not necessarily mea-sure performance; earnings related to investment offers a more realistic approach to the measurement of economic performance.

While the term "investment center" suggests that only the invest-ment in the segment of a business is measured, the true meaning actually utilizes both earnings and the investment necessary to sup-port that part of the business. On the other hand, the profit center concept measures a segment of the business that has revenue and expense responsibility, but which is not held accountable for the level of its investment.

It must be pointed out that to properly measure performance under an investment center structure, it is necessary that the head of that business segment have significant influence on the three elements of return on investment, namely, sales, earnings, and in-vestment. However, the organizational unit's return on investment can be calculated for purposes of evaluating the unit *as an economic entity* even if the unit's manager does not significantly influence return on investment. This distinction between evaluating a re-sponsibility center as an economic entity versus evaluating the per-formance of its *manager* must be made in the performance evalu-ation process, as well as when setting objectives. Caution must be taken not to criticize a manager for a disappointing return on in-vestment if that manager does not have significant influence over all three factors that make up return on investment.

What Is Return on Investment?

Return on investment (ROI) is a financial management tool that measures both past performance and future investment decisions in a reasonably systematic manner. It is what it is intended to be—a management tool using financial data. This does not mean it is to be used solely by financial people or people with some financial understanding. On the contrary, this concept is an effective tool for all levels of management in all disciplines of the organization. Used correctly, the ROI concept will assist in establishing the basic strategies for generating earnings as well as the growth and posi-tioning of the organization in the market place.

In addition, return on investment rests on the assumption that the best alternative investment is one that will maximize economic earnings and contribute to the organization. This is necessary, since within an organization, all business segments vie for funds to carry out the company's mission of generating and/or maintaining earnings standards. Also, long-term earnings result from investments made during the course of business. Investments can also be used to maintain a current position and/or strengthen the position. Without some form of investment spending, growth could be impaired.

Why Use Return on Investment?

The fundamental reason for using return on investment is that it provides management with an intelligent, yet fairly simple, way of reviewing both past and future performance. During the process, factors of intuition and judgment are reduced to an easy and understandable mathematical calculation. ROI, by taking the intuitive nature out of measuring investment performance, will enhance the ability to effectively manage the organization in the following ways:

Forces planning for growth and opportunity.

Provides a basis for decision making from the realm of intuition to economic reality.

Assists in evaluating investment opportunities.

Evaluates management performance.

Assists managers to respond to the marketplace with profitable opportunities.

What Does Return on Investment Do?

In the process of applying the ROI concept, many areas of management decision making begin to surface:

1. Problems are defined and highlighted for the attention of the decision maker.
2. Alternative investments are identified which are desirable to the organization.
3. Investments are categorized in priority by evaluating and weighing expected results of each alternative.
4. Highlighted are those nonquantitative factors needing attention

for decision making which impact on the success or failure of the investment.

Understanding the Definition

The term "return on investment" is a generic term and takes on many variations. The reasons for the variations is the fact that the equation can vary depending upon the purpose and structure of the equation. For example, the term "return on" relates to expected receipt of a sum over and above the investment over a specified period of time. This results in a ratio:

$$\frac{\text{Return}}{\text{Investment}}$$

The term "return" is an earnings figure, either before or after tax, and may include other deductions such as interest. The term "investment" would apply to the base chosen for evaluation, such as total assets, capital employed, equity capital, and so on. For example, thinking of total assets as the investment base, the term "return on total assets" arises. One can see that many definitional variations can exist which would change the calculation of the ROI fraction. The key is to define the makeup of both the numerator (earnings) and the denominator (investment) and be consistent in its use for evaluation. Any change in definition must be changed for both historical and future evaluation to reflect the proper measurement trend. Evaluation techniques must be consistent to properly measure the validity of performance.

Major Uses and Applications

To achieve planned return-on-investment performance, it is important that all parts of the organization participate in assisting to reach the required objectives. Therefore, management must be involved at all levels. It is not only top management's problem, but all managers must contribute towards the success.

The major uses and applications can be viewed to affect all disciplines. The measurement, control, and evaluation process will be interlocking in some way throughout all of the following uses and applications:

External Measurement. The evaluation of competitive data will act as a barometer in measuring a company's performance with the external environment to properly evaluate an entity's performance. A base needs to be established, and this base should relate to the community in which the entity operates, namely, its competitors.

Internal Measurement. ROI can be used in the evaluation of internal segments of a company and their effects on earnings through cost reduction and profit improvement programs, as well as the amount of investment necessary to support increased earnings contribution.

Asset Utilization. ROI analysis aids in the identification of opportunities for improving profitability through the use of assets, both current and capital assets.

Capital Investment Evaluation. ROI is the basis of the more acceptable techniques for providing the mechanism to effectively evaluate the allocation and anticipated performances of capital resources. (See Chapter 15, "Analyzing Capital Expenditure Proposals.")

Acquisitions and Divestments. The process of evaluating acquisition and divestment decisions should include analysis of the short- and long-run impact on return-on-investment performance.

Establishing Objectives. ROI provides the tool for establishing profit goals and objectives through the comparative review of both internal and external measurements.

Management Incentives. Return on investment can provide a partial basis for rewarding performance incentives.

Focus on Product Lines. The return-on-investment technique, by focusing management's attention on the profitability of existing or new product lines, can provide the basis for the elimination or addition of product lines.

Make or Buy and Lease or Purchase. Return on investment can provide the framework for financial decisions in both of these areas. (See Chapters 18 and 19.)

Evaluating Human Resources. Emerging evaluation techniques are attempting to apply the ROI concept to human resources, particularly where turnover is concerned. Since human resources constitute a large portion of the investment in an organization, using return-on-investment concepts and applications may provide a valuable tool of measurement.

Inventory Control. ROI is a useful tool for measuring the profit impact of incremental changes of inventory and those earnings generated from that additional inventory investment. An organization can more formally justify the addition of inventory by measuring its impact on the total organization's return on investment.

Pricing. Return on investment can provide a guideline for the pricing of products, including intracompany transfer prices. (See Chapter 26.)

Cautions in Using Return on Investment

Several cautions must be recognized in using return on investment. They include the interpretation of ROI data, the use of ROI data, and the consideration of other performance measurement methods.

Relying on absolute numerical results is a common fault of managers responsible for reviewing return-on-investment results. While return on investment is an excellent tool for measuring performance, too often decisions are based on absolute numerical results. This can create a false decision, since numerical results can vary with the makeup of the data in both historical and future projections.

For example, differences in accounting principles, when relating to different industries, can lead to differing return-on-investment results. In addition, one-time accounting adjustments can result in substantial differences in the final results. Therefore, before any decision is made on the return-on-investment rate, it is important to be sure everyone is well versed on the interpretation of the data being evaluated. For internal purposes, the data may be adjusted to reflect these differences, or there may simply be a general understanding that the differences are due to other factors.

Another caution involves being consistent in using both historical data and accurate forecasted data. When comparing return-on-investment rates, be sure that all historical data are uniform. Using different bases for comparison, such as total assets versus equity versus capital employed, or earnings before taxes versus earnings after taxes, will result in different return-on-investment rates. It is important that the interpreter of the data understand whether such differences are present in order to form a valid conclusion.

When forecasted data are necessary, such as for capital expenditures analysis and planning purposes, it is also important to use a similar base for the return-on-investment calculation. To properly reflect trends in the business, it is advisable to use the same historical base used for forecasting. This will highlight changing trends and provide the manager with a more accurate basis for decision making.

A final caution is not to ignore other methods of appraising performance. While return on investment is an excellent tool when used properly, there are other factors in appraising performance which may not be evaluated on a quantitative basis. Areas such as attitudes, influences on others, knowledge of the industry, and managing people may be difficult to measure numerically. In certain job functions, these other performance measurement factors may have more significance than the return-on-investment rate.

In summary, consider all facets of management, and use return on investment to assist in reaching an objective, and not as the only measurement tool.

WHAT CONSTITUTES THE INVESTMENT BASE?

The term "investment" can be construed to mean many different aggregations of accounting data. For example, when the stockholders review return on investment, they reflect on the return on *owners' equity*, or the total equity interest that the stockholders have in the business. To corporate financial officers, return on *invested capital* is important. Invested capital includes owners' equity plus long-term liabilities, the company's long-term financial commitments from owners, banks, bondholders, and so on.

Within the organization, operating managers tend to view investment as *assets*, and are expected to optimize use of these assets to generate higher earnings. Assets such as inventories, receivables, and fixed assets are used as the investment base by operating managers to generate earnings for the business. These managers are generally not responsible for the financial structure decisions and are not concerned with the manner in which the assets for which they are responsible were financed.

Investment Base Definition

Even after a company decides on the definition of "investment" that seems best suited for their purposes, there remains the problem of how to determine the amount of investment to be attributed to a *given* investment center—that is, segment of the company. These centers may be entire divisions, product lines, market segments, departments, or some other segment of the business. The only requirements are that the segment have a clearly identified manager, and that this manager have significant influence over the segment's revenues, earnings, and investment.

The determination of a given responsibility center's investment develops much controversy. The computation of net sales and net earnings is relatively easy, particularly net sales, which are generally standard as set forth by accounting and industry practices. Controversy on expense charges to a center usually focuses on allocated noncontrollable expenses, but disputes here are usually fairly easy to resolve. To compute earnings, a decision must be made as to whether they are to be calculated on a pretax or after-tax basis.

However, determining the investment base presents a more difficult problem. One must examine the purpose for which the return-on-investment rate is being used. For example, is it used as a basis for comparative performance within the industry? Is it used for setting company objectives? Or, is it used for evaluating past performance of internal operations, and perhaps also for determining a manager's bonus? Whatever the purpose, there must exist a consistency within each method so as to develop a trend which answers the question, "Where have we been and where are we going?"

Different investment base definitions will of course result in different ROI rates. The important thing to keep in mind is that performance will be evaluated using this base, and that differing investment-base definitions may lead to different decisions by investment center managers.

Here are some of the questions management must answer in computing divisional investment:

What investment should be used—total assets, fixed assets, total assets less current liabilities?

Should fixed assets be valued at gross book value or net of depreciation?[2]

---

[2] *Editors' Note:* For a detailed treatment of fixed asset valuation and depreciation alternatives, see Robert N. Anthony and John Dearden, *Management Control Systems: Text and Cases,* 3d ed. by (Homewood, Ill.: Richard D. Irwin, Inc., 1976), chap. 8. Unfortunately, the hypothetically best procedures differ so much from generally used accounting methods that they are never found in practice: for example, Anthony and Dearden conclude that annuity depreciation (rather than straight line or accelerated) is the preferable method for investment center depreciation calculations.

Should historical costs or replacement costs be the basis of asset valuation?

How should resources used by more than one investment center be included in the investment base, such as research laboratories, headquarters facilities, centralized EDP equipment, and centrally managed cash, receivables, and payables?

What time period is to be used for investment balances—beginning, ending, or an acceptable average?

The issue of the time period for measurement of the investment base, such as closing balance, opening balance, an average of the beginning and closing balances, a moving average, or several other related possibilities, can be resolved with some basic guidelines. For shorter measurement periods, period-end balances are adequate. However, for longer periods, some variation of averages should be used. Regardless of what method is used, it probably will not alter the conclusions reached, since consistency is the key element.

The concept of assigning investment to specific responsibility centers within the company has become regarded as a valuable tool for measuring performance as organizations become more decentralized. Companies are increasingly attributing their total investment to individual investment centers. Greater emphasis on future growth through long-range planning techniques has also promulgated this emphasis on decentralization.

However, it must be reemphasized that decentralization in terms of measuring investment center performance should coincide with authority over this ROI responsibility. Without this ability to control the profit and investment in the responsibility center for which the manager is responsible, ROI evaluation can lead to a sense of frustration and inequity on the part of the manager. However, if ROI measurement is appropriate, the benefits from top management's point of view are that it allows them to evaluate segment performance, take corporate corrective actions, and serve as a basis for the establishment of incentive compensation programs.

Investment Base Allocations

In many decentralized organizations, *total* corporate investments are allocated back to the operating divisions in an effort to measure the full impact on return on investment within that operating division. This allows a full evaluation of the operating division's economic performance measuring the investment that is supporting a specified or anticipated level of earnings. It enables management to measure acceptable levels of return on investment, and may lead to a decision that certain operating divisions are no longer able to meet corporate objectives. This analysis can only be done by applying the full investment that is needed to functionally operate the business. This includes the allocation of corporate-controlled investments such as centralized administrative functions, that is, cash, payables, purchasing, and so on.

The major disadvantage of allocating these investments is that they are not directly controllable by the managers of the investment centers to which they are allocated. The operating division can claim that only partial benefits are received from the allocation. This creates a situation where an operating division appears to be accountable, but is not responsible, for control over this allocated portion of its investment base. The other disadvantage of such allocations is that in order to meet corporate return-on-investment objectives, an investment center may feel it necessary to increase the price of its products. There is the risk that this action will actually reduce return on investment, because of the price increases causing a decline in volume which more than effects the per unit price increases.

As one can see, then, allocation of nonproductive "headquarters" assets can have a negative effect on the operations of the business. If the investment can be directly attributable to operations, then it is the responsibility of each operating division to earn the expected return on its investment. If not directly attributable to investment centers, other efforts should be made to control nonrevenue-generating investments, such as corporate investments in office buildings, aircraft, obsolete plant and equipment, and so on. Here, as in all performance evaluation matters, it is important that top management keep in mind the distinction between the performance of an investment center as an *economic entity* and the performance of the *manager* of that investment center.

Methods that are sometimes used for dealing with the measurement problems we have identified will now be briefly described.

Cash. Alternatives for assigning a cash balance to an investment center include: (1) use estimated cash requirements based on cash receipts and disbursements, resulting in the net cash requirements for a given period; (2) use a percent of net sales, keeping in mind credit terms; and/or (3) use a percentage of cost of goods sold, in that demands for current assets excluding cash and marketable securities, are directly affected by fluctuations in levels of sales volume. Any of these methods may result in the sum of all investment centers' imputed cash balances exceeding the actual corporate cash balance. While this bothers some managers, it is simply descriptive of the fact that centrally controlled cash requirements are less than the amount that would be necessary if each division held cash balances sufficient to provide the necessary buffer for uneven inflows and outflows.

Marketable Securities. In general, this asset should not be allocated, since in most cases, only corporate management can invest in marketable securities. If assignment to investment centers is deemed necessary, the same basis can be used as is used for cash.

Receivables. These usually can be identified by where the sales were generated. The allocation problem only arises where receivables are unidentified by an operating unit. When this is the case, they can be allocated based on operating units net sales. Some companies use a formula to allocate receivables even where sales are identifiable to divisions if the division does not control credit terms or collections. This formula should be consistent with stated credit terms, for example, one month's sales where terms are 30 days.

Inventories. Most inventories can be specifically related to a particular operating unit, and investment centers usually have direct control over the levels of their inventories. Where unidentified, production records on raw material usage, cost of goods sold, or net sales can be used. Some companies deduct accounts payable from inventories, on the grounds that this net amount represents the corporate capital investment needed to support the inventories.

Prepaid Expenses, Deferred Charges, and Other Assets. Since these items are generally not a major part of the investment base, any reasonable method may be acceptable, such as cost of goods sold and net sales.

Property, Plant, and Equipment. Most of these assets can be generally attributed to a particular operating unit. Idle plants and corporate fixed assets such as research and development laboratories, cafeterias, and joint service departments need not necessarily be assigned to investment centers, as discussed above. If they are assigned, a reasonable allocation method should be used, such as floor space used, number of employees, direct labor hours, units produced, and so on. Keep in mind that every effort should be made to make the allocation as equitable as possible, and the allocation should be periodically reviewed to ensure equitability.[3]

Pretax versus After-Tax Earnings. For purposes of management evaluation, it is preferable to use pretax earnings to measure the performance of operating units, since taxes are based on overall corporate operations and can be distorted by unique operations such as nonprofit operations, nontaxable income and expenses, effects of capital gains or losses, tax-loss carryovers, and so on. When evaluating overall company ROI, or an investment center for competitive comparisons (as well as capital expenditure proposals), an after-tax basis is appropriate.

In summary, the implementation of the ROI concept in investment centers is not easy. The subject is controversial. However, whatever the decision, the objectives should always be to provide the mechanism for achieving maximum earnings and should fit the style, needs, and objectives of the organization. Many different approaches may have to be explored to find the proper evaluation method.

The Appendix at the end of this chapter illustrates the diversity of investment center implementation approaches. Based on research performed at the University of Michigan's Graduate Business School in 1977, the Appendix includes data from over 60 percent of the *Fortune* "1,000" companies on such matters as how profit and the investment base are defined in practice.

RELATIONSHIP BETWEEN RETURN ON INVESTMENT AND THE ORGANIZATION

In analyzing return on investment, it is important to analyze each of the components which combine in making up the return-on-investment rate. The basic components are sales, net earnings, and investment. These components relate the two financial statements, namely, the earnings statement and the balance sheet. From these financial statements one can compute a series of key ratios for understanding the operations of the business. The two primary

---

[3] *Editors' Note:* For a detailed discussion of fixed asset valuation for investment center measurement, see Anthony and Dearden, *Management Control Systems,* pp. 339–44.

ratios relating to return on investment are the *profitability rate* and the *turnover rate*.

Profitability Rate

The profitability rate, also called "profit margin" or "return on sales," is computed by dividing net income by sales. It highlights the relationship of how much earnings are generated from every sales dollar. It should be noted that it is this profit margin that most Americans—and, unfortunately, some business executives—refer to when discussing whether businesses are sufficiently profitable, whereas we have seen that return on investment is the proper focus of such considerations.

Within each operating unit of a company, as well as for the total organization, one can calculate ratios which measure the company's success in controlling its costs. This analysis can be extended still further by applying various ratios barometers to each responsibility center, reflecting the fact that most operating decisions which flow together to determine profitability (and return on investment) are made at *all* managerial levels in the company. Profit margin will have the greatest leverage in generating higher returns, since, as we will see, increases in margin can generally be effected easier by way of higher revenues, lower costs, or a combination of both, than can increased investment turnover. It is possible to see the behavioral pattern of each element of the profitability rate by breaking down the elements using the following chart:

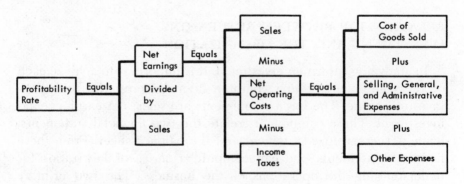

Within the above profitability rate, managers of operations who have operating responsibility can be measured as to performance by such ratios as earnings ÷ sales, gross margin ÷ sales, selling expenses ÷ sales, administrative costs ÷ sales, and so on. Also, since cost of goods sold is a function of cost of goods *produced*, traditional price and efficiency variance analyses can be conducted in much more detail than is indicated on the chart. (See Chapter 32, "Variance Analysis of Operating Results.") These analyses provide the measurement tools to determine if each operating unit is contributing adequately to overall profitability performance.

Turnover Rate

The other major ROI determinant deals with the turnover of investment, that is, sales divided by investment. As we saw above, "investment" needs to be defined; alternatives include total assets, invested capital (long-term debt plus owners' equity), and owners' equity.

Investment turnover is an indicator of how "capital intensive" a business is. For example, for a utility, asset turnover may be as low as 0.35; that is, one dollar in assets is needed to "generate" or "support" 35 cents in revenues. On the other hand, for a grocery store chain, asset turnover may be around 6.0; that is, one dollar in assets supports *six* dollars in sales. (As we shall see, these differences in turnover explain why a grocery store's profit per dollar of sales—that is, profitability rate—is much lower than that of a utility.)

To further analyze the investment turnover rate, it is possible to calculate a series of ratios called "managing ratios." These ratios assist in evaluating the various items of the balance sheet, and are used to monitor such major areas of the company as cash, inventories, receivables, plant and equipment utilization, and debt relationships. These ratios include days' cash on hand, days' receivables (collection period), days' inventory, plant and equipment "turnover" (sales ÷ plant and equipment), and the current ratio. All of these are described in finance and accounting texts.[4]

The turnover rate can also be "charted." The chart's structure depends on the investment base definition used: in this illustration, total assets is being used.

---

[4] See, for example, Chapter 12, "Financial Statement Analysis," in Robert N. Anthony and James S. Reece, *Management Accounting Principles,* 3d ed. (Homewood, Ill.: Richard D. Irwin, Inc., 1975).

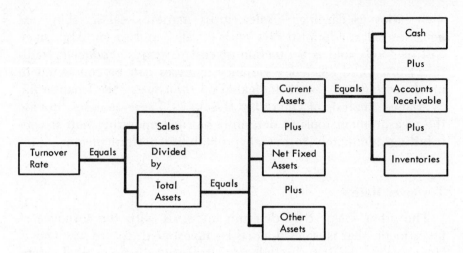

If, instead, of total assets, one uses invested capital as the concept of investment, then the chart becomes:

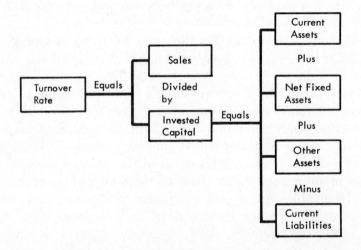

Being able to set and monitor performance standards for each of the investment components will help in attaining overall investment turnover.

The overall economic performance of an organization is measured by return on investment. The profitability and turnover ratios we have described can be multiplied together to give ROI, since:

$$\text{Return on investment} = \frac{\text{Net earnings}}{\text{Investment}} = \frac{\text{Net earnings}}{\text{Sales}} \times \frac{\text{Sales}}{\text{Investment}}$$

$$= \text{Profit margin} \times \text{Turnover}$$

This relationship is also depicted in ROI charts as follows:

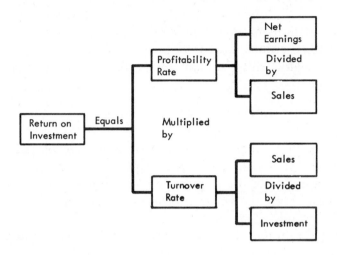

In summary, each component of return on investment, namely, the profitability rate and the turnover rate, as well as parts of those two components, can be measured throughout the organization by way of ratios. These ratios can relate to all levels of the organization, emphasizing that it is the responsibility of all levels of management to perform in such a way that overall return-on-investment performance is achieved.

COST OF CAPITAL

An important measurement tool and control concept is the *cost of capital*. It is important because it represents the average rate of earnings which investors require to induce them to provide all forms of long-term capital to the organization. Without this long-term capital, the organization would be forced to seek short-term sources of capital at a potentially higher rate, if indeed the organization could even exist without long-term capital.

It is important that corporations monitor their cost of capital, so as to ensure that their return on invested capital (before interest costs) exceeds the cost of that capital. If a person makes a 10 percent return on a $1,000 investment in the stock market but he paid 12 percent for the funds he invested, then he is economically worse off for having made the investment. The same is true for a corporation whose return on invested funds is less than its cost for using those funds. While this is generally recognized when making new plant and equipment investment decisions (by using the cost of capital as the discount rate in net present value calculations), some companies neglect this economic fact when reviewing their overall performance.[5]

Calculation

Cost of capital can be computed by using a weighted-average-cost method, in which costs are assigned to each component of invested capital, and then these are combined into a weighted-average cost using the relative proportions of the components to "weight" the individual costs.

Assigning a cost to debt capital is straightforward, but the cost of equity capital cannot be precisely measured. Just as the *cost* of debt to a company is the same as the return on investment to the *supplier* of debt (bank, bondholder, and so on), so is the cost of equity to the company the same as the return to the equity supplier —that is, shareholder. Therein lies the measurement problem: there is really no such party as a "typical shareholder," so we cannot seek out that person and ask, "What return do you expect—dividends and capital gains—on your investment in XYZ Corporation's common stock?" Nevertheless, although the cost of equity cannot be precisely measured, it *does* exist.

One method of estimating the cost of equity capital is based on future earnings per share as estimated by the investors. The stockholders invest because they expect to receive benefits which may be considered equivalent to what they would receive on an alternative investment of comparable risk. They are induced to invest because benefits derived from future dividends and capital appreciation are expected. Both of these expected benefits are derived from future earning per share, which therefore is considered a prime factor af-

---

[5] One reason for this neglect is the heavy emphasis on earnings per share as an indicator of economic performance. For examples of how this emphasis can be misleading, see Frederick W. Searby's article in the March–April 1975 *Harvard Business Review*, "Return to Return on Investment."

fecting the future price of stock. Therefore, the cost of equity capital can be approximated by using the inverse of the price-earnings ratio; for example, if a company's stock is selling at eight times earnings, its cost of equity is approximated as 12½ percent.[6]

The computation of the weighted-average cost is best explained by example:

Weighted-Average Cost of Capital Computation

Type of Financing	Amount	Proportion	After-Tax Cost	Weighted Cost
Debt...................	$ 70,000	35%	4.5%	1.58%
Preferred stock..........	20,000	10	7.5	0.75
Common equity*.........	110,000	55	10.0	5.50
Total.............	$200,000	100%	Weighted-Average Cost = 7.83%	

* Includes common stock and retained earnings.

Use of Weighted-Average Cost of Capital Computations

Upon computing the weighted cost of capital, its use can be directed in different ways. The most important and obvious use is that it provides a required minimum "cutoff" rate of return for new investments, sometimes referred to as the "hurdle rate." This rate can be adjusted for different levels of investment risk; that is, investments with low risk would have a lower hurdle rate than investments with high risk. As well as identifying different hurdle rates for different levels of project risks, different hurdle rates can also be established in accordance with different strategy objectives. Each division should have a different rate in keeping with the strategic nature of its operations.

Consequences of Not Meeting Cost of Capital

When an organization consistently earns less than its cost of capital, operational decisions are being made which result in less than favorable expectations on the part of the stockholders. For example, as earnings decrease, lower dividends are paid to the

---

[6] *Editors' Note:* Most people find the concept of the cost of equity capital confusing at first. For a more thorough treatment see J. Fred Weston and Eugene F. Brigham, *Essentials of Managerial Finance,* 4th ed. (Hinsdale, Ill.: The Dryden Press, 1977); or J. Fred Weston and Maurice B. Goudzwaard eds., *The Treasurer's Handbook* (Homewood, Ill.: Dow Jones-Irwin, 1976), chap. 32 (written by Dr. Weston).

stockholders. This earnings decrease will be related to a decrease in internally generated funds to finance expansion, so there is a slowdown in company growth. The company may also become a riskier investment for shareholders, since external financing must provide larger proportions of the company's capital needs.

With lower earnings and dividends, stockholders' returns and expectations are lowered; this results in lower market value of the stock price and an increase in the company's cost of equity capital. The company now has more risk, and stockholders will require a higher return to be induced to invest in the company.

As risk and return for the stockholders become less competitive, financing and capital costs increase, and future earnings are even more impaired. Thus, the cycle begins over, but becomes ever more severe to a point where survival is at stake.

RESIDUAL INCOME

Another approach to comparing profits and the investment needed to generate those earnings is the residual income method. This method emphasizes the maximization of dollar return over and above the cost of capital, just as ROI does; but the residual income calculation involves absolute amount of return, rather than percentages.

For example, suppose a division of a company has earned (after taxes, but before interest costs) $25 million, and that $200 million investment is tied up in the division. The company has calculated this division's cost of capital as being 8 percent (after taxes). Then residual income is calculated as follows:

$$\begin{aligned}
\text{Residual income} &= \text{Earnings (before interest)} - \text{Investment} \\
&\qquad\qquad\qquad\qquad\qquad\qquad\quad \times \text{Capital charge} \\
&= \$25,000,000 - \$200,000,000 \times 8 \text{ percent} \\
&= \$25,000,000 - \$16,000,000 = \$9,000,000
\end{aligned}$$

The interpretation is that the division's operations generated enough earnings to cover the division's capital costs *plus* an additional ("residual") $9 million.

While the residual income concept is a sound one, a majority of corporations do not employ it in measuring their investment centers' performance. There are at least three reasons for this. First, ROI is an "older" method of comparing earnings and investment, whereas residual income has received attention only in the last 25 years. Second, outside financial analysts apparently ignore residual income, and many companies' managements want to focus internally on the same measures being looked at by outsiders. Finally, because residual income is an absolute dollar amount rather than a ratio, comparisons of companies in an industry, or divisions within a single company, are more difficult, whereas ROI "normalizes" for different-sized companies or divisions.

SUMMARY

While we have focused on the return-on-investment concept as used for evaluating performance of a company or of subdivisions— "investment centers"—of that company, ROI can also be used in the areas of acquisition analysis and inventory control, and as a basis for establishing product prices.

In all uses of the ROI concept, it must be kept in mind that the practitioner must put into perspective how return on investment will assist in maximizing earnings and how this tool can be applied to each level of the organization. In particular, it is important to remember that return on investment is every manager's responsibility throughout the entire organization. An adequate ROI is essential to the success of the organization, and it is *managers*—not corporate finance staff—who determine a company's return on investment.

APPENDIX

The following 13 tables summarize the results of a survey of the *Fortune* "1,000" companies as to how these companies implement the investment center concept. The study was performed by William R. Cool, M.B.A. candidate, and Professor James S. Reece of the Graduate School of Business Administration at the University of Michigan.

TABLE A
Overall Results (total number of companies polled; 1,000; number of respondents; 620 or 62 percent)

Companies Having—	Number	Percent
No profit centers...........................	26	4.2
Profit centers, but not investment centers......................	135	21.8
Investment centers.......................	459	74.0
Total................................	620	100.0

TABLE B
Use of Profit/Investment Centers, by Sales Volume

		Companies Having—		
Sales Volume ($ millions)	Number of Respondents	No Profit Centers	Profit but Not Investment Centers	Investment Centers
$90–99.........................	25	8%	48%	44%
$100–199........................	187	4	31	65
$200–299........................	72	7	19	74
$300–499........................	92	4	24	72
$500–999........................	93	5	12	82
$1,000–1,999.....................	61	3	16	80
$2,000–2,999.....................	28	4	0	96
$3,000–3,999.....................	11	0	0	100
$4,000–9,999.....................	23	0	17	83
Over $10,000....................	8	0	12	88
Not available*..................	20	0	15	85
Total.....................	620	4%	22%	74%

* These 20 respondents chose to remain anonymous to the researchers. Sales figures were taken from *Fortune* and were not requested on the questionnaire; hence neither sales volumes nor industry codes could be attributed to the 20 companies.

TABLE C
Extent of Use of Profit and Investment Centers by Industry

Industry	Industry Codes*	Number	No Profit Centers	Profit but Not Investment Centers	Investment Centers
				Companies Having—	
Extractive..........................	10	18	17%	28%	55%
Food and tobacco.................	20,21	73	6	30	64
Textile, apparel....................	22,23	34	0	24	76
Furniture..........................	25	6	0	50	50
Paper and wood...................	26	27	0	22	78
Publishing, printing...............	27	22	0	54	45
Chemical and petroleum...........	28,29	59	3	12	85
Rubber, plastics, leather...........	30,31	14	7	7	86
Glass, concrete, abrasives, gypsum..........................	32	22	0	9	91
Metal manufacturing..............	33	49	4	14	82
Metal products....................	34	39	5	26	69
Electronics and appliances........	36	39	5	20	74
Transportation equipment........	37	10	10	20	70
Scientific, measuring, photo equipment.......................	38	24	0	4	96
Motor vehicles....................	40	24	4	13	83
Aerospace........................	41	11	9	18	73
Pharmaceuticals...................	42	14	7	21	71
Soaps, cosmetics.................	43	8	13	38	50
Office equipment, computers......	44	19	5	32	63
Industrial and farm equipment.....	45	61	7	20	74
Jewelry, silverware................	46	2	0	0	100
Toys, sporting goods, musical instrmts.........................	47	4	0	0	100
Broadcasting, motion pictures.....	48	6	0	50	50
Beverages........................	49	15	0	40	60
Not available†....................	—	20	0	15	85
Total........................		620	4%	22%	74%

* See *Fortune,* May 1976. *Fortune's* codes 10–38 correspond quite closely with SIC codes, but their codes 40–49 do not correspond at all with SIC 40–49.
 † See footnote to Table B.

TABLE D
Experience with Profit and/or Investment Centers

Question: Approximately how long has your company had profit centers?

	Number	*Percent*
Less than 2 years........	8	1.3
2–5 years................	26	4.4
6–10 years...............	98	16.5
11–25 years..............	210	35.4
Over 25 years............	226	38.0
Not sure.................	26	4.4
Total..............	594	100.0

Note that, from Table A, 135 were profit centers and 459 were investment centers, for a total of 594.

TABLE E
Determination of Profit

Question: Is profit center (or investment center) "profit" calculated in a manner consistent with the way *net income* is calculated for your shareholder reports?

	Number	*Percent*
Yes......................	239	40
No.......................	351	59
No response..............	4	1
Total..............	594	100

If "No," in which of the following ways does the profit center's calculation differ? (Check as many as apply.)

		Number*	*% of 351 Companies**
1.	No taxes are assessed to profit centers............	249	71
2.	No depreciation charge is deducted...............	11	3
3.	The depreciation calculation differs................	25	7
4.	No corporate administrative expenses are allocated to the center............................	173	49
5.	No interest charges on corporate debt are allocated to the center............................	225	64
6.	Profit center reports use direct (variable) costing, rather than full (absorption) costs.........	19	5
7.	Other differences.................................	51	15

* Columns total to more than 351 (100 percent) due to multiple responses.

TABLE F
Methods Used to Evaluate Investment Centers

Question: How is the performance of your investment centers measured?

	Number	Percent
ROI only................................	299	65
Residual income only....................	9	2
Both ROI and residual income..........	128	28
Other..................................	17	4
No answer.............................	6	1
Total.............................	459	100

TABLE G
Methods of Establishing a Target ROI

Question: If you use *ROI* (alone or with residual income), how do you set an invest-ment center's target or budgeted ROI percentage?

	Number	Percent
1. All investment centers are expected to earn the same ROI...	30	7
2. Each investment center is assigned its own target ROI, based on its profit potential...............	294	64
3. Investment centers are not given target ROIs.........	105	23
4. No answer or not applicable.........................	30	7
Total...	459	100*

* Percentages add to 101 percent due to rounding.

TABLE H
Capital Charge Rates for Residual Income

Question: If *residual income* is used (alone or with ROI) to measure your investment centers' performance:

Are different capital charges applied to different asset types?

	Number	Percent
Yes..................	26	19
No..................	111	81
Total..........	137*	100

If you answered "Yes," is the capital charge for a given asset type the same for all of your investment centers?

	Number	Percent
Yes....................	15	58
No.....................	10	38
No answer.............	1	4
Total.............	26	100

* Note, in Table F, that 137 (9 + 128) companies indicated they use residual income.

TABLE I
Assets Included in the Investment Base

Question: Which of the following items are included in the calculation of an investment center's asset base? (Check as many as apply.)

		Number*	% of 459 Companies*
1.	Cash	290	63
2.	Receivables	430	94
3.	Inventories	436	95
4.	Other current assets	348	76
5.	Land and buildings used solely by the investment center	430	94
6.	Prorata share of land and buildings used by two or more investment centers	207	45
7.	Equipment used solely by the investment center	380	83
8.	Prorata share of equipment used by two or more investment centers	188	41
9.	Other corporate ("headquarters") assets (prorata share)	73	16
10.	No answer	10	2

* Columns total to more than 459 (100 percent) due to multiple responses.

TABLE J
Valuation of Plant and Equipment

Question: In determining an investment center's asset base, how are plant and equipment valued?

		Number*	% of 459 Companies*
1.	Gross book value	63	14
2.	Net book value	389	85
3.	Replacement cost	10	2
4.	Other	2	0
5.	No answer	8	2
	Total	472	103

If *net book value* is used, is the depreciation method the same as the one used for shareholder reporting purposes?

		Number	Percent
1.	Yes	358	92
2.	No	15	4
3.	No answer	16	4
	Total	389	100

* Columns total to more than 459 (100 percent) due to these multiple responses: (1) 6 firms used gross *and* net book value: (2) 5 used replacement cost *and* net book value; and (3) 2 used replacement cost and gross book value—a total of 13 dual responses.

TABLE K
Treatment of Leases

Question: Do you include the capitalized value of leases as a part of assets employed, even though you are not necessarily required to capitalize those same leases for shareholder reporting purposes?

	Number	% of 459 Companies
Yes....................................	158	34
No.....................................	285	62
No answer or not applicable............	16	3
	459	100*

* Percentages add to 99 percent due to rounding.

TABLE L
Treatment of Liabilities

Question: Are any of the following liabilities *deducted* in calculating an investment center's asset base?

	Number Saying "Yes"	% of 459 Companies
1. External current payables................	232	51
2. Intracompany current payables..........	136	30
3. Other current liabilities..................	205	45
4. Noncurrent liabilities.....................	93	20
5. No answer..............................	16	3

TABLE M
Methods Used to Evaluate Relative Investment Center Performance

Question: How do you compare or rank your investment centers' *relative* financial performance? (Check as many as apply.)

	Number	% of 137 Companies
For 137 companies using residual income:		
1. On the basis of the amount of each center's residual income dollars....................................	63	46
2. By ranking the percentage: residual income divided by investment....................................	60	44
3. On the basis of actual residual income as a percent of budgeted residual income.....................	52	38
4. By ranking residual income as a percent of sales.........	47	34

	Number	% of 427 Companies
For 427 companies using ROI:		
5. By ranking the centers' ROI percentage...................	234	55
6. By ranking profit as a percent of sales...................	159	37
7. On the basis of actual ROI as a percent of budgeted ROI...	177	41

	Number	% of 459 Companies
For all 459 companies having investment centers:		
8. No explicit ranking of investment centers' financial performance is made..........................	133	29
9. No answer...	10	2

Note: Column totals within subgroups do not add to respondent subtotals (100 percent) due to multiple responses. Recall also from Table F, that 128 respondents used *both* residual income and ROI; these 128 are included in all three subgroups above.

ADDITIONAL SOURCES

Anthony, Robert N., and Dearden, John. *Management Control Systems: Text and Cases,* chap. 8. 3d ed. Homewood, Ill.: Richard D. Irwin, Inc., 1976.

————, and Reece, James S. *Management Accounting Principles,* chap. 12. 3d ed. Homewood, Ill.: Richard D. Irwin, Inc., 1975.

Beyer, Robert, and Trawicki, Donald J. *Profitability Accounting for Planning and Control.* New York: The Ronald Press Co., 1972.

Bierman, Harold. "ROI as a Measure of Management Performance." *Financial Executive,* March 1973, p. 40.

Carter, Albert G. "Computing Inventory ROI." *Management Accounting,* July 1973, p. 43.

Gordon, Lawrence A. "Return on Investment and the Cost of Capital." *Management Accounting,* February 1976, p. 37.

Peters, Robert A. *ROI: Practical Theory and Innovative Applications.* New York: American Management Associations, 1974.

Rachlin, Robert. *Return on Investment: Concepts and Techniques for Profit Improvement.* New York: Pilot Books, 1974.

———. *Return on Investment: Strategies for Profit Improvement.* New York: Marr Publications, 1976.

Searby, Frederick W. "Return to Return on Investment." *Harvard Business Review,* March–April 1975, p. 113.

Solomons, David. *Divisional Performance: Measurement and Control.* Homewood, Ill.: Richard D. Irwin, Inc., 1968.

Spraakman, Gary P. "Using the Return on Investment Criterion with Leased Assets." *Cost and Management,* January–February 1977, p. 18.

Weston, J. Fred, and Brigham, Eugene F. *Essentials of Managerial Finance,* chap. 20. 4th ed. Hinsdale, Ill.: The Dryden Press, 1977.

———, and Goudzwaard, Maurice B., eds. *Treasurer's Handbook,* chap. 32. Homewood, Ill.: Dow Jones-Irwin, Inc., 1976.

Williamson, Robert W. "Measuring Divisional Profitability." *Management Accounting,* January 1975, p. 29.

part five

The Management Control Process—Planning, Budgeting, and Performance Analysis

Long-Range Business Planning Systems

Lawrence M. Murray*

As the business world moves deeper and deeper into the realm of "Future Shock," the apparent need for information increases on a geometric scale. Management increasingly speaks of anticipatory management and the need for ever-improved planning. In this context, the charge of the present-day executive is to provide not only the "what" but increasingly "how," "why," and, of course, "when."

During the last several years, long-range planning (LRP) systems have increasingly been looked to for providing such answers, and to enable managers to chart the course of their own particular business ventures and goals. While the benefits continue to be debated in some quarters, the idea of LRP has received wide acceptance in government and business.

Definition

In order to set the tone of this LRP chapter, it is appropriate to define "long-range planning." First, the easy part, "long range" deals with the time frame under question or consideration. While there is no set time frame, most firms generally deal with a five-year planning horizon when talking long range. The needs of a particular business certainly dictate an appropriate horizon; for example, a utility with long lead times may find it necessary to plan 20 or more

* Mr. Murray is Assistant Corporate Controller of the Carborundum Company's Europe, Africa & Middle East Operations, London, England.

years out, while 2 years out could be considered long term for other firms.

The "planning" is a little more difficult to define, and authorities on the subject offer a wide variety of suggestions. For the purpose of this chapter, we will define planning as the *process* which *quantifies* and *defines* a firm's objectives over a specified period of time (five years in this case).

The important words are:

Process—implies a system or design for gathering information and considering alternatives.

Quantify—sets goals which can be communicated to management and establishes a benchmark for measurement.

Define—forces management to document strategies for achieving desired objectives. This step is especially critical when a formalized review process is part of the planning process.

Relationship of LRP to Strategic Planning and Budgeting

For many firms, the relationship between strategic planning, long-range (business) planning, and budgeting may be a very close one, while in others these three processes can be independent to the point that one is not even referred to in preparation of the other. In the chapter that follows this one, this subject is extensively discussed as "linkage." Basically the authors of that chapter discuss the desired objective of balancing "reach" and "realism" through loose or tight linkage in the planning/budgeting process. Loose linkage involves little relation between the two processes, which allows the manager to maximize "reach" or long-range goals, as there is no direct tie to short-range goals. The manager's primary concern is building a business for the future, which may imply short-term profit erosion for longer range considerations. On the other hand, "realism" is achieved more through tight linkage, which would normally mean the manager heavily weighs the short-term impact in building a plan. In fact, the first year or two of the long-range plan would duplicate many of the financial exhibits found in the budget, and the only difference between the two would be the degree of detail.

In order to differentiate between the strategic plan, the business plan, and budgeting, consider a typical cycle where the strategic planning would be conducted early in the year. In a static environment, the strategic plans may be updated only every two or even three years; or, as in many cases, strategic planning may be conducted on an exception basis where only strategies which *need* to be revised are submitted for review and approval. In this type of a firm, the strategic plan defines the manager's basic business with a broad perspective of what future expectations are, and how goals are to be accomplished. While numbers are generally used in defining objectives, the emphasis is on action plans and basic strategies.

Business planning, on the other hand, can best be thought of in terms of quantification of the strategic plan with a more detailed analysis of specific action plans and allocation of resources to carry out the approved strategies. This phase is generally conducted during the third quarter or early fourth quarter of the year. In addition, the business plan often may differ in time span, since strategic plans may cover ten or more years into the future even when the business plan covers only five.

Budgeting, on the other hand, is generally thought of in terms of detailing an approved business plan down to the department or expense-center level, with specific responsibility assigned for achieving short-range goals. Normally this would be for one or two years and would closely parallel the business plan content for those periods, with possible updating for known changes, or substantial changes, in the external (to the firm) economic environment. Budgets are normally highly numbers oriented and completed late in the fourth quarter or even at the beginning of the new year.

As is apparent by now, there is generally a great deal of dependency and interrelationships among the three systems, and most firms who employ all three systems basically utilize the business plan to bridge the gap between strategic planning and budgeting.

The Controller's Role in Business Planning

Business planning was previously defined, in part, as a quantification of the strategic plan. It is primarily for this reason that coordination and supervision of the planning process has long been under the direction of the controller's organization.

In most firms, finance serves as the common denominator for expressing goals, achievements, failures, measurement techniques, and strategies. Finance departments are a natural "hub" of activity and information, and as such can play a useful role in establishing a common thread in the business planning process by assuming responsibility for editing and directing to ensure that the various functional groups' plans (finance, engineering, production, marketing, and personnel) support one another and are interrelated.

Types of Business Planning Systems

When one thinks of a planning system, the first inclination is to think of a computer-based system. While computerization of planning systems is not always necessary, some form of computerization is probably necessary for firms with numerous and diverse operating divisions or product lines. Computerized planning systems may take several forms:

Econometric models. These systems range from simplistic to extremely complicated. Whatever the degree of complexity, the intent is to link the performance of the economic environment to the firm through mathematical models or equations, and to enable the firm to explore several alternatives or "what-if" situations given various economic conditions. The support necessary for such models is generally in the form of computer resources and professionals, sometimes including economists and mathematicians. While the information produced by econometric models is useful, the linkage to the budgeting process is generally "loose," and is generally used by top corporate or division management to test other types of system.

Financial models. The most common type of LRP model is based upon financial interrelationships *within* a firm. These models operate in a simulation mode and are deterministic (as opposed to probabilistic). That is, the economic environment is defined in terms of assumptions regarding rates of growth, share of the market, and so forth, and the role of the model is to project results for a given set of conditions. This approach preserves all options for the planner and enables management to consider many alternatives before selecting the one which is most likely to yield the desired results. A major benefit of this micro approach is that all the variables (pricing, fixed and variable cost, capacity utilization, resource allocation, and so on) are defined, leaving the planner free to test various alternatives with a minimum of input.

In order to utilize this type of modeling, a firm must be able to define by product line, and preferably by item or part number within a product line, the variable cost, price, and demand. Fixed cost, capacity parameters and available resources are defined by plant or location with the resource allocation algorithm defined for each.

Noncomputerized systems. Practically every business has some type of planning system, even if it is only in the head of the individual owner or manager. In the final analysis, the only difference between computerized and noncomputerized systems is the degree of detail and number of alternatives which may be considered. The manager who must depend upon manual methods to plan the course of the business must consider alternatives and be able to pick the correct one the first time.

HOW TO SET UP A LONG-RANGE BUSINESS PLANNING SYSTEM

Regardless of the type of LRP system your business requires, there are common areas which should be included, and if you establish a systematic approach, you can ensure a comprehensive, well-thought-out plan.

General Rules

In order for a plan to be successful, certain rules should be followed, perhaps the most important of which are those things that should *not* be done. Here are eight rules that the author has found useful:

1. *Top management must take responsibility.* While delegation is an integral aspect of any organization, top management must involve themselves in the planning process by:

    a. *Setting the climate.* Management may delegate many of the tasks involved in planning but not the responsibility. The unit manager must ensure coordination and continuity.

b. *Evaluation.* Any plan that is not the result of management involvement and evaluation is unlikely to get off the ground.

c. *Implementation.* Plans are made to be used, and if top management consistently fails to implement plans, then preparing successive plans will be approached with little enthusiasm.

2. *Establish adequate goals.* Goals which are vague, for example, maximize profits, minimize cost, gain share of the market, and so forth, many times lead to excessively optimistic plans which time after time wind up in failure. Goals must be measureable (e.g., increase sales 5 percent per annum and profits by 10 percent, increase share of the market from 15 to 17 percent), and top management must set the guidelines by setting the parameters *first*, before the operating units draw up their individual plans for review.

3. *Involve line management.* Plans must be carried out by line management, and their support is crucial, especially in the early stages. Significant involvement when the planning process is first introduced will enhance the probability of success—subsequent changes to the planning process may not require extensive pre-selling if the initial process is carefully done.

4. *Use plans for measuring performance.* Objectives must be based on operational needs and be measurable. Bonuses and merit increase should be tied, in part, to performance against plans, both in quantitative and qualitative aspects.

5. *Understand the process.* All persons involved in LRP must understand what is expected of them. Management can help by stimulating the imagination and creativity of those participating. "Kickoff" meetings are helpful in answering questions about the process, in identifying opportunities and threats, in soliciting ideas, and in deciding on issues which should be addressed.

6. *Make planning an integral part of the management process.* One of the basic premises behind formalized planning is to help managers make better short-range decisions in light of future events and desired results. A successful planning approach will eliminate many of the crisis decisions.

7. *Keep formality to a minimum.* Many planning systems have so many forms to fill out and so many details to explain that

participants become planning bureaucrats. In order to keep creativity and imagination in the planning process, keep planning requirements simple. Produce only the information that is necessary to achieve the objectives of the operating units. Attempt to maintain flexibility.
8. *Review LRP with operating units.* Formalized review of plans with departmental and operating unit key managers enables management to probe the credibility of the goals, the action plans designed to achieve them, and the unit managers' commitments.

Setting the Stage for a Successful Plan

Once a planning system has been decided upon, instructions and guidelines should be issued which include the following:

1. *Calendar.* Establish a calendar of significant events, and then follow it!
2. *Economic assumptions.* Broad economic assumptions should be issued to cover the planning period. Everyone's planning under the same general assumptions regarding the economic environment enables management to concentrate on key issues rather than sort out varying and conflicting economic assumptions.
3. *Basic format.* While forms should be kept to a minimum, a few basic forms will enhance the review process, especially when a multi-unit company is involved. This format may be supplemented as required by specific needs; however, brevity should be stressed to facilitate top-management review (reading time is at a premium for all managers).
4. *Budgets.* Budgetary estimates for staff functions that are charged to operating units should be established early in the process. This enables the controller's office (or whatever group is coordinating the planning) to "show support" by getting its work done on time and to keep the operating units from guessing as to the magnitude of these changes.

Plan Content

Recognizing that the needs of all businesses vary according to type and circumstance, this section will endeavor to guide the novice planner on what areas to include, or to enable the experienced planner to review an established format.

1. *Executive summary.* This section is designed to enable unit managers to put their best foot forward. It lays the foundation on which the remaining document is based. Subjects covered should include:

   a. *Introduction.* A narrative statement covering the operating unit's plans, focusing on changing trends affecting the business and new opportunities which will affect the unit's ability to realize its objectives.

   b. *Key strategies.* A brief review of those strategies and action plans necessary to successfully implement the plan, with timetables and key dates identified.

   c. *Sales and income summary.* Discussion of relevant factors affecting sales growth, profit generation, and asset utilization. Exhibits are helpful in judging planned performance against historical results. Many firms analyze the *last* five years' performance as well as the *next* five, especially when judging realism.

2. *Marketing plan.* The heart of the business plan depends upon the success of the marketing effort and careful consideration should be given to:

   a. *Environment.* An analysis of the external economic environment and its effect on each unit's ability to market successfully its services and products. The review should cover specific indices affecting the unit, leading and lagging indicators, and the social/political factors which are likely to influence performance.

   b. *Competitive analysis.* Next to the economic environment, competition is the most likely to determine success or failure of a given unit. Therefore, it is imperative that the major competitors be identified and considered as to geographical strengths, channels of distribution, market share, technical competence, and management style.

   c. *Action plans.* Discussion and summary of actions necessary to attain the planned sales and income objectives of the firm.

      (1) *Channels of distribution.* Identify methods and routes of taking the product to the marketplace. Phys-

ical distribution, marketing organization, field sales force (direct sales or distributors), and key factors affecting each should be considered.

(2) *Advertising.* Explore means of gaining maximum use of the advertising dollar, and products which are most likely to benefit from a promotional campaign. Goals should be quantified (e.g., gain 1 percent additional market share), and the return measured the same as for any other scarce resource.

(3) *Pricing.* In the context of an inflationary economy, close attention must be paid to units' pricing plans. These plans should be thoroughly analyzed as to amount, timing, frequency, effectiveness, and competitor reaction, as well as customer acceptance.

(4) *Product.* The final determination of success depends upon the firm's ability to meet the needs of its customers, and to this end all products must be examined for life trends, competitive position, causes for market growth or decline, strengths and weaknesses, introduction of new products, and customer acceptance.

3. *Technical plan.* The specific details and extent of the technical plan will depend upon the nature of business involved. However, most firms depend, at least to an extent, on some form of research and development effort in order to remain competitive in the marketplace. Projects that are necessary to obtain the objectives of the firm should be identified. At a minimum the plan should cover:

a. Description of the project, purpose, and scheduled implementation dates.

b. Key factors or external assistance which will be required to complete the project successfully.

c. A recap of the analysis performed to justify the project, including market acceptance, growth, fit, competitive reaction, and possible alternatives.

d. Financial analysis to indicate return to the unit in sales, profits, costs, and project ROI up to ten years out.

4. *Manufacturing plan.* The role of the manufacturing operations is to produce efficiently the goods and services necessary to achieve the unit's goals, particularly regarding marketing. In organizations where there is too much independence between

manufacturing and marketing, excess inventory positions and "dumping" become prevalent as the firm attempts to balance the consumers' demand and its own supply. The basic purpose of this portion is to develop those action plans necessary to carry out these objectives.

a. *Production plans.* This section should begin by identifying the required production in physical units whenever possible. Once this is accomplished, there should be comments on:

   (1) Problems which could prevent or delay delivery performance, and actions being taken to correct deficien-. cies, including state of automation.

   (2) Inventory levels and policy regarding marketing support as to:

      (*a*) Investment levels.

      (*b*) Control methods.

      (*c*) Valuation methods and cost allocations.

      (*d*) Improvements needed or planned in systems and methods.

      (*e*) Reduction in the manufacturing cycle.

      (*f*) Stockout policies.

      (*g*) Physical loss and obsolescence control.

b. *Capacity utilization.* An analysis should be performed to determine capacity available to meet current needs and future requirements as the results of customer demands covered in the marketing plan and production levels anticipated. Items to consider include: volume, mix, delivery goals, expansions, new products, production bottlenecks, and make-versus-buy considerations (subcontracting should always be considered for cost effectiveness as well as temporary demand).

c. *Capital projects.* While other functional areas may request capital funds, the manufacturing unit is responsible for the majority of funds spent and therefore this part of the plan is a logical place to review manufacturing's capital expenditure plans. Expenditures should always be based upon an independent analysis of each project based upon its merits (see Chapter 15); however, needs should be identified, costs and projected returns should be estimated over the planning period, and alternatives considered. The impact upon operations should be determined, both for the immediate future as well as for the long term (a good project may have an adverse impact in the short run).

d. *Quality control.* Quality is an important consideration for practically every firm, and a necessity for many. The plan should address the need for such a program and the specific steps being taken to ensure quality products. Items to consider include:

(1) Cost and personnel requirements of the program.

(2) Specifications that must be met in light of warranties and guarantees associated with the products.

(3) Any significant problems expected in meeting quality standards or anticipated changes in market demand (or government requirements) which are likely to impact quality requirements.

e. *Energy management.* The first objective is to secure adequate energy to meet production demands. Conservation efforts should be explored in detail as well as alternate sources, multifuel availability, and the capability to utilize them. Also to be considered are cost curtailment possibilities and inventory policy to minimize disruption where feasible.

f. *Purchasing.* Availability and delivery problems of major items should be analyzed along with price expectations. Alternatives should be covered for items with long delivery cycles, vendor reliability problems, and high-cost/high-inflation products.

g. *Cost improvement.* In order to remain competitive, unit cost improvements must be a conscious effect. These improvements should be incorporated into the annual planning process, and product quality/reliability maintained (many firms call this "value engineering"). Cost-saving goals should be identified by project as to:

(1) Labor efficiency.

(2) Material substitution.

(3) Capital investments.

(4) Methods improvements.

(5) Other.

5. *Personnel plan.* When all else is stripped away, a firm is left with its most important resource—people. In order to achieve

the goals set forth in the preceding sections of the plan, the company's personnel and organization must be examined to ensure adequacy of quantity and quality, and proper allocation. Not to be overlooked are development plans for career-minded individuals.

a. *Organization.* The present organization should be defined objectively, with a critical eye toward management succession. Each position on the organization chart should identify potential successors and explain actions being taken to:

(1) Develop personnel to succeed key management positions.

(2) Recruit or promote from within in order to strengthen void or weak areas.

In addition, anticipated reorganization plans should be explained in detail, covering the need for the reorganization, impact on personnel, and objectives to be gained from the change.

b. *Labor environment.* This section should address the problems, opportunities, and plans for the stability and adequacy of the production/clerical work force. Topics to analyze include:

(1) Availability of skilled and unskilled labor.

(2) Anticipated future needs and availability.

(3) Turnover experience, causes, and cures.

(4) Relations with unions and ways to improve strained relations.

(5) Strategy for any negotiations during the planning period with dates and trouble spots identified.

(6) Cost of the present work force and projected changes.

(7) Current safety program and any corrective action necessary during the period.

c. *Equal employment opportunity.* Plans should include an affirmative-action plan in compliance with federal government laws and regulations.

6. *Financial plan.* The objectives of the financial plan are really two fold. First, the prime objective of the financial organization (besides safeguarding of assets and financial reporting) should be to ensure that systems are in place which will routinely and quickly supply management with financial information on historical, current, and projected trends, together with associated

analysis and recommendations for corrective action. The finance group should identify the opportunities to be seized upon that impact profitability and asset utilization to assure optimum returns.

In this context, goals should be established to provide or strengthen support for problem areas, so as to enable the control group to carry out its day-to-day responsibilities. Topics to review include cost systems, inventory management, productivity measurement, asset management, production reporting, and marketing information systems.

Second, the financial plan should examine the context of the long-range plan itself and provide pertinent analysis to measure the goals and problems discussed. This section should include specific analysis based upon the needs of the business; however, some common areas covered would be:

a. Profit and loss statements, with a reconciliation of changes from year to year. It is also beneficial to provide a narrative discussion of the impact of significant factors (e.g., if raw material increases 10 percent, what impact will this have on profit?)

b. Balance sheets, the presentation of which should also include a reconciliation of significant year-to-year changes.

c. Funds flow statements, addressing the source of needed funds as well as where the money is to be expended. Alternatives should be considered, and the impact if necessary funds cannot be obtained. What trade-offs are possible to retain a balanced flow?

d. Performance measures, which are a critical factor in evaluating the plan and whose proper analysis is mandatory. Again, specific circumstances will dictate needs, but areas to consider (important to measure historical performance as well as future projections) would be:

   (1) The market environment.
      (a) What are the size and growth rates by year during the planning period?
      (b) What is the company's share of the market and how is it changing?
      (c) Who are the major competitors and what share of the market do they hold? In what direction are they moving?

(2) The firm (preferably by product line).

   (*a*) Incoming orders and backlog position.

   (*b*) Sales. The important point to consider in analyzing the sales and incoming orders is the relative growth between the firm and the market environment. Management should be prepared to explain significant shifts in market position.

   (*c*) Price index—are product prices keeping pace with inflation?

   (*d*) Profit indicators:

      Gross margin—dollars and percent to sales.

      Overhead spending—direct and allocated.

      Net profit.

      Return on investment.

   (*e*) Asset utilization:

      Working capital requirements.

      Total investment.

      Capital expenditures.

      Capacity utilization.

e. Resource allocation. The natural inclination of product managers is to add resources to their sector in order to take advantage of opportunities and to ensure continued success-

EXHIBIT 1
The Growth-Share Matrix

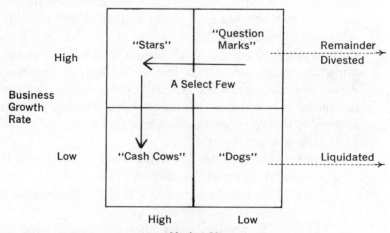

Source: Barry Hedley, "Strategy and the 'Business Portfolio,' " *Long Range Planning*, February 1977, p. 10. Mr. Hedley is a director of the Boston Consulting Group Ltd., London; this matrix was developed several years ago by BCG.

ful operations. The charge of general managers (with the the controller's assistance) is to allocate optimally their available resources, and to avoid spending excessive resources on products which have little potential. While firms use various tactics to measure potential, most attempt to combine market potential with their own business strengths. General Electric calls its approach "Stoplight Strategy" while the Boston Consulting Group calls theirs "Product Portfolio." The Boston Consulting Group's approach is shown in Exhibit 1. General Electric has expanded on the Boston Consulting Group's basic approach to include not only market share but other factors such as technology; and GE uses a "high-medium-low" scale (thus the "stop-light" approach) rather than just "high-low."

The basic approach is to chart on a grid (matrix) both a product line's market growth and the firm's position (market share). If a product line falls in the "low-low" or "dog" quadrant, minimum resources should be allocated and serious consideration should be given to liquidating that product line. If the intersection is in the "high-high" or "star" quadrant, maximum advantage should be taken of this position. A high market-growth situation with low market share should be explored for market-share development (or divestment, if the firm has no real strengths). A low market growth coupled with high share ("cash cow") is generally the sign of a successful business in a mature market, which often is the source of funds for new ventures. In this case, the company probably would not allocate many resources, but it is important to allocate enough to give this sector adequate support and service.

Revisions to the Long-Range Plan

Plans are prepared to enable management to approach in an orderly and rational manner the dynamic nature of the business world. In order to keep pace, long-range plans must periodically be updated both to incorporate the changing nature of the environment and to recognize the need for new or additional goals of the organization.

Existing plans should be updated and revised where necessary on at least an annual basis. It is not recommended that plans be revised in the interim unless a drastic change in the fundamental nature of the business occurs. While the plan is monitored on a monthly basis through financial and performance reporting, variances from the plan should be "explained" rather than be a basis for revising the plan.

The basic premise of a long-range plan is that it *is* "long range," and short-term decisions are made in light of future objectives. For this reason, revisions to the plan to reflect short-term problems or opportunities will defeat the major benefits sought from the planning process.

ADDITIONAL SOURCES

Ackoff, Russell L. *A Concept of Corporate Planning.* New York: Wiley Interscience, Inc., 1970.

Ansoff, H. Igor. "The State of Practice in Planning Systems." *Sloan Management Review,* Winter 1977, p. 1.

Argenti, John. *Systematic Corporate Planning.* New York: John Wiley & Sons, Inc., 1974.

Brickner, William H., and Cope, Donald M. *The Planning Process.* Cambridge, Mass.: Winthrop Publishers, Inc., 1977.

Boulden, James B., and McLean Ephraim R. "An Executive's Guide to Computer-Based Planning." *California Management Review,* Fall 1974, p. 58.

Chambers, John C.; Mullick, Satinder K.; and Smith, Donald D. "How to Choose the Right Forecasting Technique." *Harvard Business Review,* July–August 1971, p. 45.

Fairaizl, Alan F., and Mullick, Satinder. "A Corporate Planning System." *Management Accounting,* December 1975, p. 13.

Garretson, Donald E. "Business Planning at 3M." *Management Accounting,* November 1974, p. 33.

Gershefski, George W. *The Development and Application of a Corporate Financial Model.* Oxford, Ohio: Planning Executives Institute, 1968.

Linneman, Robert E., and Kennell, John D. "Shirt-Sleeve Approach to Long-Range Plans." *Harvard Business Review,* March–April 1977, p. 141.

Lorange, Peter, and Vancil, Richard F. *Strategic Planning Systems.* Englewood Cliffs, N.J.: Prentice-Hall, Inc., 1977.

Naylor, Thomas H., and Gattis, Daniel R.   "Corporate Planning Models." *California Management Review,* Summer 1976, p. 69.

Nelson, William G.   "The Use of the Economic Forecasting Staff." *Financial Executive,* September 1976, p. 18.

Steiner, George A.   "How to Improve Your Long Range Planning." *Managerial Planning,* September–October 1974, p. 13.

———, ed.   *Top Management Planning.* New York: The Macmillan Co., 1969.

Balance "Creativity" and "Practicality" in Formal Planning*

John K. Shank, Edward G. Niblock, and
William T. Sandalls, Jr.†

Every company engaged in long-range planning would like its efforts to attain two fundamental but often conflicting goals. On the one hand, management wants the planning function to reflect pragmatic judgments based on what is possible. On the other hand, it wants planning to reflect forward-looking, assertive, and creative thinking.

The primary way of enhancing "realism" is to give the planning function a clear action orientation. Generally, this is done by relating long-range planning closely with short-term budgetary control. And this is where the difficult lies. While close linkage between planning and budgeting puts the stress on the desired action, it also promotes a focus that can be disastrous to mind-stretching "reach."

We are making the assumption, of course, that for the formal planning system to operate effectively it must achieve a balanced compromise between realism and reach. In this chapter, we shall argue that these dual objectives need not be mutually exclusive. In fact, our purpose is to illustrate that the long-range planning system

* Reprinted by permission from the January–February 1973 *Harvard Business Review*. Copyright © 1973 by The President and Fellows of Harvard College. All rights reserved.

† Dr. Shank is the Arthur Young Professor of Accounting at Ohio State University. Mr. Niblock, who was a financial planner at Xerox Corporation, is deceased. Mr. Sandalls is Treasurer of Baybanks, Inc., Boston.

can be structured to achieve both an action orientation and a focus on mind stretching. Our discussion will proceed in two steps.

In the first stage, it is important for long-range planners to begin thinking about the realism-reach trade-off as a problem they can do something about. That "something" involves varying those aspects of the long-range planning system which relate to its interface with the short-range budgeting process. In this regard, we shall summarize the general features of the planning system which relate to plan-budget linkage, illustrating both the "tight" and "loose" form of each "linkage device."

Then, in the second step, we shall illustrate some of the most interesting devices actually being used. These reflect the experiences of six companies which we selected because they (a) are successful in terms of compound earnings growth and (b) have long-range planning systems with both action-oriented and mind-stretching characteristics.

In short, we believe that management can control the focus a planning system will exhibit with respect to the realism versus reach problem. It may not always be possible to achieve a totally satisfactory trade-off, but we shall describe the mechanisms being used by a sample of successful companies to achieve what for each of them is a satisfactory compromise.

PLAN-BUDGET DESIGN

On close examination, it quickly becomes apparent that the different aspects of plans and budgets can be linked in three distinct ways:

1. *Content linkage* relates to the correspondence between the data presented in the plan document and that presented in the budget.
2. *Organizational linkage* focuses on the relationship between the units responsible for planning and budgeting.
3. *Timing linkage* concerns the sequencing of the annual planning and budgeting cycles.

Within each of these categories, there are several specific features of the planning system that can be manipulated to influence the extent of plan-budget linkage. Let us take a closer look at each of these linkage devices.

Financial Features

One important feature of content linkage is the amount of detail in the financial statements included in the plan document. The tightest linkage would be to include statements with the same level of detail as in the monthly reporting package which compares budgeted with actual results. The loosest linkage would be not to include financial statements at all.

Another design feature related to the financial content is the level of rounding in the plan document. Although it may not seem particularly significant at first blush, there is evidence that rounding to a much higher level in the plan than in the budget (e.g., millions of dollars in the plan versus thousands in the budget) can foster a kind of mental distinction between plan and budget numbers which reduces the tendency to view the plan as solely a long-range budget. This can in turn facilitate a much more creative planning effort by making it clear that the managers do not have to commit themselves (in a budgetary sense) to delivering the planned financial results.

Still another important content feature is the conformity between plan and budget numbers for those years which are common to both documents. If the numbers differ, planning may face a credibility gap. Many companies, however, feel that allowing such differences is critical to maintaining the aggressive forward thrust of the planning effort.

For example, one conglomerate includes in the first year of its five-year plan the earnings from acquisitions that are projected to be closed during the next twelve months but which are not yet finalized. The company does not include these earnings in the budgeted results for the next year which line managers are asked to commit themselves to deliver. Several other companies show differences between planned and budgeted profit for the next year because the two documents are prepared at different times. The one prepared later in the year would reflect the latest thinking, and this might differ from projections made earlier in the year.

Situations like these may or may not be desirable, but they certainly reflect loose content linkage. If numerical differences are permitted, one way of moving back toward tightness is to require that some kind of formal reconciliation of them be included in the plan. Many companies which permit differences require such reconciliation.

Related to plan-budget conformity for years common to both documents is the issue of the uniformity of the numbers for any given year as they appear in succeeding annual plan documents. If the planned figures for any one future period change significantly each time a plan is put together, the perceived realism of the planning effort can suffer.

Our evidence suggests, however, that rarely do companies require the numbers for a given year to be "cast in concrete" the very first time that year appears in a plan document. This degree of linkage is probably unrealistically tight. As we shall illustrate later, a few companies do require formal explanations in the plan for any changes in the projections related to a given future year. This clearly reflects a tighter linkage form of this planning-system variable than would otherwise be reflected by complete freedom to change future years' projections at each iteration of the planning cycle. At least a few companies feel that some tightness at this point is desirable.

A final important design feature is the structure of the content of the plan. In most companies, the budget is structured in terms of the organizational units which will be responsible for carrying it out. Such an approach is a fundamental part of what is often referred to as "responsibility accounting." Given this situation, it is possible to restructure the plan to focus on programs rather than on the organizational units. The total expenditures for a given year are the same in either case, but there is nevertheless a distinctly looser impact on the way in which the plan document is interpreted.

Organizational Relationships

The major design feature in this category is the relationship between the organizational units responsible for the long-range planning and those responsible for the budgetary-control processes. The loosest form is to lodge planning and budgeting in separate organizational channels reporting to different top-level executives. The tightest form is to have the two functions combined in one department.

Even in those situations in which planning and budgeting are separated in terms of formal organizational relationships, there is wide latitude in the extent to which the controller is formally involved in the long-range planning effort. Naturally, the loosest link-

age situation is to have scant involvement on the part of the controller. However, because of his expertise in analyzing and communicating financially oriented data, it is probably neither possible
nor desirable to exclude him completely from the formal planning
effort.

Between this extreme of separate planning and budgeting channels and the complete integration of these functions lies a very
broad middle ground which can be probed to achieve an appropriate level of involvement for any given company. Among the relevant
questions to ask in this regard are the following:

> Does the controller provide staff support for the preparation of
> the financial data in the plan document?
>
> Does the controller review the plan document before it is final-
> ized?
>
> Does the controller have any direct or indirect responsibility for
> approving the plan?
>
> Does the controller have any direct or indirect responsibility for
> monitoring planned financial results against actual results?

The more questions of this kind that can be answered *yes*, the
tighter the plan-budget linkage, even though the functions may
officially be separate.

Timing Considerations

The most important design feature here is concerned with the
sequencing of the annual planning and budgeting cycles. If the two
cycles are carried out sequentially, which one is done first? How
much time elapses between the completion of the first cycle and the
beginning of the one which follows it? If the two cycles are undertaken concurrently, what is the relationship between initiation
dates, completion dates, and approval dates?

The loosest timing linkage is to have the planning cycle done
before the budgeting cycle and to have several months elapse between the two. One major food products manufacturer, for example,
completes the annual planning cycle in February and does not
begin the budgeting phase until November. Situations like this are
least inhibiting to the achievement of "reach" in the planning effort.

The tightest form of the design feature related to sequencing
would be to complete the budgeting cycle first and to have the plan-

ning cycle follow it with minimal elapsed time in between. Since the budgeting cycle almost always concludes in the last quarter of the fiscal year, it is rare to find a company in which the planning cycle comes last. There are, however, many companies that undertake the two cycles concurrently. In general, the more the budget process precedes the plan preparation—in terms of initiation, completion, and approval dates—the tighter the linkage, since the budgeting focus will tend to dominate the joint planning-budgeting effort.

One final timing-related design feature is the time horizon for the long-range planning effort. Usually, the shorter this span, the closer the relationship between the budget and the planning process and thus the tighter the plan-budget linkage. Conversely, the longer the time frame, the easier it becomes to clearly distinguish the process from budgeting and thus the looser the plan-budget linkage.

Nowhere in the whole range of system-design features is the trade-off between realism and reach more clearly defined than in the choice of a planning horizon. The longer the time frame, the wider the range of factors which can be varied and thus the broader the range of strategies which can be considered in moving the company toward its long-range objectives. At the same time, a longer time span increases the uncertainty regarding environmental assumptions, corporate strengths, and the financial parameters which shape the strategy formulation and evaluation process. At some point, uncertainty overcomes the gain in flexibility.

What constitutes an appropriate time horizon certainly varies from industry to industry. It is probably easier, for example, for most public utilities to do fifteen-year planning than it is for defense-aerospace companies to do five-year planning. Within the reasonable range for any given industry, however, the longer the time considerations, the looser the plan-budget linkage. Furthermore, in our opinion, a planning horizon of three or four years reflects a heavy emphasis on realism at the expense of reach, regardless of the industry.

LINKAGE EXAMPLES

In the preceding section of this chapter, we concentrated on a general framework for considering the plan-budget problem. Now, we shall turn our attention to some of the interesting devices actually being used by the six manufacturing companies that we selected as a small but representative sample of those which have (*a*) participated in formal planning studies, (*b*) earned the reputation for having both action-oriented and creative planning systems, and (*c*) been highly successful in terms of compound earnings-per-share growth. Since we believe it unlikely that their records of sustained performance could have been achieved without the help of good planning, it should be revealing to examine in some detail how these companies cope with the linkage problem.

The six companies we observed were Cincinnati Milacron, General Mills, Quaker Oats, Raytheon, Toro, and Warnaco. In them, we encountered such a large number of different linkage devices that we concluded the variety of specific links is limited only by the imagination of the personnel. We shall use the same categories as in the preceding section in reviewing the most interesting linkage practices in these sample companies.

But, first, a note of caution. It is not our intent to propose *the* right answer to the linkage problem, but only to identify some of the more important factors to be considered in determining a right answer for a given company at a specific point in time.

Content-Related Approaches

One of the most innovative attempts to use structure as a mechanism to overcome the creativity-practicality problem is the distinct separation between group and division planning at Warnaco. Each division manager prepares a three-year plan, while each group vice president plans five years out. Warnaco's objective here is to encourage the group vice presidents to think in more general and longer-range terms. They then carry this framework with them to meetings with their division managers. This encourages them to do more creative planning. It is important to note that the formats of these two plans are much different, with the divisional plans being done in much greater detail than the group plans. This serves to focus the group manager's attention on the strategy of the group itself rather than on the specific details of the divisions' operating programs.

A mechanism we mentioned earlier to overcome the problem of loose linkage is the comparison of a plan with its predecessor from a year earlier. Consider, for example, this situation taken from the planning records of a large paper manufacturer. Here are this company's profit projections for 1971 as shown in—

Five-year plan done in 1966............	$60 million
Five-year plan done in 1967............	$50 million
Five-year plan done in 1969............	$36 million
1971 budget prepared in 1970..........	$16 million

At the very least, a plan-to-plan comparison would have called the company's attention to the increasing lack of realism the further the projections extended into the future. The threat of having to formally justify this ever-receding bonanza might have served as a sobering influence to the planners.

It is also possible to use plan-to-plan comparisons to overcome the problems of overly conservative forecasting. Thus, if the paper company's profit projections had demonstrated an ascending pattern, the happy surprise of realizing more profits than expected might also have been accompanied by the undesirable development of capacity shortages and missed market opportunities. In such a case, a plan-to-plan comparison could serve as an impetus for more expansive projections.

Of the six companies we visited, only General Mills requires the reporting and justification of significant changes from the preceding year's plan. At General Mills, management feels that this checking device is sufficiently useful in preventing blue-sky fantasizing to justify its risk in terms of discouraging open-ended mind stretching.

A third content-related mechanism worth noting is the relationship between the plan and budget formats. As we noted earlier, if the two documents differ in form and style, it is more difficult to directly transpose the plan to the budget. Both Toro and Raytheon approach a program and project breakout in the budget as well as the functional allocation. In the other companies we sampled, this split is less distinct since the divisions are largely organized by program area or product line. We view this loosening device as a very significant one that has potential applicability in many companies.

Finally, all six of the sample companies vary the level of detail between the plan and the budget. It is interesting to note, however, that the absolute level of detail in the plan also varies significantly among the six companies. Cincinnati Milacron shows only very highly aggregated summary data, whereas Raytheon's plans approach the same level of detail as its budgets. The other four companies fall in between these extreme approaches.

Organization Coordination

At the corporate level, it is important to understand who is coordinating the planning and who is coordinating the budgeting. The basic question here is whether the company wants to split the two processes. The splitting of this coordination function has the effect of loosening the linkage between planning and budgeting. Both Toro and Cincinnati Milacron provide excellent examples of this.

At Toro, planning is coordinated by the Corporate Planner and budgeting by the Controller. No formal attempt is made to ensure that these two functions proceed in a similar fashion. Cincinnati Milacron handles this in much the same way that Toro does. At General Mills, the end result is the same but the mechanisms are much more complex, with coordination being handled by groups instead of individuals.

Different handling at the division level can also affect the linking process. The basic split here is between strategy formulation and the quantified explication of that strategy. While in almost all instances both are coordinated by the division manager, the degree of delegation of the quantification phase can vary significantly.

It is noteworthy that there is very little divergence in the way quantification of plan results is handled by the six sample companies. All of them largely delegate this phase to the divisional controller. This has a loosening effect by focusing the division manager's attention on policy rather than on detailed profit-and-loss information.

Although it is not a "device" in the usual sense, a company's informal communication process can function in a way that tightens the linkage between planning and budgeting. A great deal of informal information transfer across the corporate/divisional interface increases top management's cognizance of what is in the plan and how it relates to the budget. The presence of informal channels of communication may make top management appear to have an omniscient awareness of these issues, even if this is actually not the case.

At Cincinnati Milacron, where the planning and budgeting systems are very closely linked, one division manager stated that he really felt strongly committed to delivering the performance projected in his five-year plan. At Quaker Oats and Toro, where there are loose linkage systems, two division managers reported similar feelings of commitment. It is difficult for us to assess what precise influence the informal communication processes in the foregoing companies had in forging the personal commitments of these three division managers to delivering the planned results. However, the counter-intuitive coincidence of loose systems and strong commitments at least offers circumstantial evidence that this influence does exist and should not be overlooked.

Time Horizons

A separation in time between the end of the planning cycle and the beginning of the budgeting cycle, as we noted earlier, has the effect of loosening the linkage between the two processes. When the time to worry about next year's performance commitment is still several months away, it is easier to be expansive about the future. In addition, since forecast conditions are always changing, the more time that elapses subsequent to submission of the plan, the easier it is to justify a revision in the budget.

Of the six sample companies, only Raytheon pursues its planning and budgeting cycles concurrently. Cincinnati Milacron has a six-month separation between the end of planning and the beginning of budgeting. General Mills, Quaker Oats, Toro, and Warnaco all have at least a two- to three-month separation.

In general, as the number of years in the budget is extended, or the number of years in the plan contracted, the similarity between the plan and the budget increases. Different time horizons for the two processes tend to emphasize the different purposes of each. Five of the six companies we sampled have either a four- or five-year planning range and a one- or two-year budget span. The exception is Warnaco, which we noted previously.

APPROPRIATE EQUILIBRIUM

Individual linkage devices impact on the planning system by facilitating an overall planning effort which is either more creative or action oriented. As is evident from the preceding discussion, some devices serve to promote a stronger action orientation in planning while others encourage more creativity.

Since a single planning system will utilize several devices which may have opposing effects on the plan-budget balance, an "algebraic" sum of the devices is needed to determine where the planning system is located on the linkage continuum. This plays a pivotal role in achieving an appropriate equilibrium between divergent requirements for both creative and action-oriented planning.

Whether or not a particular planning balance is appropriate for a given company hinges on the corporate setting. Thus, if the underlying essence of planning is to improve a company's ability to cope with changes, it follows that, as the changes are realized, the need for specific forms of planning will also change. In other words, a dynamic corporate setting may call for heavy emphasis on creativity at one point in time and heavy emphasis on practicality at another. The implication is that, as a company's needs change, devices must be added or subtracted in order to adjust the balance between these planning objectives.

The concept of a dynamic corporate setting seems particularly relevant to the four of the six sample companies which are now diversifying extensively beyond the boundaries of their traditional industries. Consider:

> The Toro Company is changing from a manufacturer of lawn mowers and snow blowers to a broad-based participant in the environmental beautification market.
>
> General Mills's Fashion Division, which was established only three years ago, already contributes significantly to the company's sales and earnings and competes in markets dramatically different from those served by Cheerios and other ready-to-eat cereals.
>
> Quaker Oats, in its most recent fiscal year, derived 25% of its sales from nongrocery product sources, including 12% from Fisher-Price Toys. The company has since further diversified in nongrocery areas through acquisition of Louis Marx & Co. Toys and the Needlecraft Corporation of America.
>
> Cincinnati Milacron, the largest manufacturer of machine tools in the world, is seeking points of entry into the minicomputer and semiconductor markets.

A dynamic corporate setting, however, is not necessarily dependent on the diversification activity of a company. For example:

Cincinnati Milacron, with 80% of its sales in the machine tool industry, contends with market cycles which brought machine tool sales volume in 1970 down 50% to 60% below the peak reached two years earlier.

The Raytheon Equipment Division, a defense contractor, faces rapid turnover in electronics technology—a contract bidding process that sometimes makes a ticket in the Irish Sweepstakes look like a sure bet—and concomitant uncertainties and headaches in dealing with mercurial government customers.

Warnaco, competing with 30,000 other companies in the apparel industry, finds that although total sales volume is relatively stable, individual markets are highly volatile as fashions come and go in quick succession.

Whether the result of extensive diversification programs or corporate response to the challenges of traditional markets, all six companies are in a state of perpetual change.

Given this state of flux, it is significant to note that the planning systems in five of the companies have recently been changed, are in the process of being changed, or will be changed in the near future (the exception is Raytheon Equipment). To illustrate:

At Toro, David M. Lilly, Chairman and Chief Executive Officer, recently projected the development of looser linkage between the planning and budgeting systems.

At General Mills, the 1971 planning instructions announced a procedure to highlight where the 1971 plan deviated from the 1970 plan; the same instructions reemphasized a year-old procedure which required "new" businesses to be differentiated from "present" businesses.

At Quaker Oats, the corporate planner foresees the emergence of tighter linkage as the company becomes acclimated to its new divisionalized structure.

At Cincinnati Milacron, a new planning system is in its first year of operation; this system is very loosely linked to budgeting and shifts the burden of planning from the division managers to the group managers.

At Warnaco, as we noted earlier, a systems modification has been implemented; this requires group vice presidents to plan five years into the future and their subordinate division managers three years ahead.

In seeking a comprehensive explanation of the planning system changes just described, we find particularly pertinent the observation that management control systems must be consistent with top management's objectives in order to be truly effective. If the same can be said of formal planning systems, then it follows that a change in an effective planning system is usually triggered by a change in top management's objectives. The implication here is that whether or not a given change improves a planning system may be beside the point. To paraphrase Marshall McLuhan, the planning system and the changes made in it may be "the medium that is the message"—i.e., the message from top management.

Criterion of Consistency

In this section of the chapter, we shall examine more closely two of the planning system changes previously mentioned to see what inferences about top management's objectives we can draw from them.

Since 1971, Cincinnati Milacron has been pulling out of a severe recession that afflicted the entire machine tool industry. Operating management's ordeal during the past two years has been something akin to a day-to-day struggle. As the company has begun to emerge from this traumatic experience, top management has installed a new planning system to allow maximum opportunity for broad-level mind stretching. Furthermore, the burden of planning has been shifted upward to a level of management where there exists the opportunity and authority to implement a diversification program. The message of Cincinnati Milacron's two planning-system changes appears to be rather straightforward: top management wants aggressive diversification planning.

In his memorandum covering General Mills's 1971 planning instructions, James P. MacFarland, Chairman and Chief Executive Officer, indicated the need for a more aggressive capital investment program in the years ahead to achieve the company's sales and earnings objectives. He also referred to progress in the control of capital use and to a change in the planning procedures which would allow top management to focus easily on the changes made subsequent to the previous planning cycle. His general instructions described this procedural change in more detail and reiterated a year-old procedure which separated the planning for new businesses from that for current businesses.

In our judgment, it is a fair guess that it will be a tougher task to revise estimates upward in order to justify additional capital for a current business than to submit new estimates in order to justify seed capital for a new business. The message of the announcement of both a new procedure and reemphasis on an old one appears to be that the encouragement of heavier investments is intended for new and not for current businesses. (This message, incidentally, is clearly reflected in the chairman's and president's letter to General Mills's stockholders and employees in the 1971 Annual Report.)

The procedure at General Mills of separating current and new businesses is particularly noteworthy in that it creates an opportunity to differentiate the planning perspectives, and to apply different standards of expectation to each type of business. In this manner, top management can encourage a division manager to be creative in planning for his new businesses and action oriented in planning for his current businesses.

Future-oriented businesses will be best suited for loosely linked planning/budgeting systems. As the potential of a business begins to be realized, tighter linkage will be desirable in order to transform promises into results. At that point, a balance between creative planning and action-oriented planning would be especially appropriate. Later, as the business exhausts its growth potential and evolves into a "cash generator," even tighter linkage will be desirable to accommodate the corporation's capital needs for the next generation of new businesses.

In short, recognition of divergent corporate objectives for both the mature and the future-oriented business is manifested in different degrees of linkage in their respective planning/budgeting systems. As evident at Quaker Oats, for example, a divisionalized company can find itself at several points—up and down—on the linkage continuum at the same time. In evaluating whether or not any point on the continuum is "right" or "wrong," the sole criterion must be its consistency with corporate objectives.

CONCLUSION

To be effective, every formal long-range planning system must achieve a workable compromise between creativity and practicality —twin goals that are often in conflict. This problem of maintaining a satisfactory balance between "reach" and "realism" can be directly addressed by varying those design features of planning which relate to its interface with budgeting. However, in order to put in perspective the importance of loosening the plan/budget linkage, it is important to consider the role of informal communications and the personalities of management.

At the corporate/division interface, companies that have a great deal of informal communication transfer are likely to be constantly aware of what was written in the plan and how that relates to the budget. This has the effect of very tightly linking the plan and the budget, even in structurally loose systems, unless management makes a conscious effort to demonstrate that this is not wanted. Even if this intent is demonstrated at the corporate level, there still may be tight linkage built in at the division level because of the division manager's personality.

Generally speaking, the divisional planning and budgeting are either both done by the division manager himself or at least co-ordinated by him. As he coordinates the preparation of the budget, he often feels—either consciously or subconsciously—an obligation to justify the value of the plan by reflecting much of it in the budget which represents his short-term game plan for the division.

Briefly, loosening devices have much broader applications than to just those companies which have structurally tight linkage systems. In fact, some of them may be needed in any action-oriented planning system. We believe that managers should consider these devices as variables they can and should manipulate in the interest of more effective planning. Viewed in this context, the linkage continuum can be considered as a powerful interpreter of the top-management objectives implicit in the planning system.

Although at first this may seem to be counter-intuitive, we believe that it is not the planning system which generates corporate objectives but rather the corporate objectives which dictate the appropriate planning system. We are neither proposing that there is a "correct" form for any of these design features, nor that it is always possible to structure a planning system so that "realistic creativity" is ensured.

We do believe, however, that "realistic reach" in planning is not just an illusory phenomenon which exists independent of management's actions. Rather, it is well within management's control to influence the focus of the efforts by changing the structure of the planning system. That, we feel, is all any manager can ask.

ADDITIONAL SOURCES

Also see Additional Sources for Chapter 28.

Hobbs, John M., and Heany, Donald F. "Coupling Strategy to Operating Plans." *Harvard Business Review*, May–June 1977, p. 119.

30

Preparing the Annual Budget

Murray R. Mathews, Jr.*

A budget is a description in quantitative—usually monetary—terms of a desired future result. The process of preparing the budget requires management at all levels to focus on the future of the business entity. The finished product of the budgeting process is useful in communicating approved future plans, in motivating managers to achieve the desired results, and in setting a standard against which actual performance can be measured. In effect, the finished budget stipulates *what* is to be achieved in the future and *how* the desired results are to be accomplished.

Terminology

There are two commonly used terms which are *not* budgeting but which are frequently confused with it. *Forecasting* is the use of various techniques, including out-and-out guessing, which seek to estimate future events and quantitative or qualitative results in overall terms. Generally, forecasters are attempting to assess future events over which they have little or no control. While forecasting

---

* Mr. Mathews is Vice President, Control, of National Medical Care, Inc., Boston.

techniques may be—and usually are—necessary to the budgeting process, they are not in and of themselves to be mistaken for budgeting.

A *projection* results from analyzing historical events and trends which can predict the future value of the quantitative measure under analysis. A projection implies a type of forecast which is primarily dependent on historical patterns without taking planned changes in operating environment into account.

Programming is the process of deciding on specific ventures which will be undertaken by the company and the extent of the commitment (i.e., the amount of resources) to each venture. Decisions about specific product lines (and products within a line), plant construction, and research and development efforts are examples of programming decisions. Many companies make such decisions only when the need for them is perceived by management. Other companies treat programming decisions as a separate formal process and prepare *long-range plans* for periods of three to five years into the future, or even longer in the case of industries with heavy capital needs and long start-up periods such as the utility industry. However, even in those companies which do not prepare formal long-range plans, the programming process is constantly proceeding among top management.

In making programming decisions, all costs should be considered as controllable. An existing plant, the depreciation on which is properly considered to be fixed in the short run, can always be sold if the programming decision so dictates. Similarly, the customary number of quality control inspectors who insure a desired quality level can be changed to a less-expensive alternative if the cost of achieving the quality level makes the product unsalable in the marketplace.

In order to make successful programming decisions, the managers must be guided by a thorough understanding of the economics of a business and an appropriate business strategy. While the perception and development of an appropriate strategy might be considered as the more cerebral of the two requirements, the understanding of the economics of a business is very much susceptible to well-known techniques. Proficiency in these techniques prior to the preparation of the first budget is essential, as will be shown in the following sections.

Budgeting, then, is nothing more than the process of transforming a series of programming decisions into an operating plan for the constituent parts of the business entity.

BUDGETING

Since budgeting is the creation of a consistent plan for the units of a business, the first problem to be resolved is that of defining the units for which a budget is to be prepared. In general, a budget must be prepared by and for every responsibility unit which is charged with carrying out a specific function. For example, each department should have a budget for costs which are controllable by the supervisor of that department, the sum of all such budgets being the budget for the entire factory.

Similarly, budgets are prepared by those employees responsible for overall programs. For example, a budget might be prepared by the manager of Product Line X showing the expected sales, costs, and contribution to net income. Typically such budgets are useful for review of overall balance within the organization and relate back to original top-management decisions, but are not useful for control purposes since program costs cannot ordinarily be related to the responsibility of specific managers. The manager who incurs costs in most organizations is responsible to a different chain of command than is the program manager, and will be subject to an entirely different set of goals, constraints, and criteria for performance evaluation. In a true "matrix" organization, this lack of congruity between program control and responsibility control can be quite vexing and substantially complicate the budget preparation process.

Successful budgeting, then, can only be achieved through a thorough understanding of the responsibility structure of the company, for it is only through budgeting by and for those managers *responsible* for results that any measure of *control* of results can be achieved.

A second prerequisite for successful budgeting is adequate historical cost records, a timely and meaningful reporting system, and an appropriately strong level of financial analysis support. If program managers are to understand the economics of a business, its cost and financial history must be available to them in terms that are germane to their needs. Line managers must have access to historical costs for the preparation of responsibility budgets. Managers generally must have current data available if they are to use the budget to respond to changing conditions or to the failure of supervisors to perform to expected levels. If the manager does not have adequate accounting resources available, budgeting will not solve any problems and may create further problems by producing wrong or misleading indications.

Types of Costs

It is also important in budgeting that managers understand the different types of costs for which they are budgeting. These costs can be categorized as engineered costs, discretionary costs, and committed costs.

Engineered costs are elements of cost for which the "right" amount to be incurred can be estimated with reasonable accuracy. Typically such costs are referred to as *direct* or *variable* costs in that they usually vary directly with volume. For example, given a set of product specifications, production engineers can estimate the amount of direct labor time which should be spent on each production step. The total labor cost can then be estimated by applying the standard wage rate to the estimated time required to produce each part. Similarly, the amount of materials required for each item can be determined by engineering studies and priced at standard material costs (usually prepared by the purchasing department).

While it is true that production engineering is not an exact science, estimates resulting from the production engineer's analysis will generally be sufficiently precise that no reasonable grounds for disagreement will exist. However, it is essential that the production supervisor responsible for meeting the engineered standard agree with it lest he or she be insufficiently committed to achieving it.

The very same concepts and techniques which were originally derived from a manufacturing setting can be applied to the service sector of the economy. The resulting standards in a service operation will not be as precise as those which can be obtained from the observation of a manufacturing operation, primarily because the "product" is never quite the same on any two occasions. However, with a sufficiently large sample, minor differences will cancel out and the engineered cost concept will prove useful. The concept of the "learning curve" (see Chapter 5) may be more significant in the service setting because the "product" quality is more under the direct control of the operator and less a function of the variability of a machine process.

A final point to bear in mind is that in a period of rapidly changing technology, the "correct" amount of labor or materials (or their cost) may be particularly difficult to establish. Engineering cost setting is an inherently statistical process depending on the observation of large numbers of essentially identical operations. If the sample is not large enough, the possibility of statistical error will exist.

Discretionary costs are items of cost the amount of which can be varied widely at the discretion of management. The chief attribute of a discretionary cost is that there is no scientific way of determining the "correct" amount. Rather the amount which is budgeted is a function of management's perception of the effectiveness of past discretionary amounts spent and their intuitive reaction to the spending requirement for new programs or support services. Questions which are raised in reviewing discretionary costs are: What should we spend on accounting services? Should we increase the advertising budget for Product X next year? What is the proper amount to spend on research and development to maintain our marketing position? See Chapter 24 for a further analysis of this subject and suggested methods for setting discretionary cost levels in the budgeting process.

Discretionary costs tend to be more important in a service industry setting, mirroring the variability in the characteristics of the end "product" and the relatively more personal relationship of the customer with the producer of the service. Also, regardless of the setting, the budgeter of discretionary costs must be careful not to perpetuate historical mistakes. Certain cost/revenue relationships tend to become dogma with the passage of time because "we've always spent 8 percent of sales on R&D."

Committed costs are costs which are necessarily incurred as the result of a decision to pursue a program of effort. While in the long run all costs can be considered as discretionary, the short- and medium-range outlook must reflect the costs associated with management's specific decisions. Generally, committed costs are equivalent to what the accountant terms as fixed costs and arise out of the ownership of an asset (depreciation) or the entry into a binding commitment (signing a long-term lease). An otherwise discretionary cost becomes a committed cost when the decision to incur the cost becomes irrevocable. For example, the discretionary decision to use the services of an in-house attorney becomes irrevocable, from a cost point of view, when management decides to sign an employment agreement with the attorney.

Generally, the accounting/budgeting staff should be assigned the task of preparing the committed cost budget, since, by definition, such costs are no longer subject to management influence during the budget period. It is very helpful to this process if the accounting personnel are informed of all committed costs when the decision to incur them is made.

Uses of Budgets

Since a budget is nothing more than a formalized, short-term plan, the process of preparing the budget involves operating managers in *planning* specifically how programming decisions will be implemented. In the course of preparing the budget, imbalances between the various operating subdivisions of the entity and/or unsatisfactory results of programming decisions will be brought to light, and the original decisions may have to be changed. For example, if a new advertising campaign will result in substantially increased sales, the production budget may show that the cost of producing the increased quantities is so high as to make the original program decision to expand the advertising budget suspect.

The budgeting process serves to *communicate* to line managers the programming decisions of top management and factual (e.g., engineered cost) data as to number of units to be produced, materials to be used, selling prices to be sought, and so on. Policies are also communicated in the discretionary cost area, such as the willingness to support specific levels of research and development expenditures, expenditures for desired working conditions, and the amount of corporate overhead expenses to be incurred.

The process of budgeting serves as a vital link of communication in that functional managers become aware of the problems of other areas as they mutually work to complete the budget. The finished budget communicates top management's approval of the proposed plan of operations of the company.

A budget prepared in an atmosphere of commitment can serve as a powerful *motivational* tool. A carefully prepared budget will motivate operational managers, through their commitment to their own estimates, to achieve the desired result. Research has shown that the commitment to one's own goals is invariably higher than the commitment to the goals determined by others. An appropriately organized budgeting effort will involve responsible line managers at an early stage in the budget formulation process by soliciting the managers' commitment to their own goals, and by showing clearly to the line managers that top management regards the responsible setting of budgets and the achievement of budgeted goals as being of significant importance to both the company and the individual managers.

The success or failure of a line manager is measurable since the budget presents a *standard for performance measurement.* Because the budget represents the net effect of all changes in the business which could be foreseen at the time of its preparation, it measures performance against what should be done rather than against a series of cumulative mistakes, as may be the case when performance is measured against historical results. Failure to meet budget will direct attention to those areas in which corrective action should be taken.

In addition, in a period of rapid change, budgets can be easily changed to reflect management's changed expectations. Top management can thus rapidly come up with a new standard of performance against which to measure actual results.

It should also be pointed out that even the best budget will not replace an effective control system. At best, a good budget-to-actual comparison can only indicate problems after they have occurred. A good control system, however, will warn of potentially damaging transactions before they occur. The budget may give the manager an idea of transactions to watch for, either good or bad, but the control system must be depended upon to stop problems before they take place.

Although the budget serves as a standard for performance evaluation, it does not follow that performance to the budgeted standard should be considered as good performance. Failure to make budget in the face of adverse business conditions may be far better performance than making budget when conditions are ripe for substantial improvement over planned performance. On the other hand, if the company is not to become a prisoner of the budget, top management must let operating managers know quickly when its expectations have changed.

Types of Budgets

In spite of references to "the" budget, there are actually several types of budgets which make up the totality of "the" budget. These are:

1. The *operating budget*, which seeks to translate the programming decisions of top management into specific responsibility budgets of line supervisors. In addition, a supplementary budget may associate the activities of several different product lines into the total operating budget of the entity.
2. The *cash budget* translates the operating expectations of the company into financial forecasting tools for the treasurer, enabling the treasurer to determine the need for short-term financing.
3. The *capital budget* reflects the longer term programming decisions of top management, and its adoption results in the commitment of corporate funds to a specific course of action. It is useful in determining the timing and amounts of long-term financing for a company.

The operating budget consists of two portions, the program budget and the responsibility budget. The *program budget* is more net income oriented in that it attempts to measure the contribution to net income of each of the various major program decisions made by top management. Program budgets usually cut across traditional organizational lines and include appropriate elements of functional areas such as manufacturing (or service costs), marketing, selling, and advertising costs and associated revenues. In larger companies, complicated formulas have been developed to allocate divisional and corporate overhead and, in some cases, state and federal income taxes to various programs. Such budgets, primarily because they are very difficult to use as a control and evaluation tool, are most useful as a financial planning and strategy evaluation tool.

The *responsibility budget* is primarily a cost control mechanism, and is that which is most commonly referred to as "the" budget. Responsibility budgets, in contrast to program budgets, follow the formal authority structure of the company. Such budgets focus on line supervisors and attempt to motivate them to set and then meet or exceed objectives which are to the overall satisfaction of top management.

Understanding the explicit interrelationship between program and responsibility budgets requires a high level of sophistication on the part of both managers and the reporting system. Program managers who are beating their budgets based on standard costs may be living in a dream world if their accounting system is unable to inform them of significant unfavorable variances generated at the responsibility center level. Similarly, problems will ensue if responsibility centers are on budget, but the financing structure of the company has changed in such a way that high interest costs cause substantial losses.

The difficulty of relating the program decision to responsibility decisions can be complicated by purely "financial" influences which may lead to completely different answers at the program and responsibility levels. For example, a responsibility center analysis may indicate that the skilled labor force available in a developing country may be inadequate to run a projected plant profitably, but the program decision may be to proceed with the plant because of tax incentives offered by the host government. Conversely, the low labor cost which makes a plant investment appear appropriate to the responsibility manager may not be persuasive from a program point of view if the exposure to significant currency devaluation is great.

In summary, the operating budget can be "cut" two ways: towards overall programs designed to fulfill strategic objectives or towards responsibility centers which must be motivated to work towards a common goal. Program level budgets are high level and are most valuable for reviewing overall balance within the organization and for further refinement of financial and strategic plans. Responsibility budgets are prepared in detail, are useful in communicating program decisions and breaking them down into achievable pieces, and provide a useful benchmark for the evaluation of supervisory personnel.

The *variable budget* (or "flexible budget," as it is sometimes called) is a more sophisticated version of the operating budget which attempts to specify results (and expectations for responsibility centers) at differing volume levels. Successful variable budgets can result only if the budgetor has a good understanding of the changes in costs with changes in volume. Variable budgets may be expressed in solely mathematical terms, such as total costs equal fixed costs plus per unit variable costs times expected volume. A complexity is introduced by the fact that few costs vary directly with volume over a very wide range of volumes, even in a single plant. As a plant gets closer and closer to capacity, the next unit of production becomes more costly. In addition, certain costs will vary sharply as certain production levels are reached and then level out for relatively long periods of time, for example, the cost of providing second-shift janitorial services.

Variable budgets can also be expressed in discrete dollar amounts at various levels of operations. Generally only one level is used in the master budget. If actual results vary from plan, however, the "contingency" plan will be ready and managers can move quickly to react to the changed circumstances.

The cost of using variable budgets is that they are clerically cumbersome to produce, and required relatively more staff work, recordkeeping, and analysis to thoroughly understand the fixed and variable nature of cost-volume relationships. The advantage of the variable budget is that it forces management to plan for a range of possible volumes rather than fixating on a single volume estimate.

Zero-based budgets are useful for reviewing ongoing programs, usually those with high proportions of discretionary expenses. As the term suggests, a zero-based review determines from scratch such things as:

Should the activity be performed at all?

If it is to be performed, should it be done internally or contracted out?

If it is to be performed, should it be performed to the same extent as in the past? Is tradition determining current corporate strategy?

This approach is in sharp contrast to traditional budgeting, which builds on historical levels of expenditures and historical cost relationships. A zero-based review requires a comparison of present methods with various technological and organization alternatives, including the alternative of not performing the function at all. In essence, a zero-based review requires managers to justify their existence and is appropriately traumatic to the organization. Many feel that a zero-based review is so time, energy, and emotion consuming that it cannot be done annually, but that it can only be applied to specific responsibility centers on cycle basis. Proponents of the system, on the other hand, believe that it can be done every year after an initially trying period in which the basic paperwork and methods are taught to line supervisors. The reader is directed to Chapter 24 for a further explanation of the concepts and techniques of this budgeting method.

In some ways similar to zero-based budgeting is the *cost reduction program*. This often involves a zero-based review of a specific area of the business, usually as a result of a perceived crisis. In some cases, the cost reduction concept can be applied to the whole company.

A *cash budget* shows the sources and uses of cash by time period. It is particularly useful to the treasury staff in planning short-term financing needs, and is rarely prepared in any detail for more than the immediately coming year. As a financial planning tool, it has minimal operating impact, and usually is prepared by the budgeting or control staff.

The *capital budget* seeks to estimate changes in fixed or other long-term assets. Programming decisions are the major influence on capital requirements, whereas operating changes take place within the framework of available capital assets and have a minimal effect on the capital budget.

Capital budgeting decisions have, by necessity, a major impact on the long-term financing plans of an entity and hence cannot be made without an appreciation of the long-term financing constraints which impinge on the company. For an example, the decision to build a new manufacturing plant may be justified, but the resultant working capital requirements may be financable only on such onerous terms that the decision may not be workable.

The *budgeted balance sheet* combines the elements of operating budgets, cash budgets, and capital budgets. It shows the balance sheet effects of various decisions made in the subsidiary budgeting systems and is primarily of use to the financial planners. Such a budget will, for example, show that the net result of future plans may result in a default under the loan covenants of existing debt. This does not mean that the plans are unsound of themselves, but rather is a warning that the lenders will have to be involved in the decision to pursue the project.

THE MANAGEMENT PROCESS OF PREPARING THE ANNUAL BUDGET

In purely mechanistic terms, the task of preparing the annual budget can be viewed as the application of a series of techniques, the end result of which is a set of financial statements which present the planned results of actions which have not yet taken place. The greatest single task in implementing budgeting is overcoming organizational inertia and eliciting commitment from line managers to future results. It is to this set of problems which the balance of this chapter will address itself.

Organization for Budget Preparation

The *budget committee* guides the work of preparing the budget by translating strategic decisions into budget guidelines. That is, after a consultative process with the chief executive officer, which may have taken place continuously since the most recent previous budget, the budget committee disseminates approved guidelines for the current budget, reviews budget submissions, requests revisions if necessary, and resolves differences and assures balance between and among competing responsibility centers and programs.

The budget committee may vary in size from the chief executive officer only in a smaller organization, to the entire group of corporate officers (and their staffs) who report to the CEO in larger organizations. It is important, however, that the composition of the committee reflect that of the real power structure so that the completed plan reflects the commitment of those who will have to carry it out. For example, a budget committee composed of accounting-oriented individuals and salespersons in a high-technology, research-oriented organization is almost bound to fail in supervising the preparation of a budget by a group of research-oriented scientists.

While the committee cannot be too far removed from those whom it wishes to motivate, the individual members must be high enough in the organization to know what is acceptable to top management and why it is strategically required or advisable. At the same time, the committee must be sufficiently articulate to express the desired goals to subordinates without giving the impression that the budget is being imposed from the top down.

A great deal of the technical work of budget preparation is carried out by a staff under the direction of a *budget director,* who is usually an accounting-oriented individual. It is the budget director who designs the forms to be used by the line supervisory personnel, disseminates the instructions formulated by the budget committee, sees to the timely submission of a budget data by operating personnel, and provides historical data to those who require it for the preparation of their budgets. The director also provides an informal review point before individual budgets are formally submitted to the committee. Finally, the director and the director's staff perform the clerical chore of compiling the consolidated budget and analyzing the implications of decisions made in arriving at the budgeted results.

It must be emphasized that the budget director and the staff are primarily channels of communication. It is not the primary function of the budget director to pass judgment on either the strategic planning or programming decisions which went into the initial budget assumptions and objectives; nor is it the function of the director to quell a serious attempt on the part of line management to convince the committee and top management that the goals as initially stated are not achievable. For the budget process to work, the commitment must come from the managers who are responsible for controlling operations.

Content of the Budget

The question of what items to budget can be answered by determining the level of detail required to fulfill the one or more basic functions discussed in the earlier section on "Uses of Budgets." Planning financial results and the timing and amounts of financing required can usually be done with high-level budgets which present only summarized information. Similarly, the purpose of providing a medium of communications to inform line managers of overall corporate objectives in the near-term future and of motivating management to achieve those objectives can best be achieved by summarized information, since the message is general and cannot be imparted in great detail without risk of losing the point.

The establishment of a standard for specific motivation and subsequent evaluation, however, requires significant detail, since the objective is to reach down to the lowest responsibility level and set standards for performance at the level where costs are incurred. It is only through this process of working overall strategy down to the supervisory levels where the strategy is actually implemented that supervisors will know specifically what they are to do and be secure in the knowledge that their performance will be objectively judged.

Basic economic constraints must be taken into account in the appropriate level of budgeting detail. It does not make sense to develop substantial detail on those aspects of the business which are not significant to its success or failure. In a service industry, for example, labor is typically a high percentage of total costs and should receive greater attention than supplies costs, which account for a relatively small fraction of total costs.

It is also nonsensical to expend significant effort in detail budgeting of items for which reports of actual performance will be either impossible to get, or which will be so expensive or so long in preparation that they will be of no use in evaluating performance. In fact, the absence or slowness of reports of actual results will be seized upon by poor performers as excuses for their failure.

It also makes little sense to budget items over which the responsibility center supervisor has minimal or no control. Examples are transfer prices in an integrated producer which are set by historical custom or by any other nonnegotiated method, and financing costs in a capital-intensive industry, such as public utilities.

Budget Timing

Ordinarily, the basic time period for financial planning is the company's fiscal year. However, to control and monitor operations, budgets for shorter time periods are called for. At a minimum, most companies budget by quarters within the year, and many divide the quarter into calendar or fiscal (four-week) months. Some companies budget total figures by quarters, and then divide the quarterly totals into monthly amounts by means of an appropriate statistical measure such as an index of seasonality. Others specifically require the construction of budgets for each month. A further refinement of this technique requires the preparation of a revised budget for the remaining months of the company's year based on actual experience to date, or the preparation of a budget for the next twelve months based on the most recent actual figures —a so-called *rolling budget.*

In determining appropriate budget timing, one constraint to consider is the flexibility of company operations. If the nature of the business precludes rapid changes in costs, quarterly budgets may be sufficiently informative, particularly if there is a reliable statistical measure to enable the accounting department to break out quarterly budgets into expected monthly results. For example, in a geographically dispersed service industry in which local managers are given wide discretion, specific monthly budgeting may be wasteful since local managers will not change operating procedures without clear historical evidence of the need for change. Because of the time required to assemble the evidence, budgeting more frequently than quarterly in this situation does not make sense.

The frequency with which the budget is revised is also widely variable. Some companies consider the annual budget to be "locked in" and not changeable after the budget year starts. Such companies believe that the original budget best reflects the original goals of the company and the comparison with actual, even in the face of substantially changed conditions, will elicit *all* the reasons for variations. Other companies believe that comparing actual with a budget which was predicated on conditions substantially different from those actually encountered is an exercise in futility. Such companies revise the budget for the remainder of the year to reflect actual conditions.

Some companies may even maintain two budgets after the start of the year, one which was the original approved plan and one which has been revised based on results to date. In this situation, comparison of the original budget to the most currently revised budget is a measure of the change in conditions from those originally envisioned, and a comparison of the actual results to the most recent budget is a measure of the current performance of the company.

Frequent changes in the budget are helpful to financial planners, since their plans can be based on the most current situation, but frequent revisions may be clerically cumbersome, confusing to operating people who do not fully comprehend reasons for the changes, and may make the task of evaluating managers more difficult since multiple standards are involved.

A technique which is used in some large companies is to put the preparation of the budget on a cyclical basis. That is, certain of the operating units may budget by quarter for the year starting in April, others will budget by quarter for the year starting in July, others in October, and the balance will coincide with the natural calendar year of the parent company. Such a procedure has the effect of leveling out the clerical work load on the budget supervisor and his or her department and leveling out peaks in the approval process. In addition, the company can avoid the upheaval of completely revising budgets every month or quarter, but still revise overall plans and reflect the effect on each element at the point in the budget cycle when the element prepares its budget for the ensuing year. This approach is particularly appropriate in large companies where divisional enterprises have seasonal fluctuations which are not synchronous with the bulk of the business or with the parent's reporting year. The approach works best, of course, if these divisions do not have a significant number of transactions between each other.

The *sequence* of budget preparation is particularly important since many aspects of budgeting are dependent on prior steps. This becomes particularly true in large, complex businesses; and the timing of the various steps must be very carefully thought out in advance if the process is to work smoothly. One suggested series of sequential steps is as follows:

1. Decide upon and publish budget guidelines.
2. Prepare and print forms and instructions.
3. Prepare and publish the sales budget.
4. Budget all expenses in detail.
5. Negotiate disagreements and imbalances and obtain preliminary approval of the amounts agreed upon.
6. Make sure that the various program and responsibility budgets are in agreement and that no serious imbalances exist.
7. Obtain final approval of top management and, if necessary, of the board of directors.
8. Disseminate approved summary budget information to appropriate personnel for planning purposes, and details back down through the approval chain so that responsibility center managers know what is expected of them.

If the budget is for a calendar year, the process should start in the early part of the third quarter with the preparation of budget guidelines and forms and instructions for the detail work done by responsibility managers. Actual preparation of the detail is done early in the fourth quarter after third quarter results are available for guidance. Review and approval is completed in November, and the final budget is available for publication in December just prior to the start of the year. Of course, this timetable will vary, depending on such factors as uncertainties in the company's environment, how experienced company managers are with budgeting procedures, and how much budgetor-budgetee negotiation is encouraged at each level in the organization.

Budget Guidelines

The publication of guidelines to the overall goals of the company for the coming year is the typical device used to communicate programming decisions, most of which have been made well in advance of the commencement of the budgeting cycle. For example, if the program calls for the expansion of manufacturing capacity, program decisions must have been made well in advance, since changing the capacity and character of existing manufacturing facilities requires lead times of several years. Similarly, the decision to bring an entirely new product to the market can only be implemented after considerable development effort. The budget, then, is not created from scratch but is a logical outgrowth of the present operations and past strategies. Major decisions and commitments have been made well before the top-management group is faced with the task of drafting specific budget guidelines. Such guidelines can only fine-tune the strategic thinking which has already taken place and indicate how the company expects to operate in the short-run future.

Budget guidelines are generally not overly specific, since one objective of the budgeting process is to incite operating managers to commit themselves to their own goals, rather than forcing goals on the organization from the top down. However, it may be necessary to be specific in response to problem areas; for example, to reflect financing constraints, guidelines may specify an objective of reducing receivables or inventories to a mandated level. Similarly, top management may specify overall objectives for salary increases or objectives for personnel increases. In other companies, general economic assumptions may be given in great detail, while the response of program and operating managers to the assumptions may be left open to each manager's discretion.

Generally, if no guideline is specified (and if zero-based reviews are not employed), the manager can assume that present spending levels are satisfactory and can be used as a base point for figuring next year's budget. A corollary is that the budget supervisors must beware of the self-fulfilling prophecy—if the present situation is not satisfactory, appropriate changes must be called for in the guidelines or no change will be forthcoming. Alternatively, overly aggressive guidelines which are not agreed to by operating management will be ineffective, since such guidelines will not result in the commitment of individual managers to correcting the substandard result. In this latter case, budgeting becomes a number-pushing exercise and the motivational aspects of a properly devised budget are lost.

The Sales Budget

The amount and mix of sales expected for each of the company's product groups determines the constraints under which most of the responsibility managers will operate. As noted previously, there is a difference between a forecast and a budget. The former implies passive acceptance of events over which one has no real control, whereas the latter implies that the participant can actively influence events. This latter concept is used in estimating sales for the budget period. The sales supervisory force should set the budget to reflect its efforts to address weaknesses of the past and reflect whatever marketing strategy has been decided upon. Accordingly, it is appropriate at this point in the budgeting cycle to set out the main elements of the marketing campaign, and the costs which are expected to be incurred and the expected results. The full detail of individual items in the selling budget can be left to a later step in the process.

The preparation of the sales budget is typically the most difficult step in the entire budgeting process, since success or failure may be as much a function of the customers of the company as it is of the actions of the company itself. Management can plan to shift marketing emphasis and stipulate advertising expenditures, but if the customer does not respond, it may not be possible for the company to change this basic fact. On the other hand, most other expenditures are under management control (except for the prices of various raw material and labor factors) and can be varied in response to changes in the business environment.

There are two basic methods of preparing a sales estimate as the basis of a more refined sales budget:

1. A *statistical forecast* can be prepared based on historical results and ratios, governmental or trade association projections, and company estimates of future economic activity.

2. An *internal estimate* can be produced from the summarization of executive or sales personnel opinions about the level of sales which can be attained. Such a summary can be prepared by program (product line), by individual salespersons, by geographical region, or by any other supervisory hierarchy which exists.

There are advantages and weaknesses in both methods of estimating sales. Statistical methods rely on the assumption that the future will closely resemble the past. While such assumptions are frequently valid, they are most likely to be true in a mature industry where the marketing approach of the company is to change the customer's selective demand for a relatively undifferentiated product and not to expand total demand for the product line. Statistical methods also suffer the shortcoming of not explicitly recognizing the effects of product innovation and run the risk of perpetuating historical marketing weaknesses.

Internally prepared forecasts, on the other hand, can be entirely free form and recognize changes in the environment and changes in product development and innovation. Such forecasts are more effective in a primary demand situation where the strategy is to induce increased total demand for the product in question. In this case, sales results are a function of the ability of the sales staff to expose the product, and hence it is appropriate to have the sales staff commit themselves to this goal. Many companies which utilize internally prepared forecasts do not communicate revisions back to the sales staff in order to preserve the motivational aspects of the sales staff's commitment to their original estimates.

Frequently, a combination of statistical and internally prepared forecasts is used. Both types, with the judgmental factors introduced by top management, help insure that significant factors which might affect sales have not been omitted from the analysis. In addition, even when statistical forecasting methods have been established, it may be necessary to use polling forecasts at product-line levels to commit sales personnel to achieving the statistically predictable.

Regardless of the forecasting methods used, the transformation of raw forecast results into the sales budget requires the application of seasoned business judgment and the recognition of external factors which affect the ability of the sales staff to achieve its goals.

For example, the effect of regulatory lag on the timing of market introduction of a new product is a phenomenon which the sales staff may not be able to explicitly include in their budgeting, but which surely exerts a powerful force on the overall business planning of the company. An example of this is the recent experience of the medical device industry with the FDA and the time required for approval of new or revised products before they can be offered for sale. In this situation, the timing of a new product, and also the broader question of whether or not a product is marketable at all, can be answered only by the regulatory authority.

Another pitfall to be aware of in some markets is the inelastic consumer price behavior. For example, in the medical care industry, increased demand for specialized medical care services is not a function of cost, but rather is a function of the statistical incidence of the specific problem, the extent of physician knowledge of cause and cure, and the extent of reimbursement for the service by third-party payors. This is not to say that it is impossible to budget revenues in this situation, but rather to point out that sales budgets must be based on detailed knowledge of the factors which affect the demand for the service and reasonable knowledge of the way those factors might change.

Other factors which must be taken into account in the preparation of the sales budget are the effect of pricing changes and capacity shortages which will affect the availability of the product.

Cost and Expense Budgets

With preliminary approval of the sales budget, and incorporation of planned changes in the size of inventories, production managers can determine spending levels to provide the product in the mix and at the times called for in the sales budget, remembering constraints imposed by the planned manufacturing capacity.

In many ways, the expense budget is a key factor in a company's success, especially in periods of business downturn. The expense budget affects a far higher percentage of the employees and typically a far higher percentage of the supervisory personnel. Also, management typically has a greater degree of control over the incurrence of costs than they do over the purchases of their customers. The expense budget is useful in pointing out the cost of achievable imbalances between the production and sales budgets.

That is, what may be very advantageous from a marketing point of view may require unusually high manufacturing costs as a result of the peculiarities of the company's plant or operating procedures or contracts.

The techniques of expense budgeting rely more heavily on analysis of past operations and historical ratios than those which are used for sales budgeting. Approved budget guidelines and the sales budget are disseminated through the management hierarchy and are broken into successively smaller and more specific packages to correspond with the tasks assigned to each level of responsibility. At each level, responsible managers may add additional guidelines that are appropriate for the level reporting to them. Finally, at the lowest responsibility level, each departmental supervisor prepares the budget for the costs which are controllable by him or her.

The proper way to develop a cost budget is to budget items of expense in terms of physical quantities and unit prices. Since the amount of material and labor is controlled by the departmental supervisor, he or she will appropriately think in physical terms. The price to be applied to the physical quantities is ordinarily the responsibility of the purchasing agent (in the case of materials) or the labor relations department (for wage rates). Since these individuals control prices, they and not the line supervisor should budget them. If the company has a standard cost system, this step amounts to revising standard cost sheets. In so doing, it is important to keep both the physical quantities of inputs and unit prices of those inputs separate, so that, say, in a period of rapid inflation the standards can be updated by changing only the unit price components.

Usually the most currently available historical cost data is the starting point for next year's budget. Specific departmental budget guidelines may permit or require deviations from historical patterns to reflect the goals and objectives of the management levels above the department being budgeted. (For more details see Chapter 10, "Determining Standard Material and Labor Costs.")

Overhead costs which are directly controllable by the individual departmental supervisor should be budgeted as a pool of costs, and then be allocated to various activities and products of the department by the accounting department. Similarly, the budget for general factory overhead should be prepared by those who can control such costs. Individual supervisors do not need to know the details of the general overhead pool, since they cannot affect the amounts. Some companies, however, believe that informing individual supervisors of the composition and amount of the general overhead pool makes them more aware of the scope of effort required to run a production facility. In addition, when incentive compensation is involved, pressure on poor budget performers, even at the overhead level, may have some beneficial motivational influence.

Before leaving this subject, it would be well to repeat that budgeting for expenses is the most clerically burdensome aspect of preparing the budget, both for the budget staff and the supervisors who do the work. It only makes sense to keep the chore to a minimum. Budget only those items in detail that are essential to the success of the enterprise. Budget only those items for which the reporting system can provide subsequent actual data. A poorly thought-out budgeting program will not only fail to achieve the motivational and evaluative functions but will present a serious morale problem as it is extra work and time away from the primary duties of operating personnel.

Negotiation and Tentative Approval

The next step in the budgeting process, that of each supervisor's negotiating and obtaining the approval of his or her superior, is the most critical from a control and motivational point of view. It is through this process that top management's objectives are agreed to by the people who will have to carry them out. Negotiations are particularly significant to the settlement of discretionary cost amounts, since engineered costs are primarily the result of empirically observed results and committed costs (by definition) are not subject to negotiation.

Accordingly, although there is always a requirement for a negotiating process, it is proportionately more important in those industries which have relatively higher levels of discretionary expenditures. Also, the requirement for negotiations is a function of the degree of centralization in the management structure. In smaller companies with relatively unsophisticated line managers, authority to control events and responsibility for performance may be so centralized that the negotiation process may be of minimal importance. Conversely, in geographically dispersed corporations with decentralized control structures, the importance of budget negotiations is paramount if top management is to be certain that its strategies are to be carried out.

The objective of the negotiating process is to work out a compromise to an otherwise potentially unworkable situation. On the one hand, top management wants a "tight" budget to guarantee maximum return to the company. Operating personnel, on the other hand, wish to insure that the approved budget has sufficient slack in it to allow them to respond to any unforeseen problems or changes in operations. The frequently observed overemphasis on the evaluative aspects of budgeting, coupled with incentive compensation plans based on budgeted performance, mean that it is very much in the interests of operating managers to build in as much of an opportunity to meet their budgets in the face of adverse changes as they possibly can. The negotiating process is meant to reconcile these conflicting motives to the satisfaction of both parties.

During negotiations, the reviewing manager (budgetor) must keep clearly in mind the objectives as to the relative tightness or looseness of the budget, that is, the relative ease or difficulty of achieving the end budget results. An overly tight budget leads to frustration and defeatism, will conceivably give false signals to the financial planners and, in its evaluative aspects, lead to unfair criticism of operating personnel. A budget which is overly loose, on the other hand, leads to complacency, laziness, and failure to meet the otherwise achievable goals. The objective of the negotiating process is to reach a desirable middle ground in which the budget represents a goal which is difficult but which is attainable.

In some companies the concept of negotiation has fallen out of favor and the idea of a "phantom" budget has taken its place. Under this concept, top-level managers do not negotiate differences between what they want or what they really believe to be achievable and the budget submissions prepared by operating management. Rather, in place of a negotiated budget, they substitute their budget. This concept not only undermines the communicative and evaluative aspects of budgeting but, more importantly, may result in serious planning problems. If the treasurer's department is working under the assumption that the "phantom" budget will be achieved and it is either substantially lower or higher than reasonable expectations, the company may be in for a rude surprise in its cash flow and short-term financing expectations.

The tactics of negotiation are reasonably well known. The superior starts the evaluation of a proposed budget at the current level of expenditures and standard costs, primarily because there usually is not time to completely review the details of the proposed budget. One method of cutting proposed expenditures is to arbitrarily cut all submitted budgets. The problem with this approach is that it hurts efficient and inefficient subordinates unequally. In addition, if this tactic is employed repeatedly, budget preparers will combat it by padding their original submissions in the expectation that they will be arbitrarily cut.

Another frequently used tactic is insistence that historical ratios be met in the proposed budget, disregarding the fact that historical ratios may not be responsive to current conditions. The problem of perpetuation of historically occurring mistakes invariably crops up whenever historical data are relied upon extensively. This concept also fosters year-end spending patterns of a department so as to get their actual costs into line with historical precedent.

The superior should ask the budgetee to explain the reasons for changed expenditures and should also ask where costs can reasonably be expected to go down as a result of productivity gains. The requirement to defend cost assumptions introduces aspects of zero-based review to the budgetee, although the negotiation process is primarily one of an analysis of changes from period to period. This underscores the fact that budgeting is primarily an evolutionary process. There is no point in reinventing the wheel; and, similarly, there is no point, and probably no prospect, of completely reshaping the ways in which any company except the very newest does business. This must be kept in mind by both the budgetee and the superior in the negotiation process.

The result of negotiations should be a commitment on the part of all managers to meet the negotiated budget. Similarly, there is an implied commitment on the part of superiors that meeting the budget will be interpreted as good performance. The commitment may run to elements of the budget (line items on the financial report) or may run only to totals for each responsibility center. The commitment may be expressed in terms of a ceiling on expenditures, or, in other cases, may be expressed as a floor on certain types of expenditures. In still other cases, the commitment may be a range of approved expenditures. The important point is that the commitment is understood by both parties to the negotiations and is expressed in sufficiently explicit terms that there is no reasonable room for confusion.

Review and Final Approval

The review process at each step in the management hierarchy repeats this initial negotiation process. In turn, each reviewer must present his or her budget to superiors and undergo essentially the same process as have the line managers beneath the reviewer. This repetitive process tends to screen out proposals which are not in line with corporate objectives, provided that the budget guidelines have been communicated downwards clearly. It may be necessary to recycle the budget back downwards if the presentations do not measure up to corporate goals for ROI or earnings per share. In other cases where the initial submissions are not up to the desired standards, it may be necessary to decide between recycling and the setting up an "off the budget" reserve. This latter practice preserves the motivational aspects of the preceding negotiations, but the reserve puts the financial planners on notice that the budget may be overoptimistic and that they should plan accordingly. The risks in this approach have been described earlier in this chapter.

As the review process proceeds, the various elements of the budget should be compared to make sure that all are synchronized. This comparison should be done on both a responsibility-center basis and on the program level, and is generally best done by the budget staff. Any major discrepancies must be resolved, either by recycling the budget to lower levels with appropriate guidelines for corrective changes or by further negotiations between the respective budget preparers.

At the same time, a start can be made on other aspects of the complete budget—the cash flow and the budgeted balance sheet can be computed by the budget staff from the preliminary budget. Again, this serves as a further check on the profit and loss budgeting and protects management against any unpleasant last-minute surprises.

When the major functional heads have approved their respective budgets, the final step is the consolidation of the approved amounts and submission for approval by the chief executive officer. If the process has been carefully done, if guidelines were carefully prepared, and if the major conflicts and issues which emerged from the budgeting process were brought to the attention of top management as they developed, there should be no significant surprises or unresolved issues at this point and approval will be relatively automatic. The final approval process, however, is not trivial, and the chief executive should be aware that substantial effort has gone into preparation of the final document and review it with due care. The legendary experiences of ITT executives at Harold Geneen's annual budget reviews point out the fact that when subordinates realize that their budget submissions will be carefully scrutinized, they will be more thoughtful in their preparation and more careful in their presentation.

The approval of the board of directors is ordinarily sought as a matter of courtesy and good internal politics, although the board's influence should be minimal. When the budget projects results that are substantially different from what might be expected, the different results should be the result of previously considered program changes, and the Board would ordinarily have been kept advised of these as they were considered.

As a final step in the budgeting process, the approved budget must be transmitted back down through the organization so that line personnel will be aware of top-level approval of their plans or any changes which were required as a result of the series of negotiations.

It should be pointed out by each superior as he or she passes the approved plan back to the supervisors that the approved budget is not a "license to kill." While it is true that the approved budget represents mutual commitment between operating managers and the company, spending to budgeted levels without regard for established control procedures cannot be tolerated. In the unlikely event that all goes according to plan, expenditures which are equal to budget should be considered as very good performance indeed. Unfortunately, in the real world there are always differences from plans, and it is through the control mechanism that the company will be able to recognize and change circumstances. The discipline that controls engender must always be left intact. This point is sufficiently important that it bears repetition at each level at which an approved budget is passed on to a budgetee. "But we had this in the budget!" cannot be an acceptable excuse for failure to follow control procedures.

First Time Through

One of the assumptions of this chapter is that some readers may have had little or no experience with the art and science of budgeting. For those readers, a further word may well be in order as to what to expect when formalized budgeting procedures are first introduced.

Some personnel, generally those who are uncomfortable with any accounting reports, will resist the introduction of budgeting. "I know how to make widgets, not push numbers," or, "Everything went all right last year without all this hassle" are comments that will be heard more than once before the first budget is finished.

Other departments will react with enthusiasm which is all out of proportion to the benefits which can really be expected from budgeting, particularly in the first few years after the discipline has been introduced. These people will believe that with formalized budgeting there will be no more surprises during the year, or believe that they have been given the tool to do a little mischief on a rival department—"We'll finally get those clowns in the shipping department in line."

Other departments will complain that preparing complete budgets will present serious staffing and work load problems for their existing staffs. The complaint will be voiced that the budget process triples the work load. First the budget must be prepared, then actual accounting reports must be submitted, and finally the budget and the actual results must be compared and variances explained.

Another phenomenon which will be encountered is polarization between functional areas which previously did not exist. "Those _____ accountants can't make up their minds what they want (which will probably be at least partially true) and what's more they claim they don't have the information (time, personnel, etc.) to tell me what last year's Christmas party cost." This phenomenon will also crop up between operating departments, as "I made *my* budget, but those salespeople couldn't sell beer in Milwaukee and it's my bonus that's suffering because of it."

All of these scenarios will happen to a greater or lesser extent in a company which is in the throes of preparing their first budget. These arguments against budgeting can be countered by an aggressive selling campaign featuring the positive results to be derived from budgeting, such as better financial planning; by emphasizing the contributions which individual line managers can make in their commitment to their *own* goals; and by the commitment of management to spending the amounts required to do the budgeting job correctly, such as agreeing to authorize the staffing levels appropriate for the task.

Capital Budgeting

The other area of budgeting which has significant relevance for the operating manager, particularly in manufacturing management, is the formulation of capital budgets. The total capital budget is usually not prepared on the same cycle as is the operating budget, but rather individual capital project requests are prepared as they are required for the operation of the business. The total amount of capital projects which will be completed during the next operating cycle is included in the conversion of the operating budget into the cash budget, and the dollar savings expected to be realized are (or at least, should be) included in the operating budget.

Generally the capital budget request is divided into discrete projects which are approved separately, frequently by a committee which is entirely separate from the operating budget committee. Each request typically starts off with a narrative description of the proposal with emphasis on its qualitative aspects and its implications for other functional areas This is followed by financial data which set forth in some detail the expected costs and benefits of the projects with a full explanation of the assumptions used in the analysis.

Finally, the various approval levels required for the level of expenditure being requested are usually specified in the capital budgeting structure. Typically these will be dependent on the amount of money required to complete the project; the degree of risk entailed in the project (for example, the state of the art of the technology to be employed, the company's previous experience with similar projects, the loss which would be incurred if the project were less than a complete success, and so on); and, in part, on the tradition of the company. Also, in many companies, specific criteria in terms of desired rates of return, return on assets, and so on, are stipulated. The reader is directed to Chapters 15–17 for a more detailed explanation of this process.

Summary

A budget is a description in monetary terms of a desired future result. A budget is useful in communicating corporate strategy and goals to operating managers, in motivating managers to achieve the desired results and in providing a standard for performance measurement.

Most companies make longer range plans for three to five years which result in *programming* decisions related to specific ventures which will be undertaken. *Budgeting* is the process of transforming these program decisions into an operating plan, usually for a period of one year, for the constituent parts of a business entity.

In preparing the *operating budget,* a distinction is made between engineered costs, discretionary costs, and committed costs. The steps in preparing this budget are: (1) decide upon and publish budget guidelines outlining corporate goals for the coming year and general constraints which are to be followed; (2) prepare and print forms; (3) prepare the sales budget; (4) budget in detail all expenses of satisfying the sales budget; (5) negotiate agreement between superior and manager, obtaining the commitment of each to the agreed-upon amounts; (6) coordinate and review at each step in the approval process, making sure of overall balance between and among the various subdivisions of the organization; (7) obtain approval of top management and the board of directors; and (8) disseminate the approved budget back down through the organization.

The *cash budget* translates the operating budget into cash flow information which will be used by the treasurer in planning financing requirements, particularly short-term borrowings or investments. The *capital budget* is a list of the costs and benefits of various discrete projects which may be undertaken, depending on the relative value of each and the extent of the financial resources available.

ADDITIONAL SOURCES

Anthony, Robert N., and Dearden, John. *Management Control Systems: Text and Cases,* chap. 10. 3d ed. Homewood, Ill.: Richard D. Irwin, Inc., 1976.

———, and Reece, James S. *Management Accounting Principles,* chap. 21. 3d ed. Homewood, Ill.: Richard D. Irwin, Inc., 1975.

Barrett, M. Edgar, and Fraser, LeRoy B. "Conflicting Roles in Budgeting for Operations." *Harvard Business Review,* July–August 1977, p. 137.

Cherrington, J. Owen, and Cherrington, David J. "Budget Games for Fun and Frustration." *Management Accounting,* January 1976, p. 28.

Fremgen, James M. *Accounting for Managerial Analysis,* chaps. 6–8. 3d ed. Homewood, Ill.: Richard D. Irwin, Inc., 1976.

Hofstede, G. H. *The Game of Budget Control.* Assen, The Netherlands: VanGorcum & Co., 1968.

Horngren, Charles T. *Cost Accounting: A Managerial Emphasis,* chap. 5. 4th ed. Englewood Cliffs, N.J.: Prentice-Hall, Inc., 1977.

Jones, Reginald L., and Trentin, George. *Budgeting: Key to Planning and Control.* New York: American Management Association, 1971.

Judelson, David N. "Financial Controls That Work." *Financial Executive,* January 1977, p. 22.

Murphy, Richard C. "A Computer Model Approach to Budgeting." *Management Accounting,* June 1975, p. 34.

Neuner, John J. W., and Deakin, Edward B. *Cost Accounting: Principles and Practice,* chap. 14. 9th ed. Homewood, Ill.: Richard D. Irwin, Inc., 1977.

Seed, Allen H. "Utilizing the Funds Statement." *Management Accounting,* May 1976, p. 15.

Shillinglaw, Gordon. *Managerial Cost Accounting,* chap. 5. 4th ed. Homewood, Ill.: Richard D. Irwin, Inc., 1977.

Welsch, Glenn A. *Budgeting: Profit Planning and Control.* 4th ed. Englewood Cliffs, N.J.: Prentice-Hall, Inc., 1976.

Weston, J. Fred, and Brigham, Eugene F. *Essentials of Managerial Finance,* chap. 6. 4th ed. Hinsdale, Ill.: The Dryden Press, 1977.

——, and Goudzwaard, Maurice B., eds. *Treasurer's Handbook,* chap. 13. Homewood, Ill.: Dow Jones-Irwin, 1976.

31

Profit versus Profitability: Preparing Meaningful Management Reports

Helmut K. Goerling*

BASIC DEFINITIONS

Profit

Profit represents the total residual change in ownership valuation of a business enterprise as the result of operation during a specified period of time (measurement of performance). Profit is objective (based on known events of revenue and cost); and, thus, it is historic fact.

Webster's *Seventh New Collegiate Dictionary* defines profit as "the excess of returns over expenditure in a transaction or series of transactions; specifically: the excess of the selling price of goods over their cost." As the definition clearly indicates, there is not a single definition of "profit." The FASB, Financial Accounting Standards Board, urges the use of "net income" to reference the bottom line on earnings statements prepared for shareholders.

Profitability

The same dictionary defines profitability as "the potential or ability to generate profits or benefits." Unlike profit, profitability deals with uncertainty of future events, includes probabilistic judgment, and most often focuses on specific decisions (a single product

---

* Mr. Goerling is President of Davis and Goerling, Inc., management consultants, Chicago.

or service, a specific market, industry, or program) rather than the macro-environment of the entire enterprise. In short, profitability responds to the need for relevance rather than objectivity.

It is in this contrast of definitions that we find the fundamental difference between the two terms: profit is the end result, financially expressed, of an entire business operation during a specified period of time (historic), while profitability focuses on potential or (as the word can be segmented) "profit-ability," the ability of a specific business, product, service, or function to produce future profits. In short, we will have to analyze the terms profit/net income and profitability:

1. In the context of time: profit as the factual, after-the-fact scorecard of a business, while profitability emphasizes planning or future benefits that have not yet been realized; and

2. In the context of scope: profit tends to focus on the entire enterprise, while profitability often guides decisions and measures performance and costs of specific parts of an enterprise as a single product, service, or venture. In the light of these criteria, it is obvious why managers need clearest possible visibility of profitability to assure future profits: profitability looks ahead, its emphasis being not on accounting for known past expenditures but rather on the next necessary action; and profitability results from many individual decisions rather than a single event.

These differences between profit and profitability are summarized in tabular form in Exhibit 1.

EXHIBIT 1
Profit versus Profitability

Objective:	Relevant:
Factual	Probabilistic
Historic	Future
Precisely measurable	Employs estimates and projections
Looks back:	Looks ahead:
Compares to last year	Compares to plan
Emphasis on—	Emphasis on—
Total business	Single event or individual product,
(aggregate or macro)	service, venture (task)
Fixed period	Task execution time:
(comparable)	Season
	Campaign
	Project duration
Ownership oriented	Operations oriented

MULTIPLE REPORTING OBJECTIVES

The continuing discussion on definitions of profit and profitability has grown more heated than ever before during the last few years. As government agencies, shareholders, creditors, and public interest groups clamor for improved, detailed visibility on business dealings, reporting requirements have multiplied. Also, significant changes in the world economy have sired financial statements based on a myriad of differing assumptions; yet it is a moot point whether the additional volume of reports has, in fact, produced clarity and reader understanding.

Definitions abound. The careful reader of various reports ranging from news releases via annual reports and 10-Ks to tax returns cannot help but marvel at the ingenuity of financial reporters to interpret facts and draw conclusions which best suit their reporting objective and audience. The continuing worldwide inflation and its impact on business operations has given rise to a brand new set of terms (stagflation, Q's law, windfall profits, to name but a few). As a direct result—and perhaps the clearest indication of the predicament in financial reporting—the large and still-rising number of notes accompanying financial statements indicates clearly the need for clarity.

Unfortunately, many writers on the subject of financial reporting have started from the premise of proposing and virtually defending a single set of definitions and corresponding assumptions. While commendable in its attempt to simplify, such approaches are doomed from the start since they appear to overlook the very foundation of meaningful reporting; namely, the fact that financial reporting is done to meet a number of highly diverse, specific objectives and as such, of course, addresses itself to different audiences and is guided by rules, regulations, and laws which are pertinent only for specific objectives. Therefore, our task must include identification and analysis of the varying reporting objectives and tasks to develop understanding and appropriate definitions.

Last, but by no means least, many financial managers and analysts stipulate the need to reconcile all financial reports prepared by or about a single business enterprise. The point is moot and, of course, has a degree of merit since tax laws and disclosure regulations define essential relationships between business reports issued to varying audiences. For example, the rules guiding the use of Lifo inventory valuation for tax purposes preclude the use of differing methods for reports to creditors and/or investors. But by and large, differing reporting requirements exist side by side and are designed to serve their audiences in the best manner possible. Thus, it is not necessary, and possibly not even desirable, to reconcile all financial reports.

Most business enterprises, particularly publicly held ones, employ *six* identifiable processes to disseminate financial information. All of these start essentially from the same source: business transactions and investments. Yet their presentation may differ substantially, as we shall see.

External Reporting

Four of these six processes are subsumed under the general heading of "external reporting." These four are:

1. *Tax reporting* to appropriate agencies of federal, state, and municipal governments.
2. *Regulatory reporting* to government agencies which control specific aspects of business or entire industries:
   a. Civil Aeronautics Board (CAB).
   b. Department of Health, Education, and Welfare (HEW).
   c. Environmental Protection Agency (EPA).
   d. Equal Employment Opportunity Commission (EEOC).
   e. Federal Aviation Administration (FAA).
   f. Federal Energy Administration (FEA).
   g. Federal Trade Commission (FTC).
   h. Food and Drug Administration (FDA).
   i. Interstate Commerce Commission (ICC).
   j. Public Health Service (PHS).
   k. Public Utilities Commission (PUC).
3. Reports to investors and creditors, and to the Securities and Exchange Commission (SEC). Issuance of these reports is often referred to as *financial reporting*.
4. *Reporting to the public* at large. For instance, a railroad airs TV commercials emphasizing that their charge to carry essential consumer products averages less than ½ cent per pound. Energy and fuel companies run periodic campaigns highlighting the decline of known natural resources and the need for profit to finance exploration and research of alternatives. Product and

material shortages, temporary or permanent, cause and have caused massive price movement; producers of such goods hasten to advertise their plight and explain the necessity of additional revenue. Yet so-called consumer interest groups often obtain much news coverage (without cost to them) to counteract the effort. The resultant confusion about economic matters in the public sector stuns the researcher.

This last-mentioned segment is receiving growing attention in our society. Concepts and slogans (rather than terms) of "excess profits" and "windfall profits" have become synonymous with human greed, "the rich steal from the poor," and generally the root of much evil. In rebuttal, businesses and industries are making valiant, yet often futile, efforts and are spending substantial funds to inform and educate the public on the fundamentals of economics and the need for profit as the source of continued growth. After all, employment growth should constitute the primary means by which business can provide substantial contribution to public welfare.

It is certain that this segment of reporting has not yet achieved proper attention and recognition. Public opinion continues to sway legislative action. As a direct result, the public influences business incentives (favorable tax legislation) and restrictions (price controls regulations) and thus profit to a large degree.

During the last several years we have seen an increasing amount of media coverage and investigative reporting on business profits. By and large, the findings show disturbing consistency in the public's opinion of how much profit businesses actually make. Most recent surveys reported that many people, among them small shareholders, believe businesses average between 25–35 percent of every sales dollar as net income even after taxes, a percentage almost 5 times higher than the actual (less than 5 percent at the time of the survey). Specifically, the distortion in reporting and understanding centers around the *absolute* amount of money earned as opposed to its *relative* value. To most people a million dollars of profit will seem like a great deal of money; its relative value (return on invested capital) may amount to less than the interest rate paid by financial institutions on savings deposits. Further, a majority of public opinion holds that businesses should pay for desirable environmental protection and safety out of profits and additionally settle for lesser profits to provide goods and services at lower prices.

Obviously here is a total lack of recognizing the need for, and market value (or cost) of, invested capital.

A prominent network television news commentator recently alleged on the air that government agencies frequently "hear only from industry wanting bigger profits." It is sobering to reflect that the industry she was referring to has averaged a return on invested capital of less than 7 percent and is faced with additional investment requirements due to technological changes, energy conservation requirements, and vastly tightened safety and security regulations.

The task of financial reporting to the public at large requires imaginative, sincere management efforts and approaches to assure an appropriate balance in the legislative branch of government. Only an educated public which understands and appreciates more than the immediacy of take-home pay can prevent the political excesses that are likely to kill the goose that lays the golden eggs. That appropriate levels of understanding can be achieved appears frighteningly dubious at best. But if it can be done, then financial managers, as a group, must assign high priorities to inform the public in a responsible, meaningful, and consistent fashion. Without a doubt we will see increasing emphasis on this segment of reporting for years to come.

Internal Reporting

The remaining two reporting processes fall under the category of "internal reporting." These include:

1. *Reports to employees as a group.* Many companies spend considerable effort to inform their own employees about company profits or the need for cost control, particularly if the employees participate in a profit-sharing program or receive costly fringe benefits beyond take-home pay. Also, union negotiations require the dissemination of financial data as a necessary tool to arrive at equitable and affordable labor contracts.
2. *Management reports.* This reporting process must address itself to the fundamental difference between profit/net income and profitability: the need to look forward in time. While much accounting effort is spent to record, interpret, and evaluate past performance, the process of management deals with the future. Needless to say, it is important for managers to have a clear

understanding of the results of their previous decisions; yet in the final analysis a plan focuses on events yet to come, and as such on the inherent uncertainty of the future.

Conceivably reporting requirements within each of these six areas may match those in one or more other areas; yet because of the difference in audience and purpose, each audience has unique characteristics and information needs.

Attempts to define profit/net income (the "bottom line") and profitability will continue and likely increase in intensity. To expect a single "answer" which would receive universal or even broad acceptance probably constitutes the adult equivalent of a belief in Santa Claus. What is surprising, however, is the apparent concern by many financial reporters that such a solution must be found. Is it not more logical to conclude that different definitions require different terms? We believe it much more important and relevant to refine terminology and definitions. To resolve this problem we propose the use of specific terms to describe each different "bottom line," as shown in Exhibit 2.

Given so vast a scope and the diversity of purpose/objectives, it becomes obvious that accounting policies which guide investor/ creditor reporting may include accounting principles quite different from those selected for management reporting, such as depreciation or inventory valuation options. In many instances, management reporting requires complete deviation from GAAP to be meaningful, to make sense. For example, growth projections which call for increased capacity must be based on replacement cost/current cost of additional capacity increments, regardless of original cost, book value, and depreciation method of capacity in place.

Unfortunately, many financial managers remain adamantly of the opinion that any accounting policy not in total conformance with generally accepted accounting principles is, by definition, if not "illegal" at least unethical, regardless of use or need to know. Even controllers who feel perfectly comfortable in applying accelerated depreciation for tax returns as opposed to straight line for their annual report, bristle at the very suggestion of keeping more than one "set of books" as if this constituted some kind of illicit conspiracy to deceive. It should be needless to say that such reasoning is more misunderstanding than folly. Any business enterprise has the liberty, and needs the flexibility and perspective, to compile and evaluate its business data in any manner or format deemed appropriate by its managers, as long as the resulting presentation meets all requirements of purpose and audience. Obviously reports intended solely to serve managers in performance evaluation and product costing need only be relevant (pertinent, meaningful, and credible); tax laws, GAAP, and agency regulations just need not be observed

EXHIBIT 2
Proposed "Bottom-Line" Terminology

	Reporting To*	Term Which Describes the "Bottom Line"		Emphasis (objectivity or relevance)
E1	Tax agencies	Taxable income		Objectivity
E2	Regulatory	Often matches taxable income or net income. If so, those terms will be used. If different from both, use regulated income.		Objectivity
E3	Investors and creditors	Net income		Objectivity
E4 and I1	Public at large Company employees (as a group)	Profit The wide and rather indiscriminate use of this word has rendered it worthless as a technical term. However, any attempt at this time to change the term for the public at large would doubtless add to the existing confusion.		Objectivity (and interpretation)
I2	Management (profitability)	For individual products, services, or ventures	Profit contribution	Relevance
		For a division, subsidiary, or enterprise (pretax)	Earnings (or possibly bottom line)	

* "E" = external; "I" = internal.

here. The concern apparently held by a surprising number of controllers that such analyses may be accessible by representatives of government agencies would be valid only if indeed the intent is to deceive or defraud rather than to manage the business.

In summary, businesses do—and must—disclose information about their operation for many different purposes and to widely diverse audiences. As the need to know varies from audience to audience, definitions also change. But the popular notion that "profit" is an out-of-focus quantity overlooks the obvious: the difference in definitions points to the lack of sufficiently discriminatory terms. The FASB's preference for "net income" represents an important case in point; Exhibit 2 completes the essential refinement of terms. The use of too few terms has fathered confusion in describing different and differing circumstances, situations, and conditions. Thus, we propose the use of different terms for each approach. There is no conflict, no right or wrong; but rather we must accept the premise of differing needs which justifiably exist side by side in any business environment. (The discussion to this point is summarized in Exhibit 3.)

With the considerable attention focused on objective (historic) accounting, we can now identify the key tasks of this chapter:

1. To conduct an analysis of historic accounting methods and their results from the manager's point of view. Once again, there is no attempt to imply that historic accounting is meaningless or incorrect; rather we must highlight why managers need additional inputs into their decision-making process.
2. To discuss relevant techniques which quantify probable results of decisions. Conceivably these techniques do not conform to GAAP, but they provide meaningful perspective to managers.

Historic accounting gains its objectivity by eliminating uncertainty and working strictly with known events or facts. Obviously, this represents a highly commendable and reassuring aspect of historic accounting. However, a manager cannot manage the past. The management process is forward oriented: it must prepare an organization to meet the future successfully, to produce a desired result.

The incongruity is obvious: facts are history (look backward in time), while managers must look ahead. Thus, historic data prepared for managers can merely tell them what occurred in the past. But if used as the foundation of a new plan, such practice implies that history is going to repeat itself. If nothing else, the last few years have proven economic stability a fallacy. Besides, there is no assurance ever that the same result will occur from identical action taken at different points in time. It is beyond the scope of this discussion to attempt a complete analysis of factors influencing business results; however, it is a truism that historic accounting in this

EXHIBIT 3
Business Reporting Tasks

Business Investment and Transactions

Source Data for All Reporting / Type of Reporting	External					Internal
	Tax	Regulatory	Investment and Operation	Public Relations	Industrial Relations	Management
Audience	Tax agencies: Federal State Local	Regulatory agencies such as CAB, EPA, FAA, FEA, FTC, ICC, PUC	Investors, shareholders, creditors, SEC	Public at large	Company employees, unions	Operating managers
Objective/ intent	Tax optimization, cash flow	Confirmation of compliance	Proof of credit worthiness, value, potential	Educate, receive support, and approval	Inform, receive support, ideas, feedback	Cost, plan, control
Guidelines	Tax laws	Agency regulations	GAAP	Veracity, taste	Policy, union contract	Common sense, perspective (multiple input)
Emphasis	Objectivity	Objectivity	Objectivity	Interpretation	Interpretation	Relevance
Focus	Total business (aggregate), fixed time period	Specific area of control, progress toward long-range goals	Major business segment	Specific issue	General conditioning, specific issue	Single product, service, venture, "per unit"
Proposed title of "bottom line"	Taxable income	Regulated income	Net income	Profit	Profit	1. For specific tasks (individual product, service venture): *Profit contribution* 2. For divisions, subsidiary, business: *Earnings*

single aspect (time) is diametrically opposed to the marketing process. In particular the practice of comparing current period results to prior periods (objective, historic) in shareholder/investor reporting highlights the difference in emphasis between reporting for them and for management: managers must manage/execute a plan (relevant, future) and monitor their progress towards the achievement of that plan.

Depreciation

In the normal operation of a business enterprise, expenditures including capital investments do not occur synchronously to the consumption of benefits derived from such outlays of funds. The accounting principle of cost matching provides depreciation as a method to prorate the total acquisition cost of an asset over the period or periods of its useful life. Thus, the original cost of a lift truck acquired for $30,000 with an estimated life of five years (straight-line depreciation method) would be charged to operations at the rate of $6,000 per year. However, depreciation accounting also provides differing methods generically grouped as "accelerated" depreciation. Under these methods a proportionately higher percentage of original acquisition cost will be charged in the early life of the asset with a corresponding decrease of annual charge in the last periods of life. For instance, in its first year of use, the above-mentioned $30,000 lift truck would result in an annual depreciation expense of $12,000 using the double-declining-balance method, or $10,000 when employing the sum-of-the-years'-digits method. Investment tax credits may further increase the charge for the use of the lift truck in its first year (or all five years, depending on whether the "flow-through" or "deferral" method is used to account for the ITC). Accelerated depreciation methods have obvious advantages in tax reporting.

The *managerial* view of depreciation recognizes features not found in conventional historical cost accounting.

The Implied Assumption of Economic Stability. Depreciation is a method of distributing an asset's original acquisition cost over the periods of use of the asset to reflect proportionately the cost of benefits consumed. In instances of buildings, this may cover a period of 20 years or more. Thus, we conclude that depreciation of fixed assets implies economic stability for long periods of time. This assumption must be considered a fallacy in light of most recent economic developments.

Cost Obsolescence.   Accounting for the original acquisition cost clearly indicates the historic orientation of depreciation. For instance, if the $30,000 lift truck had been acquired four years ago, the depreciation expense projection (using straight-line depreciation) for next year would remain at $6,000; however, that $6,000 per year has no direct relationship to current market prices of lift trucks (nor does it claim to have, of course), or to any future price estimated to be prevailing at the time when replacement becomes necessary. In short, the cost is four years out of date, a fact that may make it very different from current market value. Yet the continued use of historical cost depreciation by operating managers, who do not necessarily understand the following implications, can mislead them during the decision process, as we shall now describe.

First, the use of depreciation expense in full costing of a product (employing methods of "absorption" costing, that is, allocating fixed costs to individual units of product) can—and often does— result in misleading cost data. Typically in periods of prolonged inflation, depreciation expense tends to undercost a product to the degree by which the current market price of a piece of equipment exceeds the actual (past) purchase price. Thus, if the lift truck purchased for $30,000 four years ago has a current price of $40,000, the *use* of this lift truck is likely to be undercosted by the difference in terms of its economic market value.

Accountants frequently are not very concerned with this aspect of product costing because they reason that the primary business objective is not the selling of long-lived productive assets. Yet it is also true that without the use of these assets, the business could not operate.

But is it *true* that businesses do not sell fixed assets as part of the normal operation? Capital-intensive service businesses (utilities, transportation, hotels, etc.) sell the use of capacity or, from the owners' point of view, make capacity available at a fee based on time used. It is semantically correct, of course, that in this instance the fixed assets which constitute such capacity are not actually sold for brief periods of time; but logically this is exactly what has happened. This becomes self-evident when specified amounts of capacity are acquired for a flat fee—Wide Area Telephone Service (WATS), for instance.

No doubt the process goes even deeper than this because of accounting's implied assumption of ownership. Assets owned by a business are depreciated (are charged to operations) based on their original purchase price; thus, the annual cost of a company's owned assets can be calculated at the time of original purchase depending on the depreciation option employed. Yet if an identical piece of equipment (such as a lift truck) is leased, that cost will most likely reflect the current market value (inflated cost) of such a lift truck.

Second, cost obsolescence and a mixture of ownership may distort return-on-investment indicators in management reporting. Often there is more involved than just a meaningful report: incentive bonus tied to "profit" could be affected. The following example demonstrates the predicament and argues for new and different approaches.

Example: The ABC retail chain operated three stores in Aville, Beetown, and Cee City. The operations are strikingly similar with respect to sales, cost of goods sold (through a central buying office), head count, operating costs, and even square footage of sales rooms. Yet the stores show significant differences in profit and return on investment. These discrepancies can be traced to the cost of facilities as follows.

The Aville store was built in the downtown shopping area in 1931. Since then, the building and all equipment have been fully depreciated; the land shows a book value of $10,000, its original purchase price, even though the current value of the site is appraised at $500,000.

The Beetown store celebrated its grand opening just before Thanksgiving last year. It is located near a new residential development. The investment in building ($500,000), equipment ($300,000), and land ($500,000) results in the following annual depreciation expense:

Item	Life	Depreciation Method	Annual Depreciation Amount
Building.........	25 years	Straight line	$20,000
Equipment.......	10 years (average)	Straight line	30,000
Land............	—	—	0
			$50,000

ABC does not own the Cee City store but leases it from XYZ Developers. The appraised value of building, equipment, and land is quite similar to the Beetown store ($1,300,000). The lease cost is calculated at 1 percent of total investment per month or 12 percent per year; thus the annual lease cost is $156,000.

In summary, the stores show the following depreciation expense and net depreciated book value:

	Investment at January 1	Current Year Depreciation Expense or Lease Cost	Net Depreciated Investment at December 31
Aville............	$ 10,000	$ 0	$ 10,000
Beetown.........	1,300,000	50,000	1,250,000
Cee City.........	0	156,000	0

Assuming each store's product inventory and working capital to be $500,000, profit before facilities cost and taxes to be $250,000 per store, and a 50 percent income tax rate, the following after-tax profits and return on year-end investment will result:

	Profit before Taxes	Net Profit	Investment	Return on Investment
Aville..........	$250,000	$125,000	$ 510,000	24.5%
Beetown.......	200,000	100,000	1,750,000	5.7
Cee City.......	94,000	47,000	500,000	9.4

Clearly, these discrepancies in reporting are no reflection or indication of differences in *managerial* performance.

ABC Company changed its management accounting (internal) methods to show actual investment at the *corporate* level, but for store reporting purposes "leased" the facilities to each store at identical per square foot lease rates to equalize the occupancy costs for purposes of measuring store manager performance. Thus, profitability can be developed reflecting correctly the use value of assets, as well as the use of assets which are not being depreciated (such as land), so that managers can make decisions about the future based on costs and capital requirements of the future rather than on the actual historical outlays for existing facilities.

Impact of Depreciation Options. The choice of an accelerated depreciation method for tax reporting needs no further discussion. But consider the *manager's* point of view if accelerated depreciation is employed for management reporting: the manager will be "paying" less in Years 2, 3, and so on for the use of an asset than was paid in Year 1. Considering the inflationary pressures of world and national economies, the result could range from mildly confusing to badly misleading.

In terms of product costing, accelerated depreciation conceivably could cause prohibitively high equipment costs to be charged to new products. Since under accelerated depreciation, the highest annual depreciation charge for equipment if needed exclusively for this new product is charged in Year 1, when product volume is still at the introductory stage, product cost per unit may appear so unattractive or unaffordable as to prevent market introduction altogether. Decelerated depreciation (units of production) may provide more meaningful numbers. (See Exhibit 4 for a pictorial representation of differing depreciation methods.) This point should not be misconstrued as an attempt to solve the entire problem of new product introduction and costing. For one thing, a risk analysis, of course, should accompany any such venture proposal. It may be decided that the entire equipment cost must be recovered in a short period due to the risk of foreign nationalization, rapid obsolescence, possibility of a fad (very short product life), or other reason.

But the impact of various depreciation options on reported profit (higher costs result in lower profits, and vice versa) casts doubt on profit as a performance measurement. Obviously the choice of depreciation method bears no relation to managerial and operational success (or its lack).

Calendar Time versus Usage. Another aspect of depreciation recognized by managers, if not by most depreciation methods, is that for depreciation purposes asset life is frequently stated in calendar time. Yet many assets depreciate in direct proportion to actual usage (such as a machine or lift truck) rather than calendar time in service. Only the so-called units-of-production method of depreciation reflects this frequent economic fact.

EXHIBIT 4
Depreciation Methods

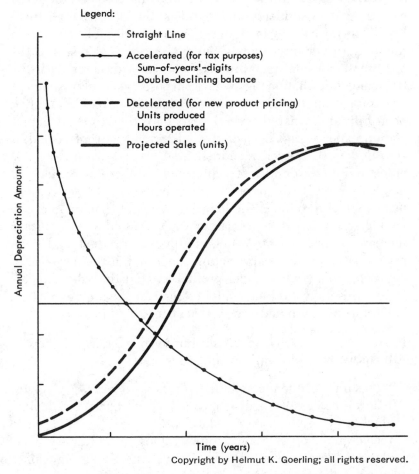

Legend:

——————— Straight Line

●——●——● Accelerated (for tax purposes)
          Sum-of-years'-digits
          Double-declining balance

— — — Decelerated (for new product pricing)
          Units produced
          Hours operated

————— Projected Sales (units)

Annual Depreciation Amount

Time (years)

Fully Depreciated Assets—A Contradiction in Terms. Since life estimates for assets are averages, and also because they are *estimates,* often equipment in manufacturing organizations operates satisfactorily after it is already fully depreciated (book value equals zero). This means that depreciation expense and thus, product cost may not reflect the value of using this machinery. This represents no problem, of course, in reporting to outsiders, but it could foreseeably understate product or service costs substantially. Plans for expansion or long-term contract negotiations need this important input.

Example: Recently the sales director of a national company asked the manufacturing manager why the cost of Product A had jumped so suddenly and significantly, even though there had been no change in design nor any noticeable change in raw material or direct labor content. After brief research the manufacturing manager provided the sales director with the following information. A special-purpose piece of machinery (used for Product A only) was well over 20 years old and had been fully depreciated several years ago; therefore, its depreciation expense had been budgeted for the current period at zero dollars. However, a sudden total breakdown of this machine required immediate replacement based on orders on hand. As a result the depreciation expense of this new equipment (which produced the identical product that the old machine had produced for so many years) resulted in a significant increase in product cost. Regrettably the product had been priced based on zero depreciation expense, but the new equipment cost made it no longer profitable. Had the sales director known this, he would have advised against buying new equipment and discontinued Product A instead.

In summary, the traditional accounting mechanism of depreciation includes the following assumptions:

1. It presumes economic stability to a large degree.
2. It accounts for original acquisition cost (backward looking), which may result in an obsolete cost.
3. Accelerated depreciation assigns values to consumed benefits which decline year after year. Against the background of prolonged inflation this practice understates product cost.
4. Depreciation emphasizes calendar time often in preference to actual usage.
5. Fully depreciated assets (zero expense) no longer add to product cost even though their use benefits the product.

Choice of inventory valuation options also affects the calculation of profit. Among GAAP options, first in/first out (Fifo), last in/first out (Lifo), and averaging find broadest application. Yet unless price trends are virtually horizontal, the choice of the inventory valuation option will impact the calculation of profit: in a rising-cost market, Fifo will result in the highest inventory value (the least-expensive, first purchases are assumed to be sold) and highest profit; conversely, Lifo results in the lowest inventory valuation and lowest profit; with averaging taking its proverbial place between the extremes in both inventory valuation and profit. Thus, companies with identical economic results may report different profit numbers if their inventory valuation options differ. Once again an accounting option affects profit calculation, raising doubts as to the validity of profit or net income (as currently reported to shareholders) as a measurement of performance.

Many pros and cons for the choice of one or the other inventory option have been voiced, including the following:

1. Fifo generally reflects physical movement of merchandise, since most businesses would endeavor to use up oldest inventory first. Yet in a rising-cost market, Fifo results in the highest inventory valuation (and correspondingly a higher profit number), which in some ways seems to violate the accounting principle of "conservatism." However, if the cost trend were to reverse itself (a phenomenon we have experienced several times during the last few years as real or presumed shortages once again moved to surplus status), of the three methods, Fifo results in the most conservative (i.e., lowest) inventory valuation.
2. In a rising-cost market, Lifo yields a lower inventory valuation than does Fifo. But under any set of circumstances, that is, rising, level, or falling costs, Lifo has the advantage of matching the most recently experienced cost of product and supplies to the revenue generated during the current period.

It is a moot point at this time whether Fifo or Lifo provides the most realistic statements. In every comparison (rising or falling cost trends, impact on balance sheet as opposed to income statement) the methods reflect opposite results when comparing cost of goods sold as compared to cost of goods not sold (inventory).

But *neither* technique considers *managerial* aspects of inventory management, which neither historical nor replacement cost can reflect. The need for alternatives shows up on seasonal or special-event merchandise. Prior to the event, a product may enjoy solid prospects of being sold. Its strategic value rises as the selling period (promotion) approaches, and peaks roughly coincident with the start of the event or season (Christmas merchandise at Thanksgiving, for instance). Then, however, the decline in strategic value is

EXHIBIT 5
Inventory Valuation: Special-Event Merchandise

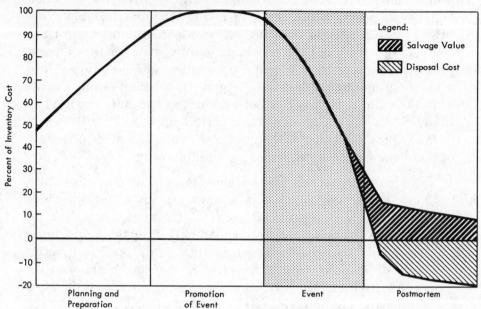

both rapid and severe as the event draws to a close, bottoming out at the salvage value more often than not. Yet some products may even require a disposal cost which could be substantial.

Suffice it to say that inventory valuation may follow a pattern (strategic value) quite apart from its historical or replacement cost, since strategy anticipates future market demand and prices. Exhibit 5 expresses in percentage terms the possible valuation pattern for strategic inventory valuation.

The Value of Land

Accounting does not provide for the depreciation of land, since most businesses use land without actually consuming it. Thus, the tax laws and GAAP do not provide for a charge against income for the use of land, unless it is used for the extraction of natural resources such as oil, gas, coal, minerals, or even top soil.

The basic reasoning is obvious and sound. While it is true that a business might not be able to operate without the use of land,

land in itself is not consumed; thus, because of the assumption that land does not lose value, management reports and product costing include no charge for the use of land. This, however, may cause the impression that land has no value at all. In most instances this practice will not have any substantial bearing on planning or product costing, but we have experienced a number of exceptions which fall essentially into three categories.

First, expansion of business volume which results in the need for additional capacity may also include the requirements for additional land. Since in many instances land has appreciated substantially over the last two to three decades, the impact could be massive. For example, a manufacturer of railroad ties (pressure treating with decay-retardant preservatives) was requested by a major customer to enlarge an existing railroad-tie plant to handle increasing demand. However, the value of surrounding property had increased from approximately $100 per acre in 1931 to well over $9,000 per acre. The question is this: Does the product cost currently charged the customer (which, of course, does not include a provision for the use of land) truly reflect the cost of doing business in that specific location today? Also, 150 acres purchased (at $100 per acre) for $15,000 result in an attractive return on investment; but the land is really worth $1,350,000.

Second, in operations which handle a mix of services or products requiring significantly varying amounts of land, not charging for the use of land could distort product cost and, of course, product profit. The example mentioned in the preceding paragraph represents a case in point. The same company also pressure-treats telephone poles in the same facility with the railroad ties. The process entails a major difference; namely, railroad ties typically are cut from hardwoods which require 5–12 months of seasoning (air drying) while they are stacked on plant property. Obviously the space requirement in a high-production plant is substantial.

By contrast, telephone poles made from pine can be conditioned in the treating cylinders immediately preceding the actual preservative-treating process. Since poles do not have to be stored the physical space requirement for the pole operation is substantially less than that for the tie operation. This can be measured based on weight, volume of wood, or sales dollars generated. We must conclude that ties reap a benefit (land for storage) without charge.

When the results of the inquiry about the cost of land were

analyzed, it became obvious that there should be a cost distinction between the treating process of poles and railroad ties respectively to reflect not only the handling cost of storage (which, of course, had been measured carefully) but also the cost of an asset (land) which had appreciated enormously since original acquisition. Today the company charges "land rent" based on area actually used to all products; obviously this is done for management reporting only.

Finally, in the typical accounting treatment of land, once again we find the implied assumption of ownership. If land is leased from someone else (not owned), the cost of the lease may be expensed. Thus, other things being equal, a company whose facilities are on land used under a 99-year lease will report lower income than a company which owns the land it uses.

Chapter 13, " 'Direct' (Variable) Costing," discusses the allocation of indirect costs to individual units of product. However, indirect costs are called "indirect" because they cannot be measured or identified with a single product unit. Therefore, any technique to assign or allocate these period costs to individual units becomes, at least to a degree, arbitrary and assumptive. Thus, the common practice of showing fixed indirect costs and profit on a per unit basis makes fixed costs *appear* as if they were variable. For instance, if Product A shows $1 for overhead *per unit*, this implies that for one unit made the overhead cost would be $1; for 2 units, $2; for 3 units, $3; and so on: that is, that the overhead is variable. What is missing, of course, is the implied volume basis over which fixed period costs have been divided. If overhead costs amount to $100,000 (all fixed) per period, then under the volume assumption of 100,000 units per period, these 100,000 units on the average would cost $1 of overhead each. With $100,000 fixed overhead costs, it is obvious that a volume of 125,000 units would result in only $0.80 per unit average; while at 80,000 units of volume the per unit average would rise to $1.25.

As a result of the above observation, we reach this conclusion: fully absorbed product unit costs, or gross margin calculated on a per unit basis, cannot be used to quantify decisions of change.

Since, by definition, direct product costs such as raw material and direct labor are specifically identifiable in each unit of product, it follows that indirect costs cannot be pinpointed to individual units; in fact, it is this very characteristic which defines the cost as being indirect. Therefore, profit or gross margin calculated using an allocation or absorption technique are not truly objective until after the fact.

The same problem plagues joint or shared processes. Slaughter and wood constitute the classic examples. For instance, butchering a cow yields hide, bones, a variety of meat cuts with differing market values, and a variety of by-products. For this process (slaughter) the raw material cost can be identified clearly (cost of animal). Also, the cost of slaughtering can be identified quite accurately. But it is quite impossible to determine precisely the cost of the hide as opposed to rump roast or filet mignon since they were bought, so to speak, in a lump and also processed in a lump. A variety of techniques have been proposed which charge each end product with a portion of the process cost. (See Chapter 9, "Joint- and By-Product Costing.") The basis of allocation can be units or pounds of output, market value of all end products, or net realizable income. These techniques are often complex and elaborate, and yet they face the identical problem: no matter how ingeniously devised, any technique that charges various products resulting from a joint or shared process is trying to do the impossible; namely, to cost units whose per unit cost by definition cannot be identified or measured.

Per unit cost and profit can only be determined with accuracy after the fact (when actual volume is known). For planning, managers need techniques which give them numbers that correctly reflect the impact of volume: marginal cost or contribution (relevant, incremental) methods fulfill this requirement.

Responsibility Accounting

Profit calculation frequently employs methods and techniques which tend to group costs. As a result, it is difficult to calculate profit of individual products, tasks, or departments. Profit, even if calculated, would by no means reflect what would happen in case of a *change* in business volume limited to only one element of business activity. Further, the assumption that discontinuance of the product, service, project, or function would eliminate calculated profit also could be misleading, largely because allocated portions of fixed costs will not disappear even if the entire product is eliminated. That also means that decisions dealing with the economic impact of a specific operation cannot be made using conventional profit measurement techniques.

Comparative performance measurements of product lines or divisions within a corporation are affected similarly. Indeed the problem is greatly amplified, as illustrated by the most common method of allocating corporate overhead to individual product lines or divisions: based on sales volume (dollars or units). This can have the following effect:

	Division A or Product A	Division B or Product B
Sales forecast...........................	$100	$100
Budgeted allocation of corporate overhead @ 10% of sales..............	10	10
Actual sales.............................	150	50
Actual allocation of corporate overhead.............................	15	5

It seems to me that this procedure imposes a penalty on success: as the successful Product Line A exceeds its forecast it is also charged a larger portion of corporate overhead, even though these corporate overhead costs tend to be largely fixed. By contrast, Product Line B benefits from lower allocations as sales fall below plan, even though corporate overhead costs could not be expected to decrease with lower sales (this is the very characteristic that makes them "fixed"). A fee program for corporate services such as legal, patent, industrial relations, and company-owned airplanes, based on competitive rates for actual use, will give a more realistic picture. (See Chapter 25, "Service Department Charge-Back Systems.") The remaining corporate administrative costs, if prorated at all, should be charged in a lump sum (fixed cost), and should be shown separately from these costs which are under the control of product or division managers.

Profitability is specifically calculated on levels which clearly identify those revenues and costs which directly pertain to a given division, department, project, product, service, or function and, therefore, remain truly measurable and identifiable for the specific responsibility of only one manager.

In summary, profit is a function of asset valuation and costing for the use of assets. The above examples by no means are intended to present every conceivable possibility, but rather to reflect a thought process which led to the developments of techniques to present more meaningful management reports. This, of course, includes a variety of methods discussed in other chapters of this Handbook. But while each technique may not be new, we have conceived novel approaches of applying these methods—approaches which operating managers who have used them consider responsive to their specific requirements and needs; the remainder of this chapter deals with them.

Accounting is generally accepted to be conservative. Thus, inventories are valued "at the lower of cost or market," for instance. Obviously this principle dictates a specific choice which deliberately deviates from the realism of today if market exceeds cost.

Yet the need for realism in accounting plays a major role in shaping and reshaping reporting requirements today. Inflation accounting techniques and the worldwide interest in "replacement cost accounting" are irrefutable evidence that the accounting profession can no longer limit itself to factual, historic accounting, but of necessity must resolve the inherent conflict of the objectivity in traditional accounting concepts with the necessary realism and relevance of today and tomorrow.

MANAGERS AND PROFITABILITY

Management reporting constitutes a most important financial reporting requirement, probably much more important than implied by the attention it has received to date. Also, management reports demand of controllers dramatically new approaches and presentations. We believe that the emergence of the controller as a quasi-line executive has its roots not only in the scorecards, which the controller must prepare after the fact, but it stems from the necessary involvement of financial and cost accounting experts in, and the application of their expertise to, the management process during planning, execution, and evaluation. It is here that the distinction between profit and profitability reigns most important. In this context, then, we must answer the questions that we raised by inference during the preceding analysis of profit/net income concepts.

Macro or Micro: The per Unit Problem

Profitability reporting represents foremost a management tool for decision making, costing, and performance evaluation. For these purposes, profitability reporting must have the ability to determine not only whether the business in its entirety is likely and/or able to produce profit in the future, but whether individual activities, products, or services are profitable and, if so, to what degree; that is, reporting should pinpoint precisely where money is made or lost, and how much.

The need for such detail visibility does not constitute a generally accepted accounting principle by any means. As recently as during the writing of this chapter, we raised the question whether for management reporting we should depreciate equipment according to its actual usage (in units produced or hours operated) rather than by time period. An accountant close to us suggested that it was immaterial; after all, he continued, "What counts is whether the aggregate depreciation charge is reasonable since depreciation on each unit would not be individually reported." This statement highlights a gross misunderstanding of management reporting needs, and simultaneously indicates the importance of distinguishing between profit and profitability. While it is quite true, of course, that for financial reporting to outsiders only the aggregate is important, for *internal* control to manage a business profitably the resultant cost differential could represent a most relevant and significant insight.

A similar example occurred recently. After the physical inventory had been taken in a major corporation, the final result indicated that the total inventory variance (book value compared to extended physical total) amounted to a scant 0.2 percent of total inventory investment. There was a considerable amount of satisfaction throughout the organization, so much so that the vice president–operations sent a congratulatory note of thanks to his inventory control staff including the director of management information systems.

It goes without saying that in many respects this result appears gratifying: processing hundreds of thousands of transactions for over 20,000 stockkeeping units (SKUs) within such close tolerance is no mean feat. Yet, when a specialized computer program compared not only the *total* inventory value but the *individual* inventory counts, against the perpetual inventory records on an item-by-item basis, the frightening fact emerged that 73 percent of all items had a physical unit count deviation of plus/minus 25 percent or more. In short, operationally, inventories were out of control. Since then the control system has seen major tightening with commensurate improvements in SKU-level accuracy.

One of the most important considerations for management reporting is the necessary emphasis on the *individual* components which in the aggregate make up total revenue, cost, or investment within a business. Total dollars can mislead. They are subject to inflation; and if summarized to too high a level, dollar amounts may hide changes in mix which could signal important shifts in demand, product, market, or customer composition. To manage a business requires visibility of sufficient detail to track profitability (or its lack) quickly and precisely to its roots.

Replacement Costing

The identical trend of emphasizing the aggregate rather than component parts showed in the FASB's 1975 price-level accounting proposal, as opposed to the SEC's 1976 requirement for 1,000 large companies to report (in their 10-Ks) inventories, plant and equipment, cost of goods sold, and depreciation not only following traditional GAAP but also based on replacement costs. While the jury is still out as to the final result and merits of replacement costing, some fundamental discussion is in order.

Replacement costing as an inflation accounting technique asks, How well is a business prepared to meet the future and assure its continuity? Business is "generally accepted" to be an ongoing concern, that is, permanent; yet conventional depreciation techniques account for past (historic) acquisition of assets up to the limit of their total original purchase price. When cumulative depreciation expense reaches that point, the asset is described as "fully depreciated" (zero net book value), even though the asset may still be in full use. The result is that after accounting for the total amount actually paid for the asset at the time of acquisition, no further charge for its use is made even if the asset still enjoys productive utilization.

Proponents of replacement costing take issue with that "free-ride concept" and simply pose the question: How much would it cost if we had to start operating from scratch today? The answer constitutes presumably the current market value of utilizing a specific asset and quantifies the benefits business operations derive from this use.

In view of prolonged inflation, this move has raised many concerns. For capital-intensive businesses, replacement costing will massively increase asset valuation and reduce the return on assets employed or invested capital in direct proportion. To wit: a recent analysis indicated that the ROI (return on investment) for a major steel manufacturer calculated against book value (net depreciated value) of his fixed assets amounted to 15.5 percent. Using replacement costs, the return on invested capital declined to a horrifying 0.3 percent.

These questions, therefore, have to be raised: How realistic are publicly reported profits for capital-intensive corporations? Is it possible that a considerable amount of the reported profits may ipso facto represent the "sale" of fixed assets with a corresponding reduction of net worth? These questions have been answered in the affirmative by a group of Dutch economists who conducted a recent study which led to the conclusion that net invested capital in all of Dutch industry has been declining consistently during the last two decades on an accelerating basis. Inflation and conventional accounting methods, so they state, have prevented this fact from receiving the immediate and massive attention it deserves.

Our task here is not one of world or national economics. But informed decision makers must realize the economic value of every element of material, labor, and asset use necessary for products or services they sell to their customers. The argument that a business does not operate with the intention of selling fixed assets must be challenged on the grounds that the *capacity* fixed assets provide is indeed sold. This conclusion convinced us to include the discussion of capacity costing, a unique method of providing additional insight into the decision process (see "Capacity Costing" below).

Perhaps a reminder is necessary one more time: under no circumstances are we suggesting that one costing method holds all the answers or invalidates all others. On the contrary, decisions which prove successful in the long run as well as in the immediate future are based on insight and understanding of many interacting forces within the real economic environment. It is the controller's task to make them visible.

Justifiable criticism of replacement costing centers on the simple truth that it is by no means easy (and may not always be practical or even possible) to determine precise replacement cost because of fundamental changes in technology. For purposes of our earlier illustration we chose a lift truck for the simple reason that the same lift truck is still being manufactured today identically as it was four years ago. But consider the case of the good old "comptometer," a device that by today's standards is obsolete: what constitutes its replacement? Is it an electronic desk calculator, which operates silently and efficiently without anywhere nearly the requirement for skilled operation? While such a jet-age marvel functionally represents its equivalent, such a contemporary device costs only a fraction of the units it replaces. Or is it likely that U.S. steel companies would build more blast furnaces rather than switch to the more cost-efficient (higher yield, higher quality) Bessemer process so effectively employed by German and Japanese steel manufacturers? It remains one of the great ironies in the steel industry that it was American money which helped build such formidable competition.

The last word is far from being spoken in the way of effective and meaningful inflation-costing techniques.

Synchronous Use Valuation

Several years ago we first began to recognize the need for forward-looking techniques which would serve managers through costing their decisions, that is, to project reliably and quantifiably the most likely result of planned action. The result was *synchronous use valuation;* we will now describe its key features.

First, it is "synchronous" because it develops revenue and cost estimates which are relevant to the period under consideration. Therefore, synchronous use valuation does not only employ replacement costing, that is, the determining of today's replacement, but also includes the anticipation costs which could be weeks or months in the future to determine the cost of the next acquisition. Here is a clear deviation from the concept of depreciation, which prorates the original cost of a benefit over subsequent periods during which the benefit is consumed. By contrast, synchronous use valuation equates the time of benefit consumption with the then-current cost (estimated if in the future) of such benefit. As such this technique anticipates the next acquisition rather than accounting for the last one.

Second, use valuation assigns a monetary value to the use of any asset at current lease or rental cost, if available from service organizations, or at the current replacement cost, if the business owns its equipment.

Third, use valuation employs the concept of direct contribution. This means that costs include only direct elements (both variable and fixed). For this purpose, the definition of "direct cost" includes all costs which are direct to the total volume of a product line or service type (rather than only a single unit). This broader definition of "direct" improves accuracy in determining costs and profitability significantly. As a technique, many writers refer to it as "relevant costing." (For details see Chapter 13, " 'Direct' (Variable) Costing.")

Fourth, to avoid the necessity of arbitrarily prorating the depreciation expense for a piece of equipment, use valuation assigns a value to units of actual usage (often expressed in time units). For instance, rather than estimating the life of a lift truck in calendar years, use valuation estimates life in the number of useful hours. Then the sum of purchase price plus maintenance cost for its entire life less salvage value will be divided by the total number of use hours to arrive at the hourly use value of such equipment.

Example:

Lift truck purchase cost	$30,000
Estimated Life	12,000 hours
Salvage value after 12,000 hours	$ 5,000
Net equipment cost	$25,000
Routine maintenance cost for entire life	11,000
Major overhaul (typically required after 8,000 hours of operation)	6,000
Total net cost for 12,000 hours	$42,000
Cost per hour (including maintenance)	$3.50 per hour

Fifth, the use value of a single hour of lift truck time would reflect the current cost of such a commodity, regardless of whether the vehicle employed is brand new, two, four, or five years old, or even older as long as it provides the identical service. Thus, a lift truck with a 20,000-pound lift capacity will be charged at the same per hour rate as long as it can lift 20,000 pounds, regardless of age or actual cost.

The capability of use valuation to determine the hourly cost of a lift truck makes this cost variable rather than fixed. To wit: if $42,000 buys 12,000 lift truck hours (the estimate of actual life may vary from brand to brand and by intended use of the equipment), then each hour of actual use will cost $3.50. This feature tends to make unit costs more complete and accurate. Also, as the lift truck price increases, so does the cost of each lift truck hour. But a single rate calculation will cover all 20,000-pound lift trucks.

Use-valuation rates which include maintenance lend themselves very well to budgeting. According to our assumptions, the total maintenance cost over 12,000 hours is estimated at $17,000. But obviously this money will not be spent at equal rates. As the assumptions stipulate, a major overhaul ($6,000) is likely to occur after 8,000 hours of use. Routine maintenance may average $0.25 per operating hour for the first 4,000 hours; $0.50 per hour from the 4,001st through the 8,000th hour; and $2.00 per hour for the last 4,000 hours of useful life. The *budget* for lift trucks will then appear as in Exhibit 6. So while each lift truck hour will cost $3.50, the

EXHIBIT 6
Components of Use Charge

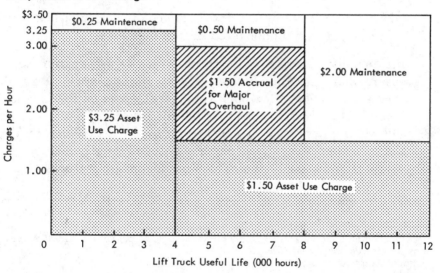

budgetary distribution differs: in the early life (first 4,000 hours) the majority of investment (replacement cost) is accumulated, while after 4,000 hours the higher expected maintenance costs account for more than half the $3.50 per hour charge. The overhaul is charged to hours 4,001–8,000, because the overhaul is expected to be performed sometime during the same calendar time period as those 4,000 hours of usage.

Use valuation may further include interest on investment or a capital use charge based on an ROI objective. All cost calculations are designed to provide this ability.

The following synopsis of a case study will illustrate this concept of synchronous use evaluation.

1. *The situation.* Initial review showed asset records for a lift truck contained these data:

> Original cost, $30,000
> Five-year life
> Straight-line depreciation
> Purchased four years ago

2. *Updating depreciation expense.* A quote from the manufacturer for the same lift truck model with identical equipment showed the current replacement value was $45,000. Based on the same five-year life, straight-line method, the annual depreciation expense should be $9,000 per year.

> *Observation:* If not updated, the service of each lift truck may be substantially understated due to inflation.

Incidentally, since the primary purpose of use valuation is to ensure that *operating budgets* reflect current costs, it is not necessary to change the book value of the asset on the balance sheet for the department using the lift truck.

3. *Calculating depreciation expense based on actual use rather than calendar time.* The company operates three plants (large, medium, and small), all of which use identical lift trucks:

	Large Plant	Medium Plant	Small Plant
Actual use hours per lift truck (as clocked on hour meter).....	5,000 per year	2,000 per year	1,000 per year
Cost per lift truck hour (@ $9,000 annual depreciation per lift truck).........................	$1.80	$4.50	$9.00

> *Observation:* The calculation of depreciation expense ($9,000) based on a fixed period (year), coupled with widely differing usage, results in very different costs per lift truck hour (directly proportionate to number of use hours). This could distort product costs among plants, and may invalidate performance evaluation among plant managers.

4. *Use Valuation versus Depreciation.* Employing use valuation, the cost of equipment becomes a function of use (hours in this case) during its expected useful life. The resultant charge for asset usage (equipment cost) shows as follows:

Lift truck cost, $45,000
Total life expectancy, 10,000 use hours
Salvage value after five years equals
    cost of major overhaul
Cost per lift truck hour:

$$\frac{\$45,000}{10,000 \text{ hours}} = \$4.50$$

	Large Plant	Medium Plant	Small Plant
Actual use hours per lift truck....	5,000 per year	2,000 per year	1,000 per year
Annual depreciation			
$4.50 per hour..................	$22,500	$9,000	$4,500

5. *Projecting future replacement cost.* Anticipating continued inflation, we forecast the price of the next lift truck to be bought to be $50,000. This raises the cost per lift truck hour immediately to $5 to accumulate sufficient funds (not through depreciation per se, but through adequate pricing based on replacement cost data) to pay for the next lift truck purchase.

Use valuation is occasionally criticized on the grounds that it could be inflationary (because "true"—and higher—costs are known, prices are set higher), or on the contention that current market prices do not support passing such increased costs to the customer in the form of higher prices. In response, it must be understood that use valuation is a costing, not a pricing, technique. But should it indeed suggest that current prices are too low to support use-valuation assumptions, then it is clear that there is no future in this business after present capacity is fully utilized and finally used up. In any event, use valuation helps managers to recognize and quantify that risk.

Capacity Costing

Capital-intensive businesses, particularly those in the service segment of our economy, have not had the benefit of the decades of diligent unit cost work that was done for manufacturing operations or generally for product-oriented industries. This obvious preoccupation with product and production (inventory, inventorying of cost, inventory valuation, absorption, burdening) that appears to permeate many areas of cost accounting tends to overlook the massive cost of fixed assets and their use. Capacity costing offers an approach that has found successful application in management reporting in many industries. We have selected two brief application histories to illustrate this approach: Example 1 comes from the construction industry; Example 2 deals with costing bank-teller services.

Capacity costing works on the premise that costs of capacity are fixed or committed (100 percent of capacity is paid for). In capital-intensive businesses, capacity costs are very high (utilities, transportation, heavy industry).

But what exactly is capacity? Webster defines it as "maximum output." Observe: maximum. Many managers fail to recognize the difference between "maximum" and the "highest actually experienced." No doubt there can exist many reasons for underutilizing capacity. But, without tough analysis to settle for less than the maximum costs money, and simultaneously increases the cost of utilized capacity, in some instances possibly to the point where a business is no longer competitive. Each capacity unit (minute, hour, day) unused remains irrevocably lost.

As an interesting observation we offer the nationwide reduction of speed limits to 55 mph (88 km per hour). In one single move the nation's over-the-road hauling capacity had been cut by 20 percent. To make up this loss truckers were granted a compensatory freight rate increase. Also, more trucks were needed to haul the same amount of goods, or (as was done in most states) the load limits had to be raised, making the trucks heavier and presumably more damaging to roads and bridges. In short, we witnessed a move that, even though well intended, turned out to be largely self-defeating.

The important question remains: How much profit is lost by a lost capacity unit? To quantify the impact of a lost capacity unit, we propose *unit contribution* as the measuring device. The contribution of a unit of capacity is defined as the difference between the revenue that can be generated from selling the product generated by that unit of capacity, less its *variable* cost of sales. In the case of an airplane seat, these variable costs include cost of a meal, the paper of a passenger ticket, incremental fuel (trivial), supplies, and other identifiable items which are a direct function of carrying the additional passenger.

This unit contribution information provides important insight when developing strategy for optimum capacity utilization. The following excerpts from two recent case studies demonstrate capacity in action.

Example 1: Capacity Costing in Asphalt Paving[1]

A 12,000-pound hot-mix batch plant with a cycle time of 40 seconds should produce 6 tons every 40 seconds or 18 tons every 2 minutes. This comes to 540 tons per hour, or 5,400 tons each ten-hour day. Thus, capacity depends both on the physical size of the unit (12,000 pounds per batch) and the time available during which this unit can be operated (ten hours per day). Capacity, therefore, is a function of physical size and available time.

Since fixed costs, by their very definition, do not change as production volume changes, it becomes obvious that total capacity (maximum output possible) must be paid for whether it is used or not. So, if the plant were to produce a batch smaller than 12,000 pounds (or a truck were to haul less than peak load), the difference constitutes a loss from the maximum possible. Similarly, every minute the plant is not actively operating at capacity results in a loss equivalent to the output that could have been generated at full production.

It is at this point that experience often restricts the thinking of many managers. A 12,000-pound batch plant, for instance, has a capacity of 540 tph or 5,400 tons per ten-hour day. Yet through a variety of circumstances (downtime, lack of trucks, full surge bins) considerable tonnage may be lost. It is entirely likely that the average loss per season could be as much as 30 to 40 percent of theoretical capacity.

Very frequently this failure to achieve the maximum obtainable influences managers to such a degree that they often do not analyze or correct specific systems weaknesses which prevent their obtaining maximum output. Yet every pound or minute of capacity not used when available means profit going to waste. After all, total capacity has already been paid for.

What does this idea of capacity mean to the asphalt-paving contractor? Mixing and laying down asphalt requires three steps: mixing, hauling, and laydown. To prevent premature cooling, asphalt

---

[1] From "How to Figure Your Real Costs to Beat Inflation." Copyright 1975 by Helmut K. Goerling.

must be laid down as soon after mixing as possible; thus, asphalt paving constitutes a system, a set of closely related, interdependent functions. Each of these steps requires special tools, such as the hot-mix plant, trucks, laydown machine, and rollers. Their cost, depreciation, rental, or lease is fixed since it does not change with volume.

The maximum output of an asphalt paving system also is determined by its smallest link ("bottleneck"), which limits sales revenue and profit contribution. Inversely, the capacity of any single component in excess of the system's bottleneck cannot be utilized and becomes waste. Yet most hot-mix plants operate below capacity. That means that any ton of plant capacity not laid down when it could have been is lost forever.

So where is its bottleneck? Laydown? No. A laydown machine of medium size can easily place 800 to 1,000 tph, obviously more than the maximum production of a 12,000-pound batch plant. Somewhat surprisingly, asphalt hauling often turns out to be the bottleneck which controls total production and, therefore, profit.

There is a need here to measure system economics. But how can we do this? Only asphalt inplace generates sales dollars, and we know the contribution of each ton laid down equals price per ton less the variable costs per ton. And lost capacity of this plant is obviously more than that of 10-hour operation if based on a 24-hour day.

The example offers some important concepts. One is that a definite value can be assigned to each minute of operation. This value is equal to the contribution that the productive capacity during this time could generate. Thus, as a minute passes idly, the potential to realize its contribution is irrevocably lost. An unused minute results in a loss. For instance, when a 12,000-pound batch plant misses one cycle, 6 tons (at $2.50 contribution each) or $15 are lost forever. Stated another way, one minute of plant time lost costs 1½ batches or $22.50.

This method provides managers with a powerful decision tool. It can be used for preparing bids, for determining the payout period of surge bins, or any problem that can be reduced to time or tons. For instance, what is the true cost of a 30-minute cleanup necessary if a dump truck unloads in front of the laydown machine? Thirty minutes of capacity at $22.50 per minute "costs" a total of $675.

The following capsule examples illustrate the technique of costing crimped capacity using the same data.

1. The incident of the side-dumped end dump.

Repair to truck.............................	$4,500
4 hours lost contribution	
(4 hours × 540 tph @ $2.50 per ton)...........	5,400
Total.................................	$9,900

2. The woes of a wobbly windrow.

Cold windrow must be removed.	
Loss of 60 tons @ $10 sales value..............	$ 600
3 hours cleanup @ 540 tph @ $2.50	
contribution per ton.......................	4,050
Total.................................	$4,650

3. The problem of the puny pickup machine. Pickup machine at laydown machine requires one hour daily repair beyond assigned maintenance time. Cost for season = 150 days @ 1 hour × 540 tons @ $2.50 contribution = $202,500 per year.
4. The trials of trucks not there. Lack of trucks causes one-hour delay at start and ten-minute plant stop per hour. One hour delay plus 9 × 10 minutes = 2½ hours at 540 tph @ $2.50 contribution = $3,375 per day.

Exhibit 2: Costing Bank-Teller Services[2]

Costing bank-teller services constitutes a task of impressive complexity. The reasons are twofold:
1. Almost all costs are totally fixed (i.e., they are independent of transaction volume actually handled).
2. The operation is subject to many volume fluctuations caused by differing period patterns. For instance, each day has a bell-shaped distribution pattern peaking between 11 A.M. and 2 P.M. (Exhibit 7-A); weekly transaction patterns show Monday and Friday to have much higher volume than midweek (Exhibit 7-B); in addition, monthly and quarterly patterns further impact transaction volume. In short, volume fluctuations are the result of varying volume patterns, not only with vast differences between highs and lows but also of divergent shapes.

---

[2] From "Costing Bank-Teller Services." Copyright 1976 by Helmut K. Goerling.

Bank-teller services must be performed on demand as customers walk into the bank lobby. As such, these services are not postponable and must be performed soon after the customer's arrival. This, of course, differs dramatically from most product-oriented businesses where production can be scheduled at consistent volume levels regardless of demand. Excess product can be inventoried, a

EXHIBIT 7
Capacity Costing

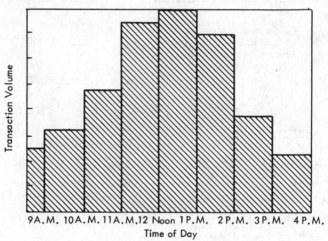

A. Daily Pattern of Transaction Volume

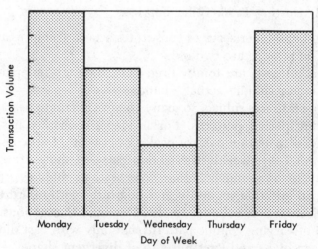

B. Weekly Pattern of Transaction Volume

EXHIBIT 7 (continued)

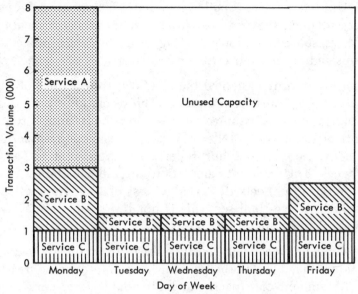

C. Example: Capacity Costing

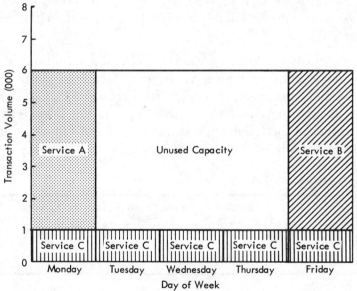

D. Example: Capacity Costing

luxury that services do not possess due to their total time dependence. Unused services "spoil" immediately: they must be used at the very moment they are available, lest they be irrevocably lost. For this reason conventional costing procedures are prone to produce misleading or even erroneous answers.

Example: In a hypothetical bank, 15,000 transactions of three different types must be processed each week. (For purposes of simplification it is assumed that services A, B, and C require identical amounts of a teller's time to process one transaction.) Total fixed costs, including teller salaries, amount to $48,000 per week. The resultant calculation (divide $48,000 by 15,000 transactions) projects the average cost of each transaction to be $3.20. As we shall see, this is not the most useful way to view cost per transaction.

The concept of capacity costing starts from the following considerations: Fixed costs provide a business enterprise with capacity. First, the amount of capacity to be available is essentially determined or even committed in advance, long before actual numbers of transactions are known. Secondly, we can observe that capacity must be adequate to handle the peaks, rather than the average volume.

Example: Retain the same volume and cost assumptions of our previous example (services A, B, and C each generate 5,000 transactions per week at a total fixed cost of $48,000). However, assume now that the transactions do not occur evenly, but rather in the following transaction pattern (shown graphically in Exhibit 7-C):

Weekly Transaction Pattern

	Monday	Tuesday	Wednesday	Thursday	Friday
A	5,000	—	—	—	—
B	2,000	500	500	500	1,500
C	1,000	1,000	1,000	1,000	1,000
Total	8,000	1,500	1,500	1,500	2,500

As a result, the processing capacity must be 8,000 per day as stipulated for Monday. Since A utilizes 62.5 percent of this peak-day's volume, B, 25 percent, and C, 12.5 percent, each service will receive the following weekly charges:

	% of Peak-Day Capacity	Total Dollars	Cost per Transaction	Average Transaction Cost
A....................	62.5	$30,000	$6.00	$3.20
B....................	25.0	12,000	2.40	3.20
C....................	12.5	6,000	1.20	3.20
Total............	100.0	$48,000		

Note: Costing provides input to, but does not dictate *pricing.*

The fact that the mix on subsequent days changes substantially and does not include any A transactions must be considered irrelevant, because if transaction type A did not exist at all, daily processing capacity could be reduced to only 3,000 daily transactions (Monday). Similarly an elimination of B transactions would result in a reduction of 2,000 transactions from the peak day, and C, in turn, would cause a decrease of 1,000 transactions.

These considerations impact service costing dramatically. Yet they are both practical and realistic: they reflect cost dependence and responsibility. Moreover, this approach (unlike conventional costing) focuses the manager's attention on the need to search for efficiencies which reduce capacity requirements for peak volumes (no benefit can be realized from improvements during off-peak periods); and to find additional volume increases for those periods when capacity is underutilized and therefore provides service potential without additional expenses (aside from truly variable costs such as the relatively small expense of special transaction forms).

The above examples illustrated the most important aspect of capacity costing. However, a complicating factor occurs as the transaction mix between services changes so that, say, A generates 5,000 transactions on Monday, B generates 5,000 transactions on Friday, with C accounting for a consistent 1,000 transactions per day. The resultant transaction pattern requires daily transaction capacity of only 6,000 transactions depicted in Exhibit 7-D, and shown here in tabular form:

Weekly Transaction Pattern

	Monday	Tuesday	Wednesday	Thursday	Friday
A....................	5,000	—	—	—	—
B....................	—				5,000
C....................	1,000	1,000	1,000	1,000	1,000
Total.............	6,000	1,000	1,000	1,000	6,000

In this pattern, the cost chargeable to A and B would be one half of 83.33 percent (5/6), or 41.67 percent each, while C will be charged with 16.66 percent. As a result each service will cost as follows:

	% of Capacity	Total Dollars	Cost per Transaction	Average Transaction Cost
A	½ of 83.33% = 41.67	$20,000	$4.00	$3.20
B	½ of 83.33% = 41.67	20,000	4.00	3.20
C	16.66	8,000	1.60	3.20
	100.0	$48,000		

SUMMARY

Profitability and profitability analysis provide the operating manager with visibility, with meaningful reports. Two points remain to be made:

1. Is it much work for the controller? Much thought—yes; new ideas—yes; more work—not necessarily. With the general availability of computers, we must design cost systems which compile cost under 6 to 12 sets of specific assumptions on command. It is not difficult, it is practical, and it works.
2. What does profitability analysis do for managers? It gives them visibility about the future. It gives them facts and quantified forecasts in useable form. It increases their response capability (quick decisions based on clear visibility). It gives them flexibility (the ability to execute alternatives under complete control).

If controllers wants to see profit for tomorrow's operation, the managers on their team must plan profitability today. Unless it happens, then the most objective reporting will not prevent disaster.

ADDITIONAL SOURCES

Anthony, Robert N., and Reece, James S. *Management Accounting Principles*, chap. 22. 3d ed. Homewood, Ill.: Richard D. Irwin, Inc., 1975.

Jones, Reginald H. "Financial Management during Inflation." *Financial Executive*, February 1975, p. 10.

King, Alfred M. "Fair Value Reporting." *Management Accounting,* March 1975, p. 25.

Neuner, John J. W., and Deakin, Edward B. *Cost Accounting: Principles and Practice,* chap. 15. 9th ed. Homewood, Ill.: Richard D. Irwin, Inc., 1977.

Silvern, David H. "Enterprise Income: Measuring Financial Management." *Financial Executive,* April 1975, p. 56.

Vancil, Richard F., and Kelly, James N. "Get Ready for Price-Level-Adjusted Accounting." *Harvard Business Review,* March–April 1975, p. 6.

Weathers, Henry T. "Managerial Profitability." *Management Accounting,* July 1974, p. 25.

32

Variance Analysis of Operating Results

Richard D. Enright*

THE CONCEPT OF PROFIT

Before digging into variances and their analysis, it would be well to understand the meaning of the word "profit." This is required because, in all but nonprofit institutions, profits and operating results are the same animal. Or, to put it another way, operating results are measured in terms of profit. Profit is the end goal, and the supreme variance is the variance in profits. All the multitudes of detailed variances are in truth merely subgroupings of the overall profit variance.

If the institution is of the nonprofit type, of course, profit is by definition not the goal. However, if one is really to do a job in this area, one should identify the goal *equivalent* to profit for the individual institution. Not only should the goal be identified but so also should the unit of measure for that goal. This is not easy, because there is rarely a unit of measure as convenient as dollars are to profits. However, with the growth of the types of services usually rendered by nonprofit institutions, the development of appropriate variance analysis to cover these services is sorely required.

---

* Mr. Enright has an accounting consulting practice in Allentown, Pennsylvania.

Profit: What Is It?

Enough digression into nonprofit institutions. Let's get back to the profit concept. The question, "What is profit?" may seem simplistic; but then profits are under attack in many quarters. In fact, much of the world seems convinced that the future belongs to an economic system which believes profits are undesirable, unnecessary, and evil. Perhaps, more ominously, many of the defenders of profits do not seem to understand what they are defending. The author has heard more than one champion of free enterprise describe profits as "that which is left over after expenses," and defend profits' existence on the grounds that "it is my property and I will do what I please with it!"

Profit is considerably more than that which is left over, and its justification lies on much firmer ground than selfish property rights. Profit is a *reward for a risk taken.* This is the essence of the concept. If one risks money or assets in a venture to produce goods and/or services to the public or some segment of it, one is entitled to a profit, if successful. The phrase "if successful" is key to the concept. It follows that if one fails, he or she is "entitled" to a loss. If this were a perfect world, then the greater the risk, the greater would be the reward. It is not a perfect world, but there is some correlation between the amount of the risk and the amount of profit or loss. Consider the fantastic profits often made on new products and try to put into perspective the large number of unheralded failures caused by new products which never left the launching pad.

Why Reward Risk Taking?

A glance at the world around us quickly demonstrates that society does not *have* to reward risk. Then why should we and others reward risk? Because society as a whole benefits from the risk takers. This is the fundamental principle of capitalism, free enterprise, and, in fact, private property itself. Society, through its agent, the government, grants charters to corporations and deeds to homeowners because it believes it will reap benefits.

What are the benefits reaped by society because of profits? The benefits are an endless stream of new products, new services, and new techniques caused because someone risked assets to bring these products, services, and techniques into the marketplace. If profits did not exist, what reward would there be for bringing these innovations into the marketplace? The alternative would be to have society itself collectively take these risks. This is what happens in those societies hostile to profits. Free enterprise rests on the assumption that the amount of risks taken and new products developed with profit as a goal will far exceed those developed by a collective social effort. The assumption is correct.

It follows that if profits made do not generate social benefits, society may curb or otherwise prevent such profits. This is the arena in which the conflict between the state and business is unresolved. To be absurd, the right to profit would not allow the sale of poison gases to the mentally disturbed. Unfortunately (or perhaps fortunately for politicians and lawyers), the rights of society as opposed to the rights of the capitalist are rarely so clear-cut.

Hopefully, we all have a good grasp of what profit is and why it exists.

How Is Profit Measured?

The most common measure of profit is as a percentage of sales dollars. It is this measure, usually supported by pie charts or bar graphs, that leads to the "profit is what is left over" syndrome. Of course, profit is what is left over, but that is the equivalent of defining blood as that which the heart pumps. Yet this is one of the two measures of profit supplied by financial journals when they report on a company's financial performance. To illustrate the weakness of this figure, compare the following hypothetical figures covering two years' activities: Year 1—Sales = $100,000, Profit = $10,000, Profit ÷ Sales = 10 percent; Year 2—Sales = $400,000, Profit = $20,000, Profit ÷ Sales = 5 percent. The briefest reflection indicates that Year 2 was the better year, even though the profit percentage is only half that of Year 1.

Profit as a percentage of sales does have some merit, however. It is a rough indicator of a safety margin. In the example, an increase in raw material or labor costs could be more harmful to Year 2 than to Year 1. In Year 1 the company has the option of just absorbing the increase and reducing profits. In Year 2 the company is almost forced to raise prices or do away with profits. Put another way, $10,000 profit which represents 10 percent of sales dollars is better than $10,000 which represents 5 percent of sales dollars.

The second measure of profit routinely supplied by financial journals is the earnings per share. This is a useful figure to the investor or potential investor, as it gives a basis to make a judgment on the price of the stock. Coupled with the amount of dividends paid or to be paid, this figure also serves as an indicator of the growth in the future value of the stock.

However, there is a measurement of profit which is not routinely reported but which is the best measure of all. This is the *return on investment.* This measures profit on the basis of the amount of investment risked. If profit is a reward for a risk taken, then its proper measure should be against the amount of risk involved. That amount is the investment or net book value of the firm. This is what the managers of the firm had to work with. The market value of the stock is usually not a tool or asset available to the managers. They only received the funds from the original sale of stock, which is represented in the owners' equity section of the balance sheet. Using the example above, assuming the investment was constant at $100,000, the return on investment for Year 1 was 10 percent and for Year 2 was 20 percent. Management did twice as well in Year 2 as in Year 1. Common sense tells us that is the truth.

There is another point involved here. Profits are a function of time. If we think of the investment as having been made in preference to the purchase of relatively riskless bonds or notes, we can perceive this better. The return on a bond is expressed as a percentage interest yield. In the example above, the profits are equivalent to interest yields of 10 and 20 percent respectively.

The importance of this time factor cannot be overemphasized. It is closely related to the break-even concept, incremental profits, and plant or space utilization. Let us illustrate this principle by assuming a situation where there are 100 machine-hours available and a choice of two products to fill this time. Product A sells at $100 and has a gross margin of $20 or 20 percent. Product B sells at $10 and has a gross margin of $1 or 10 percent. Product A is obviously the preferable choice. Or is it? Assume the production rate of Product A is 50 units per hour, and Product B is 2,000 units per hour. Then every hour running Product A yields $1,000 gross profit ($20 × 50 units) and every hour Product B is run yields $2,000 gross profit ($1 × 2,000 units). Ridiculous? Ask yourself how many errors in judgment you have seen because of the failure to recognize this concept.

As Socio-Economic Director of the Reading (Pennsylvania)

Chapter of the National Association of Accountants, for the last several years the author has been amused by the realization that almost every small business owner/manager intuitively understands this concept. On the contrary, many managers of large corporations do not. The reason is that the small business owner/manager has to see the whole picture because he or she *is* the whole picture. Corporation managers unfortunately have become too compartmentalized.

Closely allied to the return-on-investment concept is the concept of return on assets (or return on adjusted assets). This is really the same concept. The basic difference between assets and investment is represented by the financing of the assets. A firm either supports the assets by borrowing or increasing the stockholders' equity. Stockholder's equity is increased through profits retained or additional sale of stock. For the business in its *entirety*, the proper measure of its management's performance is return on investment, since management must decide between borrowing, issuing more stock, and applying retained earnings in order to support and add to the assets.

However, if the manager of a division or subgroup of the business is to be measured, then return on assets is usually the proper measure. Since the division's management is not responsible for the ratio of assets to equity, it is not fair to judge them against return on the equity. In fact, it is quite probable that the total assets should not be used in this measurement. If, for example, accounts payable are part of the division's responsibility, then the "measuring" assets should be adjusted (downward) accordingly. Similarly, if the division does not set its own credit terms or collect its own receivables, consideration should be given to omitting receivables from the division's "asset base."

One final note on profit measurement. Earnings per share *allied with* equity or assets per share can be used as a return on investment or return on assets measurement.

HOW IS PROFIT JUDGED?

The measurement of profit leads almost certainly to the judgment of profit. This section discusses some common methods to judge profits as used in industry.

Profits Compared to Prior Year(s)

Certainly the most common method of judging profits is to compare the current profit to the profit from the previous year or some part of a year. There is some merit in such a comparison. We tend to expect improvement from year to year, and this comparison tells us whether there has been any improvement. Financial journals routinely supply this comparison in their reports. If the profit for both years is coupled with an income statement prepared in some detail, the comparison will also indicate to some extent why profits have improved. Sales are up, cost of goods sold are down, selling expense has remained stable, and so on, are examples of reasons for profit improvement which can be derived from this comparison.

However, as a device for judging profits or performance, the comparison of this year's profits with last year's profits has two significant disadvantages. The first disadvantage is that last year's performance may have been very good or very bad, and therefore be an atypical standard for judging current operations. Who knows? There may have been a six-month strike last year. And even if last year was a reasonably typical year, there may be very sound reasons why the current year should not be typical.

The second significant disadvantage is that, except in the most general sense, it is not possible to determine *who* is responsible for the increase or decrease in profits. The entire "raison d'etre" of management accounting and controllership is that things do not just happen, they are caused to happen. The agents of causes are people (managers). People perform well, perform poorly, or perhaps do not perform at all. It follows that any meaningful analysis of operating results or profits must deal with the people responsible.

Comparing Profit to Others' Profits

Another rather common comparison used to judge profits is to compare the individual firm's profits against other firms' in the same industry or, less commonly, against the average profitability of all industry. The thinking here is that such a comparison eliminates the outside "uncontrollable" factors on the assumption that such factors had an effect on everybody in the industry. This idea certainly has merit. But, there are some other points to be considered. Are there really "uncontrollable" costs, or did prior decisions simply make our company too inflexible to adjust? Further, is there any benefit to management, other than the "misery loves company" theory, in knowing that their particular industry or even industry in total is failing? Probably some, but not too much.

Now let us consider the usual emphasis in this type of comparison to a specific industry group. First, comparison is only as valid as the arbitrary assignment of a particular firm to a specific industrial group. In truth, almost all firms are engaged in activities which overlap into several groups and this trend (diversification) is certainly going to continue into the foreseeable future. Second, is it reasonable to judge the management of a firm and their profits against the profits of an industrial group which routinely performs poorly? For a management team to perform 10 percent better than their specific industrial group but 20 percent below all industry indicates that they or the investors should either invest no more in that industry or (more drastically) transfer the investment already made to another, more profitable industry. The capitalistic system relies on capital being "portable." Performance below the average of industry in total caused by the conditions surrounding a specific industry leads to the question, "Why be in that industry at all?" If the answer is that the investment cannot be transferred, then this indicates that prior decisions made the business too inflexible. That was bad management. Finally, as in the comparison to prior year's judgments, it is not possible to assign responsibility for the profit performance.

Profit Compared to Goals

There is a better way to judge profit than any of the above. This method is to judge the profit against what the profit should have been. Obviously, the implication is that the firm, division, and so forth, has a profit goal. Having a profit goal implies a plan to reach the goal. Since the desirability of having a plan to reach a goal should be obvious, there really should be no problem in measuring profits in this way.

Judging profits in this way enables us to accomplish two important objectives:

1. Determine who and what caused profit to miss the profit goal.
2. Determine steps which might be taken to get profit back on the track to the profit goal.

THE INCOME STATEMENT AND BALANCE SHEET

The next preparatory step to understanding is to review the traditional presentations of operating results and financial position. These traditional presentations are the income statement or "profit and loss" statement and the balance sheet. These reports have reached a "standard" form which we are all familiar with. However, for purposes of variance analysis this "standard" form may obscure more than it reveals. This problem is caused because the "standard form" is intended for the use of "outsiders" such as stockholders, bankers, and the government. Having a different format for presenting such information for every company would lead to great confusion among these outsiders. However, variance analysis is for the benefit of "insiders"—it is a *management* accounting tool, not a shareholder reporting one. Variance analysis is a tool to be used by the individual managers of the individual company. To reach its maximum potential, this analysis should therefore be tailored to the specific company involved.

Income Statement

How does one tailor an income statement or balance sheet to a specific company? Taking the income statement first, the secret is simply to design an income statement around the responsibilities and authority of the specific company. The key for establishing these responsibilities and/or this authority is the organization chart. The organization chart represents the skeleton of the individual responsibilities, and the flesh is determined by the specific nuances of where the power and authority lie. For example, almost all companies have the credit and collection function report to the controller, treasurer, or similar position. However, it does not follow that the controller is responsible for bad debt expense. This depends upon the relative strengths of marketing and finance in establishing and implementing credit policy.

Exhibit 1 represents an organization chart for a specific company, "ABC Company." This chart and this company will be used throughout this chapter for illustrative purposes. If the organization of the ABC Company looks strange to the reader, so much the better. The whole point of redesigning the income statement is to facilitate the analysis of a specific company's operations, and

EXHIBIT 1

ABC COMPANY
Organization Chart

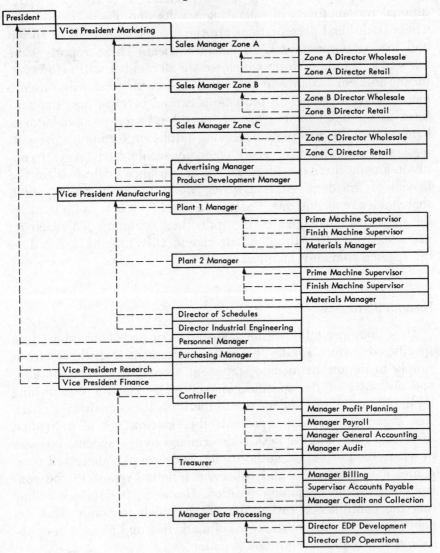

through this analysis to be able to assess credit or blame for these operating results. Thus the analysis must follow the organization chart "that is," not the chart the analyst feels "should be." The following section describes the functions and parameters of certain positions listed on the chart.

First, each sales zone has a wholesale director and a retail director. The retail director is operating a branch warehouse–sales center from which the product is distributed to the eventual user or consumer. The wholesale director is responsible for sales to independently owned warehouses and sales centers which in turn fulfill the functions of the retail directorship at a profit to themselves.

The product development manager is responsible for determining the market possibilities of new and revised products and, by close liaison with research and profit planning, expediting the development of such products. He is also responsible, subject to the approval of the VP marketing and the president, for establishing selling prices and terms.

The materials manager is responsible for the ordering of raw materials, operating supplies, and so forth, through purchasing, and for proper, safe storage of these materials until needed by production.

The director of schedules is responsible for scheduling the production equipment and the customers' shipments. He (or she) has under his control a fleet of tractors and trailers for these deliveries and the authority to shift these between plants to minimize delivery costs. It follows he also determines which plant will manufacture which order.

The personnel manager is responsible for labor negotiations with the unions, and the establishment of similar salary ranges, practices, and procedures for the nonunion work force. He (or she) administers fringe benefits and is held responsible for controlling these costs, subject to the effect of work force size changes.

The manager of profit planning is responsible for budgets, economic studies, standard costs, and similar analytical studies. The manager of general accounting is responsible for financial statement preparation, tax accounting, and the property ledgers.

The functions of the other positions on the organization chart are self-explanatory. Each position on the organization is an expense center and, if appropriate, a revenue center.

Exhibit 2 illustrates the income statement that would be developed to measure the operating results of the ABC Company. The first thing to notice is that there is a line labeled "Marketing contribution." This should warm the hearts of the sales force and marketing people. This line recognizes that the first requirement is that sales must be made. However, it also recognizes that a sales in-

EXHIBIT 2

ABC COMPANY
Internal Income Statement

	Current Year		Current Budget		Prior Year	
	Dollars	Percent	Dollars	Percent	Dollars	Percent
Gross sales		100.0		100.0		100.0
Returns and allowance						
Net sales						
Marketing expense						
Selling expense						
Advertising expense						
Product development expense						
Standard cost of goods sold						
Standard shipping expense						
Marketing contribution						
Labor usage variance						
Material usage variance						
Other manufacturing variance						
Shipping variances						
Fixed manufacturing overhead						
Total manufacturing						
Contribution after manufacturing						
Labor rate variance						
Personnel expense						
Material price variance						
Purchasing expense						
Research expense						
Finance expense						
President's expense						
Total G&A						
Income before tax						

crease is a benefit only if the costs of the product sold and the costs of making the sales increase are less than the sales dollars themselves. What has been done is to assemble all the elements of the income statement controlled or influenced by the marketing function together so that the total performance of the marketing function can be analyzed.

Of course the first item, "Marketing expense," is the direct costs of the VP marketing. This would include the salary and related fringes of the VP and the secretary and other staff people who may report to the VP. It also includes supplies, travel, and any other expenses caused by these people. The next line, "Selling expense," covers the similar expenses of the zone sales managers and their subordinate directors. Next comes the advertising expenses both of the advertising department itself and the projects designed and implemented by them. Also included are the product development costs.

Also included in calculating marketing's contribution is the standard cost of goods sold. Notice that it is the *standard* cost, not the actual cost. Marketing should not be penalized or praised for variances created in the manufacturing operations. It should also be noted that these are assumed to be *variable* production costs. The principle is clear, although it often becomes difficult in practice. Marketing is responsible for all manufacturing costs attributable to specific products and volume.

The last item listed which forms part of the marketing contribution is "Standard shipping expense." This assumes there exists a standard cost system capable of determining what expense should have been incurred to deliver the actual products sold to the actual delivery points in the actual quantities required. Note that the organization chart puts responsibility for deliveries in the hands of the director of schedules, and this individual reports to the VP manufacturing. Therefore, only the standard or "should-have-been costs" are the responsibility of marketing.

This shipping expense area also illustrates why the organization chart must be the basis of this type of analytical income statement. If we assume that delivery was a function of the marketing department, which is an assumption equally as valid as placing it within manufacturing, then the actual total shipping expense would be assigned to marketing. It all depends on responsibility. Now it is possible to decide whether to give the VP marketing a "pat on the

EXHIBIT 3

ABC COMPANY
External Income Statement

	Current Year		Current Budget		Prior Year	
	Dollars	*Percent*	*Dollars*	*Percent*	*Dollars*	*Percent*
Gross sales Return and allowances						
Net sales		100.0		100.0		100.0

Standard cost of goods
  sold
Standard shipping
  expense
Labor usage variance
Material usage variance
Other manufacturing
  variance
Shipping variance
Fixed manufacturing
  overhead
Labor rate variance
Material price variance						

Gross margin Marketing expense Selling expense Advertising expense Product development expense Personnel expense Purchasing expense Research expense Finance expense President's expense						
Total G&A						
Income before tax						

back" or a "kick in the pants," because we have determined, subject only to the limitations of the accounting function's capacity to properly classify and measure, the real contribution of marketing to profit.

If we look at Exhibit 3, a traditional income statement, we can see how difficult-to-impossible this determination would be with such a statement. The expenses are divided between the two huge groupings so that responsibility is completely lost. (Of course, Exhibit 3 shows even more detail than published income statements, which, for example, would "bury" all manufacturing variances in an actual cost of goods sold figure.)

Returning to Exhibit 2, we can see how the balance of the statement is handled. The following points should be noted:

1. The labor rate variance is assigned to G&A because it is the responsibility of the personnel function to set or negotiate these rates. If the prime responsibility for labor negotiations belonged to the VP manufacturing or a subordinate, this variance would be part of manufacturing expense.
2. Material price variances and the purchasing expenses were handled in the same manner as the labor rate variance. However, if purchasing reported to the VP manufacturing, a common practice, then both these variances would be part of manufacturing expense.
3. The G&A area could have logically been separated into groups as follows (a) research; (b) finance, controller, treasurer, and manager of data processing; and (c) president, personnel, and purchasing.

Balance Sheet

The balance sheet does not usually require a complete reorganization, but certain items—particularly in the fixed asset area—should be identified periodically by the responsible area. Whether the buildings and equipment are being utilized by marketing, manufacturing, research, or finance could make a difference in the capacity of the firm to perform or to shift its emphasis. Another area subject to this type of analysis is accounts receivable. If one of the sales zones, for example, has the bulk of the receivables, this should be pointed out to the management.

VARIANCE ANALYSIS CONCEPTS AND TECHNIQUES

There are two broad purposes for variance analysis. Simply stated, these purposes are as follows:

1. To determine why the results do not match the plan.
2. To determine what can be done to bring the results within the plan, either in the current period or future periods.

Obviously if there is a plan (budget), then one has to know why the plan was not met, or was surpassed. Was the sales budget overly optimistic or did the selling function perform poorly? And what was the cause of this poor performance: price cutting, low volume, or excessive selling expense? These are the type of questions which must be answered if the firm's planning function is to have any validity.

After these questions are answered, another set of questions presents itself. Should we cut back selling expenses or put on a major advertising or promotion program? Or perhaps a major effort should be put into new-product development? It is even possible that the question should be answered with a simple, "Go do the job." In any case, when these kinds of questions are raised and answered, the purpose of variance analysis is being served.

We shall now proceed to a more detailed consideration of how one analyzes variances in marketing, manufacturing, and general/administrative functions, as well as relationships between variances in those separate functions.

Role of the Marketing Function

Marketing has the responsibility for selling the products or services of the firm at those prices and at that product mix which will lead to the maximum possible profit contribution. Every move or decision made by the vice president of marketing should be made with this purpose in mind.

This does not mean that items such as "loss leaders," or market penetration through extensive price cutting, are improper. What it does mean is that these things are not "ends in themselves," but rather means to an end which is "maximum profit." It may well be in certain circumstances that losses may have to be incurred "now" in order to make maximum profit "then."

One of the broad purposes of variance analysis is to evaluate whether the decision to lose "now" in order to profit "then" is or was valid. Assuming a financial function both competent and appreciated, the controller would have had significant input into the decision before it was made, and certainly would examine the results as soon as they were known.

Components of the Marketing Function. Marketing has many tools or components available to enable it to meet the profit contribution assigned to it. Below will be briefly discussed the major components of the function: pricing, volume, product mix, market areas, and promotion expenses.

The first and most obvious tool available to the marketing function is the power to establish the selling price. In order to exercise this power, it is necessary to know and/or judge the following:

1. The elasticity of demand for the product(s).
2. The probable reaction of competitors.
3. Any government regulations applicable to pricing.
4. The capacity of manufacturing, warehouse, and shipping centers to handle various levels of volume for various products.

Another area where marketing has extensive power is in the area of volume. This power is of course limited by competition, general business conditions, and the capacities mentioned above. However, marketing still has the power to affect volume by the following:

1. Making more sales calls.
2. Increasing the size of the sales force or increasing sample allowances, expense allowances, and so forth.
3. Increasing the amount of advertising or other promotion of products.
4. Changing the sales price and/or terms.

Product mix is still another area where marketing must make decisions. Again, this is not an absolute power, but the following steps are available:

1. Refusing to sell, or setting a limit on sales of, a specific product(s).
2. Adjusting prices to encourage or discourage purchases of various product(s).
3. Using the advertising tool to encourage purchases of certain products.
4. Adjusting the sales effort/expense.

EXHIBIT 4
Summary of Sales/Marketing Budget (whole dollars)

	VP Mar-keting	Sales Mgr. Zone A	Zone A Whole-sale	Zone A Retail	Total Zone A	Sale Mgr Zone
1. Standard sales......................			42,342	87,884	130,226	
2. Sales price variance.................						
3. Total sales (= 1 + 2)...............			42,342	87,884	130,226	
4. Broker's commissions..............			(2,117)		(2,117)	
5. Salesperson's commissions.........				(8,789)	(8,789)	
6. Total sales revenue (= 3 + 4 + 5).....			40,225	79,095	119,320	
7. Standard manufacturing cost........			(32,579)	(52,515)	(85,094)	
8. Standard delivery cost...............			(1,725)	(2,677)	(4,402)	
9. Gross profit contribution (= 6 + 7 + 8)......................			5,921	23,903	29,824	
10. Indirect labor........................	(1,400)	(1,260)		(500)	(1,760)	(1,15
11. Supplies.............................	(140)	(126)	(50)	(100)	(276)	(12
12. Utilities..............................	(10)	(100)		(200)	(300)	(10
13. Maintenance........................	(20)	(50)		(100)	(150)	(5
14. Rental...............................	(100)	(300)		(300)	(600)	(27
15. Services.............................	(400)	(200)	(300)	(600)	(1,100)	(17
16. Travel/entertainment................	(100)	(100)	(100)	(100)	(300)	(10
17. Advertising..........................						
18. Miscellaneous.......................	(10)	(50)		(100)	(150)	(5
Total period expense (= 10–18).......	(2,180)	(2,186)	(450)	(2,000)	(4,636)	(2,02
19. Advertising allocation...............		(100)	(250)	(500)	(850)	(10
20. Adjusted period expense (= 18 + 19).	(2,180)	(2,286)	(700)	(2,500)	(5,486)	(2,12
21. Net profit contribution (= 9 – 20)......	(2,180)	(2,286)	5,221	21,403	24,338	(2,12
22. Quantity sold (lbs.)..................			77,000	132,000	209,000	
23. Standard sales per cwt. (= 1 ÷ 22 × 100).....................			54.99	66.58	62.31	
24. Gross profit contribution per cwt. (= 9 ÷ 22 × 100).....................			7.69	18.11	14.27	

Market and shipping areas and quantities constitute still another power available to marketing. Marketing can choose to sell to certain types of customers, or to customers in certain geographic areas, or only in certain quantities. They have the following tools available for this purpose:

1. The establishment of price differentials by customer class and/ or geographic areas.
2. The establishing of price differentials for shipping quantities and/or minimum order sizes.
3. Again, the advertising tool is available to promote specific customer groups or geographic areas.

It should be noted that this is an area subject to much government regulation so be careful.

Promotional expenses is obviously another area where marketing has power. The decision to incur selling expense affects the profit contribution of marketing. Of course, the effective use of the ex-

Zone B Whole-sale	Zone B Retail	Total Zone B	Sales Mgr. Zone C	Zone C Whole-sale	Zone C Retail	Total Zone C	Adver-tising	Prod Devel-opment	Grand Total
05,324	61,591	166,915		58,568	83,021	141,589			438,730
05,324	61,591	166,915		58,568	83,021	141,589			438,730
(5,266)		(5,266)		(2,928)		(2,928)			(10,311)
	(6,159)	(6,159)			(8,302)	(8,302)			(23,250)
00,058	55,432	155,490		55,640	74,719	130,359			405,169
79,212)	(35,826)	(115,038)		(44,708)	(47,880)	(92,588)			(292,720)
(5,959)	(2,550)	(8,509)		(2,328)	(2,840)	(5,168)			(18,079)
14,887	17,056	31,943		8,604	23,999	32,603			94,370
	(450)	(1,600)	(1,350)		(600)	(1,950)	(2,500)	(1,300)	(10,510)
(150)	(90)	(365)	(150)	(60)	(120)	(330)	(250)	(300)	(1,661)
	(300)	(400)	(125)		(200)	(325)	(100)	(10)	(1,145)
	(110)	(160)	(50)		(120)	(170)	(100)	(20)	(620)
	(330)	(605)	(325)		(360)	(685)	(600)	(100)	(2,690)
(900)	(500)	(1,575)	(200)	(500)	(700)	(1,400)	(400)	(800)	(5,675)
(150)	(100)	(350)	(125)	(60)	(120)	(305)	(10)	(100)	(1,255)
							(3,300)		(3,300)
	(100)	(150)	(50)		(125)	(175)	(100)	(10)	(595)
(1,200)	(1,980)	(5,205)	(2,375)	(620)	(2,345)	(5,340)	(7,450)	(2,640)	(27,451)
(600)	(400)	(1,100)	125	(500)	(700)	(1,325)	3,275		
(1,800)	(2,380)	(6,305)	(2,500)	(1,120)	(3,045)	(6,665)	(4,175)	(2,640)	(27,541)
13,087	14,676	25,638	(2,500)	7,484	20,954	25,938	(4,175)	(2,640)	66,919
92,000	85,000	277,000		107,000	142,000	249,000			735,000
54.86	72.46	60.26		54.74	58.47	56.86			56.69
7.75	20.07	11.53		8.04	16.90	13.09			12.84

penses incurred also has an effect. The point is that this is another tool or component for marketing to use in reaching its goal.

This sums up the marketing function's components. The reader should note that all of these components influence each other. A price change, for example, influences volume. None of these tools exists in isolation.

Analyzing the Marketing Function

Now we can begin to use some of the concepts and principles mentioned to perform a meaningful analysis of the marketing function. One of these principles is that profits are caused by people, so our first reports will be the reports furnished to the president of ABC Company relating to the performance of the vice president of marketing.

Marketing Budget. Exhibit 4 represents the *budget* which the vice president of marketing was expected to meet for this time period. The budget goal was a net marketing profit contribution of $66,919. Some of the concepts implied in the budget are discussed below.

The first item is "Standard sales." If there is to be really meaningful analysis of marketing, it is highly desirable to establish a standard selling price for each product. One of the most important functions of the marketing department is the establishment of selling prices and terms. It follows there should be a measurement and judgement of how well this function is performed.

Creating the proper yardstick to judge this performance does raise some questions, however. Some of the possible pricing guidelines would include:

a. The market price;
b. The company's published price list;
c. A preset markup over full costs or some portion of full costs.

Frankly, none of these appeals to the author. Market price is often difficult to determine, and for new products, impossible to determine. Published price lists already reflect the decisions we are trying to judge. Working with a markup has some validity, but it does not really recognize the meaning of profit.

At the beginning of this chapter we discussed profit as a function of time. Profits are earned and best judged in relation to time. For a manufacturing business, this means profits must be made through machine-hours. In a sense, manufacturing is the sale of machine-hours. Within any time span there is a finite number of machine-hours available. Therefore, the profit goal can and should be translated into a profit per machine-hour.

This concept gives management a measure of profit which relates *directly* to the firm's profit goal. No other measure does this. For demonstration purposes this chapter will use the standard costs in Chapter 10, "Determining Standard Material and Labor Costs": a profit contribution goal of $20 per prime machine-hour and $10 per winder-hour. The standard price will be the total of all standard variable costs plus the respective $20 and $10 per standard machine-hour. Since the standard costs are influenced by order (run) size, shipping point, and the method of distribution (wholesale or retail), the standard sales price will also reflect these items.

It should be noted that the principle applies to any type of business. By substituting such terms as man-hours, shelf-space-days,

seat-days available, and so on, for machine-hours, it can apply to a variety of business types. All businesses have a controlling element equivalent to machine-hours. The secret is to find this element(s)
Other elements in Exhibit 4 are explained as follows:

Broker's commissions are paid for all wholesale sales at the rate of 5 percent on actual sales dollars.

Salesperson's commissions are paid for all retail sales at the rate of 10 percent on actual sales dollars.

Total sales revenue represents the actual sales price less the commissions expense.

The amount shown for advertising ($3,300) represents the charges of advertising firms, and costs of supplies, and so on, which can be directly tied to specific projects or programs.

Advertising allocation represents the transfer of specific programs, projects to specific beneficiaries as follows:
   a. To specific wholesale and/or retail operations by zone;
   b. To specific zones, but not identifiable by method of distribution.

No attempt is made in the example to zero in on specific products being advertised but this would certainly be a possibility.

Actual Results. Now we can take a look at the actual results for the sample time period. Exhibit 5 is an exact duplicate of Exhibit 4 in format, but Exhibit 5 presents *actual* results rather than a budget. This latter exhibit demonstrates that the vice president of marketing has failed to reach his goal by $15,408 ($66,919 budgeted net profit contribution less actual of $51,511). In other words, if all the other departments and functions perform exactly to standard, company before-tax profits will be $15,408 short of budget.

In Exhibit 6 we have another look at the same numbers, with actuals and budgets summarized in one place. This exhibit also tells us that the unfavorable profit contribution variance is $15,408. Exhibits 4, 5, and 6 certainly tell the president how well the vice president of marketing performed vis-a-vis his budget. These exhibits will also tell the president quite a bit about the "why" of the marketing function's overall profit variance.

The most obvious problem shown in Exhibit 6 is that there was a volume shortage of 248,000 pounds. Using the budgeted gross profit

EXHIBIT 5
Summary of Sales/Marketing Actuals (whole dollars)

	VP Marketing	Sales Mgr. Zone A	Zone A Wholesale	Zone A Retail	Total Zone A	Sales Mgr. Zone
1. Standard sales.......................			20,466	89,537	110,003	
2. Sales price variance.................			(601)	74	(527)	
3. Total sales (= 1 + 2)...............			19,865	89,611	109,476	
4. Broker's commissions...............			(993)		(993)	
5. Salesperson's commissions.........				(8,961)	(8,961)	
6. Total sales revenue (= 3 + 4 + 5)......			18,872	80,650	99,522	
7. Standard manufacturing cost........			(15,782)	(53,803)	(69,585)	
8. Standard delivery cost...............			(853)	(2,720)	(3,573)	
9. Gross profit contribution (= 6 + 7 + 8)......................			2,237	24,127	26,364	
10. Indirect labor........................	(1,470)	(1,285)		(535)	(1,820)	(1,254
11. Supplies.............................	(140)	(132)	(35)	(104)	(271)	(125
12. Utilities.............................	(10)	(63)		(202)	(265)	(169
13. Maintenance........................	(18)	(44)		(99)	(143)	(8
14. Rental..............................	(97)	(153)		(300)	(453)	(148
15. Services............................	(416)	(280)	(360)	(582)	(1,222)	(322
16. Travel/entertainment................	(100)	(100)	(120)	(100)	(320)	(95
17. Advertising.........................						
18. Miscellaneous......................	(10)	(50)		(132)	(182)	(48
Total period expense (= 10–18)........	(2,261)	(2,107)	(515)	(2,054)	(4,676)	(2,169
19. Advertising allocation..............		(99)	(200)	(535)	(834)	(100
20. Adjusted period expense (= 18 + 19)........................	(2,261)	(2,206)	(715)	(2,589)	(5,510)	(2,26
21. Net profit contribution (= 9 − 20)......	(2,261)	(2,206)	1,522	21,538	20,854	(2,269
22. Quantity sold (lbs.)...................			36,000	135,000	171,000	
23. Standard sales per cwt. (= 1 ÷ 22 × 100).....................			56.85	66.32	64.33	
24. Gross profit contribution per cwt. (= 9 ÷ 22 × 100).....................			6.21	17.87	15.42	

of $12.84 hundredweight, this equates to an unfavorable volume variance of $31,843 (2,480 hundredweight × $12.84). One possible cause of a volume drop could be high prices. So we will next look to the sales price variance and the related revenue variance. Exhibit 6 tells us that the actual selling prices totaled $1,810 less than standard (based on actual volume at standard prices). Because of the resultant savings on variable commissions, this revenue decrease caused a net loss of $1,660 in revenue ($1,810 less the actual commission of 1.7 percent broker's and 6.6 percent salesperson's). We can conclude, then, that the low volume was not caused by higher than budgeted prices.

Advertising is another area that might have contributed to the volume loss. However, advertising projects are up by $665 (Exhibit 5, $3,965, less Exhibit 4, $3,300); so, at least in terms of expenditures, advertising is not a cause of the volume drop. Of course, the advertising effort might have been ineffective. Similarly, judging by actual expenses ("Total period expenses") incurred

ne B hole-sale	Zone B Retail	Total Zone B	Sales Mgr. Zone C	Zone C Whole-sale	Zone C Retail	Total Zone C	Adver-tising	Prod Devel-opment	Grand Total
2,962	74,106	127,068		42,687	66,247	108,934			346,005
	(59)	(59)		(147)	(1,077)	(1,224)			(1,810)
2,962	74,047	127,009		42,540	65,170	107,710			344,195
2,648)		(2,648)		(2,127)		(2,127)			(5,768)
	(7,405)	(7,405)			(6,517)	(6,517)			(22,883)
0,314	66,642	116,956		40,413	58,653	99,066			315,544
7,148)	(44,634)	(81,782)		(32,729)	(39,334)	(72,063)			(223,430)
2,815)	(2,790)	(5,605)		(1,804)	(1,260)	(3,064)			(12,242)
0,351	19,218	29,569		5,880	18,059	23,939			79,872
	(486)	(1,740)	(1,390)		(642)	(2,032)	(2,450)	(1,300)	(10,812)
(243)	(90)	(458)	(160)	(49)	(112)	(321)	(460)	(300)	(1,950)
	(288)	(457)	(125)		(200)	(325)	(54)	(10)	(1,121)
	(112)	(120)	(54)		(112)	(166)	(17)	(20)	(484)
	(314)	(462)	(299)		(371)	(670)	(1,014)	(100)	(2,796)
(513)	(535)	(1,370)	(80)	(20)	(672)	(772)	(400)	(800)	(4,980)
(105)	(455)	(655)	(71)	(41)	(120)	(232)	(104)	(100)	(1,511)
							(3,965)		(3,965)
	(168)	(216)	(74)		(144)	(218)	(106)	(10)	(742)
(861)	(2,448)	(5,478)	(2,253)	(110)	(2,373)	(4,736)	(8,570)	(2,640)	(28,361)
(954)	(424)	(1,478)	(70)	(770)	(763)	(1,603)	3,915		
1,815)	(2,872)	(6,956)	(2,323)	(880)	(3,136)	(6,339)	(4,655)	(2,640)	(28,361)
8,536	16,346	22,613	(2,323)	5,000	14,923	17,600	(4,655)	(2,640)	51,511
2,000	93,000	175,000		78,000	63,000	141,000			487,000
4.59	79.68	72.61		54.73	105.15	77.26			71.05
2.62	20.66	16.90		7.54	28.67	16.98			16.40

($910 over budget, including the $665 advertising), there was no letup in selling effort. Effectiveness of the sales effort should, however, certainly be questioned.

In addition to the unfavorable variance in volume ($31,843), prices net of commissions ($1,660), and period expense ($910), there was an unfavorable delivery cost variance of $244 caused by the actual shipments' being in smaller quantities and/or to more distant points than budgeted.

Of course, since the total variance is only $14,498 unfavorable, something must be favorable. Since Exhibit 4 shows that broker's commissions were affected far more than salesperson's commissions, it follows that wholesale sales were hurt more than retail sales. Since retail sales are more profitable, this helps the performance. The actual gross profit per hundredweight was $16.40 or $3.56 better than the budget of $12.84. We already know that price variance and delivery costs were unfavorable by $0.39 per hundredweight ($1,660 + $244 ÷ 4,870 hundredweight). By adding the $0.39 to

EXHIBIT 6
Profit Contribution—Sales and Marketing

	Actual		Budget		Variances	
	Dollars	Percent	Dollars	Percent	Dollars	Percent
Standard sales..............	346,005	100.0	438,730	100.0	(92,725)	(100.0)
Sales price variance.........	(1,810)	(0.5)			(1,810)	(2.0)
Total sales..................	344,195	99.5	438,730	100.0	(94,535)	(102.0)
Broker's commissions.......	(5,768)	(1.7)	(10,311)	(2.4)	4,543	4.9
Salesperson's commissions..............	(22,883)	(6.6)	(23,250)	(5.3)	367	0.4
Sales revenue..............	315,544	91.2	405,169	92.4	(89,625)	(96.7)
Standard manufacturing cost......................	(223,430)	(64.6)	(292,720)	(66.7)	69,290	74.7
Standard delivery cost.......	(12,242)	(3.5)	(18,079)	(4.1)	5,837	6.3
Gross profit contribution.....	79,872	23.1	94,370	21.5	(14,498)*	(15.6)
VP marketing expense.......	(2,261)	(0.7)	(2,180)	(0.5)	(81)	(0.1)
Zone A expense.............	(5,510)	(1.6)	(5,486)	(1.3)	(24)	
Zone B expense.............	(6,956)	(2.0)	(6,305)	(1.4)	(651)	(0.7)
Zone C expense.............	(6,339)	(1.8)	(6,665)	(1.5)	326	0.4
Advertising (net)............	(4,655)	(1.3)	(4,175)	(1.0)	(480)	(0.5)
Product development.......	(2,640)	(0.8)	(2,640)	(0.6)		
Total period expenses.......	(28,361)	(8.2)	(27,451)	(6.3)	(910)	(1.0)
Net profit contribution.......	51,511	14.9	66,919	15.3	(15,408)	(16.6)
Quantity sold (lbs.).........	487,000		735,000		(248,000)	
Standard sales per cwt......	71.05		59.69			
Sales price variance per cwt....................	(0.37)					
Standard manufacturing cost per cwt..............	(45.88)		(39.83)			
Standard delivery cost per cwt...................	(2.51)		(2.46)			
Gross profit contribution per cwt...................	16.40		12.84			

```
 * (1,660)   Price variance
  (31,843)   Vol variance
     (244)   Delivery variance
   19,249    Mix variance
  (14,498)   Total gross profit variance
```

the $0.39 to the $3.56, we have a *mix variance* of $19,249 ($3.95 ×
4,870 hundredweight).[1] (Please note that this is not a "pure"
product-mix variance, because it is caused not only by a different
mix but also by the method of distribution and the order size.)

---

[1] Strictly speaking, $3.95 × 4,870 = $19,237. However, were more decimal places
used in the variance per hundredweight, we would get $19,249. We know this latter
number is correct, since the total gross profit variance is $14,498 unfavorable, as
shown in the next paragraph. Rounding errors are always a problem in these calculations; one way to overcome them is, as here, to "plug" the final variance rather
than directly calculate it.

In summary, the $15,408 loss in net profit contribution was caused by:

1. Sales volume variance.................................. $(31,843)
2. Selling price variance (net of commissions)............. (1,660)
3. Marketing expense variance............................ (910)
4. Delivery cost variance................................. (244)
5. Mix variance.. 19,249

$(15,408)

We are also in a position to recommend to the president and marketing vice president that a serious review should be made of the selling/advertising program, because it would appear to have been somewhat ineffective.

Wholesale versus Retail. Because Company ABC has two distinct distribution methods, wholesale and retail, it would be of interest to management to see how the two methods performed. Exhibit 7 suggests some interesting things. Wholesale operations caused

EXHIBIT 7
Wholesale Total—Operating Statement

	Actual		Budget		Variance	
	Dollars	Percent	Dollars	Percent	Dollars	Percent
Standard sales...............	116,115	100.0	206,234	100.0	(90,119)	(100.0)
Sales price variance..........	(748)	(0.6)			(748)	(0.8)
Total sales...................	115,367	99.4	206,234	100.0	(90,867)	(100.8)
Broker's commissions........	(5,768)	(5.0)	(10,311)	(5.0)	4,543	5.0
Standard manufacturing cost.......................	(85,659)	(73.8)	(156,499)	(75.9)	70,840	78.6
Standard delivery cost........	(5,472)	(4.7)	(10,012)	(4.9)	4,540	5.0
Gross profit contribution......	18,468	15.9	29,412	14.3	(10,944)*	(12.1)
Total period expense.........	(1,486)	(1.3)	(2,270)	(1.1)	784	0.9
Advertising..................	(1,924)	(1.7)	(1,350)	(0.7)	(574)	(0.6)
Net profit contribution.......	15,058	13.0	25,792	12.5	(10,734)	11.9
Quantity sold (lbs.)..........	196,000		376,000		(180,000)	
Standard sales per cwt.......	59.24		54.85			
Sales price variance per cwt....................	(0.38)					
Standard manufacturing per cwt....................	(43.70)		(41.62)			
Standard delivery cost per cwt....................	(2.79)		(2.66)			
Gross profit contribution per cwt....................	(9.42)		7.82			

*	(711)	Price variance
	(14,076)	Volume variance
	(255)	Delivery variance
	4,098	Mix variance
	(10,944)	Total gross profit variance

EXHIBIT 8
Retail Total—Operating Statement

	Actual		Budget		Variances	
	Dollars	*Percent*	*Dollars*	*Percent*	*Dollars*	*Percent*
Standard sales............	229,890	100.0	232,496	100.0	(2,606)	(100.0)
Sales price variance........	(1,062)	(0.5)			(1,062)	(40.8)
Total sales................	228,828	99.5	232,496	100.0	(3,668)	(140.8)
Salesperson's						
commissions............	(22,883)	(10.0)	(23,250)	(10.0)	367	14.1
Standard manufacturing						
cost.....................	(137,771)	(59.9)	(136,221)	(58.6)	(1,550)	(59.5)
Standard delivery cost......	(6,770)	(2.9)	(8,067)	(3.5)	1,297	49.8
Gross profit contribution....	61,404	26.7	64,958	27.9	(3,554)*	(136.4)
Total period expenses......	(6,875)	(3.0)	(6,325)	(2.7)	(550)	(21.1)
Advertising................	(1,722)	(0.7)	(1,600)	(0.7)	(122)	(4.7)
Net profit contribution......	52,807	23.0	57,033	24.5	(4,226)	((162.2)
Quantity sold (lbs.)........	291,000		359,000		(68,000)	
Standard sales per cwt.....	79.00		64.76			
Sales price variance						
per cwt..................	(0.36)					
Standard manufacturing						
cost per cwt..............	(47.34)		(37.94)			
Standard delivery						
cost per cwt..............	(2.33)		(2.25)			
Gross profit contribution						
per cwt..................	(21.10)		18.09			

*	(965)	Price variance
	(12,301)	Volume variance
	(233)	Delivery variance
	9,936	Mix variance
	(3,554)	Total gross profit variance

$10,734 of the $15,408 unfavorable profit variance. Volume was short 180,000 pounds, or $14,076 in margin. There was also an unfavorable selling price variance, and advertising expenses were up. However, overall selling expenses were favorable by $784. Some questions should be asked as to the cause of this. The favorable expense variance could have contributed to the sales decline. Were the decisions on spending wise? Did the company waste the additional advertising input by not following up with the customers? The marketing vice president should answer these questions.

A glance at Exhibit 8, a statement for retail sales, shows still another tale. Standard sales only declined $2,606, so at first glance, volume does not seem to be a major factor. However, the facts are that volume is short 68,000 pounds or $12,301. The mix is significantly better because of an increase in the high-price, high-profit items. Again a question arises about the effectiveness of the sales/

advertising effort, since a significant increase in expenditures did not result in a sales increase.

Product-Line Results. Another way to analyze the results is to measure the profitability of specific products. Of course, this analysis cannot go beyond the gross profit contribution line, since the period expenses cannot be tied to specific products. (We have assumed none of the advertising is for specific products.) Exhibits 9–14 are reports on Products I–VI, respectively.

These product statements indicate that Product I is the chief culprit. Exhibit 9 tells us that there was a volume variance of $10,822, a mix variance of $689, and a selling price variance (net of sales commissions) of $544, all unfavorable. Results such as these suggest that the product should be reevaluated. Serious consideration should be given to finding a more profitable item to substitute for this product.

EXHIBIT 9
Product I Total—Profit Contribution

	Actual		Budget		Variances	
	Dollars	Percent	Dollars	Percent	Dollars	Percent
Standard sales.............	82,444	100.0	128,828	100.0	(46,384)	(100.0)
Sales price variance........	(594)	(0.7)			(594)	(1.3)
Total sales................	81,850	99.3	128,828	100.0	(46,978)	(101.3)
Broker's commissions.......	(1,283)	(1.6)	(455)	(0.4)	(828)	(1.8)
Salesperson's commissions.............	(5,613)	(6.8)	(11,966)	(9.3)	6,353	13.7
Sales revenue..............	74,954	90.9	116,407	90.4	(41,453)	(89.4)
Standard manufacturing cost......................	(53,197)	(64.5)	(76,024)	(59.0)	23,064	49.7
Standard delivery cost.......	(3,869)	(4.7)	(4,917)	(3.8)	811	1.7
Gross profit contribution.....	17,888	21.7	35,466	27.5	(17,578)*	(37.9)
Quantity sold (lbs.).........	164,000		236,000		(72,000)	
Standard sales per cwt.......	50.27		54.59			
Sales price variance per cwt...................	(0.36)		(32.21)			
Standard manufacturing per cwt...................	(32.44)		(2.08)			
Standard delivery cost per cwt..............	(2.50)		15.03			
Gross profit contribution per cwt..................	10.91					

*	(544)	Price variance
	(10,822)	Volume variance
	(689)	Delivery variance
	(5,523)	Mix variance
	(17,578)	Total gross profit variance

Exhibit 10 illustrates the profitability of Product II. The product only suffers from poor volume. A selling effort emphasizing this product, price cutting, and perhaps an advertising campaign are possible cures for this product.

The remaining products are covered by Exhibits 11–14. All have gross profit variances which are favorable. The overall problem is thus confined to Products I and II. It does not follow, however, that these products should be ignored. Quite the contrary, a push on these products might be able to compensate for the problems with Products I and II.

Product III (Exhibit 11), for example, had a gross profit contribution of 25 percent. This also happens to be its incremental profit ratio. In other words, if the run sizes, shipping points and distribution methods can be held at constant proportions, each sales increase of $100 should result in a $25 profit increase. This would

EXHIBIT 10
Product II Total—Profit Contribution

	Actual		Budget		Variances	
	Dollars	Percent	Dollars	Percent	Dollars	Percent
Standard sales...............	30,962	100.0	122,324	100.0	(91,362)	(100.0)
Sales price variance.........	19	0.1			19	
Total sales...................	30,981	100.1	122,324	100.0	(91,343)	(100.0)
Broker's commissions.......	(1,123)	(3.6)	(4,302)	(3.5)	3,179	3.5
Salesperson's commissions...............	(850)	(2.7)	(3,638)	(3.0)	2,788	3.1
Sales revenue...............	29,008	93.7	114,384	93.5	(85,376)	(93.4)
Standard manufacturing cost.......................	(21,686)	(70.0)	(85,967)	(70.3)	64,281	70.4
Standard delivery cost.......	(1,827)	(5.9)	(7,352)	(6.0)	5,525	6.0
Gross profit contribution.....	5,495	17.7	21,065	17.2	(15,570)*	(17.0)
Quantity sold (lbs.)..........	70,000		274,000		(204,000)	
Standard sales per cwt.......	44.23		44.64			
Sales price variance per cwt....................	0.03					
Standard manufacturing cost per cwt...............	(30.98)		(31.37)			
Standard delivery cost per cwt....................	(2.61)		(2.68)			
Gross profit contribution per cwt....................	7.85		7.69			

*	18	Price variance
	(15,688)	Volume variance
	49	Delivery variance
	51	Mix variance
	(15,570)	Total gross profit variance

EXHIBIT 11
Product III Total—Profit Contribution

	Actual		Budget		Variances	
	Dollars	Percent	Dollars	Percent	Dollars	Percent
Standard sales..............	36,606	100.0	18,968	100.0	17,638	100.0
Sales price variance.........	(34)	(0.1)			(34)	(0.2)
Total sales..................	36,572	99.9	18,968	100.0	17,604	99.8
Broker's commissions.......	(436)	(1.2)	(781)	(4.1)	345	2.0
Salesperson's commissions..............	(2,788)	(7.6)	(336)	(1.8)	(2,452)	(13.9)
Sales revenue..............	33,348	91.1	17,851	94.1	15,497	87.9
Standard manufacturing cost......................	(22,534)	(61.6)	(13,755)	(72.5)	(8,779)	(49.8)
Standard delivery cost.......	(1,656)	(4.5)	(952)	(5.0)	(704)	(4.0)
Gross profit contribution.....	9,158	25.0	3,144	16.6	6,014*	34.1
Quantity sold (lbs.)........	59,000		36,000		23,000	
Standard sales per cwt.......	62.04		52.69			
Sales price variance per cwt...................	(0.06)					
Standard manufacturing per cwt...................	(38.19)		(38.21)			
Standard delivery cost per cwt...................	(2.81)		(2.64)			
Gross profit contribution per cwt...................	15.52		8.73			

* (31)	Price variance
2,008	Volume variance
(100)	Delivery variance
4,137	Mix variance
6,014	Total gross profit variance

hold true until period expense has to be increased. A sales increase of $61,632 would eliminate the entire marketing variance of $15,408 (since $61,632 × .25 = $15,408).

In summary, the president and marketing vice president have a pretty thorough picture of what happened and some suggested cures:

1. A thorough review of the sales/advertising function, with a special emphasis on effectiveness (or lack of same) with respect to:
    a. Wholesale operations.
    b. Products I, II, and V and VI.
2. A program to replace Product I and possibly II.
3. A program to shift to retail; profit per hundredweight is $10 to $12 higher.

EXHIBIT 12
Product IV Total—Profit Contribution

	Actual		Budget		Variances	
	Dollars	Percent	Dollars	Percent	Dollars	Percent
Standard sales..............	42,504	100.0	42,407	100.0	97	100.0
Sales price variance.........	38	0.1			38	39.2
Total sales..................	42,542	100.1	42,407	100.0	135	139.2
Broker's commissions.......	(478)	(1.1)	(749)	(1.8)	271	279.4
Salesperson's commissions..............	(3,299)	7.8	(2,744)	(6.5)	(555)	(572.2)
Sales revenue...............	38,765	91.2	38,914	91.8	(149)	(153.6)
Standard manufacturing cost.......................	(27,632)	(65.0)	(28,470)	(67.1)	838	863.9
Standard delivery cost.......	(1,603)	(3.8)	(1,797)	(4.2)	194	200.0
Gross profit contribution.....	9,530	22.4	8,647	20.4	883*	910.3
Quantity sold (lbs.)..........	66,000		68,000		(2,000)	
Standard sales per cwt.......	64.40		62.36			
Sales price variance per cwt....................	0.06					
Standard manufacturing per cwt....................	(41.87)		(41.87)			
Standard delivery cost per cwt....................	(2.43)		(2.64)			
Gross profit contribution per cwt....................	14.44		12.72			

*	35	Price variance
	(254)	Volume variance
	125	Delivery variance
	977	Mix variance
	883	Total gross profit variance

Zone Statements. The next level of marketing responsibility is the zones themselves, plus the various support functions. A glance at Exhibits 15–23 indicates that Zone C was the most serious problem (see Exhibit 17). The major cause of Zone C's profit variance is also obvious; pounds sold were 108,000 short, which translates to a $14,137 unfavorable volume variance. The total zone variance is only $8,338 unfavorable because of a favorable mix variance which partially offset the unfavorable volume problem. The next problem is Zone A, where there is a $3,484 total variance, caused largely by a $5,423 volume variance (Exhibit 15). Zone B is also short $3,025, with a huge unfavorable volume variance of $11,761 (Exhibit 16).

In addition, the advertising manager has a $480 unfavorable spending variance, caused in part by rentals and supplies (Exhibit 22). This should probably be discussed with that manager. However, it should be remembered that (1) this variance is fairly small in absolute terms (though it is 10 percent over the budget); and (2) we are dealing here with discretionary expenses, where it is more difficult to make inferences from budgetary data (see Chapter 24).

Wholesale versus Retail—Zone Level. Each zone manager will be interested in knowing which of his or her directors fell short. Exhibits 24 and 25 show the type of information the zone manager can have. A glance at Exhibit 25 tells the Zone A manager his retail operation actually exceeded its profit budget by $135, and Exhibit 19 tells him his own expenses were $80 favorable. Therefore the problem obviously lies with his wholesale director.

Exhibit 24 shows how the wholesale director performed. There is a $3,153 unfavorable volume variance and a $571 unfavorable price variance. In short, there was both poor volume and extensive price cutting. Although prices are set by the product development man-

EXHIBIT 13
Product V Total—Profit Contribution

	Actual		Budget		Variances	
	Dollars	Percent	Dollars	Percent	Dollars	Percent
Standard sales.............	102,127	100.0	105,993	100.0	(3,866)	(100.0)
Sales price variance........	(177)	(0.2)			(177)	(4.6)
Total sales................	101,950	99.8	105,993	100.0	(4,043)	(104.6)
Broker's commissions......	(1,159)	(1.1)	(3,799)	(3.6)	2,640	68.3
Salesperson's commissions.............	(7,876)	(7.7)	(2,997)	(2.8)	(4,879)	(126.2)
Sales revenue..............	92,915	91.0	99,197	93.6	(6,282)	(162.5)
Standard manufacturing cost.....................	(67,817)	(66.4)	(76,991)	(72.6)	9,174	237.3
Standard delivery cost......	(2,387)	(2.3)	(2,672)	(2.5)	285	7.4
Gross profit contribution.....	22,711	22.2	19,534	18.4	3,177*	82.2
Quantity sold (lbs.).........	96,000		109,000		(13,000)	
Standard sales per cwt......	106.38		97.24			
Sales price variance per cwt...................	(0.18)					
Standard manufacturing cost per cwt.............	(70.64)		(70.64)			
Standard delivery cost per cwt...................	(2.49)		(2.45)			
Gross profit contribution per cwt..................	23.66		17.92			

```
*  (161)  Price variance
  (2,330)  Volume variance
     (38)  Delivery variance
   5,706   Mix variance
   3,177   Total gross profit variance
```

EXHIBIT 14
Product VI Total—Profit Contribution

	Actual		Budget		Variances	
	Dollars	Percent	Dollars	Percent	Dollars	Percent
Standard sales..............	51,360	100.0	20,205	100.0	31,155	100.0
Sales price variance.........	(1,062)	(2.1)			(1,062)	(3.4)
Total sales..................	50,298	97.9	20,205	100.0	30,093	96.6
Broker's commissions.......	(1,287)	(2.5)	(232)	(1.1)	(1,055)	(3.4)
Salesperson's commissions..............	(2,457)	(4.8)	(1,556)	(7.7)	(901)	(2.9)
Sales revenue..............	46,554	90.6	18,417	91.2	28,137	90.3
Standard manufacturing cost.......................	(30,565)	(59.5)	(11,513)	(57.0)	(19,052)	(61.2)
Standard delivery cost.......	(900)	(1.8)	(389)	(1.9)	(511)	(1.6)
Gross profit contribution.....	15,089	29.4	6,515	32.2	8,574*	27.5
Quantity sold (lbs.).........	32,000		12,000		20,000	
Standard sales per cwt.......	160.50		168.38			
Sales price variance per cwt....................	(3.32)					
Standard manufacturing cost per cwt..............	(95.52)		(95.94)			
Standard delivery cost per cwt....................	(2.81)		(3.24)			
Gross profit contribution per cwt....................	47.15		54.28			

*	(984)	Price variance
	10,858	Volume variance
	138	Delivery variance
	(1,438)	Mix variance
	8,574	Total gross profit variance

ager, it is assumed that nonstandard pricing is done at the request of the selling function. Thus the Zone A manager has a simple message for his wholesale director: (1) push for more sales; and (2) raise prices.

Zone B's manager has the same basic problem (Exhibit 26 and 27). An extensive volume variance causes wholesale operations to fail. However, the Zone B manager would probably give a pat on the back to his retail director. Retail operations benefit from both favorable volume and mix variances. Zone C tells the same basic story, except both wholesale and retail operations were unfavorable (Exhibits 28 and 29).

Summary of Marketing Analysis. In summary we have analyzed the marketing function in terms of prices, volume, mix, advertising, and selling expenses. It should be remembered, of course, that variance reports tend to *raise* questions rather than *answer* them. When we have drawn conclusions in the above analysis as to "good" or "bad" performance, it has been on the assumption that the conclusions were based on more analysis than simply reading positive or negative variances from operating statements.

Analyzing the Manufacturing Function

The manufacturing function can be described very simply: it is to manufacture salable products at the lowest possible cost, consistent with quality standards. Naturally, the amount of goods produced must relate to marketing's ability to sell, or otherwise salable products will become useless or unsalable.

EXHIBIT 15
Zone A Total—Operating Statement

	Actual		Budget		Variances	
	Dollars	Percent	Dollars	Percent	Dollars	Percent
Standard sales..............	110,003	100.0	130,226	100.0	(20,223)	(100.0)
Sales price variance.........	(527)	(0.5)			(527)	(2.6)
Total sales..................	109,476	99.5	130,226	100.0	(20,750)	(102.6)
Broker's commissions.......	(993)	(0.9)	(2,117)	(1.6)	1,124	5.6
Salesperson's commissions..............	(8,961)	(8.1)	(8,789)	(6.7)	(172)	(0.9)
Total variance expense......	(9,954)	(9.0)	(10,096)	(8.4)	952	4.7
Standard manufacturing cost.......................	(69,586)	(63.3)	(85,094)	(65.3)	15,509	76.7
Standard delivery cost.......	(3,573)	(3.2)	(4,402)	(3.4)	829	4.1
Gross profit contribution.....	26,364	24.0	29,824	22.9	(3,460)*	(17.1)
Total period expenses.......	(5,510)	(5.0)	(5,486)	(4.2)	(24)	(0.1)
Net profit contribution.......	20,854	19.0	24,338	18.7	(3,484)	(17.2)
Quantity sold (lbs.).........	171,000		209,000		(38,000)	
Standard sales per cwt.......	64.33		62.31			
Sales price variance per cwt....................	(0.31)					
Standard manufacturing cost per cwt..............	(40.69)		(40.71)			
Standard delivery cost per cwt....................	(2.09)		(2.11)			
Gross profit contribution per cwt....................	15.42		14.27			

```
*   (504)   Price variance
 (5,423)   Volume variance
     34   Delivery variance
  2,433   Mix variance
 (3,460)   Total gross profit variance
```

EXHIBIT 16
Zone B Total—Operating Statement

	Actual		Budget		Variances	
	Dollars	Percent	Dollars	Percent	Dollars	Percent
Standard sales..............	127,068	100.0	166,915	100.0	(39,847)	(100.0)
Sales price variance.........	(59)				(59)	(0.1)
Total sales..................	127,009	100.0	166,915	100.0	(39,906)	(100.1)
Broker's commissions.......	(2,648)	(2.1)	(5,266)	(3.2)	2,618	6.6
Salesperson's Commissions.	(7,405)	(5.8)	(6,159)	(3.7)	(1,246)	(3.1)
Total variance expense......	(10,053)	(7.9)	(11,425)	(6.8)	1,372	3.4
Standard manufacturing cost......................	(81,782)	(64.4)	(115,038)	(68.9)	33,256	83.5
Standard delivery cost.......	(5,605)	(4.4)	(8,509)	(5.1)	2,904	7.3
Gross profit contribution.....	29,569	23.3	31,943	19.1	(2,374)*	(6.0)
Total period expenses.......	(6,956)	(5.5)	(6,305)	3.8	(651)	(1.6)
Net profit contribution.......	22,613	17.8	25,638	15.4	(3,025)	(7.6)
Quantity sold (lbs.).........	175,000		277,000		(102,000)	
Standard sales per cwt......	72.61		60.26			
Standard price variance per cwt....................	(0.03)					
Standard manufacturing per cwt....................	(46.73)		(41.53)			
Standard delivery cost per cwt....................	(3.20)		(3.07)			
Gross profit contribution per cwt....................	16.90		11.53			

*	(56)	Price variance
	(11,761)	Volume variance
	(228)	Delivery variance
	9,671	Mix variance
	(2,374)	Total gross profit variance

In the ABC Company examples used in this chapter, there are some assumptions made which should be repeated:

1. Manufacturing includes the delivery function.
2. Purchasing and wage/salary rate setting are not manufacturing's responsibility.
3. Raw material storage, preparation, and inspection are manufacturing functions.

Components of the Manufacturing Function. The manufacturing function revolves around three primary components. The first component is the facilities or equipment required to produce. These facilities are, for any moment in time, finite and usually difficult to increase in the short run, because of the time and space requirements of obtaining new equipment.

The second component is materials. Materials can be raw, work in process created by a previous operation, or semifinished materials purchased from another manufacturer. In most instances, semifinished materials are grouped as raw materials for convenience.

The third manufacturing component is people. People can be viewed as the catalyst which causes the matching of facilities and materials to generate salable products.

Analyzing the manufacturing function is equivalent, then, to determining how well these three components were used by the company.

Manufacturing Performance Reports. Exhibit 30 is a Manufacturing Profit Contribution Report, based on the same operations and time period as the marketing reports we previously examined. First some of the items on this schedule will be explained.

EXHIBIT 17
Zone C Total—Operating Statement

	Actual		Budget		Variances	
	Dollars	Percent	Dollars	Percent	Dollars	Percent
Standard sales..............	108,934	100.0	141,589	100.0	(32,655)	(100.0)
Sales price variance.........	(1,224)	(1.1)			(1,224)	(3.7)
Total sales..................	107,710	98.9	141,589	100.0	(33,879)	(103.7)
Broker's commissions.......	(2,127)	(2.0)	(2,928)	(2.1)	801	2.5
Salesperson's commissions..............	(6,517)	(6.0)	(8,302)	(5.9)	1,785	5.5
Total variance expense......	(8,644)	(7.9)	(11,230)	(7.9)	2,586	7.9
Standard manufacturing cost......................	(72,063)	(66.2)	(92,588)	(65.4)	20,525	62.9
Standard delivery cost.......	(3,064)	(2.8)	(5,168)	(3.7)	2,104	6.4
Gross profit contribution.....	23,939	22.0	32,603	23.0	(8,664)*	(26.5)
Total period expenses.......	(6,339)	(5.8)	(6,665)	(4.7)	326	1.0
Net profit contribution.......	17,600	16.2	25,938	18.3	(8,338)	(25.5)
Quantity sold (lbs.)..........	141,000		249,000		(108,000)	
Standard sales per cwt.......	77.26		56.86			
Sales price variance per cwt....................	(0.87)					
Standard manufacturing cost per cwt..............	(51.11)		(37.18)			
Standard delivery cost per cwt....................	(2.17)		(2.08)			
Gross profit contribution per cwt....................	16.98		13.09			

* (1,009)   Price variance
(14,137)   Volume variance
  (127)   Delivery variance
  6,609   Mix variance
(8,664)   Total gross profit variance

EXHIBIT 18
VP—Marketing Operating Statement

	Actual		Budget		Variances	
	Dollars	Percent	Dollars	Percent	Dollars	Percent
Indirect labor................	(1,470)	(0.4)	(1,400)	(0.3)	(70)	(0.1)
Supplies.....................	(140)		(140)			
Utilities.....................	(10)		(10)			
Maintenance................	(18)		(20)		2	
Rental.......................	(97)		(100)		3	
Services.....................	(416)	(0.1)	(400)	(0.1)	(16)	
Travel/entertainment........	(100)		(100)			
Advertising..................						
Miscellaneous...............	(10)		(10)			
Total period expenses.......	(2,261)	(0.7)	(2,180)	(0.5)	(81)	(0.1)

EXHIBIT 19
Zone A Sales Manager—Operating Statement

	Actual		Budget		Variances	
	Dollars	Percent	Dollars	Percent	Dollars	Percent
Indirect labor................	(1,285)	(1.2)	(1,260)	(1.0)	(25)	(0.1)
Supplies.....................	(132)	(0.1)	(126)	(0.1)	(6)	
Utilities.....................	(63)	(0.1)	(100)	(0.1)	37	0.2
Maintenance................	(44)		(50)		6	
Rental.......................	(153)	(0.1)	(300)	(0.2)	147	0.7
Services.....................	(280)	(0.3)	(200)	(0.2)	(80)	(0.4)
Travel/entertainment........	(100)	(0.1)	(100)	(0.1)		
Advertising..................	(99)	(0.1)	(100)	(0.1)		
Miscellaneous...............	(50)		(50)		1	
Total period expenses.......	(2,206)	(2.0)	(2,286)	(1.8)	80	0.4

EXHIBIT 20
Zone B Sales Manager—Operating Statement

	Actual		Budget		Variances	
	Dollars	Percent	Dollars	Percent	Dollars	Percent
Indirect labor.............	(1,254)	(1.0)	(1,150)	(0.7)	(104)	(0.3)
Supplies..................	(125)	(0.1)	(125)	(0.1)		
Utilities..................	(169)	(0.1)	(100)	(0.1)	(69)	(0.2)
Maintenance..............	(8)		(50)		42	0.1
Rental....................	(148)	(0.1)	(275)	(0.2)	127	0.3
Services..................	(322)	(0.3)	(175)	(0.1)	(147)	(0.4)
Travel/entertainment.....	(95)	(0.1)	(100)	(0.1)	5	
Advertising...............	(100)	(0.1)	(100)	(0.1)		
Miscellaneous............	(48)		(50)		2	
Total period expenses.....	(2,269)	(1.8)	(2,125)	(1.3)	(144)	(0.4)

EXHIBIT 21
Zone C Sales Manager—Operating Statement

	Actual		Budget		Variances	
	Dollars	Percent	Dollars	Percent	Dollars	Percent
Indirect labor..............	(1,390)	(1.3)	(1,350)	(1.0)	(40)	(0.1)
Supplies...................	(160)	(0.1)	(150)	(0.1)	(10)	
Utilities...................	(125)	(0.1)	(125)	(0.1)		
Maintenance..............	(54)		(50)		(4)	
Rental....................	(299)	(0.3)	(325)	(0.2)	26	0.1
Services..................	(80)	(0.1)	(200)	(0.1)	120	0.4
Travel/entertainment......	(71)	(0.1)	(125)	(0.1)	54	0.2
Advertising...............	(70)	(0.1)	(125)	(0.1)	55	0.2
Miscellaneous............	(74)	(0.1)	(50)		(34)	(0.1)
Total period expenses......	(2,323)	(2.1)	(2,500)	(1.8)	177	0.5

EXHIBIT 22
Advertising Manager—Operating Statement

	Actual		Budget		Variances	
	Dollars	Percent	Dollars	Percent	Dollars	Percent
Indirect labor............	(2,450)	(0.7)	(2,500)	(0.6)	50	0.1
Supplies................	(460)	(0.1)	(250)		(210)	(0.2)
Utilities.................	(54)		(100)		46	
Maintenance............	(17)		(100)		83	0.1
Rental..................	(1,014)	(0.3)	(600)	(0.1)	(414)	(0.4)
Services................	(400)	(0.1)	(400)	(0.1)		
Travel/entertainment....	(104)		(100)		(4)	
Advertising..............	(3,965)	(1.1)	(3,300)	(0.7)	(665)	(0.7)
Miscellaneous...........	(106)		(100)		(6)	
Total period expenses...	(8,570)	(2.5)	(7,450)	(1.6)	(1,120)	(1.2)
Transfer out............	3,915	1.1	3,275	0.7	640	0.7
Net period expense.....	(4,655)	(1.3)	(4,175)	1.0	(480)	(0.5)

EXHIBIT 23
Product Development Manager—Operating Statement

	Actual		Budget		Variances	
	Dollars	Percent	Dollars	Percent	Dollars	Percent
Indirect labor............	(1,300)	(0.4)	(1,300)	(0.3)		
Supplies................	(300)	(0.1)	(300)	(0.1)		
Utilities.................	(10)		(10)			
Maintenance............	(20)		(20)			
Rental..................	(100)		(100)			
Services................	(800)	(0.2)	(800)	(0.2)		
Travel/entertainment....	(100)		(100)			
Advertising..............						
Miscellaneous...........	(10)		(10)			
Total period expenses...	(2,640)	(0.8)	(2,640)	(0.6)		

The first line, "Net profit contribution," is the same as appears near the bottom of Exhibit 6, the Marketing Summary Performance Report. In other words, because of Marketing failures, the company is $15,408 short in profit contribution. The percentages in the first line relate to the standard sales in Exhibit 6; all the other percentages on Exhibit 30 relate to "Total production earned." The last line of Exhibit 30 represents the amount of profit contribution

EXHIBIT 24
Zone A Wholesale—Operating Statement

	Actual		Budget		Variances	
	Dollars	*Percent*	*Dollars*	*Percent*	*Dollars*	*Percent*
Standard sales.............	20,466	100.0	42,342	100.0	(21,876)	(100.0)
Sales price variance........	(601)	(2.9)			(601)	(2.7)
Total sales................	19,865	97.1	42,342	100.0	(22,477)	(102.7)
Broker's commissions......	(993)	(4.9)	(2,117)	(5.0)	1,124	5.1
Sales revenue.............	18,872	92.2	40,225	95.0	(21,353)	(97.6)
Standard manufacturing cost......................	(15,782)	(77.1)	(32,579)	(76.9)	16,797	76.8
Standard delivery cost.....	(853)	(4.2)	(1,725)	(4.1)	872	4.0
Gross profit contribution....	2,237	10.9	5,921	14.0	(3,684)*	(16.8)
Indirect labor..............						
Supplies..................	(35)	(0.2)	(50)	(0.1)	15	0.1
Utilities..................						
Maintenance..............						
Rental....................						
Services..................	(360)	(1.8)	(300)	(0.7)	(60)	(0.3)
Travel/entertainment......	(120)	(0.6)	(100)	(0.2)	(20)	(0.1)
Advertising...............	(200)	(1.0)	(250)	(0.6)	50	0.2
Miscellaneous.............						
Total period expenses......	(715)	(3.5)	(700)	(1.7)	(15)	(0.1)
Net profit contribution......	1,522	7.4	5,221	12.3	(3,699)	(16.9)
Quantity sold (lbs.).........	36,000		77,000		41,000	
Standard sales per cwt......	56.85		54.99			
Sales price variance per cwt.................	(1.67)					
Standard manufacturing cost per cwt.............	(43.84)		(42.31)			
Standard delivery cost per cwt.................	(2.37)		(2.24)			
Gross profit contribution per cwt.................	6.21		7.69			

```
*  (571)  Price variance
 (3,153)  Volume variance
    (47)  Delivery variance
     87   Mix variance
 (3,684)  Total gross profit variance
```

EXHIBIT 25
Zone A Retail—Operating Statement

	Actual		Budget		Variance	
	Dollars	Percent	Dollars	Percent	Dollars	Percent
Standard sales.............	89,537	100.0	87,884	100.0	1,653	100.0
Sales price variance........	74	0.1			74	4.5
Total sales.................	89,611	100.1	87,884	100.0	1,727	104.5
Salesperson's commissions.............	(8,961)	(10.0)	(8,789)	(10.0)	(172)	(10.4)
Sales revenue..............	80,650	90.1	79,095	90.0	1,555	94.1
Standard manufacturing cost......................	(53,803)	(60.1)	(52,515)	(59.8)	(1,288)	(77.9)
Standard delivery cost.....	(2,720)	(3.0)	(2,677)	(3.0)	(43)	(2.6)
Gross profit contribution....	24,127	26.9	23,903	(27.2)	224*	13.6
Indirect labor..............	(535)	(0.6)	(500)	(0.6)	(35)	(2.1)
Supplies...................	(104)	(0.1)	(100)	(0.1)	(4)	(0.2)
Utilities...................	(202)	(0.2)	(200)	(0.2)	(2)	(0.1)
Maintenance...............	(99)	(0.1)	(100)	(0.1)	1	0.1
Rental.....................	(300)	(0.3)	(300)	(0.3)		
Services...................	(582)	(0.7)	(600)	(0.7)	18	1.1
Travel/entertainment......	(100)	(0.1)	(100)	(0.1)		
Advertising................	(535)	(0.6)	(500)	(0.6)	(35)	(2.1)
Miscellaneous.............	(132)	(0.1)	(100)	(0.1)	(32)	(1.9)
Total period expenses......	(2,589)	(2.9)	(2,500)	(2.8)	(89)	(5.4)
Net profit contribution......	21,538	24.0	21,403	24.4	135	8.2
Quantity sold (lbs.).........	135,000		132,000		3,000	
Standard sales per cwt......	66.32		66.58			
Sales price variance per cwt...................	0.05					
Standard manufacturing cost per cwt.............	(39.85)		(39.78)			
Standard delivery cost per cwt.................	(2.01)		(2.03)			
Gross profit contribution per cwt.................	17.87		18.11			

*	67	Price variance
	543	Volume variance
	27	Delivery variance
	(413)	Mix variance
	224	Total gross profit variance

available *after* manufacturing, but *before* applying costs of the G&A function. The amount is short $18,150, because manufacturing has added an additional $2,742 to the $15,408 unfavorable marketing variance. Our task is to determine why there was this $2,742 unfavorable variance.

What Manufacturing Analysis Shows

Before getting further into the "nitty-gritty" of manufacturing, it would be well to think about how manufacturing differs from other operations. Manufacturing changes the nature of things. Manufacturing could be described as the combining of various components to create a new component with characteristics and capabilities different than the characteristics and capabilities of the original com-

EXHIBIT 26
Zone B Wholesale—Operating Statement

	Actual		Budget		Variances	
	Dollars	Percent	Dollars	Percent	Dollars	Percent
Standard sales............	52,962	100.0	105,324	100.0	(52,362)	(100.0)
Sales price variance........						
Total sales................	52,962	100.0	105,324	100.0	(52,362)	(100.0)
Broker's commissions......	(2,648)	(5.0)	(5,266)	(5.0)	2,618	5.0
Sales revenue.............	50,314	95.0	100,058	95.0	(49,744)	(95.0)
Standard manufacturing cost......................	(37,148)	(70.1)	(79,212)	(75.2)	42,064	80.3
Standard delivery cost......	(2,815)	(5.3)	(5,959)	(5.7)	3,144	6.0
Gross profit contribution....	10,351	19.5	14,887	14.1	(4,536)*	(8.7)
Indirect labor..............						
Supplies..................	(243)	(0.5)	(150)	(0.1)	(93)	(0.2)
Utilities...................						
Maintenance..............						
Rental....................						
Services..................	(513)	(1.0)	(900)	(0.9)	387	0.7
Travel/entertainment......	(105)	(0.2)	(150)	(0.1)	45	0.1
Advertising................	(954)	(1.8)	(600)	(0.6)	(354)	(0.7)
Miscellaneous.............						
Total period expenses......	(1,815)	(3.4)	(1,800)	(1.7)	(15)	
Net profit contribution......	8,536	16.1	13,087	12.4	(4,551)	(8.7)
Quantity sold (lbs.).........	82,000		192,000		(110,000)	
Standard sales per cwt.....	64.59		54.86			
Sales price variance per cwt..................						
Standard manufacturing cost per cwt.............	(45.30)		(41.26)			
Standard delivery cost per cwt..................	(3.43)		(3.10)			
Gross profit contribution per cwt..................	12.62		7.75			

*	0	Price variance
	(8,525)	Volume variance
	(271)	Delivery variance
	4,260	Mix variance
	(4,536)	Total gross profit variance

EXHIBIT 27
Zone B Retail—Operating Statement

	Actual		Budget		Variances	
	Dollars	Percent	Dollars	Percent	Dollars	Percent
Standard sales............	74,106	100.0	61,591	100.0	12,515	100.0
Sales price variance.......	(59)	(0.1)			(59)	(0.5)
Total sales................	74,047	99.9	61,591	100.0	12,456	99.5
Salesperson's commissions.............	(7,405)	(10.0)	(6,159)	(10.0)	(1,246)	(10.0)
Sales revenue..............	66,642	89.9	55,432	90.0	11,210	89.6
Standard manufacturing cost.....................	(44,634)	(60.2)	(35,826)	(58.2)	(8,808)	(70.4)
Standard delivery cost.....	(2,790)	(3.8)	(2,550)	(4.1)	(240)	(1.9)
Gross profit contribution....	19,218	25.9	17,056	27.7	2,162*	17.3
Indirect labor..............	(486)	(0.7)	(450)	(0.7)	(36)	(0.3)
Supplies...................	(90)	(0.1)	(90)	(0.1)		
Utilities...................	(288)	(0.4)	(300)	(0.5)	12	0.1
Maintenance...............	(112)	(0.2)	(110)	(0.2)	(2)	
Rental.....................	(314)	(0.4)	(330)	(0.5)	16	0.1
Services...................	(535)	(0.7)	(500)	(0.8)	(35)	(0.3)
Travel/entertainment......	(455)	(0.6)	(100)	(0.2)	(355)	(2.8)
Advertising................	(424)	(0.6)	(400)	(0.6)	(24)	(0.2)
Miscellaneous.............	(168)	(0.2)	(100)	(0.2)	(68)	(0.5)
Total period expenses......	(2,872)	(3.9)	(2,380)	(3.9)	(492)	(3.9)
Net profit contribution......	16,346	22.1	14,676	23.8	1,670	13.3
Quantity sold (lbs.).........	93,000		85,000		8,000	
Standard sales per cwt.....	79.68		72.46			
Sales price variance per cwt..................	(0.06)					
Standard manufacturing cost per cwt..............	(47.99)		(42.15)			
Standard delivery cost per cwt..................	(3.00)		(3.00)			
Gross profit contribution per cwt..................	20.66		20.07			

* (53)	Price variance
1,606	Volume variance
0	Delivery variance
609	Mix variance
2,162	Total gross profit variance

ponents. Hence, materials are being used to create new materials which are then used to create still newer materials.

Exhibit 30 illustrates this concept of step-by-step usage/creation. The example is the waxed paper used as an illustration in Chapter 10; it is further assumed that there is no beginning or ending inventory involved.

The first operation is the creation of a wax mix. This involves the mixing of three ingredients (raw wax, wax additive, and a wax catalyst) to create a new material called the wax mix. Exhibit 30 assumes all performance is at standard; therefore the inventory value of the wax mix created ($1,234.25) is exactly equal to the raw materials used plus the direct labor incurred. We will call this "raw material creation." (See line 2 of Exhibit 31.) Logically it could be considered work in process creation; however, it is assumed that the company had the alternative to purchase the wax mix directly.

EXHIBIT 28
Zone C Wholesale—Operating Statement

	Actual		Budget		Variances	
	Dollars	Percent	Dollars	Percent	Dollars	Percent
Standard sales.............	42,687	100.0	58,568	100.0	(15,881)	(100.0)
Sales price variance........	(147)	(0.3)			(147)	(0.9)
Total sales.................	42,540	99.7	58,568	100.0	(16,028)	(100.9)
Broker's commissions......	(2,127)	(5.0)	(2,928)	(5.0)	801	5.0
Sales revenue..............	40,413	94.7	55,640	95.0	(15,227)	(95.9)
Standard manufacturing cost.....................	(32,729)	(76.7)	(44,708)	(76.3)	11,979	75.4
Standard delivery cost......	(1,804)	(4.2)	(2,328)	(4.0)	524	3.3
Gross profit contribution....	5,880	13.8	8,604	14.7	(2,724)*	(17.2)
Indirect labor..............						
Supplies...................	(49)	(0.1)	(60)	(0.1)	11	0.1
Utilities....................						
Maintenance...............						
Rental.....................						
Services...................	(20)		(500)	(0.9)	480	3.0
Travel/entertainment......	(41)	(0.1)	(60)	(0.1)	19	0.1 •
Advertising................	(770)	(1.8)	(500)	(0.9)	(270)	(1.7)
Miscellaneous.............						
Total period expenses......	(800)	(2.1)	(1,120)	(1.9)	240	1.5
Net profit contribution......	5,000	11.7	7,484	12.8	(2,484)	(15.6)
Quantity sold (lbs.)........	78,000		107,000		(29,000)	
Standard sales per cwt.....	54.73		54.74			
Sales price variance per cwt...................	(0.19)					
Standard manufacturing cost per cwt............	(41.96)		(41.78)			
Standard delivery cost per cwt..................	(2.31)		(2.18)			
Gross profit contribution per cwt..................	7.54		8.04			

* (140)   Price variance
  (2,332)   Volume variance
  (101)   Delivery variance
  (151)   Mix variance
  (2,724)   Total gross profit variance

EXHIBIT 29
Zone C Retail—Operating Statement

	Actual		Budget		Variances	
	Dollars	Percent	Dollars	Percent	Dollars	Percent
Standard sales.............	66,247	100.0	83,021	100.0	(16,774)	(100.0)
Sales price variance........	(1,077)	(1.6)			(1,077)	(6.4)
Total sales................	(65,170)	98.4	83,021	100.0	(17,851)	(106.4)
Salesperson's commissions.............	(6,517)	(9.8)	(8,302)	(10.0)	1,785	10.6
Sales revenue..............	58,653	88.5	74,719	90.0	(16,066)	(95.8)
Standard manufacturing cost......................	(39,334)	(59.4)	(47,880)	(57.7)	8,546	50.9
Standard delivery cost......	(1,260)	(1.9)	(2,840)	(3.4)	1,580	9.4
Gross profit contribution....	18,059	27.3	23,999	28.9	(5,940)*	(35.4)
Indirect labor..............	(642)	(1.0)	(600)	(0.7)	(42)	(0.3)
Supplies...................	(112)	(0.2)	(120)	(0.1)	8	
Utilities...................	(200)	(0.3)	(200)	(0.2)		
Maintenance...............	(112)	(0.2)	(120)	(0.1)	8	
Rental.....................	(371)	(0.6)	(360)	(0.4)	(11)	(0.1)
Services...................	(672)	(0.1)	(700)	(0.8)	28	0.2
Travel/entertainment......	(120)	(0.2)	(120)	(0.1)		
Advertising................	(763)	(1.2)	(700)	(0.8)	(63)	(0.4)
Miscellaneous.............	(144)	(0.2)	(125)	(0.2)	(19)	(0.1)
Total period expenses......	(3,136)	(4.7)	(3,045)	(3.7)	(91)	(0.5)
Net profit contribution......	14,923	22.5	20,954	25.2	(6,031)	(36.0)
Quantity sold (lbs.).........	63,000		142,000		(79,000)	
Standard sales per cwt......	105.15		58.47			
Sales price variance per cwt...................	(1.71)					
Standard manufacturing cost per cwt.............	(62.43)		(33.72)			
Standard delivery cost per cwt.................	(2.00)		(2.00)			
Gross profit contribution per cwt.................	28.67		16.90			

* (969)	Price variance
(13,351)	Volume variance
0	Delivery variance
8,380	Mix variance
(5,940)	Total gross profit variance

To be meaningful, it therefore seems better to think of wax mix as a raw material, not work in process.

Now if one jumps to the waxing operation, it can be seen that all of this wax mix is used up or consumed; and the slitting operation consumes the product of the waxing operation; and the roll-wrap operation consumes the products of the slitting operation. The last three columns (total, elimination, and adjusted total) show the

EXHIBIT 30

The Manufacturing Operation

	Wax Mix	Paper Inspection	Waxing	Slitting	Roll Wrap	Total	Elimination	Adjusted Total
Wax mix, created	1,234.25					1,234.25	(1,234.25)	
Paper A, inspected		4,212.25				4,212.25	(4,212.25)	
Total raw material created	1,234.25	4,212.25				5,446.50	(5,446.50)	
WIP, Operation 1, created			5,622.97			5,622.97	(5,622.97)	
WIP, Operation 2, created				5,858.00		5,858.00	(5,858.00)	
Total WIP, created			5,622.97	5,858.00		11,480.97	(11,480.97)	
Finished goods, created					6,444.00	6,444.00		6,444.00
Total production earned	1,234.25	4,212.25	5,622.97	5,858.00	6,444.00	23,371.47	(16,927.47)	6,444.00
Base paper A, used		(3,538.29)				(3,538.29)		(3,538.29)
Inspection paper A, used			(4,212.25)			(4,212.25)	4,212.25	
Raw wax, used	(378.84)					(378.84)		(378.84)
Wax additive, used	(600.51)					(600.51)		(600.51)
Wax catalyst, used	(41.04)					(41.04)		(41.04)
Wax mix, used			(1,234.25)			(1,234.25)	(1,234.25)	
Total raw material used	(1,020.39)	(3,538.29)	(5,446.50)			(10,005.18)	5,446.50	(4,558.68)
Operation 1 WIP, used				(5,622.97)		(5,622.97)	5,622.97	
Operation 2 WIP, used					(5,858.00)	(5,858.00)	5,858.00	
Total WIP, used				(5,622.97)	(5,858.00)	(11,480.97)	11,480.97	
Direct labor used	(213.86)	(673.96)	(176.47)	(235.03)	(586.00)	(1,885.32)		(1,885.32)
Total direct costs	(1,234.25)	(4,212.25)	(5,622.97)	(5,858.00)	(6,444.00)	(23,371.47)	16,927.47	(6,444.00)
Production pounds	5,611	16,849	21,786	20,000	20,000			
Paper A used pounds		16,849						
Raw wax used pounds	5,412							
Wax additive used pounds	541							
Wax catalyst used pounds	171							

EXHIBIT 31
Manufacturing Profit Contribution

		Actual		Budget		Variance	
		Dollars	Per-cent	Dollars	Per-cent	Dollars	Per-cent
1.	Net profit contribution.......	51,511	14.9	66,919	15.3	(15,408)	(16.6)
2.	Raw material creation.......	91,669	17.6	196,319	23.3	(104,650)	(32.4)
3.	WIP creation...............	190,870	36.6	336,769	39.9	(145,899)	(45.2)
4.	Finished goods creation.....	225,878	43.4	292,720	34.7	(66,842)	(20.7)
5.	Delivery cost earned.........	12,477	2.4	18,079	2.1	(5,602)	(1.7)
6.	Total production earned (= 2 + 3 + 4 + 5).........	520,894	100.0	843,887	100.0	(322,993)	(100.0)
7.	Raw material usage.........	(170,471)	(32.7)	(364,140)	(43.2)	193,669	60.0
8.	WIP usage.................	(304,076)	(58.4)	(403,899)	(47.9)	99,823	30.9
9.	Manufacturing direct labor usage.....................	(35,955)	(6.9)	(58,065)	(6.9)	22,110	6.8
10.	Variable delivery cost usage.....................	(13,500)	(2.6)	(18,079)	(2.1)	4,579	1.4
11.	Total direct costs (= 7 + 8 + 9 + 10)........	(524,002)	(100.6)	(844,183)	(100.0)	320,181	99.1
12.	Direct manufacturing variance (= 6 + 11).......	(3,108)	(0.6)	(296)	0.0	(2,812)	(0.9)
13.	Plant 1......................	(1,135)	(0.2)	(1,270)	(0.2)	135	
14.	Plant 2......................	(1,235)	(0.2)	(1,270)	(0.2)	35	
15.	Schedule director...........	(1,450)	(0.3)	(1,350)	(0.2)	(100)	
16.	Industrial engineer..........	(570)	(0.1)	(570)	(0.1)		
17.	VP manufacturing..........	(1,135)	(0.2)	(1,135)	(0.1)		
18.	Total manufacturing period expenses (= 13 + ··· + 17)..........	(5,525)	(1.1)	(5,595)	(0.7)	70	
19.	Grand total manufacturing (= 12 + 18)...............	(8,633)	(1.7)	(5,891)	(0.7)	(2,742)	(0.8)
20.	Profit contribution after manufacturing (= 1 + 19)...............	42,878	12.4	61,028	13.9	(18,150)	(19.6)

Note: It is assumed here, for simplicity, that all factory overhead is fixed. If there were varia-ble overheads, they would be included both in "Total production earned" and "Total direct costs" in the same manner as variable labor and materials costs.

effect. The author believes the proper production figure for analytical purposes is the total column of $23,371.47. It is recognized that there is a multiple count involved, but the following points should be made:

1. Analysis is for the benefit of insiders, so that the multiple count is harmless if recognized.
   a. Both production earned and usage are multiple counts, so the real effect is zero.

b. Since the variance is the difference between production and usage, the equation is not altered.

c. As the elimination and adjusted total columns demonstrate, it is easy to convert to the conventional format when necessary.

2. The conventional (adjusted total) method really provides no measure of effort.

a. Total production earned ($6,444) will be the same whether the roll-wrap effort was using the prior period's inventory or this period's.

b. The *real* effort of manufacturing is not just the last operation but the sum of all the operations.

3. In truth the total column reflects what really happened.

a. It demonstrates in a meaningful fashion what each operation did on its own.

b. It automatically pinpoints the point of occurrence for variances.

The next concept to be discussed is "Work in process creation" (line 3 of Exhibit 31). This is really the same principle as the raw material creation discussed above. All operations except the final one in a manufacturing plant create work in process inventory. Creating such inventory uses raw materials, perhaps work in process from a prior operation, and direct labor.

"Finished goods creation" (line 4), of course, is the production of goods ready for resale. It is valued as were raw material creation and work in process creation—at its standard *variable* cost, or its "should-have-been" costs.

"Delivery cost earned" (line 5) is also valued at standard. Each delivery made has a predetermined standard which is applied here. Of course, this cost does not go into inventory for balance sheet valuation purposes.

"Total production earned" (line 6) therefore represents the value at standard of all the variable costs of production and services rendered by manufacturing. It is the "product" of the manufacturing function, with an assigned value equal to variable standard costs.

The next section of Exhibit 31 merely represents the actual variable costs used to create this "product." If the manufacturing function has performed exactly to standard, total direct costs will exactly match total production earned. (The budgeted variance of $296 is caused by rounding errors.) Note that work in process and raw material usage can in effect be counted twice with this system if they are used to create a further stage of completion short of the finished goods stage.

Earlier the point was made that variance analysis is for use by insiders and therefore does not have to be in the traditional formats as seen by outsiders. However, we must be able to convert to this format. Below is the actual column of Exhibit 31 recast in a more traditional format:

Finished goods created......................	$225,878	
Increase (decrease) in WIP....................	(113,206)	[190,870—304,076]
Delivery costs earned.......................	12,477	
Total production earned......................	125,149	
Less: Raw material increase (decrease)....	(78,802)	[91,669—170,471]
Less: Direct labor usage....................	(35,955)	
Less: Variable delivery costs..............	(13,500)	
Direct manufacturing variance...............	$(3,108)	

The budget column in the traditional format would look like this:

Finished goods created......................	$292,720	
Increase (decrease) in WIP...................	(67,130)	[336,769—403,899]
Delivery costs earned.......................	18,079	
Total production earned......................	243,669	
Less: Raw material increase (decrease)....	(167,821)	[196,319—364,140]
Less: Direct labor usage....................	(58,065)	
Less: Variable delivery costs..............	(18,079)	
Direct manufacturing variance...............	$ (296)	

Now that we two have distinct measures of productivity, it might be interesting to make some comparisons of actual budget.

1. The *traditional* production earned is 51 percent ($125,149 ÷ $243,669).
2. Our nontraditional approach shows 62 percent productivity ($520,894 ÷ $843,887).
3. Direct labor was 62 percent of budget ($35,955 ÷ $58,065 = 62 percent).
4. Sales dropped 22 percent (from Exhibit 6, $94,535 ÷ $438,730 = 22 percent).

The author believes these figures, particularly 2 and 3 above, give a more meaningful picture of the actual productivity of manufacturing than the traditional approach does.

EXHIBIT 32
Plant 2 Operations

		Actual		Budget		Variance	
		Dollars	Per-cent	Dollars	Per-cent	Dollars	Per-cent
1.	Raw material created.......	46,843	19.9	98,087	27.0	(51,244)	(40.0)
2.	WIP created...............	115,853	49.2	180,294	49.6	(64,441)	(50.4)
3.	Finished goods created.....	72,781	30.9	85,094	23.4	(12,313)	(9.6)
4.	Total production earned (= 1 + 2 + 3)..............	235,477	100.0	363,475	100.0	(127,998)	(100.0)
5.	Paper A usage..............	(44,925)	(19.1)	(118,557)	(32.6)	73,632	57.5
6.	Paper B usage..............	(14,119)	(6.0)	(17,780)	(4.9)	3,661	2.9
7.	Raw wax usage.............	(1,702)	(0.7)	(3,884)	(1.1)	2,182	1.7
8.	Wax additive usage.........	(3,126)	(1.3)	(6,158)	(1.7)	3,032	2.4
9.	Wax catalyst................	(108)	0.0	(420)	(0.1)	312	0.2
10.	Wax mix usage.............	(5,598)	(2.4)	(12,632)	(3.5)	7,034	5.5
11.	Glue usage.................	(713)	(0.3)	(1,139)	(0.3)	426	0.3
12.	Polyethylene usage.........	(8,714)	(3.7)	(8,545)	(2.4)	(169)	(0.1)
13.	Ink usage..................	(8,603)	(3.7)	(12,820)	(3.5)	4,217	3.3
14.	Total raw material usage (= 5 + ⋯ + 13).............	(87,608)	(37.2)	(181,935)	(50.1)	94,327	73.7
15.	WIP usage.................	(132,716)	(56.4)	(155,406)	(42.8)	22,690	17.7
16.	Total material usage (= 14 + 15).................	(220,324)	(93.6)	(337,341)	(92.8)	117,017	91.4
17.	Press operator labor........	(665)	(0.3)	(920)	(0.3)	255	0.2
18.	A Machine operator labor...	(6,934)	(2.9)	(14,722)	(4.1)	7,788	6.1
19.	B Machine operator labor...	(2,629)	(1.1)	(2,629)	(0.7)		
20.	Press helper labor..........	(679)	(0.3)	(966)	(0.3)	287	0.2
21.	Machine helper labor.......	(890)	(0.4)	(1,148)	(0.3)	258	0.2
22.	Roll wrap..................	(5,260)	(2.2)	(5,812)	(1.6)	552	0.4
23.	Total direct labor (= 17 + ⋯ + 22)............	(17,057)	(7.2)	(26,197)	(7.2)	9,140	7.1
24.	Total direct costs (= 16 + 23).................	(237,381)	(100.8)	(363,538)	(100.0)	126,157	98.6
25.	Direct manufacturing variance (= 4 + 24)........	(1,904)	(0.8)	(63)	0.0	(1,841)	(1.4)
26.	Indirect labor..............	(500)	(0.2)	(500)	(0.1)		
27.	Supplies...................	(40)	(0.0)	(50)	0.0	10	0.0
28.	Utilities...................	(175)	(0.1)	(200)	(0.1)	25	0.0
29.	Maintenance................	(400)	(0.2)	(400)	(0.1)		
30.	Rental.....................	(100)	0.0	(100)	0.0		
31.	Services...................						
32.	Travel/entertainment.......						
33.	Miscellaneous..............	(20)	0.0	(20)	0.0		
34.	Total period expense (= 26 ⋯ + 33)..............	(1,235)	(0.5)	(1,270)	(0.3)	35	0.0
35.	Grand total (= 25 + 34)......	(3,139)	(1.3)	(1,333)	(0.4)	(1,806)	(1.4)

Of course manufacturing, like marketing, should be analyzed down to individual responsibility centers. We will bypass explaining most of the detail of how one can analyze a manufacturing function; this is illustrated in Exhibit 32 and 33, and is self-explanatory. We will jump to Exhibit 34. Exhibit 34 breaks the performance down to the individual machine level. The $391 total variance for all four machines is broken into components as follows: labor, $216;

EXHIBIT 33
Plant 2—Prime Machine Department

		Actual		Budget		Variance	
		Dollars	Per-cent	Dollars	Per-cent	Dollars	Per-cent
1.	WIP created..............	51,087	100.0	103,219	100.0	(52,132)	(100.0)
2.	Total production earned.....	51,087	100.0	103,219	100.0	(52,132)	(100.0)
3.	Paper A usage.............	(24,416)	(47.8)	(64,433)	(62.4)	40,017	76.8
4.	Paper B usage.............	(7,564)	(14.8)	(9,525)	(9.2)	1,961	3.8
5.	Wax mix usage............	(5,598)	(11.0)	(12,632)	(12.2)	7,034	13.5
6.	Glue usage................	(354)	(0.7)	(569)	(0.6)	215	0.4
7.	Polyethylene usage........	(4,605)	(9.0)	(4,494)	(4.4)	(111)	(0.2)
8.	Ink usage.................	(4,272)	(8.4)	(6,411)	(6.2)	2,139	4.1
9.	Total raw material usage (= 3 + ··· + 8).............	(46,809)	(91.6)	(98,064)	(95.0)	51,255	98.3
10.	WIP usage................	(1,797)	(3,5)			(1,797)	(3.4)
11.	Total material usage (= 9 + 10).................	(48,606)	(95.1)	(98,064)	(95.0)	49,458	(94.9)
12.	Press operator labor.......	(665)	(1.3)	(920)	(0.9)	255	0.5
13.	A Machine operator labor...	(1,136)	(2.2)	(2,693)	(2.6)	1,557	3.0
14.	Press helper labor.........	(679)	(1.3)	(966)	(0.9)	287	0.6
15.	Machine helper labor.......	(392)	(0.8)	(650)	(0.6)	258	0.5
16.	Total direct labor (= 12 + ··· + 15)...........	(2,872)	(5.6)	(5,229)	(5.1)	2,357	4.5
17.	Total direct costs (= 11 + 16).................	(51,478)	(100.8)	(103,293)	(100.0)	51,815	99.4
18.	Direct manufacturing (= 2 + 17)..................	(391)	(0.8)	(74)	(0.1)	(317)	(0.6)
19.	Indirect labor..............	(125)	(0.2)	(125)	(0.1)		
20.	Supplies..................	(10)	0.0	(12)	0.0	2	0.0
21.	Utilities...................	(50)	(0.1)	(50)	0.0		
22.	Maintenance...............	(100)	(0.2)	(100)	(0.1)		
23.	Rentals...................	(25)	0.0	(25)	0.0		
24.	Services..................						
25.	Travel/entertainment.......						
26.	Miscellaneous.............	(5)	0.0	(5)	0.0		
27.	Total period expenses (= 19 + ··· + 26)...........	(315)	(0.6)	(317)	(0.3)	2	0.0
28.	Grand total (= 18 + 27)......	(706)	(1.4)	(391)	(0.4)	(315)	(0.6)

EXHIBIT 34
Plant 2—Prime Machines: Machine Performance

		Waxer	Wax Laminator	Glue Laminator	Extruder	Printer	Total
1.	WIP created	25,249		4,217	10,490	11,131	51,087
2.	Paper A usage	(19,102)		(1,007)		(4,307)	(24,416)
3.	Paper B usage			(861)	(5,723)	(980)	(7,564)
4.	Wax mix usage	(5,598)					(5,598)
5.	Glue usage			(354)			(354)
6.	Polyethylene usage				(4,605)		(4,605)
7.	Ink usage					(4,272)	(4,272)
8.	Total raw material usage (=2 + ⋯ + 7)	(24,700)		(2,222)	(10,328)	(9,559)	(46,809)
9.	WIP usage			(1,797)			(1,797)
10.	Total material usage (=8 + 9)	(24,700)		(4,019)	(10,328)	(9,559)	(48,606)
11.	Press operator labor					(665)	(665)
12.	A mach operator labor	(702)		(153)	(281)		(1,136)
13.	Press helper labor					(679)	(679)
14.	Machine helper labor	(239)		(55)	(98)		(392)
15.	Total direct labor (=11 + ⋯ + 14)	(941)		(208)	(379)	(1,344)	(2,872)
16.	Total direct cost (=10 + 15)	(25,641)		(4,227)	(10,707)	(10,903)	(51,478)
17.	Direct manufacturing variance (=1 + 16)	(392)		(10)	(217)	228	(391)
18.	Crew-size variance	(132)		(17)	(37)	(38)	(224)
19.	Labor yield	(8)		2	15	33	42
20.	Labor mix						
21.	Labor performance	(9)		(3)		(22)	(34)
22.	Total labor variance (=18 + ⋯ + 21)	(149)		(18)	(22)	(27)	(216)
23.	Material yield			27	(4)	255	35
24.	Material mix	(243)		(19)	(191)		(210)
25.	Total material variance (=23 + 24)	(243)		8	(195)	255	(175)
26.	Direct manufacturing variance (=22 + 25)	(392)		(10)	(217)	228	(391)
27.	Machine-hours	102.9		24.0	42.4	83.1	252.4

Wax Laminator: (This column is blank because this machine was not operated during this period.)

and material, $175. By machine, the waxer accounts for the most variance, with the extruder's unfavorable results offset by the printer's favorable ones. Therefore we will start with the waxer to analyze the prime machine department's performance.

The waxer produced against two orders with the same standard costs per hundredweight. The first step is to break down the $392 total variance between labor and material as follows:

(Actual production × Standard labor per hundredweight)
    − Actual labor = Direct labor variance; or, in numbers,
(978.27 hundredweight × $0.81) per hundredweight − $941
$$= \$(194)$$

(Actual production × Standard material per hundredweight)
    − Actual material = Direct material variance; or, in numbers,
(978.27 hundredweight × $25.00) − $24,700 = $(243)

The $149 unfavorable direct labor variance can be broken down further. The first area to investigate is the machine rate per hour. Exhibit 4A in Chapter 10 developed a labor cost per machine-hour of $7.86, while the actual labor cost was $9.14 per machine-hour. This difference of $1.28 per hour for 102.9 machine-hours results in a variance of $132. What caused this variance? The primary cause was the fact that the wax laminator did not run at all. The standard rate assumed a helper being shared with the wax laminator. Because the wax laminator did not run, the helper was charged full time to the waxer. Exhibit 4A in Chapter 10 tells us that half the time of a helper costs $1.51 per machine-hour. The actual variance is only $1.28, because not running the full 168-hour week saved some overtime. Note that none of these variances is caused by a discrepancy in wage rates. This $132, therefore, is a crew-size variance. It is caused whenever the planned staffing cannot be met. (Another example of this type of variance would be to use a person of a higher pay than required. For example using an A-machine operator for the machine-helper task. In this instance, the variance would be a labor rate variance.)

Another cause of the $149 labor variance is the yield or waste factor. Poor yields not only effect material but also labor. Throwing away the products involves throwing away the labor already expended on the product. In this case 76,407 pounds of paper were run through the waxer, which a glance at Exhibit 6 in Chapter 10 indicates should result in 98,794 pounds production (76,407 ×

1.293). The actual production was 97,827 or 967 pounds short. The labor yield variance therefore is $8 (9.67 hundredweight × $0.81 per hundredweight).

Of course, the material effect of poor yields was much worse. A total of 101,855 pounds of paper and wax were used, which Exhibit 6 in Chapter 10 indicates should result in 98,799 (101,855 × 0.970) pounds of production. Since actual production was 97,827, there is a 972-pound shortgage, worth $243 (9.72 cwt. × $25 per hundredweight). Note this is the total material variance, because of mix was not off-standard. Also note that yield is calculated from different bases for material and labor. The labor is only based on paper used, while material is based on total ingredients used.

Now we can summarize the waxer performance as follows:

	Labor	Material	Total
Variance caused by crew-size/machine rate	(132)	—	(132)
Variance caused by poor yield/waste	(8)	(243)	(251)
Variance caused by improper mix	—	—	—
Variance caused by inefficient performance	(9)	—	(9)
Variance caused by all reasons	(149)	(243)	(392)

Some observations on this summary:

1. In our calculations, inefficient performers was "backed into;" that is, we added the crew-size, yield, and mix variances and subtracted their sum from the total to arrive at the efficiency variance. The only drawback of this approach is that a variance could have been caused by underweight rolls, which would have been a purchasing error.
2. Poor yield is certainly the major cause of the worker's variance.
3. Assuming the poor yield was not caused by "sloppy" work by the waxer crew, very little of the variance is the fault of the crew.
4. A major improvement would result from running the wax laminator, an apparently unrelated problem. Put another way, poor sales effort might be the real cause of $132 of variance.

Such a breakdown of variance prevents erroneous conclusions, such as "the waxer crew is goofing off," which would be the likely conclusion from a $149 unfavorable variance.

Now, let us turn our attention to the extruder performance, particularly the mix variance ($191). The extruder operation is basically similar to the waxer in that a coating is being placed on a roll of paper. In this case, the specifications call for a basis weight of 30 pounds, with 12 pounds of polyethylene added. Such an operation does not seem an appropriate one for discussing mix, formula, and batch variance, but it really is quite appropriate. What we are seeking is a finished product: 30/42 paper and 12/42 polyethylene. During this week, 27,933 pounds of ingredients were consumed by the extruder. The following table illustrates what happened:

	Basis Weight	Standard Mix (%)	Pounds			Cost per Pound	Material Mix Variance
			Standard	Actual	Variance		
Paper...........	30	71.4	19944	19078	866	$0.30	259.80
Polyethylene....	12	28.6	7989	8855	(866)	0.52	(450.32)
Total...........	42	100.0	27933	27933	0		(190.52)

What happened? The mix of ingredients has been changed. By exchanging more expensive polyethylene for less expensive paper, an unfavorable mix variance has been caused. This is no different than what can happen when mixing in a baking operation or a chemical plant. Indeed if the specifications allow it, the proportion can be deliberately adjusted to cut manufacturing costs.

In this extruder example, there are two other consequences worth mentioning:

1. Although there is an unfavorable material yield of $4, there is a favorable labor yield variance of $15. The reason is that the material yield is based on total ingredients, while the labor yield is based only on the paper, because only the paper is run through the machine. Obviously the yield on paper is better because more polyethylene is being added than standard as the machine runs.

2. Since the material yield is insignificant, it follows that the basis weight must have been altered. The actual usage indicates a final basis weight of 43.9 pounds, not 42.0. Although this has no labor effect at this operation, let us see what happens on the winder:

Standard

$$60,000 \div (500 \times 42.0 \times 53) = 0.054 \text{ hours per hundredweight}$$

Actual

$$60,000 \div (500 \times 43.9 \times 53) = 0.052 \text{ hours per hundredweight}$$

Because of the basis weight increase, there will be generated a favorable variance at the next operation, which should be netted against the unfavorable variance mix variance here.

Overhead Volume Variance

One category of manufacturing variance has not been mentioned. That is the *overhead volume variance*. Frankly, from an analytical perspective, it does not exist. (Note that we have consistently kept variable costs separate from fixed and treated the fixed as "period expenses.") If the firm has an absorption cost system, the expenses will still have to be separated into variable and fixed (period) types. In other words, contrary to what the IRS may think, absorption accounting is illogical and the variance analysis function must be logical. Therefore if forced to, the analyst should separate the effect on profits caused by a difference between assumed and actual volume(i.e., "volume" or "absorption" variance) as being some sort of noncontrollable, nonaccountable effect. Techniques for decomposing overhead variance in an absorption accounting system into volume and spending variances are described in all of the accounting texts listed under "Additional Sources" at the end of this chapter.

Hopefully one now understands and can utilize the concepts of manufacturing analysis, and apply them to:

1. Period (fixed overhead) expenses.
2. Direct labor expense.
   a. Caused by efficiency variations.
   b. Caused by yield variations.
   c. Caused by mix variations.
   d. Caused by crew-size/machine rate variations.

The G&A Function

The analysis of the general/administrative function is by and large the analysis of period and overhead expenses, which has been discussed earlier. The biggest problem is to find an appropriate output measure that is the equivalent of sales revenue or production earned. Some possibilities that could be used are described below.

Data processing should certainly have a standard cost per operating hour, which would include the operator and any other variable costs. Key-punching is another area subject to standard costing.

Actual results should be measured against these standards. In addition, the data processing department should be compelled to estimate the cost of new reports, systems, and so on, and should be measured (in part) on their performance against these estimates. The author is amazed at how freely American industry adds reports to its needs without ever questioning whether the benefits exceed the costs. Data processing expenditures should be justified as much as capital expenditures.

The number of payroll checks prepared would seem to be an appropriate measure of the payroll department's activity. Number of invoices or vouchers prepared would apply to billing and accounts payable. In each of these cases, a standard cost per measuring unit could be developed based upon the variable expenses involved. Although it would probably lack the precision of a manufacturing standard, it would certainly be preferable to the usual listing of expense incurred without any measure of activity (output) or performance for comparison.

Based on the assumptions at the beginning of this chapter, wage rates and fringe benefits are the responsibility of the personnel department. The variance would be determined something like this;

1. Actual hours paid × standard rate per hour........... $ XXX
2. Actual percent fringes × 1 above...................... XXX
3. Actual number of employees × fringes/employee..... XXX
4. Actual hourly fringes × actual hours worked.......... XXX
5. Less: Actual total wages and fringes paid.............. (XXX)
6. Equals: Total rate and fringe labor variance............ $ XX or (XX)

Although the author has never seen it done, he believes the concept of wage-rate variances could and should be applied to indirect labor as well as to direct labor.

Another assumption at the beginning of this chapter was that purchasing is an administrative cost category and not a manufacturing responsibility. Therefore, the purchase price variance belongs to administration. Purchasing orders issued might be the basis of a standard cost system.

In all of these G&A expenses suggestions, there is the question of what portion of labor is truly variable. Billing clerks are not variable in the sense that most manufacturing labor is. The point to remember is that the purpose is usefulness. If treating billing costs as a variable expense is useful, then do it. The key question is, "Does it enable one to understand the operation better?"

There are several areas which lend themselves to effective pre-action analysis. These belong to the project area and include such things as capital expenditures, advertising, and research/development. These should be treated as a series of individual job costs. They are recognizable by two chief characteristics: (1) large initial investment and (2) benefits in the far future. (See related chapters on capital expenditures, R&D costs, and project management.)

The proper approach to pre-analysis of these projects is to be able to know accurately:

1. What situation will exist if the expenditure is not made.
2. How this situation will change because of the expenditure.

After the project is authorized it is desirable to carefully measure and control both the costs being incurred and the results obtained. This measurement will give control and increased ability to predict accurately future projects. Most likely, such a pre-analysis program will be resisted by nonaccounting managers because they believe accountants lack the ability to perceive the intangible and the capacity to gamble on the uncertain. The accusation is often correct. To perform this function properly, the accountant must strike a rare balance between the "hard-nosed" and the "romantic." The R&D area is particularly difficult to value beforehand. The response must be that the expenditures involved and the risks incurred are too great to be ignored. Although difficult, the analysis must be performed and performed well.

The Links

Up to this point, the analysis has assumed that every variance can be tied to a specific individual without dispute. Alas, if only it were so. In this section some important interdependencies will be covered. These are variances which link two or more responsibilities. For example:

1. *Crew size/variance.* This was discussed briefly before. Is the failure of the Plant 2 wax laminator because selling failed to sell or manufacturing failed to produce? Only an analysis of the actual condition will answer this, and then, probably not completely.
2. *Sales volume.* Is it down because of a poor sales effort, or manufacturing's failure to produce?

3. *Production.* Is it down because of manufacturing, or did purchasing fail to provide the materials?
4. Assuming all facilities running at capacity, to whom does the inability to increase sales get attributed? The president, perhaps?
5. Scheduling. Exhibit 5 shows a standard delivery cost of $12,242; Exhibit 31 shows delivery costs earned of $12,477. The difference of $235 was caused because manufacturing had to ship some product from the more distant plant in order to meet the sales committment. To whom should this $235 variance be charged?
6. *Material handling.* The assumption was that certain items evaporate in storage. Presuming the longer the storage, the greater the evaporation, is excess loss the fault of: (*a*) material handling, for overordering; (*b*) purchasing, for overbuying; or (*c*) manufacturing for underusing?

By no means is the above list all-inclusive, but it does serve to illustrate how "fuzzy" the charging of responsibility can be. Intelligent variance analysis requires not only the ability to devise schedules to capture pertinent numbers but also the capacity to see beyond the numbers presented. Failure to see beyond the numbers destroys confidence in the analytical function, and having an analytical function without the confidence of its users is worthless.

The Benefits

The last section illustrates a great truth about analysis. Analysis is not a science but an art. There is nothing sacred about any of the tables and charts in this chapter. The author does not care whether the reader remembers or uses any of them. What the author does care about is that the reader thinks about *his* or *her* firm's situation, and why it does or does not reach its profit goals. If this chapter has increased the reader's capacity to perform this function for his or her firm, the author has succeeded.

In sum, analyzing operating results is useful if it is true that the firm which knows the following has the edge:

1. What its profits are?
2. What they should have been?

3. Why they are not as they should be?
4. What can be done about them?

ADDITIONAL SOURCES

Anthony, Robert N., and Dearden, John. *Management Control Systems: Text and Cases,* chap. 11. 3d ed. Homewood, Ill.: Richard D. Irwin, Inc., 1976.

————, and Reece, James S. *Management Accounting Principles,* chap. 22. 3d ed. Homewood, Ill.: Richard D. Irwin, Inc., 1975.

DeWelt, Robert L. "Labor Measurement and Control." *Management Accounting,* October 1976, p. 26.

Fremgen, James M. *Accounting for Managerial Analysis,* chap. 10. 3d ed. Homewood, Ill.: Richard D. Irwin, Inc., 1976.

Grinnell, D. Jacque. "Activity Levels and the Disposition of Volume Variances." *Management Accounting,* August 1975, p. 29.

Horngren, Charles T. *Cost Accounting: A Managerial Emphasis,* chaps. 9, 26. 4th ed. Englewood Cliffs, N.J.: Prentice-Hall, Inc., 1977.

Purdy, Charles R., and Ricketts, Donald E. "Analysis of Rate, Efficiency and Utilization Variances." *Management Accounting,* November 1974, p. 49.

Shillinglaw, Gordon. *Managerial Cost Accounting,* chaps. 21, 22, 25. 4th ed. Homewood, Ill.: Richard D. Irwin, Inc., 1977.

Sisco, Anthony F. "Overhead Variance Analysis and Corrective Action." *Management Accounting,* October 1973, p. 45.

33

Making Intracompany
Performance Comparisons *

Frank J. Tanzola†

The executives of large multidivisional companies are invariably asked two questions: how do you manage so many diverse businesses, and how do you motivate the people running the businesses, many of whom are independently wealthy because they have sold their businesses to the conglomerate? The answers to these questions are found in organization structure; comprehensive planning and accountability in the form of budgeting and monthly reporting; pooling expertise and business acumen; financial and other incentives; and, at times, downright toughness.

USI is no exception. (USI has quite a history of successful acquisition. The company has acquired more than 100 companies since 1965, with a substantial increase in net income—from $2 million in 1965 to $81 million in 1972. However, due to a worsening economy and setbacks at certain of its operations, net income has declined in the last three years.)

USI incentives for good performance have been broad. They have included contingency arrangements, whereby the total consideration paid for an acquired business depends on its profits during a number of years subsequent to the acquisition; a bonus system based on profits after a return on the corporation's investment; a

---

* This chapter is adapted from an article entitled "Performance Rating for Divisional Control," which appeared in the March 1975 issue of *Financial Executive*.

† Mr. Tanzola is Senior Vice President and Corporate Controller, U.S. Industries, Inc., New York.

stock option plan; base salary levels commensurate with position, responsibilities, and achievement; and a preference for internal promotion to higher level positions. Nevertheless, during discussions of these methods, one technique never fails to excite the questioners' interest and curiosity—USI's performance rating system.

USI's performance rating system (we also refer to it as our "achievement of objectives system") is a quantification of progress against agreed-upon standards as good, prudent measures of operating results. The rating system has been in use at USI for more than ten years, predating the acquisition period mentioned above; but it proved to be easily adaptable to a growing number of diverse businesses.

CORPORATE BACKGROUND

Before getting into the specifics of how the rating system operates, it would be helpful to an understanding of both its simplicity and flexibility if a brief overview of USI's development and diversity were presented first.

The company underwent some basic business changes since its incorporation in 1899; but it would serve no useful purpose here to review its evolution prior to 1965. It was in that year that its chairman died, and he was succeeded in that post by the current chairman, I. J. Billera. The company at that time was in four highly cyclical businesses—heavy presses for the automobile and appliance industries; ladies hosiery; oil field equipment; and offshore construction equipment dealerships. In addition, in an effort to counter the cyclicality, the former chairman had taken the company into several risky business ventures which required substantial product and market research and development, and whose payoff prospects extended well into the future. These proved to be serious cash drains, especially at times when the basic businesses were in down cycles. Two examples of these high-flying ventures were robots for handling industrial material and for packaging, and programmed teaching machines.

As a result of these factors, coupled with high overhead spending, the company was short of cash and otherwise in shaky financial condition when Billera took command. He immediately moved to restore financial stability by making drastic cuts in the overhead spending and by divesting the high-flying ventures. However, the company's vulnerability was no secret, and before the divestment program was completed, a relatively small company made a public tender offer for USI stock.

Billera successfully fought off this attack, but it did serve to underscore the need to move swiftly to complete the divestment program and then to get into businesses which would counter the company's cyclicality, but which had low capital requirements. Also, to reduce vulnerability, there was a pressing need to grow in both size and financial strength and to increase the inside holdings of the company's stock.

It became clear that the best and quickest way to accomplish all of these aims was to acquire other companies for stock. Thus was launched the acquisition program referred to at the outset of this chapter, wherein USI acquired more than 100 companies over a six-year period.

USI's Diversity

USI is now positioned in four broad business areas, but there is even diversity in each of those areas. This is clearly displayed by Exhibit 1, taken from the 1975 annual report. It does not require much study of the table in Exhibit 1 before one begins to appreciate that a set of performance measurement standards which could be

EXHIBIT 1

Operation	Principal Products and Services	1975 Sales ($ in millions)
Industrial:		
Industrial products..........	Steel warehousing, industrial fasteners, machined parts	$ 39.1
Industrial equipment........	Metal presses, forgings, precision gauges	52.8
Agribusiness.................	Egg, poultry, and livestock production, feeding and processing, irrigation systems	77.4
Energy equipment...........	Oil production equipment, heat exchangers, pressure vessels for chemical plants, refineries and nuclear power plants	93.3
Plastics.....................	Dip and injection molded plastic products, plastic resins, film, and bags	55.1
Building and furnishings:		
Building materials...........	Masonry units, doors and windows, mouldings, wire and cable, lumber, lighting fixtures and lenses	138.3

Exhibit 1 (continued)

Operation	*Principal Products and Services*	*1975 Sales ($ in millions)*
Home furnishings............	Sofas, chairs and convertibles, tables and accent pieces, modular cabinetry, outdoor furniture, lamps, housewares	95.4
Construction.................	Bridges and highways, metal buildings, electrical and foundation contracting, structural steel, air conditioning ductwork, pre-stressed concrete	103.7
Mobile homes...............	Manufacturing and retailing; mobile home hardware	46.2
Equipment distribution......	Earth-moving industrial and agricultural equipment in Philippines and Caribbean	48.7
Commercial furnishings......	Chairs, desks, and cabinets for offices and schools	43.6
Apparel:		
Women's and girls apparel...	Sportswear, screen printing, hosiery, robes, all-weather coats, children's dresses, nurses' uniforms	104.7
Men's and boys' apparel.....	Sport shirts, sweaters, leather coats, swimwear, casual socks, sport coats and suits, leisure suits	95.5
Men's and women's footwear...................	Men's work shoes, western-style boots, women's slippers, casual shoes	55.1
Junior sportswear...........	Jeans, western and regular sportswear, metal snap fasteners	88.2
Services and leisure:		
Health......................	Nationwide health spas, health spa membership finance, prescription optical dispensaries and laboratories	72.8
Leisure products.............	Pleasure boats, bicycles, sports and athletic equipment	37.6
Diversified services..........	Airport limousine services, land development, interior design, and institutional furnishings	12.8
Finance.....................	Consumer, commercial and industrial finance. Not included in total. Represents revenues of finance companies which are not consolidated for financial statement purposes.	30.3
Products divested or discontinued...............	Represents sales of businesses sold or liquidated in 1975 and 1974. Includes four from industrial, three from building and furnishings, seven from apparel and three from services and leisure.	81.3
	Net sales....	$1,341.6

equitably applicable to so many diverse businesses could be a useful management tool. This then brings us to a description of the system employed at USI.

DIVISION PERFORMANCE MEASUREMENT SYSTEM

Basis for Measurement

Each year the four groups' operating executives solicit the ideas of their division managements about appropriate measurement standards. Common standards are adopted by agreement of the group executives and corporate management. The points assigned to standards reflect those areas management decides require special attention.

The standards and point assignments are part of USI's management guide, which sets forth the corporation's policies and objectives. The guide is distributed to all top executives throughout the corporation. With the guide, all managers have a clear understanding of the challenge presented to their operation. The latest point system is outlined in Exhibit 2.

As can be seen from Exhibit 2, the measure of performance is in three broad areas. First, profits are compared to the prior year in terms of absolute dollars, margins, and return on investment. The investment community applies these yardsticks in evaluating the company as a whole. A management which regularly reports profit growth and improved results is highly regarded by investors.

Second, profits are compared to budget. Note that a point is lost for dollars of profit either too far below or too far above the amount budgeted. This is one way of discouraging divisional budgets which are either too cozy or too aggressive. There is no point for below-budget profit percent because within that sales range the division is expected to control other variables to bring at least that part of the sales dollar down to the bottom line. Realistic divisional budgets serve as a norm to identify good or poor performers or shifts in business conditions. They also provide the firm basis required for corporate planning. Theoretically, the ideal budget is one which the division does barely achieve, but through aggressive effort.

The third area measured is management of cash and capital. The emphasis here is on good management of inventory and receivables. There is no requirement to improve these compared to prior year,

EXHIBIT 2
Standards and Point Assignments

Doing better than last year:
  Pretax dollar profit:
    Exceeds same period prior year........................... 1 point
    Exceeds same period prior year by 15% or more........... 1
    Exceeds same period prior year by 25% or more........... 1
  Pretax profit percentage on sales:
    Exceeds same period prior year......................... 1
  Return on average investment:
    Exceeds same period prior year......................... 1

Planning realistically:
  Pretax dollar profit for period:
    Not less than 90% nor more than 125% of budget......... 1
  Pretax percent profit on sales for the period:
    Equals or exceeds budget.............................. 1
  Return on average capital employed for period:
    Not less than 90% of budget........................... 1

Managing cash and capital:
  Investment criteria:
    Number of months' sales in receivables equals or less
      than budget*.. 1
    Number of months' cost of sales in inventory equals or
      less than budget*................................... 1
  Cash transfers to headquarters:
    At least 75% of prior 12 months' pretax profits........ 1
    Equals or exceeds year-to-date budgeted transfers....... 2
                        Maximum per period............. 13 points†

* Provided return on capital employed is better than prior year.
† 12 points achieves standard of excellence.

so as not to penalize those divisions which have consistently controlled them at optimum levels. Also, presumably no unwarranted slippage from prior year is accepted when budgets are reviewed and approved. Sales turnover ratios are used to allow for better- or worse-than-expected business conditions and to measure management reaction to the changed conditions. Cash, of course, is the ultimate end product of business activity; its emphasis here needs no rationale other than to provide incentive to produce it so that it can be kept at work in the overall corporate structure. The 75 percent average target is calculated to cover corporate payments for taxes, overhead, and dividends. This leaves 25 percent to reinvest in the division plus depreciation and other noncash charges.

It should be noted that this approach also affords a good performance evaluation of the management of a business operating in a depressed market. While admittedly, through no fault of their own, they may not be able to earn the points based on profit comparisons to the prior year, they could nevertheless earn the points for good management of cash and capital and, to the extent they had the foresight, the points based on budgeted amounts. Thus, the managers of such a business would not be rated as poorly as they might be if they were to be judged solely on comparative profit results.

Performance Report

Each quarter, every division rates itself on a form devised and provided for that purpose and with reference to the management

EXHIBIT 3

PERFORMANCE MEASUREMENT REPORT

Company_____

_____(Date)

Group_____   (Subsidiary/division)

	This Year		Last Year's	This Year		Points	
	Actual	Budget	Actual	% of Budget	Vs. Last % Incr.	Current Quarter	Year to Date
			(dollars amounts in thousands)				
Profit objectives:							
Pretax profit:							
Current quarter	$......	$......	$......	......%	......%	☐	
Year to date	$......	$......	$......	......%	......%		☐
Net sales:							
Current quarter	$......	$......	$......				
Year to date	$......	$......	$......				
Pretax profit %:							
Current quarter	.....%	.....%	.....%			☐	
Year to date	.....%	.....%	.....%				☐
Average investment	$......	$......	$......				
Return on average investment	.....%	.....%	.....%	......%		☐	☐
Investment criteria:							
Receivables	$......	$......					
Average sales—last 3 months	$......	$......					
Number of months sales in receivable	......	......				☐	☐
Inventories	$......	$......					
Average cost of sales—last 3 months	$......	$......					
Number of months cost of sales in inventory	......	......				☐	☐
Cash transfers:							
Pure cash transfers equal to budget-year to date	$......	$......				☐	☐
Pure cash transfers and	12 Mos.	12 Mos.	12 Mos.	12 Mos.	12 Mos.		
equivalents* as % of most recent 12 months'	Cash	Equiv.	Total	PTP	Percent		
pretax profits:	$......	$......	$......	$.......	......%	☐	☐
	Total performance points						

* Consists of any direct payments for income taxes or debt.

EXHIBIT 4
Performance Standing Report

THREE MONTHS ENDED MARCH 31, 19xx
RANKED IN ACCORDANCE WITH USI MANAGEMENT GUIDE

Top 25%

Rank	Division (and points)
1	Apex (12)
2	Durel (12)
3	A E Wire and Cable (12)
4	Nashville (12)
5	Rolled Steel Products (12)
6	Daly Baking (12)
7	Hudson Chemical (12)
8	Super Automatic (12)
9	Bevy Products (12)
10	Lingus Linens (12)
11	Minute Foods (12)
12	Harvey Fasteners (12)
13	Burkey's (12)
14	Atwell (12)
15	Giner Products (12)
16	Agroi (11)
17	Mann's Supply (11)
18	Hyko (11)
19	Remson (11)

Second 25%

Rank	Division (and points)
29	Scatter Chain (9)
30	Boggs Ewell (9)
31	West-Link (9)
32	Duralee (9)
33	Specto (9)
34	Riviera (9)
35	Tacco (9)
36	Springdale (9)
37	Dusco (9)
38	Bulieg-Art (9)
39	Greenco (9)
40	Halfield (8)
41	Relayne (8)
42	Dubuque (8)
43	Relyan (8)

Third 25%

Rank	Division (and points)
57	Ramco (5)
58	Rumarko (5)
59	Regale (5)
60	Prosper-Gordon (4)
61	Relco (4)
62	Decorel (4)
63	Levivo (4)
64	Beverly (4)
65	Covia (4)
66	Recordo Devices (3)
67	Global-Reliance (3)

Fourth 25%

Rank	Division (and points)
85	Tool Steel Products (2)
86	Grand Junction (2)
87	Hamiltonian (2)
88	Georgia Belle (2)
89	Transparo Pack (2)
90	Tacoma (2)
91	Metropo (2)

20 Warston (10)	44 Bellows Falls (8)	68 Xenia (3)	92 Bow-Tel (2)
21 Philippines (10)	45 Drymouth (7)	69 Charleston (3)	93 Valiant (2)
22 Hartwell (10)	46 Girken (7)	70 Lewellyn (3)	94 Reducto (2)
23 Prince Charming (10)	47 Ledeaux (7)	71 Denver (3)	95 El-Con (2)
24 Eastern Window (10)	48 Lindenhayn (7)	72 Phoenix (3)	96 Karpo (2)
25 Royal (10)	49 Krotulis (7)	73 Car-Care (3)	97 Bel-Tone (2)
26 Keystone (10)	50 Kelly (7)	74 Desmond-Reed (3)	98 Brookings (2)
27 Southern Aire (10)	51 Duchess (6)	75 Talisman (3)	99 Konsort (2)
28 Brown Company (9)	52 Danny (6)	76 Midway (3)	100 Gurnay (2)
	53 Green Kalto (6)	77 San Miguel (3)	101 El Paso (2)
	54 Leghorn (5)	78 Temper-Tone (3)	102 Holsum Kraft (2)
	55 Recycle Products (5)	79 Real-Time (3)	103 Centrex Leasing (2)
	56 Reota (5)	80 Iron-Bilt (3)	104 D & W Fixtures (2)
		81 Reading (3)	105 National Abrading (2)
		82 Pueblo (3)	106 Thompson (2)
		83 Ark-Tite (3)	107 Portland (2)
		84 Harken's (3)	108 Southwest Reduction (2)
			109 Revolvo (2)
			110 Timer Tones (2)
			111 Halgren (2)
			112 Culver (2)

guide's point standards. These forms are forwarded to corporate headquarters, where they are reviewed and the divisions ranked, according to points earned, among all divisions in the company Where divisions have earned the same number of points, ranking in the quarterly report is according to the percent improvement of dollar profits over the prior year period. A sample of the quarterly rating form is shown in Exhibit 3.

Giving Visibility to Performance

When this information has been assembled and divisions ranked at corporate headquarters, a performance standing report is prepared and distributed throughout the company to all management guide holders during the third week following each quarter. A sample of a performance standing report is shown in Exhibit 4. (The names used are not the actual USI divisions, nor are the points shown necessarily indicative of ratings on any actual USI quarterly report.)

The same system is applied to the four USI operating groups, and they too are rated and ranked, but separately among themselves.

To provide increased visibility for performance and additional incentives, and to foster the competitive spirit implicit in the system, those divisions which were "12-pointers" are presented excellence awards in the form of "E" flags each quarter. The division and group with the highest cumulative points for the year each receives the annual first-place award—a bronze plaque. We also distribute a quarterly "Performance Awards" brochure. A full page is devoted to each of the winning organizations with photos of the key executives together with an announcement of the award and a write-up of their division or group. The first page of this brochure is a letter of congratulations from the chairman and president. What I am saying is this: It isn't enough to merely tabulate performance statistics. The results must be widely publicized, and the system must have the interest and support of top management. Additional importance is attached to it when high-point achievement is given weight in annual bonus considerations.

At USI, there is a bonus plan separate and apart from the performance ratings. The bonus pool has been calculated based on a percentage of a division's profits in excess of a required return of invested assets. Beyond this, the award can be more or less than the formula amount at management's discretion. Management assesses overall performance based on a number of considerations, and the rating report is one broad measure helpful in the deliberations. I have previously noted how a business in a depressed market would not be rated as poorly under the point system as they might be based solely on profit results.

EFFECTIVENESS OF THE SYSTEM

Managing a giant corporation from the top can be a very lonely and, at times, a frustrating and thankless job. The question of how to get line management to function most effectively in areas of corporate concern and benefit has no easy answer. The fields of employee motivation and management science are broad. Authors in those fields and practitioners offer many varied approaches adaptable to particular circumstances. At USI, we employ many of the usual approaches, but the rating system which I have described has contributed surprisingly well to our motivational efforts. I say "surprisingly" because at first blush the system may seem schoolboyish and unlikely to interest the sophisticated, successful manager. On the contrary, however, we have witnessed the extra effort and special attention to achieving goals by both our professional managers and entrepreneurs as they work to come away with the honors of the awards for their divisions or to gain a respectable ranking among all divisions. It reaffirms for us that pride and the competitive spirit are potent human drives. A motivational or incentive package which ignores or underrates them is missing a fundamental.

Side Benefits

At the risk of claiming too much for the system, it is important to list some of its secondary benefits. Starting out with the premise that the agreed-upon standards are good and prudent business measures of operating results, it follows that:

Management can see by a glance at the performance standing report which divisions are performing well and which not so well.

The lost points act as "red flags," directing management's attention to those areas.

Among the required agenda items for monthly division executive meetings is a discussion of the areas where points were lost, the reasons, and corrective actions taken. This often leads to in-depth discussion of business conditions and operating problems. Minutes of these meetings are forwarded to group and corporate headquarters where they are read by all key executives.

Included in the internal audit's review scope is a procedure where the auditor is satisfied as to the stated reasons for the division's lost points. This can lead the auditor to important findings which might otherwise escape attention.

Flexibility

The system has flexibility in regard to shifting management emphasis. It is also flexible as to its application to organizational units other than the operating division, such as departments or even business segments. In fact, a good example of adapting it for both shifting emphasis and different organization units is currently under way at USI. Management has determined that with postacquisition earnout periods largely past, and for reasons related to concentrating business expertise and operating efficiencies, the company would now be better served if it were to reorganize divisions into much fewer but larger operating units along product lines. Added benefits expected from the more simplified structure are better investor understanding of the company and better market identification. This necessitates a complete revision of the rating system to adapt it to the new structure. Nevertheless, we fully expect that the revised system will be fully operational and will be serving us as well in the future as it has in the past.

Editors' Note: The following chapter builds on this one by discussing at length the issues surrounding incentive bonuses.

ADDITIONAL SOURCES

Also see Additional Sources for Chapter 34.

Berg, Norman A. "What's Different about Conglomerate Management?" *Harvard Business Review*, November–December 1969, p. 112.

DeWitt, Frank. "Measuring Management Performance." *Management Accounting*, November 1972, p. 18.

Greiner, Larry E.; Leitch, D. Paul; and Barnes, Louis B. "Putting Judgment Back into Decisions." *Harvard Business Review*, March–April 1970, p. 59.

Thompson, Paul H., and Dalton, Gene W. "Performance Appraisal: Managers Beware." *Harvard Business Review*, January–February 1970, p. 149.

34

Incentive Bonuses as a
Management Tool

David Kraus*

You are a top executive—possibly the controller, but maybe even chairperson of the board. A large part of your job consists of getting things done through others. How do you do it?

Well, in business, you have the carrot and the stick with which to work. Most of the managerial tools for motivation fall into one or the other of these categories. This chapter deals with one of the most powerful of the "positive" motivators and one of the most significant of the management control tools in the large, modern corporation—the executive incentive bonus.

The three sections that follow review the role of incentive bonuses in the total executive pay package, discuss plan design and administration in detail, and outline bonus payout and tax implications. A fourth and final section speculates on new developments, particularly the emergence of the long-term executive incentive plan.

ROLE OF BONUSES IN TOTAL EXECUTIVE
PAY PACKAGE

The total compensation program for top executives typically consists of four main elements: base salary, incentive bonus, capital accumulation opportunity, and benefits and perquisites. Each of

---

* Mr. Kraus is a Principal of McKinsey & Company, Inc., in their Chicago office.

these elements fulfills a different purpose in meeting the three primary objectives of executive compensation, that is, attracting, retaining, and motivating (Exhibit 1).

EXHIBIT 1
Roles of Executive Compensation Elements

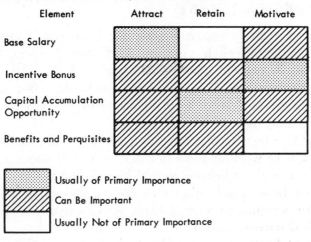

Element	Attract	Retain	Motivate
Base Salary	Usually of Primary Importance		Can Be Important
Incentive Bonus	Can Be Important	Can Be Important	Usually of Primary Importance
Capital Accumulation Opportunity	Can Be Important	Usually of Primary Importance	Can Be Important
Benefits and Perquisites	Can Be Important	Can Be Important	Usually Not of Primary Importance

Usually of Primary Importance

Can Be Important

Usually Not of Primary Importance

Base salary is most important in attracting executives to the company. Thereafter, it has some motivational impact through merit increases, but salary does not directly provide specific rewards for achievement of goals.

The incentive bonus, of course, has motivation as its primary purpose; at the same time, a bonus opportunity may also help in attracting and keeping people.

Capital accumulation opportunities (usually in the form of stock options) provide a deferred reward that is forfeited if the executive leaves the company. Thus, although a stock option might also have motivational value, its primary purpose usually is to retain executives.

Employee benefits and executive perquisites may sometimes be important in attracting and retaining key people, but they usually do not have significant motivational value, since the same provisions generally apply to all people at any given level in the organization.

Thus, incentive bonuses are the only element in the executive pay package aimed squarely at motivation. But, even so, bonuses are not necessarily appropriate for all companies, nor are they of equal importance in all companies. The balance of this section reviews where bonus plans are best used and how important they ought to be in terms of the size of bonuses and number of plan participants.

Where Are Bonuses Effective?

The most recent "Top Management Executive Compensation Survey," conducted each year by McKinsey & Company, Inc., showed that 78 percent of some 600 leading U.S. companies have incentive bonus plans. Why do these companies offer such plans while others do not? And, why do incentive plans work better in some companies than in others?

Experience suggests that ideally, five criteria should be met if a bonus plan is to work at top efficiency as a motivator. In practice, at least three of these criteria should be satisfied before a company introduces a bonus plan; otherwise, the disadvantages and difficulties of plan administration will likely outweigh the benefits. Each criterion is discussed below.

1. *Critical business factors should be controllable in the short term.* It stands to reason that bonuses can only achieve their motivational objective if the bonus recipient can indeed affect the desired outcomes. However, some businesses can be overwhelmingly influenced by outside forces. For example, banks can be at the mercy of interest rates, and activity in the construction industry depends on economic conditions. Other industries, in contrast, are naturals for incentive compensation in that short-term profit results closely reflect management's performance. These might include, for example, the cosmetics, home appliance, and apparel industries.

2. *The decision-result cycle should be one year or less for most key decisions.* Bonus plans are generally tied to the company's profit performance for the fiscal year. In order for bonuses to be meaningful, management's decisions and activities during the year should be reflected in year-end profits. But in some businesses—mainly in the capital-intensive industries—the most important decisions are very long term. For example, the success of an electric utility often depends on how well the executives have projected their customers' long-term power requirements, and on whether they have built power plants to meet those requirements and lined up fuel supplies

to produce the power. Usually, the correctness of these decisions cannot be assessed for 10 or 20 years. This is one of the main reasons bonus plans are so rare in utility companies. On the other hand, bonuses are used extensively in other industries that have shorter decision-result cycles, such as autos, fashion apparel, and retailing.

3. *Most decisions should be made by individuals.* Bonuses work best when rewards can be based on individual performance and contribution. Some companies are organized so that decisions and results are easily traceable to individual, specific people. These companies are usually well suited for an incentive bonus plan. Other companies may have "one-person rule" without any delegation of decision-making authority; or the company may rely heavily on committees that share responsibility for decisions. Either approach would probably preclude an incentive bonus from being used effectively.

4. *Information systems should provide a sound basis for judging individual performance.* Unless a company's processes for planning, budgeting, reporting profit and loss, and appraising executive performance are sound, bonuses will be based largely on discretionary judgment. While judgment is always needed, and is in fact desirable, it is critical that judgments be based on sound and objective measures in which the bonus participants have confidence. Otherwise, the bonus plan will lose its effectiveness as a positive motivational force, and become a negative, counterproductive factor.

5. *Management should be willing to make distinctions in pay among individuals.* Administering an incentive bonus plan forces management to make difficult decisions about individual bonus awards. Any tendency to treat everyone alike, in effect, penalizes the good performers and waters down the effectiveness of a bonus plan. Where the management style is extremely egalitarian, a bonus plan will likely not be a true incentive for motivating individuals, but rather a form of profit sharing aimed at rewarding the executive group as a whole.

If these criteria are generally met, a company is usually a good candidate for a bonus plan. If not, a bonus plan should probably not be introduced.

Similarly, the criteria outlined above suggest how important the incentive plan should be in terms of the size of bonuses and number of plan participants. Generally, the more the five criteria are met within a particular company, the larger the bonus should be in size and the more people should participate in the plan.

How Large Should Bonuses Be?

Measured as a percent of salary, bonuses vary considerably by industry. In industries where bonuses are important—for example, autos, retailing, and textiles—bonuses for the chief executive officer are 40 or 50 percent of salary in a normal or average year, and can run to 100 percent of salary and even beyond in an outstanding year. In banks and utilities, however, CEO bonuses—if they exist —are usually much smaller, perhaps 20 or 25 percent of salary in an average year.

This does not necessarily mean that such companies pay their executives less since, to some extent, bonuses are taken into account in establishing salary levels. That is, companies that do not have a bonus plan tend to pay higher salaries than companies that have such plans. In fact, it is usually wise to focus on total cash pay— salary plus bonus—when comparing the relative value of pay programs.

As a general rule, bonus, as a percent of salary, is largest for the top executive (CEO) and is scaled downward to the lowest level plan participant. For example, if the CEO's normal bonus opportunity is 40 percent of salary, the opportunity for the lowest level participant, perhaps a plant manager, might be 15 or 20 percent of salary.

This scaling down of the bonus opportunity from top to bottom level participants makes sense from several standpoints. First, it recognizes that decisions made at higher levels in the organization have more impact on company profits. Second, it takes into account the impact of the progressive income tax on after-tax pay. Third, it recognizes that top executives can better afford to have more of their pay at risk under a bonus plan, rather than in the more certain form of salary.

Who Should Participate?

Not surprisingly, the companies that are best suited to a bonus plan tend to have the largest plans in terms of number of participants. In general, to qualify for a bonus the individual should occupy a position that has a definite, "measurable" impact on profits. Obviously, the number of people who meet that criterion depends on the industry and the management style of the company.

In the average industrial company, we might expect only one percent of the employees to participate, that is, approximately the top 200 people in a company with 20,000 total employment. Depending on industry, organization, and other factors, however, the number of participants might be as few as 10 or 15, perhaps in a functionally organized utility, or as many as 1,000 in a diversified company broken down into many small profit centers.

PLAN DESIGN AND ADMINISTRATION ISSUES

Once a company has decided what role bonuses should play in its executive compensation program, the details of plan design and administration need to be addressed. In a one-product company, designing and administering a plan is fairly straightforward. However, large, multidivisional companies often have a complex problem on their hands when they opt for an executive incentive plan.

The example of one large midwestern corporation illustrates how bonus plans can fail to achieve the intended motivational impact. This particular company was originally in the quarry and foundry businesses. Over time, many new operations were added in a variety of diverse industries. Still, the corporation continued to rely on a single incentive bonus plan for all of its management group. The plan provided for a total executive bonus pool of up to 2 percent of all pretax profits in excess of a 10 percent pretax return on shareholders' equity.

Under this plan, the bonus fund was allocated to the plan participants by top management on a judgmental, discretionary basis, taking into account individual performance and the profit contribution of the participants' divisions. One year, which was a disappointing one for two major divisions, corporate earnings were too small to generate a bonus pool or fund under the formula. Although another smaller division had an outstanding year, no bonus funds were available to recognize its profit contribution. The next year, when corporate profits were up, executives throughout the company were rewarded—including those of several poorly performing divisions. Not surprisingly, the bonus plan was a source of discontent among many of the division executives and top management was concerned that the plan was losing its motivational value.

Many companies that have diversified and decentralized their organization face similar problems. The central question is how to reward executives fairly when their divisions participate in dissimilar industries. In terms of bonus plan design, the answer to this question depends on how the division or department bonus funds or pools are established.

Specifically, there are usually four major issues that top management needs to resolve in dealing with the question of division bonus funds:

Should there be one overall corporate incentive plan or should separate plans be established for each division?

What quantitative measure (e.g., return on investment, achievement of profit plan) should be used in establishing the incentive compensation funds?

What impact should corporate profits have on division bonuses?

What role should judgment play in establishing incentive funds?

Each of these issues is discussed in turn in the following four sections.

Overall Plan versus Separate Plans

One of the most difficult problems in designing an incentive compensation plan lies in adequately recognizing and taking into account fundamental differences that may exist among the company's businesses. The issue is whether this can be achieved with one overall corporate plan or whether separate plans need to be designed for each division.

The divisions of some companies are similar in terms of executive skills required, technology, markets, profitability, growth potential, and the like. These companies are fortunate in that one incentive plan may meet the needs of the entire company. This, of course, eases administration, simplifies communication of the plan, and provides visible evidence of internal compensation equity across the company.

But, most diversified companies need to tailor the incentive plan to the realities of each of the businesses. Differences in growth potential, variations in profitability, impact of uncontrollables, difficulty of planning, and differences in competitive pay patterns must be reflected in the incentive plan if it is to be an effective executive motivator. A sound approach often is to establish an overall program to be used throughout the company, but vary it as needed for some divisions.

For example, many diversified companies use a corporate-wide total cash compensation structure that encompasses base salary ranges and guideline bonus opportunities (Exhibit 2). Executive positions throughout the company are assigned to grades in the structure based on competitive pay levels in their particular industry and internal position evaluation. Under this approach, division in-

EXHIBIT 2
Total Cash Compensation Structure

Position Grade	Guideline Total Cash Compensation*	Salary Range Midpoint	Guideline Bonus Percentage
16.......	$50,000	$38,500	30%
15.......	42,500	34,000	25
14.......	35,000	29,000	20
13.......	29,000	25,000	15
•	•	•	•
•	•	•	•

* Salary plus bonus.

centive plans are designed to provide guideline bonuses if performance targets are met, no bonuses or less than guideline if performance falls short, and above guideline amounts if performance exceeds targets.

However, a company may have some divisions that compete in industries where bonuses are typically a large proportion of total cash compensation and others where there is less emphasis on incentives and more on salary. These differences can be taken into account using the framework of the total cash compensation structure by varying the salary and bonus components as they apply to the divisions. In the structure shown in Exhibit 2, guideline total cash compensation for Grade 15 of $42,500 is achieved through a $34,000 salary range midpoint, plus a 25 percent guideline bonus opportunity. If it wished, the company could vary the structure to suit the needs of a division where there should be greater emphasis on incentives. For example, $42,500 guideline total cash compensation could also be achieved through a salary midpoint of $29,500 plus a 45 percent guideline bonus opportunity.

A medium-size, diversified company headquartered in Texas provides another example of how, within an overall corporate approach, an incentive compensation plan can accommodate fundamental differences among its businesses. Because of the importance this com-

EXHIBIT 3
Varying Incentive Plan "Leverage" by Division

Division Bonus Fund
(percent of guideline
fund earned)

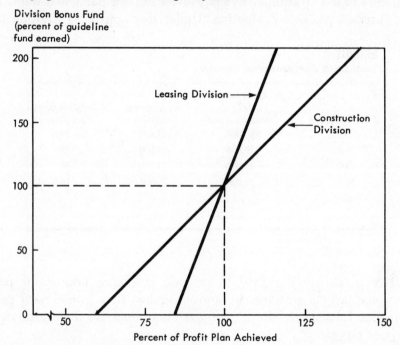

Percent of Profit Plan Achieved

pany attaches to annual profit plans, its incentive plan is based on the divisions' achievement of planned profits. However, the ability of the divisions to plan their profits effectively varies considerably. At one extreme, the construction division faces many uncontrollable influences that impact on profits and make planning difficult (strikes, weather, performance of subcontractors, and the like). For this division, profit results anywhere from 90 to 110 percent of plan are rightly regarded as "close to plan." At the other extreme, in the leasing division, most of the revenue and profits are already "locked in" at the beginning of each plan year. Consequently, annual profit planning is relatively easy—results below 90 percent of plan are regarded as disastrous and results above 110 percent are outstanding. Although the company has one overall approach, they vary the "leverage" in the incentive plan to reflect differences in difficulty of planning (Exhibit 3).

Quantitative Measures

Companies generally use one of four approaches for determining the level of bonus awards: (1) absolute profitability, (2) profit improvement, (3) performance versus industry, and (4) achievement of target or plan. One or a combination of these approaches will usually be appropriate depending on the individual company.

Absolute Profitability. It is fairly common to establish a bonus fund equal to some percentage of profits in excess of a minimum return or "set aside." Net after-tax income and return on shareholders' equity are often used in corporate plans, but these generally are not meaningful concepts at the division level. Instead, the measure usually used for divisions is pretax profits as a percentage of either gross or net assets or some other measure of corporate "investment" in the division.

This is, of course, an absolute measure, not a relative one. It ignores profit improvement relative to prior years, performance relative to the industry, and performance relative to a plan or objective. It rewards the executive group solely on the basis of whether they achieve a satisfactory rate of return. Further, it assumes that the role of division executives is to maximize the rate of return on the corporation's investment in the subsidiary or division.

This approach for division bonus plans is most suitable for the diversified corporation that operates like a holding company with a "portfolio" of businesses. However, most diversified companies do not act merely as a holding company with a portfolio of investments. To one degree or another, they manage their businesses. And, although division executives enjoy a certain degree of autonomy and retain responsibility for profits, their responsibility is in fact limited by the division's role and mission as part of a total corporation.

But even divisions whose primary role is to contribute current profits are often constrained by corporate requirements that benefit the total company but reduce short-term division profits. For example:

   Capital allocation decisions of a U.S. company with extensive mining and refining interests have favored long payback investments in a growth business over several attractive short-term opportunities in their more mature businesses.

   A Midwest retail chain with manufacturing plants levies substantial charges on divisions for products and services provided by the corporate staff and requires divisions to market exclusively the products of its "captive" plants at company-established prices.

Accordingly, it may or may not be appropriate to base division bonuses on an absolute level of profitability, depending on how the company is organized and managed. When the corporation operates like a holding company, this approach can provide a powerful incentive for division executives. But where the company is closely integrated and divisions are more actively "managed," it is usually better to establish bonuses on some other measure that focuses on the results that are controllable by division management.

Profit Improvement.   Bonus plans are sometimes based on year-to-year profit improvement. For example, one company that manufactures and sells mobile homes has an incentive pool equal to 10 percent of all pretax profits that are in excess of the previous year's pretax profits. Although it can be appropriate and often works well, this approach has two main drawbacks.

First, executives may be motivated to "manage" earnings to their advantage or may reap undeserved rewards when a disastrous year is followed by a year of only modest recovery. For example, assume the company uses the bonus formula outlined above and there has been the following record of pretax profits and bonuses:

Year	Pretax Profits	Bonus Pool
1975	$2.5 million	
1976	3.5	$100,000
1977	1.5	None
1978	2.8	$130,000

Although a larger bonus pool was created for 1978 than for 1976, actual profits were much lower in 1978. This problem can be partially overcome by using a two- or three-year base, instead of just the prior year; but this introduces another problem—that an extremely good or bad year can influence the bonus plan during the next two or three years, instead of just the following year.

Another problem inherent in the year-to-year profit improvement approach is that it can fail to recognize differences among divisions in terms of their industry growth potential. The division manager who competes in a declining industry may be unjustly penalized even though he or she earns an extremely high return on investment.

Performance Versus Industry. Another fairly common approach is to establish bonus funds on the basis of profit performance as compared with other companies in the same industry. For example, a bonus fund might be established as $25,000 for each percentage point by which the company or division exceeds its industry in return on assets or profit improvement over the previous year. The "industry" basis for comparison is usually a specially prepared index of a selected group of competitive companies.

This approach has the advantage of factoring out external influences on the industry and other uncontrollables and thereby focuses more directly on the controllable aspects of management performance. But there are also some drawbacks. Often a division is constrained by corporate strategy from competing for profitable growth as aggressively as it otherwise might. For example, if a diversified company had both a typewriter subsidiary and an adding machine subsidiary, it might constrain each one from expanding into the business of the other. Or, the corporation's strategy within an industry might be to expand geographically through acquisition, rather than to allow its divisions to pursue geographic expansion.

Basing bonuses on performance relative to the industry can also have the equally undesirable effect of focusing the executives' attention on their specific, narrowly defined industry even if, in fact, they should be thinking about opportunities beyond their traditional activities. For example, it might be a mistake to reward executives for outperforming companies in a declining or unprofitable industry if other more attractive opportunities exist in another industry.

This raises another question about the use of industry performance measures. Is it fair to shareholders to pay bonuses when profits are better than for other companies in the industry but still not up to a satisfactory level?

In addition to these considerations, there are some practical problems in implementing a bonus program based on profit performance relative to an industry group. Precise data on the profit performance of direct competitors is often difficult to obtain.

Despite these problems, tying bonuses to performance relative to the industry is the best approach in some situations. Obviously, it is only appropriate if the company's mission is to focus primarily on the opportunities in a fairly well-defined industry. It would be less suitable for companies pursuing profit-making opportunities through a wide variety of products and services. This basis for determining bonuses often works best in regulated industries, such as insurance, utilities, and banking because business activities are usually specifically defined and accounting conventions are uniform.

Achievement of Target or Plan. The fourth approach is to base bonuses on the achievement of planned profits, a profit target or objective, or a budgeted profit figure. This is consistent with the practice common among diversified companies of managing and controlling operations through a planning process. Fairly autonomous division managers prepare an annual profit plan together with a proposed program of capital expenditures. Corporate management ensures that the plan conforms to corporate strategy and establishes any necessary constraints. The profit plan then serves as a charter for division heads; their major task for the year is to achieve the plan.

Bonuses are usually tied to the planning process by establishing a "normal" or "standard" bonus pool to be awarded if the division achieves its planned profit. For example, it might be agreed that the division would receive a $60,000 bonus fund if it achieves 100 percent of its planned profit. A minimum acceptable level of performance is also established (expressed as a percentage of planned profits), below which no bonuses will be paid. Assuming that the minimum acceptable profit level is 70 percent of plan, the division would then receive a bonus fund of $2,000 for every percentage point by which its profits exceeded 70 percent of plan. Accordingly, if profits were 80 percent of plan, the fund would be $20,000; if profits were 130 percent of plan, the fund would be $120,000.

Inasmuch as profit planning is the central process through which many diversified companies are managed, it often makes extremely good sense to base incentives on achievement of planned profits. The advantage is that the profit plan itself takes into account the key factors that are beyond the control of division executives:

The division's role in the total corporation and the constraints placed on division executives by corporate management;

External conditions that can be foreseen at the beginning of the year; or

Differences in the profit opportunities available to each division.

Incentives are consistent with the company organization and central management process, and since bonuses are based on assigned tasks and objectives, the incentive plan can be a powerful managerial tool for corporate top management.

This approach is conceptually sound for diversified companies that are organized into divisional profit centers and that use business planning as the major tool controlling the activities of divisions. The main drawbacks to basing bonuses on achievement of plans stem from difficulties in administration.

In many companies, planning skills have not developed to a uniform level of effectiveness throughout the company; accordingly, division plans may differ in terms of the difficulty or may not even have sufficient meaning to serve as a basis for bonuses. Moreover, basing bonuses on achievement of planned profits can present an opportunity for "gamesmanship" on the part of both division and corporate executives. For example, unless corporate management has enough detailed knowledge to rigorously review proposed profit plans, the divisions can submit "easy" plans in order to assure themselves of bonuses.

Nonetheless, many diversified companies have found that these administrative difficulties can be overcome and that incentive compensation can reinforce planning as the central management process in the company.

Combination of Measures. Sometimes it makes sense to use more than one quantitative measure of performance. For example, a diversified company found that rapid growth and the capital requirements of a leasing business were placing a severe strain on their capital structure and decided that many of the nonleasing businesses should focus on earning a significantly higher return on assets. Accordingly, the division bonus plans, which were based on achieving planned profits, were modified so that 50 percent of the bonus fund was based on return on assets and 50 percent on achievement of planned profits. Although more emphasis on ROA could have been achieved through the profit-planning process, making this major and visible change in the division bonus arrangements provided a strong and clear signal from top management as to what they thought was important.

But adding factors to the bonus formula to achieve refinement and precision can be carried too far. As the bonus plan becomes more complex, its incentive value is usually diminished because, although one or two simple measures can be clearly communicated to and understood by plan participants, a complex series of measures and formulas is often confusing.

Impact of Corporate Results on Division Bonuses

"In our company, division bonus funds are based primarily on division performance. That way, a person's bonus is based on the results over which he or she has control. Our people know what they have to do to earn a bonus and they know that if they do the job for us, the bonuses will be there." So speaks a corporate vice president who heads a group of divisions in a major diversified company. This vice president is providing one answer to the question of whether overall corporate results should affect division bonuses and, if so, how much. But there is no universal right answer.

Some executives and company directors resist the concept of basing division bonus funds largely on division performance. But the fact is that to attract, retain, and motivate the caliber of executives needed to operate significant businesses with a high degree of autonomy, companies need to be able to grant assurances that people will be paid according to their own performance. The concept of a "total company" and its performance can be pretty obscure to an executive toiling away in a $30 million division of a $5 billion conglomerate. Tying his or her bonus to the profits of the total company is not much different than relating it to the Dow Jones stock price average.

The concept of divisional or subsidiary bonus plans is particularly relevant for the large multinational company. An executive who heads a profitable operation in Germany, for example, will have great difficulty identifying with an ailing parent headquarters company in Chicago. In this regard, it is interesting to note that many corporate executives and directors who resist the notion of incentive plans for their U.S. divisions have no difficulty with the concept when it applies to their overseas units.

Moreover, the design of the incentive bonus plan should be

viewed in the context of a total compensation program. Many executive compensation programs are deliberately designed to provide a balance among long-term, total-company incentives and short-term, division-oriented incentives. Many division executives appropriately participate in long-term, total-company incentives, such as stock options or performance shares. This stake in the total company should be taken into account when considering how much weight to give division performance in the design of the short-term annual incentive plan.

A key to gaining acceptance of the concept of division bonuses based on division performance is to distinguish clearly this arrangement from the incentive plan for corporate executives. Clearly, the pay for corporate executives, such as the chairman, the CEO, and staff whose responsibilities encompass all of the company's operations, should be tied to total-company performance.

Despite the logic of this argument, however, from a practical standpoint in some situations it may still be desirable to establish some minimum level of company performance (e.g., breaking even, maintaining the dividend) below which no bonuses will be paid—even in divisions whose performance is outstanding.

Role of Discretionary Judgment

The approaches for determining incentive funds discussed up to this point represent quantitative measures of performance that can be reduced to a formula (Exhibit 4). Indeed, most bonus plans utilize some "hard" standard to measure performance objectively and to determine arithmetically the amount of a bonus fund. But what role does discretionary judgment play in determining the amount of the bonus fund when that fund is tied to an objective measure or formula? The fact is that most companies with bonus plans either figure out in advance or learn painfully through experience that executive compensation administration, to be effective, must be a judgmental and not an arithmetical process.

In trying to deal with these complexities, a few companies have gone the route of adding more factors to their bonus formulas. But, a simple and objectively determined performance measure is the best in terms of incentive value. Accordingly, the element of judgment should be used sparingly and only where it will be understood and accepted by executives.

Not surprisingly, plans that appear to be most effective are based

EXHIBIT 4
Quantitative Approaches to Determining Bonuses

A. Profit Improvement

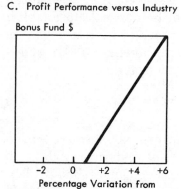

B. Absolute Profitability

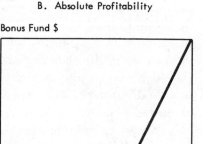

C. Profit Performance versus Industry

D. Achievement of Target or Plan

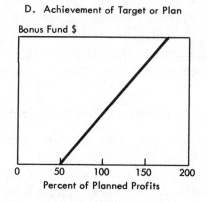

on a formula, but provide for top management adjustments on an exception basis. Under these plans, one or occasionally two of the best measures of performance are used in the formula. Then, at the end of the plan year, top management or a compensation committee of the board of directors considers other factors, and if they conclude that the formula obviously and clearly did not produce a sensible result, they adjust the bonus fund. Following are some of the factors that can be taken into account judgmentally at the end of the plan year:

Quantitative measures of performance not included in the formula, such as return on investment, meeting plan or budget, and profit improvement over the previous year;

Operating performance measures such as market share and inventory turnover;

Nonquantitative achievements, such as organization planning, executive development, and community relations;

Decisions to incur major expenses this year that benefit future profits (e.g., in maintenance or research; and, conversely, significant expenses that were avoided but should have been incurred; and

Uncontrollable external influences, such as regulatory actions, strikes, materials shortages, and accounting and tax changes.

In summary, the major issues that must be resolved in designing and administering an executive incentive plan revolve around one overall plan or separate plans for each division, appropriate quantitative performance measures, establishing the impact that corporate results should have on division bonuses, and the role of discretionary judgment. Unfortunately, there are no universal solutions or recipes, nor is it likely that what works in one company can be effectively transferred to another. Rather, each issue must be thought through and resolved to fit the unique circumstances that exist in each company. Nonetheless, the experiences of diversified companies that successfully use executive incentive bonuses suggest these general guidelines for incentive plan design and administration:

An overall corporate approach modified and tailored, as needed, to meet the needs of individual businesses;

Quantitative measures of performance that correspond to each division's role and mission within a total corporate strategy;

A mix of emphasis on corporate and division results that reflects each division's autonomy or integration within the total company; and

Provision that discretionary judgment, as well as quantitative measures, be used in reaching decisions on bonuses.

Finally, most companies are dynamic institutions, usually growing, and almost always still evolving in terms of approaches to organization and management. It only follows that the incentive compensation plan should be kept up to date to accurately reflect the goals which the executives are intended to achieve.

BONUS PAYOUTS AND TAX IMPLICATIONS

Although the success of the bonus plan will depend most heavily on the plan design and administration issues discussed above, another variable will also influence the effectiveness of the plan; that is, how and when the bonus is actually paid to the executive.

Most companies have answered the question of "how" by paying the bonus in the form of cash, although some companies prefer to use stock or perhaps giving the executive the option of taking stock if he so desires. Generally, even companies that pay stock bonuses pay part of the bonus in cash—usually half—so the executive can pay the tax on the bonus. In either case, cash or stock, the tax consequences are the same for both the executive and the company. The individual's bonus is taxed as ordinary "personal service" income subject to a maximum federal tax rate of 50 percent, while the company treats the bonus as a tax deductible expense.

As to when the bonus is paid, most companies reason that the motivational impact of the bonus is greatest when the reward follows immediately upon achievement of the goals. As a consequence, bonuses are generally distributed as quickly as possible after the end of the plan year, as soon as audited statements are available. For companies whose fiscal year is the calendar year, this usually means distribution of bonus checks in February or March.

In order to maximize the motivational mileage of the bonus plan, most companies review and discuss the participant's performance and explain how the bonus amount was determined when the bonus checks are distributed. This is also often an ideal time to discuss the individual's goals, objectives, and performance standards for the coming year.

Most companies pay the total bonus as a lump sum, but some prefer to pay the bonus in installments, over perhaps three or five years. A variation is to pay part of an executive's bonus in the form of phantom stock units, the value of which is usually paid out in installments after the individual retires.

Proponents of the deferred bonus claim that it is useful in retaining executives—that is, the plan can be designed so the executive loses any unpaid bonus installments if he leaves the company. The other supposed advantage is that the executive's income is "smoothed."

However, in most situations today, immediate payout of the entire bonus is preferable in order to underscore the motivational value of the plan. Bonuses are not the best instrument for retaining executives. Moreover, if a manager is sought by another company, or if the manager desperately wants to make a change, the loss of a deferred compensation balance usually does not stand in the way. As for income "smoothing," this runs directly counter to the purpose of the bonus, which is to provide variability in income based on performance.

Furthermore, there is usually little or no tax advantage to income deferral, and many executives would argue that because of subsequent salary increases and inflation, deferred income might even attract higher taxation later, even after retirement.

Still, companies should consider offering executives the *option* of deferring part or all of their bonus. This can occasionally be of advantage to executives who are close to retirement, and others with special personal financial situations. Moreover, such an option can usually be offered at little or no cost to the company. The company ordinarily credits interest on deferred account balances, which, in effect, compensates the executive for the company's use of his money.

LOOKING AHEAD: LONG-TERM INCENTIVE PLANS

Up to this point, this chapter has dealt with executive incentive bonus plans, as used today as a management tool. In closing, it may well be useful to look ahead a bit and speculate on what might lie ahead in the area of bonuses.

One trend is fairly clear. In private industry at least, the use of executive incentive arrangements is increasing. Each year a larger proportion of companies appears to have such plans. Perhaps as a consequence, plan design and administration are improving. Companies are becoming more sophisticated with bonuses and are getting more mileage out of bonus dollars spent. This, in turn, reflects better management practices generally, that is, in organization, planning and control, and performance appraisal, that permit sound bonus plan administration.

The increasing popularity of bonuses will probably be reflected in the number of people who participate in such plans. That is, use of bonuses will be extended not only to more companies but also to more executives within each company. This will occur as improved control systems enable the company to measure accurately the contribution of an increasing number of people within the organization.

Perhaps the most promising and interesting future trend in executive incentives is the notion of long-term incentives. Historically, practically all incentive bonus plans have been designed to function within the context of a company's fiscal year. Objectives or targets were established for a one-year time frame and performance measured and bonuses paid at the end of the year. This, of course, has been quite convenient in that:

Plans and budgets have been geared to the fiscal year;

Bonuses can be accrued and charged to earnings for the year earned, which is tidy from an accounting standpoint; and

Measurement of profit performance can be based on audited financial statements.

Despite this neatness and convenience, however, it is in reality somewhat arbitrary to base bonuses on annual performance. The year—365 days—is of critical importance to astronomers, accountants, and the IRS, but for many companies it has nothing whatsoever to do with the length of the natural business cycle, the time lag between business decisions and results, or the time frame over which planning should be done.

Fortunately, the circumstances that emerged in the early 1970s forced many companies and compensation specialists to take a new look at long-term incentives. A major precipitating event was the Tax Reform Act of 1969. This act seriously undermined the value of stock options, which have traditionally served as the primary long-term incentive plan in most corporations. In looking for a substitute for stock options, companies began to realize that stock is not the most effective incentive device, in and of itself, since the individual executive may have very little control over the stock price.

An alternative concept known as *performance shares* was developed by compensation specialists (most notably, George H. Foote of McKinsey & Company) and has emerged as an important new concept during the past four or five years. Under this approach, awards of stock shares are made to executives and "earned out" over four or five years if performance targets, say growth in earnings per share, are achieved. The performance shares have much the same appeal as stock options in that they provide a long-term, stock-related total company incentive; however, they tie the executive's reward to a variable over which the executive has more control, and they avoid the investment risks associated with traditional stock options.

While performance shares or other longer term incentive plans will probably never totally replace the annual cash incentive bonus, they will undoubtedly become more popular in the future, particularly in industries where the natural business cycle is relatively protracted. A few companies are already exploring ways to revise their annual cash bonus plans to place more emphasis on the long term.

Looking ahead, as business management becomes more complex and as business decisions extend further into the future, we can expect further development of the long-term incentive plan as a significant management tool.

ADDITIONAL SOURCES

Baker, John C. "Are Corporate Executives Overpaid?" *Harvard Business Review*, July–August 1977, p. 51.

Dearden, John. "How to Make Incentive Plans Work." *Harvard Business Review*, July–August 1972, p. 117.

Ellig, Bruce R. "Laying the Groundwork for Executive Compensation Programs." *Financial Executive*, October 1975, p. 30.

Hettenhouse, George W. "Cost/Benefit Analysis of Executive Compensation." *Harvard Business Review*, July–August 1970, p. 114.

Kraus, David. "The 'Devaluation' of the American Executive." *Harvard Business Review*, May–June 1976, p. 84.

———. "Making Executives' Incentives Effective in Diversified Companies." *Financial Executive*, June 1977, p. 32.

Murthy, K. R. Srinivasa, and Salter, Malcolm S. "Should CEO Pay Be Linked to Results?" *Harvard Business Review*, May–June 1975, p. 66.

Patton, Arch. "Executive Compensation: The Past, Present and Future." *Financial Executive*, July 1976, p. 24.

———. "Why Incentive Plans Fail." *Harvard Business Review*, May–June 1972, p. 58.

Reum, W. Robert, and Reum, Sherry Milliken. "Employee Stock Ownership Plans: Pluses and Minuses." *Harvard Business Review*, July–August 1976, p. 133.

Roberts, Reed M. "Tie Bonuses to Corporate Profits." *Financial Executive*, June 1973, p. 12.

Salter, Malcolm S. "Tailor Incentive Compensation to Strategy." *Harvard Business Review*, March–April 1973, p. 94.

35

Measuring the Profitability of Marketing

John F. Bohnsack*

Strictly speaking, marketing profits, manufacturing profits, or the profits of any single function in a business do not exist. Profits result from the integrated efforts and contributions of all activities in the business. Only the chief executive or general manager, exercising stewardship, is responsible to the owners of the business for profits of the total enterprise. It is true, however, that the top executive in the business can charge subordinates with the responsibility of contributing to the profits of the total business, but this does not abrogate or diminish total profit responsibility, and it is within this concept that the measurement of marketing profit responsibility will be discussed.

Differences among businesses are many, and diversity precludes the development of a standardized measurement approach. While research and experience have shown that the difficulties encountered in measuring the profitability of the total business become magnified when dealing with its parts, it is the author's conviction that the difficulties do not stem from technical shortcomings of designed measurements but rather from deficiencies in the planning, communicating, and integrating skills of managers. Therefore, it is the author's objective to present concepts which should be useful as theoretical underpinnings for the establishment of practical, financially oriented measurements of marketing activities. The con-

* Mr. Bohnsack is Manager, Distribution Services, Housewares and Audio Business Division, General Electric Company, Bridgeport, Connecticut.

cepts can be applied in any well-organized and managed business which has a product to market.

The Purpose, Objectives, and Goals of a Business and Their Relationship to Marketing

The post–World War II development of modern marketing theory and practice has had a significant influence on the concept of profitability and, indeed, the management of business. The marketing concept which postulates the idea that the principal purpose of a business is not to generate profits but to create and keep customers is profound; yet, in a sense, it is a perplexing and an inadequate guide to the measurement of marketing profitability.

The real objective of a business is *survival*, and profits are the necessary sustenance. Theodore Levitt pointed out:

> Profit is neither an encompassing nor prescriptive statement of business purpose. Profit is merely the result or outcome of business activity. It says nothing about what the activity itself must be. To say that a business exists to produce profits for its owners offers no prescription regarding how to do it. Profits are a consequence of business action, not a guide to what that action should be. The only legitimate guide to action, a guide as to how to balance and accommodate the inevitably conflicting requisites of the various functional entities within a large organization, is the corporate purpose, the goal and ends of the corporation and the strategies that have been devised to achieve them.
>
> Profit cannot be a corporate goal. Indeed, profit properly viewed cannot even be treated as a consequence of business action. Profit is the requisite of corporate life.[1]

The thought is similar to that expressed by Peter Drucker some years ago:

> It is the first duty of a business to survive. The guiding principle of economics, in other words, is not the maximization of profits; it is the avoidance of loss. Business enterprise must produce the premium to cover the risks involved in its operation. And there is only one source of this risk premium: Profits.[2]

---

[1] Theodore Levitt, *The Marketing Mode; Pathways to Corporate Growth* (New York: McGraw Hill, Inc., 1969).

[2] Peter F. Drucker, *The Practice of Management* (New York: Harper & Bros., 1954), p. 46.

Such concepts do not relegate profits to a place of unimportance. Indeed, Professor Frank Knight of the University of Chicago has characterized profits as the carrots that induce entrepreneurs to endure uncertainty. Professor Joseph A. Schumpeter of Harvard has described profits as the juice behind capitalism's process of dynamic innovation.[3]

Profits, yes; but how much? If we were to survey various members of our society, the responses would probably be of little help. The answers could well range from a "reasonable profit," however difficult that would be to define, to the "maximization of profits," however egocentric that might be. Contemporary business executives and economists simply do not agree. For example, few corporate executives would admit to it, but some economists have even suggested that profits are deliberately held down, although no doubt not enough to risk the wrath of creditors, stockholders, or the board of directors. This view, of course, is at variance with traditional economic theory which holds that competitive forces, not management, are the constraints which will serve to hold profits to a return in the form of interest on the capital used and a management fee.

With due respect to all the various theories concerning profits and profitability, in the final analysis the task of establishing profitability objectives falls to the owners and managers of the business. It is not only their prerogative but indeed their duty. If the enterprise is to remain viable, and the real business of business is to remain alive, profits must be sufficient enough to attract not only the necessary capital but entrepreneurial leadership as well. The first step is the establishment of profit objectives and goals. And, once they are established, they must be communicated and understood along with the other objectives of the business by cognizant managers in all functions.[4] Realistic and successful measurement of a business or its components is dependent on effective communication of the objectives and goals, and before embarking on any program of measurements it is of the utmost importance that agreement be reached among all parties measuring and being measured.

While the preceeding statements might appear redundant, the

---

[3] Leonard Silk, "Profits are Carrots, Juices and Rewards," *New York Times,* February 11, 1973.

[4] For an excellent discussion of financial measurement systems applicable to functions, see Richard F. Vancil, "What Kind of Management Control Do You Need," *Harvard Business Review,* March–April 1973.

growth of executive placement firms (and for that matter, the number of marriage counselors and divorce lawyers) attests to the fact there frequently exists a lack of understanding between partners, executives, managers, and subordinates on objectives and goals as well as methods of achievement. The definition and communication of purpose, objectives, and goals do not insure success but they form the initial steps to be taken. Though simplistic as it might sound, one cannot reach a goal without knowing where one is supposed to go and when one is to be there. As a corollary, if the promise of rewards is a proper management tool, then both the manager and the subordinate must know in advance what determines the payoff.

What Is Marketing?

We are relating marketing and profitability, and while the marketing concept is not prescriptive in the establishment of profitability goals, its understanding and application can be vital to the growth and development of the business. Yet when we try to find a suitable definition of marketing as a function we run into some difficulty.

There appears to be no universally accepted definition of the *function* that does justice to the *concept*. It has been described as a business activity, a trade phenomenon, an economic process, an area of management responsibility, and the process in society whereby demand structure for economic goods and services is anticipated through the conception, promotion, exchange, and physical distribution of such goods and services. The American Marketing Association has defined marketing as: "The performance of business activities that direct the flow of goods and services from producer to consumer or user."[5] A desirable expansion of the latter definition would focus on those activities which are directed at determining and filling customer needs and wants, "the creating and keeping of customers." It is antiquarian to suggest even remotely that the marketing job is merely to dispose of what the producer has made or can make. This does not imply that every product or service is the result of conscious identification of what a customer needs or wants, but it is a rare case where a product or service and

---

[5] Committee on Definitions, *Marketing Definitions* (Chicago: American Marketing Association, 1960), p. 15.

its market are created spontaneously. Indeed, will even a so-called "natural" product, born of pure research or discovery, ever reach its maximum potential without market development? It is quite important for the controller to have and understand the meaning of marketing in its broadest sense because the most productive and challenging work of financial analysis and measurement will occur before the product or service is even created, the first sale made, or a market developed.

A further point concerning the scope of marketing needs to be made. The marketing job is to create customers—to fill the needs and wants of *consumers* and *users*. In the process, costs are incurred and value is added in terms of time, place, and possession utility. But the process does not end at the shipping dock. The *consumer* or *user* is frequently not the first *customer* of the producer. Other agencies, including distributors, dealers, jobbers, and financing institutions, are involved. The marketing job includes all the activities involved between the producer and the end customer, and if such activities are not directly performed, someone else must be hired to do the work. An evaluation must be made as to whether the correct services are being performed and the fee for performance is right. The costs of marketing activities under the direct control of the marketer are frequently the smaller part of the total. It is myopic for a producer to look at only those activities under his or her direct control, for there have been numerous situations where potential demand was not realized because the wrong agent or channel was used to reach markets or the price paid for the services was not realistic.

Therefore, when evaluating or measuring marketing it is suggested that the following activities and functions be considered a part of the total job, even though some work elements are not the responsibility of the marketing department.

1. Selling.
2. Advertising, merchandising, and sales promotion.
3. Product planning and appearance design.
4. Marketing research and administration.
5. Order service, customer billing, credits, and collections.
6. Warehousing, transportation, and delivery.
7. Warranty and product service.
8. Distributor, jobber, and dealer operations.

Although not in the scope of this chapter, it should be pointed out that nonfinancial measures and standards of performance for each marketing activity can also be developed for the measurement of marketing. For a discussion of this aspect of measurement the interested reader is referred to an American Management Association research study on this subject.[6]

Another measurement aspect is that of cost ratios. A question which frequently is raised concerning marketing activities is the amount, in relationship to sales, that should be incurred or is spent by other companies in the same industry. One source of information is the Conference Board. For example, the Marketing Cost Institute of the Conference Board has compiled, through cooperative surveys, landmarks of prevailing costs in various industries. The cost data have been made available to manufacturers who participated in the program and who have reported their data in confidence to the Institute's data bank.

The Controller's Role in Measuring the Profitability of Marketing

A review of the relatively few books dealing with marketing-financial relationships seems to have a common thread that deals with the need for improved information for marketing decisions and the development of a symbiotic relationship between the two functions. While the development of marketing theory and practice has been making its impact on American businesses, it is doubtful that the controller has lagged behind. I suggest that there has even been a quiet revolution taking place in the finance function which has had a dynamic impact on business performance and results. Although in the past the controller had been looked upon largely as a scorekeeper concerned principally with what has happened, the changing needs of business required a change in the controller's scope of work. The progressive controller has met the challenge. This has been done by identifying the kinds of information needed to manage the business, producing the data when needed, developing improved means for processing and transmitting that data, interpreting the data, and actively participating in the day-to-day

---

[6] Ernest C. Miller, *Objectives and Standards of Performance in Marketing Management,* American Management Association Research Study No. 85 (New York: American Management Association, 1967).

decisions and forward planning. All of these actions are particularly appropriate to marketing. Are there any decisions made by marketing that do not have an impact on profitability or which could not be improved by better and more timely financial data? But the controller's job fulfillment is different from that conceived by the past. It is forward looking.

After-the-fact reporting is still necessary for legal and custodial requirements, and the controller must still maintain objectivity and nonpartisanship among functions, but no controller worth his or her salt can afford the reputation of a second guesser. When the results are recorded and being reviewed it should afford the controller and staff members the opportunity for some introspection. Let them also stand up and be counted. How did they contribute to the results?

Similarly, the controller's role in the preservation of assets is expanded, for a 100 percent score on that facet of the job is insufficient. Did the assets grow? The controller's important work is performed at decision-making time when the implicit question is asked: "Will the exchange of an asset for a cost item, or one asset for another, for example, cash for sales promotion, or the investment in extended receivables through longer terms, create a customer and help the business survive and grow?" Obviously, the controller's job, as it pertains to marketing, is not a part-time or tangential avocation. Nor is it one to be delegated to the disinterested or incompetent. Marketing people are busy people—decision makers. Their pursuits make the business move, and the exigencies of modern business frequently require fast action and always good decisions. The need for relevant and timely data and good judgment is of paramount importance.

One approach to filling the needs of marketing has been the establishment of a marketing controller[7] or marketing financial analyst position whose basic function is to advise and counsel marketing on all matters having financial implications. It is a position with high analytical content and largely freed from routine accounting work. In effect, the position is attached to the marketing department and the incumbent lives in the arena of day-to-day marketing decisions. By so structuring the job, financial advice and counsel becomes more available to marketing and the results can be outstanding.

---

[7] For a complete discussion of this concept, see *The Marketing Controller Concept: An Inquiry into Financial-Marketing Relationships in Selected Consumer Companies* (Cambridge, Mass.: Marketing Science Institute, 1970).

Standard Measures of Profitability and Their Application to Marketing

In terms of profitability, it is essential that marketing have the same objectives and goals as the total business. Otherwise, the business is not being planned and managed properly because integration is lacking. This, of course, is consistent with the views expressed earlier. Profitability objectives and goals are established by a higher level in the business hierarchy and, in turn, are communicated down through the organization, and this is where the controller's job becomes critical.

As Richard F. Vancil has pointed out: "Figuring out the best way to define and measure the financial performance for each manager is the corporate controller's most challenging and analytically demanding task."[8]

Conceptually, the job of realistic profitability measurement is not really difficult if one accepts the premises already set forth or implied: (1) profits are a requisite of business survival; (2) the owners or authorized custodians have established and communicated long- and short-range profitability objectives and goals; and (3) the objectives assigned to the various functions are in harmony with the objectives of the total business.

Traditional measures of profitability for a total business which have been employed by accountants and financial analysts serve as a starting point in developing functional measurements. These include sales, net income, percent net income to sales, investment turnover, and return on invested capital. In the post–World War II period, return on investment has been given considerable emphasis because of its great relevance to the marketing concept. If business survival and growth, creating customers and keeping those customers, is the name of the game, the need for invested capital becomes obvious.

If investors evaluate their capital risks by such a measurement as return on investment, why shouldn't those requiring and competing for such capital use the same measurement, and why shouldn't the integral parts of the business use a measurement which is consistent with the objectives of the whole business? It is not suggested that any single, rigidly defined profitability measurement can be established for any function. The objective of the discussion which fol-

---

[8] Vancil, "What Kind of Management Control Do You Need," p. 76.

lows is to point out the relevance and the interdependence of the various measurements to the central financial objective of the business.

Relating profitability measures to the marketing function can be facilitated by an analysis of the return-on-investment formula, as depicted in Exhibit 1. The significant role which marketing directly plays on total profitability will soon become apparent, and, through synthesis, supplemental measures can be developed.

EXHIBIT 1
Return-on-Investment Formula

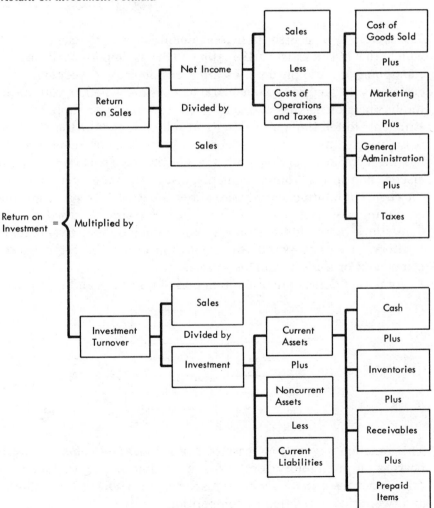

We will begin with sales. It has often been stated that nothing happens until a sale is made, and that is the first point of expansion of the measurement formula. Sales can be expressed in terms of total market and market share:

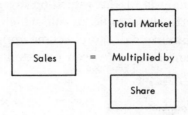

The first step, of course, is market definition and the segments in which the business is participating. This is important from the standpoint of basic purpose, creating customers and keeping those customers. In analyzing your markets, consider whether you are in the business of making and selling electric clocks or supplying instruments to tell time; of making and selling ranges or the business of supplying the means of preparing food. A clock manufacturer has the choice of serving only the electric clock market or both electric and spring wound segments, just as the range marketer has the choice of limiting activities to either the electric or gas segments or serving both segments. The market can also be divided into domestic, export, internal or external segments, and by channel, territory, and price point. An increase in either the total market component or share can increase sales.

Total sales dollars are also a function of unit sales and unit price:

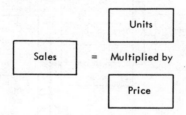

This function suggests at least two other measurements having a bearing on profitability: one, price on a time sequence, that is, a price index measured to a base year or comparison to cost indices; and two, price in relation to competition.

While the above might suggest that pricing action is a marketing responsibility, it is recognized that in some businesses final price approval is the reserved authority of general management. The fact that the positioning of pricing responsibility varies from business to business only serves to emphasize the point that measurements used to measure individuals and functions in a business must be tailored to the authority and responsibility peculiar to individual organizations.

Other related measures deal with product leadership and productivity. Product leadership, in many respects, is a measure of the innovative results of the total business. It is impossible to attribute the results in the area of product leadership to any one function of the business since, in general, the objective of a business should be to lead its industry in originating or applying the most advanced scientific or technical knowledge in the *engineering, manufacturing,* and *marketing* fields to the development of new products as well as improvement in the quality or value of existing products. With the development of the marketing concept and product planning as a marketing function, periodic product reviews have included an evaluation of the current and planned product offering vis-a-vis the best competitive offerings in terms of features, appearance, and functional design; ease and cost of manufacture; and quality and ease of maintenance. The measurement of product leadership can be expressed financially, after evaluating each product, by grouping the portion of total sales into those products which are superior, those equal to, and those inferior to the best competitive offering. A time series sequence of such data, looking both retrospectively and prospectively, will point out past performance as well as the job that needs to be done in the future.

Productivity in Marketing

Generally, productivity in a macroeconomic sense is measured by relating the *output* of goods and services to the *input* of human effort. A corresponding measurement for a particular business relates *output* (sales) to *inputs* of labor as well as other resources used. Obviously, many problems can arise in developing productivity measurements for portions of the total business and a complete discussion is beyond the scope of this chapter, but some discussion and a few words of caution are in order.

In measuring the selling activity it is sometimes proposed that sales per salesperson can be used as an index of performance. Because normally there is considerable leverage between contribution margin (sales less all variable costs) and selling costs, such a measurement could lead down the wrong path. It is quite likely that a decrease in productivity, if measured by sales per salesperson, could be desirable if it increased market penetration and improved market position. This is not to say that no attempt should be made to measure or increase the productivity of marketing, but the results should be considered in light of the other factors in the marketing mix and the effect on the total business.

Moving into the area of operations we see:

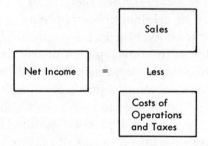

In general, it is suggested that the principle of responsibility accounting and reporting be used to measure marketing operations. Gross margin (sales less cost of goods sold) has historically been used to measure selling activities, even though marketing is not responsible for the cost of the goods; but it is believed that a more meaningful derivative measurement can be developed as a measurement of marketing profitability. The rationale for the use of this alternative measure in a consumer-oriented business is as follows.

The products to be sold are determined by the marketing function in the product planning process. The person having product responsibility will also have responsibility for determining the quantities to be sold. Therefore, during a specified time period it is reasonable for the unit cost and quantity to be established as a marketing commitment. The time frame depends on the economic production cycles of the products involved, but normally it would be a year. Following this concept, the cost of the product itself is a responsibility of marketing and it can be seen that the role of the controller and the controller's staff is a key to the successful measurement of margins, for the costs must be realistic and reflect an economic balance of the marketing requirements, production capabilities, and operating efficiencies. It is recommended that a standard variable product cost, established for the term of the operating plan, be used as the cost for which marketing is responsible. With this element of cost, sales revenue, and the marketing resources used, such as selling, advertising, and promotion, a measurement called "marketing margin" can be developed. Its general format is as follows:

```
Sales.........................................  XXX
    Less variable product cost...................  XXX
Contribution margin...........................  XXX
    Less advertising and promotion and
        marketing operations......................  XXX
    Marketing margin.............................  XXX
```

This variable product cost would include the standard variable cost of production, warranty, and distribution. The advantage of the above scheme, which must be adapted to the particular organization and responsibilities, is that it incorporates a reasonable assignment of costs for which marketing is responsible. (For an expansion of this concept, see Chapter 36.)

By using standard costs committed to by the production organization, short-term operating variances in the production process do not cloud the measurement of the marketing activities.[9] By using variable costs it gives emphasis to promotion and price opportunities for increasing margin dollars.

An integral part of any financial measurement system is the operating plan or budget. All results are compared to the predetermined plan, and variances are analyzed. When establishing the plan, comparison to prior periods are made. An analysis of contribution margin would disclose margin variances arising from deviations from the planned volume, prices, or product mix. Thus:

```
Budgeted contribution margin..........         XXXX
    Plus or minus:
        Price variance.......................  XXX
        Volume variance....................  XXX
        Mix variance.......................  XXX      XXXX
    Actual contribution margin..............         XXXX
```

---

[9] Obviously selling prices should be evaluated by using both actual and forward-looking costs. Significant cost-price imbalances which occur in a period of inflation might dictate the establishment of a new operating plan incorporating new unit selling prices and unit costs.

The concept developed above results in a slight modification of the general form for the return-on-investment formula shown previously.

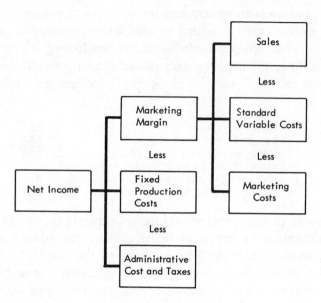

Marketing can also be measured on the utilization of capital resources. Reference is made to the "investment" portion of Exhibit 1. Generally only the utilization of certain current assets is measured. Unless marketing is responsible for the distribution system involving facilities, the measurement of investment should be limited to those items where marketing has direct influence, finished goods inventory and receivables. The management of cash and the sources of capital, creditors and shareowners, is normally outside of the marketing function's sphere of responsibility. This is not to say that if the marketing function is involved in sourcing of products that the marketing people should be unmindful of the terms on which they buy.

Some writers contend that return on investment is the most important profitability measure that the marketing person can employ for evaluation and decision making. Others have disputed this because the measure is frequently dependent on cost allocations and artificially created profit centers, transfer prices which are really not prices at all, and investment bases which are not really relevant. It is this writer's opinion that return on investment can be applied to marketing if recognition is given to the fact that all functions contribute toward the common objectives of the enterprise, and responsibilities and delegations of authority are clearly defined. Finished goods inventory and receivables in particular are largely the province of marketing, and the amount required and committed is largely the result of marketing decisions concerning levels of customer service.

Any permanent increase in these accounts should be evaluated just as carefully as the investment in a plant or distribution facility. In the short run the measurement is in relationship to the operating plan or budget. The level of receivables investment tends to become established by terms of sale; and the physical distribution system and customer service levels are the chief determinants of finished goods inventories. A monitoring of the measurements, *number of days in receivables* or *number of days inventory on hand,* and the actual amounts in the receivables and finished goods inventory accounts, will raise a warning flag of any adverse change compared to the operating plan. These two ratios can also be examined when evaluating marketing's plans, including sales budgets. (Return-on-investment measures are dealt with in more detail in Chapter 27.)

In summary, it is recommended that in the short run the measurement should concentrate on the adherence to the operating plan. Conscious deviations from the short-term plan as well as the establishment of long-range plans should be carefully evaluated like any other item of investment.

Other Key Business Measurements

Over 20 years ago in the General Electric Company, another basic management concept was developed and espoused, whose validity has increased with time. Negatively stated, this concept postulates that while lack of profitability is perhaps the most serious threat to business survival and growth, there are other key measurement areas in which a failure would have dire consequences for the business as a whole. We have already dealt with some of these measurements because they are directly related to marketing profitability. Together with the profitability measures they are called the "Key Result Areas."[10] We have already considered several of them

---

[10] There of course is not unanimous agreement on the eight areas. For a different composition and discussion see Drucker, *The Practice of Management,* p. 63.

in our discussion of profitability, but a brief summary discussion is included her because the controller, in the growing position as the information and intelligence center for the whole business, plays a key role not only in scorekeeping but also in development of the measurements.

Market Position. This measurement provides an indication of the attainment of a business' goals in terms of growth and leadership as covered previously. It reflects the value which customers have placed on the business' product and service offerings. Its usefulness depends on clear definition and delineation of the markets and offerings. Usually, quantification is expressed as some variant of "share of market."

Productivity. In a broad sense, productivity is a measurement of value created in that it relates output to input. In a business enterprise all factors of production should be considered, capital as well as human. Usually the measure is in terms of an index developed by relating input-output ratios over a period of time to a common base period. A rise in the index represents an improvement in productivity. Net sales (adjusted for inventory changes) is the business counterpart of gross national product used in the government's measure of the nation's productivity.

Product Leadership. This measurement area is sometimes referred to as innovation, inasmuch as the usual objective of the business is to lead its industry in the origination or application of advances in scientific or technical knowledge to new products or the improvement of existing ones. A suggested quantification of the measurement was presented in a prior section.

Personnel Development. Sooner or later in the course of running a business, management realizes that the shortage of qualified and trained personnel in one or more disciplines can present as serious a retardant to growth as the availability of capital resources. The important measures of this area are built around the determination of requirements and the programs designed to help fill the needs.

Employee Attitudes. Employee attitude is the disposition of the employees to make the most efficient utilization of their talents in carrying out their tasks to attain the goals of the business. Although they are not directly measurable, they are reflected in productivity and profitability. Qualitatively they can be measured by surveys. Quantitative indicators are such measurements as turnover, absenteeism, submitted ideas, and safety records.

Public Responsibility. Business must recognize its obligation to society by providing worthwhile goods and services on a continuing basis. Its principal external interfaces are with customers, vendors, and government at all levels. Few reminders of its responsibility are necessary from these members of society. But remember, business also has an obligation to other members of society to be a good citizen and even a good competitor. The growth of consumerism and other movements attests to the importance of this measurement area and the relevance of public responsibility to marketing. Measurements in this area are generally highly qualitative in nature and, like relationships with employees, rely heavily on the measurement of attitudes and the change in attitudes.

Balance between Short-Range and Long-Range Goals. Survival and growth of a business are dependent upon the decisions being made today. There are trade-offs between the *now* and the *future*. In each of the key measurement areas a balance must be struck, and this has particular relevance to marketing where short-term results are emphasized frequently. A true understanding and adoption of the marketing concept—creating customers, keeping these customers, survival, and growth—will tend to bring a balance between short-range and long-range goals in each area.

Improving Profitability through Financial Analysis for Marketing Decisions

The selection of financial and nonfinancial measurements for a business or function and the establishment of a system incorporating such measurements are in a sense secondary steps because they most often are retrospective. Earlier it was pointed out that the modern-day controller's work is as much concerned with the probabilities of what will happen as with what has happened. The controller, without abrogating independence or objectivity, should be a member of the management team and participate in the actual business decisions which will determine future results to be measured. Second-guessing should not be one of the controller's proficiencies. The controller and designees assigned to work with marketing must understand marketing problems and objectives, and how they relate to the overall objectives of the business.

Although every business has its own unique situations, problems, and opportunities, in the following abbreviated list some forward-looking decision-making areas are identified with needs for financial information. These areas represent both potential opportunities and problems.

Product and Customer Mix.   The very first marketing and business problem is to decide what will be made, to whom it will be sold, and how the markets served will be reached. An evaluation of the relative profitability of various alternatives is needed. Different segments, that is, products, customers, and channels of distribution, will have different levels of profitability; and the marketing financial analyst should participate in the selection process by furnishing needed profitability analyses. The analysis should include an evaluation of the resources required not only in the analyst's own organization but it should also identify resources required in the channels of distribution through to the end customer. It is not unusual to find that producers must finance not only their own operations but also those of their customers through such means as inventory or receivable financing.

For established businesses, periodic profitability analyses including sales, contribution margin, net income, and return on investment should be provided to marketing for products, customers, channels, territories, and other meaningful segments. Survival and growth of the business demand the most efficient utilization of the limited resources available to the enterprise, and financial analyses will greatly aid in the selection of products and customers.

Pricing.   After deciding which product and services to market, the most basic decision and the key to market penetration and profitability is pricing. Evaluation should include comparisons of unit selling prices with the cost of the product and with competitive offerings. Unit cost data on a functional basis are particularly useful in establishing prices for new offerings and when establishing legally justified price differentials under the Robinson-Patman Act. Functional cost in this context means the cost of performing any homogeneous type of work in the business process. Examples would be selling, advertising, storage, and handling. Financial evaluation of pricing will usually include the effect of alternative prices on contribution margin and net income.

Competition.   The financial analyst can furnish valuable insight into the competitive arena through evaluation of published financial statements and supplemental data such as SEC filings.

The profitability of served markets and markets to be served, as well as the strength or weakness of key competitors, can be gauged through financial analysis of the participants in the markets. Valuable lessons can be learned from both financially astute and inept competitors.

Cyclical, Seasonal, or Erratic Demand. Determining optional production schedules for seasonal businesses can be evaluated through development of unit cost data for alternative sales and marketing plans. The cost and risk of carrying higher inventory levels can be compared to the economies of leveling production throughout the year. In longer cycle businesses, the evaluation can include buy-versus-make trade-offs in providing for peak demands.

Advancing Technology. While it is impossible to predict precisely what will happen with respect to costs, the financial analyst, through expertise both as a statistician and in dealing with cost behavior and probabilities, can provide alternative projections of revenue and costs in the situations of uncertainty which occur with products dependent on rapidly advancing technology, such as electronic calculators.

Allocation of Resources. In most real-life situations both capital and human resources are scarce, or at least available in limited quantities for product alternatives. The allocation and application of resources to available alternatives are evaluated by the usual profitability and payout analyses. Return on investment is a key measurement used in these evaluations.

Distribution Logistics. The design of distribution systems has significantly advanced in recent years through the development of models which can evaluate numerous alternatives with the assistance of high-speed computers. The need for reliable cost and input-output data in the use of such models is critical. Normally the data required are unit costs for handling, storage, and transportation. Because safety stock, and thus the total inventory level, is a function of the number of stocking locations, a "cost-of-money" factor is frequently incorporated into the model. The same type of input-output data such as shipments per hour worked can be developed into productivity measurements for actual operations.

Customer Service and Product Warranty. After sales, service for a product is a function which must be covered in the selling price of the product or by a separate charge for such service. Knowledge of the cost of the service is needed when determining the price as well as when evaluating the method for providing the service, and determining the coverage and length of warranty.

Even a short list such as the above presents a challenge to the marketing financial analyst. In practice, the need for information will expand considerably. This list was furnished to illustrate the broad spectrum of needs for sound financial information in marketing planning. The innovative and creative financial expert will have many rewarding experiences applying his or her talents to aid in the solution to these and other marketing problems and opportunities.

Unless a marketing-financial relationship has already been developed, a newly designated financial analyst in the marketing area faces the problem of how to get started, how to build stature and produce useful data. The analyst, too, must do some product and market development. One approach which has been found successful is to develop a profitability study of a business segment, such as a product, a channel, or a territory. The analysis does not have to be elaborate, but seldom is one made which does not turn up information which is useful. In many cases, information developed in the course of conducting special studies provides base data which can be used in the design of deterministic and probabilistic models which are quite useful in evaluating various marketing alternatives. Once marketing sees what is available and is convinced of its utility, the analyst's problem becomes one of placing priorities on requested projects.

Some examples to illustrate the principles set forth and the broad range of financial data and analyses needed in directing marketing activities follow. The objective is to bridge the gap between the theory previously presented and actual practice, but it should be pointed out that the data included in the examples are hypothetical and the reporting format, to the author's knowledge, does not conform to any one actual situation. In most cases the reader-user would have to make some adaptation for personal real-life application.

PRODUCT PRICING AND PROGRAM DECISIONS

A series of models, utilizing time sharing, can be useful in evaluating such business decisions as price formulation and program expenditures for individual products. A sample format of a computer printout is shown in Exhibit 2. Any of the data indicated by an asterisk can be variable inputs to the system with all other vari-

EXHIBIT 2
Computer Printout from Model Used for Product Pricing and Program Decisions

	AMOUNT PER UNIT	PERCENT	TOTAL AMOUNT (000)
MODEL W21			
LIST PRICE	$19.98*		
DEALER PRICE AND MARGIN	12.95	35.2%*	
DISTRIBUTOR PRICE AND MARGIN	11.00	15.0%	
NET PRICE AND DISCOUNT	10.78	2.07	
DISTRIBUTOR PRICE	$10.78		
SALES PROGRAM ALLOWANCES	0.50*		
DISCOUNT (2.%*)	0.21		
NET SELLING PRICE	$10.07	100.0	$503.5
VARIABLE PRODUCTION OR PURCHASE COST	$ 5.00*	49.7	$250.0
WARRANTY	0.25*	2.5	12.5
VARIABLE DISTRIBUTION	0.80*	7.9	40.0
VARIABLE PRODUCT COST	$ 6.05	60.1	$302.5
CONTRIBUTION MARGIN	$ 4.02	39.9	$201.0
PROGRAMS	$ 1.52*	15.1	$ 76.0
FIXED READINESS TO SERVICE COSTS	$ 1.45*	14.4	72.5
INCOME FROM SALES	1.05	10.4	52.5
NET INCOME	0.55	5.4*	27.5

* AT VOLUME OF 50M UNITS.

able items automatically calculated by the computer. Utilizing selected programs, various alternatives can be quickly evaluated. For example:

1. How much can be spent on programs and still achieve a desired net income ratio?
2. What will be the net income, assuming specific cost factors for selected elements or estimated volumes for alternative unit price?
3. What selling price is required to make a given margin or profit, assuming a fixed amount or rate for other elements?
4. If selling prices are changed, what volume at the new price will be required to make the same current profit?

The advantage of using time-sharing models is the speed in calculation of results given judgmental evaluation of many variables. These models' usefulness in pricing decisions will be readily perceived by anyone who has had to make these decisions with imperfect information concerning future impacts of prices or promotions in the marketplace. Buyer and competitor response in most cases cannot be precisely predicted, but it can be scoped and parameters set. Getting quick answers to the many "what ifs" is a definite aid to the selection of a course of action, and a "recipe" can then be constructed from the ingredients in the marketing mix.

MEASURING INVESTMENT

It is the practice in many businesses to give extended terms, called dating, for preseason purchases. The intent of such programs is to move products to the wholesalers' and retailers' stocks; but because these programs are very difficult to evaluate in terms of precise results (such as sales) expected or actually achieved, the decision as to their use is largely a judgment evaluation. Recognizing that a marketing planner or his or her financial analyst might not be able to predict the results of such extended terms, a reasonable evaluation can be approached by determining the increased sales needed to pay for the increased interest cost on receivables lockup and the effect on selected profitability measurements such as return on investment or residual income.

In situations where the evaluation is frequently made or various terms of sale need to be evaluated, a time-sharing program can be constructed and employed. Below is shown a printout from such a program. The only inputs required are the sales and proposed terms.

```
RUN
DATING 10A09  3/12/76
SHIPMENTS—JUNE, JULY, AUGUST
PAYABLE—DECEMBER (AMOUNTS IN THOUSANDS)
```

PRODUCT LINE	AFTER-TAX INTEREST EXPENSE	SALES REQUIRED TO COVER COST	INCREASE IN AVERAGE INVESTMENT	DECREASE IN RESIDUAL INCOME
HOURGLASSES	$ 480.0	$2,181.8	$ 9,230.8	$ 553.8
WATCHES	320.0	1,684.2	6,153.8	369.2
SUNDIALS	287.9	1,370.9	5,536.9	332.2
TOTAL	$1,087.9	$5,236.9	$20,921.5	$1,255.2

```
TIME: 0.47 SECONDS.
```

The terms used in the printout are defined as follows:

After-tax interest expense is the effect on net income if borrowed funds are used to finance the extended terms of the receivables.

Sales required to cover cost is the calculated amount of "plus" sales needed to cover the additional interest cost.

Increase in average interest is the incremental average lockup in receivables.

Decrease in residual income is the reductions caused by the additional investment lockup. Residual income is defined as net income (before interest cost) less a capital charge; here the capital charge is assumed to be 6 percent.

It is important to note that an effective dating plan could have considerably less effect on operations than that shown because the alternative might be carrying inventory for a longer period. On the other hand, it must be pointed out that what is intended as a one-time effective use of extended or special terms as a selling tool can easily become the way of life in a business or even in industry. The estimated results are in relation to the normal terms of sale and give an answer to a "what if" type of question concerning financial impact of a sales plan.

DISTRIBUTION SYSTEM COSTS

The point was made earlier that the cost of marketing activities directly performed by the initial marketer is frequently the smaller part of the total cost, and that it is shortsighted for a producer to look only at those activities under his or her direct control. An analysis of a consumer product will be used to illustrate some salient points. The following table shows the allocation of retail value of a consumer product sold in three-step distribution—producer to wholesaler, to retailer, to consumer:

Percentage of Consumer Price

	Selling Price	Margin	Marketing, Distribution, and Administration	Pretax Profit
Retailer	100%	49%	37%	12%
Wholesaler	51	11	9	2
Producer	40	28	18	10

It is not uncommon to find that more than half of the costs and profit (60 percent in this example, since the producer's selling price is only 40 percent of what the ultimate consumer pays) is outside the direct control of the producer, and the cost of production (the difference between the factory selling price and margin) is a very small part of the total. In this example, only 12 cents (40 − 28) of the consumer dollar was required to produce the item. Even for activities under the producer's control, more was spent on marketing and administration than in production and, although an anomaly, it is a fact that frequently more effort is devoted to the analysis and control of manufacturing costs than to marketing, distribution and other indirect costs. But the real point is that the most important sale is the one made to the end user, and data on all costs along with other pertinent information are needed to evaluate the means of reaching that customer.

An analysis of a producer goods item sold in two-step distribution illustrates the all-too-common problem of the effect of small orders on the system:

Functional Allocation of Customer Value

	Manufacturer	Distributor	Total
Production cost	51%	—	51%
Administration-manufacturer	4	—	4
Distribution	14	25	39
Profit (loss)	15	(9)	6
	84%	16%	100%

Analysis of the distributor's costs disclosed the following:

	% of Customer Value
Selling and promotion	3.8
Transportation	1.4
Warehousing and order processing	17.4
Administration	2.6
Customer value	25.2

High warehousing and order-processing costs are typical in a situation where low-value products are being distributed in small quantities. It is possible that both the manufacturer and the distributor can take action to improve this type of situation. The distributor can price to discourage small orders, and the manufacturer might change packaging to sizes which are needed by the trade and thus prevent the high cost of breaking master cartons and repacking. In many cases, joint studies by distribtuors and manufacturers have disclosed that some products are packaged by the manufacturer in standardized quantities which could seldom be sold by the distributor. Increase in the standard pack size can have a favorable effect on costs of both the manufacturer and distributor. The cost of the total system must be observed and improvement sought. The marketer will not get the market penetration he desires unless intermediate distributors feel that the products are profitable to them.

Summary

There is no neat package of formulas which can be broadly applied to the measurement of marketing profitability. Every business has its own peculiar requirements determined by the type of business, products, and services; its organization; and the people who staff it. What has been presented are concepts and examples which can be used as guides in the development of useful measurements of the marketing functions in most businesses. Several of the concepts bear repeating:

Understanding marketing and the marketing concept is fundamental to the successful measurement of marketing profitability.

Profitability objectives and goals must be established and communicated to all cognizant managers in the business and measured at periodic intervals.

No single function is responsible for profitability. That is the province of the chief executive or general manager of the business, but a function can be charged with making a specific contribution to the profitability of the business. The charge must be clear, communicated, and understood.

The important work of the marketing controller or marketing financial analyst is in supplying financial advice and counsel for decision making.

ADDITIONAL SOURCES

Also see Additional Sources for Chapter 36.

Cox, Donald F., and Good, Robert E. "How to Build a Marketing Information System." *Harvard Business Review,* May–June 1967, p. 145.

Feder, Richard A. "How to Measure Marketing Performance." *Harvard Business Review,* May–June 1965, p. 132.

The Marketing Controller Concept: An Inquiry into Financial-Marketing Relationships in Selected Consumer Companies. Cambridge, Mass.: Marketing Science Institute, 1970.

Miller, Ernest C. *Objectives and Standards of Performance in Marketing Management.* Research Study No. 85. New York: American Management Association, 1967.

Mullins, Peter L. "Integrating Marketing and Financial Concepts in Product Line Evaluations." *Financial Executive,* May 1972, p. 32.

Scheuble, Philip A. "ROI for New-Product Planning." *Harvard Business Review,* November–December 1964, p. 110.

Shillinglaw, Gordon. *Managerial Cost Accounting,* chaps. 9, 12. 4th ed. Homewood, Ill.: Richard D. Irwin, Inc., 1977.

Spiegel, Reed S. "The Accountant, the Marketing Manager and Profit." *Management Accounting,* January 1974, p. 18.

Stephens, H. Virgil. "A Profit-Oriented Marketing Information System." *Management Accounting,* September 1972, p. 37.

Measuring the Performance
of a Product Manager

Charles F. Axelson*

Associated with the performance of a product manager are many things that do not lend themselves to precise measurement in terms of numbers. While the ultimate measurement may be the "bottom" profit line for the products for which the product manager is responsible, the day-to-day decisions that result in the final profit may not be measurable. Such things as the effectiveness of advertising, the knowledge and use of supporting corporate functions, and the benefits that may result from creative packaging are normally only indirectly measurable, if at all. Furthermore, the factors that influence the performance of a product manager may vary considerably between types of business; that is, the product manager in consumer goods is in a different situation than one in, say, heavy custom-made industrial equipment.

Some may argue that product managers should not be responsible for profit—that they are essentially staff persons who should not be distracted from more creative pursuits. In this situation, the pursuit of profit is thought of as more of a line manager's function with the product manager contributing what he or she can, but not measured against a profit goal. Perhaps this approach is valid under some corporate organizational and responsibility arrangements. Under these circumstances the measurement formats and reporting illustrated in this chapter might apply less to product managers and

---

* Mr. Axelson is Vice President, Chief Financial Officer, Lawry's Foods, Inc., Los Angeles.

more to others, but will nevertheless be useful in reaching predetermined goals. However, in these circumstances product managers,
as staff persons, will tend to be measured (if they are formally
measured at all) against nonnumerical objectives set in advance.

This chapter will concern itself largely with measuring the performance of a product manager where it is possible and desirable to
make a numerical measurement of performance; and, specifically,
with what needs to be done to make such measurement possible.
As in most measurement situations, we need predetermined goals
or objectives against which to measure performance and, for ultimate success, a computer is needed to assist in the calculations if
any degree of sophistication is introduced into the measurement
process.

It also helps to have the financial reporting of the company arranged in a manner that facilitates accountability and measurement
of performance. It does relatively little good to set goals which depend on the measurement of performance unless a company has the
ability to measure performance correctly. While goals involving
numerical measurement of performance can be set for relatively
easily measurable goals, for example, increased sales, new products
introduced, and reduction of expenses, it is the measurement of
profit at the appropriate level that really "puts it all together" and
deserves our best attention. Even a goal to increase the product
share of the market can be incorporated into a goal to attain greater
volume which can be translated into higher profit goals. Therefore,
let us first consider what is desirable in the way of financial reporting arrangements as a prerequisite to the measurement of profit
performance.

Financial Reporting Arrangements

For external purposes, a company normally follows a more-or-
less traditional prescribed format in their earnings statement. This
conventional format, followed in audit reports, published reports,
and filings with government agencies, usually starts with net sales,
after deducting allowances, cash discounts, and (where significant)
outbound freight costs. The statement then proceeds to show
amounts for major categories of expenses (cost of goods sold, selling, general and administrative expenses, and so on) before coming
down to income before taxes and, after the provision for income
taxes, on down to the "bottom line" of net income. Companies often

depart from this format for internal reporting and control purposes by expanding, rearranging, and introducing additional subtotals into the format to emphasize gross margin (net sales less cost of goods sold) and arranging other expenses according to internal lines of organization.

For effective measurement of performance at all levels, however, it is desirable to use an arrangement of the earnings statement format which separates fixed and variable expenses, identifies the contribution to the earnings of the company according to responsibilities and organizational arrangements, and ties the whole package in with product profit and other reports geared to measurement of performance. This concept involves the adoption of "direct" or variable product costing (no fixed factory overhead in product costs) for internal reporting purposes, even though variable costing is not permitted for tax or financial reporting purposes. This earnings statement format for a manufacturing company (referred to here as the "contribution measurement" format) is illustrated together with other more conventional formats in the attached exhibits. The adoption of the suggested format, of course, goes beyond the mere requirements of measuring the performance of a product manager—it is arranged in such a way as to measure performance at all levels in the company, and the product manager is thus part of a total reporting and measurement format. It would not normally seem practical to have a reporting format for a product manager which did not tie in with a general company reporting format.

It is important to remember, however, that measuring the performance of a product *manager* is not necessarily the same as measuring the economic performance of a *product* or product line. A product manager's performance is usually measured against a *plan*, even though the plan itself may be economically unsatisfactory. Thus the plan may represent an unsatisfactory return on any one or more of several bases (sales, investment, prior period dollars, and so on) due to various factors such as industry overcapacity, newly developed substitute products, maturity of product life cycle, or inherent low profit margin. However, if the product manager meets or beats his or her plan, the product manager may be doing a first-rate job. The unsatisfactory economic performance may have to be analyzed on a more encompassing basis (including long-range prospects, alternative areas of endeavor and relation to other corporate considerations) which would not be apparent in the plan.

Exhibit 1 shows a manufacturing company's earnings statement,

EXHIBIT 1
Typical Earnings Statement Format (thousands of dollars)

Line			Amount	% Sales
1.	Net sales................................		$100,000	100.0
2.	Cost of goods sold......................		79,000	79.0
3.	Gross margin on sales...................		$ 21,000	21.0
4.	Selling expenses........................	$9,500		
5.	Administrative expenses.................	5,500		
6.	Total selling and administrative expenses........................		15,000	15.0
7.	Operating income.......................		$ 6,000	6.0
8.	Interest expense........................		3,000	3.0
9.	Net operating income...................		$ 3,000	3.0
10.	Other income...........................		5,000	5.0
11.	Income before income taxes.............		$ 8,000	8.0
12.	Provision for income taxes..............		4,000	4.0
13.	Net income.............................		$ 4,000	4.0

arranged along traditional reporting lines, although the percent of sales column would not always be displayed in statements prepared for external purposes. In Exhibit 2 the figures used in Exhibit 1 have been augmented in more detail and rearranged into a "contribution measurement" format, which emphasizes the distinction between fixed and variable expenses and permits better measurement of performance. (See Chapter 13 for a detailed treatment of variable costing systems.)

Referring to Exhibit 2, it will be noted that the "contribution measurement" format commences with gross sales before any deductions (gross sales, rather than net sales, being 100.0 percent for purposes of relating costs and expenses as a percentage of sales) and then positions other items of expense so as to permit measurement and control of contribution to earnings at appropriate levels of responsibility. This will be explained more fully below.

Understanding the Contribution Measurement Reporting Format for an Earnings Statement

Before considering the ability to measure the profit performance of a product manager, it is important to understand the contribution measurement reporting format for the entire company earnings statement. This understanding will identify the applicable ground

EXHIBIT 2
Contribution Measurement Earnings Statement Format with Rearrangement of Figures Used in Exhibit 1 and Additional Figures to Illustrate Principles Involved (thousands of dollars)

	Amount	% of Sales	Line Where Included in Exhibit 1	
Gross sales..............................	$110,000	100.0	1	
Less allowances........................	6,000	5.5	1*	
Net sales................................	$104,000	94.5		
Variable expenses:				
Variable cost of goods sold.............	$ 70,000	63.7	2	
Freight expense........................	2,000	1.8	1*	
Cash discount.........................	2,000	1.8	1*	
Commissions on sales.................	3,000	2.7	4	
Loss on defective goods...............	1,000	0.9	2	
Variable warehousing expense..........	2,000	1.8	4	
Total variable expenses.............	$ 80,000	72.7		
Marginal contribution....................	$ 24,000	21.8		
Direct product expenses:				
Advertising...........................	$ 2,500	2.3	4	Level of
Other (market research, promotion				Evalu-
expenses, etc.)......................	500	0.4	4	ation for:
Total direct product expenses.......	$ 3,000	2.7		Product
Product contribution.....................	$ 21,000	19.1 ←		Manager
Product group expenses:				
Fixed factory overhead.................	8,000	7.3	2	Product
Product group contribution..............	$ 13,000	11.8 ←		Group
Division overhead:				Manager
Division administration.................	$ 1,500	1.4	5	
Division marketing.....................	1,000	0.9	4	
Fixed warehousing expense............	500	0.4	4	
Interest expense......................	3,000	2.7	8	
Total division overhead.............	$ 6,000	5.4		
Division contribution.....................	$ 7,000	6.4		
Corporate overhead (general offices,				
research and development, expenses				
of staff functions).....................	4,000	3.7	5	
Net operating income....................	$ 3,000	2.7	9	
Other income...........................	5,000	4.5	10	
Net income before income taxes..........	$ 8,000	7.2	11	
Provision for income taxes...............	4,000	3.6	12	
Net income.............................	$ 4,000	3.6	13	

*Deducted from gross sales to arrive at net sales.

rules and the way in which the profit (or "contribution") level at which the product manager is measured ties in with the total profit goals of the company. Referring again to Exhibit 2, the first line of the statement is gross sales; all costs, expenses, and profit contributions are related to *gross sales* as 100 percent. While relating to *net sales* as 100 percent is perhaps more common, starting with gross sales emphasizes the effect of allowances; these allowances may be significant, but all too often lose their visibility because they are "skimmed off the top" before the usual sequence of reporting commences starting with net sales. Also, in many industries allowances largely represent price discounts for promotions to the trade and, as such, the product manager may have a certain leeway as to whether the budget is spent for promotion allowances or in some other way. By starting with gross sales as 100 percent, allowances are more apt to be regarded on the same basis as costs and expenses and thus subject to better control, particularly if an adequate reporting system exists for allowances. While it might be argued that under this reporting format net sales is just another subtotal that should be eliminated, many allowances may be adjustments of gross sales as originally billed, so the net sales line may assume some significance under these circumstances.

Continuing down the earnings statement below net sales, the contribution measurement format is designed to identify those expenses that vary directly with gross sales on as detailed a product level as possible. Product levels may be thought of in terms of various classification gradients; that is, each container size of canned peaches may be considered a *product item code*, the adding together of all canned peaches item codes may constitute the *product* "canned peaches," and the adding together of canned peaches with other canned fruit products may result in the *product group* known as "canned fruits." If there is a special variation of canned peaches, such as those packed in a different kind of syrup, then there would be separate item codes for each container size of the special product. There are, of course, many ways in which various product item codes can be accumulated or subtotaled and the choice of alternatives (including the use of other descriptive titles such as "product line") will have to be resolved in light of all of the circumstances.

The product level at which financial data are accumulated should be the lowest level for which product item codes, price lists, and manufacturing cost classifications exist. It is only at this level that all of the variables affecting the profitability of the separate products offered for sale by the company can be identified. Subtracting these variable expenses from net sales gives marginal contribution, which is the point for measuring profitability at the detailed product item code level prior to other expenses which are not meaningful at the item code level because they do not necessarily vary with the sales of a particular item code.

The largest item included under variable expenses is usually variable cost of goods sold. This represents the variable cost of manufacture or the purchase cost (on items for resale) for specific products and excludes any fixed costs, such as factory or general overhead, that continue regardless of whether any particular product is manufactured, purchased, or sold. A company adopting this format and presently allocating manufacturing overhead to product costs which enter into inventory before being sold will need to continue including overhead in inventory for tax and financial reporting purposes, but this can be done through an adjustment at the "other income" level in the earnings statement for internal reporting purposes. The variable product cost will thus normally be the usual cost of goods sold figure with the fixed overhead portion eliminated, and should be identifiable at the product item code level.

Freight expense refers to the net cost of freight absorbed by the company which cannot be separately charged to customers (or, for inbound freight, is not assignable to the cost of purchased items). For products sold on a delivered price basis, it will usually be the entire outbound freight cost; for products sold f.o.b. shipping point, it will usually be that portion of the freight that cannot be charged to the customer. To obtain freight expense at the product item code level normally means calculating it for every line item on every invoice billed to a customer. This may require fairly sophisticated calculations and computer routines, but, if freight is significant, the effort is necessary for a proper determination of marginal contribution at the product item code level.

Cash discount and commissions on sales can normally be charged to item codes at an appropriate rate based on sales. Loss on defective goods, normally identifiable at the item code level, includes both the write-off of unsalable inventory and the markdown (to salvage value) of sales of defective goods at distress prices. Such markdowns are placed in this account, rather than in allowances, so as to segregate and emphasize the cost of defective goods. Variable warehouse expense, which excludes such fixed costs as depreciation, insurance, property taxes, salaried personnel, and so on, does not always vary *directly* with sales in any given accounting period because receiving and storage costs are usually incurred prior to shipment. Over the course of a year these expenses do vary broadly with sales, however, and are probably better handled as a variable expense assignable to product item codes than elsewhere on the statement. Such expenses are best charged to item codes on a rate basis for each location, although, again, this may necessitate fairly elaborate computations and computer programs.

When the total variable expenses are subtracted from net sales, the resulting marginal contribution is the point at which the profitability of specific products is measured. At this product item code level, each product carrying separate selling prices and/or variable expenses should be identifiable and measurable.

Proceeding on down the earnings statement below the marginal contribution level, the contribution measurement reporting format next considers those expenses which can be identified with what might broadly be considered a product without considering all the variations in size, type of container and other variables that are identified at the item code level. The direct product expenses normally would be those for which there would be no point in allocating down to the item code level because, while they vary broadly with sales of the product, they do not necessarily vary with sales of individual product item codes. Just what is includable in this category of direct product expense may vary considerably from company to company, depending on organizational arrangements and responsibilities, but would normally include product advertising expense, market research, and certain promotion expenses for products, and the expenses of a product marketing group, if such a group exists at the product level. Expenses of this nature which apply to more than one product would fit into the next category down the statement as a part of product group expenses, or perhaps in division overhead. Direct product expenses, allocated to the product level, are subtracted from marginal contribution to produce the "product contribution" level of profitability measurement. It is at this level that the performance of a manager for a product would normally be measured. At the next level and on down the statement, performance would be measured for a manager who had responsibility for a group of products.

In arriving at the "product group contribution" level, certain product group expenses are deducted from the product contribution level. These expenses are those that would normally vary broadly or relate primarily to product groups but not vary or relate to individual products within the group. Thus the fixed factory overhead for a factory manufacturing a group of similar products would be regarded as a product group expense (the variable factory overhead would be included in variable cost of goods sold). The expenses of a product group marketing staff might also be included in this category.

The "product group contribution" level represents the highest organizational level where performance associated with product or product group activity is measured. Beyond this point, the performance of the division or the company is measured and while the arrangement is briefly illustrated in Exhibit 3, this chapter will not concern itself with measurement considerations at the division or corporation level. (See Chapter 33 for a treatment of divisional performance evaluation.)

Setting Performance Goals

Once the contribution measurement reporting format is understood, goals for product managers should be set for each category on the earnings statement down to the "product group contribution" level. These goals should be set for whatever period of measurement is appropriate. Thus some companies will set annual goals (perhaps broken down into the individual months or quarters for monitoring but not for formal measurement purposes), whereas other companies may actually formally measure performance on a less-than-yearly basis.

As in many areas of business endeavor, there is no one or necessarily best way of setting these goals—each company will tend to go at it in its own way in light of its individual circumstances. The goal-setting process may be from the "top down" (more or less imposed by the chief executive), from the "bottom up" (as the result of careful consideration and buildup of data on the part of all those who are involved in making the plan), or some combination of these two extremes. Furthermore, some companies may set hard-to-attain goals whereas others are more pragmatic in what they feel can be achieved. In any event, however, the resulting plan forms the basis

EXHIBIT 3

PRODUCT GROUP RESULTS OF OPERATIONS

	Product Group Month					Cumulative Through				
	Sales		% of Sales		Variance	Sales		% of Sales		Variance
	Actual Amount	Per Unit	Actual	Plan	from Plan	Amount	Per Unit	Actual	Plan	from Plan
Units sold	1,001				(147)	6,135				437
Gross sales	$4,539	$4.53	100.0	100.0	$(523)	$27,672	$4.51	100.0	100.0	$ 1,594
Allowances	312	0.31	6.9	9.3	158	2,462	0.40	8.9	9.3	(36)
Net sales	$4,227	$4.22	93.1	90.7	$(365)	$25,210	$4.11	91.1	90.7	$ 1,558
Cost of goods—variable	$2,572	$2.57	56.7	54.2	$172	$14,292	$2.34	51.7	52.2	$ (674)
Freight	120	0.12	2.6	1.8	(28)	597	0.10	2.2	1.7	(141)
Cash discount	102	0.10	2.2	2.0	(1)	578	0.09	2.1	2.0	(56)
Commissions	139	0.14	3.0	2.8	2	814	0.13	2.9	2.8	(85)
Net loss—defective goods	48	0.05	1.1	—	(48)	63	0.01	0.2	—	(63)
Warehousing—variable	158	0.16	3.5	3.1	(3)	994	0.16	3.6	3.3	(136)
Total variable costs	$3,139	$3.14	69.1	63.9	$ 94	$17,338	$2.83	62.7	62.0	$(1,155)
Marginal contribution	$1,088	$1.08	24.0	26.8	$(271)	$ 7,872	$1.28	28.4	28.7	$ 403
Advertising	$ 182	$0.18	4.0	2.1	$ (76)	$ 601	$0.10	2.2	2.0	$ (76)
Market research	3	—	0.1	—	(2)	8	—	—	0.1	1
Promotional	33	0.03	0.7	0.4	(12)	171	0.03	0.6	0.9	65
Total direct product expense	$ 218	$0.21	4.8	2.5	$ (90)	$ 780	$0.13	2.8	3.0	$ (10)
Product contribution	$ 870	$0.87	19.2	24.3	$(361)	$ 7,092	$1.15	25.6	25.7	$ 393
Plant overhead	580	0.58	12.8	9.8	(82)	2,655	0.43	9.6	10.4	61
Product group contribution	$ 290	$0.29	6.4	14.5	$(443)	$ 4,437	$0.72	16.0	15.3	$ 454

of performance measurement. Here the controller can be most help-ful in suggesting ideas, monitoring the development of the various considerations entering into the plan, making sure that every ele-ment is consistent with overall company considerations and seeing that the plan is summarized in such a way as to facilitate review and, if necessary, further change before top management approval in final form. Presumably, attaining or exceeding the established goals is a basis, by itself or in combination with other noneconomic goals, for rewarding the product manager via a bonus or other sup-plementary incentive compensation.

Under the contribution measurement reporting format, dollar goals must be set for every category and every *product item code* down to the marginal contribution level, then for every direct prod-uct expense category and every *product* down to the product con-tribution level, and finally for every product group category and every *product group* down to the product group contribution level. In practice, it may be desirable to combine certain categories at the item code level to reduce the amount of detail. Thus, for purposes of setting goals, variable expenses might be split only into two cate-gories—variable cost of goods sold and all other variable expenses. Normally this might provide sufficient detail to arrive at a meaning-ful marginal contribution goal for each product item code. How-ever, at the product level, the amount of variable expenses may be significant enough to identify for each category, so the omission of categories for goal-setting purposes at the item code level will not permit the normal "add through" of each category of expense to the product level. In these instances, some "plugging" or special han-dling may be necessary, since it is important that the earnings state-ment ties together with the marginal contribution for each item code, and that it adds through to the total marginal contribution for each product and product group.

Product Profit Reports

Once the profit goals are set in as much detail as practicable, the measurement of profit performance against these goals becomes a matter of organizing the profit reports that supplement the princi-pal earnings statement so that they not only facilitate measurement but also adequately identify all variations from the profit plan. Com-plete identification of variances is important if areas needing im-

EXHIBIT 4
Product Results by Item Code (computer printout)

PRODUCT ITEM CODE	PRODUCT DESCRIPTION		UNITS SOLD	GROSS SALES	ALLOW- ANCE	NET SALES	VARIABLE COST OF GOODS	OTHER VARIABLE	MARGINAL CONTRIBUTION
15005	ITEM CODE "A"	ACTUAL							
		VARIATION FROM PLAN							
		PER UNIT—ACTUAL							
		PER UNIT—PLAN							
		% SALES—ACTUAL							
		% SALES—PLAN							
15006	ITEM CODE "B"	ACTUAL							
		VARIATION FROM PLAN							
		PER UNIT—ACTUAL							
		PER UNIT—PLAN							
		% SALES—ACTUAL							
		% SALES—PLAN							
15007	ITEM CODE "C"	ACTUAL							
		VARIATION FROM PLAN							
		PER UNIT—ACTUAL							
		PER UNIT—PLAN							
		% SALES—ACTUAL							
		% SALES—PLAN							
	TOTAL PRODUCT	ACTUAL							
		VARIATION FROM PLAN							
		PER UNIT—ACTUAL							
		PER UNIT—PLAN							
		% SALES—ACTUAL							
		% SALES—PLAN							

provement are to be spotted quickly for early application of corrective measures. The format of the statements used to portray profit goals, actual profits, and variations of actual from goals will depend on the amount of detail desired, computer abilities and limitations, and individual preferences. It may be desirable to computerize detail-level reports while issuing summary reports in regular printed, typewritten, or handwritten form. In Exhibits 3 and 4, sample product profit reports are shown. Exhibit 3, containing illustrative figures, could be used for a product group report or product report (with the last two lines omitted). This could be one page of an overall corporate reporting package with separate pages for other product or product groups, division totals, overall corporate financial statements, and so forth. Exhibit 4 shows the format of a computer printout report that might show results down to the marginal contribution level by individual product item code. Since variable costs, other than cost of goods sold, are lumped into one total to reduce the detail shown at this level, any questions by the report user about variances in "other variable costs" would have to be investigated by reference to supporting computer listings which would be available, although not a part of the formal reporting package.

Another measurement device that may be used, illustrated in Exhibit 5, is the analysis of variance in marginal contribution, which measures the variances from plan in terms of volume, price, and costs. Further refinements in this approach can be made to separate costs into more detail, or to make the calculations at the item code level and then summarize to the product or product group level. Calculating variances at the item code level introduces the concept of the variation due to item code mix. Also, the volumes applicable to individual item codes may be expressed in different units of quantity. Under such circumstances, the calculations can become quite extensive, requiring use of a computer. In the interests of simplicity such refinements are not illustrated here. The statement illustrated can be expanded, of course, to include analysis of variances for the cumulative period. It also may be desirable to include brief narrative comment explaining the reasons for the principal variances (and the plans for correcting unfavorable variances), although this may not be practical if the statement is computer prepared or it is not desirable to delay its release until the reasons have been determined and written down.

EXHIBIT 5

ANALYSIS OF VARIANCE IN MARGINAL CONTRIBUTION

Product Group_____

Month_____

	Actual		Plan		
	Total	Per Unit	Total	Per Unit	Unit Variance
Units..........................	1,001		1,148		(147)
Gross sales....................	$4,539	$4.53	$5,062	$4.41	$ 0.12
Allowances....................	312	0.31	470	0.41	0.10
Net sales......................	$4,227	$4.22	$4,592	$4.00	0.22
Cost of goods—variable........	2,572	2.57	2,744	2.39	(0.18)
Other variable costs...........	567	0.57	489	0.43	(0.14)
Marginal contribution..........	$1,088	$1.08	$1,359	$1.18	$(0.10)

	Favorable (unfavorable)
Reasons for Variance in Marginal Contribution	
Volume 147 fewer units @ $1.08—unfavorable........................	$(158)
Price: Gross—1,148 @ 12¢—favorable................................	$ 138
Allowances—1,148 @ 10¢—favorable...........................	115
Net—1,148 @ 22¢—favorable...................................	$ 253
Cost of goods: 1,148 @ 18¢ unfavorable.............................	$(206)
Other variable costs: 1,148 @ 14¢ unfavorable.......................	(160)
Net variation (actual, $1,088, minus plan, $1,359)....................	$(271)

Measurement of Results

Once the reports are set up and being issued on a regular basis, the information necessary for regular monitoring of results to achieve the yearly or interim goals is established. In most situations, product managers should have the maximum flexibility possible to change the components as long as they make or exceed their product contribution goal. Certain of the variable components such as cost of goods sold, cash discount, commissions, and variable warehousing expense may not be under their direct control, but they need to know these variable expenses if they are going to attain their product contribution goal. For those variable components over which they have some degree of control, they should be able to increase some and decrease others in achieving their product contribution goal. These would include gross sales (volume sold and selling prices), freight (excess cost over the lowest possible freight), loss on defective goods, and advertising and promotion expenses. This flexibility to change components need not be incorporated into a formal revision of the goals, but it may be a strong reason why variances from the goals for individual sales, cost, and expense items should not be used in measuring performance. Rather, what should be monitored is whether the manager reached the profit goal at the product contribution level by the end of the measurement period.

The measurement of results, of course, must be linked with the incentive plan adopted by the company. If a favorable variance from plan is to bring with it some reward, the details of just how the calculations are made will have to be resolved. Thus whether a minimum favorable variance is necessary for eligibility, or a maximum limitation should exist so that excessive rewards will not be paid, depends mostly on the philosophy of company management.

Conclusion

Once it is decided that a product manager should bear some responsibility for profit, it is essential that profit goals be determined and a measurement and reporting system be set up to compare actual profit performance with the profit goals. The approach and formats used in this chapter should be useful in measuring the performance of the product manager.

ADDITIONAL SOURCES

Also see Additional Sources for Chapter 35.

Buzby, Stephen L., and Heitger, Lester E. "Profit Contribution by Market Segment." *Management Accounting*, November 1976, p. 42.

Clewett, Richard M., and Stasch, Stanley F. "Shifting Role for the Product Manager." *Harvard Business Review*, January–February 1975, p. 65.

Goodman, Sam R. "Sales Reports That Lead to Action." *Financial Executive*, June 1973, p. 20.

Stevens, Ross. "Product Line Cash Income: A Reliable Yardstick." *Management Accounting*, November 1974, p. 46.

37

A Consultant's Review of Cost and Operating Controls

Thomas S. Dudick*

Editors' Note:

This chapter comprises a consultant's report to a client who has requested a survey of cost and operating controls in a major production facility. Although the company depicted is fictitious, the report is based on the author's generalized experience in conducting many such surveys.

We feel this chapter can serve any of three purposes for the reader. First, for the controller who may be considering retaining management consultants to conduct a similar survey but who has not previously hired consultants, the report gives a concrete picture of consultants' approach and of the nature and presentation format of their findings. Second, the chapter can serve as a prototype for the controller who wishes to use his or her own staff to conduct a similar survey or "management audit" of cost and operating controls. Finally, the reader may find that the consultant's recommendations are useful ideas to consider in addressing problems in the reader's firm similar to the problems in Exelon, Inc.

* Mr. Dudick is Manager, Ernst & Whinney, New York.

SAMPLE REPORT
Ernst & Whinney
153 East 53rd Street
New York, New York 10022

Mr. Ellis K. Jornsten
Vice President, Finance
Exelon, Inc.
139 Broadway
New York, N. Y. 10005

Dear Mr. Jornsten:

      We have completed our survey of cost and operating controls at the South Orange, N. J. plant and present herewith our findings and recommendations.

APPROACH AND SCOPE

The objective of our study was to examine the information systems and controls, both financial and operating, to assure that they conform to company policy and that they are responsive to the company management's current and future needs. We therefore approached this assignment through the following steps:

    1. Familiarized ourselves with corporate policy.

    2. Made a plant tour to familiarize ourselves with the manufacturing processes.

    3. Interviewed key management personnel as well as other supervisory employees in the various departments.

    4. Reviewed the various reports and source documents as well as the procedures followed in developing the reports.

    5. Upon conclusion of our field work we met with the general manager, operations manager and the controller to review our findings and recommendations.

-2-

ORGANIZATION OF THE REPORT

       This report is made up of the following sections:

    Section I   - Background

    Section II   - Cost Controls

    Section III - Operating Controls

HIGHLIGHTS OF THE STUDY

       We have capsulized below the contents of this report, which are presented in more detailed form in Sections II and III.

OVERVIEW

       We found the personnel at this plant to be technically competent. Areas of weakness were: excessive rejects, weak controls over quality of purchased parts, loose inventory controls and some erroneous costing practices.

SECTION II - COST CONTROLS

Findings   Recommendations

PRODUCT LINE INCOME STATEMENTS

Findings	Recommendations
This report, which shows gross profit by product line, is a useful report that has high acceptance by the Marketing Department.	The accuracy of this report would be improved if: . Set-up costs were identified by product line rather than being spread to all products through the conventional overhead rate application. . Tooling costs, which vary widely from product to product, should, in similar fashion, be assigned by product rather than being "leveled out" through an overhead rate application.

-3-

Findings	Recommendations

PRODUCT PROFITABILITY

In testing the profitability of several products, we found that the percentage of the selling price for product line G required to cover prime cost (material + direct labor) ranged from a low of 27% to a high of 49%. This means that in one case, 73% of the selling price is left to cover all other costs and profit; in the other case, only 51% of the selling price is left after prime costs.

We recommend that a report similar to that illustrated in Exhibit I of this report be maintained on a current basis for all products. The advantages of such a report are:
. It will indicate the relative profitability of the various items within each product line.
. It will highlight the products that have an unusually high material or direct labor cost and thus point up potential cost reduction areas.

COST ESTIMATING

In preparing cost estimates for arriving at desired selling prices, we found that the same percentage markup is applied when the product has a high material content as is applied when the material content is low. For that reason, the company finds that it cannot compete in products that have a high material content. Conversely, it is possible that products with low material content are underpriced.

Profits are normally based on converting. While some return should be expected for the investment and handling of material, the markup would normally be different for material than for the conversion cost. We recommend that a study be made to determine proper markup percentages.

OVERHEAD RATES

Although individual overhead rates are available for each of the 32 departments, this does not result in accurate costing. A number of these departments are a mixture of labor-intensive and capital-intensive operations which are not used in the same proportion by all products passing through the department.

Overhead rates should be developed for the process rather than for the department.

-4-

Findings	Recommendations

STANDARDS

In developing standards for labor, a blanket allowance is applied equally to all operations. This does not provide for certain differences in job difficulty such as heat and fumes.	Instead of overall blanket allowances, individual allowances should be assigned by the type of p.ocess. The operation of loading and unloading a furnace at over 100 degree temperatures warrants a higher allowance than an operation performed in a well-ventilated room, for example.

CONTROL OF INVENTORIES

Because of certain weaknesses in the control of inventories, which are listed below, we feel there is danger of a physical to book discrepancy.

Paperwork Controls

Documents on which issues and transfers are reported to Production Control are not being controlled.	All documents should be prenumbered and missing numbers accounted for. Submission of batches of documents should be controlled by numbering the batches sequentially.

Tie-in of Cost System to Production Control

The cost system does not follow the same physical accountability for inventory that is used by Production Control. Instead of segregating inventories on the books into Raw Material, Work-in-Process and Finished Goods, only one inventory account is maintained.	The single inventory account should be broken into three major segments. Transactions affecting Work-in-Process should recognize two separate inventories: . Components stockroom . Floor inventory
	Transfers into the stockroom should be based on good components accepted into stock. This will eliminate the dependency on accurate scrap reporting.
	Floor inventory should be valued by using the open balances of physical quantities shown on the shop orders maintained by the Production Control Department.

-5-

Findings	Recommendations

Physical Controls

Shipping areas are not fenced in. This allows easy access to areas in which finished products are available.

The shipping area should be fenced in. The gate should be kept shut except when a truck is being loaded. The same rules of access and egress should be applied at this point as in the stockrooms.

Customer Returns

Returns from customers are not being properly controlled. We found instances in which items returned by customers were disassembled and the salvaged parts moved into the components stockroom. However, the difference between the total value of the returned goods and the value of salvaged items was not removed from the finished value.

Returned goods should be accounted for in a separate inventory. When items are moved out for disassembly, the entire value should be taken out of the inventory. Then, if any components are salvaged, the salvage value should be added to the components stock.

DATA PROCESSING SUPPORT

We found instances in which reports that had been computerized caused more work rather than less. As examples,

    . In five price lists that were computerized, three different formats were used.

Price lists should be prepared in a standardized format to facilitate speed in quoting prices. The standardized format also minimizes errors.

    . Certain discount calculations that appeared on the previous lists were eliminated in the computerized version.

In computerizing, there should be no loss of information.

Written procedures are not being updated when computerization takes place. Illustrative of this is a breakdown in communications between the payroll and personnel functions, when new and recalled employees are to be added to the payroll.

Procedures in all departments in which paperwork has been automated should be revised. The work of the data processing department should not be considered complete until this has been done.

-6-

Findings	Recommendations
Certain reports, particularly operator efficiencies, are so overly detailed that foremen ignore them.	Reports should be summarized on an exception basis to facilitate review through highlighting of unusual performance.

<u>SECTION III - OPERATING CONTROLS</u>

<u>QUALITY CONTROL</u>

Scrap and rejects are too high because: . Inspectors are not catching rejects soon enough in the process. . Vendor quality is poor.	The following steps must be taken to improve product quality through reduction of the number of rejects: . Require inspectors to show an identifying mark on each item that has been inspected. This will pin down responsibility. . Eliminate the present haphazard approach to inspection of incoming material. Establish definite procedures using statistical sampling techniques.
Process controls are weak.	Hire a senior quality control engineer with the specific assignment of: . writing procedures for controlling the processes. . training personnel in the application of these procedures. . monitoring compliance.

<u>PURCHASING</u>

One-third of the parts that we sampled were purchased more than three times a year, yet they were not being included in blanket orders.	Encourage the use of blanket orders for high volume purchases.
Although many of the items purchased outside could also be made in-house, there is no make-or-buy procedure to evaluate the economics of making purchases outside.	Establish a make-or-buy committee headed by the Manager of Purchasing. Before buying on the outside, consideration should be given as to which items are best made within the plant and which are best purchased on the outside.

-7-

Findings	Recommendations
Material purchases are compared with the standard material prices only.	Buying performance should be measured against the previous prices paid as well as the standard purchase price.
Vendor performance on price and delivery not furnished to the vendor.	Vendor performance ratings should be continually monitored. This information should be reported to the vendors.

METHODS

The assembly processes are conveyorized. However, some of the products are hand-loaded on carts and wheeled to the packaging area rather than being transported on the conveyorized line.	Extend the conveyor line to the packaging area to eliminate wasteful hand loading and carting.

LAYOUT

Present layout is inefficient because of overcrowding.	Part of the new addition presently being constructed for warehousing purposes and office space should be used for production to permit a more efficient layout.

MANUFACTURING ENGINEERING

There is no program to systematically review and update standards.	A program of review should be implemented.

NEW PRODUCT DEVELOPMENT

The quality control department is not furnished with operating specifications for new products. This leaves the task of writing such specifications to personnel in the quality control department.	The new product development group which designs the new products should be held responsible for writing operating specifications for all products turned over to production.

-8-

The foregoing represent the highlights of our findings and recommendations -- the detail information is contained in Sections II and III of this report.

We appreciated the opportunity of working with you on this most important project. Should you have any questions please don't hesitate to call us.

Very truly yours,

ERNST & WHINNEY

SECTION I - BACKGROUND

The company makes ventilating fans used mostly in industrial applications. These range from the small rubber-blade types used to prevent steaming of truck windshields to the large roof exhaust fans that make up the exhaust systems of industrial buildings.

Although there are many variations in the finished product, many of which are unique to particular customers -- and therefore made to order -- most of the components parts are built for stock.

Material cost can run as high as 75% of total manufacturing cost or as low as 30%. The company has the capability of making practically all of the components except the wire, steel castings, laminations and magnets used in building the motors. In spite of this, a substantial number of components that the company can make are being purchased on the outside to satisfy peak load requirements.

Exelon manufactures approximately ten percent of the $210 million in industrial fans estimated to be sold in the United States this year. Last year's $20,971,000 in sales was made up of 62,160 customer invoices -- an average billing of $337.37 per customer.

<u>SECTION II - COST CONTROLS</u>

This section provides the details of the findings and recommendations
relative to cost controls which were summarized in the first part of
this report.

<u>PRODUCT LINE INCOME STATEMENT</u>

<u>Findings</u>

        This statement shows the profitability of the various product

lines at the gross profit level. The product lines included in this

report are:

    A. Anti-fogging fans - rubber blades
    B. Anti-fogging fans - steel blades shielded
    C. Exhaust - 627
    D. Exhaust - 885
    E. Cylinder enclosed fan
    F. Open Fans - 6306
    G. Enclosed Fans - 6388

        The statement shows the gross profit for the current month and

for year-to-date. In addition to gross profit figures, the dollar value

of inventory is also shown for each product line. This is an informative

report which is used by the marketing personnel to monitor the mark-up

factors used in pricing its products.

        Although the present report provides useful information, it

contains certain inaccuracies because of the method used in assigning

set-up and tool amortization costs to the various products. The method

followed is to include both these major items of cost in the overhead

rate. Since the overhead rate is applied on direct labor, those products

that have the largest labor content absorb the most set-up and tool amorti-

zation. This can be contrary to the true incidence of such costs.

Recommendations

Since set-up and tool amortization costs are quite large for
this operation, and since they are identifiable with the specific product
lines on which such costs are incurred, we recommend that these costs be
calculated on a per-unit basis to the appropriate product line. This
change from an overhead rate to a cost per unit by product line can have
an impact on the reported profit of some of the product lines. Product
lines C & D, for example, showed the following sales and gross profit
for March:

	Product Line	
	C	D
Sales	$152,090	$41,672
Gross Profit %	18.9%	18.2%

The sales volume of Product Line C is more than triple that of Product
Line D -- which means that actual set-up costs, on a per-unit basis, are
likely to be lower because Product Line C usually has much longer runs.

Inasmuch as Product Line C is an old product line -- while D is
new -- the tooling has been completely amortized. Although the gross
profit percentage on both C and D is reported as being almost the same,
the recommended change in application of set-up and tool amortization
would most likely show Product Line C to be far more profitable than D.

PRODUCT PROFITABILITY - CONTRIBUTION TO PROFIT

Findings

The conventional product cost includes overhead -- which is
necessary in order to determine cost/selling price relationships and
to value inventories. This does not, however, provide the type of product

profitability analysis required for determining the contribution to profit made by the various products in each line.

Recommendations

    We recommend a simplified product profitability analysis similar to that shown below:

| | SALES PRICE | STANDARD COST | | SELLING PRICE | | |
		Material	Direct Labor	Material	Direct Labor	Prime Cost
PRODUCT LINE A						
Model 4A	$ 7.63	$2.90	$ .81	38.0%	10.6%	48.6%
Model 4H	9.79	2.80	1.00	28.6	10.2	38.8
Model 5A	6.99	2.52	.92	26.1	13.2	49.3
Model 5K	8.92	2.75	.99	30.8	11.1	41.9
PRODUCT LINE B						
#44589	12.99	4.41	1.37	33.9	10.5	44.5
#56894	13.99	4.92	1.51	35.2	10.7	45.9
#67875	15.65	5.16	1.70	33.0	10.8	43.8
PRODUCT LINE C						
A-657	19.05	7.36	1.61	38.6	8.5	47.1
A-789	12.99	7.05	.71	54.2	5.5	59.7
B-456	18.65	9.02	1.15	48.3	6.2	54.5
PRODUCT LINE D						
E-8981	14.40	3.18	1.21	22.1	8.4	30.5
E-9905	16.19	3.23	1.16	20.0	7.2	27.2
J-4450	16.70	3.65	1.31	21.9	7.8	29.7
L-5430	17.60	4.62	1.40	26.3	8.0	34.3
PRODUCT LINE E						
IL-67	16.95	4.18	1.34	24.6	7.9	32.5
LE-135	16.49	7.95	.68	48.2	4.1	52.3
MO-035	19.26	5.48	1.41	28.5	7.3	35.8
MO-046	13.64	3.91	1.35	28.7	9.9	38.6

An analysis such as shown above will not only provide a clue to which products have the greatest profit contribution; it will also provide a basis for evaluating the potential for cost savings through product redesign to reduce material cost and methods improvements to reduce labor cost.

1. Profit Contribution

   The analysis, as shown above, indicates the selling price per
   unit as well as the standard material and standard labor cost
   per unit. The material and direct labor costs are calculated
   as a percentage of the selling price. This percentage
   (material + labor) indicates the portion of the selling price
   that is required to recoup the prime cost. The contribution
   to profit within each product line can be determined for individual products by comparing the percentage of the selling price
   left after prime cost. Such a comparison for Product Line E
   shows that the IL-67 is the most profitable because only 32.5%
   of the selling price is required to cover prime cost. The
   LE-135 is the least profitable of the group because the
   percentage of the selling price required to cover prime costs
   is 52.3%. In the first case, 67.5% of the selling price is
   left to cover overhead, G&A and profit; while in the second,
   only 47.7% is left.

   Comparisons such as this should be made separately for each
   product line. It would not be correct to compare Product
   Line E items with Product Line A, for example because of the
   wide differences in the nature of the processing required.
   Product Line A requires greater use of high-cost molding equipment and, therefore, should be expected to yield a higher
   percentage after recovery of prime costs.

2. Potential for Cost Savings

    This type of analysis is also useful for pointing out areas in
    which cost savings should be directed to increase the contri-
    bution to profit. Product Line D, for example, shows that
    L-5430 has a higher percentage of material to selling price
    than the other items in the same line -- which are similar
    products. A study might reveal that redesign or use of
    substitute material could reduce the percentage of the selling
    price required for material.

    The same applies to MO-035 and MO-046 in Product Line E. In this
    case, a study of methods might reveal that the labor cost of MO-046
    could be reduced to be closer to the other items in the line.

COST ESTIMATING

Findings

    Material content in Exelon products ranges from 18% of selling
price to 56%, yet the same mark-up percentage is applied to all products
irrespective of material content. This concept of marking up all elements
of cost by the same percentage can be erroneous because it assumes that
such a percentage will result in the same return on investment for both
material content and conversion cost (labor and overhead content). While
in many instances it is possible that such is the case, this should not
be left to chance.

Recommendations

We recommend that the markup percentages being used be restudied
to develop two separate factors -- one to be applied to the material content
and one to the labor/overhead content. The markup for material content
would be based on recovery of material related investment. The markup
on labor and overhead content would be related to such investment factors
as fixed assets and the conversion cost content of inventories.

While the market place generally determines what the selling
price will be, the company, in making estimates of its costs and applicable markups, should use markup percentages that are as realistic
as possible.

OVERHEAD RATES

Findings

The use of a single overhead rate for the Plastics Department
is illustrative of how a departmental rate can have a distorting effect
on product costing. This department consists of:

- Molding operations. There are 24 molding presses using
  three direct labor operators per shift on each of the
  three shifts.

- Finishing operations. The operations in this section of
  the Plastics Department consist of sanding, buffing and
  hot stamping. Eighteen direct labor operators work in
  this section on a single shift operation.

It is apparent from the above that the overhead of twenty-four
molding machines and all the related support services result in a greater
overhead cost per unit of direct labor than is incurred in finishing, which

is essentially a bench operation using relatively simple equipment and
supplies. The comparison shown below illustrates how cost distortions
can occur when a single labor-based overhead rate is used.

	HOURS PER THOUSAND PIECES			
	Handle		Control	
	Hrs.	%	Hrs.	%
Molding	2.01	56	4.54	21
Finishing	1.60	44	17.16	79
	3.61	100%	21.70	100%

These figures show that the plastic handle requires more than half of the
total hours in molding while the plastic control requires only 21%. Since
the molding overhead rate is substantially greater than the finishing rate,
a single average departmental rate overstates the cost of one product and
understates the other.

Recommendations

        Overhead rates should be established to distinguish overhead
differences in processes rather than being established on a departmental
basis. We recommend that an analysis similar to that shown above be made
for certain other departments in which there is a mixture of processes
that could contain distortions in product costing through use of an
average departmental rate.

STANDARD LABOR COSTS

Findings

        In establishing labor standards, the allowances that are added
to provide for fatigue and unavoidable delays are applied on an across-

the-board basis. Although this method simplifies the arithmetic, it
distorts costs -- not only the labor cost but the overhead, when the
overhead rate is applied on labor.

Recommendations

      A study should be made to determine what the correct allowance
is for each of the manufacturing processes. In die casting, plating,
heat treating, and painting, individual allowances should be developed to
properly equate for the greater difficulty of the operation, so that more
time will be allowed. The allowance for the remaining operations, which
would be relatively low, could be applied on an across-the-board basis.

CONTROL OF INVENTORIES

Findings

      The procedures followed by the production control department
provide the basis for valuing inventories by their natural segments;
raw material, components in the work-in-process stockroom, floor work-in-
process and finished goods. However, there is no breakdown of inventories
on the books -- only one inventory account is carried. Relief of this
inventory is based on an historical percentage of cost of sales to sales
applied to each months sales.

Recommendations

      The cost standards should be used in costing the issues and
transfers between inventories. Individual inventory accounts should be
set up on the books for:

- Raw Material
- Components in work-in-process stockroom
- Floor inventory
- Finished goods

The finished goods inventory should be broken out to show the returned goods separately to assure that there is no buildup of returns because of improper handling.

To assure that the inventories will be properly accounted for, the documents used for issues and transfers should all be prenumbered and missing numbers must be accounted for. Physical controls must be strengthened by fencing-in areas adjacent to the shipping and receiving docks.

DATA PROCESSING SUPPORT

Findings

We found the systems personnel to have a high sense of urgency in the computerization of reports for the various departments. In their effort to meet the many demands for their services, however, we found that some of the implementation was hastily done -- with the result that users' needs were not as completely satisfied as they could have been.

Recommendations

The implementation schedule should be restudied to assure that:

- proper priorities are established for the various projects that are scheduled during the coming year.

- sufficient time is alloted to each of these projects to assure that user requirements are satisfied.

It may be necessary to delay some of the planned projects of lower priority. This is preferable to assure that those projects that are completed provide users with more useful information.

SECTION III - OPERATING CONTROLS

QUALITY CONTROL

Findings

A sampling of 100 rejects of finished products revealed that
32 should have been caught by assembly line inspectors; 59 represent
defects in purchased components; and 9 were due to other causes.

There are no standard procedures for process controls; these are
communicated verbally and inconsistencies arise because of misunderstandings.

Recommendations

Line inspectors should be required to put an identifying stamp
on each item inspected. The ability to identify the inspector responsible
for allowing the defect to pass should reduce carelessness as well as
identifying those inspectors who either are not qualified or who need
training.

An incoming inspection area should be established. All purchased
components should be inspected -- using appropriate sampling techniques.

A senior quality control engineer should be added to the staff
for the specific purpose of writing and updating procedures to be followed
in the various processes. He should also be responsible for monitoring
compliance and training key personnel in the application of the procedures.

PURCHASING

Findings

   Although purchases from the outside are large, the company does
not fully avail itself of blanket orders in which lower prices can be
negotiated because of larger commitments. This was evidenced in the
finding that one-third of the items were purchased more than three times
a year, but were not covered by blanket orders.

   Decisions to buy parts on the outside that can also be fabricated
in the plant are not supported by make-or-buy studies to assure that the
economics are taken into account.

   Insufficient effort is being expended to evaluate vendor
performance. The vendor is notified of poor performance only when a
serious problem occurs.

Recommendations

   A study should be made of all orders placed during the past
year -- and contemplated in the foreseeable future -- to determine which
of these should be covered by blanket orders in the future.

   A make-or-buy committee should be established. The committee
should be headed by the purchasing manager and represented by personnel
from quality control, industrial engineering and the controller's department.

   With the establishment of the incoming inspection section, a
vendor performance report should be prepared regularly for each source.
The quality as well as delivery must be taken into account in rating
the suppliers.

PRODUCTION CONTROL

Findings

We found that inventories turn over approximately 5 times per year, an indication that the inventory level is reasonable.

Stockouts occur too often; a frequent cause is rejected purchased parts. This problem of stockouts results in:

. More frequent assembly line changeovers than planned.

. Delays while additional parts are brought to the factory from outside warehouses. These warehouses are presently located in rented areas some five miles away. A new warehouse adjacent to the factory is presently being built to centralize the inventory.

Responsibility for providing components to the factory in conformance with production schedules is split between purchasing and production control.

The Production Control system is lacking in the following:

. Capacity planning; this is done in a haphazard manner.

. There is no machine loading to identify which work centers are overloaded and which are operating below capacity.

. Manpower loading of the lines is based on rules of thumb -- so many units of product per day -- rather than evaluating the labor requirements based on the differences in requirements of the various types of products to be run.

A computerized Production Control system with weekly status reports has recently been implemented, but certain byproducts of this system have not yet been utilized.

Recommendations

Because of the lack of proper coordination between the purchasing
and production control functions, we recommend the appointment of a
materials manager who would oversee both.

With the availability of computerized information, the company
should implement:

. machine loading
. requirements planning

For better control of raw material inventory, which represents
about 65% of total inventory value, the materials should be identified by
major types. A suggested breakdown is:

. Screw machine parts
. Castings
. Plastics
. Cartons
. All other

MANUFACTURING PERFORMANCE MEASUREMENTS

Findings

The present labor efficiency report, prepared on a departmental
basis, is based on accounting standards that are frozen for inventory
valuation purposes.

Although the efficiency of labor while on standard work is being
measured, no effort is being made to determine the percentage of time that
direct labor is utilized.

Recommendations

Efficiency reports should reflect the efficiency based on current standards which are predicated on the latest methods and processes. The difference between the frozen and current standard should be calculated to determine the methods change variance.

We recommend that nonutilized direct labor (labor not on productive work) be identified through use of a special coding such as:

1. Setup
2. Material shortage
3. Equipment problem
4. Tooling problem
5. Quality problem

The present efficiency report should be revised to reflect the

. utilization of labor
. efficiency based on current standards
. change of methods variance

A suggested format for this report is shown on the next page.

METHODS

Findings

Our plant tour revealed several areas in which methods could be improved. One of these had to do with the assembly line which was conveyorized to a point just short of the packing area. At that point, the product was taken off the conveyor by material handlers and manually loaded on a cart which was wheeled fifteen feet to the packing area.

In another area we found that an operator was drilling two holes as separate operations rather than simultaneously.

EFFICIENCY REPORT

FOR _____

☐ DAILY

☐ WEEKLY

DEPARTMENT		Direct Workers Total Hours	Utiliza-tion Percent	DIRECT LABOR HOURS			DIRECT LABOR DOLLARS				Methods Variance Dollars	Effi-ciency Percent
				STANDARD		Actual	STANDARD		Actual			
No.	N A M E			Frozen	Current		Frozen	Current				
		1	2	3	4	5	6	7	8		9	10

Utilization %: Column 2 = 5 divided by 1
Efficiency %: Column 10 = 4 divided by 5
Methods variance: Column 9 = 6 plus or minus 7
(favorable variance when 7 is less)

Recommendations

       We recommend that two actions be taken:

1. A full-time industrial engineer be assigned the responsibility of soliciting and implementing methods improvements.

2. A cost reduction report be prepared each month listing all cost reduction ideas that have been proposed, their status and annual savings.

LAYOUT

Findings

       We found the areas between the workbenches crowded because of cartons of parts that were stored between the workbenches. This condition results in delays when needed material cannot be found. Frequently, to find needed material, many boxes have to be moved out of the way to locate the required part. The new warehouse under construction on the east side of the building is intended to provide additional space for storing such parts.

Recommendations

       The parts required at the workplaces could be stored more conveniently and with a smaller area requirement if shelving were constructed. This would permit cartons (or bins) to be stored on three levels rather than spread over the floor area on one level.

       Serious consideration should be given to using part of the new warehouse building for production to facilitate a more efficient material flow.

MANUFACTURING ENGINEERING

Findings

       In our review of standards, we found in a test of 20 standards taken at random from products currently in production that 4 were incorrect. Two of these were estimates that were made when the product was introduced 18 months ago; the other two were based on methods that were changed. The philosophy being followed by the chief industrial engineer is that estimates on new products should remain as estimates until a production run is made and a time study made on the basis of studying an actual run.

Recommendations

       We disagree with the philosophy of leaving an estimate in the files until an actual production run is made. Estimates are frequently made by comparing a new product with another known product that resembles it. We recommend that all estimates be reviewed when prints become available and that a serious attempt be made to arrive at the best standard that can be developed. We also recommend that when methods are changed that all standards affected by these changes be updated.

NEW PRODUCT DEVELOPMENT

Findings

       We found the liaison between the new product development group and the manufacturing plant to be poor. Lead times on several items scheduled for production were less than one week. The bills of material did not include information on packing material requirements, necessitating several time-consuming phone calls.

<u>Recommendations</u>

       The function of coordinator should be assigned to one of the individuals in the product development group. His responsibility should include, not only coordination with the plant making the product but with the marketing group.

       When changes are made, we recommend that the new prints make some indication as to where the change was made to avoid the necessity of making a complete detailed comparison of the old and the new print.

Reporting and Control in Physical Distribution

Peter K. Sour*

This chapter discusses the time-and-place utility function of industry. This logistical function is commonly called *physical distribution*. The purpose of this chapter is to show methods for fully determining what is spent in the execution of the logistics mission and what is obtained for that spending.

A distribution system is composed of many interrelated activity centers and their associated costs. Because of the intricate cost relationships between physical distribution and other corporate functional areas, the development of an efficient physical distribution system must be based on an appraisal of the total system. This total cost approach is vital to the development of a physical distribution system that achieves the goals of costs and customer service. An example of such an interrelationship is increasing the inventory in order to reduce stockouts at the warehouse. Service may not improve, but inventory carrying costs certainly will.

As indicated in the simplified illustration of the total cost concept in Exhibit 1, the individual and total costs of alternative physical distribution systems vary and are determined by the warehouse configuration and customer service level of the system. The chart illustrates what alternatives will permit a constant level of customer service. The three cost components illustrated are: inventory, which increases with the number of warehouses; transportation, the

* Mr. Sour is Group Controller, Equipment & Transportation, Dravo Corporation, and Vice President, Finance, of Union Mechling Corporation, Pittsburgh.

EXHIBIT 1
Total Logistics Cost Concept*

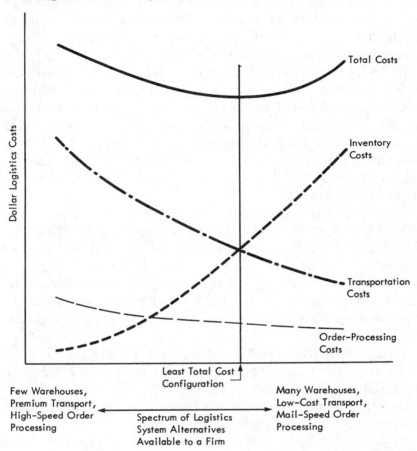

*James L. Heskett, Nicholas A. Glaskowsky, Jr., and Robert M. Ivie, *Business Logistics* (New York: The Ronald Press Co., 1973), p. 35.

premium-delivery portion of which will decrease if there are more warehouses closer to the customers; and order-processing costs. The chart illustrates that only a relatively narrow range of alternatives will produce the optimum cost structure for a given level of service.

Definition of Physical Distribution Function

In 1962 Peter Drucker wrote an article entitled "The Economy's Dark Continent."[1] Drucker wrote, "Almost 50¢ of each dollar the

---

[1] *Fortune Magazine,* April 1962, pp. 103, 265–70.

American consumer spends for goods goes for activities that occur after the goods are made, that is after they have come off of the dry end of the machine in finished form, to use the papermaker's graphic term. This is distribution, one of the most sadly neglected, most promising areas of American business."

In that 50 cents, Drucker not only included physical distribution activities but also others such as wholesaling, retailing, financing, and insuring. We will touch on that definition somewhat later. Drucker continued, "Economically, however, distribution is the process in which physical properties of matter are converted into economic value; it brings the customer to the product. But how much of the distributive cost is really 'value added,' how much is merely 'waste added?'"[2]

According to George A. Gekowitz, executive director of the National Council of Physical Distribution Management (NCPDM), they have defined *physical distribution management* as: "The term describing the integration of two or more activities for the purpose of planning, implementing and controlling the efficient flow of raw material, in-process inventory, and finished goods from the point of origin to the point of consumption." Later we will discuss each component in detail.

Perhaps a simpler definition of physical distribution would describe it as those activities necessary to connect geographically separated buyers and sellers, with the added function of offering a differentiated service response in a competitive environment which can result in a marketing advantage.

In the food industry, physical distribution has received a more than normal share of attention, principally because the profit margins of all members have been progressively shrinking. This is most obvious in food chain stores where margins have shrunk dramatically in the last few years. The result has been a rush to the panacea of sophisticated computer-based systems, an example of which is the "Cosmos" system. This was designed for The National Cash Register Company and tested in Jewel Tea's grocery stores in the midwestern United States.

The system can digest costs and revenues per square foot of shelf space and recommend to the store manager where a particular product can best be displayed and how many "facings" (how much

---

[2] Ibid.

space) should be allocated to produce a maximum profit. This analytical system, like others being considered, will reflect the full cost and profit of an item on the grocery store shelf. As an example, if one product takes less time to open, display, and price, it will have the marketing advantage and deserve a better position on the grocery store shelf. Similarly, the manufacturer who can preprint prices on the product, instead of requiring a stockroom clerk to do it, will have a competitive edge.

The kinds of pressures being felt by the typical food chain are being reflected back to the manufacturer. In fact, where the physical distribution costs are significant (e.g., 20 percent of the retail dollar), they surely will become the subject of an especially probing analytical approach. Not only have many such analyses been made but ongoing management systems have been developed.

EXHIBIT 2
Distribution Reporting and Control

Operating Cost (by function)	Customer Service (by geographical area)
Traffic/transportation	Inventory performance
Field offices	Delivery performance
Warehousing	Billing performance
Inventory carrying cost	
Administration	

In today's complex world of logistics, companies must cope with equally complex costing problems. The costing of the distribution/ logistics function must serve two fundamentally different purposes: control of the day-to-day operation of distribution and information for restructuring the distribution physical establishment.

In the discussion to follow, operating control will be discussed from the vantage point of the short-range plan and budgetary monitoring. The end of this chapter includes an introductory section on the restructuring of the distribution apparatus. The text covers the optimum location of plants and distribution centers and the modes of transportation that should be used to provide the optimum cost and service configuration.

Throughout the chapter, each one of the diagnostic tools will help the user observe two parallel factors: operating cost and customer service. These factors are delineated in Exhibit 2.

Management Decisions and Physical Distribution

In what could be considered a management primer, Bowersox, Smykay, and LaLonde define physical distribution management as "that responsibility to design and administer systems to control raw material and finished goods flow."[3]

The growth and diversification of our businesses, coupled with increased customer sophistication, have created many new demands upon our distribution systems. Further, it is becoming more and more apparent that management involvement is needed since distribution decisions will affect the total enterprise. Bernard Gallagher in his telegraphic style wrote: "Marketing to be revolutionized. Goals of marketing, sales directors to change from sales growth to profit maximization. Product managers to spend less time on promotions, more on distribution efficiencies. . . ."[4] Physical distribution is becoming more and more integrated into the marketing mix of options offered the customer. As that occurs, information about it and all its components must be developed and presented in such a way that management can see the results of its decisions in some finite and measurable way. Specifically, physical distribution must coordinate the inventory, customer deliveries, and other distribution activities, matching them to the customer-service requirements of the marketing program.

In Heskett's article, "Sweeping Changes in Distribution,"[5] he writes, "Management will devote more attention to, and change the nature of, responsibility for coordinated product flow. For example, expansions in product lines without a commensurate increase in sales produce higher inventory carrying costs as a percentage of sales. As a result, in order to maintain a given level of customer service, retailers and wholesalers are limiting their speculative risk by reducing stocks of any one item (or by investing a commensurate amount of money in inventory for a broader product line) while at the same time expecting and, in fact, depending on manufacturers' making speedy responses to their orders. This customer expectation, stated in the form of a willingness to substitute one

---

[3] Donald J. Bowersox, Edward W. Smykay, and Bernard J. LaLonde, *Physical Distribution Management: Logistics Problems of the Firm* (New York: Macmillan, Inc., 1968), p. 5.

[4] "The Gallagher Report, Inc." (New York, August 27, 1973).

[5] James L. Heskett, "Sweeping Changes in Distribution," *Harvard Business Review*, March–April 1973, p. 123.

manufacturer's product for another's in the event of the latter's inability to meet the customer's demands, in effect raises the incentive for speculation by manufacturers." Heskett goes on to talk about distribution utilities—in effect, middlemen consolidators between the producers and retailers eliminating the need for both the buyer and the seller to operate warehousing and transportation facilities.

Schiff points out that the classification of physical distribution costs in financial reports addressed to investors as well as those prepared for internal reporting on profit centers is not consistent with the organization of physical distribution as a separate business function.[6] Schiff further reports that the similarities between the physical distribution and manufacturing function are substantial and that the same kinds of data are required by both in order to optimize them.

ORGANIZATION OF THE DISTRIBUTION FUNCTION

Positioning

To study "positioning" requires a review of the many functions involved. One such function is customer service. This could conceivably be placed in the Marketing Division. Inventory management, perhaps because of the investment consideration, could be said to belong to the Financial Division. The traffic function, because of the inbound raw materials and outbound shipments, might suggest a factory orientation and could be placed within the Manufacturing Division. However, many companies are recognizing that such components can effectively be part of another rational unit; and the problem is realistically one of finding the right "fit" for the distribution responsibility.

However, if we concede that distribution is *one* function with many facets, then the positioning depends mostly on what management wants to accomplish at a particular time. Schiff, cited earlier, discusses the need for shifting the physical distribution function from manufacturing to marketing as a company enters the "new marketing concept." The whole idea in positioning distribution is to make sure it can accomplish the corporate objectives, maintain its

---

[6] Michael Schiff, *Accounting and Control in Physical Distribution Management* (Chicago: National Council of Physical Distribution Management, 1972).

integrity as a function, and retain control as an operating element. In time, no doubt, physical distribution will be the equal of the traditional functional areas. Schiff observes of the successful physical distribution manager that "success stems from the fact that he functions in his role as if he were indeed on a par with other functional areas."[7]

Degree of Centralization

It appears that consumer-products companies, or more generally, companies that have national marketing programs, find that it is more effective to centralize the physical distribution function. However, products which are not marketed nationally, and which are either a commodity or low cost, may be more effectively decentralized.

However, generalization is almost impossible, and any structure has to be tailored to the needs of the operation. Certain components can be centralized, at least from a control point of view. These include the data processing function, where centralization can be significant to achieve maximum utilization of the hardware involved. Inventory management and inventory planning are also candidates for centralized control.

Functional Components

Before proceeding to a description of the system to monitor and manage these components, it is appropriate to provide a brief description of each major functional component.

Traffic. Traffic, or "transportation," as it is becoming known, is that area of management and expenditure which deals with the physical flow of products. Under the direction of a general or national traffic manager, this function generally accounts for the largest single component of distribution costs. If we look at a traditional finished goods flow chart, we will note that there are three major flows: (1) customer shipments, either from a distribution center, a mixing point, or a factory; (2) warehouse supply, from factory or other suppliers; and (3) the return of goods from the customer. The general tendency has been to emphasize the cheapest mode of transportation. There are many technical points to traffic

---

[7] Ibid., p. 17.

management, such as freight-rate management, commerce commission rights, and permits, to name but a few.

Any firm in the *Fortune* "500" list must handle at least one-quarter million shipments annually with a cost equal to at least 3 percent of the sales dollar. Finite costs, proper allocation to cost centers, and standard costs have lagged behind considerably in their application to physical distribution. The principal reason for the lag is the problem of processing such a massive amount of data. However, in the last few years computer systems have been developed in which are filed all rates and applicable tariffs. Such data processing systems are now on the market and eliminate the need for internal development. The selection of a traffic data retrieval system can be further complicated by the other options now available. These can include bank-freight payment plans and freight reporting systems. Systems exist which will calculate and pay for the shipment without a freight bill, which entitles the shipper to a cost reduction. In fact, certain motor carrier tariff bureaus are considering a $1 reduction for each shipment for which they get paid but for which they do not have to prepare a freight bill.

Field/Customer Service Offices. Typically, field offices are remote from headquarters, receive the customers' orders, process them, and prepare them for the warehouses. The offices can have several basic functions: order processing, accounting, and accounts payable. They often are "landlords" for local sales offices. Many of these transactions can be isolated, identified, and productivity measures and standards applied. Normally this function has been neglected because it seems so fragmented.

Warehouses. Productivity measures are also key to successful warehouse operation. The older manager with 20 years of service knew how these factors worked: they point out the problems that occur in trying to serve customers in the response time allotted. Naturally, the degree of specialization within the warehouse can contribute significantly to its productivity as can the layout of the facility itself. The equipment, too, influences productivity and efficiency of the operation. These components must be considered to gauge rationally the success of one warehouse compared to its previous performance, to other warehouses in the system, or to engineered standards.

The most common reason for engineered standards is to form a base for a productivity-oriented incentive payment system. However, incentives should be avoided unless there will be no substantial changes in work methods; nothing can more effectively hamper innovation in work methods than an incentive system. For example, the author has witnessed an incentive system which links a warehouseman's pay to productivity in loading railcars. This incentive plan was designed in the era before the forklift truck. The forklift truck driver who became the successor to this task earned more, not only because of the work but also because management gave the truck driver a tool they had not imagined when they designed the incentive system for loading railcars.

Inventories. Stocks of finished goods form a buffer between plants and customers because the customer's requirement seldom is tailored exactly to the plant's capacity. But different production strategies will have different inventory results. Does the change in Year 2 production strategy shown in Exhibit 3 justify the increased inventory?

In a competitive environment, the time utility (i.e., speed of delivery) function becomes important to respond to an identified customer's service requirement. Presently, customers are tending to reduce inventory levels. Thus, inventories are now stored closer to the customer's location at the manufacturer's field warehouses.

EXHIBIT 3
Effects of Alternate Production Strategies

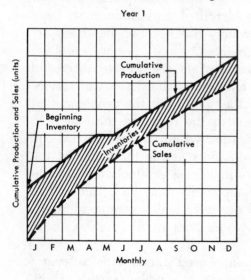
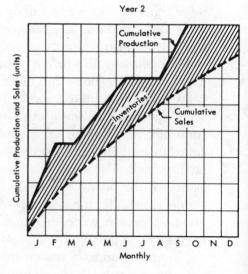

From any inventory management system, to whatever degree automated, we must learn, too, how efficient inventory-level policies are. The system must reveal that part of the inventory that is essentially fixed, and the component which is discretionary and related to the level of customer service required.

Administration. Behind all these components is a centralized administrative function which must direct the day-to-day operations as well as provide the plans necessary for the future. This centralized bureaucracy also has a productivity, perhaps more difficult to evaluate. Nonetheless, administration does have a cost function that can get out of control.

NEED FOR A SYSTEM

Purpose

The purpose of a system of cost and service reporting is to provide management at different levels with an integrated, methodical approach toward realistic measurement and evaluation of the distributive system's total performance. Manufacturing standard cost systems are well developed, established, and accepted. This relatively new process "industry" also needs controls. In fact, viewing the distribution function as a process will make it much easier to systematize.

Additionally, this system is expected to fill a long-recognized gap in management's ability to discharge fully its responsibility, to exercise its options in the field of distribution, and to be advised on the results of its actions. The president of the largest food company in the world wrote, "In recent years, the importance of distribution has been steadily growing . . . for these reasons, I feel that distribution as a whole warrants more attention and so it has been decided to distribute this manual on distribution controllership."

It is distribution controllership that any system must provide, including selected information keyed to different levels of management in relevant terms. Because both of the above-mentioned elements (costs and service) are inseparable in any useful evaluation, the results must be reported jointly. This permits management to take results-directed action without the risk of jeopardizing other valuable objectives.

Justification

To illustrate the need for a system, it might be useful to compare the traditional treatment of distribution expense with this proposed approach.

The Traditional Method. This method primarily serves financial-reporting requirements rather than operational needs. As a result, distribution expenses or parts of it are found scattered under headings as "corporate overhead," "manufacturing costs," "factory overhead," "selling expense," "cost of goods," or "distribution expense." Total distribution costs are not readily visible and, therefore, are difficult to measure and control. Also, meaningful comparisons between different operations may not be possible. Similarly, new-product distribution and resultant costs would be difficult to anticipate.

Illustrated in Exhibit 4 are some of the ways that traditional profit and loss statement captions can disguise distribution costs. As an example, freight costs for moving raw material can be hidden in the line labeled "Cost of goods sold." For years it has been very "neat" accounting to absorb the freight on inbound materials with the production costs. This practice, however, has made it difficult for distribution managers to determine the transportation costs in

EXHIBIT 4
Typical Product Profit and Loss Statement

	Actual	Variance	Costs Not Readily Seen
Revenues	$XX	$XX	
Discounts	XX	XX	
Net sales	$XX	$XX	
Cost of goods sold	XX	XX—	{ Freight on raw material
Freight and warehousing	XX	XX	{ Packaging material
Variable profit	$XX	$XX	
Advertising	XX	XX	
Promotion	XX	XX	
Market research	XX	XX	
Other marketing	XX	XX	
Fixed factory costs	XX	XX	
Product contribution	$XX	$XX	
Marketing expense	XX		{ Field offices
Administration and general	XX	XX—	{ Distribution headquarters
Operating income	$XX	$XX	{ Depreciation of owned
Depreciation	XX	XX—	{ facilities
			{ Cost of excess inventory
Interest	XX	XX—	{ Product damage
Income before taxes	$XX	$XX	

order to optimize them. Purchasing managers need to be sure that the delivered price they get is the best corporate "buy," but they must include transportation costs. This is difficult for them to do without the support of distribution managers. Similarly, packaging material savings can result in increased product damage. Most accounting systems make no attempt to link these, nor can traditional systems do the job.

The freight and warehouse category seems straightforward. But does it in fact include warehousing at the production factory? Are data really available in a useful format, or do the data exist but not address the distribution manager's cost information needs?

The corporate "Administrative and general" category may include distribution management and the field office operation, with little information, certainly, on their relative productivity.

Depreciation might well cloud management's ability to see the difference between leased and owned facilities. All leased warehouses' costs would be included in the fifth line of the Exhibit 4 profit and loss, while owned facilities would show a substantial charge to depreciation.

The cost of carrying excess amounts of finished goods inventory is not the kind of accounting entry a corporate controller can make. Excessive inventory can help smooth production and compensate for sales forecast errors; or it can be used to make life excessively simple—a luxury that cannot be afforded in today's business environment.

The New Approach.   Under this approach, all elements of distribution costs are brought under a single management heading. A logical grouping by function can give them the required visibility, such as:

Distribution management and administration;

Warehousing of finished goods at factories;

Warehouse replenishment;

Warehouse operations;

Customer delivery;

Unit load means (containers, pallets, etc.); and

Inventory carrying costs.

Under this approach the total system cost is readily available and presented in comprehensive and understandable form. The tracing of interactions between different cost elements becomes possible. Additionally, meaningful comparison can now be made between different operations or even different divisions within the same company; further, the cost of new-product distribution and delivery channels can be more accurately determined.

Today's managers surely will have devised some sort of a reporting system. These "bootleg" reports are necessary until a system such as the one discussed here is installed—a system which satisfies their needs.

Potential

The potential benefits from the distribution costing system, as experience has shown, are many. Among them are:

It motivates distribution management to take controlled action in applying existing marketing policies.

It encourages marketing management to conduct profit-oriented reviews of existing marketing and stock policies with advanced knowledge of the costs.

It permits conclusive analysis of different distribution patterns out of which more differentiated customer service policies may develop.

Based upon the author's experience, it can be safely stated that cost reductions ranging from 5 to 10 percent can be expected within three years of introduction. For large and complex firms, realizable savings have been found to be even on a greater scale. To take advantage of this potential requires certain internal capabilities and resources which may have to be developed, as the system not only provides the necessary information but obliges the users to take action. The author has witnessed successful installations throughout Europe and the Americas.

The Distribution Controller

At this point the reader will recognize that a large business must make a large commitment in organizing data to properly inform distribution management. One way to recognize this is to establish a distribution controllership function. Major effort has been expended by a number of firms to establish a distribution cost system. However, accountants cannot be asked to modify a bookkeeping system solely for operational needs, nor can systems developed solely by distribution managers answer with credibility questions by others within the business firm.

Distribution managers develop their own systems and often succeed in challenging and stimulating the corporate accountant. Much of the data used by the distribution manager must of necessity tie into the books of the company; therefore, the distribution manager must have access to corporate accounting systems through someone properly skilled.

Whether the direct control of the skilled person lies with the distribution manager or the corporate controller, and the "dotted line" to the other, is of little importance. The major objective is that a connecting link between the distribution manager and the corporate accounting structure must be forged. Most frequently the distribution controller reports to the distribution manager. Thus, the distribution manager can design the cost control mechanisms and set the priorities for the distribution controller. This leaves the corporate controller in a position to critique the technical efforts of the distribution controller.

SYSTEM DESCRIPTION

Performance Measurement and Evaluation

Effectiveness and cost of distributive systems are not easily measured and evaluated. There are several reasons for this. To a large extent, this is due to numerous and varying external influences which force marketing to continually reevaluate its customer-service policies. For example, what may be deemed acceptable performance today could be considered unacceptable tomorrow because of competitive activity.

Another problem is that distributive capability cannot be stored awaiting surges in customer demand. Instead, it is expended on a day-to-day basis. Capability to deliver must, in most cases, respond to peaks in demand. Conversely, rapid communications and a corresponding reporting frequency on operations and costs are essential. Extensive use of ratios is made with the underlying philosophy that the information reported should be expressed in meaningful terms to make it actionable. Experience in multiple installations of such a system has shown that a certain amount of expertise is required in working with ratios; this experience can be developed through practice. Generally, a set of ratios is needed to analyze the expense. For example:

1. Costs as a percent of net sales may decrease; and
2. Cost per ton may increase.

This case illustrates the need to understand if price increases are masking increased distribution costs. A distribution manager certainly can use these data.

Costs. The principal distribution cost components, as we have discussed earlier, are freight, warehousing, administration, and inventory carrying cost. All but the last of these are normally accumulated within an accounting system and can be extracted to suit the particular needs of distribution management. None is meant to be the sole measure of productivity, but each one may be a key indicator. With these figures it is possible to evaluate not only the cost of each transaction, which will differ among locations based on a number of factors, but also a productivity index which can yield a more objective comparable tool than costs alone.

Exhibit 5 shows a summary ratio table for field operations, both offices and warehouses. The office section essentially covers the administrative group where, in a typical distribution operation, customer orders, adjustments, or invoice corrections are being processed. Not only must managers see cost per document but they must also see the numbers of transactions performed per hour. This will provide appreciation of the efficiency of the operation and differences between operations.

In the example shown, Location 1 processes 2.9 documents per man-hour but they cost $5.31 each. Location 3, on the other hand, has only about half the productivity, but less than one third the cost of Location 1. The purpose of this reporting system fundamentally is to provide a basis for asking questions. Its purpose is not to provide all the answers.

On the warehouse side of this form you will note that the cost of Warehouse 3 was 175 percent of budget and twice the cost per case of Warehouse 1. Certainly each summary of the sort illustrated above will have to have base data work sheets which we will not attempt to illustrate here.

EXHIBIT 5

VARIABLE COST PERFORMANCE
January–December

Period _____

Location	Offices								Warehouses				
	Cost $(000)			Variable Cost per Document	% versus Total Budget	Documents per Hour		% versus Total Budget	Cost $(000)			Variable Cost Company Wholesale Only	
	Variable	Fixed	Total			This Month	Year to Date		Variable	Fixed	Total	Per Case	Per Ton
1	$ 509.3	$ 48.5	$ 557.9	$5.31	100	2.9	2.9	106	$ 311.8	$ 174.4	$ 486.2	$0.028	$3.17
2	$ 105.1	$ 7.6	$ 112.8	$4.32	87	7.9	2.7	104	$ 147.0	$ 87.9	$ 235.0	$0.030	$2.99
3	$ 24.8	$ 2.2	$ 27.0	$1.62	78	1.7	1.5	175	$ 193.0	$ 151.3	$ 344.4	$0.056	$5.32
4	$ 131.4	$ 20.8	$ 152.3	$3.76	105	2.7	2.1	105	$ 168.0	$ 72.8	$ 240.9	$0.036	$3.18
Other Locations													
National	$2,999.9	$211.4	$39,211.3	$4.70	99	2.2	1.9	112	$2,471.7	$2,000.8	$4,472.5	$0.042	$4.16

Occasionally, productivity of a warehouse can be significantly affected by certain limiting factors which are not totally controllable by either the warehouse or the office. In these cases it is important that the manager know the magnitude of these inhibiting forces in order to properly assess them. Illustrated in Exhibit 6 are the operating limitations for warehouses and then net productivity.

The operating limitations shown in this example are restricted to the things that the warehouse does not control. Inbound palletization rate illustrates the amount of physical work that must be done. Since all the inbound materials do not come readily prepared for handling, the warehouse must load the product onto pallets by hand. The other example shown is stenciling. Illustrative of this is that Warehouse I must do a considerable amount of stenciling; other warehouses do not report that much. The stenciling refers to a legal requirement in some market zones to label each case with the customer's name and address. The effect on productivity should be readily discernible. However, Location 1 shows up well on the productivity report (last two columns of Exhibit 5). Have they found an efficient way to handle this process?

Inventory Status. Inventory levels of finished goods change as the result of specific actions, some of which are intended to improve customer service. Exhibit 7 shows the inventory coverage in weeks for the period just ended, as well as near-term projections.

The coverage figure portrays the amount of time the inventory should last against projected sales. Stock availability is the customer service measurement for inventories and is defined as the percent of stock instantly available to fill customer orders.

To illustrate, Product 1 has stock availability of 98.4 percent for the year to date with slightly more than three weeks coverage. Product 7, a very seasonal summer product, has a year-to-date stock availability of 91.6 percent. This was inferior to last year, yet the product has seven weeks of inventory. Certainly this would suggest that this inventory was not where and when it was needed.

It is possible to have less than 100 percent stock availability with, say, six weeks of inventory. With more than one warehouse, there is a chance that the stock is in transit or that it has been put in the wrong place because of an error in the forecasted sales. While this forecast error can be measured and compensated for, it will occur.

Exhibit 7 illustrates that Product 1 had a lower stock availability, partly because there was a three-week inventory in the last month.

EXHIBIT 6

WAREHOUSE RATIO TABLE
December
Period _____

Company-Operated Warehouse	Operating Limitations								Productivity in Net Distribution Hours			
	Inbound Palletization Rate (1)				Outbound Stenciling Rate (2)				Case per Hour		Tons per Hour	
	Cases		Tons		Cases		Tons					
	This Month	Year to Date	This Month	Year to Date	This Month	Year to Date	This Month	Year to Date	This Month	Year to Date	This Month	Year to Date
1	46.4	81.3	86.2	88.2	14.2	9.8	13.3	9.1	621.7	402.7	4.0	3.6
2	92.5	95.9	92.4	96.4	—	—	—	0.1	462.3	414.8	3.9	4.2
3	99.5	91.8	99.5	93.7	—	0.5	—	0.5	245.4	249.7	2.9	2.8
4	93.3	94.0	53.3	87.4	—	2.5	0	4.0	489.0	313.0	7.0	3.7
Other Locations												
National	82.5	91.9	87.4	92.8	11.8	11.4	11.8	11.1	451.3	362.0	4.3	3.7

EXHIBIT 7

INVENTORY STATUS

December Report

Coffee Products	Percent Stock Availability				Coverage in Weeks — Projected				
	Last Year		This Year		December	January	February	March	April
	Year to Date	Month	Year to Date	Month					
1	98.4	98.4	98.4	98.3	3.	6.	6.	5.	7.
2	90.4	86.4	96.9	92.6	4.	4.	7.	8.	8.
3	97.6	99.7	97.6	93.8	7.	7.	9.	8.	9.
4	86.9	84.8	96.4	95.5	12.	15.	14.	17.	13.
5	98.6	98.3	98.6	99.5	3+	4+	5+	6.	7.
6	98.7	74.5	98.7	98.3	6+	6+	6+	6+	7+
7	98.8	100.0	91.6	92.0	7+	7+	7+	7+	7+
8	88.8	88.7	96.7	98.9	13.8	16+	16+	16+	16+
Total Coffee Products	97.8	98.3	97.8	96.2					
Other Products									

This "low" inventory situation will be improved, the report shows, in the future.

Service. Shown in Exhibit 8 are billing and delivery problems which are illustrative of service functions which need to be monitored. For the office we show these billing errors that are caused by the distribution department as well as those that are caused by other factors. An example of those that are not related to, nor caused by, distribution is the late notification of a change in price or promotional package being offered to customers at the last moment. There is no question that this may be dictated by the marketplace. The distribution group must correct the initially incorrect bill. In the illustration, Location 2 has created twice as many "distribution" errors in December as any other location. While the December errors significantly increased that location's annual error rate, it is Location 3 that should be looked at first, because of their high annual error rate. Are the errors theirs, or are they caused by influences beyond their control?

Warehouse service situations can vary considerably by type. To illustrate, stockouts are shown to see if there is a location which is a key cause to those national problems shown earlier in the inventory status report. Location 2 seems to have more out of stock and may be more difficult to forecast. Is the proper response more safety stock or just closer supervision?

Now turning to customer refusals, we see illustrated that Location 4 has a higher level of customer refusals than any other location shown. This may be a function of poor order processing, order picking, or even of late delivery. Regardless of the cause, it will certainly need to be investigated.

Customer returns are another mirror on shipment performance. High returns may be the result of merchandise arriving too late or not living up to specifications. "Customer L&D" refers to those claims presented by customers for loss or damage of products shipped to them and subsequently billed to them. Any location with an unusually high level of customer L&D, such as illustrated by Location 4, warrants a close scrutiny to determine the principal causes.

The customer service interface is multifaceted and truly includes not only the successful and timely shipping of orders but the rendering of correct invoices. Each firm will have to define for itself the key categories on which to focus initially, but they will generally

EXHIBIT 8

RATIO TABLE CUSTOMER SERVICE PERFORMANCE

December

Period _____

Location	Office Billing Errors (1)						Warehouse Service Situations (2)							
	Distribution		Nondistribution		Total		Stockout		Customer Refusal		Customer Return		Customer L&D (3)	
	This Month	Year to Date	This Month	Year to Date	This Month	Year to Date	This Month	Year to Date	This Month	Year to Date	This Month	Year to Date	This Month	Year to Date
1	0.8	1.3	3.0	2.4	12.9	9.3	7.2	6.2	0.4	1.1	4.3	1.3	1.1	.6
2	2.0	1.5	2.5	2.1	19.5	18.4	15.1	14.0	0.9	0.5	1.0	1.5	2.5	2.4
3	1.0	2.2	2.3	3.9	16.6	14.4	9.3	7.8	0.4	0.2	1.1	1.6	5.8	4.8
4	0.6	1.3	3.0	2.2	30.2	15.8	10.4	8.0	2.4	1.0	3.2	1.6	14.1	4.4
Other Locations														
National	1.2	1.5	1.9	2.0	20.3	15.4	14.9	11.1	0.6	0.5	1.1	0.9	3.7	2.9

include the items which are shown in Exhibit 8 on customer service. On-time shipment and/or deliveries may also warrant inclusion. Each of the ratios is developed from the number of incidents versus the number of customer shipments which actually occurred.

Logistics System Changes

Logistics managers periodically face decisions as to how the logistics system must be changed to respond to changes in the demands on the system. For example, the interrelationship of number of factories and their location with the number of warehouses is a matter requiring periodic reconsideration. As one geographic area expands in its consumption of a particular product, the marketers are relatively quick to respond. However, distribution management, too, needs information in order to reshape the distribution system.

A nineteenth-century German philosopher, Johann von Thunen, began the work that currently is described as transportation theory. In this theory, he recognized the fact that the further from the market the producer was, the less competitive he became. This theory can be explored more systematically and rigorously because of the development of two different mathematical techniques which can be used (among other things) to help evaluate distribution strategies of the business firm. These two techniques are called "simulation" and "linear programming." It is not our aim here to describe either technique in detail.[8] Rather, we will briefly treat them from their data input point of view.

Linear programming is a technique used to find a mode of operation which will maximize profit (or minimize costs) given (1) a set of resources which can be applied to that operation and (2) a set of requirements (such as customer demands) which must be fulfilled. A special class of linear programming problem is the "transportation problem." This is best understood by considering a simple example:

Example: Farmer Smith and Farmer Jones belong to a dairy cooperative which operates two milk processing plants. Smith's farm produces 20,000 gallons a day, while Jones's produces 80,000. Each of the two plants, located at Payson and Spring-

---

[8] For more information on these techniques, see: Harold Bierman, Jr., Charles P. Bonini, and Warren H. Hausman, *Quantitative Analysis for Business Decisions*, 5th ed. (Homewood, Ill.: Richard D. Irwin, Inc., 1977).

ville, can process 50,000 gallons a day. Smith's farm is 2 miles from Payson and 5 miles from Springville, while Jones's farm is 4 miles from Payson and 8 miles from Springville. Since the cooperative reimburses the farmers for transporting milk to the plants, it is in the two farmers' best interests to minimize the total hauling (gallon-miles) for the cooperative, as opposed to minimizing the hauling for either farmer viewed individually.

Linear programming can be used to minimize total gallon-miles in this problem. The minimum is 540,000 gallon-miles, and is attained by having Smith ship all his milk to Springville, while Jones ships 30,000 gallons to Springville and 50,000 gallons to Payson. Note that this "optimal solution" might not be apparent to Farmer Smith, since it involves his shipping to the plant which is 3 miles more distant from his farm.

Although the problem is more complex, the same technique can be applied to the situation shown in Exhibit 9, where a company is shipping from 11 factories to 17 warehouses. If the company can determine the production capacity of each plant, the demand at each warehouse, and the transportation cost between each plant

EXHIBIT 9
Location of Field Distribution Centers

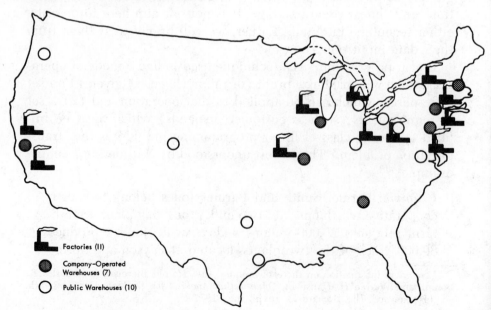

Factories (11)

Company–Operated Warehouses (7)

Public Warehouses (10)

and each warehouse, then a linear programming approach can be used to determine what goods to ship from which plant to which warehouse in order to minimize total transportation costs.

An even more elaborate problem related to Exhibit 9 is as follows. The company feels that it is spending too much on public warehouse costs and wants to drop the use of some public warehouses and build one or more additional company warehouses. The company can formulate a linear programming problem for each warehouse configuration it wants to evaluate. For example, a problem can be formulated which drops both Texas public warehouses and replaces them with a new company warehouse in, say, Arlington, Texas. The minimum total transportation cost for this configuration can be compared with the original configuration in Exhibit 9 to see if there are in fact cost savings from the new configuration and, if so, if these savings are sufficient to justify investment in the new company warehouse. Similarly, any number of alternative configurations can be evaluated, including, for example, dropping all public warehouses and adding company warehouses in several locations. This methodology will not necessarily result in finding the "ideal" configuration, but it will identify the best of all the alternatives considered, *before* a decision has to be made on any one of these alternatives. (Incidentally, there are very sophisticated techniques which *can* come quite close to finding the "ideal" configuration.)

The "simulation" technique involves describing some real-world process in mathematical terms. How well the simulation model describes the real-world process can be tested by feeding into the model actual input data from past experience and seeing if the model is a good predictor of the known actual results.

For example, a model can be built to simulate a plant's operations. Data can then be fed into this model about what the plant is required to produce (say, last year's actual production), and then the model will predict the materials, man-hours, and other resources needed for this level of production, along with the total costs of these resources. The model can then be "fine tuned" so that the production costs it predicts are virtually the same as the plant's actual costs for that level of production—that is, until the model correctly simulates the actual production situation.

However, the real value of a simulation model comes not from its ability to simulate the past. Rather, the value comes from its ability to predict some future result, given assumptions about future conditions. In our example, this means using the plant model to predict costs of *next* year's planned production, taking into account, of course, any anticipated increases in material costs, labor rates, worker efficiency, and so on.

Simulation can be used in a number of distribution problems where it is desirable to be able to predict the results of making a decision *before* the decision has to be made. Consider the following example:

> *Example:* Acme Steel Supply Company is considering how many trucks to lease for the coming year. These trucks are used exclusively to deliver steel products from Acme's one warehouse to its customers. It is important in this business to be able to deliver quickly, as the customers, which are relatively small steel users, tend to want shipment within one or two days of placing their orders so as to minimize their own inventory investment. Thus, while there is clearly an out-of-pocket cost to adding trucks to the fleet, there is also the possibility of a "cost" in the form of profits on lost sales if a competitor can deliver more quickly than Acme because Acme has too few trucks.
>
> Acme analyzed its past sales data to determine probability distributions for the number of truckloads required per day and the trip time per truckload. Also identified were lease costs per truck per year, and an "imputed" goodwill-loss cost for each day beyond 24 hours a shipment was delayed. These data were sufficient to design a simulation model, which simulated a year's sales, and calculated total leasing and lost-customer goodwill costs, first for a fleet of two trucks, then three trucks, then four trucks, and so on. The simulation showed the best fleet size was eight trucks.

Similar applications simulation include: deciding how many loading docks to have at a warehouse; determining whether an airport should have parallel runways to permit virtually simultaneous takeoffs; deciding how many elevators a high-rise building needs; and so on.[9]

---

[9] In Chapter 16 the reader can learn how simulation can be used to reflect uncertainties in capital budgeting problems. For another application of simulation to a logistics problem, see Harvey N. Shycon and Christopher R. Sprague, "Put a Price Tag on Your Customer Servicing Levels," *Harvard Business Review*, July–August 1975, p. 71.

Physical Distribution Cost Dynamics

The total cost of the physical distribution system is directly related to the customer service offered by the system and by its configuration. Within the system configuration and between its components exists a network of cost interrelationships which changes with every change in the system. Therefore, fewer warehouses want larger and costlier deliveries. However, *aggregate* costs are what management needs to know in order to decide on a final system configuration.

Transportation expenses are usually the largest cost component and are greatly affected by the number and location of warehouses in the system. (See Exhibit 10.) Generally, as the number of warehouses in the system increases, the distance to the customer is reduced. The transportation costs can be reduced if these costs are

EXHIBIT 10
Transportation Costs in Relation to Number of Warehouses

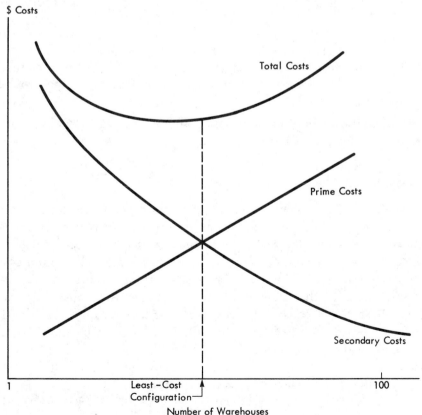

Number of Warehouses

linear in their relationship to distance. However, as the number of warehouses increases, the factory shipment to the warehouse decreases in size, with an increase in unit cost because of the loss of economies of scale.

Because the cost of operating a warehouse is greatly influenced by its size, the number of warehouses in the system has a direct relationship with the average size of the warehouse. A smaller number of warehouses in the system will result in a lower total-cost level,[10] again due to the economy of scale rules.

The inventory should be held to the minimum level necessary for providing the prescribed customer service level. An increase in the number of warehouses will increase the total safety-stock requirements and the amount of inventory required. An increased number of warehouses from 1 to 10 must be matched by a commensurate increase in safety stock from, say, 1,000 units to 10,000 units. This would have no commensurate increase in total sales or service. The cost system must properly identify these increased inventory carrying costs.

> We attempt to identify each cause of extra cost in physical distribution. In almost every case, the solution is a trade-off. The system is so interrelated that a push in one place causes a bulge in another. If the bulge you get is smaller than the push you had, then you've made progress.[11]

The simulation technique mentioned above is useful in dealing with these complex interrelationships.

SUMMARY

The physical distribution cost system must stand the test of use. It must be able to answer why costs are up for transportation, warehousing, and office operations. The manager must be able to see if the customer service requirements justified the use of premium-cost modes of shipment. The manager must see if a geographical change in sales changes the transportation and warehousing cost. If, however, most of the causes of change in cost levels cannot be identified by the reporting system, then the system must be modified to respond to those questions.

---

[10] Bowersox et al., *Physical Distribution Management*, p. 226.

[11] John H. Gerstenmaier, president, Goodyear Tire & Rubber Company, unpublished "Presidential Issue: Handling and Shipping," September 1976, p. 7.

The accounting system cannot be expected to answer for every customer, item, and location, but must provide the base to permit the business to respond competitively and profitably. The cost reporting system we have discussed is meant to provide clear insight into the costs, to isolate these costs into meaningful groups, to provide a cost accountability against standards and/or budgets, and to provide an interface with profitability studies. The long-term effect looked for by distribution managers can influence the type of packaging material used, and even the class of trade to be solicited by their company's marketing effort.

We must acknowledge that there are differences in delivering goods between downtown Kansas City and downtown New York City. To presume one standard delivery cost may result in failure of a product. This could be because these factors were not properly assessed.

Management of the firm expects certain distribution costs to remain fixed, especially the administrative apparatus. However, management can expect certain costs to rise directly as a function of sales, while some costs rise less quickly than the increase in sales. Flexible budgeting can profitably be introduced for distribution cost control, and can adjust to the changes in sales volumes without the costs' appearing as nothing more than another cost increase.

Control of the distribution function can only be achieved if service and cost data are organized into a useful, timely, and understandable system of reporting, and management takes appropriate action—for without action, there is no need for a system.

ADDITIONAL SOURCES

Aretos, Gust M. "Developing Warehouse Costs." *Management Accounting,* October 1972, p. 46.

Bierman, Harold, Jr.; Bonini, Charles P.; and Hausman, Warren H. *Quantitative Analysis for Business Decisions,* chaps. 12–16, 21. 5th ed. Homewood, Ill.: Richard D. Irwin, Inc., 1977.

Bowersox, Donald J.; Smykay, Edward W., and LaLonde, Bernard J. *Physical Distribution Management: Logistics Problems of the Firm.* New York: Macmillan, Inc., 1968.

Burdeau, Howard B. "Planning and Control of Distribution Costs." *Managerial Planning,* July–August 1973, p. 37.

Enright, Richard D. "Standard Costs for Delivery Systems." *Management Accounting,* January 1974, p. 34.

Friedman, Walter F. "Physical Distribution: The Concept of Shared Services." *Harvard Business Review*, March–April 1975, p. 24.

Goeffrion, Arthur M. "A Guide to Computer-Assisted Methods for Distribution Systems Planning." *Sloan Management Review*, Winter 1975, p. 17.

Haskett, James L. "Sweeping Changes in Distribution." *Harvard Business Review*, March–April 1973, p. 123.

————; Glaskowsky, Nicholas A.; and Ivie, Robert M. *Business Logistics*. New York: The Ronald Press Co., 1973.

Lewis, Ronald J. "How Accountants Can Help Physical Distribution Management." *Cost and Management*, May–June 1972, p. 18.

Neuner, John J. W., and Deakin, Edward B. *Cost Accounting: Principles and Practice*, chap. 19. 9th ed. Homewood, Ill.: Richard D. Irwin, Inc., 1977.

Neuschel, Robert P. "Physical Distribution—Forgotten Frontier." *Harvard Business Review*, March–April 1967, p. 125.

Schiff, Michael. *Accounting and Control in Physical Distribution Management*. Chicago: National Council of Physical Distribution Management, 1972.

Shycon, Harvey N., and Sprague, Christopher R. "Put a Price Tag on Your Customer Servicing Levels." *Harvard Business Review*, July–August 1975, p. 71.

Stern, George L. "Traffic: Clear Signals for Higher Profits." *Harvard Business Review*, May–June 1972, p. 72.

Stolle, John F. "How to Manage Physical Distribution." *Harvard Business Review*, July–August 1967, p. 93.

39

Order Entry and
Inventory Control

Harrison H. Appleby*

"Nothing happens around here until somebody sells something."
Unfortunately, in some cases nothing much happens even then.

In a well-run company adopting a physical distribution management outlook, the first statement will likely be true and the second not true. When somebody sells something, things should indeed happen. Though this statement is obvious, there are no automatic results. To produce results, a company will have to relate its business systems to its physical distribution activities. This chapter discusses the value of establishing that relationship.

PHYSICAL DISTRIBUTION ACTIVITIES

Unfortunately, there does not appear to be a universal method for undertaking physical distribution systems analysis, although there does appear to be a hierarchical ordering of activities that can be sequenced as follows:

Order entry.
Inventory control.
Sales forecasting.

---

* Mr. Appleby is a Principal with Touche Ross & Company in Chicago.

Order Entry

An *order-entry system* is the cornerstone of all business systems. Statistics obtained from accepting and processing an order, its subsequent shipment, and billing, form an information base for managing the entire company. For example:

Order-entry statistics are utilized in computerized forecasting models to determine future requirements for finished goods and plant capacity.

Order-entry statistics are utilized to project external requirements such as finished goods, warehousing, and transportation.

The shipment of an order results in transportation/traffic statistics required for plant and warehouse site selection.

The shipment of an order results in an invoice (record of sale) which, in turn, provides the statistical data utilized for sales analysis, sales compensation, promotions, advertising, and cash flow planning.

For these reasons and others too numerous to detail here, order entry is clearly the single most important focal point in the systems analysis effort associated with the development of physical distribution systems.

The approach utilized in developing an order-entry system must be tailored to the needs of the individual enterprise. The factors to determine the right approach to follow would include:

Frequency of demand.

Number of customers.

Lead-time demand.

Customer delivery requirements.

Geographical considerations.

To illustrate the application of these factors, consider the case of a large, regionally oriented enterprise with annual sales of $500 million. Based on this sales volume alone, there might be an inclination to consider developing a very sophisticated online order-entry system. However, in this particular case, a closer look revealed that the company had a comparatively small product line and relatively few customers, all of whom purchased in large, bulk quantities. In this situation, it simply would not have been practical to recommend development of a large, complex computer system for order entry.

On the other hand, a large, national distribution organization with thousands of customers and many thousands of order-entry transactions could easily justify a large, complex, online system, even if overall sales volumes were not larger than those of the company cited above. The determining factors are order-entry volume, the necessity to deliver small orders to a large group of customers, geographic dispersion, customer-service criteria, customer stocking habits, and so on.

Another important element of an order-entry system is the task of *order fulfillment.* Order fulfillment encompasses the activities and procedures necessary to process an order through a warehouse or factory, pick the required merchandise, assemble and package the order if necessary, and dispatch the goods to designated destinations.

Techniques for order fulfillment will vary with type of industry, physical characteristics of product, size of distribution center, geographic location, and size and frequency of individual customer orders. In general, the larger the facility and the greater its order volume, the more organized and automated the order fulfillment process will be. For example, the wholesale grocery industry has adopted allocation modeling techniques under which warehouse locations correspond with anticipated volumes, seasonal demands, and other factors. In industries where orders are traditionally limited to case lots, such as liquor wholesaling and others, many companies have adopted the practice of installing computers which generate tags for individual cases. In other situations, companies are experimenting with and installing computer-controlled, automated warehousing facilities.

Order fulfillment is becoming an area of increasing concern and specialization as the costs of finding, assembling, and delivering goods mount. This function is also important because of its interrelationships with a number of other "down-stream" systems. As is demonstrated in subsequent discussions, completion of the order-fulfillment cycle generates a series of other transactions, including invoicing and inventory record updating. The inventory updating, in turn, ultimately triggers the stock replenishment cycle as discussed later in this chapter.

Inventory Control

Inventory control and inventory management methods have probably suffered more from "oversophistication" than any other single systems area. Many articles and books have been written about inventory control and inventory management techniques. For the most part, these publications have concentrated on the mathematical and technical niceties related to the control and management of inventories. There appears to have been a trend toward developing complex algorithms as solutions to virtually any inventory problem.

In point of fact, experience has shown that there can be a falling off in benefits if a company attempts to oversophisticate its inventory control systems at a level which may be beyond its actual needs or abilities to comprehend.

In today's data processing environment, even relatively small companies can justify the use of computers to manage their inventory investments. In general, the trick is to avoid approaches which try to do too much, which become so sophisticated that people who work with the systems don't understand them, and can't use them effectively. Experience has shown that relatively unsophisticated, standardized computer inventory models can, in most instances, produce almost as many benefits, at far lower costs, than can be realized with complex, sophisticated systems. Certainly it is safe to say that a vast majority of the benefits to be obtained from computerized inventory recordkeeping are achievable through the use of relatively simple systems. These approaches are built around training, discipline, and the development of understandable procedures which are implemented by people. The judgment of experienced people who know the business of the individual company can be far more effective in controlling and managing inventories than highly complex, nonjudgmental algorithms.

To make any inventory control and management system work, experience has shown, one must first begin by developing a basic stock-status reporting system. Simply having the right information available at the right time and asking experienced managers to exercise their sound judgment makes it possible to realize many of the benefits that would be attainable through the implementation of more sophisticated systems. At a minimum, such status reporting would include the following information for each inventory item stocked:

Warehouse location.

Stockkeeping unit (SKU) identification.

On-hand quantity—available for shipment.

On-hand quantity—unavailable for shipment.

On-order quantity.

Supplier code.

Replenishment order identification.

Expected delivery dates of replacement orders.

Normal replenishment lead time.

Reorder point.

Reorder quantity.

The primary sources of data for the stock-status system are, obviously, the company's order-entry and order-fulfillment systems.

Sales Forecasting

Sales forecasting, like inventory management, is an area replete with complicated solutions to simple problems. This topic, too, has attracted a series of books and highly complex algorithms for the extrapolation of existing sales data and projection of sales forecasts. Our experience has led us to the same general conclusion as discussed for inventory control systems; that is, relatively simple, readily available computerized systems can produce a high, immediate yield. The fine tuning available through the use of more complex systems can then be considered at a more leisurely pace and evaluated in terms of costs and projected benefits.

Typically, a company will forecast sales on a long-range basis for cash flow purposes, material planning, capacity planning, and other planning functions. Short-range sales forecasts are also utilized in many companies. These are generally prepared for a series of weeks, a series of months, or a season. In general, these forecasts will be utilized for short-term production planning, scheduling, purchasing, warehouse planning, and management of sales activities. Data generated from short-term sales forecasts provide inputs to a company's requirements-planning process.

Thus, where physical distribution management is concerned, sales forecasting is a basic input to the physical distribution planning process. Operationally, the key lies in the reporting/feedback mechanism which measures and reports on forecast errors. Sales forecasts, therefore, are continually being updated in the light of actual, current experience. Physical distribution systems, then, must be designed so that they are flexible enough to tolerate and adapt to forecasting errors.

This is one of the important challenges faced by physical distribution managers. They must be prepared, on an instant's notice, to adjust their own operations while providing feedback information to the other functions of the enterprise so that overall plans can be adjusted on the basis of current realities.

SYSTEMS DEVELOPMENT

The Beginning

Systems for physical distribution begin with order entry. Without order entry, there really would not be any business systems. Without orders of some form, there would be no reason for a company's existence.

Schematically, the central importance of order entry as a beginning point for systems development and implementation is shown in Exhibit 1. The enterprise's order-entry system is at the hub of the systems activity. Supporting and dependent organizational activities are shown in surrounding, contributing, and dependent positions. The interrelationship of these activities with the order-entry system and its derivations is self-evident. Exhibit 1 illustrates this relationship by showing physical distribution management as the rim of a wheel and order entry as its hub. Elimination of the rim leads to fragmentation of the elements it holds in place. Elimination of the hub leads to collapse.

System Interrelationships

These principles and relationships apply as well to the work of designing an order-entry system. The system itself stems from the basic transaction of accepting, entering, and fulfilling an order. Ramifications from this key business transaction then flow into the life stream of the entire company, affecting shipments, invoicing, accounts receivable, bills of lading, marketing forecasts, product

EXHIBIT 1
The Physical Distribution Wheel

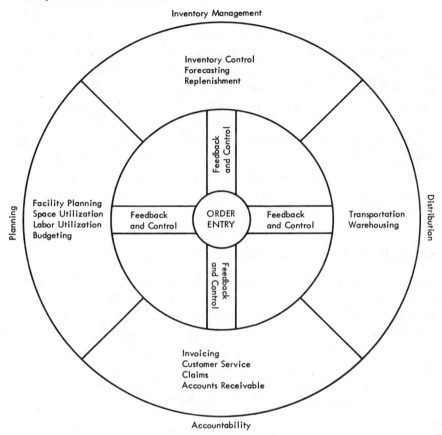

Inventory Management

Inventory Control
Forecasting
Replenishment

Feedback and Control

Planning

Facility Planning
Space Utilization
Labor Utilization
Budgeting

Feedback
and Control

ORDER
ENTRY

Feedback
and Control

Transportation
Warehousing

Distribution

Feedback and Control

Invoicing
Customer Service
Claims
Accounts Receivable

Accountability

forecasts, financial forecasts, purchasing, finished goods inventories, and production planning.

Obviously, all order-entry systems will have this impact. The difference in approach lies somewhere between the fragmentation of normal operations and integration under a physical distribution management concept. Under a fragmented system, timeliness is virtually impossible. There are just too many things to do to one stream of data. There are too many places to look for meaningful information.

The consequences of fragmentation are self-evident. In a poorly structured enterprise, it is not uncommon to find several managers in a management meeting quoting statistics based on single sources that they have developed independently with regard to the order-entry activity. For example, the marketing manager might speak glowingly of the success of a promotion based on orders his or her people had booked. Looking at the same promotion, the accounting manager would feel the promotion had been a failure because invoicing, lagging behind sales, lead him or her to believe that sales had declined. The distribution manager, on the other hand, might have little or no reaction because his or her reporting indicated that warehouse shipments had remained at a steady level.

With just this simple illustration, it can be seen that three reporting systems were funneled into three different facets of the business —marketing, accounting, and distribution—and actions taken by these departments, based on entirely different readings of the same business facts, were often contradictory.

DELICIOUS FOODS—A CASE STUDY

In order to illustrate the importance of the order-entry function in a centralized company, as this function relates to physical distribution concepts, the author has drawn on his experience in the development and implementation of large physical distribution systems. The following case study describes the efforts of a large national manufacturer and distributor of specialty foods in overcoming its distribution problems. The company name, Delicious Foods, is obviously a disguise.

The Order-Entry System

Following a significant amount of time spent in planning and analysis, Delicious Foods elected to centralize their order-processing systems. The centralized approach was developed to replace the rather loose-knit procedures under which salespersons submitted orders to the nearest Delicious Foods warehouse in their territory.

Under these former procedures, warehouses filled orders directly. Each warehouse maintained its own inventory records. None had control over the replenishment activity. When customer orders were shipped, each of the 30 warehouses mailed copies of these orders to the corporate offices for invoicing and accounts receivable processing. Invoices were issued as soon as possible, but delays were inevitable because of lack of control over delivery of source documents. Further, a large segment of invoices in process were tied up while error notices and new inputs were snarled up in the mails.

The New Approach

Under revised procedures, all of the company's sales and distribution points are linked into a single communications network, with corporate headquarters at the hub. (This network is diagrammed in Exhibit 2, which the reader is urged to consult as he or she reads about the system.) Each warehouse in the system has a batch-oriented data terminal built around a minicomputer that is linked, via communication lines, with a centralized minicomputer which polls the field and collects data from, and transmits data to, the field. The centralized minicomputer, in turn, is linked through shared, online storage devices to the company's large central computer.

Data on orders, finished goods inventory receipts, shipments, and other transactions affecting inventory are now captured on magnetic storage media at the warehouses as part of the daily order-entry process. The captured data are collected by the central data processing facility four times a day, at scheduled intervals.

At the central data processing facility, incoming data from warehouses are processed immediately on the large, central computer. Files affecting every facet of the physical distribution side of the business are updated in a single processing sequence. This initial processing step also identifies exception items among incoming orders and generates error-notification messages, which are transmitted automatically back to the originating warehouses. Because all files are updated centrally and on a current basis, the centralized system now represents a *data bank* for the entire company. Managers in field warehouses or at central locations can enter inquiries with transaction batches and receive return messages on the status of individual orders, customers, and product inventories.

All told, Delicious Foods processes some 2,000 orders *daily* from its 30 locations under this system. This, in itself, says something about both company operations and data processing requirements. If a food company moves $600 million in annual sales on 2,000 orders daily, these orders must be large ($1,200 per order average) and involve a relatively large number of line items. It is not unusual for the larger of these individual orders to cover entire carloads of

EXHIBIT 2
Delicious Foods—Order Entry Flowchart

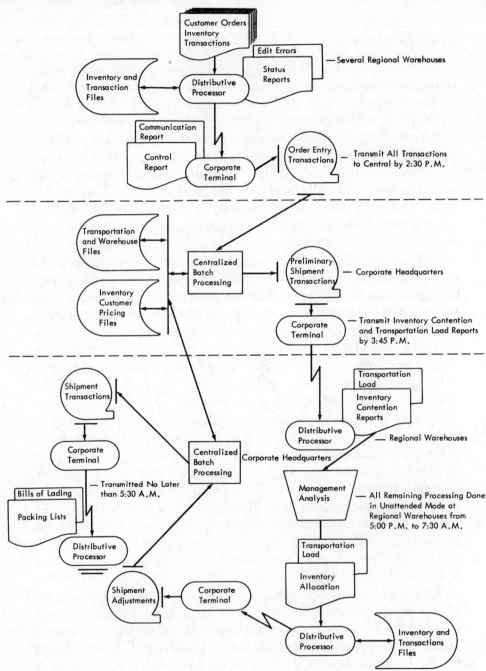

merchandise. It becomes understandable, then, that in revising the order-entry system, management was anxious that the new procedures be highly responsive to customer demands and activities.

At 3 P.M. daily, Delicious Foods ends its order-entry day. Input is cut off at the central computer facility. Based on final processing of the data accumulated throughout the day, the central computer compares outstanding orders with available inventories and generates two reports to each field warehouse:

1. An *Inventory Contention Report* identifies specific situations where the warehouse will not have sufficient supplies to fill current orders from existing stocks. For each short item in each warehouse, the report lists the amount of stock available and all outstanding orders, by customer. Personnel in the field can then make the basic decisions on how to prioritize the distribution of available stocks to customers.
2. A *Carrier-Loading Report* groups on-order merchandise on a bill-of-lading basis according to outbound destination and optimum shipping lots—truckload or carload. This report, obviously, becomes a tool for planning the next day's shipments from each warehouse.

Correction or adjustment messages, based on analysis of the inventory contention and carrier-loading reports, are transmitted at a scheduled time back to the central computer. Each evening, then, the computer updates its files and transmits all of the order-fulfillment paperwork each warehouse will need. Printed at the warehouse terminal are two types of items:

Picking slips, which serve as the basis for picking merchandise in predetermined stock locations from storage and locating it at specified outbound loading dock areas, are printed out.

As appropriate, the computer also generates one or all of three types of bills of lading—consolidated, master, or detailed—required for shipment.

This documentation is transmitted to each warehouse automatically. Terminals are in an unattended mode during this operation. Customer orders are picked and shipped the following day, with all shipments completed within 24 hours of the daily 3 P.M. cutoff.

Shipment transactions are communicated to the central location in order to trigger the invoicing and accounts receivable systems. Inventory and production planning systems also stem from this basic order-entry processing cycle.

Decision Criteria

As indicated earlier, one of the main management objectives in the design of this system was customer responsiveness. With management's emphasis on this consideration, during the system study which led to the development and implementation of this order-entry system, management expressed strong interest in, and support for, a fully interactive, online, real-time system. Under this approach, each order or other transaction would have been entered on a terminal and communicated directly into the central computer. Each order would have been processed centrally at the time it was entered, with picking and shipping documents being produced immediately on the terminals in the field.

This approach unquestionably would have resulted in greater responsiveness. But the consulting team engaged by Delicious Foods recognized the potential for overkill. It was their opinion that this level of responsiveness would have to be acquired at much too high a cost considering the relatively low volume of orders involved. Studies showed that acquisition and operation of a real-time order-processing system would have cost between three and four times as much as the data-collection-oriented batch system now in use.

(Significantly, the same consulting team *did* recommend a real-time order-entry system in another case. In this case, orders involved comparatively few line items and small dollar amounts. However, order volume was an entirely different picture, averaging some 30,000 to 40,000 orders daily. In this particular case, a batch approach would have swamped any reasonable data-collection capabilities. A description of this approach follows the Delicious Foods case study.)

At Delicious Foods, management's interest in a real-time service capability resulted in initiation of an in-depth analysis of just how orders were being handled in the field. Consultants studying sales operations learned that it had become a habit for most salespersons to collect orders as they made their rounds on three- or four-day trips, bringing the entire collection in with them. Thus, average delays of from one to two days were being experienced before orders got from the customer to the warehouse.

The customer response level desired by management was achieved simply by installing WATS or METRO telephone services at each warehouse. Each order is now phoned in as soon as the salesperson leaves the customer's premises. Under the new system, all merchandise is shipped within 24 hours of receipt of an order. Average response-time improvement was approximately one to two days. Management achieved its goals at about 30 to 40 percent of what it would have cost to implement a real-time system. Further, simple introduction of real-time techniques would not have solved the problem of salespersons who squirreled orders away in their briefcases.

As a bonus accruing from the setting up of a data-communication network separate from the central computer, Delicious Foods was able to use its order-entry communications network for administrative messages within the company as well. In effect, part-time use of this same equipment gives the company an internal message-switching network capability, since, as will be described below, the implementation of the inventory control system led to the inclusion of the company's plants in the same data communication network.

Inventory Control

Outputs from the order-entry system described above flowed naturally into—and were capitalized upon for—creation of a system for inventory control within Delicious Foods. Data on orders, shipments, receipts, customer returns, and other transactions affecting inventory are used to update inventory status records within the same central computer system. These stock-status records include data on stock on hand, stock on order, stock in transit, reorder points, reorder quantities, and other statistical parameters required for stock replenishment.

As indicated previously, the data-communications network was expanded to include Delicious Foods' manufacturing plants. Note that in a system where finished goods are purchased from outside vendors, the same type of file and processing procedures would generate purchase orders for replenishment purposes. In the case of Delicious Foods, orders are transmitted to data terminals in the plants to initiate replenishment activities. With this integrated capability, Delicious Foods was able to refine its inventory control system to take in the full spectrum of physical distribution management concepts.

Orders transmitted to plants reflect a consolidation of product mixes for optimizing shipments of finished goods from plant to warehouse. In effect, the plant replenishment cycle is analyzed and controlled according to cubic content of the replenishment orders. Products are consolidated on manufacturing orders according to stipulated cubic dimensions and weight allowances of the railcars or trucks which will be used for shipment.

By tying replenishment orders and shipment volumes together in this way, Delicious Foods was able to impact the manufacturing warehouse operation directly. Applying space-management concepts throughout its operations, Delicious Foods is able to maintain its computerized inventory records on a cubic-space accountability basis. That is, the computer shows more than just *how much* of a given product is in a specific warehouse. Inventory records indicate exactly *where* merchandise is located, identified down to manufacturing lot number and production date.

This continuity of operations, a trademark of physical distribution concepts, carries through—from the moment of entry of production orders in the plants—to the shipment of each palletized unit of merchandise in the field warehouses. As replenishment orders are placed, plant terminals print out labels for each pallet load of merchandise required by the field. As merchandise is assembled for shipment, one of these labels is affixed to each pallet load of product. These labels contain the product code and the exact storage location at the receiving warehouse where the merchandise is to be stored.

Following the shipment of the replenishment merchandise from a plant, a message is transmitted to the central data processing facility, indicating by product and individual pallet number the manufacturing date and lot number of the merchandise shipped. These data are maintained on each stockkeeping unit in the field, providing a basis for space management of field warehouses and a product recall capability essential to the stringent quality-control characteristics of the food manufacturing industry. Data transmitted at the time of shipment from a plant also include information on carrier, trailer, or car number, and the seal number affixed to the door of the car (if rail shipment is made).

Preparedness documentation, transmitted to the consigned warehouses, includes all of this relevant information. Warehouse managers can then utilize this information to plan for the receipt of replenishment merchandise ahead of time.

Another example of how this continuity of operational systems is applied under physical distribution concepts is in the area of controlling freight-car demurrage costs. On rail shipments, each warehouse is advised when an inbound car arrives in a railroad's local switching yard. This information is, in turn, transmitted to the central computer, which then advises the warehouse which cars to schedule in for unloading on a day-to-day basis. The computer subsystem considers both current order status and demurrage costs and/or penalties in determining these schedules. This subsystem has reduced demurrage costs considerably, while at the same time improving the material flow into the warehouse.

When a shipment arrives at the warehouse, pallets are unloaded and stored in the location specified on their labels. Receiving and storage information, including any changes in space utilization determined at the individual warehouse, are input to the central computer system as part of the three daily batches processed under the order-entry system. This information then updates inventory and space-utilization files, making the merchandise available for use in order processing.

As a further extension of the inventory control (status-keeping) capabilities of the system, each plant transmits every day to the central computer inventory-control data on finished goods that were produced that day, and the production schedule for the following day. At the end of each week, each plant transmits data on its production schedule for the following week.

INTERNATIONAL DISTRIBUTING—A CASE STUDY

There will be those who after reviewing the foregoing case study will reflect that what was presented was all well and good for a centralized organization but has no meaning in terms of a decentralized organization. This is not true; although the techniques that will be described in the following case study (also disguised) are different as they relate to processing of data, the underlying principles of simplicity and order remain.

Order Entry—An Online Approach

The earlier discussion on the situation of Delicious Foods explained that management was originally predisposed to an online system, but that the study showed the company's economics to be elsewhere. For comparative purposes, the significance of the International Distributing situation is that this is probably a classic environment for an online order-entry system. Two predominant factors applied in this situation:

1. The company is in a service-critical business. The customers themselves operate in a condition of constant emergency. In addition, this is a large industry, sufficiently large so that International Distributing has many eager competitors. These circumstances combine to require an ability to react to incoming orders in a matter of hours.

2. The participating divisions of International Distributing process between 30,000 and 40,000 orders daily, with an average of three to four line items each. With this kind of volume, any attempt to accumulate orders in batches would simply have resulted in a swamping of the entire system. Further, because of the volumes involved, the incremental costs for the computer processing of orders are extremely small, making it easy to justify the overhead of an online communication system.

The system actually implemented at International Distributing (shown schematically in Exhibit 3) is designed so that any order, entered from any point in the country, is processed completely, with picking and packing slips in the hands of the shipping warehouse, within a maximum of 15 minutes. The distribution system at International Distributing includes some 110 warehouse shipping points operated by a variety of divisions and some 140 sales points, many of them located at warehouse sites. In addition, a comparatively large number of customers, running into the hundreds, installed remote data-entry devices tied into their local International Distributing sales offices. Standard order items, then, can be entered into these remote devices, transmitted to the local sales office, and processed by the centralized system within an hour at most.

This nationwide order-entry network is linked into a large computer installation which includes two central computers at corporate headquarters. The two computers are interconnected under an ar-

EXHIBIT 3
International Distributing—Order-Entry Flowchart

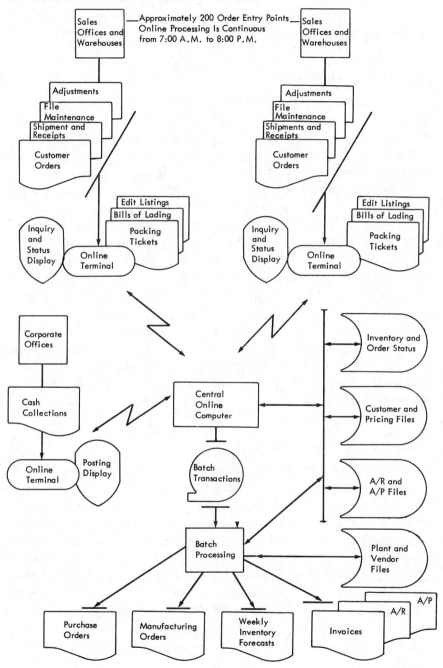

rangement where one computer serves the online network while the other performs offline jobs but still monitors the situation of the online system. Should the online computer go down for any reason, the backup unit will take over the processing load automatically.

Communication Network

Communication linkage between the computers and the order-entry points is tailored to the volumes and complexities of the segments of the business served. High-volume order points are linked, in several cases, through leased-line circuits. In lower volume situations, the system uses AT&T's WATS service with the central computer polling order-entry points in rotation and accepting transactions as they are encountered. Direct-dial order-entry input is also accommodated from a number of points through Telstar, including International Distributing facilities in Canada, Hawaii, and Alaska.

Individual order-entry points also use a variety of terminals, depending chiefly upon the volumes involved. High-volume locations utilize cathode ray tube (CRT) terminals tied directly to the central computer for interactive conversational inquiry or order entry. Lower volume sites use punched-card readers for order input. Orders are processed on card punches, with the cards left in terminals for transmission as the affected stations are polled. At these locations, separate teletypewriters print responses or directions from the central computer.

Standardized Transmittal Approaches

All orders, whether they originated from cards or CRT terminals, are structured to correspond with standard formats for the entire system. Data-entry requirements, however, are minimized by the structure of the system itself. For example, where a customer has a remote-entry device, this has its own coded identity which is recognized by the central computer. The central computer then fills in all of the laborious customer identification and shipping instructions. Similarly, orders processed at sales locations can simply be encoded with a customer's number and the central computer will fill in customer identification and shipping descriptions.

Within the centralized computer system, obviously, are all of the requisite data elements and files described previously. In this case, the files include complete records for some 80,000 inventory items and 100,000 customers. Records are also organized according to individual warehouse. All of these files are interrelated by system software, making it possible for the computer to determine which warehouse will ship each ordered item. The computer can search its own files looking for an item at the nearest location to the customer first, then moving to the next closest site if the item is not at the first one, and so on. This is an important capability in meeting the basic management objective of customer responsiveness. Many companies will put an item on back order if it is not available at a point convenient to the customer's place of business. However, in implementing this system, International Distributing advertised and sold the idea of a full distribution network, stressing that the company was willing to absorb the extra cost of shipment from a remote point if inventory did not exist locally. The ultimate appeal to the marketplace in this case was that the customers did not have to overstock items to protect themselves against stockouts by local distributors.

In the process of selecting the shipment point for each ordered item, the computer obviously must review inventory files. In this process of assigning shipment responsibility, the computer also deducts the item from the appropriate inventory, updating these files as it goes. Following the processing of each order, a packing slip is generated on a terminal at the designated warehouse. If items covered in a single order are to be shipped to two or more different points, individual, nonduplicate packing slips are generated on a terminal at the designated warehouse. If items covered in a single order are to be shipped from two or more different points, individual, nonduplicate packing slips are generated at responsible warehouses.

All of this is done on a real-time basis with all order documentation and packing slips generated at action points within 15 minutes of order entry. This is notably different from the systems described earlier at Delicious Foods, where orders were collected throughout the day and complete requirements were communicated to warehouses at 3 P.M. At International Distributing, the printers at busy warehouses actually operate continuously, with warehouse personnel packing and shipping a few orders at a time. At the same time as packing slips are being generated for the warehouses, the sales entry point receives a master order listing indicating the status and disposition of each item entered.

When the goods are to be shipped from more than one warehouse, individual warehouse points are noted as part of the description for each item. The meticulous detailing associated with intercompany transshipments of merchandise is accounted for and processed automatically by the computerized system, which contains a direct interface to the company's computerized general ledger.

Obviously, another capability of the order-entry system lies in accepting transactions describing warehouse receipts or returns. Again, correcting or adjusting transactions to the system's files are picked up and processed automatically. For example, a transaction covering usable merchandise returned by a customer would generate a credit to the customer's file and update the inventory record. When a transaction recording merchandise receipts at a warehouse is entered into the system, the computer tests first to see if there are any outstanding back orders. If so, these are deducted first, before the merchandise is added to inventory records for availability to the system.

Each time an order is shipped, a notification transaction is entered at the terminal in the shipping location. In addition to describing the merchandise shipped, this transaction also adds freight cost and any other appropriate shipping information not incorporated in the packing list. Shipping notification transactions also indicate any shortages or quantity adjustments made in processing the order. These data are used to correct online inventory files and are also utilized to trigger International Distributing's invoicing system.

It is worth noting at this point that the invoicing system, as well as the inventory management, purchasing, back-order processing, accounts payable, accounts receivable, and sales analysis applications, all of which derive their inputs from order entry, are processed offline through use of information captured from the order-entry cycle. Processing is done on an available time and overnight basis. Each evening, voluminous reports needed in the field, such as detailed stock-status listings, are captured on microfiche and air-shipped overnight to the remote location. Summaries of offline processing runs are created automatically and read into the online computer files for transmission of messages to the field locations the following day.

Error Correction and Control

Considering the importance of service levels at International Distributing, one of the important roles of the online system is that it becomes possible to identify, retain a record of, and correct each error very quickly. Although errors represent only a small part of total order-entry transactions, the very volume of the system itself makes for a problem in error processing. For example, considering initial order-entry transactions are 99 percent accurate, when a system handles 40,000 orders a day, the remaining 1 percent represents 400 orders a day which must be put in a holding file and followed up until they are corrected. Maintaining an open-error file in this way forms an important element of internal control within the order-entry system. Errors are followed up until they are corrected. Duplicate orders cannot be entered to circumvent the error file or to circumvent such conditions as exceeded credit limits. Further, there are no manual exception situations at International Distributing. None are necessary because the online system is sufficiently responsive to handle any situation.

A correcting entry serves to remove an order from the error file and enter it, along with other good orders, into an open-order file maintained on a corporatewide basis. The open-order file, itself, is a major control device. All orders accepted for processing are logged into this file by date and time received. The open-order file is updated when merchandise is shipped, and the item is removed from the open-order file six weeks after an invoice is issued. In the interim, field offices can inquire at any time to track the exact status of any order entered into the system. The system also produces exception reports on delays in shipment or invoicing. It also accumulates data on, and reports exceptions by, frequency of occurrence. Open-order processing also performs an important accounting control function in that transactions from this file serve as both authorization and validation of inventory transactions.

Another accounting-type control is applied by the computerized system to assure International Distributing of a certain, minimum profit margin on each sales transaction. A basic pricing file is incorporated within the computer system. If the salesperson does not price an ordered item, the computer enters the appropriate amount, including discount by customer classification or annual control price, from its files. However, in special situations, the salesperson does have the ability to override standard prices and provide customers with special quotations. When this is done, the special prices are entered and processed. However, the system has been programmed so that International Distributing always realizes a certain, minimum margin of profit on each transaction. If this condition has not been met, the computer will refuse the order, processing it as an error.

Maintaining Decentralized Authority

Override capabilities have been built into every facet of the International Distributing systems. This is in keeping with the basic philosophy that that organization will remain decentralized and that the centralized computer activities will be of a support nature only. Thus, operating decisions, along with accompanying profit responsibilities, remain with division managers. To implement this philosophy, division managers need the flexibility to be able to override the centralized systems when conflicts occur. For example, under the order-processing cycle described above, an item out of stock at one warehouse might automatically be ordered from another, where inventory is available. However, when the order is received, the division manager may determine that this particular merchandise is in short, critical supply and that he or she cannot afford to fill the order. In such situations, division managers retain the authority to refuse the order, notifying the computer system of their decision.

Because this flexibility and support of decentralized authority have been built into the system, the override capabilities are used only infrequently. Confidence that inequities of a mechanized system can be overcome leaves managers secure that they are in charge of their own operations. Hence, they don't feel called upon to prove that they are in charge.

Other Online Services

In implementing an online order-entry system, International Distributing created capabilities to support a number of other communication dependent services for its field organization. These include two major inquiry features:

1. A comprehensive, online inquiry capability that permits the field to make inquiries against customers, orders, and invoicing files; and
2. An inquiry hold feature that permits the field to reserve quantities for potential customer orders.

Online Inquiry. The ability to inquire on order status from field locations already has been cited. In addition, field personnel dealing with customers can inquire about the status of inventories for specific items desired, assuring customers of when they can be shipped and from where. In the course of such discussions, a salesperson can also check the customer's current credit status or any other customer or inventory information he may desire. If an inquiry deals with an open order, the salesperson or other field personnel can inquire against the open-error file to see if an order is being held up because of incorrect entries. In reports responding to status inquiries, a salesperson can be informed to any level appropriate to the situation. For example, the salesperson may wish to know if the merchandise is on hand in a local warehouse. If it is not, the salesperson can present a national-level inquiry and find out just where the item is in stock, letting the customer know exactly where an item can be shipped from and how long it will take.

Inquiry Hold. This transaction is structured to help field offices cope with the real work of a company processing 40,000 orders daily. In a fast-moving situation like the one at International Distributing, it could be entirely possible for a salesperson at a field location to assure the customer that merchandise is in stock, only to have it sold out and unavailable by the time the order was placed, even just a few minutes later. Therefore, in dealing with a customer on a real-time basis, the salesperson can put items about which an inquiry had been made "on hold," pending entry of an order. The computer will then protect this merchandise, making it unavailable for other orders entered subsequently. The computer times and keeps track of the inquiry-hold transactions. If a confirmation against a "hold" is not received and processed within one hour, it is dropped and the merchandise is made generally available to the system.

Other Services Provided by the System

There are still additional services provided by International Distributing's system:

Message switching: Under this feature, the communication system is used on an "as-available" basis for automatic routing and transmission of administrative messages between various plants within the company. At International Distributing, the system has been designed to "explode" message distribution. Based on coding incorporated in the messages themselves, transmissions will be generated automatically to all encoded levels within the organization.

Back-order releases: Each evening, all open back orders are processed against the day-end inventory balance file. When current balances fill back-order requirements, the materials are allocated to the back orders and a file is established releasing them for processing the next day. This file is processed on the online system the first thing the following morning.

Directed transfer orders: In addition to being able to search for, find, and allocate merchandise from other warehouses in response to customer orders, the International Distributing system will also respond to management-directed merchandise transfer messages. For example, if a warehouse manager receives a report in the morning indicating that the facility has had several transshipment orders for out-of-stock items, the warehouse manager may elect, if the replacement situation warrants, to override the systems distribution matrix and order a transfer of supplies from another warehouse. If this is done, the transaction requires specific approval from the manager of the other warehouse. Without such approval, the transaction will not be processed.

GENERAL SUMMARY

There are some important lessons to be learned from these two case studies. Discounting the variations in processing approaches, the basic approaches to the development of these systems were the same:

Recognition of the fact that order-entry transactions were the key to current operations and future sophistication.

Recognition of what was needed to satisfy customer-service criteria within sound economic parameters.

Recognition of organizational differences (centralized versus decentralized) in the design of these systems.

Recognition of the need to communicate between various organizational elements of an otherwise fragmented physical distribution organization.

However, the most important lesson that can be learned from this chapter is that the old adage, "You have got to crawl before you can walk," is as true under today's modern technology as it was in granddad's time. The message, then, is: get the basics completed before you take on the more sophisticated, albeit more stimulating, approaches to physical distribution management.

A simple and well-thought-out order-entry and inventory-control system (stock status) will provide somewhere between 80 and 90 percent of the benefits (improved customer service levels and reduction in inventory investment) that can be achieved from the implementation of physical distribution systems. The remaining 10 to 20 percent of benefits can be milked through the application of more sophisticated management sciences techniques. However, their attainment is predicated on the soundness and completeness of the basic order-entry and inventory-control systems.

ADDITIONAL SOURCES

Davis, Gordon B. *Computer Data Processing.* 2d ed. New York: McGraw-Hill, Inc., 1973.

————. *Introduction to Management Information Systems: Conceptual Foundations, Structure and Development.* New York: McGraw-Hill, Inc., 1974.

Eliason, Alan L., and Kitts, Kent D. *Business Computer Systems and Applications.* Chicago: Science Research Associates, Inc., 1974.

Hax, Arnoldo C. "Planning a Management Information System for a Distributing and Manufacturing Company." *Sloan Management Review,* Spring 1973, p. 85.

Mockler, Robert J. *Information Systems for Management.* Columbus, Ohio: Charles E. Merrill Publishing Co., 1974.

Prince, Thomas R. *Information Systems for Management Planning and Control.* 3d ed. Homewood, Ill.: Richard D. Irwin, Inc., 1975.

40

Identifying and Controlling
Inventory Losses

Thomas S. Dudick*

One area of vulnerability to the controller is improper accountability for inventories. Many companies have found an 11-month profit suddenly revert to a loss because of a large unfavorable "book-to-physical" adjustment. Profits, which had been overstated all year because of incorrect accountability of inventory must now be corrected. While the size of this adjustment may appear to be miniscule when compared with the total throughput, unfortunately, in the pressure of meeting financial targets, the impact on profits counts for more than the relationship to throughput.

Controllers who have experienced large book-to-physical adjustments generally do not publicize this experience: therefore the frequency with which this occurs is not a matter of general knowledge. Because of complexities in the method of manufacture and continual growth of business, vulnerability to inventory discrepancies is on the uptrend.

This chapter will identify some of the reasons that inventory discrepancies occur and the preventive action that must be taken.

WHAT CAUSES INVENTORY DISCREPANCIES?

Inventory adjustments or discrepancies are of two general types: (1) disappearance through theft and (2) improper accounting. Dis-

---

* Mr. Dudick is Manager, Ernst & Whinney, New York.

crepancies due to disappearance are generally smaller than those due to improper accounting. However, disappearance through theft is a true loss, while improper accounting essentially results in the mismatching of revenues and costs during the year with a large correcting adjustment at year-end.

Disappearance through Theft

Detecting inventory theft losses through the accounting records is usually difficult because of the many different types of transactions, the normal errors in identification, and, possibly, incomplete paperwork. Prevention, rather than after-the-fact bookkeeping, should therefore be the approach to take in avoiding inventory theft losses.

> *Example.* One manufacturer of small automotive accessories dismissed the possibility of employee theft on a large scale because the plant and its employees were all new—presumably too new to make the proper connections needed to dispose of stolen inventory. It was no small surprise to the company officials when the highway patrol found some employees on the night shift passing cartons over the fence and loading up a car. Since the average-sized car need load up only once a week to accumulate $5,000 in merchandise, the annual loss on that basis could be as much as a quarter of a million dollars. The company recognized that while the accounting records would certainly reflect the loss, more direct preventive measures were required.

What specific steps can management take to reduce inventory shrinkage resulting from employee theft? According to the private security firm of Pinkerton's, Inc., prevention should begin with the hiring of new employees. The background of job applicants should be thoroughly investigated where practical since employee training costs money and pre-employment checks can save money. Further savings can be realized by background investigations of persons already employed who are being considered for positions of greater trust and responsibility.

As we know, laxity of internal control is the primary factor that invites employee dishonesty. To help tighten up internal security, periodic internal surveys should be made to detect misdeeds and improve management communications. The results can be crucial in checking inventory loss and improving profits.

Improper Accounting

Improper accounting, which can result in large—usually unfavorable—differences between physical and book inventories, can be grouped into two basic categories:

Overstatement of input (i.e., amounts put into inventory).

Understatement of relief (i.e., amounts taken out of inventory).

Overstatement of Input. Input can be overstated through (1) overreporting of production, (2) improper handling of customer returns, or (3) improper coding. Let's look at some examples of each of these pitfalls.

Overreporting of Production. When products, or the components making them up, prove to be defective, they are frequently reprocessed to correct the defect. If not properly accounted for, such rework might be counted as good production *twice*—with the result that the book value of inventory will be overstated when compared with the year-end value of the physical inventory.

Example. One company had well-written procedures for handling defective units. A rework tag was attached to the batch of units requiring reprocessing. Upon completion of the rework, the batch was moved back into the stream of production and the tag was used as the signal that the batch had *already been counted* as production at that operation. It was found, however, that employees were sometimes improperly detaching tags as the parts entered the line. The result was that many of the reworked items did not have tags and were therefore counted as good production a second time. Because of this, the year-end inventory discrepancy amounted to $190,000.

While the procedures were fine—as far as they went—they lacked an important control feature which was readily available. Although the rework tags were prenumbered, no effort was being made to assure that all tags were accounted for. As a result of the large inventory discrepancy, the procedure was changed so that all tag numbers were logged when issued and checked when they were returned from the production line.

Thus, if a tag was improperly detached in the rework process (so that the goods were counted twice), the missing number would be brought to the attention of the accounting personnel and the amount represented by the missing tag would be subtracted from the reported production for that month.

Improper Handling of Customer Returns. If sales returns are not handled properly, it is possible to have duplicate inventory input entries which can produce substantial distortions.

Example: A company experienced a substantial jump in customer returns due to incorrect design of a new product. Each month an inventory of all items returned during the month was taken and these totals were added to the book inventory. But, as these defective units were processed, credits were issued to the customers. These credits resulted in an automatic entry into inventory a second time—resulting in a duplication totaling $290,000.

The procedure was changed so that items were added to inventory only upon issuance of the credit to the customer. (This was more logical since the units were not the property of the company until a credit was actually issued.)

Improper Coding. Errors in coding can also result in substantial inventory distortion.

Example: A company charged its labor and overhead directly into inventory rather than first clearing these items through a variance account. In computing its payroll, it incorrectly coded its overtime pay as direct labor. As a result, the inventory value on the books was $410,000 higher than the value of the physical inventory at year-end. The reason was that overtime premium was also included in the overhead rate—a second time. Therefore, this item of cost was charged into inventory twice —once as overhead and once as direct labor.

Understatement of Relief. Understatement of relief is another way in which inventory shortages can appear. Thus, inventories can be overstated if (1) the company costs its shipments as a percentage of sales and this percentage is too low, or (2) losses in production are not accounted for.

Incorrect Cost of Sales Estimates. Companies that have thousands of items in inventory, but lack the capability to cost each of these items, frequently resort to the use of a percentage that is applied to the month's sales. This percentage is usually determined from historical experience. It may be an overall percentage applied to total sales or it may be a series of individual percentages, one for each product family.

Such a percentage method might work well for a time. Some firms even add a contingency factor to the percentage to assure that if an error does occur, it will be on the favorable side. The problem with this method is that the basic factors affecting the percentage are subject to change, and the effects of such changes cannot be measured with precision at interim dates.

Example: A company using this percentage-of-sales method found that its mix of sales had gradually changed—and so did the percentage cost of sales. Although the change appeared to be imperceptible, it resulted in a percentage-of-sales increase from 58 percent in the previous year to 65 percent in the current year. Because 58 percent was used in the current year, the relief to inventory was so understated that an 11-month profit of $1,650,000 actually turned out to be only $375,000 at year-end.

There was no easy remedy because the inventory consisted of 500 items in raw material, 18,000 parts in work in process stock, and 4,500 products in finished goods. The solution was a long-term program to computerize the cost system so that individual items could be costed without resort to estimated percentages.

Losses in Production. Companies whose input into inventory is based on standards applied to production must rely on accurate reporting to adjust the inventory for production losses. These losses are made up of such items as:

Excess usage of raw materials—the amount of material in excess of normal requirements that is spoiled during the manufacturing operation.

Yield loss—the material and conversion costs that are lost because the quantity of good production is less than can normally be expected from the input quantity.

Manufacturing defects—parts that do not meet the inspection requirements and cannot be reworked.

Rare is the company that can attest to the accuracy of its reporting or production losses. A company that can account for two thirds of such losses is doing well. The reason is economics. In many instances, the unit cost of the items produced is so small that the cost of an accurate reporting system would be prohibitive.

The answer, when the economics permits, lies in a "shop-order" system whereby the production control department monitors physical quantities through work in process. Under this method, production quantities are recorded by operation. To account for all the losses, the number of units accepted into stock is subtracted from the number started, the reported rejects are accounted for, and year-end inventory is adjusted for the unaccounted-for balance.

This "shop-order" system is illustrated in Exhibit 1. The total

EXHIBIT 1
Illustration of Shop-Order Quantity Control (Shop Order No. 10908)

Cost Center	Operation	Started	Completed	Reported Rejects	Unaccounted-for Losses
20	1	75,500*	74,800	300	400
21	2	74,800	67,600	4,500	2,700
23	3	67,600	65,000	1,500	1,100
26	To stock-room	65,000			
				6,300	4,200

* Starting quantity.

units started into production were 75,500 while the numbers of units actually accepted into the stockroom were 65,000, a loss of 10,500 units. Of this 10,500 a total of 6,300 units were reported to the accounting department and were relieved from inventory. The unaccounted-for losses of 4,200 units that are still residing in the book inventory must be removed, otherwise there will be a discrepancy between physical and book inventory at year-end.

GOOD INVENTORY ACCOUNTING PROCEDURES

The key to good inventory accounting procedures is a realistic *cost flow*, which in turn should be based on a realistic *production flow*. And, of course, the production flow should depend upon the type of product or service involved. When the product or service is unique and its specific cost must be known, as in the case of a custom-made product, the *job* cost system is mandatory. On the other hand, in a process-type business in which standardized products are built to stock rather than to order, a *process* cost system is more suitable. (Where a company makes custom products from standard components which are interchangeable, the production flow to make the custom components can be quite similar to the flow in making standard products. However, for the purpose of our discussion, we will disregard this hybrid type of production flow.) Using Exhibit 2 to illustrate these two types of cost flow, let's examine each of them in turn.

EXHIBIT 2
Two Basic Cost Flows

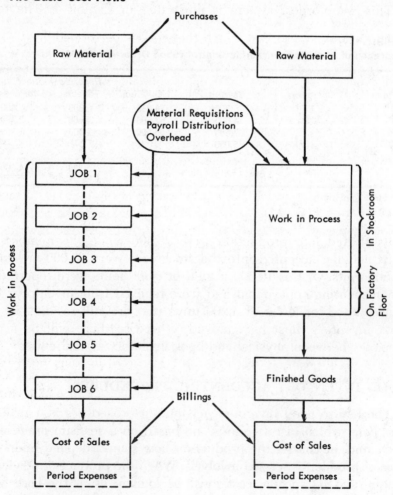

Job Costing

The production flow in a job cost system is built around making a specific product for a specific customer. The flow of material, labor, and overhead is directed toward satisfying the requirements for making that particular product. When completed, the product is shipped to the customer out of work in process.

A job costing system utilizes two basic inventory accounts: (1) raw material and (2) work in process (or jobs in process). There is usually no finished goods inventory. While purchases are normally directed into the raw material inventory account and then issued to jobs as needed, this is not always the case; material purchased specifically for a job can bypass the raw material inventory account and be charged directly to work in process. Direct labor is charged directly against the job on which the work is performed.

Inventory accounting under job costing has the advantage of being relatively simple. As each job is completed, all accumulated costs that were charged to that job are cleared out of inventory, leaving no unaccounted-for residual quantities. However, there is also a major disadvantage to the job costing method. Such a system requires substantially more work than a process cost system. (As an example, a company with annual sales of less than $10 million might have as many as 500 jobs in process.) Another disadvantage is that there is a tendency in job shops to "borrow" from one job to meet priority requirements of another. When such borrowing is done without paperwork documentation, the accuracy of the inventory accounting becomes questionable, particularly with respect to the actual costs of individual jobs.

Process Costing

The production flow in a process cost system can be pictured as a steady stream of material, labor, and overhead flowing into work in process through the various operations. From work in process, the flow is through the finished goods inventory, out of which shipments are made.

In a process-type business, the three basic inventory accounts are raw material, work in process, and finished goods. The work in process account is usually further broken down into: components parts in stockroom (parts fabricated in advance for use in later assembly operations, which are held in the stockroom until needed) and factory floor inventory (work in process around the work areas). Although the production control department segregates these two types of work in process, most accounting departments do not make this segregation in their records. While the balance sheet would not reflect this breakdown of work in process, the supplementary inventory records should.

Why Base Inventory on Production Flow?

Accounting systems in which no breakdown is made between raw material, work in process, and finished goods inventories are most vulnerable to year-end discrepancies between physical and book. The reason is that in many circumstances, input is based on costs that have been actually incurred with little or no further accountability until the inventory is sold. If a breakdown of the inventory components is maintained, the costs applicable to the inventory can be tracked with greater accuracy.

Further, as noted before, the relief values in such instances are estimates based on broad averages, such as percentages applied to sales to estimate the inventory cost of shipments. While this approach runs against the grain of an accountant, there are many instances in the real world where there is no other approach short of a long-term program to establish a computerized cost system in which individual items are costed through the use of standards. Such a program would divide the single inventory account into its three basic segments: raw material, work in process, and finished goods. Each of these can then be monitored individually.

Many companies that have computerized their cost system—and have thereby greatly improved the credibility of their financial statements—are still vulnerable to year-end discrepancies because of incipient problems which are not reflected in the paperwork that documents the various transactions affecting the inventory. Such discrepancies might stem from:

> Overreporting of production, for example, when reworked items are counted a second time and when returns from customers are erroneously added to inventory while the product is still the property of the customer.

Excessive use of material that is unreported, for example, when material is taken out of stockrooms by unauthorized personnel without accounting for it.

Unaccounted-for rejects, for example, when losses in production are not reported.

Most of the foregoing problems that result in underrelief of inventory occur in the work in process inventory account. Efforts to correct the reporting frequently become highly frustrating because the cost of the cure often far exceeds the benefits. This is particularly true when low unit values are involved. What, then, is the answer?

Breaking Down Work in Process

The answer, stated briefly, is to correlate the cost flow with the production flow—that is, to break out work in process inventory so as to identify the "components stockroom" portion separately from the "floor inventory" portion and to account for each separately.

Components Stockroom Inventory. When the desired shop order controls needed to identify production losses are not available, an alternative method can be used. Rather than input labor and overhead costs into inventory on an operation-by-operation basis (and then be concerned with the problem of reducing the input by losses that are difficult to account for), it would be far better to input labor and overhead into inventory only when the completed components are accepted into the components stockroom. Then, the number of good units accepted into stock multiplied by the standard labor and standard overhead would determine the proper input value into inventory of these two elements. This would conform to normal production control procedures in which perpetual inventories by stockrooms are maintained. The same paperwork that supports the physical units being accepted into stockrooms would be used to support the input into the books of account.

Floor Inventory. The floor inventory, which is usually a relatively small segment of total work in process, would be accounted for separately. Many production control departments maintain a list of the balances of the various items in process. These balances reflecting the latest operation, extended by the standard cost would provide the book value of this segment of work in process. Each month the prior month's entry would be reversed and the new balance recorded.

In the event that this type of control of floor inventory is not maintained, two other alternatives are available: (1) establishing a constant value and (2) taking a monthly physical inventory.

Establishing a constant value should be satisfactory if the floor inventory is represented by a type of pipeline inventory which remains fairly constant irrespective of changes in volume of production.

Taking a monthly physical inventory is advisable if inventories are accumulated at various points on the factory floor as reservoirs for subsequent operations, since using a constant value on the books will result in distortions on the financial statements. It is often possible that the physical could be limited only to those areas in which fluctuations occur.

The Practical Approach

Most managers, fortunately, have not experienced the shock of a large inventory discrepancy. However, the dangers are very real. Controllers cannot remain oblivious to the realities around them. When they know the obvious—that completely reliable reporting of production losses can't be enforced because of the economics—they must look for other solutions.

Solutions can be found if the proper effort is made. Controllers should be aware that those in charge of controlling production and meeting customer orders must know the true status of physical quantities in inventory. It then behooves them to find ways of tying in their inventory costing procedures with the actual physical movement of production through the factory.

ADDITIONAL SOURCES

Neuner, John J. W., and Deakin, Edward B.   *Cost Accounting: Principles and Practice*, chap. 18. 9th ed. Homewood, Ill.: Richard D. Irwin, Inc., 1977.

Pattinson, W. Richard.   "Excess and Obsolete Inventory Control." *Management Accounting*, June 1974, p. 35.

41

Controlling Research and
Development Costs

Marion W. Ray, Jr.*

Research and development is supported and funded through many sources, which include profit-making organizations, governmental agencies, private and institutional grants, and so on. Accordingly, the financial control of funds expended must vary due to the type of funding and restrictions placed by the supporter or supplier of funds. In this chapter the basics to be considered in establishing controls for research and development will be discussed. Accounting methods will not be reviewed since normally accepted accounting procedures can be applied in effecting adequate controls.[1] In general, the minimum controls considered absolutely necessary for research and development in a profit-making organization will be dealt with. The controls briefly outlined herein can easily be modified to meet the financial control objectives for research and development in not-for-profit organizations.

Research Definition

Initially, it is important to define the type of research that technical operations or functions perform. Definitions usually assist management or individuals outside the technical organization in understanding the technical or scientific function being supported. These

---

* Mr. Ray is Assistant Treasurer of The Hearst Corporation, New York.

[1] *Editors' Note:* The following chapter, "Project Management Systems," goes into detail on individual project controls.

individuals are generally not scientifically oriented and, therefore, categorizing and defining technical programs can enhance receiving continuing support.

Groupings for types of research fall into the following categories: (1) pure research, (2) basic research, (3) applied research, (4) development, and (5) technical services. The flow of research usually follows the order indicated. Pure research, however, is primarily performed through public and private grants in universities or special laboratories. The only control exercised over pure research costs is the total amount of money to be spent. Therefore, pure research presents no serious control problems. No attempt will be made here to define each research type, since any definition offered could be argumentative. Each technical organization should define its activities into the types best suited for its efforts and functions under the broad definitions existing in many publications.

The only valid justification for research, development, and technical services in a profit-making organization is their ultimate contribution to earnings. To assure the success of profits and programs, proper policies and procedures are required to guide technical expenditures and effectively measure the net result. The overall purpose of the technical function is to help meet earnings goals and growth objectives competitively with the principal activities being (1) to serve operations in process with product problems and new developments and (2) to conduct longer range research in areas of present or potential commercial interest. This is true not only for industrial organizations but for other profit-making organizations whose primary product is the development and sale of technology and technical services.

Most companies which fund monies for research and development expenses assign members of management to approve, review, and guide their technical efforts. Usually these members of management are constituted as a committee and are senior executives. This committee will be referred to hereafter as the Technical Committee.

One of the main functions of this management Technical Committee is the determination of the level of funds the company can afford in research and development expenditures. Therefore, the Technical Committee should consist of senior management members, that is, the senior operating officer, senior marketing executive, chief financial officer, and technical director, each of whom can contribute expertise in the review process as to the needs and overall value of technical programs and projects from a short- and long-range perspective. If the company is medium to small in size, or if it is highly technically oriented, thus requiring high levels of research and development expenditures, or if its principal existence depends upon its research efforts, then the chief executive officer is essential to the committee membership. The chief executive officer's inputs and guidance are imperative.

It is suggested that the committee be chaired by either the senior operating executive or the senior marketing executive, if the chief executive officer is not on the committee. Specifically, the Technical Committee has the following management responsibilities: (1) decide the total amount of money to be spent on research; (2) determine the direction of the expenditures; and (3) evaluate the research efforts and effectiveness periodically. Some industries are highly technically oriented and therefore require a high level of research and development expenditures in contrast to other industries which have fairly standard production processes. For analogy, one would expect a company that is consumer oriented usually to spend larger sums for advertising than a company which is only indirectly consumer oriented. The same is true with a technically oriented company which must spend large sums in research and development for survival.

Financial procedures for control or research and development costs are discussed herein under the general headings of Budgets, Project or Program Authorization and Control, and Financial Responsibility and Reporting.

Budgets

For each calendar or fiscal year the total expenditure authorization for research and development should be established by the company (through the Technical Committee) after giving proper consideration to the demand for research and development and technical assistance, the financial resources available, the stability of the technical staff, the availability of technical facilities, the long-range plans of the company, and so on.

The decision as to the amount of money to be spent for research and development is sometimes poorly handled due to inadequate financial information. However, the decision as to the total amount to be spent should not be influenced strongly by temporary con-

1084 Controller's Handbook

siderations such as the profit outlook of the company at the time the budget is approved. Probably the most inefficient way to spend research and development money is by the "on-again off-again" method. The correct way is to hold the overall costs relatively constant and change on a slow and systematic basis. Inefficiencies in research programs usually result from establishing research funding levels by a formula approach, for example, relating research spending to annual sales volume. However, priorities and direction of efforts in programs and projects should be reviewed periodically (quarterly) for maximizing effectiveness of the R&D effort.

Within the overall limitation of total funds available and with the approval of the company or committee, budgetary planning and control should be provided by means of two separate budgetary systems, with each providing for the total of all proposed expenditures in the research and development activities.

The first budget, a "line-item budget," should consist of an expense budget which lists all anticipated expenditures during each calendar month (if desired), quarter and year, by type of expense, that is, salaries, wages, benefits, travel, equipment, material, utilities, depreciation, and so on. This budget details and outlines the financial commitments in total and by type of expense for the year. Monthly expense budgets for research and development functions are sometimes unnecessary due to the nature of funds flow and work flow peculiar to technical accomplishments. Quarterly detailed expense budgets are usually more desirable. The expense budget should separately identify expenses which are directly chargeable to specific projects or programs, and those expenses of fixed or supporting nature which are not directly assignable to specific projects.

A second budget, a "projects budget," should be developed consisting of a series of separate budgets for each calendar quarter reflecting: (1) project expenditures scheduled by project and categorized by type of activity, that is, basic research, applied research, development, and so forth; (2) project expenditure schedules for the functions that support the technical activity, that is, corporate office, division, plant, and so on; and (3) unallocated funds available for new projects or programs that may be authorized during the year. The total of this projects budget must be equal to and be consistent with the dollar levels in each type of expense in the line-item budget.

Project or Program Authorization and Control

With respect to individual projects, the financial control system should provide separate project designation for each specific investigation or venture taken.

Authorization. The Technical Committee should establish dollar levels of authorization for the approval of individual projects. In general it would be expected that such approvals of dollar levels will follow specific guidelines; that is, (1) internal research and development projects to be charged to an operating or production unit would be authorized jointly by the requesting operations head and the technical director of the department providing technical operations; (2) projects which are corporate in nature and not expected to exceed a specific dollar figure determined by the Technical Committee could be authorized by the technical director; and (3) projects whose total cost is expected to exceed a specific dollar figure should be authorized by the Technical Committee through its designee.

Projects which can be programmed and where the scope and expected final cost can be reasonably anticipated should be budgeted and approved for their full cost by quarter and year. Projects of an exploratory nature and involving basic and applied research should be approved on a step-by-step basis. When budgeted funds have been expended, new fund appropriations should be sought through appropriate review and revision of the original justification.

A formal request for project approval should be initiated in soliciting and documenting approval for each project. A sample form is shown in Exhibits 1 and 2 for guidance in design of such forms. They should be brief, simple, and all inclusive. It is further suggested, for simplicity, that Exhibit 2 be printed on the reverse side of Exhibit 1, so that one sheet of paper would be a total summary of information and financial data pertinent to the project. Supplemental information can always be attached for complex projects, as desired for the reviewer's perusal.

Depending upon the nature and scope of the project, the financial evaluation should be supported, when applicable, by profitability forecasts, estimates of ultimate production costs, and requirements for market research, product development, trial runs, capital expenditures, and so on. A sample project appraisal summary is shown

EXHIBIT 1
Annual Project Authorization Form

ANNUAL PROJECT AUTHORIZATION FORM

ANNUAL PROJECT AUTHORIZATION FORM

DATE:

PROJECT TITLE

PROJECT NO.

PROJECT OBJECTIVE

FINANCIAL GOAL

SCOPE

PRECEDING PROJECT NO.	ANNUAL ESTIMATED COST	ADDITIONAL PERSONNEL REQUIRED	ADDITIONAL CAPITAL EQUIPMENT REQUIRED	REVIEW DATE
	$		$	

BACKGROUND INFORMATION

PROJECT RESPONSIBILITY	CORP.CHG. ☐ DIV.CHG. ☐	OPERATING DIVISION
		PRINCIPAL CONTACT

DISTRIBUTION LIST:

EXHIBIT 2
Annual Project Authorization Form

ANNUAL PROJECT AUTHORIZATION FORM			PROJECT NO.	
FINANCIAL DETAILS			BUDGET	
			PERSON-MONTHS	DOLLARS
DIRECT COSTS	PERSONNEL—PROFESSIONAL			$
	PERSONNEL—TECHNICIAN			
	EXPERIMENTAL EQUIPMENT AND RAW MATERIAL			
	OTHER DIRECT COSTS			
	DIRECT COSTS—TOTAL			
INDIRECT COSTS				
• TOTAL PROJECT COST				$
FINANCIAL COMMENTS:				
OTHER NOTATIONS				
— APPROVALS —				

TECH. COMPTR.	SECTION MGR.	DEPT. DIRECTOR	DIR. TECH.	TECH. DIR.-DIV.	GEN. MGR.-DIV.
DATE	DATE	DATE	DATE	DATE	DATE

SENIOR V.P.	EXEC. V.P.	EXEC. V.P.			
DATE	DATE	DATE	DATE	DATE	

EXHIBIT 3
R&D Project Appraisal Summary

PROJECT TITLE: _____   R&D PROJECT APPRAISAL SUMMARY   PROJECT NO. _____

	CHARACTERISTIC	POOR	FAIR	GOOD	EXCELLENT
MARKETING ASPECTS	Effect on Sales of Present Products (sold in same trade area)	Reduce sales of present products.	No effect on sales of existing products.	May help sales of present products.	Will substantially help sales of present products.
	Suitability of Present Sales Force; Product and End-Use Familiarity	Unsuitable; new sales and technical service groups will be required.	Present force inadequate; additional personnel required.	Present force generally adequate – some retraining necessary.	Present sales and technical service force very adequate.
	Market Trend	Declining market or high obsolescence risk.	Stable, basic market.	Growth market.	New potential market.
	Product Competition	Highly competitive end-use; several competing products.	Several competing products; product needed to hold market position.	No competing products at present; competitors active in this area.	No competitive product.
	Product Advantage	Higher price and equal quality.	Competitive price and quality.	Either price or quality advantage.	Both price and quality advantage.
	Merchandisability	Common product; no promotional value.	Some promotional value; has already been exploited by competition.	Average promotional value; or felt to be ahead of competition.	High promotional or prestige value.

	Less than 0.20 Less than 0.50	0.20 – 0.50 0.50 – 0.75	0.50 – 0.75 0.75 – 0.90	More than 0.75 More than 0.90
Probability of Successful Res.: Technology Dev.:				
TECHNOLOGICAL ASPECTS — Time Required for Commercialization	More than 5 years	2 – 5 years	1 – 2 years	Less than 1 year
Personnel Required	Considerable; must hire new personnel.	Considerable; will force suspension of other projects.	Moderate; will delay some projects.	Slight; personnel available.
Capability	Must hire new personnel with specific skills.	Intensive training of personnel required.	Necessary skills available within the company.	Necessary skills available in appropriate organizations.
Patentability	Nil. All features present in prior art.	Minor features possibly patentable. Competition not blocked off.	Strong process and product patents likely. Competition under definite handicap.	Basic product and process patent expected. No competition except under license.
GENERAL — Raw Material Availability	Limited availability or only one supplier.	Available from several suppliers.	Possibly available within the company.	Readily available within the company.
Equipment Availability	All new facilities needed.	Some new facilities needed.	Modify presently available facilities.	Necessary facilities presently idle.
Process Familiarity	Entirely new process with expected above-average new process operating problems.	Entirely new process with average new process operating problems.	Similar to existing process.	Routine process at another location.
FINANCIAL ASPECTS — Profitability Index	Considerably less than standard on similar products. Less than____%	Less than minimum desired. ____% to ____%	Better than minimum desired. ____% to ____%	Considerably better than minimum. Above____%

R&D Costs of $____M recovered in ____years.
Capital Costs of $____M recovered in ____years.
(Cash Inflow Expected $____in ____yrs.)

EXHIBIT 4
Project Review Form

PROJECT REVIEW FORM DATE:				
PROJECT TITLE				PROJECT NO.
ANNUAL ESTIMATED COST $	COST TO DATE THIS YEAR $	COST THIS REPORT PERIOD $	DATE OF NEXT REVIEW	DATE OF PREVIOUS REPORT
PROJECT REVIEW				
PROJECT RESPONSIBILITY	CORP. CHG. ☐ DIV. CHG. ☐	OPERATING DIVISION		
		PRINCIPAL CONTACT		
DISTRIBUTION LIST:				

EXHIBIT 5
Project Review Form

PROJECT REVIEW FORM			PROJECT NO.		
FINANCIAL DETAILS			BUDGET		ACTUAL DATE
			PERSON–MONTHS	DOLLARS	DOLLARS
DIRECT COSTS	PERSONNEL–PROFESSIONAL			$	$
	PERSONNEL—TECHNICIAN				
	EXPERIMENTAL EQUIPMENT AND RAW MATERIAL				
	OTHER DIRECT COSTS				
	DIRECT COSTS—TOTAL				
INDIRECT COSTS					
• TOTAL PROJECT COST				$	$
FINANCIAL COMMENTS:					
OTHER NOTATIONS					
TECH. COMPTRLR. DATE	SECTION MGR. DATE		DEPT. DIRECTOR DATE		DIR. TECH. DATE

in Exhibit 3. This illustrative appraisal form is for the reader's guidance, and should be modified to fit specific needs of the reviewing management. Companies or laboratories use various methods in appraising technical programs. Many projects, depending upon their purpose and stage of development, cannot realistically be appraised for profit potential.

Project Review and Analysis. Each project authorization should specify the approximate date for the project's initial review. Although most projects should be reviewed at least quarterly, the specific review interval assigned must depend on the nature of the project, and project work schedule, and the availability of materials, supplies, and equipment. Some equipment required in laboratory experiments cannot be purchased, and alternative sources must be arranged by improvisation.

A formal project review should be utilized in keeping all interested or supporting parties informed. The formal review process can be supplemented through oral presentation. However, a basic written report covering each interim and final review should be completed and documented. Exhibits 4 and 5 reflect an illustration in format that may be utilized for written review material. Again, the report should be brief and inclusive of all pertinent information. Exhibits 4 and 5 can also be printed back to back on one piece of paper.

The final review report of any project deemed to be successful should set a date for eventual follow-up and issuance of a postcompletion audit evaluation of benefits derived, particularly for actual financial benefits. The postcompletion audit can provide management with some indication of the technical project's return on "expense investment," and can also highlight weaknesses and overoptimistic monetary benefits estimated during the period when the project's funding was authorized. Obviously, some monetary-benefit projections must be somewhat "blue sky" for some projects in the basic research stage. However, the fact that a postcompletion audit will be performed will provide effective control.

Financial Responsibility and Reporting

To insure that a technical activity or function benefits fully from the knowledge and services available in the financial area, and to enable the technical staff to devote their full time to the technical effort, it is important to assign the full responsibility for all financial matters pertaining to the technical activities to a professionally qualified financial administrator or controller. This individual has a twofold purpose in assisting the Technical Committee in evaluating the research activity: (1) to see that the committee is not given misleading budget reports; and (2) to provide them with relevant information for periodic project evaluation. The principal functions of this responsibility should as a minimum include the following:

1. On the basis of estimates as to the use of personnel, materials, and so forth, to develop, in collaboration with the responsible technical staff, the project budget.
2. To determine whether sufficient funds are available for projects after the overall expense budget has been determined.
3. To assist in the development of the immediate and long-range financial objectives of technical efforts and projects, and to be responsible for the complete and accurate reflection of the stated technical estimates.
4. To maintain permanent files of all project estimates, approvals, reviews, and expense, both technical and financial.
5. To prepare monthly reports for each active project reflecting the actual expenditures, cumulative expenditures year to date, and the comparative budgets, and to maintain cumulative expenditures since the start of the project in case of year-to-year project life "overlapping."
6. In the case of organizations where technical expenses are to be transferred to other units, that is, operating or production departments, to charge these costs in accordance with company accounting procedures after approved authorization, and to issue such supporting informational data as may be deemed to be in order and necessary.

It is the experience of the author that the purchasing function in technical operations should be under the administration and control of the controller. This serves many purposes, the principal one being to ensure that project purchases are authorized before they are made and to accurately record authorized project expenses.

Although many of the expenditures in the technical operations necessarily involve both fixed costs and nonproject services which cannot be charged to specific projects on a direct basis, it is essential for proper evaluation of project profitability that (*a*) all direct charges to projects, including salaries and wages, be recorded on an actual basis; and (*b*) all expenses for fixed costs and supporting activities be prorated equitably among the active projects. In this connection, further analysis may indicate that an appropriate allocation of fixed and nonproject costs should be charged to "free time" for unscheduled investigations of scientists and engineers. Depending upon the technical activities, it may be advisable to exclude this type of expense from individual project costs since the so-called "free time" is spent maintaining up-to-date technical expertise.

Since salaries normally constitute the bulk of research and development expenditures, nonproject expenses can normally be allocated on that basis. However, some technical activities or operations may dictate other more realistic methods of allocation. When technical activities are performed for external purposes or sales, it is important that the allocations and costing procedures be adequate, accurate, and realistic. If the technical information is being prepared for and funded through governmental agencies, costing techniques must meet the standards and requirements set forth by the agencies.

A Caution

Research and development departments constitute discretionary expense centers. Accordingly, all of the problems associated with control of discretionary expenses, as described at the outset of Chapter 24, apply in the area of R&D management. This is especially true for projects nearer the research end of the research-development spectrum. (Projects nearer the development end become more susceptible to the type of project controls described in the next chapter.)

In particular, in evaluating the performance of the R&D department and its head, it is important not to overemphasize the budgeted-versus-actual cost comparison. Any R&D department manager can (and should) keep the department's total expenses within budget. If pressure is put on the manager to "beat" the budget, this can be done, too—by layoffs or not filling vacant positions, and by stretching schedules or reducing the level of effort on certain projects. The problem is that there is not a clear or precise input-output relationship in R&D efforts. Thus a budget underrun of 10 percent may or may not mean that 10 percent less research output was accomplished. Similarly, a budget overrun (if authorized) may or may not mean that more research results were produced. In other words, the notion of "efficiency" is very hard to apply here, and "effectiveness" is often hard to measure.

Thus a considerable amount of judgment must be exercised when evaluating the R&D function. It is largely a judgment, rather than a measurement, as to whether the R&D function is sufficiently effective and efficient. And there is a delicate balance between these two evaluation criteria: an overemphasis on budgetary control can lead to demoralization among the researchers, and the loss of the best of them to other organizations; while an overemphasis on producing quick research results can lead to an unacceptably high level of R&D cost and perhaps to the buildup of hard-to-discover "fat" in the R&D organization.

While measurements and forms of the kind described in this chapter are certainly a must for R&D management, when all is said and done the most important R&D control probably is selection of the head of R&D. It is important that top management feel R&D managers are both technically and managerially competent, and that they are exercising good judgment in maintaining a balance between costs (inputs) and results (outputs).

Summary

As initially indicated, the intent of this chapter is not to give a specific method of controlling research and development costs, since the type of technical activity and organization varies dramatically. Some R&D control methods can be relatively "loose," as is usually the case in industrial organizations. Other methods are relatively rigid, especially when the work is sponsored under grants or supported principally through governmental agencies. Many technical activities are very small in dollar size, while others may appear staggering. Under these conditions, no one method is always realistic and practical. The controls must be in conformity to meet specific needs.

However, in all instances it is necessary to adopt a system that develops information for the Technical Committee that assists them in determining the following: (1) how much money should be spent; (2) where should the money be spent (which projects or programs); and (3) how good a job the research and development activity is doing. The impact of an error in judgment concerning either the amount or direction of R&D expenditures can be very great. It may take a long time to correct the effects of any error and its impact on profits, and competitive considerations can be large. However, it is hoped that with moderate modifications, the procedures (and cautions) contained herein will provide the framework for effective control.

ADDITIONAL SOURCES

Also see Additional Sources for Chapter 42.

Cook, Leslie G. "How to Make R&D More Productive." *Harvard Business Review,* July–August 1966, p. 145.

Dearden, John. "Budgeting and Accounting for R&D Costs." *Financial Executive,* November 1963, p. 20.

Hughes, Everett C. "Preserving Individualism on the R&D Team." *Harvard Business Review,* January–February 1968, p. 72.

Quinn, James Brian, and Cavanaugh, Robert M. "Fundamental Research Can Be Planned." *Harvard Business Review,* January–February 1964, p. 111.

Thompson, Paul H., and Dalton, Gene W. "Are R&D Organizations Obsolete?" *Harvard Business Review,* November–December 1976, p. 105.

Watson, Spencer C. "A Vote for R&D Profit Centers." *Management Accounting,* April 1975, p. 50.

42

Project Management
Systems

L. W. Johnson*

The project management system to be described in this chapter is the system being used by Control Data's Aerospace Division in its monitoring and controlling of performance on significant government contracts. It should be pointed out, however, that the concepts and procedures described are applicable to all types of project efforts. Other commercial Control Data divisions do, in fact, use the same system, with minor variations, on development projects.

The original concepts and procedures described below were developed in mid-1974 and were applied on a pilot basis to a relatively large contract in the fall of 1974. The system and the pilot program experience were reviewed by a Management System Task Force which was established to increase the effectiveness of the division's management systems. This task force gave its approval in mid-1975 to use the system on all new programs.

CHARACTERISTICS OF PROJECT
MANAGEMENT SYSTEMS

A project management system has certain essential characteristics. The elements we used for developing our project management system are also applicable to management systems in general. Each of these four characteristics will now be described.

* Mr. Johnson is Manager of Program Control, Aerospace Division, Control Data Corporation, Minneapolis.

The first important characteristic of such a system is that it identify the key factors in the business operation that must be controlled to achieve a given overall result. For a project, the factors are technical performance (the quality of the end product), schedules, and costs. In the project plan, the overall project objectives are further broken down and delineated with the result that the key factors are very specifically defined for all project elements. At the end of the planning phase, the critical factors are known and documented, thus assuring that the project manager can concentrate on those areas which critically affect the project.

Second, the system should specify the basis for establishing performance criteria for each key factor. In manufacturing, for example, there are various standards which may be used to judge performance. Development efforts, because they are one-time, one-of-a-kind projects, do not have historical information on which to base standards. There must be, however, *some* baseline, some yardstick, to use to determine if the progress being made is satisfactory or not. The plan must serve as this frame of reference because it has defined the objectives and the intermediate steps and actions (defined in terms of what? who? how? when? and how much?) which must be taken to achieve the end objectives. Progress against the plan, then, is the only criterion available to judge the project performance. It is not possible to ascertain whether the performance required by the plan is above or below average because there are no objective standards on which to base such a judgment. Inherent in the plan, however, is the fact that the end objectives will be reached only if the performance levels specified within the plan are achieved. Any deviation beyond tolerable limits from the original plan requires managerial action to bring the actual performance back within the planned limits, to develop an alternative approach to achieving the objectives, to change the end objective, or to abandon the project.

To give an example, if the plan required a software project to be completed in six months at a cost not to exceed $250,000, there is no way of knowing if most other software development groups would take less or more time, or would incur costs greater or less than this. But, in the planning process, the achieving of the end objective is predicated upon all organizations, including software, achieving a certain level of performance. The availability of performance standards would offer a more effective measure; however, the performance levels specified in the plan are sufficient for the success of the program—success being defined in terms of achieving stated objectives. For control purposes, all that need concern the project manager is that performance does not fall below the planned level.

From this, it may be seen that well-formulated plans are essential to the control process. This control is one of the primary reasons for planning, and plans must be formulated with this objective in mind. (This is not the only objective of planning; it is only one of several primary purposes.)

A third aspect of designing a project management system is defining the information—the cost accounting records, the operating data, and the statistics—that must be accumulated to measure status and performance. Much of this information is universally defined for all projects. In this category are technical information (how well are specifications being met), schedule data (PERT or other networking, milestone reporting, and so on), and cost information (actuals, budgets, and so forth). Some of this information will be unique to particular projects. Examples of items in this category are forecasted manufacturing costs or forecasted reliability. The plan is the source for some of this information. Budgets, schedules, and specifications have already been defined in the plan, at least in a gross manner. The only information left to collect is the actual performance data which are received in the form of test results, accounting data, and schedule completions.

A fourth project management characteristic is the establishment of a reporting structure that identifies performance in each control area; relates causes and effects; signals trends; and identifies results by responsibility under the plan of organization. Some of these structures are in existence (accounting reports, PERT reporting), and some must be devised by the project manager to satisfy his (or her) or the project's unique requirements. The unique requirements are spelled out in the plan, and from these the project manager is able to determine what type of reporting structure will be needed to monitor this performance.

It is doubtful if the reporting structure itself will relate causes to effects. Symptoms of problems will be reported, but it will be the task of the project manager to use the information disseminated by the reporting system to define and isolate the true problem. Because the plan has delineated organizational responsibilities, it is easy to define results by organization.

The signaling of trends early enough in the project cycle for corrective action to be taken has always been a significant requirement for performance measurement systems. In a project environment, the capability of spotting problem areas early can be accomplished relatively easily. The plan must define in enough detail what is expected to be accomplished within what time and at what costs. Frequent checkpoints must be established throughout the life of the project. If the checkpoints are defined at, say, six-month intervals, there is no possible way to measure performance at points earlier than six months. If checkpoints are defined at one- or two-month intervals then status can also be obtained at those intervals. To get early warning of significant trends, then, it is absolutely necessary to define in terms of technical, schedule, and cost objectives what must be accomplished early in the project.

From the foregoing, it is easy to see that without a plan, there can be no control. Additionally, the effectiveness of project control is directly related to the soundness and completeness of the plan, as well as the design, implementation, and use of the monitoring system itself.

Interrelationship of Cost, Schedule, and Technical Objectives

As mentioned above, the management parameters which must be controlled in any project are time, cost, and technical performance, and these three factors are interdependent. In the planning phase, these parameters are balanced against each other in order to achieve a desired result based upon marketing needs and the competitive situation. For instance, if the market requires that a new product be introduced as quickly as possible, the time factor will be emphasized at the expense of cost and technical features. It is important for project managers constantly to keep in mind the particular emphasis within any project because in managing and controlling their projects they will constantly be faced with trade-off decisions which must be made in order to achieve optimum project results.

It is easy to see how the costs and time requirements would be affected if the technical objectives were changed. For instance, if it has been determined that the costs and/or time must be reduced, a decision could be made to reduce the testing requirements with a resultant increase in the risk of the product not performing properly. Similarily, time requirements could be reduced by increasing the costs. In a project management system, the three factors must be integrated and their specific relationships always understood. In the system to be described, the reporting of schedule and cost status is integrated, but the technical performance is not. This is due primarily to there being no simple, effective technique available. While there is no objective reporting technique that integrates technical performance with cost and schedule performance, the manner of documenting the project requirements provides a subjective method of integrating the three.

Because this Handbook deals primarily with financial controls, the cost monitoring feature of the project management system will be emphasized. Schedule and technical performance control systems, such as PERT, Line-of-Balance, and Technical Performance Trend Charts, will therefore not be treated in detail. It must be remembered, however, that they are essential elements of a comprehensive, integrated project management system and that their omission in this chapter is no indication of their relative importance. Schedule and technical performance will be addressed only when it is necessary to relate them to cost performance.

PERFORMANCE MEASUREMENT CAPABILITIES

As stated before, the CDC Aerospace Project Management System has the capability of measuring objectively the cost and schedule performance, but not the technical performance of projects. This system enables a continuous measuring process throughout the life of the project.

Exhibit 1–A is an illustration of the traditional cost performance data for a particular project. It reflects the summarization of the bits and pieces of data processed within the project management system.

Traditional Evaluation

The conventional method of cost monitoring in the past has been the comparison of actual costs (indicated by the solid line in Exhibit 1–A) with the budgeted costs (indicated by the dashed line) at a particular point in time. This comparison is at best worth little,

EXHIBIT 1–A
Project Budget Graph

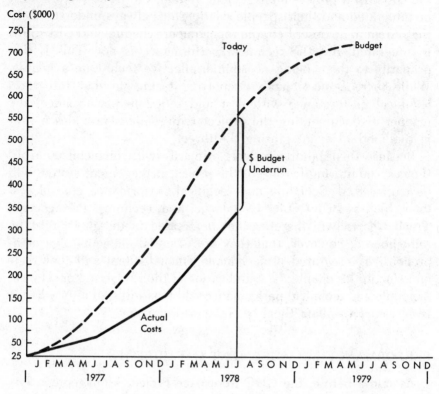

Cost ($000)

and at the worst is deceptive, because it takes no account of the amount of work accomplished. In other words, it does not integrate task costs with task accomplishments.

The deficiency inherent in comparing the cumulative actual costs incurred at a point in time with the costs budgeted to have been incurred by that time is caused by the fact that the budget line is a function of the project *schedule*. The work is first scheduled and then the associated costs are time phased according to that schedule. Of course, it is an unusual project which has all of its work proceeding on exactly the original schedule. Hence the actual costs shown are the costs for all work completed through the reporting date regardless of when this work was scheduled to have been performed. The actual versus budget comparison is an indication of the actual *rate of spending* as compared to the planned rate of spending. It does not indicate whether the work is being accomplished within the budgeted allocations. To do this, it is necessary to have some measure of the work performed.

In the following paragraphs, a monitoring system that overcomes the drawbacks discussed above will be described conceptually. This system is called the Accomplishment/Cost Procedure (ACP). This title was borrowed from an article in the *Harvard Business Review* by Ellery B. Block, which was used as one source of information in developing the CDC Aerospace Project Management System.[1]

Relating Costs and Accomplishment

ACP is a technique that portrays the relationships among dollars spent, dollars budgeted, amount of work accomplished, and amount of work expected—all at once—in a single picture. Exhibit 1–B illustrates some of the features of ACP. In the illustration, the project depicted would be described by the traditional method as having a very favorable cost variance, because the actual costs through today are approximately $350,000, while the budgeted costs are $575,000. Thus the project budget would be said to be underrun by approximately $225,000.

By using the dotted line on the graph, an entirely different cost status is indicated. The dotted line indicates the value of the work *accomplished*. In the illustration, the value of the work accomplished is $275,000. Because it has cost $350,000 to accomplish work that was originally planned to cost $275,000, it can be seen that at this point in time the project is actually *overrun* by $75,000. In this case, the comparison of actual costs to the budget is deceiving because the project, rather than being in a favorable financial condition, has overrun its costs on the work that has been accomplished.

The term "value of work accomplished" is used because it is analogous to a contract price (before profit). If it were possible to negotiate a price or value with a customer for the work that was completed as of the reporting date, the resulting value would be that which is depicted on the chart, that is, $275,000. The value would be predicated upon the cost estimates for the work. This measure of value received would then be compared to the actual costs incurred to determine the profitability of the work completed to date.

---

[1] Block, Ellery B. "Accomplishment/Cost: Better Project Control," *Harvard Business Review*, May–June 1971, p. 110.

EXHIBIT 1–B
Project Summary Graph Using Accomplishment/Cost Procedure

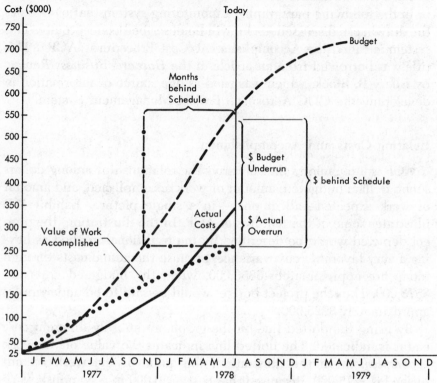

Another way of looking at the value of work accomplished is to treat it as the sum of the budgets for the work completed to date, regardless of when this work was scheduled for completion. Accordingly, in some systems this amount is called the "budgeted cost of work accomplished," or the "earned value."

The ACP chart can also give indication of project schedule status. The budget line is really the scheduling of the dollar value of the work to be accomplished based upon the costs estimated in the planning phase. In the illustration, the value of the work scheduled to have been completed by "today" is $575,000, while the actual value of the work accomplished is $275,000. In dollar terms, the project is $300,000 worth of work behind schedule.

The number of months behind schedule is obtained by horizontally projecting the accomplishment point to the budget line to determine the point in time when the realized accomplishments were actually scheduled to have been accomplished. From the chart, it can be seen that $275,000 worth of work was scheduled to be accomplished by November 1977. Time "now" is July 1978; the project is therefore eight months behind schedule.

Again the analogy with contract value can be used. In the example, it was anticipated that $575,000 of value would have been received from the customer through today. As it is, only $275,000 would have been received. It may also be stated that parcels of work whose budgets total $575,000 were scheduled for completion, while parcels of work whose budgets total $275,000 were actually completed. It should be emphasized that original budgets are used to give value to the work accomplished and scheduled because the original plan is used as the frame of reference for performance measurement.

Obviously, the crux of ACP is the value of the accomplishments and how this value is determined. The method of determining the value will be treated more extensively in the section on Cost/Schedule Performance Monitoring.

PLANNING CONCEPTS AND PROCEDURES

The one element of project management which is perhaps the most misunderstood and neglected is project planning. Without viable, integrated, well-constructed plans, project direction will be lacking and there will be no usable frame of reference against which to monitor and control the project. Planning is an absolute necessity in project management, and, if done effectively, will provide a high rate of return on the resources used. Because planning is more abstract and does not result in tangible work accomplishments that immediately contribute to the specific requirements of the project, very often it is not done at all or is done only very superficially. Many times only a perfunctory planning process is carried out to satisfy the requirement that planning be done. But after this type of plan is completed, it is put on a shelf to gather dust and is never used again. The plan is not "worked" and not used for control. Effort devoted to this kind of plan is usually mostly wasted, and it is this type of planning that results in future resistance to planning of any kind.

Planning, to be useful, requires dedicated and intensive effort. Because the anticipated effort to achieve the project objectives must be specified in the plan, many false starts can be avoided and major problem areas defined before they make a major, adverse impact upon the project.

Effective project planning requires that four sequential steps be completed. These must be completed in the sequence indicated below in order for the resulting plan to be completely integrated. These steps are:

1. Develop the project "work breakdown structure" (WBS).
2. From the WBS, specify the "work packages" which are the short-term jobs required to complete the contract.
3. Schedule the project by using the work packages to define the schedule network and then provide time estimates for each work package (activity).
4. Determine the project time-phased budget through the application of the necessary resources to complete the defined work.

Many times, poor or no planning is done because the project personnel have no structured, disciplined approach to follow. The further elaboration on these four steps that follows will provide the necessary guidelines for an effective planning process.

Work Breakdown Structure

Central to the project planning process is the definition and organization of the work necessary to accomplish the project objectives. This must necessarily be the first step, and it forms the basis for all subsequent planning effort.

A technique essential in the work definition is the development of a work breakdown structure (WBS). An example of a typical WBS is given in Exhibit 2. The WBS is essentially the logical subdividing of the work to be performed. It assists the project personnel by providing a structured means of defining and organizing the work. It makes the work to be accomplished more understandable by identifying nice, neat tasks within a bewildering array of objectives, alternatives, and activities. Additionally, the WBS provides the integrating mechanism and framework for controlling the technical, cost, and schedule parameters.

The determination and definition of objectives is the initial and the most important step in the management process. This is achieved through the WBS by assigning technical, cost, and sched-

EXHIBIT 2
Typical Work Breakdown Structure

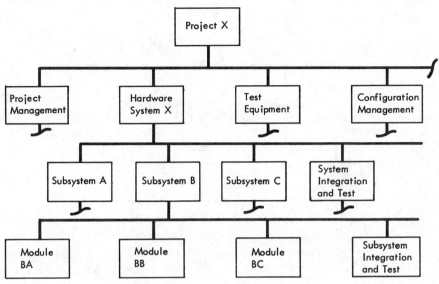

ule objectives to each element in the WBS. First, the overall project objectives are established and then subobjectives, which are linked or related to the project objectives, are extended downward to the lower detailed levels. This approach assures that:

Project objectives will be achieved through the accomplishment of lower level objectives;

The project structure is fully integrated, and each part of the structure is consistent with and related to the project as a whole; and

Project information will be usefully summarized.

The WBS, then, provides for the logical determination of objectives and subobjectives and provides the means for the distribution of specific and coordinated objectives from higher to lower levels of management.

From the example in Exhibit 2, it can be seen that the WBS is an end-item oriented "family tree" composed of hardware, software, services, and other work tasks. It is necessarily end-item or product oriented, as opposed to functional-organization oriented, because the outputs or "products" of the project, and not the functions which are performed, must be defined.

EXHIBIT 3
Incorrect WBS

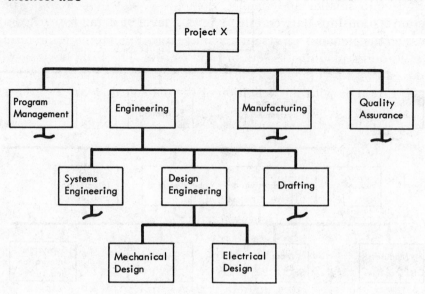

A common mistake in developing work breakdown structures is shown in Exhibit 3. In this example, the functional organizations are defined, but the actual definition of the subdivision of the work and structure of the project itself is not given. End-item orientation and the top-down approach of breaking down of the end item into products or physical entities is required because:

It provides a sound basis for assuring that the technical objectives are related or linked from one level to the next. The functional and performance requirements for the system are allocated to the next lower level and so on down through the structure.

Technical, schedule, or cost problems can be ascribed to a particular entity. This makes problem isolation and solution much easier.

Historical data is collected and retained on a product basis which makes for more meaningful information for estimating and controlling future projects.

Responsibility can be assigned to individuals for the successful completion of the individual products, even though there may be different performing organizations.

The WBS is developed by successively dividing the total project effort into smaller and smaller elements, taking into account the interrelationships between them, until a level of detail is reached at which the elements represent a manageable set of activities in terms of visibility, planning, execution, and control. The WBS begins with the end result to be accomplished as a product of the total project effort. It ends with the definition of the manageable tasks.

While the definition of "manageable task" is subjective, factors to be considered in establishing the WBS' configuration content and detail are:

The size of the project;

The complexity of the project; and

The organizational structure of the organization involved.

The lowest elements of the WBS are considered the manageable task—the effort described can be managed, that is, organized, planned, directed, coordinated, and controlled by one person. No further delegation of managerial authority or responsibility is necessary nor desirable to successfully complete the task. While there may be other individuals or organizations responsible for work defined in the task (work packages), they are not responsible for the managerial functions of organizing, planning, and so on.

The work pacakages, which are subsumed under the manageable tasks but which do not become a part of the WBS, are the specific elements or parcels of work required to accomplish the manageable tasks. Examples of these are electrical design, mechanical design, layout, assembly, inspection, and so forth.

The manageable task is analogous to the first-level or lowest level organization in the organizational hierarchy. The organization is essentially subdivided by function until a function whose scope can be managed by one person is defined. This person is the first-line supervisor. If the business expands, further subdivision may be necessary to reduce the functional scope and a lower level of supervision is defined. The organization hierarchy is subdivided by function; the work breakdown structure is subdivided by product or end result.

These manageable tasks are also treated as the lowest level cost accounts. They are the focal point for collecting costs of work and, normally, these tasks also constitute the lowest level in the structure at which comparisons of applied direct costs to budgeted costs are required.

The WBS must describe the way the work is actually to be accomplished and will therefore be a logical, natural breakdown of the work. If it is artificially constructed just to satisfy an administrative requirement, it will lose its benefits—the objectives established will be meaningless and any control information will be artificially generated and of little value. In developing the WBS, there is a trade-off involved between a desirable level of control and the associated administrative effort. The more levels a particular project has, the more control is possible, but also the administrative costs are higher and the sorting out of the detail information becomes more difficult.

There are no restrictions on the number of levels in the WBS, and all manageable tasks need not occur at the same level. A "dictionary" defining the functions and performance requirements of each block on the WBS is prepared. For services, a description of all required services is specified.

A well-conceived, properly constructed WBS offers many advantages and benefits:

It provides the structure for actually managing the project. Complex mathematical problems are solved by breaking the problem into its solvable parts; large complex projects can be managed by breaking them down into their manageable parts. By effectively managing the manageable tasks, the entire project will be effectively managed. Small projects of low complexity are easily managed. The WBS breaks the project down into these small projects of little complexity. The secret of success, then, is the definition of the manageable tasks. It is no easy task to break down the overall project objectives into meaningful subobjectives but, if it is not done correctly and is not all-inclusive, the project has little chance of success. The project manager must be willing to accept the time and costs required to perform this difficult task properly.

It forces a discipline whereby all the work must be completely and adequately described and documented before work actually begins. It reduces and minimizes the probability of surprises in the form of unanticipated work or technical requirements after the work has begun.

It provides a sound basis for the original estimation of costs. It is much easier and more accurate to estimate the cost of the manageable pieces of work than that of a large monolithic project.

It enhances control because problem areas are more precisely defined. The control data are organized to provide better concentration.

It forms the basis for the development of a specification tree. System engineers can use the WBS for the allocation of function and performance requirements consistent with the end product's specifications. By breaking the end product down into its subsystems, devices, modules, and so on, it is possible to define the requirements which must be met at each level in order to achieve the higher level requirement.

It integrates the cost, schedule, and technical parameters of the project. Each block has its technical specification and statement of work, its associated cost and schedules.

Definition of Work Packages

The second step in developing the project plan is the definition of work packages. The work packages are descriptions of the functional effort—the actual work—which must be performed to accomplish the result required of the manageable task. An example of work packages is given in Exhibit 4.

EXHIBIT 4
Work Packages

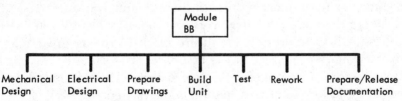

Work packages must have the following characteristics:

They represent work at levels where performance is managed.

The performance of the work described is assignable to a single first-level organization.

They should be of relatively short duration.

They should describe a unit of work required to complete a specific job, such as a report, a drawing, a piece of hardware or a service.

In defining work packages during the planning process, the requirement that they be of short duration is important for two reasons. First, when monitoring progress against a plan, checkpoints have to be chosen with such frequency that an objective evaluation can be made in sufficient time that any necessary corrective actions can be taken. These checkpoints cannot be arbitrarily chosen to correspond to a specific length of time, but must be chosen to correspond to the completion of an event which will give an objective measure of the work completed. Examples of such checkpoints are the completion of a drawing or a report, piece of hardware or a service. These intermediate objectives must be established to determine if the pace of work is rapid enough to achieve the project's end objective. In other words, the plan says that if we are to have the finished product of Project X by an established date, the drawing for Module BB must also be completed by a certain date. If the drawing is late, the management must quicken the pace of work in certain later tasks in order to meet the overall deadline.

Obviously, a year is too long a time duration for a work package. It would be very difficult to determine whether the pace is adequate until the better part of the year had passed. Toward the end of the year, it would probably be possible to determine whether the work would be completed on time; but if it is determined, say, in the 11th month that that pace is not adequate, it may be impossible to compress the remaining month's work enough to meet the work package's deadline. But if a work package is only two months in duration, the compression of future work is not as great and recovery is more probable. In the first case, approximately a year has passed before it is apparent that corrective action is needed; in the second case, less than two months have passed.

Second, for cost control it is necessary to relate work accomplished to the costs. When the work packages are long, it is necessary to use subjective or arbitrary formulas to assess the amount of work accomplished. For short work packages, on the other hand, little or no assessment of the work in process is necessary because the measure of the work accomplished is determined mainly by completed work packages. Optimum cost monitoring is achieved when a work package is started in one accounting period and ends in the next. Because accounting periods are usually one month long, the optimum length of work packages would be two months or less.

While no specific guidelines can be established for the length of work packages, from the foregoing it would appear that two months or less would be a reasonable criterion. However, such an arbitrary requirement should be avoided and the decision on length should be made on the basis of the criticalness of the work, the precision with which the work package can be defined (too restrictive definition of work packages in dynamic and changeable areas may require extensive redefinition), and the natural subdivisions of the work. Sometimes it is impossible to define a short-term work package. In those cases every effort should be made to establish objective interim milestones on which an objective measure of progress can be made.

Not all work established by the work breakdown structure will be work packages. Some tasks cannot be associated with tangible output; these are support activities which are "level-of-effort" tasks. Project management and engineering support are examples. Level-of-effort tasks are included in the WBS but are not scheduled. Additionally, there is no objective way to measure accomplishments for these tasks other than to value them according to their time-phased budgets. (This will be treated later.) Additionally, there may be situations early in the project where it is infeasible or impossible to define all the short-term work packages that will be performed later in the project. In those cases it will be necessary initially to define the larger effort of the manageable tasks. After the project is underway, however, all work packages should be described approximately six months before they are scheduled to occur.

The key feature of a work package, then, is the description of discrete, short-term elements of work with definable and measureable results assignable to a particular first-level or lowest level organization. The work package provides the integration with the organizational structure to provide the means for measuring organizational performance (see Exhibit 5). The work package can be

EXHIBIT 5
Work Packages Assignment

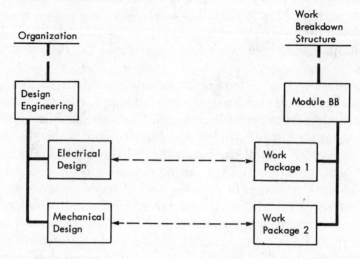

assigned to only one performing organization; but, of course, a particular organization can be assigned more than one work package within a project.

Project Scheduling

Once the work packages have been defined, they must be tied together through a scheduling network. The best-known network system is PERT (Program Evaluation and Review Technique), but there are several different variations with essentially the same basic underlying concepts. Because it is the best known, PERT will be used to explain the basic principles of networking. It is beyond the scope of this chapter to provide an extensive treatment of the mechanics of PERT. Only the basic underlying concepts will be treated; the reader is referred to other literature (listed at the end of this chapter) if a fuller treatment is desired or if more information on other network systems such as the critical path method (CPM) is required.

Basic to any network analysis technique is the concept of the "arrow diagram" or the "network," as it is commonly called. The network is a graphic model showing interdependencies between various project activities by means of a simple charting technique.

In a network, the circles represent events and the lines connecting any two circles represent activities.

An activity is defined as the work necessary to progress from one event to another. Activities consume time, money, and personnel. An activity connecting any two events defines a precedence relation between those events. In Exhibit 6, Event 2, system testing complete, cannot be completed before Event 1, integrated system available, has occurred. These events occur at the beginning and end of Activity 1–2, run system tests. For this activity, Event 1 is called the predecessor event and Event 2, the successor.

The activities in a project are related to each other in various ways. These relationships are termed interdependencies. Dependen-

EXHIBIT 6
Network Example (1)

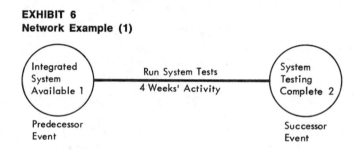

cies between activities result from precedence relationships which constrain an activity from starting until the product of the preceding activity is available. For the purpose of illustration, consider the interdependencies depicted in Exhibit 7, which shows a very simple network consisting of four activities and four events. Events 2 and 3 are both dependent on the occurrence of Event 1. Event 4 cannot occur until activities 1–2, 1–3, 2–4, and 3–4 all have been performed.

The network is thus a logic diagram of a project. It overcomes many of the weaknesses of bar charts and milestone charts. The network shows all interrelationships between activities and thus reveals, in the planning stages, the factors which constrain the beginning or end of any activity or group of activities in the project. The network shows all the events or milestones of interest to management and thereby facilitates progress reporting and control.

The Concept of Critical Path. Each activity consumes resources and has a time dimension. The time required to complete an activity, with a given level of personnel, is shown in suitable time units along the activity lines of the network. In PERT, the activity duration is specified in terms of three time estimates: most optimistic, most likely, and most pessimistic durations; however for the sake of clarity, only a single time estimate will be used here.

In any network, there is always at least one connected path (made up of activity lines and events) that goes from the start event to the end event. In the network shown in Exhibit 7, there are two such paths: 1–2–4, and 1–3–4. Each of these begins at 1, which is the start event, and ends at 4, which is the terminal event.

EXHIBIT 7
Network Example (2)

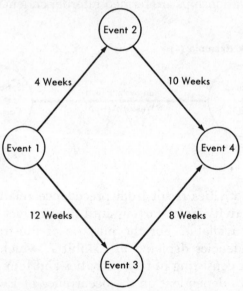

Now, if activity duration times along each such complete path are summed, the network will usually reveal one path that takes the longest to reach from start to end in terms of time units. This longest path is called the *critical path*. This is an exceedingly important concept underlying network analysis. For the network in Exhibit 7, the sums of the activity times are as follows:

Path 1–2–4:   4 + 10 = 14 weeks
Path 1–3–4:   12 + 8 = 20 weeks

By definition, then, the critical path for this network is identified as 1–3–4, having a total time requirement of 20 weeks.

The critical path provides very vital planning and control information. For example, it shows that:

1. Given the network logic and the activity time duration, the project will take 20 weeks to complete.
2. If an activity slips while on this path, the end event will slip by a corresponding amount, increasing the project duration.
3. The activities on this path are thus the most critical from a schedule standpoint.
4. The management should focus its attention on the activities that fall on the critical path. These activities have the greatest impact on the total project schedule and, as such, are most responsive to management's effort to improve the project schedules.

The activities that do *not* lie on the critical path have varying amounts of "slack" times associated with them. Slack means the length of time by which a particular activity can slip without having any delaying effect on the end event. In the example of Exhibit 7, Activities 1–2 and 2–4 have *combined* slack of six weeks; that is, either individually or in combination these activities' schedules can be "slipped" six weeks without delaying the scheduled deadline for Event 4. Note that if this six-week slippage *did* occur, path 1–2–4 would also become critical.

The critical path concept is important because the performance measuring system compares the value of work accomplished with all the work scheduled, regardless of whether it is on the critical path or not. It would be possible for the system to show a significant behind schedule situation and yet the end date would not be in jeopardy because all the slipped effort is on noncritical paths. If a schedule variance is indicated on the performance measurement chart, the network must be consulted to fully understand the implications.

Cost Estimating

Network scheduling systems calculate the start and end dates for the activities (or work packages) from the estimated times (i.e., activity durations) and the start date of the beginning event. Once the schedule is determined, each work package's cost is estimated. When this estimating process is completed, a project time-phased budget is developed as illustrated in Exhibit 8.

EXHIBIT 8
Accomplishment/Cost

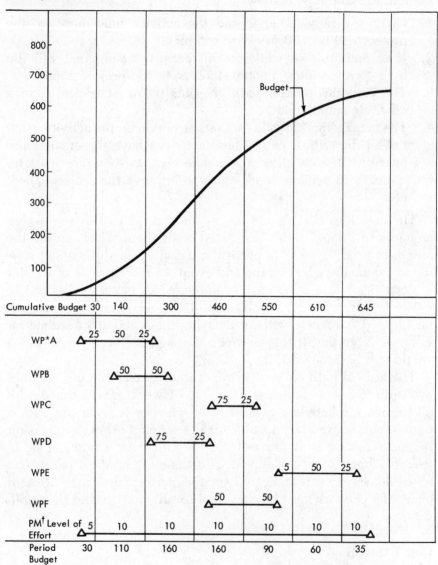

| Cumulative Budget | 30 | 140 | 300 | 460 | 550 | 610 | 645 | |

WP*A △—25—50—25—△

WPB △—50—50—△

WPC △—75—25—△

WPD △—75—25—△

WPE △—5—50—25—△

WPF △—50—50—△

PM† Level of Effort △—5—10—10—10—10—10—10—△

| Period Budget | 30 | 110 | 160 | 160 | 90 | 60 | 35 | |

* Work project.
† Project management.

In the lower half of this illustration, the resources required for each work package (WP) are indicated by time period. For example, Work Package A has $25 budgeted in the first time period, $50 in the second, and $25 in the third. The total resources estimated for each work package become the amount allocated (budgeted) and should be viewed as the cost target for the work package.

As may be seen from the upper half of Exhibit 8, the time-phased budget integrates the budgeted costs with the schedule objectives. It is a measure of the schedule in that it depicts the value of work scheduled in terms of the cumulative budgeted amounts; that is, it depicts the total amount of work which is scheduled to be accomplished through each point in time. In effect, each work package is weighted according to its value, and this weighting will be used in determining the amount of work actually accomplished. To measure the work, it would be insufficient to measure the absolute number of work packages completed, because some will cost more (i.e., have a higher weight) than others. Work packages, then, are measured in terms of dollars, which provide a common denominator in measuring schedule and cost performance. (Throughout the discussion, dollars are used as the unit of measure. If desirable, hours would also be an appropriate unit.)

The Project Management (PM) level of effort at the bottom of Exhibit 8 cannot be associated with any particular milestone, and is thus shown as a budget over the life of the project. It does not have the short duration restriction imposed upon it. The time-phased budget becomes the baseline against which the actual performance is compared.

The work packages illustrated in Exhibit A are examples of labor. Material for a particular work breakdown structure element would also be planned, except it would be planned when it is expected to be issued or used at a particular point in time, and not over several periods of time. Again, the value is the original estimate for the required materials.

Project Changes and Management Reserves. The planning baseline should remain unchanged over the life of the project (unless the project's scope is changed—this is discussed below.) This baseline reflects the summarization of cost and schedule objectives. Performance monitoring is concerned with comparing the actual performance against the objectives. It is management's responsibility to assure the objectives are met and to overcome obstacles that stand in the way.

Some project management systems monitor the actual cost performance against the *latest* cost estimates. Performance monitoring in these systems does not provide good cost control because the objectives are always changed to reflect what has actually happened. If an overrun has occurred, the new baseline is established to reflect this. (This is sometimes referred to as the "rubber baseline" phenomenon.) Poor performance is obscured because the frame of reference is changed to reflect what actually happened. In this type of system there is no motivation to concentrate on finding ways of achieving the original objectives. It reflects a philosophy that the costs and schedules will be what they will be and there is nothing that can be done about variances from the original plan. The extension of this rationale would be a good argument against the need for management. If the path of a project were inexorably set from the beginning, the need for managerial direction would be eliminated.

The estimates made during the planning phase should be considered as a way of establishing reasonable objectives. Once the project is begun, the estimates are transformed into objectives. Commitment to these objectives is important, and a determination of how well managers do their jobs is how well they meet those objectives. Objectives should not be considered estimates which can be updated. Of course, if the budget is exceeded, some control must still be exercised on the overrun costs. This is accomplished by distinguishing between the budget and the funding authorization. The funding authorization is the dollar amount which may be spent on the particular task, and this funding would exceed the budget if an overrun were authorized. The budget amount would still be used to measure performance.

The cost and schedule baseline will also change if the description of the work were to change. For purposes of this discussion, it is necessary to distinguish between *internal* scope changes and *external* scope changes. Internal scope changes are those which are necessary to meet the original specifications of the contract, or the agreement with top management for internally funded projects. These changes are necessary because the work as described in the original plan is not sufficient to meet the requirements of the contract or management agreement.

Funds which are used to cover this type of change normally come from a management reserve or management contingency fund. That is, funds are set aside at the origination of the program to cover unforeseen work.

There are two primary ways to provide funds for reserve purposes. The first, and easiest, is to include them in the original estimate as a separate item when negotiating with the customer or top management. However, when they are highly visible, there is a good probability they will be disallowed, especially by government and military contract negotiators.

The second method is to hold back a portion of the budgets from each of the tasks; that is, allocate budgets which are less than the estimates. The total difference between the budgets allocated and the original estimates will be the reserve or contingency. The rationale behind this method assumes that the original estimates include a factor for unforeseen circumstances; for example, the estimates assume that a normal number of things will go wrong. The amount that is actually allocated to a task, however, is the amount that would be required to do the job if nothing went wrong. It is difficult if not impossible to objectively determine this, so subjective percentage estimates are used. This, then, provides the project manager with the control of the funds which were originally estimated for problems. The funds would be used where and when required and at the project manager's own discretion.

Additionally, it is assumed that on project efforts some tasks will overrun and some will underrun, but that there will be an offsetting effect, with the result that the total project will come in on target. However, in reality most of the tasks either meet or exceed their budgets with very few tasks underrunning. This is so because the conscious effort is normally toward just achieving the goal and plans are not made to perform better than the goal. To motivate managers, more stringent budgets are allocated than were originally estimated. If the budgets are achieved, then the funds put aside in establishing these budgets may be used to cover the problem areas in other tasks.

Management reserves should not be used to cover cases of poor performance. Only if the scope of work changes should the budgets be increased. To do otherwise would negate the purposes of the performance measurement in that it must show performance against the original goals.

The external scope change arises when the customer or top management changes the description of the product or products produced by the project. In these cases, additional funds must be obtained from the customer or management and then allocated to affected tasks. For good cost control, timely incorporation of these changes is a must. New tasks and/or work packages with their associated budgets may need to be created, and/or existing budgets for tasks/work packages may need to be changed. Otherwise, overruns or schedule problems can be blamed on the changes for which work is progressing, but which have not been incorporated into the WBS or reporting system.

COST/SCHEDULE PERFORMANCE MEASUREMENT

Extremely important in the project performance measurement system is an objective determination of the value of the work performed—in other words, the budgeted objectives for the work performed. Exhibit 9 illustrates one method of calculating this value. (This exhibit is for the same hypothetical project which was budgeted in Exhibit 8.) The darkened triangles indicate completion of the milestone.

For completed work packages (A and B), the value of work performed is simply the original budget for the work package. For in-process work packages, there are several methods of calculating the value of work performed:

Percent Complete Estimates. This is a very unreliable method because, of necessity, it must be subjective. There is often little to guide the manager, other than the passage of time (i.e., time to date versus total estimated time for the task), in his or her determination of percent complete; and if passage of time is used, a behind schedule situation can be masked.[2] For short-term work packages (two to three months), this may be an acceptable method because the error cannot become too large.

50/50 Technique. With this method, half the value (work package budget) is credited as complete when the work package is started, and the other half when it is completed. This is the easiest method to handle administratively, but it can introduce significant

---

[2] Essentially equivalent to passage of time is cumulative expenditures divided by the work package budget. But this can be similarly misleading—because 70 percent of the budget is spent does not necessarily mean the task is 70 percent complete.

EXHIBIT 9
Accomplishment/Cost (schedule status)

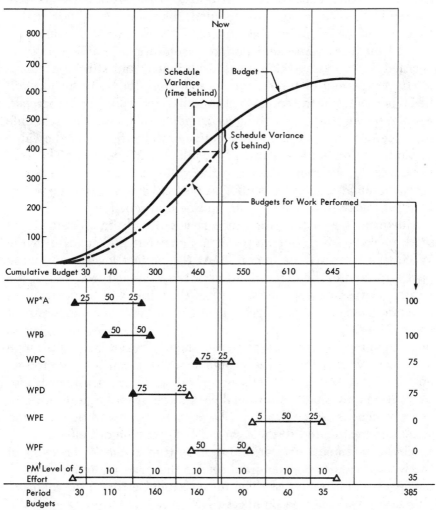

* Work project.
† Project management.

errors, especially on long work packages. These errors are somewhat overcome, however, if there are a large number of work packages in process since, in effect, this method counts them as *collectively* being half finished. Ideally, the use of this technique should be restricted to work packages that start in one accounting period and end in another.

The error that can be introduced by this method can be seen by looking at Work Package A in Exhibit 9. If the work package were started in the first period as scheduled, the value given to it at that time would be 50 percent complete. If work was still being performed on it in the second period, no additional value would be accrued, but costs and time-phased budget would still be accumulated. At the end of the second period then, the value would still be 50 percent, but the actual costs and budget would be 75 percent, assuming everything was going as originally planned. The schedule variance, which is the difference between the budget and the value or budgets for work performed, would be 25 percent. The cost variance, the difference between the value earned and the actual costs, would also be 25 percent. This particular work package would be erroneously shown as overrun and behind schedule.

However, because performance is not usually measured at the work package level, but rather at a somewhat higher level in the WBS, this error may be tolerable. At the project level, many work packages go into the determination of the value earned. And, if the work packages are kept short, most of the value will be determined by completed work packages in which there is no measurement error. This is especially true after the project has been in progress more than three months. In this case, the total value earned through in-process work packages is proportionately small and, therefore, any error introduced in estimating in-process work packages is also proportionately small. Additionally, if there are a large number or work packages, some work packages will be overestimated and some underestimated so there would be a washingout effect.

These statements may or may not be true at the lower levels of the work breakdown structure, because there are many fewer work packages within each task. The measurement error at the manageable task level could be significant.

Interim Milestone. This technique requires that milestones be defined for each reporting period covered by the work package. The total value would be the budget through the reporting period in which the last milestone was completed. If there was a milestone indicated in the second period and if that milestone were completed as in the previous example, the value earned would be 75 percent. This method of determination was used for Work Packages C and D in Exhibit 9. While this method is probably more precise, some error can still be introduced. For example, if Work Package C were

EXHIBIT 10
Process Flowchart

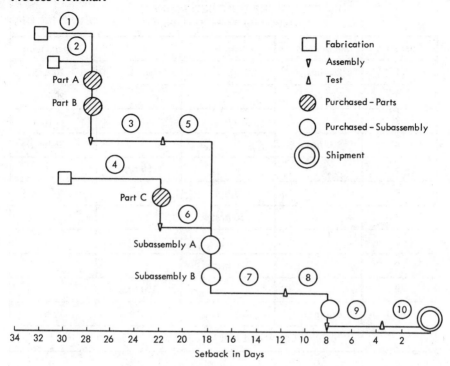

Setback in Days

actually started the last day of the reporting period, its earned value would be overstated.

Equivalent Unit. If the project were concerned with production efforts, the equivalent unit method would be appropriate. In this case, the work package would be completed units. If there is not a lot of in-process work involved, the number of completed units could be the earned-value criterion. However, in most cases the completed units do not give a true picture of the actual effort because of the buildup of work in process.

The process flowchart of Exhibit 10 indicates that 32 days of manufacturing effort are required before a unit is completed. If the earned-value determination were based on completed units, in a continuous manufacturing operation, up to 32 days of work which was incurred would have no associated value. To get around this problem, a value determination is made for each of the ten operations (circled numbers) involved in the production of the unit.

EXHIBIT 11

EQUIVALENT UNIT DETERMINATION (standard hours/operation)				
Operation	Fabrication	Assembly	Test	Inspection
1	200 hrs.			20 hrs.
2	175 hrs.			20 hrs.
3		100 hrs.		
4	300 hrs.			30 hrs.
5			50 hrs.	
6		75 hrs.		
7		150 hrs.		
8			75 hrs.	
9		120 hrs.		
10			100 hrs.	
Total	675 hrs.	445 hrs.	225 hrs.	70 hrs.
Equivalent unit = 1,415 hours				

This is done by an objective weighting of the operations and then determining the total number of operations completed.

Exhibit 11 shows a method of determination of equivalent units by using standard hours which give a measure of the relative weight of each operation. Estimated hours would serve the same purpose. From the chart, it may be seen that an equivalent unit is defined as 1,415 standard hours. The completion of Operation 1 would be equivalent to the completion of 0.155 units ($220 \div 1,415$) or the completion of Operation 1 approximately $6\frac{1}{2}$ times would be the equivalent of 1 unit.

At the end of each reporting period, the equivalent units are calculated as shown in Exhibit 12. A more precise measurement, if desired, can be accomplished by accruing value at 50 percent when the operation is started and 50 percent when it is completed.

The standard hours are used only as a basis for weighting each operation and, normally, the earned standard hours cannot be used as a direct comparison with the actual hours. The estimated hours are usually determined by adding a productivity factor to the standard hours which will cause the actual hours to be greater. However, it is possible to determine the actual hours budgeted for the number of equivalent units completed, and this can be compared to the actual hours. To make the comparison with the project baseline, the equivalent units are converted into earned dollars (or hours) based upon the value per equivalent unit. A learning curve can be used if it significantly affects the results by giving an appropriately larger value to the earlier units.

Level of Effort.　As previously mentioned, level of effort cannot be associated with a specific output or milestones. An example is

EXHIBIT 12
Equivalent Unit Accomplishment

Operation	Standard Hours	Units Complete	Hours Earned
1...............	220	10	2,200
2...............	195	9	1,755
3...............	100	6	600
4...............	330	5	1,650
5...............	50	3	150
6...............	75	3	225
7...............	150	1	150
8...............	75	0	0
9...............	120	0	0
10...............	100	0	0
			6,730

$$\text{Equivalent units complete} = \frac{6,730}{1,415} = 9.5$$

shown in Exhibit 9. Value is accrued according to the budgets for each period. In Exhibit 9, the budget through the reporting period is 35, and this is the value earned.

Because all the methods of determining the in-process value of work performed are approximations, and because it is desirable to plan in short-term work packages, the most practicable method is the 50/50 formula. This causes the least disruption to project personnel and requires a minimal administrative effort. With short-term work packages, the in-process error is, in most cases, tolerable. The in-process work cannot be completely ignored, however, and the methods described are used to make a reasonable determination of its value.

Schedule Variance

It has been shown that the time-phased budget reflects the cumulative budgets of the work packages through time, and that the dollar budgets were used to weight each work package. In measuring schedule performance, the same basis—original budgets—must be used in determining the amount of work accomplished. It would be inappropriate to use actual costs because the variance obtained when comparing these to the budget would be comprised of a schedule and cost variance, and it would be impossible to separate the two. What is required is a pure schedule variance.

From Exhibit 9 it may be seen that work had been *scheduled* through time "Now" whose total budgeted cost was $460. The work that was *actually* completed had a budget of $385. The project is therefore $75 behind schedule: $75 less in budgeted work was completed than was scheduled. The variance in terms of time may be approximated by determining the point in time at which the value of the work actually accomplished was scheduled to be accomplished. This is done by projecting horizontally the value of the work accomplished until it intersects the time-phased budget. The difference in time between this point and the current period is the time variance. In the example illustrated in Exhibit 9, the variance is two to three weeks behind schedule if it is assumed that each period is one month in length. This means that $385 of budgeted work *should* have been completed two to three weeks ago.

It is also possible to determine what specific work packages are causing the variance; for example, $25 can be attributed to Work Package D and $50 to Work Package F.

Caution must be exercised in using the accomplishment/cost charts to estimate schedule status. The original budget indicates the cumulative value of all the work scheduled up to a point in time. It takes no account of the critical path. Any slippage shown on the charts does not necessarily indicate total project slippage with regard to the anticipated completion date, because some or all of the work slipped may not be on the critical path. All that can be said of any indicated slippage is that the work scheduled was not completed on time; it does not give any indication of whether the work may be rescheduled without affecting the end date. Because ACP does not eliminate the need for a separate scheduling system, PERT, CPM, or another scheduling system is necessary for a complete schedule analysis.

Cost-to-Date Variance

The basis for measuring the cost-to-date variance is the total of the budgets for the work actually performed. This is illustrated in Exhibit 13 (which uses the same example as previously). In the illustration, work that was actually performed had a total budget of $385 while the actual costs were approximately $300. Since $385 was budgeted for work which actually cost $300, the project (to

EXHIBIT 13
Accomplishment/Cost (cost status)

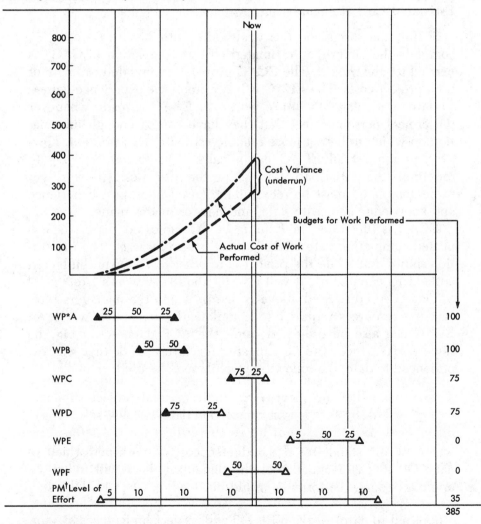

* Work project.
† Project management.

date) is underrun by $85. Normally, costs are not collected against individual work packages, which in a large and complex project may be at the sixth or even lower levels on the work breakdown structure. The lowest cost-account level is usually the manageable task, and this is therefore the lowest level for which cost variances can be determined. The manageable task manager, since he or she is close to the work, will know without a formal reporting system which work packages are causing the problem.

Estimated Cost at Completion

So far, the discussion has dealt only with historical costs. To complete the picture, an estimated cost at completion (ECAC) is needed for the project. The ECAC provides an updated estimate of total project costs. The ECAC is based upon the experience gained to date as it relates to future work. An ECAC is made whenever the project personnel feel that they have gained enough information on which to base a more reliable estimate. It is prudent, however, to request an ECAC periodically. This forces everyone to reexamine the initial basis for making the estimates. The work yet to be completed must be reexamined, based upon past experience and knowledge gained to date, and new estimates made.

ECAC is illustrated in Exhibit 14. As indicated there, the expected completion date of the project is also forecast. The illustration shows that while the project is forecast to underrun budgeted costs at its completion, it will also be about five weeks late.

The ECAC discussed above is one in which the managers forecast the resources required to complete the remaining work. An ECAC can also be projected using the ACP data. Assuming the same performance is to be expected for future work that was experienced to date, the following formula may be used:

$$\text{ECAC} = \frac{\text{Actual to date}}{\text{BCWP}} \times \text{Total project budget}$$

where BCWP stands for the budgeted cost of work performed to date. Or, if it is assumed that the remaining work will follow its original budget, the formula would be:

$$[(\text{Actual to date}) - \text{BCWP}] + \text{Total project budget} = \text{ECAC}$$

EXHIBIT 14
Accomplishment/Cost (cost-at-completion status)

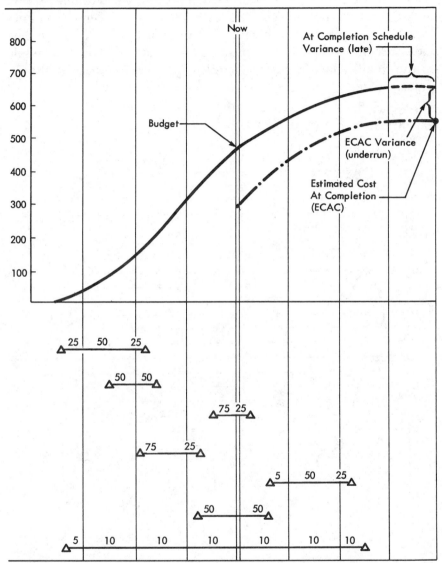

Trends

It is sometimes desirable to inspect the trend of the performance data in order to detect deteriorating conditions or to see if a corrective action plan is causing the desired improvement. An example of such a chart is given in Exhibit 15. Each point on the chart shows the status at the end of each reporting period (one month, on the illustration). The cost and estimated cost at completion lines indicate the percentage overrun or underrun; the schedule line indicates the percentage of the dollars ahead or behind schedule to the total dollars of work scheduled for completion as of the reporting date.

EXHIBIT 15
Trends

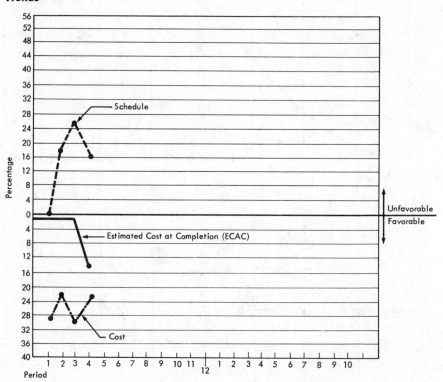

Certain trend conditions indicate conditions which require explanation. For example, if the cost trend is deteriorating while the ECAC is remaining steady, it implies that better than budgeted performance is anticipated. The project manager should determine if this forecast is based upon some specific actions or is just a pious hope.

Analysis and Corrective Action

It is not sufficient just to provide data on the cost/schedule performance. Data showing poor performance should be treated as a symptom of an underlying problem or problems.

At the beginning of a project, variance thresholds are established which, if exceeded, require a variance report. For instance, if 10 percent were established as the threshold for the cost to date on a manageable task, a variance analysis report is required for each manageable task whose variance exceeds 10 percent (either underrun or overrun). Variance thresholds may be established at different rates for overruns and underruns (5 percent for an overrun condition and 10 percent for an underrun); or they may be established at different rates for the various levels of the work breakdown structure (5 percent at project level and 15 percent at manageable task level). Also, a greater variance may be tolerated at the beginning of a project when more options are available than at the middle or closing phases of a project.

In the variance analysis report, the reasons for the variance must be identified. Variances fall into two major classifications: rate and usage. Using higher paid personnel than originally anticipated will cause a rate variance; using more labor hours than anticipated will cause a usage variance. (See Chapter 32 for a more detailed discussion of variance analysis.) It is not satisfactory, however, simply to identify variances as rate or usage variances. If more labor hours are being used than budgeted, the specific reasons must be ascertained.

While determining the reasons for variance is a necessary feature of good cost/schedule control, in itself it is not sufficient. A plan to correct any unsatisfactory performance is also required. Again, this plan needs to be specific in terms of "why?" "what?" "when?" and so on.

Isolating areas of poor performance is relatively easy in this system which is based upon a work breakdown structure. Poor performance at the project level can be traced down through the structure, and the elements showing poor performance can be isolated. The examples in the illustration showing how variances are determined would be appropriate for any level of the work breakdown structure. Of course, the actual value of work accomplished is determined only through work packages and work packages occur only within manageable tasks. Data for elements of the work break-down structure higher than the manageable task are the summary of the data for the elements which are contained within them.

EVALUATION OF THE SYSTEM

Experience gained in using this system at the Aerospace Division of Control Data Corporation has shown it to be a good indicator of performance relatively early in the life of a project. The data generated has been shown to represent correctly the status of the project.

To realize the cost control benefits of some of the disciplines required by the system, a good working knowledge of the system is required. Training was given to project personnel prior to the implementation of the system, but it was discovered that while it was necessary, it was not sufficient in achieving the understanding necessary to effectively utilize the system. Only through actual experience by project personnel was a good working knowledge of the system attained. In implementing this system, close surveillance was initially required to assure all aspects were properly implemented.

As for any system, the backing of top management is a prerequisite for success. The system had such backing, and the data generated were used for top-management reporting. This reporting required project personnel to understand the concepts of the system.

There was some resistance to the detailed planning required at the beginning of the project. The argument really reduces to whether or not planning produces desirable results and is worth the expenditure of the required resources. In other words, is cost control worth its cost? Experience has shown that the detailed planning required by this system reduces or eliminates the cost associated with the various exercises required to determine the status of a project which is without such a detailed plan. Once the plan is established, status is obtained routinely with very little impact upon project personnel. One of the primary advantages of this system is the ease with which a very accurate picture of the project status is obtained.

Although the system requires procedures which promote good cost/schedule control, it cannot truly be defined as a cost/schedule control system. It is a performance monitoring system which provides a measure of how well the cost/schedule control is working and, as such, is only a tool for cost/schedule control.

Before the management parameters can be controlled, there must be sensing and measuring techniques used to monitor the project performance. These monitoring techniques are sometimes erroneously called "control systems," but they do nothing but measure and report performance during the project life cycle. They do nothing in themselves that will impact the project; they may report poor performance, but do nothing to automatically correct this poor performance. The project manager must personally exercise the control. The control to be exercised cannot be specified or predetermined as can the features of the reporting system.

The problems related to control are usually unique and require the resourcefulness, ingenuity, innovativeness, and organizing ability of the project manager for a solution. If this were not true and control problems could be reduced to set formulas, a computer could easily replace the project manager. The monitoring techniques, if used properly, can reduce some uncertainty and provide the basis for better judgment. It must be kept constantly in mind, however, that they are only tools and their value is realized only when they are properly used.

Finally, if cost/schedule control is to be achieved, the budgets and schedules established in the original plan must be viewed as objectives and a firm commitment made to their achievement. The individual's performance is then measured on how well these objectives are achieved.

Most performance measurement systems do not achieve their original expectations because cost overruns and late deliveries continue to occur after their implementation. Of course, the original expectations are that the system itself would, as if by magic, correct management deficiencies. To achieve cost/schedule control, the objectives specified in the plan must be met. It is management's functions to assure the objectives are met. The system described assists managers by providing them with well-defined, achievable objectives and tells them how well the objectives are being accomplished.

ADDITIONAL SOURCES

Also see Additional Sources for Chapter 7.

Anthony, Robert N., and Dearden, John. *Management Control Systems: Text and Cases,* chap. 16. 3rd ed. Homewood, Ill.: Richard D. Irwin, Inc., 1976.

Archibald, Russell D., and Villoria, R. L. *Network-Based Management Systems*, New York: John Wiley & Sons, Inc., 1967.

Bierman, Harold; Bonini, Charles P.; and Hausman, Warren H. *Quantitative Analysis for Business Decisions*, chap. 22. 5th ed. Homewood, Ill.: Richard D. Irwin, Inc., 1977.

Block, Ellery B. "Accomplishment/Cost: Better Project Control." *Harvard Business Review*, May–June 1971, p. 110.

Clough, Richard H. *Construction Project Management*. New York: John Wiley & Sons, Inc., 1972.

Crowston, Wallace B. "Models for Project Management." *Sloan Management Review*, Spring 1971, p. 25.

Dusenbury, Warren. "CPM for New Product Introductions." *Harvard Business Review*, July–August 1967, p. 124.

Gemmill, Gary, and Wilemon, David L. "The Power Spectrum in Project Management." *Sloan Management Review*, Fall 1970, p. 15.

Hathaway, Bruce R. "Controlling New Facilities Costs." *Management Accounting*, April 1975, p. 47.

Hoare, Henry R. *Project Management Using Network Analysis*. New York: McGraw-Hill, Inc., 1973.

Howard, David C. "Cost/Schedule Control Systems." *Management Accounting*, October 1976, p. 21.

Jonason, Per. "Project Management, Swedish Style." *Harvard Business Review*, November–December 1971, p. 104.

Levin, Richard I., and Kirkpatrick, C. A. *Planning and Control with PERT-CPM*. New York: McGraw-Hill, Inc., 1966.

Middleton, C. J. "How to Set Up a Project Organization." *Harvard Business Review*, March–April 1967, p. 73.

Morley, Eileen, and Silver, Andrew. "A Film Director's Approach to Managing Creativity." *Harvard Business Review*, March–April 1977, p. 59.

Saitow, Arnold R. "CSPC: Reporting Project Progress to the Top." *Harvard Business Review*, January–February 1969, p. 88.

Schoderbek, Peter P., and Digman, Lester A. "Third Generation, PERT/LOB." *Harvard Business Review*, September–October 1967, p. 100.

Shillinglaw, Gordon. *Managerial Cost Accounting*, chap. 23. 4th ed. Homewood, Ill.: Richard D. Irwin, Inc., 1977.

43

Measuring and Controlling
the Cost of Advertising

Jerome M. Minkin*

Typically, books on corporate budgeting and control have little to say about the control of advertising[1] expenses, and books on advertising usually have little or nothing to say about budgeting and control. The controller is interested in operating a system that provides for orderly financial planning, measurement of results, comparison of plans and results to identify variances, explanations giving the causes of the variances, and evaluations of the anticipated impact of the variances over the fiscal period. The advertising manager is interested in identifying reachable customer audiences, developing effective message strategies, selecting the right combination of media to transmit the messages, and implementing programs which will effectively communicate the messages to the proper groups of customers or prospective customers.

Within these two frameworks, the controller may be treating total "advertising" as one category of expense with one variance from plan or, at best, one for each division or major product line, while the advertising manager knows that in reality he or she is dealing with many segments of many programs that are generating a myriad of variances for many reasons. The controller understandably wants advertising expenses to behave in an orderly fash-

---

* Mr. Minkin is Director of Operations Planning and Control, Schering Division, Schering-Plough Corporation, Kenilworth, New Jersey.

[1] Throughout this chapter, the term "advertising" is used to signify "advertising and sales promotion."

ion, but the advertising manager knows that expenses booked in any given period can be paying for parts of programs completed and used in the past, as well as for current activities, and also for some items for use in the future.

Not only is it true that the advertising expense booked in any one month can apply to time periods different from that month but it is also true that the revenue resulting from advertising can cover still another entirely different series of time periods. In most companies, the sales revenue booked in any month cannot be said to have been generated by the advertising expense booked in the same month. For this reason, the profit variance from plan for that month, which the controller has to explain, may be a misleading or even a meaningless figure. (The significance of this problem is a function of the size of the advertising budget as a percent of sales volume.) Likewise, the explanation of the monthly advertising expense variance may not be too meaningful because of the conditions described above.

By attempting to force the treatment of advertising expense into the same mold as the more routine types of expense, controllers may be trying to explain the wrong variances, or nagging the advertising people to explain them, while advertising managers are wishing someone would help measure whether they are reaching their markets and whether the right message is getting across. With such divergent viewpoints, it is little wonder that controllers and advertising people do not properly deal with each other in the books they write about themselves.

Nevertheless, there must be proper measurement and control of advertising expense. To accomplish this requires, first of all, an understanding of how advertising expense behaves, and secondly the development of an appropriate system to control it in its own terms as well as integrating it into total company control. It is the purpose of this chapter to explore these two aims and offer an example of a workable system.

WHY ADVERTISING EXPENSE *IS* DIFFERENT

Some of the major characteristics that distinguish advertising expense, with regard to measurement and control, are: its use of lead times and advance commitments, its special role in strategic planning, its high degree of variability, and its amenability to control despite its complexity. Each of these characteristics is worthy of comment.

Lead Times

Because of the usual time needed for planning, preparation, review, and approval, work on advertising pieces for use in January, for example, may need to be started around the previous June or July (with marketing planning well under way long before that time). In order to have the necessary materials in hand on time, suppliers have to be lined up, purchase or production orders issued, and commitments made well in advance.

Once advertising funds are committed, they are as good as gone from the advertising budget and should be so removed for purposes of both planning and control. It is well to remember that "committed is as good as spent." The significance of this condition is that the advertising department needs a budgetary control system based on what funds are *committed* and what the balance remaining to work with is, rather than on what funds have been *expensed* on the books.

The case for such a system is strengthened when it is realized that because of lead-time requirements, it is sometimes necessary to make substantial commitments before the budget for the coming year has been approved. The well-run advertising department may by midyear have planned for—or, in effect, "spent"—90 percent or more of its annual budget because there is little left for it to do regarding planning for the current year since it has already started on the following year's work. Yet the usual expense variance report it receives half way through the year will show that perhaps only 40 to 45 percent of its budget has been expensed. Since such reports are of little or no use in managing advertising, it is not uncommon for advertising departments to set up their own budgetary control systems and employ accountants to run them. Controllership may be missing an opportunity to be of service in such cases.

Strategic Aspects

Advertising is not only an expense; it is a resource for generating business. The typical statement of profit and loss implies that advertising is a charge against sales. More properly stated, advertising and selling effort *yield* gross sales (recognizing, but leaving aside here, that such other factors as research and development, product improvement, increased distribution and better understanding of product also yield gross sales).

Instead of starting the P&L with "sales, less production cost of sales" to find the gross production margin, it might be more helpful to net the expenses of advertising and selling against sales to determine "promotion contribution margin." By estimating the effect on sales volume of varying amounts of advertising or of changing media mixes within product, it is possible, within the limitations of estimating ability, to plan the contribution margin (sometimes loosely referred to as "profit planning"). Thus it can be seen that advertising is an integral element of margin planning and can be used as such to assess alternate strategies.

Variability and Flexibility

But how much in advance should the profit plan be fixed? Should the total amount of the advertising budget be assigned down to the product level for the upcoming budget year? The answers to these questions depend on the dynamics of the enterprise and on the flexibility of the accounting system. In a rapidly growing or changing business, a certain amount of the advertising budget should be held aside to permit quick responses to market challenges without upsetting ongoing advertising programs. Funds intended for launching new products should likewise be held in reserve. By the same token, it may be desirable to provide for the switching of advertising funds among products or expense categories as needed as the year unfolds.

To utilize such flexibility to the greatest advantage requires the operation of a quick-responding control and reporting system. Here is a case of flexibility and control going hand in hand. Highly variable expenses are usually anathema to the controller. But the variability of advertising expense, when properly controlled, can be turned into the advantage of permitting desired flexibility.

Controllability

Advertising expense comprises a myriad of minutiae. Situations involving large numbers of variables are usually difficult to control.

Such need not be the case with advertising expense, however, because with the proper system, every element of advertising can be related back to a given product, campaign, or other planned activity. In fact, far more meaningful detail is possible with advertising expense than with many other types of expense because the total can be "atomized" and very carefully controlled when all the pieces are identified and measured.

BEFORE-THE-FACT CONTROL OF ADVERTISING EXPENDITURES

Because of its lead-time requirements, large amount of detail, variability, and complexity, advertising expense cannot properly be controlled under the traditional system of reporting expenses after they have occurred. What is needed for the adequate control of advertising expense is a before-the-fact accounting system.

Budgeting and Reporting

Basic to any control system is a budget or plan, prepared in advance, containing as much detail as is feasible at the time. An annual budget laid out by quarter or deal period, by product or campaign, and by advertising medium is a minimum requirement. Exhibit 1 shows a typical grid sheet for quarterly advertising budgeting for a given product. It is assumed that the supporting documents to the grid sheets (perhaps the marketing plans) identify the objectives for the product and the resources allotted for achieving those objectives.

The Budget Grid Sheet is necessary but not adequate for control. Also needed is an ongoing system of expense appropriations which provides a more timely and more specific description of what is being done to implement the advertising program. Exhibit 2, Expense Appropriation Request, shows a financial summary format suitable for use as a quarterly expense appropriation. The supporting documents would spell out additional detail. Direct mail expense, for example, would be backed up by a direct mail schedule specifying audiences to be reached, number of pieces, mailing dates and costs. The total direct mail expense would relate back to the grid sheet.

As is true with any sizable control system, all expenses must be

EXHIBIT 1

BUDGET GRID SHEET					
Product and Code_____ Program and Code _____					
197X Working Budget_____ ($000)					
	1st	2d	3d	4th	TOTAL
INCENTIVES					
DIRECT MAIL					
JOURNALS					
CONVENTIONS					
COOP ADVERTISING					
DISPLAYS					
Etc.					
TOTAL					

Date Prepared: _____
Prepared by   : _____   Revision No.:_____
Approved by : _____

EXHIBIT 2

EXPENSE APPROPRIATION REQUEST	FOR EXPENSE ITEMS OR PROJECTS OF $500 OR MORE.	NO.
DEPARTMENT	EXPENSE CENTER NAME	EXP. CTR. NO.
	PRODUCT	QUARTER	BUDGET YEAR

DETAILS OF EXPENSE REQUEST

REQUEST FOR APPROVAL	EXPENSE ACCOUNT		TOTAL EXPENDITURE	CURRENT YEAR BUDGET			TOTAL NEXT YEAR
	NUMBER	DESCRIPTION		ORIGINAL	REVISIONS	TOTAL	
OPERATING EXPENSE							
TOTAL OPERATING EXPENSE							
RELATED EXPENSES:							
PERSONNEL EXP. (CURRENT YR.)							
PERSONNEL EXP. (ANNUALIZED)							
CAPITAL EXPENSES							
GRAND TOTAL							

JUSTIFICATION (USE ATTACHMENTS IF NECESSARY)

FOR BUDGET MANAGER'S USE ONLY					APPROVALS AND ROUTING ☑ INDICATES ROUTING AND APPROVAL REQUIRED	
QTR.	BUDGET	PRIOR APPROVALS	THIS REQUEST	BUDGET BALANCE	ORIGINATED BY ☑	DATE
1					DEPARTMENT HEAD ☑	DATE
2					_____ VICE PRESIDENT ☑	DATE
3					BUDGET MANAGER ☑	DATE
4					CONTROLLER ☑	DATE
TOTAL					VICE PRESIDENT – GENERAL MANAGER ☐	DATE

AFTER APPROVALS RETURN TO BUDGET MANAGER FOR DISTRIBUTION

COPY DISTRIBUTION:

☑ BUDGET MANAGER   ☐ _____   ☐ _____   ☐ _____   ☐ _____

identified by product or program. It is vital to the success of the system that all purchase orders, work orders, production orders, assignments, vouchers, invoices, and so on, be accurately coded by product or program (e.g., audience segment) as well as by advertising medium (expense account number).

In addition to the budget (grid sheet) and the backup detail to the quarterly expense appropriation, the third element required for controlling advertising is a method of updating cost estimates constantly throughout the year. Periodic expense variance reports are necessary for control purposes but not sufficient because they do not take into account commitments and changes in estimates.

Once the budget is prepared, the budget itself represents the best estimate of the cost of advertising for the year. As expense appropriations (based on more detailed, up-to-the-minute plans) are made, however, the total of the appropriations plus the unappropriated part of the budget becomes the best annual estimate. After all of the appropriation requests for the first quarter of the year have been written, for example, the best estimate of the annual expense is the sum of the first quarter's appropriation requests plus the budgets for the remaining three quarters. This total may differ from the initial budget, and may require adjustments in the appropriation requests, or in the profit plan, depending on the magnitude of the difference and the operating style of the company. Note that since first-quarter appropriation requests can be completed in the third or fourth quarter of the preceding year, there may be no actual expense incurred up to this time. In fact, the budget year has not yet begun, but under this system of updating estimates, there is already a new estimate better than the original budget.

As appropriations are assigned for production (either internally or through suppliers or agencies), the cost estimates on the assignments update those on the appropriations. Exhibit 3 illustrates the type of detail that may be found on an agency estimate sheet. Assuming that we are in the middle of the first month of the fiscal year and that all assignments for the first quarter and expense appropriations for the second quarter have been written, the sum of these two plus the budgets for the third and fourth quarters are now the best estimate of annual advertising cost. This estimate is better than the budget alone because it is based partly on more specific and more recent information. In this example, no expense

EXHIBIT 3

AGENCY ESTIMATE SHEET

Date _____

Job number _____ Product _____

Format or description _____

Number of colors _____ Size _____

Cost estimates

	Initial estimate	Rev. #1	Rev. #2	Rev. #3
Copy				
Layout–design				
Artwork				
Photography				
Model fees				
Props				
Dye transfers				
Retouching				
Typography				
Mechanicals				
Photostats				
Engravings				
Electros				
Printing				
Reprints				
Sub–totals				
Agency commission				
Sales tax				
TOTAL				
Approved by				

Work schedule

Stage	Original	Revised
C/L		
Approval		
Stats		
Approval		
Mech. released		
Printed mat.		

Agency budget _____

Total budget _____

Estimated creative cost to date

	Initial	Rev. #1	Rev. #2	Rev. #3
Copy				
Layout				

Comments _____
_____
_____
_____
_____
_____
_____
_____
_____
_____
_____
_____
_____
_____

EXHIBIT 4

			ADVERTISING PROJECT ASSIGNMENT	
			PROJECT NO.	-0

AVOID MAKING ERASURES ON THIS FORM, WHEN DATES OR ESTIMATES CHANGE, DRAW A LINE THROUGH OLD FIGURE AND WRITE NEW FIGURE NEARBY

QUANTITY	PRODUCT	DOSAGE FORMS	FORMAT	SUGGESTED SIZE
COLORS	STOCK		DATE ISSUED	DATE WANTED
EXP. CTR./ACCT./PROD. CODE		AGENCY	SUGGESTED OR REQUESTED BY	
NO. OF PAGES	NO. PER PSR	MAILING LIST CODE(S)	EXPENDITURE APPROVAL NO.	QUARTER

COPY SLANT, SPECIAL INSTRUCTIONS, ETC.:

	WANTED	REVISED	REC'D.	FORWARD	COMMENTS	SUMMARY OF COST FINDINGS	COMMITTED	FINAL CHARGE INCL. COMM.
PRELIM. COPY						AGENCY		
LAYOUT						ART-TYPE COPY		
APPROVED COPY/LAYOUT						PRINTING		
STAT						PRINTING		
MECH. RELEASE						POSTAGE		
PRINTED MATERIAL						SAMPLES		
MAILING DATE						OTHER		

PURCHASE ORDER NUMBER:

1.	REQUEST PROD. MG.	OTHER
	TRAFFIC	
2.		OTHER
	ADVERT.	AGCY. PRINT. COMM.
3.	AGENCY	
	SPACE	TOTAL
4.	ART	
		DATE COMPLETED — BUDGET
5.		APPROVED BY — DATE
	ENV.	

reports have yet been issued because the first month has not closed, but measurement and control of advertising expenses have already begun because the estimates have been constantly updated.

Agreed-upon assignments become commitments. Exhibit 4, Advertising Project Assignment, shows the recording of commitments under "summary of cost findings." Finally, when some of the early commitments are completed and invoices or other charges start to come in, the best annual estimate of advertising cost becomes the total of the following:

Actual expenses paid, plus

Commitments not yet completed or billed, plus

Assignments not yet committed, plus

Expense appropriations not yet assigned, plus

Budget not yet appropriated.

One of the keys to the successful operation of this system is, of course, accurate *estimating*. The initial advertising expense budget is an aggregation of estimates—some very rough—not adequate for control purposes. At the next step, the more detailed expense appropriations are somewhat more refined estimates of what the advertising will cost. Appropriations are written into assignments in close consultation with advertising production personnel or suppliers. When costs contained in assignments are examined, it is sometimes found necessary to modify assignments to stay within appropriations—or to find offsets in other assignments where cost estimates have come through from the budget or appropriation stage. (Note the provision for cost revisions in Exhibit 3.)

Assignments thus contain better estimates than do appropriations. Assignments become commitments when the exact nature of the work and its cost estimate are agreed on and the activity given out for completion. Commitments contain the best estimates possible because they specify the particular jobs to be accomplished. Commitments, therefore, form the basis for the measurement and control of advertising expense.

An Illustration

The operation of the system can best be illustrated by seeing what happens when an invoice or charge for an item of advertising expense is received by the unit performing the advertising measurement/control function. These are the questions that are asked:

1. To what specific job on which assignment does the charge refer? (The coding system referred to earlier, using purchase or work order numbers, and so forth, will have had to be established in advance.)
2. Does this charge cover the whole job (i.e., is the job completed)?
   a. If so, how does the charge compare with the control estimate on the commitment?
      (1) If the charge is the same as the estimate, that item on the assignment is closed out.
      (2) If the charge is different (either higher or lower) from the estimate, how does this affect the total advertising budget? Does this job occur again later in the year for this product or even for other products? If so, appropriate adjustments in other appropriations, assignments, and commitments may have to be made. This step is one of the important features of this system which distinguishes it from the conventional accounting practice of merely reporting expenses after the fact.
   b. If the job is not complete, what will the remaining charge be? How will the total charge compare with the control estimate? Is the difference large enough to flash a warning signal regarding other work in process?

Overall Control

With a large number of estimates subject to continuous change, a means of assessing the impact of the total of all the estimates is required to assure overall control. What is needed is an orderly way of recording and summing all the estimates at a point in time. The Product Promotion Expense Status Report, Exhibit 5, shows one possible framework for filling that need.

The report starts with recording the expense appropriations (labeled "Exp. Approvals" on Exhibit 5) by quarter, by product, and by promotional medium. The blocks marked "Estimate" are filled in from the flow of assignments and commitments. Before

EXHIBIT 5

		PRODUCT PROMOTION EXPENSE STATUS REPORT																	PRODUCT		
		AS OF_____																			
		INCENTIVES	DIRECT MAIL	JOURNALS	CONVENTIONS	COOPERATIVE ADV.	DISPLAYS	Etc.													TOTAL
1ST QUARTER	EXP. APPROVALS																				
	ACTUAL																				
	ESTIMATE																				
	UNDER (OVER) COMMITTED																				
2D QUARTER	EXP. APPROVALS																				
	ACTUAL																				
	ESTIMATE																				
	UNDER (OVER) COMMITTED																				
3D QUARTER	EXP. APPROVALS																				
	ACTUAL																				
	ESTIMATE																				
	UNDER (OVER) COMMITTED																				
4TH QUARTER	EXP. APPROVALS																				
	ACTUAL																				
	ESTIMATE																				
	UNDER (OVER) COMMITTED																				
YEAR TO DATE	EXP. APPROVALS																				
	ACTUAL																				
	ESTIMATE																				
	UNDER (OVER) COMMITTED																				

there is any actual expense recorded, the differences between appropriations and estimates indicate conditions of under- or overcommitment. Large differences may require investigation and corrective action.

When actual charges start to appear on the report, the corresponding estimates grow smaller until they disappear altogether when the final payment is made. When both an actual and an estimate are shown together because additional charges are expected, the total of the two is compared with the appropriation to determine the degree of under/overcommitment. When the programs for the quarter have been finished and completely billed, the estimate block is blank, the total cost being shown as "actual." It is important to recognize that not all charges received during a given quarter are posted to that same quarter's "actual." For the system to provide the proper amount of control and operating guidance, each charge must be examined to determine which quarter's *approved expense appropriation* it refers to, and be posted appropriately.

How do differences in timing usually occur? Sometimes work is submitted in advance of when it is expected. The usual reason for this is to effect economies of scale. Two similar items needed for two consecutive quarters, for example, are produced simultaneously. It is far more common for expenses to come later rather than earlier. This is not only because of work falling behind schedule, but this can also occur simply because invoices are slow to arrive.

Whatever the reason, if some promotional expenses currently received are posted to quarters other than the current one because they pertain to programs planned and approved for those other quarters, then the total "actual" on the advertising report (Exhibit 5) for a given quarter will in all likelihood not agree with the amount expensed on the company's books for that quarter. Yet it is the difference or variance between the amount expensed on the books and the budget which must be accounted for for control purposes. By not forcing agreement by quarter between "advertising" and "controller," this system provides for something more valuable than nominal agreement: it provides for those elusive explanations of expense variances due to differences in timing.

In terms of the advertising report itself (Exhibit 5), it is to be expected that there may be many, albeit hopefully minor, differences between planned costs and actual costs by medium by quarter. If the differences move in both directions, some plus and some minus, and tend to offset each other in aggregate, then the over/undercommitted entries found in the year-to-date section along the bottom of the report and in the total column on the far right-hand side of the report will generally be smaller than in the individual quarters and media. Certainly the variances caused by differences in timing referred to above will offset each other if they are confined within one year.

At any point in time, the advertising report (Exhibit 5) shows what the planned variance is expected to be if all activities are carried out as planned at that time. The amount of planned variance which is acceptable without change is up to each company to determine for itself. The degree of offsetting or netting of expense variances, either within the scope of one product or among a number of products, should also be determined in the design of a control system.

Change Approval

Within the system described here, "change in plan" is not an acceptable explanation for the appearance of two large offsetting variances. Significant changes must be submitted for approval and reflected in the system when approved. Exhibit 6, Amendment to Expense Appropriation Request, is an example of a document that could be used to reflect a change in plan that would otherwise result in offsetting variances among media, quarters, or products. Since it only shifts funds already approved, it cannot be used to increase the budget or the level of approved expense appropriations. When amendments are processed, the affected blocks marked "Exp. Approval" on Exhibit 5 are changed to incorporate them. The corresponding over/undercommitted entries are thus offset.

Multiproduct Summaries

In multiproduct companies, the individual product sheets (Exhibit 5) need to be summarized to provide an assessment of the total picture. An example of such a summary form is presented in Exhibit 7, Product Promotion Expense Status Report Summary. Four of the columns are the same as the four total columns in the lower right-hand corner of Exhibit 5. That is, they show, for the year to date for each product, the total expenses appropriated, charges actually booked, estimated costs outstanding, and amounts over/undercommitted.

For ease of understanding, the summary also shows a total of the actual and estimate for each product, since it is the total which is subtracted from the expense appropriation to determine the degree of over/undercommitment. Of interest also is the change in the commitment variance since the prior report. For this reason, the summary reproduces the over/undercommitment column by product from the earlier report. For the proper functioning of the system, it is necessary that the summary be accompanied by writ-

EXHIBIT 6

AMENDMENT TO EXPENSE APPROPRIATION REQUEST		E.A.A. Number _____	
	FROM	**TO**	
Account	E.A. # _____ Qtr. _____ Prod. _____ $ _____	E.A. # _____ Qtr. _____ Prod. _____ $ _____	
Incentives			
Direct Mail			
Journals			
Conventions			
Coop Advertising			
Displays			
Etc.			
Etc.			
TOTAL			

Reason for Transfer: _____

Originated by: _____ Product Promotion Manager
Approved by: _____ Adv. and Sales Promotion Manager
Approved by: _____ Adv. Admin. Manager
Approved by: _____ Product Manager
Approved by: _____ Group Marketing Manager
Issued by: _____ Oper. and Plan. Dept.

NOTE: Switches totaling more than $5,000 must be countersigned by the
appropriate Group Marketing Manager.

EXHIBIT 7

| PRODUCT/PROGRAM | CURRENT REPORT | | | | | Previous Report |
	Exp. App.* thru ____Qtr.	Actual thru ____	Estimate thru ____Qtr.	Total Actual & Estimate	Under (over) COMMITTED	Under (over) COMMITTED
GROUP TOTAL						
GROUP TOTAL						
GRAND TOTAL						
*Includes EA#						
EAA#						

PRODUCT PROMOTION EXPENSE STATUS REPORT SUMMARY

($000)

ten commentary explaining the significance of the commitment variances and the changes since the last report.

System Administration

Although the data on the exhibits are shown as being on a quarterly basis, the reports themselves can and should be issued at least once a month. The reports described here are not dependent on any other reporting except for the information on actual expenses which, it is assumed, will be produced as part of the monthly closing. Ideally, all items of "actual" should be listed and coded so that they are readily identifiable by medium and expense appropriation which would automatically indicate product, program, and quarter.

In a fully integrated automated accounting system, the "actual" could be accumulated and printed out directly into the appropriate blocks on the Product Promotion Expense Status Report (Exhibit 5) for each product each month. Data for approved expense appropriations and amendments could be inputted routinely as requests are approved. Because it involves judgment, the "estimate" data would have to be worked up manually each time. Following this step however, the rest of the report and summary could be machine generated.

Even with full automation, though, this system would still require that all invoices and other charge documents be routed through the advertising department so that their effect on estimates might be determined. Aside from the mechanical considerations of careful and proper expense coding, the success of this system hinges on the expertise of the advertising cost estimators.

SUMMARY

The system described in this chapter offers many opportunities for control, but control can and does run much deeper than is indicated above. Exhibit 8, which portrays one possible sequential flow in the creation of advertising material, shows the potential for at least four additional budget review checkpoints: (1) when assignments are broken down in subassignments, (2) when copy and layout are approved, (3) when mechanicals and stats are submitted, and (4) when approved mechanicals are released.

EXHIBIT 8
Activity Flowchart (six months time lapse)

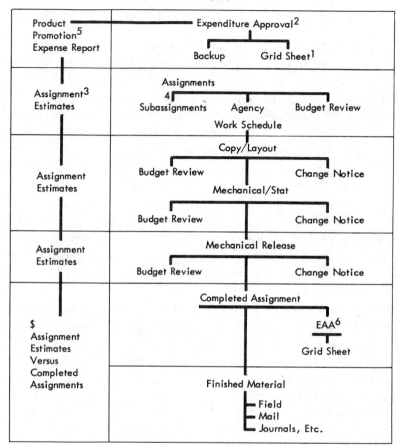

At each of these checkpoints, more is known about how much the advertising will cost. And each review provides an opportunity for making the changes needed to help keep advertising expenses in line. On Exhibit 8, assignment estimates are shown at four different stages to indicate that they can undergo controlled modifications by means of the issuance of official Change Notices at various Budget Review points. The numbers on Exhibit 8 refer to the first six exhibits used in this chapter which are as follows:

1. Budget Grid Sheet.
2. Expense Appropriation Request (expenditure approval).
3. Agency Estimate Sheet.

4. Advertising Project Assignment.
5. Product Promotion Expense Status Report.
6. Amendment to Expense Appropriation Request (EAA).

Fraught with so much inherent variability, advertising expense can be *expected* to show variances from budget, at least over short periods. One of the distinguishing benefits of the system described above is that, with commensurate effort, it provides a guide to the explanation of expense variances down to any level of detail required by the corporation. Assuming the advertising budget is broken out by category of expense (magazines or trade journal ads, selling aids, direct mail, and so on) within product and program and by month or quarter, it is possible to use the proposed system to explain any expense variance by comparing the budget "cell" first with the Expense Appropriation Request, to see if a difference occurred at this stage when the program was first being better defined, and then, if necessary, with the resulting assignments, commitments and completions to see what changes may have occurred.

Because it exercises before-the-fact control of expenditures, this system is different from those usually employed in the control function. This one is more akin to the more familiar process of using interim projections for planning purposes. But by combining the ideas of projection and control, it presses a planning device into the service of control.

This is made both possible and necessary by the peculiar qualities of advertising expense. Since "committed is as good as spent," and commitments are generally needed well in advance, a complete and accurate record of commitments provides an excellent basis for projecting advertising costs.

While the system presented here may not be appropriate for every company or division that has a problem in measuring and controlling the cost of advertising, it is illustrative of the kinds of considerations which should be taken into account in designing a solution to the problem.

ADDITIONAL SOURCES

Bogart, Leo. "Mass Advertising: The Message, Not the Measure." *Harvard Business Review*, September–October 1976, p. 107.

Friedman, Lawrence.　"A Variable Budgeting System for Consumer Advertising." *Sloan Management Review,* Winter 1971, p. 77.

Hurwood, David L.　"How Companies Set Advertising Budgets," *The Conference Board Record.* New York: National Industrial Conference Board, March 1968.

————.　"Budgeting for Advertising: Eight Company Cases," *The Conference Board Record.* New York: National Industrial Conference Board, April 1968.

Krugman, Herbert E.　"What Makes Advertising Effective?" *Harvard Business Review,* March–April 1975, p. 96.

Minkin, Jerome M.　"Developing the Marketing Budget," *Handbook of Modern Marketing,* New York: McGraw-Hill Book Co., Inc., 1970.

Newton, Derek A.　"Advertising Agency Services: Make or Buy?" *Harvard Business Review,* July–August 1965, p. 111.

Riso, Ovid.　*Advertising Cost Control Handbook.* New York: Van Nostrand Reinhold Co., 1973.

44

Effecting Administrative Cost Reductions

Donald N. McKay*

Costs in the administrative area are susceptible to the same types of budgetary control procedures and to the same analytical approach to improvements in efficiency as are commonly applied to the operating areas of business enterprises. These management techniques have not been consistently employed in the administrative areas, however, with the result that the initiative for reducing costs in these areas more often than not comes from general management. Under such circumstances the administrative department heads may find themselves required to operate within a set of arbitrary expense limitations which fail to take into account the realities of the work loads existing in the administrative area.

To avoid these types of situations, which compromise the management status of the administrative department heads, disrupt their planning, and damage morale in their organizations, a program has to be developed whereby management can be shown what types of costs are being incurred, how these are being controlled, and how they are related to providing the services and support expected from the administrative areas. Against this background of information, steps can be taken to reduce expenses through improving employee productivity, eliminating all identifiable excess or unnecessary costs, and through developing the most economical and efficient working methods. When further cost reductions

* Mr. McKay is Director of Budgets and Profit Planning for Phelps Dodge Corporation, New York.

beyond those to be generated through these improvements in efficiency are required, these can then be logically related to eliminating or curtailing the scope of specific types or levels of administrative service or support programs.

As a key executive in the administrative area and as that executive most concerned with cost, the controller ought to take the lead in bringing about this type of rational approach to the task of planning for and controlling administrative expenses.

FOUR-POINT PROGRAM FOR CONTROL

While recognizing the fact that what may be classified as administrative functions and how these may be assigned on a departmental basis may vary from company to company, the following four-point program for the systematic control of administrative expenses would appear to have universal application. This program calls for the controller to:

1. Make certain that the cost accounting system provides a suitable apparatus for the accurate identification, reporting, and measurement of control of administrative expenses.
2. Initiate actions necessary to improve productivity in the administrative areas.
3. Initiate actions to eliminate excess costs in the administrative area.
4. On a longer term basis, initiate the systems studies necessary to insure that the output of the administrative departments is essential, is tailored to the requirements of the users, and is produced in the most efficient manner possible.

The organization of a particular company might initially restrict the total application of this program to those areas for which the controller is directly responsible. Once implemented, however, the program cannot fail to have a significant beneficial impact on all areas of administrative responsibility.

1. Providing a Suitable Cost Accounting Apparatus

The accounting system must provide a coding structure by which costs can be identified by function and by responsibility within that function. For example, costs incurred by the accounting department in the course of performing accounting operations must be identified with and charged to the accounting department. If there is a further breakdown of responsibilities within the accounting department, on a subfunction or cost center basis, the system needs to recognize this further identification of costs. In general, for the purposes of effective control, cost centers should be recognized down to the lowest effective decision-making level.

For planning and control purposes, the system should also provide for the breakdown of costs within each cost center by types of costs or cost elements. The coding structure should be so established as to provide identifiable cost elements down to the level where the amount to be charged in any one cost center can be considered significant. Thus, while an accounting department having only salaried employees would be satisfied with only one cost element for labor, an administrative services group having responsibility for hourly paid maintenance workers or security personnel would require that the labor cost element be further broken down between salaried and hourly personnel.

In order for this coding structure to be understood and used correctly in all areas of cost responsibility, a chart of accounts which clearly defines the function and the parameters of each cost center, and explicitly describes the makeup and nature of each element of expense, has to be made available to each cost center head. The system must further provide for the periodic reporting to the responsible cost center heads of the costs charged to them on a cost center and cost element basis. For the system to be effective for planning and control purposes, however, these reported costs need to be measured against some predetermined standard of performance. The most effective device for this purpose is the administrative expense budget.

These budgets can usually be prepared with considerable accuracy at the department head level or even by budget specialists reporting directly to top management. The greatest benefit appears to be derived, however, when these budgets are prepared initially at the cost center level and are then reviewed and given final approval at higher levels. The obvious advantages to this latter approach are the following:

1. The cost center heads *must* plan. They are forced to make a critical examination of the types of work their section is ex-

pected to perform, make an assessment of the volume of work, consider the timing requirements, and, finally, estimate on a quantitative basis what will be required in terms of personnel, equipment, supplies, and other support to accomplish the work required.

2. Cost center heads tend to develop a sense of personal commitment for the successful attainment of their work objectives within the cost framework which they themselves have established. This presumes, however, that any modifications to their budget which may result from a higher level review are thoroughly explained and are logical and reasonable. If arbitrary changes are made at higher levels, the budget, in effect, becomes a budget imposed from above for which the cost center head no longer has any feeling of responsibility. Cost center budgets are most effective if they include only those costs directly controllable by the cost center's head.

3. The fact that the budget must be reviewed and accepted at a higher level tends to emphasize to the cost center head the fact that management is aware of, and has an interest in, the work performed and the costs incurred in his or her section.

4. The detailed planning and review process often produces an immediate and beneficial fallout in terms of work simplification and improvements in working methods.

The final reporting system requirement is that the system must be one which not only reports costs against a budget or other standard of performance but which also provides for the systematic review of any variances and requires explanations or indications of remedial action being taken when these appear to be called for. There are a variety of ways in which this review procedure can be organized. One approach is that of requiring comments on the performance of his or her section by each cost center head on a regular basis. Less cumbersome and probably much more likely to be effective is the management by exception principle, where the performance reports are reviewed at a higher level and questions raised only on variances which appear to be significant. The regular review and analysis of cost variances is an indispensible feature of any effective cost control system. This procedure serves the dual purpose of keeping management informed on a continuing basis of major development or trends in the cost area, and of providing a constant reminder to the cost center head of the need for the careful management of those costs for which he or she is responsible.

2. Increasing Productivity in the Administrative Areas

One of the benefits to be expected from the longer term systems studies would certainly be an improvement in employee productivity. There are actions which can be implemented currently, however, which can lead to a betterment of employee output, quantitatively, and qualitatively, which in turn can lead to reductions in overtime, in the need for temporary help, and perhaps even to reductions in the number of full-time employees. These actions involve increasing the amount of time spent by employees in productive work and improving the caliber of the supervision provided.

The potential for the recovery of a substantial amount of lost working time exists in virtually every office through the simple device of enforcing established rules governing office discipline. At the stated time for the start of work, employees should be in their work areas rather than in the elevator, at the front door, or driving into the parking lot. Similarly, they should still be in their working areas at quitting time. Lunch periods and any break periods need to be used with reasonable fairness. The intent of any effort to improve office discipline is not that of making a taut ship out of a happy one, but is merely that of insuring that hours paid for are, in fact, hours worked.

For such an effort to be successful, it must be a continuing one and one applied consistently throughout the administrative areas. The controller will thus require the support of other members of *top* management and the cooperation of other administrative department heads.

Critical to the success of any program for a better conformity with working rules, however, is the attitude of the first-line supervisor. It is this supervisor, more than anyone else, who by example and actions can make or break the program. A single "good guy" supervisor who tries to curry favor with employees by tolerating sloppy work habits can completely undermine the conscientious efforts colleagues may be making in what is not always an easy task.

Recapturing lost productivity time will serve no useful purpose, however, unless all productive time is being managed effectively. In this connection, an evaluation needs to be made of how well each supervisory function is being carried out. Supervisory positions should be looked at to see if they are so structured that persons in the positions can in fact supervise; can devote the major portion of their time to planning, directing, and reviewing the work of others, and to making major decisions on the work performed in their areas; and can concern themselves with matters related to the working conditions, equipment, and other support required by their people and with their attitudes, deportment, and morale. In some instances, the work load of the position may have so evolved that the so-called supervisor is expected to perform so many specific duties personally that he or she can function only as a lead clerk. The solution to this type of problem may involve a recognition of the fact that the cost center is not actually a true cost center and should be folded into another cost center under different supervision. Or what may be required is that additional or more highly qualified personnel will have to be added to the cost center to relieve the supervisor of the excess work load. In any case, the job content of the position in question will have to be redefined.

Under other circumstances, the failure of the supervisor to supervise properly may rest with the individual rather than with the job makeup. Additional training for the supervisor may be all that is required to correct this situation. If this is not sufficient, recognition will have to be given to the fact that the particular individual, regardless of how proficient he or she may be, is simply not ready or able to lead other people and will have to be reassigned and replaced.

In any type of business undertaking, the best efforts of well-qualified and highly motivated subordinates can be blunted by ineffective leadership. This is no less true in the administrative area than it is in manufacturing, marketing, or any other major segment of the business. Unfortunately, however, supervision in the administrative areas often tends to be taken for granted, supervisory positions are not always well defined, and specialized knowledge tends to be confused with the ability to lead and direct. Only by going through the process of determining what each supervisor should be expected to do, and by taking the actions required to insure that the right person is in each supervisory position, can the quality of supervision needed to meet the goal of high productivity be attained.

3. Eliminating the Expense of Wasteful Work Practices

The opportunities for salvaging profit dollars through eliminating unnecessary expenses in administrative work will vary from organization to organization and will be influenced by such factors as the size of the company and the efficiency of its management; but these opportunities are always to be found. How effective the controller can be in capitalizing on these opportunities for saving is subject to two constraints. The first is that of the "life style" which management has selected for the company. If the management philosophy is one of "always going first class," the climate for any determined effort to eliminate all types of unnecessary expenses may not exist. If, on the other hand, management is more concerned with essentials than with frills, it can be expected to give its full support to any programs calculated in the long run to cut down on the drain on profit dollars.

The second constraint is the practical one of the extent to which the controller can make his or her influence felt throughout the administative departments and, indeed, throughout all of general management. The greater the area of responsibility and the more services or functions falling under the controller's direct control, the easier that task will be. Even under the most adverse conditions, however, few managements are likely to object to reasonable proposals which are intended to save money for the company.

Recognizing that there may be these constraints, the administrative areas nevertheless offer a fertile field for cost reduction action if an objective look is given to the organizational way of life, and questions are raised as to the real need for doing everything that is being done, and for doing it in quite the manner in which it is being done. Since companies are so diverse and their business practices and procedures are so different, no specific proposals are offered here. Rather, a few of a potentially great number of common or traditional business practices are suggested as being worthy of closer scrutiny.

The High Cost of Showmanship. Certain reports or presentations may have to be directed outside the company under circumstances where the element of selling is involved. Under these circumstances, a slickly packaged, highly professional presentation may well be an absolute necessity. For internal presentations, however, the same degree of showmanship amounts to a flagrant waste

of effort and expense. The following tests might be applied to reports prepared for purely internal use, bearing in mind the fact
that there is a cost associated with every step taken in putting a
report package together:

1. Must the report be bound or covered? Hard usage, adverse
    storage conditions or lengthy periods of storage, or special
    identifying features making the report readily distinguishable
    from other reports are valid considerations. Merely improving
    the appearance of the report adds nothing to the value of its
    content.
2. Are excess copies being circulated?
3. Has the report been sufficiently condensed and summarized so
    that no extraneous information is being circulated?
4. Must the information presented be typed, or are handwritten
    figures or tab runs acceptable? In this connection, it should be
    remembered that data processing output can now be dressed
    up to meet the most exacting appearance requirements.
5. Must a report be prepared at all or can the salient elements of
    information be presented verbally?

Intracompany business meetings ought to be brief and to the
point. They probably would be if they were job costed and charged
on a time basis with the salaries of the participants. In fact, there
would probably be a sharp reduction in the number of such meetings. Assuming, however, that the need for a meeting is real and
that the purpose could not be accomplished through informal discussions, through telephone conversations, or through the exchange
of memos, great care needs to be taken lest those making any kind
of presentation at the meeting go overboard in the use of charts,
slides, and other visual aids or in the use of handout materials. All
too often, there is a real effort among groups making such presentations to be the first to use the latest products of the research and
development departments of the audio visual industry, or to outdo
one another in the size and appearance of their handout packages.

Business meetings need to be kept in perspective. People are
being brought together for the interchange of information, ideas,
and opinions so that judgments can be made, recommendations developed, and decisions reached. Persons attending a meeting are
presumed to be intelligent and knowledgeable in the subject being
reviewed or they would not be there. They should, therefore, not

be shown or given anything which they already know, and, conversely, they should be shown or given only information essential to the understanding and resolution of the problem being discussed.

The cost of visual or audiovisual displays increases in direct proportion to the degree of sophistication. The preparation of even a simple chart big enough to be seen by a group of people involves an outlay for materials and time, and usually the time of skilled draftsmen. Care has to be exercised in the use of slides and movies lest the exposure time be so brief that the viewers, however conscientiously they may try, simply cannot comprehend everything that is being shown.

Handout materials should outline the verbal presentation or support it by providing explanatory data not treated in detail in the presentation, or by providing data which need to be referred to in the course of the discussion. The handout package which, in effect, virtually duplicates the presentation, ought instead to be sent out in advance of the meeting in sufficient time for the participants to review and react to it. Any subsequent meeting could then be a condensed one convened for the purpose of clarifying or discussing any salient points raised and of deciding on whatever further course of action may be required.

Calculating the cost of visual aids and other materials used in business meetings is entirely feasible and highly desirable. Where it is not already being done, the practice ought to be introduced if only on a memo basis. This is an item of expense which can be budgeted for and where a reasonable assessment of value received in relation to the cost incurred is entirely possible.

The "Adam and Eve Complex." In the divine order of things, it was decreed that Adam needed an Eve, and this presumably is the basis for the hallowed business tradition that every executive must have a secretary whether one is needed or not. In a typical business organization, even the most casual observation will bring to light countless nonproductive hours of secretarial time. It can be conceded at the outset that there are many executive positions where a secretary is an absolute necessity. It is equally true that there are probably a great many more positions where the executives, because they are traveling, attending meetings, on vacation, holding discussions with visitors in their office, studying material sent for their review, devising solutions to problems, drafting reports, or just plain thinking, simply cannot generate enough work of the type a secretary can help them with to occupy more than a few hours of the secretary's time each day.

Management consulting firms which specialize in finding ways to improve office efficiency invariably zero in on these one-to-one relationships and earn substantial fees for suggesting the judicious use of executive secretarial pools, something which management ought to be able to see the value of without outside help. There may be a reluctance on the part of management to deprive executives of one of their status symbols, and there may be some concern lest the damage to their morale will effect their attitude or performance. This persumed reaction is entirely mythical. Typically, executives wll give their support to any step which helps the bottom-line dollar figure, and as long as they get their mail opened and sorted, their typing and filing taken care of, and their telephone messages taken when they are out of the office, they are not too concerned as to whether it is "my" secretary or "our" secretary who does the work.

Apropos of secretaries and telephones, it is interesting to speculate on the amount of time spent by business people in talking to those secretaries who make a fetish of taking all telephone calls for their bosses, even those which are obviously intraoffice calls. For executives who dial their own calls—and a surprisingly large number have learned how to do this—the constant routine of identifying themselves and waiting for their colleagues to be told that it is now safe for them to pick up the receiver can be a frustrating experience. The executive can, of course, have his or her secretary call the other person's secretary, but somehow, getting four people involved in the completion of one telephone call seems counterproductive. There is no problem, of course, if it is company practice for each person to answer his or her own telephone.

The Printing Department "Open House."   With the constantly increasing cost of commercial printing, more and more companies have their own in-house facilities or, at the least, make use of varying types of copying machines. Normally, an attempt is made to exercise some degree of control over those larger printing devices which require the services of full-time operators. As the case of the "Pentagon Papers" a few years ago so admirably demonstrated, however, control over the do-it-yourself copiers is somewhat more difficult to manage, to the ultimate benefit of numerous churches, civic groups, scouting organizations, football pool organizers, and a host of other worthy groups who, incidentally, make no contribution to corporate profits.

Quite often, it is company policy to give this type of support to outside organizations provided that the sponsoring employee requests permission and gives an indication of the size of the job to be done. Where there is no such policy and where, in fact, the use of such equipment for personal business is discouraged, difficult control problems may exist. Solutions involving limitations on the hours when the equipment can be used, or requiring approval of the material to be reproduced, negate the advantages of speed, simplicity, and convenience which these machines offer. Relocating these units into supervised printshop work areas, or into relatively high traffic areas where the type of job being worked on is given some degree of exposure, can serve as a satisfactory deterrent to their indiscriminate use for noncompany purposes. Worthy of consideration for business purposes also is the practice followed in many universities of making such equipment available as a convenience to their students, with coin-operated controls which provide for the recovery of their cost of operation.

With supervised printshop operations, control procedures are usually better established. Work normally is covered by requisitions approved at specified levels of authority. These requisitions describe the job to be worked on, specify the type of printing, the number of copies needed and the priority to be given the work. As a rule, the original of the requisition is retained by the print shop and a copy is returned with the completed work. Merely establishing the requisition file in the print shop is not enough to establish any form of control, however. The file has to be reviewed and the work followed up with the originators to confirm that the number of copies requested is actually required, to reduce the incidence of reruns to correct incomplete, premature, or erroneous submissions, and to identify those jobs where the problems originated with poor work in the print shop itself. Priorities assigned need to be realistic. Those which will lead to overtime in the print shop should be cleared at a higher level in the using department. This work-load review also helps in planning ahead for repetitive jobs and in scheduling personnel and machine availabilities to avoid bottlenecks and overtime. To be guarded against are requests for pre-printing forms which bear the names of individuals or show complete dates. Turnover and the passage of time will all too quickly make such forms obsolete.

Printing and reproduction costs are not of the magnitude where they will make or break the company. Nevertheless, however large of small they may be, they should be so controlled that they are never larger than they have to be. In this connection, it might be interesting to determine how necessary is the widespread practice of providing virtually every administrative employee with supplies of personally imprinted "From the Desk of" pads.

Equipment Overkill. In the area of equipment selection, there seems to be an almost universal tendency to lease or buy equipment with interesting but unneeded features. A classic case in point is the desk calculator. For most business purposes, all that is needed is a tool for the basic arithmetic functions of addition, subtraction, multiplication, or division. To admit this, however, is tantamount to a confession of mental inadequacy, so on numerous desks in numerous offices sit trim, handsome—and expensive—machines with multiple memory banks, the capacity to solve the most intricate mathematical problems, and other exotic features, whose control keys will never be touched by human hand except by accident.

Equipment is sometimes acquired which is patently time saving and practical—except for the employee to whom it is assigned. The employee may have requested a particular piece of equipment only because a counterpart in another company or another department had one, or the equipment may have been thrust upon the employee by a superior who thought the employee ought to have one. In any case, many a dictating unit, tape recorder, or pocket calculator, after a brief period of desultory use, is quietly stored away in a desk drawer or a filing cabinet.

There can be a quantitative as well as a qualitative overkill with office equipment. Even the most portable of units may somehow lose all mobility once it has been delivered. This inability to move the machine from one department to another or even from one desk to another in the same department naturally requires the purchase of additional units.

Data processing equipment is a subject in itself and one best discussed by experts. Suffice it to say that it is a rare company which has determined beforehand exactly what it expects from the use of such equipment, has updated and streamlined all of the manual systems to which the equipment will be applied, and has then selected that equipment which will exactly handle its foreseeable needs.

The Transmittal Letter. Transmittal letters are typically brief, easy to write, and a waste of time unless they explain the purpose of, add information to, or otherwise improve the usefulness of the document or report which they accompany.

There are many other areas where gentle probing might produce some interesting answers. For example, questions might be raised as to why so much of a company's business with outsiders has to be transacted over business luncheons, and why so many company employees, and why the same employees, need to be involved; or why, when it has been deemed necessary to send five or six persons to a technical meeting in a distant city, not one will report back on the great amount of new knowledge gained from such a meeting.

Before leaving the subject of wasteful office practices, mention should be made of cost-saving suggestions which originate with employees. Whether the much-ridiculed suggestion box or some other means is used, employees should be encouraged to submit their cost-saving proposals. The ideas suggested, since they are usually developed on the basis of actual work experiences, can be practical and productive. The encouragement of such proposals may be tied in with a system of monetary rewards or may simply involve giving the employee some degree of recognition. At the very least, such suggestions should be taken seriously and should be acknowledged; and the employee should be told if his or her idea is going to be used or, if it is not, be given an explanation as to why it is not possible to put it into effect.

4.   Initiating Systems Studies to Improve Working Efficiency

Systems studies calculated to establish the real work loads of the administrative departments and to determine the most economical and efficient ways to manage these work loads offer the greatest long-term potential for controlling and reducing administrative expenses. This sort of comprehensive analysis of work requirements and working methods in the administrative departments requires careful advance planning. Before any systems study program can be adopted, the following steps need to be taken:

Definition of System Study Scope. The decision as to what por- tion of the work of the administrative departments is to be covered will in turn influence considerations of cost and of the time ex- pected to be required for the completion of the study and the implementation of the actions decided upon as a result of the study. Again, assuming that it is the controller who has taken the initiative in deciding that a systems study will be of benefit to the company, the position which the controller's department occu- pies within the organization can in itself influence the scope of the undertaking. If the greater part of the activities and specialized functions of the administrative area fall within the controller's department, the study could well be one confined to that depart- ment. If, on the other hand, there are other strong and independent administrative departments, confining the study to the controller's department could limit its effectiveness and reduce the ultimate benefit to the company.

Because of the interrelationships which the controller's depart- ment, regardless of its size, has with other administrative depart- ments and with general management, a reasonable approach seems to be that of establishing the scope of the study to include the con- troller's department, together with all output from that department used elsewhere in the organization. This will require that other departments and the appropriate levels of general management be informed as to the purpose of the study, be alerted as to the areas of their work on which the study could have an impact, and be encouraged to provide the necessary liaison support.

Provision of Adequate Study Leadership. A study of this type necessarily involves the detailed review of the work being done and the methods used to do it in all of the areas included within the scope of the study. This review will require the interest and the complete cooperation of every department head and cost center head involved, together with the same degree of support from the personnel actually performing the work. In order to achieve the necessary quality of support, direction of the project has to be assigned at a sufficiently high level in the organization so that all participants can readily understand that the program is a serious one and that management has a real concern for its success. For this purpose, the use of a steering committee headed by the controller is recommended. Other members of the committee should include: those of the controller's principal assistants whose work is most likely to be affected by the study; high-ranking members of the other departments involved; and the individual, whether from inside or outside the company, who has been designated as the person actually heading up the study.

A steering committee is a real necessity for an undertaking of this sort. While one of its functions is certainly that of giving the project the visible and actual backing it needs in order to succeed, it is not a figurehead group and must function as a working committee in defining objectives, establishing priorities, and in following the progress of the work. One of its major and more difficult responsibilities is that of seeing that the primary objectives of the study are not lost sight of, and that the study group is not allowed to be diverted from the main goals by intriguing or challenging secondary problems. Keeping the project on track and on schedule requires that the committee be provided with regular and complete progress reports and that it meet regularly to review and act on the information it has been given.

Establishment of a Schedule for the Study and Implementation of its Recommendations.   To a great extent, the scope of the project will influence the determination of the target dates for the completion of the systems study. The nature and extent of the recommendations developed will in turn determine the sort of schedule to be followed in implementing these recommendations. The variable here is the degree of urgency which management decides to give to the project, and the resources it is willing to commit. A crash program offers the prospect of the earlier realization of the expected benefits but carries with it the risk of problems brought about by hasty planning. The condition of the existing systems may well be such, however, that prompt and drastic action will be worth whatever risks are entailed.

Whether the study is to be an all-out effort or something less, the principal systems and subsystems involved need to be identified. The sequence in which each is to be reviewed should be established and, depending on the personnel to be available, dates for the completion of each section of the overall study should be set. The dates should be so selected that there is always some degree of pressure for the completion of the work. They must be realistic, however, in giving recognition to the fact that most of the employees providing background information for the systems study will also have the task of meeting the requirements of their day-to-day work loads.

In-House Study versus Outside Consultants. If the company has an established systems group, or in the absence of such a group, if there are enough people within the organization with systems backgrounds, an in-house study can be undertaken with some probability of success. This approach has the advantage of saving the time which consultants would require in getting oriented. It may offer other advantages with respect to convenience, flexibility, and easier direct control of the project. There may be a cost advantage as well, but this might or might not materialize, depending on the circumstances applying to each systems study.

In any in-house study there has to be a hard core of analysts assigned full time to the project. This project team may have to be augmented from time to time with personnel temporarily assigned from the department under review. The key members of the project team must be relieved of all other duties and responsibilities if the study is to be carried out with any hope of success.

If the company lacks personnel with systems capabilities, a consulting firm should be used. The firm chosen should have a proven record of successful systems installations, supported by recommendations from previous customers in the same industry or with similar types of businesses. By using outside professionals, the company gets the benefit of the experience they have gained in the systems area—experience paid for by other companies. The company also benefits from the availability of as many highly qualified systems experts as may be needed to do the job. Cost may be a factor, but the fees charged would have to be considered in relation to the estimated internal cost for doing the same work; the likelihood, based on the consulting firm's record, of an entirely satisfactory job; and the possibility for a decreased need for direct involvement of management with the detailed development of the project. It is a sad truism that consultants are often paid well for suggesting measures which employees may have advocated for years, and there thus may be a further benefit from the use of consultants because of the higher degree of credibility which management may give to their conclusions and recommendations.

If consultants are used, it must be made clear to them that they are subject to the authority of the steering committee and that they must provide the committee with progress reports and all other required information. Even if consultants are used, it may be found desirable to set up an internal project team to assist them and to expedite their work. Conversely, if the in-house systems study is decided on, it may be found beneficial to engage a consultant for purely advisory purposes.

Obtaining Top Management's Support.   On a very small-scale systems study conducted entirely within the controller's department, the approval of the controller, who is part of senior management, may well be sufficient. On the great majority of projects, however, the interaction between the work of the controller's department and that of other departments, and the extent of the resources to be committed, will probably dictate that the project be given the same management overview as that given to a capital project of like magnitude. This would require that management be informed as to what it is that is to be done, why it is being done, the benefits expected to be gained, when those benefits are expected to be realized, and the estimated cost of the project. In the case of a project of especially great size, management may feel that it is desirable to advise the board of directors of its plans or request its approval of those plans.

In addition to creating a climate of better interest and understanding at the top-management level, the fact that management is fully informed on and supports the project will help to insure greater responsiveness and cooperation at all levels and will be particularly helpful in matters involving interdepartmental relationships.

Conducting the Study   Once the scope and timing of the project have been decided upon, a steering committee selected, a consultant selected, or an in-house systems group activated, and management's full support obtained, the actual work can be started. With or without a consultant, the general procedure will be much the same. What is involved are the following:

1.   A survey which completely and precisely defines the output of the administrative groups included in the scope of the study, and which delineates in detail the procedures followed in developing that output.
2.   A qualitative analysis of the current output to determine what changes, if any, are required in order to better meet the actual

requirements of the users of that output. This would be analogous to the product research constantly carried on by marketing organizations.

3. A determination of the simplest and most effective means for developing the newly defined or redefined output requirements. This effort would parallel those of the industrial engineering or operations research people in the manufacturing area.
4. Development of a specific set of recommendations for action, together with a timetable for their implementations.
5. The actual implementation of the approval program for action.

The comprehensive survey needed to establish what work is being done and how it is being done can be carried out by the project team by interviewing each employee individually, or it can be accomplished through means of a self-analysis type of survey. This would still be under the direction of the project team, but the actual work information would be supplied by the employees themselves, with review, approval, and final summarizations being done at the cost center head or department head levels.

The latter method is much less time-consuming and has the advantage of getting the active rather than the passive participation of the employees involved. It can also have the advantage of helping department and cost center heads update their knowledge of the detailed work being done in their areas and may bring to light needed work-load redistributions or opportunities for eliminating work, or simplifying procedures, which can be acted on immediately without waiting for the completion of the total systems study.

Typically, a self-analysis survey will begin with an introductory or initiation phase. In this first phase, cost center and department heads are told, first by letter and then in follow-up discussions, of the purpose, scope, and planned timing for the systems study. The plans for the work-load and methods survey are then explained. In this phase, the liaison between the project team and the department is established through the designation of the organizational representative. This will be either the department or cost center head or a knowledgeable employee who, as required, can be made available to assist the project team in its understanding of the information given it.

In this first phase also, the controls for the survey are set up through the submission by the department head of a personnel listing and a departmental activity or function listing. The personnel listing should identify all supervisors and their subordinates by name and classification. This will provide the project team with a checklist for the individually prepared work description listings to be submitted in the implementation phase of the survey.

In the departmental activity or function listing, the department head numbers sequentially and lists each major identifiable activity of his area. All subsequent information provided by individual employees on work performed and documents used will be keyed to these activity numbers.

In the action or implementation phase, each employee and supervisor typically submits, for the department head's review and concurrence, a description of what he or she does and of the document flow involved in the work performance. Exhibit 1 illustrates the type of form which might be used by an employee or supervisor in analyzing the work load. In the "Listing of Duties or Task Description," the employee describes what is done on each of identifiable job and the use and disposition of each of the documents handled. Each task, as defined, must in turn be related to a departmental activity.

Exhibit 2 illustrates a Document Inventory and Flow List which would be turned in by the employee in support of the Employee Duty/Task List. The example shown illustrates incoming documents. Similar forms would be needed for internal documents such as journals, ledger sheets, and so forth, for which the final column would show the purpose or end use of the document rather than the source; and for externally distributed documents for which the last column would then indicate the recipient of the form, either inside or outside the department or company. Each of the Document Inventory and Flow Listings should be accompanied by copies of all the documents referenced with the possible exception of confidential documents. These should be actual working copies which illustrate the actions cited in the task descriptions.

The third phase of the survey would be the review and summarization phase at the cost center or department head level. Each of the submissions by the individual employees will have to be checked for consistency, completeness, and accuracy. When this has been done and any necessary revisions or corrections made, the information on tasks performed and documentation required should be summarized on a departmental or cost center basis in relation to

EXHIBIT 1

	Organizational Unit					
	Employee Name					
EMPLOYEE DUTY/TASK LIST	Position Title		Grade			
	Name of Supervisor					
	Date		Approved By			

Task No.	Listing of Duties/Task Description	Hrs. per Task	Task Frequency				Activity No.	Average Hours per Month
			Daily	Weekly	Monthly	Yearly		

INSTRUCTIONS

1. Number each task—print legibly
2. Start with task you perform most frequently
3. Start with verb—describe in detail each task and documents used
4. Report task time in units of 1/4 hours
5. Reference task to activity number on Activity List

the control list of activities developed by the department head.

Exhibit 3 illustrates for a typical department how the persons involved in the completion of each departmental activity are identified by name, how the role each person plays in the completion of the activity is delineated, and how the time spent per month on the activity by each person is shown. It should be noted here that this departmental work distribution chart thus gives a good indication

EXHIBIT 2

						Page of
DOCUMENT INVENTORY & FLOW LIST Incoming Documents			Organizational Unit			
			Date		Approved By	
Log No.	Activity No.	Title or Description	Freq.	No. of Copies	Receive from Company/Department/Person	

NOTES	INSTRUCTIONS
Freq. Codes: D–Daily W–Weekly (2W=twice weekly) M=Monthly (2M=twice monthly) Q=Quarterly A=Annually S=As Specified	1–Submit copies of filled in documents. 2–LOG NO.––Leave blank (to be filled in by project coordinator).

EXHIBIT 3

DEPARTMENT WORK DISTRIBUTION CHART

Page ___ of ___   SECTION ___

Organizational Unit Charted: ___

Existing Organization: ___   Date: ___

Charted By: ___   Approved By: ___

Activity No.	ACTIVITY/FUNCTION	Avg. Hrs. per Mo.	Name: ___ Position: ___ Grade: ___ DUTIES/TASKS	Avg. Hrs. per Mo.	Name: ___ Position: ___ Grade: ___ DUTIES/TASKS	Avg. Hrs. per Mo.	Name: ___ Position: ___ Grade: ___ DUTIES/TASKS	Avg. Hrs. per Mo.	Name: ___ Position: ___ Grade: ___ DUTIES/TASKS	Avg. Hrs. per Mo.

of the cost of carrying out each of the activities shown, since the hours shown as being spent by each employee can easily be converted into equivalent salary dollars and since, for a great many of these activities, labor is easily the major element of expense.

In similar fashion, the documentation associated with each departmental activity should be summarized with incoming, internal, and external documents listed in separate columns. These summaries then will give the department head an organized visual presentation of both the work load and the flow of paper within the department. It is at this stage of the survey that the opportunities for immediate improvements are most likely to be uncovered.

After the departmental survey material has been delivered to the project team and has been gone over by them with the organizational representatives, the project team can begin its analysis work. At some risk of oversimplification, this analytical process involves three steps. The first step involves the qualitative review of the output. This requires getting together with the users of the output to determine how well the output meets their actual needs. As the result of this review, report format or content may be modified, timing requirements may be changed, two or more reports may be combined, certain reports may be done away with altogether, and so on.

The second step involves the identification of the major systems and their supporting systems which will be used in the generation of data for the output as redefined. These systems will then have to be tracked back through each department or cost center and related to the appropriate departmental activity with its associated schedules of employee actions and document flow.

The third step calls for the step-by-step review of employee actions and document flow from the first point at which any action is initiated, on through to the final output as it now has been defined. The object of this review is that of determining what improvements are possible at each level with respect to work-load content, working methods and document design, content, and flow. In all of this effort, the emphasis is on the one-time input of information or data into the system, on summarizing or otherwise reworking the data into usable form at the lowest possible level, and on moving it forward through the system toward the final output in the most direct manner possible.

In the development of its recommended programs for management action, the project team has an obligation to present what it considers to be the optimum solution to the problems brought out by the study, together with an alternate set of proposals. This will give management the opportunity to decide how far and how fast it wants to go and what resources it is willing to commit. If management should decide on something less than the total program, it will still have available a blue-print for implementing other phases of the program in the future.

The project team should continue to play an active role in seeing that the programs which it has recommended are put into effect according to the timetable suggested and are debugged and modified as required to make them completely workable as far as the using departments are concerned. Since the work requirements in the administrative area are subject to constant change and since new and improved working methods are constantly being developed, it may be found to be well worthwhile to provide for some continued monitoring of systems so that desirable changes can be introduced as the requirement for them develops, and the need for future large-scale systems overhauls thus be done away with.

SUMMARY

The controller will have a firm and sound grasp of the cost situation in the administrative area when his or her cost accounting and cost control systems are in place, when administrative area personnel are working to capacity under effective leadership, when wasteful and inefficient work practices have been identified and eliminated, and when the work loads have been redefined and updated and working methods streamlined. Under these conditions, the controller can be certain that work requirements are being met with the least possible cost. If further curtailments in these expenses should then become necessary, the controller will be in a good position to recommend to management, on a logical basis, the reductions in those specific areas of support which will accomplish management's cost reduction objectives.

ADDITIONAL SOURCES

Also see Additional Sources for Chapter 24.

Bumbarger, W. B. "O.F.A.: Key to Lasting Overhead Productivity Improvement." *Financial Executive*, September 1977, p. 40.

Greer, Willis R.   "Standard Costing for Non-Manufacturing Activities." *Cost and Management,* November–December 1975, p. 12.

Neuman, John L.   "Make Overhead Cuts That Last." *Harvard Business Review,* May–June 1975, p. 116.

Trentin, H. George, and Jones, Reginald L.   *Budgeting General and Administrative Expenses.* New York: American Management Association, 1966.

45

Controlling Service Organizations

Paul G. Hines*

Service organizations dominate our economy. The number of people employed in service organizations was only slightly larger than the number employed in manufacturing organizations at the end of World War II. Currently, service employees exceed manufacturing employees by over 33 million people, with nearly 90 percent of new employees each year going to work in service industries. That probably 90 percent of the controllership and cost accounting literature deals with the manufacturing-firm minority is therefore ironic. What follows is a humble effort toward beginning the process of redressing this literary imbalance.

DISTINGUISHING CHARACTERISTICS OF SERVICE ORGANIZATIONS

There are several somewhat concrete features differentiating service organizations from manufacturing concerns. The foremost feature is that service organizations, to varying degrees, are labor intensive. Unlike the machinery and equipment associated with a manufacturing firm, people are the major producing asset in service organizations. The expertise of its employees is at the heart of such service organizations.

A second feature of service organizations is the normal absence of physical inventories which can be stored. Surely a consulting firm

---

* Mr. Hines is Senior Vice President, Corporate Development and Control, at E. F. Hutton, New York.

cannot save up the hours of its professional staff to be used for a rainy day. A brokerage firm could not easily sacrifice today's transactions and assume they could make them up on another day. On the other hand, manufacturing firms, more often than not, have a supply of a finished products which can be sold months, or even years, after they are produced.

A third feature differentiating manufacturing and service organizations revolves around their relative abilities to precisely measure their product. A widget manufacturer has the inherent ability to gather product data as to specific costs and inputs, physical location, and final sales and revenues. Spoilage of defective widgets is identifiable, and therefore widgets can easily be returned for one's money back or exchanged for another fungible widget. But such joys of precise measurement are not always as apparent for services provided. For example, schools and colleges are service organizations. What is the value of education? How do you value degrees in the same curriculum from different schools as to which presents more value to the matriculant? The course descriptions may be the same, the professors equally credentialed and the costs the same, yet the comparative value can be far different.

In addition to these features, service organizations generally fall under one of two revenue earning categories: time-based or transaction-based revenue earning companies. The former group's services are normally paid for according to their time value, although fixed-price arrangements for continuing service are common. The product sold is the expertise of the individuals in the firm, and the major constraint on revenues is available staff hours and available opportunities to bill those services. The transaction-based group acts frequently as an agent or middleman, attempting to create higher revenues through adding value by bringing buyers and sellers together. For instance, a grocer creates revenues by making the farmer's product available to the consumers. A stock broker's job involves coordinating transfers of stock and other financial instruments among individuals, institutions, and other brokers. Real estate agents are conduits between home sellers and home buyers.

Time-Based Service Organizations

One way to classify time-based service organizations is by their required level of employee professionalism. For example, there are organizations which consist primarily of licensed and certified professionals. These include lawyers, engineers, architects, certified public accountants, and other forms of consultants. In these days of specialization, groups of consultants can be found offering wide varieties of expertise ranging from applied mathematics to organizational behavior.

A common goal in these organizations is optimizing the use of the available human resources. In quasi-Orwellian terms, professionals are professionals, but not all professionals are equal. Thus, the cost of the services of these professionals is normally a function of daily billing rates. A billing rate is normally a function of an individual's compensation level, which in turn is a function of an individual's experience.

Frequently, the "rule of three" is used as a method for setting up the billing structure for client business. For normal business, each employee would be billed out at three times his or her hourly rate. The hourly rate is derived by dividing the employee's available hours in the year into his or her salary, which is usually a factor of approximately 2,000 hours. Often a firm will pool together the available man-hours and salaries to compute a single billing rate for each experience level. The implications behind the "rule of three" are as follows:

⅓—For the employee.

⅓—To cover firm overhead.

⅓—For partners (as salaries and profits) or equity holders (as dividends and retained earnings).

One must remember that the "rule of three" is merely a rough estimate of overhead and profits, since their percentage can vary at any point in time.

Obviously these billing rates imply an organizational hierarchy of professionals. The management objective is to allocate optimally the time-value resource these people represent. The more junior a person, the greater portion of his or her time is devoted to billable assignments, while further up the hierarchy, time is allocated to nonbillable but profitable pursuits such as client servicing and new-business prospecting. These firms are generally managed against budgets where the billable-nonbillable norms vary by experience (billing) level and by firm. Among management consultants, it is fairly common to try to keep associates 85 percent billed, project managers 75 percent billed, and producing partners 50 percent billed. Variations on the general theme include separate revenue budgets for new and existing clients. Time not billed is a most valuable resource which is often controlled as tightly as is billable time. Such nonbilled time is spent on personal development, managing the service business itself, and developing new business.

The task of budgeting internally for revenue and expenses in a time-based service firm is often as much of an art form as it is a precise science. For example, Exhibit 1 represents a biweekly employee performance report generated for a CPA (public accounting) firm. It could be used as an example not only for CPA firms but also for law and consulting firms. Since most time-based professionals keep a detailed record of where their time was spent, it is easy to identify which hours were chargeable versus nonchargeable to the clients. A chargeable (billable) percentage either to standard hours available or actual hours worked can be computed, thus indicating the utilization of each employee during an accounting period. Further, nonchargeable hours are separated into controllable and noncontrollable categories. The former classification includes hours spent on business development, firm projects, training classes, and professional reading, while the latter classification consists of sick days and vacation days.

Typically, a CPA firm has a busy season from September through April followed by a slow season during the summer months. Obviously, the billing rates must be based on a full year's worth of peaks and troughs. Profits are extremely sensitive to the employee utilization rate, which in itself can vary widely due to seasonality and the demand for various experience levels. In Exhibit 1, the desired utilization rate, which this firm defined to be billings divided by salaries, was set by management at 2.5. One would expect a CPA firm to be running below the desired utilization rate in July, as this group of staff assistants is doing at 1.77. If the "rule of three" were used for billing purposes, then the staff would have needed 83⅓ percent of its hours to be billable in order to meet the 2.5 target.

Exhibit 2 demonstrates the sensitivity of profits when employee utilization is less than planned. The profit margin planned by management is 5.9 percent ($28,350 ÷ $480,000.) But if the same employee utilization mix falls below 94.4 percent ($480,000 ÷ $508,350) of the budgeted billable hours, then this firm will lose money rather than earn a profit. A higher desired multiple would

EXHIBIT 1
Employee Performance Report in a Public Accounting Firm*

Midwest Region
Detroit Office
Staff Assistants

Biweekly
Period Ending 7/14/77

| Employee | | Hours | | | Nonchargeable | | Staff Utiliza- | Chargeable % | | Average Bill | Fees at | Salary |
No.	Name	Standard	Total	Charge-able	Control-lable	Non-control	tion Rate†	To Standard	To Total	Rate	Standard	
1005	Bryan, H.........	70.00	71.00	36.50	13.50	21.00	1.54	52.14	51.41	$28.00	$1,022.00	$ 665.00
1102	Gates, S.........	70.00	72.00	57.00	1.00	14.00	2.55	81.43	79.17	28.00	1,596.00	626.23
1119	Porter, C.........	70.00	70.00	42.50	13.50	14.00	1.70	60.71	60.71	25.20	1,071.00	630.00
1328	Brown, J.........	70.00	76.00	59.00	3.00	14.00	2.57	84.29	77.63	28.00	1,652.00	643.47
1424	Kendal, B.........	70.00	70.00	37.50	18.50	14.00	1.58	53.57	53.57	25.20	945.00	597.70
1734	Stoner, E.........	70.00	0.00	0.00	0.00	0.00	0.00	0.00	0.00	0.00	0.00	619.23
1816	Tunney, J.........	70.00	70.00	54.00	2.00	14.00	2.24	77.14	77.14	28.00	1,512.00	675.78
1817	Adams, J.........	70.00	70.00	52.75	10.25	7.00	2.71	75.36	75.36	25.20	1,329.30	490.00
1844	Toole, R.........	35.00	28.00	5.75	22.25	0.00	0.51	16.43	20.54	25.20	144.90	282.70
	Totals..............	595.00	527.00	345.00	84.00	98.00	1.77	57.98	65.46	$26.88	$9,272.20	$5,230.11

* This is an actual report, though the names and office location are disguised and the firm prefers to remain anonymous.
† This firm defined staff utilization rate to be Billings ÷ Salaries. It can be shown as follows that this is equivalent to billable (chargeable) percent times billing multiple:

$$\text{Staff utilization rate} = \frac{\text{Billings}}{\text{Salaries}} = \frac{\text{Billable hours}}{\text{Total hours}} \times \frac{\text{Billing rate}}{\text{Hourly salary}} = \text{Billable percent} \times \text{Billing multiple}$$

EXHIBIT 2
Sensitivity of Profits to Employee Utilization

Position	No. of People	Total Base Salaries	Overtime Pay	Total Salaries	Available Hours	Fraction Billable	Billable Hours	Direct Labor Cost	Hourly Cost	Billing Rate	Available Billings
Partner	1	$70,000	—	$ 70,000	2,080	0.50	1,040	$ 35,000	$33.65	$100.96	$105,000
Manager	1	36,000	—	36,000	2,080	0.70	1,456	25,200	17.31	51.92	75,600
Senior	2	42,700	$4,300	47,000	4,160	0.85	3,536	39,950	11.30	33.89	119,850
Assistant	5	71,500	5,500	77,000	10,400	0.90	9,360	69,300	7.40	22.21	207,900
				$230,000				$169,450			$508,350

Calculation of multiple = $508,350 / $169,450 = 3.0

Salaries + Overhead* = $480,000
Therefore a $28,350 normal profit results.

Position	No. of People	Total Base Salaries	Overtime Pay	Total Salaries	Available Hours	Fraction Billable	Billed Hours	Direct Labor Cost	Hourly Cost	Billing Rate	Actual Billings
Partner	1	$70,000	—	$ 70,000	2,080	0.45	936	$ 31,500	$33.65	$100.96	$ 94,500
Manager	1	36,000	—	36,000	2,080	0.65	1,352	23,400	17.31	51.92	70,200
Senior	2	42,700	$4,300	47,000	4,160	0.80	3,328	37,600	11.30	33.89	112,800
Assistant	5	71,500	5,500	77,000	10,400	0.85	8,840	65,450	7.40	22.21	196,350
				$230,000				$157,950			$473,850

Salaries + Overhead* = $480,000
Therefore a $6,150 loss results.

* Assumed overhead = $250,000.

be expected from firms with fewer recurring projects, such as architectural and engineering firms and general-management consultants. A CPA firm or legal firm, which depends mainly on continuing client relationships, could afford to settle for a lower utilization rate, since the variance from budgeted billable hours should not be as volatile as firms with constant client turnover.

From the lower portion of Exhibit 2, we can see that circumstances can arise where the average billed time drops below that required to break even. Faced with excess people capacity, a time-based service firm has two major options. The first option is to retain its employees and continue training them for future assignments. When business picks up again, the firm will be prepared with qualified people at its disposal. The added expense of retaining employees is hopefully made up later in time saved from experience and better quality in the work performed. The other option to combat excess capacity is to lay off employees. The obvious savings are visible immediately by way of lowered expenses. But several drawbacks arise from using this method for optimal labor utilization. When business turns upward again, the cost of training new employees is incurred another time.

Several large CPA and consulting firms found even greater problems resulting from staff purges in the early 1970s. Their ability to recruit qualified people has been hampered because the layoffs have tarnished their image. And four or five years later, these same firms found a gap whereby fewer employees were capable and available to handle middle-management responsibilities. The obvious lesson to be learned is that even managements of service organizations must recognize the difference between managing profits and managing the business.

The time analysis can be broken down further by examining actual hours versus budgeted hours by client. Progressing to a more sophisticated level, actual hours can be compared to earned hours.[1] Suppose, for example, that the following situation existed for a consulting firm:

---

[1] Since budgeted hours represent 100 percent of the expected time necessary for the project, then the earned hours represent the portion of the total job which has been completed. At a project's completion, budgeted hours will equal earned hours since 100 percent of the job has been finished. Earned hours are an evaluation of where one stands at a point in time in relation to the final product. Expressed as a percentage of budgeted hours, earned hours are often called "percent completed."

Project	Total Budgeted Hours	Actual Hours to Date	Earned Hours to Date
No. 1...................	60	32	35
No. 2...................	40	37	40
No. 3...................	80	60	20

The value of including earned hours to date is apparent. Project No. 1 is running close to plan, and Project No. 2 was completed slightly under budget. On the other hand, Project No. 3 indicates that problems have arisen or that the original budget was unrealistic. Seeing that 25 percent accomplishment of Project No. 3 has taken 75 percent of total budgeted hours should warn management that possible changes in emphasis are necessary, *before* the project runs over budget.

It is crucial that honest appraisals of hours earned are made if this method of analysis is to be a useful tool for management. Here the concept is the other side of the "cost to complete" concept. That is, the project work may be one quarter done based upon managerial appraisal while the project budget has been three quarters consumed. Such is the position inexperienced project managing consultants can find themselves in if they do not tightly manage their assignment. In this example, project managing consultants either have to figure a way to justify a 50 percent higher charge to the client (six quarters) or a 50 percent write-off to their partners. Neither position is a nice one in which to be.

All of the above is no doubt more than the general reader needs and wants to know about professional service firms. However, as the services descend the hierarchial ladder of professionalism from highest and most premium priced through the journeyman middle of blue-collar professionals such as electricians and plumbers and other middle professionals to the lower skilled services such as guards and scrub persons, the managerial concept is still basically the same. That concept is achieving the greatest yield on the human resources employed.

As discussed, the managerial concept in other kinds of labor-intensive service organizations is to optimize the utilization of employees at a billing rate or fee for their services. The managerial task is to balance the opportunities to produce revenue with the capacity to service the revenue opportunities. Obviously, service firms achieve the strongest economic results when all billable individuals are fully utilized. The worst economic environment for a service firm is one where the ability to earn revenue and the capacity to produce revenue become grossly imbalanced. As the examples showed, there can be substantial positive as well as negative leverage in a service firm. Depending on the characteristics of the firm, to earn a nominal profit the staffs have to be 80–90 percent billed. A small drop in junior staff utilization can eliminate the profit margin. A large drop in utilization creates losses in the absence of layoffs.

Some professions, but not all, have premium-pricing opportunities which tend to occur in isolated instances. Premium pricing occurs when the price paid bears no relation to the economic value of the service provided. This concept is tricky because economic value is not established in relation to the work done but rather in relation to the next best employment value of the human resources.

Contingent legal fees are an example of such premium-pricing arrangements. In these cases the fee is a function of the settlement and not the purchased cost of the legal services provided. Corporate finance fees paid for merger and acquisition services are another such example. These fees are often more a function of the size of the deal than of the cost of the professional services required to complete the transaction had they been purchased at a price related to their cost. Thus in these cases, notions of cost-based pricing are the last thing of interest. Rather the focus is on optimizing premium-pricing opportunities. Obviously professionals are only motivated to "premium price" when the expected value of the premium price exceeds the time-value price. Equally as obvious, not all premium billing opportunities yield revenues in excess of their time value.

Some professions, such as certified public accountants and physicians, do not allow contingent fees. A further pricing variation is that some consultants, including physicians and accountants, have dual pricing schedules whereupon higher rates are charged for work where the consultant possesses unique expertise. Specializd tax practitioners are one such example where a CPA's tax skills may have a higher value than his or her audit skills. To the extent a CPA cannot be fully utilized on tax work and there exists audit work to be done, a lower fee will be charged for his or her audit services. The idea here is not that the tax work is per se more valuable than audit work, but that a professional may be better at one thing than another and command a premium for what the professional is good at. CPA firms often are contracted to work on special projects because the expertise in the company's business has already been gained during the course of the audit. For such highly professionalized services the consistent managerial thread is that of the optimum use of the human resources in relation to their values. Values may be a function either of premium-pricing opportunities, unique-expert values, or of cost-based schedules such as in the rule of three.

Many corporations have internal departments consisting of these same kinds of professionals. There are lots of reasons for the existence of these departments. The usual primary reason is to retain the one third of the billing rate that represents profit and executive (partner) compensation. Another reason is for continuity of staff to avoid the cost of having to educate outsiders to recurring problems. The decision of whether or not to have such departments is often approached as a make-or-buy decision where the internal full cost of servicing certain of the firm's professional needs on a continuous basis is less than the cost of purchasing them outside of the firm on a cost-based pricing schedule under most conditions, and under an expert- or a premium-priced schedule under all conditions.

Transaction-Based Service Organizations

Unlike the time-based consulting firms, there are many service organizations which incur large expenses above and beyond their direct labor costs. Transportation companies and wholesale and retail traders all must consider the substantial cost in excess of labor when pricing transactions. The employee mix in such firms is quite complex, thus eliminating simple pricing methods such as the rule of three. But pricing theory for transaction-based service organizations can sometimes have a child-like simplicity as well. For example, the classic methodology for establishing product prices is to calculate the full cost of a product including a normal profit, and to divide by the normal volume to arrive at the required price. Factors which tend to make pricing most difficult in practice include:

1.   The availability of a number of different methodologies for defining full cost plus normal profit, especially in complex multi-product organizations.

2. The position of the product to be priced within a firm's product mix.
3. The importance of pricing strategy as a component of the product's overall marketing strategy.
4. The competitive environment.
5. The political/cultural environment.

Currently, because of the uncertainty of the impact of negotiated rates, the securities industry provides an excellent laboratory for experiencing how these factors combine to cloud the conceptual simplicity of cost-based pricing. Prior to negotiated rates, the securities industry had within its institutional segment a conditon where the full-cost-plus-normal-profit value for the services provided appeared less than the available revenue. The most visible outward manifestations of this perceived imbalance were the large numbers of individuals performing functions including investment research, sales, and stock trading, whose annual incomes were multiples of those paid to individuals performing similar functions in banks and insurance companies. Under the assumption that the nonsecurities industry individuals were equally qualified, the casual observer could conclude that indeed an economic disequilibrium did exist.

Pricing the service provided, based upon the salaries paid for the investment research, sales, and trading functions in banks and insurance companies, would result in a lower cost than that which prevailed before negotiated rates. The fact that many transactions were initiated by institutions themselves based upon their own decisions to buy or sell specific stocks, and not upon the recommendations of the investment researchers, salespersons, and traders at the servicing brokers, raised the further issue that sometimes the institutions were paying for services they did not want even at lower prices. This line of logic led to a concept that there should exist a price for execution only, which excluded the cost of investment research, sales, and trading. That is, the value of a transaction initiated by a client where the execution was ordinary, rather than a complex execution, had a value substantially less than even the lower full-cost-plus-normal-profit cost previously defined.

Pressures by institutions for cost-based pricing have forced the rates charged by institutions' brokers down from an approximate average of 26 cents per share to less than 10 cents per share between the inception of negotiated rates in May 1975 and the present.

The approximate *variable* cost per share for execution only from an efficient broker may be about 5 cents per share. The *full* cost, excluding a normal profit, for execution only by an efficient broker may be about 12 cents per share. Thus, currently the pressure of powerful buyers has reduced the charge for the simplest transaction to a level which may approximate full cost plus normal profit for only the most efficient execution-only brokers.

The facts are that most brokers operate an economic system which has evolved in such a way that it is not possible truly to separate the cost of execution only from those of custody, trading, and sales, including investment research. As a result, many of the firms whose assumption was that a package of investment research, sales, and trading was a valuable service have either gone out of business, merged, or are in the process of changing the basic nature of their business. At the extremes, one of the largest and best-known institutional brokers is rumored currently to have more retail revenue than institutional revenue and appears to be pursuing an active, aggressive strategy to allocate its assets away from the securities industry and into investment in profitable firms in other industries.

The events which have transpired in the securities industry between May 1975 and the present provide an outstanding real-time laboratory for studying the interplay of very basic supply-and-demand economics and their pricing consequences. While this chapter is not the place for a complete discussion of the events which have transpired in the securities industry, nevertheless the cost characteristics of the industry and the pressures on those characteristics from the environment provide a living, classic laboratory for the study of pricing.

The presence of high variable or high fixed-cost structures is one of the major differences among transaction-based service organizations as opposed to those with highly individualized professional content. Extreme examples of each type would be a guard service, with nearly all costs variable, and a computer service center, with the major cost, that of the computer, being a fixed cost. In such industries, maintaining a proper balance between the ability to create revenues and the capacity to process revenues is critical for survival.

The securities industry provides a good in-between example with the variable sales costs being approximately one third of revenue, and the fixed location, communications, and operations costs ranging between 40 and 60 percent of product and service revenues in good and bad times. The largest variable cost is the salesperson whose cost goes upward from 25 percent of revenue. Sales volume is largely not under the control of firms in the industry. Thus, a difficult task in the securities industry has been managing an optimal balance between the capacity to produce revenue given the opportunities to produce revenue and the capacity to process those available revenues. The nonprojectable short-term behavior of stock-market volumes make the ability to define the required level of processing capacity very difficult. For example, in most years there are periods where the average transaction volumes over, say, a month's extended time is double the longer term average volume. This volatility of volume problem has resulted in the securities industry's creating an excess of highly automated transactions-processing capacity, with attendant high levels of fixed cost. Thus, the cost per securities transaction is more a function of volume processed than of any other factor.

A SERVICE FIRM CONTROLLER'S FUNCTION

Identifying and working with the truly controllable dimensions of the service organization's underlying economics is the service firm controller's main function. How well controllers specifically do this and how they see their function philosophically will largely determine their effectiveness. Thus while there may be considerable consensus around the basics of the control function, how controllers actually behave in the function will be a major determinant of their operative effectiveness. Operative effectiveness is measured by what changes are made in the organization as a result of the way controllers themselves use information within the firm.

Control Philosophy

For purposes of illustration, there seem to be at least two possible extremes of control philosophy and behavior open to controllers in service organizations (or any organization, for that matter). One is measurement centered, while the other is behaviorally centered. Measurement-centered control focuses primarily on the calculation of differences between what happened and what was supposed to happen in an accounting period. Controllers in this group reflect the evolution of controllership and cost accounting from its manufacturing roots. Many of the more quantitative contemporary management science techniques are applied by measurement-centered controllership staffs. The primary role of this form of controllership is to provide understanding of why what was supposed to happen did not happen or, in rare cases, did happen. This is consistent with the need for structure and definiteness that often is a characteristic of the personalities of people attracted to controllership careers.

On the other hand, behaviorally oriented control persons view their task as one of using quantitative tools and techniques to *change behavior* in the firm. That is, changing behavior is primary, and controllership methodology is secondary. Over time, this type of controller strives to improve the quality of executive decision making in the firm. Information generated by the behaviorally oriented controller is used to challenge the firm's assumptions about its objectives and strategies. Often behaviorally oriented controllers are challengers of the status quo. They find quantifiable measures of a firm's objectives and track how well it is achieving those objectives, as well as monitor the adequacy of those objectives themselves, in a changing environment. When a firm is not performing as it should, they challenge both the firm and the objectives themselves. Frequently, such challenging leads to internal organizational changes as well as to changes in the objectives themselves. These organizational and objective changes then require changes in the reporting and compensation systems.

When controllers are challenging performance and objectives, they are really challenging the competency of the firm or division or department as an effective human organization. In most cases, poor performance is an organizational problem and not only a quantitative one. There is an old saying among consultants that "when a fish has an odor, the odor begins in the head." Consultants often resort to this bit of homily among themselves when faced with difficult and sensitive poor performance symptoms of serious organizational problems. More often than not, the quote fits the organizational reality.

As a result, controllers who look at their position not only from the traditional role of safeguarding the firm's assets but also from the more contemporary role of status-quo challenger can positively affect the firm as it moves through time and in an ever-changing environment. Of course, behaviorally oriented controllers must use quantitative techniques. However, they use them to surface dysfunctional human performance.

Where performance is so much a function of human competence, such as in service organizations, the behaviorally oriented controller has a most valuable contribution to make. Besides, in the service firm there are fewer opportunities to apply the sophisticated management science techniques so useful in manufacturing controllership. In a service organization, the behaviorally oriented controller constantly challenges the ability of the organization to perform in relation to the goals set for it. This task is quite different from the more traditional manufacturing controller, whose task is to ensure that the product cost is achieved as planned and if it is not, to know why.

The service controller operates in a somewhat different environment than a manufacturing controller. Some of manufacturing's most valuable control techniques, such as variance analysis, often require a different emphasis in service organizations. For example, in the brokerage industry there is an obvious and high correlation between volumes, price movements, and revenues. But as already mentioned, there can be more than a 100 percent difference between a high- and a low-volume day. There can be as much as 65 percent volume variance between successive quarters, as occurred between the final quarter of 1975 and the first quarter of 1976 at the author's firm. Such swings cause havoc with even the most sophisticated flexible budgeting system. Huge volume variances are created which are of relatively little analytic use.

On the other hand, for certain parts of a service firm, variance analyses can be very useful, both on a continuing basis and on a project basis. It is always useful to know the components of change even if the causes of change are not directly controllable. And sometimes, merely the knowing of why what happens happens can be useful in gaining control of areas previously believed to be noncontrollable in the normal sense.

For example, the operations divisions of brokerage firms have often used the huge volume fluctuations as reasons for not applying standard costing and flexible budgeting techniques to their operations. Nevertheless, one firm did install a flexible budgeting and standard costing system in its operations divisions. That system was found to be most beneficial for two reasons. First, the system helped them deal with issues of capacity management and control. Over time, they were able to use actual versus standard and over- and underabsorption of costs as reliable indices for making corrections to processing department manning levels. It also allowed them to develop a better understanding of the learning curves they were experiencing. As a result of knowing its costs from the standard costing system, the firm was able to develop a pricing and marketing strategy for correspondent services, which helped the firm to quickly become one of the largest and most profitable brokers' brokers in the securities industry. Thus, the firm transcended the standard wisdom and used well-known manufacturing cost analysis and control techniques to its benefit.

This feat is unusual in the securities industry, since a piece of industry folklore is that virtually all of the companies in the securities industry which employed formal costing and budgeting systems went out of business. Obviously the two are not cause-and-effect related. Rather, firms with weak underlying economics cannot look to budgeting as a lifesaving remedy, which is like ingesting a placebo to cure an incurable illness.

Thus, faced with any service controllership problem, the controller must be very clear on several issues. One of the most important issues is understanding the underlying economics of the business. Another issue focuses on the definition and identification of the controllable economic dimensions. Further issues concern the required understandings of the competitive and regulatory environment in which the company operates. More issues relate to the internal organization, how decisions are made, and who makes them.

Economic Issues

Experience in the design of decision-oriented planning, budgeting, and control systems has shown that the most critical factor in the success or failure of such systems is that they be *real* to the users. "Real" means that the systems developed accurately reflect the underlying economics of the decision units. Decision units are where revenues are created, because there are third-party arm's-length customers where costs are incurred and/or where capital is committed. Units with all three characteristics are capable of being tracked as investment centers (see Chapter 27). Units which create revenues and incur modest costs in relation to those revenues, that is, branch sales offices, are revenue centers. Units with no customers and which incur costs only are cost (expense) centers.

This last description is a gross oversimplification of responsibility accounting terminology, but it is useful if for only one reason: most managers, even ones who should know better, want to be judged on profits or return on capital. Unless the unit is a true profit or investment center, the only way to "manufacture" the desired profit-center result is through some usually complicated set of revenue transfer and cost and capital allocation methodologies which sometimes obscure more than they reveal. All of which is to say that the author's bias is toward holding managers responsible only for that which they control, and for not trying to make managers look like something they are not.

The ability to measure clearly the quality of executed management decisions is what we are after. Decisions can often be looked at in different ways. For example, many service firms have separate sales and product-management organizations where optimizing the sale of the product in any particular location is the job of a local salesperson, and at the corporate or division level there are complex product/market-management matrices. The controller's task is to be able to measure in quantifiable terms who is doing the best *product* job as well as who is doing the best *place* job.

Likewise, cost decisions are made at different levels and have different effects on the firm. The main cost control issues are to define at what level in the organization what costs are controlled and what the costs should be. This process is often not as simple as it sounds. As an example, branch sales managers will have their location costs charged directly to them, yet the decision to incur those costs was made at an entirely different organizational level. The decision to open a new branch is made at a much higher level and is controlled at a much higher level than the branch manager. The decision to close an office to save branch location costs is not one management could reasonably expect of the branch manager, or perhaps even of the district or regional manager. Sales managers inherently dislike closing offices. As a result, such decisions often must be made at higher organizational levels than would appear necessary. For this reason, it is very important for the controller not only to possess the theory of where decisions should be made but also to know where they are actually made.

Decisions which commit capital are frequently easier in manufacturing companies than in service companies because the capital consequences are more definitive. One such example is the decision to expand productive capacity in the face of increased product demand. These classes of decision making lend themselves to the well-known techniques of capital budgeting analysis (see Chapter 15). On the other hand, service firms of most types do not need much capital. A possible exception is accounts receivable financing as a service firm is growing. However, most highly labor-intensive service firms just do not have much need for the "brick-and-mortar" class of investment.

A good example of an "involuntary" capital investment can occur in the securities industry when the securities markets become both attractive and active at the same time. One thing that happens is that the public becomes more active and opens new margin accounts, while those investors who already have margin accounts increase their balances. The result can be an increase of several hundred million dollars in customer margin accounts, which have a related regulatory capital need. If the regulatory capital need goes up faster than the related product revenues and profits, then the return on capital will decline. This phenomena was actually experienced by the securities industry during 1972 and 1977.

The major distinctions between the assets of service firms and the assets of manufacturing firms is probably found in the predominance of short-term assets on a service firm's balance sheet compared to a manufacturing firm. This difference extends to the equities side of the balance sheet. As a result, service firms of most types do not need much long-term capital, although they may require substantial amounts of short-term borrowings to finance their current assets. On the other hand, most manufacturing companies have substantial amounts of fixed plant and equipment financed through long-term borrowings.

For many service firms, the management of accounts receivable is most important. Obviously, for the service firm to actually earn a profit, it must actually collect its billings. The balance sheets of professional firms frequently show approximately 80 percent of total assets in the form of accounts receivable and unbilled work in process. Clearly the service firm must carefully manage the billing and collection of these amounts. Accounts receivable management in a service firm is quite different from accounts receivable management in a manufacturing firm. In a manufacturing firm, the collectability is hardly ever in question, assuming product delivery and credit worthiness of the buyer. In fact, in a nonservice firm, accounts receivable management is often primarily a credit management function. On the other hand, in a service firm, collectability is frequently more a function of the ability to manage projects against agreed to budgets and the human relationship between the client and the senior service firm representatives. In some instances, such as in a law firm doing highly specialized work, the amount actually billed may not be a function of aggregate time value accrued but of the premium value of the service performed. Managing the quality of the work in process inventory and the ultimate collectability of accounts receivable is one of the primary functions of experienced client-managing service professionals.

One example of poor management of accounts receivables occurred at a law firm where hours billed against client matters were aggregated and extended at appropriate billing rates, but where the billing process itself was determined at a monthly partners' meeting. At that meeting the amounts to be billed appeared more a function of the amounts required to maintain the firm at a consensus-desired level of profitability than of a managed billing and collection process. A study of the firm's earned but unbilled backlog revealed opportunities to collect literally hundreds of thousands of dollars of unbilled fees from major clients. This law firm was being run more like a country store than a serious professional partnership. One of the main reasons for this situation was the reluctance of the partnership tax attorneys to reflect, even on a memo-accounting basis, the earned but unbilled accounts receivable. Their reluctance stemmed from a fear of being taxed on an accrual basis rather than on a cash basis. This fear was not shared by other similar law firms. Yet very conservative tax accounting ended up costing the partnership the ability to manage themselves as well as they represented their clients by obscuring rather than illuminating their fee opportunities.

Backlog Management

Managing the firm's available but unearned backlog is extremely important. Conceptually, the available but unearned backlog may be the most valuable asset of a time-based revenue earning service organization. This asset does not appear on any conventional periodic accounting statement, although it must be reported as part of the firm's financial management and control reports. Adroit management of this asset is critical to achieve targeted profit objectives. Managing this resource is critical because of its relationship to the firm's ability actually to earn and eventually to collect the target revenues.

There is a rule, similar to the rule of three billing rate rule, that is useful in managing the available but unearned backlog. The experience of some service firms has been that in order to keep staff and managers billed at budgeted rates, the available but unearned backlog must be approximately four times the monthly billing budget. An available but unearned backlog of less than the four months' billing budget is frequently a warning that intensive efforts are required to build the backlog. Staff reductions must be seriously considered when the backlog falls below an amount adequate to meet billing budgets.

Obviously, many methodologies can be applied to successfully manage this important asset. Some firms schedule managerial assignments in detail for six months and staff assignments in detail for three months against the available backlog. Then decisions to acquire or release staff are made based on the available backlog of unearned billings in the second and third months.

Partners in consulting firms who are responsible for creating new client relationships and maintaining existing ones frequently find that their own monthly billings have a consistent relationship between new and existing clients which reflects their backlog-building responsibilities. In equilibrium, management consultants should be adding approximately one month's backlog each month, and at least 25 percent of their own billings should come from new clients. Managing the processes of backlog accumulation, fee earning, and collection are the main responsibilities of senior managers and partners in time-based revenue earning service organizations.

Obviously intuitive notions like the billing rate rule of three and the backlog rule of four will be different for different kinds of service organizations. The difference will be a function of many factors such as the kind of service rendered, the mix of new and existing clients, client turnover, the average length of client projects, and other factors unique to the economics of the specific services rendered. Among the service controller's tasks are defining the rules relevant to his or her own organization and using them to improve the quality of the staffing decisions made.

Controllership Methodologies

The controller's job is to communicate the economic consequences of executive decisions. There can be no reasons, only invalid excuses, for controllers not fully understanding the interplay of economics and management decisions in the firm or division of which they are the controller. In some sense controllers are a collection of solutions looking for problems to solve. Controllers, perhaps especially in a service organization, have at their command an army of controllership methodologies whose usefulness varies as the environments facing their firms varies.

Other chapters in this book cover in great detail those controllership methodologies most relevant to other than service organizations. This section will attempt to focus on those management science techniques most relevant to service organizations. The section will avoid detailed discussion of well-known techniques such as budgeting, variance analysis, and capital budgeting.

A technique of great usefulness in service organizations is program planning. This technique traces its lineage (or at least its title) to the Defense Department in the 1960s, and was ordered imposed within the civilian agencies in 1968 by President Johnson. Despite its hawkish lineage, it is a valid concept. The concept tried to identify the costs and benefits of government programs such that choices could be made among programs competing for limited resources based upon the excess of benefit over cost. The problem in government was the inability to measure the benefit of social programs. In business this shortcoming can often be overcome by using lucre as the measure of benefit.

The power of the concept lies in looking at the incurrence of costs in relation to the achievement of identifiable results. A specific example is the pricing of available management and staff time and related expenses against measurable achievement such as promotional objectives, that is, attracting new clients. Research and development management also is, in a stretched sense, a service activity, often discretionary in direction and amount, that lends itself to the program planning conceptual framework. Benefit measures are applied to project budgets in a manner which allows systematic analyses and trade-offs.

Questions asked or challenges made are of the nature of "What revenue streams can be/have been achieved as a result of the Franistran research/promotion effort?" Or, "Last year we spent $X million on travel and entertainment expense. Of that, 20 percent was spent on prospecting for new clients and only 20 percent was spent on developing existing clients; the remaining 60 percent was spent on firm meetings. I [the president or division sales manager] want that changed. What will be the impact of spending the same amount, but reallocating the total amount between existing and new clients? What is the optimal way of programming this expenditure?"

All of this might sound like old wine in cracked bottles, yet the power of the program performance idea for nonfinancially oriented managers is very powerful. Also the benefit measure does not always have to be lucre, which means that service organizations within larger companies can use this technique. Nonmonetary performance measures can be set to measure the benefits performance of staff organizations. The program planning literature itself offers many examples of such benefit measurement.

A later, yet similar, concept discussed elsewhere in this handbook (Chapter 24) is zero-base budgeting. The concept here is extremely powerful, being based on that most essential of all questions, "Do we have to do that?" The concept has great power because it is so basic and simple. It is so powerful as to be unavoidable in the sense that ZBB is what good managers have been doing for years; in many ways, ZBB's jargon articulates and structures the obvious. The concept is so good that, when well implemented, it is hard to imagine an instance where the effort's cost would not be repaid in rich multiples.

The concept raises budgeting to the level of that old advertising homily, "Do you know a company that doesn't need to advertise?" Once a seasoned advertising agency head replayed that back as "Do you know a company that doesn't need to plan?" Today the question has got to be rephrased as, "Do you know a company that can't benefit from zero-base budgeting thinking?" The answer has got to be a resounding "No." ZBB is the most promising aggregation of available budgeting techniques to come along in years for controllers and managers. It is a kind of EST for controllers; that is, it beneficially challenges the status quo—and it is easy.

Modeling is another controllership method which holds great promise. The trick with modeling is not to fall victim to the temptation to oversophisticate the effort. Modeling literature includes the following as the most important characteristics of models:

1. Simplicity—understandable to users.
2. Adaptability—to changed environmental assumptions.
3. Complete—on all important issues.
4. Credibility—incapable of producing nonsensical answers.

A model formulated along these dimensions tends to minimize the model's risks. Model risk can come in several forms, including excessive cost and lack of credibility.

Possibly the most crucial characteristic is that the model be real to the users. Being "real," in this instance, means understandable and acceptable to managers, whose decisions can be improved as a result of using the model for that class of decisions for which models are helpful. Those classes of decisions include assisting the formulation of responses to various "what if?" scenarios. Such scenarios are encountered in forecasting long-term capital requirements, forecasting the impact of changes in product mix and volume on profitability, new-product cost and profitability studies, and the myraid of other uses for corporate modeling.

Financial models can be most useful in the sensitivity analyses of the critical controllable and noncontrollable elements in a business plan. There are many fine books and consulting practitioners of the modeling art available as resources to controllers with an urge to model.

However, before one succumbs to that urge, a few words of caution are in order. Most modelers tend to be primarily operations researchers, mathematicians, or econometricians. They tend not to be burdened with great knowledge of how mundane debits and credits flow through a firm, especially a specific firm, and as a result, some tend to model pieces rather than closed systems. The point here is that allegiance to the beautiful symmetry of the accounting equation can be a most powerful tool in validating models. The author's experience is that most successful model applications for executive decision making are kept within the boundaries of the simplistic discipline of double-entry trial balances.

CONCLUSION

Many of the materials presented in this chapter are based on a philosophy of the role of controllership in a firm of whatever type. That philosophy is in turn based on conclusions regarding what differentiates great performing firms from mediocre ones. Neither a great controller alone nor the application of contemporary management science alone can create a great performing firm. Rather, great performance seems more a function of a combination of competences in management.

These competences are human, organizational, and functional. It takes great human competence to attract, motivate, and retain really good people, as we all know. Assembling competent people and melding them into a competent organization may well be the most important executive function. Therefore, organizational skills are the second but equally important competence.

Next in importance come the functional skills such as finance, production, marketing, and administration, and all their offshoots including controllership. Fortunately, functional skills can be purchased. There are growing numbers of skilled practitioners of these functions as evidenced by the growing numbers of masters degrees in business being awarded.

These graduates are often packages of functional and management science solutions looking for problems to solve. Many are armed with very high-level computer and quantitative skills. Some of the business schools glorify these quantitative and computer skills to the point where it appears that business school faculties are competing with the pure sciences such as mathematics and physics for contributions to basic knowledge.

Somehow a point is being missed in all this. That point deals with the primacy of leadership as the key executive competence. Superior executive leadership means attracting, motivating, and retaining superior people. Executive leadership also means providing direction, demanding standards, and infusing the organization with an appropriate sense of urgency. The effective executive (including the controller) must be competent in human and organizational skills. Obviously good controllers require these same skills in order to create control organizations capable of changing behavior in a firm.

Another way to look at the controllership opportunity is in relation to the three-legged stool analogy. One leg is the *objectives/ strategy* leg, or the business policy leg. There questions such as "What are we trying to do?" (objectives) and "What do we have to do in time-phased detail to reach our objectives?" (strategies) are addressed. Another leg is the *organizational* leg. There the questions are "What kinds of skills and in what quantities and in what arrays (organizations) are required to achieve the strategies within the time desired?" The third leg is the *information and reward/ punishment* leg. That leg's questions center around: "What do you need to know to determine whether or not the organization is doing what it must do in order to achieve its goals?"

Obviously, this third leg is the controllership function. When controllers look at the world in this way, they are functioning as what was earlier termed behaviorally oriented controllers. Looked at another way, the business policy organization and information legs are interconnected. Information is the integrating factor between the policy and organization legs. The controller is the integrator. For the author, being a constructive integrator is the most rewarding aspect of controllership. Effective integration can cause constructive change in the direction and organization of a firm such that over time, executives are helped and can make more-informed decisions.

ADDITIONAL SOURCES

American Institute of Architects. *Financial Management for Architectural Firms*. Washington, D.C., January 1970.

Anthony, Robert N., and Dearden, John. *Management Control Systems: Text and Cases*, chaps. 14, 15. 3d ed. Homewood, Ill.: Richard D. Irwin, Inc., 1976.

———, and Herzlinger, Regina. *Management Control in Nonprofit Organizations*. Homewood, Ill.: Richard D. Irwin, Inc., 1975.

Jones, Reginald L., and Trentin, H. George. *Management Controls for Professional Firms*. New York: American Management Association, 1968.

Levitt, Theodore. "The Industrialization of Service." *Harvard Business Review*, September–October 1976, p. 63.

———. "Production-Line Approach to Service." *Harvard Business Review*, September–October 1972, p. 41.

McDonald, Howard E., and Stromberger, T. L. "Cost Control for the Professional Service Firm." *Harvard Business Review*, January–February 1969, p. 109.

Sasser, W. Earl. "Match Supply and Demand in Service Industries." *Harvard Business Review*, November–December 1977, p. 133.

Sibson, Robert E. *Managing Professional Services Enterprises.* New York: Pitman Publishing Corp., 1971.

Wilson, Aubrey. *The Marketing of Professional Services.* London: McGraw-Hill, 1972.

Wittreich, Warren J. "How to Buy/Sell Professional Services." *Harvard Business Review,* March–April 1966, p. 127.

46

Planning and Control in International Operations

George M. Scott*

Planning and control in international companies differ significantly in several respects from these same activities in domestic companies, and planning and control systems must be designed to cope with a variety of conditions that are unique to or exacerbated by international operations. This chapter examines the nature of the planning and control systems and processes of companies with manufacturing and distribution activities in foreign countries. These systems must enable companies to achieve efficiency in the dynamically changing international environment, to grapple with restrictions which are different in every country, to capitalize on advantages inherent in these differences between countries and to gain the economies of scale of an international marketplace.

THE INTERNATIONAL ENVIRONMENT

Of paramount importance to the planning and control of international companies are the complexities of the international environment, complexities that are individually niggling, but which can combine to present major obstacles to planning and control. The major factors affecting complexity of the international environment are communications differences, cultural differences, environ-

* Dr. Scott is Professor of Accounting at the College of Business Administration of The University of Oklahoma, Norman.

mental changes, differing price levels, and the diversity of economic, political, and business operating conditions encountered.

Communications Differences

Communications become immensely more complicated and time-consuming in international operations. Planning and control involve extensive face-to-face interaction and written communication, and the lack of a common language throughout the corporate system can reduce the effectiveness of these activities. The need to translate company documents from multiple languages also inevitably takes its toll. The language aspect of communications was thought to be so important that Philips Lamp (a Netherlands-based company with operations in about 120 countries) has adopted English as the official company language for management purposes in all of its countries of operations.

Communications in international operations are also complicated by greater distances and commensurately greater travel and message transmission costs, the existence of national boundaries which can reduce communications capability, and the existence of different technical characteristics of communications systems in each country. Differing levels of expertise in various areas of the world among computer and other information systems and communications technicians can also have an impact.

Cultural Differences

Cultural factors also affect control activities. Managers in most international companies are in agreement that if qualified local managers are available they should be preferred to expatriates. Nevertheless, managers from different cultures have culture-related attributes which reduce the effectiveness of planning and control processes. As examples, they may have a fundamental antipathy to the concept of control, believing it to be an unjust and demeaning infringement on private prerogatives; they may have different concepts of time as it relates to the importance of budget preparation deadlines; they may have different conceptions of the role of planning meetings, perhaps viewing them as trivial or, at the other extreme, very important for social rather than management purposes; they may have too little empathy for cultures other than their own, which can affect their relations with associates in other countries; they may have different attitudes toward collaborative efforts, preferring to undertake independent action; and they may have high resistance to change, which is especially critical in international companies because of the constant flux in the international environment.

Environmental Changes

Change and diversity can be found within an individual country's environment, but within one country the environment tends to be relatively constant and to change slowly. The combination of operations in several countries and the need to conduct operations between and among countries serves to amplify greatly the environmental diversity and its effects on planning and control. For international operations, the total environment is more difficult to define, more turbulent. In international operations the environmental constraints are not homogeneous between countries and even cease to be constants—they must be treated as variables which affect the choice of planning and control methods and approaches.

The individual country environments are different at a point in time and also change relative to one another through time, providing a dynamic element to international operations that is not found in domestic operations. Further, environments not only change relative to one another but also change at different rates of speed. The result is greater dynamism of the total environment of international companies; controls and plans implemented today may be appropriate now but obsolete tomorrow, next week, or next month when the environments have changed relative to each other.

Differing Price Levels

For planning and control, one of the most difficult aspects of this environmental change and diversity to deal with is the problem of inflation. Inevitably, inflation impinges on the management, control, and coordination processes in multinational enterprises; not only does inflation affect the *ability* to control and coordinate but it also affects the *need* for these activities. A high rate of local inflation means that local managers are preoccupied with the continuous necessity to find new sources of working capital, with protecting the values of local monetary assets, with frequent re-assessments of product prices, and with the necessity continuously to reevaluate product-line composition as inflation causes structural changes in the various economies. With this onerous burden, managers are inclined to slight normal managerial chores during periods of high local inflation, such as those of maintaining production and distribution efficiency and controlling and coordinating routine operations.

Nevertheless, it is precisely during periods of inflation that global coordination is most needed. Inflationary conditions in local countries mean that local operations can benefit greatly from assistance from headquarters and from subsidiaries in other countries. Tight coordination of the operations in an inflationary environment with operations in other parts of the network can provide sources of inexpensive working capital and can even reduce the amount of working capital required. Coordination with other components of the system can also help to protect inflation-endangered local resources and provide less-expensive sources for raw materials as local prices rise.

Significant inflation is not a phenomenon to be reckoned with in just one country of the multinational enterprise's system—it occurs in several or even most countries simultaneously. This multi-country inflation greatly complicates the coordination processs necessary for coping with inflation itself as well as for coordination of other activities. Most notably, differential rates of inflation mean that real costs of production and other factors change dynamically relative to one another so that a global system must be continuously cost balanced, resulting in the shifting of production and other resources among countries as relative costs change.

Diversity of Conditions

The diversity of the economic, political, and business operating conditions in multiple countries also contributes substantially to the complexity of international operations. Legal and tax systems, business customs and practices, types of government and governmental regulation, and a variety of other matters are quite different among countries and serve to take their toll on the ability to control local operations. To maintain control and to plan coherently in the face of such environmental dynamics, controllers—both at headquarters and locally—must understand the fundamental structure of each of their company's multiple environments and must be aware of the forces which bring about environmental changes as well as be attuned to the changes themselves. Additionally, the international company's management processes must be carefully structured so that flexibility of management and ability to adapt rapidly to change are incorporated into these processes; this means that planning and control functions also must adapt continuously as the directions of the company change.

THE MHC AND THE ME

Two general types of companies are found in international operations, the "multinational holding company" (MHC) and the "multinational enterprise" (ME).[1] Their differences are matters of degree and center on differences in modes of operations, which in turn necessitate divergences in the nature of their planning, control, and evaluation systems.

Characteristics of an MHC

The MHC style of operations permits a fair degree of local autonomy of operations in each host country. Each MHC subsidiary is likely to manufacture and sell in the local country many or most of the products manufactured and sold by the parent in the parent's country. As a consequence, there is little exchange of products among the various countries—local manufacture is intended primarily as a substitute for importing products from the parent. With little product exchange, financial flows between countries are also not likely to be great. Generally these will consist primarily of payments to the parent of dividends, interest, and royalties and an occasional loan to the foreign subsidiary.

Since operations are not very interactive between countries, managerial autonomy is more easily granted and each subsidiary is expected to maximize its own return on its own resources as a profit or investment center (although even for the MHC the international environments impose grave difficulties on ability to properly meas-

---

[1] The distinctions made here between these types of enterprises are made in much the same way by most authors; however, some use "international company" to represent what is here called an MHC, and many refer to the ME as a "multinational corporation" (MNC).

ure this return, as will be discussed at a later point). The parent company may promulgate policies and directives to its foreign subsidiaries, but these generally pertain to standardization of quality, customer relations, and similar matters rather than to management methods. Sears, Roebuck and Company appears to be a typical example of an MHC, although assuredly not a pure case.

Characteristics of an ME

An ME has a distinctly different and more complex mode of operations that may be characterized as "global coordination." This mode requires that a substantially different set of measurements be utilized for planning, control, and evaluation, as will be shown. The ME attempts to manage all operations together to optimize *global* returns. To achieve this the operations in all countries are integrated vertically and horizontally and coordinated on a worldwide basis to the extent that this is possible within the constraints imposed by national governments' policies and the limitations of managerial and information systems technology.[2]

This integration and coordination of the subsidiaries of the ME means that the autonomy of local subsidiaries must be severely constrained. However, the system cannot be managed in a centralized fashion, since headquarters managers do not have detailed knowledge of local conditions and cannot be continuously aware of changes in these conditions. Attempts to achieve flexibility and adaptability via centralized management are doomed to failure since it is the subsidiary managers who have the knowledge of the local conditions to which the ME must adapt.

On the other side, local managers are not in a position to assess the big picture or to evaluate their country's conditions vis-a-vis those of other localities in order to determine what decisions will be in the best interest of the entire system. Thus a decentralized form of management also cannot function effectively because it does not provide the required system-wide cohesion and adaptability in response to environmental changes.

It can be seen that headquarter managers and local managers

---

[2] Counter trends can be identified in some of these countries: national governments are imposing more restrictions on ME operations, which makes global coordination more difficult; but at the same time, MEs are developing the previously rudimentary managerial expertise, techniques, and information systems needed to integrate and coordinate still more comprehensively.

each have vital elements of the managerial information and expertise necessary to conduct operations in a coordinated, adaptive fashion. The management process must be structured so that the vital ingredients provided by each group are pooled and integrated in a fashion which allows the ME to manage all operations together and adapt these operations rapidly. The result is neither centralization nor decentralization—it is a form of coordinated management. This means that not only are the operations of an ME integrated but so too is its management. This integration of management tends to facilitate good planning processes but often serves to frustrate the purposes of traditional control systems, which tend to be structured to hold one manager (rather than two or more) responsible for one management activity.

To illustrate this global integration of operations and management, raw material may be purchased or extracted by a subsidiary in the least-cost world location and shipped to a subsidiary in the country with the lowest cost of fabrication for the particular component; the component might then be shipped to a subsidiary in the world location with the lowest cost of assembly, and finally the finished product is shipped to the most promising markets of the world. As costs and market conditions change throughout the system the ME attempts to adapt by restructuring itself to take advantage of the new lowest-cost raw materials sources and production centers. Similarly, the financing function may seek the lowest cost capital in the world, lend excesses in the market of best return, and construct a cash management system which optimizes global cash flows via concentration accounts in countries without currency restrictions, as well as by other techniques.

In the above scenario the local managers must constantly keep tabs on local costs, local markets, and local political and economic developments and apprise headquarter managers of these changed conditions to facilitate making the decisions which effect the adaptive restructuring. It is not just facts that local managers communicate to headquarters; they also have the considerable responsibility of formulating and communicating "the feel for the situation." This involves a good bit of "uncertainty absorption" in their formulation of judgments, that is, they must synthesize the facts and communicate their opinions rather than communicate the facts in detail.[3] A

[3] The phenomenon of uncertainty absorption is treated in James G. March and Herbert A. Simon, *Organizations* (New York: John Wiley & Sons, Inc., 1958).

great deal of corporate inculation, teamwork and mutual reliance, and joint decision making is required to make this system effective. It is in the sense of this paragraph that the managements of MEs are integrated.

Transportation, border and conversion costs, national restrictions imposed on international operations, regional trade agreements, and other considerations serve to limit the extent to which global coordination is possible for MEs, so that it becomes a partial approach or is regional in nature. For example, transportation costs may dictate that a product can be marketed economically in a region encompassing only several countries. Accordingly the product might also be produced in other regions. Other variations, such as allocation to a region of global responsibility for a particular product line, are also found.

Combinations of MHC and ME Attributes

MHCs and MEs have thus far been portrayed in their extreme and mutually exclusive forms. In fact, however, few companies can be classified as either a pure MHC or a pure ME; a particular company may have any combination of the attributes of both. For example, many companies coordinate their financial function on a global basis in much the manner of an ME, but conduct their materials sourcing, manufacturing, and distribution activities as does an MHC. Such companies are likely to integrate their cash borrowing/lending functions and their currency forecasting, exchange risk, exposure determination, and currency hedging activities, but grant more autonomy to local managers for production, marketing, and local financial functions.

It is exceedingly difficult to say with precision that a particular company is or is not now an ME; this can only be determined by an evaluation of many considerations. Further, multinationalism is a matter of degree. If a subjective assessment were made as to the extent of integration and coordination of companies, they could be arrayed along a spectrum as in Exhibit 1. Perhaps 20 to 40 well-known American companies, including Exxon, IBM, ITT, Mobil Oil, and W. R. Grace, to name a few, as well as perhaps a dozen European companies, such as Philips Lamp, Nestle, Shell, and Unilever, could be identified as being clustered well along toward multinationalism at about point 1. Several hundred others in the United States could be placed between the midpoint (*M*) and point 1; as the top-level managers of these companies perceive the benefits of coordination, and as the managerial and information systems required for coordination are gradually developed, the autonomy of their foreign subsidiaries is eroded and replaced by an ME mode of operations. Several hundred large- and middle-size companies are probably currently in this state of transition. A company's form of organization, the nature of its products, its managerial traditions, and the relative power status of the largest subsidiaries vis-a-vis the parent are all variables important in determining the rapidity and extent to which a company evolves toward the status of an ME.

EXHIBIT 1
Spectrum of Multinationalism

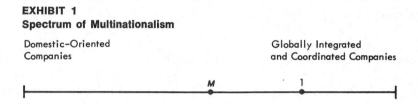

Domestic–Oriented
Companies

Globally Integrated
and Coordinated Companies

For a few companies the evolution is planned. For most, it is a natural result of adapting to their environment in an *ad hoc,* hit-or-miss, error-prone fashion. The companies with planned evolutions and a fortunate few of the companies evolving in an *ad hoc* fashion will quickly become MEs; for the remainder, the process will be slow and the outcome uncertain.

Not only is multinationalism a matter of degree among companies, it is also a matter of degree within a company. Different functions, divisions, and product lines, and even individual managers within each of these, have the spirit of multinationalism to differing extents or may even be oblivious to multinationalism. To a great extent, the degree of sympathy for multinationalism is a function of the degree and type of organizational differentiation influencing managers' perspectives. It is not uncommon for the treasurer's function at the headquarters of many companies to have a global focus but for other functions to remain parochial; in many of these same companies even the treasurers in the overseas operations "think local" and so intentionally or inadvertently obstruct the headquarters' financial coordination efforts. To move all functional areas within a company toward multinationalism in a systematic and balanced fashion is a major challenge of planning for multinationalism and is itself a program that must be globally coordinated.

The final section of this chapter outlines a program for development of planning and control systems for companies just entering international operations as well as for those with foreign operations that are evolving toward greater integration and coordination. With foreign multinational companies rapidly closing the technological gaps and becoming much more competitive with U.S. companies in the international marketplace, it appears that the U.S. picnic in foreign operations is over, and that the major competitive advantage in the future, if one will exist, will repose in the superior management, control, and coordination processes that are now under development in U.S. multinationals.[4]

Coordination in Multinational Enterprises

Coordinated operations emerged gradually in international operations as companies began to perceive that by careful management of international complexity, the differences among the country environments could be turned to advantage. The potential benefits of extensive coordination are greater internationally than domestically because of these greater differences in environments—for example, the differences in labor costs among foreign countries are many orders of magnitude greater than the differences within the United States. As companies gradually learn to manage the complexity, these perceived benefits from coordination begin to be realized, which encourages still more integration and coordination.

How are the operations of MEs coordinated? One's first inclination may be to say, "Surely they must be centrally coordinated." However the answer is not so simple; indeed, it is exceedingly complex.

As is suggested by the regionalism already mentioned, some aspects of operations are coordinated at regional centers with only loose coordination (perhaps as a part of long-range planning)

---

[4] The development of these planning, control, and coordination systems is a major theme in the author's forthcoming book, *Management, Control, and Coordination of Multinational Enterprises*. The role of these systems in providing a competitive advantage to U.S. companies also will be explored in this book, which also will deal in detail with most of the topics presented in this chapter.

among the regional centers. It is also necessary to distinguish direct coordination by global or regional centers from indirect coordination and from horizontal coordination. With the direct variety, the central decision makers are actually making the decisions such as "ship 50 units of Product A from our Country X subsidiary to our Country Z subsidiary." In the more complex situations of the larger MEs, the sheer numbers of such decisions which must be made result in overload of the headquarters managers and of the communications channels which provide the information for the decisions. Therefore indirect coordination is often resorted to, at least until more efficient information systems can be developed.

Indirect coordination consists of policy guidelines issued by headquarters which direct that, for example, "whenever inventory of Product A in Country X reaches a level of 100 units, all additional output is to be shipped to Country Y or Z, whichever has the lower quantity on hand." Such guidelines can be provided in a great many areas of operations; these guidelines are then adhered to by the country managers. In this fashion, headquarters is relieved from making large numbers of operating-level decisions, but has assumed two additional functions: headquarters must now monitor and control key activities (usually via periodic reports) to ensure that guidelines are being adhered to; and in the dynamic international arena, headquarters must also frequently and systematically evaluate the continuing suitability of its own guidelines.

Horizontal coordination is the direct coordination of flows between two or more host-country subsidiaries by managers within these subsidiaries. Recalling that the MHC has fewer interactions among host-country subsidiaries than does the ME, there is correspondingly little need for horizontal coordination in MHCs. In MEs, however, the interactions are extensive and involve, as examples, coordination of production schedules and of intercompany product shipments. Many of these interactions are at the operations level rather than at the level of upper management, and information timeliness tends to be measured in hours and days rather than weeks and months. To coordinate by sending information up one chain of command and down another would be too time-consuming and would further clutter these already busy channels. Hence, a system of measures and managerial reports which constitutes a lateral information network among the various country subsidiaries is necessary. International variables introduce complexities into lateral information systems which would not be encountered in similar systems among subsidiaries in the same country.

Budgeting and long-range planning systems are integral components of coordination. Other ingredients include specific managerial techniques applied to specific coordination problems (such as computer simulation used for global cash management) and management policies which serve as general guidelines for managerial action in complex situations.

Much of the coordination technology required by MEs is yet to be developed. It seems reasonable to expect that the effects of coordination systems that are designed especially for MEs will be to reduce the costs of coordination and increase the benefits of coordination, increasingly so as a function of the managerial learning curve.

With the preceding as background, it is not difficult to see that the measurement, planning, control, and reporting systems involved in the highly coordinated operations of the ME are both different from, and more complex than, those of the MHC. The former must (1) measure and integrate costs and revenues from many locations into a framework which facilitates evaluation of the trade-offs involved in determining the location of the various aspects of operations; (2) provide the information to support extensive coordination and planning (although less information is needed centrally for coordination than for direct control by management); (3) provide feedback by control systems about the effectiveness of coordination; and (4) measure results for performance evaluation purposes. At present these systems are successful to a degree in MEs even though they are still considerably less than fully developed in most MEs. Certainly, the results already achieved in MEs should provide the incentive for other companies to adopt more coordination.

The Nature of Control Systems in MEs

As a consequence of the complexity of the international environments and the differences in goals between those of local subsidiaries and those of headquarters that are often present, the demands placed upon the control system in MHCs are severe. Because of the additional consideration in MEs of their utilizing extensive coordination, the demands placed on their control systems are much greater. Controllers who design and implement the planning and control systems must understand the nature of the business, the nature of and differences among the foreign environments, and the management strategies being pursued, if they are to establish a set of controls and financial reports which motivate and guide the managers of foreign subsidiaries˙ and fairly measure their performance.

Control System Elements. For purposes here, the control system of an international company is considered to be composed of the accounting system generally; the budgeting/profit planning and long-range planning systems; the forecasting systems; the reporting systems; the policies, guidelines, and other rules and understandings that influence managers' conduct; the mechanisms utilized to gain manager commitments to the company's goals; and the various management and performance evaluation processes. Collectively, these elements provide unified direction, coordination, and feedback which enables a company to utilize its resources efficiently in the pursuit of its goals within the guidelines established during the planning processes. While the control system relates to all corporate functions, attention here will be concentrated on financial control.

The control system elements interact extensively so that, for example, it is difficult to pinpoint where profit planning leaves off and performance evaluation begins. While the control system of an international company is not unlike that of a domestic company with respect to the attribute of articulation of its elements, the systems of the international company must possess some special characteristics. Indeed, the company that simply utilizes its domestic control systems abroad, as many U.S. companies have been wont to do, will experience grave control problems in its international systems, and will find itself unable to operate as a coordinated ME.[5]

System Requisities. Because of the dynamics of the international environments, prime requisites of control systems in international operations are *flexibility* and *adaptability.* Two of the most commonly encountered types of control systems must be avoided if flexibility and adaptability are to be maintained as a company's foreign operations increase in size. These are direct centralized control, and the system of control based on guidelines promulgated by headquarters.

---

[5] David Hawkins elaborates on the difficulties caused by using abroad the control systems designed for domestic U.S. operations: "Controlling Foreign Operations," *Financial Executive,* February 1965.

When companies initially undertake foreign operations, headquarters executives are not fully conversant with the special problems or the unique opportunities of foreign operations and do not realize that the financial control function of these operations requires special attention. Typically control is exercised by a very small staff supervised by one executive for whom international operations is but a small part of his or her duties.[6] Foreign subsidiaries are left to manage themselves, and no coordination is attempted. But as the benefits which accrue to coordination become increasing apparent (often as companies' foreign operations become more significant and advantages of scale can accrue), companies tended to "overcontrol" by gradually pulling financial and other functions into headquarters and attempting centrally to direct those local activities which provide payoffs to coordination. As the scope of centralized control expands and as the size and number of foreign subsidiaries increase, the sheer weight of the thousands of daily decisions that must be made at headquarters begins to take its toll. Communications channels become clogged, crucial decisions are delayed, and the company pays a high price for not utilizing the local managers' intimate knowledge of local conditions. The inflexibility of this centralized control has a paralyzing effect on the entire corporate network, and the control system is itself out of control.

Alternatively, or as a corrective restructuring of the preceding condition, many international companies that recognize the need for tight control and coordination based on the broader orientation and financial experience of headquarters financial specialists have implemented a type of indirect control. This indirect control is based on policy guidelines and other forms of rules which determine reporting procedures, permissible financing means and mechanisms, procedures for intercompany transactions, and a host of other matters. Local managers are delegated discretionary authority, but only with respect to certain activities and within the limited range permitted by the guidelines. Headquarters managers directly call the tune on the major decisions of local subsidiaries.

This type of control system is awkward, unwieldly, and bureau-

---

[6] A Conference Board study found in 1970 that of about 300 industrial companies with international operations, few had a separate international financial executive. National Industrial Conference Board, *Managing the International Financial Function* (New York, 1970).

cratic. As with most bureaucracies, the control system stifles initiative, reduces personal commitment, and dramatically reduces the response time of the company to changed conditions that were not anticipated by the rulemakers. While the headquarters staff attempts to take local differences into account in formulations of the rules, this is difficult to do except by adjusting the guidelines as conditions change. The consequence is that headquarters staff members are continuously revising the guidelines, but with a time lag, so that often a suitable new rule does not appear until conditions have changed again.

MEs have now begun to develop a control approach that consists of a symbiotic merging of the talents of headquarters and local managers in a way that permits control systems to be flexible and responsive to changed conditions. This approach involves the extensive interaction of headquarters and local managers to effect a joint managing and controlling of operations. The mechanisms for achieving this are varied and include frequent headquarters observation or performance-review visits to foreign operations, frequent visits and temporary assignments of foreign managers to U.S. headquarters, and frequent planning, control, and performance-evaluation meetings. Of these, it is the meetings which are likely to be by far the most important, and they may take place for several days each month.[7]

The result is a form of international participative management, which might be called "coordinative management." Embodied in this style of management is a substantial element of control. Partly this is derived from the recognition accorded local managers as team members, which enhances their morale and commitment; and partly it stems from a form of corporate inculcation which enables local managers to act independently but in ways which they know will be acceptable to headquarters. Increasingly, this local-headquarters collaboration appears to be resulting in a formal matrix organization or joint assignment of responsibilities in some areas.

---

[7] ITT appears to be a pioneer in this interactive management, holding meetings of its senior managers around the world for several days each month. See, for example, "How ITT Manages Itself by Meetings," *International Management,* February 1970. The description of the elaborate performance review system for overseas operations utilized by 3M Company serves as one example of extensive interaction between headquarter and local managers; John J. Mauriel, "Evaluation and Control of Overseas Operations," *Management Accounting,* May 1969 (Appendix).

BUDGETING (PROFIT PLANNING) IN
FOREIGN OPERATIONS

In most major companies, budgeting has long been accepted as a management tool for planning, control, and evaluation. The budget provides a forecast of expected results, and a comparison of actual results to the plan produces variances useful for control and evaluation purposes. Budgeting is often integrated with the management process so that budgeting is transformed into a dynamic goal-setting and comprehensive planning process which is often termed "profit planning."

In international operations certain aspects of profit planning are more difficult. Important behavioral considerations lurk behind the budgeted figures, and so local customs, mores, and social norms affect the profit planning process as well as its impact on productivity. Further, when budgeting is initially introduced in foreign operations, local personnel may not be acquainted with budgeting concepts, which will make acceptance and implementation of budgeting systems a difficult and slow process. Finally, local reporting regulations can render transnational profit-plan standardization possible only at the cost of duplication of reporting systems.

However, profit planning is even more important in international operations than in domestic operations. One reason is that the planning process gives managers the opportunity to state how well they think they should do and so provides performance standards; these standards (if properly determined) are all the more important in the international environment where top management is not so familiar with the level of performance that can be achieved and with what the standards should be. A related reason is that the relative ignorance of headquarters about local conditions means that company-wide planning must rely to a greater extent on budget preparation in the local country subsidiaries, since this is a major tool facilitating corporate planning. Also, since (as will be shown) profit centers have less utility in international operations, control and performance evaluation by headquarters must be on other bases. One of the most important of these bases is detailed analysis of the budget variances which are controllable at the host-country level.

As previously noted, communications is one of the most difficult problems because of language and cultural differences. Goal conflicts also present problems in international operations. Profit plans are important in assisting with both of these problems. Company objectives must be explicitly considered by participating personnel in construction of profit plans, and must be approved by each next higher level of management and ultimately by top management. Profit plans thus serve admirably well for communication of the system's goals, policies, and strategies to each local subsidiary to guide local managers in goal setting and plan development; in turn these plans are an excellent vehicle for communication of intentions, commitments, and detailed strategies back to headquarters. This form of communication provides a degree of assurance, higher than that provided in most other ways, that everyone at headquarters and local subsidiaries is fully informed about expectations. Each party, by agreeing to the plan, is in essence saying, "We understand each other."

The profit plan is thus a mechanism which is almost unequivocal in its clarity, is entirely systematic in establishing communications, and automatically provides a basis—as well as topics (variances from plan)—for future dialogues that can be invaluable in keeping the communications lines open between managers from different cultures who speak different languages.

MHC-ME Profit Planning Differences

Profit planning is significantly different for MEs from profit planning for MHCs in three important respects. First, the coordination efforts of MEs require that a large quantity of detailed information be forwarded to and utilized by the coordination centers on a continuous basis, whereas the budget detail for a MHC subsidiary is likely to be used only by the local managers to control local operations. Local variances which in a MHC might have only been used locally, or might have been forwarded only quarterly or annually to headquarters, may have significance in an ME for system-wide coordination on a weekly or monthly basis. As examples, a variance in a production schedule plan can affect product supply elsewhere on the globe, and increased costs over the plan may indicate that materials sources in another country should be tapped or that the component can now be manufactured more cheaply in another country.

Second, profit plans (as well as long-range plans) are a primary tool to effect coordination of the global (ME) system. Careful attention must be given during plan preparation to the range of possible physical and financial flows among subsidiaries as well as between subsidiaries and headquarters so that these interrelationships can be incorporated into the plans on which subsequent actions are based. In MHCs these potential interactions are largely ignored.

Finally, profit plans may require frequent revision in MEs. In the integrated ME, adaptations to a change in the environment of one country are likely to elicit new strategies in several countries rather than only in that country. Thus, the profit plans of several countries become obsolete and require either revision or replacement. Especially valuable in these circumstances are computerized budgets that are structured so that the affected variables can be quickly altered and new plans can be quickly generated.

The planning processes (including long-range planning) provide a fringe benefit. Planning is a part of a greater process which inculcates managers with the common norms, philosophies, approaches, and expectations which enable them to work together more efficiently in a coordinated system. Thus planning contributes substantially to development of a company-wide "style of management," or, in the case of MEs, to development of coordinative management.

LONG-RANGE PLANNING IN
INTERNATIONAL OPERATIONS

Formal long-range planning systems are a fairly recent phenomenon even in the most managerially advanced companies; it has been only in the last decade that most of the concepts and procedures have been developed. Growing out of increasing commitments to planning generally, and an increasing awareness that management can effectively guide a company toward specific goals three, five, or even ten years hence even in the face of dynamic environments, the movement toward long-range planning represents one facet of an evolution toward management by planning at the top levels of major companies. Effective long-range planning systems are dovetailed with budgeting systems so that, as examples, no goal conflicts exist between them, and information from the budget is available when it is a necessary input to the long-range plan and vice versa. This means that senior managers devote much or most of their time to the planning processes, and planning thus becomes their management mode; that is, they manage by planning. This further enhances the importance of profit plans, since they become linchpins for long-term plans.

MHC-ME Planning Differences

The focus of long-range planning differs between MHCs and MEs. In MHCs, a significant proportion of long-range planning is likely to take place at the host-country level, since local entities enjoy a fair degree of autonomy of operations. Thus, planning for product introduction, capital investment, product mix, product prices, product diversification strategy, and market penetration may be done locally. The corporate long-range plan tends to be an aggregation of these individual local plans, although local entity wishes typically will be acquiesced to only within a range.

Long-range planning in the ME places emphasis on what the entire global network should look like at the end of the planning horizon, and the long-range planning necessary to maneuver the entire company into the desired global markets, product lines, and position vis-a-vis competition is likely to be spearheaded by the headquarters staff. Capital budgeting is viewed as a subprocess of long-range planning, and capital allocations are controlled centrally to provide the future production and distribution capacity in the locations thought to best serve the global markets selected in the long-range plan. Additionally, headquarters in MEs intends that this capacity be provided in a flexible manner so that one facility can provide backup capacity for another country and so that the shifting of production to different nodes in the global network is facilitated as cost and other factors change. The extraordinary adaptive ability attributed to the ME is in part the result of its coordinated planning processes.

Long-range planning is often described either as "top down" in nature whereby global goals are formulated by a headquarters planning staff to serve as guidelines for more detailed plans formulated at local levels; or as "bottom-up" plans whereby the local objectives and plans are first established by local managers and then filter upward for approval. While "bottom up" is reasonably representative of the typical MHC's long-range planning processes, the top-down approach does not accurately portray the processes in MEs. Long-range planning in MEs is more properly described as joint and simultaneous participation in long-term planning by both headquarters and local entity planners.

While long-range planning is spearheaded by the planning staff at headquarters of MEs, this planning is heavily dependent on evaluations by local managers of expected local cost, revenue, and market patterns, and typically the local managers participate directly—and often deeply—in the formulation of the long-range plan. Additionally, measurements directed by the local manager which pertain to the local environment become a part of a central data bank for use in examining various alternative configurations of long-range plans.

THE INTERNATIONAL FINANCIAL FUNCTION

An integrated international financial function is evolving in MEs. There have always been elements of such a function, but heretofore it has tended to be a divided responsibility carried out on an *ad hoc* basis without benefit of carefully formulated guiding principles.

It is this financial area where the ME is most readily seen to be an integrated and coordinated entity. Increasingly, all aspects of financial operations involving multiple currencies and the risk of currency value changes are coordinated together. In many MEs, as well as in a few MHCs, one headquarters executive is assigned to coordinate this financial function on a global basis. In some companies this function also encompasses responsibility for certain of the more traditional financial activities, such as subsidiary borrowing and lending, and coordination of international cash stocks and flows.

Tremendous advantages can accrue to coordinated cash management, as one example. Multinational enterprises are evolving toward global or regional cash "pools" whereby operations in several countries draw upon and replenish a cash concentration account according to their needs and surpluses. However, a variety of impediments in the international environments inhibit the full development of multinational cash pools at the present time.

Foreign Exchange Management

The specific objectives of the foreign exchange aspect of the international financial function are to:

Minimize exchange risks and exchange losses;

Minimize the deleterious impact on global operations of individual country exchange and remittance controls, tariffs, and other impediments to the free exchange of money and goods;

Minimize currency conversion costs; and

Accomplish these objectives within the broader financial framework of cash management and capital market activities.

The above objectives involve trade-offs. To make these trade-offs, specialized information about all countries of operation must be gathered and integrated for use in a systematic fashion. This information acquisition and integration function is performed by the company's information system.

The foreign exchange aspect of the international financial function entails direct control and coordination of international variables, which brings about direct benefits in the nature of cost savings. It also provides information input useful for managing operating cash and financing international operations. The major thrust of this management activity is to balance losses from nontrivial currency realignments against trade-offs involving loss avoidance costs (such as hedging costs) as well as other needs for company resources.

Determination of Exchange Gains and Losses. Over the last decade many companies with extensive international operations have developed sophisticated systems for avoiding exchange losses. These systems usually include all or some of the ingredients shown in Exhibit 2. As yet few companies have completely rationalized their approach to protecting against exchange losses, and a particularly nettlesome problem is the determination of the exchange loss for the entire system of an ME when an exchange rate changes. This question is addressed elsewhere by the author:

> Several internal economic phenomena affect exchange rates. Certain of the phenomena may affect local operations and their subsequent profitability, and certain of them may not. To a great extent, this is a function of the situation of the particular operation and will vary widely from one local company to another. Even assuming timely and appropriate movement of exchange rates in response to economic stimuli, the pressures by real economic factors for exchange rate changes may affect different companies' operations in radically different ways. In a particular country, the net effect of rate changes may be deleterious to operations of some companies,

EXHIBIT 2
Elements of an Exchange Loss Avoidance System

---

1. A surveillance information system to monitor political, economic, military, and financial developments in all of the countries in which operations are conducted. Balance-of-payments status and trends are examples of the types of information which must be gathered.
2. A system to predict the probable timing and extent of fundamental currency realignments and the probable nature and severity of accompanying exchange controls. (No systems have yet been devised that can reliably predict a currency realignment and its approximate size and timing; however the systems presently in use are much better than guesswork, and they are continuously being refined.)
3. An evaluation system to match the asset and transaction-in-process status of each company's operations with the predictions for currency realignments and controls in order to derive an expected exchange loss, given the "exposed" status. This expected loss can be measured on a statistical "expected value" basis.
4. An array of preplanned compensator (hedging or risk avoidance) actions intended to reduce the exposed status (and hence any exchange loss) or to provide an offsetting exchange gain. Most of these actions have costs which can be calculated and compared to the expected value of the exchange losses to be avoided.
5. Decision criteria to determine which hedging activity, if any, is to be utilized for each "expected value" exchange loss.
6. A postaudit feedback system to measure and evaluate the success of the approach.

Source: Adapted from George M. Scott et al., *An Introduction to Financial Control and Reporting in Multinational Enterprises* (Austin, Texas: Bureau of Business Research, University of Texas, 1973), p. 38.

may affect others' operations little or not at all, and may be greatly beneficial to the operations of other companies within the economy.[8]

The difficulty in determining economic gains and losses resulting from exchange rate changes can be traced in part to accounting translation procedures. At the present time, using historical costs and generally accepted accounting principles, accounting rules devised for currency translation purposes are applied to measure exchange gains and losses. As a consequence of these rules, managers are likely to hedge or take other actions to reduce exposure and avoid an apparent loss. Such losses are unlikely to be a reflection of changes in the underlying economic operating conditions of the local subsidiary that deleteriously affect operations of that subsidiary to about the same extent as the recorded losses; indeed, the

---

[8] George M. Scott, "Currency Exchange Rates and Accounting Translations: A Mis-Marriage?" *ABACUS*, June 1975, pp. 66–67.

changes which result in the recorded loss, or in hedging to avoid the loss, may on balance be beneficial to the local subsidiary.

As an example, a lack of international competitiveness in the primarily manufacturing export sector of a foreign economy will adversely affect the economy's exchange rate. However, a local subsidiary which produces cereal in that foreign economy for local consumption will be affected by an exchange rate change only indirectly or not at all. There is not likely to be a direct relationship between an exchange rate change and the profitability of the local cereal operations. Indeed, the impact on the cereal producing company of a real or threatened devaluation is unlikely to be easily ascertainable and could be positive, negative, or neutral. The impact on operations in this example, as in many situations, would be likely to be largely the result of many specific internal price and supply/demand changes of the type which would flow through and be measured in the normal course of operations by an increased or decreased net income.

It is increasingly recognized that exchange gains and losses may not be measured properly by accounting rules.[9] However no satisfactory alternatives have yet been developed. The best approach is to exercise caution, not accept the conventional wisdom on the topic, and keep alert to the underlying economics of every exchange risk situation.

In the author's opinion, current-value accounting has the potential to revolutionize the way managers view the impact of exchange rates fluctuations on operations and the way in which translation gains and losses are determined. The author's research on current-value accounting leads to the tentative conclusion that exchange rate gains and losses may be viewed as the difference in the current value of local resources and obligations before and after an exchange rate change.

Exchange rate gains and losses should be related to economic

---

[9] One author states that "The debatable assumption that these translation adjustments are always real losses or gains lies at the heart of the accountants' current translation dilemma." Donald J. Hayes, "Translating Foreign Currencies," *Harvard Business Review*, January–February 1972, p. 12. Another author asserts, "It is important to realize that translation losses in many cases are not real economic losses, just book losses. A devaluation can, in fact, improve the subsidiary's competitive position by making its goods less expensive in world markets." As quoted in "Multinational Report," *Fortune*, July 1971, p. 37. See also Gunter Dufey, "The Outlook for the International Monetary System and Implications for Subsidiary Valuation," *The International Journal of Accounting*, Fall 1970, pp. 25–33.

reality. Economic reality necessarily means *economic value*. Economic value, in turn, means *current value*. Therefore, measurement of economic reality must necessarily consist of measurement of current-value changes attributable to exchange rate changes.[10]

PROFIT CENTERS IN INTERNATIONAL OPERATIONS

The concept of a profit center is that of an entity manager's making the major expenditure, pricing, and other decisions which affect the profitability of his or her "profit center." Since the manager thereby directly influences the results of operations, he or she is accountable for and evaluated on the basis of those results, which are the profit center's profits.[11]

Although profit centers are often faulted for their theoretical deficiencies, they have been widely implemented and are generally considered successful in domestic operations. Profit centers permit senior managers to rely to a great extent on the "bottom-line" profit result for control and evaluation so that careful scrutiny of budget variances and attention to other detailed and time-consuming analyses of performance are not required.

Unfortunately, the same degree of success of profit centers cannot be found in the international operations of either MHCs or MEs for reasons implicit in the preceding sections of this chapter. First, the profit centers of a company with only domestic operations enjoy a uniformity of environment and depth of understanding of that environment on the part of headquarters managers which do not exist for foreign profit centers. With greatly differing inflation rates and other economic as well as political and social differences among countries, top management is unable to understand fully each country's situation, and therefore is less able to evaluate what is a good or bad profit performance abroad. For this reason, profit centers inherently have less utility for international operations than for domestic operations.

The second reason relates to the severe transfer pricing problems encountered in international operations. Products, management

---

[10] For further discussion of these points, see George M. Scott, "An Academic's View of Accounting Translation," *Proceedings of The Conference on Currency Translation in Business Operations* (Miami: Florida International University, March 1977).

[11] A distinction is properly made between cost centers, profit centers, and investment centers. However, for the purposes of this chapter these distinctions are not crucial.

services, royalties on processes and patents, insurance, administrative and other services, dividends, interest, and overhead charges are forms of intracorporate transfers which result in accounting entries as costs to one unit and revenues to another unit. These charges have come to be called "transfer prices." Although no cohesive and acceptable theory of transfer pricing has been developed, in domestic-only enterprises the transfer pricing policy generally followed is that of establishing prices which seem to be "fair" or equitable to the organization units involved. Transfer prices directly affect organization units' costs and revenues and so their profit; if corporate units are controlled and evaluated as profit centers, then profit center managers are naturally concerned that the transfer prices be equitable.

In international operations (and especially in MEs) equity usually ceases to be the prime consideration in establishing transfer prices and is replaced by some other objective, the most frequent of which is tax minimization. In certain circumstances, currency and profits remittance restrictions of a country may make primal the objective of charging high prices into the country so that permitted payments for goods received will extract greater remittances from the local country. For the ME, transfer prices with the greatest utility for resource allocation decisions also compete for primacy, since extensive resource allocations between subsidiaries are continuously being made as a part of the global coordination process. Thus in different affiliates or even within the same subsidiary, different transfer price policies may be used simultaneously for different goods and services to accomplish different purposes, and the policies may change as the circumstances change.

Transfer prices set to accomplish objectives other than equity serve to bias the indicated profits of a profit center. Additionally, if transfers constitute a significant portion of total operations, then the resulting profit does not have relevance as a performance measure. Transfers do constitute significant portions of the international operations for many, if not most, foreign subsidiaries.[12]

The combination of major differences in environments among countries and transfer pricing policies which emphasize objectives other than equity among foreign subsidiaries results in profit centers

---

[12] One study indicates that transfers between related subsidiaries account for more than 30 percent of *all* international trade. T. A. Bisat, "An Evaluation of International Intercompany Transfers" (Ph.D. diss., American University, 1967).

abroad which may be profit centers in name only, although in the least coordinated companies some utility may remain. Nevertheless, many companies continue to foster the illusion that foreign operations are bona fide profit centers. One reason is that this permits local managers to appear to be more independent from foreign control.

A further blow is dealt to profit centers in the situation of MEs by their management style of coordination. The independence of profit center managers in making the major decisions affecting profits, which is vital to profit centers, is the very antithesis of what is found in MEs. Not only are the units of an ME integrated (versus independent), but also the units are managed as a coordinated whole, and the major decisions affecting local profit are strongly influenced by headquarters or are made in some cooperative fashion. The profit center concept is simply irrelevant to MEs except at the global or (for some MEs) at the regional level or on a global product-line basis.[13]

This inability to use profit centers for control purposes in international operations leaves a tremendous void in financial control. This void must be filled by greater emphasis at headquarters on expense budgets and other control mechanisms. To appreciate the magnitude of the control problem in the absence of profit centers, it is worth recalling that profit centers evolved in part because of top managements' inability to directly control far-flung and complex domestic operations. Yet foreign operations are more far-flung and more complex. This suggests (correctly) that foreign operations are seldom as well controlled by headquarters as are domestic operations of the same company.

THE PROBLEM OF PERFORMANCE EVALUATION

Performance evaluation is inextricably intertwined with planning and control. The control aspect of performance evaluation relates to garnering clues from past performance about how to improve future performance, and to encouraging greater efforts this period

---

[13] Where facilities and personnel are clearly separable along product lines and strong interactions exist between activities relating to the same product lines in different countries, but only weak interactions exist among different product lines, the product-line profit center approach can have viability. Relatively few companies, however, have product lines which are so separate that global product-line profit centers will be logical.

because it is known that in the future the present period's performance will be assessed.

Performance evaluation also is related to planning. Past results provide a starting point for comprehensive company-wide managerial and strategic planning and for integrating the activities of all managers into a company-goal oriented effort.

It can be seen that in international operations, performance evaluation is more important than as just a basis for adjustment of managers' renumeration and for promotion decisions. It affects the future well-being of the network of companies because it affects motivation, resource allocations and coordination.

However an assortment of considerations makes difficult the evaluation of performance in international operations; they sum to the complexities of international operations and the operating styles of MEs. Complexity causes difficulty in setting reliable performance goals, and it obfuscates tracing local managers' decisions and other activities to specific operating results. The major performance evaluation considerations which are peculiar to international operations (and most of which have already been discussed in this chapter in other contexts) are:

1. *Differential rates of inflation.* No systematic inflation adjustments are made by most MEs, with the consequence that intercompany comparability is destroyed. Inflation biases introduced into profit and rate-of-return calculations are different in each country.

2. *Different currencies and the need for currency translation.* Scarcely anyone is convinced that present accounting translation procedures are entirely neutral with respect to affecting reported after-translation performance that took place in one currency and is reported in another. Evaluation of performance inevitably must suffer from this nonneutrality.

3. *Currency devaluations and revaluations.* Experts cannot agree about which gains and losses caused by currency adjustments are real and which are specious, nor is there always agreement as to whether the recorded gains and losses should be the responsibility of headquarters or of local managers.

4. *Transfer pricing.* In MEs the proportion of goods and services transferred is often high and the bases for setting transfer prices may be varied. The setting of transfer prices to facilitate performance evaluation appears to be a low priority in most international companies.

5. *The different economic environments of different countries.* As examples only: different taxation systems impose different burdens and often elicit managerial activity that impairs operating performance (such as disposing of property holdings in some circumstances to avoid property taxes); larger inventory may be required because of fear of impending import restrictions or longer and more erratic supply lines; working capital management may consume a disproportionate amount of local managerial effort to the detriment of other aspects of operations; and factor proportions and costs may vary dramatically from country to country. These considerations and many others contribute to the inherent noncomparability of operations in different countries and serve to make comparative performance evaluation exceedingly difficult.

6. *Different political environments.* A host of political considerations affects costs, revenues, and opportunity costs differentially between countries, and accordingly these considerations impact on performance evaluation. One, for example, is the need to tailor actions and even products to suit the development plans of local country governments or to ensure a continuing welcome by a country's government.

7. *The definition of performance.* Should the profits used for evaluation of the performance of local operations be local earnings in local currency, translated local earnings, earnings available for remittance, earnings actually remitted, earnings remitted to a third country, or some combination? Further, should management-service fees, royalties, interest, and so on be included in measurements of return on capital? The answers depend in part on the purpose of the evaluation. Different companies reach different conclusions about how to treat these matters for evaluation purposes.

8. *The coordinative mode of operations of MEs.* The existence of coordination affects performance evaluation in two ways. First, MEs' global operations must be carefully tuned to achieve optimum performance of the totality, so that the contribution required of each entity is not the same as it would be if that entity were seeking its own local optima; the marginal utility of various alternatives can be quite different for the global system than it is for the local entity.

Second, the integration and coordination of operations severely circumscribe the areas of operations controllable entirely by a country manager in an ME. Evaluation of the manager on the basis of accountability is therefore difficult at best, and this difficulty is compounded because the manager may now participate in, and should be evaluated partly on, the basis of activities which have a beneficial or detrimental impact on operations other than his or her own.

Measures Used

Whereas in situations where profit centers are effective the entity's performance is a virtual identity with the profit center manager's performance and both can be measured by profit, in international operations profit is rarely an adequate performance measure for either. Other measures must be used, and increasingly managers are being evaluated on a variety of bases.

Budgets are emerging as key elements, with the emphasis on careful analysis of budget variances and the circumstances which account for these variances. For evaluation of whether or not the entity resources made a satisfactory contribution, all variances are considered, but for evaluation of the manager's performance only those variances that are controlled by the manager are included. The evaluation is often conducted as a part of formal performance reviews.

Nonfinancial statistical indicators also are used with increasing frequency to evaluate managers. These include employee turnover, percentage of the market, labor hours lost, and progress on personnel training programs, to cite but a few. Managers are also evaluated on the basis of the extent and quality of their cooperation with, and participation in, the global activities of planning and coordination; in practice the summary indicator of this amorphous criterion sometimes appears to be how well the manager is prepared for the periodic planning, control, and coordination meetings and how much of a contribution he or she makes to the deliberations during those meetings.

THE INFORMATION SYSTEM OF THE ME

Multinational enterprises have been characterized as being highly integrated and coordinated across national boundaries. This mode of operations has a "push and pull" relationship with the management information systems (MIS) of MEs. On the one hand, a given level of integration and coordination tends to elicit an MIS which supports this management approach; for example, a great deal of information must be channeled to headquarters and must be passed between subsidiaries. On the other hand, a highly developed global MIS facilitates a still higher degree of integration and coordination, and a sophisticated MIS can constitute a major competitive advantage in international operations.

While the MIS serves all levels of companies, the portion of the MIS that is of greatest concern here is that which serves top management and its staff. In MEs, this top management is pluralistic. Each ME has not one but several top managements: a top management for each country of operations, one for headquarters, and one for each regional headquarters (if these exist).

One direction of sophistication required of an MIS for integrated and coordinated operations is that of integration of the MIS.[14] The need for information integration in IBM is highlighted as follows:

> Now, in an integrated operation, each country has to get information from the other countries. Information has to cross borders, not only for finished product, but also for parts and raw materials requirements.
>
> Traditional information systems were capable of handling information requirements only for some international operations. But with the advent of long-range requirements and added international operations and integration it became necessary to develop a new concept. For example, today the daily input for only one of our major applications consists of 500,000 pieces of information to be distributed internationally; so we had to design a multinational system to convey the information faster and more selectively from the source to where it was needed.[15]

Integration is most evidenced by the need for interacting EDP systems. This is brought about by extensive data transmission between organization units and by a system of international data bases that permits data at one location to be quickly available in the form needed to all locations.[16]

---

[14] For discussion of MIS integration, see George M. Scott, "Information Systems and Coordination in Multinational Enterprises," *The International Journal of Accounting Education and Research,* Fall 1974.

[15] Paul Hoffman, "Designing the Multinational Information System," *International Management Information Systems* (New York: American Management Association, 1967), p. 6.

[16] For a managerial perspective and tutorial on data bases, see George M. Scott, "A Data Base for Your Company?" *California Management Review,* July 1976.

Integration of data originating in different countries, either by accumulating the data in a central location or by separate data bases linked to the global system, is not as easy as integration within one nation. Transmission of data over longer distances, across national frontiers, and across oceans entails greater cost as well as technical and political problems. But global teleprocessing networks are feasible now, and several have been implemented.

General Electric's time-sharing Mark III system provides an excellent example of an existing multicountry telecommunications network for data processing.[17] Although a time-sharing service, it may be a portent of future global systems. Transmission lines, undersea cables, and satellites link over 100 Mark III computers to provide a teleprocessing network which encompasses all medium and large U.S. cities as well as 50 urban centers in Western Europe, Australia, and Japan. The system spans 17 time zones. All processing (except local preprocessing) for the network's customers takes place at GE's "Super Center" in Ohio.

PREPARING FOR CONTROL AND COORDINATION IN INTERNATIONAL OPERATIONS

Both large and small companies can gain the benefits of the careful and close control and coordination of foreign operations that is normally associated with large MEs. If the reader's company is planning to enter international operations by establishing operating units abroad, or already has operating units abroad but is expanding or integrating these, or is dissatisfied with its control over these foreign operations, now is the time to initiate a program for development of the control and coordination systems of these foreign operations. A program that is appropriate for most circumstances is as follows:

Step 1. Begin by encouraging the control personnel to gain a thorough appreciation of the lore of multinationalism. This entails studying the concept of multinationalism, considering the costs and benefits trade-offs involved, and in these and other ways acquiring a "multinational attitude." This multinational frame of mind will permit the combined U.S. and foreign operations to be viewed as one articulating global system rather than as a domestic company

---

[17] George J. Feeney, "The Computer Utility," *PMM World*, Spring 1974.

with foreign auxillaries or appendages. With this perspective, control personnel are better able to anticipate the control and coordination systems and the information flows that will be required in the future.

While the controller's area is unlikely to be the driving force in moving toward integration and coordination, a lack of a global perspective should not be permitted to cause this area to be the constraining factor. However, it is necessary to bear in mind that effective multinationalism does not flower immediately no matter how fertile the environment—multinationalism is the result of a long evolutionary process.

Step 2. Determine the probable direction in which your company will evolve with respect to international operations—what products it will take abroad, whether they will be exported or manufactured abroad, in which countries operations will be conducted, how access to those countries will be gained (acquisitions, joint ventures, etc.), the probable distribution channels, the probable time schedule, and so on. To accomplish this, consider the interests, competences, and predispositions of the managers who occupy the top three or four levels in each area of the company, and if possible talk to these managers to ascertain their plans, hopes, and aspirations for international operations; review the company plans and particularly the strategic and long-range plans; observe the company's more progressive competitors and other companies in related areas; and look carefully for the future implications of requests for new and different types of information and reports. Then synthesize these sources of information to chart what the company's probable future is in international operations. In turn, this forecast will be invaluable for establishing the nature of the control systems that will be required.

Step 3. Take steps to ensure that the controller's and other groups involved with the control system begin to acquire the managerial and technical knowledge that will be needed in new areas as the company becomes more integrated and coordinated. As examples, control-related personnel should acquire knowledge in the following areas:

a. Management style—style affects the control processes and the kind of control systems needed.
b. The intricacies of international trade—exchange rates, hedging and covering techniques, and so on.

c. Distributed information systems and mini-computers—distributed systems appear to be more compatible with coordinative management than are centralized systems.
d. Large-scale data bases and the logical integration of geographically decentralized data bases.
e. Intelligence information systems.
f. Coordination—both the concept and the techniques.
g. How organizations are designed and evolve, and the nature of change and its impact on people and organizations.
h. The environments of the local countries—their tax codes, legal systems, history and culture, and so on. An important fringe benefit of this is that one is likely to learn to genuinely admire the people of the country of operations, a fact that will not be overlooked by the local personnel and will go far toward making local subsidiaries as cooperative as are domestic subsidiaries.

Step 4. Inventory the present status of the company's financial control systems and evaluate their strengths and weaknesses. Are standard and marginal-cost systems in place? Are the budgeting and planning systems well developed and effective? Are the personnel who run these systems far-sighted, adaptable, open to new ideas, and spirited enough to leap at new challenges and opportunities? Are there capable project managers in the group? And so on. This inventory and assessment should be in depth and formal, and it should not gloss over shortcomings. A serious corporate involvement in international operations can founder for want of adequate control systems, and the control group—as well as top management—should know how well-prepared the company's control systems are for international operations.

Step 5. Establish concrete goals with respect to the desired nature of the control and coordination system at specific future dates. The fact that the direction in which the company is going cannot be predicted in detail should not be permitted to delay the development of specific goals. The goals selected will, of course, vary widely from one situation to another, but the following serve as illustrations:

a. Goal: Introduce standard costing systems in all production centers by 19XX.
b. Goal: Rotate all foreign controllers through the U.S. headquarters for one year periods before 19XX.

c. Goal: Establish standardized and interactive data bases in all major locations by 19XX.
d. Goal: Acquire five internal auditors with fluency in a relevant foreign language by 19XX.
e. Goal: Achieve complete standardization of all accounting reports submitted to headquarters by 19XX.

Step 6. Develop specific strategies to guide the control and coordination systems from their present status to the future goals in an orderly, systematic fashion. These strategies relate to such matters as personnel hiring and training, equipment acquisitions, how to integrate planning and budgeting systems, and so on. Each strategy will require that specific actions be taken. By incorporating these strategies into the control group's budgets and long-range plans, senior management is alerted to the steps being taken and why, and the resources to undertake the strategies will be allocated as a matter of course.

ADDITIONAL SOURCES

Anthony, Robert N., and Dearden, John. *Management Control Systems: Text and Cases*, chap. 13. 3d ed. Homewood, Ill.: Richard D. Irwin, Inc., 1976.

Barrett, M. Edgar. "Case of the Tangled Transfer Price." *Harvard Business Review*, May–June 1977, p. 20.

Brooke, Michael Z., and Remmers, H. Lee. *The Strategy of Multinational Enterprises*. New York: American Elsevier Publishing Co., Inc., 1970.

Granick, David. "National Differences in the Use of Internal Transfer Prices." *California Management Review*, Summer 1975, p. 28.

Hays, Richard D.; Korth, Christopher M.; and Roudiani, Manucher. *International Business: An Introduction to the World of the Multinational Firm.* Englewood Cliffs, N.J.: Prentice Hall, Inc., 1972.

Mason, R. Hal. "Conflicts between Host Countries and the Multinational Enterprise." *California Management Review*, Fall 1974, p. 5.

Perlmutter, Howard V. "The Tortuous Evolution of the Multinational Corporation." *Columbia Journal of World Business*, January–February 1969.

Prindl, Andreas R. *Foreign Exchange Risk*. New York: John Wiley & Sons, Inc., 1976.

————. "Guidelines for MNC Money Managers." *Harvard Business Review,* January–February 1976, p. 73.

Robbins, Sidney M., and Stobaugh, Robert B. *Money in the Multinational Enterprise.* New York: Basic Books, Inc., 1973.

Scott, George M., et al. *An Introduction to Financial Control and Reporting in Multinational Enterprises.* Austin, Texas: University of Texas Bureau of Business Research, 1973. (Originally published in the *1973 Supplement to The Accounting Review.*)

Stopford, John M., and Wells, Louis T. *Managing the Multinational Enterprise.* New York: Basic Books, Inc., 1972.

Walton, Horace C. "Foreign Currency—To Hedge or Not to Hedge." *Financial Executive,* April 1974, p. 48.

Weston, J. Fred, and Goudzwaard, Maurice B., eds. *Treasurer's Handbook,* chap. 4. Homewood, Ill.: Dow Jones-Irwin, 1976.

index

Index